SCHMITTHOFF'S I

BY THE SAME AUTHOR

The English Conflict of Laws; 3rd ed., 1954.
The Sale of Goods; 2nd ed., 1966.
Legal Aspects of Export Sales; 3rd ed., 1978 (First edition translated into Spanish).
Palmer's Company Law; 24th ed., 1987 (General Editor).
Charlesworth's Mercantile Law; 14th ed., 1984 (Co-Editor).
The Sources of the Law of International Trade; 1964 (Editor).
The Harmonisation of European Company Law; 1973 (Editor).
Commercial Law in a Changing Economic Climate; 2nd ed., 1981, (translated into Korean).
Agency Agreements in the Export Trade (1980).
Extrajudicial Dispute Settlement (1985).
International Carriage of Goods: Some Legal Problems and Possible Solutions (The International Commercial Law Series, Vol. 1, Co-Editor, 1988).

AUSTRALIA AND NEW ZEALAND

The Law Book Company Ltd.
Sidney : Melbourne : Perth

CANADA AND U.S.A.

The Carswell Company Ltd.
Agincourt, Ontario

INDIA

N. M. Tripathi Private Ltd.
Bombay

and

Eastern Law House Private Ltd.
Calcutta and Delhi
M.P.P. House,
Bangalore

ISRAEL

Steimatzky's Agency Ltd.
Jerusalem : Tel Aviv : Haifa

PAKISTAN

Pakistan Law House
Karachi

SCHMITTHOFF'S
EXPORT TRADE

THE LAW AND PRACTICE OF INTERNATIONAL TRADE

BY

CLIVE M. SCHMITTHOFF

LL.M., LL.D. (London), Dr. jur. (Berlin), Dres. h.c., F.I.Ex., Barrister, Hon. Professor of Law at the University of Kent at Canterbury, Professor Emeritus of the City of London Polytechnic, Hon. Professor of Law at the Ruhr-Universität Bochum.

with assistance from

JOHN ADAMS, LL.B.
Barrister,
Professor in Commercial Law at the University of Kent at Canterbury.

NINTH EDITION

What would this island be without foreign trade, but a place of confinement to the inhabitants, who (without it) could be but a kind of hermites, as being separated from the rest of the world; it is foreign trade that renders us rich, honourable and great, that gives us a name and esteem in the world.

Charles Molloy,
De Jure Maritimo et Navale, 1676

LONDON
STEVENS & SONS
1990

First Edition	*1948*
Second Edition	*1950*
Third Edition	*1955 (translated into Russian 1958)*
Fourth Edition	*1962 (translated into Japanese 1968)*
Fifth Edition	*1969 (translated into French 1974)*
Sixth Edition	*1975*
Second Impression	*1977*
Seventh Edition	*1980 (translated into Chinese, Peking, 1985)*
Reprinted	*1982, 1983 and 1985*
Eighth Edition	*1986*
Reprinted	*1988 and 1989*
Ninth Edition	*1990*
Reprinted	*1992*

Published in 1990 by
Stevens & Sons Limited
part of
Sweet & Maxwell Limited
South Quay Plaza
183 Marsh Wall, London
Computerset by
LBJ Enterprises Ltd.
Hampshire & Somerset
Printed in England by Clays Ltd, St Ives plc

British Library Cataloguing in Publication Data

Schmitthoff (Clive Maximilian)
Schmitthoff's export trade: the law and
practice of international trade.—9th ed.
1. Great Britain. Exporting. Law
I. Title
344.103878

ISBN 0-420-48180X
ISBN 0-420-481907 pb

**TO
TWINKIE**

PREFACE

THE aim of this book is to give, as concisely as possible, an account of the law and practice of international trade. The book is intended for the use of businessmen and their professional advisers, and the growing number of students who study the law of international trade as part of their syllabuses in legal and business studies. The fact that it is written for lawyers and laymen alike has not presented a serious difficulty. In my experience businessmen engaged in the promotion of overseas trade are able to appreciate the meaning of legal principles, if explained to them without undue stress on legal terms of art; they talk the same language as commercial lawyers, dealing with the same subject from a different angle. I have endeavoured to give guidance to the newcomer and the expert by describing the elements of legal institutions with which I have to deal, before treating their special functions in the practice of international trade.

Export law or, as some prefer to call it, the law of international trade, covers an unusually wide spectrum of business activity. This is reflected in the arrangement of this work. Its eight Parts deal with The International Sale of Goods; Marketing Organisation Abroad; Finance of Exports; Insurance of Exports; Transportation of Exports; International Commercial Dispute Settlement; Construction and Long Term Contracts; and Customs Law.

In the Preface to the preceding—eighth—edition, published in 1986, I described the changes which had taken place in international trade as revolutionary. This development has continued. It is amazing to note the many advances made in the brief interval since the publication of the last edition. Two trends stand out and should be mentioned here.

First, the global integration of international trade law has made rapid progress. The trading nations appear to realise that in our shrinking world the global unification of international trade law is of immense practical benefit to the international business community. The nations are now more inclined than before to lend support to international conventions aimed at global unification. The Vienna Convention on Contracts for the International Sale of Goods (1980) became operative on January 1, 1988; it has been ratified, acceded or approved by some 20 countries, amongst them the USA, the People's Republic of China, Australia, France and West Germany, and it is only a question of time when it will form part of English law. Several other Conventions, which deal with special subjects, are aligned to the Vienna Convention, and are ready for implementation, amongst them the Limitation Convention (1974), the Geneva Convention on Agency in the International Sale of Goods (1983), the Hague Convention on the law applicable to Contracts for the International Sale of Goods (1986) and the two Ottawa Conventions on International Factoring and International Financial Leading (1988). The Vienna Convention will thus become the centre piece of a network of related conventions. Another convention which has been completed after a long period of gestation is the Convention on International Bills of Exchange and International Promissory Notes (1988).

Secondly, on the regional level, the move towards the establishment of a Single Market in the European Community by December 31, 1992 has led to a considerable penetration of the subject by EC law. The Brussels Judgments Convention (1968) was given effect in the United Kingdom by the Civil Jurisdiction and Judgments Act 1982, which came into operation on January 1, 1987; this important enactment deals *inter alia,* with service out of the jurisdiction and dispenses with leave of the court in actions founded on contract if the defendant is domiciled in another EC country. The ambit of the 1968 Convention will soon be extended to the EFTA countries when the so-called Parallel Convention of Lugano (1988) will come into operation. Further, the Rome Convention on the Law applicable to Contractual Obligations (1980) is likely to be given effect to in the United Kingdom; a Bill providing for this is at present before Parliament. In addition to these key matters, the penetration of EC law is noticeable in many topics. Mention may be made of the EC Directive on Product Liability (1985), to which effect was given in the United Kingdom by Part I of the Consumer Protection Act 1987, which came into operation on March 1, 1989. Further, a block exemption to Article 85(1) admits the validity of certain franchising agreements (1988). A new form of joint export cooperation is sponsored by the Community and is admitted in United Kingdom law; this is the European Economic Interest Grouping (EEIG, 1989). The proposal for the creation of a European company statute, which was dormant for more than ten years, was revived in 1988 and the Tenth Draft Directive on Company Law Harmonisation (1985) proposes to admit cross-border mergers of public limited companies; this Directive, when approved and implemented, will facilitate acquisitions of companies in other EC countries.

These two main trends, the global integration of international trade law and the penetration of the subject by EC law, are given due weight in this edition, in addition to the obvious task of updating the book, by indicating the effect of new international and national legislation and of the avalanche of new decisions which the English, American and Commonwealth courts, as well as the European Court of Justice, produce in this lively branch of law. Two new chapters had to be added in this edition, one on Product Liability (Chap. 11) and the other on the Complaints Procedure under GATT (Chap. 33). The former chapter deals with the EC Directive on Product Liability and then surveys the English law on the subject; a brief note on American law is added. The latter chapter is founded on the resolutions for a streamlined complaints procedure by GATT adopted by the Uruguay Round in May 1989. It is realised that the ordinary exporter has no *locus standi* in GATT but cases have occurred in which it had to be considered whether an approach should be made to the Department of Trade and Industry to initiate the complaint procedure under the GATT rules. Further, some international trade practices have gained in importance and require fuller treatment in this edition; into this category fall the various forms of countertrade; licensing and franchising agreements, equity and contractual joint ventures; factoring, forfaiting and financial leasing. Other topics have lost some of their practical significance and here some judicious pruning of the text was appropriate. In the result, although two new chapters are added, the present edition is one chapter shorter than its predecessor.

The study of international trade law provides, in my view—and I plead guilty to the charge of bias—the most fascinating approach to the understanding of modern commercial law. The reasons are not far to seek. They are that international trade law deals with the actualities of business life and the interaction of legal institutions which are usually considered only in isolation, such as sales, finance, insurance, transportation, arbitration and litigation. The main feature of modern international trade law is its sophistication and refinement. If this feature is ignored, the complex nature of modern trade cannot be understood. The lawyer and the businessman should be sensitive to this characteristic of the subject. The lawyer—and in particular the law student—should realise that, in this multiform subject, the slightest mutation of facts may lead to a distinction from precedent, and the businessman who wants to succeed in the competitive conditions of modern export trade should be aware of the great variety of possibilities which the law places at his disposal; they are, after all, the tools of his trade.

It is my pleasant duty to record sincere thanks to the many persons and organisations who assisted in the preparation of this edition by willingly giving information, advice and help. My special thanks are due to Professor John Adams, of the University of Kent at Canterbury, who prepared the drafts of the sections on Licensing and Franchising (which are now included in the chapter on Sole Distribution Agreements (ch. 15)), of the chapter on the Competition Law of the EC and the UK (ch. 19); and of the chapter on Marine Insurance (ch. 26); he also made valuable suggestions for the improvement of other parts of the work and read the proofs. Special thanks are also due to Mr. Peter T. Muschlinski, Lecturer in Law, London School of Economics and Political Science, who successfully revised and updated the difficult chapter on Customs Law (ch. 35), adding references to the SAD (the Single Administrative Document) and other measures of Customs formalities simplification; Mr. A. Paul Dobson, Programme Director for Law, Polytechnic of North London, assisted in checking on the numerous cross-references. My former pupil and present Professor of Law at DePaul University, Chicago, Mr. Stephen J. Leacock, kindly gave me up-to-date information on various aspects of American law, to which I have referred in this edition. My thanks are also due to Mr. Arnold W. G. Kean, C.B.E., the retired Legal Adviser to the Civil Aviation Authority, who assisted in the revision of the chapter on Carriage of Goods by Air (ch. 29); Mr. Harold Caplan, Director of International Insurance Services Ltd., who helped in the preparation of the section on Aviation Insurance; Mr. Christopher M.C. Cashmore, Senior Lecturer in Law at the City of London Polytechnic, for his assistance on Carriage by Land; Mr. Malcolm Evans, Secretary General of UNIDROIT (Rome); Dr. Gerold Herrmann of UNCITRAL (Vienna); Mr. Derrick Langham, Director General of the Institute of Export; Mr. R. A. Pilcher, Chief Executive of the Export Finance Company Ltd. (EXFINCO), and Dr. Ivo Schwartz, Director of the Directorate Approximation of Laws of the EC Commission (Brussels). The Export Credit Guarantees Department very kindly assisted in bringing the chapter on Export Credit Guarantees up to date. I am grateful to Mr. Robert Spicer, barrister, for having provided a comprehensive index to this work. I wish also to express sincere thanks to the readers and reviewers who drew my attention to changing trade practices and shortcomings of previous editions.

The law of the export trade is, as already observed, the most active branch of commercial law and changes and new developments occur constantly. It is, therefore, important that the reader should be in possession of the latest information as soon as possible. The present edition will be kept up to date by articles on the subject and by notes on the section on the Export Trade in the *Journal of Business Law* which is published by Messrs. Stevens & Sons Ltd. in London.

The law is stated as on October 1, 1989 unless another date is given.

C.M.S.

29 Blenheim Road,
Beford Park,
London, W4 1ET.
December, 1989

CONTENTS

PART ONE

THE INTERNATIONAL SALE OF GOODS

PART TWO

MARKETING ORGANISATION ABROAD

PART THREE

FINANCE OF EXPORTS

PART FOUR

INSURANCE OF EXPORTS

PART FIVE

TRANSPORTATION OF EXPORTS

PART SIX

INTERNATIONAL COMMERCIAL DISPUTE SETTLEMENT

PART SEVEN

CONSTRUCTION AND LONG-TERM CONTRACTS

PART EIGHT

CUSTOMS LAW

CASES

Cases other than those decided by the European Court of Justice and the EEC Commission; for these see p. lxxi, post.

DECISIONS OF THE EUROPEAN COURT OF JUSTICE AND THE EC COMMISSION

STATUTES

STATUTORY INSTRUMENTS

RULES OF THE SUPREME COURT

EUROPEAN COMMUNITIES LEGISLATION

UNITED STATES LEGAL MATERIALS

UNIFORM CUSTOMS AND PRACTICE FOR DOCUMENTARY CREDITS (1983 Revision)

INTERNATIONAL CONVENTIONS AND OTHER FORMULATIONS OF INTERNATIONAL TRADE LAW

ABBREVIATIONS

AAA	American Arbitration Association
ABE	Associated Borrower Endorsement (a facility available from ECGD)
A.C.	(Law Reports) Appeal Cases
ACL	Atlantic Container Line
ACN	Air Consignment Note
ACP States	African, Caribbean and Pacific States
Adp	Automatic data processing
AG	Aktiengesellschaft
All E.R.	All England Reports
ATA	Admission temporaire—temporary Admission
ATP	Aid and Trade Provision
AWB	Air waybill
BOTB	British Overseas Trade Board
BV	besloten vennotscha
c and f	cost and freight
CABF	contre attestation de blocage des fonds
CAP	Common Agricultural Policy
CARDIS	Cargo Data Interchange System
CBI	Confederation of British Industry
CCC	Customs Co-operation Council (Brussels)
CCT	Common Customs Tariff
CFR	Cost and Freight
CFS	container freight station
CHIEF	Customs Handling of Import and Export Freight
c.i.f. and c	cost, insurance, freight and commission
c.i.f. and e	cost, insurance, freight and exchange
c.i.f. and c. and i	cost, insurance, freight and commission and interest
CIP	Freight/Carriage and Insurance paid to
CFS	Container freight station
Ch.	(Law Reports) Chancery Division
C.i.f.	Cost, insurance, freight
CIM	Convention internationale concernant le transport des marchandises par chemin de fer
CMEA	Council for Mutual Economic Assistance
CMI	Comité Maritime International
CMR	Convention relative au contrat de transport international de marchandise par route
c.o.d.	cash on delivery
com. document	community document
COMECON	(also called CMEA) Council for Mutual Economic Assistance
COMPRO	Common Market Facilitating Procedures Committees (for the other Member States of the EEC)
COTIF	Convention relative aux transports internationaux ferroviaires (Convention concerning International Carriage by Rail)
CPT	Carriage paid to
CRN	Customs Registered Number
CST Guarantee	Comprehensive short-term guarantee (issued by ECGD)
CT	Community Transit (Certificate)
CT	Combined Transport
CTO	Combined Transport Operator

CY	Container yard

DAF	Delivered at Frontier
D/A	Documents to be delivered on acceptance of bill of exchange
DCP	Freight/Carriage paid to
DDP	Delivery duty paid
DDU	delivery duty unpaid
DEQ	delivered ex quay
DES	delivered ex ship
D/P	Documents to be delivered on payment of bill of exchange
DTI	Department of Trade and Industry

EC	European Economic Community
ECE	United Nations Economic Commission for Europe
ECGD	Export Credits Guarantee Department
ECS	Echantillon Commerciaux—Commercial samples
ECSC	European Coal and Steel Community
ECU	Economic Community Unit
EDF	European Development Fund
EEC	European Economic Communities
EEIG	European Economic Interest Grouping (EEC law)
EFT	Electronic fund transfer
EFTA	European Free Trade Association
e.g.	exempli gratia (namely)
EIB	European Investment Bank
EIS	Export Intelligence Sevice (of BOTB)
Essays	"Clive M. Schmitthoff's Select Essays on International Trade Law," edited by Professor Chia-Jui Cheng, 1988 (Martinus Nijhoff and Graham and Trotman)
eta	expected time of arrival
ETS	estimated time of sailing
EURI (and EURZ)	customs forms used for EC preference arrangements
EXFINCO	Export Finance Co. Ltd.
EXS	Ex ship
EXQ	Ex quay
EXW	Ex works
e. and o.e.	Errors and omission excepted

F.a.s.	free alongside
FCA	free carrier
f.i.	free in (meaning f.o.b. stowed)
FIATA	Fédération Internationale des Associations de Transitaires et Assimilés
FIATA-FCR	FIATA—Forwarder's Certificate of Receipt
FIATA-FCT	FIATA—Forwarder's Certificate of Transport
FBL	FIATA—Negotiable Combined Transport Bill of Lading
FCL	Full container load
FCR	Forwarder's certificate of receipt
FINCOBE	Finance Contracts (Overseas Banks) Endorsement (a facility available from ECGD)
f.o.a.	free on airport
F.o.b.	Free on board
F.o.r.	Free on rail
FOSFA	Federation of Oils, Seeds and Fats Association
F.o.t.	Free on truck
FRC	Free carrier
FTA	Free trade agreement

GAFTA	Grain & Free Trade Association
GATT	General Agreement on Tariffs and Trade
g.a.	General average
GmbH	Gesellschaft mit beschrankter Haftung
GIE	Groupement d'Intérêt Economique (French law)

HMSO	Her Majesty's Stationery Office
IATA	International Air Transport Association
IBRD	International Bank for Reconstruction and Development
ICLQ	International and Comparative Law Quarterly
ICD	Inland clearance depot
I.C.R.	Industrial Case Reports
ICSID	International Centre for Settlement of Investment Disputes
IDA	International Development Association
i.e.	id est
IMCO	Inter-governmental Maritime Consultation Organisation
IMDG	International Maritime Dangerous Goods Code
Inc.	Incorporated
Inco	International Chamber of Commerce
ISO	International Organisation for Standardisation
JBL	Journal of Business Law
KG	Kommandit-Gesellschaft (German law)
LASH	Lighter aboard ship
LCIA	London Court of International Arbitration
LCL	Less than full container load
LDCs	less developed countries of Africa, Asia and Latin America
LOI	Letter of indemnity
Ltd	Limited
MEGS	Market Entry Guarantee Scheme (of BOTB)
m.f.c. price	most forward customer price
MIEx(Grad)	Member of the Institute of Export (Graduate)
MIGA	Multilateral Investment Guarantee Agency
mpt	multipurpose transport document
M.R.	Master of the Rolls
M/T	Mail transfer
m.v.	motor vessel
NICs	newly industrialised countries
NV	naamloze vennotschap
NVD	No value declared
O.	Order
OCL	Ocean Container Lines
OCT	overseas countries and territories
OECD	Organisation for Economic Co-operation and Development
OGEL	open general expert licence
OJ	Official Journal of EEC
OTAR	Overseas Tariffs and Regulations Section (of the Department of Trade and Industry)
PCT	Patent Co-operation Treaty
P & I Club	Protection and Indemnity Associations (marine insurance)
plc	public limited company
PPI	Policy proof of interest
PSI	preshipment inspection
Pte	Proprietary company
Q.B.	(Law Reports) Queen's Bench Division
r.	rule
RHA	Road Haulage Association
Reg.	Regulation
Ro/Ro	roll on/roll off
RSA	Refined Sugar Association
R.S.C.	Rules of the Supreme Court

SA	société anonyme
SAD	Single Administrative Document (Customs)
Sarl	Société à responsabilité limitée
SCP	simplified clearance procedure
SDRs	Special Drawing Rights
SGS	Société Générale de Surveillance S.A.
S.I.	Statutory Instrument
SITPRO	UK Simplification of International Trade Procedures Board
S.S.Co.'s bill of lading	steamship bill of lading
ST	Short term guarantee (see CST policy of ECGD)
s.t.c.	said to contain
sub.	substituted vessel
SWIFT	Society for Worldwide Interbank Financial Telecommunication
t.b.a. l/u	terms to be agreed with leading underwriters
TDR	Transnational Data Report on Information, Politics and Regulation
THE	Technical Help for Exporters
TIR	Transport International Routier
T/T	telegraphic transfers
UCC	(US) Uniform Commercial Code
u.c.e.	unforeseen circumstances excepted
UCP	Uniform Customs and Practice for Documentary Credits (1983 Revision), ICC Brochure No. 400
U.K.	United Kingdom of Great Britain and Northern Ireland
UN	United Nations
UNCITRAL	United Nations Commission on International Trade Law
UNCTAD	United Nations Conference on Trade and Development
Unidroit	International Institute for the Unification of Private Law (Rome)
UNITAR	United Nations Institute for Training and Research
UNTDED	Trade Data Elements Directory (ISO 7372)
UNTDID	United Nations Trade Data Interchange Directory
VAT	Value added tax
WIPO	World Intellectual Property Organisation
W.L.R.	Weekly Law Reports

PART ONE

THE INTERNATIONAL SALE OF GOODS

CHAPTER 1

INTRODUCTION

INTERNATIONAL trade transactions relate to the exportation of goods or services from one country to another, which is the importing country. These transactions are referred to in this work as *export transactions*. The conduct of export transactions can be divided into two categories: transactions founded on the contract for the international sale of goods and those having as their object the supply of services abroad, such as the construction of works and installations in another country.

Export transactions founded on the contract of sale

These transactions are carried out in two ways. An exporter may sell goods directly to an importer abroad or he may build up a marketing organisation abroad and transact business through distributors, agents, branch offices or subsidiary companies.

Both forms of export sales have their justification. The former type is more appropriate to cases where the export of goods is secondary to the home trade or where export connections are so slender as not to warrant the establishment of a permanent representation abroad. The second type, which is particularly favoured by medium and large-scale enterprises, offers definite advantages where export trading assumes a more than casual character. Considerable variety exists within these two categories. Direct export sales may be transacted regularly or may be isolated ventures into the overseas market. Trading through representatives abroad may be carried out under the direct control of an enterprise in the United Kingdom, as in the case of overseas branch offices and subsidiaries, or may be transacted on the basis of looser arrangements, as in the case where the overseas representative is an independent distributor who represents other firms in addition to the United Kingdom principal; it may likewise be carried out by establishing a joint venture with an undertaking in the country to which the exports are directed.

Trading by means of sales contracts and through representatives abroad are not exclusive methods of export trading; they are, in fact, complementary. The exporter who has appointed permanent representatives abroad normally carries out individual export transactions with them, or through them, by virtue of contracts of sale. For example, an exporter who has established a subsidiary company in Canada and granted exclusive sales rights to an importer in Sweden exports goods to those

3

countries by selling them to the Canadian company and to the Swedish importer.

It is intended in this Part to examine export trading based on the contract of sale, and in the following Part[1] to deal with export trading carried out through marketing organisations in other countries.

Export transactions for the construction of works and installations

These transactions are often major export projects involving a considerable amount of capital. They occur particularly frequently where organisations in the developing countries wish to procure the establishment of new industries in their own countries and in this case are a means of transferring technology from the industrialised to the developing countries. The construction contract proceeds often by invitation of tenders but there exist also other procurement methods.

Construction contracts and contracts founded on export sales are not mutually exclusive. Often the procurement contract provides that, when the construction is in progress or has been completed, machinery or other equipment shall be supplied by the contractor on the basis of export sales.

It is, therefore, appropriate to deal with transactions for the construction of works and installations abroad after those founded on export sales and their financial, insurance and transportation implications have been considered. Construction contracts will be discussed in Part 7.[2]

EXPORT MERCHANTS AND MANUFACTURERS; BANKERS, INSURERS, CARRIERS AND FREIGHT FORWARDERS

The persons concerned with the export trade are chiefly manufacturing or trading enterprises and export merchants.

Export merchants carry on their business under various descriptions, such as Export Houses, Confirming Houses or Merchant Shippers.[3] None of these descriptions has a definite legal or commercial meaning and it is important to ascertain in every instance whether the exporter who buys goods from a manufacturer in this country does so as a principal or as agent for his customer abroad.[4] In the former case his profit consists often[5] in the profit made on the turnover of the goods when reselling

---

[1] See p. 257, *post*.
[2] See p. 729, *post*.
[3] They have formed the British Exporters' Association, whose address is 16 Dartmouth Street, London SW1H 9BL.
[4] See p. 296, *post*.
[5] But not invariably; *e.g.* a confirming house may buy goods in this country in its own name or may make itself personally responsible to the seller and, yet, its profits may be the commission payable by its overseas customer; see *Rusholme & Bolton & Roberts Hadfield Ltd.* v. *S. G. Read & Co. (London) Ltd.* [1955] 1 W.L.R. 146; *Sobell Industries Ltd.* v. *Cory Brothers & Co. Ltd.* [1955] 2 Lloyd's Rep. 82; and p. 300, *post*.

them to the importer abroad; in the latter case his profit is represented by the buying commission which the overseas principal has agreed to pay. A vast proportion of the export trade is handled by export houses, and it cannot be denied that the merchant system has been responsible to a large degree for the expansion and prosperity of British foreign trade during the last two centuries.

Today many manufacturers, particularly large business houses, sell directly to customers in other countries and maintain their own export organisation. In particular, the form of the multinational enterprise is often used in the export trade, both within the EC and outside. A multinational enterprise consists of several national companies, connected by shareholdings, managerial control or contract and acting as one economic unit in world trade. Usually there is the parent company in the home country and its subsidiaries in the host countries. In the EC, after 1992 when the single market will be established,[6] the method of direct marketing will be widely used.

Other categories of persons closely connected with the export trade are bankers, finance houses, insurers, carriers and freight forwarders. The assistance which they give to the exporter will be surveyed later.[7]

EXPORTERS AND THE NATIONAL INTEREST

The promotion of exports is a matter of national importance. The national interest is reflected in arrangements made by the government with a view to assisting the exporter and in statutory regulations. First, the Department of Trade and Industry has provided extensive information services for exporters. Secondly, the Export Credits Guarantee Department, a separate government department under the Secretary of State for Trade and Industry, provides insurance facilities covering export risks not normally covered by commercial insurance. Thirdly, the government exercises some control over certain aspects of exporting, mainly by means of export licences and Customs regulations. Fourthly, the law relating to restrictive trade practices recognises the special importance of exports for the national economy by exempting many exclusive export agreements from the duty of notification to the Director General of Fair Trading or registration by him. These topics will be treated later in their appropriate places.[8]

---

[6] The creation of the single market is provided by the Single European Act, signed in Luxembourg and The Hague on February 17 and 28, 1986; this is not a UK enactment but it is an international treaty amending the EC Treaty. Effect is given in the UK to certain provisions of the Single European Act by the European Communities (Amendment) Act 1986.

[7] On finance of exports, p. 377, *post*; on credit insurance, p. 471, *post*; on other insurance of exports, p. 488, post; on carriage by sea, air and road, p. 535, *post*, on freight forwarders, p. 302, *post*.

[8] Government information services, p. 81, *post*; Export Credits Guarantees, p. 471, *post*; government regulation of exports, p. 757, *post*; restrictive trade practices, p. 363, *post*.

THE EXPORT TRANSACTION

The export transaction is normally founded on a contract for the international sale of goods. From the legal point of view, it is essential to distinguish this contract which has as its object the exportation of goods from this country, from other contracts of sale relating to the same goods but not being the direct and immediate cause for the transportation of the goods to another country. We are concerned only with the contract of sale under which the goods leave this country, be it by sea, air or road, in containers or as ordinary cargo. All other contracts of sale, though preparatory to the ultimate exportation of the goods, are home transactions and outside our purview. When an exporter in the United Kingdom buys, for the purpose of export, goods from a manufacturer in this country, the contract of sale is a home transaction, but when he resells these goods to a buyer abroad that contract of sale has to be classified as an export transaction. When a buyer in another country orders goods directly, or through an agent, from a manufacturer in the United Kingdom, we deal, strictly speaking, with an export transaction although it makes a great difference in law whether the contract has to be performed by delivery of the goods ex works or the goods have to be sent free of charge to the address of the buyer. In practice there is no difficulty in determining whether the contract of sale has as its objective the exportation of goods from this country because the terms of the export contract contain provisions dealing with the place of delivery of the goods and the mode of their transportation to the place of destination, and the buyer, or the person authorised by him to receive the goods, invariably resides abroad. It is evident that a bewildering variety of transactions has to be classified as export sales and that the rights and duties of the contracting parties vary greatly according to the arrangement which they make with respect to the place and method of delivery of the goods and the payment of the purchase price. Fortunately the custom of the merchants has developed a number of stereotyped trade terms peculiar to the export transaction and it is possible, by a separate examination of these terms, to reduce to order the numerous export arrangements which the exporter is at liberty to make with his overseas buyer.[9]

Contracts for the international sale of goods exhibit a characteristic which is not present in contracts for the sale of goods in the home market. They are entwined with other contracts, in particular with the contract of carriage by sea, air or road, under which the goods are exported, and the contract of insurance, by which they are insured. In many export transactions the delivery of the shipping documents to the buyer or his agent plays, as will be seen,[10] an important role in the

---

[9] These Special Trade Terms are considered in Chapter 2, p. 9, *post*.
[10] See p. 37, *post*.

performance of the contract of sale; the shipping documents consist normally of a transportation document, *e.g.* the bill of lading, a marine insurance document and the invoice and thus represent elements of the three contracts referred to. The situation is even more involved when payment is made under a bankers' letter of credit because this frequent method of payment in the export trade requires the addition of further contracts to the export transaction, namely the contracts of the bank or— more frequently—the banks with the buyer and seller respectively.[11] In short, the export transaction presents itself to the businessman as a natural and indivisible whole[12] and he is apt to pay little attention to its constituent parts, like the motorist who thinks of the components of his car only when he notices a fault in them. We have to analyse the individual contracts which constitute the export transaction because this is the best method of appreciating the functioning of the machinery of exports as a whole. From this point of view, the contract for the international sale of goods is the principal and central legal arrangement underlying the whole export transaction, and all other contracts, such as contracts of carriage, insurance and credit, have a supporting and incidental character.[13]

THE UNITED KINGDOM SALE OF GOODS ACT 1979

The United Kingdom enactment on which the law relating to the contract for the sale of goods is founded is the Sale of Goods Act 1979. The regulation provided by this Act is further governed by enactments dealing with contracts generally, *viz.* the Misrepresentation Act 1967 and also the Unfair Contract Terms Act 1977, which, however, exempts international supply contracts[14] from its limits on the restriction of liability of contracting parties. There is also in force the Uniform Laws on International Sales Act 1967[15] which, however, is of little practical importance. In addition, a number of enactments aim principally at the protection of the consumer;[16] they are rarely of practical importance in international trade transactions.

---

[11] See p. 400, *post.*
[12] This concept underlies the treatment of export transactions in the U.S. Uniform Commercial Code, see General Consent preceeding the U.C.C., p. 21, and Soia Mentschikoff, "Highlights of the Uniform Commercial Code" (1964) 27 M.L.R. 167, 168.
[13] These matters are dealt with in Parts 3 to 6 of this work.
[14] See p. 100, *post.*
[15] See p. 241, *post.*
[16] The Supply of Goods (Implied Terms) Act 1973 (in so far as not repealed); the Consumer Credit Act 1974; the Supply of Goods and Services Act 1982 (which however, is inapplicable to contracts for the sale of goods); and the Consumer Protection Act 1987.

PRODUCT LIABILITY

So far, the contractual relations into which an exporter may enter have been indicated. The law of many countries, however, holds the producer of defective goods which have caused injury or damage liable even if he is not in contract with the injured person. Product liability, if not founded on contract, is of tortious or statutory character.

In the United Kingdom product liability is regulated by Part I of the Consumer Protection Act 1987. The subject of product liability will be considered in a later chapter.[17] It is sufficient here to state that the exporter of goods from the United Kingdom may be subject to the—very wide—provisions of the Consumer Protection Act 1987 and also to the law of the country to which his exports are directed. An importer of defective goods into the United Kingdom may likewise be liable by virtue of the 1987 Act although he has not manufactured or produced the goods in question.[18]

---

[17] See Chapter 11, p. 165, *post*.
[18] See p. 171, *post*.

CHAPTER 2

SPECIAL TRADE TERMS IN EXPORT SALES

EXPORT transactions based on the contract of sale usually embody trade terms which are not customary in the home trade. The most common of these terms are the f.o.b. and the c.i.f. clause, but there are other clauses which likewise call for attention.

These trade terms have been developed by international mercantile custom and have simplified, and to a certain extent standardised,[1] the sale of goods abroad. They are in universal use in international trade transactions, both in the countries which have adopted the market economy and in the socialist countries.[2] They are, however, sometimes interpreted differently in various countries and their meaning may be modified by agreement of the parties, the custom of a particular trade or the usage prevailing in a particular port.

The United Kingdom exporter, who wishes to avoid a misunderstanding with his buyer abroad, should make clear the meaning of a special trade term which he intends to adopt. There are various ways of achieving this aim. He may insert a term into the contract to the effect that the contract shall in all respects be governed by the law of his own country[3]; or, when referring to a trade term, he may add explicitly what he understands by it, a precaution which is often adopted in the commodity trade conducted on standard contract forms issued by trade associations; or he may refer in his own conditions of sale[4] to *Incoterms*,[5] a set of standard trade terms sponsored by the International Chamber of Commerce. The edition in use at present[6] is *Incoterms 1980* but a revision

---

[1] See p. 63, *post.*
[2] *The Sources of the Law of International Trade* (Clive M. Schmitthoff ed., 1964) p. 3.
[3] See pp. 204–239, *post.*
[4] See p. 75, *post.*
[5] Incoterms were first published in 1936. Revisions and additions were made in 1953, 1967, 1976 and 1980 and a further revision will, be issued in 1990. (ICC Brochure No. 460). In some countries Incoterms are given statutory force and in others they are recognised as custom of the trade (see p. 66, *post*). In the United Kingdom neither of these is the case. Incoterms can be obtained from ICC United Kingdom, which is the British National Committee of the International Chamber of Commerce, address on p. 66, *post.*
[6] December 1, 1989.

of this edition is in preparation, it will be known as *Incoterms 1990* and is intended to be operative at some date in 1990. The Incoterms referred to in this work are those of the 1980 edition.[7]. An exporter who wishes to make use of this valuable facility, should refer to Incoterms either generally in his standard terms of business or in his contractual arrangement with a buyer abroad should add such a reference, *e.g.* "c.i.f. New York (Incoterms)" or "delivery free carrier Birmingham (Incoterms)."[8]

The special trade terms are primarily designed to define the method of delivery of the goods sold. They are, however, often used for another purpose, namely to indicate the calculation of the purchase price and, in particular, the incidental charges included therein.[9] It is evident that the seller, when quoting f.o.b., will ask for a lower price than when quoting c.i.f. because in the latter case he would include insurance and freight charges in the purchase price while he would not do so in the former case. The seller's price list or catalogue might quote ex works prices for the advertised goods, and the buyer abroad might order goods accordingly, but the parties might agree that the goods shall be dispatched by mail by the seller, who undertakes to pack, invoice, frank and insure them; here the term "ex works" refers to the calculation of the purchase price only,

---

[7] The substance of the trade term definitions in the 1990 Revision is the same as that in the 1980 Revision but the wording is sometimes different. The 1990 Revision includes the same terms as the 1980 Revision, except that the term FOR/FOT (free on rail/free on truck) of the 1980 Revision is omitted in the 1990 Revision (because it is thought to be covered by the term "free carrier"), and that the new term "delivered, duty unpaid" is added.

The 1990 Revision is arranged in a more logical manner than its predecessor. It proceeds from the terms applicable to the departure through the whole range of terms to those suitable for the destination. The 1990 Revision is laid out in a semi-tabular form which will make it easier for the uninitiated businessman to appraise his obligations under a particular term.

The following table set out the proposed arrangement of the 1990 Revision. This is followed by a reference to the treatment of the term in this work.

Arrangement of 1990 Revision	*See on page, post:*
Ex works (EXW)	11
Free Carrier (FCA)	60
Free alongside (FAS)	13
Free on board (FOB)	16
Cost and freight (CFR)	55
Cost, insurance, freight (CIF)	33
Carriage paid to (CPT)	162
Carriage and insurance paid to (CIP)	61
Delivered at frontier (DAF)	158
Delivered ex ship (DES)	56
Delivered ex quay (DEQ)	58
Delivered duty unpaid (DOU)	—
Delivered duty paid (DDP)	59

[8] In *Universal Petroleum Co. Ltd.* v. *Handels und Transport GmbH* [1987] 1 W.L.R. 1178 Incoterms 1980 were embodied into a contract for the sale of a cargo of oil.

[9] See Roskill, L.J. in *The Albazero* [1975] 3 W.L.R. 491, 523, reversed [1977] A.C. 774 (H.L.).

while the delivery of the goods is governed by other terms. In the British Customs and Excise practice, the export value is based on the f.o.b. value and the import value on the c.i.f. value, irrespective of the terms of delivery arranged by the parties. We shall now proceed to deal with terms referring to the actual delivery of the goods and the attendant responsibilities of the parties, but these observations likewise apply, *mutatis mutandis*, to clauses describing the elements of price calculation.

Ex WORKS, Ex FACTORY, Ex WAREHOUSE, OR Ex STORE
(where the goods are situate)

This is the most favourable arrangement which can be obtained by a seller desirous of conducting an export transaction as closely as possible on the lines of an ordinary sale of goods in the home market. The term denotes that the overseas buyer, or his agent, has to collect the goods at the locality at which the seller's works, factory, warehouse or store are situate.

The obligations of the parties under an ex works contract in the United Kingdom are described in detail in Incoterms[9a] as follows:

A. The seller must:
1. Supply the goods in conformity with the contract of sale, together with such evidence of conformity as may be required by the contract.
2. Place the goods at the disposal of the buyer at the time as provided in the contract, at the point of delivery named or which is usual for the delivery of such goods and for their loading on the conveyance to be provided by the buyer.
3. Provide at his own expense the packing, if any, that is necessary to enable the buyer to take delivery of the goods.[10]
4. Give the buyer reasonable notice as to when the goods will be at his disposal.[10]
5. Bear the cost of checking operations (such as checking quality, measuring, weighing, counting) which are necessary for the purpose of placing the goods at the disposal of the buyer.
6. Bear all risks and expenses of the goods until they have been placed at the disposal of the buyer at the time as provided in the contract, provided that the goods have been duly appropriated to the contract, that is to say, clearly set aside or otherwise identified as the contract goods.
7. Render the buyer, at the latter's request, risk and expense, every assistance in obtaining any documents which are issued in the country of delivery and/or of origin and which the buyer may require for the purposes of exportation and/or importation (and, where necessary, for their passage in transit through another country).

[9a] The reference is to Incoterms 1980, see p. 10, *ante*.
[10] It is thought that in the British practice these obligations arise only if stipulated in the contract. On the duty of the seller under an ex works contract not specifying the locality of the seller's works to notify the buyer of that locality, see p. 12, *post*.

B. The buyer must:

1 Take delivery of the goods as soon as they are placed at his disposal at the place and at the time, as provided in the contract, and pay the price as provided in the contract.

2. Bear all charges and risks of the goods from the time when they have so placed at his disposal, provided that the goods have been duly appropriated to the contract, that is to say, clearly set aside or otherwise identified as the contract goods.

3. Bear any Customs duties and taxes that may be levied by reason of exportation.

4. Where he shall have reserved to himself a period within which to take delivery of the goods and/or the right to choose the place of delivery, and should he fail to give instructions in time, bear the additional costs thereby incurred and all risks of the goods from the date of the expiration of the period fixed, provided that the goods shall have been duly appropriated to the contract, that is to say, clearly set aside or otherwise identified as the contract goods.

5. Pay all costs and charges incurred in obtaining the documents mentioned in article A.7, including the cost of certificates of origin, export licence and consular fees.[10]

The purchase price becomes due on delivery of the goods unless other arrangements have been made. As the contract is both concluded and to be performed in this country, it is normally governed by English law.

In an ex works contract a dispute arises sometimes as to who has to bear the cost of packing. This question has to be decided by reference to the terms of the contract of sale between the parties, but, as stated in Article A3 of Incoterms, normally the seller is under an obligation to pack the goods, and in this case the customary method of packing has to be adopted. The seller has, however, only to provide the packing necessary to enable the buyer to take delivery; unless otherwise stipulated in the contract,[11] he is not bound to provide export packing or to bear the cost of such packing.

The ex works clause may either contain the address of the premises from which the goods are to be collected or refer only to the town where the seller's works, factory, store or warehouse is situate. The latter form appears preferable when the seller's business is carried on at various premises in the same locality and it is desired that the sale shall not interfere with the disposition of the goods in the seller's business before they are collected. The seller is then bound to inform the buyer or his agent in time of the local address at which the goods are ready for collection; if he fails to give the buyer notice of the locality at which the goods are to be delivered he might lose his claim for damages for non-acceptance and be himself liable in damages. In one case[12] Brett J. said: "The words are 'ex quay or warehouse Liverpool.' Liverpool is a large place, and is there not, then, an implied condition for notice to be given?"

---

[11] In *Commercial Fibres (Ireland) Ltd.* v. *Zabaida* [1975] 1 Lloyd's Rep. 27 the sellers undertook to provide export packing at the expense of the buyers.
[12] *Davies* v. *McLean* (1873) 21 W.R. 264, 265.

An ex works contract does not necessarily qualify as an international supply contract within the meaning of section 26 of the Unfair Contract Terms Act 1977,[13] even if the seller knows that the goods are destined for export. Consequently the consumer protection provisions of that Act may apply to an ex works contract in appropriate circumstances.[14]

The expressions "ex store" and "ex warehouse" are synonymous and denote the place for the storage of goods on land[15]; the terms do not normally include the storage of goods afloat, *e.g.* in a lighter, because in this case the goods, when insured, represent a marine risk, whereas goods stored on land are a land risk.[16] The term "ex store" may refer, in certain circumstances, to a particular kind of storage: if *e.g.* frozen meat is sold "ex store," the term might have to be construed as meaning "ex refrigerating store."[17]

F.A.S. (named port of shipment)

This acronym stands for "free alongside ship." This term embodies elements not to be found in a sale on the home market. The seller's responsibility and risk in respect of the goods is discharged when they are carried alongside the ship so that they can be placed on board either in the ship's tackle, or by a shore crane or some other means. The actual loading of the goods over the ship's rail is the buyer's, and not the seller's, responsibility and the charges for it have to be borne by the buyer. Where the ship is berthed alongside a wharf or quay, the goods have to be placed ashore near her anchorage; where the ship cannot enter the port or is anchored in the stream, the seller has to provide and pay for lighters which will take the consignment alongside the ship, unless the parties agree that delivery should be made "free on lighter," in which case the responsibility of the seller ends when the goods are delivered over the lighter's rail.

---

[13] See p. 100, *post.*

[14] See *Rasbora Ltd.* v. *J. C. L. Marine Ltd.* [1977] 1 Lloyd's Rep. 645. (This case was decided under the Sale of Goods Act 1893, s.62(1), as amended, which provision was superceded by the Unfair Contract Terms Act 1977, ss.26 and 31(4).)

[15] *Fisher, Reeves & Co.* v. *Armour & Co.* [1920] 3 K.B. 614.

[16] The term "warehouse" has been interpreted in a case concerning burglary insurance as a building and not an enclosed yard (*Leo Rapp Ltd.* v. *McClure* [1955] 1 Lloyd's Rep. 292, 293). The same interpretation need not necessarily be given to the term in a contract of sale.

[17] The definition "free on rail" and "free on truck", which are contained in the 1980 Incoterms but omitted in the 1990 Revision are not treated here as they have become obsolete by the use of the term "free carrier".

According to Incoterms,[18] the obligations arising under an f.a.s. contract[19] are the following:

A. The seller must:

1. Supply the goods in conformity with the contract of sale, together with such evidence of conformity as may be required by the contract.
2. Deliver the goods alongside the vessel at the loading berth named by the buyer, at the named port of shipment, in the manner customary at the port, at the date or within the period stipulated, and notify the buyer, without delay, that the goods have been delivered alongside the vessel.
3. Render the buyer at the latter's request, risk and expense, every assistance in obtaining any export licence, or other governmental authorisation necessary for the export of the goods.[20]
4. Subject to the provisions of articles B.3 and B.4 below, bear all costs and risks of the goods until such time as they shall have been effectively delivered alongside the vessel at the named port of shipment, including the costs of any formalities which he shall have to fulfil in order to deliver the goods alongside the vessel.
5. Provide at his own expense the customary packing of the goods, unless it is the custom of the trade to ship the goods unpacked.
6. Pay the costs of any checking operations (such as checking quality, measuring, weighing, counting) which shall be necessary for the purpose of delivering the goods alongside the vessel.
7. Provide at his own expense the customary clean document in proof of delivery of the goods alongside the named vessel.[21]
8. Provide the buyer, at the latter's request and expense (see B.5), with the certificate of origin.[21]
9. Render the buyer, at the latter's request, risk and expense, every assistance in obtaining any documents other than that mentioned in article A.8, issued in the country of shipment and/or of origin (excluding a bill of lading and/or consular documents) and which the buyer may require for the importation of the goods into the country of destination (and, where necessary, for their passage in transit through another country).

B. The buyer must:

1. Give the seller due notice of the name, loading berth of and delivery dates to the vessel.
2. Bear all the charges and risks of the goods from the time when they shall have been effectively delivered alongside the vessel at the named port of shipment, at the date or within the period stipulated, and pay the price as provided in the contract.
3. Bear any additional costs incurred because the vessel named by him shall have failed to arrive on time, or shall be unable to take the goods, or shall close for cargo earlier than the stipulated date, and all the risks of the goods from the time when the seller shall place them at the buyer's disposal provided, however, that the goods shall have been duly appropriated to the contract, that is to say, clearly set aside or otherwise identified as the contract goods.
4. Should he fail to name the vessel in time or, if he shall have reserved to himself a period within which to take delivery of the goods and/or the right to choose the

---

[18] The reference is to Incoterms 1980, see p. 10 *ante*.

[19] For an illustration of an f.a.s. contract see *Metro Meat Ltd.* v. *Fares Rural Co. Pty. Ltd.* [1985] 2 Lloyd's Rep. 14.

[20] Under the agreement of the parties, the duty to obtain an export licence falls normally on the seller, see pp. 16 and 30, *post*.

[21] It is thought that in the British practice these obligations arise only if stipulated in the contract.

port of shipment, should he fail to give detailed instructions in time, bear any additional costs incurred because of such failure and all the risks of the goods from the date of expiration of the period stipulated for delivery, provided, however, that the goods shall have been duly appropriated to the contract, that is to say, clearly set aside or otherwise identified as the contract goods.

5. Pay all costs and charges incurred in obtaining the documents mentioned in articles A.3, A.8 and A.9 above.

Strictly speaking, port rates fall due when the goods are "exported," *i.e.* when the ship carrying them leaves port. But in practice this obligation is often varied by the rules or custom of the port of shipment. In this respect the obligations under the clause f.a.s. are the same as under that of f.o.b. Thus, it is thought that the port rates are included in the charges demanded by the Port of London Authority.[22] In order to avoid any dispute as to the responsibility for the payment of port rates, this liability should be covered by express agreement of the parties.[23] Thus, the term f.a.s. London (including port rates) would indicate that the export seller wishes to conform with the practice mentioned earlier.

Dock dues payable when the goods enter the docks, as well as wharfage, porterage, lighterage and similar charges, have to be borne by the seller,[24] in the absence of a contrary agreement or custom of the port. Where the parties agree that the goods are to be delivered "free to docks" or the phrase "delivery to docks" is used, these charges fall upon the buyer.

The seller need not provide a dock or wharfingers' receipt unless this is stipulated in the contract in terms or required by the custom of the trade.

Under the f.a.s. contract, as under the strict f.o.b. contract,[25] the duty to nominate a suitable ship falls on the buyer unless the parties have made other arrangements.[26]

The question whether under an f.a.s. contract an export licence has to be obtained by the seller or the buyer is subject to the same considerations as are explained later with reference to the f.o.b. contract.[27] In the leading case of *M. W. Hardy & Co. Inc.* v. *A. V. Pound & Co. Ltd.*[28]

---

[22] See Tariff of the Port of London Authority.

[23] On f.o.b. contracts, see p. 18, *post.*

[24] The seller has likewise normally to pay or refund to the buyer the "f.o.b. service charge" which freight forwarders often charge. It would appear to make no difference whether the forwarder was chosen by the seller or by the buyer.

[25] See p. 20, *post.*

[26] *Anglo-African Shipping Co. of New York Inc.* v. *J. Mortner* [1962] 1 Lloyd's Rep. 610. In *Gill and Duffus Landauer Ltd.* v. *London Export Corporation GmbH* [1982] 2 Lloyd's Rep. 627 a contract "f.a.s. California" was in issue and Goff J. held, *inter alia*, that the place of performance was in California and the law governing the contract was Californian.

[27] See p. 30, *post.*

[28] [1955] 1 Q.B. 499, 512; affirmed by the House of Lords [1956] A.C. 588.

(which dealt with an f.a.s. contract) Lord Goddard C.J. when examining this question said: "that in the present case the contract was f.a.s. and not f.o.b. is in my opinion immaterial."

The f.a.s. contract thus creates many, though not all, rights and duties germane to the f.o.b. contract,[29] and it is not surprising that in the American Uniform Commercial Code these two trade terms are treated in the same paragraph.[30]

In container transport the parties sometimes arrange for delivery "free arrival station," meaning that the carrier undertakes to deliver the containers to the arrival station specified in the contract, ready for Customs clearance and emptying by or on behalf of the importers.[31] They may abbreviate this term "f.a.s." but it has, of course, an entirely different meaning from the term here discussed and its meaning should be expressed in unambiguous terms. This type of contract is, in effect, an arrival contract.[32]

F.O.B. (named port of shipment)

Definition

The seller when selling f.o.b. ("free on board") assumes still further responsibilities than in the preceding instances.[33] He undertakes to place the goods on board a ship that has been named to him by the buyer and that is berthed at the agreed port of shipment. All charges incurred up to and including the delivery of the goods on board ship have to be borne by the seller while the buyer has to pay all subsequent charges, such as the stowage of the goods in or on board ship,[34] freight and marine insurance as well as unloading charges, import duties, consular fees and other

---

[29] See p. 24, *post.*
[30] UCC s.2–319, entitled "F.o.b. and f.a.s. terms." The f.a.s term is defined in s.2–319(2).
[31] *Kuehne and Nagel Ltd.* v. *W. B. Woolley (Scotland) Ltd.* (1973), unreported, Westminster County Court, see p. 611, *post.*
[32] See p. 56, *post.*
[33] On the history of f.o.b. and c.i.f., see David M. Sassoon, "The Origin of f.o.b. and c.i.f. Terms and the Factors influencing their Choice" in [1967] J.B.L. 32. See also Frank Wooldridge, "The Kinds of f.o.b. Contracts" in *Law and International Trade*, Festschrift für Clive M. Schmitthoff, Frankfurt, 1973, 383.
[34] The parties may, however, agree on "f.o.b. stowed" or "f.o.b. stowed/trimmed" or "f.o.b. in": *President of India* v. *Metcalfe Shipping Co.* [1970] 1 Q.B. 289 (C.A.); *David T. Boyd & Co. Ltd.* v. *Louis Louca* [1973] 1 Lloyd's Rep. 209; *The Filipinas I* [1973] 1 Lloyd's Rep. 349; *Kollerich & Cie S.A.* v. *The State Trading Corporation of India* [1980] 2 Lloyd's Rep. 32; *Compagnie de Renflouement etc. Baroukh* v. *W. Seymour Plant Sales & Hire Ltd., etc.* [1981] 2 Lloyd's Rep. 466, 470; *Gill & Duffus SA* v. *Société pour L'Exportation des Sucres SA* [1985] 1 Lloyd's Rep. 621; *Pagnan SpA* v. *Tradax Ocean Transportation SA* [1987] 2 Lloyd's Rep. 342 (tapioca pellets, "f.o.b. stowed/trimmed").

incidental charges due on arrival of the consignment in the port of destination.[35] The transaction differs considerably from an ordinary sale in the home market where no dealings in a port have to be carried out, and yet it does not exhibit the foreign complexion which is a true characteristic of an export transaction.

The following meaning is attributed to the term f.o.b. by Incoterms:[35a]

A. The seller must:

1. Supply the goods in conformity with the contract of sale, together with such evidence of conformity as may be required by the contract.
2. Deliver the goods on board the vessel name by the buyer, at the named port of shipment in the manner customary at the port, at the date or within the period stipulated, and notify the buyer, without delay that the goods have been delivered on board.
3. At his own risk and expense obtai any export licence or other governmental authorization necessary for the export of the goods.
4. Subject to the provisions of articles B.3 and B.4 below, bear all costs and risks of the goods until such time as they shall have effectively passed thed ship's rail at the named port of shipment, including any taxes, fees or charged levied because of exportation, as well as the costs of any formalities which he shall have to fulfil in order to load the goods on board.
5. Provide at his own expense the customary packing of the goods, unless it is the custom of the trade to ship the goods unpacked.
6. Pay the costs of any checking operations (such as checking quality, measuring, weighing, counting) which shall be necessary for the purposes of delivering the goods.
7. Provide at his own expense the customary clean document in proof of delivery of the goods on board the named vessel.
8. Provide the buyer, at the latter's request and expense (see B.6), with the certificate of origin.
9. Render the buyer, at the latter's request, risk and expense, every assistance in obtaining a bill of lading and any documents, other than that mentioned in the previous article, issued in the country of shipment and/or of origin and which the buyer may require for the importation of the goods into the country of destination (and, where necessary, for their passage in transit through another country).

B. The buyer must:

1. At his own expense, charter a vessel or reserve the necessary space on board a vessel and give the seller due notice of the name, loading berth of and delivery dates to the vessel.
2. Bear all costs and risks of the goods from the time when they shall have effectively passed the ship's rail at the named port of shipment, and pay the price as provided in the contract.
3. Bear any additional costs incurred because the vessel named by him shall have failed to arrive on the stipulated date or by the end of the period specified, or shall be unable to take the goods or shall close for cargo earlier than the stipulated date or the end of the period specified and all the risks of the goods from the date of expiration of the period stipulated, provided, however, that the goods shall have been duly appropriated to the contract, that is to say, clearly set aside or otherwise identified as the contract goods.
4. Should he fail to name the vessel in time or, if he shall have reserved to himself a period within which to take delivery of the goods and/or the right to choose the

---

[35] The f.o.b. buyer under an f.o.b. contract has to bear the charges for obtaining the bills of lading. Unless otherwise agreed, the f.o.b. buyer has also to bear the costs for obtaining documents such as certificates of origin, consular documents or other documents which he may require for importation into his country or for transit through other countries.

[35a] The reference is to Incoterms 1980, see p. 10, *ante.*

port of shipment, should he fail to give detailed instructions in time, bear any additional costs incurred because of such failure, and all the risks of the goods from the date of expiration of the period stipulated for delivery, provided, however, that the goods shall have been duly appropriated to the contract, that is to say, clearly set aside or otherwise identified as the contract goods.

5. Pay any costs and charges for obtaining a bill of lading if incurred under article A.9 above.
6. Pay all costs and charges incurred in obtaining the documents mentioned in articles A.8 and A.9 above, including the costs of certificates of origin and consular documents.

In addition to the obligations of the seller set out in Incoterms, according to English law the f.o.b. seller has to give the buyer in certain circumstances due notice enabling him to insure the goods in sea transit; this duty is provided by the Sale of Goods Act 1979, s.32(3) which states:

"Unless otherwise agreed, where goods are sent by the seller to the buyer by a route involving sea transit, under circumstances in which it is usual to insure, the seller must give such notice to the buyer as may enable him to insure them during their sea transit, and, if the seller fails to do so, the goods shall be deemed to be at his risk during such sea transit."

The liabilities of the parties arising under a contract of sale on f.o.b. terms are sometimes defined by usage prevailing in a particular trade or a particular port. Thus, in the oil trade a trade usage exists according to which an f.o.b. buyer has to give the seller timely notice of loading.[36] In the port of Stockholm, if wood products are sold "f.o.b. Stockholm," the buyer has to bear the loading costs into the vessel; by this trade usage the f.o.b. delivery is converted into an f.a.s. delivery.[37]

Where a contract is stated to be on f.o.b. terms, the presumption is that the parties intend to give it its established meaning; the seller's instructions to the shipping agents not to hand over the goods until payment has been secured, do not nullify the normal consequence that the seller has completed the delivery of the goods when they are placed on board ship in the port of despatch.[38]

The responsibilities of the parties for the payment of port rates, dock dues, wharfage, porterage and similar charges are the same as were explained in connection with a sale on f.a.s. terms on p. 15 *ante*.

American practice

In the United Kingdom and the Commonwealth "f.o.b." is understood as meaning "f.o.b. vessel." In the American practice "f.o.b." has become a general delivery term which, if used in the form "f.o.b. place of

---

[36] *Scandinavian Trading Co. A/S* v. *Zodiac Petroleum SA and William Hudson Ltd. The Al Hofuf* [1981] 1 Lloyd's Rep. 81, 84. On notice of readiness to load, see p. 29, *post*.
[37] Clive M. Schmitthoff, *International Trade Usages*, ICC Brochure No. 440/4, 1987, 27.
[38] *Frebold an Sturznickel* (*Panda O.H.G.*) v. *Circle Products Ltd.* [1970] 1 Lloyd's Rep. 499, 504.

destination," even denotes free delivery at that place.[39] The equivalent to the English meaning of "f.o.b." is the American term "f.o.b. vessel." The American regulation can be gathered from the following provisions of the Uniform Commercial Code[40]:

> Unless otherwise agreed the term f.o.b. (which means "free on board") at a named place, even though used only in connection with the stated price, is a delivery term under which—
>
> (a) when the term is f.o.b. the place of shipment, the seller must at that place ship the goods . . . and bear the expense and risk of putting them into the possession of the carrier; or
>
> (b) when the term is f.o.b. the place of destination, the seller must at his own expense and risk transport the goods to that place and there tender delivery of them . . . ;
>
> (c) where under either (a) or (b) the term is also f.o.b. vessel, car or other vehicle, the seller must in addition at his own expense and risk load the goods on board. If the term is f.o.b. vessel the buyer must name the vessel and in the appropriate case the seller must comply with the provisions of this Article on the form of bill of lading . . . .

The term f.o.b. has spread from maritime to air transport.[41] Further, in container transport the term f.o.b. is sometimes used as a general delivery term, *e.g.* in such phrases as f.o.b. container freight station, but this is confusing and should be avoided. It is better in this case to use the term "free carrier" suggested by Incoterms.[42]

Types of f.o.b. clauses

The term f.o.b. is used in transactions of different character and the responsibilities which arise under the clause differ according to the nature of the transaction in which the clause occurs. The incidental obligations which the clause f.o.b. implies have to be ascertained by an analysis of the express or implied intention of the parties.[43]

The clause f.o.b. may be used by an exporter who buys from a manufacturer or merchant in the United Kingdom and who intends to resell the goods abroad; this supply transaction may, *e.g.* be concluded f.o.b. London. Further, an exporter may sell or resell goods to an overseas buyer f.o.b. London; in this case the f.o.b. clause is used in the export transaction. The exporter should be aware of the fact that the f.o.b. clause when used in the supply transaction may carry different incidental obligations from such a clause when used in the export

---

[39] In this sense the term was used by a Canadian company in *Northland Airliners Ltd.* v. *Dennis Ferranti Meters Ltd.* (1970) 114 S.J. 845.

[40] S. 2–319(1).

[41] On f.o.b. airport, see p. 32, *post.*

[42] See p. 60, *post.*

[43] The different types of f.o.b. clauses and the incidents of the f.o.b. contract in general are analysed in Sassoon and Merren, *C.I.F. and F.O.B. Contracts* (*British Shipping Laws*, Vol. 5, 3rd ed. 1984).

transaction. This point was made clear by Singleton L.J. in *M. W. Hardy & Co. Inc.* v. *A. V. Pound & Co. Ltd.*,[44] who explained that this difference might be material for the decision whether an export licence had to be obtained by the seller or the buyer.[45]

A further distinction of considerable practical importance is that between three types of f.o.b. contract, and, here again, it depends on the intention of the parties which of these types is used.

The first type is the *strict or classic f.o.b. contract*.[46] Under this arrangement the buyer has to nominate a suitable ship.[47] When it arrives in the port of shipment, the seller places the goods on board under a contract of carriage by sea which he has made with the carrier, but this contract is made for the account of the buyer. The seller receives the bill of lading which normally shows him as consignor and is to his order, and he transfers it to the buyer. Marine insurance is normally arranged by the buyer directly, if he wishes to insure, but he may also ask the seller to arrange marine insurance for his—the buyer's—account.

The second type is the *f.o.b. contract with additional services*. Under this arrangement the shipping and insurance arrangements are made by the seller, but this is done for the account of the buyer. In this type of f.o.b. contract the buyer is not under an obligation to nominate a suitable ship but the nomination is done by the seller. Again, as in contracts of the first type, the seller enters into a contract with the carrier by sea, places the goods on board ship and transfers the bill of lading to the buyer.

The third type may be described as the *f.o.b. contract (buyer contracting with carrier)*.[48] Here the buyer himself enters into a contract of carriage by sea directly or through an agent, *e.g.* a forwarder. Naturally the buyer has nominated the ship, and when it calls on the port of shipment, the seller puts the goods on board. The bill of lading goes directly to the buyer, usually through an agent of the buyer in the port of shipment, such as a freight forwarder, and does not pass through the seller's hands.

---

[44] [1955] 1 Q.B. 499, 508, 510; affirmed by the House of Lords [1956] A.C. 588.
[45] See p. 31, *post.*
[46] McNair J. in *N.V. Handel My. J. Smits Import-Export* v. *English Exporters (London) Ltd.* [1957] 1 Lloyd's Rep. 517, 519. In *Scandinavian Trading Co. A/B* v. *Zodiac Petroleum S.A. and William Hudson Ltd. The Al Hofuf* [1981] 1 Lloyd's Rep. 81 an f.o.b. clause used in the oil trade was in issue. Mocatta J. referred to the clause as of the classic type (on p. 84), but it is more likely that the clause was of a type described here as a f.o.b. (buyer contracting with carrier) clause. The terminology is not quite settled. Other cases in which the contracts of sale were strict f.o.b. contracts are *Lusograin Comercio Internacional De Cereas Ltda.* v. *Bunge AG* [1986] 2 Lloyd's Rep. 654, 658, and *Spiliada Maritime Corporation* v. *Cansulex Ltd.* [1987] A.C. 460.
[47] See p. 27, *post.*
[48] Although in this type of f.o.b. contract the buyer concludes the contract of carriage with the carrier directly, this type of f.o.b. clause, like any other type of this clause, is, of course, a term of the contract of sale between the seller and buyer and determines the ship's rail as the critical point for the delivery of the goods.

Considerable legal differences exist between these three types of f.o.b. contract. They indicate the flexible nature of this arrangement. Indeed, variations and combinations of these types of f.o.b. contract are met in practice. In f.o.b. contracts of the first and third type the duty to nominate the ship falls on the buyer, but in those of the second type it falls on the seller. In contracts of the first and second type the seller is in contractual relationship with the sea carrier, and for this reason the second type has been described as a variant of the first type.[49] In a contract of the third type, on the other hand, the contract of carriage by sea is made directly with the buyer and the seller is not a party to it.

The three different types of f.o.b. contract are described by Devlin J. in *Pyrene Co. Ltd.* v. *Scindia Navigation Co. Ltd.* as follows[50]:

> The f.o.b. contract has become a flexible instrument. In . . . the classic type . . . for example, in *Wimble, Sons & Co. Ltd.* v. *Rosenberg & Sons*,[51] the buyer's duty is to nominate the ship, and the seller's to put the goods on board for account of the buyer and procure a bill of lading in terms usual in the trade. In such a case the seller is directly a party to the contract of carriage at least until he takes out the bill of lading in the buyer's name. Probably the classic type is based on the assumption that the ship nominated will be willing to load any goods brought down to the berth or at least those of which she is notified. Under present conditions, when space often has to be booked well in advance, the contract of carriage comes into existence at an earlier point of time. Sometimes the seller is asked to make the necessary arrangements; and the contract may then provide for his taking the bill of lading in his own name and obtaining payment against the transfer, as in a c.i.f. contract. Sometimes the buyer engages his own forwarding agent at the port of loading to book space and to procure the bill of lading; if freight has to be paid in advance this method may be most convenient. In such a case the seller discharges his duty by putting the goods on board, getting the mate's receipt and handing it to the forwarding agent to enable him to obtain the bill of lading.

This statement has been referred to with approval by the Court of Appeal in *The El Amria and El Minia*[52]:

> In *Pyrene & Co.* v. *Scindia Steam Navigation Co.*[53] Mr. Justice Devlin instanced three types of f.o.b. contract. In the first, or classic type, the buyer nominates the ship and the seller puts the goods on board for account of the buyer, procuring a bill of lading. The seller is then a party to the contract of carriage and if he has taken the bill of lading to his order, the only contract of carriage to which the buyer can become a party is that contained in the bill of lading which is endorsed to him by the seller. The second is a variant of the first, in that the seller arranges for the ship to come on the berth, but the legal incidents are the same. The third is where the seller puts the goods on board, takes a mate's receipt and gives this to the buyer or his agent who then takes a bill of lading. In this latter type the buyer is a party to the contract of carriage *ab initio*.

In the *Pyrene* case an f.o.b. contract of the third type was in issue. The plaintiffs, Pyrene Co. Ltd., sold a number of fire tenders to the Government of India for delivery f.o.b. London. The buyers nominated a

---

[49] By Donaldson L.J. in *El Amina and El Minia* [1982] 2 Lloyd's Rep. 28, 32.
[50] [1954] 2 Q.B. 402, 424.
[51] [1913] 3 K.B. 743.
[52] [1982] 2 Lloyd's Rep. 28, 32.
[53] [1954] 2 Q.B. 402, 424.

ship belonging to the defendants and through their forwarding agents made all arrangements for the carriage of the goods to Bombay. While one of the tenders was being lifted into the vessel by the ship's tackle the mast broke and the tender, which had not crossed the ship's rail, was dropped on the quay and damaged; it was repaired at the cost of £966 and later shipped in another vessel. The sellers claimed the cost of the repair from the defendants who admitted negligence but pleaded that, being carriers, their liability was limited under the regulation then in force[54] to £200. Devlin J. held that the sellers although not parties to the contract of carriage by sea (which was concluded between the buyers and the defendants) participated in the contract so far as it affected them, and took the benefits of the contract which appertained to them subject to the qualifications imposed by the contract, *i.e.* subject to the maximum limits of liability. The learned judge held further that as far as the defendants as carriers were concerned the "loading" for which they were responsible was the whole loading operation undertaken by them, and not only that stage of the loading occurring after the goods crossed the ship's rail. Devlin J. gave judgment for the sellers for £200.[55] But the position may be different in multimodal transport, where different international conventions apply to different stages of the loading operation. In *Thermo Engineers Ltd.* v. *Ferrymasters Ltd.*[56] the issue was whether damage suffered by the cargo during its loading on board ship was governed by the CMR, which applies to the carriage by road,[57] or by the Hague Rules, which then applied to the carriage by sea.[58] The cargo was a huge heat exchanger which had been sold by an English company to buyers in Copenhagen. The exchanger was carried in a trailer and when the trailer drove on the ship, the protruding superstructure of the exchanger struck the bulkhead of the lower deck and was damaged. The trailer had already passed the outward ramp of the vessel and crossed the line of the stern.

---

[54] That regulation was art. IV(5) of the Schedule to the Carriage of Goods by Sea Act 1924, as supplemented by the British Maritime Law Association Agreement of 1950; The 1924 Act is now superseded by the Carriage of Goods by Sea Act 1971; see p. 562, *post.*
[55] It has been questioned whether *Pyrene Co. Ltd.* v. *Scindia Navigation Co. Ltd.* is good law, in view of the decision of the House of Lords in *Midland Silicones Ltd.* v. *Scruttons Ltd.* [1962] A.C. 446. It is thought that this question has to be answered in the affirmative; see Viscount Simonds on p. 471. This view is supported by the fact that in the U.S.A. where the Supreme Court in *Robert C. Herd & Co. Inc.* v. *Krawill Machinery Corpn.* (1959) 359 U.S. 297; [1959] 1 Lloyd's Rep. 305 decided similarly to *Midland Silicones*, a New York court gave later a decision similar to *Pyrene* in *Carle & Montanari Inc.* v. *American Export Isbrandtsen Lines Inc.* [1968] 1 Lloyd's Rep. 260; see also *New Zealand Shipping Co. Inc.* v. *A. M. Satterthwaite & Co. Ltd. The Eurymedon* [1975] A.C. 154 and the other cases cited on p. 605, *post*; also *The Mormaclynx* [1970] 1 Lloyd's Rep. 527, 536; *Burke Motors Ltd.* v. *Mersey Docks & Harbour Co.* [1986] 1 Lloyd's Rep. 155, 158–159; *The Kapetan Markos* [1986] 1 Lloyd's Rep 211; *The Kapetan Markos (No. 2)* [1987] 2 Lloyd's Rep. 321, 325.
[56] [1981] 1 Lloyd's Rep. 200; *The Captain Gregos, Financial Times,* December 22, 1989.
[57] See p. 635, *post.*
[58] When the accident happened the unamended Hague Rules, and not the Hague-Visby Rules, applied; see p. 563, *post.*

Neill J. held that the carriage by road had ceased, although the trailer and its load had not been secured in the ship, and that the damage was governed by the Hague Rules. If in this case the damage had occurred before the trailer crossed the ship's rail, the CMR would have applied.

F.o.b. values

The f.o.b. clause is frequently taken as a basis for the calculation of the goods sold and not as a term defining the method of delivery.[59] Thus, in the practice of the United Kingdom Customs and export licensing authorities, the export value of the goods is founded on an f.o.b. calculation, whatever the agreed terms of delivery.[60]

Arrangement of freight and marine insurance

When goods are sold on f.o.b. terms it is in principle the duty of the buyer to arrange the freight and marine insurance cover. The f.o.b. (buyer contracting with carrier) contract[61] is thus the most typical form of f.o.b. contract.[62]

This arrangement is often felt to be inconvenient because the seller who conducts his business in the country where the goods are situate before dispatch has better facilities for arranging these items than the buyer. This has given rise to the other two types of f.o.b. contract, the classic f.o.b. contract and the f.o.b. contract with additional services.[63] In these two types the parties have agreed that the seller shall enter into a contractual relationship with the carrier and arrange the carriage. In both these types of f.o.b. contract the seller will do so normally in his own name. But in all types of f.o.b. contract the costs of the freight and insurance have to be borne ultimately by the buyer.[64]

In the f.o.b. contract with additional services the seller may take out the bill of lading in his own name or as an agent of the buyer.[65] In accordance with general principle, the seller is entitled to charge the

---

[59] See p. 11, *ante.*

[60] *Ibid.*

[61] See p. 20, *ante.*

[62] If the seller under an f.o.b. contract has given the buyer credit, it may be in his interest to take out a contingency insurance relating to the goods because he may have to exercise his right of stoppage in transit. See p. 508, *post.*

[63] See pp. 20–21, *ante.*

[64] *N. V. Handel My. J. Smits Import-Export* v. *English Exporters Ltd.* [1957] 1 Lloyd's Rep. 517, and Herring C.J. in *The Mahia (No. 2)* [1960] 1 Lloyd's Rep. 191, 198 (Sup. Ct. Victoria).

[65] On Agency, see p. 279, *post.*

buyer for the freight and insurance premium, if on the instructions of the buyer he has taken out insurance, and with incidental expenses. He may further charge a commission for having procured the contracts of carriage by sea and marine insurance unless the parties have agreed otherwise or there is a custom of the trade to the contrary. In this case the seller may make out two invoices, one showing the f.o.b. values of the goods including all expenses up to the delivery of the goods over the ship's rail, and another invoice showing the additional services which he performed by request of the buyer, and in particular the costs of prepaid freight and marine insurance and any commission which might be due to him.[66]

Responsibilities of the parties

Under the f.o.b. clause the cost of loading the goods into the ship has to be borne by the seller[67] but normally this is included in the freight which has to be paid by the buyer.[68] The risk with respect to the consignment passes from the seller to the buyer when the goods are shipped; normally this means when they are delivered over the ship's rail.[69]

Passing of property

In an f.o.b. contract, if the goods are unascertained, as is the case when they are shipped in bulk but parts of the bulk consignment are sold to several buyers, the property does not pass to these buyers until the various portions are appropriated to them.[70] This is so even if the parties have agreed in their contract that the property shall pass upon the cargo being loaded on board the carrying vessel.[71]

If the goods are ascertained, under an f.o.b. contract property in them passes when they are shipped unless the passing of title is postponed by

---

[66] In the certificate of value required by some Customs authorities the second invoice should be mentioned under "special arrangement."

[67] This distinguishes the f.o.b. contract from the f.a.s. contract under which the buyer has to pay the cost of loading.

[68] Exceptionally the parties may agree that the seller shall bear the cost of stowing goods in the ship's hold; this clause is sometimes referred to as "f.o.b. stowed" or—rather ambiguously—as the f.i. ("free in") clause; see p. 617, *ante*.

[69] *Carlos Federspiel & Co. S.A.* v. *Charles Twigg & Co. Ltd.* [1957] 1 Lloyd's Rep. 240; see p. 119.

[70] See p. 117, *post*.

[71] *Obestain Inc.* v. *National Mineral Development Corporation Ltd. The Sanix Axe.* [1987] 1 Lloyd's Rep. 465, 467. See also *Vitol SA* v. *Esso Australia Ltd. The Wise, The Times*, February 1, 1988.

express or implied stipulation; thus, the seller may have reserved the right of disposal of the goods until the contract terms of payment have been performed.

Where the seller is in contract with the carrier and obtains the bill of lading, as is the case in the strict f.o.b. contract and in the f.o.b. contract with additional services,[72] the question arises whether title to the goods passes on shipment or on transfer of the bill of lading. The answer depends on the intention of the parties. Normally their intention will be that the passing of the title is postponed until the seller makes available the bill of lading to the buyer or his agent,[73] but the facts may disclose a different intention.[74]

When the seller has not, by express stipulation or implication of the law, retained the property in the goods sold after delivery to the carrier, he may in certain circumstances[75] be entitled to claim the rights of the unpaid seller, and in particular a lien on the goods or the right of stoppage in transit.

Examination of the goods

The place of examination of the f.o.b. goods depends on the arrangement of the parties and the circumstances of the case. The parties may have agreed on pre-shipment inspection,[76] which plays an increasing role in modern export trade. Where they have not so agreed and the custom of the trade does not provide for it, the buyer is not obliged to inspect the goods when shipped and, if he fails to examine them on that occasion, will not lose his right of rejection if they do not conform to the contract. In this case usually "the only possible place of inspection would be on arrival of the goods at their place of destination."[77] If, however, the goods are bought by the overseas buyers with a view to resale, the court might regard as sufficient an inspection which is carried out at the place where the ultimate buyer resides.

The loading operation

If loading on board the vessel is completed without hitch, it is permissible and, indeed, convenient to refer to the ship's rail as the legal

---

[72] See p. 20, *ante*.

[73] *E.g.* the advising bank under a letter of credit, see p. 403, *post*.

[74] In *Mitsui & Co. Ltd.* v. *Flota Mercante Grancolombiana SA. The Ciudad De Pasto and Cuidad De Neiva* [1988] 2 Lloyd's Rep. 208 the Court of Appeal held that, according to the intention of the parties, the passing of property was postponed until the balance of the purchase price was paid; the bills of lading were deliverable to the order of the sellers and the court considered that the presumption of s.19 of the Sale of Goods Act 1979 was not replaced. See also *The Kapetan Markos (No. 2)* [1987] 2 Lloyd's Rep. 321.

[75] On the rights of the unpaid seller, see p. 148, *post*.

[76] On pre-shipment inspection, see p. 128, *post*.

[77] *Per* Atkin L.J. in *Boks & Co. Ltd.* v. *J. H. Rayner & Co. Ltd.* (1921) 37 T.L.R. 800, 801; on examination of the goods, see p. 137, *post*.

frontier dividing the responsibilities of the f.o.b. seller and his buyer. If, however, during the loading operation an accident occurs, *e.g.* the ropes break when the cargo is lifted from the shore into the ship, a closer analysis is required to determine the critical point at which the risk, and possibly the property, passes to the f.o.b. buyer. Such an accident affects two legal relationships; the contract of sale and the contract of carriage by sea. It is, of course, purely fortuitous whether the cargo drops down this side of the ship's rail or that. Devlin J. indicated the fortuitous character of the event in the *Pyrene* case[78]:

> Only the most enthusiastic lawyer could watch with satisfaction the spectacle of liabilities shifting uneasily as the cargo sways at the end of a derrick across a notional perpendicular projecting from the ship's rail.

Devlin J. held in this case, as already observed,[79] that in the contract of carriage by sea the loading operation had to be considered as an indivisible whole and the carrier's liability for negligence extended to all stages of that operation irrespective of whether they occured before or after the crossing of the ship's rail.[79a]

But what about the contract of sale? When does the risk, and possibly the property, pass to the f.o.b. buyer if the parties have failed to regulate this point in their contract?

Here two views are possible.[80] It has been suggested that in an f.o.b. contract the goods are at the buyer's risk when they pass the ship's rail and it is irrelevant whether they reach the ship safely on completion of the loading operation or as the result of an accident. According to this view, "loading" has a different meaning in the contract of sale from that attributed to it in the contract of carriage by sea.

Alternatively, it can be argued that the seller has fulfilled his obligations under an f.o.b. contract only if the goods are deposited safely on board the vessel and the loading operation is completed. Here the same meaning is attributed to the concept of loading in both types of contract.

It is thought that the second view is correct. The fortuitous element which Devlin J. righly rejected as a test for the contract of carriage by sea, should likewise be rejected for the contract of sale. It is relevant in this connection that Incoterms define the duty of the f.o.b. seller to "deliver the goods *on board* the vessel"[81] and that the American Uniform

---

[78] [1954] 2 Q.B. 402, 419.
[79] See p. 21, *ante.*
[79a] Stowage is part of the loading operation if the goods are taken from their position in the docks directly into the ship's holds or tanks, as is the case, *e.g.* when grain or oil is loaded. Where the goods are first deposited on deck and then taken below deck (or, if the parties have agreed on deck cargo, are then properly secured on deck), stowage is a separate operation, following the loading operation, and is at the risk of the buyer, unless the parties have arranged "f.o.b. free stowed" or a similar term.
[80] See Sasson and Merren, *C.I.F. and F.O.B. Contracts,* 3rd ed., 1984, para. 577.
[81] See p. 17, *ante.*

Commercial Code refers to his duty to "load the goods *on board.*"[82] The point will eventually have to be settled by authority.[83]

Nominating a suitable ship

The ship or line upon which the goods are to be delivered is sometimes specified in the contract. Where this is not done, it is, in principle, the duty of the buyer to inform the seller of the name of a suitable ship in which the goods can be carried.[84] Lord Hewart C.J. defined this duty in the following words[85]

> It was the duty of the purchasers to provide a vessel at the appointed place at such a time as would enable the vendors to bring the goods alongside the ship and to put them over the ship's rail so as to enable the purchasers to receive them within the appointed time . . . the usual practice under such a contract is for the buyer to nominate a vessel and to send notice of her arrival to the vendor, in order that the vendor may be in a position to fulfil his part of the contract.

The buyer is under a duty to nominate a suitable ship in a strict f.o.b. contract and an f.o.b. (buyer contracting with carrier) contract. He is not necessarily under this duty in f.o.b. contracts with additional services because in this type of contract he may leave the choice of the ship to the seller.

In an f.o.b. contract the time to nominate a suitable ship is normally of the essence of the contract, in other words, it is a condition. The seller is entitled to treat the contract as repudiated if the buyer fails to nominate the ship in the stipulated time or, if no time is stipulated, in a reasonable time.[86] The seller has the same right if the nomination is manifestly artificial and fanciful, in the sense that it is practically unrealistic that the vessel can carry out the function of a suitable ship.[87]

---

[82] See p. 19, *ante.*

[83] For the second (alternative) view see McCardie J. in *Colley* v. *Overseas Exporters* [1921] 3 K.B. 302, 307. *Thermo Engineers Ltd.* v. *Ferrymasters Ltd.* [1981] 1 Lloyd's Rep. 200 (see p. 22, *ante*) does not support the first view stated in the text because the case did not raise an issue concerning the passing of the risk but dealt with the application of international conventions. See also Lloyd L.J. in *Cie. Commerciale Sucres et Denrees* v. *C. Czarnikow Ltd., Financial Times,* July 26, 1989.

[84] A suitable ship is sometimes referred to, in antiquated language, as an "effective ship."

[85] In *J. and J. Cunningham Ltd.* v. *Robert A. Monroe & Co. Ltd.* (1922) 28 Com. Cas. 42, 45; see also Scrutton L.J. in *H. O. Brandt & Co.* v. *H. N. Morris & Co. Ltd.* [1917] 2 K.B. 784, 798. For a detailed nomination clause see *Bremer Handelsgesellschaft mbH* v. *J. H. Rayner & Co. Ltd.* [1978] 2 Lloyd's Rep. 73, 85–86. Also *Miserocchi and C. S.p.A.* v. *Agricultores Federados Argentinos S.C.L.* [1982] 1 Lloyd's Rep. 202, 207; *Gebrüder Metelmann G.m.b.H. & Co. K.G.* v. *N.B.R. (London) Ltd.* [1984] 1 Lloyd's Rep. 614; *Bunge A.G.* v. *Sesostrad S.A. The Alkeos* [1984] 1 Lloyd's Rep. 687, 688.

[86] *Olearia Tirrena S.p.A.* v. *N. V. Algermeene Oliehandel; The Osterbeck* [1972] 2 Lloyd's Rep. 341. On the onus of proving that the buyer would not have been able to provide a suitable ship in time, see *Petraco (Bermuda) Ltd.* v. *Petromed International SA* [1988] 2 Lloyd's Rep. 357.

[87] *Texaco Ltd.* v. *The Eurogulf Shipping Co. Ltd.* [1987] 2 Lloyd's Rep. 541, 545 (such a nomination is sometimes described as a "Mickey Mouse" nomination).

What is a suitable ship?

A ship is suitable if it is able, ready and willing to carry the goods from the port of shipment to the port of destination. If, *e.g.* refrigeration is required for the carriage of fresh vegetables and the refrigeration installation of the ship is insufficient, the ship is not an "able ship." In one case[88] the cargo consisted of huge pipes which had been used for drainage and were cut into large pieces. They were sold as scrap metal and had to be carried under an f.o.b. contract from a place in South Africa to a scrap mill in Turkey. The buyers nominated *The Vicmar Navigator* to carry the goods and the sellers accepted the nomination. Mustill J. said[89]:

This raises only one issue of principle, which is short but not easy. As I have already stated *Vicmar* was not a suitable ship for her task and the tender of this ship was prima facie a breach of contract. Yet [the sellers] expressly accepted her at the time when she was fixed, subject to shipper's approval.

Failure to nominate a suitable ship

The seller is entitled to claim damages for the failure of the buyer to nominate a suitable ship or for the buyer's delay in doing so, but he cannot claim the purchase price because he still has the goods. When claiming damages, the seller must mitigate them by deducting the value of the goods which he has retained. The amount which has to be deducted depends on whether the goods have a marketable value or whether they are built to the specification of the buyer. The rule that if the buyer breaks his obligation to nominate a suitable ship, the seller is only entitled to damages applies even where the buyer's failure to name the ship is due to a chain of unfortunate circumstances.[90] In view of this position the seller is well advised to insist on a contract clause to the effect that the purchase price becomes due on a fixed date, whether a suitable ship has been named or not.

The contract sometimes expressly provides that the buyer shall give the seller notice within a stated time of the probable readiness of the nominated vessel to load, so that the seller can have the goods ready for

---

[88] *Compagnie de Renflouement de Récuperation et de Travaux Sous-Marins V.S. Baroukh et Cie.* v. *W. Seymour Plant Sales & Hire Ltd.* [1981] 2 Lloyd's Rep. 466, (A.C.)
[89] On p. 482.
[90] In *Colley* v. *Overseas Exporters* [1921] 3 K.B. 302.

loading.[91] In the oil trade there exists a custom of the trade obliging the buyer to give the seller timely loading notice.[92]

Where the f.o.b. clause is combined with a clause allowing a shipment period, *e.g.* shipment in August and September, the buyer has to nominate a suitable ship at a time which allows shipment within the stipulated shipment period. In such a case the buyer has the option of determining the time for loading (within the stipulated period of shipment) and in this respect the goods are at "the buyer's call." The seller is obliged to load the goods if the ship thus nominated by the buyer is ready to receive them but he is not obliged to have the goods ready for shipment before that time.[93] To give business efficacy to this type of contract, a term may have to be implied into the contract providing that, before the buyer need nominate a suitable ship, the seller shall notify him when, or approximately when, the seller is ready to load.[94]

Nomination of substitute ship

Where the nominated ship is withdrawn or the nomination fails for another reason the buyer is obliged to name a substitute vessel as soon as possible and to bear the additional expense caused by the substitution. This rule is, however, subject to a qualification: if the contract of sale provides that the buyer shall nominate a ship within a stated time or the goods shall be delivered to the ship within a stated time, it is thought that he can nominate a substitute ship only if he is within the contract time.[95]

---

[91] On this type of loading notice see *Bunge Corporation* v. *Tradax Export S.A.* [1980] 1 Lloyd's Rep. 294 (C.A.) where it was held that the obligation to give such notice was a condition, and not an innominate term, because in mercantile contracts stipulations as to time are usually of the essence of the contract. Similarly *Gill & Duffus SA* v. *Société pour l'Exportation des Sucres SA* [1985] 1 Lloyd's Rep. 621 where in an f.o.b. contract with additional services the duty to nominate the load port within a specified time fell on the seller and his failure to do so was held to be a breach of a condition relieving the buyer from his obligation to perform. Also *Lusograin Comercio Internacional De Cereas Ltda.* v. *Bunge AG* [1986] 2 Lloyd's Rep. 654 (where it was also held that in the case of non-accepted repudiation the seller's damages have to be calculated as on the date of failure to ship, and not as on the date of failure to give notice). Further, *Lombard North Central plc* v. *Butterworth* [1987] Q.B. 527, 543, *per* Nicholls L.J.); *Cargill UK Ltd.* v. *Continental UK Ltd.* [1989] 2 Lloyd's Rep. 290 (if the contract contains a nomination clause requiring provisional and final notices and the buyer gives these notices with respect to vessel A but later substitutes vessel B without giving notices for B, he is in breach of contract although time was too short to comply with the notice requirements for B).

[92] *Scandinavian Trading Co. A/B* v. *Zodiac Petroleum S.A. and William Hudson Ltd. The Al Hofuf* [1981] 1 Lloyd's Rep. 81, 84.

[93] *The Belgrano, Financial Times*, November 26, 1985. The term "at buyer's call" means "on demand" of the buyer and a three days' delay of delivery, on the part of the seller, after the ship is ready to load, would entitle the buyer to repudiate the contract: *Tradax Export SA* v. *Italgrani di Francesco Ambrosio, Sosimage SpA* [1983] Com.L.R. 116. See also *Cie. Commerciale Sucres et Denrees* v. *C. Czarnikow Ltd., Financial Times*, July 26, 1989.

[94] *Harlow & Jones Ltd.* v. *Parex (International) Ltd.* [1967] 2 Lloyd's Rep. 509, 526–527.

[95] *Agricultores Federados Argentinos Sociedad Cooperativa Limitada* v. *Ampro S.A. Commerciale Industrielle et Financiere* [1965] 2 Lloyd's Rep. 757, 767.

Unless a term can be implied into the contract allowing the substitution beyond the contract time[96] or a trade custom or practice exists to that effect—which in any event would allow the substitution only within a reasonable time[96a]—the buyer would be in default if the second nomination carried him beyond the contract time.

Multi-port f.o.b. terms

The contract provides sometimes for delivery at one of several ports which are defined regionally, *e.g.* "f.o.b. United Kingdom port," or "f.o.b. European continental port."[97]

Such a term has to be interpreted according to the intention of the parties. Where the contract is a strict f.o.b. contract or an f.o.b. (buyer contracting with carrier) contract it is thought that the buyer's duty to nominate a suitable ship normally includes his duty to elect the port of shipment within the range stipulated in the contract and to inform the seller accordingly in good time.[98] Where the contract is an f.o.b. contract with additional services, the duty to select the appropriate port falls on the seller. In short, the party responsible for the shipment has normally the choice of the port of shipment.

Duty to procure an export licence[99]

Normally the parties agree expressly or by implication that any export licence that may be required shall be procured by the seller. If the contract does not expressly provide for it[1], such implication is readily

---

[96] An express contract clause allowing substitution does not, it is thought, normally extend the shipment time: see *Finnish Government (Ministry of Food)* v. *H. Ford & Co. Ltd.* (1921) 6 Ll.L.R. 188. But such clause may in appropriate cases reveal that intention of the parties; see *Thomas Borthwick (Glasgow) Ltd.* v. *Bunge & Co. Ltd.* [1969] 1 Lloyd's Rep. 17 (however, this was a c.i.f. contract).

[96a] On the notice of readiness for the substitute vessel see p. 29 n. 91 (the *Cargill* case).

[97] *Fielding & Platt Ltd.* v. *Najjar* [1969] 1 W.L.R. 357.

[98] *David T. Boyd & Co. Ltd.* v. *Louis Louca* [1973] 1 Lloyd's Rep. 209; *Muller Brothers* v. *G. M. Power Plant Co.* [1963] C.L.Y. 3114. However in *Miserocchi and C. S.p.A.* v. *Agricultores Federados Argentinos S.C.L.* [1984] 1 Lloyd's Rep. 202 it was held that, although the buyer had to nominate a suitable ship, the choice of the port of shipment under the multi-port f.o.b. clause was intended to be made by the seller. In *Lusograin Comercio Internacional De Cereas Ltda.* v. *Bunge AG* [1986] 2 Lloyd's Rep. 654 the contract gave the sellers an option to choose the port of shipment from the ports specified in the contract.

[99] On export and import licences generally and frustration, see pp. 186 and 192, *post*.

[1] Thus, in *Compagnie Continentale d'Importation Zurich S.A.* v. *Ispahani* [1962] 1 Lloyd's Rep. 213, the contract provided that export duties should be based on current rates and that "change of export duties [should be] for buyers' account." Export duties were abolished after part of the shipment was made. The Court of Appeal held that the buyers were entitled to recover from the sellers a sum equivalent to the export duties saved.

prompted when the f.o.b. clause occurs in an export, and not a supply, transaction[2] and, to the knowledge of both parties, regulations requiring an export licence are in existence in the country of shipment at the date of the contract and according to which regulations the seller, or his local supplier, is the only party competent to apply for the licence. In *A. V. Pound & Co. Ltd.* v. *M. W. Hardy & Co. Inc.*[3] an American company agreed to buy from the sellers, an English company, 300 metric tons of Portuguese gum spirits of turpentine f.a.s. buyers' tank steamer at Lisbon. The sellers knew at the time they entered into the contract that the buyers contemplated a port in East Germany as the destination of the goods. The sellers then bought the goods from Portuguese suppliers subject to export licence which, however, was refused. The buyers had nominated a tank steamer which arrived in Lisbon in time and was ready to load but as they refused to name another destination and a licence for East Germany was not forthcoming, the goods were not loaded. It was proved that by Portuguese law only the Portuguese suppliers could obtain the export licence and the goods could not be put alongside and cleared through the Customs house before a licence was obtained. The House of Lords, treating the case as being subject to the same rules as apply to an f.o.b. contract, held that, in the circumstances of the case, the parties intended and impliedly agreed that it was the duty of the sellers, and not of the buyers, to obtain the export licence. The court held that the sellers had to do their best to obtain the licence[4] and that as, it was not granted, inspite of the efforts to obtain it, the contract was frustrated and they could not recover damages from the buyers.

Where the parties have neither expressly nor impliedly agreed that the f.o.b. seller should obtain the licence and where the transaction is an export transaction, the duty to obtain the export licence is on the seller, and not the buyer. The seller is normally the only person who is sufficiently acquainted with the licensing practices in the country of exportation and is able to obtain the licence. The view expressed here is also adopted by Incoterms.[5] Only if the transaction is a supply transac-

---

[2] See pp. 19–20, *ante*.

[3] [1956] A.C. 588.

[4] But there is a duty on both parties to co-operate reasonably in obtaining the licence; *A. V. Pound & Co. Ltd.* v. *M. W. Hardy & Co. Inc.* [1956] A.C. 588, 608, 611; see p. 189, *post*.

[5] The position may be different, however, in very rare circumstances, such as prevailed in *H. O. Brandt & Co.* v. *H. N. Morris & Co.* [1917] 3 K.B. 784, where an American buyer, acting through Manchester agents, bought goods from a Manchester seller, the contract providing for delivery f.o.b. Manchester. In consequence of the outbreak of the first world war, an export licensing system was introduced. An application for a licence could only be made by a person resident in the United Kingdom, and in this case both the seller and the buyer's agents were resident in the United Kingdom. No licence was granted and the contract was not performed. In a dispute on who had to obtain the licence, the Court of Appeal held that this duty fell on the buyer because the licence was required when the ship carrying the goods left the country. It is submitted that even in the circumstances then prevailing the decision was wrong because the seller could not have placed the goods on board ship without an export licence.

tion, *e.g.* if a United Kingdom exporter buys goods from a United Kingdom supplier f.o.b. Liverpool, would the duty to obtain the export licence fall on the buyer, *i.e.* the exporter.

F.o.b. airport[6]

The term f.o.b airport, sometimes expressed as f.o.a., was incorporated into Incoterms in 1976 and is, of course, retained in the current edition. The obligations of the seller and the buyer under this term are set out in Incoterms at great length. The main duties of the parties are stated therein as follows:

A. The seller must:
1. Supply the goods in conformity with the contract of sale, together with such evidence of conformity as may be required by the contract.
2. Deliver the goods into the charge of the air carrier or his agent or any other person named by the buyer, or, if no air carrier, agent or other person has been so named, of an air carrier or his agent chosen by the seller. Delivery shall be made on the date or within the period agreed for delivery, and at the named airport of departure in the manner customary at the airport or at such other place as may be designated by the buyer in the contract.
3. Contract at the buyer's expense for the carriage of the goods, unless the buyer or the seller gives prompt notice to the contrary to the other party. When contracting for the carriage as aforesaid, the seller shall do so, subject to the buyer's instructions as provided for under Article B.1, on the usual terms to the airport of destination named by the buyer, or, if no such airport has been so named, to the nearest airport available for such carriage to the buyer's place of business, by a usual route in an aircraft of a type normally used for the transport of goods of the contract description.

4–14. . . .

B. The buyer must:
1. Give the seller due notice of the airport of destination and give him proper instructions (where required) for the carriage of the goods by air from the named airport of departure.
2. If the seller will not contract for the carriage of the goods, arrange at his own expense for said carriage from the named airport of departure and give the seller due notice of said arrangements, stating the name of the air carrier or his agent or of any other person into whose charge delivery is to be made.
3. Bear all costs payable in respect of the goods from the time when they have been delivered in accordance with the provisions of Article A.2 above, except as provided in Article A.5 above.

4–9. . . .

Two points should be noted. First, in f.o.b. airport the critical point between the responsibilities of the seller and the buyer is the point at which the air carrier takes delivery of the goods at the airport (clause A (2)). That will normally be the air carrier's transit shed at the airport. If the goods are lost or damaged between that point and before they are lifted into the aircraft, *e.g.* in the carrier's transit shed or on the tarmac,

---

[6] See also "Air Trade Terms," by Leslie T. Pal, in [1973] J.B.L. 9.

such loss or damage would fall on the buyer and he should insure against it. Secondly, Incoterms provide that, unlike under f.o.b. vessel, the seller shall be entitled to arrange for air carriage, of course at the buyer's expense, if he or the buyer has not given prompt notice to the contrary (clause A (3)). Whether in British practice the seller has that right is doubtful and depends on the intention of the parties.

The term f.o.b. aircraft, under which the seller would be responsible until the goods are lifted into the aircraft, is unusual.

C.I.F. (named port of destination)

This is the most characteristic export term which the custom of the merchants has evolved. Lord Wright[7] observed that the term c.i.f. ("cost, insurance, freight"[8]) "is a type of contract which is more widely and more frequently in use than any other contract used for purposes of seaborne commerce. An enormous number of transactions, in value amounting to untold sums, is carried out every year under c.i.f. contracts." Lord Porter[9] indicated the general characteristics of the c.i.f. stipulation in the following passage:

> The obligations imposed on a seller under a c.i.f. contract are well known, and in the ordinary case, include the tender of a bill of lading covering the goods contracted to be sold and no others, coupled with an insurance policy in the normal form and accompanied by an invoice which shows the price and, as in this case, usually contains a deduction of the freight which the buyer pays before delivery at the port of discharge.[10] Against tender of these documents the purchaser must pay the price. In such a case the property may pass either on shipment or on tender, the risk generally passes on shipment or as from shipment, but possession does not pass until the documents which represent the goods are handed over in exchange for the price. In the result, the buyer, after receipt of the documents, can claim against the ship for breach of the contract of carriage and against the underwriters for any loss covered by the policy. The strict form of c.i.f. contract may, however, be modified. A provision that a delivery order may be substituted for a bill of lading or a certificate of insurance for a policy would not, I think, make the contract be concluded on something other than c.i.f. terms.

And Donaldson J. observed in one case[11]:

> The contract called for Chinese rabbits, c.i.f. Their obligation was, therefore, to tender documents, not to ship the rabbits themselves. If there were any Chinese rabbits afloat, they could have bought them. . . .

---

[7] In *T. D. Bailey, Son & Co.* v. *Ross T. Smyth & Co. Ltd.* (1940) 56 T.L.R. 825, 828.

[8] T. S. Eliot's explanation (in Notes on *The Waste Land*, 1.210) that c.i.f. denotes "carriage and insurance free," is by way of poetical licence.

[9] In *Comptoir d'Achat* v. *Luis de Ridder* [1949] A.C. 293, 309; Blackburn J. in *Ireland* v. *Livingston* (1872) L.R. 5 H.L. 395, 406; Sellers J. in *André et Cie S.A.* v. *Vantol Ltd.* [1952] 2 Lloyd's Rep. 282, 291.

[10] See p. 35, n. 20, *post.*

[11] *P. J. van der Zijden Wildhandel N.V.* v. *Tucker & Cross Ltd.* [1975] 2 Lloyd's Rep. 240, 242.

The nature of the c.i.f. contract is best understood if its economic purpose is kept distinct from the strict legal effect of the transaction.

Definition

From the business point of view, it has been said that the purpose of the c.i.f. contract is not a sale of the goods themselves but a sale of the documents relating to the goods. "It is not a contract that goods shall arrive, but a contract to ship goods complying with the contract of sale, to obtain, unless the contract otherwise provides, the ordinary contract of carriage to the place of destination, and the ordinary contract of insurance of the goods on that voyage, and to tender these documents against payment of the contract price."[12] McNair J.[13] described the ordinary c.i.f. contract as a contract in which "the seller discharges his obligations as regards delivery by tendering a bill of lading covering the goods." The buyer's aim is to obtain, as early as possible, the right of disposal of the goods in order to resell them or to secure a bank advance on them, and to obtain either the goods or, if they are lost, the insurance money. The seller's aim is to accommodate the buyer and to secure for himself increased profits by providing carriage and insurance cover, to part with the right of disposal of the goods only against payment of the purchase price and not to be answerable for loss of or damage to the goods during the voyage. The aims of both parties are attained when the buyer—or a banker nominated in the contract if the contract so provides—effects payment in the stipulated manner against delivery of the documents relating to the goods. The fact that the delivery of the shipping documents is, "in a business sense, the equivalent of the goods,"[14] is, as will be seen later,[15] of great importance when the goods are lost in transit but the shipping documents have been delivered to the buyer or can still be delivered to him.

The sale on c.i.f. terms involves the exporter in calculations and operations which, being different from those applied in the home market,

---

[12] *Per* Scrutton, J. in *Arnold Karberg & Co.* v. *Blythe, Green Jourdain & Co.* [1915] 2 K.B. 379, 388. The phraseology, but not the substance, of Scrutton J.'s observations has been subjected to certain criticism in the Court of Appeal: [1916] 1 K.B. 495. See also Diplock J. in *Tricerri Ltd.* v. *Crosfields and Calthrop Ltd.* [1958] 1 Lloyd's Rep. 236, 242 and Sir John Donaldson M.R. in *Congimex* v. *Tradax Export SA* [1983] 1 Lloyd's Rep. 250, 253.

[13] In *Gardano and Giampieri* v. *Greek Petroleum George Mamidakis & Co.* [1962] 1 W.L.R. 40, 52. Further, Roskill J. in *Margarine Union GmbH* v. *Cambay Prince Steamship Co.* [1967] 2 Lloyd's Rep. 315, 332; Lord Morris of Borth-y-Gest in *Kendall & Sons* v. *William Lillico & Sons Ltd., etc.*, appeals from *Hardwick Game Farm* v. *Suffolk Agricultural Poultry Producers' Association* [1969] 2 A.C. 31, 101; Lord Diplock in *Berger & Co. Inc.* v. *Gill and Duffus S.A.* [1984] 2 W.L.R. 95, 100.

[14] Lord Wright in *T. D. Bailey, Son & Co.* v. *Ross T. Smyth & Co. Ltd.* (1940) 56 T.L.R. 825, 829.

[15] See pp. 50–51, *post*.

require expert knowledge and experience. Export managers and confirming houses naturally possess this expert knowledge and are often in a position to make favourable arrangements as regards freight and insurance. In particular, they will often secure reductions in these charges when engaged in substantial or regular trade with the buyer's country, or they may be able to group several consignments to the same consignee or a number of consignments to different consignees in order to make the best use of the available shipping space[16]; in these cases the c.i.f. clause offers them distinct advantages.

From the legal point of view, the situation is complicated because the c.i.f. transaction embodies, by necessity, elements of three contracts, *viz.* the contract of sale, the contract of carriage by sea and the contract of marine insurance. These complications have in the past often given rise to litigation, but most of them can now be regarded as settled by precedent.[17]

The seller's obligations under a c.i.f. contract have been defined as follows[18]:

1. To ship at the port of shipment goods of the description contained in the contract.[19]
2. To procure a contract of carriage by sea under which the goods will be delivered at the destination contemplated by the contract.
3. To arrange for an insurance upon the terms current in the trade which will be available for the benefit of the buyer.
4. To make out an invoice which normally will debit the buyer with the agreed price, or the actual cost, commission charges, freight, and insurance premium, and credit him for the amount of the freight which he will have to pay to the shipowner on delivery of the goods at the port of destination.[20]
5. To tender these documents to the buyer, so that he may know what freight he has to pay and obtain delivery of the goods, if they arrive, or recover for their loss, if they are lost on the voyage.

The duties of the buyer are defined in Incoterms[20a] as follows. The buyer must:

1. Accept the documents when tendered by the seller, if they are in conformity with the contract of sale, and pay the price as provided in the contract.
2. Receive the goods at the agreed port of destination and bear, with the exception of the freight and marine insurance, all costs and charges incurred in respect of the goods in the course of their transit by sea until their arrival at the port of destination, as well as unloading costs, including lighterage and wharfage charges, unless such costs and charges shall have been included in the freight or collected by the steamship company at the time freight was paid.

---

[16] On groupage bills of lading and container shipment, see p. 609, *post.*
[17] These problems form the subject-matter of Sassoon and Merren, *C.I.F. and F.O.B. Contracts* (*British Shipping Laws*, Vol. 5, 3rd ed., 1984).
[18] By Lord Sumner (then Hamilton J.) in *Biddell Brothers* v. *E. Clemens Horst Co.* [1911] 1 K.B. 214, 220. See, further, Sellers J. in *André et Cie S.A.* v. *Vantol Ltd.* [1952] 2 Lloyd's Rep. 282, 291.
[19] Or to procure and tender to the buyer goods afloat which have been so shipped. See p. 49, *post.*
[20] This definition is founded on the assumption that the parties have arranged "freight collect" and that the freight has not been prepaid by the seller; see p. 553, *post.*
[20a] The reference is to Incoterms 1980, see p. 10.

If war insurance is provided, it shall be at the expense of the buyer . . .
Note: if the goods are sold "c.i.f. landed," unloading costs, including lighterage and wharfage charges, are borne by the seller.

3. Bear all risks of the goods from the time when they shall have effectively passed the ship's rail at the port of shipment.
4. In case he may have reserved to himself a period within which to have the goods shipped and/or the right to choose the port of destination, and he fails to give instructions in time, bear the additional costs thereby incurred and all risks of the goods from the date of the expiration of the period fixed for shipment, provided always that the goods shall have been duly appropriated to the contract, that is to say, clearly set aside or otherwise identified as the contract goods.
5. Pay the costs and charges incurred in obtaining the certificate of origin and consular documents.[21]
6. Pay all costs and charges incurred in obtaining the documents mentioned . . . above.
7. Pay all Customs duties as well as any other duties and taxes payable at the time of or by reason of the importation.
8. Procure and provide at his own risk and expense any import licence or permit or the like which he may require for the importation of the goods at destination.

Businessmen will adapt these legal definitions to the particular transaction which they wish to carry out, and will vary and supplement them whenever necessary. They will, in particular, define exactly in their contract the requirements of the shipping documents which the seller has to tender to the buyer, and the terms, time, place and currency of payment of the purchase price. They have, however, to take care that these amendments and variations do not destroy the essential characteristics of the c.i.f. stipulation which are that as the result of the transfer of the shipping documents a direct relationship is established between the buyer on the one hand and the carrier and insurer on the other, so as to enable the buyer to make direct claims against these persons in case of loss of, or damage to, the goods. If the parties vary this quality of the shipping documents, *e.g.* by providing that the seller shall be at liberty to tender, instead of a bill of lading, a delivery order on his agent in the port of destination or the goods themselves, the contract ceases to be a true c.i.f. contract in the legal sense.[22]

The shipping documents

The shipping documents thus stand in the centre of the c.i.f. transaction. The shipping documents consist, in principle, of—

1. A clean bill of lading evidencing a contract of carriage by sea to the agreed place of destination.
2. A marine insurance policy or certificate covering the usual marine risks and any agreed additional risks.

---

[21] It will often be the intention of the parties that these costs and charges have to be borne by the seller, as they are pre-shipment charges (C.M.S.).
[22] See p. 51, *post*.

3. The invoice in the stipulated form.

Two of these shipping documents, *viz.* the bill of lading and the insurance policy, provide a continuous cover from the port of shipment to the port of discharge, "so that the c.i.f. buyer, whatever happens to the goods, will have either a cause of action on the bill of lading against the ship or a cause of action against the underwriters on the policy."[23]

It is usual to send the buyer at least two sets of documents, one set by one airmail, and the other by a subsequent one, and it is advisable to arrange that both airmail letters should be sent by registered post.[24] The buyer's order may, *e.g.* provide—

Shipping documents—Originals by first airmail and duplicates by the following airmail.

The bill of lading

The individual documents included in a set of shipping documents are examined later[25]; it is sufficient here to make the following observations. The bill of lading, which the seller has to procure, must be a clean bill, *i.e.* a bill which must not contain a qualification of the statement that the goods are shipped in apparent good order and condition.[26] It depends, in the absence of express agreement between the parties, on the custom prevailing in the particular trade whether a "received for shipment" bill or a delivery order on the ship may be substituted for a "shipped" bill.[27] Sometimes the seller will include in his conditions of sale an express clause to the effect that a "received for shipment bill of lading, if tendered, shall be accepted by the buyer." If the terms of the contract are silent and no contrary trade custom applies, the buyer is entitled to a "shipped" bill but in container shipment the intention of the parties is invariably that a "received for shipment" bill of lading may be tendered. The parties may further agree that the seller shall be entitled to substitute a delivery order for a bill of lading. Unless the parties have defined the delivery order differently, this means a ship's delivery order, *i.e.* a delivery order addressed to the ship and, if properly acknowledged —"attorned"—by the carrier,[28] giving the buyer a direct right of action against the carrier to receive the goods from the ship.[29] A contract which

---

[23] *Per* Roskill J. in *Margarine Union G.m.b.H* v. *Cambay Prince Steamship Co. Ltd.* [1969] 1 Q.B. 219, 245.
[24] On sending a set of shipping documents in the ship's bag, see p. 543, *post.*
[25] On bills of lading, p. 561, *post*; on marine insurance policies, p. 488, *post*; on invoices, p. 102, *post.*
[26] On clean bills, see pp. 543 and 584, *post.*
[27] On "shipped" and "received" bills, see p. 569, *post*; on delivery orders, see p. 581, *post.*
[28] Even before the formal attornment the contract has to be treated as a genuine c.i.f. contract.
[29] *Colin & Shields* v. *W. Weddel & Co. Ltd.* [1952] W.N. 420; *Margarine Union GmbH* v. *Cambay Prince Steamship Co. Ltd.* [1969] 1 Q.B. 219; on the various types of delivery orders, see p. 581, *post.*

provides that the seller may substitute a delivery order of different character, *e.g.* an order addressed to one of his agents or to a warehouse-man, would not be a true c.i.f. contract.[30] The seller under a c.i.f. contract must ship the goods within the agreed shipping period[31] or by the agreed shipping date. They have to be shipped by the customary route, except if a particular route of shipment is stipulated in the contract. If the customary route is blocked, the seller is not relieved of his contractual obligation but must ship the goods by any reasonable and practicable route.[32]

The insurance document

The marine insurance policy or certificate, which the seller has to tender to the buyer, should provide cover against the risks which it is customary in the particular trade to cover with respect to the cargo and voyage in question.[33] The parties should not place too much reliance on the custom of the trade, which sometimes varies at the ports of shipment and destination and may be differently interpreted by merchants and courts; they should, in appropriate cases, agree in the contract of sale on the nature of the insurance policy which the seller has to tender, *e.g.* whether the policy should be an all risks policy in the form of Institute Cargo Clause A to Lloyd's Marine Policy,[34] or should cover war risks. It has been held that a seller, who undertakes to insure "on usual Lloyd's conditions," has not discharged his obligations unless the insurance cover which he obtains is as comprehensive as that provided by the customary transit clause.[35] Another point which should be covered by agreement of the parties to the c.i.f. contract is the value of the insurance cover which the seller has to obtain. The parties often agree on the calculation of that value. Their contract normally provides that the insurable value shall be the invoice value of the goods plus incidental shipping and insurance charges plus a specified percentage of say 10 or 15 per cent., representing the buyer's anticipated profits.[36] It should be noted that the law requires the seller, in the absence of a clear custom of the trade to the contrary, to insure merely the reasonable value of the goods at the place of shipment.

---

[30] See p. 51, *post.*
[31] On shipment within the shipment period but under a falsely dated bill of lading see *Proctor & Gamble Philippines Manufacturing Corporation* v. *Kurt A. Becher GmbH & Co. KG* [1988] 1 Lloyd's Rep. 88, 91 and [1988] 2 Lloyd's Rep. 21 (C.A.); see p. 582, *post.*
[32] *Tsakiroglou & Co. Ltd.* v. *Noblee Thorl GmbH* [1962] A.C. 93, 113 (Lord Simonds), 121 –122 (Lord Radcliffe); see p. 141, *post.*
[33] *Reinhart Co.* v. *Joshua Hoyle & Sons Ltd.* [1961] 1 Lloyd's Rep. 346, 352.
[34] See p. 512, *post.*
[35] Which incorporates the "warehouse to warehouse" clause; see p. 514, *post.*
[36] See p. 493, *post.*

Normally this means the cost price of the goods including commission, shipping charges and insurance premium but excluding any rise in the value of the goods, anticipated profits of the buyer and the freight (which, unless it is advance freight,[37] will not be payable if the goods fail to arrive). It is therefore necessary for a buyer, who wishes to obtain cover for any of these interests, to make express arrangements to that effect with the seller at the time when the contract of sale is concluded.[38]

The seller will often have arranged an open cover[39] which covers an unspecified quantity of goods that are to be shipped within a fixed time, and describes the insurance in general terms only, and he then will effect the insurance of the ordered goods by sending the insurers a declaration relating to the details of the consignment in question. In this case he will not receive an insurance policy which he can tender to the buyer, but he will merely receive a broker's cover note or certificate or himself issue an *insurance certificate.*[40] It was held in older English decisions[41] that these documents are not in law equivalent to an insurance policy. The American practice differs from the English practice: in the United States an insurance certificate issued by or on behalf of an insurance company may invariably be tendered in lieu of a policy of insurance[42] but "the term 'certificate of insurance' . . . does not of itself include certificates or 'cover notes' issued by the insurance broker and stating that the goods are covered by a policy."[43] However, it is thought that in modern English practice an insurance certificate or other document entitling the insured (or transferee) to demand the issue of a policy is regarded as equivalent to a formal policy, by implied agreement of the parties, unless their contract stipulates that the seller shall tender a formal policy. The decisive criterion is that the document tendered entitles the holder at any time to demand the issue of a formal policy. A cover note which does not have this quality need not be accepted by the buyer unless he has so agreed or there is a course of dealing or custom of the trade which otherwise provides. The requirement that an effective insurance policy has to be obtained to cover the goods when in transit is an essential condition of the contract, and the buyer under a c.i.f. contract would be

---

[37] See p. 552, *post.*
[38] On insurable value, see p. 492, *post.*
[39] See p. 497, *post.*
[40] See p. 501, *post.*
[41] *Wilson, Holgate & Co.* v. *Belgian Grain and Produce Co.* [1920] 2 K.B. 1. It was held in *Donald H. Scott & Co.* v. *Barclays Bank* [1923] 2 K.B. 1 that a certificate of insurance is not an "approved insurance policy"; and it was decided in *Harper & Co.* v. *Mackechnie & Co.* [1925] 2 K.B. 423 that, even where the buyer accepts a certificate of insurance, the seller impliedly warrants that the assertions in the certificate are correct and that he will produce the insurance policy referred to in the certificate. See also *Promos S.A.* v. *European Grain and Shipping Co.* [1979] 1 Lloyd's Rep. 375. The definition of c.i.f. in Incoterms 1980 likewise requires an insurance policy.
[42] Uniform Commercial Code, s.2–320(2)(c).
[43] Comment to the section quoted in the preceding footnote, para. 9.

entitled to refuse the acceptance of uninsured goods even when they arrived safely at the port of destination.[44]

The invoice

The invoice must be completed in strict agreement with the terms of the contract. Even the slightest variation may cause difficulties, in particular with the bank which will, in that case, be reluctant to make available finance under the letter of credit.[45] The legal requirements for the trading invoice have been described earlier[46]; they apply unless abrogated by the agreement of the parties or the custom of the trade. On occasion the invoice has to satisfy official requirements of the country of importation of the goods; we shall deal with these requirements later.[47]

Attention should be paid to the proper linkage of the invoice with the other documents tendered.[48] It must be clear that they all identify the goods sold although some latitude is admitted with respect to their description in the other documents.

Other documents

The parties may further agree that, in addition to the three principal documents, other documents shall be included in the shipping documents, such as certificates of origin, or quality, or of inspection.[49] Failure to tender these documents in the proper form will normally have the same consequences as a failure to tender the appropriate principal documents.[50]

The right to reject the documents and the right to reject the goods

In a c.i.f. contract the right to reject the documents is distinct from the right to reject the goods. Devlin J. observed in *Kwei Tek Chao* v. *British*

---

[44] *Orient Company Ltd.* v. *Brekke & Howlid* [1913] 1 K.B. 531; *Diamond Alkali Export Corp.* v. *Fl. Bourgeois* [1921] 3 K.B. 443; *Koskas* v. *Standard Marine Insurance Co. Ltd.* (1927) 32 Com.Cas. 160.

[45] See p. 406, *post*.

[46] See p. 35, *ante*, and p. 102, *post*.

[47] See p. 105, *post*.

[48] *Banque de L'Indochine et de Suez S.A.* v. *J. H. Rayner (Mincing Lane) Ltd.* [1983] Q.B. 711. See also p. 415, *post*.

[49] On these certificates see p. 125, *post*. A certificate of quality to be obtained on discharge of the goods is not a certificate which can be tendered with the shipping documents: *Gill & Duffus S.A.* v. *Berger & Co. Inc. (No. 2)* [1984] A.C. 382, 389.

[50] *Re Reinhold & Co. and Hansloh* (1869) 12 T.L.R. 422.

Traders and Shippers Ltd.[51] that "the right to reject the documents arises when the documents are tendered, and the right to reject the goods arises when they are landed and when after examination they are not found to be in conformity with the contract."

In principle, the right to reject the documents is lost when the buyer or the bank which advises a letter of credit for the payment of the price takes up the documents, even if inaccurate, and pays against them without objection. The documents are inaccurate if, when taken together,[52] they disclose a defect to a person who reads them or could have read them. Thus, in *Panchaud Frères S.A.* v. *Establissements General Grain Co.*,[53] a contract for the sale of a quantity of Brazilian maize, c.i.f. Antwerp, provided for shipment in June/July 1965. The goods were shipped on August 10 to 12 but the bill of lading was backdated to July 31, 1965. The superintendents who supervised the loading of the maize issued a certificate of quantity in which they stated that they had drawn samples on August 10 to 12. That certificate formed part of the shipping documents which were taken up and paid for by the buyers. Later the buyers sought to complain about the false dating of the bill of lading and the delayed shipment. The Court of Appeal rejected this claim. Lord Denning M.R. said[54]: "By taking up the documents and paying for them, they are precluded afterwards from complaining of the late shipment or of a defect in the bill of lading." But, as observed, the loss of the right to reject the documents, does not mean that the buyer has lost the right to reject the goods after their arrival on the ground that they do not conform with the specification in the contract. Hobhouse J. observed in one case[55]:

> The exercise of the right to reject the goods is one which the buyer is entitled to postpone until the goods arrive. He can make up his mind then to exercise the right as it suits him best. He may lose his right meanwhile if he deals with the goods or documents so as to disable himself from restoring title to the sellers or by actual waiver. . . .

The rejection must be "clear and unequivocal;"[56] it must indicate that the buyer wants to have nothing to do with the documents or goods. If it

---

[51] [1954] 2 Q.B. 459, 481; *Proctor & Gamble Philippine Manufacturing Corporation* v. *Kurt A. Becher GmbH & Co. KG* [1988] 2 Lloyd's Rep. 21, 26.

[52] On the rule that all documents forming part of the shipping documents have to be read together, see p. 414, *post*.

[53] [1970] 1 Lloyd's Rep. 53 (C.A.).

[54] On p. 58. On the question of waiver see also *Bunge GmbH* v. *Alfred C. Toepfer* [1978] 1 Lloyd's Rep. 506; *Bunge S.A.* v. *Schleswig-Holsteinische etc.* [1978] 1 Lloyd's Rep. 480. The distinction between the doctrines of waiver and equitable estoppel is discussed on p. 147, *post*.

[55] *Bergerco U.S.A.* v. *Vegoil Ltd.* [1984] 1 Lloyd's Rep. 440, 446.

[56] *Per* Saville J. in *Vargas Pena Apezteguia y Ciasaic* v. *Peter Cremer GmbH* [1987] 1 Lloyd's Rep. 394, 398. Saville J. correctly distinguished this case from *Kwei Tek Chao* (see text, above) because in the case before him the buyers' loss was not caused by the loss of the right to reject the documents, but it was caused by the fall of the market when the buyers resold the goods. (In *Vargas* the sales contract was on f.o.b. terms, not on c.i.f. terms.)

is couched in ambiguous terms or the buyer engages in contradictory action, such as the resale of the goods, it is ineffective.[56]

Exceptionally, however, where the buyer or his agent could not realise that the documents were inaccurate, he does not lose his right to claim damages for a breach of a condition relating to the documents on the ground that he has lost his right to reject the goods.[57] In *Kwei Tek Chao v. British Traders and Shipper Ltd.* London exporters sold goods to merchants in Hongkong c.i.f. Hongkong, shipment from continental port not later than October 31, 1951. Unknown to the sellers, the goods were shipped in Antwerp after that date but the bill of lading was forged and showed October 31 as the date of shipment. The buyers, who were unaware of it, accepted the documents and disposed of the goods after their arrival by placing them into a go-down and by pledging the go-down warrants with a bank by way of security. Later the buyers discovered the forgery of the bill of lading and sued the sellers for damages. Devlin J. held that, the two rights to reject the documents and to reject the goods being distinct in a c.i.f. contract, the disposal of the goods by the buyers did not result in the loss of their right to reject the documents as not being in accordance with the contract and that they were entitled to claim damages for being prevented from rejecting the documents; the amount of damages which they could recover was substantial; it consisted of the difference between the contract price of the goods and the value of the goods when the buyers discovered the breach of the sellers' obligation.[58]

Responsibilities of the parties

Under the c.i.f. clause, the seller's responsibility for the goods ends when he delivers them at the port of shipment on board ship into the carrier's custody; the goods travel at the buyer's risk although the seller is responsible for the payment of the freight and the marine insurance premium. Despite the presumption of section 32(1) of the Sale of Goods Act 1979, the goods are deemed to be delivered to the buyer when the bill of lading is delivered to him.[59] The risk passes to the buyer on

---

[57] On the right to refuse acceptance of the goods, see pp. 132 and 137, *post.*

[58] [1954] 2 Q.B. 459. The *Kwei Tek Chao* case was referred to in *Empresa Exportadora de Azucar* v. *Industria Azucarera Nacional S.A.* (*The Playa Larga and Marble Islands*) also known as *Cubazucar* v. *Iansa* [1983] 2 Lloyd's Rep. 171, 179; *Gill & Duffus* v. *Berger & Co. Inc.* [1984] 2 W.L.R. 95, 103; *Bergerco U.S.A.* v. *Vegoil Ltd.* [1984] 1 Lloyd's Rep. 440, 445, and in other cases.

[59] *Biddell Bros.* v. *E. Clemens Horst Co.* [1912] A.C. 18, 22. In exceptional cases, however, the goods may be released by the seller to the buyer before delivery of the bills of lading. Such procedure may raise the presumption that property in the goods has been effectively withheld by the seller: *Cheetham & Co. Ltd.* v. *Thornham Spinning Co. Ltd.* [1964] 2 Lloyd's Rep. 17; *Ginzberg* v. *Barrow Haematite Steel Co. Ltd.* [1966] 1 Lloyd's Rep. 343. See p. 120 *post.*

shipment, but the property in the goods sold does not normally pass on shipment, and in so far as the two incidents of the passing of the risk and of the property are separated under the c.i.f. clause, contrary to the provisions of the Sale of Goods Act, s.20.[60] The property usually passes when the bill of lading is delivered to the buyer or to the bank if payment is arranged under a letter of credit and the buyer thereby acquires the right of disposal of the goods,[61] but normally he acquires only conditional property, *viz.* property subject to the condition subsequent that the goods shall revert to the seller if, upon examination, they are found to be not in accordance with the contract.[62] The buyer's right to inspect the goods is governed by the same rules as apply to these incidents under the f.o.b. stipulation.[63]

Import duties and consular fees have to be paid, in the case of the c.i.f. contract, by the buyer while export licences have to be obtained by the seller who likewise would be responsible for export duties in the rare cases where they are levied; but these rules of law apply only where the parties have not agreed on another arrangement.[64]

A seller of feeding stuff under a c.i.f. contract who transfers the bills of lading and other shipping documents to his buyer in England, is liable to him under the warranty implied by what was then section 2(2) of the U.K. Fertilisers and Feeding Stuffs Act 1926[65] which provides that the goods must be suitable for their use as feeding stuff and not contain a prohibited ingredient.[66] The decisive feature here is that the transfer of the shipping documents takes place in England; the physical situation of the goods themselves at the date of transfer of the documents is irrelevant.

---

[60] See p. 124 *post.*

[61] Whether property passes in ascertained goods depends on the intention of the parties (Sale of Goods Act 1979, s.16). The parties may therefore make other arrangements than the normal arrangements set out in the text. They may arrange that property shall pass on shipment (*per* Roskill L.J. in *The Albazero* [1975] 3 W.L.R. 491, 523, reversed by the House of Lords [1977] A.C. 774; *per* Donaldson J. in *Golodetz & Co. Inc.* v. *Czarnikow-Rionda Co. Inc.*; *The Galatia* [1980] 1 Lloyd's Rep. 453, 455). Or they may arrange for the property to remain in the seller until he receives the purchase price in cash, see also p. 121 *post.*

[62] *Kwei Tek Chao* v. *British Traders and Shippers Ltd.* [1954] 2 Q.B. 459, 487; *Gill & Duffus S.A.* v. *Berger & Co. Inc.* [1984] 2 W.L.R. 95, 104. On defeasible property, see also *McDougall* v. *Aeromarine of Emsworth Ltd.* [1958] 1 W.L.R. 1126.

[63] See p. 25 *ante*; on examination of the goods, see p. 137 *post.*

[64] *Produce Brokers New Co. (1925) Ltd.* v. *British Italian Trading Co.* [1952] 1 Lloyd's Rep. 379. *Cf.* this case with *Compagnie Continentale d'Importation Zurich S.A.* v. *Ispahani* [1962] 1 Lloyd's Rep. 213; see p. 31, *ante*. See also *D. I. Henry Ltd.* v. *Wilhelm G. Clasen* [1973] 1 Lloyd's Rep. 159 (C.A.) ("Cape surcharge buyer's account").

[65] Now s.72 of the Agriculture Act 1970.

[66] *Henry Kendall & Sons* v. *William Lillico & Sons Ltd., etc.*; appeals from *Hardwick Game Farm* v. *Suffolk Agricultural Producers' Association* [1969] 2 A.C. 31, 120–122, 127.

Contractual relations of seller and carrier[67]

In a c.i.f. contract *the seller* (consignor) concludes the contract of carriage with the carrier and rights and duties arise from this contract between these parties unless and until they are transferred from the seller to the buyer by virtue of the Bills of Lading Act 1855.[68] After such statutory transfer the seller can no longer sue the carrier on the contract of carriage.[69]

Contractual relations of buyer and carrier

Contractual relations between *the buyer* (consignee)[70] and the carrier exist in two cases.

1. If the requirements of the Bills of Lading Act 1855 are satisfied, the right to sue the carrier and the liabilities in respect of the goods[71] are vested in the consignee or indorsee of the bill of lading. This situation will be considered later.[72]

2. If the requirements of the Bills of Lading Act 1855 are not satisfied but the buyer takes delivery of the goods in his own right,[73] a contract may be implied between the buyer and the carrier in the terms of the bill of lading. This was decided in *Brandt* v. *Liverpool, Brazil and River Plate Steam Navigation Co. Ltd.*[74] But the rule in *Brandt's* case applies only if a

---

[67] The cases in which a claim may be made by the shipper (seller) or the consignee (buyer) for damage to goods on board ship are summed up by Staughton L.J. in *Mitsui & Co. Ltd.* v. *Flota Mercante Grancolombiana S.A. The Ciudad de Pasto and Ciudad de Neiva.* [1988] 2 Lloyd's Rep. 208, 211.

[68] See p. pp. 551 and 558, *post.*

[69] *Albacruz (Cargo Owners* v. *Albazero (Owners)* [1977] A.C. 774; see p. 559, *post.*

[70] Or another person, having acquired title from the consignee, such as an indorsee of the bill of lading or a pledgee (who has a special property in the bill of lading).

[71] Mainly the obligation to pay the freight but sometimes also to pay demurrage. The liability of the consignor as original party to the contract of carriage is preserved by the Bills of Lading Act 1855, s.2.

[72] See p. 558, *post.*

[73] And not as agent of the seller (consignor).

[74] [1924] 1 K.B. 575. In this case the action for damages to the goods was brought by a pledgee who was neither the consignee nor an indorsee of the bill of lading but who tendered the carrier the bill of lading, which was in his possession, paid the freight and received the goods; his action was successful. It was held in *Cremer* v. *General Carriers SA* [1974] 1 W.L.R. 341 that the tender of a ship's delivery order was as good as that of a bill of lading. But the implication of a contract under the *Brandt* v. *Liverpool* rule must be by *necessary* implication (*The Moorcock* (1889) 14 P.D. 64. *Liverpool City Council* v. *Irwin* [1977] A.C. 239). Normally such a contract can only be implied *after* delivery of the goods to the recipient. But there may be exceptional cases in which such a contract must be assumed to be concluded by necessary implication *before* or *without* delivery of the goods: see the dictum of Staughton J. in *Kaukomarkkinat O/Y* v. *"Elbe" Transport Union GmbH. The Kelo.* [1985] 2 Lloyd's Rep. 85, 87–88 and of Evans J. in *The Aramis* [1987] 2 Lloyd's Rep. 59, 62 (overruled by the C.A. on other grounds, [1989] 1 Lloyd's Rep. 213, 230.).

contractual intention can be inferred from the tender of the bill of lading by its holder and the delivery of the goods by the carrier; *e.g.* if the holder, when tendering the bill, impliedly undertakes to pay the freight for which the carrier may have a lien on the goods. In practice the cases in which the rule in *Brandt's* case can be invoked are more frequent than one should expect. The goods may arrive before the bill of lading and the buyer obtains their delivery against his own or a bank indemnity; or the property in the goods does not pass under the bill of lading but has passed before or is passing after that event or the goods are unascertained (part of a bulk cargo)[75] or the seller has reserved title until he has received the price.[76]

Liability of carrier in tort

As we have seen, under a c.i.f. contract the risk of loss of or damage to the goods passes to the buyer on shipment; the buyer—or his insurer—thus undoubtedly has an interest in the goods. The question arises whether this interest—the bearing of the risk—is sufficient to sustain an action in the *tort of negligence* by the buyer against the carrier. The question is relevant if the buyer cannot sue the carrier in contract because the requirements of the Bills of Lading Act 1855 or of *Brandt's* case are not satisfied and the goods are lost or damaged owing to the negligence of the carrier,[77] but for one reason or another the seller cannot or will not sue the carrier in contract. This problem may arise if the goods, at the time of the loss or damage, are unascertained goods[78] or are subject to a reservation of title in favour of the seller; in these cases property has not passed at the time of the loss or damage. A similar situation exists if, on arrival of the goods, the buyer takes delivery of them as an agent of the seller, and not in his own right.[79] It was held by the House of Lords in *The Aliakmon*[80] that the fact that the buyer bore the risk was not sufficient to

---

[75] See Sale of Goods Act 1979, s.16 (p. 117, *post*) and *The Aramis*, see preceding note.

[76] See p. 121, *ante*.

[77] Or his servants or agents.

[78] The buyer may have bought a portion of a bulk cargo: *Obestain Inc.* v. *National Mineral Development Corporation Ltd. The Sanix Ace.* [1987] 1 Lloyd's Rep. 465 (Property in unascertained goods cannot pass until the goods are appropriated; see p. 117, *post*).

[79] This excludes the application of the rule in *Brandt's* case.

[80] *Leigh and Sillivan Lt.* v. *Aliakmon Shipping Co. Ltd.* [1986] A.C. 785. Before this decision the issue was controversial. Roskill J. held in *Margarine Union GmbH* v. *Cambray Prince Steamship Co. Inc. The Wear Breeze* [1969] 1 Q.B. 219 that a plaintiff in the tort of negligence had to have the property in or a possessory title to the goods, but Lloyd J. had held in *Schiffahrt & Kohlen GmbH* v. *Chelsea Maritime Ltd. The Irene's Success* [1982] Q.B. 481 that the fact that the c.i.f. buyer bears the risk on the shipment of the goods was sufficient to give him a right of action though he had not become the owner of the goods or entitled to their possession. The decision of Lloyd J. in *The Irene's Success* was followed by Sheen J. in *The Nea Tyhi* [1982] 1 Lloyd's Rep. 606, 612. In *The Aliakmon* the House of Lords rejected the view of Lloyd J. in the *Irene's Success* and decided in favour of Roskill's view in *The Wear Breeze*.

enable him to bring an action in negligence and that only a person who had legal ownership of or a possessory title to the goods could bring such an action. In *The Aliakmon* English buyers bought a quantity of steel coils from a Japanese company. The contract provided that the goods should be shipped from South Korea c. and f. free out to the English port of Immingham. The sellers arranged for the shipment from South Korea under a clean bill of lading which showed the buyers as consignees and the sellers as notified party. The ship which carried the goods was *The Aliakmon*. Before the goods arrived, the buyers found it impossible to resell the goods, as they had intended, owing to a fall in the market. The parties then agreed that on presentation of the bill of lading to the ship the buyers should take delivery of the goods as agents of the sellers, that they should store them separately from their own goods to the order of the sellers, and that the title in the goods should be reserved to the sellers. The buyers carried out this agreement and paid the purchase price to the sellers. On discharge from the ship it was found that the goods were damaged in transit. Lord Brandon summed up the legal position thus:

In the present case, what had been originally a usual c. and f. contract had been varied to become a contract of sale ex warehouse. Under an ordinary contract of sale ex warehouse, risk and property pass at the same time. Under the varied contract, however, the risk had already passed on shipment because of the original c. and f. contract, and there was nothing in the new terms which caused it to revert to the sellers.

The buyers sued the carrier in the tort of negligence but the House of Lords held that this claim could not be sustained because, at the time of the damage, the buyers did not have property of or a possessory title to the goods[81] and the fact that they bore the risk was not sufficient to support their claim. Lord Brandon added that buyers in such a position could easily have secured to themselves the remedy which they required. His lordship was thinking of an arrangement whereby the seller assigned his contractual claim against the carrier to the buyer. The decision of the House of Lords in the *Aliakmon* case was not welcomed by those engaged in international trade; they attach great importance to the passing of the risk, as is shown by the fact that this incident is often regulated by express provisions in their contracts.

It should be noted that according to the test adopted by the House of Lords in *The Aliakmon* the buyer is entitled to sue the carrier in the tort

---

[81] See also Lord Brandon in *Candlewood Navigation Corporation Ltd.* v. *Mitsui OSK Lines Ltd. The Mineral Transporter.* [1986] A.C. 1, 4. In this case it was held that a person who has merely contractual rights relating to the goods cannot bring an action in negligence against the carrier. See A. M. Tettenborn, "Sellers, Buyers and Negligent Damage to Goods" in [1983] J.B.L. 459.

Martin Davis and Guy Lawson in "Limiting Shipowners' Liability for Economic Loss" in 16 *Aust. Bus. Law Review* (1988) 271 contend that the rule in *The Aliakmon* and *The Mineral Transporter* may not be followed in Australia.

of negligence if he has "a possessory title" to the goods.[81a] He need not be in actual possession of them, it is sufficient if he has "an immediate right to possession."[81b] He would have such right, *e.g.* if the carrier has attorned to him; *i.e.* if he has acknowledged to the buyer that he will deliver the goods according to his instructions.

Payment of the price

In a c.i.f. contract, unless the parties have otherwise agreed, the payment of the price becomes due when documents conforming to the contract are tendered.

But delay in presenting the shipping documents may entitle the buyers to rescind the contract. Thus in a case[82] concerning the sale of Canadian rapeseed by German sellers to Dutch buyers on a contract form issued by the Oils, Seeds and Fats Association (FOSFA) the contract provided: "Payment: net cash against documents and/or delivery order on arrival of the vessel at port of discharge but not later than 20 days after date of bill of lading. . . ." The bills of lading were dated December 11, 1974 but the arrival of the ship, which had run aground and had to be repaired, was delayed without fault of the sellers, who received the bills in January 1975 and presented delivery orders on the ship in February 1975. The buyers rejected them on the ground that the presentation was out of time. The Court of Appeal held that in a commodity contract provisions as to the time of shipment were prima facie conditions and that the payment clause imposed not only an obligation on the buyers to pay within the stipulated time but also an obligation on the sellers to present the documents within that time; these were correlative obligations and rights. The buyers had therefore rightly rejected the documents. If no time is stipulated for the tender of the documents or the payment of the price, the seller should tender the documents within a reasonable time.[83]

Port of shipment and port of destination

Stipulations in a c.i.f. contract as to the time and place of shipment are, as already observed, ordinarily conditions of the contract, a breach of which entitles the buyer to refuse acceptance of the documents when

---

[81a] Or if he has the property in the goods.
[81b] Slade L.J in *Transcontainer Express Ltd.* v. *Custodian Security Ltd.* [1988] 1 Lloyd's Rep. 128, 132; see p. 306, *post.* See also *Chitty on Contracts*, 26th ed., 1989, Vol. 2, para. 3189.
[82] *Toepfer* v. *Lenersan-Poortmann N.V.* [1980] 1 Lloyd's Rep. 143 (C.A.).
[83] *Biddell Bros.* v. *E. Clemens Horst Co.* [1912] A.C. 18, 22.

presented.[84] The contract may provide for shipment in a specified ship "or substitute"[85] or in a "direct ship," *i.e.* a ship which may not call on an intermediate port.[86]

Where a c.i.f. contract provides for shipment from a specified port and *prohibits the transhipment* of the goods, the buyer is normally[87] entitled to a bill of lading evidencing the continuous carriage from the port of shipment to the port of destination; in this case the bill of lading should not contain a transhipment clause; if the goods are shipped from another port or are transhipped, contrary to the contract of sale, the buyer would be entitled to reject the bill of lading.[88]

Where the contract of sale *does not prohibit transhipment* the buyer can claim a bill of lading issued by the ship carrying the goods to the port of destination because it is only on presentation of such bill that he will receive the goods. In this case indirect shipment or transhipment (under an appropriate and usual clause in the bill of lading) is admitted. If in such a case the goods are transhipped owing to an emergency, *e.g.* because the first ship cannot continue the voyage in consequence of a mishap, and the oncarrying ship does not issue a bill of lading but its master would deliver the goods on the presentation of a bill issued by the first ship, the tender of such bill is sufficient although it is not issued by the carrying ship.[89]

Where it is intended that transhipment shall be prohibited and payment is to be made under a letter of credit, the instructions to the bank should state the prohibition in very explicit terms because the UCP (1983 Revision), which apply to most bankers' credits, provide in Article 29[90];

   (a) For the purpose of this article transhipment means a transfer and reloading during the course of carriage from the port of loading or place of dispatch or taking in charge to the port of discharge or place of destination either from one conveyance or vessel to another conveyance or vessel within the same mode of transport or from one mode of transport to another mode of transport.

   (b) Unless transhipment is prohibited by the terms of the credit, banks will accept transport documents which indicate that the goods will be transhipped, provided the entire carriage is covered by one and the same transport document.

   (c) Even if transhipment is prohibited by the terms of the credit, banks will accept transport documents which:

---

[84] Donaldson J. in *Aruna Mills Ltd.* v. *Dhanrajmal Gobindram* [1968] 1 Lloyd's Rep. 304, 311; *Thos. Borthwick (Glasgow)* v. *Bunge & Co.* [1969] 1 Lloyd's Rep. 17, 28; *Alfred C. Toepfer (Hamburg)* v. *Verheijdens Veervoeder Commissiehandel Rotterdam*, The Times, April 26, 1978.

[85] *Thos. Borthwick (Glasgow)* v. *Bunge & Co.* [1969] 1 Lloyd's Rep. 17. On the substitute clause see also p. 29, *ante.*

[86] *Bergerco U.S.A.* v. *Vegoil Ltd.* [1984] 1 Lloyd's Rep. 440, 443. *State Trading Corporation of India Ltd.* v. *M. Golodetz Ltd.* [1988] 2 Lloyd's Rep. 182, 183–184.

[87] Unless the contract makes special arrangements or a trade custom or practice exists to the contrary.

[88] *Continental Imes Ltd.* v. *H. E. Dibble* [1952] 1 Lloyd's Rep. 220, 226.

[89] *Holland Colombo Trading Society Ltd.* v. *Segu Mohamed Khaja Alawdeen* [1954] 2 Lloyd's Rep. 45.

[90] On the Uniform Customs and Practice for Documentary Credits see p. 401, *post.*

(i) incorporate printed clauses stating that the carrier has the right to tranship, or

(ii) state or indicate that transhipment will or may take place, when the credit stipulates a combined transport document, or indicates carriage from a place of taking in charge to a place of final destination by different modes of transport including a carriage by sea, provided that the entire carriage is covered by one and the same transport document, or

(iii) state or indicate that the goods are in a container(s), trailer(s), "LASH" barge(s), and the like and will be carried from the place of taking in charge to the place of final destination in the same container(s), trailer(s), "LASH" barge(s), and the like under one and the same transport document.

(iv) state or indicate the place of receipt and/or of final destination as "C.F.S." (container freight station) or "C.Y." (container yard) at, or associated with, the port of loading and/or the port of destination.

Where the tendered bill of lading or delivery order does not name as the terminus of the carriage the port stipulated in the contract as destination, it may be rejected by the buyer. In an import transaction in which hides were bought c. and f. Liverpool but were shipped to Manchester and were from there transhipped to Liverpool in a dumb barge, a delivery order addressed to the master porter of the hide berth in the North Carriers Dock of Liverpool was held to be rightly rejected by the buyers.[91]

Tender of goods afloat

Normally the seller under a c.i.f. contract has the option either to arrange the actual shipment of the goods in a ship chosen by him or to purchase goods which are already afloat; in either case the seller has to tender to the buyer the appropriate bills of lading.[92]

The buyer cannot compel the seller to adopt one or the other of these alternatives; the choice is with the seller. If, however, one alternative becomes impossible, in principle the seller is obliged to use the other one to perform; if, *e.g.* the goods cannot be shipped at the contemplated port of shipment because the Government places an embargo on them the seller is bound to procure the goods afloat and to tender the buyer bills of lading relating to them.[93]

In practice, however, the situation will often be different. The c.i.f. contract may provide expressly or by necessary implication that the goods shall be "shipped" from a particular port. If the despatch from that port

[91] *Colin & Shields* v. *W. Weddell & Co. Ltd.* [1952] W.N. 420.
[92] *Vantol Ltd.* v. *Fairclough Dodd & Jones Ltd.* [1955] 1 W.L.R. 642, 646; *Pyke (Joseph) & Sons (Liverpool)* v. *Cornelius (Richard) & Co.* [1955] 2 Lloyd's Rep. 747, 751; *P. J. van der Zijden Wildhandel N.V.* v. *Tucker & Cross Ltd.* [1975] 2 Lloyd's Rep. 240, 242.
[93] *Per* Lord Denning M.R. in *Tradex Export S.A.* v. *Andre & Cie S.A.* [1976] 1 Lloyd's Rep. 416, 423.

becomes impossible owing to a frustrating event, the seller is not obliged to buy goods afloat[94] and the effect of frustration takes place.[94a] Commercial considerations may compel this interpretation of the contract. In many circumstances buying afloat would be impracticable and commercially unsuitable. Lord Denning M.R. observed in one case[95]:

> Take the usual case of a string of contracts between the shipper and the receiver. If there were an obligation to buy afloat, who is to do the buying? Is each seller to do so in order to fulfil his obligation to the buyer? If that were so there would be . . . "large numbers of buyers chasing very few goods and the price would reach unheard of levels." Alternatively, is the first seller in the string to do so? Or the last seller? No one can tell. It seems to me that if there is prohibition of export or *force majeure*, the sellers are not bound to buy afloat in order to implement their contract.

On the other hand, the c.i.f. contract may expressly provide that the goods should be shipped "afloat," with or without reference to a particular ship.[96]

Loss of goods

It follows from the peculiar character of the c.i.f. contract that, if the goods are shipped and lost during the ocean transit, the seller is still entitled to tender proper shipping documents to the buyer and to claim the purchase price. Donaldson J. said[97]:

> . . . the fact that the ship and goods have been lost after shipment or that a liability to contribute in general average or salvage has arisen is no reason for refusing to take up and pay for the documents.

It has been held[98] that these rules apply even when the seller at the time when offering the shipping documents knows that the goods are lost. It is

---

[94] *Vantol Ltd.* v. *Fairclough Dodd & Jones Ltd.* [1955] 1 W.L.R. 642, 647; *Lewis Emanual & Son Ltd.* v. *Sammut* [1959] 2 Lloyd's Rep. 62; *Tradex Export S.A.* v. *Andre & Cie S.A.* [1976] 1 Lloyd's Rep. 416; *Toepfer* v. *Schwarze* [1977] 2 Lloyd's Rep. 380, 390; *Exportelisa S.A.* v. *Rocco Giuseppe & Figli Soc. Coll.* [1978] 1 Lloyd's Rep. 433, 437; *Bremer Handelsgellschaft mbH* v. *Vanden Avenne-Izegem P.V.B.A.* [1978] 2 Lloyd's Rep. 109; *Bunge S.A.* v. *Kruse* [1980] 2 Lloyd's Rep. 142.
[94a] See p. 197, *post.*
[95] *Per* Lord Denning M.R. in *Tradex Export S.A.* v. *Andre & Cie S.A.* [1976] 1 Lloyd's Rep. 416, 423. See also *Bunge S.A.* v. *Kruse* [1980] 2 Lloyd's Rep. 142.
[96] See, *e.g. Mash & Murrell Ltd.* v. *Joseph I. Emanuel Ltd.* [1961] 1 W.L.R. 862, 863; [1962] 1 W.L.R. 16. In *Eurico SpA* v. *Philipp Brothers. The Epaphus.* [1987] 2 Lloyd's Rep. 215, 217 the buyers bought a cargo of rice afloat. See also *State Trading Corporation of India Ltd.* v. *M. Golodetz Ltd.* [1988] 2 Lloyd's Rep. 182.
[97] In *Golodetz & Co. Inc.* v. *Czarnikow-Rionda Co. Inc. The Galatia* [1979] 2 Lloyd's Rep. 452, 455, affd. by C.A. in [1980] 1 Lloyd's Rep. 453. See also MacCardie J. in *Manbre Saccharine Co.* v. *Corn Products Co.* [1919] 1 K.B. 198, 204.
[98] In *Manbre Saccharine Co.* v. *Corn Products Co.* [1919] 1 K.B. 198; *State Trading Corporation of India Ltd.* v. *M. Golodetz Ltd.* [1988] 2 Lloyd's Rep. 182, 183.

immaterial whether before the tender of the documents the property in the goods is vested in the seller or the buyer or a third person or whether the goods are unascertained or have been appropriated. "The seller must be in a position to pass the property in the goods by the bill of lading if the goods are in existence but he need not have appropriated the particular goods in the particular bill of lading to the particular buyer until the moment of the tender, nor need he have obtained any right to deal with the bill of lading until the moment of the tender."[99]

The buyer's remedy, in case of loss of the goods in transit, is normally a claim against the carrier or the insurer. The legal causes of action available for the buyer's claim against the carrier have been considered earlier,[1] but normally the buyer will claim against the insurer, in which case he has only to prove that the loss is caused by a risk covered by the policy. The insurer, when paying, will demand the assignment of the claim against the carrier to him or is subrogated to it and, if necessary, wiill pursue this claim which will only be successful if it is proved that the carrier was negligent.

Cases may arise where the goods are lost in transit owing to causes which do not entitle the buyer to make a claim against the carrier or insurer. In these cases the significance of the statement becomes evident that under a c.i.f. contract the buyer, and not the seller, bears the risk from the moment when the goods are delivered to the carrier. It means that, even in these cases, which sometimes involve hardship for the buyer, the buyer has to pay the purchase price to the seller upon tender of the duly made out shipping documents or, if he has already paid, cannot recover the price on the ground that there was a total failure of consideration.

Contracts expressed to be c.i.f. but not being true c.i.f. contracts

These strict rules are peculiar to the c.i.f. contract and do not apply to other contracts, in particular not to arrival contracts[1] and other contracts which are not true c.i.f. contracts though they may be so described by the parties. It should be noted that the terminology employed by the parties is not always a safe guide to their real intentions. In *Comptoir d'Achat* v. *Luis de Ridder*; *The Julia*[2] the sellers who sold on c.i.f. terms reserved the

---

[99] Atkin J. in *C. Groom Ltd.* v. *Barber* [1915] 1 K.B. 316, 324.
[1] See pp. 44–47, *post*.
[2] [1949] A.C. 293. See further, *Re Denbigh, Cowan & Co. and R. Atcherley & Co.* (1921) 90 L.J.K.B. 936; *The Parchim* [1918] A.C. 157, 163; *Colin & Shields* v. *W. Weddel & Co. Ltd.* [1952] W.N. 420; *John Martin of London* v. *A. E. Taylor* [1953] 2 Lloyd's Rep. 589; *Holland Colombo Trading Society Ltd.* v. *Segu Mohamed Khaja Alawdeen* [1954] 2 Lloyd's Rep. 45; *H. Glynn (Covent Garden) Ltd.* v. *Wittleder* [1959] 2 Lloyd's Rep. 409, 413; *Gardano and Giampieri* v. *Greek Petroleum George Mamidakis & Co.* [1962] 1 W.L.R. 40 ("Delivery ex Eleussinia Installation"); *Margarine Union GmbH* v. *Cambay Prince Steamship Co. Ltd.* [1969] 1 Q.B. 219 (delivery orders not on ship).

right to substitute a delivery order on their agents at the port of destination for the bill of lading; the buyers accepted the delivery order and paid the purchase price but the order could not be implemented because the ship carrying the goods had to be diverted owing to circumstances connected with the Second World War. The House of Lords held that the buyers were entitled to the return of the purchase price because an analysis of the customary course of trading of the parties showed, in the words of Lord Porter,[3] that "payment was not made for the documents but as an advance payment for a contract afterwards to be performed"; the contract was, thus, no true c.i.f. contract and the sellers' inability to deliver the goods at the port of destination resulted in a total failure of consideration for the payment of the purchase price by the buyers. The contract was, in law, an "arrival" contract.[4]

Where a contract expressed to be on c.i.f. terms provided that "any tender or delivery of the goods or of the bill of lading" should constitute a valid tender or deliver, the Judicial Committee of the Privy Council, on appeal from Ceylon (now Sri Lanka), advised that the contract was not intended to be a true c.i.f. contract since the tender of the goods was admitted as an alternative to the tender of the documents.[5]

A transport document which on transfer does not give the transferee a direct contractual right against the carrier to claim delivery of the goods does not satisfy the requirements of a genuine c.i.f. contract. Thus, a bill of lading issued by a freight forwarder[6] is not sufficient unless he is himself a carrier by sea. But according to the UCP (1983 Revision) certain specified transport documents, which do not qualify as marine bills of lading, will be accepted by a bank unless it is instructed by the credit that the seller shall tender a marine bill of lading. A contract using the term c.i.f. in connection with air transport is not a true c.i.f. contract, as Graham J. correctly held in a case[7] which provided for delivery of goods sent from Holland to purchasers in the United Kingdom "c.i.f. Gatwick."

Refusal to accept the goods

The peculiar features of the c.i.f. contract do not prevent the buyer from rejecting the goods[8] when, on delivery and inspection, he finds that

---

[3] [1949] A.C. 293, 310.

[4] See p. 56, *post*. In *The Aliakmon* (p. 000, *ante*) an original c. and f. contract was converted by agreement of the parties into an ex warehouse contract.

[5] *Holland Colombo Trading Society Ltd.* v. *Segu Mohamed Khaja Alawdeen, supra.*

[6] See p. 302, *post*.

[7] *Morton-Norwich Products Inc.* v. *Intercen Ltd.* [1976] F.S.R. 513; [1977] J.B.L. 182.

[8] On the refusal to accept the documents, see p. 41, *ante*.

they are not in accordance with the terms of the contract, *e.g.* that they are of an inferior quality or damaged owing to insufficient packing. The payment of the purchase price on delivery of the shipping documents is subject to the condition subsequent that the goods are in accordance with the terms of the contract of sale.[9] If they fall short in that respect, the condition is discharged and the position is the same as in every other contract of sale. If the agreement of the parties as to the quality of the goods was a condition of the contract of sale and not merely a warranty,[10] as is normally the case, the buyer may rescind the contract and recover the purchase price.[11]

The buyer's right to inspect and examine the goods is similar to that of a buyer under an f.o.b. contract.[12]

Variants of the c.i.f. contract

Two variants of the contract, even if called by the parties "c.i.f.," do not, as already observed,[13] satisfy the essential legal requirements of the c.i.f. contract. First, if according to the intention of the parties the actual delivery of the goods is an essential condition of performance, the contract is not a c.i.f. contract. Secondly, if on transfer of the shipping documents no direct relation is constituted between the transferee, on the one hand, and the carrier and insurer, on the other, the contract lacks the essential legal features of a c.i.f. contract.

The following variants of the c.i.f. contract are admissible; they are reconcilable with the legal nature of that type of contract:

1. *c. and f.*; *c.i.f. and c.*; *c.i.f. and e.*; *c.i.f. and c. and i.* These variants are discussed in the following paragraphs.
2. *date of arrival of goods is mere determinant for payment of price.* The parties agree sometimes on c.i.f. terms, adding "payment on arrival of goods," or "payment x days after arrival of goods."

   This clause is ambiguous and its meaning has to be ascertained from the intention of the parties.

   The parties may have intended that the arrival of the goods shall be a condition for the payment of the price. In this case the contract is not a c.i.f. contract. The English practice was formerly inclined to interpret the clause in this manner,[14] but the better view

---

[9] See p. 43, *ante.*
[10] On conditions and warranties in contracts of sale, see p. 133, *post.*
[11] See pp. 134 and 142, *post.*
[12] See p. 25, *ante*; on examination of goods, see p. 137, *post.*
[13] See p. 51, *ante.*
[14] *Dupont* v. *British South Africa Co.* (1901) 18 T.L.R. 24; *Polenghi* v. *Dried Milk Co.* (1904) 10 Com.Cas. 42.

is that this interpretation should only be adopted if this intention of the parties can clearly be gathered from the contract.[15]

Alternatively, the parties may have intended that the clause shall only refer to the time at which payment has to be made. In short, if the goods do not arrive, payment shall be made on tender of the documents at the date at which the goods would normally have arrived. In this case the clause refers only to the incident of payment but not to that of delivery and the contract is a proper c.i.f contract. The American practice is inclined to this interpretation, as appears from the Uniform Commercial Code, section 2–321(3):

> Unless otherwise agreed where the contract provides for payment on or after arrival of the goods the seller must before payment allow such preliminary inspection as is feasible; but if the goods are lost delivery of the documents and payment are due when the goods should have arrived.[16]

3. *"net landed weights," "delivered weights," "out-turn," quantity or quality.* These or similar clauses are normally intended only to relate to the determination of the price.[17] They do not affect the character of the contract as a true c.i.f. contract.

These clauses mean that after the goods are landed the seller must allow a price adjustment.[18] If the goods are lost and the buyer has already paid an estimated price on tender of the documents, he is not entitled to an adjustment unless he can prove that the shipped goods were less in quantity or quality than he paid for.

4. *a specified element of the charges to be borne by the buyer.* A clause such as "increase of export duties for buyer's account"[19] or "Cape surcharge buyer's account"[20] again refers only to the ascertainment of the charges and is entirely reconcilable with the character of the contract as a c.i.f. contract.

c. and f. (named port of destination)

C. and f. stands for "cost and freight." Under this clause the seller has to arrange the carriage of the goods to the named foreign port of

---

[15] Sassoon and Merren, *C.I.F. and F.O.B. Contracts* (*British Shipping Laws*), Vol. 5, (3rd. ed., 1984), para. 15.

[16] The term "no arrival, no sale," under which the seller is not obliged to ship, appears to be used in the American practice (Uniform Commercial Code, s.2–324) but is not customary in the English practice.

[17] Uniform Commercial Code, s.2–321(1).

[18] See *Oleificio Zucchi S.p.A.* v. *Northern Sale Ltd.* [1965] 2 Lloyd's Rep. 496, 518, where a contract c.i.f. Genoa provided for allowances if the goods (Canadian rapeseed screenings in bulk) arrived damaged. Further: *Oricon Waren-Handels GmbH* v. *Intergraan N.V.* [1967] 2 Lloyd's Rep. 83, 94 ("gross delivered weight"). In *Gill & Duffus S.A.* v. *Berger & Co. Inc.* [1984] 2 W.L.R. 95 the parties agreed that "quality final at port of discharge as per certificate of General Superintendance Co. Ltd."

[19] *Produce Brokers New Co.* (*1924*) *Ltd.* v. *British Italian Trading Co.* [1952] 1 Lloyd's Rep. 379.

[20] *Henry* (*D.I.*) *Ltd.* v. *Wilhelm G. Clasen* [1973] 1 Lloyd's Rep. 159 (C.A.).

destination at his expense (but not at his risk which ceases when he places the goods on board ship at the place of shipment), but he is not obliged to arrange marine insurance which is the concern of the buyer and, if effected, has to be paid by him.[21] In this respect the clause differs from the ordinary c.i.f. clause, but in all other respects the liabilities and duties of the parties are the same as under a c.i.f. contract.[22]

The c. and f. seller should bear in mind the provisions of section 32(3) of the Sale of Goods Act 1979.[23] If he fails to give the buyer such notice as may enable him to insure the goods,[24] the goods would, exceptionally, travel at the seller's, and not at the buyer's risk.

A c. and f. contract sometimes contains the words "insurance to be effected by buyer," or words to this effect. It has been held[25] that these words are not merely declaratory but constitute a contractual obligation of the buyer to take out the usual insurance policy, *i.e.* a policy which, if the contract had been on c.i.f. terms, would have to be taken out by the seller.

The term c. and f. is not frequently adopted by export merchants, except in the case of some countries which, for political reasons or owing to lack of foreign exchange, require their importers to insure at home rather than to buy on c.i.f. terms. The c. and f. clause leads to an artificial separation of the arrangements for insurance and freight, whereas the c.i.f. stipulation, like the f.o.b. clause, provides a natural division of responsibilities between the export merchant and the overseas buyer.

c.i.f. and c., c.i.f. and e., c.i.f. and c. and i.

Other variants of the ordinary c.i.f. stipulation are the terms *c.i.f. and c., c.i.f. and e., and c.i.f. and c. and i.* The first of these abbreviations stands for "cost, insurance, freight and commission," in the second the letter "e." means "exchange," and in the third the letters "c. and i." denote "commission and interest." These terms should only be used when it is clear that the other party is acquainted with their meaning because they are often misunderstood. If there is any danger of a

---

[21] Where the c. and f. seller has given the buyer credit, it may be advisable for him to take out a contingency insurance covering the goods in transit, see p. 608, *post.*

[22] In particular, the price is payable on tender of the correct shipping documents (exclusive, of course, of an insurance document), even though the parties are aware that the vessel carrying the goods has sunk and the goods are at the bottom of the sea: *State Trading Corporation of India Ltd.* v. *M. Golodetz Ltd.* [1988] 2 Lloyd's Rep. 182, 183.

[23] See p. 18, *ante.*

[24] And unless the parties have otherwise agreed.

[25] *Reinhart Co.* v. *Joshua Hoyle & Sons Ltd.* [1961] 1 Lloyd's Rep. 346, 354, 357, 359. See also *Golodetz & Co. Inc.* v. *Czarnikow-Rionda Co. Inc.*; *The Galatia* [1979] 2 Lloyd's Rep. 450, affd. [1980] 1 Lloyd's Rep. 453 (C.A.).

misunderstanding, it is advisable to state expressly the additional terms which it is desired to introduce into the conventional c.i.f. clause. The commission referred to in the c.i.f. and c. clause is the export merchant's commission which he charges when acting as buying agent for the overseas buyer. Export houses claim this commission as a matter of course and quote their prices "c.i.f. and c." because they wish to inform their customers abroad that the prices include their commission. The expression "exchange" is ambiguous; it is sometimes said to refer to the banker's commission or charge, while others maintain that it refers to exchange fluctuations. In the former case it denotes that the banker's charges are included in the price calculation when "c.i.f. and e." prices are quoted. In the latter case it means that the purchase price is not affected by the subsequent rise or fall of the stipulated currency of payment against the pound sterling. It is thought that the former interpretation is more common and that arrangements about currency fluctuations are usually made explicitly. The clause "c.i.f. and c. and i." is used when goods are exported to distant places where some time elapses before the bill drawn on the customer abroad is settled. When the seller negotiates the bill to his bank, the latter charges him commission and interest until payment has been received on the draft in this country, and the seller, by adding, in his contract of export sale, the letter "i." to the clause, indicates to the buyer that the quoted price includes the bank's interest and commission; this arrangement is used in the export trade with India, Pakistan, Bangladesh, Burma and the Far East; if the buyer pays the bill before maturity he is often allowed a rebate by the eastern exchange banks.

ARRIVAL, OR EX SHIP (named port of arrival)

This clause[26] has been defined by the Judicial Committee of the Privy Council as denoting that "the seller has to cause delivery to be made to the buyer from a ship which has arrived at the port of delivery and has reached a place therein which is usual for the delivery of goods of the kind in question."[27] The clause is also defined in Incoterms and in the American Uniform Commercial Code.[28] Under this clause the seller has to pay the freight or otherwise to release the carrier's lien, and the buyer

---

[26] Contracts containing this clause are sometimes referred to as "delivery contracts." This description is ambiguous and should be avoided.

[27] *Yangtsze Insurance Association* v. *Lukmanjee* [1918] A.C. 585, 589; Mustill J. in *Industria Azucarera Nacional S.A. (IANSA)* v. *Expresa Exportadora de Azucar (Cubazucar)* [1982] Com.L.R. 171; affd. by C.A. in [1983] 2 Lloyd's Rep. 171 (the case is known as *Cubazucar* v. *IANSA*).

[28] UCC, s.2–322.

is only bound to pay the purchase price if actual delivery of the goods is made to him at the stipulated port of delivery.

The difference between the arrival (or ex ship) contract and the c.i.f. contract is that in the former case the documents do not stand in the place of the goods, but that delivery has to be made *in specie, i.e.* the goods sold have to be delivered to the buyer at the named port of delivery. Consequently, if the goods are lost in transit, the buyer is not obliged to pay the purchase price upon tender of the documents, and can, in certain circumstances, claim return of the price he paid in advance. The delivery of the indorsed bill of lading from the seller to the buyer is not given with the intention of passing the property in the goods, but, unless otherwise agreed, the property will pass only when the goods are handed over to the buyer after arrival of the ship at the agreed port of destination. As the goods are not at the buyer's risk during the voyage, the seller is not under an obligation to the buyer to insure the goods. Where the seller actually insures them and they are lost or damaged in transit, the buyer cannot claim the insurance money from the insurance company because he has no insurable interest in the goods but he may have an insurable interest in the profits which he hoped to make on the goods and he may either himself or through the seller acting as his agent in this behalf insure this interest.[29] The seller must discharge all liens arising out of the carriage and, if he has not transferred the bill of lading to the buyer, must give him a delivery order on the ship.

The ex ship clause relates exclusively to the place of delivery of the goods and does not bring into play the special method of payment of the purchase price against delivery of the shipping documents. In an ex ship contract the elements of the contract of sale are not combined with those of the contracts of carriage and insurance in the manner characteristic of the c.i.f. contract.

The reference in a contract of sale to the goods being purchased "ex" or "afloat per" a particular ship is part of the description of the goods and if the goods are not shipped in that ship a condition of the contract of sale is broken.[30] Likewise the reference to the approximate date of arrival of the named ship is part of the description of the goods: "there is good commercial sense in that, inasmuch as a description of the goods being 'afloat per SS. *Morton Bay* due approximately 8th June' does give the buyers, not an absolute guarantee of arrival on June 8, but at least some indication of the date on which they may be expected in London."[31]

---

[29] *Yangtsze Insurance Association* v. *Lukmanjee* [1918] A.C. 585, 589.
[30] s.13 of the Sale of Goods Act 1979; see p. 133, *post.*
[31] *Per* McNair J. in *Macpherson Train & Co. Ltd.* v. *Howard Ross & Co. Ltd.* [1955] 1 W.L.R. 640, 642.

Ex Quay (named port of destination)

Under this term, which should not be confused with the term "free to docks" or "franco quay" combined with a named port of *shipment*,[32] the seller's duties are the same as under the arrival term but, in addition, the seller accepts responsibility for import duties and unloading charges payable at the port of destination, such as lighterage, dock dues and porterage. "Ex quay" combined with the port of destination, which is also defined in Incoterms, is rarely used in British export practice because the seller will not normally accept responsibilities arising from the landing of the goods unless he has a representative or agent at the port of destination who is acquainted with the local habits. The buyer remains, under this clause, liable for the carriage on and from the quay to the ultimate place of destination of the goods, which may be situate inland.[33]

Delivered at Frontier (named point at frontier)

This term is frequently used in the Continental export trade where no sea or air carriage is involved. It is also defined in Incoterms.[34] United Kingdom importers of Continental vegetables and fruit sometimes buy "delivered at frontier" also described as "franco frontier," of the country where the fruit originates.

The term, when used in a contract of sale, should specify not only the frontier but also the named place of delivery, *e.g.* "Delivered at Franco-Italian frontier (Mondane)." The term does not oblige the seller to obtain an insurance policy for the buyer's benefit; the parties should lay down in the contract of sale the duties which they should assume with respect to insurance.

Delivered Free Duty Paid
(named place of destination in the country of importation)

This, term sometimes expressed as "franco domicile" or "free delivery," represents the most favourable terms which the buyer can obtain and the

---

[32] On this clause, see p. 15, *ante.*

[33] In *Bunten & Lancaster (Produce)* v. *Kiril Mischeff* [1964] 1 Lloyd's Rep. 386 an import contract provided for "landed duty paid ex quay Liverpool." Also *Glass's Fruit Markets Ltd.* v. *A. Southwell & Son (Fruit)* Ltd. [1969] 2 Lloyd's Rep. 398.

[34] In the *General Conditions of Delivery of Goods* 1968 adopted by the USSR and the other members of the Council of Mutual Economic Assistance (see p. 70, *post*) "delivered at frontier" is the standard arrangement for all deliveries by rail.

most onerous arrangement for the seller. The term is rarely found in the practice of the British export trade, except where the parties have agreed on the delivery of goods of relatively small size by air or mail. The obligations arising under this clause are stated in Incoterms.

Under this term the goods have to be placed at the seller's risk and expense at the buyer's disposal at the named place of destination. The seller's obligation is to pay all charges up to the delivery of the goods at the buyer's address, including import duties and inland carriage in the buyer's country. An import licence has to be obtained by the seller, unless otherwise agreed.

In the absence of agreement to the contrary, the buyer is not obliged to pay the purchase price on presentation of the bill of lading or a consignment note, but payment can only be demanded against delivery of the goods themselves.

The French equivalent to this term is *rendu droits acquittés*.

CONTAINER TRADE TERMS

Incoterms contain three trade terms[35] which, though they can be used for all modes of transport, are particularly suitable for container transport and all forms of multimodal traffic, including roll on—roll off operations by trailers and ferries.[36]

The main object of these terms is to take account of the growing use of modern methods of transportation. These terms shift the "critical point," when the risk and possibly other legal incidents pass from the seller to the buyer, away from the ship's rail to an earlier point, *viz.* when the first carrier takes charge of the goods. When shipping goods in containers, whether as full container load (FCL) or less than full container load (LCL),[37] the exporter should give preference to one of the container terms rather than use a term appropriate to non-container shipment. The UCP provide that transport documents used in container transport are acceptable to banks under letters of credit unless the credit calls for a marine bill of lading, a post receipt or a certificate of posting.[38]

If the parties to the contract of export sale have agreed on one of the container terms, *e.g.* "free carrier," specifying that Incoterms shall apply, their mutual rights and duties are regulated with a high degree of precision.

---

[35] Container terms were first added by the 1980 Revision of Incoterms. This revision added the terms "free carrier (named point)" and "freight or carriage and insurance paid to" and amended the older version of "freight or carriage paid to."

[36] On container transport see Chapter 28, on p. 609, *post.*

[37] See p. 610, *post.*

[38] Art. 25 of the UCP. The Article states the conditions on which these documents are acceptable to the banks and gives a catalogue of these documents; see p. 413, *post.*

Free carrier (named point of delivery to carrier)

This is the most important and most frequently used container term. It is based on the same main principle as f.o.b.,[39] except that the seller fulfils his obligations when he delivers the goods into the custody of the carrier at the named point. If no precise point can be mentioned at the time of the contract of sale, the parties should refer to the place or range where the carrier should take the goods into charge. The risk of loss of or damage to the goods is transferred from the seller to the buyer at that point.

Incoterms[39a] define the rights and duties of the parties under a "free carrier" contract as follows:

A. The seller must:
1. Supply the goods in conformity with the contract of sale, together with such evidence of conformity as may be required by the contract.
2. Deliver the goods into the charge of the carrier named by the buyer on the date or within the period agreed for delivery at the named point in the manner expressly agreed or customary at such point if no specific point has been named, and if there are several points available, the seller may select the point at the place of delivery which best suits his purposes.
3. At his own risk and expense obtain any export licence or other official authorization necessary for the export of the goods.
4. Subject to the provisions of article B.5 below, pay any taxes, fees and charges levied in respect of the goods because of exportation.
5. Subject to the provisions of article B.5 below, bear all costs payable in respect of the goods until such time as they will have been delivered in accordance with the provisions of article A.2 above.
6. Subject to the provisions of article B.5 below, bear all risks of the goods until such time as they have been delivered in accordance with the provisions of article A.2 above.
7. Provide at his own expense the customary packing of the goods, unless it is the custom of the trade to dispatch the goods unpacked.
8. Pay the cost of any checking operations (such as checking quality, measuring, weighing, counting) which shall be necessary for the purpose of delivering the goods.
9. Give the buyer without delay notice by telecommunication channels of the delivery of the goods.
10. In the circumstances referred to in article B.5 below, give the buyer prompt notice by telecommunication channels of the occurrence of said circumstances.
11. At his own expense, provide the buyer, if customary, with the usual document or other evidence of the delivery of the goods in accordance with the provisions of article A.2 above.
12. Provide the buyer with the commercial invoice in proper form so as to facilitate compliance with applicable regulations and, at the buyer's request and expense, with the certificate of origin.
13. Render the buyer, at his request, risk and expense, every assistance in obtaining any document other than those mentioned in article A.12 above issued in the country of departure and/or of origin and which the buyer may require for the importation of the goods into the country of destination (and, where necessary, for their passage in transit through another country).

---

[39] See p. 16, *ante.*
[39a] The reference is to Incoterms 1980, see p. 10, *ante.*

B. The buyer must:
1. At his own expense, contract for the carriage of the goods from the named point and give the seller due notice of the name of the carrier and of the time for delivering the goods to him.
2. Bear all costs payable in respect of the goods from the time when they have been delivered in accordance with the provisions of article A.2 above, except as provided in article A.4 above.
3. Pay the price as provided in the contract.
4. Bear all risks of the goods from the time when they have been delivered in accordance with the provisions of article A.2 above.
5. Bear any additional costs incurred because the buyer fails to name the carrier, or the carrier named by him fails to take the goods into his charge, at the time agreed, and bear all risks of the goods from the date of expiry of the period stipulated for delivery, provided, however, that the goods will have been duly appropriated to the contract, that is to say, clearly set aside or otherwise identified as the contract goods.
6. Bear all costs, fees and charges incurred in obtaining the documents mentioned in article A.13 above, including the cost of consular documents, as well as the costs of certificates of origin.

Freight/carriage and insurance paid to (named point of destination)

This term is framed on the model of the c.i.f. contract but, as it is explained below, whether it is a genuine c.i.f. contract or an arrival contract,[40] depends on the documents which the seller is obliged to tender.

The seller pays the freight for the carriage of the goods to the named destination. He has also to procure transport insurance against the risk of loss of or damage to the goods during the carriage at his expense. He contracts with both the carrier and the insurer. The risk of loss of or damage to the goods is transferred from the seller to the buyer when the goods have been delivered into the custody of the first carrier. Any increase in the freight and insurance charges between the conclusion of the contract of sale and the delivery of the goods to the first carrier has to be borne by the seller.

The rights and duties of the seller and buyer under this clause are defined in Incoterms.

The contract is a genuine c.i.f. contract if, according to the terms of the contract of sale, the seller is obliged to tender a genuine marine bill of lading or a delivery order on the ship and, on the transfer of these documents and the insurance document,[41] the buyer or his transferee is

---

[40] See p. 51 *ante*.
[41] In Incoterms 1980 there is a distinction in the definition of the insurance instrument between the terms c.i.f. and freight or carriage and insurance paid. In the former term, which is the older, a policy of insurance is required but in the latter, which is the newer, an insurance policy or other evidence of insurance cover is declared to be sufficient, provided that the transport insurance gives the buyer or other person having an insurable interest a direct claim against the insurer. See p. 39, *ante*.

placed into direct contractual relationship with the carrier and the insurer. In all other cases the contract of sale is not a true c.i.f. contract; in practice the latter arrangement is likely to occur more frequently than the former.

Freight/carriage paid to (named point of destination)

This term corresponds to the c. and f. contract.[42] In other words, the seller is not obliged to procure insurance cover for the transport. In other respects the observations made on the term "freight/carriage and insurance paid to" apply.

Here again, the mutual rights and duties of the parties to the contract of sale are defined in Incoterms.

---

[42] See p. 55, *ante.*

CHAPTER 3

STANDARDISATION OF TERMS IN INTERNATIONAL SALES

WHEN discussing in the previous chapter the trade terms used in the export trade, it was stated that these terms were not always interpreted in the same manner in all countries and that this may lead to misunderstandings among those engaged in international trade.[1] To avoid them, frequent attempts have been made to standardise the terms on which export and import business is transacted.

These attempts can be classified into three groups[2]: *Uniform rules of general character* have been issued which are intended to apply to all types of international trade transactions. Sometimes the uniform terms have, or are intended to have, the force of law; sometimes they are intended to apply only if adopted by the parties to the contract. Further, in some types of business, mainly in the trade in commodities or in capital goods, *standard contract forms applying to specified international transactions* are in existence which normally apply only if used by the parties to the contract. Thirdly, exporters and importers frequently embody *general terms of business* into their contracts. They are intended to apply to all transactions to which these persons become a party unless they are expressly excluded. This chapter further contains references to the attempts to simplify export documentation and to introduce electronic data interchange (EDI) into international trade transactions.

UNIFORM RULES OF GENERAL CHARACTER

The most important sets of uniform rules applying to international trade transactions are formulated by international organisations which have as their object, or as one of their objects, the harmonisation of international trade law. These organisations are intergovernmental,[3] regional,[4] or non-governmental.[5] They prepare international conventions, formulate rules for adoption by the parties in their contract, or engage in other harmonising activities. They are known as the *formulating agencies*.[6] The

---

[1] See p. 9, *ante.*

[2] See Mario Matteuci, "The Unification of Commercial Law," in [1960] J.B.L. 137.

[3] *e.g.* UNCITRAL and Unidroit.

[4] *e.g.* the EC and CMEA.

[5] *e.g.* The International Chamber of Commerce.

[6] See Clive M. Schmitthoff, *Commercial Law in a Changing Economic Climate*, (2nd ed., 1981), 24 *Essays*, 219. A full list of formulating agencies and their activities is contained in the Report of the Secretary-General of UNCITRAL on *Co-ordination of Work—Register of Organisations* of March 2, 1988 (A/CN.9/303).

most important of them and the measures promoted by them are noted in the following.

Many of the measures sponsored by the formulating agencies are accepted and applied by the international business community. The activities of these organisations are of accelerating importance, in view of the progressive global integration of international trade. But the documents which the formulating agencies have produced are numerous and sometimes not easily accessible. Many of them are conveniently collected in Professor Cheng's "Basic Documents on International Trade Law."[7]

United Nations Commission on International Trade Law

In 1966 the United Nations decided to take an interest in the progressive harmonisation of the law of international trade. They constituted the United Nations Commission on International Trade Law (UNCITRAL) which became operative on January 1, 1968.[8] The Commission consists of representatives of 36 States; they are arranged in the following five groups:

African States (9 States);
Asian States (7 States);
Eastern European States (5 States);
Latin American States (6 States);
Western European and other States (9 States).

The objects of UNCITRAL are "to further the progressive harmonisation and unification of the law of international trade."[8a] The seat of UNCITRAL is in Vienna.

UNCITRAL has published a *Handbook*[9] and is also issuing regularly a *Yearbook*.[10] The Handbook is a document of considerable interest. It gives a brief summary of the constitution of UNCITRAL, its working methods and activities, and surveys the various topics on the programme of harmonisation by the Commission. It contains in the Annexes the text of all conventions and other measures prepared and finalised by the

---

[7] Chia-Jui Cheng, Basic Documents on International Trade Law, 2nd ed., 1990.
[8] C. M. Schmitthoff, "The Unification of the Law of International Trade," in [1968] J.B.L. 105 *Essays*, 206.
[8a] There exists also the *International Trade Centre UNCTAD/GATT (ITC)*. It was founded in 1964 as a joint subsidiary organ of GATT and the United Nations, acting through UNCTAD. Its seat is in Geneva. Its principal functions is the promotion of international trade, particularly by providing assistance to the developing countries. As the ITC is not engaged in the harmonisation and standardisation of international trade law, its constitution and activities are not considered here.
[9] Published in 1986. United Nations Sales No. E.86.V.8. Obtainable from the Sales Section of the United Nations in New York or Geneva or the distributors of United Nations Publications throughout the world.
[10] Obtainable from the same suppliers as stated in the previous footnote.

Commission. The most important of these texts are listed in the following.[11]

The *Convention on the Limitation Period in the International Sale of Goods*, recommended by the United Nations in 1974. This Convention was amended for the purpose of aligning it with the Vienna Convention on Contracts for the International Sale of Goods (1980) by a Protocol to the Convention.[12]

The *UNCITRAL Arbitration Rules*, recommended by the United Nations in 1976. They provide a framework for international commercial arbitration and are applied where parties have agreed in writing that disputes shall be settled under them.[13] They are widely used by individual parties and also as a model for the arbitration rules of arbitral institutions. In 1980 the *UNCITRAL Conciliation Rules* were recommended by the United Nations.[14] A *Model Law on International Commercial Arbitration* was recommended by the United Nations in December 1985.[15] It has been used as a model for national legislation by Canada and Cyprus.[16]

The *Convention on the Carriage of Goods by Sea*, adopted by a United Nations conference at Hamburg in March 1978. The so-called Hamburg Rules adopted by that Convention were prepared by UNCITRAL and UNCTAD jointly. They are intended to replace the Hague Rules and the Hague-Visby Rules relating to Bills of Lading.[17] The Hamburg Rules have not yet been given effect in the United Kingdom.

A *Convention on Contracts for the International Sale of Goods* was adopted by the United Nations in April 1980 at Vienna.[18] It is intended to supersede the two Hague Conventions on the Uniform Laws on International Sales of 1964.[19] The Vienna Convention came into operation on January 1, 1988, after the required number of ratifications and accessions was received. It has not been given effect in the United Kingdom yet.[19a]

A *Convention on International Bills of Exchange and International Promissory Notes* was adopted by the United Nations on December 9, 1988.

UNCITRAL is engaged in many other projects aimed at the harmonisation of international trade law. For example, it has issued a *Legal Guide on Drawing up International Contracts for the Construction of Industrial Works* (1988).[20] and a *Legal Guide on Electronic Funds*

---

[11] Position: October 1, 1988.
[12] See p. 254, *post.*
[13] See p. 673, *post.*
[14] See p. 674, *post.*
[15] See p. 675, *post.*
[16] Position: October 1, 1988.
[17] See p. 563, *post.*
[18] See p. 249, *post.*
[19] See p. 241, *post.*
[19a] But in June 1989 the DTI issued a consultative document relating to it.
[20] See pp. 75 and 732 *post.*

Transfers (1987) and is considering issues arising from countertrade and automatic data processing. It is further working on a Convention for the acceptance of a universal unit of accounts for international conventions—probably the Special Drawing Right (SDR) of the International Monetary Fund—, and is studying the nature and effect of contract clauses stipulating liquidated damages and penalties.

Mention should also be made of the *Convention on International Multimodal Transport of Goods*. This Convention was promoted by UNCTAD and adopted by the United Nations in Geneva in May 1980.[21] It has made little practical impact although an international regulation of multimodal container transport would be desirable.

International Chamber of Commerce publications

The International Chamber of Commerce, which has consultative status under the Charter of the United Nations, has contributed valuable publications which ease the flow of international trade and are from time to time referred to in this work. It is convenient to list the most important of them here.[22]

Incoterms, which have the sub-title *International Rules for the Interpretation of Trade Terms*, were published by the International Chamber of Commerce and have been amended from time to time[23]; the edition in use at present is the 1980 edition but the 1990 Edition is in an advanced state of preparation and is likely to come into operation on April 1, 1990. Exporters and importers who wish to use them for an individual contract should specify that the contract is governed by the provisions of "*Incoterms.*" Sometimes exporters, notably on the continent of Europe, provide in their general terms of business that all their contracts shall be governed by *Incoterms*, unless otherwise agreed in a particular instance.[24] In some countries *Incoterms* have been given statutory effect, *viz.* in Spain[25] and in Iraq.[26] In the U.S.A., where formerly other trade terms

---

[21] See p. 613. *post.*

[22] A complete list of ICC publications can be obtained from the National Committees of the ICC or its headquarters in Paris (38 Cours Albert 1er, 75008 Paris, tel. 261.85.97, Telex 6507701CCHQ).

[23] Brochure No. 350. See p. 9, n. 5. *ante. Incoterms* can be obtained from ICC United Kingdom, Centre Point, 103 New Oxford Street, London WC1A 1QB, Telephone 01–240 5558, Telex 21332. ("ICC United Kingdom" is the name of the British National Committee of the ICC. There exists also a *Guide to Incoterms* (ICC Brochure No. 354).

[24] See, *e.g., The Albazero* [1975] 3 W.L.R. 491, 498.

[25] In Spain this applies to contractual terms in import and export transactions; Royal Decree of September 14, 1979, preceded by the Ministrial Ordinance of September 25, 1968 and the decision of November 30, 1968. The reference in the Royal Decree is to Incoterms 1953; see C. M. Schmitthoff, *International Trade Usages*, 1987, p. 28, para. 39 (ICC Publication No. 440/4).

[26] In Iraq this applies to all foreign trade transactions; see ICC Information, December 1971, p. 3.

were used,[27] interested trade circles are now recommended to use *Incoterms*. In France and West Germany *Incoterms* are regarded by some authorities as the international custom of the trade.

The Uniform Customs and Practice for Documentary Credits (1983 Revision)[28] are widely adopted throughout the world; the list of countries in which the UCP have either been adopted by banking associations or by individual banks includes 175 countries,[29] amongst them the United Kingdom, the United States of America and the Soviet Union. The *Uniform Rules for Collections* (1978)[30] are also used widely.

The Problem of Clean Bills of Lading (1974) which contains a list of superimposed clauses declaring a defective condition of the goods or packaging put by carriers on bills of lading for reference and optional use.[31]

The ICC Rules of Conciliation and Arbitration, in force as from January 1, 1988.[32] The ICC Court of Arbitration is the most popular arbitral tribunal for the settlement of disputes arising from international commercial contracts but it has jurisdiction only if the parties have agreed on ICC arbitration. Arbitration may be preceded by optional conciliation.

Commercial Agency, A Guide for the Drawing Up of Contracts between Parties residing in Different Countries (1983).[33] This publication deals with the problems which have to be considered when agency agreements in the strict legal sense are drawn up.

Uniform Rules for a Combined Transport Document (1975).[34] This publication proposes the adoption of a single combined transport document for the transportation of goods in containers by means of two or more modes (multimodal) of transport. The issue of such a document would avoid the need to issue a series of separate transport documents for each stage of the transport.[35]

---

[27] The Revised American Foreign Trade Definitions 1941, adopted by a joint committee representing the Chamber of Commerce of the United States of America, the National Council of American Importers, Inc., and the National Foreign Trade Council, Inc.

[28] See p. 401, *post*. There exist also two further documents. *viz. Documentary Credits, Standard Documentary Credit Forms Guidance Notes—Recommendations* (ICC Publication No. 416) and *Documentary Credits, Standard Documentary Credit Application. Guidance Notes for Credit Applicants* (ICC Publication No. 416A).

[29] The list of countries is obtainable from the National Committees of the ICC or its headquarters in Paris.

[30] Brochure No. 322 see p. 396 *post*.

[31] Brochure No. 283 On clean bills of lading, see pp. 542–543, and 571, *post*.

[32] ICC Publication No. 447. This publication supersedes No. 291. See p. 676, *post*.

[33] Brochure No. 410. See p. 279, *post*.

[34] Brochure No. 298 (Reprinted March 1985).

[35] The ICC document is discussed on p. 615, *post*. On the UN Convention on International Multimodal Transport of Goods, see p. 613, *post*. On container transport see p. 609, *post*.

Extortion and Bribery in Business Transactions (1977).[36] This brochure contains, first, recommendations to governments, to be adopted nationally and internationally to promote the elimination of bribery and extortion in business transactions, and secondly, rules of conduct for voluntary application by enterprises.[37]

Uniform Rules for Contract Guarantees (1978)[38] deal with the issue of performance and bank guarantees supporting obligations arising in international contracts. A new edition of this document is expected to be issued in 1990.

Adaptation of Contracts. Rules. Standard Clauses. Application to Standing Committee (1978).[39] This document deals with the adaptation of long-term contracts to changing economic and political circumstances. It enables parties who wish to continue their contractual relations in spite of changed conditions, to have recourse to a third party intervener. He may make recommendations on the adaptation of the terms of the contract or give a definite ruling, according to the agreement of the parties to the contract. If need be, the third party intervener can be appointed by a Standing Committee of the ICC constituted to provide this service.

Force Majeure and Hardship (1985).[40] This brochure offers suggestions for the adoption of force majeure and hardship clauses, particularly in long term contracts or contracts involving complex projects, such as turn-key contracts or public works. The arrangements suggested in this document are intended to enable the parties to provide in their contract for any unforeseen eventuality.

UNCID Uniform Rules of Conduct for Interchange of Trade Data by Teletransmission (1988)[41] This code of conduct is discussed later in this chapter.[42]

Uniform Laws on International Sales

In 1964 a diplomatic conference at the Hague approved two Uniform Laws, one on the International Sale of Goods and the other on the Formation of Contracts for the International Sale of Goods. These Uniform Laws have been introduced into the law of the United Kingdom by the *Uniform Laws on International Sales Act 1967*. This Act was put into operation on August 18, 1972 and is considered in a later chapter.[43]

---

[36] Brochure No. 315.
[37] There exists also a *Guide to the Prevention of International Trade Fraud* (ICC Publication No. 420).
[38] Brochure No. 325. See p. 447, *post*.
[39] Brochure No. 326. See p. 750, *post*.
[40] Brochure No. 421. See pp. 199 and 751, *post*.
[41] Brochure No. 452.
[42] See p. 78, *post*.
[43] See Chapter 14, on p. 241, *post*.

The Hague Conventions have also been introduced into the law of Belgium, W. Germany, Israel, the Netherlands, Gambia and San Marino.[44]

The two Uniform Laws approved at The Hague will be superseded by the Vienna Convention on Contracts for the International Sale of Goods (1980), prepared by UNCITRAL, which came into effect on January 1, 1988. The countries which have ratified the Vienna Convention include the United States and China.[45] It is to be hoped that this attempt to achieve a unification of the law of international sale on a global basis will be more successful than the Hague Conventions which, however, prepared the ground for the Vienna Convention. The Vienna Convention is assuming the character of the central Convention to which other conventions connected with the supply of goods in international trade are aligned.[46]

American Uniform Commercial Code

The characteristic feature of the American unification of commercial law is that it was not carried out by the federal legislation but that it came about by the adoption of a uniform law, the Uniform Commercial Code, by all the 50 States of the Union with the exception of the State of Louisiana. Work on the Uniform Commercial Code commenced in 1942 as a joint project of the American Law Institute and the National Conference of Commissioners on Uniform State Laws. In 1951 the first official text of the Code was adopted by the two sponsoring organisations.[47] The present Official Text dates from 1987.[48] The Uniform Commercial Code has been described as one of the outstanding developments of commercial law in the twentieth century.[49] It has been highly successful. It owes its success to its inherent quality. "It has three outstanding merits: it is modern in spirit, pragmatic in treatment, and comprehensive."[50]

The Code deals, *inter alia*, with sales (including the terms of export sales discussed in the preceding chapter),[51] commercial paper (bills and

---

[44] Italy had originally acceded to the Hague Uniform Laws but discontinued its adherence when it acceded to the Vienna Convention of 1980.
[45] See p. 249, *post*.
[46] *E.g.* the Hague Convention on the Law applicable to Contracts for the International Sale of Goods of 1985 (see p. 207), *post*, and the Conventions on International Factoring and International Financial Leasing of 1988 (see pp. 458 and 463, *post*).
[47] *Cf.* Clive M. Schmitthoff, "American and European Commercial Law," in *Journal of Legislation; University of Notre Dame Law School*, Vol. 6, 1979, 44; *Essays,* 108.
[48] *Selected Commercial Statutes*, 1989 edition, West Publishing Co.
[49] Clive M. Schmitthoff, *Commercial Law in a Changing Economic Climate* (2nd ed., 1981), p. 13.
[50] *Ibid.* p. 15.
[51] Article 2 of the Uniform Commercial Code.

notes),[52] collections and documentary letters of credit,[53] bills of lading and other documents of title.[54] The 1987 Revision includes a new article on leasing and replaces the article on "bulk transfer" of a person's business assets by a new regulation.

General conditions of the Council for Mutual Economic Assistance

The member countries of the Council for Mutual Economic Assistance,[55] the regional economic organisation of Eastern European and other socialist countries, have adopted a series of General Conditions. They have the nature of intergovernmental Conventions containing recommendations which are given effect in the Member States of CMEA.[56] The General Conditions are widely used by the foreign trade corporations.[57] of the Eastern European countries and normally govern the individual export transactions between those corporations.

The most important of these General Conditions are:

General Conditions of Delivery of Goods 1968–1975 (in the 1979 version as amended in 1989)[58]
General Conditions for Assembly and Rendering of other Technical Services in Connection with Deliveries of Machines and Equipment between the Organisations of the CMEA member countries (1973).

---

[52] Article 3.

[53] Articles 4 and 5.

[54] Article 7.

[55] The member countries of the Council for Mutual Economic Aid are at present Bulgaria, Cuba, Czechoslovakia, the German Democratic Republic, Hungary, Mongolia, Poland, Romania, The USSR and Vietnam. CMEA is sometimes referred to as Comecon.

[56] Thomas W. Hoya, *East-West Trade*. Comecon Law. American-Soviet Trade. 1984, Oceana Publications Inc.; Trajan Ionasco and Ian Nestor, "The Limits of Party Autonomy" in The Sources of the Law of International Trade (ed. Schmitthoff), London, 1964, p. 177. Jerzy Rajski, "L'Unification du droit des pays membres du Conseil d'Assistance Economique Mutuelle* 1977–1983" in *Uniform Law Review*, 1984, Vol. II, p. 56; Dietrich Maskow, "Main Aspects of the General Conditions of Delivery of the Council for Mutual Economic Assistance," in *Law and Legislation in the German Democratic Republic*, 1–2/84, p. 5.

[57] On foreign trade corporations in the socialist countries see in detail Thomas W. Hoya in the work referred to in the preceding footnote; also Viktor Knapp, "The Function, Organisation and Activities of Foreign Trade Corporations in the European Socialist Countries" in *The Sources of the Law of International Trade*, referred to in the preceding footnote.

[58] See Thomas W. Hoya, *op. cit.*; also Iván Szász, "CMEA Uniform Law on International Sale of Goods," (Akadémiai Kiadó, Budapest, 1985) (this work contains an English translation of the General Conditions of Delivery of Goods); Jerzy Rajski, "Le rapprochement et l'unification du droit dans le cadre du Conseil d'Aide Economique Mutuelle" (1976), *Revue internationale de droit comparé*, Paris, 30; Jyula Eörsi, "The 1968 General Conditions of Delivery" in [1970] J.B.L. 99. The CMEA Conditions 1968 were preceded by those of 1958. The CMEA Conditions in the 1979 version can be obtained from the CMEA Secretariat in Moscow. The 1989 amendment provides that the unilateral act of a State authority shall not act as a frustrating event: Fritz Enderlein in *Rabels Zeitschrift*, vol. 53, 1989, 383.

General Conditions for Customer Service for Machines, Equipment and other Products delivered between the Organisations of the CMEA member countries (1973).
General Conditions of Specialisation and Cooperation in Production between Organisations of member countries of CMEA (1979).

The member countries of CMEA have also adopted a Convention on the Settlement by Arbitration of Civil Law Disputes between Economic Organisations of the Member States; this Convention was signed in Moscow on May 26, 1972 and came into force on August 13, 1973. Uniform Rules for Arbitration Tribunals at the Chambers of Commerce of the CMEA countries were recommended by CMEA on February 28, 1974 and adopted by these chambers of commerce with certain variations; modifcations of these Rules were recommended by CMEA on January 21, 1987.

Further, upon the recommendation of CMEA in 1966, the Member States of CMEA and Yugoslavia have adopted General Principles concerning Supply of Spare Parts in their Mutual Trade. In 1978 Finland and the Council of CMEA approved General Conditions for the Delivery of Goods; these General Conditions were recommended for acceptance in individual contracts between foreign trade organisations of the Member States of CMEA and enterprises in Finland.[59]

Codifications of international trade law in the socialist countries

Czechoslovak International Trade Code

This enactment which came into force on April 1, 1964, has been described as "a municipal regulation which forms part of the Czechoslovak legal order but at the same time governs exclusively international trade relations between parties to international commercial contracts."[60]

The Code is applied by courts or arbitration tribunals in or outside Czechoslovakia, if

1. the issue is a matter of international trade, as defined by the Code, and
2. subject to a few exceptions, the parties are resident in different countries, and
3. the contract in question is governed by Czechoslovak law.[61]

East German Law on International Economic Contracts

The German Democratic Republic adopted this Law on February 5, 1976.[62] The Law regulates international contracts in general and deals,

---

[59] Reino Erma, "General Conditions for the Delivery of Goods between Finland and the CMEA" in [1981] J.B.L. 161.
[60] Translated into English, with an Introduction and commentary by Dr. Ludvík. Kopáč See also Pavel Kalenský, "The New Czechoslovak International Trade Code" in [1966] J.B.L. 179, 181.
[61] I owe this wording of the application of the Czechoslovak Code to Dr. Boris Illner, Prague.
[62] *Gesetz über internationale Wirtschaftsverträge* (GIW), in *Gesetzblatt*, 1976, Pt. I, 61. A German-English text of this Law was published in 1979 by the Staatsverlag of the Deutsche Demokratische Republik in Berlin.

more specifically, with contracts of sale, services, construction, agency, forwarding, warehousing, credit, insurance, leasing, licensing, guarantees and securities. The Law is intended to apply if the parties adopt the law of the German Democratic Republic or if that law applies according to the rules of the conflict of laws.[63] But international arrangements are not affected; consequently in dealings between East German State enterprises and those of the other Member States of CMEA the General Conditions of CMEA,[64] and not the provisions of the East German international trade code, apply.

Yugoslav General Usages of Trade 1954 [65]

These are the uniform practices of international trade as applied in Yugoslavia, subject to the provisions of the Yugoslav Code of Obligations of 1978: The General Usages are a well-drafted[66] code of the law of international trade; they are founded on the universally accepted rules of the export trade.

The General Usages apply to foreign trade transactions between a Yugoslav and another party if the proper law of the contract is that of Yugoslavia or the parties have agreed on arbitration by the Yugoslav Foreign Trade Court of Arbitration unless the parties have excluded the application of the General Usages in whole or in part.

Yugoslavia enacted also a Foreign Investment Law, which came into operation on January 1, 1989.[66a]

STANDARD CONTRACT FORMS APPLYING TO SPECIFIED INTERNATIONAL TRANSACTIONS

The international trade in many commodities and capital goods is conducted on the basis of standard contract forms. Some of them are issued by international trade associations of which those of the United Kingdom have worldwide reputation. Others are drafted by the United Nations Economic Commission for Europe. Others again are used in construction contracts for works and installations abroad.

---

[63] See p. 204, *post.*
[64] See p. 70, *ante.*
[65] Obtainable in English from the Yugoslav Chamber of Economy, P.O. Box 47, Belgrade, Yugoslavia.
[66] They are the work of Professor A. Goldštajn, one of the outstanding modern authorities on the law of international trade.
[66a] Obtainable in English from Publishing House Jugoslovenski pregled, Moše Pilade 8/1, Beograd, Yugoslavia.

All types of standard contracts have in common that they apply only if the parties to a contract of sale adopt them and that they normally can be varied by agreement of the contracting parties.

Standard conditions issued by trade associations

The most important standard commodity contracts are the various forms provided by the following trade associations.[67]

the British Wool Confederation;
the Cocoa Association of London Ltd.;
the Federation of Oil, Seed and Fats Associations (FOSFA);
the Grain and Feed Trade Association (GAFTA);
the International Wool Textile Organisation;
the Liverpool Cotton Association;
the General Produce Brokers' Association of London;
the London Jute Association;
the London Metal Exchange;
the London Rubber Trade Association;
the Refined Sugar Association;
the Timber Trade Federation of the United Kingdom.

Many of these, and some other trade associations, are members of the British Federation of Commodity Associations.

Model contracts sponsored by the United Nations Economic Commission for Europe

Various sets of general conditions of sale and standard forms of contract have been drafted by working parties convened by the United Nations Economic Commission for Europe.[68]

Notable amongst them are:
Form   188—For the Supply of Plant and Machinery for Export;
  ,,   574—For the Supply of Plant and Machinery for Export;
  ,,   188A—For the Supply and Erection of Plant and Machinery for Import and Export;
  ,,   574A—For the Supply and Erection of Machinery for Import and Export;

---

[67] A list of these markets and trade associations is provided in the Arbitration (Commodity Contracts) Order 1979 (S.I. 1979 No. 754).
[68] The UN ECE forms can be obtained from HMSO. On the preparation and aim of these contract conditions and forms: see Peter Benjamin, "The General Conditions of Sale and Standard Forms of Contract drawn up by the United Nations Economic Commission for Europe," in [1961] J.B.L. 113; André Tunc, "L'élaboration des conditions générales de vente sous les auspices de la Commission Economique pour l'Europe," in (1960) 12 *Revue Internationale de Droit Comparé* 108; Clive M. Schmitthoff, "The Unification or Harmonisation of Law by Means of Standard Contracts and General Conditions" (1968) 17 I.C.L.Q. 551; *Essays* 188; Henry Cornil, "The ECE General Conditions of Sale" in 3 *Journ. of World Trade Law* (1969) 390.

,,　　188B—Listing Additional Clauses for Supervision of Erection of Engineering Plant and
　　　　　Machinery abroad;
,,　　574B—Listing Additional Clauses for Supervision of Erection of Engineering Plant and
　　　　　Machinery abroad;
,,　　188D—Listing Additional Clauses for Supervision of Erection of Engineering Plant and
　　　　　Machinery abroad;
,,　　730　—For the Export of Durable Consumer Goods and Engineering Articles.

Form 188 and its variations are used between enterprises of free market economy, and Form 574 and its variations are for use between enterprises of socialist economy and for the East-West trade, while Form 730 can be used for international trade between any enterprises.[69]

In addition to these sets of model contracts, the Economic Commission for Europe has sponsored model contracts for the sale of cereals, citrus fruit, sawn softwood, solid fuels, potatoes and steel products.

Further, the Economic Commission for Europe has published a series of interconnected Guides dealing with major international contracts for the construction of works and installations.[70]

Model contract forms used in construction contracts

The most frequently used model contract forms dealing with the erection of works and installations abroad are:

Conditions of Contract for Works of Civil Engineering Construction (4th ed., March 1987). These Conditions are sponsored by the *Fédération Internationale des Ingénieurs-Conseils (FIDIC)*.[71]
General Conditions of Contract.
These Conditions are recommended by the Institution of Mechanical Engineers, the Institution of Electrical Engineers and the Association of Consulting Engineers.[72]

Form B1—Export contracts with delivery f.o.b.,c.i.f. or f.o.r. (5th ed., 1981);
Form B2—Export contracts, delivery f.o.b.,c.i.f. or f.o.r., with supervision of erection (5th ed., 1981);

---

[69] On the difference between these forms, see [1965] J.B.L. 100 and [1966] J.B.L. 71. Of further importance is the "Preface to the General Conditions of Sale, Standard Forms of Contract and Commercial Arbitration Instruments prepared under the auspices of the United Nations Economic Commission of Europe."
[70] Guide for use in drawing up contracts relating to the international transfer of know-how in the engineering industry (Trade/222/Rev. 1); Guide on drawing up contracts for large industrial works (ECE/Trade/117); Guide on drawing up international contracts on industrial co-operation (ECE/Trade/124); Guide for drawing up international contracts between parties associated for the purpose of executing a specific project (ECE/Trade/131); Guide for drawing up international contracts on consulting engineering, including some related aspects of technical assistance (ECE/Trade/145); Guide on drawing up international contracts for services relating to maintenance, repair and operation of industrial and other works (E.87.II.E.2); Guide on new forms of industrial co-operation (1988); Juridical Guide for the creation of East-West joint ventures on the territory of socialist countries (1988).
[71] Obtainable from The Federation of Civil Engineering Contractors, 6, Portugal Street, London W.C.2. There exist also the FIDIC Conditions (International) for Electrical and Mechancial Works (including Erection on Site), 3rd ed., 1987 (FIDIC E&M).
[72] Obtainable from the Institution of Electrical Engineers, Savoy Place, London WC2R OBL.

Guidelines for Procurement under IBRD Loans and IDA Credits, May 1985.[73]
*General Conditions for Public Works and Supply Contracts financed by the European
Development Fund,* applied to contracts financed in the Associated Overseas
Countries and Territories, February 14, 1974.[74]

The model contract forms sponsored by the United Nations Economic
Commission for Europe, which are listed in the preceding paragraph, are
likewise used in international construction work. UNCITRAL has also
published a *Legal Guide on Drawing up International Contracts for
Construction of Industrial Works.* (1988).

The main model forms used in construction contracts will be considered
in a later chapter of this work.[75]

GENERAL TERMS OF BUSINESS ADOPTED BY INDIVIDUAL EXPORTERS

The importance, for international sales, of well-drafted general terms of
business can hardly be exaggerated. They are particularly important
where neither uniform conditions of export sales nor standard contract
forms are used. Litigation can often be avoided when the seller is able to
refer the buyer to a clause in his printed terms of business which was
embodied in the quotation or acceptance, and the fact that these terms
apply to all transactions concluded by the seller adds persuasive force to
his argument.

Some important clauses

The most important clauses which the exporter should embody in his
general terms of business are:

1. *General clause.* Every contract of sale is subject to the seller's conditions of sale;
2. *Retention of title clause.* Until the seller receives the purchase price fully in cash,
   (a) the seller retains the legal property in the goods and is given the
       irrevocable right to enter the premises of the buyer at any time and without
       notice in order to retake possession of the goods; and
   (b) the buyer may resell the goods only as an agent of the seller and only in the
       ordinary course of business to a bona fide repurchaser, and, if he does so,
       shall receive the proceeds of the resale as an agent of and trustee for the
       seller and shall place the said proceeds in a separate account in the name of
       the seller.[76];

---

[73] There exist also Guidelines for the Use of Consultants by World Bank Borrowers and by
the World Bank as Executing Agency (August 1981). Those documents are obtainable from
the World Bank Headquarters, 1818 H Street, N.W., Washington D.C., 20433, U.S.A., or
the European Office of the World Bank at 66, avenue d'Jéna, 75116 Paris, France.
[74] Obtainable from the EC Commission, 200 rue de la loi, Brussels, Belgium.
[75] See Chapter 34, on p. 737, *post.*
[76] For a discussion of the various types of reservation of title clauses see p. 121, *post.* The
clause suggested in the text is the simple clause with an extension. It is thought that this
form of clause does not require registration as a charge by virtue of section 396 of the
Companies Act 1985. If it is intended to use further extensions of the reservation of title
clause, it is advisable to register the clause as a charge.
  The clause in the text is founded on *Aluminium Industrie Vaassen B.V.* v. *Romalpa
Aluminium Ltd.* [1976] 1 W.L.R. 676 and *Clough Mill Ltd.* v. *Martin* [1985] 1 W.L.R. 111.

3. *Price escalation clause.* Unless firm prices and charges are agreed upon, the seller shall be entitled to increase the agreed prices and charges in the same proportion in which the prices or charges of the goods or their components including costs of labour to be paid or borne by the seller have been increased between the date of the quotation and the date of the delivery.[77]

4. *Interest.* All moneys due under or in connection with this contract, including moneys due by way of damages, shall bear interest until the date of payment at a [specified] rate above a [specified] United Kingdom clearing bank's base lending rate.[78]

5. *Force majeure clause.* (An illustration of this clause is given later on)[79];

6. *Choice of law clause.* The validity, construction and performance of this contract shall be governed by the law of England.

7. *Arbitration.* All disputes arising in connection with the present contract shall be finally settled under the Rules of Conciliation and Arbitration of the International Chamber of Commerce by one or more arbitrators appointed in accordance with the said Rules.[80] The arbitration shall be held in London and shall be in the English language.

These essential clauses are indicated here only in general terms. The particular requirements of the exporter's business may demand a fuller treatment or the insertion of additional clauses in the general terms of business. The exporter is well advised to ask his solicitor to frame general terms of business appropriate to his activities and to revise them from time to time.

Standard terms in home transactions

The Unfair Contract Terms Act 1977 provides[81] that where one of the contracting parties deals on the other's written standard terms of business, the party who inserted the standard terms cannot rely on them in order to exclude or restrict his liability, except if the standard term in question satisfies the *test of reasonableness*. The same rules apply if the party who inserted the standard terms wishes to rely on them in order to avoid performance of the contract.

---

[77] Several variants of the price escalation or "rise and fall" clause are in use. Sometimes a "rise" clause is inserted into a c.i.f. contract; the clause provides for an increase of the purchase price if the freight and insurance charges are raised. See also Lars Gorton, "Escalation and Currency Clauses in Shipping Contracts" 12, *Journal of World Trade Law* (1978), p. 319.

It may also be necessary to insert provisions dealing with the exchange rate risk (or at least to cover this risk by an appropriate financial arrangement, see p. 224 *post*, and *Exchange Rate Risks in International Contracts*, ICC Publication No. 440/3 (1987).

[78] *e.g.* 3 per cent. above the base lending rate of the National Westminster Bank plc.

[79] See pp. 199–200, *post*.

[80] This is the arbitration clause recommended by the Rules for the ICC Court of Arbitration; see p. 676, *post*. The adoption of the ICC arbitration clause is recommended in major export transactions. In transactions of lesser importance it is recommended not to adopt an arbitration clause but to use a choice of jurisdiction clause in favour of the English courts. This clause should be worded: "The English courts shall have exclusive jurisdiction to settle all disputes arising out of or in connection with this contract." On the question whether arbitration or litigation is preferable, see p. 647, *post*.

[81] In s.3.

These provisions will not, however, normally concern the exporter because they do not apply to international supply contracts, as defined in section 26 of the Act.[82]

SIMPLIFICATION OF EXPORT DOCUMENTS

The United Kingdom Simplification of International Trade Procedures Board (SITPRO)[83] has developed the United Kingdom aligned system of export trade documents now set out in the publication entitled "*TOP-FORM.*" This work is the result of international co-operation carried out under the auspices of the United Nations Economic Commission of Europe. *SITPRO* works in close co-operation with the Department of Trade and Industry.[84]

The object of SITPRO's system of export documentation is to save clerical labour by admitting the completion of export documents by the single-run process. This system is based mainly on photocopiers for reproducing documents. A master stencil is prepared from which, after masking the parts not required, every document is run off. The documents which can be run off from the master include bills of lading, certificates of insurance, certificates of origin, Customs and exchange documents, port forms and EC movement certificates. If these documents are prepared in the form suggested by the single-run process they are referred to as "the aligned series." The aligned series technique has important advantages for undertakings in international trade and is widely used. It can save up to 50 per cent. of administration costs.

SITPRO has also developed a range of methods from one typing set through to microcomputer systems. The Organisation plays an important role, nationally and internationally, in the development of electronic data interchange (EDI)[85], the use of electronic messages instead of paper-based documentation. Of the other document simplification tasks undertaken by SITPRO mention should be made of its work on the problem of incorrect or late documents presented under letters of credit. SITPRO has published four letter of credit checklists and guides for exporters, export sales executives and export customers, plus "How to control floating money."

SITPRO co-operates closely with the COMPROs, the various national facilitation committees of the other European countries. The activities of the national facilitation committees are co-ordinated by the UN Economic Commission for Europe, which has its own facilitation pro-

---

[82] See p. 100, *post.*
[83] Address; 26–28 King Street, London SW1 6QW.
[84] See p. 82, *post.*
[85] See p. 78, *post.*

gramme.[85a] The UN Economic Commission for Europe takes also part in the UN's initiative to develop EDI. The Commission itself has a trade facilitation programme.

The tendency towards paperless electronic communication of messages, which in international banking has led to the adoption of SWIFT,[86] has also extended to international trade. The teletransmission of trade data is commonly referred to as EDI or EDP.[87] Several organisations work on the standardisation of EDI, notably UNCITRAL, the International Chamber of Commerce, the UN Economic Commission for Europe and SITPRO. However, progress is slow and a generally accepted consensus of the business community has not emerged yet.

The present efforts exist on two levels; formal and substantive. The former aims at the standardisation of the *methods* of trade data communication by EDI, the latter at the standardisation of the *substantive contents* of such communications.

Standardisation of EDI methods of communication

The UNCID Rules

Here a certain finality has been achieved by the publication, in January 1988, of the UNCID Rules, sponsored by the International Chamber of Commerce and the UN Economic Commission of Europe.[88] The full title of the UNCID Rules is *Uniform Rules of Conduct for Interchange of Trade Data by Teletransmission*.

The aims of the UNCID Rules are indicated in Article 1:

> These Rules aim at facilitating the interchange of trade data effected by transmission, through the establishment of agreed rules of conduct between parties engaged in such

---

[85a] The UN Economic Commission for Europe has published, *inter alia,* a "Layout for Standard Consignment Instructions" in March 1989; this is Recommendation No. 22 adopted by the working party on facilitation of international trade procedures (ECE/Trade 168).

[86] "SWIFT" stands for *Society for Worldwide Interbank Financial Telecommunications.* Its headquarters are in Brussels and it has regional offices in Belgium, the Netherlands, and the United States. Only banks can be members of SWIFT.

[87] EDI stands for electronic data interchange, and EDP for electronic data processing; see Roy M. Goode, in *Legal Problems of Multimodal Transport,* in International Commercial Law Series, Vol. 1 (1988), . . .

[88] Published as ICC Brochure No. 452 (1988).

transmission. Except as otherwise provided in these rules, they do not apply to the substance of trade data transfers.

The UNCID Rules provide e.g. that the sender of a transfer may stipulate that the recipient should acknowledge receipt of it. They also contain some — rudimentary – provisions for the protection of trade data in the "computer document", which consists of magnetic impulses and of which the print-out is merely a copy.[89]

The UNCID Rules, like most ICC codes, are voluntary and apply only if the parties adopt them by means of a specific communication agreement, referred to in the Rules as "trade data interchange application protocol (IDI–AP)."

The UNCID Rules are intended to be the first step of a series of documents aimed at the general acceptance of EDI in international trade communications.

The UN/EDIFACT Rules

A further step in this direction is the adoption of UN/EDIFACT by the UN Economic Commission for Europe in April 1988.[90] UN/EDIFACT stands for *United Nations Rules for Electronic Data Interchange for Administration, Commerce and Transport*. UN/EDIFACT is defined as "the computer to computer transfer of commercial or administrative transactions using an agreed standard to structure the data pertaining to that transaction."[91] In plain language, this means that these Rules are designed to enable the computer of the sender of the message to communicate with the computer of its recipient in a language which the latter can understand. The adoption of these Rules is again voluntary and it remains to be seen whether they find general acceptance by the trade.

Teletransmission of letters of credit

A particular problem arises in letter of credit transactions. When the issuing bank (usually in the buyer's country) instructs another bank (in

---

[89] See Kurt Grönfors, *Legal Problems of Multimodal Transport, supra*, n. 84. p. 20 See also *Reg.* v. *Gold* [1988] 2 W.L.R. 984.
[90] There exist also EDIFACT Syntax Guidelines and EDIFACT Syntax Implementation Guidelines. Information on these documents can be obtained from SITPRO in London or from the International Standards Organisation (ISO).
[91] UN Paper Trade/R. 544 (July 13, 1988), para. 19, page 7. This paper is an Information Note on UN/EDIFACT, prepared by the Secretariat for the 37th Session of the Committee on the Development of Trade of the UN Economic Commission for Europe, held in December 1988.

the seller's country) to advise the credit and these instructions are sent by teletransmission, it may be doubtful whether the telex or other telecommunication is the operative instrument or whether it is only an indication that a letter will follow, which will set out the terms of the credit and is intended to be the operative document. There may be variations in the terms of the telecommunication and the subsequent letter. If the letter of credit is subject to the UCP—like most letters of credit—the answer is provided by Article 12 of the UCP.[92] This article states that, if the issuing bank instructs an advising bank by telecommunication and wishes the subsequent mail confirmation to be the operative credit instrument, it should state so in express terms in the telecommuncation or at least state "full details to follow," or words to similar effect; otherwise the telecommunication is regarded as the operative credit instrument.

Standardisation of substantive EDI communications

The International Organisation for Standardisation (ISO), in co-operation with other international organisations, has produced a Trade Data Elements Directory (UNTDED), which is published in English, French, Russian and Spanish.[93] This document was adopted in 1985 as ISO 7372. It contains about 500 trade terms with numeric tags. UNTDED gives coded references to the following[94]

> trade documents names;
> dates and periods of time;
> names of countries and some geographical entities;
> names of places of relevance to international trade (ports, airports, etc.);
> the Incoterms of the ICC;
> conditions of payment;
> modes of transport (water, rail, road, air, etc.);
> unit loads in transport, package forms and package materials;
> units of measurements (metric and imperial);
> units of currency.

UNTDED is supplemented by a Trade Data Interchange Directory (UNTDID) which describes the use of standardised trade terms in electronic procedures.

---

[92] For the full wording of Art. 12 of the UCP see p. 416, *post.*
[93] See Barbo Beer, "Informatics in International Trade" in 19 *Journal of World Trade Law* (1985), 570. On electronic transfer of shipping documents see also p. 539, *post.* Apart from the communications system produced by the ISO, other communications systems may be used by the parties, *e.g.* the U.S.A. system of CARDIS (Cargo Data Interchange System).
[94] Beer, *ibid.* 574.

CHAPTER 4

MARKET INFORMATION FOR EXPORTERS. MARKET RESEARCH

Direct market research

An enterprise which wants to engage in export transactions, whether on the global or EC level, will first engage in an exploration of the markets to which it wishes to target its exports.

The exporter may engage in his own market research. He may have in-house experts or he may call in independent marketing experts or other consultants. He may visit the overseas markets himself or send out appointed representatives. He may have received approaches or inquiries from importing or commission houses abroad or may have been contacted directly by overseas customers who have read his advertisements in the home or overseas press or may have obtained his address by other means.

In his direct market research the exporter can obtain valuable assistance from his local chamber of commerce, which is likely to have an export department, or from his trade association.

Government assisted market research

In many instances the exporter will make use of the highly developed Government services for exporters[1] promoted by the British Overseas Trade Board (BOTB).[2] They include facilities for market research. As a preliminary step he may visit the *Statistics and Market Intelligence Library* and the *Product Data Store* of the BOTB which both provide him with excellent facilities for desk research.[3] He can also approach various other market advisory services offered by the Board or the chambers of commerce. The *Export Marketing Research Scheme* which is now administered by the chambers of commerce, will in suitable cases arrange for financial assistance towards the cost of export marketing research projects, whether carried out by consultants or in-house staff, and towards

---

[1] See below in the text.
[2] The address of the Headquarters of the BOTB is 1 Victoria Street, London SW1H 0ET.
[3] Their addresses and those of the other organisations mentioned in this paragraph are the same as that of the Headquarters of the BOTB.

the salary and overhead costs incurred on marketing research projects during the first year of setting up a new export marketing research department.

Within the framework of its broadly based *Enterprise Initiative* the Department of Trade and Industry promotes a number of services for the exporter. They are retitled *Export Initiative*. In particular, the Department promotes an *export counselling service*, which is run by the leading chambers of commerce in the United Kingdom; this service is free to businesses but the Department charges for additional services. The management of the Department's export marketing research scheme is contracted out to the Association of British Chambers of Commerce. The *Small Firms Service,* which is run by the Department of Employment, also provides counselling through its Small Firms Centres; this advice extends to building up business abroad.

GOVERNMENT SERVICES FOR EXPORTERS

The Department of Trade and Industry

This Department has four Overseas Trade Divisions.

Overseas Trade Division 1
   Projects and Export Policy (PEP).
   PEP is the focus of Government support for firms and consortia pursuing major project business overseas. The Division is also responsible for departmental interest in export financing the use of aid and general export policy.
   PEP is divided into industry sectors.

Overseas Trade Division 2
   North America Branch.
   South Asia and Far East Branch.
   China and Hong Kong Branch; Export Controls.

Overseas Trade Division 3
   Export Promotion Policy Branch.
   Fairs and Promotions Branch.
   Exports to Europe Branch.
   Export Data Branch.
   Eastern Europe Branch.

Overseas Trade Division 4
   Middle East Branch.
   Latin America, Caribbean and Australian Branch.
   Sub-Saharan Africa Branch.

The British Overseas Trade Board

The BOTB[4] controls the whole of the export promotion work of the Department of Trade and Industry (DTI). The Board consists of busi-

---

[4] For address see n. 2, *ante.* The BOTB was constituted on May 11, 1971, under the name of the British Export Board. Its name was changed to the present name on March 1, 1972.

nessmen and a representative each from the Foreign and Commonwealth Office, the Export Credits Guarantee Department and the British Invisible Exports Council. The Board's main task is to ensure that the official export promotion activities are conducted with due regard to the needs of industry and commerce and to utilise the available Government resources to the best advantage.

The function of the BOTB is to give direction to the official export promotion services with which it closely co-operates. The day-to-day work, which is of primary interest to the exporter, is handled by the various Branches of the Overseas Trade Divisions of the DTI and the other Government offices concerned.

The DTI has seven Regional Offices in England; in addition, there exist offices in Scotland, Wales and Northern Ireland. They should be approached by the exporter, who wishes to avail himself of the services of the Department or the BOTB. The Board has also 17 Area Advisory Groups which are arranged according to overseas markets. They can likewise be consulted.

BOTB services offered to the exporter

The many and varied services which the BOTB offers to the exporter are listed in the brochure *Export Initiative*[5]. In addition to those in the important field of preliminary market research, which were referred to earlier,[6] the following should be mentioned.

Major contract projects

They are the concern of the Projects and Export Policy Division (Overseas Trade Division 1). There exists an *Overseas Projects Board,* consisting of senior businessmen and advising on general trade policy and individual projects; this Board is set up by the BOTB.

The Government also provides support to companies through the *Aid and Trade Provisions* (ATP) to help United Kingdom companies match their overseas competitors' concessionary financing terms. The projects so supported have normally a United Kingdom element of at least £20 million but consultancies with a lower value are also considered. Arrangements exist between the World Bank and the Government for co-financing; they are founded on an agreement of 1986 which allows up to

---

[5] The addresses of the DTI Regional Offices are listed in the *Export Initiative*; about this publication, see p. 85 *post.*
[6] See p. 81, *ante.*

£200 million of United Kingdom exports to be supported by ATP. There exist also other multilateral aid programmes, *e.g.* those promoted by the European Development Bank.[7]

The Projects and Export Policy Division has also issued a publication entitled *Countertrade. Some Guidance for Exporters.*[8] Countertrade, which is of growing importance, is international trade by reciprocal trading arrangements.[9]

The Export Intelligence Service

The Export Intelligence Service (EIS) is controlled by Overseas Trade Division 3 but is managed by *Export Opportunities,* a subsidiary of *Export Network,* a private sector company. Its function is described in a previous publication of the BOTB as follows[10]

The Export Intelligence Service (EIS) issues details of overseas trade opportunities and market and economic information to subscribers. The information, mostly drawn from the flow of items of commercial intelligence reported daily from nearly 200 overseas posts throughout the world, is selectively matched by computer to subscribers' chosen requirements.

Outward and inward missions; fairs and exhibitions

This activity is the concern of the Fairs and Promotions Branch of Overseas Trade Division 3 of the DTI. Assistance is given to BOTB outward missions of British exporters; to BOTB inward missions of overseas buyers or others who can influence purchases, on the suggestion of British firms wishing to bring these potential overseas customers to the UK; to trade fairs, seminars and symposia overseas; to overseas store promotion and similar activities. As regards firms taking part in international trade fairs, space and shelf stand and stand services can be arranged on favourable charges in the case of a joint venture scheme sponsored by an approved non-profit-making body, usually a trade association or a chamber of commerce. Assistance is also provided for British Pavilions organised by the Fairs and Promotions Branch.

---

[7] The amount not covered by ATP may be insured with ECGD under a Project Financing Cover, see p. 478 *post.*

[8] August 1988. This Document is revised from time to time. It can be obtained from the Projects and Export Policy Division Branch 3A, Department of Trade and Industry, 1–19 Victoria Street, London SW1H 0ET.

[9] On Countertrade see Chap. 10, p. 154, *post.*

[10] Export Handbook, p. 19 (discontinued). Further information can be obtained from the Regional and the Scottish, Welsh and Northern Irish Offices of the DTI, see p. 83, *ante.*

Simplification of export documentation

The operation of SITPRO, already noted earlier,[11] is likewise a BOTB activity.

Technical help to exporters

The technical standards required in the various countries vary considerably. It is of great importance to the exporter to comply with the standards of the country to which his exports are directed. Some national requirements are mandatory, but even in cases in which they are not mandatory the export effort is facilitated if the exporter can offer goods which comply with the national standards. A consultancy service known as *Technical Help to Exporters* (THE) provides information on the various national standards.[12]

EXPORT PUBLICATIONS

Many excellent trade publications exist which keep the exporter informed of the constantly changing market conditions in the overseas markets and the legal and consular requirements abroad. It is perhaps invidious to specify some of these publications but it is believed that the following are particularly useful for the exporter.

DTI/BOTB publications

They include:[13]

The Export Initiative: Guide to Export Services

This brochure describes the range of DTI services for exporters.[14]

---

[11] See p. 77, *ante*.
[12] Address: Linford Wood, Milton Keynes, MK14 6LE, Tel.: 0908 320066.
[13] See also the publication *Countertrade*, referred to on p. 84, *ante*. The DTI/BOTB also publish occasional papers.
[14] (2nd ed., 1988). This Guide can be obtained free of charge from the DTI headquarters (Hotline 01–200 1992) or one of its regional offices.

Hints to exporters

This is a series of booklets, each about exporting to a different country (or countries) abroad. They are regularly updated and contain valuable information on currency and exchange regulations, passport and entry formalities, methods of doing business, local holidays, economic factors, social customs and many other useful tips for visiting British businessmen and women.

Market reports

DTI Market Branches publish an extensive range of information on individual overseas markets.

Export guides for smaller firms

The three short guides in this series introduce smaller firms to the key principles of successful exporting.

Overseas trade

Overseas Trade magazine provides regular news of export practice, opportunities and successes, as well as the range of support services. It is mailed to export firms free of charge.

Croner's Reference Book for Exporters

This is a comprehensive loose-leaf publication[15] which consists of two Parts. Part 1 contains valuable general information relating to export control, Customs procedures and other matters of export practice. Part II contains a detailed countries survey. An index is also provided.

The work is kept up-to-date by regular releases providing an amendment service of the main volume and by the monthly publication *Export Digest.*[16]

---

[15] Obtainable from Croner Publications Ltd., Croner House, 173 Kingston Road, New Malden, Surrey KT3 3SS, Tel.: 01–942 8966, Telex 267778 Croner G.

[16] Another reference work is *Export Data,* published by Benn Publications Ltd. It is in loose-leaf form and is kept up to a date by the monthly publication *Export Notes.* Further, the following work should be helpful: Janet Phillips, *Dictionary of Trading Terms* (obtainable from Broomhills Publishing, 23 Park Street, Old Hatfield, Hertfordshire AL9 5AT, England).

London Commerce

This journal, published monthly by the London Chamber of Commerce, contains, a section on International Markets which gives much valuable information to the exporter.[17] The same is true of journals published by other chambers of commerce. Many trade journals likewise publish export information.

The Association of British Chambers of Commerce publishes a weekly called "Business Briefing." It has taken the place of "British Business", formerly published by the DTI and now discontinued. The new publication contains general information on British business.

Export Today

This is the official journal of the *Institute of Export*,[18] the foremost educational organisation providing professional examinations leading to graduate membership of the Institute (MIEx.(Grad.)).

Export Today is published every two months. It contains valuable articles of topical interest to the exporter and other useful information.

Eurostat

The EC operates a Statistical Office known as *Eurostat*. It publishes updated information on all economic and social activities of the EC and the Member States, as well as their main trading partners. This information is available to the public.[19]

---

[17] A list of London Chamber of Commerce services and publications can be obtained from the Publications Department of the London Chamber of Commerce, 69 Cannon Street, London EC4N 5AB.
[18] Address: Export House, 64 Clifton Street, London EC2A 4HB, Tel.: 01–247 9812.
[19] The address of Eurostat is: The Statistical Office of the European Communities, Bâtiment Jean Monnet, Rue Alcide de Gasperi, L–2920 Luxembourg.

CHAPTER 5

FORMATION OF CONTRACT

THE NEGOTIATIONS

Inquiries and invitations to contract

NEGOTIATIONS between the parties may or may not lead to the conclusion of a legally binding contract. The first contact between the parties may take the form of an inquiry or an invitation to contract,[1] such as contained in a catalogue, advertisement or invitation to submit tenders for construction or other work. Statements made in the course of negotiation are not contractual statements, like an offer and acceptance, unless embodied into the contract.[2] But they are not without legal effect; if a contract results, a pre-contractual statement may have to be characterised in law as a misrepresentation,[3] and even if a contract does not ensue, the information imparted during the negotiations may have been of a confidential nature and its misuse may give rise to a legal remedy.[4]

The quotation

Whether a quotation is merely an invitation to contract or constitutes an offer depends on the intention of the parties, and pre-eminently on that of the person submitting the quotation. Normally a quotation is only an invitation to contract. In this case the person to whom the quotation is addressed makes the offer and it is for the sender of the quotation to decide whether to accept or reject it. In one case[5] carriers were invited by exporters to undertake the shipment of waste paper from New Zealand to India. The carriers sent the exporters a telex stating the periods of the intended shipments, the freight rate and the manner of stowage, but the

[1] In older terminology called "an invitation to treat."
[2] In insurance practice the statements on the proposal form are often incorporated into the contract by a "basis of contract" clause.
[3] Misrepresentation Act 1967.
[4] The cases on confidentiality generally are referred to on p. 285, *post.*
[5] *Scancarriers A/S* v. *Aotearoa International Ltd.* 135 N.L.J. (1985), 799. See also *The Gudermes*, [1985] 2 Lloyd's Rep. 623.

telex did not state the quantity of the cargo, the number of shipments, the dates and the intervals between them. The exporters presented 919 tonnes of paper for shipment, and this quantity was shipped in two vessels. The exporters failed to pay the freight charges for these consignments and the carriers refused all further bookings. The exporters claimed damages from the carriers for breach of contract. The Privy Council, on appeal from New Zealand, held that the carriers' telex was no more than the quotation of a freight rate and that it was not an offer. Consequently there was no binding contract and the exporters' claim for damages failed.

On the other hand, a quotation may contain all the elements of an offer and may qualify in law as such. The decisive test it, may be repeated, is the intention of the person submitting the quotation.

Failure to agree on essential points

Sometimes lengthy and detailed negotiations take place between the parties, particularly if a major contract is negotiated. In these cases it is on occasion difficult to determine whether the parties have reached agreement or the negotiations have failed because they have not been able to overcome the "sticking point."[6]

If the parties have agreed on all essential points but left details to be settled later, a valid contract is concluded. Such an arrangement is sometimes referred to as *heads of agreement*.[7] However, "it is for the parties to decide whether they wish to be bound and, if so, by what terms, whether important or unimportant;"[8] Of course, if the agreement of the parties does not extend to all terms which are necessary to make it enforceable there is no "contract" in the legal sense[9]

THE OFFER

The offer is a statement intended to result in a binding contract if duly accepted by the offeree. The seller should make certain that the essential

---

[6] In *J. Milhem & Sons* v. *Fuerst Brothers & Co. Ltd.* [1954] 2 Lloyd's Rep. 559, the court held that the parties were never *ad idem*. Another case in which the negotiations of the parties did not advance to a binding contract was *Pagnan SpA* v. *Granaria BV* [1986] 2 Lloyd's Rep. 547. *Mitsui & Co. Ltd.* v. *Flota Mercante Grancolombiana S.A. The Ciudad de Pasto and Ciudad de Neiva* [1987] 2 Lloyd's Rep. 392, 399; *Pagnan SpA* v. *Feed Products Ltd.* [1987] 2 Lloyd's Rep. 601.
[7] But not all so-called heads of agreement are intended to be binding.
[8] *Per* Lloyd L.J. in the *Pagnan* case, on p. 619, quoted in no. 6, *ante*. The learned judge dealt mainly with contracts concluded by correspondence.
[9] *Ibid*.

elements of the contract are clearly stated in the communications exchanged by the parties. These elements are:

1. the goods ordered which should be described without ambiguity;
2. the purchase price and the terms of payment; and
3. the terms of delivery, including instructions for packing and invoicing, transportation and insurance.

Firm offers

In English law an offer can be revoked until it is accepted, unless it is supported by consideration (when it is so supported, it becomes an option) or is expressed in the form of a deed. It can even be revoked if it is given as a "firm offer,", *i.e.* if it states that the offeror will consider himself to be bound by it for a specified time.

Other legal systems adopt a different — and less dogmatic — attitude to the firm offer and consider it as binding in certain circumstances. Thus, the UCC, s.2–205, provides that a firm offer for the purchase or sale of goods given by a merchant in a signed writing is not revocable for lack of consideration. The Vienna Convention on Contracts for the International Sale of Goods goes further; it provides in Article 16(2) that a firm offer shall be binding but, unlike the UCC, does not require that it is made by a merchant and in a signed writing.

THE ACCEPTANCE

The acceptance must be unconditional and unqualified

The acceptance must be unconditional and unqualified. If it is otherwise, it constitutes a rejection of the original offer, combined with a counteroffer. It follows that, if the original offeror receives a qualified acceptance and does not express agreement, there is no contract; he is not obliged to reply to the modified acceptance, although complete silence, after its receipt, hardly constitutes good business practice. Thus, in *Northland Airliners Ltd.* v. *Dennis Ferranti Meters Ltd.*[10] the sellers, a company in North Wales, negotiated with the buyers, a Canadian company, for the sale of an amphibian aircraft. The sellers sent the following telegram: "Confirming sale to you Grummond Mallard aircraft . . . , Please remit £5,000." The buyers replied: "This is to confirm your

---

[10] (1970) 114 S.J. 845; *The Times*, October 23, 1970.

cable and my purchase Grummond Mallard aircraft terms set out your cable . . . £5,000 sterling forwarded your bank to be held in trust for your account pending delivery . . . Please confirm delivery to be made thirty days within this date." The sellers did not reply but sold the aircraft to a third person at a higher price. The Court of Appeal held that there was no contract. The buyers' reply introduced two new terms, one as to payment and the other as to delivery, and the sellers were not bound to reply to this counteroffer.

The rule that a modified acceptance always constitutes a counteroffer and can be rejected by the original offeror by mere silence is too rigid in its generality. According to the Uniform Law on the Formation of Contracts[11], which applies to international sales, an acceptance which contains additional or different terms that do not materially alter the offer constitutes a valid acceptance with the proposed modifications, unless promptly objected to by the original offeror.[12] The American Uniform Commercial Code contains a similar—though not identical—regulation. It provides[13]:

The additional terms are to be construed as proposals for addition to the contract. Between merchants[14] such terms become part of the contract unless:

    (a) the offer expressly limits acceptance to the terms of the offer;
    (b) they materially alter it; or
    (c) notification of objection to them has already been given or is given within a reasonable time after notice of them is received.

Acceptance subject to seller's general conditions

The acceptance should invariably embody the seller's general conditions of business and here the earlier observations on general terms of business adopted by individual exporters[15] should be kept in mind.[16] When previous export transactions have taken place between the parties and their contracts are governed by the same conditions of sale, the buyer can be presumed to have placed his orders subject to those conditions[17] and the unqualified acceptance by the seller will clinch the bargain. In most cases, however, the seller's conditions of sale will be unknown to the

---

[11] UCC s.2–207(1)(2).
[12] Uniform Laws on International Sales Act 1967, Sched. 2, art. 7(2). The UN Convention on Contracts for the International Sale of Goods (Vienna, 1980) contains the same regulation in Art. 19(2).
[13] In s.2–207(2).
[14] A "merchant" is defined in s.2–104(1).
[15] See p. 75, *ante.*
[16] If the general conditions of the seller conflict with those of the buyer a "battle of forms" may ensue, see p. 99, *post.*
[17] See *The Kite* [1933] P. 154, 164; *Hardwick Game Farm* v. *Suffolk Agricultural Poultry Producers Association* [1969] 2 A.C. 31.

buyer when making his offer, and the acceptance by the seller "subject to our conditions of sale" represents in strict law a rejection of the buyer's offer combined with a counteroffer by the seller although the courts will be reluctant to reach this conclusion if the transaction and the subsequent conduct of the parties disclose a clear intention to be bound by their agreement. In these cases the seller who wishes to be on safe ground should obtain the buyer's unqualified confirmation before carrying out the contract, particularly when the negotiations were conducted by correspondence. In practice, the strict requirements of the law are sometimes disregarded; this is understandable, but may lead to unfortunate consequences.[18] The reasonable exporter should at least insist on strict observance of the legal requirements in the case of orders that are not routine transactions.[19]

Communication of acceptance

The general rule is that a contract is made when the acceptance is communicated to the offeror. If it is necessary to determine where a contract is formed, it is logical that this is the place at which the acceptance is communicated.[20] "Communication" is a technical term of art; it means that the addressee must have been able to take notice of the statement in question. The statement is duly communicated if it has been received by the addressee, even if for one reason or the other he has not read it, *e.g.* because in his internal office organisation it has not reached him.

---

[18] Even where the court holds that there was a valid contract between the parties as in *Macpherson Train & Co. Ltd.* v. *J. Milhem & Sons* [1955] 2 Lloyd's Rep. 396 and *Brown & Gracie Ltd.* v. *F. W. Green & Co. Pty. Ltd.* [1960] 1 Lloyd's Rep. 289, costly and protracted litigation might result from the disregard of the simple rules on offer and acceptance or from ambiguity.

[19] When the question of construction of a contract document is in issue, a so-called parol (extrinsic) evidence rule does not exist, see Law Commission Report No. 154 on Parol Evidence (January 1986, Cmnd. 9700). The true purpose of construction of a document is to ascertain the intention of the parties. Sometimes they intend that the document should contain everything, and then extrinsic evidence is not admissible. In other cases their intention is that the document should be read together with their previous negotiations, and then it has to be construed in what Lord Wilberforce called in *Prenn* v. *Simmonds, infra,* "the commercial, or business, object of the transaction." See *Prenn* v. *Simmonds,* [1971] 1 W.L.R. 1381 at 1385; *Partenreederei M.S. Karen Oltman* v. *Scarsdale Shipping Co. Ltd. The Karen Oltman* [1976] 2 Lloyd's Rep. 709; *Reardon Smith Line Ltd.* v. *Yngvar Hansen-Tangen. The Diana Prosperity.* [1976] 1 W.L.R. 989; *Barlee Marine Corporation* v. *Trevor Rex Mountain. The Leegas.* [1987] 1 Lloyd's Rep. 471.

[20] Lord Wilberforce in *Brinkibon Ltd.* v. *Stahag Stahl und Stahlwarenhandels GmbH* [1983] 2 A.C. 34, 41; Neill J. in *Bunge Corpn.* v. *Vegetable Vitamin Foods (Private) Ltd.* [1985] 1 Lloyd's Rep. 613, 617. For a critical review of *Brinkibon* see John Wightman "Does Acceptance Matter?" in *Essays for Clive Schmitthoff* (ed. John Adams, 1983), p. 145.

This rule is applied to *instantaneous contracts*. These are contracts made verbally, by telephone or by telex, and it is thought by facsimile (fax).[21]

If the acceptance is by *post or telegram*, it depends on the intention of the parties whether the general rule for the communication of the statement shall apply or whether the mere posting of such an acceptance, and not its arrival at the address of the offeree, shall be sufficient. Normally the intention of the parties will be that the general rule shall apply[22] but in exceptional circumstances it can be inferred from the terms of the offer that mere posting of the acceptance shall be sufficient.[23] To exclude ambiguity, the offer should state that the offeror will only be bound if he actually receives the acceptance.

Telex communications

Contracts made by telex, as already observed, are normally regarded as instantaneous contracts. But the rule is not of universal application, as the following observations of Lord Wilberforce in the *Brinkibon* case[24] show:

> . . . there are many variants on it. The senders and recipients may not be the principals to the contemplated contract. They may be servants or agents with limited authority. The message may not reach, or be intended to reach, the designated recipient immediately: messages may be sent out of office hours, or at night, with the intention, or upon the assumption, that they will be read at a later time. There may be some error or default at the recipient's end which prevents receipt at the time contemplated and believed in by the sender. The message may have been sent and/or received through machines operated by third persons. And many other variations may occur. No universal rule can cover all such cases: they must be resolved by reference to the intentions of the parties, by sound business practice and in some cases by a judgment where the risk should lie.

Telex in letter of credit transactions

If the issuing bank sends the credit instructions to the advising bank by telex, which is later followed by a mail confirmation, the question arises

---

[21] *Brinkibon Ltd.* v. *Stahag Stahl und Stahlwarenhandels GmbH* [1983] 2 A.C. 34, *Entores Ltd.* v. *Miles Far East Corpn.* [1955] 2 Q.B. 327; *The Brimnes*, [1975] Q.B. 929. An allegedly false or negligent misrepresentation requires publication and, if made by a person abroad to a person in England by telephone or telex, the place where the tort is committed is the place at which the communication is received, *i.e.* England: *Diamond* v. *Bank of London and Montreal Ltd.* [1979] Q.B. 333. It was held in *R.* v. *Governor of Pentonville Prison, ex parte Osman, The Times*, April 13, 1988, that the theft of bank funds by telex was committed at the place where the telex was sent (Hong Kong), but the possibility was not ruled out that the appropriation likewise took place at the locality where the telex was received (New York).
[22] *Howell Securities Ltd.* v. *Hughes* [1974] 1 W.L.R. 155.
[23] *Household Fire and Carriage Accident Insurance Ltd.* v. *Grant* (1879) 4 Ex.D. 216, 223.
[24] See n. 21, *ante;* p. 42 of Lord Wilberforce's judgment in the *Brinkibon* case. See also John Wightman, *op. cit.* in n. 20, *ante.*

whether the telex or the mail confirmation is the operative credit document. This situation is regulated by Article 12 of the UCP (1983 Revision) and has been considered in an earlier chapter.[25]

Forms of acceptance

The Confirmation Slip

Where a contract is negotiated verbally or by correspondence and later one party sends the other an order or acceptance on a printed form with an attached confirmation slip, which has to be returned duly signed by the other party, it is always a matter of construction, which in some cases is not easy to resolve, whether the parties have agreed to the terms of the contract with sufficient precision and what those terms are.[26] Even though the confirmation slip is not returned there may be a binding contract between the parties.[27] "The court will always lean towards giving legal effect to documents which the parties themselves regard as constituting a binding contract in law."[28]

The countersigned acceptance form

Another method of obtaining the offeror's written agreement to the terms of acceptance is to send him two forms of acceptance acknowledging his order and to ask him to return one, duly signed by him. This method is frequently used in the export trade particularly where the goods ordered represent a considerable value or have to be built to the buyer's specification.

In this case it is essential that the two forms of acceptance should contain identical terms or, at least, that the form retained by the offeror should have a "red hand" clause,[29] drawing attention to the fact that the form which he has signed and returned contains further clauses not included in the form retained by him. In one case[30] an English buyer bought two large machines from a German manufacturer, the machines to be installed on the premises of the buyer. The seller sent the buyer two

---

[25] See pp. 79–80 *ante*. The full text of Art. 12 is reproduced on p. 416, *post*.
[26] On the parol (extrinsic) evidence rule, see p. 92, n. 19, *ante*.
[27] *Compagnie de Commerce et Commission S.A.R.L.* v. *Parkinson Stove Co. Ltd.* [1953] 1 Lloyd's Rep. 532.
[28] *Ibid.* p. 542, *per* Pilcher J.
[29] On the "red hand" clause, see p. 97, *post*, n. 39.
[30] *Harvey* v. *Ventilatorenfabrik Oelde GmbH, Financial Times*, November 11, 1988.

forms of acceptance (both in German), the original which contained the seller's terms of business on the reverse, and a copy on which the reverse was left blank. In accordance with the directions of the seller, the buyer returned the original duly signed and retained the copy, assuming that the two forms were identical. Later the buyer, who claimed that the goods were unsatisfactory, commenced proceedings in the English courts but the seller asked that the proceedings be conducted in the German courts; he relied on a clause printed on the reverse of the signed original. It was conceded that the buyer was not conversant with the German language. The Court of Appeal held that the buyer was misled into believing that the two documents were identical and in all the circumstances it would be wrong to hold that he was bound by the German jurisdiction clause on the document returned by him.[30a]

Comfort letters

A typical situation in which a comfort letter is given arises if a company wishes to obtain a loan from a bank and the latter asks for some assurance from the company's parent company. The parent company may be unwilling to guarantee the loan because, if it does so, it would have to show the guarantee as a contingent liability in its balance sheet but it is willing to lend its support to the subsidiary by giving the bank a letter of comfort.

In most cases a comfort letter is intended to create only moral, and not legal, obligations for the parent company. In these cases it is couched in general terms, *e.g.* that the directors of the parent company are aware of the loan facility sought by the subsidiary. In other cases the parent, by the comfort letter, accepts a legal obligation, though not of a financial nature, *e.g.* it undertakes not to sell or otherwise to dispose of the shares in the subsidiary as long as the loan is outstanding.[31]

On occasion, however—and these cases will be rare—the comfort letter is worded in terms which place the parent company under a financial obligation to the bank. In one case[32] the two comfort letters which the parent gave the bank with respect to loans to the subsidiary contained this statement:

[30a] The case was not decided under the Civil Jurisdiction and Judgments Act 1982 (see p. 709, *post*).

[31] In *Chemco Leasing SpA* v. *Rediffusion plc*, [1987] F.T.L.R. 201, the comfort letter did not create legal rights; the letter, written by the defendants, the parent of a subsidiary, stated that the defendants would "take over" the subsidiary's liability to the plaintiffs if they—the defendants—disposed of their interest in the subsidiary and the new shareholders were not acceptable to the plaintiffs; the Court of Appeal held that the defendants' offer of liability was not accepted by the plaintiffs within a reasonable time.

[32] *Kleinwort Benson Ltd.* v. *Malaysia Mining Corporation Berhad* [1989] 1 W.L.R. 379.

> It is our policy to ensure that the business of [the subsidiary] is at all times in a position to meet its liabilities to you under the above arrangements.

The trial judge (Hirst J.) held that the parent was liable on these undertakings but he was reversed by the Court of Appeal. Ralph Gibson L.J. said:[33]

> . . . in this case it is clear . . . that the concept of a comfort letter . . . was known to both sides at least to extend to or to include a document under which the defendants would given comfort to the plaintiffs by assuming, not legal liability to ensure repayment of the liabilities of the subsidiary, but a moral responsibility only.

SPECIAL PROBLEMS RELATING TO GENERAL CONDITIONS

The buyer's agreement to the seller's standard terms

The general terms of business should be printed on price lists, catalogues, estimates, offers, and all contract documents emanating from the seller, such as acceptances, in a clear, legible and conspicuous manner. They should be embodied in the context of the seller's offer or acceptance but, where that is not feasible, the context should at least contain a clear and conspicuous reference to the fact that conditions of sale are printed on the reverse or on an attached sheet. It is also necessary to obtain the agreement of the buyer to the general terms of business of the seller. It is desirable that the buyer should agree in writing and the question has already been examined how to obtain the buyer's written consent.[34]

Particular care should be taken in this connection with the *choice of jurisdiction clause.*[35] The EC Convention on Jurisdiction and the Enforcement of Judgments in Civil and Commercial Matters of September 27, 1968, to which effect is given in the United Kingdom by the Civil Jurisdiction and Judgments Act 1982,[36] provides in Article 17(1) that a contractual agreement conferring jurisdiction on a court in a Contracting State "shall be either in writing or evidenced in writing or, in international trade or commerce, in a form which accords with practices in that trade or commerce of which the parties are or ought to have been aware." The Court of the European Communities insists that these requirements should be complied with strictly,[37] but the last words of the

---

[33] On p. 391.

[34] See p. 94, *ante.*

[35] See p. 76, n. 80, *ante*, and p. 711, *post.*

[36] This Act came into force on January 1, 1987. See also p. 709, *post.*

[37] See, *e.g., Galeries Segoura S.p.r.l.* v. *Firma Rahim Bonakdarian* [1977] 1 C.M.L.R. 361. It was held by the EC Court of Justice in *F. Berghoefer GmbH & Co. KG* v. *ASA SA* (Case 221 /84) [1986] 1 C.M.L.R. 13 that an express oral agreement (on the jurisdiction of a court), if later confirmed in writing by one of the parties and not objected to by the other, satisfied the requirements of Article 17. In *Iveco Fiat SpA* v. *Van Hool NV* (Case No. 313/85 judgment of November 11, 1986) the EC Court held that, where a written agreement contained a jurisdiction clause but was continued orally in a manner valid according to the relevant national law (Belgian law), the jurisdiction clause still satisfied the requirements of Article 17 and applied to the continued (oral) agreement.

article, *viz.* the reference to the practices of international trade, save the validity of a jurisdiction clause in a document in common use, even though it is not signed by both parties, *e.g.* in a bill of lading or a standard contract form sponsored by a trade association operating in the field of international commerce.[38] An arbitration agreement by telex or other electronic communication will also normally accord with the practices of international trade.

In certain foreign countries, the courts will not admit general terms of business which are embodied in the contract only by reference. In English common law it is immaterial that the buyer, in a particular case, did not read the conditions or had to refer to other documents in order to ascertain them; but it is necessary that the fact should be clearly brought to his notice that such conditions exist and that the contract is concluded subject to them.[39] The law of Texas requires a foreign law clause to be printed in boldfaced print.[40] In Italian law certain exempting or limiting clauses contained in general conditions of contract are only valid if expressly approved in writing by the other party.[41]

It may happen that the general terms of business of the two parties to the contract conflict. This problem, known as the *battle of forms,* pertains to the law of offer and acceptance and will be treated later.[42]

A verbal contractual promise may override general conditions

It is a general principle of law that where the parties have embodied general terms in a written document—and printed general conditions are

---

[38] The last words of Article 17(1) were added when the Article was amended by the Convention of Accession to the 1968 Convention by Denmark, Ireland and the United Kingdom of October 9, 1978. The case of *Partenreederei ms. Tilly Russ v. Haven & Vervoerbedrijf Nova NV* [1985] 3 W.L.R. 179, decided by the European Court of Justice, deals with the unamended form of Article 17 and cannot be regarded as relevant to the problems discussed in the text after the amendment of that Article.

[39] The rule that notice must be given to unusual contract terms is sometimes referred to as the "red hand" rule; the expression has its origin in a dictum of Denning L.J. in *Spurling* v. *Bradshaw* [1956] 1 W.L.R. 461 that "such clauses would need to be printed in red ink with a red hand pointing to it before the notice would be sufficient." See also *Phoenix Insurance Company of Hartford* v. *De Monchy* (1929) 45 T.L.R. 543. See further *MacLeod Ross & Co. Ltd.* v. *Compagnie d'Assurances Générales L'Helvetia of St. Gall* [1952] W.N. 56; see p. 498, *post. Interfoto Picture Library Ltd.* v. *Stiletto Visual Programmes Ltd.* [1988] 2 W.L.R. 615; Elizabeth Macdonald, "The Duty to give notice of Unusual Contract Terms" in [1988] J.B.L. 375.

[40] Texas State Law effective September 1, 1987, H.B. 1881, see *Forum USA,* Vol. 5 No. 1, 1988, 3. This statutory requirement applies where the contract is executed by an individual resident in the state or a corporation incorporated in Texas or having its principal seat of business in Texas. The foreign law clauses to which the Act applies are clauses providing that the contract is governed by the law of another State or that the courts of another State shall have jurisdiction, or that an arbitration shall be held outside Texas.

[41] Italian Civil Code, art. 1341, see *The Saudi Prince (No. 2)* [1988] 1 Lloyd's Rep. 1, 6.

[42] See p. 99, *post.*

a written document—a special agreement in their contract normally[43] overrides these general terms. Furthermore, verbal evidence is usually not admissible to vary or qualify the written agreement. However, this rule is subject to a number of exceptions.[44] In particular, where a party has given another a verbal promise not to rely on a term in the general conditions and that promise has been accepted by the other party, he cannot rely on that term if it would make the verbal contractual promise wholly illusory. In one case[45] English importers of an Italian injection moulding machine in negotiations with their freight forwarders insisted that, if the machine was to be shipped in a container, the latter should be carried below deck because they feared that the machine might get rusty. The manager of the forwarders assured the importers orally that "if we use containers, they will not be carried on deck." When the machine was shipped from Rotterdam to Tilbury, the Dutch associated company of the forwarders failed to ensure that the container in which the machine was carried was shipped below deck. The ship met with a slight swell and the container which contained the machine and was shipped on deck fell off and became a total loss. In an action for damages by the importers, the forwarders sought to rely on their printed general conditions which gave them complete freedom as to the method of transportation. The Court of Appeal held that the verbal promise of the forwarders not to ship the goods on deck constituted an enforceable contractual promise which overrode the relevant term in the printed general conditions. The court gave judgment for the importers.

Incorporation of current edition of general conditions

General conditions are revised from time to time in the light of experience. They should provide that the edition current at the date of the conclusion of the contract shall apply. But even where such a clause is not included, one would, in the absence of indications of another intention of the parties, arrive at the same result. Where the contract provided that it was subject to general conditions "available on request," it was held[46] that that was a reference to the current edition. "It is common experience that the general conditions of various undertakers are revised from time to time, and anyone requesting a copy of such

---

[43] But not invariably. It depends on the intention of the parties, see *Fratelli Moretti SpA* v. *Nidera Handelscompagnie BV* [1981] 2 Lloyd's Rep. 47, 51 where it was held that the parties intended that a general clause adopted by incorporation should prevail over the special clauses in the contract.

[44] On the admission of extrinsic evidence, see p. 92, n. 19, *ante*.

[45] *J. Evans & Son (Portsmouth) Ltd.* v. *Andrea Merzario Ltd.* [1976] 1 W.L.R. 1078. See also *The Ardennes* [1951] 1 K.B. 55, pp. 545–546, *post*.

[46] *Smith* v. *South Wales Switchgear Co. Ltd.* [1978] 1 W.L.R. 165.

conditions would reasonably expect to receive the current up-to-date edition."[47]

The battle of forms

It sometimes happens that one party sends the other an offer on his general conditions of business and the other accepts subject to his own general conditions. The two sets of conditions will normally not agree and the question may arise whether the parties are in contract and, if so, whose general conditions apply. This situation is sometimes referred to as *the battle of forms*.[48]

No battle of forms will arise if one party has taken the precaution of obtaining the other party's consent to his own conditions by a suitably worded confirmation slip or a signed acceptance, as recommended earlier. Thus, in one case[49] the sellers quoted for a machine. Their general conditions which were printed on the reverse of the quotation contained a price escalation clause. The buyers ordered the machine on their general conditions which did not contain a price escalation clause. On the foot of the buyers' order was a tear-off slip stating that the order was accepted by the sellers "on the terms and conditions stated therein." The sellers signed the slip and returned it to the buyers. The Court of Appeal held that the contract was concluded on the buyers' terms and that the sellers were not entitled to increase the price by virtue of the escalation clause. In another case[50] between Californian sellers and English buyers Parker J. avoided an apparent conflict of forms by finding that the contract was made by exchange of telex messages prior to the exchange of formal documents. The learned judge came to the conclusion that the "small print clause [in the sellers' formal acknowledgment of the order] is, in the context, meaningless. . . . The reference to the original offer was for identification only. . . ."

A real difficulty arises in the battle of forms situation if the operation of the general conditions of one of the parties is not placed beyond doubt by a signed confirmation or acceptance of the other party or if it cannot be established that the contract was concluded by other means than the exchange of formal documents. Here one would only with reluctance arrive at the result that there is no contract, as the strict application of the offer-acceptance-counteroffer analysis may demand, because that is not what the parties intended. One would have to analyse the other terms of

---

[47] *Ibid. per* Lord Keith of Kinkel, 177.
[48] John Adams, "The Battle of Forms" in [1983] J.B.L. 297.
[49] *Butler Machine Tools Co. Ltd.* v. *Ex-Cell-O Corporation (England) Ltd.* [1979] 1 W.L.R. 401.
[50] *G.T.M. Ltd.* v. *Hydranautics* [1981] 2 Lloyd's Rep. 211, 215.

the contract and the subsequent conduct of the parties in order to ascertain whether the conditions of the man "who fired the last shot" or those of the man "who got in the first blow"[51] were intended to apply. If such analysis does not resolve the problem of the battle of forms but there is a clear intention of the parties to be in a contractual relationship, the best course is to ignore the contradictory "small print" in the forms as meaningless and to decide according to the law.[52]

INTERNATIONAL SUPPLY CONTRACTS

In order to protect contracting parties of relatively weak bargaining power and, in particular, the consumer, the Unfair Contract Terms Act 1977 and other enactments[53] prohibit or restrict certain contract terms, such as clauses exempting a party from his liability under the general law. Normally the exporter will not be concerned with the provisions of the Unfair Contract Terms Act[54] because the contracts which he concludes with his overseas customers will qualify as international supply contracts[55] and, as such, are exempted from the protective provisions of that Act.[56] Exceptionally, however, as we have seen,[57] an export contract may not qualify as an international supply contract.

An international supply contract is defined by the Unfair Contract Terms Act 1977, s.26(3) and (4), as having the following characteristics:

   (*a*) either it is a contract of sale of goods or it is one under or in pursuance of which the possession or ownership of goods passes; and
   (*b*) it is made by parties whose places of business (or, if they have none, habitual residences) are in the territories of different States (the Channel Islands and the

---

[51] Lord Denning M.R. in the case quoted in n. 49.

[52] In *British Steel Corporation* v. *Cleveland Bridge & Engineering Co. Ltd.* [1982] Com.L.R. 54, the issue of conflicting general contract terms was dropped and the question for the decision of the court was whether the communications between the parties constituted a contract. Robert Goff J. found that this was not the case but allowed the party who had supplied the goods compensation on the quasi-contractual ground of *quantum meruit*. The decision is not very satisfactory.

[53] The Sale of Goods Act 1979, the Supply of Goods and Services Act 1982, and the Supply of Goods (Implied Terms) Act 1973 (as far as not repealed), the Consumer Credit Act 1974 and the Consumer Protection Act 1987.

[54] See p. 7, *ante*.

[55] Numerous definitions of international sales contracts exist, see Uniform Law on the International Sale of Goods (1964), art. 1 (see p. 204, *post*) and UN Convention on Contracts for the International Sale of Goods (Vienna, 1980), art. 1. On the definition of an international contract in American and French law, see G. R. Delaume "What is an International Contract? An American and a Gallic Dilemma" 29 I.C.L.Q. (1979), 258.

[56] Unfair Contract Terms Act, s.26(1) and (2).

[57] See p. 13, *ante*. The international supply contract is also not exempt from the provisions of the Supply of Goods and Services Act 1982, ss.13 to 15. But the Secretary of State may grant exemption by statutory instrument (s.12(4) and (5)). To date (October 1, 1989) no such exemption has been granted for international contracts for the supply of services.

Isle of Man being treated for this purpose as different States from the United Kingdom).

In addition, the contract must satisfy the following requirements:

(*a*) the goods in question are, at the time of the conclusion of the contract, in the course of carriage, or will be carried, from the territory of one State to the territory of another; or

(*b*) the acts constituting the offer and acceptance have been done in the territories of different States; or

(*c*) the contract provides for the goods to be delivered to the territory of a State other than that within whose territory those acts were done.

CHAPTER 6

INVOICES AND PACKING

INVOICES

CORRECT invoicing is a matter of great importance in the export trade. The smooth performance of the contract of sale will often depend on it. The seller may sometimes regard the buyer's instructions on this point as too exacting, but he should not forget that the buyer requires these details in order to comply with the regulations in force in his own country applying to such topics as import licences, Customs duties and exchange restrictions. This explains why the buyer in certain circumstances will ask for a *pro forma invoice* in advance or for the invoice to be dated a month, or some other fixed time, later than the date of the last invoice.

The invoice must be true and correct

The exporter should make it a firm principle of business policy in international sales and other international supply contracts only to issue invoices which are correct in all respects.

He is sometimes requested by the buyer abroad to insert inaccurate particulars into the invoice. The buyer may ask that the price for the goods be understated in the invoice because he wants to reduce or evade taxes or import duties in his country.[1] Or, vice versa, he may ask that the invoice price be increased above the true purchase price and the excess be transferred to an account outside his country because he wishes to evade local exchange control on the transfer of funds abroad.[2]

False invoicing has almost invariably an improper motive. A contract in which the parties agree that a false invoice be issued is often unenforceable in law.

---

[1] *Euro-Diam Ltd.* v. *Bathurst* [1987] 1 Lloyd's Rep. 178 (where a UK exporter, complying with the request of a German importer, underpriced in the invoice goods (diamonds) delivered to the importer on sale or return terms and thereby committed an offence under the German tax code. Nevertheless, when the unsold goods were stolen in Germany, he could recover from the UK insurer because the insurance contract was not tainted by the illegality of the sale or return contract).

[2] *United City Merchants* (*Investments*) *Ltd.* v. *Royal Bank of Scotland The American Accord.* [1983] 1 A.C. 168; see p. 112, *post*.

The exporter should, in his own interest, decline to accommodate the buyer if he requests that the invoice should contain false statements. If the seller agrees to the request, knowing that the contract stipulating for a false invoice is illegal under the buyer's law, the English courts will refuse to enforce the contract because they give no legal assistance to a party who intends to break the laws of a friendly foreign country.[3] If in these cases the buyer fails to perform his obligations, the seller may be without a contractual remedy in the English or foreign courts, unless in English proceedings the court holds that the remainder of the contract can be severed from the illegal part.[4] Moreover, false invoicing may infringe English law directly. Overpricing in the invoice in order to evade foreign exchange control may contravene the Bretton Woods Agreements[5] which form part of English law. If this is the case, the contract is unenforceable in the English courts as far as the excess price is concerned.[6]

The refusal of the exporter to be a party to the issue of a false invoice will thus avoid a potential source of subsequent legal embarrassment to himself. Normally the seller's statement that the issue of a false invoice is contrary to his business practice will be accepted by the buyer.

The commercial invoice

The trading invoice should state the names and addresses of the seller and buyer, the date and reference number of the buyer's order, a description of the goods sold, details of package (including the weight of every bale or case), exact marks and numbers appearing on the package, and the price. If possible, the details of shipping (including the name of the steamer and the route) should be added. It is not unusual for the invoice to contain the note "*e. and o.e.*" (errors and omissions excepted). A typical reference to the shipping details would be—

> INVOICE of 4 Cases Worsted Tweeds supplied by Messrs. Bubble and Squeak, of Liverpool, to Messrs. Bow and Line, of Sydney, Australia, to be shipped in *SS. Aurora* from Liverpool. Order Number XYZ/1345.

The invoice price has to be stated in accordance with the agreed terms of the contract as explained earlier; it may be the ex works price, or the

---

[3] See p. 235, *post.*

[4] *Fielding & Platt Ltd.* v. *Najjar* [1969] 1 W.L.R. 357, 362 (where the court found that the British manufacturer had no knowledge of the illegality under the buyer's law); see also *The American Accord* n. 2, *ante.*

[5] The United Kingdom is a member of the Bretton Woods Agreements. The Bretton Woods Agreements Act 1945 was repealed by the Overseas Development and Co-operation Act 1980, s.18(1) and Sched. 2, but the Bretton Woods Agreements Order in Council 1946 (S.R. & O. 1946 No. 36) is still in operation.

[6] *United City Merchants (Investments) Ltd.* v. *Royal Bank of Canada; The American Accord* [1983] 1 A.C. 168; see p. 112, *post.*

f.o.b. price, or the c.i.f. price and so on. In the case of a c.i.f. contract, the price calculation in the invoice has to comply, in the absence of an agreement of the parties to the contrary, with the principles explained earlier.[7] The buyer will often ask that a detailed statement of the elements of the price be shown on the invoice, setting out the actual net price ex factory and the further charges separately, because these details are required for submission to his own authorities. In an f.o.b. contract with additional services[8] the seller is requested by the buyer to arrange freight and insurance for the consignment. As this goes beyond the normal duty of the f.o.b. seller and represents a separate arrangement, the buyer should be debited for these items not on the goods invoice but on a separate invoice which would cover the prepaid freight, the insurance premium and the incidental commissions and charges.[9]

Invoices in letter of credit transactions

Where payment under a letter of credit is agreed, it is normal that the commercial invoice is one of the documents which have to be tendered to the advising bank. Here the invoice is an important—if not the most important—document. Great care should be taken that it contains the correct description of the goods and any other particulars relating to them, as specified in the contract of sale. These details are likely to be transmitted by the buyer (the applicant for the credit) to the issuing bank when instructed to open the credit; they are passed on to the advising bank and the documents may be rejected by either bank if the required details are not stated, or are stated incorrectly, in the invoice. Article 41 of the UCP (1983 Revision) provides:

(a) Unless otherwise stipulated in the credit, commercial invoices must be made out in the name of the applicant for the credit.

(b) Unless otherwise stipulated in the credit, banks may refuse commercial invoices issued for amounts in excess of the amount permitted by the credit. Nevertheless, if a bank authorised to pay, incur a deferred payment undertaking, accept, or negotiate under a credit accepts such invoices, its decision will be binding upon all parties, provided such bank has not paid, incurred a deferred payment undertaking, accepted or effected negotiation for an amount in excess of that permitted by the credit.

(c) The description of the goods in the commercial invoice must correspond with the description in the credit. In all other documents, the goods may be described in general terms not inconsistent with the description of the goods in the credit.

The details in the invoice have also to correspond with the general description of the goods in the other documents tendered to the bank.[10]

---

[7] On p. 35, *ante*. Blackburn J. in *Ireland* v. *Livingston* (1872) L.R. 5 H.L. 395, 406.

[8] See p. 20, *ante*.

[9] See p. 24, *ante*.

[10] On the linkage of documents tendered to the bank see p. 415, *post*.

Official requirements for invoices

Although consular invoices, which had to be completed on an official form and to be certified by the local consul, are now abolished, some countries prescribe that the commercial invoice should be in a particular form or should satisfy certain requirements, *e.g.* that it should be combined with a certificate of value and/or origin. The commercial invoice for imports into Barbados has to contain the following declaration:

> It is hereby certified that this invoice shows the actual price of the goods described, that no other invoice has been or will be issued and that all particulars are true and correct.
>
> (Signature and status of authorised person)

The requirements of foreign laws in respect of invoices vary greatly and are altered from time to time. The exporter who does not employ the services of a freight forwarder should keep himself informed of these changes and make certain that he dispatches the goods in accordance with the latest invoice requirements in force in the country of destination. They are recorded in *Croner's Reference Book for Exporters* and the other trade publications mentioned earlier.[11] In case of doubt the exporter can obtain the desired information from the consulate of the country of destination, his chamber of commerce or the appropriate Regional Office of the Department of Trade and Industry.

PACKING

The obligation to provide suitable packaging

The exporter has to give careful consideration to the packing of the goods to be shipped abroad. Unless otherwise agreed in the contract of sale, it is his duty to pack the goods in a manner which assures their safe arrival and facilitates their handling in transit and at the place of destination. Neglect in this respect will invariably result in delay in the delivery of the goods and might entitle the overseas customer to reject the goods or to claim damages. The legal position is aptly described in the General Conditions of Delivery of Goods 1968–1975 of CMEA[12] in a provision which, it is believed, has general application[13]:

---

[11] See pp. 85–87, *ante*.
[12] See p. 70, *ante*.
[13] General Conditions of Delivery of Goods 1968–1975 (1979 Revision), para. 20(1).

1. If there are no special directions in the contract concerning packing, the seller must ship the goods in packing used for export goods in the seller's country, which will assure preservation of the goods during transportation, taking into account possible transshipment, and proper and usual handling of the goods. In appropriate cases the duration and methods of carriage must also be taken into account.
2. Before packing, machines and equipment shall be properly greased to assure their preservation from corrosion.

Packing in the sale of goods

The buyer is in certain circumstances entitled to refuse the acceptance of the goods if they are not packed in accordance with his instructions or with the custom of the trade. Where a particular package is stipulated, the packing of the goods often forms part of the *description* of the goods within the meaning of section 13 of the Sale of Goods Act 1979. It may be essential for the overseas buyer that the goods should be supplied in the stipulated packings.[14] If he has ordered jam in one and two pound jars, the contract is broken if the jam is supplied in 10 pound tins. According to section 13(1) of the Act it is an implied condition, where goods are sold by description, that the goods shall correspond with the description. This however, has to be read in the light of the modern doctrine of the innominate term,[15] according to which it depends on the nature and gravity of the breach whether it entitles the buyer to rescind the contract or whether the contract still subsists and he is only entitled to damages.[16] If the deficiency in the packing affects the "substantial identity" of the goods, it will be treated as a breach of the condition implied by section 13(1). In that case the buyer is entitled to reject the goods, and where goods, which are packed in the stipulated manner, are mixed with other goods, the buyer may reject the whole consignment or, if he prefers, only that part of it that is packed contrary to the agreement (Sale of Goods Act 1979, s.30(4)).

These rules have been repeatedly applied by the courts. In one case, where the description qualified as a condition, the buyer of Australian canned fruit was held to be entitled to reject the whole consignment

---

[14] Although in *M/S Aswan Engineering Establishment Co.* v. *Lupdine Ltd.* [1987] 1 W.L.R. 1 the failure to perform the contract for the sale of a liquid waterproofing compound by a UK seller to a buyer in Kuwait was due to the quality of the packing (heavy duty pails purchased for export collapsed in intensive heat in Kuwait), the issues in this case did not concern the point here treated; they were whether the pails were of merchantable quality within section 14(2) of the Sale of Goods Act 1979 (which the court held they were) and whether the buyer had a claim in the tort of negligence against the manufacturer of the pails (which the court rejected).

[15] See p. 135, *post.*

[16] Lord Wilberforce in *Reardon Smith Line Ltd.* v. *Yngvar Hansen-Tangen* [1976] 1 W.L.R. 989, 998.

because the cases did not all contain 30 tins each, as agreed upon, but there were included in the consignment smaller cases containing 24 tins each, and this, although an umpire had declared that there was no difference in the market value of the goods whether packed 24 or 30 tins in a case.[17] This case, if it was decided correctly, would indicate a remarkable extension of the rule. In an earlier case, where Siam rice was rejected because it was supplied in single bags instead of double bags, (*i.e.* gunny bags) as stipulated, the buyer was required to prove that the rice was more easily saleable in double bags,[18] and today this kind of evidence or other evidence as to the gravity of the breach is necessary to establish that the breach has to be qualified as breach of a condition. When goods are sold on f.o.b. or c.i.f. terms, the price quotation includes export packing charges unless it is stated expressly that an extra charge will be made for package. The exporter, who wishes to make an extra charge for package, should state so clearly when sending out the quotation or confirmation.

Packing in the law of carriage of goods

In the law of carriage of goods by sea, freight is paid on the weight or measurement or value of the cargo and the carrier is entitled to demand the calculation of the freight at the highest rate.[19] The seller should consult his freight forwarder in order to ascertain the mode of packing which is required to secure a favourable rate of freight, but he should not place this consideration higher than the safety of the consignment and the convenience of the customer whose agents have to handle the packages on arrival. Where stowage on deck (*cargaison de tillac*) is agreed upon, presumably stronger package will have to be provided than where the goods are stowed in the holds unless the goods are stowed in containers. The master of the ship will refuse to sign a clean bill of lading if the package is defective, and the seller, who under his contract with the buyer may be obliged to tender him a clean bill, will be unable to do so. The individual packages should be marked and branded in strict compliance with the directions of the buyer who is entitled to refuse the acceptance of a bill of lading which refers to goods that are marked and branded differently. The description of the goods in the bill of lading or other transport document should, at least in general terms, correspond to

---

[17] *Re an Arbitration between Moore & Co. Ltd. and Landauer & Co.* [1921] 2 K.B. 519. It is doubtful if this case would be decided in the same manner today; it is possible that the term in question may be classified as an innominate term. See also *Manbre Saccharine Co.* v. *Corn Products Co.* [1919] 1 K.B. 198, 207.

[18] *Makin* v. *London Rice Mills Co.* (1869) 20 L.T. 705.

[19] See p. 547, *post.*

that in the invoice and other documents, so that an identification of the goods throughout the whole set of documents is possible.

Under Article IV(5)(*a*) of the Hague-Visby Rules, to which effect was given in the United Kingdom by the Carriage of Goods by Sea Act 1971, the liability of the carrier for loss of or damage to the goods in transit is limited in amount; unless the nature and value of the goods have been declared before shipment and inserted in the bill of lading, the liability does not exceed 666.67 units of account per package or unit or two units of account per kilo of gross weight of the goods lost or damaged, whichever is higher.[20] In the case of transportation by air, the statutory maximum limitation of liability of the carrier is calculated by weight and not by the number of packages.[21] In the international transport by road, it is likewise expressed by reference to weight, and not to package or unit.[22]

Packing in containers

In container transport by sea a difficult legal problem arises: is the container itself a "package" within the meaning of Article IV(5)(*a*) of the Hague-Visby Rules, or is each of the pieces of cargo carried in the container a separate "package" within the meaning of that provision? The practical importance of this problem is obvious. If the container is the "package," the liability of the carrier is limited as indicated earlier. But if each part of its contents is a "package," and the container, *e.g.* carries 100 pieces of cargo, the maximum liability of the carrier under the Hague-Visby Rules would be 100 times higher than in the former case.

This question is discussed later, when the legal aspects of container transport are treated in general.[23] Reference is made there in particular to the decisions of the courts which have considered this question.

Packing in insurance law

Insufficient packing may in certain circumstances be regarded as inherent vice of the goods and deprive the assured of the protection of an all risks cover under Cargo Clauses A attached to Lloyd's Marine Policy.[24]

---

[20] The units of account are the SDRs of the World Bank. For the conversion of the SDRs into pounds sterling see p. 602, *post*.
[21] Carriage by Air Act 1961, Sched. 1, art. 22(1). This Schedule will be superseded by Sched. 1 of the Carriage by Air and Road Act 1979 when this Act will be put into operation; see pp. 628 and 632, *post*.
[22] Carriage of Goods by Road Act 1965, Sched. 1, art. 23(3), as amended by section 4(2) of the Carriage by Air and Road Act 1979; see p. 641, *post*.
[23] See p. 618, *post*.
[24] *F. W. Berk & Co. Ltd.* v. *Style* [1956] 1 Q.B. 180; see p. 517, *post*.

Import regulations relating to packing

Further, the package should conform with the legislation in force in the country of destination. In some countries, certain types of packing are prohibited or restricted: *e.g.* the import regulations of New Zealand prohibit the use of hay, straw, chaff, flax rug or rice husks as packing material and special requirements apply to other packing material, particularly wood. Australia imposes similar restrictions on the use of packing material; if wood is used for packing cases or in connection with other means of packing, it must be fumigated or otherwise treated in accordance with the Australian Quarantine Regulations and a certificate of packing on the company's headed paper and signed by a senior member of the export company must give precise details of the method of treatment and has to be sent with the other documents to the consignee. In some foreign countries, import duties are levied on a particular kind of packing material, *e.g.* glass containers or metal sheeting. Many countries have nowadays strict regulations about the marking and branding of packages. The seller, if in doubt, should obtain full instructions from his buyer or, if it is more convenient, consult the trade publications or inquire of the institutions referred to earlier.[25]

Dangerous goods

There exist stringent legal requirements for the packing and labelling of dangerous goods in transit.[26] These regulations are different for the transportation by sea, air, road and rail.[27] Information about these requirements can be obtained from firms specialising in export packing, freight forwarders and in the *Hints to Exporters* booklets mentioned earlier.[28]

As far as sea transport is concerned, detailed information including classifications of dangerous goods is contained in the *Blue Book* (Report of the Standing Advisory Committee on the Carriage of Dangerous Goods in Ships)[29] and in the *IMDG Code* (International Maritime Dangerous Goods Code).[30]

---

[25] See Chapter 4, p. 81, *ante.*
[26] Merchant Shipping Act 1948, s.446, Merchant Shipping (Safety Convention) Act 1949, Merchant Shipping (Dangerous Goods) Regulations 1981 (S.I. 1981 No. 1747) and Merchant Shipping (Dangerous Goods) (Amendment) Regulations 1986 (S.I. 1986 No. 1069).
[27] See *Croner's Reference Book for Exporters.*
[28] See p. 86, *ante.* Guides to Packaging Dangerous Goods for Transport can also be obtained from Aurigny Ltd., P.O. Box 12, Guildford, Surrey GU4 7PL, England, or in North America from Hazardous Materials Advisory Council, Suite 907, 1012 Fourteenth Street N.W., Washington D.C., 20005, USA.
[29] Obtainable from HMSO.
[30] Obtainable from International Maritime Organisation, Imco House, Albert Embankment, London SE17. 1990 edition.

CHAPTER 7

MODES OF PAYMENT

THIS topic will be considered fully when the various methods of financing exports are analysed.[1]

It will be seen that in international trade certain standardised methods of payment for exports have been evolved, that extensive use is made in this connection of the bill of exchange as an instrument of payment,[2] and that in particular, the goods themselves, as represented by the bill of lading, can be used as a security for financing exports, *e.g.* by arranging payment under a bankers' letter of credit.[3] If payment is not made under a letter of credit, particular caution is called for in two cases: if credit is allowed,[4] or if the purchase price is paid in advance[5]; in the latter case, if the seller becomes insolvent, the buyer might find that he has no title to the goods and that his claim for recovery of the price is practically worthless.

British exchange control

Exchange control has been abolished in the United Kingdom since 1979. In that year the statutory instruments regulating exchange control were revoked.[6] Later the Exchange Control Act 1947 which authorised the Treasury to operate an exchange control system was repealed.[7]

---

[1] See Part 3, pp. 376 *et seq.*, *post.*
[2] See p. 379, *post.*
[3] See p. 400, *post.* Other methods of obtaining payment are likewise used, *e.g.* collection arrangements (p. 395, *post*) or non-recourse finance, such as factoring or forfaiting (p. 453, *post*).
[4] See p. 148, *post.*
[5] See p. 116, *post.*
[6] This was done by statutory instruments with effect from October 24, 1979, except Southern Rhodesia (Exchange Control (Revocation) Directions 1979) (S.I. 1979 No. 1339) and from December, 1979 with respect to Southern Rhodesia (Exchange Control (Revocation) (No. 2) Directions 1979) (S.I. 1979 No. 1662). These statutory instruments were consolidated on December 6, 1979 into an instrument granting general exemption (Exchange Control (General Exemption) Order 1979) (S.I. 1979 No. 1660).
[7] By the Finance Act 1987, s.68. After the repeal of the Exchange Control Act 1947, the scheduled territories were defined, for the purposes of the Borrowing (Control and Guarantees) Act 1946, by the Control of Borrowing (Amendment) Order 1988 (S.I. 1988 No. 295) as follows: The United Kingdom, the Channel Islands, the Isle of Man, the Republic of Ireland and Gibraltar.

Foreign exchange control

Exchange contracts under the Bretton Woods Agreements

Some foreign countries still maintain exchange control regulations for the protection of their currency. If such a country is a member of the Bretton Woods Agreements—the United Kingdom is also a member—a contract qualifying as "exchange contract" which involves the currency of the foreign country in question and is contrary to its exchange control regulations is unenforceable in the English courts. This is provided by the Bretton Woods Agreements Order in Council 1946[8] which gives force in England to article VIII, section 2(b) of the Bretton Woods Agreement of 1944.[9] This provision is in the following terms:

> Exchange contracts which involve the currency of any member and which are contrary to the exchange control regulations of that member maintained or imposed consistently with this agreement shall be unenforceable in the territories of any other member. . . .

An exchange contract within the meaning of this provision is in principle only a monetary deal in currencies.[10] It does not comprise a genuine commercial contract for the sale and purchase of merchandise or commodities, although the price is expressed in a foreign currency. Thus, a contract whereby Italian buyers purchased metal from English dealers but which had not been authorised by the Italian authorities did not qualify as an "exchange contract" and was enforceable against the buyers.[11]

Disguised exchange contracts

But an exchange contract may be made in the disguise of an innocent merchandise contract and would then be unenforceable. If a Member State of the Bretton Woods Agreements operates exchange control, a

---

[8] S.R. & O. 1946 No. 36. This Order in Council was made under the Bretton Woods Agreements Act 1945 which was repealed by the Overseas Development and Co-operation Act 1980. The Order in Council of 1946, however, is still in force. It has not been repealed and is apparently saved by section 9(6)(a) of the 1980 Act.

[9] The international monetary system set up by the Bretton Woods Agreements in 1945 broke down in 1971 and was replaced by a generalised system of floating exchange rates (see Bruno Oppetit, in *Exchange Rate Risks in International Contracts*, ICC Brochure No. 440/3, 1987, p. 5), but, as stated in the preceding note, the legal regulation relating to the Bretton Woods Agreements has not been repealed in the United Kingdom.

[10] *Sharif* v. *Azad* [1961] 1 Q.B. 605; *Sing Batra* v. *Ebrahim, The Times*, May 3, 1977.

[11] *Wilson, Smithett & Cope Ltd.* v. *Terruzzi* [1976] Q.B. 683; see Sir Joseph Gold, "Exchange Contracts, Exchange Control, and the IMF Articles of Agreement; Some Animadversions on *Wilson, Smithett & Cope Ltd.* v. *Teruzzi*" in 33 I.C.L.Q. (1984), 777.

buyer in that State may induce the seller to invoice the goods at a higher price than the true price and ask him to transfer the excess to the buyer's account outside his, the buyer's, country. As far as the excess over the true price is concerned, the transaction is an exchange contract because it involves the transfer of currency from the buyer's country in breach of that country's exchange control regulations. This part of the contract is unenforceable in the English courts but the part which represents the genuine merchandise transaction is enforceable. This was decided in *United City Merchants (Investments) Ltd.* v. *Royal Bank of Canada; The American Accord.*[12] In this case Glass Fibres and Equipment Ltd., an English company, sold a glass fibre manufacturing plant to Vitrorefuerzos S.A., a Peruvian company. At the request of the buyers the sellers stated double the genuine purchase price in the invoice which showed a price of, $662,086 f.o.b. UK port. The arrangement between the parties was that the excess over the genuine purchase price should be transferred by the sellers to the U.S.A. into a "draw down" account, which was at the disposal of the buyers. The House of Lords held that the transaction, as far as the excess over the genuine purchase price was concerned (£331,043), was an exchange contract in disguise and unenforceable as contravening the Bretton Woods Agreements Order in Council 1946. Lord Diplock observed that the court must take this point itself, even if not pleaded, and added:

> But this does not have the effect of making an exchange contract that is contrary to the exchange control regulations of a Member State other than the United Kingdom into a contract that is illegal under English law or render acts undertaken in this country in performance of such a contract unlawful. Like a contract of guarantee of which there is no note or memorandum in writing it is unenforceable by the courts and nothing more.

Similarly, an agreement whereby airline tickets were bought in Iran (a member of the Bretton Woods Agreements) with Iranian currency for the purpose of obtaining a refund on them in pounds sterling in England was a disguised exchange contract and an action on a cheque given by the defendant who allegedly had obtained the refund would have amounted to enforcing an unenforceable contract and would have to be dismissed, provided, of course, that the transaction contravened Iranian exchange control regulations and these regulations were consistent with the Bretton Woods Agreements.[13]

---

[12] [1983] 1 A.C. 168. In this case another important point arose which relates to letters of credit; this point is treated on p. 443, *post*. See also *Overseas Union Insurance Ltd.* v. *AA Mutual International Insurance Co. Ltd.* [1988] 2 Lloyd's Rep 63, 70. (Reinsurance agreements did not contravene South African exchange control and were not disguised exchange contracts).

[13] *Mansouri* v. *Singh*, [1986] 1 W.L.R. 1393 (C.A.).

Foreign exchange control regulations recognised but not enforced by the English courts

The exchange control regulations of a foreign country, whether a member of the Bretton Woods Agreements or not, are *recognised* by the English courts in so far as they will not enforce a contract deliberately aimed at the infringement of these regulations. But the English courts refuse to *enforce* in the English jurisdiction foreign exchange control regulations, particularly at the suit of the foreign revenue authority.

This subject is treated in a later chapter.[14]

English judgments and arbitration awards in a foreign currency

Where the currency of the contract is expressed in the money of a foreign country or damages have been suffered substantially in such country, the English courts and arbitration tribunals are prepared to express their decisions in the foreign currency in question. This subject will be treated later on.[15]

---

[14] Chapter 13, pp. 233 and 235, *post.*
[15] See pp. 224–246, *post.*

CHAPTER 8

PERFORMANCE OF THE CONTRACT

THE disposal of the goods by the seller in performance of the contract of sale has to pass through three phases, namely, the delivery of the goods, the passing of the property in the goods and the passing of the risk. In the normal cases of overseas sales, in particular on f.o.b. and c.i.f. terms, these three phases do not coincide and should be clearly distinguished.

ENGLISH AND FOREIGN SALES LAW

The first question which has to be examined when a dispute arises between the parties about the delivery of the goods, the passing of the property or of the risk, is whether the matter is to be considered from the point of view of English law or of the foreign law prevailing in the country of the buyer. This question pertains to the branch of law known as the conflict of laws which will be discussed later.[1] The answer which the rules on the conflict of laws may provide is evidently that the issue is decided either by English law, in which case the provisions of the Sale of Goods Act 1979 will apply,[2] or by the foreign law in question. If the latter conclusion is reached, the English courts may still have jurisdiction to hear the case; the substantive question of the law applicable to the contract is distinct from the procedural one of jurisdiction of the court and these two questions should not be confused; the only inference which has to be drawn from the application of foreign law to a particular contract is that the rules of the relevant foreign law displace the provisions of the Sale of Goods Act 1979, and that foreign law can be relied upon in the English courts if its rules can be proved by expert witnesses or in another admissible manner.[3] A third, though from the practical point of view remote, possibility is that the parties agree in their contract to apply the Uniform Laws on International Sales; in this case the provisions of the Uniform Laws on International Sales Act 1967 apply.[4]

---

[1] See p. 204, *post*.
[2] See p. 7, *ante*.
[3] See p. 204, *post*.
[4] See p. 241, *post*. The Uniform Laws on International Sales will in due course be replaced by the UN Convention on Contracts for the International Sale of Goods (Vienna 1980) but this Convention has not been given effect in the United Kingdom yet (Position: October 1, 1989).

If the contract of sale is governed by foreign law, it should be borne in mind that the rules of foreign law may be different from those of English law. Thus, in some continental countries, such as France, Italy, Germany and Greece, if the seller delays the delivery of the goods and no time is fixed for the delivery, the buyer must normally demand delivery and allow the seller a reasonable time for performance (*délai de grâce*; *Nachfrist*) before he can treat the contract as repudiated[5]; this requirement of *mise en demeure* is unknown in Anglo-American law which is much stricter in this respect and entitles the innocent party at once to treat the contract as repudiated when a reasonable time for delivery has expired, provided that time is of the essence of the contract, as is normally the case.[6] While in English law a buyer who wishes to reject goods which are not in accordance with the contract has to inform the seller of this intention within "a reasonable time,"[7] in Swiss and Scandinavian law the defects have to be notified to the seller "at once" (*sofort*); in German law, if the parties are businessmen "without delay" (*unverzüglich*); in Italian law, in principle, within eight days; in Spanish law, as regards packed goods, within four days and as regards hidden defects (*vicios internos* or *occultos*) within 30 days[8]; and in French law the buyer has to start proceedings "within a short time" (*dans un bref délai*).[9] According to the Convention on the Limitation Period in the International Sale of Goods sponsored by UNCITRAL and signed in 1974,[10] the limitation period in respect of a claim arising from a defect or lack of conformity of goods in an international sale shall, in principle, be four years.

Further, under the laws of England, the United States of America, France, Belgium, Italy and Portugal the property in the goods sold passes when the parties intend it to pass, whether the delivery of the goods did or did not take place. The position is different under the laws of the Netherlands, Spain, Germany, the Argentine, Brazil, Chile and Columbia where the property passes, as a rule, only if the intention of the parties that it should pass is supported by the actual delivery of the goods. These very considerable differences in the national sales laws are not helpful to international trade. The general adoption of the UN Convention on Contracts for the International Sale of Goods (Vienna, 1980) which came into operation on January 1, 1988, would be of great benefit to the international trading community.

---

[5] The requirements of the various laws as regards *délai de grâce* vary.
[6] *Toepfer* v. *Wenersan-Portman N.V.* [1980] 1 Lloyd's Rep. 143, 147–148 (C.A.). See p. 136, *post*.
[7] See pp. 140 and 142, *post*.
[8] In some South American laws the periods are shorter than in Spanish law.
[9] Sometimes trade usages applying to certain commodities provide for another regulation as regards the notification of defects.
[10] See p. 254, *post*. This Convention and the Protocol amending it (Vienna, 1980) have not been given effect in the United Kingdom yet (Position: October 1, 1988).

Let us assume that the United Kingdom exporter has avoided the pitfalls of foreign law—which, incidentally, sometimes operate in his favour—by the simple device of having embodied in his contract an express stipulation that the contract shall be governed, in all respects, by English law.[11] In this case, the Sale of Goods Act 1979 applies, which contains a definition of the term "delivery" and a number of rules on the passing of the property and the risk.

DELIVERY OF THE GOODS

According to section 61 of the 1979 Act "delivery" means the "voluntary transfer of possession from one person to another." The goods are normally delivered to the buyer when he, or his agent, acquires custody of the goods or is enabled to exercise control over them.[12] In cases in which no bill of lading is issued, delivery to the carrier for the purposes of transmission to the buyer is prima facie deemed to be delivery to the buyer.[13]

The place and time of delivery are, in export sales, usually defined by the special trade terms which have been considered earlier; these special arrangements displace the provisions of the Sale of Goods Acts 1979 on delivery which are mainly contained in sections 27 to 37. In particular, where the seller has obtained a bill of lading, as is the case in classic f.o.b. contracts and f.o.b. contracts with additional services, or in c.i.f. or c. and f. contracts, the goods are deemed to be delivered when the bill of lading is delivered to the buyer.[14] If the parties have agreed on one of the container delivery terms,[15] delivery takes place when the carrier takes charge of the goods, except in the rare cases in which the seller has undertaken to tender a marine bill of lading; in these cases the same considerations apply as explained above.

PASSING OF THE PROPERTY

The rules of the Act on the passing of the property in the goods sold are likewise often modified by special arrangements made between the

---

[11] Such a clause is called "a choice of law clause," see p. 211, *post*.
[12] See *E. Reynolds & Sons (Chingford) Ltd.* v. *Hendry Bros. Ltd.* [1955] 1 Lloyd's Rep. 258, 259; *Commercial Fibres (Ireland) Ltd.* v. *Zabaida* [1975] 1 Lloyd's Rep. 27 (delivery ex warehouse or ex dock at place of shipment).
[13] s.32(1). The same applies where the goods are shipped not to the buyer but to a bank to which they are pledged by way of security (*Kum* v. *Wah Tat Bank Ltd.* [1971] 1 Lloyd's Rep. 439).
[14] *Biddell Bros.* v. *E. Clemens Horst Co.* [1912] A.C. 18, 22.
[15] See p. 59, *ante*.

parties to an export sale. The Act provides here two fundamental rules, namely that, where the contract is for the sale of unascertained goods, the property does not pass to the buyer unless and until the goods are ascertained (s.16) and, where the contract is for the sale of specific or ascertained goods, the property passes at such time as the parties intend it to pass (s.17(1)).

Unascertained goods

The rule that no property can pass in unascertained goods[16] causes, on occasion, difficulty. This is so particularly in two sets of circumstances, *viz.* where a buyer buys part of a bulk consignment, *e.g.* 10,000 tonnes of crude oil out of a consignment of 200,000 tonnes carried in a supertanker, or where the buyer has paid the purchase price in advance and the seller becomes insolvent before delivery of the goods. Thus, in *Re Wait*[17], which concerned an import transaction, a British merchant bought 1,000 tonnes of wheat on c.i.f. terms from American suppliers and resold a parcel of 500 tonnes to another British firm which paid the purchase price in spot cash; the wheat was then shipped in bulk to the merchant who went bankrupt before the ship arrived. The trustee in bankruptcy successfully resisted the sub-purchaser's claim for delivery of 500 tonnes of the bulk cargo; the court held that his parcel consisted of unascertained goods and the property in them had not passed to the sub-purchaser as there had never been an appropriation or identification of the 500 tonnes of wheat which represented the sub-purchaser's goods. But unascertained goods may become ascertained by a *process of exhaustion* and then property may pass in them. Thus, in *The Elafi*[18] the ship carried 22,000 tonnes of copra in bulk. The claimants, Karlshamns Olje Fabriker, acquired bills of lading relating to 6,000 tonnes and later by a separate contract an additional 500 tonnes of the bulk consignment. The vessel discharged first at Rotterdam and then at Hamburg and the cargo remaining on board consisted only of the copra purchased by the claimants under the two contracts. When the vessel arrived at Karlshamn, water entered one of the holds and the copra therein was damaged. The claimants founded their action against the shipowners on the tort of negligence, claiming that they had become owners of the damaged goods.[19] Mustill J. held that

---

[16] "As a general principle, the passing of full title to the goods depends upon the ability to identify the goods," *per* Hobhouse J. in *Obestain Inc.* v. *National Mineral Development Corporation Ltd. Sanix Ace.* [1987] 1 Lloyd's Rep. 465, 469.

[17] [1927] 1 Ch. 606; *The Aramis*, [1989] 1 Lloyd's Rep. 213 (C.A.).

[18] *Karlshamns Olje Fabriker* v. *Eastport Navigation Corporation. The Elafi* [1981] 2 Lloyd's Rep. 679. See John Adams in 45 M.L.R. (1982) 690.

[19] The claim was also founded on the Bills of Lading Act 1855; see p. 558, *post.*

the goods which remained in the vessel after discharge in Hamburg had become ascertained goods by exhaustion and the claimants had acquired property in them; it was irrelevant that they were acquired under two separate contracts.

The rule in *Re Wait* is unsatisfactory. Mustill J. rightly qualified it in *The Elafi* by admitting ascertainment by exhaustion but the facts will rarely allow the application of this qualification. A more equitable solution of the problem of undivided shares in bulk would be if the law provided that persons interested in the bulk should be regarded as owners in common pro rata their interest. The common ownership rule was indeed adopted by Staughton J. in *The Ypatianna*,[20] a case concerned with a different issue; the defendants, who were the owners of the vessel *Ypatianna*, loaded crude oil, which was the property of the plaintiffs, into their vessel in the port of Novorossisk in the Soviet Union and mixed it in the vessel with their own crude oil. The learned judge found that the mixture could not be separated and that the defendants had not acted "for some commercial motive." It was held in some old cases, going back to 1594, that, if an owner mixed his goods with those of another in an inextricable manner, the whole of the goods belonged to the other. Founded on those cases, the plaintiffs claimed the value of the whole consignment in *The Ypatianna*. Staughton J., in an erudite judgment, distinguished the old cases and held that the mixture of crude oil was in the common ownership of the parties; the result was that the plaintiffs were only entitled to the value of their portion in the mixture. To revert to the question here discussed, the common ownership rule is adopted by the American Uniform Commercial Code, s. 2–105(4):

> An undivided share in an identified bulk of fungible[21] goods is sufficiently identified to be sold although the quantity of the bulk is not determined. Any agreed proportion of such a bulk or any quantity thereof agreed upon by number, weight or other measure may to the extent of the seller's interest in the bulk be sold to the buyer who then becomes an owner in common.

Although *The Elafi*, to a limited extent, reduces the effect of the rule in *Re Wait*, the rule is not abolished in English law and its ambit remains controversial. It is hoped that the rule will be further modified by the higher courts and, if necessary, by Parliament.[21a]

Another case which indicates the precarious position in which a buyer who has made an advance payment finds himself if the seller becomes

---

[20] [1987] 2 W.L.R. 869.

[21] "Fungible" is defined in the UCC, s.1–201 (17) thus: " 'Fungible' with respect to goods or securities means goods or securities of which any unit is, by nature or usage of trade, the equivalent of any other like unit. Goods which are not fungible shall be deemed to be fungible for the purposes of this Act to the extent that under a particular agreement or document unlike units are treated as equivalents."

[21a] The reform of section 16, as far as relating to rights to goods in bulk, is discussed in working paper No. 112 of the (English) Law Commission, 1989, and discussion paper No. 83 of the Scottish Law Commission, both of 1989.

insolvent before passing the property in the goods sold is *Carlos Federspiel & Co. S.A.* v. *Charles Twigg & Co. Ltd.*[22] In this case, which concerned an export transaction, a Costa Rican company bought from an English company 85 bicycles f.o.b. British port and paid the price for them in advance. The bicycles were packed into cases, marked with the buyers' name and registered for shipment in a named ship which was to load at Liverpool but they had not yet been sent to that port and were not yet shipped. A receiver and manager appointed by the debenture holders of the sellers claimed that the bicycles, like the other assets of the sellers, were charged in favour of the debenture holders. Pearson J. held that that contention was correct because the property in the bicycles had not yet passed; in the view of the learned judge the common intention of the parties was that the property should pass on shipment, or possibly later. This decision, it is thought is unsatisfactory.

Ascertained goods

In the case of specific or ascertained goods the task is to ascertain the intention of the parties, who are at liberty to fix the time when the property passes. This is not an easy task, since the clues which the Act furnishes in section 17(2) for ascertaining that intention are couched in vague and general terms, and the five specific presumptions which are laid down in section 18 are not appropriate to the particular circumstances of an export sale. Two possibilities exist here which require separate consideration: the seller may reserve the property in the goods (or, as businessmen sometimes call it, the right of disposal of the goods) until certain conditions have been fulfilled, or he may not have made the transfer of the property conditional.

In the first contingency, property does not pass to the buyer until the conditions imposed by the seller are satisfied, and that will even be the case where the goods have been delivered to the buyer, his agent, or a carrier for transmission to the buyer (s.19(1)). Such a condition may be imposed by the seller inserting into the contract of sale a retention of title[23] clause, *i.e.* a clause making the passing of the property conditional on the receipt of the purchase price in cash — a not unusual condition, particularly in overseas sales unless it is clear that the seller intends to give unsecured credit. The law provides two rebuttable presumptions in favour of a conditional transfer of the property: first, where goods are shipped and by the bill of lading the goods are deliverable to the order of

---

[22] [1957] 1 Lloyd's Rep. 240.
[23] The terms "title" and "property" are often used interchangeably; see the UCC s. 2 –401(1).

the seller or his agent, it is presumed that the seller reserves the property in the goods until he or his agent delivers the bill to the buyer or his agent (s.19(2))[24]; and secondly, where the seller has drawn a bill of Exchange on the buyer for the purchase price and transmits that bill and the bill of lading together to the buyer to secure acceptance or payment of the bill of exchange, the property does not pass to the buyer, if he does not honour the bill of exchange, and in this case he would have to return the bill of lading (s.19(3)). These provisions apply to f.o.b. and c.i.f. contracts alike.

The second contingency arises where the seller has failed to make the passing of the property conditional and where neither of the legal presumptions provided by subsection (2) or (3) of section 19 can be invoked to remedy that failure. Where, *e.g.* the seller has taken out a bill of lading to the order of the buyer or his agent, all depends on whether the seller delivers the bill to the buyer; it has been held[25] that taking out a bill of lading in the name of the buyer does not necessarily reveal the seller's intention of passing the property to him. Where the bill is delivered to the buyer or his agent, the inference is almost[26] irresistible that the seller intended to transfer the property in the goods to the buyer.[27]

These rules apply to all contracts under which it is the seller's duty to deliver a bill of lading. In cases where that duty does not exist, *e.g.* in ex works, f.o.b. (buyer contracting with carrier) or free delivered contracts, the physical delivery of the goods to the buyer or to the carrier is presumably the act which passes the property to the buyer.

Where under a c.i.f. or c. and f. contract, or under an f.o.b. contract under which the seller has taken out the bill of lading, the bill is delivered to the buyer or his agent, the inference is that the property which is intended to pass to the buyer is only *conditional*, *viz.* that the property in the goods shall revert to the seller if upon examination they are found to be not in accordance with the contract.[28]

In exceptional cases the c.i.f. seller may release the goods to the buyer before handing over the bill of lading to him, by giving the buyer a delivery order on the ship. It depends here on the intention of the parties

---

[24] *Mitsui & Co. Ltd.* v. *Flota Mercante Grancolombiana S.A. The Ciudad de Pasto and Ciudad de Neiva* [1988] 2 Lloyd's Rep. 208, 213. The presumption of s.19(2) is rebutted between related companies: *The Albazero* [1975] 3 W.L.R. 491, 512, 513; reversed on other grounds by H.L. in [1977] A.C. 274.
[25] *The Kronprinsessan Margareta* [1921] 1 A.C. 486, 517; *The Glenroy* [1945] A.C. 124.
[26] Exceptionally the circumstances may support another inference, see the observation of Roskill L.J. in *The Albazero*, [1975] 3 W.L.R. 491, 523, reversed in [1977] A.C. 774 (H.L.).
[27] In *The Albazero* [1977] A.C. 774, Brandon J., the Court of Appeal and the House of Lords agreed that by virtue of the transfer of the bill of lading the property and possession had passed to the consignees. See also *The San Nicholas* [1976] 1 Lloyd's Rep. 8, 11, 13.
[28] *Kwei Tek Chao* v. *British Traders and Shippers Ltd.* [1954] 2 Q.B. 459, 487; *Gill & Duffus S.A.* v. *Berger & Co. Inc.* [1984] 2 W.L.R. 95, 104 (H.L.). Another case in which the property passed only defeasibly was *McDougall* v. *Aeromarine of Emsworth Ltd.* [1958] 1 W.L.R. 1126.

whether this procedure is adopted in performance of the c.i.f. contract or merely as "mechanics of delivery."[29] The deliberate retention of the bill of lading by the seller may indicate an intention of the parties that property shall not pass to the buyer on such an anticipated delivery.[30] Further, the fundamental principle should not be overlooked that, from the commercial point of view, the retention of title to the goods is regarded as "security" for the payment of the price, if this "security" is furnished in another way, *e.g.* by the provision of a standby letter of credit by a reputable bank, the intention of the parties may well be that property in the goods shall pass when the bank issues the credit.[31]

The retention of title clause

It has already been stated[32] that English law admits a clause which provides that the seller retains the property in the goods sold until he receives the purchase price in cash. The clause makes the passing of property conditional on a specified event, *viz.* the receipt of the price by the seller. It is clear from section 19(1) of the Sale of Goods Act 1979 that the clause is effective and defeats the general presumption that the property passes when the bill of lading is transferred from the seller (or his agent) to the buyer (or his agent).[33]

Retention of title clauses can be divided into two classes, *viz.* simple and extended clauses.

The simple retention of title clause

This clause provides that the seller retains the property in the goods sold until a specified condition is satisfied, *e.g.* that he receives the purchase price in cash. This type of clause causes little difficulty in law but it is normally considered insufficient by the seller. The validity of the

---

[29] McNair J. in *Ginzberg* v. *Barrow Haematite Steel Co.* [1966] 1 Lloyd's Rep. 343, 353.
[30] *Cheetham & Co. Ltd.* v. *Thornham Spinning Co. Ltd.* [1964] 2 Lloyd's Rep. 17; *Ginzberg* v. *Barrow Haematite Steel Co. Ltd.* [1966] 1 Lloyd's Rep. 343.
[31] *The Filiatra Legacy, Financial Times,* November 21, 1989.
[32] See p. 75, *ante.*
[33] A definition of a "retention of title agreement" is provided in section 251 of the Insolvency Act 1986. It runs as follows:

"retention of title agreement means an agreement for the sale of goods to a company, being an agreement—
    (a) which does not constitute a charge on the goods, but
    (b) under which, if the seller is not paid and the company is wound up, the seller will have priority over all other creditors of the company as respects the goods or any property representing the goods."

simple retention of title clause cannot be doubted because, as has already been observed,[34] section 19(1) of the Sale of Goods Act 1979 admits it expressly. This clause does not require registration as a charge under section 396 of the Companies Act 1985.

There exists a *Draft European Convention on the Simple Reservation of Title*, sponsored by the Council of Europe in 1982.[35] This Convention has not been finalised yet.[36]

The extended retention of title clause

Of greater practical importance is the extended retention of title clause but it raises difficult legal problems. Two types of extended clauses are used but other clauses may also be devised. In particular, a combination of the features of the two main types is sometimes found in practice.

First, the clause may provide that the buyer, if he sells the goods, shall do so as an agent of the seller and shall be a trustee of the proceeds of sale for the benefit of the seller. This clause gives the buyer a licence to sell and, at the same time, attempts to safeguard the position of the seller. The buyer is made the bailee of the goods supplied by the seller who is in the position of a bailor. This is the most common type of extended retention of title clause. It has been recommended earlier that the exporter shall include this clause into his general conditions of business.[37] These extended clauses are frequently used in Germany and the Netherlands; they are also used in France where they are regulated by a law of May 12, 1980.[38] In the United Kingdom such a clause has been upheld in the *Romalpa* case.[39] Aluminium Industrie Vaassen BV (AIV), a Dutch private company, sold a quantity of aluminium foil to Romalpa, an English company. The terms of delivery were ex works AIV in Holland and the price was expressed in Dutch currency. The contract contained an extended title clause which was worded in great detail.[40] A receiver was appointed for Romalpa. Although the contract was closely connected

---

[34] See p. 119, *ante*.
[35] See Patrick Latham, "Retention of Title. Recent Developments in Europe" in [1983] J.B.L. 81.
[36] Position: September 1, 1989.
[37] See p. 75, *ante*.
[38] The French law is known as the *loi Dubanatet*. See also [1980] J.B.L. 388.
[39] *Aluminium Industrie Vaassen BV* v. *Romalpa Aluminium Ltd.* [1976] 1 W.L.R. 676. Also *Hendy Lennox (Industrial Engines) Ltd.* v. *Graham Puttick Ltd.* [1984] 1 W.L.R. 485; *Clough Mill* v. *Martin* [1985] 1 W.L.R. 111 (C.A.); *In re Andrabell Ltd.*, [1984] 2 All E.R. 407. See further the Report by Professor Aubrey L. Diamond on "A Review of Security Interests in Property," submitted to the Minister for Corporate and Consumer Affairs on November 7, 1988. Professor Diamond's Report is discussed by Mark Lawson in "The Reform of the Law relating to Security Interests in Property" in [1989] J.B.L. 287.
[40] The clause is reproduced fully in [1976] J.B.L. 209–210.

with Dutch law, that law was not pleaded and the case was decided according to English law. The Court of Appeal held that AIV were entitled to the property in the goods supplied by them and still being in existence. As regards the goods resold by Romalpa, the court held that Romalpa had acted as agents for AIV and were, therefore, in a fiduciary relationship to them; that admitted the application of the equitable doctrine of tracing, as developed in *Re Hallett's Estate*.[41] But it was held by Slade J. in *Re Bond Worth Ltd*.[42] that, where the property in the goods was transferred unconditionally to the buyer and the latter was not constituted an agent for the seller, the reservation of title clause constituted a floating charge on the goods and on the money obtained on their resale and, as such, was registrable under what is now the Companies Act 1985, s.396; the *Bond Worth* clause was worded differently from the *Romalpa* clause. In *Pfeiffer* v. *Arbuthnot Factors Ltd*.[43] a German retention of title clause was in issue, but the case was decided according to English law; the clause was worded similar to, but not identical with, that in *Romalpa*; Phillips J., in an unconvincing judgment, distinguished Romalpa and held that the retention of title clause was invalid because it had not been registered as a charge. Essentially the issue is one of construction of the clause. It is thought that the retention of title clause does not require registration under the Companies Act if it contains two essential provisions:[44] *first*, that the seller retains the *legal* property in the goods (possibly with the supporting provisions that the goods shall be kept separate from other goods in the possession of the buyer and its storage be marked with the seller's name), and *secondly* that the buyer may resell them only as agent of the seller and receive the repurchase price as agent for and on behalf and on account of the seller (possibly with the supporting provision that the buyer shall keep the proceeds of resale in a separate account kept in the seller's name). But in the present state of authorities the requirements of a non-registrable extended retention of title clause cannot be stated with absolute certainty. If only a simple retention of title clause is adopted, an extension to the proceeds of sale is not implied by the law. Such extension must be expressly provided in the clause.[45] Where under a retention of title clause of the type here discussed the buyer obtains possession of the goods and has a licence to resell them, a purchaser in good faith is protected by section 25(1) of the Sale of Goods Act 1979, if the requirements of this

---

[41] (1880) Ch.D. 696.
[42] [1980] Ch. 228. See also [1979] J.B.L. 216, where the reservation of property clause in *Bond Worth* is reproduced in full.
[43] The full title of this case is *E. Pfeiffer Weinkellerei-Weineinkauf GmbH & Co.* v. *Arbuthnot Factors Ltd.* [1988] 1 W.L.R. 150.
[44] See the retention of title clause suggested on p. 75, *ante*.
[45] *Hendy Lennox (Industrial Engineers) Ltd.* v. *Graham Puttick Ltd.* (1984) 81 L.S. Gaz. 585.

provision are satisfied; in this case the title of the original seller is defeated.[46]

Secondly, the clause sometimes states that if the goods sold are used in the production of other goods, either by admixture or another manufacturing process, the property in the goods so produced shall vest in the seller. This clause is ineffective if the new product has a different commercial identity from the material sold under the reservation of title clause. Thus, if a clause purporting to extend to the new product occurs in a contract of sale of resin it does not extend to chipboard into which the resin is incorporated[47]; and if it occurs in a contract for the sale of leather, it does not extend to handbags manufactured of the leather.[48] In any event, even if the clause extended to the finished product, it would be registrable as a charge under section 396 of the Companies Act 1985.

PASSING OF THE RISK

The risk of accidental loss of the goods sold passes prima facie when the property passes (s.20(1)). This is an antiquated rule of the Sale of Goods Act 1979, derived from its predecessor, the Act of 1893. Modern texts, *e.g.* the Uniform Commercial Code (s.2–509) and the Vienna Convention on Contracts for the International Sale of Goods (art. 67), provide that, as a rule, the risk shall pass on delivery of the goods.[48a]

In the law of international trade, contrary to the presumption of section 20(1) of the Sale of Goods Act, the two concepts of the passing of the risk and the transfer of property are regularly separated and the statutory presumption is displaced by agreement of the parties. Here again, special arrangements are admitted between the parties; in the absence of them[49] the risk will generally pass in a contract for the sale of goods abroad when the goods leave the custody of the seller. In ex works the risk normally passes when the goods are delivered to the buyer or his agent; in f.a.s. contracts it passes when the goods are placed alongside the ship and in f.o.b. and c.i.f. contracts normally when they are delivered over the ship's rail. If the contract provides for delivery franco domicile of the buyer, the intention of the parties as regards the passing of the risk can

---

[46] *Cf. Four Point Garage Ltd.* v. *Carter, The Times*, November 19, 1984.
[47] *Borden (U.K.) Ltd.* v. *Scottish Timber Products and McNicol Brownlie Ltd.* [1981] Ch. 25.
[48] *In Re Peachdart Ltd.* [1984] Ch. 131.
[48a] Clive M. Schmitthoff, "The Risk of Loss in Transit in International Sales" in *Unification of the Law Governing International Sales of Goods, in The Comparison and possible Harmonisation of National and Regional Unification*, Paris, 1966, pp. 169–199; *Essays*, 277.
[49] In *President of India* v. *Metcalfe Shipping Co.* [1969] 2 Q.B. 123; affirmed by C.A. in [1970] 1 Q.B. 289, passing of the risk (and of the property) under an f.o.b. contract was postponed until delivery of bills of lading.

often be gathered from the terms of payment and the insurance arrangement: if the price is prepaid and the buyer is responsible for insurance, there is hardly a doubt that the goods travel at his risk; the result would be reversed if the price were collected on delivery and the seller had to cover the insurance risk. In the container delivery terms the risk passes normally when the goods are delivered into the custody of the carrier.

The risk, unlike the property, may pass to the buyer although the goods are unascertained goods which have not been appropriated, but only if some "special facts" can be established.[50]

A buyer to whom the risk, but not property or a possessory title, is transferred by the seller, is not entitled to sue the carrier in the tort of negligence.[51]

The risk of accidental loss should not be confused with the risk of deterioration of the goods in transit. In f.o.b. and c.i.f. contracts relating to perishable goods and containing an implied condition that the goods shall be of merchantable quality,[52] the seller undertakes, by further implication, that the goods shall be in a merchantable state not only when they are loaded but also upon arrival at destination and a reasonable time thereafter, allowing for their normal disposal,[53] but this implied condition does not apply where the deterioration of the goods is due to an abnormal delay in their transit or disposal[54] Diplock J. stated this rule thus[55]:

> It is the extraordinary deterioration of the goods due to abnormal conditions experienced during transit for which the buyer takes the risk. A necessary and inevitable deterioration during transit which will render them unmerchantable on arrival is normally one for which the seller is liable.

---

[50] *Sterns Ltd.* v. *Vickers Ltd.* [1923] 1 K.B. 78. Special facts are, *e.g.* the acceptance, by the buyer, of the seller's delivery warrant instructing a storekeeper to deliver to the buyer part of the bulk, particularly if by the terms of the warrant the buyer is liable to pay the charges for his portion of the bulk. See also Croom-Johnson, J. in *Comptoir d'Achat* v. *Luis de Ridder* [1947] 2 All E.R. 443, 453. But where no special facts can be established, the property and the risk in the sold part of a bulk stored with a third person pass only when the third person has separated that part from the bulk and acknowledges that he holds that part as the buyer's goods; *Wardar's (Import & Export) Co. Ltd.* v. *W. Norwood & Sons Ltd.* [1968] 2 Q.B. 663. Compare Vienna Convention, Art. 67(2).

[51] *Leigh and Sullivan* v. *Aliakmon Shipping Co.* [1986] A.C. 785; see p. 46, *ante.*

[52] See ss.14(2) and 15(2)(c) of the Sale of Goods Act 1979. s.14(6) which contains the following definition of merchantable quality, is quoted on pp. 168–169, *post.* For an explanation of the term "merchantable quality" see *Cehave N.V.* v. *Bremer Handelsgesellschaft mbh. The Hansa Nord* [1976] 1 Q.B. 44 and *M/S Aswan Engineering Establishment Co.* v. *Lupdine Ltd.* [1987] 1 W.L.R. 1; see p. 106, n. 14 and 169, n. 20, *ante.* See also John Livermore, "Merchantable Quality" in [1985] J.B.L. 217, 294.

[53] *Mash & Murrell Ltd.* v. *Joseph I. Emanuel Ltd.* [1961] 1 W.L.R. 862; reversed on appeal on the facts [1962] 1 W.L.R. 16. See also *Rogers* v. *Parish (Scarborough) Ltd.* [1987] Q.B. 933.

[54] *Broome* v. *Pardess Co-operative Society* [1939] 3 All E.R. 978, 985; *Ollett* v. *Jordan* [1918] 2 K.B. 41, 47.

[55] *Mash & Murrell Ltd.* v. *Joseph I. Emanuel Ltd., supra,* n. 52, on p. 871.

CERTIFICATES OF QUALITY AND OF INSPECTION

Certificates of quality

Certificates of quality, which should not be confused with certificates of origin,[56] are used in the export trade from time to time. The parties may, *e.g.*, arrange that the seller should provide a certificate of quality "by experts,"[57] a government certificate that certain army surplus goods were "new,"[58] that the goods—fruit—should be covered by "phytopathological certificates of freedom from disease"[59] or by a certificate certifying that the goods were of the quality of a trade association's "standard sample,"[60] or that "certificates for maize in government elevators"[61] should be produced; the parties may also agree that a certificate as to composition or quality should be given by the seller himself.[62]

Certificates of quality are of two types: certificates of standard quality addressed to all the world (also known as certificates *in rem*) and certificates of contract requirements addressed to the parties to the contract (so-called certificates *in personam*).[63] What type of certificate is required depends on the intention of the contracting parties. Examples of certificates of standard quality are a certificate of a public analyst or of a recognised engineering, shipbuilding or surveying classification organisation,[64] *e.g.* a Lloyd's certificate. Sometimes a certificate of quality issued by an inspection organisation, such as SGS,[64a] is required.[65]

Certificates of quality *in personam* state sometimes that they shall be "*final, as to quality.*" In this case the certificate is binding on the seller

---

[56] On certificates of origin, see p. 105, *ante*.

[57] *Equitable Trust Company of New York* v. *Dawson Partners Ltd.* (1926) 27 Lloyd's Rep. 49; see p. 407, *post*.

[58] *Bank Melli Iran* v. *Barclays Bank (Dominion, Colonial and Overseas)* [1951] 2 Lloyd's Rep. 367; see p. 409, *post*.

[59] *Yelo* v. *S. M. Machado & Co. Ltd.* [1952] 1 Lloyd's Rep. 183; *Phoenix Distributors Ltd.* v. *L. B. Clarke (London)* [1966] 2 Lloyd's Rep. 285.

[60] *F. E. Hookway & Co.* v. *Alfred Isaacs & Sons* [1954] 1 Lloyd's Rep. 491.

[61] *South African Reserve Bank* v. *Samuel* (1931) 40 Ll.L.R. 291. See: *Re Reinhold & Co. and Hansloh* (1896) 12 T.L.R. 422; *Foreman & Ellams Ltd.* v. *Blackburn* [1928] 2 K.B. 60; *Panchaud Frères S.A.* v. *Etablissements General Grain Co.* [1969] 2 Lloyd's Rep. 109.

[62] *Groupement National d'Achat des Tourteaux* v. *Sociedad Industrial Financiera Argentina* [1962] 2 Lloyd's Rep. 192.

[63] *Ibid*.

[64] *Minister Trust Ltd.* v. *Traps Tractors Ltd.* [1954] 1 W.L.R. 963, 977–979.

[64a] This acronymn stands for *Société Générale de Surveillance SA* (Geneva).

[65] *Berger & Co. Inc.* v. *Gill & Duffus S.A.* [1984] 2 W.L.R. 95. (The certificate referred to in this case was stated to be issued by "General Superintendence Co. Ltd." This company changed its name later to "S.G.S. Inspection Services Ltd." The certificate required in this case was a post-shipment certificate as it had to be issued in the port of discharge. It could therefore not be tendered as one of the shipping documents under the contract which was on c.i.f. terms.). On the distinction between an official natural weight certificate of wheat and the certificate of an independent laboratory see *Ets Soules & Cie* v. *International Trade Development Co. Ltd.* [1979] 2 Lloyd's Rep. 122, 133.

and buyer even though the certificate was inaccurate or the certifier acted negligently; but it ceases to be binding if it is set aside by a court or arbitration tribunal or revoked by the certifier.[66] Further, the parties to a contract of sale may draw a distinction between the quality of the goods and their condition and in such a case the certificate, though stated to be final, has to be construed restrictively as referring to the quality of the goods only and does not prevent the buyer from raising a complaint with respect to the condition of the goods.[67] If the parties have omitted to draw that distinction, then "quality of goods" includes their state or condition.[68]

Certificates of inspection

A certificate of inspection is not identical with a certificate of quality although the latter may be issued by an inspection organisation, if the contract so provides. The minimum requirements for such a certificate are that the inspector has visually inspected the goods and found them to be in apparent good condition. If a particular method of inspection shall be adopted or particular information as the result of the inspection shall be recorded, such as the test results of electrical appliances, the buyer must expressly stipulate this.[69] Of the numerous inspection organisations dealing with general merchandise, four may be mentioned here, as they are represented in many commercial centres of the world: Société Généréle de Surveillance SA (SGS) which has its head office in Geneva, it claims to be the world's largest independent inspection organisation and operates in Great Britain through SGS Inspection Services Ltd., London; further, Cargo Superintendents Ltd., London; Superintendence Co. Inc., New York; and Bureau Veritas of France.

The contract between the inspection organisation and the client is known as the *contract of goods inspection*.[70] The inspector is under a

---

[66] *Alfred C. Toepfer* v. *Continental Grain Co.* [1973] 1 Lloyd's Rep. 289; *Berger & Co. Inc.* v. *Gill & Duffus S.A.* [1984] 2 W.L.R. 95. See also *N. V. Bunge* v. *Compagnie Noga d'Importation et d'Exportation S.A. The Bow Cedar.* [1980] 2 Lloyd's Rep. 601, 605 (Certificate of chemical analysis did not cover description of the goods): similarly *Ch. Daudruy van Cauwenberghe & Fils S.A.* v. *Tropical Products Sales S.A.* [1986] 1 Lloyd's Rep. 535. See also *Jones* v. *Sherwood Computer Services plc.*, The Times, December 14, 1989.
[67] *Cremer* v. *General Carriers S.A.* [1974] 1 W.L.R. 341, 354.
[68] See Sale of Goods Act 1979, s.61.
[69] *Commercial Banking Co. of Sydney Ltd.* v. *Jalsard Pty. Ltd.* [1973] A.C. 279; *International Petroleum Refining and Supply Sociedad Ltd.* v. *Caleb Brett & Son Ltd.*; *The Busiris* [1980] 1 Lloyd's Rep. 569.
[70] See A. Goldštajn, "The Contract of Goods Inspection" in (1965) 14 Am.J.Comp.Law 383. For third party inspection of goods in dispute see Uniform Commercial Code, s.2–515(b).

contractual duty to use reasonable care. In one case[71] an inspector was appointed to take tests of oil on its loading at the port of dispatch. The oil was liquid when it was loaded but arrived at its destination in a solidified state. Proceedings were taken against the inspector and the Court of Appeal held that he had failed in his contractual duty because he did not take sufficient samples when the oil was loaded, did not take them in regular intervals and did not check its gravity. He was also liable in tort for negligence on the principle in *Hedley Byrne & Co. Ltd.* v. *Heller & Partners Ltd.*[72] In another case[73] the parties agreed on pre-shipment inspection which was to be carried out by one of two nominated inspection organisations referred to in the contract as "firms of international repute." One of them was appointed to carry out the inspection but delegated it to another unspecified company. It then adopted the certificate of the unspecified company as its own certificate without further check. The court held that the nominated organisation was in breach of the contract of inspection. By the terms of this contract it had to carry out the inspection through its own organisation and was not authorised to delegate this duty.

Pre-shipment inspection

This type of inspection, briefly referred to as PSI, is of growing importance in modern export trade. It is usually carried out by an independent inspection organisation. If the inspector is properly instructed, pre-shipment inspection is very useful. It avoids later disputes between the seller and buyer on whether the goods are in accordance with the contract. It also avoids disputes between the insured and the insurer on whether any loss of or damage to the goods occurred before or after the risk attached.[74] Certain overseas countries, including Nigeria, Kenya and Bolivia, insist on pre-shipment inspection. The information on each country in *Croner's Reference Book for Exporters* states whether a pre-shipment certificate is required for imports into the country.

The normal procedure is, to have the goods physically inspected when they are delivered to the carrier. The inspection relates normally to the quantity and condition of the goods but the mode of inspection depends

---

[71] *International Petroleum Refining and Supply Sociedad Ltd.* v. *Caleb Brett & Son Ltd.*; *The Busiris* [1980] 1 Lloyd's Rep. 569.
[72] [1964] A.C. 465.
[73] *Kollerich & Cie S.A.* v. *The State Trading Corporation of India* [1980] 2 Lloyd's Rep. 32 (this case arose between the seller and the buyer and it was held that the certificate was false and the seller had failed to tender a correct certificate).
[74] *Cf. Fuerst Day Lawson Ltd.* v. *Orion Insurance Co. Ltd.* [1980] 1 Lloyd's Rep. 656, 664 (in this case there was, in fact, a pre-shipment certificate but the court considered it to be insufficient).

on the terms of the contract of goods inspection. Some inspection organisations maintain laboratories and other testing facilities and are prepared to carry out more elaborate tests if instructed.

Sometimes the inspection organisation is instructed, in addition to the quality control, to carry out a price control. In this case they have to advise the buyer whether the price charged is comparable to prices charged by other suppliers for similar goods. Some countries in the course of development will not grant import licences unless an inspection organisation has issued a clean pre-shipment certificate covering price control. In some cases exporters have complained that the inspection organisation insisted on an unjustified reduction of a price firmly agreed with the overseas buyer or that it demanded the disclosure of a price calculation regarded as confidential. Such interference by a third party with the contractual relations of the seller and the buyer may raise legal problems unless it is clearly agreed upon in advance in the contract of sale.

The complaints of exporters about the interference by inspection organisations with freely negotiated contracts have not been without effect. A few countries, notably West Germany,[75] have introduced a strict regulation of PSI, including price comparison. But as the exporters of many countries, including the USA, are affected, the solution has to be sought on an international level. Among the international bodies considering the problem are GATT, the ICC, the EC, and the UN Economic Commission for Europe. The SGS has published a brochure explaining to exporters the procedure which it applies when carrying out PSI, including the principles which to which it has resort in price comparison.[76]

LIQUIDATED DAMAGES AND PENALTIES

The parties are at liberty to provide in their contract that in the case of non-performance or delayed performance the party in default shall pay a fixed sum, the amount of which may be calculated either as a lump sum or on a scale varying with the length of the default.[77]

In British contracts concerning the export of merchandise, clauses fixing the amount recoverable on breach are seldom met but they are common in international standard contract forms, such as those used in the commodity trade[78] or sponsored by the United Nations Economic

---

[75] This regulation is founded on a provision introduced in 1983, viz. Article 44a of the *Aussenhandel-wirtschaftsverordnung* (BGBl. No. 2 of February 22, 1983).

[76] SGS, Clean Report of Findings, "Preshipment Inspection of Imports: Guidelines for Exporters," January 1988. Obtainable from the local SGS office or from the head office of SGS, at 1 place des Alpes, Case postale 898, Ch–1211, Geneva 1, Switzerland.

[77] As, *e.g.* in case of demurrage.

[78] See p. 73, *ante*.

Council for Europe,[79] or in the General Conditions of Delivery of Goods used in the countries of CMEA.[80]

In English law[81] a fixed sum payable on breach of contract may either be *liquidated damages* or a *penalty*. It is the former if the contract, upon its proper construction, reveals the intention of the parties genuinely to pre-estimate the damages suffered by the breach of contract; it is the latter if the intention of the parties is to secure the performance of the contract by the imposition of a fine or penalty; such intention is, in particular, evident if the fixed sum is disproportionate to the possible or probable amount of damages, *i.e.* if it is extravagant or unconscionable.[82] The genuine intention of the parties has to be ascertained; the use of the terms "liquidated damages" or "penalties" in the clause, though indicative of the parties' intention, is not conclusive. If the sum fixed in the contract qualifies as liquidated damages, the court will award that sum and it is no obstacle to its recovery that the consequences of the breach are such as to make the pre-estimate of damages almost an impossibility; it is equally irrelevant that the loss actually suffered is lower or higher. But a liquidated damages clause cannot be relied upon if the plaintiff himself has contributed to the breach.[83] On the other hand, if the fixed sum qualifies as a penalty, it will be ignored by the court.[84] The differences between these two types of clauses are also important in the law of procedure: if the clause stipulates liquidated damages, the party who claims damages need not prove the amount of damages but if it is a penalty clause (which, as has been seen, is ignored) he has to prove the amount of damages which he wants to recover.

A liquidated damages clause makes it unnecessary for the parties to have the damages fixed by the court. The quantification of damages is a matter of mathematical calculation. The clause offers advantages not only to the buyer but also to the supplier because it limits his liability.

---

[79] See pp. 73–74, *ante.* In the ECE contract forms the fixed sums are described as "allowances."

[80] See p. 70, *ante.* In the General Conditions for Delivery the fixed sums are described as "sanctions" and are payable in case of delayed performance.

[81] See *Dunlop Pneumatic Tyre Co. Ltd.* v. *New Garage and Motor Co. Ltd.* [1915] A.C. 70, 87; further, *Ford Motor Co.* v. *Armstrong* (1915) 31 T.L.R. 267; *Law* v. *Redditch Local Board* [1892] 1 Q.B. 127, 132; *Lombard North Central plc.* v. *Butterworth* [1987] Q.B. 527, 540 (*per* Nicolls L.J.); *Jobson* v. *Johnson* (1988) 4BCC 498 (C.A.).

[82] An indemnity clause does not operate as a penalty. This was decided in *Exports Credit Guarantee Department* v. *Universal Oil Products Co.* [1983] 1 W.L.R. 399 where a clause providing that ECGD should be indemnified by the defendants for payments made to bankers who had financed a construction project of the defendants was upheld by the House of Lords. Carrying charges in the Argentine maize trade are not a penalty: *Fratelli Moretti S.p.A.* v. *Nidera Handelscompanie B.V.* [1981] 2 Lloyd's Rep. 47. In a shipbuilding contract a clause providing for immediate payment of all moneys outstanding if the purchasers of the vessel defaulted on a long term loan granted by the shipbuilder, was not a penalty clause: *Oresundsvarvet Aktiebolag* v. *Marcos Diamantis Lemos. The Angelic Star.* [1988] 1 Lloyd's Rep. 122.

[83] *Astilleros Canarios S.A.* v. *Cape Hatteras Shipping Co. Inc.*; *The Cape Hatteras* [1982] 1 Lloyd's Rep. 518, 526.

[84] *Lamdon Trust Ltd.* v. *Hurrell* [1955] 1 W.L.R. 391.

As regards the treatment of penal contract clauses in other legal systems, Mr. Peter Benjamin refers to[85]—

> the extreme complexity of French, German or Soviet law on the subject of penal clauses, for starting from the principle that penal clauses are or are not subject to modification, each system has grafted on the rule it has adopted a whole series of exceptions that give rise to considerable uncertainty in practice. . . .

These observations do not, however, apply to the common law countries, such as Australia, New Zealand or the United States of America, in which the English distinction between liquidated damages and penalties is accepted. On the whole, there is justification in Mr. Benjamin's conclusion that in international commercial transactions "these clauses, which appear so attractive at first sight, are a deadly weapon, due to the confusion and uncertainty engendered thereby in commercial relations," and that it is doubtful whether their procedural advantage is "a sufficient counterbalance to their uncertainty from the point of view of substantive law."

---

[85] "Penal Clauses in Commercial Contracts" in (1960) 9 I.C.L.Q. 600, 627.

CHAPTER 9

ACCEPTANCE AND REJECTION OF GOODS.
RIGHTS OF THE UNPAID SELLER AGAINST THE GOODS

IN the performance of a contract of international sale the rules relating to the examination, acceptance and rejection of the goods are of great practical importance. If the contract is governed by English law,[1] these rules are founded on the Sale of Goods Act 1979.[2] The parties to an international sale may also adopt the Uniform Laws on International Sales, appended to the Uniform Laws on International Sales Act 1967; they and the Vienna Convention on Contracts for the International Sale of Goods (1980), which eventually will take their place,[3] will be treated later.[4]

The general principle on which the regulation of the Sale of Goods Act rests is that if the buyer is deemed to have accepted the goods he loses his right to reject them. But he does not lose all rights with respect to them. Although he is now bound to retain them he can still claim damages if the value of the goods which were actually delivered is less than the value of the goods which the seller promised to supply. This claim for damages is not lost as the result of legal rules peculiar to the sale of goods. It is governed by general legal principles; thus, it is not lost by lapse of time until it becomes barred under the Limitation Act 1980; since most mercantile contracts are in the nature of simple contracts the seller is normally[5] entitled to plead the defence of limitation after the lapse of six years from the breach of contract.

The tendency of English sales law is to discourage the rejection of goods by the buyer but to admit, without serious restriction or qualification, his claim for damages if he has overpaid their value, as expressed in the contract price.

---

[1] See p. pp. 114–115, *ante*, and p. 204 *post*.
[2] See pp. 7 and 100, *ante*, where the other enactments which may affect an international contract of sale are listed.
[3] This Convention came into operation on January 1, 1988, but has not been given effect in the United Kingdom yet (Position: October 1, 1988).
[4] See p. 240, *post*.
[5] The period of limitation may be longer if there is a new accrual of the action as the result of an acknowledgment in writing or part payment, or in case of fraud or of similar circumstances.

CONDITIONS, WARRANTIES AND INNOMINATE TERMS

According to the Sale of Goods Act 1979, the terms of the contract of sale are either *conditions* or *warranties*. This simple classification has proved to be insufficient in modern commercial circumstances and the courts have supplemented it by recognising a third type of contractual term, the *innominate term*, also referred to as the intermediate term.[6]

We shall first consider the distinction between conditions and warranties and then deal with the innominate term.

Conditions and warranties

The buyer is entitled to reject the goods if a condition relating to them is broken, *e.g.* if they are not in accordance with their description in the contract (s.13(1)); if they are unsuitable for the particular purpose for which, with the knowledge of the seller, they are bought (s.14(3)); if they do not correspond with the sample (s.15)[7]; or with sample and description (s.13(2)); or in some of these cases, if they are not of merchantible quality.[8] These conditions are implied by law into contracts of sale but, subject to the Unfair Contract Terms Act 1977 (which does not apply to international supply contracts),[9] may be contracted out or varied (s.55).

Defects of this type have one feature in common: a *condition* of the contract of sale is broken. A condition is a term to which the parties, when making the contract, attribute such importance that it can truly be described as being of the essence of the contract.[9a] A condition has to be distinguished from a *warranty*, a contract term of less significance which relates to matters collateral to the main purpose of the contract (s.61). In the case of breach of a warranty the buyer is not entitled to reject the goods. He has to retain them but may claim damages which, if the goods have an available market, are prima facie the difference between the value of the goods as delivered and the value they would have if they had answered to the warranty (s.53(3)).[10] As a condition is of higher legal quality than a warranty, every condition includes a warranty—a statement

---

[6] See Mustill L.J. in *Lombard North Central plc.* v. *Butterworth* [1987] Q.B. 527, 537.
[7] Provided that the contract, by its terms, is by sample (s.15(1)).
[8] See s.14(2); and (6); and s.15(2)(*c*) and (3); on merchantable quality see also *Bernstein* v. *Pamson Motors (Golders Green) Ltd.* [1987] 2 All E.R. 220 (concerning a home market transaction) and p. 125, n. 52, *ante.*
[9] See p. 100, *ante.*
[9a] For a discussion whether a term of the contract is a condition, see *Trading Corporation of India Ltd.* v. *M. Golodetz Ltd. The Sara D.,* [1989] 2 Lloyd's Rep. 277.
[10] If he has not yet paid the full price, he may set off his claim for damages against the price in diminution or extinction of the latter (s.53(1)(*a*)).

which cannot be reversed. The buyer is, therefore, at liberty to treat a broken condition as a broken warranty and, instead of rejecting the goods, he may keep them and claim the difference between those two values by way of damages (s.11(2)). If the buyer is deemed by the law to have accepted the goods (s.35) and if, consequently, he has lost his right to reject them, he is bound henceforth to treat what originally was a condition as a warranty and his only claim is for damages for breach of warranty (s.11(4)).

In the eyes of the law the breach of a condition operates as a repudiation of the contract by the party who broke the condition.[11] Consequently, a buyer who is entitled to reject the goods is in the same position as a buyer to whom the goods were not tendered[12] at all unless the broken term has to be treated as an innominate term,[13] or the rule of insignificance[14] or special considerations, such as a trade custom or an agreement of the parties to the contrary,[15] apply. In the normal case the buyer is entitled to claim damages from the seller for the non-delivery of the goods (s.51).[16] If he has paid the purchase price in advance he can recover it by way of damages, and if he has suffered other reasonably foreseeable loss, he can recover damages likewise. The motivation for the buyer's desire to reject the goods is usually that the non-conforming goods which the sender has tendered are useless to him and that the claim for damages is his only remedy. The practical point in the distinction between the buyer's right to reject the goods on the ground that a condition of the contract is broken and his right to claim damages for breach of warranty is that in the former instance the buyer can often claim damages on a considerably higher scale than in the latter. Where a party is entitled to damages, he is bound to take reasonable steps to mitigate the damages[17] but he is not bound "to go hunting the globe" to find a market in a distant country,[18] nor can it be held against him, if he has acted reasonably, that a method of mitigation more favourable to the defaulting buyer existed.[19]

---

[11] See s.11(2).
[12] The seller may, however, make a second tender of new goods if the time for delivery has not expired. See p. 143, *post.*
[13] See p. 135, *post.*
[14] *De minimis non curat lex*; see *Moralice (London) Ltd.* v. *E. D. and F. Man* [1954] 2 Lloyd's Rep. 526; *Rapalli* v. *K.L. Take Ltd.* [1958] 2 Lloyd's Rep. 469.
[15] The conditions of trade associations which, *e.g.* in the commodity trade, are widely adopted, sometimes exclude the rejection of goods.
[16] The measure of damages is the difference between the contract price and the market price, if there is an available market for the goods (s.51(3)). The relevant market price is that ruling at the date of delivery or, failing delivery, that at the date of refusal to deliver.
[17] *The Solholt* [1983] 1 Lloyd's Rep. 605.
[18] *Lesters Leather and Skin Co.* v. *Home and Overseas Brokers Ltd.* (1948) 64 T.L.R. 569.
[19] *Gebrüder Metelmann GmbH & Co. KG* v. *NBR (London) Ltd.*, [1984] 1 Lloyd's Rep. 614.

The innominate term

This is a contractual term which is neither a condition nor a warranty. Its characteristic is that, if the contract is broken, the effect of the breach depends on the nature and gravity of the breach.[20] If the breach is grave, the innocent party can treat the contract as rescinded but if the breach is not serious the contract subsists and the innocent party can only claim damages for any loss which he may have suffered.

The concept of the innominate term was developed in shipping contracts with respect to the stipulation that the ship should be seaworthy.[21] Unseaworthiness could be of serious or trifling character and its effect on the contract varied according to the facts which made the ship unseaworthy. The concept of the innominate term has been extended to other types of contract, notably to the contract of sale.[22] Lord Wilberforce referred to it as "the modern doctrine" when he said[23]:

> The general law of contract has developed along much more rational lines . . . , in attending to the nature and gravity of a breach or departure rather than in accepting rigid categories which do or do not automatically give a right to rescind, and if the choice were between extending cases under the Sale of Goods Act 1893 into other fields, or allowing more modern doctrine to infect those cases, my preference would be clear.

An illustration of the application of the innominate term to the law of international sales is provided by *Cehave N.V.* v. *Bremer Handelsgesellschaft mbH, The Hansa Nord.*[24] Bremer Handelsgesellschaft, a German company, sold a quantity of U.S. orange pellets c.i.f. Rotterdam to Cehave, a Dutch company. The pellets were to be used in the manufacture of cattle food. The contract was made on a form of the Cattle Food Trade Association which contained the term "Shipment to be made in good condition." The consignment in issue was about 3,400 metric tonnes and was carried in *The Hansa Nord*. The contract price,

---

[20] *Hongkong Fir Shipping Co. Ltd.* v. *Kawasaki Kisen Kaisha Ltd.* [1962] 2 Q.B. 26; *United Dominions Trust (Commercial) Ltd.* v. *Eagle Aircraft Services Ltd.* [1968] 1 W.L.R. 74, 80, 82; *The Mihalis Angelos* [1971] 1 Q.B. 164; *Cehave N.V.* v. *Bremer Handelsgesellschaft mbH, The Hansa Nord* [1976] 1 Q.B. 44, 60, 70, 82–83; *Reardon Smith Line Ltd.* v. *Yngvar Hansen-Tangen* [1976] 1 W.L.R. 989, 998; *Compagnie General Maritime* v. *Diakan Spirit S.A. The Ymnos* [1982] 2 Lloyd's Rep. 574 (container guarantee clause, guaranteeing the suitability of a chartered ship for container transport); *Phoenix General Insurance Co. of Greece S.A.* v. *Halvanon Insurance Co. Ltd.* [1985] 2 Lloyd's Rep. 599, 614.
[21] *Hongkong Fir Shipping Co. Ltd.* v. *Kawasaki Kisen Kaisha Ltd.* [1962] 2 Q.B. 26.
[22] *Cehave N.V.* v. *Bremer Handelsgesellschaft mbH, The Hansa Nord* [1976] 1 Q.B. 44: see below in the text.
[23] In *Reardon Smith Line Ltd.* v. *Yngvar Hansen-Tangen* [1976] 1 W.L.R. 989, 998; see also Lord Wilberforce in *Bremer Handelsgesellschaft mbH* v. *Vanden Avenne Izegem PVBA* [1978] 2 Lloyd's Rep. 109, 113, and p. 201, *post*; *Krohn & Co.* v. *Mitsui and Co. Europe GmbH* [1978] 2 Lloyd's Rep. 419; *Antaios Compania Naviera S.A.* v. *Salen Rederierna A.B.* [1984] 3 W.L.R. 592, 597.
[24] [1976] 1 Q.B. 44.

converted into pound stirling, was about £100,000 but the market price at the time of arrival of the ship had fallen considerably. On discharge from *The Hansa Nord* the cargo ex hold no. 1 (1,260 tonnes) was found to be damaged but the cargo ex hold no. 2 (2,053 tonnes) was in good condition. The buyers rejected the whole consignment. The Rotterdam court ordered its sale. It was purchased by a middleman for a sum which, after deduction of the expenses, amounted to an equivalent of £29,903. The middleman sold the pellets the same day for the same price to the original buyers who took them to their factory and used them for the manufacture of cattle food although they received a somewhat smaller quantity of pellets than they would have done if part of the consignment had not been damaged. The total result of the transaction was that the Dutch buyers received goods which they had agreed to buy for £100,000 at the reduced price of about £30,000. The case went to arbitration and then to the courts. The Court of Appeal held that the contractual term "shipment to be made in good condition" was not a condition within the meaning of the Sale of Goods Act but was an innominate term. Lord Denning M.R. said[25]:

> If a small proportion of the goods sold was a little below that standard, it would be met by commercial men by an allowance off the price. The buyer would have no right to reject the whole lot unless the divergence was serious and substantial.

The court held that the buyers were not entitled to reject the whole consignment but were entitled to damages for the difference in value between the damaged and sound goods on arrival in Rotterdam. The case was remitted to the arbitrators for the determination of these damages.

However, the use of the concept of the innominate term should not be overdone. Many terms are regarded by the parties to the contract as so essential that they qualify as conditions in the legal sense. This applies in particular to most time clauses in commercial contracts,[26] *e.g.* in an f.o.b. contract a clause that "buyers shall give at least [15] consecutive days' notice of probable readiness of vessel(s). . . ."[27] Similarly, in a c. and f. contract a clause that the ship shall sail directly from the port of loading to the port of discharge (direct shipment clause), was held to be a condition and not an innominate term.[28]

---

[25] *Ibid.* 61.

[26] *Lombard North Central plc.* v. *Butterworth* [1987] Q.B. 527; but not every time clause is a condition, see Kerr L.J. in *Trading Corporation of India Ltd.* v. *M. Golodetz Ltd. The Sara D., Financial Times,* June 16, 1989 (CA).

[27] *Bunge Corporation, New York* v. *Tradax Export S.A., Panama* [1981] 1 W.L.R. 711, 716 (H.L.); *Société Italo-Belge pour le Commerce et l'Industrie S.A.* v. *Palm and Vegetable Oils (Malaysia) Sdn. Bhd; The Post Chaser* [1982] 1 All E.R. 19; *State Trading Corporation of India Ltd.* v. *M. Golodetz Ltd.* [1988] 2 Lloyd's Rep. 182, 187; *British and Commonwealth Holdings plc.* v. *Quadrex Holdings Inc., Financial Times,* November 30, 1988 (where no date is fixed for performance and time originally is not of the essence, it may become so by reasonable notice requesting performance).

[28] *Bergerco U.S.A.* v. *Vegoil Ltd.* [1984] 1 Lloyd's Rep. 440, 444; *State Trading Corporation of India Ltd.* v. *M. Godoletz Ltd.* [1988] 2 Lloyd's Rep. 182, 183–184.

EXAMINATION OF GOODS

When the seller tenders delivery of the goods, the buyer, unless otherwise agreed, is entitled to request that he be given a reasonable opportunity of examining the goods for the purpose of ascertaining whether they are in conformity with the contract (s.34(2)). A buyer who has not previously examined the goods[29] is not deemed to have accepted them and, consequently, has not lost his right to reject them unless and until he has had a reasonable opportunity of examining them (s.34(1)).

There exists, thus, a prima facie presumption that the place and time of examination are the place and time of delivery of the goods. This presumption is, however, displaced where the arrangements of the parties, the circumstances of the sale or a trade custom point to a different intention of the parties. Bailhache J. observed in one case[30]:

> In order to postpone the place of inspection it is necessary that there should be two elements: the original vendor must know, either because he is told or by necessary inference, that the goods are going farther on, and the place at which he delivers must either be unsuitable in itself or the nature or packing of the goods must make inspection at that place unreasonable.

An illustration of exceptional circumstances in which the place and time of examination were postponed occurred in *B. & P. Wholesale Distributors* v. *Marko Ltd.*,[31] in which the sellers, importers of meat, sold one tonne of fat salted backs with rind to the buyers who were wholesale purveyors of meat. The buyers had an opportunity of inspecting the meat cursorily at the docks in London when it arrived, but failed to avail themselves of it and had it taken to their depot in Chester. In the depot the buyers noticed that the meat was not in accordance with the contract; they rejected it and stopped the cheque for the price which they had given the sellers. The latter sued the buyers on the cheque and the buyers counterclaimed for damages for non-delivery of the goods. Pearson J. decided in favour of the buyers. The learned judge held that the place of delivery was the docks in London but that the place of examination was postponed to the buyers' depot in Chester. He observed that the true meaning of section 34 of the Sale of Goods Act (as then in force) was that it must be practicable to make a proper examination of the goods, and until such opportunity was afforded to the buyers they were not deemed to have accepted the goods within the meaning of section 35. In further support of his judgment, the learned judge could now refer to the additional words contained in section 35 of the Sale of Goods Act 1979[32];

---

[29] On pre-shipment inspection, see p. 128, *ante*.
[30] *Saunt* v. *Belcher and Gibbons* (1920) 26 Com.Cas. 115, 119; see also *Perkins* v. *Bell* [1893] 1 Q.B. 193 and *Bergerco U.S.A.* v. *Vegoil Ltd.* [1984] 1 Lloyd's Rep. 440, 446; *Cie. Commerciale Sucres et Denrées* v. *C. Czarnikow Ltd.*, *Financial Times*, July 26, 1989.
[31] *The Times*, February 20, 1953.
[32] In s.35 the reference to s.34 (see p. 140, *post*) was already added by the Misrepresentation Act 1967, s.4(2).

these words make it clear that the buyer's right to reject exists until he is given a genuine opportunity of examining the goods.

In export sales the place and time of examination are frequently not those of delivery but are postponed. In a contract of export sale the place and time of delivery is, as we have seen,[33] usually defined by the special trade clause which the parties have adopted. Where the seller is not obliged to tender a bill of lading to the buyer, as in sales ex works, f.a.s., f.o.b. (buyer contracting with carrier), or in container delivery contracts, physical delivery of the goods takes place in his—the seller's—country,[34] and where bills of lading have to be tendered, as in f.o.b. contracts of the classic type or providing additional services, c.i.f. contracts, and c. and f. contracts, the delivery of the goods is constructive and completely divorced from the actual situation of the goods. Whether in an export sale the delivery is physical or constructive, the two conditions postulated by Bailhache J. in the case referred to earlier[35] for the postponement of the place of examination are normally satisfied: the goods are usually ordered and packed for export, and these facts alone indicate to the seller that they are going farther on, and the locality at which the delivery takes place is usually unsuitable for the examination of the goods, so that it is unreasonable to expect the buyer to carry out the examination there. Consequently, in an export sale, unless the parties have otherwise agreed, *e.g.* by arranging pre-shipment inspection,[36] or a trade custom provides a different regulation, it has to be assumed that the parties intend that the examination of the goods shall be postponed until the goods have arrived at the place of their destination and that that place is the agreed place of examination.[37] Thus, in a case concerning a c. and f. contract Hobhouse J. said[38] that "the exercise of the right to reject goods is one which the seller is entitled to postpone until the goods arrive." Further, in *Molling & Co. v. Dean & Son Ltd.*[39] the sellers, colour printers in Germany, sold the buyers 40,000 toy books which, as they knew, the buyer had resold to sub-purchasers in the United States of America. The books were packed specially for carriage to America and the buyers, without opening the cases, sent them on to their sub-purchasers who rejected them rightly as not being in conformity with their contract and reshipped them to the

---

[33] See p. 9, *ante.*

[34] Normally when the goods are delivered to the carrier for transmission to the buyer (s.32).

[35] *Saunt v. Belcher and Gibbons*, note 30, *supra.*

[36] See p. 128, *ante.*

[37] *Molling v. Dean* (1902) 18 T.L.R. 217; *Boks v. Rayner* (1921) 37 T.L.R. 800; *Bragg v. Villanova* (1923) 40 T.L.R. 154; *Scarliaris v. Ofverberg & Co.* (1921) 37 T.L.R. 307 (C.A.); *Biddell Bros. v. E. Clemens Horst Co.* [1911] 1 K.B. 934, 960; *Kwei Tek Chao v. British Traders and Shippers Ltd.* [1954] 2 Q.B. 459; *Bergerco U.S.A. v. Vegoil Ltd.* [1984] 1 Lloyd's Rep. 440.

[38] *Bergerco U.S.A. v. Vegoil Ltd.* [1984] 1 Lloyd's Rep. 440, 446. For a fuller quotation from this judgment see pp. 41–42, *ante.*

[39] (1902) 18 T.L.R. 217.

original buyers (their sellers). It was held that the place of examination was postponed to America and that the buyers were entitled to reject the books and to claim by way of damages the cost of sending them to America and from there back to England, as well as the duty paid on them in New York.

In international sales, where the wharf at which the goods are landed or the Customs house into which they are taken after landing is unsuitable for examination, the place of examination is the business premises of the buyer[40] (or his agent in performance of the contract[41]). Where the place of destination is situated inland and the goods, after having been landed, have to be taken to that locality, the intended place of examination will normally be the place of ultimate destination.

It should be noted that the Act does not make the examination of the goods a condition precedent of the acceptance. It merely requires that the buyer be given a *reasonable opportunity* of examining the goods and provides that he is not deemed to have accepted the goods until he is given that opportunity (s.34(1)). Whether the buyer avails himself of that opportunity or waives his right of examination is for him to decide. He waives this right, *e.g.* by refraining from inspecting the goods when given that opportunity. In such a case the buyer loses his right to reject the goods. Thus, a buyer who after arrival of the goods orders them to be taken to his warehouse without inspecting them cannot reject them when many months later he discovers that they are faulty, because the retention of goods after the lapse of a reasonable time[42] without intimation that the goods are rejected is deemed to be an acceptance of the goods (s.35). It is always prudent to examine the goods as early as practicable after their arrival at the place of examination, whether that is the place of delivery, the place of final destination or another place.

Where the goods have hidden defects, "not discoverable by any reasonable exercise of care or skill on an inspection,"[43] the time of examination with respect to that defect is postponed to the time at which such examination could have been carried out effectively; if the defect can only be discovered when the goods are used, but not on prior examination, the buyer would still be entitled to reject them on discovery

---

[40] This follows from *B. & P. Wholesale Distributors* v. *Marko Ltd.*, *The Times*, February 20, 1953; see p. 137, *ante*.

[41] As contrasted with an agent for the purposes of transmission (whose authority is limited to that purpose), such as a carrier, forwarder or warehouseman. (Unless, exceptionally, a buyer has a reasonable opportunity of inspecting the goods in the possession of any of those persons.)

[42] Assuming that he kept the goods in his warehouse unexamined an unreasonably long time.

[43] *Per* Brett J. in *Heilbutt* v. *Hickson* (1872) L.R. 7 C.P. 438, 456.

of the defect, provided that he has not kept them for longer than a reasonable time.[44]

ACCEPTANCE OF GOODS

The acceptance of the goods should not be confused with their receipt or with their approval. The test adopted by section 35 is whether the buyer is "*deemed* to have accepted" the goods.[45] The receipt of the goods is less than acceptance and the section does not provide that the mere receipt of the goods shall be deemed to be acceptance. On the other hand, approval is not always required by the section: in two of the three cases postulated by section 35 less than approval satisfies the statutory test and a buyer is deemed to have accepted the goods though he may not have approved them.

The buyer is deemed to have accepted the goods (s.35)—

1. When he intimates to the seller that he has accepted them;
2. Except where section 34 otherwise provides,[46] when the goods have been delivered to him, and he does any act in relation to them which is inconsistent with the ownership of the seller; or
3. When, after the lapse of a reasonable time, he retains the goods without intimating to the seller that he has rejected them.

The first of these three cases is obvious and does not call for comment. As regards the third one, it should be noted that indecision on the part of the buyer may lead to the loss of his right to reject the goods, namely, if he retains them unreasonably long without intimating that he has rejected them. The Act refrains from requiring a fixed period of time within which the buyer has to intimate his rejection. "Reasonable time" is a flexible requirement which varies according to the circumstances of the case; the question of what is a reasonable time is always a question of fact (s.59). The prudent buyer will, as observed earlier,[47] examine the goods as soon as they arrive at the place of examination and will then decide whether to reject them or to keep them.

Of particular importance is the second case. First, this contingency arises only after the buyer has been afforded a reasonable opportunity of examining the goods; the reference to section 34 makes this clear.

---

[44] In *Bernstein* v. *Pamson Motors (Golders Green) Ltd.* [1987] 2 All E.R. 220 Rougier J. held, obiter, that a buyer could be deemed to have accepted the goods by retention although he had no knowledge of the defect; this statement might be too general; in the case before him the judge found, as a fact, that the buyer retained the goods although he had an opportunity of discovering the defect.

[45] See Ian Brown, "Acceptance in the Sale of Goods" [1988] J.B.L. 56.

[46] These words were added by the Misrepresentation Act 1967, s.4(2). S.34 provides that goods are not deemed to have been accepted until the buyer has had a reasonable opportunity of examining them. On s.34, see p. 137, *ante.*

[47] See p. 139, *ante.*

Secondly, "an act inconsistent with the ownership of the seller" is deemed to be an acceptance of the goods only after the goods have been delivered to the buyer, but the delivery need not be physical: a delivery to a carrier for transmission to the buyer, *e.g.* under an f.o.b. or c.i.f. contract, would be sufficient (s.32).[48] An act inconsistent with the ownership of the seller is any act by which the buyer behaves as if he were the owner of the goods. Any disposal of the goods, *e.g.* a resale and dispatch or delivery of the goods to a sub-purchaser, or the pledging of them as a security, is an act inconsistent with the ownership of the seller, because thereby the buyer accepts the title to the goods although he might not have accepted their quality.[49] Assuming an exporter in London sells by sample 20 pieces of cotton goods to an importer in Sydney, Australia. He then buys the goods in the same manner from a manufacturer in Lancashire under a contract which provides for delivery (not packed for export) at his, the exporter's, premises in London. On arrival of the goods the exporter notices that they do not correspond with sample. Although, according to section 15(2)(*a*), entitled to reject the goods, he decides to ship them to Australia, hoping that his customer will accept them in performance of the contract. The Australian importer, however, rightly rejects the goods. By having dispatched the goods to Sydney, the exporter has done an act inconsistent with the ownership of the manufacturer and, by virtue of section 35, he is deemed to have accepted the goods. The exporter can still claim damages from the manufacturer for breach of warranty,[50] the measure of damages being the difference in the value of the goods as contracted for and the value of them as delivered to him. If after the export order was placed the market in cotton goods slumped in Australia but was maintained in London, the exporter can recover only the difference between the London value of the inferior goods and the value of the sound goods. The exporter may in this case suffer serious financial loss, and not merely inconvenience, as the result of losing his right to reject. He cannot avoid this result by protesting to the manufacturer or by intimating to him, before shipping the goods to Australia, that he rejects them if his customer in Australia rejects them to him. In this respect English law and the legal systems of Commonwealth countries which found their sales law on English law are more strict than other legal systems.[51] If the exporter, on discovering the defects of the goods, rejects them to the manufacturer as once and,

---

[48] *Kwei Tek Chao* v. *British Traders and Shippers* [1954] 2 Q.B. 459; *Bergerco U.S.A.* v. *Vegoil Ltd.* [1984] 1 Lloyd's Rep. 440, 445. See also *Benaim* v. *Debono* [1924] A.C. 514, p. 216, *post*.

[44] But a mere resale of the goods (unaccompanied by a disposal or an attempted disposal of them, such as a dispatch to the sub-purchaser), or an inquiry whether the goods are saleable, is not an act inconsistent with the ownership of the seller.

[50] See p. 134, *ante*.

[51] As is demonstrated by *Benaim* v. *Debono* [1924] A.C. 514, which is discussed on p. 216, *post*.

before shipping them to Australia, obtains his agreement that the goods be shipped without prejudice to his, the exporter's, right to reject them in the case of the Australian customer rejecting them to him, he preserves his right. In short, a buyer who contemplates passing on the goods to his sub-purchaser or disposing of them otherwise cannot by a *unilateral* act preserve his right to reject the goods to his supplier but may do so *by a new agreement* made before the disposal of the goods.

In the illustration just discussed the place of examination of the goods was London. The position would be different if under the contract of sale between the exporter and the manufacturer the examination is postponed to Australia. It has been observed earlier[52] that this is the normal arrangement in international sales; it would, *e.g.* apply if the exporter sells the goods to his Australian customer f.o.b. English port and buys them from the manufacturer in this country f.o.b. Manchester, and the manufacturer, in accordance with instructions received by the exporter, has to deliver the goods, packed for export, to a forwarder in Manchester for transmission to Sydney. In this case the exporter to whom the customer in Australia has rejected is still entitled to reject the goods to his manufacturer.

If the contract is indivisible and the buyer has accepted part of the goods, he can no longer reject the other part of the goods (s.11(4)).[53] The position is different, however, if the seller tenders the wrong quantity of goods or tenders the contract goods mixed with others; in any of these cases the buyer is entitled to reject the whole consignment or to accept the contract goods and to reject the others, but if he accepts a smaller or larger quantity than he bought he has to pay for what he accepted (s.30). Where the buyer has bought "assorted" goods but is tendered only one type of goods he is entitled to accept a reasonable percentage of the tendered goods and to reject the remainder.[54]

REJECTION OF GOODS

A buyer who wishes to reject the goods has to intimate within a reasonable time[54a] to the seller that he refuses to accept them (s.36). This notice should be clear and definite and should not be contradicted by an act relating to the goods by which the buyer denies the title of the seller to the goods. No form is prescribed for the notice of rejection; it may be given verbally, by telex, fax or in writing but the buyer should make certain that it reaches the seller, otherwise it is ineffective.

---

[52] See p. 138, *ante.*
[53] *J. Rosenthal & Sons Ltd.* v. *Esmail* [1965] 1 W.L.R. 1117 *lf. Gill & Duffus S.A.* v. *Berger & Co. Inc.* [1984] 2 W.L.R. 95. See also p. 144, *post.*
[54] *Ebrahim Dawood* v. *Heath (est.* 1927) [1961] 2 Lloyd's Rep. 512.
[54a] On "reasonable time" see p. 140, *ante.*

The buyer who rejects the goods is not bound to return them to the seller unless this is agreed (s.36) but, being a bailee, he has to exercise reasonable care with respect to them. Subject to this obligation, if the goods are rejected for good reason and in good time, the risk of loss of, or damage to, the goods is with the seller.

Unless a different intention of the parties is expressed in the contract or can be gathered from its terms by necessary implication, the buyer's right to reject the goods is postponed until the goods arrive and he has a reasonable opportunity of examining them.[55] But in appropriate cases the buyer may reject the goods even before having received them, namely, if he notices from a provisional invoice or advice note that the seller has dispatched goods which are not in accordance with the contract.[56] A seller, except in c.i.f. sales,[57] who has tendered goods not in accordance with the contract may cancel the original tender and make another tender but only if he can make the other tender within the time stipulated in the contract.[58] Branson J. said in one case[59]:

> It does not prevent the seller, if he has time within which to do so, from tendering another parcel of goods, which may be goods which accord with the contract, and which the buyer must, therefore, accept and pay for. . . . It cannot be predicated in any particular case that, if the first tender is not a proper tender, there may not yet be another tender which is a proper tender.

Right of rejection in c.i.f. contracts

Some observations have to be added on c.i.f. contracts. As has been explained earlier,[60] the characteristic feature of these contracts is the importance attributed to the shipping documents. It has been held, *obiter*, in *Kwei Tek Chao* v. *British Traders and Shippers Ltd.*[61] that a disposal of the bill of lading (which is part of the shipping documents) is not necessarily an act inconsistent with the seller's ownership of the goods and that, in principle, a c.i.f. buyer does not lose his right to reject the goods by dealings with forged documents, *e.g.* by pledging the bill of lading to a bank. In that case, the question whether by dealing with the documents the buyers had done an act inconsistent with the sellers' ownership in the goods did not arise, but in the interest of "those who may be concerned" Devlin J. observed that so long as a buyer was merely

---

[55] *Bergerco U.S.A.* v. *Vegoil Ltd.* [1984] 1 Lloyd's Rep. 440, 446; see p. 137, *ante*.
[56] *E. E. & Brian Smith (1928) Ltd.* v. *Wheatsheaf Mills Ltd.* [1939] 2 K.B. 302.
[57] Where it is important that *the tendered documents* are in order.
[58] *Ibid.*; and *Borrowman* v. *Free* (1878) 4 Q.B.D. 500; Lord Devlin "The Treatment of Breach of Contract" [1966] Cam. L.J. 192.
[59] *E. E. & Brian Smith (1928) Ltd.* v. *Wheatsheaf Mills Ltd.* [1939] 2 K.B. 302, 314.
[60] See p. 34, *ante*.
[61] [1954] 2 Q.B. 459; see also p. 42, *ante*.

dealing with the documents, he did not commit an act inconsistent with the seller's ownership in the goods and retained the right of rejecting the goods if upon examination after their arrival they were found not to be in conformity with the contract. The formidable argument that the buyer, when reselling the bill of lading or pledging it to a bank, intended to give the sub-purchaser or pledgee a proprietary interest in the goods and passed title to him, was rejected by Devlin J. on the grounds that the buyer himself had only *conditional* property, *viz.* property conditional on the goods being in accordance with the contract and that therefore he could not deal with more than conditional property. Devlin J. said[62]:

> I think that the true view is that what the buyer obtains when the title under the documents is given to him, is the property in the goods, subject to the condition that they revest if upon examination he finds them to be not in accordance with the contract. That means that he gets only conditional property in the goods, the condition being a condition subsequent. All his dealings with the documents are dealings only with that conditional property in the goods. It follows, therefore, that there can be no dealing which is inconsistent with the seller's ownership unless he deals with something more than the conditional property.

Rejection where each delivery to be treated as separate contract

The contract may provide that "each delivery is to be treated as a separate contract."[63] Unless delivery by instalments is arranged, this term gives the seller an option; he may deliver in one consignment, in which case there is one indivisible contract, or he may make several deliveries, in which case there are several separate contracts. The seller exercises this option by the mode of performance.[64] Where the contract is on c.i.f. terms, the fact that the seller has shipped under separate bills of lading in different vessels indicates clearly that he has exercised the option in favour of several contracts. Difficult is the position if he ships under separate bills of lading in the same vessel; here it is a question of intention of the parties, *i.e.* whether they intend that there should be one transaction or several contracts. In one case[65] a seller in Hong Kong sold 140 bales of grey cotton poplin to cotton converters in Manchester. The contract was c.i.f. Liverpool and provided that each delivery was to be treated as a separate contract. The seller shipped the whole consignment in the same ship but for reasons connected with the quota regulation in Hong Kong the goods were shipped under two bills of lading, each relating to half the consignment. The buyers accepted one bill of lading

---

[62] [1954] 2 Q.B. 459, 487.
[63] In *Cehave N.V.* v. *Bremer Handelsgesellschaft mbH, The Hansa Nord* [1976] 1 Q.B. 44 the contract provided: " . . . each shipment shall be considered a separate contract."
[64] *J. Rosenthal & Sons Ltd.* v. *Esmail* [1965] 1 W.L.R. 1117.
[65] *Ibid.*

and rejected the other. The House of Lords held that in the special circumstances of this case—the buyers requiring the goods for their own use and not for resale—the parties, in spite of the shipment under two separate bills of lading, treated the transaction as one, and the buyers, having accepted part of the goods, could no longer reject the other part.[66] This case, however, was founded on special facts. Normally, when the contract contains a separation clause and the goods are shipped under separate bills of lading, it has to be inferred that the parties intend that there should be several contracts.[67]

Property in rejected goods

The property in the rejected goods revests in the seller when he accepts the rejection.[68] When he does not accept the rejection, it is believed that, if it is later decided by the court or arbitration tribunal that the rejection was justified, the property likewise revests in the seller because, as Devlin J. observed in the *Kwei Tek Chao* case,[69] the property passes to the buyer subject to a condition subsequent, namely, that on examination the goods are found to be in accordance with the contract. A buyer who has paid the price in advance and then rejects the goods is not entitled to retain them by virtue of an "unpaid buyer's lien"[70] until the price is refunded. In the case of c.i.f. contracts, dealings with the documents do not affect the right of the buyer to reject the goods, which right normally arises only after the arrival of the goods when they can be examined.[71]

Rejection and estoppel

If the buyer has a valid ground for the rejection of the goods but so conducts himself as to lead the seller to believe that he is not relying on

---

[66] See p. 142 *ante.*
[67] A different question is whether shipments under several bills of lading constitute "partial shipments" for the purposes of letters of credits, entitling the bank to reject such bills of lading. Here the UCP (1983 Revision) provide in art. 44(a) that partial shipments are allowed unless the credit stipulates otherwise. Further, it is provided in art. 44(b) that "shipments by sea, or by more than one mode of transport but including carriage by sea, made on the same vessel and for the same voyage, will not be regarded as partial shipments, even if the transport documents indicating loading on board bear different dates of issuance and/or indicate different ports of loading on board."
[68] *J. L. Lyons & Co.* v. *May & Baker* [1923] 1 K.B. 685, 688.
[69] [1954] 2 Q.B. 459; see p. 144, *ante.*
[70] An analogy to the unpaid seller's lien (see p. 150, *post*) is not admissible: *J. L. Lyons & Co.* v. *May & Baker* [1923] 1 K.B. 685.
[71] See p. 143, *ante.*

that ground, he is estopped—precluded—from setting up that ground of rejection when it would be unfair or unjust to allow him so to do.[72] On the other hand, if a buyer has rejected the goods on a ground which he has notified to the seller, he is not confined to that ground and can later rely on other grounds for the rejection.[73]

Rejection and frustration

If owing to a frustrating event the rejection of the goods becomes impossible, it would appear that the buyer has lost the right to reject the goods.[74]

RELAXATION OF STRICT PERFORMANCE OF CONTRACT[75]

It happens sometimes that a party to a contract of international sale does not insist on strict performance of the contract when the other party asks for indulgence. The buyer may ask the seller to defer the date of delivery of the goods or the date of payment of the price, or the seller may ask for extension of the shipping time. The party to whom such request is addressed may fully realise that, according to the terms of the contract, he is entitled to refuse it and, if the other party does not perform, he may treat the contract as repudiated and claim damages. But he may not wish to stand on his rights for reasons of business policy. From the legal point of view this reasonable attitude might cause considerable difficulty. If the party who has been asked to relax the terms of the contract asks for a consideration in return for the favour, there is a true contract to vary the terms of the original contract and the new agreement is binding on both parties; but if the favour is merely a voluntary forbearance to insist on strict performance, the position is different. In that case, if "one party has by its conduct led the other to alter his position"[76] it is probable that the former party cannot change his mind at once and insist again on his strict rights. For instance, an overseas buyer of computers asks the export seller to defer shipment for one month, and the seller agrees. It is probable that the seller cannot arbitrarily set aside this arrangement. This view is founded either on what has become known as the doctrine of *waiver* or

---

[72] *Panchaud Frères S.A.* v. *Etablissements General Grain Co.* [1970] 1 Lloyd's Rep. 53, 57.
[73] *Ibid.* p. 56.
[74] *Mackay* v. *Dick* (1881) 6 App.Cas. 251; *Colley* v. *Overseas Importers* [1921] 3 K.B. 302.
[75] This paragraph is founded on Clive M. Schmitthoff, *Legal Aspects of Export Sales*, published by the Institute of Export, 3rd ed., 1978, pp. 14–16.
[76] *Per* Lord Simonds in *Tool Manufacturing Co. Ltd.* v. *Tungsten Electric Co. Ltd.* [1955] W.L.R. 761, 764.

on that of *equitable estoppel*.[77] The latter was formulated by Denning L.J. in a commercial case[78] as follows:

> If one party, by his conduct, leads another to believe that the strict rights arising under the contract will not be insisted upon, intending that the other should act on that belief, and he does act on it, then the first party will not afterwards be allowed to insist on the strict rights when it would be inequitable for him to do so.

But this does not mean that the terms of the original contract are varied, and can no longer be relied upon. Goddard J. (as he then was) said in this connection[79]:

> If what happens is a mere voluntary forbearance to insist on delivery or acceptance according to the strict terms of the written contract, the original contract remains unaffected and the obligation to deliver and to accept the full contract quantity still continues.

And Lord Simonds observed[80]:

> I would not have it supposed, particularly in commercial transactions, that mere acts of indulgence are apt to create rights.

If, therefore, in the above example the buyer, after expiration of one month, is still unwilling to accept delivery of the goods, the seller would be entitled to revert to the original terms of the contract. Goulding J. said in one case[81]:

---

[77] These two doctrines are frequently equated and usually overlap but strictly speaking they are distinct and separate doctrines, see Denning L.J. in *Panchaud Frères S.A.* v. *Etablissements General Grain Co.* [1970] 1 Lloyd's Rep. 53, 57, and John Adams, "Waiver Redistributed" (1973) 36 *Conveyancer* 245. On the doctrine of equitable estoppel see also *Janred Properties Ltd.* v. *Ente Nazionale per il Turismo* (*No. 2*), *Financial Times*, December 17, 1985; *The Wise, Financial Times,* July 18, 1989.

Different from equitable estoppel is estoppel by previous conduct, technically known as "estoppel by convention." This arises where the parties have acted on an agreed assumption that a state of facts is true (see *Chitty on Contracts* (26th ed., 1989, para. 221). A party who has acted in such a manner would not act in good faith if he suddenly decided to act contrariwise (*venire contra factum proprium*). Entirely different from the problems discussed here is the procedural problem of "issue estoppel"; on this see p. 705, *post*.

[78] *Plasticmoda S.p.A.* v. *Davidsons* (*Manchester*) *Ltd.* [1952] 1 Lloyd's Rep. 527. There are numerous older cases on this subject; the most famous of them is *Central London Property Trust Ltd.* v. *High Trees House Ltd.* [1947] K.B. 130. The modern cases include: *Panchaud Frères S.A.* v. *Etablissements General Grain Co.* [1970] 1 Lloyd's Rep. 53; *Woodhouse A.C. Israel Cocoa Ltd. S.A.* v. *Nigerian Produce Marketing Co. Ltd.* [1972] A.C. 741; *W. J. Alan & Co. Ltd.* v. *El Nasr Export & Import Co.* [1972] 2 W.L.R. 800, 814; *Bremer Handelsgesellschaft GmbH* v. *Vanden Avenne-Izegem PVBA* [1978] 2 Lloyd's Rep. 109; *Société Italo-Belge pour le Commerce et l'Industrie S.A.* v. *Palm and Vegetable Oils (Malaysia) Sdn. Bhd.*; *The Post Chaser* [1982] 1 All E.R. 19; *K. Lokumal & Sons (London) Ltd* v. *Lotte Shipping Co. Pte Ltd. The August Leonardt* [1985] 2 Lloyd's Rep. 28, 35; *Government of Swaziland Central Transport Administration* v. *Leila Maritime Co. Ltd. The Leila* [1985] 2 Lloyd's Rep. 172; *Tai Hing Cotton Mill Ltd.* v. *Liu Chong Hing Bank Ltd.* [1985] 3 W.L.R. 317, 333; *Sea Calm Shipping Co. S.A.* v. *Chantiers Navals de L'Esterel S.A. The Uhenbels.* [1986] 2 Lloyd's Rep. 294, 298; *The Antares* (*No. 2*) [1986] 2 Lloyd's Rep. 633, 639; *In re Exchange Securities & Commodities Ltd.* [1987] 2 W.L.R. 893, 899; *Nichimen Corporation* v. *Gatoil Overseas Inc.* [1987] 2 Lloyd's Rep. 46, 52; *Proctor & Gamble Philippine Manufacturing Corporation* v. *Kurt A. Becher GmbH & Co. KG* [1988] 2 Lloyd's Rep. 21, 27.

[79] *Bessler Waechter Glover & Co.* v. *South Derwent Coal Co.* [1938] 1 K.B. 408, 416.

[80] In *Tool Manufacturing Co. Ltd.* v. *Tungsten Electric Co. Ltd.* [1955] 1 W.L.R. 761, 764.

[81] (1973) 26 P.C.R. 89; quoted with approval by Kerr L.J. in *Nichimen Corporation* v. *Gatoil Overseas Inc.* [1987] 2 Lloyd's Rep. 46, 53.

> Indeed, the mere extension of the period to a new fixed period would on the authorities have preserved the position that time was of the essence without fresh stipulation to that effect.

Moreover, if no time limit is provided for the indulgence, the party who has agreed to relax the strict terms can likewise unilaterally notify the other party that the indulgence is over and that the strict terms of the contract shall apply again. Normally the party who has shown indulgence has to give the other party notice of reasonable length "for readjustment before he is allowed to enforce his strict rights"[82]; but such notice is not always essential: it is not required if it is clear from the circumstances that the period of suspension is over or that, even if notice had been given, the other party could not have complied with it. Thus, in one case[83] a French company bought goods from an English company under an f.o.b. contract which provided that the price should be paid in sterling under a banker's letter of credit to be opened in London "within a few weeks." The time for the opening of the credit expired, as the court found, on August 19; there were extensions, and on October 22 the sellers informed the buyers peremptorily that, having regard to the delay in the establishment of the credit, they considered the contract cancelled. Devlin J. held that the peremptory notice of October 22 was sufficient and that the sellers were not obliged to give the buyers further time because even if they had given them, say, a fortnight's notice the buyers could not have complied with it as they could not obtain transferable sterling from their bank; the legal principle was expressed by the learned judge[84] as follows:

> The position of a party who has started out with a contract where time is of the essence and has allowed the time to go by is, I think, quite clearly laid down in the authorities. He has got to make time of the essence of the contract again in the normal case, and that means that he has to give notice giving the other side what is a reasonable time in all the circumstances to comply with their obligations. . . . But in my judgment, although that is the ordinary doctrine, the giving of a notice is not always essential.

These equitable principles are of great importance in international sales. They enable a seller who has voluntarily forborne to insist on the strict performance of the contract, to reintroduce those strict terms again if the necessity arises.

THE RIGHTS OF THE UNPAID SELLER AGAINST THE GOODS

In international sales transactions the seller normally parts with the possession of the goods before receiving the purchase price because he

---

[82] Lord Tucker in *Tool Manufacturing Co. Ltd.* v. *Tungsten Electric Co. Ltd.* [1955] 1 W.L.R. 761, 785; *S.C.C.M.O. (London) Ltd.* v. *Société Générale de Compensation* [1956] 1 Lloyd's Rep. 290, 300.
[83] *Etablissements Chainbaux S.A.R.L.* v. *Harbormaster Ltd.* [1955] 1 Lloyd's Rep. 303; *British and Commonwealth Group plc.* v. *Quadrex Holdings Inc.*, *The Times*, December 8, 1988. See also *Nichimen Corporation* v. *Gatoil Overseas Inc.* [1987] 2 Lloyd's Rep. 46 (failure to open letter of credit was breach of a condition of the contract of sale and this position was not changed by the sellers granting the buyers indulgence for the opening of the credit).
[84] In the *Chainbaux* case at p. 312.

wants to dispatch the goods with due expedition. Even where the sale is on a cash basis, some time will elapse before the buyer's remittance reaches the seller. Where the sale is a credit transaction more time will pass before the bill of exchange drawn by the seller on the buyer is settled. Much may happen during that time; the buyer may become insolvent, he may issue debentures taking priority over ordinary trading debts, he may amalgamate with a firm that is heavily indebted, or the buyer's country may prohibit payment in the stipulated currency, *e.g.* sterling. It is imperative that the seller should be properly protected here.

The law would fail in its task if it omitted to devise special rules for the protection of the seller during the vulnerable period which commences when he gives up possession of the goods and continues until he has received the price. However, here again, the best protection is the seller's forethought. The seller who parts with his goods before obtaining the price should insert into the contract of sale a clause reserving the title in the goods until he receives the purchase price. Such a clause was suggested earlier when the general conditions of sale were discussed.[85] Section 39(2) of the Sale of Goods Act 1979 entitles the unpaid seller, who has reserved the property in the goods, to withhold their delivery, and provides that[86] his rights against the goods shall be similar to and coextensive with the rights of lien and stoppage in transit which can be claimed by an unpaid seller who has not retained title in the goods.

The rights of the unpaid seller

Where the seller has failed to reserve the property in the goods, the rights of the unpaid seller are defined in sections 38–48 of the Sale of Goods Act 1979. These rights, which can be claimed by implication of the law, are (s.39(1)):

1. A lien on the goods for the price while he is in possession of them.
2. In case of the insolvency of the buyer,[87] a right of stopping the goods in transit after he has parted with the possession of them.
3. A right of resale, as limited by the Act.

The Act provides also in section 38 a definition of that unfortunate person, the unpaid seller, who becomes such:

---

[85] See p. 75. The retention of title clause is discussed on p. 121, *et seq.*, *ante.*
[86] In addition to his other remedies.
[87] The Sale of Goods Act 1979, in s.61(4), as amended by the Insolvency Act 1985, Sched. 10, defines insolvency thus: "A person is deemed to be insolvent within the meaning of this Act if he has either ceased to pay his debts in the ordinary course of business or he cannot pay his debts as they become due. Insolvency of companies and individuals is regulated by the Insolvency Act 1986.

1. When the whole of the price has not been paid or tendered, or
2. When a bill of exchange or other negotiable instrument has been received as conditional payment and the condition on which it was received has not been fulfilled by reason of the dishonour of the instrument or otherwise.

The rights of the unpaid seller may likewise be claimed by an agent of the seller to whom the bill of lading has been indorsed or by a consignor or confirming agent who has himself paid or is directly responsible for the price or who, for other reasons, is in the position of a seller (s.38(2)).[88]

The unpaid seller's lien

The unpaid seller can exercise his lien on the sold goods only if he still has actual possession of them. Where he has delivered them to a carrier for the purpose of transmission to the buyer, or to the buyer or his agent, the lien on the goods is lost (s.43). If the goods still pass through the channels of communication and have not yet been delivered into the possession of the buyer or his agent authorised to accept them on his behalf, the question arises whether the unpaid seller can exercise his right of stoppage in transit. This question will be examined in the next section. It will be seen that the conditions on which the Act admits stoppage in transit are very strict. In international sales transactions the unpaid seller's lien on the goods plays a relatively minor role.

The seller's right of lien is merely a right to retain the goods until the purchase price is paid and is not a right to resell them. He has, however, in certain contingencies such a right under the Act[89]; sometimes such right is given by mercantile custom, *e.g.* in the tea trade. The lien cannot be claimed for storage charges incurred when the goods are stored during the buyer's default.[90]

In the case of a credit sale, the unpaid seller has no right of lien during the credit period unless, during that period, the buyer becomes insolvent (s.41(1)(c)). After the expiration of the credit period he can exercise the lien in any event. The seller is entitled to the lien even if he is in possession of the goods as an agent for the buyer (s.41(2)); a confirming house, which acts as agent for a principal abroad, may exercise the lien on goods bought on behalf of the principal if he fails to pay the commission or incidental charges.

Stoppage in transit

This right is of much greater practical value for the exporter than the right of lien, particularly as it has always been interpreted favourably for

---

[88] See p. 298, *post.*
[89] See p. 153, *post.*
[90] *Somes* v. *British Empire Shipping Co.* (1860) 30 L.J.Q.B. 229.

the seller by the courts, but it should be noted that it can only be claimed if the buyer is *insolvent*.[91] Stoppage in transit operates, as it were, as the seller's outstretched arm, which snatches back goods, over which he has lost control, from the danger route leading to the insolvent buyer.

This right can only be exercised *during the transit* of the goods. This period begins when the goods have left the possession of the seller or his agent, and ends when the goods have reached the possession of the buyer or his agent who is authorised to accept the goods on his behalf. The Act defines the duration of transit as the time when the goods "are delivered to a carrier by land or water, or other bailee . . . for the purpose of transmission to the buyer, until the buyer or his agent in that behalf takes delivery of them from such carrier or other bailee. . . ."[92] It follows that the term "transit" has in law a technical meaning which is entirely different from its natural meaning. Goods may be "in transit" although not in motion, and goods which are in motion may never have been "in transit" in the eyes of the law. If, *e.g.* the seller under an ex works contract delivers the goods to the buyer's purchasing agent in this country, the goods pass from the possession of the seller directly to that of the buyer, and the seller cannot claim a right of stoppage while the goods are being shipped to the place of destination. Only where the goods, after having left the seller's possession, are in neutral hands, *e.g.* in the custody of a carrier, shipping agent or other independent intermediary, and only so long as they are in those hands for the purposes of transmission, can the right of stoppage be claimed. The right operates against the goods themselves; its aim is to revest possession of the goods in the seller as long as they are in the course of transit and to enable him to retain them and claim a lien on them until the purchase price is paid (s.44). If the goods are damaged, the seller who exercises his right of stoppage has no claim for the insurance money as was decided in a case concerning the importation of timber from Sweden.[93] The plaintiff, a timber merchant in Sweden, sold timber to a firm in London; the timber was duly shipped but damaged during the voyage. The buyers, who had the timber insured, stopped payment before the timber arrived in England. The seller gave notice of stoppage to the captain of the ship, and the question was whether he was entitled to the insurance money which had been paid for the damage to the timber. It was held that the claim was untenable; in the words of Lord Cairns L.C.:

> The right to stop in transitu is a right to stop the goods in whatever state they arrive. If they arrive injured or damaged in bulk or quality the right to stop in transitu is so far impaired; there is no contract or agreement which entitles the vendor to go beyond those goods in the state in which they arrive.

The right of stoppage in transit is exercised by the seller giving notice of his claim to the carrier or the carrier's principal, or by the seller taking

---

[91] See p. 149, n. 87, *ante*.
[92] s.45.
[93] *Berndtson* v. *Strang* (1868) L.R. 3 Ch.App. 588.

actual possession of the goods if he can do so without breach of the peace. The notice to the carrier's principal, *e.g.* the line in whose ships the goods are carried, is only effectual if given in such time and under such circumstances that the principal, by the exercise of reasonable diligence, can communicate it to his servant or agent in time to prevent a delivery to the buyer (s.46(1)).

The right of stoppage in transit, which originally arose by custom of the merchants, gave rise to much litigation before it was cast in its present form. It is outside the scope of this work to dwell on further details. Three points, however, may shortly be indicated.

First, delivery of the goods to a carrier or agent, who takes his instructions from the buyer, does not necessarily lead to a loss of the right of stoppage; in connection with that right, section 32(1) of the Act, which has been discussed earlier,[94] does not apply. If the carrier or agent is merely the buyer's agent for the purposes of transmitting the goods, the right of stoppage in transit can still be claimed, provided that the goods are still in the agent's possession; if, on the other hand, the agent is authorised to accept delivery of the goods in accordance with the terms of the contract of sale and has to dispose of them in compliance with the instructions of the buyer, the right is lost. The courts will generally lean in favour of the view that the master of the ship obtains possession of the goods in his capacity as carrier and not as agent of the buyer to take delivery under the contract of sale, and this applies even where the goods are delivered on a vessel chartered by him. Thus, where the seller, under an ordinary f.o.b. contract, delivers the goods to the master of the ship, who makes out the bill of lading in the buyer's name, the goods are still "in transit," and the right of stoppage can be exercised by the seller. But where, in the course of the shipment[95] or after arrival of the goods at the place of destination, the carrier acknowledges—"attorns"—to the buyer or his agent that he holds the goods on his behalf, the transit has come to an end even if the buyer orders the transshipment of the goods to another place (s.45(3)).

Secondly, the right of stoppage is not lost when the bill of lading is made out in the name of the buyer (or his agent), or, if originally made out in the seller's name, is delivered to the buyer. The latter act is, as has been seen,[96] decisive for the passing of the property unless the seller has reserved the right of disposal; but these acts are irrelevant for the exercise of the right of stoppage. In fact, that right acquires particular practical importance after the bill of lading has reached the buyer and he has thus obtained the right of disposal of the goods.

Thirdly, while normally the unpaid seller's lien or right of stoppage in transit is not affected by a sale or other disposition which the buyer has

---

[94] See p. 116, *ante.*
[95] *Reddall* v. *Union-Castle Mail Steamship Co. Ltd.* (1915) 84 L.J.K.B. 360.
[96] See p. 120, *ante.*

made with respect to the goods without the seller's assent (s.47(1)),[97] the position is different in one case: if the bill of lading was delivered to the buyer and he has indorsed it for·valuable consideration to a third person who is acting in good faith, the unpaid seller's rights are defeated and the third party acquires a valid title to the goods.[98] This rule is now laid down in section 47(2) of the 1979 Act; it was first established in 1794 in the celebrated case of *Lickbarrow* v. *Mason*,[99] after six years of litigation.

The right of resale

The Sale of Goods Act gives the unpaid seller the right to resell the goods[1]:

1. Where they are of a perishable nature, without further notice to the buyer; or
2. Where they are not perishable, after he—the unpaid seller—has given notice to the buyer of his intention to resell, and the buyer has not within a reasonable time paid or tendered the price.

By the exercise of the right of resale the unpaid seller has put it out of his power to perform the original contract which is rescinded.[2] The property in the goods has reverted to the seller who transfers it to the second buyer. The seller is entitled to retain the proceeds of the resale, whether they be greater or less than the original contract price.[3] If the seller makes a loss on the resale, he can recover damages from the defaulting buyer for breach of contract (48(1)). A third person who buys the goods on resale acquires a good title to them as against the original buyer (s.48(2)).

---

[97] A case in which the seller assented to the sale by the buyer and thereby lost his rights against the goods was *D. F. Mount* v. *Jay & Jay (Provisions) Co. Ltd.* [1960] 1 Q.B. 159.

[98] The same rule applies to other documents of title, *e.g.* a delivery order addressed to a wharfinger; but the third person who acquires the goods from the buyer is only protected if the buyer indorses to him the same delivery order which he himself received from the seller; the third person is not protected by s.47(2) if the buyer delivers to him a "back-to-back" delivery order, *i.e.* a new delivery order corresponding to that received by the buyer from the seller; in that case the third person may, however, claim the protection of what under the 1979 Act is s.25(1) if the requirements of that section are satisfied: *D. F. Mount* v. *Jay & Jay (Provisions) Co. Ltd.* [1960] 1 Q.B. 159.

[99] (1794) 5 T.R. 683. A delivery order addressed to a warehouseman is either a promise by the seller that the goods be delivered to the buyer or a mere authority to the buyer entitling him to receive the goods; whether it is one or the other, depends on the intention of the parties: *Alicia Hosiery Ltd.* v. *Brown Shipley & Co. Ltd.* [1970] 1 Q.B. 195.

[1] An unpaid seller who has not exercised the right of lien or stoppage in transit but is still in possession of the goods has likewise a right of resale: Diplock L.J. in *R. V. Ward Ltd.* v. *Bignall* [1967] 1 Q.B. 534, 545.

[2] *R. V. Ward Ltd.* v. *Bignall* [1967] 1 Q.B. 534. The exercise of the right of lien or retention or stoppage in transit—as contrasted with the exercise of the right of resale—does not rescind the contract (s.48(1)).

[3] *Ibid.*

CHAPTER 10

COUNTERTRADE

COUNTERTRADE is a collective term which denotes various methods of linking two export transactions, one emanating from the exporter's country and the other from that of the importer. The simplest forms of countertrade are reciprocal sales and barters but, as will be seen later, other types of countertrade are also in use, some of great complexity.

Contracts of sale and of barter

Normal dealings in international trade are founded on the concept of the sale of goods. The sale of goods means an exchange of goods for money. The money consideration is called the price.[1] It is irrelevant whether the price is payable on delivery of the goods,[2] or in advance, or whether credit is allowed. In English law, unlike some other legal systems,[3] it is equally irrelevant that the price is not fixed in the contract of sale or that the contract does not contain machinery for the determination of the price. The Sale of Goods Act 1979 admits "open price" contracts and states[4] that in these cases the buyer must pay "a reasonable price." But if the contract provides for an exchange of goods for goods or services, it is not a contract of sale in the legal sense, but it is a barter.[5]

The rules governing a contract of barter are not well defined in English law.[6] It is obvious that the Sale of Goods Act 1979 does not apply

---

[1] The Sale of Goods Act 1979, s.2(1) provides: "A contract of sale of goods is a contract by which the seller transfers the property in goods to the buyer for a money consideration, called the price."

[2] Unless otherwise agreed, the price is so payable. In the terminology of the Sale of Goods Act 1979, unless otherwise agreed, the delivery of the goods and payment of the price are "concurrent conditions" (s.28).

[3] e.g. French law (Civil Code, art. 1583) requires the fixing of the price, or a method of ascertaining it, in the contract of sale. USA law, like English law, admits "open price" contracts (Uniform Commercial Code, s.2-305(1)), in which case a "reasonable price" is payable. The Uniform Law on the International Sale of Goods (Hague Convention, 1964), art. 57, and the UN Convention on Contracts for the International Sale of Goods (Vienna, 1980), art. 55, follow, in principle, the UK and USA regulation. On "open price" contracts generally see *R. & J. Dempster Ltd.* v. *Motherwell Bridge and Engineering Co. Ltd.* 1964 S.C. 308.

[4] In s.8(2).

[5] See *Re Westminster Property Group plc*, [1985] 1 W.L.R. 676. The American concept of the contract of sale is wider than the English concept. The UCC, s.2-304(1) provides that "the price can be made payable in money or otherwise." A contract of barter is thus a contract of sale in American law.

[6] See *Benjamin's Sale of Goods* (3rd ed., 1987), para. 35, p. 32; Law Commission's Report on Implied Terms in Contracts for the Supply of Goods (Law Com. No. 95, HMSO, 1979), paras. 48–55. See also *Esso Petroleum Co. Ltd.* v. *Customs and Excise Commissioners* [1976] 1 W.L.R. 1, 11.

directly. But the provisions of the Supply of Goods and Services Act 1982, Part I,[7] apply to a contract of barter. By virtue of this Act the contract of barter is assimilated to the contract of sale, as far as the terms implied by the law into the contract are concerned.[8] The property in the goods, supplied in a barter by each party to the other, passes when the parties intend it to pass.[9] In this respect, as in others not covered by the 1982 Act, many provisions of the Sale of Goods Act 1979 apply to barter by way of analogy.[10]

The economic background

Countertrade, though, as will be seen, a practice of dubious benefit to international trade, is of growing importance. According to a publication of the Department of Trade and Industry,[11] the number of countries which have regulations for countertrading has risen from 27 in 1979 to approximately 100 at the end of 1986. The main growth comes from the less developed countries (LDCs) in Latin America, Africa and Asia and the newly industrialised countries (NICs), which include Brazil, Mexico, India, Taiwan and South Korea. Countertrade arrangements are also required by the Member States of CMEA[12] and some oil exporting countries. Australia and New Zealand demand offset arrangements for public sector purchases. In other countries of Western market economy governmental requirements for countertrade arrangements are not usual but in practice they are sometimes asked for, particularly in major transactions, such as defence, aviation and high technology deals.

The reasons for countertrade arrangements are not difficult to find. Some countries, particularly the LDCs, lack hard currency and credit facilities to pay for their imports. Some countries wish to expand their own export markets by demanding these facilities. The oil exporting countries want to establish stability of market conditions and use the oil which they produce as consideration in kind for industrial and other products which they require. Among the LDCs, Indonesia has introduced

---

[7] Which came into operation on January 1, 1983; see [1982] J.B.L. 357–358.

[8] These terms relate to title, etc. (s.2), description (s.3), quality of fitness (s.4), sample (s.5), and the exclusion of implied terms by express agreement, course of dealing or usage binding both parties. (s.11).

[9] *cf. Koppel* v. *Koppel* [1966] 1 W.L.R. 802, 811 (not a very clear precedent).

[10] *Buckley* v. *Lever Bros. Ltd.* [1953] 4 D.L.R. 16.

[11] "Countertrade. Some Guidance for Exporters," 1987 edition, published by the Project and Export Policy Division of the Department of Trade and Industry. See also "Draft outline of the possible content and structure of a legal guide on drawing up international countertrade contracts," Report of the Secretary-General, UNCITRAL, June 2, 1989, Ref.: A/CN.9/322. For a study of countertrade in French, see Marcel Fontaine, *"Aspects juridiques des contrats de compensation"* in D.P.C.I. 1981, p. 181.

[12] See p. 70, n. 55, *ante.*

a detailed statutory regulation requiring countertrade measures in government procurement transactions.[13] In some countries administrative rules having a similar effect are applied.

Countertrade is not the most desirable form of international trade. It is not in harmony with the concept of an open, cash-based, multilateral trading system, which the General Agreement on Tariffs and Trade (GATT) and the Organisation for Economic Co-operation and Developments (OECD) aim to maintain and promote. It is stated in the DTI publication referred to earlier[14]:

> Countertrade, by emphasising closed goods-based reciprocal transactions, risks prejudicing the long-term advantages to all parties concerned from multilateral trade. Countertrade replaces the pressures of competition and market forces with reciprocity, protection and price setting. It is for these reasons that the GATT and OECD have expressed concern at the growth of countertrade in recent years.

In spite of these general objections, in practice importers in many overseas markets will insist on countertrade measures. The large or medium-sized exporter cannot ignore this trend. He should realise than countertrade arrangements often involve considerable additional risks. The disposal of the countertraded goods may cause difficulty, in particular if they cannot be sold at a readily available commodity market. The exporter may require for their disposal the services of a third party, such as a trading house, and he may be charged for the countertraded goods more than the goods will fetch when sold. This price difference, plus the trading house's commission, is known as the *disagio*; it may be considerable and has to be calculated into the price for which the exporter is prepared to sell his goods. Sometimes the exporter may find it difficult to turn the countertraded goods into money in consequence of exchange control restrictions or other trade barriers which exist between various countries, and it may be necessary for him to engage in a complicated swap transaction involving a third country in order to obtain the consideration due to him for the export sale. Finally, ECGD cover is not available for a countertrade transaction, except in the case of a reciprocal sales agreement under which the ordinary export sale is unconnected with the countersale[15]; private insurance may offer more favourable terms. Some of these additional risks can be reduced or avoided, if the exporter enters into a factoring agreement with a confirming house, broker, bank or other finance institution.[16] The exporter then assigns his obligations to the factor and is no longer involved in the countertrade transaction. The factor provides him at once with cash, charging, of course, a fee for his services and sometimes demanding a bank guarantee from the exporter.

---

[13] They and a description of the Australian offset policies are reproduced in the DTI brochure, referred to in n. 11.
[14] On pp. 5–6 of the brochure referred to in n. 11.
[15] See p. 158, *post.*
[16] On factoring, see p. 453, *post.*

An exporter who has to agree to the demand for countertrade is well advised to make use of the specialist services available to assist him. Reference has already been made repeatedly to the informative brochure, *Countertrade. Some Guidance for Exporters*, published by the Project and Export Policy Division of the Department of Trade and Industry (1987 edition). Appended to this brochure is a list of some British companies experienced in countertrading with addresses and information about their activities.

TYPES OF COUNTERTRADE TRANSACTIONS

The forms which countertrade transactions assume are infinite and vary from country to country and case to case. But some types of countertrade transactions can be discerned. Normally it is advisable to conclude a *framework agreement*, within which the individual transactions shall operate. The essential features of the framework agreement will be considered later.[17] Exceptionally no separate framework agreement is necessary. Thus, in a long-term or major construction contract[18] it is usual to build the countertrade provisions into the main contract. To give a hypothetical example, if a company in country A undertakes to build a mine for a public undertaking in country B and it further contracts to buy back the output of the mine, the buy-back clauses are likely to be included in the mining contract. Strictly speaking, these clauses, although appearing as terms of the main contract, constitute a framework agreement for the individual contracts whereby the company in country A will purchase the minerals from the public undertaking in country B.

Reciprocal sales agreements

Under this arrangement the export seller enters into a separate contract with the overseas buyer whereby he (the export seller) or another person undertakes to purchase certain specific goods produced in the buyer's country. There are thus two parallel contracts of sale, the export contract and the countersale. It is left to the agreement of the parties whether the countersale shall cover the total value of the export sale or only part of it.[19] In the latter case the balance has to be paid by the overseas buyer in cash or additional goods have to be supplied in order to achieve

---

[17] See p. 163, *post*.
[18] See p. 731, *post*.
[19] In *State Trading Corporation of India Ltd.* v. *M. Golodetz Ltd. The Sara D* [1989] 2 Lloyd's Rep. 277 the countersale covered only 60 per cent. of the principal sale.

equivalence. The reciprocal sales agreement is the most frequently used form of countertrade.

Two variants of reciprocal sales agreements exist. In the first the obligation of the export seller to enter into the countersale is linked with the countersale only in the framework agreement but, apart from this linkage, the two contracts of sale are entirely independent of each other. In the second variant, the export sale is conditional on the export seller entering into, or possibly performing, the countersale. The first variant is preferable for two reasons. First, the exporter can obtain cover for the export sale from ECGD under a comprehensive short-term guarantee (CST guarantee).[20] Secondly, the usual bank guarantees, letters of credit and/or performance bonds are more easily arranged for the export sale if it is entirely independent of the countersale.[21] Even if the first variant is chosen, the linkage between the export sale and the countersale is so close that, if one of these contracts cannot be performed, *e.g.* because it is frustrated, there is strength in the argument that the parties intended the other contract likewise to be invalidated.

The remedies of the parties to the export sale and the countersale for non-performance or breach of contract are exactly the same as in a single sales transaction.

A reciprocal sales agreement was contemplated in *Pagnan SpA* v. *Granaria BV;*[22] one contract was for the sale of Thai Tapioca and the countersale for Chinese manioc.[23] The parties negotiated but, according to the findings of the court, never entered into binding contracts. In the course of his judgment, Sir John Donaldson M.R. said[24]:

> The idea was that each would buy from the other and that there would therefore be a "swap" transaction. I think it is inherent in that concept that if either of these contracts were still under negotiation at the crucial moment, they both were.

The definition of the countersale buyer

In reciprocal sales agreements a difficulty arises. Only in rare cases will the export seller wish to acquire the countersold goods for his own use.

---

[20] See p. 474, *post*.

[21] In *State Trading Corporation of India Ltd.* v. *M. Golodetz Ltd. The Sara D,* [1989] 2 Lloyd's Rep. 277 a reciprocal sales agreement, in which the sale and the countersale were independent, was in issue. Unfortunately there was a linkage of the financial arrangements. The buyers were obliged to open a letter of credit and the sellers were to give a so-called countertrade guarantee with respect to their obligations under the countersale. To make things worse, both the obligations of the buyer and those of the seller had to be performed simultaneously. The buyers failed to open the letter of credit and the sellers failed to give the countertrade guarantee. The Court of Appeal held that the seller's obligation to procure the countertrade guarantee was not a condition precedent to the buyer's obligation to open the letter of credit and that the buyers were in breach of contract owing to their failure to open the credit.

[22] [1986] 2 Lloyd's Rep. 547.

[23] Which is another name for tapioca although there is a difference in quality between the Chinese and the Thai product.

[24] *Ibid.*, on p. 549.

Normally he wants to dispose of them and to turn them into money. This means that he has to find a trader who is willing to buy the countersold goods. This difficulty is particularly great if the goods do not have a readily accessible commodity market. Usually the exporter, before agreeing to a countertrade transaction in goods not traded at a commodity market, will approach a trading house specialising in these transactions in order to ascertain whether it is willing to purchase the countertraded goods.

From the legal point of view, the important question is: who is the buyer in the countersale? Often exporter A will conclude the contract of export sale with overseas importer B and importer B will sell by way of countersale to trading house C in the exporter's country, C acting as a principal in the countersale transaction. But it is also possible that importer B will insist that C should act as agent of A, in which case the countersale contract is concluded between B and A.

Sometimes, even though the reciprocal sales agreements are independent of each other, the exporter will insist that the countersold goods are shipped before he is willing to ship his goods. But the foreign importer will be unwilling to ship unless he is sure of his money. The foreign counterseller may have to provide a performance guarantee[25] but it is more usual to resolve this difficulty by constituting an *escrow account* with a bank. Under such an arrangement the bank undertakes to pay out the money only if certain specified conditions are satisfied, *e.g.* the counterpurchaser would pay the price for the counterbought goods into the escrow account, and the bank would release it to the counterseller or his bank when notified that the countersold goods are shipped.

Barter

This term is employed loosely in commercial circles. It is sometimes used—incorrectly—for all types of countertrade, irrespective of the legal nature of the arrangements made by the parties.

In law a barter, as already observed,[26] is an exchange of goods for goods or services, *e.g.* sugar from Cuba is exchanged for screws produced in Britain.

A barter arrangement is sometimes described as a *compensation contract* because the delivery of the goods by one of the parties is "the compensation"—in legal terms "the consideration"—for the delivery of the goods by the other. If one of them fails to make delivery in accordance with the contract, this may provide a ground for the non-performance by the other.

---

[25] See p. 451, *post*.
[26] See p. 154, *ante*.

Here again, two types can be distinguished. In the true barter, there is a simple exchange and no value is placed on the goods exchanged. For example, the owner of a motor cycle arranges with his friend to exchange it for the friend's minicar. In the second type, some value is put on the exchanged goods. It is obvious that in commercial transactions only the valued barter is used.

A valued barter is not the same as a reciprocal sales contract although in some cases the courts have been inclined to treat it as such.[27] The essential difference is that a valued barter, like an unvalued one, is a one-contract transaction in which the obligations of the parties are made dependent on each other, whereas the reciprocal sales agreement is always a two-contract arrangement, even if the contracts are linked together in the manner indicated earlier.[28]

In the valued barter two problems arise. The first is the disposal of the goods received by the exporter from the overseas customer. The position is here the same as has been discussed for the reciprocal sale.[29] In other words, the exporter will normally deal with these goods by way of a disposal or swap transaction, requiring the services of a third party who will charge a fee, commission or disagio. Secondly, arrangements have to be made for the payment of the settlement balance which at the end will arise in favour of one of the parties to the barter. A *settlement account* or *evidence account* will have to be constituted, preferably in a hard currency country which does not operate an exchange control system. The value of the bartered goods is set off in the settlement account and on termination of the transaction the credit balance is paid in cash or kind to the party entitled thereto.

The buy-back agreement

This kind of arrangement is made in mining, oil exploration or other major export transactions. The contractor who carries out the work agrees that the purchase price be paid in full or partly by his purchase of the produce of the installation. The buy-back clauses, which may be lengthy, are normally incorporated into the main contract.[30]

The buy-back terms will often contain a most favoured customer (m.f.c.) clause, according to which the employer (the seller of the produce) will grant the contractor (the buyer) the most favourable price which he charges another customer purchasing goods on comparable

---

[27] *Aldridge* v. *Johnson* (1857) 7 E. & B. 885; see *Benjamin's Sale of Goods* (3rd ed., 1987), para. 36, p. 32.
[28] See p. 158, *ante*.
[29] *Ibid*.
[30] See p. 157, *ante*.

conditions.[31] The m.f.c. price will be reduced by a discount which includes the amortisation element for the installation price. In view of the need to include the amortisation factor, the duration of the buy-back agreement may be lengthy.

Offset arrangements

An offset transaction is an arrangement by which the exporter of goods is obliged to incorporate in the goods specified materials, components or sub-assemblies produced in the importing country or otherwise to perform specified services in that country. Offset arrangements are an established feature in the sale of advanced technology products, such as defence systems and aircraft. Sometimes the exporter is required in the importing country to open or equip a factory producing components or to maintain an assembly plant.

In Australia offsets are required for public sector purchases by the Federal Government and the State Governments.[32] The main types of offsets acceptable to the Federal Government are:

1. Technology transfers.
2. Research and development and training.
3. Part production or assembly.
4. Production in Australia of related goods or services for sales overseas.
5. Overseas marketing.
6. Joint or collaborative ventures.
7. Purchase of Australian-made products and services.
8. Gifts and donations to local companies, *e.g.* in form of money, equipment, software, and resources.
9. Direct loan or equity investment in local firms.

The offset of the State Governments are similar.

Disposal and switch transactions

In reciprocal sales and barter agreements the disposal of the countertraded goods causes, as already discussed,[33] a problem. Here two situations have to be distinguished: the goods may have an easily

---

[31] For an example of a m.f.c. clause see pp. 266–267, *post.*
[32] The DTI Brochure on Countertrade quoted on p. 155, n. 11, *ante* gives a detailed survey of the Australian preference and offset policies.
[33] See pp. 158–159, *ante.* There may be other problems. Some of them came to light in *Pagnan SpA* v. *Granaria BV* [1986] 2 Lloyd's Rep. 547, 549, viz. the price differential between the sold and the countersold goods, the differential in the dates of payment, and the different requirements of an export certificate. There may be also problems relating to the exchange rate, see "Exchange Rate Risks in International Contracts," edited by Professor Bruno Oppetit, ICC Brochure No. 440/3, 1987.

accessible commodity market at which the goods are regularly traded[34] or they may not be so easily marketable.

If the goods have a commodity market, like oil or many commodities, the exporter will ask a dealer at the market to sell the goods. If, *e.g.* an aircraft manufacturer sells aircraft to an oil producing country, which pays in oil, it is relatively easy for the manufacturer to sell the oil through a dealer at the oil market in Rotterdam. Even such a simple disposal may involve a string of dealers. In these string contracts the property in the countertraded goods (the oil), which may be still afloat, is passed by transfer of negotiable bills of lading.

More complicated is the position if no commodity market exists for the goods. The U.K. exporter may be unable to obtain payment from the overseas importer because the importer's country may not permit the transfer of the price to the U.K., owing to lack of hard currency or for other reasons. On the other hand, the importer's country may have a bilateral clearing arrangement with a third country, which has a credit surplus with the importer's country. Here this credit surplus can be utilised by way of a swap transaction for the payment of the price due to the U.K. exporter. This would involve a triangular swap. The U.K. exporter arranges the countersale in the following manner. He sells his goods to the overseas buyer in country A. The overseas buyer sells produce of his own country to country B which has the clearing arrangement with A. The buyer in country B (which has no currency restrictions against the U.K.) then pays the U.K. seller. In this manner the U.K. exporter is paid out of the credit surplus accumulated by country B in its trade with country A. Other forms of swap transactions are also in use. They need not always be triangular and some of them are simply currency swaps. It is obvious that swap deals in any form require the assistance of an experienced countertrade expert.

Oil countertrade

In the oil business, countertrade transactions are frequently used. For this reason the illustrations given in the preceding sections refer often to oil transactions. Countertrade in oil usually takes the form of reciprocal sales contracts or barter transactions. The disposal of the countertraded goods is relatively easy as oil has a commodity market, but sometimes the services of an oil distributing company are required to carry out the disposal of the oil.

---

[34] In commercial terminology, these markets are referred to as "terminal commodity markets."

The framework agreement

In countertrade transactions great importance should be given to the proper drafting of the initial framework agreement, sometimes also referred to as the *countertrade agreement.*

Sometimes this agreement takes the form of a letter of intent. This is unsatisfactory because a letter of intent is not enforceable in law.

The framework agreement should be a contract enforceable in law. It should contain a clear definition of the mutual obligations of the parties. The countertraded goods should be specified and it should be provided whether their value should be ascertained on an f.o.b. or c.i.f. basis. Arrangements should be made for a settlement account or evidence account and for the payment or other settlement of the credit balance at regular intervals and on termination of the agreement. The agreement should also provide that the exporter's obligations under the countertrade contract may be performed by an affiliated company or another company nominated by him. The framework agreement should also allow the transferability of the obligation to counterpurchase. This will enable the exporter to transfer these obligations to a third party, such as a trading house, which will then become the buyer of the countersold goods in the capacity of principal. There should further be no restrictions relating to the markets in which the countersold goods can be traded. Sometimes the countries which insist on countertrade offer a variety of their produce for countertrade and in this case the U.K. exporter should attempt to secure for himself the widest choice of countertraded goods as possible.

The framework agreement should also contain a link between the reciprocal sales agreements, if this form is chosen. It should, *e.g.* be provided that the exporter's countersale obligations shall only become effective when the main export contract is concluded or the counterseller has provided a performance guarantee.

If the exporter intends to realise the countertrade proceeds at once by a disclosed factoring arrangement,[35] the factor should be a party to the framework agreement.

The framework agreement often contains penalty provisions for non-performance of the countertrade obligations by the exporter. The conditions on which these penalties become payable should be kept separate from and independent of the exporter's obligations under the contract of export sale. In other words, if the countertrade transaction is in the form of a reciprocal sales arrangement, the penalty provisions should only relate to the countersale but should not relate to the export sale.

In addition, the framework agreement should contain the terms normally inserted into an international trade contract.[36] In particular, a

---

[35] See p. 456, *post.*
[36] See p. 75, *ante.*

choice of law clause should be provided. It simplifies matters if all contracts, *viz.* the framework agreement, the export sale and the counter-sale, are submitted to the same legal system. There should also be an arbitration clause which should be wide enough to cover any dispute arising out of or in connection with the framework agreement itself and all connected contracts. The parties may provide ad hoc arbitration, *e.g.* so-called "neutral arbitration,"[37] but, speaking generally, their best course would be to agree on arbitration under the rules of the ICC Court of Arbitration. In any event, the arbitration clause should lay down the venue and the language of the arbitration.

---

[37] This normally means arbitration in Switzerland, Sweden or the Netherlands.

Chapter 11

PRODUCT LIABILITY

By product liability[1] is understood the liability of the producer of a product[2] which, owing to a defect, causes injury, damage or loss to the ultimate user. The defect may consist in the quality—or rather lack of it— of the product itself, but it may also be due to insufficiency in the instructions for use or in the failure to give adequate warning of a dangerous propensity of the product.

It is obvious that the potentiality of product liability is a matter of great concern to the manufacturer who sells part of his produce abroad, and, in certain circumstances, also concerns other suppliers. Of equal importance to them is the question whether they can insure this risk and, if so, on which terms.

A claim for damages caused by a defective product may be founded on contract, tort, a statutory right, or a combination of these causes of action.

THE BASIS OF PRODUCT LIABILITY

Liability for defective products is based on one of these principles:

1. strict liability;
2. qualified liability; or
3. fault liability.

In all three types of product liability the claimant has to prove that the product was defective and that he has suffered damage. But the difference is this:

If a legal system adopts the principle of *strict liability*, all the claimant has to prove—additionally to the facts mentioned above—is causation,

---

[1] For further reading: Greville Janner, *Janner's Complete Product Liability* (1988); Brian W. Harvey and Deborah L. Parry, *The Law of Consumer Protection and Fair Trading*, (3rd ed., 1987), Chap. 6; C. J. Miller (ed.), *Comparative Product Liability* (1986); G. Woodroffe (ed.), *Consumer Law in the EEC*, (1984); C. J. Miller, *Product Liability and Safety Encyclopaedia* (loose-leaf); Department of Trade and Industry, *An Implementation of the EC Directive on Product Liability*, An explanatory and consultative note (November 1985); Leslie Sheinman, "*The EEC Directive on Product Liability*," [1985] J.B.L. 504; *Product Liability*, ed. by Alex Schuster, 1989, Irish Centre for European Law, Trinity College.

[2] "Product" has a wider meaning than "goods"; it includes electricity. On the definition of "product" in the EC Directive and in the Consumer Protection Act 1987, see pp. 166, and 170, *post*.

i.e. that the damage was caused by the defect of the product. If he succeeds in discharging this onus of proof, the producer has no defence and, in principle, is liable.

If the principle of *qualified liability* is applied, the claimant has, of course, likewise to prove causation but the producer has the defence that in the state of scientific or technical knowledge existing at the time when he put the product into circulation, he could not have been expected to have discovered the defect. This defence is known as the *development risk defence* or state of art defence.

If a claim is founded on *fault liability*, the claimant, in addition to the facts mentioned before, has to prove that the producer was at fault, *e.g.* that he was negligent in the production of his product.

In English law, all three principles are applied. The strict principle applies if the action can be founded on contract. The qualified principle applies if it is founded on the Consumer Protection Act 1987. The fault principle is applied if the action has to be founded on the tort of negligence. However, before the position in English law can be considered it is necessary to deal with certain international measures, and, in particular, the EC Directive on Product Liability. This is necessary because an important aspect of English law, *viz.* the statutory right of action provided by the Consumer Protection Act 1987, is founded on the EC Directive.

The EC Directive on Product Liability

This Directive was approved by the Council of Ministers on July 25, 1985.[3] Effect has so far[4] been given to it by:

Greece[5];	Luxembourg[7a];
Italy[6]; and	Denmark,[7b];
The United Kingdom.[7]	Portugal[7c]
	West Germany[7d]

A "product" is defined in the Directive thus (Art. 2):

> For the purpose of this Directive "product means all movables with the exception of primary agricultural products and game, even though incorporated into another

---

[3] 85/374/EEC; O.J. 1985 No. L260/29.
[4] Position: February 5, 1990.
[5] By the decree of March 31, 1988, published in the Greek Official Journal of April 22, 1988. The only option which Greece has exercised is in favour of limiting the financial liability (Art. 16).
[6] By the Decree No. 224 of May 22, 1988, published in the Italian Official Journal of June 22, 1988. Italy has not exercised any option under the Directive.
[7] By the Consumer Protection Act 1987, see p. 169, *post.*
[7a] By a Law of April 21, 1989.
[7b] By a Law of June 7, 1989.
[7c] By a decree of November 6, 1989.
[7d] By a Law of December 15, 1989.

movable or into an immovable. "Primary agricultural products" means the products of the soil, of stock-farming and of fisheries, excluding products which have undergone initial processing. "Product" includes electricity.

The harmonisation of the national laws of the Member States by the EC Directive was no easy task.[8] The two main difficulties were: to agree on the basis of product liability by resolving the conflict between strict and fault liability, and to determine whether the liability of the producer should be capped, *i.e.* whether a maximum limit of liability should be imposed.[9] The first of these problems raised a particularly delicate issue of policy; in the countries of Western Europe traditionally tort liability was founded on fault but modern technological progress made this attitude unrealistic and favoured the introduction of strict liability in one form or another, and this demand became even more acute since the United States accepted the principle of strict liability.[10] The problem for the EC was to adopt a system which, though admitting strict liability, did not discourage progress in scientific and technological development.

The Directive solved these difficulties by adopting a system of "options." In the main areas of dispute it adopts its own regulation but it allows the Member States to "opt" for another regulation. As regards the basis of liability, it adopts the principle of qualified liability (Art. 7(e)); this is a compromise between strict and fault liability with a strong leaning towards strict liability; but it allows Member States to opt out of this regulation by adopting the principle of unqualified strict liability (Art. 15(i)(b)); an option in favour of fault liability is not admitted.

As regards the limits of liability, the Directive provides that the producer's liability shall not be limited or excluded by a provision limiting his liability or exempting him from liability (Art. 12), but a Member State may admit a limitation to an amount of not less than 70 million ECUs[11] in case of damage resulting from death or personal injury (Art. 16).

A third option is provided by the Directive with respect to primary agricultural products and game. The definition of "product" in the Directive excludes these items[12] but a Member State may opt to include them (Art. 15(i)(a)).

It should be noted that when the Directive is given effect by all Member States—and this is only a question of time—the principle of qualified liability will be the minimum standard of product liability throughout the whole European Community.

---

[8] The preparation of the Directive took nine years.

[9] As is provided, *e.g.* by international conventions relating to nuclear damage, see Nuclear Installations Acts 1965 and 1969. The EC Directive does not apply to injury or damage arising from nuclear accidents and covered by international conventions ratified by the Member States (Art. 14).

[10] See p. 175, *post.*

[11] ECU stands for Economic Community Unit; it is the accounting currency of the EEC.

[12] See p. 166, *ante.*

The European Convention on Products Liability in regard to Personal Injury and Death

This Convention was adopted by the Council of Europe at Strasbourg and opened for signature on January 27, 1977.[13] It has so far[14] been signed by Austria, Belgium, France and Luxembourg.

The Convention is founded on the principle of strict liability (Art. 3). As the Convention does not permit the introduction of a development risk defence, and as there are a number of other potential inconsistencies between the Convention and the Directive,[15] the United Kingdom does not propose to sign the Convention in its present form.[16] It is, however, possible that, when the EC Convention is implemented by all Member States of the EC, the Council of Europe may consider a revision of the Convention in order to bring it into line with the EC Convention.

ENGLISH LAW

Liability arising from the contract of sale

Turning now to English law, we have first to consider the liability for defective goods of the seller under the Sale of Goods Act 1979 and of the transfer of property in the goods under the Supply of Goods and Services Act 1982. Liability under these two enactments is not limited to the producer of goods. Under these enactments it is irrelevant whether the supplier is a manufacturer selling his own goods or a merchant selling goods produced by others.

These Acts provide two implied conditions as to quality or fitness, if the sale (or transfer) is in the course of a business. These conditions are that, subject to certain requirements, the goods must be of merchantable quality[17] and that they are fit for the particular purpose for which they are acquired.[18]

Goods are of merchantable quality if they are[19]:

---

[13] The Convention is attached to C. J. Miller (ed.), *Comparative Product Liability* (London, 1986), as Appendix B.

[14] Position: January 19, 1989.

[15] See Ferdinando Albanese, "Legal Harmonisation in Europe, Product Liability. A Comparison between the Directive of the European Communities and the Council of Europe Convention," in C. J. Miller (ed.), *op. cit.* in n. 11, 15.

[16] Explanatory and Consultative Note of Dept. of Trade and Industry on "Implementation of the EC Directive on Product Liability," November 1985, Annex II.

[17] Sale of Goods Act 1979, s.14(2); Supply of Goods and Services Act 1982, s.4(2).

[18] Sale of Goods Act 1979, s.14(3); Supply of Goods and Services Act 1982, s.4(4).

[19] 1979 Act, s.14(6) and 1982 Act s.4(9). In the text, the word in square brackets refers to the 1982 Act.

as fit for the purpose or purposes for which goods of that kind are commonly bought [supplied] as it is reasonable to expect having regard to any description applied to them, the price (if relevant) and all the other relevant circumstances.

The implied condition of fitness for a particular purpose applies when the buyer (or transferee), expressly or by implication, makes known:

(*a*) to the seller (or transferor), or
(*b*) where the price (or consideration) or part of it is payable by instalments and the goods were previously sold by a credit-broker to the seller (or transferor), to that credit-broker

any particular purpose for which the goods are being bought (or acquired).[20]

If the goods are defective and the defect qualifies as lack of merchantable quality, or makes them unfit for the particular purpose for which they are acquired, the buyer (or transferee) is entitled to reject them and to claim damages for breach of a condition of the contract. The seller's (or transferor's) liability is in the nature of strict liability, in the sense in which this term was used earlier.[21] The strictness of this regulation is mitigated, to some extent, by the application of the concept of the innominate term.[22]

As against a consumer, the implied conditions of merchantable quality and fitness for a particular purpose cannot be excluded or restricted by a contract term.[23] In other sales or supply contracts and, in particular, in international supply contracts,[24] contractual exemption and restriction clauses are admissible.

The Consumer Protection Act 1987

This Act, which became fully operative on March 1, 1989,[25] aims in Part I, entitled "Product Liability,"[26] at giving effect to the EC Directive on this subject.[27] Indeed, it provides in section 1(i):

This Part shall have effect for the purpose of making such provision as is necessary in order to comply with the Product Liability Directive and shall be construed accordingly.

---

[20] See p. 125, *ante*, and *Frost* v. *Aylesbury Dairy Co. Ltd.* [1905] 1 K.B. 608; *Vacwell Engineering Co. Ltd.* v. *B.D.H. Chemicals Ltd.* [1969] 1 W.L.R. 927; *McAlpine & Sons Ltd.* v. *Minimax Ltd.* [1970] 1 Lloyd's Rep. 397. See also *Brown (B.S.) & Son Ltd.* v. *Craiks Ltd.* [1970] 1 W.L.R. 752; *Ashington Piggeries Ltd.* v. *Christopher Hill Ltd.* [1972] A.C. 441.

[21] See pp. 165–166, *ante*. Cf. also the observations of Sellers J. in *Nicolene Ltd.* v. *Simmonds* [1958] 2 Lloyd's Rep. 419, 425, quoted on p. 181, *post*. Unlike the common law, in the civil law liability in damages for breach of contract is often founded on the fault of the contract breaker.

[22] See p. 135, *ante* and *Cehave N.V.* v. *Bremer Handelsgesellschaft m.b.h.*, *The Hansa Nord* [1976] 1 Q.B. 44, treated there.

[23] 1979 Act, s.55(1); 1982 Act, s.11(1), and Unfair Contract Terms Act 1977, s.6(2)(*a*).

[24] Unfair Contract Terms Act 1977, s.26; see p. 100, *ante*.

[25] Consumer Protection Act 1987 (Commencement No. 3) Order 1988 (S.I. 1988 No. 2076).

[26] Part II deals with Consumer Safety, Part III with Misleading Price Indications and Parts IV and V with enforcement and miscellaneous matters.

[27] See p. 166, *ante*.

The Act follows closely the provisions of the Directive. The liability of the producer is founded on the principle of qualified liability (s.4(1)(*e*)). The United Kingdom has not availed itself of any of the options admitted by the Directive,[28] but it has reserved the right to do so any time by Order in Council (s.8).

Definition of "Producer"

The Act applies in principle only to the manufacturer—"producer"—of an article. It does not apply to a merchant or dealer who distributes the goods of others. But, as will be seen from the next paragraph, the statutory right of action provided by the Act is available also against certain persons other than the producer; such a person is referred to as the "supplier."

The term "producer" is defined in section 1(2) of the Act thus:

> "producer," in relation to a product, means
> (*a*) the person who has manufactured it,
> (*b*) in the case of a substance which has not been manufactured but has been won or abstracted, the person who won or abstracted it;
> (*c*) in the case of a product which has not been manufactured, won or abstracted but essential characteristics of which are attributable to an industrial or other process having been carried out (for example in relation to agricultural produce), the person who carried out that process.

The statutory right of action

The Act gives a statutory right of action to a user[29] who suffers damage caused wholly or partly by a defect in a product (s.2(i)). "Product" is defined in the Act thus[30]:

> "product" means any goods[31] or electricity and (subject to subsection (3) below[32]) includes a product which is comprised in another product, whether by virtue of being a component part or raw material or otherwise.

As regards the position of a product which comprises a defective component or defective raw material, according to section 1(2) the victim

---

[28] See p. 167, *ante*.

[29] The user may be a natural or a legal person, such as a company.

[30] This definition should be compared with that in the Directive, see p. 166, *ante*.

[31] As regards "goods," s.45 states that " 'goods' includes substances, growing crops and things comprised in land by virtue of being attached to it and any ship, aircraft or vehicle." This definition of "goods" differs from that in s.61(1) of the Sale of Good Act 1979.

The liability for defective products does not extend to any game or agricultural produce, except if it has undergone an industrial process (s.2(4)).

[32] Subsection (3) of section 1 reads: "For the purposes of this Part a person who supplies any product in which products are comprised, whether by virtue of being component parts or raw materials or otherwise, shall not be treated by reason only of his supply of that product as supplying any of the products so comprised."

can sue the producer of the defective component or raw material (if he knows him) or the producer of the final product, or both who would be liable jointly and severally (s.2(5)).[33] The victim may also sue the supplier under section 2(3),[34] but the supplier (as contrasted with the producer) is not liable only on the ground that the component part or raw material was defective (s.2(3)); obviously the supplier does not have the same opportunity of examining the ingredients of the final product as a producer.

If a component was made according to the design or instructions of the producer of the final product and the defect in the design or instructions was not discoverable, the producer of the defective component is not liable.

The action may be brought against any of the following (s.2(2) and (3))[35]:

1. The producer[36] of the product;
2. The person who, by putting his brand name on the product has held himself out to be the producer;
3. The importer into a Member State of the EC; or
4. a supplier, who when asked by the claimant within a reasonable period to identify the producer of the defective product, fails to give this information within a reasonable time.

The "supplier" under heading 4, above, may be a wholesaler, distributor or retailer. This is a safety network provision which is of particular importance if the producer is unknown or cannot be traced.

A "defect" of a product is present if the safety of the product is not such as persons generally are entitled to expect (s.3).

The right of action for damages caused by a defective product provided by the Act is without prejudice to any other cause of action which the claimant may have (s.2(6)). Thus, if he can rely on breach of contract, the producer cannot claim the development risk defence. The statutory cause of action provided by the Act is treated as an action founded in tort for jurisdictional purposes (s.6(7)); the action is quasi-tortious.

The liability of a person under this Part of the 1987 Act cannot be limited or excluded by a contract term, by any notice or by any other provision (s.7).

Defences

The defences to the statutory action for damages for a defective product—apart from those denying the pre-conditions of the action—are

---

[33] The provisions of the Civil Liability (Contribution) Act 1978 may apply.
[34] On the meaning of "supplier," see *infra* .
[35] For detailed definition see the wording of the sections mentioned in the text.
[36] For the definition of "producer" see p. 170, *ante*.

listed in section 4(1) of the 1987 Act. They are so important that this
provision has to be quoted in full:

> In any civil proceedings by virtue of this Part against any person ("the person
> proceeded against") in respect of a defect in a product it shall be a defence for him to
> show—
>> (a) that the defect is attributable to compliance with any requirement imposed
>> by or under any enactment or with any Community obligation; or
>> (b) that the person proceeded against did not at any time supply the product to
>> another; or
>> (c) that the following conditions are satisfied, that is to say—
>> (i) that the only supply of the product to another by the person proceeded
>> against was otherwise than in the course of a business of that person's; and
>> (ii) that section 2(2) above does not apply to that person or applies to him
>> by virtue only of things done otherwise than with a view to profit; or
>> (d) that the defect did not exist in the product at the relevant time; or
>> (e) that the state of scientific and technical knowledge at the relevant time was
>> not such that a producer of products of the same description as the product
>> in question might be expected to have discovered the defect if it had
>> existed in his products while they were under his control; or
>> (f) that the defect
>> (i) constituted a defect in a product ("the subsequent product") in which
>> the product in question had been comprised; and
>> (ii) was wholly attributable to the design of the subsequent product or to
>> compliance by the producer of the product in question with instructions
>> given by the producer of the subsequent product.

Two points should be noted: the development risk defence is stated in
subsection 1(e) of section 4, and it is a defence that the transfer of
property was by way of a gift or other non-business transaction (subsection 1(c)).

Examples

Three hypothetical examples may illustrate the position. First, a boy of
six years of age bought a catapult from a stationer[37]; when he used it in
the ordinary way, it broke in his hands as it was made in an indifferent
manner and part of it ruptured the boy's eyes. The stationer had bought a
quantity of these catapults from a wholesaler who had bought them from
an importer; the catapults were manufactured abroad. Under the 1987
Act the boy can sue the importer directly, basing his claim on the
statutory right of action.[38]

Secondly, a manufacturer of commercial storage freezers markets them
in the United Kingdom and in his export markets under his own brand
name, but indicating that they are made for him abroad by another

---

[37] This example is modelled on the facts of *Godley* v. *Perry* [1960] 1 W.L.R. 9.
[38] In 1959, when *Godley* v. *Perry* was decided, the liability was founded on the chain of
contracts, *i.e.* the boy had to sue the stationer, the latter the wholesaler and he in turn the
importer who may have had a contractual claim against the supplier abroad.

manufacturer. One of these freezers is wrongly wired and malfunctions; the food stored therein perishes and its loss causes the shopowner considerable damage; the manufacturer is liable because the defective product was marketed under his brand name.

Thirdly, a pharmaceutical manufacturer produces a drug which has an excellent therapeutic effect; after long and careful tests, and being satisfied that it is harmless, he puts it on the market; after some time it is unexpectedly discovered that the drug has a harmful side-effect on a small number of users alergic to one of its components; under the Act the manufacturer may be able to avail himself of the development risk defence.

General rules on damages

In principle, damages shall not be awarded under the Act for any loss or damage to property if the amount to be awarded is £275 or less (not including interest) (s.5(4)). Further, the person against whom an action can be brought under section 2,[39] is not liable under the Act for loss of or damage to the defective product itself, but may, of course, be so liable under other causes of action.

Contributory negligence

It is controversial whether in 'proceedings under the 1987 Act a defendant who is liable under the Act may plead contributory negligence on the part of the plaintiff by virtue of the Law Reform (Contributory Negligence) Act 1945.

The answer should be in the negative for the following reasons. First, the defence can hardly be admissible in cases in which the action itself is founded on strict liability, or a variation of it, such as qualified liability, where an element of fault on the part of the defendant need not be pleaded. Secondly, its admission would contravene section 7 which prohibits the exclusion or limitation of liability.[40] Thirdly, this defence is—obviously deliberately—not included into the statutory list of defences.[41]

In crass cases, absolutely irrational behaviour of the plaintiff may, however, affect the requirement of causation between the loss and the defective product.[42]

---

[39] See p. 170, *ante*.
[40] See p. 171, *ante*.
[41] See pp. 171–172, *ante*.
[42] See p. 165, *ante*.

Physical and economic loss

Where the action can be founded on breach of contract, damages for physical loss, *i.e.* for death, personal injury or damage to property, as well as for economic loss, *i.e.* loss of profit or other financial loss, can be recovered.[43] Where the action is founded on the Consumer Protection Act 1987, physical damage is recoverable but not economic loss; this is expressly provided in section 5(i) of the 1987 Act.

If the action for damages for a defective product is founded on the tort of negligence, it is clear since *Donoghue* v. *Stevenson*[44] that damages for physical loss, both with respect to the person and to property, are recoverable. As regards the recovery of economic loss, the position is less clear. Lord Wilberforce applied in *Anns* v. *Merton London Borough Council*[45] the so-called two-stage test of sufficient proximity (which was founded on reliance and was almost of contractual nature) and absence of considerations negativing or restricting the scope of the duty of care.[46] The House of Lords in *Junior Books Inc.* v. *Veitchi*,[47] on the facts of the case, held that Lord Wilberforce's test was satisfied and admitted the recovery of economic loss. But in subsequent decisions[48] the courts have restricted the principle in *Junior Books* considerably.[49] The present law is, it is thought, stated correctly by Purchas L.J. in the *Greater Nottingham Co-operative Society Ltd.* case,[50] when observing[51] that an action in negligence for the recovery of economic loss is only admissible if it is "possible to cull from the close relationship of the parties the assumption by the tortfeasor of a duty not to cause pecuniary loss to the victim."

---

[43] *Czarnikow Ltd.* v. *Koufos* [1969] 1 A.C. 350. Also *Victoria Laundry* v. *Newman Industries* [1949] 2 K.B. 528.

[44] [1932] A.C. 562.

[45] [1978] A.C. 728, 751.

[46] Such as an exclusion of liability clause.

[47] [1983] 1 A.C. 520.

[48] Particularly in *Muirhead* v. *Industrial Tank Specialities Ltd.* [1986] Q.B. 507; *Yuen Kim Yeu* v. *Attorney-General of Hong Kong* [1988] A.C. 175 (and the cases referred to in this decision of the P.C.); *Simaan General Contracting Co.* v. *Pilkington Glass Ltd.* (*No. 2*) [1988] 2 W.L.R. 761; *D. & F. Estates Ltd.* v. *Church Commissioners for England* [1988] 3 W.L.R. 368; and *Greater Nottingham Co-operative Society Ltd.* v. *Cementation Piling and Foundations Ltd.* [1988] 3 W.L.R. 396; *Banque Keyser Ullman SA* v. *Skandia (U.K.) Insurance Co. Ltd.* [1989] 3 W.L.R. 25, 72 (recovery of economic loss in contracts of utmost good faith).

[49] The main reason of the courts for this attitude is a policy consideration. They fear that a general admission of recovery of damages for purely economic loss in a negligence action may open "the floodgates" of litigation for an indeterminate class of cases. From the legal point of view, the floodgates argument is not convincing; see David Oughton, "Liability in Tort for Economic Loss suffered by the Consumer of defective goods," in [1987] J.B.L. 370, 372–373, but there is the economic ground that risks of that kind would hardly be insurable.

[50] *Ibid.* see note 48.

[51] On p. 413. Purchas L.J. called this type of proximity the *Hedley-Byrne* type of relationship, after *Hedley Byrne & Co. Ltd.* v. *Heller & Partners Ltd.* [1964] A.C. 465.

Where the action is founded on a defect of a product, this will be possible only in rare circumstances;[52] such exceptional circumstances may perhaps be present if it can clearly be established that the user of the defective product relied solely on the "brand loyalty" of the product.[53]

Limitation of actions

Where an action for damages caused by a defective product is founded on breach of contract or on the tort of negligence, it is subject to the ordinary time limits set out in the Limitation Act 1980, amended, with respect to negligence actions, by the Latent Damage Act 1986.[54]

Where the action is founded on the statutory right of the Consumer Protection Act 1987, the action must be brought within three years from the date when the cause of action occurred or of knowledge of the cause of action.[55] But there is an overriding time bar of ten years from "the relevant time"; this is essentially the time when the product is supplied or in relation to electricity, when it is generated.[56]

AMERICAN LAW

A brief survey of the legal position in the United States has to be added, and this for two reasons. The United States are an important export market and the British exporter and his legal adviser should be aware of the problems which arise in that market.[57] Further, the early adoption of strict liability by the United States[58] has greatly influenced the acceptance of the qualified principle by the EC.

---

[52] See Bingham L.J. in *Simaan Contracting Co.* v. *Pilkington Glass Ltd.* (*No.* 2) [1988] 2 W.L.R. 761, 777.

[53] Oughton, *op. cit.* in n. 49, p. 375.

[54] Speaking generally, the ordinary time limits for claims founded on simple contract are six years from accrual of the cause of action and twelve years upon a deed, but there are longer periods for actions founded on fraud, concealment or mistake. Negligence actions involving damage to property must be brought within six years from the accrual of the cause of action or three years from knowledge, but there is an overriding bar of 15 years from the damage-causing event. Claims for personal injury must be brought within three years from accrual or knowledge, and for death within three years from accrual or knowledge of the personal representative.

[55] Sched. 1, para. 1 of the Consumer Protection Act 1987, which has inserted a new section 11A into the Limitation Act 1980; the Schedule has also made consequential amendments of the 1980 Act.

[56] The "relevant time" is defined in s.4(2) of the Act.

[57] They are perceptibly examined from time to time by Derrick Owles in the legal press, see, *e.g.* his notes on "Strict Liability in the USA" in the 138 N.L.J. (1988) 648, and on "Pure economic loss in the United States" in 138 N.L.J. (1988) 917, and "Product Liability" in 139 N.L.J. (1989) 1120.

[58] See Stephen J. Leacock, "A General Conspectus of American Law on Product Liability," in [1989] J.B.L. 273.

Restatement (Second) of Torts, section 402A

The law on product liability of all the American States is founded on section 402A of the Restatement (Second) of Torts, which was published in 1965. This provision adopts the principle of strict liability, by expressly providing (in sub-section 2(*a*)) that the rule applies although "the seller[59] has exercised all possible care in the preparation and sale of his product."[60]

Section 402A states[61]:

> **402A.** Special Liability of Seller of Product for Physical Harm to User or Consumer
> (1) One who sells any product in a defective condition unreasonably dangerous to the user or consumer or to his property is subject to liability for physical harm thereby caused to the ultimate user or consumer, or to his property, if
>> (*a*) the seller is engaged in the business of selling such a product, and
>> (*b*) it is expected to and does reach the user or consumer without substantial change in the condition in which it is sold.
> (2) The rule stated in Subsection (1) applies although
>> (*a*) the seller has exercised all possible care in the preparation and sale of his product, and
>> (*b*) the user or consumer has not bought the product from or entered into any contractual relation with the seller.

The section provides only liability for physical damage to a person or his property. As regards purely economic damage, in the words of an American author,[62] "the decisions are in disarray," but the preponderance of judicial opinion seems to favour the view that purely economic loss is not recoverable without privity of contract.[63]

The reform of American Law

In the United States the reform of the law relating to product liability is widely discussed. The conflicting lobbies of producers and consumers are strong and so far no definite federal reform legislation has emerged. But

---

[59] Unlike the position in English law, the term "seller" in the American Restatement applies to any person engaged in the business of selling, including a manufacturer, wholesaler or retail dealer or distributor, even the operator of a restaurant (Comment to s.402A(f)).

[60] But American law admits the defence of "unavoidably unsafe products." This defence applies, in particular, to experimental drugs. If such a product, properly prepared and accompanied by proper directions and warning, is used by a knowing user, it is not considered as defective or unreasonably dangerous and the "seller" (see note 59) would escape strict liability (comment (k)).

[61] This rule is, as is usual in the Restatement, followed by an extensive Comment which is not reproduced here.

[62] Jerry J. Phillips, "The Status of Products Liability Law in the United States of America," in *Comparative Product Liability* (ed. C. J. Miller, 1986), 143, 145.

[63] See Stephen J. Leacock, *op. cit.* in n. 58; the author refers, in particular, to the judgment of Chief Justice Trayner in *Seely* v. *White Motor Co.* 63 Cal. 2d. 9 (1965).

in 1986 more than three-fifths of the States had enacted some form of tort reform legislation,[64] and this trend is likely to continue. Many States have introduced "caps," *i.e.* maximum limits of liability for specified cases of non-economic damages, *e.g.* for damages for pain and suffering, while others have capped all derivative non-economic damages.[65] The situation varies from State to State and a uniform regulation by a federal enactment would be in the interest of international trade.

PROCEDURAL ASPECTS

Disputes concerning product liability—or insurance or re-insurance covering the risk—often raise procedural issues.

If the defective product is produced in the United Kingdom and exported to another country, where it is ultimately acquired by a user who suffers damage, the question arises whether the user may sue in this country or in his own country. This may raise an issue of concurrent jurisdictions, and, in particular, the issue which court is *forum non conveniens.*[66]

Further, in cases to which the Brussels Convention on Jurisdiction and Enforcement of Judgments in Civil and Commercial Matters of 1968 applies,[67] the victim has a choice: he may either sue in the courts of the producer's country or in his own courts.

These procedural aspects are treated later in this work.[68]

PRODUCT LIABILITY INSURANCE

A manufacturing exporter will have to give serious consideration to the question whether he should cover the risk caused by a defective product by insurance,[69] bearing in mind that even the best run and most carefully supervised production line on occasion turns out a "rogue elephant." The same considerations apply to other persons who may be sued under the

---

[64] Nancy L. Manzer, "1986 Tort Reform Legislation: A Systematic Evaluation of Caps on Damages and Limitations on Joint and Several Liability," in 73 *Cornell Law Review* (1988), 628.

[65] Nancy L. Manzer, *op. cit.* in preceding note, 637–648.

[66] See p. 698, *post,* Also *E. I. Du Pont De Nemours & Co.* v. *I. C. Agnew (No. 2)* [1988] 2 Lloyd's Rep. 240.

[67] The Convention is given effect in the United Kingdom by the Civil Jurisdiction and Judgments Act, 1982, see p. 709, *post.*

[68] On concurrent jurisdictions, see p. n. 66, above. On the Convention, see n. 67, above.

[69] A full examination of this subject is outside the ambit of this Work. For an excellent treatment of product liability insurance, see Peter Madge, in *Janner's Complete Product Liability* (1988), Part VII.

Consumer Protection Act 1987[70] or may otherwise become liable for the supply of a defective product. Product liability insurance can be obtained, but at a price. For this reason very large manufacturers cover this risk by self-insurance.[71] But the ordinary manufacturer who exports part of his produce should—and does—cover product liability by insurance. Mr. Peter Madge, an eminent insurance expert, observes correctly[72] that "product liability has made enormous advances in the last 25 years as consumerism and increasing claim-consciousness on the part of the general public have created a demand for protection."

There are two types of product liability cover. The cover may be contained in a separate product liability policy or it may be added, by way of an amendment, to a general public liability policy.[73]

The following is a general example of an insurance clause in a separate product liability policy, but the conditions and exceptions of the policy are not reproduced here[74]:

> The Company will subject to the terms exceptions and conditions of this policy indemnify the Insured against all sums which the Insured shall become legally liable to pay as damages in respect of
> (1) accidental bodily injury (including death or disease) to any person
> (2) accidental loss of or damage to property
> happening anywhere in the world elsewhere than at premises owned or occupied by the Insured during the Period of Insurance and caused by any Goods sold supplied repaired altered treated or serviced by or on behalf of the Insured from or in Great Britain, Northern Ireland, the Channel Islands and the Isle of Man in connection with the Business.

This policy does not provide complete cover. The word "accidental" appearing under headings (1) and (2) means "fortuitous"; it excludes liability for negligence. Liability for economic loss, if admitted by the courts, is likewise not covered. Further, although according to this policy it is irrelevant where in the world the injury, damage or loss is sustained, the policy covers only goods emanating from Great Britain or another part of the British Isles, but it does not cover goods produced by a subsidiary in another country. On its face, the policy also does not cover a reasonably negotiated settlement with the claimant which the insured may prefer to a formal court or arbitral ruling that he is "legally liable" to pay damages. If the exporter considers it necessary that insurance should extend to any of these contingencies, he should ask the insurer for a suitable amendment of the policy but the insurer may not be willing to

---

[70] See p. 171, *ante.*

[71] Jerry J. Phillips, *op. cit.* in n. 62, p. 146. But, from the economic point of view, self-insurance is non-insurance.

[72] Peter Madge, *op. cit.* in n. 69, p. 181.

[73] The public liability policy normally excludes liability arising out of any goods sold or supplied by the insured and for this reason the amendment is necessary, Madge, *loc. cit.* p. 181.

[74] Reproduced from Peter Madge's work on Product Liability Insurance (Part VII of *Janner's Complete Product Liability*, 1988) by kind permission of the author. A detailed explanation of the clauses of this policy will be found in Madge's work.

accept the risk, *e.g.* for economic loss, and if he does accept a particular risk he will charge an additional premium.

All product liability insurance is limited in amount and, in principle in time. The time limit is normally a year but, of course, the policy is renewable, though not necessarily on the same terms as the lapsed one.

Exports to the USA or Canada sometimes contain special exclusion clauses[75]; *e.g.* punitive damages are excluded, disease risks such as asbestosis are excluded; legal costs for defence or settlement are included into the overall limitation of the amount covered, and are not in addition thereto.

The general principles of insurance law likewise apply to product liability insurance, foremost of them the duty to disclose, the requirement of an insurable interest on the part of the insured and the object of insurance as indemnity for the loss sustained by the insured. These principles are discussed later in the chapter on Marine and Aviation Insurance.[76]

---

[75] Madge, *op. cit.* in n. 694, pp. 208–209.
[76] Chapter 26, on p. 488, *post*; Duty to disclose, on p. 502, *post*; insurable interest, on p. 506, *post*; indemnity principle, on p. 529, *post*.

CHAPTER 12

FRUSTRATION OF CONTRACT

IT may happen that the commercial aims which the parties pursued when
concluding the contract are defeated through no fault of their own but by
force of supervening circumstances. The situation existing at the conclusion
of the contract may subsequently have changed so completely that the
parties, acting as reasonable men, would not have made the contract, or
would have made it differently, had they known what was going to happen.
All legal systems take notice of this situation. They admit the excuse for
non-performance in certain circumstances. But the conditions on which this
defence is admitted, vary in the various legal systems. English law has
developed the doctrine of frustration which will be considered in this
chapter. The American Uniform Commercial Code admits the excuse of
commercial impracticability,[1] French law admits it in case of *force majeure*,[2]
German law uses the notion of *Wegfall der Geschäftsgrundlage* (collapse of
the basis of the transaction),[3] and the CMEA General Conditions of
Delivery[4] relieve a party from liability in case of "circumstances of insuper-
able force," which are defined as events of an extraordinary character that
were unforeseeable and unavoidable.[5]

In English law the principles on which the doctrine of frustration is
founded are well settled. But whether in a particular case the circumstances
qualify as a frustrating event, is often difficult to decide. The question of
frustration is, in the words of Lord Diplock in the *Nema*[6]:

> . . . never a pure question of fact but does in the ultimate analysis involve a conclusion of
> law as to whether the frustrating event or series of events has made performance of the
> contract a thing radically different from that which was undertaken by the contract.

But if arbitration is arranged, the courts will normally leave it to the
arbitrator to decide, on the facts found by him, whether the contract is

---

[1] UCC, s. 2–615. The impracticability must affect the "basic assumption" on which the contract
was made.
[2] Or *cas fortuit*, see CC, art. 1148. The doctrine of imprévision appears to be still restricted
to administrative contracts: *Amos and Walton's Introduction to French Law*, (3rd ed., 1967), p.
165.
[3] Zweigert-Kötz, *An Introduction to Comparative Law* (translated by Tony Weir, 1977),
Vol. II, pp. 193–195. This test is used in addition to that of objective impossibility of
performance laid down in BGB, para. 323.
[4] See p. 70, *ante*.
[5] CMEA General Conditions, para. 68 (1) and (2); see Hoya, *East-West Trade* (1984), pp.
418–419.
[6] *Pioneer Shipping Ltd.* v. *B.T.P. Tioxide Ltd. The Nema* [1982] A.C. 724, 738. Also
Tsakiroglou & Co. Ltd. v. *Noblee Thorl GmbH* [1962] A.C. 93.

frustrated and will intervene only if he has failed to apply the correct legal test or has reached a conclusion which no reasonable person, on the facts found, could have reached.[7]

By virtue of this doctrine the parties are free from liability for acts of performance not yet due when their contract is regarded by the law as frustrated. The doctrine is exceptional because "in the ordinary way . . . it does not matter whether the failure to fulfil a contract by the seller is because he is indifferent or wilfully negligent or just unfortunate. It does not matter what the reason is. What matters is the fact of performance. Has he performed or not?"[8]

The doctrine of commercial frustration is of great importance in international trade transactions because they imply a greater element of uncertainty than home transactions in consequence of the fact that they are subject to political and economic influences in foreign countries. It is no accident that the doctrine in its present form emerged from litigation which was primarily concerned with transactions of international trade. It is intended to deal first with the conditions upon which the doctrine of commercial frustration may be invoked, and then with the effect of its application.

LEGAL MEANING OF FRUSTRATION

Frustration occurs only where, subsequent to the conclusion of the contract, a fundamentally different situation has unexpectedly emerged. Not every turn of events which the parties did not expect satisfies this test; such uncontemplated development might make the performance of the contract more difficult, onerous or costly than was envisaged by the parties when entering into the contract; it may be due to a sudden, and even abnormal, rise or fall in prices or to the necessity of obtaining supplies from other, and dearer, sources of supply than those anticipated.[9] These events, as such, do not operate as frustrating a contract of export sale; only where they are of such magnitude as to create a fundamentally different situation do they result in the frustration of the contract. This is clearly stated by Lord Radcliffe and Lord Simon. Lord Radcliffe said in a passage which has become the classic statement of the doctrine of frustration[10]:

---

[7] Lord Roskill, in the *Nema, supra*, p. 753; and *Kissavos Shipping Co. S.A.* v. *Empresa Cubana de Fletes. The Agathon.* [1982] 2 Lloyd's Rep. 211, 213.

[8] Sellers J. in *Nicolene Ltd.* v. *Simmonds* [1952] 2 Lloyd's Rep. 419, 425.

[9] The doctrine of frustration can be applied to a c.i.f. contract relating to unascertained goods but, in view of the nature of such contract and the possibility of buying goods afloat, it is more difficult to find a frustrating event in this case than in others: *Lewis Emanuel & Son Ltd.* v. *Sammut* [1959] 2 Lloyd's Rep. 629.

[10] *Davis Contractors Ltd.* v. *Fareham Urban District Council* [1956] A.C. 696, 729; *National Carriers Ltd.* v. *Panalpina (Northern) Ltd.* [1981] A.C. 675. See also *Condor* v. *The Barron Knights Ltd.* [1966] 1 W.L.R. 87.

> . . . frustration occurs whenever the law recognises that without default of either party a contractual obligation has become incapable of being performed because the circumstances in which performance is called for would render it a thing radically different from that which was undertaken by the contract. *Non haec in foedera veni*. It was not this that I promised to do.

Lord Simon stated in a leading case[11]:

> The parties to an executory contract are often faced, in the course of carrying it out, with a turn of events which they did not at all anticipate—a wholly abnormal rise or fall in prices, a sudden depreciation of currency, an unexpected obstacle to execution, or the like. Yet this does not in itself affect the bargain they have made. If, on the other hand, a consideration of the terms of the contract, in the light of the circumstances, existing when it was made, shows that they never agreed to be bound in a fundamentally different situation which has now unexpectedly emerged, the contract ceases to bind at that point— not because the court in its discretion thinks it just and reasonable to qualify the terms of the contract, but because on its true construction it does not apply in that situation.

It is evident from these observations that the modern international merchant is expected to have a considerable degree of foresight. He should therefore guard himself against an unexpected, but in the view of the law, foreseeable turn of events by ordinary commercial safeguards, such as an appropriate *force majeure* clause,[12] insurance or a hedging transaction.

Frustration may be a matter of degree

It is further evident that frustration in the legal sense occurs in some cases at a stage—often not easily predictable—in a sequence of events which are in gradual transition and that it is a matter of degree whether an uncontemplated event does, or does not, amount in law to frustration. Lord Roskill stated this rule as follows[13]:

> . . . in some cases where it is claimed that frustration has occurred by reason of the happening of a particular event, it is possible to determine at once whether or not the doctrine can be legitimately invoked. But in others, where the effect of that event is to cause delay in the performance of contractual obligations, it is often necessary to wait upon events in order to see whether the delay already suffered and the prospects of further delay from that cause, will make any ultimate performance of the relevant contractual obligations "radically different" . . . from that undertaken by the contract.

Denning L.J. recognised this in one case[14] in which the Court of Appeal held that the sellers of Brazilian piassava under a c.i.f. contract containing the clause "subject to any Brazilian export licence" were not relieved from

---

[11] *British Movietonews Ltd.* v. *London and District Cinemas Ltd.* [1952] A.C. 166, 185.
[12] See p. 199, post.
[13] *Pioneer Shipping Ltd.* v. *B.T.P. Tioxide Ltd, The Nema* [1982] A.C. 724, 752; *Kissavos Shipping Co. S.A.* v. *Empresa Cubana de Fletes, The Agathon* [1982] 2 Lloyd's Rep. 211, 213
[14] *Brauer & Co. (Great Britain) Ltd.* v. *James Clark (Brush Materials) Ltd.* [1952] 2 All E.R. 497, 501. See also *Hong Kong Fir Shipping Co. Ltd.* v. *Kawasaki Kisen Kaisha Ltd., The Antrim* [1962] 2 Q.B. 26 (C.A.); *Exportelisa S.A.* v. *Rocco Guiseppe & Figli Soc. Coll.* [1978] 1 Lloyd's Rep. 433.

their obligation to obtain the licence by a rise in prices by 20 to 30 per cent. in excess of the prices agreed upon with their buyers. Denning L.J. said: "Was that [payment of the higher price] a step which they could reasonably be expected to take? This depends on how much was the price they had to pay to get the licence. If it was . . . 100 times as much as the contract price, that would be 'a fundamentally different situation' which had unexpectedly emerged, and they would not be bound to pay it."[15] Consequently, regarding in that case the scale of rising prices, somewhere between a rise of 30 per cent. and one of 10,000 per cent. frustration occurred.

A similar question of degree arises where it is alleged that a contract is frustrated as the result of a government prohibition of exportation or importation, or as the result of a strike[16] or other industrial action.[17] In those cases the contract might, at the beginning of the event in question, merely be suspended and might become frustrated only after the lapse of a reasonable time when it becomes clear that the delay caused by the intervening event affects the foundation of the contract.[18] What is a reasonable time is again a question of degree.[19] In these cases it is not necessary to ascertain the exact date on which the contract was frustrated but it is sufficient to state that the contract was frustrated by not later than a certain date.[20]

Frustration by delay

Whether delay for which neither party is responsible operates as a frustrating event, is a matter of degree and has been considered, as such, in the preceding paragraph.

However, the following has to be added. Arbitration is sometimes promoted with such inordinate delay that a party contends later in court proceedings that the arbitration agreement is "frustrated" because a fair trial before the arbitrator is no longer possible.[21] Lord Diplock observed[22] that

---

[15] Denning L.J. supported this statement by a reference to *British Movietonews Ltd.* v. *London and District Cinemas Ltd.* [1952] A.C. 166.

[16] Lord Roskill in *The Nema*, p. 752. If a party fails to take reasonable steps to avoid a strike, he may not be able to rely on a *force majeure* clause: *B. & S. Contracts and Design* v. *Victor Green Publications* [1982] I.C.R. 654

[17] On the effect of war as a frustrating event, see p. 185, *post.*

[18] *Reardon Smith Line Ltd.* v. *Ministry of Agriculture, Fisheries and Food* [1962] 1 Q.B. 42; reversed in part on different grounds [1963] A.C. 691.

[19] Andrew J. Bateson, "Time as an Element of Frustration" in [1954] *Business Law Review*, p. 173; see also the same, "Time in the Law of Contract" in [1957] J.B.L. 357.

[20] *Marshall* v. *Harland & Wolff Ltd.* [1972] 1 W.L.R. 899, 904.

[21] *Bremer Vulkan Schiffbau und Maschinenfabrik* v. *South India Shipping Corporation Ltd.* [1981] A.C. 909; *Paal Wilson & Co. A/S* v. *Partenreederei Hannah Blumenthal* [1983] 1 A.C. 854. In *Food Corporation of India* v. *Antclizo Shipping Corporation ("The Antclizo.")* [1988] 2 Lloyd's Rep. 93, 95 101, the House of Lords expressed concern about so-called "sleeping arbitrations" and suggested that, by a legislative measure, the court should be empowered to dismiss arbitrations for want of prosecution.

[22] In the *Hannah Blumenthal* case, *supra*, p. 919.

the virtual impossibility of having a fair trial in consequence of inordinate dilatoriness on the part of the parties is "incapable of qualifying as a frustrating event, even if it has come about without default by either party." Inordinate delay in arbitration proceedings may allow the inference that the parties have abandoned the arbitration by mutual agreement or that one party has repudiated it and the other has accepted the repudiation.[23] In both cases the arbitration has come to an end but neither case constitutes "frustration" in the legal sense.

Self-induced frustration

An act or omission of one of the parties rendering the performance of the contract impossible or otherwise creating a fundamentally different situation does not qualify as a frustrating event. The first requirement of the doctrine of frustration is that the frustrating event must be an event beyond the control of the parties, *i.e.* an event for which neither of them is responsible.[24] The event must, in the words of Lord Brandon of Oakbrook in the *Hannah Blumenthal* case,[25] be "some outside event or extraneous change of situation." The expression "self-induced frustration" is thus a contradiction in terms—as incidentally is the expression "invalid contract"—but it is widely used and has the advantage of being shorter than the correct phrase "self-induced inability to perform."

The onus of proving that the "frustrating" event was self-induced, rests on the party raising this point.[26]

CONDITIONS UPON WHICH THE CONTRACT IS FRUSTRATED

It is obviously impossible to give a complete catalogue of frustrating events. The following are typical sets of circumstances in which it has been contended—often successfully—that the contract was frustrated.[26a]

---

[23] See p. 264, n. 12, *post*. Silence and inactivity may, in a particular case, constitute an offer and acceptance to discontinue the arbitration but the clearest possible evidence is required that this was the intention of the parties: *Excomm Ltd. Guan Guan Shipping (Pte) Ltd. The Golden Bear* [1987] 1 Lloyd's Rep. 330, 341. See also *Tankrederei Ahrenkeil GmbH* v. *Frahuil S.A. The Multitank Holsatia.* [1988] 2 Lloyd's Rep. 486, 493, where that intention of the parties was not proved.
[24] *Bank Line Ltd.* v. *A. Capel & Co.* [1919] A.C. 435, 452: "Reliance cannot be placed on self-induced frustration" (*per* Lord Sumner); *Maritime National Fish Ltd.* v. *Ocean Trawlers Ltd.* [1953] A.C. 524. See also *J. Lauritzen A/S* v. *Wijsmuller BV, The Times,* October 17, 1989.
[25] *Paal Wilson & Co. A/S* v. *Partenreederei Hannah Blumenthal* [1983] 1 A.C. 854, 909.
[26] *Joseph Constantine Steamship Line Ltd.* v. *Imperial Smelting Corporation* [1942] A.C. 154, 179.
[26a] On the view of the European Court of Justice on frustration see *Joannis Theodorakis Viomikhania Eleou AE* v. *The State (Greece)* [1989] 2 C.M.L.R. 166 (109/86).

Destruction of subject-matter

The simplest case of frustration occurs where the performance depends on the continued existence of a given person or thing and, after the conclusion of the contract, that person or thing has been physically destroyed. In these cases, "a condition is implied that the impossibility of performance arising from the perishing of the person or thing shall excuse the performance."[27]

Thus, during the war between Iraq and Iran in 1986, a vessel which was to carry the sold goods—premium motor spirit—from a port at the Gulf to ports in Australia was hit by an Exocet missile on the voyage in the Gulf; delivery of the goods in Australia had become impossible and the buyers successfully claimed that the contract of sale was frustrated.[28] Further, where a ship was chartered but failed to load because it had been disabled by an explosion which was not due to the negligence of the shipowners or their servants, the commercial object of the contract of carriage by sea was held to be frustrated.[29] When the subject-matter of the contract is the sale of specific goods, as, *e.g.* is the case in the sale of secondhand machinery or antiques, this effect is expressly provided for by section 7 of the Sale of Goods Act 1979 which lays down:

> Where there is an agreement to sell specific goods, and subsequently the goods, without any fault on the part of the seller or buyer, perish before the risk passes to the buyer, the agreement is thereby avoided.

But frustration cannot be pleaded if the event which made performance impossible existed already *before* the conclusion of the contract and could have been covered by an appropriate clause in the contract.[30]

Illegality

Outbreak of war

When, after the parties have entered into the contract, war breaks out, the question arises whether the performance of the contract is rendered illegal by that event or is only indirectly affected by the outbreak of war.

---

[27] Blackburn J. in *Taylor* v. *Caldwell* (1863) 3 B. & S. 826, 839. See Leon E. Trakman, "Frustrated Contracts and Legal Fictions" (1983) 46 M.L.R. 39.

[28] *Vitol S.A.* v. *Esso Australia Ltd. The Wise, The Times,* February 1, 1988.

[29] *Joseph Constantine Steamship Line Ltd.* v. *Imperial Smelting Corporation Ltd.* [1942] A.C. 154. Frustration also takes place where parties enter into a joint venture agreement for the development of an oilfield in a foreign country and subsequently the foreign government expropriates the interests of the parties in the oilfield: *B.P. Exploration Co. (Libya) Ltd.* v. *Hunt (No. 2)* [1979] 1 W.L.R. 783.

[30] *Eurico SpA* v. *Philipp Brothers. The Epaphus.* [1987] 2 Lloyd's Rep. 215 (A c. and f. contract for the sale of rice provided for delivery per vessel *Epaphus* "at one main Italian port." The buyers, who under the contract were entitled to nominate the port of delivery, nominated Ravenna, but the draught of the vessel was too deep for this port and the port authorities refused permission for the *Epaphus* to discharge. The vessel went to Ancona, where it was lightened by partial discharge of the cargo. The court refused to imply a term prohibiting the buyers to nominate an Italian port where discharge was impossible).

If a United Kingdom exporter has sold goods to an importer in another country and unfortunately war breaks out between the United Kingdom and that country, the performance of the contract by the United Kingdom exporter has become illegal because it would constitute an act of trading with the enemy, and the contract is frustrated. The same is true if in the course of the war the importer's country has passed under the control of the enemy. Thus, in the *Fibrosa* case,[31] a Polish company had ordered certain flax-hackling machines from manufacturers in Leeds shortly before the outbreak of the Second World War. The machines had to be delivered c.i.f. Gdynia within a certain time and the contract provided that in case of war or other events beyond the control of the parties a reasonable extension of the time of delivery should be granted. After the outbreak of the war, Gdynia was occupied by the Germans. It was held by the House of Lords that the contract was frustrated owing to war and the British manufacturers were discharged from delivering the machines; even the clause allowing for extension of the time of delivery did not save the contract because it was intended to cover merely minor delay as distinguished from a prolonged and indefinite interruption of contractual performance.

If, on the other hand, the contract is for the exportation of goods from the United Kingdom to country X and war breaks out between country X and country Y, the outbreak of war affects the contract only indirectly. In this case the legality of performance is not affected by the war and the contract does not automatically become frustrated by that event. It is, of course, an entirely different question whether in those circumstances the contract might be frustrated for other reasons, in particular on the ground that its performance is prohibited by the government of the United Kingdom or of country X, or that in consequence of the effect of war[32] there has been a vital change in circumstances. These questions will be examined later.[33]

Export and import prohibitions

Apart from the case of war, a contract may be frustrated because subsequent to its conclusion the government has prohibited its performance, *e.g.* by placing an embargo on the exportation or importation of the goods sold.[34]

---

[31] *Fibrosa Spolka Akcyjna* v. *Fairbairn Lawson Combe Barbour Ltd.* [1943] A.C. 32. The effect of frustration on the *Fibrosa* case is discussed on p. 197, *post*.

[32] The effect of war is here contrasted with the outbreak of war, see *Kodros Shipping Corporation* v. *Empresa Cubana de Fletes, The Evia (No. 2)* [1983] 1 A.C. 736; *International Sea Tankers Inc.* v. *Hemisphere Shipping Co., The Wenjiang (No. 2)* [1983] 1 Lloyd's Rep. 400; *Finelvet A.G.* v. *Vinava Shipping Co. Ltd., The Chrysalis* [1983] 1 W.L.R. 1469; and see pp. 189–192, *post*.

[33] See *supra* and pp. 190–191, *post*.

[34] On the requirement of export and import licences and quotas, p. 192 *post*.

Here, however, great care should be applied. Not every governmental prohibition has the effect of rendering the contract illegal. Sometimes the effect is merely to suspend and postpone the performance of the contract. It is always necessary to relate the prohibition to the terms of the contract, especially those governing the time of performance. The prohibition operates as a frustrating event only if it is final and extends to the whole time still available for the performance of the contract. If these conditions are not satisfied a party would be well advised to wait until the time of performance has expired before treating the contract as frustrated because the prohibition may be removed in time to allow performance.[35] If the government prohibition extends beyond the stipulated time for performance it is normally safe to assume that the contract is frustrated because there is an implied condition in every contract that its performance shall be legal at the date when the contract is to be performed.[36]

The rule that a subsequent government prohibition operates as a frustrating event only if it covers the whole of the contract period applies likewise if the prohibition does not come into operation at once and exporters are allowed a time of grace during which they may perform existing contracts. In one case[37] the contract provided for the shipment of horse beans from a Sicilian port c.i.f. Glasgow during October and November 1951. By an Italian regulation dated October 20, 1951, the exportation was prohibited as and from November 1, 1951, except under special licence. The sellers failed to ship and the buyers claimed damages. Devlin J. held that they were entitled to succeed. The prohibition did not operate as a frustrating event; it merely reduced the time of shipment from two months to one month and after the issue of the Italian regulation the sellers had still 10 days' grace within which they could have effected shipment. If the prohibition of export had been instantaneous it would have operated as a frustrating event, and the same would have been the case if the sellers could have proved that they had no shipping facilities during the remaining 10 days.

Further, sometimes the government prohibition may allow exporters to perform at least some of the contracts into which they have entered. It may thus leave "loopholes." It may, *e.g.* allow exporters who have goods already on lighters or have begun to load them on vessels to fulfil their contracts. In these cases an exporter who wishes to plead frustration has the heavy

---

[35] *Andrew Millar & Co. Ltd.* v. *Taylor & Co. Ltd.* [1916] 1 K.B. 402; *Austin, Baldwin & Co.* v. *Wilfred Turner & Co.* (1920) 36 T.L.R. 769; *Atlantic Maritime Co. Inc.* v. *Gibbon* [1954] 1 Q.B. 105, 114, 132; *Compagnie Algerienne de Meunerie* v. *Katana Societa di Navigatione Marittima S.p.A., The Nizetti* [1960] 2 Q.B. 115, 125–126.

[36] *Walton (Grain & Shipping Ltd.)* v. *British Italian Trading Co. Ltd.* [1959] 1 Lloyd's Rep. 223. Cf. *Nile Company for the Export of Agricultural Crops* v. *H. & J. M. Bennett, Commodities Ltd.* [1986] 1 [1986] 1 Lloyd's Rep. 555, 582.

[37] *Ross T. Smyth & Co. Ltd. (Liverpool)* v. *W.N. Lindsay Ltd. (Leith)* [1953] 1 W.L.R. 1280; explaining *Re Anglo-Russian Merchant Traders Ltd., and John Batt & Co. (London)* [1917] 2 K.B. 679.

burden of proving that he could not avail himself of one of these "loopholes."[38]

Government prohibitions affecting State trading corporations

The question has arisen whether a State trading corporation can plead a government prohibition of exports as a frustrating event. Normally the State trading corporation which has separate legal personality will not be so closely connected with its own government as to be precluded from relying on the prohibition, but there might be exceptional cases in which it can be proved that the foreign government had taken action in order to extricate the State enterprise from its contractual obligations and in these cases the courts might arrive at a different conclusion. These rules can be inferred from a case[39] in which a Polish State trading corporation sold a quantity of sugar to English sugar merchants. The contracts, which were subject to the standard rules of the Refined Sugar Association (RSA), were made in May and July 1974 and provided for delivery in November/December of that year. The Polish State corporation had been authorised to enter into these contracts and the sugar which formed the subject matter of the contracts was intended to be Polish beet sugar. The force majeure clause of the RSA provided, *inter alia*, that if "government intervention" occurred, there should be an extension and ultimately a cancellation of the contracts. Owing to heavy rains in August, the sugar crop failed in Poland and on November 5 the Polish Minister of Foreign Trade signed a decree making the export of sugar illegal by Polish law. This export ban remained in force until July 1975. The State corporation failed to deliver the sugar and pleaded force majeure. The House of Lords held that the claim was justified. The State trading corporation was independent of the government and the evidence showed that the export ban was imposed in order to avoid serious domestic, social and political unrest; that was "government intervention" within the meaning of the force majeure clause in the rules of RSA. It would thus appear that the courts are entitled to inquire into the motives of the government prohibition preventing the State trading organisation from performing its contract[40]; but they will be reluctant to exercise this jurisdic-

---

[38] *Per* Lord Denning M.R. in *Bunge S.A.* v. *Deutsche Conti Handelsgesellschaft mbH* [1979] 2 Lloyd's Rep. 435, 437; *Bremer Handelsgesellschaft mbH* v. *C. Mackprang Jr.* [1979] 1 Lloyd's Rep. 221, 223. (These are two of the *Soya Bean Meal* cases considered on p. 201, *post*).

[39] *C. Czarnikow Ltd.* v. *Rolimpex* [1979] A.C. 351. See also the cases referred to in the next footnote.

[40] In addition to *C. Czarnikow Ltd.* v. *Rolimpex*, *supra*, see *I Congreso del Partido* [1983] 1 A.C. 244; *Empresa Exportadora de Azucar* v. *Industria Azucarera Nacional S.A.* (*Iansa*), *The Playa Larga and the Marble Islands* [1983] 2 Lloyd's Rep. 171, 189.

tion if they think that it may constitute an unwarranted interference with a foreign State's sovereignty.[41]

An amendment of 1989 to the General Conditions of Delivery of CMEA provides that in contractual relations, to which the General Conditions apply, a unilateral act of a State authority interferring with the performance of the contract shall not be regarded as a frustrating event, unless the measure in question has general effect affecting all transactions of that kind.[41a]

Duty of parties reasonably to co-operate

Where, subsequent to the conclusion of the contract, the exportation or importation of goods is prohibited except by government licence, a condition is often implied into the contract obliging the parties to collaborate in all reasonable endeavours to obtain the licence. This condition will be discussed later on[42] when licensing and quota regulations and the effect of their change subsequent to the conclusion of the contract will be examined.

Fundamental change in circumstances

A contract is further frustrated if, after it was made,[43] such a radical change of circumstances has occurred that the foundation of the contract has gone and the contract, if kept alive, would amount to a new and different contract from that originally concluded by the parties. To hold the parties to their original bargain after the original common design is gone would mean that a different contract was substituted for their original contract.

While it is usually relatively easy to ascertain whether a contract is frustrated by impossibility, physical (destruction of the subject-matter) or legal (illegality), it is often extremely difficult to decide whether in cases in

---

[41] In *Settebello Ltd.* v. *Banco Totta and Acores* [1985] 1 W.L.R. 1050 the Court of Appeal refrained from expressing a view on the question whether the English courts should analyse the motivation of foreign legislation, which allegedly was designed to interfere with contracts concluded by a State trading corporation and its guarantors, but the court decided that letters of request relating to these issues should not be addressed to the courts of a friendly foreign State if the request would be "deeply embarrassing and indeed offensive" to those courts. It is doubtful whether the "act of State" doctrine applies to commercial transactions, see p. 227 *post*.

[41a] See p. 70, *ante,*

[42] See p. 194, *post.*

[43] That circumstances existing *before* the conclusion of the contract cannot constitute frustration, was discussed on p. 185, *ante*. They may, of course, constitute a common mistake (*Solle* v. *Butcher* [1950] 1 K.B. 671); *Associated Japanese Bank International Ltd.* v. *Credit du Nord SA.* [1988] 3 All E.R. 902.

which performance would still be possible a fundamentally different situation has unexpectedly arisen in which the contract ceases to bind.[44] The English decisions show that the courts consider the principle of sanctity of contracts as of infinitely higher importance than the requirements of commercial convenience and that they will not lightly assume that a contract which is still capable of performance is frustrated. Only if the change in circumstances is so profound that the parties would have replied to another person—"the officious bystander"—when the contract was made: "of course, if that event happens, the contract is off," is the contract regarded as frustrated.[45]

If, *e.g.* the performance of a contract for the supply of goods is delayed inordinately for reasons beyond the control of the parties and consequently the prices which were fixed in relation to the then existing conditions of labour and costs of raw material are entirely outdated, it may well be argued that the foundation of the contract has gone.[46] Into this category fall further cases in which the contract aimed at the execution of a particular object which has been defeated by supervening events. Normally an event which was within the contemplation of the parties when they entered into the contract does not operate as a frustrating event even though they did not expect or consider it probable that it would happen[47]; but in exceptional cases the doctrine has been applied where the parties were aware of the possibility that the frustrating event might occur but omitted to provide for that eventuality.[48]

How difficult it is to contend successfully that a change in circumstances is so fundamental that it results in frustration, may be seen from the so-called *Suez Canal* cases.[49] These arose in connection with the closure of the Suez Canal on November 2, 1956, as the result of military operations between Egypt and Israel. In these cases exporters in East Africa had sold certain goods for shipment c.i.f. specified European destinations; the contracts were made before the date of the closure of the Canal but had to be performed after that date. On the date of performance the Canal was no longer open for shipment but it was still possible to ship the goods to their destination via the Cape of Good Hope. That route was very much longer than the voyage

---

[44] See the statements referred to on pp. 181–182, *ante*, by Lord Radcliffe in *Davis Contractors Ltd.* v. *Fareham U.D.C.* [1956] A.C. 696, 729, and Lord Simon in *British Movietonews Ltd.* v. *London and District Cinemas Ltd.* [1952] A.C. 166.

[45] McNair J. in *Carapanayoti & Co. Ltd.* v. *E.T. Green Ltd.* [1959] 1 Q.B. 131, 148; Pearson J. in *Lewis Emanuel & Son Ltd.* v. *Sammut* [1959] 2 Lloyd's Rep. 629.

[46] *Metropolitan Water Board* v. *Dick, Kerr & Co.* [1918] A.C. 119, 139.

[47] *Davis Contractors Ltd.* v. *Fareham U.D.C.* [1956] A.C. 696.

[48] *W. J. Tatem Ltd.* v. *Gamboa* [1939] 1 K.B. 132.

[49] *Tsakiroglou & Co. Ltd.* v. *Noblee Thorl GmbH* [1962] A.C. 93 (H.L.); *Gaon (Albert D.) & Co.* v. *Société Interprofessionelle des Oléagineux Fluides Alimentaires*; *Tsakiroglou & Co. Ltd.* v. *Noblee Thorl GmbH* [1960] 2 Q.B. 318 (C.A.); *Carapanayoti & Co. Ltd.* v. *E. T. Green Ltd.* [1959] 1 Q.B. 131 (McNair J.); *The Eugenia* [1964] 2 Q.B. 226 (C.A.) and *The Captain George K.* [1970] 2 Lloyd's Rep. 21 (where contracts of affreightment were in issue).

via the Canal and caused considerable additional expense. It was clear that the additional expense was not of such magnitude as to support the view that the contracts were frustrated on that account. More difficult was the question whether the necessity to ship by the alternative route round the Cape constituted a radical difference in the character of the seller's obligation. The House of Lords[50] answered that question in the negative; the court held that the sellers were under a duty, when the usual route—via the Canal—was no longer available to send the goods by a reasonable and practicable route; such a route was in the present case still available in the route around the Cape. In the Court of Appeal Harman L.J. stated the general attitude of the English courts to issues of frustration in the following terms[51]:

> Frustration is a doctrine only too often invoked by a party to a contract who finds performance difficult or unprofitable, but it is very rarely relied upon with success. It is, in fact, a kind of last ditch, and, as Lord Radcliffe says in his speech in the most recent case,[52] it is a conclusion which should be reached rarely and with reluctance.

Another line of cases, the so-called *Shatt-al-Arab* cases,[53] indicates that frustration is a legal conclusion which should not be reached lightly or prematurely. When war broke out between Iran and Iraq in September 1980, a large number of vessels was trapped in the Shatt-al-Arab, a waterway separating the two hostile countries. Legal disputes concerning some of these vessels arose, mainly on the issue when the charterparties relating to these vessels were frustrated.[54] The opinions of the maritime arbitrators who dealt with these cases varied between October 4, 1980 and December 9, 1980,[55] but many considered November 24, 1980 as the date of frustration. The House of Lords in *The Evia (No. 2)*[56] declined to lay down one date for all these cases because the factual matrix of them might be different, the charterparties may be of different length, the discharge of the cargo may have been completed on different dates, the masters and crews of the various vessels may have left their vessels on different dates. The only principle which emerges from the *Shatt-al-Arab* cases is that already noted,[57] *viz.* that *outbreak* of war between two foreign countries does not normally

---

[50] In the *Tsakiroglou* case, *supra*. In the court of first instance there was a considerable difference of opinion. McNair J. in *Carapanayoti's* case decided in favour, and Diplock J. in *Tsakiroglou's* and Ashworth J. in *Gaon's* case against frustration; see [1959] J.B.L. 366.

[51] [1960] 2 Q.B. 318, 370. An event affecting only a minor aspect of performance does not necessarily frustrate the contract: *Congimex Compania Geral de Commercio Importadora e Exportadora S.a.r.l.* v. *Tradax Export S.A.* [1983] 1 Lloyd's Rep. 250.

[52] In *Davis Contractors* v. *Fareham U.D.C.* [1956] A.C. 696, 727.

[53] *Kodros Shipping Corporation of Monrovia* v. *Empresa Cubana de Fletes, The Evia (No. 2)* [1983] 1 A.C. 736; *International Sea Tankers Inc.* v. *Hemisphere Shipping Co., The Wenjiang (No. 2)* [1983] 1 Lloyd's Rep. 400; *Finelvet AG* v. *Vinava Shipping Co. Ltd., The Chrysalis* [1983] 1 W.L.R. 1469.

[54] But other issues, such as whether the ship was directed to a "safe port," also arose; see *The Evia (No. 2), supra*.

[55] See *The Wenjiang* [1982] 1 Lloyd's Rep. 128, 130.

[56] See n. 53, *supra*.

[57] See pp. 185–186, *ante*.

act as a frustrating event, but that the *effect* of such war may lead to frustration. Mustill J. summed up the position in the *Chrysalis*[58] thus:

> Except in the case of supervening illegality, arising from the fact that the contract involves a party in trading with some one who has become an enemy, a declaration of war does not prevent the performance of a contract; it is the acts done in furtherance of the war which may or may not prevent performance, depending on the individual circumstances of the case.

Export and import licences and quotas

Considerable difficulty is often caused by the imposition or strengthening of restrictive government regulations affecting the exportation and importation of goods, such as licences and quotas. Where a contract cannot be performed because the licence is not granted or the quota is too small, it is often contended that the contract is frustrated.[59] Here the following propositions should be borne in mind:

(1) *Where the contract of sale does not contain the terms "subject to licence," "subject to quota" or a similar term making it conditional,* the question arises whether the parties intended that the party on whom the duty falls to obtain the licence or quota[60] shall be bound absolutely by his undertaking or whether he merely shall use due diligence and take all reasonable steps to obtain the licence or quota.[61] The legal position is different in both cases. Where a party has absolutely undertaken to perform, he has warranted to obtain the licence or quota and if he fails to do so he is in breach, but where he has merely undertaken to take all reasonable steps the contract is frustrated if he can prove that he has discharged that duty but failed. The question is one of construction of his contractual undertakings.

If a party has failed to make the nature of his obligation explicit in the contract by using such a phrase as "subject to"—"a piece of phraseology," as Devlin J. observed,[62] "with which all commercial men must be very familiar"—it is very doubtful and depends entirely on the circumstances of

---

[58] [1983] 1 W.L.R. 1469, 1481.

[59] On government prohibitions rendering performance illegal, see pp. 186–188, *ante*.

[60] On the duty to procure an export licence under an f.o.b. contract, see p. 30, *ante* (where *A. V. Pound & Co. Ltd.* v. *M. W. Hardy & Co. Inc.* [1956] A.C. 588, is treated). On the question whether in a c.i.f. contract the seller is bound to procure goods afloat if he cannot ship from the port of shipment, see pp. 49–50, *ante*.

[61] *Re Anglo-Russian Merchant Traders Ltd., and John Batt & Co. (London) Ltd.* [1917] 2 K.B. 679, 685, 689; *Diamond Cutting Works Federation Ltd.* v. *Triefus & Co. Ltd.* [1956] 1 Lloyd's Rep. 216, 224; *Pagnan Spa* v. *Tradax Ocean Transportation S.A.* [1986] 2 Lloyd's Rep. 646, 650.

[62] In *Peter Cassidy Seed Co. Ltd.* v. *Osuustukkukauppa I.L.* [1957] 1 W.L.R. 273, 279. It should not be thought that the phrase "subject to" is a general escape clause enabling the party in whose favour it is directed to withdraw from the contract in any circumstances; see *Hong Guan & Co. Ltd.* v. *R. Jumabhoy & Sons Ltd.* [1960] A.C. 684; p. 199, *post*.

the case what interpretation the courts will place on this undertaking. Devlin J. once said[63] that "when nothing is said in the contract it is usually, indeed I think it is probably fair to say almost invariably, the latter class of warranty that is implied," *i.e.* the warranty to use all due diligence, and Steyn J. said[64]:

> In accordance with the principles governing the implication of terms, the court will usually incline towards implying the minimal provision necessary to give business efficacy to the contract, *viz.*, that the duty is one of reasonable diligence only.

But there are also dicta of other judges[65] to the contrary, and, in view of the widespread use of the phrase "subject to" by exporters there is always considerable risk that, in the absence of such a phrase, the court may hold the undertaking to be absolute.

Three illustrations of absolute undertakings by the seller may be added. In one case[66] Indian sellers of jute who had sold the goods under c.i.f. contracts not containing the clause "subject to quota" found themselves unable to supply the whole quantity of goods because the quota allotted to them was too small; when the contracts were made the exportation of jute from India was prohibited except under licence and a quota system was already in force; the sellers contended that an implied term should be read into the contracts that they were subject to the necessary licences and quotas being obtainable. The House of Lords rejected this view and held that the obligation of the sellers to deliver the goods was absolute. In another case[67] sellers in Finland sold to an English company a quantity of ant eggs f.o.b. Helsinki, "delivery: prompt, as soon as export licence granted." The sellers were unable to obtain the export licence and to ship, although they used all due diligence, because they were not members of the Finnish Ant Egg Exporters' Association. Devlin J. held that "as soon as" was not the same as "subject to" and that the sellers had undertaken absolutely to obtain the licence earlier or later; the learned judge upheld an award holding the sellers liable to pay damages to the buyers. The third case[68] concerned the exportation of Thailand tapioca pellets to the EC, which operated a quota system restricting the importation of these goods into the EC. The contract of sale, which was on GAFTA Form 119, contained a special condition according to which the sellers had to provide a Thai export certificate enabling the buyers to import the goods into the EC at a reduced Customs rate. The sellers failed to obtain the certificate and the buyers claimed

---

[63] [1957] 1 W.L.R. 273 at p. 277; see also the cases quoted in note 60 above.
[64] *Pagnan SpA* v. *Tradax Transportation S.A.* [1986] 2 Lloyd's Rep. 646, 650.
[65] See Jenkins L.J. (approved by the House of Lords) in *Partabmull Rameshwar* v. *K. C. Sethia (1944) Ltd.* [1951] 2 Lloyd's Rep. 89, 97–98; Denning L.J. in *Brauer & Co. (Great Britain) Ltd.* v. *James Clark (Brush Materials) Ltd.* [1952] 2 All E.R. 497, 501.
[66] *Partabmull Rameshwar* v. *K. C. Sethia (1944) Ltd.* [1951] 2 Lloyd's Rep. 89, 97–98.
[67] *Peter Cassidy Seed Co. Ltd.* v. *Osuustukkukauppa I.L.* [1957] 1 W.L.R. 273. In *Atisa S.A.* v. *Aztec AG* [1983] 2 Lloyd's Rep. 579 the sellers specifically undertook to obtain the export licence; consequently the contract was not frustrated when the licence was refused.
[68] *Pagnan SpA* v. *Tradax Ocean Transportation S.A.* [1986] 2 Lloyd's Rep. 646.

damages. Steyn J. held that the special condition constituted an absolute undertaking on the part of the sellers to obtain the export certificate.[69]

(2) *Where the contract of sale contains the term "subject to licence," "subject to quota" or a similar term making it conditional*, this clause gives the seller some, but not complete, protection: the seller is free from his obligation to deliver the goods but only if he can show that although he used *due diligence and took all reasonable steps* he was unable to obtain the licence or to comply with the government regulation, or that he could do so only on prohibitive terms which he could not reasonably be expected to accept. If he remains inactive and makes no attempt to obtain the licence because, as he alleges, such an attempt would have been useless, the burden that the attempt would have failed rests on him and, in the words of Devlin J., it "is always a difficult burden for a party to assume."[70] If the seller is ignorant of a local requirement of an export licence and therefore has failed to obtain such licence when, in all probability, he might have been granted it, he has not used his best endeavours to obtain the licence.[71]

The duty to co-operate in order to comply with government requirements regulating the exportation or importation of goods arises from a general condition implied into every contract that the parties shall reasonably co-operate to ensure the performance of their bargain.[72] This duty rests on the seller and buyer alike. In one case[73] buyers of cotton seed which was to be shipped from Syria failed to send the seller a certificate stating that they did not intend to re-export the goods to Israel (against which Syria maintained an embargo) and consequently the seller was unable to obtain a Syrian export licence and to ship the goods. The court dismissed the action by the buyers against the seller for damages for non-performance because the buyers themselves had failed to co-operate by sending the seller the necessary information to obtain the export licence which, as both parties knew, was required.

While, as has already been observed,[74] it is always wise to stipulate expressly "subject to licence or quota," it is possible in appropriate cases to

---

[69] But the claim of the buyers for damages failed; Steyn J. held that the special condition did not override the clause in GAFTA 119 providing for cancellation of the contract in case of restriction of exports by governmental action of the country of origin, and the sellers, though in breach of their absolute obligation, were excused of performance by virtue of that clause.

[70] Devlin J. in *Charles H Windschuegl Ltd.* v. *Pickering & Co. Ltd.* (1950) 84 Lloyd's Rep. 89, 93; Sellers J. in *Société D'Avances Commerciales (London) Ltd.* v. *A. Besse & Co. (London) Ltd.* [1952] 1 T.L.R. 644, 646; Denning L.J. in *Brauer & Co. (Great Britain) Ltd.* v. *James Clark (Brush Materials) Ltd.* [1952] 2 All E.R. 497, 501; *Joseph Pike & Sons (Liverpool) Ltd.* v. *Richard Cornelius & Co.* [1955] 2 Lloyd's Rep. 747, 750; *Aaronson Bros. Ltd.* v. *Maderera del Tropico S.A.* [1967] 2 Lloyd's Rep. 159, 160; *Smallman* v. *Smallman* [1972] Fam. 25, 32.

[71] *Malik Co.* v. *Central European Trading Agency Ltd.* [1974] 2 Lloyd's Rep. 279, 283.

[72] See p. 189, *ante*. Andrew J. Bateson, "The Duty to Co-operate" in [1960] J.B.L. 187.

[73] *Kyprianou* v. *Cyprus Textiles Ltd.* [1958] 2 Lloyd's Rep. 60.

[74] See p. 182, *ante*.

imply such term into the contract by way of necessary implication in order to give it business efficacy.[75] In this case the obligations of the parties are the same as if the term had been expressly adopted.

Partial frustration

Where a contract gives a party the right of electing one of several modes of performance and one mode has become frustrated, the contract is not completely destroyed but has to be performed in one of the remaining modes.[76] Thus, under a contract concluded shortly before the Second World War goods were to be shipped from Calcutta to Hamburg, Antwerp, Rotterdam or Bremen and the buyers had to declare the port of destination; the outbreak of war did not frustrate the contract as delivery in Antwerp and Rotterdam (which at that time were not occupied by Germany) was still legal.[77] Further, where United States/Brazilian soya bean meal—a commodity having a world market—was sold c.i.f. Lisbon under a GAFTA contract but the Portuguese authorities refused an import licence, the contract was held not to be frustrated because it was not proved that the prohibition would have prevented the reshipment or transhipment to a non-Portuguese destination.[78]

If in a c.i.f. contract shipment at the contemplated port of shipment has become frustrated, the seller might often not be obliged to acquire the goods afloat and to tender bills of lading relating to them to the buyer.[79]

Apportionment of performance

It has been seen that self-induced frustration does not qualify as frustration in the legal sense, *i.e.* it is not admissible as an excuse for non-performance.[80]

This rule creates a difficulty if a person has entered into several contracts but, owing to a supervening event, which qualifies in law as frustration, is

---

[75] *Re Anglo-Russian Merchant Traders Ltd., and John Batt & Co. (London) Ltd.* [1917] 2 K.B. 679, 685, 689; *Diamond Cutting Works Federation Ltd.* v. *Triefus & Co. Ltd.* [1956] 1 Lloyd's Rep. 216, 225; *Peter Cassidy Seed Co. Ltd.* v. *Osuustukkukauppa I.L.* [1957] 1 W.L.R. 273; *Pagnan SpA* v. *Tradax Ocean Transportation S.A.* [1986] 2 Lloyd's Rep. 646, 650 (see the quotation on p. 193, *ante*).
[76] *Waugh* v. *Morris* (1873) L.R. 8 Q.B. 202; *Reardon Smith Line Ltd.* v. *Ministry of Agriculture, Fisheries and Food* [1963] A.C. 691; see the notes by Raoul P. Colinvaux on this case in [1960] J.B.L. 236 and [1961] J.B.L. 407.
[77] *Hindley & Co. Ltd.* v. *General Fibre Co. Ltd.* [1940] 2 K.B. 517; see also *Ross T. Smyth & Co. Ltd. (Liverpool)* v. *W.N. Lindsay Ltd. (Leith)* [1953] 1 W.L.R. 1280; p. 153, *ante.*
[78] *Congimex* v. *Tradax Export S.A.* [1983] 1 Lloyd's Rep. 250, 253.
[79] See p. 50, *ante.*
[80] See p. 184, *ante.*

unable to perform them all. To give an example, an exporter sells 1,000 tonnes of sugar to A and another 1,000 tonnes of sugar to B. Subsequently the government introduces unexpectedly a quota system and allocates only 1,000 tonnes to the exporter. What is he to do? Shall he pass on the quota rateably to A and B, shipping 500 tonnes to each? Or shall he follow the chronological order and supply fully the first customer, whose order he has accepted, and ship nothing to the other?

The older view was that, whatever a party in this quandary did, was a matter of his own volition and consequently self-induced frustration. This meant that, whatever he did, he could not escape liability.[81] This result was unsatisfactory and can now be regarded as discarded.

The modern view, founded on the decision of the Court of Appeal in *Intertradax S.A.* v. *Lesieur-Tourteaux Sarl*,[82] is that the party who cannot perform all contracts into which he has entered because a frustrating event prevents him from doing so, should act in a fair and reasonable manner and, if he does so, may plead frustration in so far as he cannot perform all contracts. In this case Lord Denning M.R. quoted with approval the following observations of the judge of first instance, Donaldson J.[83]:

> . . . if the seller appropriates the goods in a way which the trade would consider to be proper and reasonable—whether the basis of appropriation is pro rata, chronological order of contracts or some other basis—the effective cause is not the seller's appropriation, but whatever caused the shortage.

But when apportioning, the seller should only take into account his legal commitments. He must disregard any moral commitments, even to regular customers with whom, at the relevant time, he is not in contract.[84]

It is appropriate here to refer to American law. The Uniform Code provides[85]:

> Where the causes mentioned in paragraph (a) affect only a part of the seller's capacity to perform, he must allocate production and deliveries among his customers but may at his option include regular customers not then under contract as well as his own requirements for further manufacture. He may so allocate in any manner which is fair and reasonable.

English law thus adopts now the same principle of apportionment as American law, namely that it has to be done in a fair and reasonable manner and, if so done, does not disentitle the seller from raising the plea of frustration in respect of the part which he has not performed. But there is an important difference between English and American law. English law does not allow the seller to take into account moral commitments to his regular customers but American law does so.[86] Further, the English courts have not

---

[81] This view was founded on *Maritime National Fish Ltd.* v. *Ocean Trawlers Ltd.* [1953] A.C. 524. See also *The Eugenia* [1964] 2 Q.B. 226.

[82] [1978] 2 Lloyd's Rep. 509.

[83] *Ibid.* 513.

[84] *Pancommerce S.A.* v. *Veecheema B.V.* [1983] 2 Lloyd's Rep. 304, 307.

[85] UCC, s.2–615(b).

[86] Sir John Donaldson M.R. emphasised this point in *Pancommerce S.A.* v. *Veecheema B.V.*, *supra*, on n. 84.

yet been called upon to decide whether a seller in this situation may include his own requirements in the apportionment. It is very doubtful that they will allow him to do so when he is under contractual obligations to others. Here again, there may be a significant difference between English and American law.

EFFECT OF FRUSTRATION

In general

The consequences of frustration have been stated by Lord Simon L.C.[87] with admirable brevity: "When frustration in the legal sense occurs, it does not merely provide one party with a defence in an action brought by the other. It kills the contract itself and discharges both parties automatically." The contract is consequently avoided as from the date when the frustrating event occurs: the liability of the parties in respect of the future performance of the contract is discharged, and all that remains to be done is to provide for an adjustment of their mutual rights and liabilities which arose under the contract prior to the time of discharge. This adjustment may involve difficult problems. Thus, in the *Fibrosa* case[88] the Polish buyers had paid £1,000 on account of the purchase price of £4,800 when the frustrating event took place, and the British manufacturers had incurred considerable expense in building the machines, which were of an unusual type, to the specification of the buyers. In such a case, can the buyer recover the advance paid on the purchase price? Is the seller entitled to retain his expenses, and, if so, how have they to be calculated? These and similar problems arise when the adjustment is made between the parties.

The Law Reform (Frustrated Contracts) Act 1943

When the contract is discharged by frustration, the adjustment of the contractual rights of the parties has to be carried out in most cases[89] in compliance with the provisions of the Law Reform (Frustrated Contracts) Act 1943. This Act was passed following the *Fibrosa* litigation with the aim of enabling the courts to adjust these differences on the basis of equity and justice.[90] Under section 1(2) of the Act, all advances paid before the time of

---

[87] *Joseph Constantine Steamship Line Ltd.* v. *Imperial Smelting Corporation Ltd.* [1942] A.C. 154, 163.

[88] See p. 186, *ante*.

[89] For exceptions, see *infra*.

[90] In the *Fibrosa* case it was held that the Polish buyers could recover the deposit of £1,000 on the ground that there was total failure of consideration. This rigid rule was abrogated by the Act of 1943.

discharge can be recovered by the party that paid them, but the recipient of the money is entitled to retain such expenses incurred before that time in or for the purpose of the performance of the contract as the court may consider just. Where no advance was paid and consequently expenses cannot be retained, the court may allow a claim for payment of just expenses against the party who, at the time of the discharge of the contract, had obtained a valuable benefit at the cost of the claimant (s.1(3)). The Act provides expressly that overhead expenses and personal labour may be included in the claim for retention or recovery of expenses (s.1(4)) and that, when the adjustment is made, the court shall not take into account the fact that a party may have insured voluntarily against the frustrating event and obtained the insurance money, but, if the insurance was effected in consequence of an express term of the frustrated contract (or under an enactment), *e.g.* if it was a c.i.f. contract, the insurance money has to be taken into account when the adjustment is made (s.1(5)). The Act aims at the prevention of unjust enrichment of either party at the expense of the other.[91]

The Act does not apply in the following exceptional cases:

(1) Where the contract is not governed by English law (s.1(1)). This provision lacks precision because it does not state what is to happen when different aspects of the contract are governed by different laws.[92] Where, *e.g.*, a contract is concluded in England but is to be performed in Brazil, the essential validity of the contract is likely to be governed by English law, but the incidents of performance by the law of Brazil. It is believed that such a contract, if frustrated, cannot be adjusted under the provisions of the Act, but that those provisions apply only where English law governs the performance of the contract.

(2) Where section 7 of the Sale of Goods Act 1979 applies (s.2(5) of the Law Reform (Frustrated Contracts) Act 1943). Section 7 provides for the avoidance of a contract for the sale of specific goods which have perished before the risk passed to the buyer.[93] In this case, advances paid on the purchase price can be recovered by the buyer, but the seller is not entitled to retain or recover just expenses.

(3) Certain contracts of insurance; certain charterparties and other contracts of carriage by sea (s.2(5)). The contracts dealing with these topics normally contain special provisions for the adjustment of the rights of the parties when frustration occurs.

(4) When the contract contains provisions which are intended to have effect in the event of commercial frustration; in this case the court has to give effect to the contractual provisions and to apply the provisions of the Act only to such extent as appears to be consistent with the contractual provisions (s.2(3)).

The Act provides especially (s.3(2)) that it shall likewise apply when the dispute is to be determined by an arbitrator. An arbitration clause is normally not invalidated when a party maintains that the contract is frustrated, and the arbitrator has to decide a dispute between the parties on the question whether the contract has been frustrated or not.[94]

---

[91] *B.P. Exploration Co. (Libya) Ltd.* v. *Hunt (No. 2)* [1979] 1 W.L.R. 783, 799; [1983] 2 A.C. 352 (H.L.). See also *Bank of Boston Connecticut* v. *European Grain and Shipping Ltd. The Dominique.* [1989] 2 W.L.R. 440, 454 (HL). See further A. M. Haycroft and D. M. Waksman "Frustration and Restitution" in [1984] J.B.L. 207.

[92] See p. 210, *post.*

[93] See p. 185, *ante.*

[94] *Heyman* v. *Darwins Ltd.* [1942] A.C. 356; see further, p. 651, *post.*

Force Majeure Clauses

The attentive reader will conclude that it is not always easy to say whether in an individual case the contract has or has not been frustrated. He will reflect that it may be wiser for the parties to introduce a clause in their agreement defining in advance their mutual rights and duties if certain events beyond their control occur, whether or not such events result, in the eyes of the law, in the frustration of the contract or not.[95] Such clauses are, in fact, frequently employed in practice; they are known as *force majeure clauses* and vary considerably in ambit and effect.[96]

Different kinds of force majeure clauses

As regards the ambit of the clause, *i.e.* the events covered by the clause, it is sufficient to state simply that it shall apply in case of force majeure. This term has a clear meaning in law[97]; it includes every event beyond the control of the parties. Sometimes, however, the parties modify the normal meaning of the clause and it is, therefore, necessary to construe the clause in each case "with a close attention to the words which precede or follow it, and with a due regard to the nature and general terms of the contract. The effect of the clause may vary with each instrument."[98] Sometimes the parties define the ambit of the clause in considerable detail, as may be illustrated by the following clause[99]:

---

[95] Lord Tucker in *Fairclough Dodd & Jones Ltd.* v. *J. H. Vantol Ltd.* [1957] 1 W.L.R. 136, 143. See also Bernard J. Cartoon, "Drafting an Acceptable Force Majeure Clause," in [1978] J.B.L. 230.

[96] A force majeure clause differs from an exception clause in that the latter is intended to protect a party who is in breach, whereas the former applies when a certain event happens, whether or not, in consequence of that event, the party would be in breach; see Lord Tucker, *ibid*.

[97] Although Donaldson J. said in *Thomas Borthwick (Glasgow) Ltd.* v. *Faure Fairclough Ltd.* [1968] 1 Lloyd's Rep. 16, 28 that "the precise meaning of this term, if it has one, has eluded the lawyers for years." For the interpretation of the force majeure clause by the EC Court see *Theodorakis* v. *Hellenic Republic* (case 109/86 [1989] 2 CMLR 166 and *The Greek State* v. *Inter-Kom Emboriki kai Viomikhaniki Epikhirisis Eleon* (case 71/87), unreported at date of writing (October 1, 1989).

[98] McCardie J. in *Lebeaupin* v. *Crispin* [1920] 2 K.B. 714, 720. The protection of the clause "subject to force majeure and shipment" is not available to a seller who has, in fact, received a shipment of the goods sold from his supplier but uses it for the performance of other commitments: *Hong Guan & Co. Ltd.* v. *R. Jumabhoy & Sons Ltd.* [1960] A.C. 684. A party who has not taken reasonable steps to avoid a strike may not be able to rely on a force majeure clause: *B. & S. Contracts and Design* v. *Victor Green Publications* [1984] I.C.R. 419.

[99] This clause is founded on the model of force majeure clauses in *Baltimex Ltd.* v. *Metallo Chemical Refining Ltd.* [1955] 2 Lloyd's Rep. 438, 446, and *Sonat Offshore S.A.* v. *Amerada Hess Development Ltd. and Texaco (Britain) Ltd.* [1988] 1 Lloyd's Rep. 145, 148.
Another (more complicated) form of a force majeure clause is suggested in ICC Brochure No. 421 on *Force majeure and Hardship* (1985).

> Strikes, lockouts, labour disturbances, anomalous working conditions, accidents to machinery, delays en route, policies or restrictions of governments, including restrictions on export or import or other licences, war (whether declared or not), riot, civil disturbances, fire, act of God, or any other contingency whatsoever beyond the control of either party, to be sufficient excuse for any delay or non-performance traceable to any of these causes.

This force majeure clause, like most clauses of this type, consists of two parts, *viz.* a catalogue of "the various catastrophes there listed"[1] and at the end a general clause operating as a safety net to include any event not listed in the catalogue; in the preceding illustration the general clause is worded "any other contingency whatsoever beyond the control of either party."[2]

As regards the effect of the force majeure clause, sometimes these clauses provide for the extension of the time of performance, or the automatic suspension or cancellation of the contract in case of the occurrence of the disturbing element; sometimes they give each party or one party only an option of suspending or cancelling the contract in that event. Expressions such as "force majeure excepted" or "subject to force majeure" mean that in the event of force majeure the parties shall be excused from further performing the contract, subject to their obligation to co-operate reasonably to ensure the performance of their bargain.[3]

The two-stage force majeure clause

The form of force majeure clause which in modern international trade is increasingly used provides for two stages with respect to the effect of force majeure. In the first stage the time for the performance of the contract is extended for a specified period, *e.g.* 28 days. If the event which constitutes force majeure continues after the expiration of that period, each party is entitled to cancel the contract.

Sometimes it is provided that the party claiming extension of the time for performance shall give the other party notice or even several notices, such as a warning notice and a final notice. These provisions, as those relating to the exercise of the option to cancel the contract, have to be complied with carefully.[4]

---

[1] *Per* Purchas L.J. in the *Sonat* case (n. 99, *ante*), on p. 158.

[2] In the *Sonat* case the general clause was worded "or other cause beyond the reasonable control of such party"; the Court of Appeal held that these words had to be construed *ejusdem generis,* and not disjunctively, with the words in the catalogue, and did not extend to breakage or failure of drilling equipment of an oil rig caused by alleged negligence or wilful default of a party.

[3] See p. 194, *ante.*

[4] *Bremer Handelsgessellschaft mbH* v. *Vanden Avenne Izegem PVBA* [1978] 2 Lloyd's Rep. 109. In *Tradax Export S.A.* v. *Andre & Cie S.A.* [1976] 1 Lloyd's Rep. 416 the Court of Appeal held that a "rolled up" notice, *i.e.* a notice combining several required notices, was sufficient, as long as it contained all the required information. In *Johnson Matthey Bankers Ltd.* v. *State Trading Corporation of India Ltd.* [1984] 1 Lloyd's Rep. 427 a provision in a force majeure clause that the seller, an Indian State trading company, if unable to deliver the goods—silver bullion—should pay damages to the buyers was held not to be against Indian public policy when the contract was frustrated by an export prohibition of the Indian government.

Force majeure clauses in standard contracts used in the commodity trade

Sometimes contracts, particularly standard contracts in the commodity trade, contain a more elaborate regulation. Thus, a contract[5] on a form of the London Oil and Tallow Trades Association provided for the shipment of Egyptian cottonseed oil from Alexandria to Rotterdam during December and January. The contract contained two force majeure clauses, one to the effect that in case of war or other specified events *preventing* shipment the contract should be cancelled, and the other providing that if another event *delayed* shipment, the period of shipment should be extended by two months. The Egyptian Government prohibited the exportation of the goods from December 12 to January 3 (during which period the sellers, in fact, intended to ship) but shipment was possible on January 31 when the shipment period expired. The sellers did not ship within the original shipment period, and the buyers claimed damages. The defence of the sellers was that, by virtue of the second clause, the performance of the contract was extended by two months. The House of Lords held, on the construction of the force majeure clause, that that contention was correct and that the clause became operative through the intermittent delay although the delay was no longer in existence at the end of the shipment period.

Elaborate force majeure and cancellation clauses were in issue in the so-called *Soya Bean Meal* cases, which concerned the interpretation of standard contract forms of the Grain and Feed Trade Association (GAFTA).[6] In the *Vanden Avenne* case Bremer Handelsgesellschaft, of Hamburg, sold a quantity of soya bean meal of American origin to Vanden Avenne, of Antwerp. The contracts, which were dated April 5, 1973 and provided for

---

[5] In *Fairclough Dodd & Jones Ltd.* v. *J. H. Vantol Ltd.* [1957] 1 W.L.R. 136.
[6] *Bremer Handelsgesellschaft mbH* v. *Vanden Avenne Izegem PVBA* [1978] 2 Lloyd's Rep. 109; *Alfred C. Toepfer* v. *Peter Cremer* [1975] 2 Lloyd's Rep. 118; *Tradex Export S.A.* v. *André & Cie S.A.* [1976] 1 Lloyd's Rep. 416; [1977] 2 Lloyd's Rep. 484; [1978] 1 Lloyd's Rep. 639; *Toepfer* v. *Schwarze* [1977] 2 Lloyd's Rep. 380; *Bunge S.A.* v. *Schleswig-Holsteinische Landwirtschaftliche Hauptgenossenschaft Eingetr. GmbH* [1978] 1 Lloyd's Rep. 480; *Bunge GmbH* v. *Alfred C. Toepfer* [1978] 1 Lloyd's Rep. 506; *Bunge S.A.* v. *Deutsche Conti Handelsgesellschaft mbH* [1979] 2 Lloyd's Rep. 435; *Continental Grain Export Corpn* v. *S.T.M. Grain Ltd.* [1979] 2 Lloyd's Rep. 460; *Bremer etc.* v. *Toepfer* [1980] 2 Lloyd's Rep. 43 (The two offices of Bremer in Hamburg and Munich treated as separate entities for the purposes of a string contract); *Bremer etc.* v. *C. Mackprang Jr.* [1979] 2 Lloyd's Rep. 221; [1981] 1 Lloyd's Rep. 292; *Bremer etc.* v. *Westzucker GmbH* (*No.* 1) [1981] 1 Lloyd's Rep. 207; (*No.* 2) [1981] 1 Lloyd's Rep. 214; *Bremer etc.* v. *Bunge* [1983] 1 Lloyd's Rep. 476; *Bremer etc.* v. *Raiffeisen Hauptgenossenschaft eG* (*No.* 1) [1982] 1 Lloyd's Rep. 210; (*No.* 2) [1983] 1 Lloyd's Rep. 434. *Raiffeisen etc.* v. *Louis Dreyfus & Co. Ltd.* [1981] 1 Lloyd's Rep. 345; *André et Cie S.A.* v. *Tradax Export S.A.* [1983] 1 Lloyd's Rep. 254; *Cook Industries Inc.* v. *Meunerie Liegeois* [1981] 1 Lloyd's Rep. 359; *Tradax Export S.A.* v. *Rocco Giuseppe & Figli* [1981] 1 Lloyd's Rep. 353; *Mitsubishi International GmbH* v. *Bremer etc.* [1981] 1 Lloyd's Rep. 106; *Vanden Avenne-Izegem PVBA* v. *Finagrain S.A.* [1985] Lloyd's Rep. 99; *Cook Industries Inc.* v. *Tradax Export S.A.* [1985] 2 Lloyd's Rep. 454; *André et Cie* v. *Cook Industries Inc.* [1987] 2 Lloyd's Rep. 463.

monthly instalment deliveries c.i.f. Rotterdam, were made on GAFTA form no. 100 which in clauses 21 and 22 contained detailed prohibition of exports and force majeure clauses. Owing to the flooding of the Mississippi in the spring of 1973 the export of soya bean meal by American shippers was greatly impeded and the shortage caused the market price to rise sharply. On June 27, 1973 the United States Government imposed an embargo on the export of soya bean meal but after a few days, on July 2, it allowed exporters a quota by which they could export 40 per cent. of their contracted obligations. The sellers claimed that by virtue of the prohibition and force majeure clauses in GAFTA form no. 100 they were relieved from their obligation to ship the prohibited portion of the June 1973 instalment and the House of Lords, interpreting clauses 21 and 22, upheld that contention. One of the arguments of the buyers was that clause 21 (which provided for notices) was a condition precedent, the onus of satisfying it was on the sellers and, since the findings of fact by the arbitrators did not deal with that point, the case had to be remitted to them. The House of Lords rejected this argument. Lord Wilberforce said that clause 21 was an innominate term[7] and not a condition precedent and that no such finding was necessary. The court further held that there was no obligation on the sellers to purchase the goods afloat,[8] and decided in favour of the sellers.[8a]

Another illustration of a detailed force majeure clause in a commodity contract is provided by the Polish sugar beet case[9] where the contract was subject to the standard rules of the Refined Sugar Association.

Force majeure clauses which are too vague

While, as has been seen, the meaning of the phrase "force majeure" is clear in law, although perhaps not in all its implications, and its use does not render the agreement of the parties invalid on the ground of uncertainty, the position is different where the contract contains an unspecified reference to the "usual" force majeure clause and it is impossible to state with certainty which of the numerous force majeure clauses used in practice the parties had in mind. In these cases the courts have held that the clause is too vague; if it is of the essence, it makes the whole contract in which it occurs invalid,[10] but if the meaningless clause is severable from the other terms of the contract it is ignored and leaves the other obligations unaffected and

---

[7] See p. 135, *ante.*
[8] See p. 49, *ante.*
[8a] In some of the cases listed in n. 6, *ante,* the facts were found to be different from those in *Vanden Avenne,* and the decision was for the buyers.
[9] *C. Czarnikov Ltd.* v. *Rolimpex* [1979] A.C. 351, see p. 188, *ante.*
[10] *British Electrical and Associated Industries (Cardiff) Ltd.* v. *Patley Pressings Ltd.* [1953] 1 W.L.R. 280, 285.

enforceable.[11] The position is different if the phrase "usual force majeure clause," by necessary implication, has a definite meaning, *e.g.* if it clearly refers to a clause usual in a particular trade; in that case it has full legal effect.

Further, it would be unwise for the parties to adopt words which have no clear legal connotation. Thus, in one case[12] a judge had to decide whether a contract embodying the clause "u.c.e." (unforeseen circumstances excepted) was discharged when unforeseen circumstances prevented the seller from obtaining the goods, which he had sold to the buyer, from the source of supply contemplated by him; the judge observed:

> It is a pity that merchants will continue to use shorthand expressions of this kind, if I may so term them, without a definition of them in the contract, and thus leave them to be interpreted by the court,

and held that the clause did not mean that the seller should be free if the goods could not be obtained from that particular source of supply but were still obtainable elsewhere.

Force majeure clauses defeated by events

Exceptionally a force majeure clause may be defeated by events. The courts have disregarded such clauses where the supervening event rendered the performance of the contract illegal or was of such an unforeseeable magnitude that the contract, if upheld, would have constituted a new and different contract from the original one.

A force majeure clause does not protect a seller who claims that he is not bound to deliver the goods for the reason that he cannot obtain an export licence unless he pays a price 20 to 30 per cent. higher than the contract price; this is not a case of force majeure, there is no physical or legal prevention of the exportation, such as a prohibition or an embargo.[13]

---

[11] *Nicolene Ltd.* v. *Simmonds* [1953] 1 Q.B. 543.

[12] Greer J. in *George Wills & Sons Ltd.* v. *R.S. Cunningham, Son & Co. Ltd.* [1924] 2 K.B. 220, 221.

[13] *Brauer & Co. (Great Britain) Ltd.* v. *James Clark (Brush Materials) Ltd.* [1952] 2 All E.R. 497, 499; see pp. 182–183, *ante*.

CHAPTER 13

ENGLISH LAW AND FOREIGN LAW

THE exportation of goods from this country embodies, by necessity, a foreign element and falls, in so far, within the province of English law known as private international law or the conflict of laws. This branch of law applies to transactions extending over several countries and determines in an individual case the law applicable to the dispute between the parties and the jurisdiction of the courts which have to adjudicate upon the issue. These two questions do not coincide; it is conceivable that according to the rules of the conflict of laws the dispute has to be heard by the English courts but that these courts have to apply a foreign system of law. In the eyes of the English lawyer and the English courts, every system of law applied in another country is considered to be foreign law, and no difference is made in this respect between the laws prevailing in the countries which have founded their law on the common law, the Member States of the EC, and other countries. "In the English courts, English law is the municipal system of law while the laws of Scotland, New Zealand or China are alike foreign laws."[1]

It is of great importance for the parties to know whether their contract is governed by English law or the foreign system of law prevailing at the place where the buyer resides or to which the goods have ultimately to be shipped. In fact, from the legal point of view, this is the central problem arising in an export transaction. It has been pointed out before that the rules of English and foreign law are often at variance; the expression f.o.b. has a different meaning in English and American law[2]; the Sale of Goods Act 1979 applies when an international contract is governed by English law but does not apply when it is governed by foreign law[3]; a contract may be regarded as frustrated by English law but as valid by foreign law; the provisions of the Law Reform (Frustrated Contracts) Act 1943 apply only to contracts governed by English law[4]; and so forth.

Proof of foreign law

However, even if it is clear that the contract is governed by a foreign system of law, this does not mean that the judge or arbitrator has to

---

[1] Clive M. Schmitthoff, *The English Conflict of Laws* (3rd ed., 1954), p. 5.
[2] See p. 19, *ante.*
[3] See p. 114, *ante.*
[4] See p. 198, *ante.*

ascertain the rules of that legal system *ex officio*. English judges and arbitrators regard foreign law as a question of fact which has to be proved to their satisfaction by expert witnesses or other admissible evidence.[5] If a party fails to adduce such evidence, English law will be applied. Consequently, a party in English proceedings will plead foreign law only if this is to his advantage; otherwise it is cheaper for him to have the issue decided in accordance with English law. Thus, in the *Romalpa* case[6] it was probable that the contract was governed by Dutch law but as neither party pleaded Dutch law, the case was decided according to English law. In many continental countries, judges and arbitrators have to ascertain the foreign law, which in their view applies, *ex officio*.

MEASURES OF CONFLICT AVOIDANCE

The need to avoid, or at least to reduce, the dangers of a conflict of laws in international commercial transactions is obvious. Remedial action is taken on several levels.[7] International Conventions have been adopted with this end in sight; the most important affecting international sales law are noted below. On the private level, general conditions of sale and model contract forms[8] normally embody a choice of law clause.[9]

The Hague Uniform Laws and the Vienna Convention on Contracts of International Sale

In particular, the two Hague Uniform Laws on International Sales appended to the Uniform Laws on International Sales Act 1967 attempt

---

[5] The House of Lords, however, in an English or Northern Irish appeal, takes judicial notice of Scots law and vice versa. Moreover, by the Civil Evidence Act 1972, s.4(2), where any question of foreign law has been determined by a specified higher court in England or by the Privy Council, then any finding or decision on that question is admissible in evidence in subsequent proceedings and the foreign law shall be taken to be in accordance with that finding unless the contrary is proved, provided that the finding or decision is reported or recorded in citable form, *i.e.* in a form in which it can be cited as an authority in an English court.

J.H.C. Morris, in his *The Conflict of Laws* (3rd ed., 1984), p. 37, rightly observes that the rule that foreign law is a question of fact, is "paradoxical," but it is firmly established in English law. But, as has been said by Megaw L.J. in *Dalmia Dairy Industries Ltd.* v. *National Bank of Pakistan* [1978] 2 Lloyd's Rep. 223, 286 "it is a finding of fact of a very different character from the normal finding of fact"; also Lloyd L.J. in *The Saudi Prince (No. 2)* [1988] 1 Lloyd's Rep. 1, 3.

[6] *Aluminium Industrie Vaassen BV* v. *Romalpa Aluminium Ltd.* [1976] 1 W.L.R. 676; see p. 121, *ante*.

[7] See Clive M. Schmitthoff, "The Law of International Trade", Chap. 2 in *Commercial Law in a Changing Economic Climate* (2nd ed., 1981), p. 18; *Essays* 219.

[8] See p. 76, *ante*.

[9] See p. 211, *post*.

to reduce the possibility of a conflict of laws. These measures will be considered in the next chapter[10] but it should be mentioned here that the Hague Uniform Law on the International Sale of Goods states in article 2:

> Rules of private international law shall be excluded for the purposes of the application of the present Law, subject to the contrary in the said Law.

The Uniform Laws were not widely accepted[11] but they formed the foundation of the Vienna Convention on Contracts for the International Sale of Goods of April 11, 1980, promoted by the United Nations. This Convention has every prospect of being widely accepted, particularly after it was ratified by the United States and China,[12] but at the date of writing[13] it has not been introduced into United Kingdom law yet.[13] It will likewise be considered in the next chapter. Unlike the Hague Laws, it does not contain a general clause excluding the application of private international law; on the contrary, taking a more realistic view, it provides[14] that resort to the rules of private international law may be had to fill gaps in the Convention.

The Hague Convention on the Law applicable to International Sales of Goods

This Convention, which came into operation on June 15, 1955,[15] pursues a less ambitious aim than the measures just discussed. Unlike them, it does not aim at a world-wide unification of the law of international sales. The 1955 Convention recognises that, as things are today, the possibility of a conflict of laws in the area of international sales cannot be excluded. Its object is to provide uniform rules for deciding which national law shall apply to international sales transactions if a dispute arises between the parties. It thus deals only with a question of private international law. The simple principle adopted by the Convention is that, if the parties have not agreed on the law governing their contract, the seller's law shall apply, but some exceptions are admitted. The main rules of the Convention have been summed up as follows[16]:

---

[10] See p. 240, *post.*
[11] See pp. 240–241, *post.*
[12] See p. 249, *post.*
[13] Position: October 1, 1989.
[14] Particularly from art. 7(2); see p. 251, *post.*
[15] This Convention was adopted by the 7th Session of the Hague Conference on Private International Law in 1951. At the 14th Session (1985) a declaration was adopted according to which the 1955 Convention does not prevent States, which are parties to the Convention, from applying special rules to consumer sales but it is recommended that they should inform the Bureau of the Conference of this fact.
[16] By Dr. G.C. Cheshire, "International Contracts for the Sale of Goods," [1960] J.B.L. 282.

1. A contract for the sale of goods is regulated by the domestic law designated by the parties;
2. Failing such designation, the domestic law of the country in which the seller has his habitual residence applies;
3. The preceding rule is subject to two exceptions:
    (*a*) where the order is received by a branch office of the seller, the contract is regulated by the domestic law of the country in which such branch is situated;
    (*b*) where the order is received by the seller or his agent in the buyer's country, the domestic law of the country in which the buyer has his habitual residence applies.

The Convention has been given effect[17] by Belgium, Denmark, Finland, France, Italy, Niger, Norway, Switzerland and Sweden, but not by Great Britain. The principle that, unless otherwise agreed, the seller's law shall apply is likewise accepted by the CMEA General Conditions of Delivery of Goods 1968–1975 (1979 version) which apply to the trade between the Comecon countries.[18]

The 1955 Convention will be superseded by the *Hague Convention on the Law applicable to Contracts for the International Sale of Goods,* of December 22, 1986. This measure was necessary in order to bring the provisions of the 1955 Convention into line with those of the Vienna Convention on Contracts for the International Sale of Goods of 1980. The 1986 Convention will enter into force after ratification by five signatory or acceding States (art. 27); at the date of writing,[19] it has not come into operation yet and the 1955 Convention still applies. When the 1986 Convention has come into force, it will automatically replace the 1955 Convention for the States which have adopted the latter (art. 28). The principles on which the 1986 Convention is founded are essentially the same as those of the 1955 Convention, but in a modified form. The main rules of the 1986 Convention are:

1. A contract for the international sale of goods is governed by the domestic law chosen by the parties (Arts. 7 and 15).
2. In the absence of such choice, the contract is governed by the domestic law of the State where the seller has his place of business at the conclusion of the contract (Arts. 8 and 15). If a party does not have a place of business, reference is to be made to his habitual residence (Art. 14 (2)).
3. By way of exception, where, in the light of the circumstances as a whole, for instance any business relations between the parties, the contract is manifestly more closely connected with another law the, the contract is governed by the other law. (Art. 8(3)).
4. The application of a law determined by the Convention may be refused only where such application would be manifestly incompatible with public policy (*ordre public*) (Art. 18).

The EC Convention on the Law applicable to Contractual Obligations

This Convention, also called the Private International Law Convention or the Rome Convention, was adopted by the Council of the EC on June

---

[17] Position as on October 1, 1988.
[18] CMEA General Conditions of Delivery of Goods, para. 110.
[19] See n. 17 *supra*.

19, 1980 in Rome.[20] Its object is to provide in all Member States of the EC uniform rules for the ascertainment of the law governing an international contract. The provisions of the Rome Convention are likely to be introduced into UK law in 1990.[21] The main provisions of the Convention will be surveyed later.[22]

The EC Convention on Jurisdiction and the Enforcement of Judgments in Civil and Commercial Matters

This Convention, also called the Judgments Convention or the Full Faith and Credit Convention, was adopted by the six original members of the EEC on September 27, 1968 in Brussels. Following the accession of Denmark, the Irish Republic and the United Kingdom to the EC, it was amended in 1978.[23] The Convention is given legislative force in the United Kingdom by the Civil Jurisdiction and Judgments Act 1982.

The Convention deals with procedural matters. It defines the international jurisdiction of the courts of the Member States by excluding—not wholly successfully—concurrent jurisdictions which invite "forum shopping," *i.e.* the choice by the litigant of the most favourable of several competent courts. The Convention also introduces an expeditious procedure for the recognition and enforcement of judgments of certain courts of the Member States throughout the EC. The Convention will be considered later.[24]

THE LAW GOVERNING THE CONTRACT

The international Conventions noted in the preceding paragraphs do not exclude the possibility of a conflict of national laws in the field of international commercial transactions. Even if they are fully implemented, this possibility will still persist. In a branch of law such as that relating to letters of credit, in which far-reaching uniformity is achieved by the almost universal—voluntary—acceptance of the Uniform Customs and Practice for Documentary Credits (1983 Revision),[25] conflict problems still arise occasionally.[26]

---

[20] O.J. 1980, L. 266.
[21] See p. 222, *post.*
[22] *Ibid.*
[23] By the Convention on the Accession to the 1968 Convention and the 1971 Protocol. The Accession Convention was signed on October 9, 1978 in Luxembourg.
[24] See p. 709, *post.*
[25] See p. 401, *post.*
[26] See p. 419, *post.*

To solve these problems, we have to turn to private international law. We have to examine the rules which the English courts apply when faced with the task of ascertaining the law governing an international contract.

The principle

According to English law, a contract is governed by the law which the parties intend to apply to their agreement or, if they have not formed such an intention, the law with which the contract is most closely connected. This law is, for brevity's sake, called the *proper law of the contract*. Lord Simonds[27] stated these rules in the following words:

> The proper law of the contract [is] the system of law by reference to which the contract was made or that with which the transaction had its closest and most real connection.

Ascertainment of the proper law

The proper law is ascertained by reference to a system of law and not to a particular country,[28] but that legal system is normally[29] the legal system applied in a particular country or locality. It is ascertained in relation to the situation at the time when the contract is made and factors after this event cannot be taken into account retrospectively.[30] But, as Ackner L.J. observed in one case,[31] "it is unusual for a clause to provide expressly or by implication for two proper laws—one to be applied in one event and another to be applied if that event is negatived, . . . But I cannot see why there cannot be sound commercial sense in a fall-back provision of the kind which this clause seems to me to represent."[32]

---

[27] *Bonython* v. *Commonwealth of Australia* [1951] A.C. 201, 219. See also *Whitworth Street Estates (Manchester) Ltd.* v. *James Miller & Partners Ltd.* [1970] A.C. 583; *Amin Rasheed Shipping Corporation* v. *Kuwait Insurance Co.* [1984] A.C. 50.

[28] May L.J. in *Amin Rasheed Shipping Corporation* v. *Kuwait Insurance Co.* [1983] 1 W.L.R. 228, 241; affd. by H.L. in [1983] 3 W.L.R. 241 (see Lord Diplock on p. 246).

[29] But the English courts would not object if the parties leave the choice of law to the arbitrators and the arbitrators, without contravening the law governing the arbitration procedure (in the case in question Swiss law), adopted "the internationally accepted principles of law governing contractual obligations," *i.e.* an anational law (the international *lex mercatoria*): *Deutsche Schachtbau-und-Tiefbohrgesellschaft mbH* v. *R'As al-Khaima National Oil Co.* [1987] 3 W.L.R. 1023, 1032 (*per* Sir John Donaldson M.R.); reverd. in part on another point by H.L. in [1988] 3 W.L.R. 230; see p. 655, *post*.

[30] *Amar Shipping Co. Ltd.* v. *Caisse Algérienne d'Assurance et de Réassurance* [1981] 1 W.L.R. 207, 215.

[31] *Astro Venturoso Compania Naviera* v. *Hellenic Shipyards S.A.*, *The Mariannina* [1983] 1 Lloyd's Rep. 12, 15.

[32] The clause in question occurred in a bill of lading and provided for arbitration in London but added that, if it was ruled by a competent authority that the arbitration provision was unenforceable, Greek law should apply and the Greek courts of Piraeus should have jurisdiction.

The parties may also provide that, if proceedings are commenced by the purchasers, the sellers' law shall be applied but if they are started by the sellers, the purchasers' law shall be the proper law.[33] But "there cannot be a time during the life of the contract when it has no ascertainable proper law."[34]

Application of several proper laws to the same contract

Although it is usual to talk of the proper law of the *contract* or to state that a contract is an English contract or a French contract or that a bill of exchange is an English or a French bill, it may happen that a particular aspect of the contract is governed by one legal system and the other aspects are governed by another law. The proper law of the contract may thus be split by applying the laws of different countries to various aspects of the same contract; this split is also called *dépeçage*.[35]

It is conceivable that a manufacturer in Birmingham, through an agent in Melbourne, sells machine tools to an Australian buyer f.o.b. London. The parties may well have intended that the form and essential validity of the contract shall be governed by the law of the State of Victoria (Australia) in the territory of which Melbourne is situate, while the performance of the contract shall be governed by English law because the contract has to be performed in London. In short, "in English law a transaction may be regulated in general by the law of one country although as to parts of that transaction which are to be performed in another country, the law of that other country may be the law admissible."[36]

Thus, in *M.W. Hardy Inc.* v. *A.V. Pound & Co. Ltd.*,[37] although the proper law of contract for the sale of goods f.a.s. Lisbon was held to be English law, its performance was held to be regulated by the law of Portugal, and according to that law, only the Portuguese supplier could obtain the export licence. Another split of the proper law occurs where a bank customer, under the same agreement, maintains accounts with the bank in New York and at its London branch; as the contract between the bank and the customer is, in principle, governed by the law of the place where the account is kept, the New York account is governed by the law of New York and the London account by English law; consequently, a

---

[33] *Black Clawson International Ltd.* v. *Papierwerke Waldorf-Aschaffenburg A.G.* [1981] 2 Lloyd's Rep. 446, 449.

[34] *Per* Mustill J., *ibid.* 456.

[35] On *dépeçage* see Aubrey L. Diamond, "Harmonisation of Private International Law relating to Contractual Obligations", in Academy of International Law, *Recueil des cours*, Vol. 199 (1986–IV), 259, 285.

[36] *Per* Lord Roche in *R.* v. *International Trustee* [1937] A.C. 500, 574.

[37] [1956] A.C. 588; see p. 20, *ante*.

freezing order of the US President did not affect the assets in the London branch.[38]

But the courts will not subject different incidents of the contract to different laws readily or without good reason.[39]

THE LAW INTENDED BY THE PARTIES

The parties to a contract for the sale of goods abroad are well advised to provide expressly which legal system they desire to be applied to their contract. Difficulties will be avoided subsequently if attention is given to this point in time, and with this aim in view it has been suggested that the British exporter should, in his general terms of sale, make express provision for the application of English (or Scottish) law to the contract in question, in short he should embody a *choice of law clause* into his contract. Due attention should be given to the wording of that clause. Sometimes a short clause is chosen to the effect that the contract shall be governed by English law and sometimes the words "in all respects" are added to this clause; this form, without such an addition, is, in fact, adopted by section 1(1) of the Law Reform (Frustrated Contracts) Act 1943. This terminology is not commendable because it can be argued— not necessarily successfully—that the clause is intended to cover the formation of the contract only, and not its performance. This argument is avoided if the parties state in the choice of law clause that both the conclusion and the performance of the contract shall be governed by English law.[40]

The parties may submit their contract to any legal system which they like to elect[41] and, in particular, they are not limited to a legal system with

---

[38] *Libyan Arab Foreign Bank* v. *Bankers Trust Co.* [1988] 1 Lloyd's Rep. 259 (Credit balance in U.S. dollars (Euro-dollars) in London branch of U.S. bank not affected by U.S. order freezing all Libyan assets); *Libyan Arab Foreign Bank* v. *Manufacturers Hanover Trust Co.*, [1988] 2 Lloyd's Rep. 494; *ibid (No. 2)* [1989] 1 Lloyd's Rep. 608. See also *Forsikringsaktieselskapet Vesta* v. *J.N.E. Butcher Bain Dawes Ltd. and the Aquacultural Insurance Service Ltd.* [1989] 1 Lloyd's Rep. 331 (HL) (English reinsurance of Norwegian original insurance covering a fish farm in Norway; although the reinsurance agreement was governed by English law, a clause providing for a 24 hours watch of the fish farm in the reinsurance contract had to be construed according to the law governing the original insurance, *i.e.* Norwegian law, because the reinsurance contract expressly incorporated the clauses of the original insurance).
[39] Lord MacDermott in *Kahler* v. *Midland Bank* [1950] A.C. 24, 42.
[40] See p. 76, *ante*.
[41] But submission to the law of a particular legal system does not necessarily mean that there is a submission to the jurisdiction of the courts of that country. If that is intended it should be expressly stated: *Dundee Ltd.* v. *Gilman & Co. (Australia) Pty. Ltd.* [1968] 2 Lloyd's Rep. 394 (Sup.Ct. of N.S. Wales). (on p. 215, *post*). See also *Amin Rasheed Shipping Corporation* v. *Kuwait Insurance Co.* [1984] A.C. 50, where it was held that the proper law was English law but that the courts of Kuwait had jurisdiction.

which the circumstances surrounding their contract have an actual connection.[42] In one case[43] goods were shipped from a port in Newfoundland
to New York in a vessel owned by a Nova Scotian (Canadian) company
but the bill of lading embodied a clause providing that the contract should
be governed by English law. The shippers brought an action in the courts
of Nova Scotia against the shipowners in respect of damage to the goods,
and the shipowners pleaded that they were exempt from liability by virtue
of the Hague Rules,[44] which formed part of English law. It was contended
on behalf of the shippers that the choice of English law in the bill of
lading failed as there was nothing to connect the contract in any way with
English law. The Judicial Committee of the Privy Council, which heard
the case on appeal from the Supreme Court in Nova Scotia, rejected this
argument in no uncertain terms.[45]

> Connection with English law is not as a matter of principle essential. The provision
> in a contract (*e.g.* of sale) for English arbitration imports English law as the law
> governing the transaction, and those familiar with international business are aware how
> frequent such a provision is, even where the parties are not English and the
> transactions are carried out completely outside England.

The discretion of the parties to elect the law applicable to the contract is,
however, not entirely unlimited: the parties must exercise this discretion
bona fide and for a legal purpose. They cannot adopt a particular legal
system, *e.g.* American law, for the majority of their stipulations and
submit one provision, *e.g.* a restraint of trade, to another law, *e.g.*
English law; in this case the choice of English law would not be exercised
bona fide and for a legal purpose and the arrangement would fail if it
would be evident that it was adopted with the aim of evading the
American Anti-Trust Acts.

In United Kingdom law, the mandatory provisions of the Unfair
Contract Terms Act 1977[46] cannot be contracted out by a choice of law
clause adopting foreign law if:

> (*a*) the term [*i.e.* the choice of law clause] appears to the court, or arbitrator or
>   arbiter to have been imposed wholly or mainly for the purpose of enabling the
>   party imposing it to evade the operation of this Act; or
> (*b*) in the making of the contract one of the parties dealt as a consumer, and he was
>   then habitually resident in the United Kingdom, and the essential steps necessary

---

[42] The position in the USA is somewhat different. The UCC section 1–105 (1) requires that
"a reasonable relation" should exist between the chosen law and the transaction and the
New York courts have so decided in numerous cases. But, in order to make New York law
and the New York forum more acceptable in large commercial transactions, the law was
changed in New York by adding Title 14 to the General Obligations Law; this change came
into effect on July 19, 1984; this law provides that, where the parties in a non-consumer
contract agree on New York law, their choice shall be honoured and, where they have
agreed to the jurisdiction of the New York courts, the defence of *forum non conveniens*
shall not be available; see Graham A. Penn and Thomas W. Cashel, "Choice of Law under
English and New York Law" in [1986] J.B.L. 500.
[43] *Vita Food Products Inc.* v. *Unus Shipping Co.* [1939] A.C. 277.
[44] See p. 562, *post*.
[45] *Vita Food* case, at p. 290.
[46] Sections 2 to 7 and 16 to 21. See also Sale of Goods Act 1979, s.56.

for the making of the contract were taken there, whether by him or by others on his behalf.[47]

But these mandatory provisions do not apply to international supply contracts, as defined in section 26.[48] On the other hand, if the parties to a contract which would be governed by foreign law agree on a choice of law clause adopting English or Scots law, the mandatory provisions of the Unfair Contract Terms Act 1977 do not apply.[49] The intention of the legislator is to exempt all international supply contracts from the operation of the mandatory provisions of the Act.

Other mandatory provisions which cannot be contracted out are contained in the Carriage of Goods by Sea Act 1971. This enactment gives effect in the United Kingdom to the Hague-Visby Rules relating to Bills of Lading.[50] These Rules lay down certain maximum limits of the carrier's liability for loss of or damage to the goods.[51] It was held by the House of Lords in *The Hollandia* (also called *The Morviken*)[52] that a choice of law clause subjecting the contract of carriage to a foreign law admitting lower limits of liability of the carrier was invalid because these provisions of the Hague-Visby Rules were mandatory.

Where the parties have not expressly stated which law shall govern their contract, it may still be possible to gather their intention from other contract clauses. Thus, in one case[53] concerning the insurance of ships 30 per cent. of the cover was placed in London, 39 per cent. in the United States, and the balance in other countries. The insurance was effected in the United States, in particular by brokers in San Francisco. The policies contained a "follow London" clause which began: "Assurers herein shall follow Lloyd's underwriters and/or British insurance companies in regard to amounts, terms, conditions, alterations, additions, extensions, endorsements, cancellations, surveys and settlements of claims hereunder. . . ." But it contained also a "New York suable clause" which enabled the assured to sue at their option in New York or any other American

---

[47] s.27(2).
[48] See p. 100, *ante*.
[49] s.27(1).
[50] See p. 564, *post*.
[51] See p. 602, *post*.
[52] [1983] 1 A.C. 565; see also *The Benarty*, [1984] 3 W.L.R. 1082. This subject is treated on p. 566, *post*.
[53] *Armadora Occidental S.A.* v. *Horace Mann Insurance Co.* [1977] 2 Lloyd's Rep. 406. See also *Cantieri Navali Riuniti SpA* v. *NV Omne Justitia. The Stolt Marmaro (formerly Stolt Argobay).* [1985] 2 Lloyd's Rep. 428. These cases concerned insurances underwritten by several underwriters in different countries and dealt, inter alia, with the construction of the "follow London" clause.
    Particular difficulty arises in reinsurance contracts which may be governed by a different law from that of the original insurances (but may, on occasion, incorporate the law of the original insurance for the construction of certain clauses), see *Citadel Insurance Co.* v. *Atlantic Union Insurance Co. SA* [1982] 2 Lloyd's Rep. 543; *Forsikringsaktieselskapet Vesta* v. *J.N.E. Butcher Bain Dawes Ltd. and the Aquacultural Insurance Service Ltd.* [1988] 1 Lloyd's Rep. 19 (see p. 211, *ante*).

State. The assured—the shipowners—were keen to bring proceedings in the English courts and applied for leave to serve proceedings out of the jurisdiction. The English courts would assume jurisdiction only if the assured could bring their case under the Rules of the Supreme Court 1965, Ord. 11, r. 1(1)(*f*) which provide that the contract "by its terms or by implication [is] governed by English law."[54] The Court of Appeal held that the "follow London" clause revealed such intention. Lord Denning said[55]: " . . . the New York suable clause does not alter in any way the effect of the 'follow London' clause. The judge said, and I would entirely agree with him, that the clause is of paramount importance. It shows that the contract is to be construed, interpreted and applied according to English law."

THE LAW WITH WHICH THE CONTRACT IS MOST CLOSELY CONNECTED

If the parties have omitted to state the law which is to govern their contract and if their intention cannot be gathered from the terms of the contract, it is the task of the courts to ascertain the legal system with which the contract is most closely connected.[56] All the circumstances surrounding the contract have to be examined to ascertain that law.

> The single facts to which the courts have attached importance are manifold. Amongst them are: the place where the contract has been concluded, the place where the contract has to be performed, the language and terminology employed by the parties, the form of the documents made with respect to the transaction, the personality of the parties, the subject-matter of the contract, a submission to arbitration, the situation of the funds which are liable for the discharge, or security of the obligation, a connection with a preceding transaction, the effect attributed to the transaction by a particular legal system.[57]

The question is which of these facts, or combination of facts, shall prevail in indicating the law of the closest connection. Some of these factors require more detailed examination.

The form of the contract

The form of the contract may give a clue to the ascertainment of the law of the closest connection but, as such, it carries as little weight as the

---

[54] See p. 695, *post*. The reference to Order 11, r.1(1)(f) is to the arrangement of the Order before the relevant provisions of the Civil Jurisdiction and Judgments Act 1982 came into operation. The reference would now be to Order 11, r.1(1)(d)(iii).
[55] [1977] 2 Lloyd's Rep. 406, 412.
[56] *Re United Railways of Havana and Regla Warehouse Ltd.* [1961] A.C. 1007 (overruled on another point by *Miliangos* v. *George Frank Textiles Ltd.* [1976] A.C. 443); also *Bonython* v. *Commonwealth of Australia* [1951] A.C. 201; *Offshore International S.A.* v. *Banco Central S.A.* [1976] 2 Lloyd's Rep. 402, 404; *Amin Rasheed Shipping Corporation* v. *Kuwait Insurance Co.* [1984] A.C. 50, 71. Also *Citadel Insurance Co.* v. *Atlantic Union Insurance Co. S.A.* [1982] 2 Lloyd's Rep. 543. *Libyan Arab Foreign Bank* v. *Bankers Trust Co.* [1989] 3 W.L.R. 314 (the law governing the relationship of the bank and its customer is normally the law of the location of the bank).
[57] Clive M. Schmitthoff, *The English Conflict of Laws* (3rd ed., 1954), pp. 110, 111.

language which the parties have used. Lord Wilberforce said in *Amin Rasheed Shipping Corporation* v. *Kuwait Insurance Co*[58]: "The simple proposition that because a form of contract has to be interpreted in accordance with English rules, or even decisions, the proper law must be English would have very unfortunate consequences."[59] In this case the plaintiffs, a Liberian shipping company, insured a cargo vessel, the *Al Wahab*, with the defendants, an insurance company in Kuwait. At that time, no marine insurance law existed in Kuwait and the insurers used their standard policy which was in the English language and followed meticulously (with minor and immaterial omissions of express references to London) the old Lloyd's S.G. policy.[60] The *Al Wahab* became a total loss. The assured wished to litigate in the English courts and asked for leave to serve a writ on the insurers out of the jurisdiction. The House of Lords held that the proper law of the contract of insurance was English law but, in the exercise of its discretion, refused leave to serve the writ out of the jurisdiction. The result was that the case had to be decided by the Kuwaiti courts but that, in the opinion of the House of Lords, these courts would have to apply English law. The House of Lords founded the view that the law of the closest connection of the contract of insurance was English law, not solely on the form and language of the policy but it applied "the classic process of weighing the factors . . . with all the difficulties inherent in the process."[61] The main consideration of the learned law lords was that the S.G. policy could only be interpreted by reference to the U.K. Marine Insurance Act 1906 and the judicial exegesis of its provisions.[62]

The place where the contract was concluded

The place where the contract was concluded is an indication of considerable importance in cases in which the contract has to be performed in the same place or a place of the same jurisdiction. Here the

---

[58] [1984] A.C. 50, 70.

[59] Thus, in *Compagnie Tunisienne de Navigation S.A.* v. *Compagnie d'Armement Maritime S.A.* [1971] A.C. 572 (see p. 217, *post*) an English standard form—a tanker voyage charterparty—was used, to which some clauses were added in French. The House of Lords held that, in spite of the use of the English form, the proper law of the contract was French law.

[60] This form is now obsolete, see p. 512, *post*.

[61] *Per* Lord Wilberforce [1984] A.C. 50, 71.

[62] If the determination of the proper law solely depends on the construction of English legal documents and no oral evidence on the meaning of them is offered, the English courts are more suitable to construe these documents than foreign courts which may not be acquainted with the English rules of construction: *Seashell Shipping Corporation of Panama* v. *Mutualidad de Seguros del Instituto Nacional de Industria, The Times*, August 11, 1988. On concurrent proceedings, see p. 698, *post*.

form, construction and essential validity of the contract is likely to be governed by the law of that country.[63] But the evidence may show that the parties intended the application of another legal system to their agreement.[64]

When, as frequently is the case in export sales, the contract is concluded between persons who are not present in the same locality, the contract is deemed to be concluded at the place where its definite and unequivocal acceptance is effected because this act transforms the arrangement from mere negotiations to an enforceable legal obligation.[65] Thus, if a merchant in London receives a shipment order from a buyer in India on terms c.i.f. Calcutta and accepts this order, the courts are likely to hold that the contract is governed by English law, for it is concluded in this country and to be performed here by delivery of the goods on board a ship sailing for the agreed port of destination.[66]

The place where the contract is to be performed

The place of performance is a very weighty factor to be taken into consideration when determining the law of the closest connection, even in cases where it is not the same as the place at which the contract was concluded. In a case[67] where a merchant residing in Malta bought goods from merchants carrying on business in Gibraltar, the contract, which provided for delivery f.o.b. Gibraltar, was concluded in Malta. The Maltese buyer rejected the goods on the ground of their inferior quality but he had, before rejecting them, tendered them to his sub-purchasers, who refused to accept them. According to the law of Gibraltar (which in this respect was identical with English law, now the Sale of Goods Act 1979, s.35), the buyer had lost the right of rescission because by tendering the goods to his sub-purchasers he had done an act inconsistent with the ownership of the seller in the goods; by the law of Malta (which is the civil law) the buyer was still entitled to rescind. The Privy Council which heard the case on appeal from Malta, concluded that under the f.o.b clause the contract "was to be performed by the delivery of the goods on

---

[63] *Jacobs* v. *Credit Lyonnais* (1884) 12 Q.B.D. 589; *Citadel Insurance Co.* v. *Atlantic Insurance Co. S.A.* [1982] 2 Lloyd's Rep. 543 (reinsurance contract concluded in London through London brokers); *Islamic Arab Insurance Co.* v. *Saudi Egyptian American Reinsurance Co.* [1987] 1 Lloyd's Rep. 315 (reinsurance contract concluded in London; Bingham L.J. (on p. 320): "It now seems more likely that perfection of the contracts in London was not a purely formal act.")

[64] *N.V. Handel My. J. Smits Import-Export* v. *English Exporters Ltd.* [1955] 2 Lloyd's Rep. 317, 323.

[65] See p. 90, *ante.*

[66] *Johnson* v. *Taylor Bros. & Co. Ltd.* [1920] A.C. 144.

[67] *Benaim & Co.* v. *Debono* [1924] A.C. 514; *Compagnie Tunisienne de Navigation S.A.* v. *Compagnie d'Armement Maritime S.A.* [1971] A.C. 572 (H.L.).

board a ship at Gibraltar selected by the buyer," and that the buyer's right of rescission was consequently to be determined by the law of Gibraltar.

In *Compagnie d'Armement Maritime S.A.* v. *Compagnie Tunisienne de Navigation*[68] a Tunisian company, Compagnie Tunisienne, and French shipowners, Compagnie d'Armement Maritime, concluded a contract through brokers in Paris for the transport of specified quantities of crude oil from one Tunisian port to another. The brokers used an English printed standard form, a tanker voyage charterparty, and adapted it for this transport by adding some clauses. The contract was negotiated and signed in France and the freight was payable in Paris in French francs. Two clauses in the charterparty were relevant. One of them provided that the contract should be governed by the laws of the flag of the vessel carrying the goods, and the other stipulated that disputes should be settled by arbitrators in London. The French shipowners found that their own vessels flying the French flag were not large enough to carry the cargo and chartered six other vessels to perform the contract. These vessels were Norwegian, Swedish, Liberian (two), French and Bulgarian. Disputes arose between the parties and it had to be determined, as a preliminary question, which law governed the contract. The arbitrators and the judge in the Commercial Court held that French law was the proper law. The Court of Appeal reversed the learned judge and held that it was English law because the choice of law clause referring to the law of the flag had failed by employing substitute vessels flying different flags and the choice of London as the place of arbitration carried with it the implied choice of English law as the substantive law governing the contract. The House of Lords reversed this decision and held that the proper law of the contract was French law. This conclusion was unanimous but the judges were not in agreement in their reasoning. Lord Morris of Borth-y-Gest, Viscount Dilhorne and Lord Diplock thought that the clause in favour of the law of the flag was decisive because the parties intended that the contract should primarily be performed by the vessels of the shipowners which flew the French flag. Lord Reid and Lord Wilberforce considered French law as the law of the closest connection.[69] All members of the House of Lords were agreed that the arbitration clause was no more than one indication which—as in the present case— had to give way to other indications.

Where an irrevocable and unconfirmed letter of credit[70] was issued, the law of the place where the advising bank carried on business was, as regards the relationship between that bank and the seller (the beneficiary

---

[68] [1971] A.C. 572.
[69] The case was argued in the English courts on the assumption that the law of Tunisia was the same as French law because they were both based on the Napoleonic Code.
[70] See p. 419, *post*. The same principle applies, *a fortiori*, to a confirmed credit.

under the credit), the law of the closest and most real connection.[71] Otherwise "the advising banks would have constantly to be seeking to apply a whole variety of foreign laws."[72] But the law governing the relationship between the buyer and the seller, or between the buyer and the issuing bank, or between the issuing and advising bank may well be another system of law.[73]

The place where an arbitration is to be held

The general principles

An export sale often embodies a clause providing for an arbitration to be held by a particular arbitrator or at a particular place. The contract may, *e.g.* provide that any difference or dispute shall be referred to the arbitration by the London Court of International Arbitration.[74] In arbitrations, three problems relating to the conflict of laws may arise:

1. is a contract clause providing for arbitration to be held at a specified place an indication that the substantive law of the contract shall be the law of that place;
2. what is the law governing the arbitration agreement; and
3. what is the law applicable to the arbitration procedure (the curial law)?

"In the great majority of cases, these three laws will be the same. But this will not always be so. It is by no means uncommon for the proper law of the substantive contract to be different from the *lex fori*; and it does happen, although much more rarely, that the law governing the arbitration agreement is also different from the *lex fori*."[75]

As regards the law governing the substantive contract

As regards the first of these questions, an arbitration clause stating a venue for the arbitration is an indication—and a fairly strong one— supporting the inference that the parties intend to submit their substantive contract to the law of the place of arbitration because it can be assumed that they intend that the arbitrator should apply the law with

---

[71] *Offshore International S.A.* v. *Banco Central S.A.* [1976] 2 Lloyd's Rep. 402.
[72] *Per* Ackner J., *ibid.* 404.
[73] This topic is treated more fully on pp. 419–420, *post*.
[74] See p. 680, *post*.
[75] *Per* Mustill J. in *Black Clawson International Ltd.* v. *Papierwerke Waldhof-Aschaffenburg A.G.* [1981] 2 Lloyd's Rep. 446, 453: *Naviera Amazonica Peruana SA* v. *Compania Internacional de Seguros del Peru* [1988] 1 Lloyd's Rep. 116, 119.

which he is best acquainted.[76] In one case[77] the arbitration clause contained the usual reference to the English Arbitration Acts[78]; it was ruled that that reference supported the inference that the arbitration was to be conducted according to English law and that, consequently, the substantive contract itself was to be governed by English law. In another case[79] Swedish sellers of a ship agreed with the Greek buyer that disputes should be settled by arbitration in the City of London and the Court of Appeal held, in the words of Lord Denning M.R.,[80] "that, by choosing the City of London as the place of arbitration, the parties have impliedly chosen English law as the proper law of the contract." But it should not be forgotten that the place of arbitration is only one of the factors to be taken into account in determining the law of the closest connection. Other factors have also to be taken into consideration and it may well be that in "the classic process of weighing the factors"[81] the other factors will prevail. This, indeed, happened in the *Compagnie Tunisienne* case.[82]

If the parties have agreed on ICC arbitration,[83] two possibilities exist. They may have agreed that such arbitration should be held at a certain place, *e.g.* Geneva, or they may simply have agreed on ICC arbitration, leaving it to the Court of Arbitration of the ICC to fix the venue. In the former case the place of arbitration may have some indicative value though it is best in these cases to determine the law of the closest connection of the substantive contract by reference to other indications but the use of the place of arbitration as one of them is not excluded. Thus, an alleged agency agreement between a Milanese insurance company and underwriting agents who were a company incorporated in the British Virgin Islands and managed from the Channel Islands, provided for ICC arbitration in Geneva.[84] Lloyd J. held that the contract—if there was one—was governed by Italian law and continued[85]:

> If I were wrong in thinking that Italian law governed, I would choose the next law of the Canton of Geneva. I would do that because although the law of the place where the arbitration is to take place is no longer conclusive, it is still a very strong factor particularly in contracts between the nationals of different States. Why should the parties have chosen arbitration under the ICC Rules in Geneva rather than, say, in

---

[76] *Maritime Insurance Co. Ltd.* v. *Assecuranz Union von 1865* (1935) 52 Ll.L.R. 16; *Hamlyn & Co.* v. *Talisker Distillery* [1894] A.C. 202. See further, *Kianta Osakeyhtio* v. *Britain & Overseas Trading Co. Ltd.* [1954] 1 Lloyds Rep. 247; *Tzortzis* v. *Monark Line A/B* [1968] 1 W.L.R. 406 (C.A.); *Steel Authority of India Ltd.* v. *Hind Metals Inc.* [1984] 1 Lloyd's Rep. 405, 409.

[77] *Spurrier* v. *La Cloche* [1902] A.C. 446.

[78] The reference was to the predecessors of the Acts referred to on pp. 656–657, *post.*

[79] *Tzortzis* v. *Monark Line A/B* [1968] 1 W.L.R. 406.

[80] *Ibid.* 412.

[81] Lord Wilberforce in the *Amin Rasheed* case, on p. 215, *ante.*

[82] See p. 217, *ante.*

[83] See p. 676, *post.*

[84] *Atlantic Underwriting Agencies Ltd.* v. *Compagnia de Assicurazione di Milano SpA* [1979] 2 Lloyd's Rep. 240.

[85] *Ibid.* 245.

Paris, unless they intended Swiss law to apply to the substance as well as to the procedure, especially as procedure is to some extent governed by the ICC Rules themselves?

If the parties have agreed on ICC arbitration without fixing a venue, the place of arbitration is purely coincidental and does not support the inference that the parties intended the law of the place of arbitration to govern their contract.

As regards the law governing the arbitration procedure

The law governing the arbitration agreement and the arbitration procedure are normally the same but may, as already observed, be different from the substantive law of the contract. Every arbitration has a "seat" or venue or forum.[86] "[I]n the absence of any contractual provision to the contrary, the procedural (or curial) law governing arbitrations is that of the forum of the arbitration . . . since this is the system of law with which the agreement to arbitrate in the particular forum will have its closest connection."[87]

As every arbitration must have a local seat, "de-localised" arbitration is not recognised in English law.[88] However, this statement should not be misunderstood. If the parties have adopted the UNCITRAL Arbitration Rules, *e.g.* in an ad hoc arbitration[89] or have agreed on a system of institutional arbitration, *e.g.* under the Rules of the ICC Court of Arbitration,[90] a practically self-contained code of arbitration procedure applies, and the need to refer to the local procedural regulation of the seat arises only if the code contains gaps or any of its provisions are inapplicable.

The place where the arbitration is actually held need not be the seat of the arbitration. The arbitrator and the parties may agree that, for reasons of convenience, the hearings shall take place at another locality. In this case the arbitrator has to apply the procedural rules of the seat of

---

[86] *Naviera Amazonica Peruana SA* v. *Compania Internacional de Seguros del Peru* [1988] 1 Lloyd's Rep. 116. 119.
[87] *Per* Kerr L.J. in *Bank Mellat* v. *Helliniki Techniki SA* [1984] Q.B. 291, 301. Also *Whitworth Street Estates (Manchester) Ltd.* v. *James Miller & Partners Ltd.* [1970] A.C. 583; (see p. 654, *post*). *Black Clawson International Ltd.* v. *Papierwerke Waldhof-Aschaffenburg A.G.* [1981] 2 Lloyd's Rep. 446.; *Naviera Amazonica Peruana SA* v. *Compania Internacional de Seguros del Peru* [1988] 1 Lloyd's Rep. 116. There are, however, rare exceptions from the rule that the law of arbitration procedure is that of the venue of the arbitration; see *Dallal* v. *Bank Mellat,* [1986] Q.B. 441 *cf.* pp. 654–655 *post*. On the application of the transitional lex mercatoria, see p. 654, *post*.
[88] Kerr L.J. in the *Naviera Amazonica Peruana* case, on p. 119; Mustill L.J. in Bos and Browlie's "Liber Amicorum for Lord Wilberforce." 1987, 149.
[89] See pp. 653 and 674, *post*.
[90] See p. 616, *post*.

arbitration, and not those of the place where the arbitration is held. In one case[91] a construction contract between the Turkish government and an English company provided for arbitration in Ankara; at the first hearing, which took place in Ankara, the arbitration tribunal and the parties resolved that for reasons of convenience further hearings should be held in Frankfurt, where the chairman of the arbitration tribunal was resident, but the rules of procedure which the tribunal, sitting in Frankfurt, applied were the Turkish rules of arbitration procedure.

The Foreign Limitation Periods Act 1984

The preceding observations dealt mainly with the ascertainment of the *substantive law* applicable to the contract. We have seen that a different problem is the ascertainment of the *procedural rules* applying to a case pending before the courts or an arbitrator, and that the judge or the arbitrator will normally apply his own rules of procedure, *i.e.* the *lex fori.*

Here the following problem arises. Every legal system provides a time bar for commencing proceedings in litigation or arbitration. In English law the periods of limitation are laid down in the Limitation Act 1980. Speaking generally, they are in actions founded on a simple contract six years after the cause of action accrued and in actions upon a deed twelve years from that date. Special provisions apply for actions founded on tort or in actions based on fraud. Foreign legal systems provide other—and sometimes longer—periods of limitation. The attempt to unify at least the limitation periods in the international sale of goods is not far progressed.[92]

In English private international law the limitation of actions is classified as pertaining to the procedural rules but in many foreign legal systems it forms part of the substantive law. Consequently, if proceedings were brought in England upon a contract governed by foreign law, the judge or arbitrator had to apply the English periods of limitation, as laid down in the Limitation Act 1980, as part of the *lex fori.* A plaintiff could thus lose the benefit of a longer period of limitation which he may have enjoyed under the foreign law applying to the substantive contract or a defendant the benefit of a shorter period of limitation. To remedy this injustice, Parliament passed the *Foreign Limitation Periods Act 1984,* which came into operation on October 1, 1985.[93] The Act provides that, in principle, where a foreign law has to be applied by the English courts or an arbitrator in England, the foreign rules of limitation shall likewise apply (s.1(1)). The same is the case if both the law of England and Wales and

---

[91] An unreported case; the author was a member of the arbitration tribunal.
[92] See p. 254, *post.*
[93] Foreign Limitation Periods Act 1984 (Commencement) Order 1985 (S.I. 1985 No. 1276).

that of a foreign country have to be taken into account (s.1(2)). But there
are exceptions to this principle; the foreign limitation rules shall not apply
to the extent to which they conflict with English public policy (s.2(1)); it
is expressly provided that such a conflict exists if the application of the
foreign limitation rules "would cause undue hardship[93a] to a person who
is, or might be made, a party to the action or proceedings" (s.2(2)). The
reference to the foreign law is to the internal foreign law and does not
include a reference to the foreign private international law (s.1(5)).[94]

Conversely, the decision of a foreign court on a limitation point shall
be regarded as a decision "on the merits," *i.e.* on a substantive point of
law, and this includes even a decision of the foreign court on the English
rules on limitation (s.3).

As already indicated, the provisions of the Act apply to arbitration
proceedings (s.5).

THE EC CONVENTION ON THE LAW APPLICABLE TO CONTRACTUAL OBLIGATIONS

As already observed,[95] this Convention was adopted by the EC on June
19, 1980 in Rome it has been ratified by the following Member States

Belgium, Denmark, France, Germany (West), Greece, Italy and Luxembourg.

The Rome Convention will probably be ratified by the United
Kingdom soon and its provisions will be introduced into UK law by
an enactment likely to be known as the *Contracts (Applicable Law)
Act 1990*.[96] The aim of the Convention is to provide a uniform
regulation for the ascertainment of the law governing contracts in all
Member States of the EC.[97] But the Convention regulates not only
conflict situations between the laws of the Member States. It will
apply also to cases in which the law of a Member State conflicts with
that of a non-Member State.[98]

[93a] On the interpretation of "undue hardship" see *Jones* v. *Trollope Colls Cementation
Overseas Ltd, The Times*, January 26, 1990; and *The Komninos S, Financial Times*, January
16, 1990.
[94] This provision is intended to exclude *renvoi* from the foreign law to English law.
[95] See p. 207, *ante.*
[96] A Bill to this effect was introduced by the Government into Parliament on November 28,
1989. The Rome Convention is appended to the Bill as Schedule 1. On this Convention, see
Dicey and Morris, on The Conflict of Laws, (11th ed., 1987), p. 1253. Further P.M. North,
"The EEC Convention on the Law Applicable to Contractual Obligations" in [1980] J.B.L.
382. Aubrey L. Diamond, "Harmonisation of Private International Law relating to
Contractual Obligations," Hague Academy of International Law." *Recueil des cours* Vol.
199 (1986—IV), 235.
[97] It was originally intended that the Convention should also regulate the law applicable to
claims arising in tort but this plan was abandoned.
[98] Art. 1(1).

The provisions of the Convention do not apply to bills of exchange, cheques and promissory notes, to agreements for arbitration or the choice of a court, to insurance contracts covering risks situated in an EC country,[99] to the internal law of companies, to trusts and to the question whether an agent is liable to bind a principal to a third party.[1]

Two basic principles are adopted by the Convention. They are the same as those developed by the English courts and explained earlier. The first is that of freedom of choice: the proper law of the contract shall be the law intended by the parties.[2] The second is that, if the parties have failed to choose the proper law, it shall be the law with which the contract is mostly closely connected.[3] But the rules provided by the Convention for the application of these principles may in some cases lead to results different from those at which English law would arrive.

As far as the first of these basic principles is concerned, the Convention imposes similar restraints on the freedom of choice as exist in English law, *viz.* the parties cannot contract out of the mandatory provisions of the law of a particular country if all the other elements at the time of the choice are connected with that country only.[4]

As regards the ascertainment of the law of the closest connection, there exist considerable differences from English law. Here the Convention establishes a—rebuttable—presumption[5] that that law shall be the law of the "characteristic performance."[6] This is a concept so far unknown in English law. The Convention provides:

> . . . it shall be presumed that the contract is most closely connected with the country where the party who is to effect the performance which is characteristic of the contract has, at the time of conclusion of the contract, his habitual residence, or, in the case of a body corporate or incorporate, its central administration. However, if the contract is entered into in the course of that party's trade or profession, that country shall be the country in which the principal place of business is situated or, where under the terms of the contract the performance is to be effected through a place of business other than the principal place of business, the country in which that other place of business is situated.

It should be noted that the law of characteristic performance is not the law where performance has to be carried out but it is the law of the place

---

[99] But contracts of reinsurance fall under the Convention even in these cases.
[1] For a complete catalogue of the transactions to which the Convention does not apply, see art. 1(2) and (3).
[2] Art. 3(1). Dépeçage (see p. 210, *ante*) is admitted by this provision.
[3] Art. 4(1). Here again, dépeçage is admitted.
[4] Art. 3(3).
[5] Modern English law has abandoned the use of presumptions for the determination of the law of the closest connection because, in surveying the whole array of factors and indications, they introduce an element of rigidity. This—the desire to make the law certain—is exactly the reason why the Convention has reintroduced the old notion of presumptions.
[6] Art. 4(2).

where the party who has to effect the characteristic performance has his seat of business. This presumption may change the balance of indications which English law would apply. If, *e.g.* an oil company in Paris sells oil f.o.b. Rotterdam to an oil company in Italy, the presumption of the Convention would point to French law, and not to Dutch law. In a contract of sale, the characteristic performance is effected by the seller who has to deliver the goods, and not by the buyer who has to pay the price.

The Convention contains special rules applying to certain consumer contracts[7] and individual employment contracts.[8] They provide, in essence, that a consumer or an employee shall not be deprived by a choice of law of the parties of the protection afforded by the mandatory rules of the country in which he has his habitual residence. The Convention also provides that the application of a rule of a foreign law, which by virtue of the Convention would apply, may be refused if such application is "manifestly incompatible" with the public policy (*ordre public*) of the forum.[9]

A problem arises when the law determining the existence and validity of a contract or a contractual term is in issue. Here the Convention provides that this shall be the law which would govern the contract or term on the assumption that it would be valid.[10] This law has been called the putative proper law.[11]

A controversial provision of the Convention is article 7. It states that, when applying the law of a country, the judge or arbitrator may give effect to the mandatory rules of another country with which the situation has *a close connection*, "if and so far as, under the law of the latter country, those rules must be applied whatever the law applicable to the contract." This extension of the effect of mandatory rules goes beyond the effect of those rules in the law of the *closest connection* and might even admit the extraterritorial effect of mandatory rules of a third country. Objection is raised to this extension in the United Kingdom and the Bill at present before Parliament (see p. 222 n. 96, *ante*) proposes that article 7 shall not apply in the United Kingdom.[12]

MONEY OF ACCOUNT AND OF PAYMENT; RECOVERY IN FOREIGN CURRENCY

The parties may agree that a monetary obligation, *e.g.* the purchase price, shall be expressed in one currency but the debtor shall be at liberty

---

[7] Art. 5.
[8] Art. 6.
[9] Art. 16.
[10] Art. 8.
[11] *Dicey and Morris on the Conflict of Laws*, 11th ed, 1987, p. 1253.
[12] Clause 1(2)(2).

to discharge this obligation in another. The currency in which the debtor's liability is measured is the *currency of account*, and the currency in which he may pay is the *currency of payment*. The effect of this distinction is that, if at the date of discharge the rate of exchange of the currency of payment has fallen against the currency of account, the buyer must acquire more currency of payment in order to satisfy his obligation. Thus, in one case[13] the Nigerian Produce Marketing Board sold Woodhouse a quantity of cocoa under contracts providing for delivery c.i.f. Liverpool. The purchase price was expressed in Nigerian currency, at that time the Nigerian pound,[14] which was equivalent to the pound sterling. In response to the request of the buyers, the sellers agreed that the buyers may pay the price in pounds sterling. Before payment was made, the pound sterling was devalued but the Nigerian pound retained its value. The House of Lords held that the money of account was still the Nigerian currency, notwithstanding the sellers' agreement to accept pounds sterling in discharge of the buyers' liability.

The distinction between the money of account and the money of payment has lost some of its importance because it is now possible to obtain judgments in foreign currency in the English courts if the contractual obligation is expressed in that currency or payment in a foreign currency was reasonably in the contemplation of the parties at the time when the contract was concluded; the conversion into pounds sterling then takes place at the date when enforcement of the foreign currency judgment is sought.[15] Arbitration awards can likewise be obtained in foreign currency in appropriate cases.[16] Further, judgments on a bill of exchange expressed in a foreign currency but payable in England may be obtained in the foreign currency.[17] It is also possible to recover damages in contract or tort in foreign currency if the loss was sustained in that currency.[18] Unless the contract provides that damages shall be paid in

---

[13] *Woodhouse A.C. Israel Cocoa S.A.* v. *Nigerian Produce Marketing Co.* [1972] A.C. 741; see also *W. J. Alan & Co. Ltd.* v. *El Nasr Export & Import Co.* [1972] 2 Q.B. 189; *President of India* v. *Lips Maritime Corporation. The Lips.* [1987] 3 W.L.R. 572 (freight and demurrage under a charterparty fixed in U.S. dollars but payable in "British external sterling; delay in payment of demurrage is not a cause of action in damages).

[14] It is now called Naira.

[15] *Miliangos* v. *George Frank Textiles Ltd.* [1976] A.C. 443; *Schorsch Meier GmbH* v. *Hennin* [1975] Q.B. 416.

[16] *Jugoslavenska Oceanska Plovidba* v. *Castle Investment Co. Inc.* [1974] Q.B. 292.

[17] *Barclays Bank International Ltd.* v. *Levin Brothers (Bradford) Ltd.* [1977] Q.B. 270. That is so notwithstanding that according to the Bills of Exchange Act 1882, s.74(4), such a bill shall be payable at the "rate of exchange for sight drafts at the place of payment on the day the bill is payable."

[18] *Jean Kraut A.C.* v. *Albany Fabrics* [1977] Q.B. 182; *The Despina R.* [1978] 3 W.L.R. 804. *Services Europe Atlantique Sud* v. *Stockholm Rederiaktiebolag Svea, The Folias* [1978] 2 W.L.R. 887. *George Veflings Rederi A/S* v. *President of India; The Bellami* [1978] 1 W.L.R. 982; *B.P. Exploration Co. (Libya) Ltd.* v. *Hunt (No. 2)* [1979] 1 W.L.R. 783, 837; *Société Française Bunge SA* v. *Belcan NV. The Federal Huron* [1985] 2 Lloyd's Rep. 189; *Metaalhandel J.A. Magnus BV* v. *Ardfields Transport Ltd; Financial Times*, July 21, 1987 (damages in foreign currency refused because they could not have been in the contemplation of the parties).

the currency of account, the court or arbitrator should fix the damages in the currency which best expresses the party's loss.[19] The *Practice Direction (Judgment: Foreign Currency)*[20] states, *inter alia*:

> The writ or statement of claim in which a claim is made for payment of a debt or liquidated demand in foreign currency must contain the following statements, namely: (i) that the contract under which the debt is claimed in the foreign currency is governed by the law of some country outside the United Kingdom; and (ii) that under *that* contract the money of account in which the debt was payable was the currency of that country or of some other foreign country.

But the creditor is not obliged to claim payment in the foreign currency. If he prefers, he may make his claim in sterling.[21] In the words of Donaldson J.[22]:

> . . . it is for the plaintiff to select the currency in which to make his claim and it is for him to prove that an award or judgment in that currency will most truly express his loss and accordingly most fully and exactly compensate him for that loss . . . while the currency of account is a factor of considerable importance, it is not decisive of the currency in which the plaintiff should make his claim and in which judgment should be given.

In the winding-up of an insolvent company a foreign currency debt, and interest thereon, are converted into sterling on the date of the commencement of winding-up.[23] In the words of Mervin Davies J.,[24] the original " 'money of account' has, as against the bank [the creditor], by virtue of the liquidation, become sterling." The reason is that all creditors of the company should be treated equally in the winding-up. But in the winding-up of a wholly solvent company the position may be different; if the creditor is paid less than his full contractual foreign currency claim, the liquidator may well be obliged to make good the shortfall before distributing the surplus assets to the shareholders.[25]

FOREIGN STATE IMMUNITY

When an enterprise contracts with a foreign State[26] or a foreign State corporation and disputes occur, the question arises whether, if proceed-

---

[19] *The Despina R* [1979] A.C. 685. Where the contract specifies an exchange rate between the moneys of account and payment, that rate must be applied: *The President of India* v. *Taygetos Shipping Co. S.A., The Times*, October 16, 1984. See also *The Lash Atlantico* [1985] 2 Lloyd's Rep. 464.

[20] Issued December 18, 1975; see [1976] 1 W.L.R. 83.

[21] *Ozalid Group (Export) Ltd.* v. *African Continental Bank Ltd.* [1979] 2 Lloyd's Rep. 231.

[22] *Ibid.* 234.

[23] *Re Dynamics Corporation of America* [1976] 1 W.L.R. 757; *Re Lines Bros. Ltd.* [1983] Ch. 1; *Re Lines Bros. Ltd. (No. 2)* [1984] 2 W.L.R. 905.

[24] *Re Lines Bros. Ltd. (No. 2)*, *supra*, 914.

[25] Brightman L.J. in *Re Lines Bros. Ltd.*, *supra*.

[26] The EC is not a "State" within the meaning of the State Immunity Act 1978 and cannot claim immunity under it: *Maclaine Watson & Co. Ltd.* v. *Department of Trade and Industry*, [1988] 3 W.L.R. 1033, 1107 (CA).

ings are commenced, the foreign State or State corporation can plead sovereign immunity and thereby evade its commercial obligations. Here two theories are advanced. Under the doctrine of *absolute immunity* the foreign State or State corporation can always plead immunity. Under the doctrine of *restrictive immunity* a distinction is drawn between acts in the exercise of sovereign authority (*acta jure imperii*) and ordinary commercial transactions (*acta jure gestionis*). Immunity is accorded to the former but refused to the latter.[27]

The State Immunity Act 1978[28] gives effect to the doctrine of restrictive immunity.[29] Section 3 of the Act provides:

(1) A State is not immune as respects proceedings relating to—
    (*a*) a commercial transaction entered into by the State; or
    (*b*) an obligation of the State which by virtue of a contract (whether a commercial transaction or not) falls to be performed wholly or partly in the United Kingdom.

(2) This section does not apply if the parties to the dispute are States or have otherwise agreed in writing; and subsection (1)(*b*) above does not apply if the contract (not being a commercial transaction) was made in the territory of the State concerned and the obligation in question is governed by its administrative law.

(3) In this section "commercial transaction" means—
    (*a*) any contract for the supply of goods or services;
    (*b*) any loan or other transaction for the provision of finance and any guarantee or indemnity in respect of any such transaction or any other financial obligation; and
    (*c*) any other transaction or activity (whether of a commercial, industrial, financial, professional or other similar character) into which a State enters or in which it engages otherwise than in the exercise of sovereign authority;

---

[27] English common law has adopted the principle of restrictive immunity: *I Congreso del Partido* [1983] 1 A.C. 244. Before this decision the restrictive doctrine was already applied by the Privy Council in *The Philippine Admiral* [1977] A.C. 373 and the Court of Appeal, *obiter*, in *Trendtex Trading Corporation* v. *Central Bank of Nigeria* [1977] Q.B. 529. On the concept of sovereignty ("*par in parem*") see Lord Wilberforce in *I Congreso del Partido*, on p. 262c. See further Charles J. Lewis, *State and Diplomatic Immunity* (2nd ed., London, 1985).

An entirely different matter is the rule of public international law sometimes referred to as the act of State doctrine, according to which the courts will not adjudicate on transactions between foreign sovereign States: *Buttes Gas and Oil Co.* v. *Hammer (No. 3)* [1982] A.C. 888. In *MacLaine Watson & Co. Ltd.* v. *International Tin Council*, [1989] Ch. 253 (affd. by H.L. in [1989] 3 W.L.R. 969), Kerr L.J. expressed doubt that the act of State non-justiciability rule could be extended to claims based on commercial agreements. Also Evans J. in *Amalgamated Metal Trading Ltd.* v. *Department of Trade and Industry, The Times*, March 21, 1989 In the USA the Supreme Court admitted the commercial activity exception to the act of State doctrine in the leading case of *Alfred Dunhill* v. *Republic of Cuba*, 425 U.S. 682 (1976); see Stephen J. Leacock, "The Commercial Activity Exception to the Act of State Doctrine revisited: Evolution of a Concept," in 13 *North Carolina Journal of International Law & Commercial Relatons*, 1988, 1.

[28] Which came into operation on November 22, 1978 (The State Immunity Act 1978 (Commencement) Order 1978 (S.I. 1978/1572 (C.44)). See Gillian White, "The State Immunity Act 1978," in [1979] J.B.L. 105.

[29] The Act starts, as Lord Diplock observed in *Alcom Ltd.* v. *Republic of Colombia* [1984] 2 W.L.R. 750, 755, by restating the absolute principle in s.1(1) but it makes the principle subject to wide-ranging exceptions (ss.2–17). In view of the wide extent of these exceptions, the statement in the text is justified.

but neither paragraph of subsection (1) above applies to a contract of employment between a State and an individual.

It should be noted that in the cases mentioned in section 3(3)(*a*) and (*b*) the purpose of the transaction is irrelevant. Thus, a foreign State cannot claim immunity if it has purchased equipment for its army. But in the case of section 3(3)(*c*) transactions *jure imperii* are excluded and the State can rely on its immunity in such transactions.

The Act further deals with State corporations which enjoy separate legal personality.[30] Such a separate entity does not enjoy immunity, except if:

(*a*) the proceedings relate to anything done by it in the exercise of sovereign authority; and

(*b*) the circumstances are such that a State (or in the case of proceedings to which section 10 above applies, a State which is not a party to the Brussels Convention) would have been immune.

The central bank or other monetary authority of a foreign State is not regarded a separate entity within the meaning of these provisions, even if under its own law it has that character, and its property is immune.[31] Where a State has agreed in writing to arbitration, it is not immune as respects proceedings in the courts of the United Kingdom which relate to arbitration; such an agreement may be entered into even before a dispute has arisen.[32]

It is possible to execute a judgment or arbitration award in respect of State property which is for the time being in use or intended for use for commercial purposes[33] and such property is likewise subject to execution if it is intended to enforce a foreign judgment or arbitration award in the United Kingdom, provided that the conditions for such enforcement are satisfied. It is not, however, possible to obtain an injunction against a foreign State even in commercial matters[34]—a decided shortcoming of the Act. It is, however, thought that one can obtain an injunction against a third party, *e.g.* a bank, which holds commercial property of the State because that possibility is not expressly barred by the Act. The account of a foreign diplomatic mission with a commercial bank cannot be attached by way of execution of a judgment[35] against the mission, if the money in the account is intended to be used for the day-to-day expenditure of the mission because this is not a "commercial purpose" within section 13(4) of the Act; but the position is different if the judgment creditor can prove

---

[30] In s.14(2).

[31] s.14(4). *Hispano Americana Mercantil S.A.* v. *Central Bank of Nigeria* [1979] 2 Lloyd's Rep. 277 (the immunity of a central bank under the U.K. Act of 1978 goes further than that under the U.S. Foreign Sovereign Immunities Act 1976 which protects only property of the bank "held for its own account").

[32] s.9.

[33] s.13(4). *Cf. Alcom Ltd.* v. *Republic of Colombia* [1984] A.C. 580.

[34] s.13(2)(*a*).

[35] Such attachment is done by way of garnishee proceedings.

that the account was designated solely (subject to the *de minimis* rule[36]) to meet liabilities incurred in commercial transactions.[37]

In the United States the restrictive theory is likewise adopted[38] and forms the basis of the Foreign Sovereign Immunities Act 1976.[39]

EXTRATERRITORIAL EFFECT OF FOREIGN STATE MEASURES

Extraterritorial effect may be claimed by a State for its legislative or administrative measures or by a court for its judgments or orders. Extraterritorial claims of this character are attempts at exercising an "exorbitant" jurisdiction and should, in principle, be avoided but, in practice, are sometimes encountered, in order to give effectiveness to domestic law or for other—possibly economic or political—reasons. Foreign claims of extraterritoriality have, on occasion, come into conflict with the sovereignty of the United Kingdom and her trading interests.

Protective measures have been taken on two levels: Parliament has enacted the Protection of Trading Interests Act 1980 and the courts have rejected extraterritorial claims of foreign courts conflicting with British sovereignty.

The Protection of Trading Interests Act 1980

The main provisions of this Act, as amended,[40] are:

1. Where an overseas country takes, or proposes to take, measures regulating or controlling international trade and these measures damage or threaten to damage the trading interests of the United Kingdom, the Secretary of State may order that persons carrying on business in the United Kingdom should notify him of such measures and he may issue directions prohibiting compliance with them.[41]

---

[36] *De minimis non curat lex* (the law takes no account of trifles).
[37] *Alcom Ltd.* v. *Republic of Colombia* [1984] A.C. 580. See also *Maclaine Watson & Co. Ltd.* v. *International Tin Council (No. 3)*, [1989] 3 W.L.R. 969 (H.L.).
[38] In the U.S. the changeover from the absolute to the restrictive doctrine was accelerated by the so-called Tate letter of May 19, 1952, addressed by Mr. J.B. Tate, acting legal adviser to the State Department, to the then acting Attorney-General. The restrictive theory was applied by the Supreme Court in *Alfred Dunhill of London Inc.* v. *Republic of Cuba* (1976) 96 S.C. 1854.
[39] See Kazimierz Grzybowski, "The United States Foreign Sovereign Immunities Act 1976" in [1978] J.B.L. 111.
[40] By the Magistrates Courts Act 1980, Scheds. 7 and 9, and the Civil Jurisdiction and Judgments Act 1982, s.38. For a consideration of the Protection of Trading Interests Act 1980 see Lawrence Collins, "Blocking and Clawback Statutes: The United Kingdom Approach" in [1986] J.B.L. 372, 452.
[41] s.1. Orders under this section were made in connection with the Trans-Siberian Pipeline (S.I. 1982 No. 885; see [1982] J.B.L. 360) and the *Laker* litigation (S.I. 1983 No. 900; this S.I. was considered in *British Airways Board* v. *Laker Airways Ltd.* [1985] A.C. 58).
Non-compliance with a requirement of the Secretary of State under s.1 without reasonable excuse is punishable (s.3).

2. If a request is made on a person inside the United Kingdom to produce to any court or authority of an overseas country a commercial document which is not within the territorial jurisdiction of that country or to furnish any commercial information to such overseas court or authority, or if such a requirement is imposed on a person inside the United Kingdom, the Secretary of State may prohibit compliance with such requirement if it is inadmissible by the Act.[42]

Section 2(2) provides that such requirement is inadmissible:

> (a) if it infringes the jurisdiction of the United Kingdom or is otherwise prejudicial to the sovereignty of the United Kingdom; or
> (b) if compliance with the requirement would be prejudicial to the security of the United Kingdom or the relations of the government of the United Kingdom with the government of any other country.

Subsection (3) of this section provides, with respect to a request made by a person in an overseas country, that the requirement shall be inadmissible:

> (a) if it is made otherwise than for the purposes of civil or criminal proceedings which have been instituted in the overseas country; or
> (b) if it requires a person to state what documents relevant to any such proceedings are or have been in his possession, custody or power or to produce for the purposes of any such proceedings any documents other than particular documents specified in the requirement.[43]

3. The Act further provides that a court in the United Kingdom shall not assist an overseas court[44] to obtain evidence in the United Kingdom if it is shown that the overseas request infringes the jurisdiction of the United Kingdom or is otherwise prejudicial to the sovereignty of the United Kingdom; and a certificate signed by or on behalf of the Secretary of State to that effect shall be conclusive evidence.[45]

4. The Act further contains provisions directed against the recovery of multiple damages in the United Kingdom in excess of damages attributable to compensation. Such damages may be awarded in particular by the United States courts in anti-trust proceedings; they contain a punitive element, whereas damages in the United Kingdom are, in principle, of compensatory nature. The provisions of the Act relating to multiple damages are considered later on in another connection.[46]

---

[42] s.2. Again non-compliance without reasonable excuse is punishable (s.3).

[43] This provision is directed against so-called fishing expeditions, particularly in pre-trial proceedings which are widely admitted in the United States; the purpose of such proceedings is to ascertain whether the enquirer has enough evidence to commence proceedings; on the other hand, the English courts will not restrain a litigant before them from making use of his right to obtain information by way of pre-trial proceedings in the American courts: *South Carolina Insurance Co.* v. *Assurantie Maatschappij "De Zeven Provincien" NV* [1987] A.C. 24. But the problem may also arise in other contexts, see *Lonrho Ltd.* v. *Shell Petroleum Co. Ltd.* [1980] 1 W.L.R. 627 (H.L.); *In re State of Norway's Application (No. 2)* [1988] 3 W.L.R. 603; reversed by H.L. in [1989] 2 W.L.R. 458 (see pp. 231–232, *post*).

[44] Under the Evidence (Proceedings in Other Jurisdictions) Act 1975; see p. 231, *post*.

[45] s.4.

[46] See p. 375, *post*.

Rejection of foreign extraterritorial claims by the courts. Letters of request.

The English courts reject claims by foreign courts or authorities if these claims, in the judgment of the English courts, infringe the sovereignty of the United Kingdom.[47] In particular, they will reject claims by United States courts or authorities to assist in the enforcement of United States anti-trust laws of extraterritorial character in the United Kingdom.[48]

Here, however, a difficulty arises. The English courts are bound by the Hague Convention on the Taking of Evidence Abroad in Civil or Commercial Matters of March 18, 1970, to which effect is given in the United Kingdom by the Evidence (Proceedings in Other Jurisdictions) Act 1975, to assist foreign courts when requesting assistance in obtaining evidence situate in England and Wales. The request of the foreign courts is called *letters of request* or *letters rogatory*. The requirements of the 1975 Act for letters rogatory are strict; the procedure under this Act can only be used to obtain *evidence* but not to make *discovery*.[49] One of the requirements of the Act is that, if the production of documents is required, they must be sufficiently particularised.[50] But the letter of request procedure must not be used for an improper purpose. In one case,[51] where it was used on the intervention of the United States Department of Justice as a request for evidence for a grand jury investigation into an alleged anti-trust arrangement, letters rogatory were refused because, as Lord Wilberforce observed,[52] "the attempt to extend the grand jury investigation extraterritorially . . . was an infringment of United Kingdom sovereignty." Another illustration is provided by the *State of Norway's Application* cases.[53] A wealthy Norwegian shipowner

---

[47] On the rejection of foreign revenue laws, penal laws, certain public laws, expropriatory laws claiming extraterritorial effect and certain discriminatory laws, see pp. 233–235, *post.*

[48] *British Nylon Spinners Ltd.* v. *Chemical Industries Ltd.* [1953] Ch. 19; *Re Westinghouse Electric Corporation Uranium Contract Litigation M.D.L. Docket No. 235 (No. 1 and No. 2)* [1978] A.C. 547. See also *Radio Corporation of America* v. *Rauland Corporation* [1956] 1 Q.B. 618 (request for pre-trial discovery in a U.S. patent action); *X A.G.* v. *Bank A* [1983] 2 All E.R. 464 (injunctions ordering non-compliance with subpoena of US court). But the English courts will not restrain a litigant before them from making use of the American pre-trial discovery procedure, see the *Zeven Provincien* case quoted in n. 43, *ante.*

[49] *Re International Power Industries Inc. NV* [1985] BCLC 128. See the seminal article by Lawrence Collins on "Problems of Enforcement in the Multinational Securities Market. A United Kingdom Perspective" in 9 *University of Pennsylvania Journal of International Business Law* (1987), 487.

[50] *Re Asbestos Insurance Coverage Cases* [1985] 1 W.L.R. 331. Evidence under the 1975 Act for a foreign court may be taken by videotape although such evidence might be inadmissible in the English courts: *J. Barber & Sons* v. *Lloyd's Underwriters* [1987] Q.B. 103.

[51] The *Westinghouse* case; see n. 48. The *Westinghouse* case was decided before s.4 of the Protection of Trading Interests Act 1980 (above in the text) came into force.

[52] *Ibid.* 616.

[53] *In re State of Norway's Application* [1987] Q.B. 433; *Re State of Norway's Application (No. 2)* [1988] 3 W.L.R. 603 and [1989] 2 W.L.R. 458 (H.L.).

had died domiciled in Norway. The Norwegian revenue alleged that he was the beneficial owner of a trust created in England and that he was liable to tax on his interest in the trust which he had failed to declare but the representatives of the deceased denied these allegations and proceedings were pending on these matters in a city court in Norway. That court requested the English courts to examine a director and an employee of an English merchant banking house which had acted as bankers to the trust. In the first case[54] the Court of Appeal, by a majority judgment, refused to comply with the letter of request on the ground that the request was too general and compliance with it would unjustifiably cause the bank to break its duty of confidentiality to a customer. The Norwegian court then particularised its request meticulously and repeated it and, in the second of these cases, was successful in the House of Lords.[55] The highest court held that the proceedings in the city court of Norway fell within the definition of a civil or commercial matter both in English and Norwegian law. The House of Lords further held that the rule that the English courts would not assist in the direct or indirect enforcement of a foreign revenue law,[56] did not extend to the seeking of assistance in obtaining evidence to be used for the enforcement of a foreign revenue law in the foreign State.

Conversely, the English courts will refuse an application for (English) letters of request to be sent to a foreign court if the request is likely to cause embarassment to the foreign court;[57] the grant of the application would contravene the comity of nations and would not be in accordance with the mutual respect which the courts of friendly nations show—or ought to show—to each other. The English courts will also refuse, save in exceptional circumstances, to make an order infringing a foreign State's sovereignty.[58]

The Exclusion of Foreign Law

The English courts recognise, in principle, the validity of the laws of a foreign country and will give effect to them in their jurisdiction. This is a matter of international comity. English law expects to be accorded the same treatment by the foreign courts.

Exceptionally, however, the English courts will refuse to recognise or enforce foreign laws. The ultimate reason for such a refusal is that, in the

---

[54] *In re State of Norway's Application* [1987] Q.B. 433.
[55] *In re State of Norway's Application (No. 2)* [1989] 2 W.L.R. 458 (H.L.).
[56] See p. 233, *post.*
[57] *Settobello Ltd.* v. *Banco Totta and Acores* [1985] 1 W.L.R. 1050; see p. 231, *ante.* See also *Buttes Gas and Oil Co.* v. *Hammer (No. 3)* [1982] A.C. 888; *Maclaine, Watson & Co. Ltd.* v. *International Tin Council,* [1989] 3 W.L.R. 969 (see p. 227, n. 27).
[58] *Mackinnon* v. *Donaldson, Lufkin and Jenrette Securities Corporation* [1986] Ch. 482.(Order refused to produce under the Bankers' Books Evidence Act 1879 documents kept by a foreign bank abroad).

judgment of the English courts, the foreign law in question is inconsistent with the public policy of English law. The situations in which the English courts refuse the application of foreign law can be grouped as follows.

Foreign confiscatory or nationalisation laws

While the English courts admit the validity of nationalisation or other expropriatory laws of a foreign State recognised by the government of this country,[59] as far as property situate at the time of the expropriation in the territory of the foreign State is concerned,[60] they refuse to recognise the application of such laws to property situate at that time outside the territory of the foreign State, even if the expropriatory law claims to have extraterritorial effect.[61] Such a claim would be an excess of national sovereignty and an interference with the sovereignty of other States and this is contrary to the generally accepted principles of international law.

Foreign revenue laws, penal laws and other public laws of political or administrative character

The English courts will not enforce, directly or indirectly, revenue laws of another country even if that country is a member of the Commonwealth or the EC.[62] This rule applies to taxes, rates, Customs duties or other impositions levied in the overseas country.

Penal laws of a foreign country are likewise not enforceable in the English jurisdiction. "Penal laws" in the strict sense are "criminal laws"[63] but the term is given a wider meaning and includes discriminatory laws directed against a particular person,[64] family or business enterprise,[65] especially if these discriminatory measures are directed against a person or corporation resident in the United Kingdom[66] or if they contravene

---

[59] *Carl Zeiss Stiftung* v. *Rayner & Keeler (No. 2)* [1967] 1 A.C. 853; *Gur Corporation* v. *Trust Bank of Africa Ltd.* [1987] Q.B. 599. Jersey is not a sovereign State for the purposes of the CMR: *Chloride Industrial Batteries Ltd.* v. *F. & W. Freight Ltd*, [1989] 1 W.L.R. 45; see p. 635, *post*.

[60] *Luther* v. *Sagor* [1921] 3 K.B. 532; *Princess Paley Olga* v. *Weisz* [1929] 1 K.B. 718.

[61] *Lecouturier* v. *Rey* [1910] A.C. 262; *Frankfurther* v.*W.L. Exner Ltd.* [1947] Ch. 629; *Redler Grain Silos Ltd.* v. *BICC Ltd.* [1982] 1 Lloyd's Rep. 435, 438.

[62] *Re Visser* [1928] Ch. 877; *Indian Government* v. *Taylor* [1955] A.C. 491. See also the *In the State of Norway's Application* cases quoted on p. 232 n. 56, *ante*.

[63] *United States of America* v. *Inkley* [1988] 3 W.L.R. 304 (Florida judgment in civil proceedings for enforcement of a bail bond refused because the bail bond was given in penal proceedings).

[64] *Banco de Vizcaya* v. *Don Alfonso de Borbon y Austria* [1935] 1 K.B. 140.

[65] *The Rose Mary* [1953] 1 W.L.R. 246 (see on this case *Re Helbert Wagg & Co. Ltd.'s Claim* [1956] Ch. 323, 346).

[66] *Folliott* v. *Ogden* (1789) 1 H.Bl. 123.

fundamental human rights. But, apart from the two last-mentioned cases, the English courts recognise, on the principle in *Luther* v. *Sagor*,[67] a penal law in the wider sense if the foreign State has perfected its title to the expropriated assets in its own territory, *e.g.* if it has expropriated the shares of a local company even though the company has valuable assets outside the territory of the expropriating State.[68]

Whether the English courts should refuse recognition to other public laws of a foreign country is controversial.[69] It is thought that there are two kinds of public laws, those which are of political or administrative[70] character and those which are not. The latter class includes statutes designed to protect the natural environment or to prevent the exportation of national art treasures without licence.[71] Public laws of the former type should be refused recognition but there is no justification in extending this refusal to public laws of the latter type, particularly as this country has enacted legislation having the same aims.

Other cases of public policy

It should, however, be emphasised that, to vary the words of a famous judge,[72] the categories of public policy are never closed. The English courts have a residual discretion to refuse the application of foreign laws in cases other than those mentioned in the preceding paragraphs if they conclude that recognition would contravene heads of public policy which

---

[67] See n. 60, *supra*.

[68] *Williams and Humbert Ltd.* v. *W. & H. Trade Marks (Jersey) Ltd.*; *Rumasa SA* v. *Multinvest (U.K.) Ltd. (The Dry Sack litigation)* [1986] A.C. 368 (H.L.).

[69] See Staughton J. in *Attorney-General of New Zealand* v. *Ortiz* [1982] Q.B. 349 who thought that they should not refuse such recognition; the House of Lords in this case ([1984] A.C. 1, 46) did not express an opinion on this point; *Kingdom of Spain* v. *Christie, Manson & Woods Ltd.* [1986] 1 W.L.R. 1120; both these cases are noted on pp. 781–782 and 784 respectively, *post*.

[70] The EC Convention on Jurisdiction and the Enforcement of Judgments in Civil and Commercial Matters of 1968, to which effect is given in the United Kingdom by the Civil Jurisdiction and Judgments Act 1982, states in art. 1 that it shall not extend "to revenue, Customs or administrative matters."

[71] There exists an International Convention on the means of prohibiting and preventing the illicit import, export and transfer of ownership of cultural property, of November 14, 1970. The United Kingdom has not acceded to it.

[72] Lord Macmillan in *Donoghue* v. *Stevenson* [1932] A.C. 562, 619.

are not purely domestic.[73] Not only the courts have this discretion, but
Parliament has it too. An application of these considerations are the
measures which Parliament has adopted for the protection of British
trading interests,[74] particularly against excessive extraterritorial claims in
United States anti-trust proceedings, and the attitude of English judges if,
in their view, a foreign claim infringes the sovereignty of the United
Kingdom.[75]

FOREIGN ILLEGALITY

Civil consequences

The English courts will not enforce "a contract where performance of
that contract is forbidden by the law of the place where it is to be
performed."[76] Thus, if the parties to a contract of export sale knowingly
and deliberately agree to break the laws of a friendly country, *i.e.* a
country with which the United Kingdom is not at war and the Government of which is recognised by the Government of this country,[77] the
English courts will not enforce such contract at the suit of one of the
parties because to do so would disregard the rules of international comity.
This applies even if the laws which the parties intended to infringe were

---

[73] *Lemenda Trading Co. Ltd.* v. *African Middle East Petroleum Co. Ltd.* [1988] 2 W.L.R.
735 (Alleged influence on foreign official for pecuniary gain held to contravene English
public policy; Phillips J. (on p. 745): "Some heads of public policy are based on universal
principles of morality . . . Where a contract infringes such a rule of public policy the English
court will not enforce it, whatever the proper law of contract and wherever the place of
performance") See also *Mitsubishi Corporation* v. *Alafonzos, Financial Times,* October 28,
1987; *E.I. Du Pont de Nemours* v. *I.C. Agnew, Financial Times,* July 24, 1987 (English
court better placed to decide a point on English public policy than foreign court); *Ali* v.
Carrier Transcontinental Co. Ltd., Financial Times, October 25, 1989 (contract contained
clause that it should be void if it contravened US Foreign Corrupt Practices Act 1977; the
English court, interpreting the US Act, held the contract to be invalid because it provided
for the payment of a promise of a secret commission).
[74] See p. 229, *ante.*
[75] See p. 231, *ante.*
[76] Lord Wright M.R. in *International Trustee* v. *R.* [1936] 3 All E.R. 407, 428; *Ralli Brothers*
v. *Compania Naviera Sota y Aznar* [1920] 2 K.B. 287. Supervening government prohibition,
without fault of either party, may result in frustration (see p. 186, *ante*) or be a force
majeure event (see p. 200, *ante*). But the mere fact that the contract is, or becomes, illegal
by the law of the country in which the person who has to perform resides, is not sufficient
unless that country is also the country in which the actual performance has to take place:
Toprak Mahsulleriofisi v. *Finagrain Compagnie Commerciale, Agricole et Financière* [1979] 2
Lloyd's Rep. 98, 107. See also *Kleinwort Sons & Co.* v. *Ungarnische Baumwolle Industrie
A.G.* [1939] 2 K.B. 678; *Libyan Arab Foreign Bank* v. *Bankers Trust Co.* [1988] 1 Lloyd's
Rep. 259, 268. (These cases were decided before the introduction of the concept of
"characteristic performance" into English law, see p. 223, *ante.*)
[77] See p. 232 n. 57.

the revenue laws[78] of another country, *i.e.* laws relating to Customs duties and quotas, import or export prohibitions, exchange control regulations[79] or taxation.

In *Regazzoni* v. *K.C. Sethia (1944) Ltd.*[80] the Government of India prohibited the direct or indirect exportation of specified goods, including, jute bags, to among others, South Africa because differences had arisen between the Governments of the two countries with respect to the treatment of Indian nationals in South Africa. Regazzoni, a Swiss merchant, bought from the defendants, a company incorporated in England and having Indian connections, a large quantity of jute bags c.i.f. Genoa; thence the goods were, as both parties knew, to be transhipped to South Africa. Both parties intended, as the court found, to infringe the prohibition of Indian law. The contract which was governed by English law was not carried out because the Indian Government did not sanction the exportation of the goods to Genoa, and the action by the buyer against the sellers for damages for non-delivery of the goods was dismissed by the English courts on the ground that it was against English public policy to enforce a contract intended by the parties to involve the breach of the laws of India.

The rule of which the *Regazzoni* case is an illustration is subject to certain qualifications and exceptions.[81] First, the validity of the contract is not affected where only one party, but not the other, is aware of the illegality.[82] Secondly, where the transaction in issue is completed and the illegality arises thereafter, or the illegality precedes the transaction and is exhausted before the parties contract, their bargain is unaffected by the illegality[83]; an ordinary sale in England of goods which, as the seller knows or suspects, will be smuggled by the buyer into another country is likely to be valid. Thirdly, foreign illegality affects only the contract in which it arises but not supporting contracts; thus, the fact that export invoices were falsified in order to deceive the Customs authorities of the

---

[78] But the English courts will not enforce revenue laws at the suit of an overseas government or government department; see p. 233, *ante*.

[79] In *United City Merchants (Investments) Ltd.* v. *Royal Bank of Canada* [1983] 1 A.C. 168 a different point arose. The agreement of the parties to infringe Peruvian exchange control regulations was invalid because it infringed *English* law, *viz.* the Bretton Woods Agreements Order 1946, and *not* because it aimed at the infringement of the laws of a *foreign* country, *viz.* Peru; see p. 112, *ante*.

[80] [1958] A.C. 301; see also *Foster* v. *Driscoll* [1929] 1 K.B. 470.

[81] Apart from the cases in which the English courts refuse to recognise or enforce foreign law, see p. 232, *ante*.

[82] *Archbolds (Freightage) Ltd.* v. *S. Spanglett Ltd.* [1961] 1 Q.B. 374; *Fielding & Platt Ltd.* v. *Najjar* [1969] 1 W.L.R. 357; *Phoenix General Insurance Company of Greece SA* v. *Halvanon Insurance Co. Ltd.* [1987] 2 W.L.R. 512, 561; *S.C.F. Finance Co. Ltd.* v. *Masri (No. 2)* [1987] 2 W.L.R. 58, 78.

[83] *Regazzoni* v. *K.C. Sethia (1944) Ltd.* [1958] A.C. 301; also *Mackender* v. *Feldia A.G.* [1967] 2 Q.B. 590. But in *Geismar* v. *Sun Alliance and London Insurance Ltd.* [1978] Q.B. 383 it was held that a contract of insurance of goods illegally imported into this country was unenforceable on grounds of public policy.

importer's country did not prevent the exporter from recovering damages in this country from carriers, when the exporter's goods were stolen from their lorry in transit to the docks of London[84]; further, where diamonds were exported to West Germany on a sale or return basis and their price was understated in the invoice to save German turnover tax, and part of the consignment was stolen in West Germany, the English insurance contract, under which the diamonds were insured at their correct value, was not tainted by the German illegality and the insurers were liable under the policy.[85]

Criminal consequences[86]

Different from the civil consequences of foreign illegality is the question whether a British exporter who has committed a criminal offence under the laws of another country or has conspired to commit such offence can be convicted of it and punished in England.[87] Here the position is this:

1. The courts of this country do not enforce the criminal law of another country at the suit of that country, either directly or indirectly[88];
2. As a rule, an act committed abroad is not punishable in England.
3. Exceptionally, however, certain acts committed abroad are made offences by the common law of England or United Kingdom statutes and are punishable in the English courts;
4. Where an offence falls within the list of extradition crimes, and the United Kingdom has reciprocal arrangements for extradition with a foreign country, a person accused or convicted of such crime may be extradited to the country in question. Extradition to most foreign countries is regulated by the *Extradition Acts 1870 to 1932*,[89] and the Orders in Council made thereunder, and to Commonwealth countries or to those foreign countries to which

---

[84] *Pye Ltd.* v. *B.G. Transport Service Ltd.* [1966] 2 Lloyd's Rep. 300.
[85] *Euro-Diam Ltd.* v. *Bathurst* [1988] 2 W.L.R. 517.
[86] On Customs offences, see p. 781, *post.*
[87] See C.M. Schmitthoff, "Criminal Offences in Export Trade Law" in [1957] J.B.L. 146.
[88] Denning L.J. in *Regazzoni* v. *K.C. Sethia (1944) Ltd.* [1956] 2 Q.B. 490, 515; affd. [1958] A.C. 301, 318. See p. 235, *ante.*
[89] The rule against the enforcement of foreign revenue laws does not apply to an extradition under the Extradition Acts if the offence committed in the foreign State is an extraditable offence, though directed against the foreign revenue authority: *R.* v. *Chief Metropolitan Stipendiary Magistrate, ex parte Secretary of State for the Home Department* [1988] 1 W.L.R. 1204. Conspiracy to import dangerous drugs into a foreign country (the US) is an extraditionable offence under the Extradition Acts and the bilateral treaty with the foreign country: *Government of the United States* v. *Bowe, The Times,* September 13, 1989 (PC on appeal from the Bahamas).

the Acts are made applicable by the Fugitive Offenders Act 1967.[90] Both these Acts are amended by the Suppression of Terrorism Act 1978, the Taking of Hostages Act 1982 and other enactments.

The third of these rules, *viz.* that an act committed abroad may be punishable in England by virtue of English law, was at least indirectly involved in *R.* v. *Reiss and John M. Potter Ltd.*, decided by Barry J. at Leeds Assizes on December 10, 1956.[91] The accused had exported wool tops from Uruguay directly to Italy and Greece under certificates of origin obtained from the Bradford Chamber of Commerce and certifying falsely that the wool tops were of United Kingdom manufacture. The certificates of origin were obtained in this manner: the accused submitted the usual application forms to the Chamber of Commerce which, in perfect good faith and not suspecting that they contained false details, verified them. The legislation then in force[92] stated that it was an offence for any person who, being within the United Kingdom, aided and abetted, "*without the United Kingdom*," any act which, if committed in the United Kingdom, would be a misdemeanour. The accused were prosecuted and fined £5,000. The Trade Descriptions Act 1968, which has taken the place of that legislation, does not have extra-territorial effect and even provides that there shall be no prosecution in the United Kingdom if a false description is attached to goods intended for dispatch to a destination outside the United Kingdom.[93]

If goods are purchased in the United Kingdom under the false representation that they will be resold in an export market but they are intended to be sold in the home market and the seller, relying on the misrepresentation, charges the (lower) export price, the fraudulent purchaser has committed the offence of obtaining property by deception, contrary to section 15 of the Theft Act 1968.[94] He further commits the tort of deceit and is liable to the seller in damages, which are assessed at the full market value of the goods.[95]

A person dispatching from England a forged end-user certificate purporting to be issued by a foreign authority can be convicted for uttering a forged document in England, contrary to the Forgery Act 1913, s.6(2), if he knows that the document is a forgery.[96] A conspiracy to

---

[90] The 1967 Act still applies to Fiji although this country is no longer a member of the Commonwealth: *R.* v. *Governor of Brixton Prison, ex parte Kahan, The Times* December 19, 1988.

[91] Unreported. The case is discussed in [1957] J.B.L. 147.

[92] s.11 of the Merchandise Marks Acts 1887 and 1953. These enactments were repealed by the Trade Descriptions Act 1968.

[93] Trade Descriptions Act 1968, s.32, as amended (other particulars may be dispensed with by the Board of Trade).

[94] *R.* v. *Dearlove and Drucker* (the Oxo cubes case) [1988] Crim. L.R. 323; [1988] J.B.L. 167 (CA). The offence is even committed if the dual price structure contravenes Article 85(1) of the EC Treaty.)

[95] *Smith Kline & French Laboratories* v. *Long* [1989] 1 W.L.R. 1 (CA).

[96] *Board of Trade* v. *Owen* [1957] A.C. 602.

commit an export offence abroad is only punishable as such if it constitutes, at the same time, a conspiracy to commit a crime in England, *e.g.* the crime of obtaining a pecuniary advantage by deception in England.[97] This rule applies even if the effect of the conspiracy to commit a crime abroad might cause economic loss to somebody in the United Kingdom. Thus, in one case[98] two persons conspired in the United Kingdom to affix on goods situated abroad faked labels of highly reputed merchandise produced in the United Kingdom and to sell these inferior goods under the false labels to a foreign buyer. The damage of such conspiracy to the British export trade was obvious. Nevertheless, the Court of Appeal held that the two wrongdoers could not be prosecuted in England. This decision is regrettable and it is to be hoped that it will be reversed by the House of Lords if the highest court has an occasion to consider this matter.

Conversely, a conspiracy entered into abroad to commit a crime in England, continues in existence so long as there are two or more parties to it intending to carry out its design; if the conspirators, having still that intention, come to England, the English courts have jurisdiction to try them for conspiracy.[99] In exceptional cases a dishonest or improper deal abroad by a person resident in England may be punishable in England as conspiracy to commit a public mischief to the prejudice of honest British traders but the courts approach this crime with caution and circumstances must be very strong to persuade them that it has been committed.[1]

---

[97] *R.* v. *Peter Stanley Cox* [1968] 1 W.L.R. 88; *R.* v. *Governor of Brixton Prison, ex p. Rush* [1969] 1 W.L.R. 165; *Attorney-General's Reference* (*No. 1 of 1982*) [1983] Q.B. 751.
[98] *Attorney-General's Reference* (*No. 1 of 1982*) [1983] 3 W.L.R. 72.
[99] *R.* v. *Doot* [1973] A.C. 807.
[1] See *R.* v. *Newland* [1954] 1 Q.B. 158; *Board of Trade* v. *Owen* [1957] A.C. 602. This principle was not applied in *Attorney-General's Reference* (*No. 1 of 1982*) [1983] Q.B. 751.

CHAPTER 14

THE UNIFICATION OF INTERNATIONAL SALES LAW

IT has already been pointed out[1] that it would be of great value to the international business community if the law relating to international sales were unified and no longer determined by different national legal systems which provide different answers to questions such as when an offer or acceptance becomes effective, when possession, property or risk in the goods sold passes, what the rights of a buyer are when goods not conforming to the contract are tendered, and similar questions. A unification of the law of international sales would reduce the danger of a conflict of laws in a particularly sensitive area of international business relations. Aware of the value of a unified sales law for the international business community, the International Institute for the Unification of Private Law in Rome, on the suggestion of the great German comparatist Ernst Rabel, drafted two Uniform Laws on International Sales and after 30 years' preparation these Laws were adopted by a conference at The Hague on April 25, 1964.[2]

The two Uniform Laws are *The Uniform Law on International Sale of Goods* (Uniform Law on Sales) and *The Uniform Law on the Formation of Contracts for the International Sale of Goods* (Uniform Law on Formation).[3] The former aims at the unification of the substantive law of international sales, in particular the obligations of the buyer and seller, and the passing of the risk. The latter is complementary to the former; it attempts to reconcile the differences of the common and civil law on offer and acceptance leading to the conclusion of an international contract[4]. The two Uniform Laws are given effect in United Kingdom law by the Uniform Laws on International Sales Act 1967. This Act will be considered later.[5]

The number of countries which have ratified the Hague Conventions of 1964 is disappointingly small. UNCITRAL has therefore made the unification of international sales law one of its priority subjects. Its efforts

---

[1] See p. 114, *ante.*

[2] The two Uniform Laws are embodied in two Conventions, referred to here as the First Convention and the Second Convention.

[3] Both Conventions are appended as Schedules to the Uniform Laws on International Sales Act 1967; see *infra.*

[4] A. Szakats, "The Influence of Common Law Principles on the Uniform Law on the International Sale of Goods" in (1966) 15 I.C.L.Q. 749; the same author, "The Sale of Goods Act 1893 and the Uniform Law on the International Sale of Goods" [1968] J.B.L. 235; and the note by J. D. Feltham in (1967) 30 M.L.R. 670; R. H. Graveson, E. J. Cohn and D. Graveson, *The Uniform Laws of International Sales Act 1967,* 1968.

[5] See *infra.*

were successful and in 1980 the UN Convention for the International Sale of Goods was approved in Vienna by a diplomatic conference.[6] The Vienna Convention came into effect on January 1, 1988[7] but, at the date of writing,[8] has not been introduced into English law yet.[9] It is founded on the two Hague Conventions but combines them into one instrument. The Vienna Convention and another Convention, the UN Convention on the Limitation Period in the International Sale of Goods, will be reviewed later[10].

THE UNIFORM LAWS IN THE UNITED KINGDOM

The Uniform Laws on International Sales Act 1967

This enactment introduces the two Uniform Laws adopted by the Hague Conference of 1964 into the law of the United Kingdom. They are appended to the Act as Schedules 1 and 2. The Act of 1967 was activated and the two Uniform Laws came into force in the United Kingdom on August 18, 1972.[11]

Contracting States for the purposes of the Uniform Law on the International Sale of Goods (the First Convention) are[12]:

Contracting State	Effective date of ratification
Belgium	August 18, 1972
Gambia	September 5, 1974
West Germany	April 16, 1974
Israel	August 18, 1972
The Netherlands	August 18, 1972
San Marino	August 18, 1972
United Kingdom	August 18, 1972

Italy was a Contracting State from August 23, 1972 to January 1, 1988 but then discontinued adherence to the Uniform Laws and adopted the Vienna Convention instead.

---

[6] See *infra* in text.

[7] The Convention came into effect after having been ratified or acceded to by 10 States (art. 99).

[8] October 1, 1989. But the UK is at least considering whether to give effect to the Vienna Convention. The DTI published in June 1989 a consultative document on this subject.

[9] According to English law, an international convention, even if ratified by the Government (at the date of writing the Vienna Convention has not been ratified), becomes part of the law of the country only if given effect by an Act of Parliament. In USA law, as in the law of many European continental countries, an international convention is self-executing, *i.e.* it becomes part of the municipal law as soon as it is ratified.

[10] Vienna Convention, p. 249, *post*; Limitation Period Convention, p. 254, *post*.

[11] The Uniform Laws on International Sales Order 1972 (S.I. 1972 No. 973).

[12] The Uniform Laws on International Sales Order 1987 (S.I. 1987 No. 2061). This Order provides a replacement schedule to that appended to the 1972 Order.

Application of Uniform Laws only if adopted by parties

The Order in Council which gives effect to the two Uniform Laws provides that the Uniform Law on Sales shall only apply if it has been chosen by the parties to the contract[13]; the Uniform Law on Formation has only ancillary character and applies only to contracts to which the Uniform Law on Sales is applied.[14]

While such a restriction considerably reduces the usefulness of the Uniform Laws, it might lead to a difficulty if one party to the contract is resident in the United Kingdom and the other in a country in which the Uniform Laws apply automatically (unless excluded by the parties). This raises a problem of private international law, *viz.* it has to be determined whether the proper law of the contract is English or foreign law.[15] In the latter case the Uniform Laws apply to an English party who has not adopted them in the contract but in the former case they apply only if adopted by the parties.

Mandatory provisions of proper law cannot be contracted out

When the parties adopt the Uniform Laws—and they may adopt them even if the conditions for the application of the Uniform Laws are not satisfied—the parties cannot, by so doing, contract out of the mandatory provisions of the law which would have been applicable if they had not chosen the Uniform Laws.[16] As far as the law of the United Kingdom is concerned, the only provisions which are mandatory by statute[17] are those aiming at the protection of the consumer in the domestic sale of goods, namely those contained in the Unfair Contract Terms Act 1977, ss.2 to 7. These provisions apply, as already stated, only to domestic sales. They do not apply to international supply contracts.[18] As regards the latter type of contract, exemption clauses, if freely negotiated, are perfectly valid. The definition of international supply contracts was given earlier.[19]

Further, by adopting the Uniform Laws, the parties cannot contract out of provisions directly founded on public policy.

---

[13] This regulation was admitted by the 1967 Act s.1(3). The United Kingdom was entitled to restrict the scope of the Uniform Law on Sales in this manner by virtue of art. V of the First Convention.

[14] 1967 Act, Sched. 2, art. 1.

[15] See p. 204, *ante.*

[16] Uniform Laws on International Sales Act 1967, s.1(4); this section was amended by the Unfair Contract Terms Act 1977, Sched. 4, and by the Sale of Goods Act 1979, Sched. 2, para. 15. Also Uniform Law of Sales, art. 4.

[17] Unfair Contract Terms Act 1977, s.27(2).

[18] Unfair Contract Terms Act 1977, s.26.

[19] See p. 100, *ante.*

GENERAL LIMITATIONS OF UNIFORM LAWS

Two of these general limitations have already been considered in the preceding paragraphs. They are the restriction of these Laws to cases in which the parties have chosen them as the proper law of contract[20] and the rule that the parties cannot exclude the mandatory provisions of the proper law by their adoption of the Uniform Laws.[21] There are, however, further limitations which may be introduced by States when ratifying the Conventions to which the Uniform Laws are appended.

Restriction to contracts between parties in Convention States

The Uniform Laws, as drafted, apply to all cases in which the parties to the contract have their places of business in the territories of different States or, if they have no place of business, are habitually resident in different States.[22] The Laws do not require that the places of business or habitual residence should be in the territories of Contracting States; in brief, they do not require reciprocity in that respect. However, a State, when ratifying the Conventions embodying the Uniform Laws, may stipulate that it will apply them only if each of the parties to the contract has his place of business or habitual residence in the territory of a different State which likewise has ratified the Conventions.[23] The United Kingdom when enacting the Uniform Laws of International Sales Act 1967, has made use of this qualification.[24] For this reason it was necessary to state earlier[25] which States have become "contracting States" for the purposes of the Uniform Laws on International Sales.

A State which adopts this qualification introduces into its law an unfortunate complication. It has two legal regimes applying to international sales contracts, one in respect of residents in Convention States and the other in respect of residents in other foreign countries.

Restriction to proper law under the Hague P.I.L. Convention

A difficulty arises for the countries which have adopted the Hague Convention of June 15, 1955, on the Law applicable to International

---

[20] Uniform Law on Sales, art. 4.
[21] Art. II of both Conventions.
[22] Uniform Law on Sales, art. 1(1) and (2).
[23] Both Conventions, art. III.
[24] 1967 Act, s.1(1). See also the reference to "Contracting Parties" in art. 1(1) of the First Convention, contained in Sched. 1 of the 1967 Act.
[25] See p. 241, *ante*.

Sales of Goods, which in due course will be superseded by the Hague Convention on the Law applicable to Contracts for the International Sale of Goods of December 22, 1986 (The Hague P.I.L. Convention).[26] It will be recalled that this Convention provides, in essence, that, failing an agreement by the parties, the seller's law shall be the proper law of the contract. The difficulty is here to align the Uniform Laws with the P.I.L. Convention. This has been done by providing that a State which previously has adopted the P.I.L. Convention may declare, on ratification of the Conventions embodying the Uniform Laws, that these Laws shall only apply if the P.I.L. Convention requires their application.[27] If a State adopts this qualification, the application of the Uniform Laws will be restricted to contracts in which they are automatically the seller's law under the legal regulation applicable in the seller's country or to contracts in which they are chosen as the proper law of contract by the parties. In other cases falling under the P.I.L. Convention the Uniform Laws are inapplicable. By such a declaration the P.I.L. Convention is given precedence over the Uniform Laws and the field of application of the latter is severely restricted. In the domain in which the two Uniform Laws apply, however, the rules of private international law are excluded.[28]

The United Kingdom, it will be recalled, has not adopted the Hague P.I.L. Convention.

Effect of limitations

Even if a great number of States had given effect to the Uniform Laws, the unification achieved would be partial only and not complete. The United Kingdom exporter would be faced with a situation in which some of his contracts may be governed by the Uniform Laws and others not, and even more complicated will be the situation with regard to international sales contracts concluded by his foreign subsidiaries. Even if it appears that the Uniform Laws apply, the further question has to be examined whether they apply subject to a particular qualification.

It follows that the United Kingdom exporter should, at least for the time being, aim first at the adoption of English law as the law governing the transaction and only in the second place agree with the overseas importer on the adoption of the Uniform Laws.

CONTRACTS OF INTERNATIONAL SALE

The Uniform Laws apply only to contracts for the international sale of goods. They do not apply to home transactions.[29]

---

[26] See p. 206, *ante.*
[27] Both Conventions, art. IV.
[28] Uniform Law on International Sales, art. 2.
[29] Unless a State introduces legislation applying them to home transactions or the parties to home transaction adopt them.

A contract of international sale, within the meaning of the Uniform Laws in the form adopted by the 1967 Act, is defined[30] as a contract of sale of goods entered into by parties whose places of business are in the territories of "different contracting States,"[31] in each of the following cases:

(a) where the contract involves the sale of goods which are at the time of the conclusion of the contract in the course of carriage or will be carried from the territory of one State to the territory of another;

(b) where the acts constituting the offer and the acceptance have been effected in the territories of different States;

(c) where delivery of the goods is to be made in the territory of a State other than that within whose territory the acts constituting the offer and the acceptance have been effected.

Where a party to the contract does not have a place of business, the habitual residence of the party shall determine his situs. The nationality of the parties is irrelevant for the determination of the international character of the contract.[32] Further, the Uniform Laws apply to contracts of sale regardless of the commercial or private character of the parties.[33]

THE UNIFORM LAW ON INTERNATIONAL SALES

The Uniform Law on Sales does not define the trade terms customary in international trade[34] but provides[35]:

1. The parties shall be bound by any usage which they have expressly or impliedly made applicable to their contract and by any practices which have been established between themselves.

2. They shall also be bound by usages which reasonable persons in the same situation as the parties usually consider to be applicable to their contract. In the event of conflict with the present Law, the usages shall prevail unless agreed by the parties.

3. Where expressions, provisions or forms of contract commonly used in commercial practice are employed, they shall be interpreted according to the meaning usually given to them in the trade concerned.

Consequently, where the parties have agreed on a trade term, such as f.o.b. or c.i.f., the regulation intended by that term takes precedence

---

[30] Uniform Law on Sales, art. 1. This definition should be compared with that of the international supply contract in section 26 of the Unfair Contract Terms Act 1977; see p. 100, *ante.*

[31] Two or more States may declare that they do not consider themselves as "different States" for the purposes of the Uniform Laws because their law of sale and their law on the formation of the contract of sale are substantially the same; see the two Conventions, art. II, and the two Uniform Laws, art. 1(5). Such a declaration of conformity can, *e.g.* be made between the United Kingdom, on the one hand, and Australia, New Zealand and Canada (with the exception of Quebec) on the other hand, if the latter States decide to adopt the Uniform Laws.

[32] Uniform Law on Sales, art. 1(3).

[33] *Ibid.* art. 7.

[34] See p. 9. *ante.*

[35] In art. 9 of the Uniform Law on Sales. (All references to articles in this section are to the Uniform Law on Sales (1967 Act, Sched. 1), unless stated otherwise.)

over the provisions of the Law. Further, the Law does not prevent the parties from agreeing on a uniform interpretation of these trade terms, *e.g.* by embodying into their contract Incoterms or a similar text.

The Uniform Law does not use the distinction between conditions and warranties which, as we have seen,[36] the Sale of Goods Act, 1979 adopts. It distinguishes, however, between two types of breach of contract, *viz.* a fundamental and a non-fundamental breach. A fundamental breach occurs[37]:

> wherever the party in breach knew, or ought to have known, at the time of the conclusion of the contract, that a reasonable person in the same situation as the other party would not have entered into the contract if he had foreseen the breach and its effects.

The principle of the Law is that where a breach is of fundamental nature, the person who suffers it may declare the contract as avoided but if the breach is not fundamental the contract continues to be in existence, subject to the right of the wronged party to claim damages. This is similar in effect to the modern English concept of the innominate term, discussed earlier.[38] These rules may be illustrated by reference to the case of a seller who has failed to deliver the goods timely, *i.e.* at the date agreed in the contract. It depends here on the importance which the parties have attached to timely delivery. If the failure to deliver timely constitutes a fundamental breach, the buyer has the choice between requiring performance of the contract or declaring the contract avoided; if he does not exercise this choice within a reasonable time, the contract is automatically avoided.[39] On the other hand, if the failure to deliver timely does not amount to a fundamental breach, the buyer may grant the seller an additional period of reasonable length, and failure to deliver within this period would turn the non-fundamental breach into a fundamental breach.[40]

Of further interest are the provisions of the Uniform Law on the rights of the buyer if the seller tenders or delivers "non-conforming goods," *i.e.* goods which fail to conform with their description in the contract or with the stipulated quantity or quality. Such a failure will normally constitute a fundamental breach of the seller's obligation to deliver the goods contracted for.[41] In these cases the buyer loses his right to rely on lack of conformity—

---

[36] See p. 133, *ante.*
[37] Art. 10.
[38] See p. 135, *ante.*
[39] See art. 26(1). This rule is subject to exceptions, see art. 26(2) and (3). "Avoidance of the contract" does not mean that the contract is null and void from the beginning, it merely releases both parties from their obligations thereunder (art. 78). In the case of avoidance of the contract the buyer may be entitled to damages (art. 84).
[40] See art. 27. The requirement of an additional period follows the German requirement of a *Nachfrist*; see p. 115, *ante.*
[41] Art. 33.

1. if he fails to notify the seller promptly[42] after he has discovered that lack or ought to have discovered it, but in no circumstances, not even in the case of hidden defects, can notice of lack of conformity be given after two years from the date when the goods were handed over, unless a longer guarantee was stipulated in the contract.[43] The notice of lack of conformity must specify the nature of the defects,[44] or
2. if he fails to take the matter to the court, by action or defence, within one year after having given notice of lack of conformity, except if he has been prevented from relying on lack of conformity by fraud on the part of the seller or if he claims reduction of the price in an action for payment of the price by the seller.[45]

If the buyer has given due notice of lack of conformity, he is entitled—

1. to demand performance of the contract by the seller.[46] But where the court would not order specific performance in respect of similar contracts not governed by the Law—as is the case in England—it is not compelled by the Law to order specific performance of an international contract[47]; or
2. to declare the contract as avoided, but only if the lack of conformity constitutes a fundamental breach[48]; or
3. to reduce the price[49]; and
4. in addition, to claim damages.[50]

If the lack of conformity does not constitute a fundamental breach, the seller is entitled, even after the date fixed for the delivery of the goods, to make a second tender of conforming goods or to remedy the defect, "provided that the exercise of this right does not cause the buyer either unreasonable inconvenience or unreasonable expense."[51] Here again, however, the buyer can turn the non-fundamental breach into a fundamental one by fixing an additional period for further delivery or for remedying the defect.[52]

THE UNIFORM LAW ON FORMATION

This Law, as adopted by the U.K. Uniform Laws on International Sales Act 1967, is ancillary to the Uniform Law on Sales, *i.e.* it applies only to

---

[42] *i.e.* "within as short a period as possible" (art. 11).
[43] Art. 39(1).
[44] Art. 39(2).
[45] Art. 49.
[46] Art. 41(1)(*a*).
[47] First Convention, art. VII.
[48] Art. 41(1)(*b*).
[49] Art. 41(1)(*c*).
[50] Art. 41(2).
[51] Art. 44(1).
[52] Art. 44(2).

contracts of international sale "which, if they were concluded, would be governed by the Uniform Law on the International Sale of Goods."[53] This curious provision postulates a retrospective consideration: one has first to assume that the contract was validly concluded, then to satisfy oneself that it falls within the ambit of the Uniform Law on Sales, and if that condition is satisfied, one has to revert to the primary assumption and to examine whether the contract was or was not validly concluded.

Three provisions of the Law on Formation deserve special mention. First, the Law attempts to reconcile the different attitude of English and European continental law to the problem of the firm offer. In English law an offer can, in principle, always be revoked until it is accepted; in short, unless the offer is by deed, rendered irrevocable by statute,[54] or supported by consideration, the concept of a binding offer is not admitted in English law.[55] In most European continental laws, on the other hand, an offeror is bound by his offer unless he has excluded its binding character. The compromise adopted by the Uniform Law on Formation is that in principle an offer can be revoked but such a revocation is excluded—

1. if the offer states a fixed time for acceptance or otherwise indicates that it is firm or irrevocable; or
2. if the revocation is not made in good faith or in conformity with fair dealing.[56]

Secondly, the Uniform Law on Formation attempts to solve the problem of an acceptance containing additional stipulations. In English law, if such stipulations are contained in the acceptance, the offer is normally regarded as rejected and the acceptance constitutes a counter-offer which may or may not be accepted by the original offeror. Logical as this rule is, it is iniquitous if the additional terms are only immaterial or trifling.[57] The Uniform Law provides that in principle an acceptance containing additions, limitations or other modifications shall be a rejection of the offer and a counter-offer, but if these additional or different terms do not alter the terms of the offer materially, the reply including these additions or modifications shall constitute the acceptance unless the offeror promptly objects to the discrepancy.[58]

Thirdly, the Uniform Law deals with the case of the late acceptance. Here it is provided that such an acceptance may be treated by the offeror

---

[53] Uniform Law on Formation, art. 1. (All references to articles in this section are to the Uniform Law on Formation (1967 Act, Sched. 2), unless stated otherwise.)

[54] See Companies Act 1985, s.82(7).

[55] American law differs in this respect from English law; the Uniform Commercial Code (1987 Official text), s.2–205, admits in certain circumstances firm offers.

[56] Art. 5(2) and (3).

[57] Here again, modern American law adopts a different solution in the Uniform Commercial Code (1987 Official Text), s.2–207.

[58] Art. 7. This provision is referred to in *Butler Machine Tool Co. Ltd.* v. *Ex-Cell-O Corporation (England) Ltd.* [1979] 1 W.L.R. 401, 406; see p. 99, *ante*.

as having arrived in due time if he promptly so informs the acceptor.[59] Further, if the delay in the receipt of the acceptance is due to unusual circumstances and the communication of the acceptance would have arrived in time if the transmission had been normal, the acceptance is deemed to have been communicated in due time, unless the offeror has promptly informed the acceptor that he considers his offer as lapsed.[60]

UN CONVENTION ON CONTRACTS FOR THE INTERNATIONAL SALE OF GOODS (1980)

The Vienna Convention and the Hague Uniform Laws

It has already been observed[61] that the Vienna Convention came into operation on January 1, 1988.[62] The States which have ratified it or acceded to it are[63]:

> Argentina, Australia, Austria, Byelorussian SSR, China, Denmark, Egypt, Finland, France, German Democratic Republic, Hungary, Italy, Lesotho, Mexico, Norway, Sweden, Syria, USA, Yugoslavia and Zambia.

Although founded on the Hague Uniform Laws, the Vienna Convention differs from them in form and, in some respects, in substance.

As regards form, the subject-matter of the two Uniform Laws is contained in the Vienna Convention in one document. The Vienna Convention consists of four Parts:

I. Sphere of Application and General Provisions.
II. Formation of the Contract.
III. Sale of Goods.
IV. Final Provisions.

Part II deals with offer and acceptance and the conclusion of the contract and is founded on the 1964 Uniform Law on Formation.[64] Part III, which is based on the 1964 Uniform Law on International Sales,[65] is subdivided into the following chapters:

---

[59] Art. 9(1).
[60] Art. 9(2).
[61] See p. 206, *ante*.
[62] The main literature on the Vienna Convention (in English) is: John O. Honnold, *Uniform Law for International Sales under the 1980 United Nations Convention*, 1982; C. M. Bianca and M. J. Bonell (eds.), *Commentary on the International Sales Law. The 1980 Vienna Sales Convention*, 1987; Peter Schlechtriem, *Uniform Sales Law. The UN Convention on Contracts for the International Sale of Goods;* Hamzeh Haddad, *Remedies of the Unpaid Seller in International Sale of Goods under ULIS and 1980 UN Convention*, 1985.
[63] Position: October 9, 1989. With respect to the UK, see p. 241, n. 8.
[64] See p. 247 *ante*.
[65] See p. 244 *ante*.

I. General Provisions.
II. Obligations of the Seller.
III. Obligations of the Buyer.
IV. Passing of the Risk.
V. Provisions common to the obligations of the Seller and the Buyer.

Chapter V of Part III contains provisions on anticipatory breach,[66] damages and exemptions,[67] and avoidance of contract[68]; it also contains provisions on the preservation of the goods.[69]

The Convention provides that a Contracting State, by declaration on accession, may adopt only Part II (on formation of contract) or Part III (on sale of goods).[70]

As regards substance, the Vienna Convention has greatly simplified the regulation contained in the Uniform Laws and has made it more flexible. A German scholar comments on these features of the Convention[71]:

> The tendency to avoid inflexible and irrevocable legal remedies . . . influenced the formulation of the remedy provisions in the 1980 Convention. The need for greater judicial discretion in particular cases also became clear, such as in the requirement that a measure or waiting period should be 'reasonable.' The new provisions on time limitations for giving notice in a timely manner (Articles 39 and 44) show especially clearly the strongly felt need for flexible rules to accommodate the buyer's difficulties.

Applicability of the Vienna Convention

The sphere of application of the Vienna Convention[72] is different from that of the Uniform Laws. While the latter are intended to apply in principle to all international sales but enable an acceding State to restrict their application to sales contracts between parties who have their place of business or habitual residence in Contracting States,[73] the Vienna Convention—realistically—restricts its application to contracts between parties who have their place of business in different Contracting States or to cases in which the proper law of the contract is that of a Contracting State. Article 1(1) of the Convention provides:

> This Convention applies to contracts of sale of goods between parties whose places of business are in different States:
>   (*a*) when the States are Contracting States; or

---

[66] Arts. 71 and 72.
[67] Arts. 74 to 77, 79 and 80.
[68] Arts. 81 to 84.
[69] Arts. 85 to 88.
[70] Art. 92.
[71] Peter Schlechtriem, *loc. cit.* in n. 62, p. 22.
[72] The Convention, by virtue of Article 2, does not apply to sales (a) of goods for personal, family or household use (with a slight qualification); (b) by auction; (c) on execution or otherwise by authority of law; (d) of stocks, shares, investment securities, negotiable instruments or money; (e) of ships, vessels, hovercraft or aircraft; (f) electricity.
    The Convention likewise does not apply to barter arrangements.
[73] The United Kingdom has made use of this qualification, see p. 243, *ante*.

(b) when the rules of private international law lead to the application of the law of a Contracting State.

An important feature of the Vienna Convention is that it does not admit a State which wishes to become a party to it and to introduce it into its national law to provide that the Convention shall only apply if the parties to the contract have adopted it.[74] But the Convention allows the parties to exclude its application or to derogate from or vary the effect of its provisions by their contract.[75] The effect of this regulation in the United Kingdom is this: under the 1967 Act the Uniform Laws apply only if the parties "contract in" but if the Vienna Convention is introduced into United Kingdom law, parties who do not wish to be subject to the Convention regulation would have to "contract out."

The Vienna Convention and the national law

While the Uniform Law on International Sales is intended to be a self-contained code as regards the topics regulated by it and expressly excludes the rules of private international law[76] in so far, the draftsmen of the Vienna Convention were aware that measures of conflict avoidance can reduce the dangers of a conflict of laws but cannot completely exclude them. For this reason they have linked the Vienna Convention with the national systems of private international law. This linkage occurs in two respects.

First, the Vienna Convention (like the Uniform Sales Law) does not regulate *all* incidents of the international sales transaction. It does not regulate:

(a) the special trade terms for the delivery of goods and the fixing of the price[77]; and
(b) the passing of property in the goods.[78]

Secondly, the Convention contains an express reference to national systems of private international law for the filling of gaps in the Convention. Article 7(2) provides:

Questions concerning matters governed by this Convention not expressly settled in it are to be settled in conformity with the general principles on which it is based or, in the

---

[74] This qualification is admitted by art. V of the First Convention of 1964 and the United Kingdom availed itself of it by the Uniform Laws on International Sales Act 1967, s.1(3); see p. 242, *ante*.
[75] Art. 6.
[76] See p. 206, *ante*.
[77] See p. 9, *ante*.
[78] Art. 4(b). The reason for this exclusion is that the regulation of the passing of property in the various legal systems is so different that a uniform rule could not be established; see p. 115 *ante*.
   In addition, the Convention does not regulate the law governing the alleged invalidity of a contract on general grounds, such as fraud, misrepresentation, incapacity and so on (Art. 4(a)). Product liability is likewise not regulated by the Convention (Art. 5).

absence of such principles, in conformity with the law applicable by virtue of the rules of private international law.

A good illustration of the linkage between the Vienna Convention and national law is provided by American law. The Convention is part of the federal law of the USA[79] and, as such overrides the Uniform Commercial Code, which is state law in the States which have given effect to it,[80] except if the parties have excluded the application of the Convention in whole or part[81] or in so far as a particular topic is not regulated by the Convention; these topics include important parts of Article 2 of the UCC—this is the Article dealing with Sales—, such as the special trade terms[82] and the provisions on passing of title, reservation for security and good faith purchasers.[83] The same relationship exists between the Vienna Convention and other national systems of law. It will therefore be necessary in many cases to ascertain the national law governing the international sales contract.

The central position of the Vienna Convention

The Vienna International Sales Convention is intended to be the centre piece of international harmonisation of trade law. A number of other satellite-Conventions is aligned with it, each dealing with a specialised subject and being self-contained but taking account of the provisions of the International Sales Convention. Thus, the UN Limitation Period Convention of 1974 was amended by the Vienna Conference of 1980 on the same day as the Conference approved the International Sales Convention, in order to make it conform to the latter.[84] Other of these aligned Conventions are the Hague Convention on the Law applicable to Contracts for the International Sale of Goods of 1986[85] and the Geneva Convention on Agency in the International Sale of Goods in 1983.[86] The

---

[79] *Selected Commercial Statutes* 1989 ed. West Publishing Co., p. 1087.

[80] These are all USA States and jurisdictions, except Louisiana. The effect is that the Vienna Convention is law in Louisiana but Article 2 of the UCC is not.

[81] By virtue of Article 6 of the Convention. If the parties adopt in their contract the law of a Contracting State, their adoption would include the adoption of the State's private international law and they would then again adopt the Convention; if they wish to exclude the Convention, they have to adopt the *domestic* law of the Contracting State. Thus, a choice of law clause in favour of the law of New York makes the Convention applicable, but a choice of law clause in favour of New York *domestic* law does not have this effect.

[82] Ss.2–319 to 2–324 of the UCC.

[83] Ss.2–401 to 2–403. s.2–402 deals with the rights of the seller's creditors against the sold goods.

But the provisions of s.2–201 of the UCC, which requires evidence in writing for sales contracts of $500 or more, is excluded by Art. 11 of the Vienna Convention and the USA has not declared Art. 11 to be inapplicable.

[84] See on p. 154 *post.*

[85] See p. 205 *ante.*

[86] See p. 312 *post.*

two Ottawa Conventions on International Factoring and International Financial Leasing of 1988[87] are likewise aligned to the Vienna Convention.

Some features of the Vienna Convention

Fundamental and non-fundamental breach

The Convention adopts many concepts of the Uniform Sales Law of 1964, but has refined them and made them more acceptable. It retains the distinction between fundamental and non-fundamental breach of the sales contract but defines fundamental breach in a more objective manner.[88] The definition of fundamental breach in the Vienna Convention,[89] should be compared with that of the Uniform Law on International Sales.[90] The definition of the Vienna Convention is this:

> A breach of contract committed by one of the parties is fundamental if it results in such detriment to the other party as substantially to deprive him of what he is entitled to expect under the contract, unless the party in breach did not foresee and a reasonable person of the same kind in the same circumstances would not have foreseen such a result.

From the practical point of view, the objective test of fundamental breach considerably restricts the cases in which avoidance of the international sales contract can be claimed under the Vienna Convention.

Specific performance and repair of non-conforming goods

The Vienna Convention entitles the buyer to demand specific performance, delivery of substitute goods for non-conforming goods and even repair of such goods. Article 46 of the Convention provides:

> (1) The buyer may require performance by the seller of his obligations unless the buyer has resorted to a remedy which is inconsistent with this requirement.
> (2) If the goods do not conform with the contract, the buyer may require delivery of substitute goods only if the lack of conformity constitutes a fundamental breach of contract and a request for substitute goods is made either in conjunction with notice given under Article 39[91] or within a reasonable time thereafter.

---

[87] See p. 453 *post*.
[88] The definition of fundamental breach in the Uniform Sales Law has been criticised as being too subjective.
[89] Art. 25 of the Vienna Convention.
[90] Art. 10 of the Uniform Law; see p. 246, *ante*.
[91] Article 39 provides that the buyer loses the right to rely on non-conformity if he does not give the seller notice specifying the defects within a reasonable time, and in any event he loses that right if he does not given such notice within two years from the date when the goods were handed over, unless a longer guarantee was given.

> (3) If the goods do not conform with the contract, the buyer may require the seller to remedy the lack of conformity by repair, unless this is unreasonable having regard to all the circumstances. A request for repair must be made either in conjunction with notuce given under Article 39[92] or within a reasonable time thereafter.

These remedies are different from those normally available in English law. In English law the normal remedy for the breach of a condition, such as the supply of non-conforming goods, is a claim for damages. A claim for the repair of such goods is unknown to the common law.

UN CONVENTION ON THE LIMITATION PERIOD IN THE INTERNATIONAL SALE OF GOODS (1974)

This Convention was signed June 14, 1974 in New York. It was the first project of UNCITRAL which reached fruition. This Convention was amended by a Protocol, adopted by the UN Conference at Vienna on April 11, 1980, the same day when the Convention on Contracts for the International Sale of Goods was approved. The purpose of the Protocol is to align the provisions of the Limitation Convention with those of the Contracts for the International Sale of Goods Convention. The Limitation Convention has been ratified or acceded to by the following countries[93]

> *Argentina, Czechoslovakia, Dominican Republic, *Egypt, *German Democratic Republic, Ghana, *Hungary, *Mexico, Norway, Yugoslavia, and *Zambia.

The United Kingdom has not ratified the Limitation Convention.[94]

The Convention is intended to replace a variety of conflicting national laws which provide limitation periods ranging from six months to 30 years. The basic aim of the Convention is to establish a uniform time limit that prevents the pressing of claims at such a late date that evidence has become unreliable.

The Convention[95] limits to four years the period within which a buyer or seller may press claims based on a contract for the international sale of goods.[96] The sphere of application of the Limitation Convention is

---

[92] Michael Will, the commentator of Article 46 in *Bianca and Bonell* (see n. 62, *ante*), 334, correctly states that the common law admits a claim for specific performance in equity only if damages would be an inadequate remedy; he then states: "interestingly enough, the two opposing approaches appear to be less different in practice." It is thought that this comment is correct because the aggrieved buyer will normally prefer to claim damages.

[93] Countries preceded by * have ratified or acceded to the Protocol of 1980, and such a ratification makes them automatically Contracting States of the Limitation Convention (Arts. XI and XIV of the Protocol).

[94] Position: October 9, 1988.

[95] The Convention, as amended by the 1980 Protocol, does not apply to the sales to which the International Sales Convention does not apply; see n. 72, *ante*. The exclusions in the unamended Limitation Convention are worded slightly differently.

[96] Art. 8 of the Limitation Convention.

assimilated by the 1980 Protocol to that of the International Sales Convention of that year.[97]

The Convention contains provisions specifying exactly when the limitation period begins to run, which is usually the case when the claim becomes due. It also states when the limitation period ceases to run, under what circumstances it can be extended, how it can be modified by the parties and how it is calculated. In the case of a breach of contract, the limitation period begins on the date of the breach. When the buyer finds a defect in the goods supplied or discovers that they do not otherwise conform to the terms of the contract the limitation period starts from the date when the goods were handed over to him or its delivery is refused by him. The limitation period for claims based on fraud begins on the date on which the fraud is discovered or reasonably could be discovered.

The limitation period ceases to run when one party begins judicial or arbitral proceedings against the other. In the case of other proceedings, including those in which a party presses a claim upon the death or insolvency of the other party, the period ceases to run once the claim is asserted. When a party making a claim is prevented by circumstances beyond his control from starting legal proceedings, he may have a one-year extension from the time when those circumstances cease to exist. The overall limit for extensions of the limitation period is 10 years from the date when the period began to run. A circumstance occurring in another Contracting State that affects the cessation or extension of the limitation period, shall be taken into account, provided that the creditor has taken all reasonable steps to inform the debtor of it as soon as possible.

---

[97] See p. 250, *ante*. In the unamended Limitation Convention the sphere of application was different.

PART TWO

MARKETING ORGANISATION ABROAD

CHAPTER 15

SOLE DISTRIBUTION AGREEMENTS. LICENSING AND FRANCHISING

THE main concern of the exporter who is intent on expanding his sales abroad is to devise a well-planned marketing strategy. Obviously he will first engage in intensive market research, utilising the sources of information described in an earlier chapter.[1] But he will soon discover that the economic, social and political conditions in the various overseas countries are so different that his approach to marketing his goods abroad must be very flexible. An organisational scheme suitable for one country may be totally unsuitable for another.

The establishment of a single market in the EC in 1992[2] will, it is hoped, create a favourable climate for direct purchases by buyers in a Member State from sellers in others, but even in the countries of the Community differences founded on linguistic problems, customary sales techniques and traditional customer preferences will remain; it may therefore be necessary for the exporter even in this regional market to contemplate the establishment of local outlets for his products.

In the present Part of this work the various legal forms of overseas marketing will be considered. They can be grouped as follows:

1. The exporter may conclude a *sole distribution* or a *licensing* or *franchising agreement* with an importer abroad; or
2. he may entrust his respresentation to an *exclusive agent* abroad or ask his overseas customers to use the services of a *confirming house* in this country; or
3. he may provide his own unincorporated or corporate marketing organisation in the overseas country by establishing a *branch office* or *subsidiary* there, or by a *foreign acquisition, i.e.* by acquiring an enterprise already carrying on business in the target country and possibly having established market outlets there; or
4. he may combine with an enterprise in the overseas country in a *joint venture* or adopt another form of joint export organisation, *e.g.* the *European Economic Interest Grouping (EEIG)*.

It is intended to deal in this chapter with the first types of marketing organisation and to examine the other types in the following chapters of

---

[1] Chapter 4, on p. 81 *ante.*
[2] Provided by the Single European Act 1986; see p. 5, n. 6, *ante.*

this Part. Since the choice of the marketing organisation most appropriate to the circumstances is greatly influenced by the competition law of the EC and the United Kingdom, a chapter dealing with these topics is included in this Part.

NATURE OF SOLE DISTRIBUTION AGREEMENTS

Sole and exclusive agreements

In distribution agreements, which are considered in this chapter, and in agency agreements, which are treated in the next one, the distributor or agent is often granted "sole" or "exclusive" rights of representation. The law does not attach a definite meaning to these terms. It has, therefore, to be ascertained in every case what the parties meant by them. The best course for the parties is to spell out in their agreement the precise rights which they intend the representative to have. If these rights are not defined in the contract, it should be borne in mind that in modern commercial usage the following meaning is often attributed to the terms "sole" and "exclusive:"

1. Both terms imply that the principal shall not be entitled to appoint another distributor or agent for the territory of the representative.
2. If the representation is "sole," the principal himself may undertake sales in the territory of the representative on his own account without any liability to the representative.
3. If the representation is "exclusive," the principal is not allowed himself to compete with the representative in the allotted territory. This interpretation is supported by the definition of the word "exclusive" in the Patents Act 1977, s.130, where the term "exclusive licence" is defined.

Sometimes a distribution or agency agreement provides that the representative shall have "sole and exclusive" rights of representation.

Sole distribution agreements distinguished from contracts of sale and from agency agreements

Sole distribution agreements,[3] as customary in the export trade, are different from contracts of sale and agency agreements. They provide, in

---

[3] See Roberto Baldi, *Distributorship, Franchising, Agency. Community and National Laws and Practice in the EEC.* English translation, 1987. Also *Guide to Drafting International Distributorship Agreements,* ICC Brochure No. 441, December 1988; Rudolf Graupner, "Sole Distributorship Agreements—a Comparative View" (1969) 18 I.C.L.Q. 879; J. A. Wade, "The Sole Distributor in Comparative and Private International Law, in *Hague-Zagreb Essays* 4 *on the Law of International Trade,* p. 213, edited by C. C. A. Voskuil and J. A. Wade (1983, T.M.C. Asser Instituut, The Hague). On exclusive sales agreements in French law and on the law of the EC, see R. Plaisant, *Les contrats d'exclusivité* in (1964) 17 *Rev.Trim. de Droit Commercial* 1; Thomas E. Carbonneau, "Exclusive Distributorship Agreements in French Law." (1979) 28 I.C.L.Q. 91.

essence, that the seller, a United Kingdom manufacturer or merchant, grants the buyer, an overseas merchant, sole trading rights within a particular territory with respect to goods of a specified kind while the buyer may undertake to rely on the seller as the sole source of supply whenever desirous of buying goods of the specified kind in the United Kingdom.[4] Where such a contract is concluded between a manufacturer of computers in the United Kingdom and an Indian importer, the former is not entitled to appoint another distributor for his computers in India, nor, if that is the intention of the parties, is the latter at liberty to buy competitive makes of computers in this country. The sole distribution agreement is not a contract of sale of specific goods. It merely lays down the general terms on which later individual contracts of sale will be concluded. Sometimes the sole distribution agreement contains a stipulation on the part of the buyer to buy a quantity of specified goods which have to be delivered by instalments or on call. Even where such a stipulation is not agreed upon, the sole distribution agreement is not merely a contract to conclude a contract, but an agreement which is presently effective. Although its mandatory clauses are dependent on the conclusion of individual contracts of sale in the future, its restrictive clauses are immediately effective and remain in force for the duration of the agreement even when individual sales are never concluded. Where the exclusive buyer resides in a region or country which has strict laws safeguarding competition, such as the EC or the United States, great care has to be taken that the proposed agreement does not infringe these laws.[5]

Further, the sole distributor is not an agent of the British manufacturer or merchant in the legal sense, although in commercial parlance he is sometimes loosely referred to as such.[6] Unlike an agent in the legal sense, the sole distributor does not act on behalf of the British principal and is not accountable to him for the profits derived from the resale of the goods in his own territory. The profit of the sole distributor is normally the difference between the buying and selling price whereas the profit of the agent is usually the commission which he earns when concluding a sales contract on behalf of his principal or when the principal concludes a sales contract with a customer introduced by the agent.

The sole distribution agreement has some affinity with a contract granting exclusive agency rights; in both contracts an area or territory is defined where the exclusive trading rights are to be operative. The sole distribution agreement differs from the exclusive agency agreement also in another aspect; the contracts which are concluded within its framework are proper contracts of sale by which the overseas merchant—the

---

[4] For details see p. 267, *post.*
[5] See p. 346, *post.*
[6] See p. 279, *post.*

distributor—buys in his own name and when he resells the goods in his territory no contractual bond is established between the re-purchaser and the British exporter.[7] The sole distribution agreement has thus a distinct advantage over the exclusive agency agreement: the British exporter is not concerned with the credit of a multitude of buyers in the foreign territory, but he sells to one person only whose credit and commercial standing is well known to him or is at least relatively easily ascertainable.

Sole distribution agreements and licensing and franchising agreements

The sole distribution agreement is sometimes described by commercial men as the grant of a sales licence. From the legal point of view, this is an inaccurate description because the distribution agreement provides for the conclusion of straightforward contracts of sale and not for the grant of licences.

Licensing and franchising agreements are very different from sole distribution agreements. By a licensing agreement the owner of an intellectual property right authorises another person, the licensee, to use that right, subject to certain conditions. The intellectual property right may be a patent, trade mark, (unregistered) business name or a particular business method. A franchise agreement is a contract whereby the franchisor grants the franchisee a licence to carry on a particular business under a name belonging to the franchisor and making use of his business methods, which the franchisor communicates to the franchisee. Normally the franchisor is entitled under this agreement to exercise a strict degree of control over the franchised business during the period of the licence.[8] Licensing and franchising agreements will be considered later on.[9]

Export distribution agreements

A sole distribution agreement might further be concluded between an exporter in this country and a manufacturer or wholesaler here. In this case the exporter, who is sometimes referred to as "exporter distributor," is granted the exclusive right of distributing the manufacturer's goods abroad, either anywhere or in a specified market. Two types of export

---

[7] A commission agent or *commissionaire* in the continental sense (see p. 293, *post*) is not a sole distributor because, although he resells the goods in his own name, he acts on behalf of his principal and is accountable to him for the profits of the transaction. He is a true agent, as this term is understood in English law. He receives usually a commission.

[8] John Adams and K. V. Prichard Jones, *Franchising* (1987), p. 8.

[9] See p. 271, *post*.

distribution agreements are in use and the contract should make it clear in unambiguous terms which type is intended: under some export distribution agreements the distributor undertakes to place annually orders of a fixed amount with the manufacturer, and under other agreements he merely undertakes to place such orders if and when he receives them from his customers abroad; although in the latter case—as in the former—the export distributor undertakes to place the order in his own name (and not as agent of the overseas customer) and to hold himself personally liable for the price, the nature of his obligation differs; in the latter case the distributor is only liable if he fails diligently[10] to pass on to the manufacturer such customers' orders as are received by him while in the former case he is liable to order goods of the stipulated value whether he receives such orders or not. The importance of this distinction became evident in the following case[11]: the defendants, a confirming house, undertook to act as exclusive export distributors of the plaintiffs, manufacturers of water taps and other sanitary fittings, for certain foreign countries. The agreement was for 15 years but could be cancelled at the end of 10 years by giving six months' notice. Under clause 2(*k*) of the agreement the export distributors undertook to "pass on to the manufacturers customers' orders for the goods amounting to not less in volume than the volume of goods which at present price would amount to the value of £80,000." The agreement continued in operation for about 15 months when the amount of orders had fallen short of the stipulated value, mainly because in some foreign countries the issue of import licences for the goods in question was suspended. A dispute arose between the parties on the exact meaning of clause 2(*k*). The manufacturers maintained that the distributors were bound to place annually £80,000 worth of orders while the latter contended that they were only obliged to give them whatever orders they received from their customers. The manufacturers contended that the distributors had repudiated the agreement and claimed damages resulting, first, from the breach of clause 2(*k*) during the currency of the agreement and, secondly, from the repudiation of the entire contract. The Court of Appeal held that clause 2(*k*) obliged the export distributors to place annually £80,000 worth of orders with the manufacturers whether they received such orders from their customers or did not receive them, but that the construction which the distributors put on the clause, though being erroneous, was adopted in good faith and did not evince an intention to repudiate the entire

---

[10] He must use his best endeavours; see *Ault & Wiborg Paints Ltd.* v. *Sure Service Ltd.*, *The Times*, July 2, 1983; see p. 267, *post*.
[11] *James Shaffer Ltd.* v. *Findlay Durham & Brodie* [1953] 1 W.L.R. 106. See also the Canadian case of *Wingold* v. *Wm. Looser & Co.* [1951] 1 D.L.R. 429 and the Scottish case *R. J. Dempster Ltd.* v. *Motherwell Bridge and Engineering Co. Ltd.* 1964 S.C. 308.

contract.[12] The court awarded the plaintiffs damages for non-performance of the distributors' undertakings during the 15 months during which the contract was in operation, but dismissed the claim for damages resulting from the repudiation of the contract which, in view of the long currency of the contract, would have been heavy.

When interpreting the clauses of a sole distribution agreement, it must be borne in mind that the parties intend to build up an enduring relationship. Minor deviations from the terms of the contract cannot be used as an excuse to treat the whole contract as repudiated although they may give rise to a claim for damages. This is particularly true if, without obligation on his part, the sole distributor has incurred considerable expense in order to promote the sales of the producer's goods. Thus in *Decro-Wall S.A.* v. *Marketing Ltd.*[13] Decro-Wall, a French company, gave the sole distributing rights of their goods—decorative tiles—in the United Kingdom to Marketing, a small but reputable company. The sole distribution agreement was of indefinite duration and thus determinable by reasonable notice. Marketing was highly successful in building up a market in the United Kingdom. Two years after the conclusion of the agreement there were already 780 points of sale of Decro-Wall products in the United Kingdom. Marketing spent some £30,000 on advertising Decro-Wall products and had engaged at least six extra salesmen. There were, however, some minor differences between the parties due to slow payment by Marketing, although in the end it always paid fully; Marketing also alleged delayed deliveries by Decro-Wall. The managing director of Marketing thereupon submitted a new plan for smaller but more regular deliveries but that plan was rejected by Decro-Wall. Decro-Wall then appointed another company in the United Kingdom its sole concessionaire. Decro-Wall alleged that its contract with Marketing had been repudiated by the latter by its failure to pay the bills punctually and purported to accept that repudiation. Decro-Wall sued Marketing in the English courts for the outstanding bills and also for a declaration that

---

[12] Repudiation occurs only if there is clear and unequivocal conduct of a party evincing his intention of not to be bound by the contract, see *The Mercanaut* [1980] 2 Lloyd's Rep. 183, 185; *Woodar Investment Development Ltd.* v. *Wimpey Construction U.K. Ltd.* [1980] 1 W.L.R. 277 (H.L.). The repudiation must be accepted in order to terminate the contract; such acceptance does not, of course, mean abandonment of the claim for damages by the aggrieved party: *MSC Mediterranean Shipping Co. SA* v. *B.R.E.-Metro Ltd.* [1985] 2 Lloyd's Rep. 239. There can be no acceptance without knowledge of the innocent party that a repudiation has occurred; the innocent party must have the option of electing whether to accept the repudiation or not: *Fercometal Sarl* v. *Mediterranean Shipping Co. SA. The Simona.* [1988] 3 W.L.R. 200, 206 (H.L.); *State Trading Corporation of India Ltd.* v. *M. Golodetz Ltd.* [1988] 2 Lloyd's Rep. 182, 1988. For the measure of damages in repudiation cases see *Lusograin Comercio Internacional de Cereas Ltda.* v. *Bunge AG* [1986] 2 Lloyd's Rep. 654.

[13] [1971] 1 W.L.R. 361; see also *Evans Marshall & Co. Ltd.* v. *Bertola S.A.* [1975] 2 Lloyd's Rep. 373 (the contract of sole distributorship contains an implied term according to which the supplier must not charge the distributor prices which would prevent him from making a reasonable commercial profit).

Marketing had ceased to be its sole concessionaire in the United Kingdom. Marketing, by its counterclaim, asked for a declaration that it was still the sole concessionaire of Decro-Wall in the United Kingdom. The Court of Appeal held that Marketing had not repudiated the agreement by its failure to pay outstanding bills punctually, as time was not of the essence of the payments, that the agreement between the parties still subsisted and could only be terminated by reasonable notice and that, in the circumstances, the length of such notice was twelve months.

CLAUSES IN SOLE DISTRIBUTION AGREEMENTS

Sole distribution agreements require careful drafting. An infinite variety of arrangements is possible here. The parties have complete liberty of contracting and should use that discretion for the purpose of creating by their contract a charter of trading which is fair and equitable to both of them, and closely adapted to the particular requirements of their trade and can be relied upon, whether the market is a seller's or a buyer's market. In view of the variety of forms admitted by the law, it is impossible to give an exhaustive catalogue of the clauses embodied in these agreements; it is believed that the main points to be considered are indicated under the following heads which are illustrated by contract clauses when necessary.

Definition of the territory

The following points have to be considered by the parties:

(1) The geographical definition of the territory which may consist of several political units, *e.g.* the Scandinavian countries, or of one political unit, *e.g.* Sweden, or of part of a political unit, *e.g.* the city of Stockholm.

(2) The extension of the territory at a future date. Sometimes such extension is merely expressed as a moral claim, sometimes the buyer—the sole distributor—is given a legal right to claim the extension on the happening of certain events, *e.g.* when the sales in his own territory have reached a certain amount over a fixed period.

(3) The seller's obligation not to sell directly to customers in the territory. In earlier agreements it was usual to provide that the seller should insert a clause into his contracts with his home buyers and overseas buyers (other than the contracting party) prohibiting the direct or indirect sale of the goods in the territory of the

exclusive dealer. In modern practice such an undertaking is normally omitted, as far as the Member States of the EC are concerned, because such restrictions are likely to infringe the competition law of the EC.[14]

(4) The seller's obligation to refer direct inquiries from consumers in the territory to the buyer.

(5) The buyer's obligation to pass on enquiries from outside the territory to the seller.

(6) The buyer's obligation to keep customers'—retailers'—lists and to supply them to the seller on request.

(7) The territory in which the buyer is bound to buy exclusively from the seller. Here again, the former practice of providing that the buyer shall not buy any goods of the specified description from another source of supply than the buyer is now usually abandoned in the EC because of the danger that such restrictions may contravene the provisions of the EC Treaty or of national legislations.

Definition of the price

Sometimes the distribution agreement contains provisions relating to the ascertainment of the price which the distributor shall pay when ordering goods under that agreement. The difficulty is here that the distribution agreement is intended to be of considerable duration but that the prices of the goods, which shall be bought from time to time by way of individual sales contracts under the terms of the distribution agreement may be affected by inflation or other events or may fluctuate if quoted on world markets, as, *e.g.* is the case with crude oil, minerals or commodities.

The parties refer sometimes in the distribution agreement to a definite price ruling on a particular date, such as the date of conclusion of the sales contract or the delivery of the goods, *e.g.* the f.o.b. spot price for crude oil of the grade in question quoted at Rotterdam at the date of the bill of lading. In other cases the parties agree that the distributor shall pay the *most favoured customer (m.f.c)* price, *i.e.* the best price which the supplier would obtain from another customer at the critical date, possibly subject to a rebate. When an m.f.c. price is agreed upon, it is usual to allow the supplier a list of exempted customers and to provide that sales to them shall not be taken into account when determining the m.f.c. price. This list includes, among others, the holding company, the subsidiaries, associated and connected companies of the supplier. An example of an m.f.c. price clause is this:

---

[14] See p. 357, *post.*

For the supplies in accordance with clause 1 of this agreement [the distributor] will pay [the supplier], unless otherwise agreed, the lowest f.o.b. price charged under comparable conditions to any customer of [the supplier], except if supplied to a company on the attached list, such price to be reduced by a rebate of 18 per cent.

Definition of the goods

(1) The contract may only refer to some lines produced or traded by the seller and not to his whole range of production or trade.

(2) A good method of defining the goods in question is to append to the contract a schedule of identifying them by the seller's catalogue number.

(3) Sometimes goods are described generally as "all kinds and types of goods, machinery and equipment designed for use in the . . . industry."

(4) The contract should cease to apply with respect to goods which the seller discontinues to manufacture or trade.

(5) The contract should allow for an extension to new lines manufactured or traded by the seller where the new lines are used in the same trade as the goods covered by the agreement.

Sole buying and selling rights

(1) A contract need not provide for sole buying and selling rights as concurrent terms and is valid if only establishing sole selling rights or sole buying rights. In practice, reciprocal agreements provide mutual satisfaction and are preferable to agreements whereby only one party is granted sole trading rights; but all depends here on the requirements of the particular trade. Where these matters are not regulated expressly in the distribution agreement, a term may have to be implied that the distributor shall use his best endeavours to promote the supplier's goods. It was held in one case[15] that in the circumstances of the contract such implied term was not inconsistent with the distributor being at liberty to promote similar goods made by competitors of the supplier but required him to treat the supplier favourably, at least as favourably as he treated the competitors. The decision demonstrates the need for regulating

---

[15] *Ault & Wiborg Paints Ltd.* v. *Sure Service Ltd., The Times,* July 2, 1983 (C.A.; (the case dealt with a home transaction)). What constitutes a breach of the contractual obligation on the part of the distributor to use his best efforts on behalf of the supplier, was discussed in the Australian case *U.S. Surgical Corporation* v. *Hospital Products Ltd.* [1983] 2 N.S.W.L.R. 157.

these matters expressly in the contract, subject, of course, to the mandatory provisions of the competition rules of the EC and the national legislation.[16]

(2) The contract should put it beyond doubt that the overseas importer acts as buyer and not as agent of the seller. The following clause illustrates this point:

> It is agreed and understood that the buyer is not the agent or representative of the seller for any purpose whatever, and that the buyer has no authority or power to bind the seller, or to contract in the name of, and to create a liability against, the seller in any way or for any purpose, but on the other hand it is understood that the buyer stands in the relation of an independent contractor with the exclusive rights to buy the seller's . . . machinery, and to resell, handle and deal in the same on his own account and responsibility in the said territory as hereinbefore set forth.

(3) The seller may ask for a clause obliging the buyer to offer the seller's goods in the market. The following clause is here sometimes found:

> During the life of this contract the buyer agrees vigorously, diligently, and in good efficient salesmanlike manner, to solicit orders for and to bring to the attention of buyers or potential buyers within the territory, the seller's entire line of . . . machinery and equipment, all to the end that as large a volume of sales of the seller's said machinery and equipment can and will be made to the ultimate users thereof in the territory as the circumstances of competition and general business from time to time permit.

(4) The seller asks sometimes that orders representing a minimum value shall be ordered within a fixed time; sometimes the agreement gives the seller an option of giving notice of termination if the orders placed by the buyer do not represent a minimum value for a fixed period.

Advertising, market information, protection of patents and trade marks

(1) The seller is normally not interested in the proceeds of the sale of goods in the territory, as his overseas contractor stands in the position of a buyer and not of an agent. The seller is, however, interested in seeing a demand created in the overseas market for his goods and having his trade mark advertised if the goods are distributed under that mark. The buyer is, therefore, sometimes asked to undertake certain minimum obligations with respect to the advertising of the goods. The following clause illustrates this point:

---

[16] See p. 346, *post.*

> All exhibiting, soliciting of orders, and advertising either by circulars or by paid advertisements in journals or magazines circulating in the territory, of the . . . machines and equipment of the seller shall be under the exclusive control and at the expense of the buyer, but the buyer agrees during the life of this contract to provide and pay for not less than 12 full-page advertisements per annum, appearing at regular monthly intervals in the national journals or magazines of the . . . industry circulating generally throughout the territory, and the buyer at his own expense will at the time of issue dispatch to the seller a copy of each such monthly journal or magazine in which such advertisements of the seller's machinery or equipment appears.

(2) It is sometimes provided that the distributor shall visit certain prospective customers at regular intervals.[17]

(3) The buyer is often asked to provide the seller with market information which is accessible to him, *e.g.*:

> The buyer agrees to the best of his ability to provide the seller at intervals or at such reasonable times as the seller may request information concerning any developments in the territory relating to the demand, the reactions of the ultimate users, the activities of the competitors, or other matters or circumstances relating to this contract as far as such information is reasonably accessible to the buyer, and the latter agrees to do all such acts and things as may be necessary or helpful to extend and improve the sale of the seller's . . . machinery and equipment in the territory, and to extend and maintain the public goodwill towards the seller's said machinery and equipment.

(4) Due protection should be provided for the seller's patents and trade marks,[18] and the seller sometimes asks generally for an undertaking on the part of the buyer not to make, imitate or copy the goods.

Other clauses

(1) The contract should embody the appropriate provisions of the seller's general conditions of sale which have been discussed earlier.[19]

(2) The contract is usually concluded for an indefinite time, and either party is given the right of terminating the agreement upon a fixed date, *e.g.* the end of every calendar year, on having given notice a

---

[17] In *L. Schuler A.G.* v. *Wickman Machine Tool Sales Ltd.* [1974] A.C. 235 the sole distributor agreement concerned panel presses and the sole distributor undertook to visit the six largest United Kingdom motor manufacturers at least once every week. Failure to comply with this clause was held not to be a breach of a condition although the clause was described in the contract as a condition.

[18] In *Sport International Bussum BV* v. *Hi-Tec Sports Ltd.*, *The Times*, June 23, 1987, the Dutch owner of a trade mark granted a distributor the exclusive right to use his trade mark in the UK; the Court of Appeal held that a term had to be implied into the distribution agreement that after its termination the distributor was not only prevented from using the owner's trade mark in the UK but also from using it in any other country without licence by the owner.

[19] See p. 75, *ante*.

fixed number of days or months prior to that date. Sometimes the seller's right to terminate the agreement depends on the purchases by the buyer falling below a certain minimum value over a fixed period.

Where the contract contains no provision for its termination, a party is entitled to give the other party notice of reasonable length.[20] In agreements in the commercial field, such as exclusive sales agreements, there is no presumption in favour of permanence.[21]

Laws Relating to Restrictive Practices

The sole distribution agreement must further conform with the laws relating to restrictive trade practices and restraints of trade, as in force in the EC, the United Kingdom and in the countries in which the agreement is intended to operate.

As far as EC law is concerned, an exclusive sales agreement may contravene the prohibitions of Articles 85(1) and 86 of the EC Treaty. Great care has to be taken when it is drafted to avoid this danger. The regulation of EC law, as far as affecting exclusive sales and agency agreements, will be examined later on.[22] So will be the relevant competition law of the United Kingdom, as far as this is possible in its present[23] state of flux.[24] In common law a clause in restraint of trade is invalid unless it can be justified as reasonable in the circumstances of the case; restraints of trade which can be shown to be reasonable will be enforced by the English courts.[25] In the United States of America "restraint of trade," "tying requirements" and "exclusive dealings" have, in individual cases, been declared invalid as representing unfair practices and may also infringe the various Anti-Trust Acts[26] in force.

Foreign Legislation Protecting Sole Distributors

Some countries, including the United Kingdom,[27] protect certain classes of employees from unfair dismissal and, unlike the United Kingdom,

---

[20] See *Decro-Wall S.A.* v. *Marketing Ltd.* [1971] 1 W.L.R. 361, discussed on p. 264, *ante.*
[21] *Martin-Baker Aircraft Co. Ltd.* v. *Canadian Flight Equipment Ltd.* [1955] 2 Q.B. 556, 571; *Tower Hamlets London Borough Council* v. *British Gas Corporation* (1982) 79 L.S.Gaz. 1025; *The Times,* March 23, 1982.
[22] See p. 346, *post.*
[23] October 1, 1989.
[24] See p. 361, *post.*
[25] See p. 371, *post.*
[26] On the extraterritorial effect of the American anti-trust legislation, see pp. 229–231, *post.*
[27] Employment Protection (Consolidation) Act 1978, Part V, as amended. For foreign protective legislation affecting employees, see p. 333, *post.*

even grant agents a claim for compensation after termination of the contract of agency, subject to certain conditions.[28] But no country, except Belgium, extends these protective measures to sole distributors.

A Belgian Law of July 27, 1961, amended by a Law of April 13, 1971, aims at the protection of sole distributors carrying on business in Belgium.[29] The protection of this Law is extended to sole, exclusive and quasi-exclusive distributors, whether their trading privilege is of contractual or factual nature. The Law provides that exclusive distributorships of indefinite duration cannot be terminated without giving reasonable notice, except if one of the parties seriously defaults in his duties, and that, if terminated without such notice, the distributor is entitled to an equitable compensation. Moreover, even if it is terminated properly, an equitable compensation may be payable in certain circumstances. The highest Belgian court, the Court of Cassation, held in one case[30] that these provisions cannot be contracted out, particularly not by submitting the contract of sole distributorship to a non-Belgian law or by adopting arbitration outside Belgium. It may, however, be possible to avoid this result by inserting into the contract a clause providing for exclusive jurisdiction of a court in another EC country.[31] The Court of Cassation also held in the case referred to that an exclusive distribution agreement limited in time but repeatedly renewed was to be treated as an indefinite distributorship.

LICENSING AND FRANCHISING AGREEMENTS

Licensing agreements

Frequently the owner in a particular territory of patents, trade marks, and other forms of intellectual property wants to exploit them abroad through licensing, rather than by using them himself. The advantage of this is that the licensee provides the capital needed and carries the commercial risk of the transactions. The two principal matters which need to be attended to when drawing up the licence are quality control and

---

[28] See p. 310, *post.*

[29] Charles Price "Selling through a distributor or licensee in Belgium" in [1983] J.B.L. 443. The Belgian law is reproduced on p. 178 of Roberto Baldi's book, quoted on p. 260, n. 3, *ante.*

[30] In *S.A. Adelia Petit* v. *Audi-NSU*, judgment of July 28, 1979, see [1980] J.B.L. 132.

[31] Charles Price, *op. cit.* 449. The Belgian courts apparently consider themselves to be bound by art. 17 of the Brussels Convention on Jurisdiction and the Enforcement of Judgments in Civil and Commercial Matters of September 27, 1968; the United Kingdom has given effect to this Convention by the Civil Jurisdiction and Judgments Act 1982, see p. 710, *post.*

taxation. Failure to provide for adequate quality control can damage not only the owner's reputation, but also some of the intellectual property rights themselves. Various strategies to control quality are employed, according to the type of business involved, but frequently sampling will suffice.

The principal concern, so far as taxation is concerned, is whether or not tax is deductible at source. The fact that tax is deductible at source can create serious difficulties for a licensor, because it will affect his cash flow, and because it may prevent him from minimising his liability to taxation.

It is also important, especially when licensing in third world countries, to ensure that the licence complies with the provisions of any technology transfer legislation. In general, this is legislation designed to redress the inequality of bargaining power which often exists between the owners of intellectual property in advanced countries and the potential licensees in less developed countries.[32] This legislation provides guidance to the potential licensees, as to the terms they should be seeking to negotiate. It is also important to ensure that the licence does not infringe any relevant antitrust legislation.[33]

The licensing transaction described here is sometimes referred to as ordinary licensing. It should not be confused with financial licensing, which is a financial credit transaction.[34]

Franchising agreements

The course of business

Where is is important for marketing purposes that the licensee operates under the licensor's corporate image, the particular form of licensing known as "franchising" may be adopted. Under this type of arrangement, the franchisee carries on the licensed business under the franchisor's name, marks, etc., in accordance with a system developed by the franchisor. Almost every aspect of the licensed business is controlled by the franchisor, the object of the system being to preserve strict uniformity between outlets so that customers are unable to distinguish between the various franchised outlets, and between franchised outlets and company-owned outlets. In every respect, but one, the franchised outlet resembles a company-owned outlet. The one respect in which it does not is, however, crucial: the franchisee owns the outlet, and risks his own

---

[32] See Guillermo Cabanellas "Antitrust and Direct Regulation of International Transfer of Technology Transactions" (1982).
[33] See p. 346, *ante*.
[34] See pp. 462–465, *post*.

capital; he therefore has a great incentive to make a success of the business. The system is particularly valuable in industries such as catering where labour problems are endemic and employee behaviour is difficult to monitor, but it is applicable to very many other types of business. Although it is very commonly associated with what are called "fast food" restaurants, this is only a small part of the industry. Moreover, the franchise industry is not solely involved in supplying goods and services to consumers. Many businesses exist which deal principally or exclusively with other businesses. Where there is a local franchise association, it will usually be desirable that the franchisor should join it. These associations in general subscribe to the Code of Ethics established by the International Franchise Association. Would-be franchisees will usually expect reputable franchisors to belong to the local association. Strict control over every aspect of the way in which the franchisee carries on the business is crucial in franchising, and a franchisee who fails to comply with the terms of the agreement can expect to have it terminated. The agreement is for a fixed number of years, during which the franchisee expects to be able to recoup his initial investment and to make a profit (often quite large). It is not usual for a franchisor to make any payment to the franchisee at the end of the term in respect of the assets of the business. Sometimes a franchisee will be given the option of a second term, but usually he will be required to execute a new agreement.

Franchising agreements in the EC jurisprudence

Franchising has raised difficult problems in the competition law in the EC. The first decision of the EC Court of Justice on this subject was given in *Pronuptia de Paris GmbH* v. *Schillgalis*.[35] It was followed by the decision of the Commission in *Computerland*[36] and *Yves Rocher*,[37] which involved distribution franchises, and *ServiceMaster*[38] which involved a service franchise. As a result of these cases, the block exemption,[39] and the recent decision in *Charles Jourdan*,[40] the application of EC competition law to the many business format franchise agreements is now somewhat clearer.

In the *Pronuptia* case the plaintiffs were Pronuptia de Paris GmbH, which were a subsidiary of Pronuptia de Paris SA in France. The company traded in wedding dresses and other products connected with

[35] Case 161/84, [1986] 3 ECR 353; [1986] 1 C.M.L.R. 414.
[36] O.J. 1987 L222/12. [1989] 4 C.M.L.R. 259.
[37] Case 87/100 O.J. 1987 L8/49 [1988] 4 C.M.L.R. 592.
[38] O.J. 1988 L332/38. [1989] 4 C.M.L.R. 581.
[39] Regulation 4087/88 O.J. 1988 L359/46.
[40] 1989 O.J. 35/31 [1989] 4 C.M.L.R. 591.

weddings under the trade mark "Pronuptia de Paris." The defendant Irmgard Schillgalis was a franchisee of the GmbH and had been granted exclusive rights to use the Pronuptia de Paris trade mark for marketing the Pronuptia goods and services in the districts of Hamburg, Oldenburg and Hanover. The franchisors undertook not to open up any other Pronuptia shops or to provide goods or services covered by the agreement to third parties in the districts mentioned. A dispute arose between the franchisors and the franchisee with respect to the licensing fees. This highest court in West Germany, the *Bundesgerichtshof,* referred the question to the EC Court. The Court held that, in principle, a franchising agreement, whose purpose it was to protect the franchisor's know-how or the identity and reputation of his distribution network, did not infringe Article 85(1), but clauses in the agreement which resulted in a division of markets between franchisor and franchisee or between franchisees could constitute restrictions of competition, contrary to that Article. In particular, the clause in the agreement prohibiting the sale of Pronuptia goods or offering Pronuptia services on premises other than specified in it might be restrictive because it would prevent the defendant from opening a second shop in her district.

The EC block exemption concerning franchising

In this block exemption,[40a] the EC Commission distinguishes three types of franchise: industrial franchises involving the manufacturing of goods; distribution franchises, involving the sale of goods; and service franchises involving the supply of services. It is important to note at the outset that the block exemption only covers *retail distribution of goods and service franchises.*[41] These are franchise agreements whereby one of the parties supplies goods or provides services to end-users.[42] Industrial franchise agreements, consisting of manufacturing licences based on patents, technical know-how, trade marks etc. are not covered[42a] (though they may benefit from other block exemptions). The Regulation covers agreements whereby a combination of goods and services are provided to end-users e.g. where goods are processed or adapted to fit the specific needs of customers. It also applies to cases where the relationship between the franchisor and franchisee is created through a master franchisee. It does not cover wholesale franchise agreements.[43]

Article 2 contains a list of restrictions of competition in these agreements which are exempted. These may be summed up thus:[43a]

[40a] See p. 273, n. 39.
[41] Article 1(3), Recitals (4) and (5).
[42] *Ibid.*
[42a] *Ibid.,* and Recital (6).
[43] *Ibid.* and Recital 5.
[43a] For the exact wording see the Article itself.

1. sole and exclusive terms with regard to the franchise territory;
2. an obligation on master franchisee not to conclude franchisor agreements with third parties outside their territory.
3. an obligation for the franchisee to exploit the franchise only from the contract premises;
4. restraints on the franchisee seeking sales outside his territory;
5. an obligation not to sell or use in the course of providing services goods competing with the franchise goods (this obligation may not be imposed, however, in respect of spare parts or accessories).

Following the usual pattern of block exemptions, Article 3 then sets out a list of *"white clauses,"* *i.e.* clauses which are permissible in so far as they are necessary to protect the franchisor's industrial and intellectual property, or to maintain the common identity and reputation of the franchised network. The obligations which may be imposed on franchisees, and which have conditional clearance, may be summarised as follows:[43b]

1. to sell or use exclusively goods meeting the franchisor's quality specifications;
2. to sell only goods manufactured by the franchisor or designated suppliers, where it would be impractical, owing to the nature of the goods, to apply objective quality specifications;
3. not to compete with other franchised outlets in the business (including the franchisor), and for a reasonable period after termination which, however, may not exceed one year in the territory where the franchisee exploited the franchise;
4. not to acquire financial interests in competitors, which would provide influence over them;
5. to sell the goods which are the subject-matter of the franchise only to end users, other franchisees or to resellers within other distribution channels supplied by the manufacturer of the goods or with its consent;
6. to use their best endeavours to sell the goods or provide the services which are the subject-matter of the franchisee and to meet certain other requirements, including minimum range stocks and turnover requirements, as well as customer warranty services;
7. To pay advertising contributions paid to the franchisor or to carry out some specified advertising.

Other clauses listed in Article 3(2) have unconditional clearance. These are:

1. confidentiality requirements both during the course of the agreement and after termination;
2. feedback of information requirements, by which the franchisee is required to communicate its experience in exploiting the franchise and to permit the franchisor and other franchisees to benefit from that experience;
3. requirements that franchisees provide assistance in pursuing infringers;
4. requirements that franchisees use any know-how[44] only in exploiting the franchise, and not to use it after termination (until presumably it becomes generally known outside the trade in question);
5. requirements that franchisees attend training courses arranged by the franchisor;
6. requirements that franchisees use the franchisor's business methods (which will be set out in the manual);
7. requirements that franchisees adhere to the franchisor's standards of cleanliness, presentation and quality control;

[43b] Art. 3(1).
[44] "Know-how" is used is a grade, non-technical sense.

8. requirements that franchisees allow the franchisor to carry out spot checks;
9. prohibitions on the change of the location of the franchise without the franchisor's prior consent;
10. prohibitions on assignment without the franchisor's consent.

The obligations referred to above in Article 3(2) are exempted even if they fall within the scope of Article 85(1).[45]

Article 4 then sets out the conditions on which any of the exemptions shall apply; these conditions are:

1. The franchisee must be free to obtain the goods subject to the franchise from other franchisees, where such goods are also distributed through another network of authorised distributors, the franchisee must be free to obtain goods from them;
2. where the franchisee must honour guarantees for the goods, it must honour similar guarantees from other suppliers of the goods within the EC;
3. the franchisee must be required to indicate its status as an independent undertaking (in the UK this obligation is usually complied with in any event because of the requirements of the Business Names Act 1985).[46]

The *"black list"* is contained in Article 5. The following will prevent the exemption from applying:

1. market sharing agreements whereby undertakings producing goods or providing services which are identical, or are considered by users as equivalent (*i.e.* they are goods or services in respect of which there is in the economist's phrase "consumer substitutability"), enter into franchise agreements with each other in respect of such goods or services;
2. subject to certain exemptions, foreclosing the possibility of the franchisee obtaining equivalent goods from other suppliers;
3. subject to a specified exemption,[47] foreclosing supplies, *i.e.* where the franchisor refuses for reasons other than the protection of its intellectual property, or maintaining the identity and reputation of the franchised network, to permit the franchisee to obtain supplies from a third party designated by the franchisee;
4. post-termination use of know-how once it has become generally known or easily accessible);
5. resale price maintenance (recommended prices are permitted);[48]
6. no challenge clauses in respect of intellectual property of the franchisor (though the agreement can be made to terminate on a challenge);
7. prohibitions on the supply of users resident outside the territory (though, as noted above, the franchisee can be restrained from actively seeking customers outside his territory).

Agreements within the guidelines provided by the Regulation need not be notified. Agreements which are not within the guidelines, must be notified, but by Article 6 are subject to the opposition procedure whereby, provided that the agreement contains no clauses within Article 5, it will be exempted unless the Commission does not oppose exemption within six months. The six months runs from the date of receipt of notification by the Commission, or the date of the postmark if notification

---

[45] Art. 3(3).
[46] See Adams and Prichard Jones *Franchising* (2nd ed. 1987) ss.6.24 *et seq.*
[47] Article 2(e).
[48] Unless they amount to a concerted practice, see art. 8(d).

is sent by registered post. Express reference to Article 6 must be made in the notification, and complete information must be furnished with it. Where agreements were notified prior to the coming into force of the Regulation (February 1, 1989) the opposition procedure can be invoked by submitting a communication to the Commission referring expressly to Article 6 and to the notification. Member States can oppose exemption within three months of the notification being forwarded to them. The information furnished to the Commission must be treated by it as confidential (Article 7).

The benefit of the exemption can be withdrawn if the effect of parallel networks established by competing manufacturers or distributors is to restrict competition, if the goods or services enjoy a *de facto* monopoly in the EC, if the franchisor or franchisees prevents end users from having access to parallel imports or otherwise isolates markets within the EC, if there is evidence of horizontal concerted practices to maintain prices, and if there are unjustified controls over franchisees for reasons other than the protection of the franchisor's legitimate trading interests.[49] The Regulation came into operation on February 1, 1989 and is to continue in force until December 31, 1999.

De minimis guidelines

The guidelines contained in the Commission Notice of September 3, 1986 on agreements of minor importance are applicable to franchising agreements.[50] The principal practical problem with these, however, is to determine the relevant market. Thus, Charles Jourdan had a negligible share of the French and Community markets in shoes, but if the market is medium and top quality shoes, the share rose to 10 per cent. of the French market, and 2 per cent. of the Community market, so that its agreements would be outside the guidelines. Agreements within the guidelines do not have to be notified.

---

[49] Article 8.
[50] See p. 352 *post.* Though when franchising networks become normal in a particular market, even small new networks may not fall within the Notice, see ibid, para. 16.

CHAPTER 16

AGENCY ARRANGEMENTS

SELF-EMPLOYED AGENTS ABROAD

THE peculiar feature of this form of marketing is that the exporter enters into direct relations with the customer abroad, by means of a contract procured or concluded, on behalf of the exporter, by a representative who resides abroad and is not his employee.[1] The remuneration of the self-employed agent is usually based upon a commission on the price of the goods sold by or through, him, while the remuneration of the employee normally is a fixed salary sometimes enlarged by bonuses or commissions.

Great care should be taken by an exporter who wishes to market his goods in a foreign country through the instrumentality of a self-employed agent. A contract of agency is a confidential relationship, and the agent has, in certain conditions, implied authority to dispose of the principal's goods, to allow a customer credit terms or to receive the purchase price from him. The exporter should make searching inquiries about the personal reputation and financial standing of the agent before reposing his trust in him. These inquiries are often made through the exporter's bank or through his forwarder. When they result in a satisfactory reply, two further points should be observed. First, a precautionary measure is usually included in the contract, *e.g.* a short probationary period precedes the long-term commitment, or a minimum turnover is stipulated for a certain period, or the termination of the contract is admitted upon short notice but here the minimum periods of notice prescribed by some foreign laws[2] will have to be allowed. Secondly, personal contact should be established and maintained between the principal and agent; no agency agreement of consequence should be concluded before the principal has met the agent in person; and regular visits of the principal to the agent, or vice versa, should maintain the high standard of mutual confidence which is an essential element in every successful agency agreement.

---

[1] But the United Kingdom exporter does not enter into relations with the overseas customer if his representative abroad is a *commissionaire*. Most European continental laws admit the concept of the *commissionaire*. On this concept and that of the commission agent in English law, see p. 292, *post.*

[2] See p. 310, *post.*

An exporter who wishes to find a local agent or distributor in a particular country may use the *Export Representative Service* of the BOTB which can be approached through its regional offices.[3] The Board will contact the Commercial Department of the British Embassy or other diplomatic post in the country selected and the report of the BOTB will list businessmen in that country interested in representing the exporter. The *Export Intelligence Service*[4] offers the exporter similar opportunities.

THE CONTRACT OF AGENCY

The legal nature of the contract of agency

An agent in the legal sense is a person who has authority from another person, the principal, to represent him or act on his behalf in relation to third persons. In the export trade, the authority which the exporter gives the self-employed agent abroad normally takes one of two forms: the agent may be authorised to *introduce* third parties in his territory to the principal, leaving the decision whether he wants to contract to the latter,[5] or the agent has authority to *conclude* contracts with third parties on behalf of the principal. In law, the term "agent" has thus a different meaning from that sometimes attributed to it in commercial parlance: it is wider in so far as it covers employees who conclude contracts with third parties on behalf of their employers, and it is narrower in so far as it does not include representatives who buy and sell in their own name. Scrutton L.J. in one case[6] referred to the well-known fact "that in certain trades the word 'agent' is often used without any reference to the law of principal and agent" and added that many difficulties have arisen from the habit of describing a purchaser as an agent.[7]

A sole distributor is not an agent in the legal sense because he does not act on behalf of the supplier and is not accountable to him. He buys

---

[3] See p. 83, *ante.*

[4] See p. 84, *ante.*

[5] For a case in which the agent had only authority to introduce customers to his principal but not, without his prior consent, to accept orders, see *Vogel* v. *R. and A. Kohnstamm Ltd.* [1973] Q.B. 133. See also *Alpha Trading Ltd.* v. *Dunnshaw-Patten Ltd.* [1980] 2 Lloyd's Rep. 284; see p. 291, *post.* The EC Court of Justice held in a case concerning a German agent having only authority to introduce (*Vermittlungsvertreter*) that such type of agency did not constitute "a branch, agency or other establishment" for the purposes of Art. 5(5) of the Convention on Jurisdiction and the Enforcement of Judgments in Civil and Commercial Matters of 1968: *Blankaert and Willems PVBA* v. *Trost* [1982] 2 C.M.L.R. 1.

[6] *W. T. Lamb & Sons* v. *Goring Brick Co.* [1932] 1 K.B. 710, 717; *The Regenstein* [1970] 2 Lloyd's Rep. 1, 5.

[7] On the drawing-up of agency agreements see Clive M. Schmitthoff, "Agency Agreements in the Export Trade," published by The Institute of Export, London, 1980. Also ICC publication No. 410 on *Commercial Agency*, 1983, *Cf.* further the Geneva Convention on Agency in the International Sale of Goods of February 17, 1983, see p. 312, *post.*

goods from the supplier and resells them to his customers for his own profit.[8]

More difficult is it to define the legal character of a person who describes himself as a procurement agent. His business is to obtain goods for another person who has instructed him. The term "procuring agent" is ambiguous. He may act as an agent in the legal sense for the instructing party or he may sell the goods to him. Whether he acts in the one or the other capacity depends on the construction of the contract between him and the instructing party.[9]

An agent who discloses his representative capacity to the customer to whom he sells the goods acts merely as the mouthpiece or conduit pipe of the principal, provided that he has acted within the scope of his actual or ostensible authority.[10] The contract of sale is concluded between the latter and the customer, and the agent disappears completely from the picture.[11] Every agency agreement creates three relationships:

1. That existing between the principal and the agent,
2. That existing between the principal and the third party, and
3. That existing between the agent and the third party.

The first is the internal arrangement between the principal and the agent, the contract of agency proper; it settles the rights and duties of these two parties, the scope of authority granted to the agent and the remuneration due to him. The second is a normal contract of sale, but superadded thereto are certain features which are due to the fact that the seller concluded the contract through an agent. The third relationship comes into play only in exceptional circumstances.

Disclosure of principal

The agent is not obliged to disclose his representative capacity to the third party. From the viewpoint of the third party, *viz.* the customer abroad, the following possibilities exist here:

---

[8] On sole distributors, see p. 259, *ante.*

[9] *Bowstead on Agency*, (15th ed., 1985), p. 21. On confirming houses, see p. 296, *post.*

[10] On actual and ostensible authority, see p. 282, *post.*

[11] Except if the agent undertakes personal liability to the third party, see *e.g.* the liability of the confirming agent to the supplier in the U.K., p. 297, *post.* If the agent signs a deed in his own name he is personally liable even if he signs as "agent": *Plant Engineers (Sales) Ltd.* v. *Davies*, (1969) 113 S.J. 484. In accordance with the principle stated in the text, if an allegation of negligent misrepresentation is made by the third party and a claim is raised under the Misrepresentation Act 1967, s.2(1), the principal, and not the agent, would be liable: *Resolute Maritime Inc.* v. *Nippon Kaiji Kyokai, Skopas* [1983] 1 W.L.R. 857. On the liability of the principal if the agent has made a fraudulent misrepresentation causing loss to the third party, see *Armagas Ltd.* v. *Mundogas SA* [1986] 2 W.L.R. 1063, 1073 (H.L.). A sole Customs agent who innocently submits documents falsely showing the EC origin of goods and is personally liable to his Customs authorities for the differential import duties, cannot claim a waiver of the differentials under EC law: EC Court of Justice in *Van Gend en Loos NV* v. *EC Commission* (Cases 98/83 and 230/83) [1984] E.C.R. 3763.

1. The agent does not disclose the existence of his principal and concludes the contract in his own name. Here he acts for an *undisclosed* principal, or
2. The agent discloses his principal's existence but not his name, *e.g.* by signing a contract "on behalf of our principals." In this case he acts for an *unnamed* principal, or
3. The agent discloses both the existence and the name of his principal. Here he acts for a *named* principal.

The first of these three cases is of considerable importance as it reveals the difference in the concept of agency in the common law countries, including England, from that prevailing in the civil law countries, including most European continental countries. In English law, provided the agent was duly authorised by the principal,[12] if he concludes the contract with the third party in his own name, *i.e.* without revealing his representative capacity, two rights arise: the third party's right of *election* and the principal's right of *intervention*. The third party (the customer), when discovering the true facts, may elect to sue the principal or the agent. This election must be unequivocal. If the third party commences proceedings against either of these persons, this is strong evidence that he has elected to hold him alone liable but this evidence may be rebutted, *e.g.* if the third party was not in possession of all relevant facts, and he can then still bring an action against the other.[13] If, however, the third party proceeds to judgment against either person that would terminate his right to elect and an action against the other would then be barred. Correspondingly, the undisclosed principal has the right to intervene and to make a direct claim against the customer. The customer's right of election and the principal's right of intervention thus enable these parties even in the case of undisclosed agency to constitute a direct contractual bond between them.[14]

In the other two cases the customer can only sue the principal; he can sue the agent only if the law in force in the territory in question provides a different regulation or the agent has undertaken personal liability to the

---

[12] Although normally "ratification relates back and is deemed equivalent to an antecedent authority" (*per* Jenkins L.J. in *Danish Mercantile Co. Ltd.* v. *Beaumont* [1951] Ch. 680, 686), it has been decided that if the *undisclosed* "agent" exceeds his authority or otherwise concludes a contract without authority, the "principal" cannot ratify the "agent's" act and sue the third party directly: *Keighley Maxsted & Co.* v. *Durant* [1901] A.C. 240.

[13] *Clarkson-Booker Ltd.* v. *Andjel* [1964] 2 Q.B. 775. See also *Chevron International Oil Co. Ltd* v. *A/S Sea Team. The T. S. Havprins.* [1983] 2 Lloyd's Rep. 356 (Third Party knew that agent acted for undisclosed or unnamed principal; principal's standard contract terms apply); *Asty Maritime Co. Ltd.* v. *Rocco Guiseppe & Figli. The Astyanax* [1985] 2 Lloyd's Rep. 109, 113 (contract between agent and third party must not be inconsistent with undisclosed agency relationship). Further D. J. Hill, "Some Problems of the Undisclosed Principal" in [1967] J.B.L. 122.

[14] See Clive M. Schmitthoff, "Agency in International Trade, A Study in Comparative Law" 129 *Recueil des Cours*, Academy of International Law (1970, Vol. 1), 107, 141–143 *Essays*, 306.

third party or is liable by custom of the trade. The agent who does not disclose the *existence* of his principal does not normally escape liability (if the third party elects to sue him) by merely adding to his firm style a descriptive term such as "export and import agencies."[15] If, however, he signs the contract with the customer "as agent," or addresses letters to him "on behalf of our principals," or "on account of our principals," no personal liability attaches to him, even if he does not disclose the *name* of the principal.[16] Sometimes it is clear from the circumstances that the person who acted did so as an agent although he did not indicate that he acted in that capacity, *e.g.* if the third party knew that he was merely a broker; in that case only the principal, but not the agent, is liable.[17]

The principal is in all three cases entitled to sue the third party in his own name. It has already been observed that, according to English law, he has this right even where the agent concluded the contract without disclosing the existence of the principal, provided that the agent was duly authorised to act on his behalf.[18] Thus, where an English export house or other person has acted as agent in the legal sense for a foreign undisclosed principal and the goods do not conform with the contract, the latter has a direct claim against the supplier in this country.[19] Some foreign laws differ in this respect from English law and provide that, when the contract is concluded by the agent in his own name, only he and not the undisclosed principal can sue on it. In view of this divergency, the exporter who wishes to reserve the right to sue the customer abroad for the purchase price should expressly provide in the contract which he concludes with the agent that the agent should disclose his representative capacity when selling to the customers, or should, at least, ask the agent for an undertaking to assign to him any claims against customers if so required.

Actual and ostensible authority

An agent may have actual or ostensible authority. Actual authority is the authority given to him by contract with the principal expressly,

---

[15] *The Swan* [1968] 1 Lloyd's Rep. 5, 13.

[16] Halsbury, *Laws of England* (4th ed.), Vol. 1, para. 854. An agent who sells goods in his own name which involve a breach of the law relating to weights and measures is criminally liable even if he is not guilty of negligence. But he is not liable if he sells them as agent for a named principal: *Lester* v. *Balfour Williamson Merchant Shippers Ltd.* [1953] 2 Q.B. 168. An agent acting for an unnamed or undisclosed principal cannot appoint himself as principal, except in the rare cases in which the identity of the principal is immaterial: *Gewa Chartering BV* v. *Remco Shipping Lines Ltd.*, *The Remco.* [1984] 2 Lloyd's Rep. 205.

[17] *N. & J. Vlassopulos Ltd.* v. *Ney Shipping Ltd.*; *The Santa Carina* [1977] 1 Lloyd's Rep. 478.

[18] See p. 281, n. 12, *ante.*

[19] *Teheran-Europe Co. Ltd.* v. *S. T. Belton (Tractors) Ltd.* [1968] 2 Q.B. 545 (C.A.).

impliedly, or by conduct, or conferred on him by law, as in the case of agency by necessity. "Ostensible or apparent authority is the authority of an agent as it *appears* to others."[20] "Actual authority and apparent authority are quite independent of one another. Generally they co-exist and coincide, but either may exist without the other and their respective scopes may be different."[21] Four conditions must be satisfied for a third party to rely successfully on the ostensible authority of an agent: (1) a representation must have been made to the third party; (2) it was made either by the principal or a person who had actual authority; (3) the third party relied on the representation; and (4) the principal had capacity to contract.[22] Ostensible authority may sometimes be inferred from the position into which the agent has been placed. Thus, it has been held that a company secretary had ostensible authority to enter into contracts of an administrative—but not of a managerial—nature on behalf of his company,[23] and that a documentary credit manager of a bank had ostensible authority to sign a bank guarantee alone although internal bank regulations required two signatures.[24] Sometimes it is difficult to determine whether the position, into which the principal has placed the agent, (giving him only limited authority), clothes the agent with ostensible authority enabling him to commit his principal beyond those limitations.[25] The onus of proving that the "agent" had ostensible authority is on the person alleging it.[26]

---

[20] *Per* Lord Denning M.R. in *Hely-Hutchinson* v. *Brayhead Ltd.* [1968] 1 Q.B. 549. Browne-Wilkinson L.J. in *Ebeed* v. *Soplex Wholesale Supplies Ltd.*, *Financial Times*, December 11, 1984, thought that the doctrine of ostensible authority was a form of estoppel; among academic writers this is controversial, see *Bowstead on Agency* (15th ed.), 1985, 290–292.

[21] *Per* Diplock L.J. in *Freeman & Lockyer* v. *Buckhurst Park Properties (Mangal) Ltd.* [1964] 2 Q.B. 480, 504.

[22] *Ibid.* It is not sufficient for the representation to the third party to be made by the agent, who is acting without actual authority; it must have been made either by the principal or a person having actual authority; *United Bank of Kuwait Ltd.* v. *Hammoud* [1988] 1 W.L.R. 1051, 1064.

[23] *Panorama Developments (Guildford) Ltd.* v. *Fidelis Furnishing Fabrics Ltd.* [1971] 2 Q.B. 711.

[24] *Egyptian International Foreign Trade Co.* v. *Soplex Wholesale Supplies Ltd. and P. S. Refson & Co. Ltd. The Raffaelia.* [1985] 2 Lloyd's Rep. 36.

[25] Ostensible authority admitted by the courts: *Freeman & Lockyer*, n. 20, *supra*; *Panorama Developments*, n. 23, *supra*; *The Rafaellia*, n. 23 *supra*; *The Nea Tyhi* [1982] 1 Lloyd's Rep. 606; *Liquidators of M. F. Howard & Sons Ltd.* v. *H. L. Goode*, *Financial Times*, March 30, 1983; *United Bank of Kuwait Ltd.* v. *Hammoud* [1988] 1 W.L.R. 1051; also *Shearson Lehman Brothers Inc.* v. *Maclaine, Watson & Co. Ltd. (No. 2)* [1988] 1 W.L.R. 16, 28 (H.L.).
Ostensible authority rejected by the courts: *British Bank of the Middle East* v. *Sun Life Assurance Co. of Canada (U.K.) Ltd.* [1983] 2 Lloyd's Rep. 9; *Rhodian River Shipping Co.* v. *Halla Maritime Corpn.*, [1984] 1 Lloyd's Rep. 373, 379; *Armagas Ltd.* v. *Mundogas SA*, [1986] 3 W.L.R. 1063, 1068 (H.L.).

[26] *United Bank of Kuwait Ltd.* v. *Hammoud* [1988] 1 W.L.R 1051, 1065.

Duties of the agent

The following are the principal duties of the agent, as far as relevant here:

(i) *To use reasonable diligence.* The agent has to carry out the duties which he has undertaken, with customary and reasonable care, skill and diligence, and is responsible to the principal for any loss caused by a failure to observe these standards. A selling agent has no authority to give the buyer a warranty with respect to the goods sold unless such authority is given him expressly or impliedly or arises from a trade custom.[27]

(ii) *To disclose all material facts.* The agent is obliged to disclose all facts to his principal which are likely to influence the latter when deciding whether to accept the customer's order or not. If, *e.g.* the principal has instructed the agent not to sell to X, and Y, a subsidiary company of X, ordered the goods from the agent, the latter, when forwarding the order to the principal, would have to point out that Y is known as being controlled by X. In particular, the agent is obliged to disclose to the principal any personal interest which he might have in the transaction. He must not buy the principal's goods without having first obtained the consent of the principal, nor must he act as agent for the buyer and receive double commission on the transaction without prior disclosure to the principal.[28] A contract in which the agent has an undisclosed personal interest is voidable at the option of the principal.

(iii) *Not to accept bribes or to make secret profits.* The agent must not accept a bribe nor in other respects make a secret profit out of his representative position. Where a bribe has been promised, the principal can claim it from the third party or, if it has been paid over, from the agent[29]; further, he is entitled to dismiss the agent without notice, or to avoid the contract with the third party, or to refuse to pay commission on the tainted transaction, or to claim damages for any loss which he has

---

[27] *Benmag* v. *Barda* [1955] 2 Lloyd's Rep. 354 where McNair J. found on the facts that the seller had authorised his agent to warrant to the buyer that a consignment of goat hair was of the same quality as an earlier consignment.

[28] *Anglo-African Merchants Ltd.* v. *Bayley* [1970] 1 Q.B. 311 (insurance broker).

[29] *Reading* v. *Att.-Gen.* [1951] A.C. 507; *Grinstead* v. *Hadrill* [1953] 1 W.L.R. 696; *T. Mahesan S/O Thambia* v. *Malaysia Government Officers' Co-operative Housing Society Ltd.* [1978] 2 W.L.R. 444. On the converse case of the liability of a principal whose agent bribes the servant of the third party, see *Armagas Ltd.* v. *Mundogas SA* [1985] 3 W.L.R. 640, 663; affd. [1986] 2 W.L.R. 1063 (H.L.); *Islamic Republic of Iran Shipping Lines* v. *Denby* [1987] 1 Lloyd's Rep. 367 (although the principal may recover the bribe from the agent, the latter does not hold the bribe as constructive trustee and consequently the principal is not entitled to the profits made by the use of the bribe (a very doubtful decision)). Also *Lemanda Trading Co. Ltd.* v. *African Middle East Petroleum Co. Ltd.* [1988] 2 W.L.R. 735 (see the note on p. 000 n. 71); and *Logicrose Ltd.* v. *Southend United Football Club Ltd.*, [1988] 1 W.L.R. 1256.

sustained through entering into the contract; and the bribe which the principal has recovered is not taken into account when the damages are assessed. These consequences ensue even when the bribe or secret profit has been accepted by the agent with the definite intention not to be influenced by it in his judgment, or when it can be proved that the interests of the principal have not been injured.[30] It is a matter of business morality as well as of the law that the standards of honesty required of the agent should be exacting; they are relaxed only if the principal knows that the agent receives a remuneration from the third party and has given his informed consent.

(iv) *Not to divulge confidential information.* The agent must not divulge confidential information or material, which he has obtained in the course of his employment, to third parties during the existence or after termination of the agency agreement, nor must he use such information himself unfairly in order to compete with the principal.[31] He cannot, on the other hand, be restrained from using the skill and experience, which he gained when acting for the principal, after termination of the agency agreement, unless the parties agreed upon a reasonable restraint of trade.[32] Further, the agent may divulge confidential information concerning the principal to the police, a public authority or, it would appear, even the press if the facts in question constitute a crime or fraud committed by the principal, or a serious matter contravening the public interest.[33]

In one case[34] an international trade directory was published by a British publisher who employed agents in certain districts of the European Continent allotted to them exclusively. They were remunerated by a commission on the amounts received for advertisements; apparently it

---

[30] In certain circumstances criminal proceedings may be instituted against the agent under the Prevention of Corruption Act 1906 and here again, "if a person does what is called a double-cross, and does not do what he was bribed to do, that is no reason why he should be acquitted of taking a bribe"; *R.* v. *Carr* [1957] 1 W.L.R. 165, 166.

[31] On confidentiality generally see *Seager* v. *Copydex Ltd.* [1967] 1 W.L.R. 923; *Thomas Marshall (Exports) Ltd.* v. *Guinle* [1979] Ch. 227; *Fraser* v. *Thames Television Ltd.* [1984] Q.B. 44; on the duty of confidentiality of an employee to his employer (and former employer) see *Faccenda Chicken Ltd.* v. *Fowler* (C.A.), 136 N.L.J. (1986), 71; see also *Speed Seal Products Ltd.* v. *Paddington* [1985] 1 W.L.R. 1327 (injunction granted although allegedly confidential information already published earlier; a very exceptional case); *Johnson & Bloy (Holdings) Ltd.* v. *Wolstenholme Rink plc.*, *Financial Times*, October 9, 1987 (C.A.). See also M. W. Bryan, "Restraint of Trade: Back to a Basic Analysis" in [1980] J.B.L. 326.

[32] *Roger Bullivant Ltd.* v. *Ellis* [1987] I.C.R. 464 (injunction restraining confidential information after termination of contract restricted to contractual prohibition period). On the measure of damages for breach of confidentiality see *Dowson & Mason Ltd.* v. *Potter* [1986] 1 W.L.R. 1419. On confidentiality after termination of contract generally, see *Lock International plc* v. *Beswick*, (1989) NLJ 644.

[33] *Initial Services Ltd.* v. *Putterill* [1968] 1 Q.B. 396.

[34] *Lamb* v. *Evans* [1893] 1 Ch. 218. See also *Nordisk Insulinlaboratorium* v. *C. L. Bencard* [1934] Ch. 430; *British Syphon Co. Ltd.* v. *Homewood* [1956] 1 W.L.R. 1190; *L. S. Harris Trustees Ltd. (Trading as L. S. Harris & Co.)* v. *Power Packing Services (Hermit Road) Ltd.* [1970] 2 Lloyd's Rep. 65; *Baker* v. *Gibbons* [1972] 1 W.L.R. 693.

was their habit to take down, in their own notebooks, the material relating to the advertisers in their district which later was produced in the directory. On terminating the agency agreement, the publisher successfully applied for an injunction to restrain the agents from using the material collected in their notebooks in their own interest or that of a rival publisher. It was argued on behalf of the agents that the advertisements after publication in the directory could be reprinted by anybody unless they were protected by copyright, but Kay L.J. dealt with this argument as follows:

> The jurisdiction against these defendants is because these materials which they want to use were obtained by them when they were in the position of agents for the plaintiff, and, although the plaintiff might not be able to prevent anybody else in the world from publishing or using such materials as he is trying to prevent these defendants from using, that would be no answer, because these defendants, from the position in which they were in, are put under a duty towards the plaintiff not to make this use of the material.

In very exceptional circumstances, where the principal has an overwhelming prima facie case that actual or potential damage to him would be serious and there is clear evidence that the agent possesses vital confidential material which he might destroy or dispose of, the court may make an order to permit the principal's representatives, usually accompanied by his solicitor, to enter the agents premises to inspect and remove the confidential material; in these exceptional cases such an order may be made even on an *ex parte* application of the principal. This order is known as an *Anton Piller injunction*, taking its name from the case in which the court issued it by virtue of its inherent jurisdiction.[35] Now the Supreme Court Act 1981, s.33(1), empowers the court to issue these injunctions. Anton Piller injunctions are issued for various reasons.[36] They may be granted to preserve evidence which might otherwise be removed, destroyed or concealed.[37] And they have also been granted where it was alleged that the principal's confidential drawings may be secretly passed on to the competition,[38] where allegedly confidential information, including lists and evaluations of customers, may be used

---

[35] *Anton Piller KG* v. *Manufacturing Processes Ltd.* [1976] Ch. 55. Also *Lock International plc* v. *Beswick*, [1989] 1 W.L.R. 1268, 1277.
[36] Particularly to seize allegedly pirated video tapes (*Rank Film Distributors Ltd.* v. *Video Information Centre (A Firm)* [1982] A.C. 380) or allegedly counterfeit goods (*Sony Corporation* v. *Time Electronics* [1981] 1 W.L.R. 1293). Where the court grants an Anton Piller (or Mareva) injunction, it may in appropriate cases order the defendant not to leave the jurisdiction and to give up his passport: *Bayer AG* v. *Winter* [1986] 1 W.L.R. 497. If documents are seized in Anton Pillar proceedings and held by solicitors until further order, the court will not order their release to the Customs in criminal proceedings against alleged VAT offenders: *E.M.I. Records Ltd.* v. *Spillane* [1986] 1 W.L.R. 967. Some of the principles decided on *Mareva* injunctions (see p. 701) apply to *Anton Piller* proceedings.
[37] *Crest Homes plc* v. *Marks* [1987] A.C. 829; *Columbia Picture Industries Inc.* v. *Robinson* [1987] Ch. 38.
[38] See n. 35, *supra*.

improperly,[39] and even after judgment in aid of execution in order to prevent the defendant from destroying or hiding certain documents.[40]

(v) *To account to the principal.* An agent is obliged to keep proper accounts of all agency transactions and to produce them to the principal in accordance with the terms of the agency agreement or upon request by the principal. The agent has to keep the customary office records and should keep the money and property of the principal separate from his own. He has to pay over to the principal all moneys actually received on behalf of the latter but, in the absence of contrary provisions in the agency agreement, is, in appropriate cases, entitled to a set-off or a lien on the principal's goods or money.[41] These rights of the agent can be exercised where money is owing from the principal but the agent cannot claim these rights to retain arbitrarily expenses which have not been agreed upon.

Duties of the principal

The following are the main duties of the principal as far as relevant here:

(i) *To pay commission.* The principal has to pay the agent the agreed remuneration which customarily, but not by force of law, is a commission payable on the purchase price of the goods actually sold by the agent. This method of remuneration is intended to operate as an incentive for the agent, but it sometimes tempts an unscrupulous agent to pay greater attention to the volume of effected sales than the financial soundness of the customers whose orders he solicits. The principal who wishes to protect himself against this contingency has several possibilities. The most effective is to lay down in the contract of agency that the commission shall be earned when the purchase price is received by the principal in cash, a frequent provision of this type is that

> commission shall be paid at a rate of . . . per cent. on all moneys received by the principal as purchase price for goods sold by the agent.

Another possibility is to arrange *del credere* terms[42] whereby the agent, usually on payment of an additional commission, undertakes to indemnify the principal for any loss sustained through an insolvency of customers introduced by him.

It is advisable to state expressly when the commission is earned. If the contract is silent on this point the normal intention of the parties is that

---

[39] *Vapormatic Co. Ltd.* v. *Sparex Ltd.* [1976] 1 W.L.R. 939.
[40] *Distributori Automatici SpA* v. *Holford General Trading Co. Ltd.* [1985] 1 W.L.R. 1066. The English court may allow documents obtained under an Anton Piller order to be used in foreign proceedings: *Bayer AG* v. *Winter (No. 3)* [1986] F.S.R. 357.
[41] *Rolls Razor Ltd.* v. *Cox* [1967] 1 Q.B. 552.
[42] See p. 294, *post.*

the agent can claim the commission when the contract of sale is concluded, *e.g.* when the principal accepts the customer's order.[42a] It is customary to distinguish the date when the commission is payable from that when it is earned, and to provide that the commission shall be payable some time later than it was earned or at certain fixed dates; if the contract does not deal with this matter and no contrary trade usages exist, the agent can claim commission immediately it is earned. Advances on unearned commission must normally be repaid on termination of the agency agreement.[43]

An agent is only entitled to commission if he introduces a ready, willing and able purchaser[44]; if the buyer has no money to pay the price, he is not an able purchaser, and if after the termination of the agency the principal and the buyer enter into new negotiations and the former enables the latter by financial assistance to conclude the contract of sale, the effective cause of the sale is not the introduction by the agent, although to some degree it remained, but the provision of finance by the principal, and the agent is not entitled to commission.[45]

The principal must not prevent the agent from earning his commission by a wrongful act, *e.g.* by wilfully breaking his contract of sale with a third party whom the agent has introduced and whom he has accepted.[46]

Three points require particular attention when the agent's commission is discussed by the parties: the reimbursement of the agent for expenses, the payment of commission on orders emanating from the agent's territory but received directly by the principal, and commission due on repeat orders. These matters should be dealt with in the contract in precise terms. The law does not provide detailed rules on these topics; it is based on the arrangement reached by the parties and, if the negotiating parties have expressed themselves thereon merely in general assertions of mutual good will, the court has the difficult task of inferring their presumed intention from the surrounding circumstances—a laborious process which sometimes leads to unsatisfactory results.

[42a] The position is different with respect to a shipbroker acting for the seller in the sale of a ship. There the intention is that the broker—an agent of the seller—is only entitled to his commission when the contract has been completed by delivery and payment of the purchase price: *Marcan Shipping (London) Ltd.* v. *Polish Steamship Co. The Manifest Lipkowy* [1989] 2 Lloyd's Rep. 138, 142 (in this case the court refused to imply a term into the agency contract, according to which the principals (the sellers) would not by any breach of the contract of sale deprive the agent of his commission).

[43] *Bronester Ltd.* v. *Priddle* [1961] 1 W.L.R. 1294.

[44] *Luxor (Eastbourne) Ltd.* v. *Cooper* [1941] A.C. 108; *Christie Owen & Davies* v. *Rapacioli* [1974] 2 W.L.R. 723.

[45] *Jack Windle Ltd.* v. *Brierley* [1951] 2 All E.R. 398.

[46] See pp. 290–291, *post.* If the agent himself is in breach of his obligations under the contract of agency but nevertheless a contract of sale has been concluded between the principal and the third party, the agent is still entitled to his commission if the breach was done honestly and in good faith, but he forfeits this claim if he has acted in bad faith: *Robinson Scammell & Co.* v. *Ansell*, [1985] 2 E.G.L.R. 41.

It happens sometimes—though more often in the home trade than in the export trade—that the principal agrees to pay the agent a fixed sum at monthly or other intervals "on account of the commission which will accrue to him"; such an arrangement would make the agent a servant of the principal rather than constitute him an independent contractor. If, in such a case, on the termination of the agency the payments by the principal exceed the commission earned by the agent, the agent has to repay the principal the excess unless the agency agreement contains an express or implied provision to the contrary.[47] As this point often gives rise to disputes, it is advisable to cover it in advance by an express term in the agency agreement.

(ii) *Agent's expenses and indemnity.* The self-employed sales agent abroad who solicits orders for an exporter cannot claim his trading expenses from the principal unless this is expressly agreed upon in the contract of agency. If the agent, with the approval of the principal, incurs liabilities in the course of his duties, *e.g.* if he sues a defaulting customer in the courts of the country where the customer resides, he is entitled to be indemnified for any losses sustained or liabilities incurred by him.

(iii) *Orders emanating from agent's territory but not procured by him.* In principle, the agent is entitled to commission if the transaction for which commission is claimed is the direct result of his efforts. The agent can therefore claim commission if the customer with whom he has negotiated eventually orders goods directly from the principal, or if the customer whom he introduces offers a lower price than the list price and the principal decides to accept the offer at the lower price. He cannot claim commission if the customer places an unsolicited order with the principal, or if the order has been obtained by the principal himself or other agents. These rules of law are frequently modified by the contract parties or a custom of the trade, which may provide that the agent shall be entitled to commission on all transactions emanating from his territory. These arrangements are particularly frequent when an agent is appointed as exclusive agent for a defined territory.

(iv) *Repeat orders.* It depends on the intention of the parties as evinced in the agency agreement whether the agent is entitled to commission on repeat orders. Two questions have to be distinguished here: is the agent entitled to commission on repeat orders during the currency of the agency agreement, and is he so entitled after its termination?

As regards the first of these questions, the parties frequently arrange in the agency agreement expressly that commission shall be payable on repeat orders, *e.g.* by providing that the agent shall be entitled to commission on "repeats on any accounts introduced by" him,[48] or

---

[47] *Rivoli Hats Ltd.* v. *Gooch* [1953] 1 W.L.R. 1190; *Clayton Newbury Ltd.* v. *Findlay* [1953] 1 W.L.R. 1194.
[48] *Levy* v. *Goldhill* [1917] 2 Ch. 297.

sometimes by stating generally that commission shall be due "on all orders from customers introduced by him."[49] If the parties have failed to make express provision on this point, the principles stated above under (iii) apply. In other words, if the first order was the direct result of the agent's efforts, he is entitled to commission on the repeat order because they have to be considered as the continued effect of his original efforts. It is irrelevant whether these repeat orders are placed with the agent or with the principal directly.

The second question raises more difficult legal problems. The difficulty arises if, after termination of the agency contract by notice, mutual agreement or death of the agent, the principal has accepted repeat orders which, if the agency had not been terminated, would have carried a commission for the agent. Here it can well be argued that the principal appropriates the fruits of his former agent's labours after termination of his relationship with him. Nevertheless, unless the parties have otherwise provided in the agency agreement, the rule is that no remuneration is payable on transactions between the principal and third parties arising after termination of the authority, whether such transactions are due to the agent's introduction or not.[50] But the rule admits exceptions and it is not easy to determine whether in a particular case the rule applies or an exception should be admitted. Speaking generally, where the agency agreement was concluded for a limited time, the rule applies,[51] but where it was concluded for an indefinite time, on occasion exceptions from the rule have been admitted.[52] However, the question is always one of construction of the relevant contractual terms and the modern tendency is not to admit commission on repeat orders after termination of the agency agreement but, as observed, each case has to be decided on its own merits.[53] Even in the cases in which according to these principles the agent is entitled to commission after termination, his claim is only for a lump sum representing monetary compensation for loss of commission on the repeat orders; he cannot claim a declaration and an account for the future because that would amount to an annuity "to the crack of doom."[54]

(v) *Principal's discretion to accept orders.* When the agent has only authority to introduce customers, the principal has full discretion to accept or reject the customer's order, and the agent cannot claim

---

[49] *Salomon* v. *Brownfield* (1896) 12 T.L.R. 239; *Bilbee* v. *Hasse & Co.* (1889) 5 T.L.R. 677; *Wilson* v. *Harper, Son & Co.* [1908] 2 Ch. 370; *Roberts* v. *Elwells Engineers Ltd.* [1972] 2 Q.B. 586.
[50] *Halsbury's Laws of England* (4th ed.), Vol. 1, para. 804.
[51] *Weare* v. *Brimsdown Lead Co.* (1910) 103 L.T.R. 429.
[52] *Levy* v. *Goldhill* [1917] 2 Ch. 297; *Bilbee* v. *Hasse & Co.* (1889) 5 T.L.R. 677; *Salomon* v. *Brownfield* (1896) 12 T.L.R. 239; *Wilson* v. *Harper, Son & Co.* [1908] 2 Ch. 370; *British Bank Ltd.* v. *Novimex Ltd.* [1949] 1 K.B. 623; *Sellers* v. *London Counties Newspapers* [1951] 1 K.B. 784.
[53] *Crocker Horlock Ltd.* v. *B. Lang & Co. Ltd.* [1949] W.N. 97.
[54] *Roberts* v. *Elwells Engineers Ltd.* [1972] 2 Q.B. 586.

commission on orders which the principal elects to refuse, unless the parties have agreed on special terms, *e.g.* that commission shall be paid on the introduction of or inquiries from potential customers, or established trade usages can be proved allowing commission on a reduced scale. But the principal must not prevent the agent by a wrongful act or omission from earning his commission, and the agent can recover damages for the actual loss sustained if the principal contravenes this rule of law; these damages may in appropriate cases be commensurate to the lost commission. In one case[55] a principal was introduced by an agent to a Dutch buyer who wanted to buy a quantity of cement that was to be shipped c. & f. to a port in Iran. The principal accepted the introduction and contracted with the buyer accordingly. The buyer opened a letter of credit in favour of the seller (the principal) and the latter provided a performance guarantee in favour of the buyer. Later the principal decided not to perform the contract of sale. He met a claim by the buyer by forfeiting the performance guarantee and making an additional payment. The agent claimed damages for the lost commission. The court held that he was entitled thereto. It was an implied term in the contract of agency that the principal would not deprive the agent of his commission by breaking the contract with the third party. Lawton L.J. expressed this principle in a graphic manner[56]:

> The life of an agent in commerce is a precarious one. He is like the groom who takes a horse to the water-trough. He may get his principal to the negotiating table but when he gets him there he can do nothing to make him sign, any more than the groom can make a horse drink. . . . Once the signing has been done, the agent is in a different position altogether, because by that time the principal has accepted the benefit of the agent's work. In these circumstances, he ought not to be allowed to resile from his obligations to the agent . . . the whole relationship of principal and agent depends upon the principal accepting his obligations to the agent once the agent has done his work and the principal has accepted the benefit of it.

Where commission is to be paid on the purchase price received by the principal, and the customer repudiates the contract before paying the price, the principal is not bound to sue the customer in order to enable the agent to earn his commission, but if he receives some compensation from the customer the agent would appear to be entitled to a reasonable remuneration which may be a good deal less than full commission.[57]

Exclusive trading rights

The agency agreement may provide that the self-employed agent shall have sole, or exclusive, or sole and exclusive trading rights in a particular

---

[55] *Alpha Trading Ltd.* v. *Dunnshaw-Patten Ltd.* [1981] Q.B. 290. However, in *The Manifest Lipkowy* (*ante*, n.42a) the CA refused to imply such a term (the explanation of this discrepancy is probably the special nature of the contract of ship brokerage).
[56] *Ibid.* 308.
[57] *Boots* v. *E. Christopher & Co.* [1951] 2 All E.R. 1045.

territory.[58] The character of the agency is here territorial and not personal. The agent is normally paid commission on all sales emanating from his territory whether procured by his own efforts or those of other persons, and he usually undertakes to promote systematically in the territory reserved to him the distribution of the principal's goods by an organisation of subagents, advertisements or other means. Agency agreements are, as far as the exclusivity of trading rights is concerned, similar to distribution agreements, but the essential difference between an agent, who contracts on behalf of a principal, and a distributor, who contracts on his own account and for his own benefit, remains.[59] In particular, the contract of agency should state expressly that the agent has to sell in the principal's name. In one case,[60] the terms of an exclusive agency contract were summed up by Lord Simon L.C. as follows:

> By a written contract dated February 19, 1938, the respondents, manufacturers of steel in Sheffield, as principals appointed the appellants, whose business address was in New York, to be sole selling agents of their tool steels in a wide area of territories including the western hemisphere (excluding U.S.A. and Argentine), Australia, New Zealand and India. The appellants were to sell in the name of the respondents, the respondents fixing f.o.b. prices and the appellants charging the purchaser with such excess price over f.o.b. prices as they could obtain. Any excess price over the f.o.b. price was for the credit of the appellants and the respondents were to account to the appellants in respect of such excess price after the respondents had received payment in full from the purchaser. The duration of the agreement was to be for three years from April 1, 1938, as a minimum. The agreement contained an arbitration clause.

An exclusive agency agreement, as such, is not prohibited by Article 85(1) of the EC Treaty but may contravene it if it contains clauses which have as their object or effect the distortion of competition in the common market. However, the EC Commission has granted important exemptions *en bloc* from the general prohibition of Article 85(1). The regulation of European Community Law, as far as affecting exclusive distribution and agency agreements, will be considered later on.[61]

SPECIAL TYPES OF AGENTS

Commercial practice has evolved certain types of agency agreements which play an important role in the export trade.

The commission agent

The agent whom the British exporter appoints in an overseas country, may be classified by the agent's own law as a *commissionaire*. Most

---

[58] On the meaning of the terms "sole" and "exclusive," see p. 260, *ante.*
[59] See p. 261, *ante.*
[60] *Heyman* v. *Darwins Ltd.* [1942] A.C. 356, 357 (in this case the remuneration of the agent did not consist of a commission).
[61] See p. 346, *post.*

European continental countries and other legal systems founded on the civil law[62] recognise *commissionaires* as a special class of self-employed commercial agents. The term *"commissionaire"* is sometimes rendered in English as "commission agent" or "commission merchant" but this translation is confusing because the civil law and common law concepts of this type of agency are fundamentally different.

A *commissionaire* is a person who internally, *i.e.* in his relationship to his principal, is an agent but externally, *i.e.* in his relationship to the third party, is a seller or buyer in his own name.[63] Where a *commissionare* has acted for the principal, no privity of contract can be constituted between the principal and the third party.[64] As an agent, the *commissionaire* is accountable to his principal for the profit from the transaction, must use reasonable diligence in the performance of his duties, and must not make an undisclosed profit or take a bribe. The principal, on the other hand, cannot claim the price from the third party directly nor is he liable in contract for any defects of the goods.

In the civil law countries a distinction is drawn between direct and indirect agency. A direct agent is an agent who discloses his agency quality to the third party, an indirect agent is a person who, though being an agent, treats with the third party in his own name. The *commissionaire* is an indirect agent.

This form of commercial activity is, of course, also known in English law. Indeed, it is widely used, *e.g.* by confirming houses.[65] In English law, the institution of an agent acting for an undisclosed principal[66] fulfils the function of the *commissionaire* in the civil law. If duly authorised, he is a true agent of his principal but he appears to be a seller or buyer in his own name, as far as the third party is concerned.

There is, however, a fundamental difference between the *commissionaire* of the civil law and the English commission agent.[67] The *commissionaire* relationship is always a two-contract relationship and, as we have seen, privity of contract can never be established between the principal and the third party.[68] But the undisclosed principal can enter

---

[62] The English lawyer distinguishes between the civil law countries whose law is derived from the *corpus juris civilis* of Emperor Justinian (529 A.D.), and the common law countries, whose law is derived from English law. The civil law countries are most European continental and Latin American as well as other countries. The common law countries are England and Wales, Scotland, Ireland, the U.S.A. (except Louisiana), Canada (except Quebec), Australia, New Zealand, India and many other countries.

[63] The French Commercial Code, art. 94, defines a *commissionaire* thus: *"Le commissionaire est celui qui agit en son propre nom ou sous un nom social pour le compte d'un commettant."*

[64] Except by assignment.

[65] See p. 296, *post.*

[66] See p. 281, *ante.*

[67] See Clive M. Schmitthoff, "Agency in International Trade. A Study in Comparative Law," Academy of International Law, 129 *Receuil des Cours*, (1970, Vol. 1), 109, 135. *Essays*, 306.

[68] See n. 64, *supra.*

into direct contractual relationship with the third party by election or intervention[69] and thus a one-contract relationship can be constituted between them.

A commission agent who has himself paid the price to the third party, has the same rights as an unpaid seller, *viz.* the right of lien, stoppage in transit and resale. This is provided by the Sale of Goods Act 1979, s.38(2).[70] These rights are of great value to him if his principal does not repay him or cannot do so because he has become insolvent.

The del credere agent

A *del credere* agent is an agent who undertakes to indemnify the principal for any loss which the latter may sustain owing to the failure of a customer, introduced by the agent, to pay the purchase price. The advantages of the *del credere* arrangement are evident: the principal is not sufficiently in touch with the foreign market in which the agent operates to judge the financial soundness of the customer who orders goods; credit terms cannot always be avoided if it is desired to market the goods on a competitive basis, and even where no credit terms are granted the exporter might find himself entangled in complicated and costly insolvency proceedings if the customer fails. These pitfalls are avoided by the agent agreeing to accept the *del credere* for the customers introduced by him and, incidentally, the principal can be assured that the agent will not place considerations of turnover higher than the solvency of the customers whose orders he solicits. It is usual to pay an additional commission, called the *del credere* commission, to the agent who accepts a *del credere* responsibility. The *del credere* agreement need not be evidenced in writing; it is a contract of indemnity and not a contract of guarantee.[71] The *del credere* agent undertakes merely to indemnify the principal if the latter, owing to the insolvency of the buyer or some analogous cause, is unable to recover the purchase price, but the agent is not responsible if a perfectly solvent buyer refuses to pay the price on the ground that the principal has not duly performed the contract.[72] Lord Ellenborough expressed this rule in 1817 as follows[73]: "The (*del credere*) commission imports that if the vendee does not pay, the factor will; it is a guarantee from the factor to the principal against any mischief to arise from the

---

[69] See p. 281, *ante.*
[70] See p. 150, *ante.*
[71] Consequently, s.4 of the Statute of Frauds 1677, which provides, *inter alia*, that a contract of guarantee, to be enforceable, must be evidenced in writing, does not apply. (This provision of s.4 is not repealed by the Law Reform (Enforcement of Contracts) Act 1954.)
[72] *Gabriel & Sons* v. *Churchill & Sim* [1914] 3 K.B. 1272.
[73] In *Hornby* v. *Lacy* (1817) 6 M. & S. 166, 171.

vendee's insolvency. But it varies not an iota the rights subsisting between vendor and vendee."

By an announcement of December 24, 1962,[74] the EC Commission indicated that it did not consider exclusive dealing arrangements with commercial agents as falling within the prohibition of Article 85(1) of the EC Treaty, provided that the agent did not assume a financial risk other than that implied in the usual *del credere* obligation.[75]

The agent carrying stock (the mercantile agent)

Agents resident abroad have either authority to solicit or accept orders and pass them on to the principal who then dispatches the goods to the customer directly, or they are entrusted with a store or consignment of stock lines, spare parts, etc. and have authority to supply customers directly from their store. Agents of the latter type are *mercantile agents* within the meaning of the Factors Act 1889. According to the Act, a mercantile agent is an agent who in the customary course of his business has authority sell goods, or to consign goods for sale, or to buy goods or to raise money on the security of goods.[76] The problem that arises with respect to these consignment agents is that they may dispose of their principal's goods contrary to his instructions and without due authority. Great uncertainty would be imported into business transactions if the deals of consignment agents in goods entrusted to them were invalid for lack of authority, particularly as these agents often do not disclose their representative capacity and the third party has no means of ascertaining the internal arrangement between the principal and agent. The Factors Act 1889 aims at the protection of third parties dealing in good faith with the consignment agent and provides in particular that, where such an agent, in his capacity of mercantile agent,[77] with the consent of the

---

[74] See p. 353, *post.*

[75] This announcement does not bind the Commission or the courts. In particular, the legal form of agency must not be used as a device to evade the competition rules of the EC; the Commission and the EC Court of Justice will always look at the realities of the situation: *Re Pittsburgh Corning Europe* [1973] C.M.L.R. D.2; *Re Sugar Cartel* [1975] E.C.R. 1663; [1976] 1 C.M.L.R. 295.

[76] s.1(1). The expression "factor" in the title of the 1889 Act is an antiquated term which is not used in the Act itself. The Act refers to "mercantile agents."

[77] *Astley Industrial Trust* v. *Miller* [1968] 2 All E.R. 36. (It is doubtful whether this case was correctly decided and whether it was really necessary that the consent of the owner to the factor's possession must extend to such possession *qua* factor); see *Worcester Works Finance Ltd.* v. *Cooden Engineering Co. Ltd.* [1972] 1 Q.B. 210.

If A's goods are stolen and, having passed through several hands, are sold by a mercantile agent (acting in good faith) to B (who buys them likewise in good faith), A can recover the goods from B; B is not protected by s.9 of the Factors Act 1889 because there was no consent of the owner—A—when the goods passed from his possession: *National Employers' Mutual General Insurance Association Ltd.* v. *Jones* [1987] 3 W.L.R. 901 (A.C.).

principal is in possession of goods or documents of title to the goods, any sale or other disposition transacted by him in the ordinary course of business in respect of these goods is as valid as if it were expressly authorised by the principal, provided the third party did not know of the lack of the mercantile agent's authority.[78] The Act cannot be invoked often in export transactions because the contract between the agent residing abroad and the customer there is normally governed by the law of the foreign country where the contract is concluded or to be performed,[79] but the laws of many foreign countries embody rules corresponding to the provisions of the Factors Act 1889. On the other hand, the Act provides a valuable protection in import transactions, as shown in the following case[80]: importers obtained an advance from Lloyds Bank on the security of bills of lading in respect of certain merchandise and the bank returned the bills of lading to the importers in order to enable them to sell the goods; on receipt of the bills of lading, the importers gave the bank a trust receipt[81] wherein they acknowledged their holding of the documents under lien of the bank and agreed to clear the goods as trustees of the bank; the importers who were in financial difficulties pledged the bills of lading, in breach of trust, with the Bank of America which was unaware of the true position. The court decided that the importers received the documents of title as mercantile agents of Lloyds Bank and that the pledging of the documents with the Bank of America was valid as against Lloyds Bank.

The confirming house

It happens often in the export trade that an overseas importer buys in the United Kingdom through a confirming house resident in the United Kingdom.[82] In modern practice these confirming houses are called *export houses.*[83] Business enterprises carrying on these activities are, of course, also established in other countries, notably the USA.

---

[78] s.2(1). The mercantile agent must be in possession of the goods or documents of title when he disposes of them: *Beverley Acceptances Ltd.* v. *Oakley* [1982] R.T.R. 417. See also *Four Point Garage Ltd.* v. *Carter* [1985] 3 A11 E.R. 12 (on a similar point under s.25(1) of the Sale of Goods Act 1979).

[79] See pp. 215–218, *ante.*

[80] *Lloyd's Bank* v. *Bank of America National Trust and Savings Association* [1937] 2 K.B. 631; [1938] 2 K.B. 147.

[81] On release under a trust receipt see p. 398, *post.*

[82] The following observations are founded on my *Legal Aspects of Export Sales* (3rd ed. 1978), pp. 8–10.

[83] Their trade association is the British Exporters' Association, 16 Dartmouth Street, London SW1 89BL. This Association has published a brochure describing the services offered by its members.

Nature of the confirming house

The term "confirming house" has no definite meaning in law or in commercial practice. A confirming house enters usually into two legal relationships, namely, to its overseas customer who asks it to procure certain goods for him, and to the seller in the home market with whom it places the order or indent. The relationship to the overseas customer is normally that between principal and agent whereas the relationship to the seller in the home market depends on the nature of the contract which the confirming house concludes with him. Three possibilities exist in that respect: *first*, when placing the order with the seller, the confirming house may buy from the seller; in that case it enters into a direct contract of sale and is liable for the price and for the acceptance of the goods as a buyer; the fact that the seller knows that the goods are destined for export and even knows the name of the overseas buyer is not relevant. The *second* possibility is that the confirming house places the order with the seller "as agents on behalf of our principals," either naming them or not; in that case the contract of sale is made directly between the seller and the overseas buyer and the confirming house does not intend to make itself liable for the price. The first and the second possibility are diametrically opposed; in the first case the confirming house places its client's order as a principal and in the second it does so as an agent. A *third* arrangement is possible and, indeed, this is the typical confirming arrangement: the confirming house may place the client's order as agent of the overseas importer but may indicate at the same time that it intends to hold itself personally responsible for the price; this type of confirmation is described by McNair J.[84] as follows:

> The critical question is: What is the meaning of "confirming order" or what is the meaning of "confirming house"? . . . It seems to me, using the word in its ordinary sense, "to confirm" means that the party confirming guarantees that the order will be carried out by the purchaser. In that sense he adds confirmation or assurance to the bargain which has been made by the primary contractor, just as a bank which confirms that a credit has been opened by the buyers in favour of the seller guarantees that payment will be made against the credit if the proper documents are tendered.

This third arrangement produces, as far as the liability for the price is concerned, the same effect as the first one; it is the normal and typical confirmation transaction into which the confirming house enters.

In practice, confirming houses when carrying out orders received from their customers abroad use two types of forms, one in which they order the goods from the supplier in the home market under their own liability,

---

[84] In *Sobell Industries Ltd.* v. *Cory Bros. & Co. Ltd.* [1955] 2 Lloyd's Rep. 82, 89; Donaldson J. in *Teheran-Europe Co. Ltd.* v. *S.T. Belton (Tractors) Ltd.* [1968] 2 Q.B. 53 (this part of the judgment was affirmed by the Court of Appeal in [1968] 2 Q.B. 545). See also *International Ry.* v. *Niagara Park Commission* [1941] A.C. 328, 342; and the American case of *Schoenthal* v. *Bernstein*, 93 N.L.S. 2d 187, 190 (1949).

and another in which they merely pass on the order of the overseas importer as his agent; they use whatever form is appropriate in the case in question.

It should be noted that in the first of these cases the confirming house acts as agent and buyer at the same time. It is clearly established that a person may combine these two qualities in the same transaction. Thus, Roche J. said[85]:

> Between a commission agent . . . and the foreign principal there is no relation except that of agency; but as between the British seller and the commission agent . . . as buyer there is no party to the contract except the commission agent . . . on that side.

Further, the Sale of Goods Act 1979 makes express provision for the protection of an agent, such as the confirming agent, who has himself paid, or is directly responsible for, the price: section 38(2) of that Act provides that he shall have the same rights against the goods as an unpaid seller: namely, the rights of lien, of stoppage in transit, and resale.[86]

The activities of export houses are of great benefit to international trade. By entering into an absolute obligation to the supplier, either by ordering the goods in its own name or by confirming the overseas order, the export house provides, in effect, non-recourse finance to the supplier. At the same time it often allows the overseas purchaser credit and thus enables him to place the order at all.

Obligations of confirming house

The confirming house, which has made itself liable to the supplier, is under a personal obligation to the supplier to pay the price for the goods. If before the execution of the transaction the overseas customer cancels the order without valid reason, the confirming house is still bound to pay the price to the supplier; its position is similar in this respect to that of the confirming bank under a bankers' letter of credit.[87] If the confirming house has performed this obligation, it is entitled to be indemnified by the customer for what it has paid to the supplier and, in appropriate cases, can recover damages.[88]

---

[85] In *R. & J. Bow Ltd.* v. *Hill* (1930) 37 Ll.L.R. 46 (the learned judge referred in this case to the famous case of *Ireland* v. *Livingstone* (1872) L.R. 5 H.L. 395); see further *Basma* v. *Weekes* [1950] A.C. 441, 454; *Brown & Gracie Ltd.* v. *F. W. Green & Co. Pty. Ltd.* [1960] 1 Lloyd's Rep. 289, 303; *Format International Security Printers Ltd.* v. *Mosden*, [1975] 1 Lloyd's Rep. 37.
[86] This interest can be covered by the confirming house by insurance, p. 508, *post*. On the rights of the unpaid seller against the goods see p. 148, *ante*.
[87] *Hamzeh Malas & Sons* v. *British Imex Industries Ltd.* [1958] 2 Q.B. 127; see p. 426, *post*.
[88] *Anglo-African Shipping Co. of New York Inc.* v. *J. Mortner Ltd.* [1962] 1 Lloyd's Rep. 610 (C.A.).

As regards the client, the confirming house undertakes to give the supplier proper shipping instructions but—and this has to be emphasised —it does not undertake liability for the conformity of the goods with the contract, and in particular for their quality and quantity.[89] If a dispute of this character arises, the customer must make a direct claim against the supplier; in this respect the confirming house, if it has merely confirmed the customer's order, has acted for an undisclosed principal.[90] In order to have certainty about the confirming house's position in this type of case, it is advisable for confirming houses, which intend to hold themselves personally responsible to the supplier, to use the third form of transaction—the actual confirmation—rather than the first form under which they are buyers from the supplier.[91]

Confirming houses often insert express clauses in their contracts with the customer and the supplier, to make this position clear. A typical clause is this:

> By confirming the order, we undertake full responsibility to pay the supplier for all goods delivered in accordance with our confirmation, but it is expressly agreed that we are to incur no other liability whatsoever in respect of the said contract and are not to be made parties to any litigation or arbitration relating thereto.

As already observed, the confirming house has a special lien on the goods and bills of lading *vis-à-vis* the customer and is, in this respect, in the same position as an unpaid seller.[92] But where the confirming house has allowed the customer credit, it does not have a general lien entitling it to retain goods or bills of lading for an indebtedness of the customer resulting from earlier transactions, unless such a general lien is contractually granted to the confirming house; the confirming house is not in the position of a factor, who by custom of trade, has a general lien.[93]

The contracts into which an English confirming house enters provide often that they shall be governed by English law and that the parties submit to the jurisdiction of the English courts.

Insolvency of the confirming house

If the confirming house becomes insolvent, the question arises whether the seller can still claim the price from the overseas buyer. If the confirming house has re-ordered the goods from the seller, the answer is clear: the seller can claim the price from the buyer on the contract of purchase originally placed by the buyer. If the confirming house has

---

[89] Provided that it has passed on the instructions of the customer correctly to the supplier.
[90] *Teheran-Europe Co. Ltd.* v. *S. T. Belton (Tractors) Ltd.* [1968] 2 Q.B. 545 (C.A.).
[91] See p. 297, *ante.*
[92] Sale of Goods Act, 1979, s.38(2).
[93] *Tellrite Ltd.* v. *London Confirmers Ltd.* [1962] 1 Lloyd's Rep. 236.

confirmed the buyer's order the position is more difficult. If the intention of the parties was that the obligation of the confirming house shall be the sole obligation to the seller, there would be no claim against the overseas buyer. That conclusion would, however, be exceptional. Normally the confirmation by the confirming house, like the confirmation of the advising bank under a letter of credit, provides only conditional discharge and the seller has still his claim against the overseas buyer.[94]

Illustrations

Two illustrations of transactions in which the confirming agent was held to be personally liable to the supplier may be added. In *Rusholme's* case[95] the plaintiffs, manufacturers in England, received in May 1951, through their Australian agents, orders for shirting material from an Australian importer; the orders provided "terms—confirmation and payment by" the defendants, a confirming house in London. The confirming house then ordered the shirting material from the manufacturers. The order stated "Purchased by [the confirming house], holders of Purchase Tax No. Central 2/3793 of goods as stock intended for export." There was nothing on the order to show that it had reference to another transaction except the words: "In confirmation of your agents' Indent No. 14." The order was accepted by the manufacturers by a letter of June 7 in these words: "We thank you for the above order for [name of the Australian importer] and have pleasure in confirming same herewith": then the terms of the contract were set out. Owing to an Australian trade recession before the delivery date the Australian importer cancelled the orders and the confirming house refused to accept delivery. Pearce J. found that the manufacturers would not have accepted the orders without the interposition of an English confirming house and held that the orders by the confirming house to the manufacturers constituted the true contracts between the parties and that the confirming house was liable to pay damages for non-acceptance of the goods. The learned judge said with respect to that order form:

> The document means what it says, namely, that the defendants are assuming liability as between themselves and the plaintiffs. It would have been easy for the defendants to put a different wording in the document had the intention been otherwise. The defendants at first claimed that their wording "Purchased by S. G. Read & Co. (London) Ltd." was inserted on the compulsion of the Board or Trade as a condition of the defendants holding a purchase tax certificate; but in cross-examination Mr. Read had to admit that this was not so. He could have set out in terms that they were purchasing only as agents.

In *Sobell Industries Ltd.* v. *Cory Bros. & Co. Ltd.*,[96] Sobell obtained a considerable order for radio sets from a firm in Istanbul and insisted on

---

[94] *Cf.* pp. 439–440, *post.*
[95] *Rusholme & Bolton & Roberts Hadfield Ltd.* v. *S. G. Read & Co. (London) Ltd.* [1955] 1 W.L.R. 146.
[96] [1955] 2 Lloyd's Rep. 82.

confirmation by Cory who, in addition to other activities, carried on the business of export merchants and shippers. Cory thereupon placed an order for the same goods in their own name with Sobell. The Turkish buyers accepted only part of the goods and the confirming house—Cory—likewise refused to accept the balance of the goods. The sellers successfully sued the confirmers for damages for non-acceptance of the goods. McNair J. founded his judgment on a very short point; he held that the contract was contained in the order by the confirming house to the sellers and that it was clear from that order that the confirming house acted as principal.

Whether an English confirming house is personally liable to a supplier in this country depends entirely on the terms of the contract between him and the confirming house. If the contract discloses an intention to constitute privity of contract between these two parties, the confirming house is liable but if the contract shows that privity of contract shall only be constituted between the customer and the supplier, the confirming house acting merely as agent of the customer, there is no liability on the part of the confirming house.

No presumption of liability of English agent acting for foreign principal

In older decisions the courts held that an English agent who acted for a foreign principal was presumed to constitute privity of contract between himself and the English supplier. In modern practice such a presumption no longer exists.[97] "The most that can now be said is that in deciding whether privity of contract exists between an English supplier and the foreign principal of an English agent, [is that] the fact that the principal is foreign is a factor to be taken into account although its weight may be minimal."[98] These principles likewise apply where the foreign principal is unnamed (*e.g.* the English agent has acted "for our clients") or, it is thought, even where he is undisclosed.[99]

Confirmation by confirming house and by bank

It should not be thought that the confirmation by a confirming house has the same effect as that by a bank in all circumstances. Where the

---

[97] *Teheran-Europe Co. Ltd.* v. *S.T. Belton* (*Tractors*) *Ltd.* [1968] 2 Q.B. 53; affirmed on this point by C.A. in [1968] 2 Q.B. 545.
[98] *Per* Donaldson J., *ibid.*, at p. 62.
[99] *Teheran-Europe Co. Ltd.* v. *S.T. Belton* (*Tractors*) *Ltd.* [1968] 2 Q.B. 53; affirmed on this point by C.A. in [1968] 2 Q.B. 545.

confirming house merely adds its own confirmation to that of the customer,[1] that is true to a certain extent, although the confirming house gives shipping instructions to the supplier and the bank does not do so. But where the confirming house itself places the order with the United Kingdom supplier,[2] the position is fundamentally different. In this case the confirming house, in the words of McNair J.,[3] confirms "the contract as a whole." The confirmed credit has, thus, the merit of safety, in view of the financial status of the confirmer, but the acceptance of personal liability of the confirming house by way of a purchasing order has the additional merit of giving the seller protection in contingencies which are not purely financial.

The freight forwarder

The services of freight forwarders are of great value to those engaged in the export trade, and particularly to small firms which do not possess their own export organisations and shipping department.[4] Forwarders have a specialised knowledge of the intricacies of carriage by sea, air and land[5] and are, in particular, acquainted with the constantly changing Customs formalities at home and abroad, the rates and rebates of freight, the practices of sea and air ports, the groupage of sea or air cargoes in container transport[6] and the package and handling of export goods. They also undertake on occasion the inspection of goods[7] and the collection of debts from customers abroad.

The forwarder acting as principal or as agent

A forwarder may act as a principal or as an agent. Historically, forwarders acted as agents on behalf of their customers[8] but the practice has changed and in modern circumstances they often carry out other services, such as packing, warehousing, cartage, lighterage, insurance, or, in container transport, the groupage or consolidation of parcels of various

---

[1] See p. 297, *ante*.
[2] *Ibid*.
[3] In *Sobell Industries Ltd.* v. *Cory Bros. & Co.* [1955] 2 Lloyd's Rep. 82, 89.
[4] See D. J. Hill, *Freight Forwarders*, Stevens, London, 1972.
[5] The activities of forwarders in connection with the reservation of freight space for cargoes are described on p. 540, *post*.
[6] On container transport, see p. 609, *post*; on groupage bills of lading, see p. 579, *post*.
[7] *P.S.A. Transport* v. *Newton, Lansdowne & Co.* [1956] 1 Lloyd's Rep. 121 (port dues and wharfage charges payable before release of the goods for inspection not included in agents' agreed charges and agents entitled to be reimbursed).
[8] For this reason they were known as forwarding agents.

customers into one container. Often they act as carriers. It follows that, in law, they qualify more often as principals than as agents. Nevertheless, it has to be ascertained in every individual case in which legal capacity the forwarder acted. The answer depends on the construction of the contract between the forwarder and his customer and the facts of the case.

If the forwarder acts as the customer's agent, his duty is to procure with due diligence others who perform the carriage, storage, packing or handling of the goods. The customer, through the intermediaryship of the forwarder, enters into direct contractual relations with the others. In this case the forwarder is under the usual duties of an agent, unless they are modified by his contract with the customer. In particular, he is accountable to him, but, as will be seen, this duty is usually qualified by the trading conditions of the forwarder.

If the forwarder acts as a principal, he enters into a contract of services with the customer. He is the only person with whom the customer is in contractual relations, even though the actual services, which the forwarder has undertaken, are carried out by others. The profit which the forwarder makes, when contracting with the actual operators, is his own affair and he is not accountable for it to the customer.

The forwarder, when acting as agent, will often charge a commission, and, when acting as principal, an "all-in" price. But the method of remuneration is not the decisive factor and not even an indicative guide; it is just one of the details which, in the factual matrix of the case, have to be taken into consideration. In modern practice a forwarder acting as agent may charge a fixed price, known as an uplift price, and, vice versa, a forwarder acting as principal may describe his remuneration as commission. In one case[9] Donaldson J. said: "The reference to a commission is equivocal" and held that, although the remuneration was described as commission, the forwarder had acted as principal.

The *Standard Trading Conditions* (1984 edition) of the Institute of Freight Forwarders Ltd., to which reference will be made below, recognise that today the activities of the forwarder as principal and as agent are of equal importance.[10] They give the forwarder an option, unless the contract with the customer otherwise provides, to act in the one or the other capacity; they provide in clause 16:

> (A) . . . in the absence of specific agreement between the Customer and the Company, the Company shall be entitled to procure the carriage, storage, packing or handling of the goods as an Agent subject to these Conditions or to provide any or all of its services as a principal contractor.

The capacity of the forwarder is particularly difficult to determine when he is instructed to arrange for the *carriage* of goods, and this is obviously

---

[9] *Salsi* v. *Jetspeed Air Services Ltd.* [1977] 2 Lloyd's Rep. 57, 60.
[10] The 1981 Edition of the *Standard Trading Conditions* contained a presumption that the forwarder acted as agent but this presumption is discontinued in the 1984 edition.

the most frequent practical problem. The question is here whether the forwarder has acted as carrier, *i.e.* as principal, or as forwarding agent whose duty was only to procure carriage on behalf of the customer.[11] The difficulty is enhanced by the distinction drawn in modern international transportation Conventions[12] between the contractual and the actual carrier. The contractual carrier is a person who has contracted to move the goods from one place to another, although he does not carry out the transportation himself but leaves this task to the actual carrier with whom he has contracted. The CMR Convention, which deals with the international carriage of goods by road,[13] provides[14] that, where a carriage governed by a single contract is performed by successive carriers, each of them shall be responsible for the performance of the whole operation, and it has been held[15] that a forwarder who merely contracted to move the goods from one country to another, was a carrier within the meaning of the Convention. But in other cases the courts held[16] that the forwarder had acted as agent. It is also possible for the forwarder to act in a "hybrid" character,[17] *e.g.* as a carrier for the land segments of the journey and as forwarding agent for the sea leg.[18] As already observed, it is always a question of construction of the contract and the facts whether the forwarder has acted as a carrier or as forwarding agent in a particular case. Bean J. expressed this conclusion, when observing[19] that "at the end of the day it was very much a matter for the trial judge whether forwarding agents were in fact acting as principals or agents."

---

[11] Rowlatt J. in *Jones v. European & General Express Co. Ltd.* (1920) 90 L.J.K.B. 159, 160. Also *Chas. Davis (Metal Brokers) Ltd. v. Gilyott & Scott Ltd.* [1975] 2 Lloyd's Rep. 422; *Elektronska Industrija Oour TVA v. Transped Oour Kintinentalna Spedicna* [1986] 1 Lloyd's Rep. 49 (defendants describing themselves as "full load and groupage services specialists to Yugoslavia—full loads to all European countries" held to have contracted as carriers within the CMR). Also, *passim, Sidney G. Jones Ltd. v. Martin Bencher Ltd.* [1986] 1 Lloyd's Rep. 54, 64.

[12] Guadalajara Convention of 1961 (air transport; see pp. 620 and 623, *post*); CMR (road transport; see pp. 634 and 636, *post*).

[13] Effect is given to this Convention in the United Kingdom by the Carriage of Goods by Road Act 1965; see p. 634, *post*.

[14] In art. 34.

[15] *Ulster-Swift Ltd. v. Taunton Meat Haulage Ltd.* [1977] 1 Lloyd's Rep. 346; *Tetroc Ltd. v. Cross-Con (International) Ltd.* [1981] 1 Lloyd's Rep. 192.

[16] *Marston Excelsior Ltd. v. Arbuckle, Smith & Co. Ltd.* [1971] 2 Lloyd's Rep. 306; *Hair & Skin Trading Co. Ltd. v. Norman Airfreight Carriers Ltd.* [1974] 1 Lloyd's Rep. 443; *Motor Vespa SA v. Mat (Brittania Express) Ltd.* [1979] 1 Lloyd's Rep. 175, 179. In *Harlow & Jones Ltd. v. P. J. Walker Shipping & Transport Ltd.* [1986] 2 Lloyd's Rep. 141 Bingham J. held that the forwarders acted as agents, and not as principals, but that, in their capacity as agents, they had warranted that the freight would not exceed a stated sum, so that the risk of excess freight had to be borne by them.

[17] *Per* Beattie J. in *The Maheno* [1977] 1 Lloyd's Rep. 81, 86, 88 (N.Z.). See also *Burke Motors Ltd. v. Mersey Docks & Harbour Co.* [1986] 1 Lloyd's Rep. 155, 161–162.

[18] *Ibid.*

[19] In *Hair and Skin Trading Co. Ltd. v. Norman Airfreight Carriers Ltd.* [1974] 1 Lloyd's Rep. 443, 445.

The *Standard Trading Conditions* provide[20] that, when the forwarder contracts as a principal, he is not a common carrier. He is, therefore, not liable absolutely for loss of or damage to the goods in his possession.[21]

The Standard Trading Conditions of the Institute of Freight Forwarders

Most forwarders in the United Kingdom embody the *Standard Trading Conditions* sponsored by the Institute of Freight Forwarders Ltd. into the contracts with their customers although they do not apply automatically by usage of the trade.[22] The present edition is the 1984 Edition.[23]

The forwarder has a particular lien by virtue of the law, and the *Conditions* give him a general lien; under which he may retain the customer's goods and documents relating to the goods in his possession until all debts due from the customer are paid.[24] The conditions authorise the forwarder to retain and be paid all brokerages, commissions, allowances and other remunerations customarily retained or paid to shipping and forwarding agents or insurance brokers, *e.g.* rebates under shipping conference arrangements entered into by the forwarding agent and not by the customer, or commissions on insurance.

---

[20] In clause 34. On the liability of the forwarder for lost or stolen goods, see D. J. Hill, "Loss in Transit" [1969] J.B.L. 100.

[21] An inland carrier who has contracted under the Road Haulage Association Ltd.'s Conditions of Carriage is normally authorised to sub-contract unless the nature of the load or the surrounding circumstances exclude such authority: *John Carter (Fine Worsteds) Ltd.* v. *Hanson Haulage (Leeds) Ltd.* [1965] 1 Lloyd's Rep. 49, 60; *Garnham, Harris & Elton Ltd.* v. *Alfred W. Ellis Ltd.* [1967] 2 Lloyd's Rep. 22–27.

[22] *Salsi* v. *Jetspeed Air Services Ltd.* [1977] 2 Lloyd's Rep. 57, 60. But the application of the Standard Trading Conditions may arise from a previous course of dealing, in which they have been clearly indicated, particularly as they are "not particularly onerous or unusual and, indeed, are in common use" (*per* Taylor L.J. in *Circle Freight International Ltd.* v. *Mideast Gulf Exports Ltd.* [1988] 2 Lloyd's Rep. 427, 433).

[23] These conditions are revised by the Institute of Freight Forwarders Ltd. from time to time. See *E. W. Taylor & Co. (Forwarding) Ltd.* v. *Bell* [1968] 2 Lloyd's Rep. 63.

[24] Clause 42; see *J. O. Lund Ltd.* v. *Anglo-Overseas Transport Co. Ltd.* [1955] 1 Lloyd's Rep. 142. The forwarder has no general lien by custom of the trade; if he wants to claim a general lien, he must provide for it in his contract with the customer, *e.g.* by incorporating the *Conditions*: *Langley, Beldon & Gaunt Ltd.* v. *Morley* [1965] 1 Lloyd's Rep. 297. Where the customer is a company and a receiver is appointed, the general lien is operative on goods reaching the forwarder's possession after the appointment of the receiver, provided that the contract under which the general lien arises was made before that event: *George Barker (Transport) Ltd.* v. *Eynon* [1974] 1 W.L.R. 462. Where a forwarder promised the customer that his goods, though shipped in containers, would be shipped under deck, he was held to be liable when they were shipped on deck and part of them fell overboard owing to a swell at sea: *J. Evans & Son (Portsmouth) Ltd.* v. *Andrea Merzario Ltd.* [1976] 1 W.L.R. 1078. Where forwarders deposited goods into a warehouse for consolidation in containers, the contractual general lien of the warehousemen did not operate against the owners of the goods (who did not know that the consolidation was carried out by the warehousemen): *K. Chellaram & Sons Ltd.* v. *Butlers Warehousing and Distribution Ltd.* [1978] 2 Lloyd's Rep. 412 (C.A.).

The *Conditions* contain detailed provisions limiting the liability of the forwarder when contracting as principal. They provide, inter alia, that the forwarding company accepts only liability for loss of or damage to goods "taken into its charge occurring between the time when it takes the goods into its charge and the time when the company is entitled to call on the customer, consignee or owner to take delivery of the goods."[25] The *Conditions* also provide maximum limitations of liability, calculated by reference to Special Drawing Rights (SDRs)[26] and a list of exemptions from liability.[27]

Further, according to the *Conditions* "no insurance will be effected [by the forwarder] except upon express instructions given in writing by the customer"[28]; in this connection it should be mentioned that insurance brokers instructed to effect marine insurance are normally not obliged, in the absence of express instructions, to insure the goods in the hands of forwarders or packers and are not liable if they fail to do so.[29] If, however, the forwarder has undertaken to insure the goods during storage by him, he must store them in such a manner that they are covered by his insurance policy; otherwise he is liable in damages.[30] If the forwarder has undertaken to make a claim under an air waybill for missing goods but fails to do so in good time, he is liable to the owner.[31]

The forwarder as bailee

If a dispute involving the forwarder as carrier cannot be resolved by reference to the provisions of the international convention applying to the particular mode of transport[32] or the Forwarders' Standard Trading Conditions or other terms of the contract, it may become necessary to resort to the common law concept of bailment because the carrier, who has possession of the owner's (bailor's) goods, is undoubtedly the bailee of those goods. A bailment arises if a person (the bailee) has possession

---

[25] Clause 33(A). The predecessor of this clause was clause 13 of the 1974 Conditions; this clause was interpreted by Bingham J. in *Swiss Bank Corporation* v. *Brink's-Mat Ltd.* [1986] 2 Lloyd's Rep. 79, 91.
[26] Clause 37; on SDRs see p. 602, *post.*
[27] Clause. 36.
[28] Clause 21(A); see p. 491, *post.* Clause 12 of the 1974 Conditions, which was worded exactly like the present clause 21, was referred to in *Swiss Bank Corporation* v. *Brink's-Mat Ltd.* [1986] 2 Lloyd's Rep. 79, 92.
[29] *United Mills Agencies Ltd.* v. *R. E. Harvey, Bray & Co.* [1952] 1 T.L.R. 149. But insurance brokers are under a duty to use reasonable care to the customer; if the latter thinks that he is insured but the insurance has been cancelled, they are bound to advise him at once; *London Borough of Bromley* v. *Ellis* [1971] 1 Lloyd's Rep. 97; see also p. 491 *post.*
[30] *Firmin & Collins Ltd.* v. *Allied Shippers Ltd.* [1967] 1 Lloyd's Rep. 633, 639.
[31] *Marbrook Freight Ltd.* v. *K.M.I. (London) Ltd.* [1979] 2 Lloyd's Rep. 341.
[32] See p. 537, *post.*

of another person's (the bailor's) goods by consent of the latter and undertakes to deal with them as directed by the bailor. The carrier, the warehouseman, the goods repairer are typical examples of bailees, as long as they have the bailor's goods in their charge. The main duty of a bailee for reward was defined by Lord Denning M.R.[33] as the "duty to take reasonable care to keep [the bailor's goods] safe."

Difficulties arise, in particular, if the bailee, with the consent of the bailor, allows a sub-bailee to take charge of the bailor's goods. In *Transcontainer Express Ltd.* v. *Custodian Security Ltd.*[34] Duty Free Distributors (UK) Ltd., an English company, bought 400 cases of brandy from a French supplier in Machecoul. Duty Free contracted with Transcontainer to carry the brandy from Machecoul to Feltham in Middlesex. Transcontainers sub-contracted the leg of carriage from Dover to Feltham to Crossland Haulage Ltd. The warehouse in Feltham was not able to take delivery of the goods and the driver of Crossland took them to the East India Dock where the defendants Custodian Security Ltd. provided a security service. There the brandy was stolen. Transcontainer paid Duty Free £5,620.16 (exclusive of duty) by way of damages and the duty of £49,458.46 to Customs and Excise. Transcontainer claimed to recover these sums from the defendants Custodian, founding their claim on the tort of negligence. The Court of Appeal dismissed the action because, according to the principle in *Aliakmon*,[35] they were not entitled to sue in negligence since they were neither the owners of the goods nor did they have possession of them but it was doubtful whether they had "an immediate right of possession" which would have given them a "possessory title"; as this question was not argued in the court of first instance, the Court of Appeal left this important point undecided. The sub-bailee is under the same duty to take reasonable care as the main bailee.[36]

A further problem is whether a defence available to the sub-bailee against the main bailee can be pleaded by him against the bailor. This question has to be answered in the affirmative if the sub-bailee is employed by the main bailee with the consent of the bailor. In *Singer Co. (UK) Ltd.* v. *Tees and Hartlepool Port Authority*[37] Singer contracted with J. H. Bachman (U.K.) Ltd. to crate and deliver machines to UK ports;

---

[33] In *Morris* v. *C. W. Martin & Sons Ltd.* [1966] 1 Q.B. 716, 726.

[34] [1988] 1 Lloyd's Rep. 128.

[35] See p. 46, *ante*.

[36] In *Metaalhandel J. A. Magnus BV* v. *Ardfields Transport Ltd.*, *Financial Times*, July 21, 1987, Metaalhandel, a Dutch company asked the forwarder (Ardfields) to store some tungsten near London. Ardfields contracted with Jones Transport to store the goods in Ashfield, Middlesex. The goods were handed over by Jones's employee to an unauthorised person and disappeared. Although Ardfields never had possession of the goods they were held liable as "quasi-bailees" because they had failed to check the system of safeguarding applied by the sub-bailee (Jones).

[37] [1988] 2 Lloyd's Rep. 164.

the machines were to be shipped from there to Brazil. Bachman took the machines to one of the defendants' docks for loading on the vessel *Serra Dourada* but in the loading process the machines were badly damaged. Singer claimed damages from the defendant port authority which denied that its employees had been negligent. Bachman had acted as principal, and not as agent of Singer. The Court of Appeal held that Bachman had implied authority from Singer to employ the port authority for the loading of the machines; the limitation of liability provisions in the port authority's (sub-bailee's) general conditions could be pleaded against Singer (the bailor), and these limitation provisions were reasonable and not invalid under the Unfair Contract Terms Act 1977. In the result, Singer's claim was dismissed.

Further duties of the forwarder

Further, where shipping agents were employed by importers for the clearance of imports through Customs but, in the course of dealing with their customers, did not make Customs entries without specific instructions from their customers, they were held not to be liable for failing to make such Customs entries before the date when the import duty for the goods went up.[38] Where a freight charge quoted by a forwarder to his customers is based on the weight and measurement of the goods, the customers are liable to make additional payment to the forwarder if he has to pay higher freight on the ground that the measurements of the goods are greater than originally stated.[39]

According to the custom of the London freight market, forwarders, who by request of their customers book freight space on board a ship, are personally liable for dead freight to the carrier if the customers fail to load the goods and the ship sails with the space unfilled; in this case the forwarders are entitled to be indemnified by their customers.[40]

---

[38] *World Transport Agency* v. *Royte* [1957] 1 Lloyd's Rep. 381.

[39] *Brushfield Sargent & Co. Ltd.* v. *Holmwright Engineering Co. Ltd.* [1968] 1 Lloyd's Rep. 439. But the forwarder cannot claim additional freight when he has given a firm quotation without finding out whether the goods which he has undertaken to transport have any peculiar characteristics: *S. Zimmermann & Son Ltd.* v. *Baxter, Hoare & Co. Ltd.* [1965] 1 Lloyd's Rep. 88. If, after a firm charge has been agreed, the forwarder demands a surcharge and this demand amounts in law to economic duress (a concept which English law recognises and which is much more severe than commercial pressure), the customer need not pay the surcharge: *Atlas Express Ltd.* v. *Kafco (Importers and Distributors) Ltd.* [1989] 3 W.L.R. 389.

[40] *Anglo-Overseas Transport Co. Ltd.* v. *Titan Industrial Corporation (United Kingdom) Ltd.* [1959] 2 Lloyd's Rep. 152. Similarly, air agents who undertake personal liability are entitled to be indemnified by the customer, if the latter ought to have known that the air agents rendered themselves personally liable: *Perishable Transport Co. Ltd.* v. *Spyropoulos (London) Ltd.* [1964] 2 Lloyd's Rep. 379.

The agent of necessity

Where an agent is in possession of his principal's goods and has a limited authority only, *e.g.* not to sell from his stock unless expressly authorised by the principal, or to return the consignment to the principal or, perhaps, to dispatch to him goods bought on his behalf, circumstances of such urgent necessity might occur as to justify the use of exceptional measures for the protection of the principal's property. Mercantile law has evolved the doctrine of agency of necessity under which an agent is allowed—but not obliged—to exceed his authority in an emergency and to do what is required for safeguarding his principal's property, including the sale of it where there is danger of deterioration or loss. But the conditions upon which an agency of necessity can be exercised are difficult to establish, and the courts are not prepared to extend them unduly.[41] These conditions are, first, that the excess of authority is required by an actual and definite commercial necessity,[42] and secondly that the agent cannot communicate with the principal and obtain his instructions before disposing of the goods.[43] In 1920[44] London export merchants sent a parcel of goods to Batum through British carriers, who had establishments in Batum and Constantinople (now Istanbul), with instructions to deliver the goods to a local merchant. When the goods arrived, Batum was on the verge of serious disturbances; British residents had to evacuate the town and a clash between Soviet and White Russian forces seemed imminent. The carriers thereupon removed the goods to Constantinople when evacuating Batum and did not deliver them to the local merchant. The court ruled that they acted as agents of necessity and were not liable for any loss suffered by the exporters owing to the removal of the goods to Constantinople. Bailhache J. expressed the decisive test as follows[45]:

> I have come to the conclusion that under all circumstances there never was a point of time that I can put my finger on and say "here the defendants ought to have communicated with this country and if they had done so at that particular date there was a reasonable chance of getting a reply."

It is extremely difficult to establish agency of necessity where there is no pre-existing agency relationship.[46] The only exception is that, if the

---

[41] *John Koch Ltd.* v. *C. & H. Products Ltd.* [1956] 2 Lloyd's Rep. 59, 65–66 (*per* Singleton L.J.).

[42] *Sachs* v. *Miklos* [1948] 2 K.B. 23; *Munro* v. *Willmott* [1949] 1 K.B. 295.

[43] The term "agency of necessity" should, for reasons of clarity, be confined to a situation in which these two conditions are satisfied. It should not be applied to a situation in which a bailee incurs expenses to save the bailor's goods from deterioration; here less stringent conditions apply and, in particular, inability to communicate with the owner of the goods is not a condition precedent of the bailee's own right to reimbursement of his expenses: *China Pacific SA* v. *Food Corporation of India, The Winson.* [1982] A.C. 939, 958, 962, 964.

[44] *Tetley & Co.* v. *British Trade Corporation* (1922) 10 Ll.L.R. 678.

[45] At p. 681.

[46] *Re Banque de Moscou, Royal Exchange Assurance* v. *The Liquidator* [1952] 1 All E.R. 1269, 1278.

two conditions for agency of necessity are satisfied, the master of a vessel has power to act for the cargo owner although he had not been in an agency relationship to him before.

Further, in the modern state of telecommunications cases in which the agent is unable to communicate with the principal and to obtain his instructions with respect to the goods will arise rarely. But it is not beyond imagination that such a situation may still develop suddenly.

FOREIGN AGENCY LAWS

National enactments protecting agents

In English law the enactments protecting the position of employees[47] do not apply to independent agents and there are no special legal rules protecting their position.[48]

Some foreign laws,[49] however, provide far-reaching protection for the independent agent in a manner which cannot be contracted out. In particular, they entitle the agent after termination of the agency to claim compensation from the principal for the goodwill which he has created and which continues to accrue to the principal, but the conditions for claiming compensation differ in the various countries.[50] A claim for compensation (*Ausgleichsanspruch, indemnité de cliènte, indemnitá*) is admitted in Germany,[51] Switzerland,[52] France, Italy and Austria.[53] In Belgium legislation exists for the protection of sole distributors whose contracts with the suppliers are of indefinite duration; this legislation has been considered earlier.[54]

A difficult question is whether the United Kingdom exporter can avoid the overseas agent's claim for compensation by providing that the agency agreement shall be governed by English law. As far as German law is concerned, such a clause is effective and, consequently, bars the agent's

---

[47] These enactments are mainly the Employment Protection (Consolidation) Act 1978, as amended by the Employment Acts 1980 and 1982, and other enactments.
[48] On their right to commission for orders placed after the termination of the agency contract, see p. 289 *ante*.
[49] See Clive M. Schmitthoff, "Agency in International Trade, A Study in Comparative Law" 129 *Recueil des Cours*, Academy of International Law (1970, Vol. 1), 109, 165 *Essays*, 306; Ole Lando, "The Commercial Agent in European Law" in [1965] J.B.L. 179, 374 and [1966] J.B.L. 82; Roberto Baldi, *Distributorship, Franchising, Agency*, 1987, p. 29.
[50] [1966] J.B.L. 84.
[51] H.G.B. s.89b (introduced by an Act of August 6, 1953).
[52] OR, s.418u (as revised in 1953).
[53] Lando, *loc. cit.* p. 85. In France the agent may be entitled to compensation amounting to two year's earnings on termination of the agreement.
[54] See p. 271, *ante*.

claim,[55] but in other legal systems it is uncertain whether the agent's claim for compensation, which is mandatory, can be excluded by submitting the contract of agency to English law. If the agency contract does not provide which law shall apply, many laws assume that that shall be the law of the place where the agent carries on his business; this is the view of the courts in France, Germany, Denmark, Holland and Switzerland, and presumably Belgium, Sweden and Norway.[56] In Italy the Civil Code states that the contract shall be governed by the law of the place where it was concluded.[57] In England, the proper law of the contract between the principal and the agent has to be ascertained in the manner discussed earlier[58]; this is in general the law of the country where the relation of principal and agent is created; it is likely to be the law of the principal, particularly if the agent has sought out the principal in that country, but in other circumstances it may well be the law of the country of the agent.[59]

INTERNATIONAL MEASURES AIMING AT THE UNIFICATION OF AGENCY LAW

Two international measures aimed at the unification of the law of agency should be mentioned. As neither of them has become law in the United Kingdom yet,[60] reference to them can be brief.

The EC Directive relating to Self-employed Commercial Agents

This Directive was adopted by the Council of Ministers December 18, 1986.[61] The United Kingdom and the Republic of Ireland have until January 1, 1994 to adapt their laws to give effect to this Directive.[62]

The Directive aims at regulating the basic principles applying to the relation of principal and agent. It applies to self-employed agents having

---

[55] German Federal Supreme Court, judgment of January 30, 1961.

[56] Schmitthoff, *loc. cit.*, p. 170; Lando, *loc. cit.*, p. 89.

[57] CC, *disp. prel.*, art. 25.

[58] See p. 209, *ante*.

[59] Dicey and Morris, *Conflict of Laws*, 11th ed., 1987, Rule 200, pp. 1339–1340. The contract between the principal (acting through the agent) and the third party is, it is thought, governed by its own proper law which may be entirely different from the law applicable to the contract between the principal and agent, *i.e.* the agency contract proper; see Dicey and Morris, *Conflict of Laws*, Rule 201, pp. 1341–1347.

[60] Position: October 1, 1989.

[61] 86/653/EEC; O.J. of December 31, 1986, No. L382/17. See Department of Trade and Industry, "Implementation of EC Directive on Self-employed Commercial Agents." An explanatory and consultative Note, July 1987. See further Frans van Kraay, "The EEC Directive on Self-employed Agents" in [1988] J.B.L. 267.

[62] The other Member States must implement the Directive by January 1, 1990 but Italy has until January 1, 1993 to implement Article 17.

authority to negotiate contracts on behalf of the principal as well as to agents having authority to conclude such contracts. The agent may be a natural person, partnership or company.

Two provisions of this Directive require mention here. The first relates to repeat orders.[63] Here it is provided that the agent shall automatically be entitled to commission on orders placed by customers "acquired," *i.e.* introduced, by him, though the orders are not placed through him. This appears to be an unexceptionable regulation. It is further provided that Member States, when giving effect to this regulation in their territories, shall have the option of introducing one of the following alternatives: the agent shall be entitled to commission on all orders emanating from the area or group of customers allocated to him, whether "acquired" by him or not; or he shall only be so entitled if he is given the *exclusive* right in this respect. It is probable that the United Kingdom, when giving effect to this Directive, will adopt the second alternative.

The second problematic provision of the Directive concerns the right of the agent to a termination indemnity.[64] The introduction of such a right will constitute a new feature in the English law of agency, though the termination indemnity is known to many other European laws.[65] Here again the Member States have the option of introducing one of two alternatives into their national law. The first of them is to provide an "indemnity" by way of recompense for contribution to the principal's continuing goodwill, and the second is a "compensation for damage" for loss of the agency.[66] The Directive contains a list of circumstances in which no indemnity or compensation is payable,[67] but it does not require a minimum period of currency of the agency agreement in order to entitle the agent to indemnity or compensation. The amount of the indemnity— but not the claim for damages—shall not exceed a figure equivalent to the agent's remuneration for one year calculated on the average annual remuneration over the preceding five years.[68] The parties may not derogate from the provisions relating to the agent's claim to indemnity or compensation to his detriment before the expiration of the agency agreement.[69]

The Convention on Agency in the International Sale of Goods

This Convention, promoted by Unidroit, was adopted by a diplomatic conference at Geneva on February 17, 1983. So far[70] it has been ratified or acceded to by:

---

[63] Art. 7 of the Directive.
[64] Art. 17.
[65] See p. 310. *ante*.
[66] Art. 17(3) specifies the circumstances in which damages may be demanded.
[67] Art. 18.
[68] Art. 17(2)(b).
[69] Art. 19.
[70] Position: September 28, 1988.

South Africa (January 27, 1986), Italy (June 16, 1986), France (August 7, 1987), Mexico (December 22, 1987) with reservations.

It will come into force only when it is ratified or acceded to by 10 States.[71] The Convention is intended to be complementary to the Vienna Convention on Contracts for the International Sale of Goods.[72]

The Convention applies where the principal and the third party have their places of business in different States and the agent has authority from his principal to conclude a contract of sale of goods with a third party, but it is also intended to cover agency agreements authorising the agent only to introduce customers to the principal. It applies irrespective of whether the agent acts in his own name or in that of the principal. It deals with the relations between the principal and the agent, and also with the relations affecting the third party.[73]

Three features of the Convention may be mentioned. First, the Convention admits the principle of ostensible authority.[74] It provides[75]:

> . . . where the conduct of the principal causes the third party reasonably and in good faith to believe that the agent has authority to act on behalf of the principal and that the agent is acting within the scope of that authority, the principal may not invoke against the third party the lack of authority of the agent.

Secondly, the Convention adopts, at least as a matter of last resort, the rules on intervention and election where a duly authorised agent has concluded the contract with the third party in his own name.[76] In this respect the Convention follows English law and does not adopt the rigid rules of the civil law on the *commissionaire*.[77] Thirdly, in accordance with the principle of autonomy of the parties' will, which is a fundamental maxim in the law of contract of all countries of the world, the principal, or an agent acting in accordance with the express or implied instructions of the principal, may agree with the third party to exclude all or any provisions of the Convention.[78]

Speaking generally, the Convention is a skilful combination of the principles of the civil and common law on agency in the international sale of goods. It is to be hoped that the Convention will be given effect in due course. This would be a valuable step towards the unification of the law of international trade.[79]

---

[71] Art. 33(1).
[72] See p. 252, *ante*.
[73] Art. 1.
[74] See p. 282, *ante*.
[75] Art. 14(2).
[76] Art. 13.
[77] See pp. 281 and 293, *ante*.
[78] Art. 5.
[79] Clive M. Schmitthoff, "The Codification of the Law of International Trade" [1985] J.B.L. 34.

TRAVELLING REPRESENTATIVES ABROAD

Another form of marketing is for an exporter to send travelling representatives abroad. Their task is to solicit orders from new customers or to maintain contact with already existing customers. They usually produce on their visits samples of their principal's goods or exhibit them in local showrooms. The customer, who wishes to place a repeat order, normally sends it directly to the principal's head office. Travelling representatives often visit their customers at regular intervals in order to show them a new range of samples.

When the single market is established in the EC in 1992, visits by travelling representatives in this regional "home" market may become more widely used than at present. But, speaking generally, this method of marketing is not as effective as maintaining a permanent presence in the target territory, by independent distributors or self-employed agents, or, better still, by local branches or subsidiaries.

Travelling representatives and their luggage are subject to the laws of the overseas countries which they visit, and these laws vary greatly. Three points have to be borne in mind here: does the traveller require a licence when soliciting or accepting orders, are taxes payable by the principal in respect of the traveller's activities, and is Customs duty payable on the samples which he carries?

In most countries a business traveller representing a principal resident abroad does not require a Government licence when pursuing his activities. That is certainly true with respect to the Member States of the EC which are visited by the travelling representative of a principal resident in another Member State, but it also applies in the case of United Kingdom travelling representatives visiting countries outside the EC, such as Australia, New Zealand, Canada, the United States, Brazil and Peru. Only in some African and South American countries does such a travelling representative have to obtain a licence before engaging in business.

In some countries transient traders' taxes are levied on principals represented by travelling representatives. Sometimes these taxes are State and sometimes municipal revenues. They provide a serious obstacle to the free movement of international trade. The Conventions on relief from double taxation, which the United Kingdom Government has concluded with various overseas governments, aim at the exemption of United Kingdom firms from this form of taxation.

The Customs regulations of most countries provide special facilities for the importation of bona fide trade samples by travelling representatives. In some countries samples which are of no commercial value are admitted free of duty. Generally, however, trade samples are liable to Customs duties but it is often sufficient for a deposit to be paid to the Customs authorities; in other cases where the duty has to be paid, a refund or drawback is allowed when the samples are exported within a stated time, *e.g.* six or 12 months.

ATA carnets

The importation of commercial samples and other goods temporarily required for exhibitions, scientific, professional and other purposes is regulated by a number of international Conventions sponsored by the Customs Co-operation Council which has its seat in Brussels but is not connected with the EC.[80] The Convention which is of particular interest here is that dealing with the issue of ATA carnets for the temporary admission of goods of December 6, 1961.[81] All Member States of the European Community, including the United Kingdom, and many other countries have given effect to the ATA Convention.[82] When the single market will be established in the EC in 1992, the ATA procedure should become superfluous within the territory of that regional market but it is important in the European market during the run up to 1992 and it will remain of great practical value for business in non-EC countries.

The carnets facilitate Customs clearance of certain classes of temporary importations and exportations by replacing:

(*a*) normal Customs documentation in the country of temporary exportation, and
(*b*) normal Customs documentation and security (*e.g.* by bond or deposit) in the country of temporary importation.

ATA carnets may be used for the temporary exportation from the United Kingdom of:

(*a*) commercial samples and advertising films (16mm);
(*b*) goods for international exhibition;
(*c*) professional equipment, *viz*:
Articles for meetings for a charitable purpose or to promote any branch of learning: art; craft; sport; religion, *etc*.; equipment for the press; also sound and television broadcasting equipment; musical instruments; costumes; scenery; and other stage properties; cinematographic equipment; professional equipment for testing, maintaining, or repairing machinery, *etc*.; equipment for use by surgeons, archaeologists, zoologists, entertainers, lecturers, *etc*.; vehicles especially adapted for use in connection with any of the above, including travelling workshops and laboratories.

Carnets are issued by chambers of commerce or similar organisations approved by the Customs authorities of the country in which they operate. The decision whether to issue a carnet is entirely a matter for the organisation concerned. Inquiries about the issue of carnets to cover goods to be sent abroad should be made to the London Chamber of

---

[80] See Claude Jacquemart, *La Nouvelle Douane Européenne.* Collection "Exporter," Editions Jupiter, 1971, paras. 277–281.
[81] The letters ATA stand for *Admission Temporaire—Temporary Admission.* ATA carnets have superseded the ECS carnets which were issued by virtue of a Convention of March 1, 1956. ECS (*Echantillons Commerciaux—Commercial Samples*) carnets are now obsolete.
[82] According to a note in *London Commerce* of June 1988, 40 countries have adopted the ATA procedure and in 1987 some 250,000 carnets were issued around the world covering goods worth almost £2 billion.

Commerce[83] or to certain chambers of commerce in the larger provincial cities. These organisations will also give the names of chambers of commerce abroad which will issue carnets for the temporary importation of goods into the United Kingdom. Carnets may not be used for goods sent to or from the United Kingdom by post.

The carnet system operates in the following manner: the chamber of commerce, which issues the carnet, guarantees to the Customs of the overseas country, into which the goods are temporarily imported, that all duties, taxes, etc. will be paid to them if the conditions, under which the temporary importation of the goods is permitted, are broken. The chamber of commerce requires a corresponding security from the applicant for the carnet. The security may be given in cash, by a banker's draft or in the form of a guarantee issued by a bank or an approved insurance company. The guarantee is given on the official form of the chamber of commerce. The guarantee period is 31 months. The reason for this length of the guarantee is that the chamber of commerce is under a liability during this period. It comprises the carnet validity period of 12 months, plus a further 12 months during which claims against the carnet must, under the international Convention, be received by the issuing chamber, plus a seven months' allowance for finalising claims. If the carnet is used within a shorter time and returned to the issuing chamber, a conditional discharge is given by the chamber at its discretion and the guarantee will be released earlier. Regular users of the carnet system may give the chamber a continuing guarantee.

The period of temporary importation allowed by the overseas Customs varies but, speaking generally, is 12 months for commercial samples and six months for exhibition goods and professional equipment. In no circumstances does the validity of a carnet exceed one year.

If the goods covered by the carnet are lost or stolen whilst in the overseas country, they will automatically become liable to Customs duty, etc. This is the liability of the carnet holder who will have to reimburse the chamber of commerce for any payment it makes to the overseas Customs.

The ATA consists essentially of a booklet which includes a list of the goods covered and a number of vouchers and corresponding counterfoils that have to be completed when goods leave and enter a country. The Customs of the overseas country detach and retain the appropriate voucher, and check that a temporary importation voucher is later discharged by a corresponding re-exportation voucher.

---

[83] Address: 69 Cannon Street, London EC4N 5AB.

CHAPTER 17

BRANCH OFFICES AND SUBSIDIARIES ABROAD. FOREIGN ACQUISITIONS

The most effective method of overseas marketing is undoubtedly the establishment of a local branch or subsidiary in the country to which the exports are directed. The progressive intensification of international trade and, on the regional level, the establishment of a single market by the EC in 1992 favour this form of marketing. In many countries national corporations expand into transnational groups of companies,[1] sometimes of global dimension. But the medium-sized exporter should not ignore this form of overseas marketing; he will often find that trading through overseas branches or subsidiaries opens new markets for his products, is profitable and contains a considerable growth element.

In the EC a national of a Member State—this includes a company having its seat in it[2]—is entitled to establish agencies, branches or subsidiaries in any other Member State and Article 52 of the EC Treaty provides that, within the framework of the Treaty, any restrictions of this right shall be abolished.[3] This freedom of establishment has been characterised by the Court of Justice of the European Communities as "one of the fundamental principles of the Community;"[4] the Court has also pointed out that the provisions of the Treaty guaranteeing this freedom are of direct application[5]; consequently, national restrictions of this right are, in principle, invalid.

---

[1] See "Groups of Companies," edited by Clive M. Schmitthoff and Roy M. Goode, Vol. 2 of the International Commercial Law Series, 1990.

[2] Article 58 of the EC Treaty.

[3] For a discussion of the right of establishment of companies see *R.* v. *H.M. Treasury and Commissioners of Inland Revenue, ex parte Daily Mail and General Trust plc.* (Case 81/87) [1988] 3 C.M.L.R. 713; in this case the European Court of Justice held that the freedom of establishment did not entitle a national company to transfer its residence—the central management and control—from a Member State to another, and a provision in the tax law of the Member State of origin of the company requiring consent of the Treasury to such a transfer did not contravene the prohibition of Articles 52 and 58.

[4] In the *Daily Mail* case. See also *Re Tax Credits. EC Commission* v. *France* (Case 270/83) [1987] 1 C.M.L.R. 401 (tax credit discrimination against foreign EC branches and subsidiaries infringes Article 52 and the risk of tax evasion could not derogate from the effect of Article 52); *D.H.M. Segers* v. *Bestuur van de Bedrijfsvereniging voor Bank-en Verzekeringswezen, Groothandel en Vrije Beroepen.* (Case 79/85). [1987] 2 C.M.L.R. 247 (sickness benefit could not be refused in the Netherlands to a director (who was a Dutch national) of a company incorporated in England on the grounds that the company was not incorporated in the Netherlands).

[5] In the *Daily Mail* case, n. 4, *supra.*

BRANCH OFFICES AND SUBSIDIARIES ABROAD

The choice between branches and subsidiaries

The exporter who wishes to establish a permanent presence in an overseas country will ask himself whether it is more advantageous to establish a branch office in that country or to work through a subsidiary incorporated there. There is no general answer to this question and all depends on the circumstances of the individual case. Two considerations have to be taken into account: first, whether the local legislation, particularly relating to employment, companies, taxation and foreign investment, is more favourable to one of these alternatives; and secondly, whether the exporter wishes to co-operate with local interests. In the latter case, if he does not wish to adopt the form of joint venture or another form of joint export co-operation,[6] the form of a local subsidiary is preferable though the exporter should aim at obtaining the control over it, *e.g.* by retaining the majority of votes. But even if he does not intend such co-operation, the preference may well be for a wholly-owned subsidiary.

The legal distinction between branches and subsidaries

The decisive difference between these two types of business organisation is that the subsidiary has a separate and independent legal personality in the overseas country, in which it is incorporated, but a branch office is merely an emanation of the exporter in the overseas country and, through it, he is himself present in that country.

A subsidiary which requires bank credit might be unable to offer sufficient security and the bank may ask for a guarantee by the parent company to secure the debts of the subsidiary.[7] No such guarantee is required in the case of a branch office because its debts are automatically those of the head office.

A particular problem arises in the EC. In this region some Directives aiming at harmonisation of the national company laws of the Member States impose strict requirements of disclosure and accountability on companies incorporated in them.[8] The national laws giving effect to these

---

[6] On joint ventures and other forms of joint export cooperation, see p. 338, *post.*

[7] Sometimes the bank will accept a "letter of comfort" from the parent company but normally such a letter does not constitute an obligation of the latter to be liable for the debts of the subsidiary; see p. 95 *ante.*

[8] Particularly the First, Fourth and Seventh Directives; see *Palmer's Company Law*, Vol. I, 24th ed., 1987, para. 2–15.

Directives apply to subsidiaries incorporated in a Member State but do not automatically apply to branches of a company incorporated in another Member State or in a non-EC country. To fill this gap, the EC Commission submitted in 1986 to the Council of Ministers a Draft Directive aimed at imposing on branches operating in a Member State the same requirements of disclosure as apply to companies incorporated in that Member State.[9] This Draft Directive is not operative yet[10] but if and when it becomes effective it assimilates the disclosure requirements of branches to those of subsidiaries. As far as United Kingdom law is concerned, the adoption of this Directive would not make a material difference because a company incorporated outside Great Britain and having an established place of business in Great Britain has to register as an "oversea company" and, as such, has already now to give far-reaching disclosure.[11]

BRANCH OFFICES ABROAD

Jurisdiction over the head office

The difference between branches and subsidiaries abroad is also important if a plaintiff in the overseas country, in which the permanent representation is established, wishes to commence proceedings against the exporter's enterprise. The jurisdiction of the courts in the overseas country is governed by the procedural law of those courts.[12] The considerations which may be relevant are indicated when the reverse case is examined, *viz.* the case of an overseas enterprise establishing a permanent presence in the United Kingdom.

The "oversea company" in UK bar

If a company incorporated in a country other than Great Britain establishes a branch office, *i.e.* a place of business, in this country, the

---

[9] The Eleventh Draft Directive of July 29, 1986, see *Palmer. Ibid.*

[10] Position: October 1, 1989.

[11] Companies Act 1985, s. 691 *et seq.*; see p. below in text. *post.*

[12] If the overseas country is an EC Member State and has given effect to the Brussels Convention on Jurisdiction and Enforcement of Judgments in Civil and Commercial Matters of 1968, Article 5(5) may be relevant, which provides that, as regards a dispute arising out of the operation of a branch, agency or other establishment, the courts of the place in which the branch, agency or other establishment is situated shall have jurisdiction; see p. 214, *post.*

company must register as an "oversea company" under the Companies Act 1985.[13] One of the requirements of the Act is that it shall deliver to the Registrar of Companies the name and address of a person resident in Great Britain and authorised to accept service of proceedings and notices on behalf of the oversea company.[14] In brief, the oversea company, which has established a branch office in Great Britain, can be sued in the English courts like any other person ordinarily resident here.

The subsidiary registered in this country of a company incorporated elsewhere will have its registered office either in England and Wales or in Scotland and can be sued in the courts of these countries like any other company registered here.

Dealings between branches

Exceptionally, *e.g.* in string contracts[15] in the commodity trade, dealings between two branches of the same legal entity are treated like dealings between two separate legal entities, provided that these dealings are regarded in the trade as genuine trading transactions.[16]

SUBSIDIARY COMPANIES ABROAD

The favoured form of intensive export marketing is the establishment of a subsidiary company in the country into which exports are directed.

The overseas subsidiary

The overseas subsidiary is incorporated under the law of that country; it possesses, as we have seen, independent and separate legal personality

---

[13] ss.691 *et seq*.

[14] s.691(1)(*b*)(ii). If the company has made default of this obligation, the document may be sent by post to its place of business (s.695); for details see *Palmer's Company Law* (24th ed.), para. 91–07. As the law stands at present, an oversea company, which has duly nominated a person authorised to accept service, can be served with process on him even after it has notified the Registrar of Companies that it has discontinued to have a place of business in Great Britain: *Rome* v. *Punjab National Bank (No. 2)* [1989] 1 W.L.R. 1211 (CA).

[15] A string contract is a series of contracts under which a dealer (A) sells goods to another dealer (B), and so on, possibly through the whole alphabet, and only the last in the series takes delivery of the goods. In the oil trade, these contracts are colloquially called "daisy chain contracts:" *Voest Alpine Intertrading GmbH* v. *Chevron International Oil Co. Ltd.* [1987] 2 Lloyd's Rep. 547.

[16] *Bremer Handelsgesellschaft mbH* v. *Toepfer* [1980] 2 Lloyd's Rep. 43, 47, 51 (the case concerned a soya meal transaction under a GAFTA form). See also *Prince* v. *Oriental Bank Corporation* (1878) 3 App.Cas. 325, 332 (separate branches of bank in negotiable instruments transactions) and *Bank of Tokyo Ltd.* v. *Magid Karoon*, (Note) [1987] A.C. 45 and *Libyan Arab-Foreign Bank* v. *Barbers Trust Co.* [1989] 3 W.L.R. 314, 332.

and enjoys in the country of its incorporation the same status as an indigenous trading corporation.[17] The control of the overseas subsidiary is vested in the parent firm which *e.g.* is resident in the United Kingdom; it is exercised by various means, such as holding a majority of shares in, or a majority of the voting power of, the subsidiary company, or by reservation of the right to appoint its directors or managers, but these examples are illustrative only and not exhaustive.[18] In Nigeria a foreign company can only carry on business through the incorporation of a domestic company.[19]

The overseas subsidiary is capable of entering into the same contractual relations with the parent firm as can be entered into by every other enterprise trading in the overseas country. The relations between these two enterprises may be ordinary contracts of sale concluded on f.o.b. terms, c.i.f. terms or other trade terms; or the parent firm may arrange a sole distribution agreement with the subsidiary or employ it as its commission agent or resident representative abroad; the observations made earlier in regard to these different forms of trading apply here, *mutatis mutandis*. The form of a subsidiary company is particularly well suited when several United Kingdom exporters combine in export marketing or when a United Kingdom exporter associates with an overseas concern in the production or distribution of certain goods. The overseas subsidiary is, thus, the ideal trading instrument for joint ventures[20]; in view of the wide discretionary powers admitted by the company laws of most countries, it is not difficult to arrange the distribution of control in the subsidiary and the participation in its profits and losses in harmony with the agreement between its constituent members.

A different question is whether the parent company can be regarded as being within the jurisdiction of the court by virtue of the subsidiary having place of business there. As the parent and the subsidiary are two different legal persons, the question has, in principle, to be answered in the negative. But exceptionally the courts are prepared "to lift the veil of corporateness", *e.g.* if it can be proved that the subsidiary acted as agent of the parent or was merely a sham or façade.[20a]

---

[17] Robert R. Pennington and Frank Wooldridge, *Company Law in the European Communities* (3rd. ed., 1982); *Die Gründung einer Tochtergesellschaft im Ausland*, ed. Marcus Lutter, (Berlin, 1988).

[18] *British American Tobacco Co. Ltd.* v. *Inland Revenue Commissioners* [1943] A.C. 335.

[19] Nigerian Decree No. 51 of 1968.

[20] On joint ventures, see p. 338, *post.*

[20a] There exist many cases and voluminous literature on "lifting the veil." Only the following may be mentioned here: *SA des Minerals* v. *Grant Trading Inc. The Ert Stefanie* [1989] 2 Lloyd's Rep. 349; *Adams* v. *Cape Industries plc., The Times,* August 5, 1989; *Palmer's Company Law,* 24 ed. para. 18–22; Clive M. Schmitthoff, "The Wholly Owned and the Controlled Subsidiary" in [1978] J.B.L. 218, *Essays,* 742.

The multinational enterprise

By establishing one or several subsidiaries overseas, the British parent company becomes a multinational or, as it is sometimes called, transnational enterprise. Such an enterprise has been defined "as a combination of companies of different nationality, connected by means of shareholdings, managerial control, or contract and constituting an economic unit."[21]

On the international level no effective regulation of multinationals is established yet. The United Nations have constituted two bodies, a Commission and a Centre on Transnational Corporations; both have been operative since 1975. The aim is to produce a UN code of conduct of multinational enterprises. But many other UN organisations and agencies and regional groupings have made proposals or published codes in this area.[22] The picture which emerges from this situation is one of confusion, none of these measures having gained general recognition. On the other hand, OECD published *Guidelines for Multinational Enterprises* on June 21, 1976; these Guidelines are widely accepted by the practice.[23]

On the national level two legal problems arise with respect to multinational enterprises. First, the interests of the *host country* in which the subsidiary is formed may conflict with those of the *home country* in which the controlling company has its seat. If a subsidiary is involved in such a conflict, the public policy of the host country must, in principle, prevail over that of the home country[24]; if the United Kingdom is the host country, the Protection of Trading Interests Act 1980 enables the Secretary of State to prohibit the United Kingdom subsidiary of an overseas parent to comply with the directions of its parent if he considers that compliance would damage the trading interests of the United Kingdom.[25]

Secondly, in some circumstances the veil of separate legal status of the various constituent companies of the multinational enterprise is pierced and the multinational is treated as an economic unit. In particular, in the competition law[26] of the EC the European Court has assumed jurisdiction[27] over a parent company incorporated in a non-Member State and

---

[21] Clive M. Schmitthoff, "The Multinational Enterprise in the United Kingdom," in *Nationalism and Multinational Enterprise*, edited by H. R. Hahlo, J. Graham South and Richard W. Wright, Sijthoff, Leiden, 1973, 24 *Essays*, 717.

[22] See Desirée Sauermann, "The Regulation of Multinational Corporations and Third World Countries," in *South African Yearbook of International Law*, Vol. II, 1985–1986, 55.

[23] Clive M. Schmitthoff, *Commercial Law in a Changing Economic Climate* (2nd ed., 1981), p. 51.

[24] See Clive M. Schmitthoff, "Multinationals in Court," [1972] J.B.L. 103, 104 *Essays*, 709; *affaire Fruehauf, ibid.*; *Decro-Wall S.A.* v. *Marketing Ltd.* [1971] 1 W.L.R. 361; *Acrow (Automation) Ltd.* v. *Rex Chainbelt Inc.* [1971] 1 W.L.R. 1676.

[25] See pp. 229 *ante*.

[26] Articles 85–90 of the EC Treaty; see pp. 346 *et seq.*, *post*.

[27] In *I.C.I. Ltd. and Others* v. *E.C. Commission* (48–57/69) [1972] C.M.L.R. 557; and *Europemballage Corporation and Continental Can Company Inc.* v. *E.C. Commission* (6/72) [1973] C.M.L.R. 199; *Commercial Solvents Corporation* v. *Commission* [1973] C.M.L.R. 309; *Hoffmann-La Roche* v. *Commission* [1979] 3 C.M.L.R. 211.

having a subsidiary in a Member State if that subsidiary "does not determine its behaviour on the market in an autonomous manner but essentially carries out the instructions of the parent company."[28] The English courts, on the other hand, prefer the principle of separate legal personality to that of treating the group as an economic unit, with results which are not always happy.[29]

The proposed European comany

The EC authorities propose to create a new form of company, namely that of the European Company (*société Européenne, societas Europea, SE*). The proposal was first made in 1970 and then amended in 1975.[30] The latest version is the proposal submitted by the Commission to the Council on August 25, 1989.[30a]

According to the latest proposal, the SE can be formed by at least two public limited companies having their central administration in different Member States. These companies may create an SE either by merging or by making it their holding company. An SE itself may take part in the formation of another SE, and it may also constitute another SE as its subsidiary. An SE will have the status of a public limited company in every Member State; it must have a capital and shares.

An SE is formed by registration in the appropriate register of a Member State, but where it has a branch in another Member State, it has also to register the branch in that State.

Although the proposal of 1989 refers in its preamble to the desirability of admitting the form of the SE when the single market is established in 1992, it is thought that the admission of the creation of the SE is still a long term project.

OVERSEAS SUBSIDIARIES IN ENGLISH AND FOREIGN LAW

Overseas subsidiaries in English law

According to the United Kingdom Companies Act 1985 an overseas subsidiary of a British company is, in principle, treated in the same manner as if the subsidiary was incorporated in the United Kingdom.[31]

---

[28] In the *I.C.I.* case, on p. 629.
[29] *Multinational Gas and Petrochemical Co.* v. *Multinational Gas and Petrochemical Services Ltd.* [1983] Ch. 258; this decision is criticised by Lord Wedderburn in (1984) 47 M.L.R. 87.
[30] *Proposal for a Council Regulation on the Statute for European Companies*, May 13, 1975, *Bulletin of the European Communities*, Supplement 4/75. See further the Consultative Document of the Department of Trade and Industry and the Employment Department on "EC Memorandum concerning Formal Proposals for a European Company Statute" of September 1988.
[30a] O.J. 1989 No. C263/41, of October 16, 1989. In December 1989 the Departments of Trade and Industry and of Employment published a Consultative Document on "Proposal for a European Company Statute."
[31] Overseas subsidiaries are sometimes promoted as partnerships, and not as companies.

The Companies Act 1985 provides[32] in section 736(1) that a company shall be deemed the subsidiary of another (the holding) company if—

1. The holding company either
   (a) is a member of it and controls the composition of its board of directors, or
   (b) holds more than half in nominal value of its equity share capital, or
2. The company is a sub-subsidiary of the holding company.

The composition of a company's board of directors is deemed to be controlled by the holding company if the latter has power, without consent of any other person, to appoint or remove all or a majority of the directors (s.736(2) and (3)). The equity share capital is defined in section 744 as the issued share capital excluding any part thereof which, neither as respects dividends nor as respects capital, carries any right to participate beyond a specified amount in a distribution; consequently, non-participating preference shares do not form part of the equity share capital.

The 1985 Act further provides for an extension of publicity of the company's affairs and lays down in particular that, as a matter of principle, group accounts shall be presented by the holding company (s.229). Group accounts have to consist of—

(1) a consolidated balance sheet dealing with the state of affairs of the company and all the subsidiaries to be dealt with in group accounts;
(2) a consolidated profit and loss account dealing with the profit or loss of the company and those subsidiaries (s.229(5)).

The Act admits several exceptions from the obligation to include subsidiaries into the group accounts.

The European Community has issued various Company Directives affecting the relationship of parent and subsidiary companies. The Seventh Company Directive[33] deals with consolidated accounts and the Eighth Company Directive[33a] with the qualifications and the position of auditors of companies.[33b] The Companies Act 1989,[33c] seeks inter alia, to implement in the United Kingdom the Seventh and Eighth EC Company Directives: this legislation introduces, for the purposes of group accounts, the new concepts of parent and subsidiary undertakings (which are wider than those of holding and subsidiary companies in the 1985 Act) and recasts the provisions of the 1985 Act dealing with accounts and audit contained in Part VII of the Act, in order to make them conform with the requirements of the two EC Directives.[33d]

---

[32] A detailed treatment of this subject is contained in Palmer's *Company Law,* 24th ed., Chap. 74.

[33] Of June 13, 1983 (83/349/EEC).

[33a] Of April 10, 1984 (84/253/EEC).

[33b] The Ninth Company Directive will deal with the conduct of groups of companies. Its Draft has not been submitted by the Commission to the Council yet.

[33c] Which received the Royal Assent on November 16, 1989.

[33d] The sections of the 1985 Act most affected by the implementation of the Seventh and Eighth EC Directives by the Companies Act 1989 are sections 221 to 262; the 1989 Act substitutes new sections for the old ones and also adds some new sections. (see Part I of the 1989 Act).

Overseas Subsidiaries in foreign law

When it is intended to establish a subsidiary in an overseas country, the legal position in that country is an important factor to be considered, in addition to extra-legal factors, such as the political and economic stability of the country, the cost of labour, raw material and transport, the size of the market and the membership of the country to a regional trade group.

Broadly speaking, there are four branches of foreign law to which the United Kingdom exporter must give attention when deciding to form an overseas subsidiary; *viz.* the law relating to companies, employment, taxation and foreign investment. A detailed treatment of these topics is beyond the compass of this work, inasmuch as the foreign regulations change constantly. Obviously the exporter has to obtain competent advice on the legal position in the overseas country in which he intends to set up a subsidiary. In the following it is intended to indicate in a general way the different attitude which legal systems may adopt in the areas mentioned.

Foreign company law

The principle of free registration of a company under the general laws of the country, without the requirement of a special Government licence, is recognised in many overseas countries, including the countries of the Commonwealth, the United States, France, Spain and West Germany. In another group of countries a Government permission has to be obtained for the formation of the company but can be refused only for specified reasons; hereunder fall the laws of the Netherlands[34] and Finland although such a permission is in most instances a mere formality. In a third group of countries, a Government licence is required which may be refused on grounds of administrative expediency and discretion; this is the position in Turkey, Indonesia, Argentina, Bolivia, Chile, Guatemala, Haiti and Honduras.

Generally speaking, apart from a few specified activities, the laws of the Member States of the EC, of many Commonwealth countries, and of Austria and Israel do not restrict the participation of non-residents or foreign shareholders or directors. In other countries, however, whether industrially developed or in the course of development, legal restrictions exist.

According to a number of national laws, the majority of shares must be held by nationals of the country in question. In Mexico and the United

---

[34] See H. C. S. Warendorf and R. L. Thomas, *Companies and other legal persons under Netherlands Law and Netherlands Antilles Law*, 1988 (looseleaf).

Arab Republics, as a rule, 51 per cent. of the share capital, must be owned by nationals. In Nigeria, in certain specified enterprises, no alien can engage unless the equity interest of Nigerian citizens or associations is not less than 60 per cent., and in other specified enterprises aliens must not hold more than a 60 per cent. equity interest.[35] Restrictions of alien equity participation exist also in other countries of independent black Africa. In the countries of Eastern Europe restrictions exist in joint venture companies on the equity participation of foreign partners.[36] In view of the changing economic conditions in those countries, it is not possible to make general statements relating to those restrictions. They have to be ascertained by way of negotiation in every individual case and they may vary in the country in question from case to case. The same is true with respect to the position in the People's Republic of China.

In Sweden and Finland the articles must require that at least four-fifths of the capital are owned by nationals and cannot be transferred to aliens; if the articles do not so provide, restrictions are imposed on the company's right to own land.[37] Restrictions on ownership of land and mineral rights in the case of foreign participation are also found in other laws, notably those of Canada, Mexico and the Philippines.

In Sweden all the founders of the company must be resident Swedish subjects. Similar provisions requiring the majority of promoters to be American citizens exist in some of the United States, notably in the States of New York and Pennsylvania. Often these restrictions can be lawfully avoided by the use of nominees or "dummies."

In several countries special qualifications are required as regards the nationality or residence of the directors and managers of a domestic company. Thus, in Sweden, Norway, Finland and Switzerland all or the majority of the members of the board of directors must be resident nationals of the respective country, but in some cases the Government may dispense with this requirement. In Iraq[38] companies are obliged to employ national lawyers as secretaries or legal advisers respectively.

Foreign employment law

The laws of foreign countries often contain employee protection legislation. Such legislation applies to a subsidiary incorporated in the

---

[35] Nigerian Enterprises Decree 1977.

[36] UN Economic Commission for Europe, "East-West Joint Ventures domiciled in Eastern Europe and Yugoslavia: Current Status of Legislation and Enterprise Response," Note by the Secretariat, October 9, 1984 (Trade/R. 489), paras. 58 and 59.

[37] That makes it impossible to use bearer shares without permission of the Government. As regards Finland, see Dr. V. Reinikainen in "Aspects of the Right of Establishment by Aliens in Finland" in *Economic Review* (Helsinki), 1964, No. 3, pp. 119–139.

[38] [1961] J.B.L. 211.

country in question and controlled by aliens in the same manner as to individual alien employers. The general trend of this protectionist legislation will be surveyed later.[39]

Foreign tax law

The provisions of foreign tax law applying to overseas subsidiaries of British concerns vary considerably in the various countries. It is obvious that the incidence of taxation is one of the major considerations when a decision is taken whether to set up a subsidiary in the target country. It is perhaps less obvious that what matters is not merely the legal regulation but the realities of the tax position, and, in particular, the administrative discretion vested in the revenue authorities which in many foreign countries are not supervised by the ordinary courts. In some countries the revenue authorities have little discretion in the assessment and collection of taxes; in others a foreign enterprise is treated apparently or actually preferentially because it is the policy of the country to attract foreign capital, and in one or two instances, notably in Liechtenstein, the rates of taxation can be settled by negotiation before the foreign subsidiary is formed. In other countries, on the other hand, while the rates of taxation for foreign and domestic enterprises are the same and the law does not admit open discrimination, the practical effect of taxation is such that its impact is stronger on foreign than on domestic enterprises and, from the practical point of view, a considerable degree of discrimination may result.

Sometimes the operations of an overseas subsidiary attract taxation both in this country and in the country in which it is constituted; in these cases the question arises whether the exporter qualifies for double taxation relief in this country.

In the USA, some States apply to branches or subsidiaries carrying on activities in the State the concept of "unitary business," *i.e.* they treat the branch or subsidiary and the parent as a unit and claim to tax the income of the whole enterprise, irrespective of whether it is earned inside or outside the State. The Supreme Court upheld a unitary tax imposed by California in 1983,[40] and even after the passing of the Outer Continental Shelf Act,[41] which in principle prohibits the application of State tax laws to the Outer Continental Shelf, admitted a unitary tax law imposed by Iowa.[42] This claim of extraterritorial application of tax law is a serious obstacle to the free flow of international trade.

---

[39] On pp. 335–337, *post.*
[40] *Container Corporation of America* v. *Franchise Tax Board* 463 U.S. 159 (1983).
[41] 67 Stat. 29, 43 U.S.C. para. 1331 *et seq.* (1982 ed. and Supp. III).
[42] *Shell Oil Company* v. *Iowa Department of Revenue* Supreme Court Opinion of November 8, 1988; see 57 LW 4001 (1988), in this case which concerned Outer Continental gas, the court held that the Act was not applicable

Foreign investment law

National investment legislation. Many overseas countries which wish to develop their own industry with the help of foreign private investors have enacted legislation granting special privileges to foreign interests prepared to transfer technology by building up an industry in the country in question, either on their own or in collaboration with local industrialists. Amongst these countries are Egypt, Ghana, Greece, India, Israel, Italy, Nigeria, Pakistan, Portugal, Thailand, Turkey and Yugoslavia.

The investment privileges which national legislations normally provide, subject to many conditions and often not as generous as they appear at the first glance, relate to—

1. *Exchange control regulations.* The investor is allowed to transfer home profits and to repatriate his invested capital and any capital gain;
2. *Customs regulations.* Free entry or entry at a reduced rate is allowed for machinery required to set up or expand the new industry and sometimes also for the goods produced;
3. *Relief from taxation.* Hereunder fall relief from, or preferential rates of, national or municipal taxation, stamp duties and similar imposts; such relief is normally limited to a specified "running in" period; and
4. *Public credit facilities.* Thus in Italy financial grants or loans can be obtained from the *Cassa del Mezzogiorno*,[43] particularly if the location of foreign industry is in specified areas of Southern Italy.

The industrial development of the developing countries, particularly in Asia and Africa, which provide great potential markets for industrial goods, is only possible if private investors in the developed countries are prepared to risk their capital and—more important than finance—to apply their knowledge and experience to the development of industries in those parts of the world. Here the danger exists that the exporter, possibly after having been invited into the capital-importing country by favourable investments legislation and having sunk considerable capital into his subsidiary in that country, is threatened by "creeping" or overt expropriation and thereby deprived of the fruits of his investment.[44]

Various measures have been adopted to alleviate that fear. The United States have tried to protect American investors risking their funds and energies elsewhere against losses resulting from expropriation, inconvertibility of currency and war damages by inserting appropriate clauses into

---

[43] Mario Fiore, " The Italian Location of British Industry in the Common Market" in [1960] J.B.L. 299, 305.
[44] E.I. Nwogugu, *The Legal Problems of Foreign Investments in the Developing Countries*, Manchester, 1964; C.M. Schmitthoff, "The Law of International Trade and Investments" in (1967) 6 *Il Diritto negli scambi internazionali* 169; the same author, "British Aid to the Developing Countries" (1967) 1 *Journal of World Trade Law* 564; Karl E. Lachmann, "The Role of International Business in the Transfer of Technology to Developing Countries" in [1967] J.B.L. 346; G. Schwarzenberger, *Foreign Investments and International Law*, 1969; P. Kahn, "The Law applicable to Foreign Investments" in (1968) 49 Indiana L.J. 1; G.R. Delaume, "Public Debt and Sovereign Immunity" [1974] J.B.L. 175.

bilateral treaties of friendship, navigation and commerce and into so-called investment guarantee agreements which they have concluded with other countries.[45] In some cases Governments have undertaken in concession agreements or other contracts with foreign private investors not to expropriate their assets except in the case of overriding public interest and in that event to pay just and fair compensation without delay. However, these arrangements do not provide effective protection to the foreign investor. If they are broken by the Government which made them or—more likely—by its successor, the private investor is often helpless.

The general rules of international law afford at present little protection to the private investor. In the absence of an undertaking to the contrary, international law considers a sovereign State to be at liberty to carry out non-discriminatory measures of any kind in its own territory, including measures amounting to the expropriation of property of aliens, but in the modern view the expropriating state must pay the alien full, fair and speedy compensation. The English courts consider as effective an expropriation or nationalisation decree of a foreign country the Government of which is recognised by the Crown unless—

1. the decree or order attempts to attach property situate outside the territory of the expropriating State;
2. the decree is unenforceable under other rules of English private international law[46]; or
3. the decree constitutes a breach of international law, *e.g.* a breach of an undertaking or obligation of that State.

Attempts have been made to extend the protection which international law provides for the private investor by creating an *international investments code*, a multilateral Convention, the signatories of which would undertake definite obligations protecting foreign private investment in their countries. Projects of such a code have been advanced by the Prime Minister of Malaya, the Council of Europe, the ICC, the OECD and various other organisations, but so far these plans have not yet led to an international convention.

In view of this lack of international protection, manufacturers are often reluctant to invest capital in the building of factories in a less developed country unless the investment is grant aided[47] or the political risk is covered by insurance; in the United Kingdom such cover might be provided by the Export Credits Guarantee Department.[48]

The settlement of international investment disputes. An attempt has been made to approach the protection of foreign investors from the procedural

---

[45] "The Role of Private Enterprise in Investment and Promotion of Exports in Developing Countries," 1968, United Nations Publications, Sales No. E.68 II D9.
[46] See p. 232, *ante.*
[47] *e.g.* by a loan of the World Bank, a credit of IDA, or a grant from the European Development Fund, see *post.* See further *The Law of Financing and Payment in International Trade* (ed. Norbert Horn), ch. 11, 1989 (Vol. 5 of Studies in Transnational Economic Law).
[48] See p. 471, *post.*

angle, by providing machinery for the settlement of international investment disputes by means of arbitration. In 1965 a *Convention on the
Settlement of Investment Disputes between States and Nationals of Other
States* was concluded in Washington. The United Kingdom gave effect to
it by the *Arbitration (International Investment Disputes) Act 1966*,[49] as
amended.[50] This Act will be considered later in the context of arbitration
generally.[51]

The procedure under the Washington Convention is not the only
method of settling international investment disputes by arbitration. The
agreement under which the investment is carried out sometimes provides[52]
that in the case of disputes an ad hoc arbitration tribunal[53] shall be
constituted or the dispute should be settled under the rules of the ICC
Court of Arbitration.[54]

FOREIGN ACQUISITIONS

An enterprise which is cash rich or has a leverage facility[55] may consider
expanding its export potential by acquiring a company established in an
overseas country. It can then utilise the marketing outlets of that
company for the distribution of its own products and need not build up a
permanent representation from the beginning in that market.

The usual—and best—method of a foreign acquisition is that of an
agreed take-over bid.[56] The bidding company will purchase the equity—or
at least the majority of the voting shares—in the target company from its
shareholders. The effect of this transaction is that the target company has
become a subsidiary of the bidding company and the observations made
earlier on subsidiary companies abroad[57] apply to the acquired company.[58]

---

[49] The Convention entered into force for the U.K. on January 18, 1967 (Treaty Series No.
25/1967); Cmnd. 3255. The Convention has been extended to various colonies, etc.; see
S.I.s 1967 Nos. 159, 249, 585.
[50] By the Evidence (Proceedings in other Jurisdictions) Act 1975, s.8(2) and Sched. 2; the
Administration of Justice Act 1977, s.4 and Sched. 5; the Judicature (Northern Ireland) Act
1978, Sched. 5; and the Supreme Court Act 1981, Sched. 5.
[51] See p. 682, *post.*
[52] Or the parties so agree when the dispute has arisen.
[53] See p. 653, *post.*
[54] See p. 676, *post.*
[55] Leverage means financing an acquisition by means of capital borrowed from a bank. This
is also called debt financing.
[56] If the target company is a public company the shares of which are traded at a stock
exchange, there may, of course, also be a hostile take-over.
[57] See p. 320 *ante.*
[58] There exist also other methods of foreign acquisitions, including mergers across the
borders; they are proposed for the EC by the Tenth Draft Directive on Company Law
Harmonisation; this Draft Directive was submitted by the Commission to the Council in
1985.
An EC Regulation on Preliminary Control of European Mergers was adopted by the
Council of Ministers on December 21, 1989; it will come into operation on September 21,
1990 (Europe Documents No. 1591 of December 29, 1989).

In addition to the general considerations which have to be taken into account, if it is intended to establish a permanent representation abroad,[59] two special areas of law have to be examined: the local law relating to take-overs and the competition law of the country in question.

The law relating to take-overs

Many countries have laws and regulations dealing with this subject. In the United Kingdom, if a foreign company makes a take-over bid on a company incorporated in this country, the provisions of the Companies Acts 1985 and 1989 have to be considered[60]; they apply to all types of companies, whether public or private companies. If the company to be acquired is a public company the shares in which are traded at the International Stock Exchange, the provisions of the City Code on Take-overs and Mergers and the Rules governing Substantial Acquisitions of Shares, as well as the Regulations of the Stock Exchange, have to be taken into consideration.[61]

A United Kingdom company, which wishes to acquire a foreign company, has to obtain expert advice on the acquisition law of the country in question. Some of these laws are remarkable. Thus, some States of the USA have enacted laws controlling hostile take-overs; these States include Indiana,[62] Delaware, New York and New Jersey.[63]

Competition law and foreign acquisitions

In the case of a foreign acquisition, great care has to be taken that the bid does not infringe the relevant competition law, particularly that of the country of the target company. Apart from the United Kingdom law on restrictive trade practices which applies if a foreign enterprise acquires a United Kingdom enterprise,[64] two areas of law should be mentioned: the competition law of the EC and the antitrust law of the USA.

The competition law of the EC, which is of great practical significance in all Member States of this regional organisation, is surveyed in a later

---

[59] See p. 325, *ante*.
[60] Particularly sections 428 to 430F; they aim mainly at the protection of minority shareholders in the offeree company.
[61] See *Palmer's Company Law*, Vol. I, (24th ed.), 1987, Chap. 81.
[62] See Stephen J. Leacock, "Restricting Hostile Take-over in America," in [1987] J.B.L. 514. The Indiana law was upheld by the Supreme Court in *CTS Corp.* v. *Dynamics Corp. of America* 55 L.W. 4478 (1987). As regards US Federal Law, see the Exon–Florio Amendment to the Trade Act.
[63] See John F. Lowry, "Curbs on Corporate Raiders," in [1989] J.B.L. 91.
[64] See p. 361, *post*.

chapter.[65] In the United States, the Sherman Act has, since the *Alcoa* case,[66] some extraterritorial effect, which, however, was restricted by the so-called rule of reason[67] and later legislation[68]. Further, as has been seen,[69] in the United Kingdom the extraterritorial effect of American antitrust law, where it is still claimed is further restricted to some extent by a "blocking" statute, the Protection of Trading Interests Act 1980[70] and can be completely nullified if necessary by a measure of delegated legislation made under this Act.

THE PERSONNEL EMPLOYED IN OVERSEAS BRANCHES AND SUBSIDIARIES

A branch or subsidiary abroad is normally staffed by two types of employees who work in co-operation, namely United Kingdom personnel which the exporter has sent abroad and local personnel. From the legal point of view, this distinction is important. The contracts of employment with the former type of employees have to satisfy the requirements of the English law of employment as well as of the law of the country in which the branch or subsidiary is situate, but the contracts with the latter type of employees have only to comply with the local foreign law, unless the parties have agreed that they shall be governed by English law in which case only the mandatory provisions of foreign law apply.[71]

Arrangements between exporters and employees on overseas service[72] vary widely according to the nature of the goods intended to be exported and the circumstances existing in the country where the branch office is situate. Sometimes the United Kingdom executive has merely to supervise the staff of local sales agents and to assist them with his technical knowledge, but sometimes he is engaged in the marketing operations directly. In some companies it is usual to post rising young managers on foreign service for a limited period of time, to give them an opportunity of gaining experience and proving that they are worthy to be considered for further promotion.

The contract between the exporting enterprise and the employee serving abroad sometimes requires the employee to provide security by

---

[65] See chapter 19, *post.* p. 346.
[66] *United States* v. *Aluminium Co. of America* 148 F. 2d 416 (2d Cir. 1945).
[67] *Timberlane Lumber Co.* v. *Bank of America* 549 F.2d 597 (9th Cir. 1976).
[68] Title IV of the Export Trading Company Act of 1982. The Foreign Trade Antititrust Improvements Act.
[69] See p. 229, *ante.*
[70] See Ralph H. Folsom, Michael Wallace Gordon and John A. Spanogle Jr., *International Business Transactions*, 1986, Chap. 16, pp. 1094 *et seq.*
[71] *Cf. Sayers* v. *International Drilling Co. N.V.* [1971] 1 W.L.R. 1176 (Dutch company recruiting European personnel to work on oil rig; contract between Dutch employers and English employee governed by Dutch law).
[72] See William Hedley, "Sales Representatives Abroad" in [1958] J.B.L. 347.

giving a bond in his own name or procuring a fidelity guarantee from an insurance company or third parties. This is particularly required in cases in which the employee is given a considerable degree of discretion to make financial decisions up to a certain amount.

English employment law

The contract of service between a United Kingdom enterprise and an employee ordinarily resident in the United Kingdom but posted on foreign service is normally governed by English—or Scots—law, either because the contract contains a choice of law clause to that effect or that legal system is the law of the closest connection.[73] But two additional aspects have to be taken into account: first, the provisions of the British employee protection legislation, many of which cannot be contracted out,[74] may apply; and secondly, in some overseas countries protective employee provisions, which likewise are of mandatory character, are also applied to employees who are not ordinarily resident in the country in question but have worked there for some time.

As far as UK law is concerned, the Employment Protection (Consolidation) Act 1978[75] constitutes a comprehensive code containing provisions for the protection of employees ordinarily working in Great Britain. It demands the delivery, to the employee, of written particulars of the terms of employment, prescribes minimum periods of notice for the termination of the contract of employment (varying between one week and 12 weeks or more, depending on the length of employment), contains provisions for unfair dismissal,[76] redundancy payment, maternity pay and the right to return to work, and deals with other rights arising in the course of employment, such as, *e.g* the right to have time off for trade union activities. It also secures to some extent the position of the employee in the insolvency of the employer.[77] The Race Relations Act 1976 may likewise be relevant.[77a]

---

[73] See p. 209, *ante*.

[74] See Employment Protection (Consolidation) Act 1978, s.140, as amended by the Employment Act 1980, Scheds. 1 and 2.

[75] As amended, particularly by the Employment Acts 1980, 1982 and 1989.

[76] In principle a two years qualifying period of continuous employment is required for a complaint to an industrial tribunal for unfair dismissal (Unfair Dismissal (Variation of Qualifying Period) Order 1985 (S.I. 1985 No. 782, varying s.64A of the Employment Protection (Consolidation) Act 1978).

[77] The provisions of the Employment Protection (Consolidation) Act 1978, ss.121 to 127 are partly repealed and partly amended and in any event should be read together with the Insolvency Act 1986, Sched. 6, Category 5.

[77a] *Kapur* v. *Barclays Bank plc., Financial Times,* July 5, 1989 (CA). (Asian employees who had served with the bank in East Africa and opted for transfer to the UK alleged that the bank did not count their African service for pension purposes whereas they did so in the case of European employees; held that if the plaintiffs could prove these facts, the bank would have discriminated continuously against them, so that they could pursue their claim although out of time, (*i.e.* out of the three months period for complaints under the Race Relations Act 1976).

These protective provisions apply to employees ordinarily working in Great Britain. The Act provides[78] that the following shall not apply "to employment where under his contract of employment the employee ordinarily works outside Great Britain": maternity benefits, unfair dismissal, and time off for trade union activities and other rights arising in the course of employment. The provisions relating to the protection against insolvency of the employer do not apply where the employee ordinarily works outside the territory of the Member States of the EC.[79] As regards redundancy payment, the Act provides[80]:

> An employee shall not be entitled to a redundancy payment if on the relevant date he is outside Great Britain, unless under his contract of employment he ordinarily worked in Great Britain.

As regards the requirement to give written particulars of the terms of employment and the calculation of the period of notice, it is stated[81] that the periods during which the employee is engaged in work wholly or mainly outside Great Britain shall not be included into the calculation "unless the employee ordinarily works in Great Britain and the work outside Great Britain is for the same employer."

Persons partly employed in Great Britain and partly outside

Where the employee, by the terms of his contract of employment, is wholly employed at the overseas branch of a United Kingdom enterprise, it is clear that the provisions of the Employment Protection (Consolidation) Act 1978 do not apply.

A difficulty arises, however, where an employee is partly employed in Great Britain and partly outside. Here the courts apply the so-called base test.[82] Megaw L.J. expressed this test as follows:[83]

> . . . the correct approach is to look at the terms of the contract, express and implied . . . in order to ascertain where, looking at the whole period contemplated by the contract, the employee's base is to be. It is, in the absence of special factors leading to a contrary conclusion, the country where his base is to be which is likely to be the place where he is to be treated as ordinarily working under his contract of employment. Where his base, under the contract, is to be will depend on the examination of all relevant contractual terms. These will be likely to include any such terms as expressly

---

[78] s.141(2).
[79] s.141(2A).
[80] s.141(3).
[81] s.141(1).
[82] *Wilson* v. *Maynard Shipbuilding Consultants A.B.* [1978] Q.B. 665; *Todd* v. *British Midland Airways Ltd.* [1978] I.C.R. 959; *Janata Bank* v. *Ahmed* [1981] I.R.C. 791.
[83] *Wilson* v. *Maynard Shipbuilding Consultants A.B.* [1978] Q.B. 665, 676–677; *Scrivner* v. *Chief Adjudication Officer, The Times,* November 7, 1989 (whether contributions to national insurance in another EC Member State (Belgium) should be taken into account the calculation of UK unemployment benefit).

define his headquarters, or which indicate where the travels involved in his employment begin and end; where his private residence—his home—is, or is expected to be; where, and perhaps in what currency, he is to be paid; whether he is to be subject to pay national insurance contributions in Great Britain. These are merely examples of factors which, among many others that may be found to exist in individual cases, may be relevant in deciding where the employee's base is for the purpose of his work, looking to the whole normal, anticipated, duration of the employment.

Restraint of trade clauses

A stipulation restraining the employee from trading after the termination of the contract is invalid in English law if the stipulation is unreasonably wide in the area of application or in point of time, or covers more goods or kinds of transactions than is reasonable.[84]

Foreign employment law

Free movement of employees in the EC

Where it is intended to employ United Kingdom personnel in an overseas branch or subsidiary, the first question is whether that branch or subsidiary is established in another Member State of the EC or in a country which is not a member of the Community.

In the former case, the EC Treaty and the secondary legislation made thereunder apply. The Treaty provides valuable privileges for workers of the Member States of the Community[85]. It is laid down that progressively the free movement of persons shall be secured within the Community and discrimination based on nationality shall be abolished between workers of the Member States as regards employment, remuneration and other conditions of work and employment[86]. Moreover, the Treaty provides that the restriction of the freedom of establishment of nationals of a Member State in the territory of another Member State shall be abolished and states:[87]

---

[84] See p. 371 *post.*

[85] The Treaty draws a distinction between persons in salaried or wage-earning employment who are described as workers and are given the freedom of movement, and self-employed person who have the freedom (or right) of establishment. Articles 48–51 apply to the former, and Articles 52–58 to the latter.

[86] EC Treaty, Art. 48.

[87] *Ibid.* Art. 52; by virtue of Art. 58, this provision applies to companies. See *Reyners* v. *Belgian State* [1974] 2 C.M.L.R. 305; *van Duyn* v. *Home Office* [1975] 1 C.M.L.R.1; *van Binsbergen* v. *Bestuur van de Bedrijfsvereniging voor de Metaalnijverheid* [1975] 1 C.M.L.R. 298; *Thieffry* v. *Conseil de l'Ordre des Avocats à la Cour de Paris* [1977] 2 C.M.L.R. 373; *Patrick* v. *Ministre des Affaires Culturelles* [1977] 2 C.M.L.R. 523; *R.* v. *H.M. Treasury and Commissioners of Inland Revenue, ex parte Daily Mail and General Trust plc* [1989] 2 W.L.R. 908.

> Such progressive abolition shall also apply to restrictions on the setting up of agencies, branches or subsidiaries by nationals of any Member State established in the territory of any other Member State.

It follows that no discriminatory requirements can be imposed in any of the other Member States of the Community against the employment of United Kingdom personnel in branches or subsidiaries of British enterprises, except if limitations are justified on grounds of public policy, public security or public health[88].

The articles of the EC Treaty, guaranteeing employees the freedom of movement, like those guaranteeing enterprises the right of establishment are "fundamental principles of the Community"[89] and any national prohibition or discriminatory measure infringing them is invalid.

Aliens legislation in non-EC countries

In the countries which are not Member States of the EC, the business activities of United Kingdom citizens are governed by the aliens legislation. The permission to enter the country does not, as a matter of course, imply the right to engage in business there. Aliens legislation varies greatly in different countries; the alien is usually required to obtain a permission from a government department before allowed to commence business.

Attention should, further, be paid to the foreign tax legislation. In the United States British exporters conducting business through established branch offices or resident employees are subject to federal income tax while they are not liable to tax when conducting business through independent commission agents who keep no stocks in the United States and are merely authorised to solicit but not to accept orders on behalf of the principal; here the definition of a "permanent establishment" in the Double Taxation Relief Convention with the United States applies.[90]

Foreign legislation protecting security of employment

It has already been noted[91] that in many countries, including Great Britain,[92] legislation exists aimed at the protection of the employee in the

---

[88] Art. 48(3); see *van Duyn* v. *Home Office* [1975] 1 C.M.L.R.I.; *Roland Rutili* v. *French Minister of the Interior* [1976] 1 C.M.L.R. 140; *Defrenne* v. *Sabena* [1981] 1 All E.R. 122. See also *Stanton* v. *INASTI* [1989] 3 C.M.L.R. 761 (person self-employed in one Member State and employed in another).

[89] *The Daily Mail* case, above; see p. 317 *ante*.

[90] See Schmitthoff and Hall, "The Taxation of Exports" in [1969] J.B.L. 276.

[91] See p. 332 *ante*.

[92] See p. 333, *ante*.

event of the termination of his service agreement, by providing that he shall be entitled to notice of a specified length or to compensation, but the qualifying conditions, the periods of notice and the amounts of compensation frequently differ from those applicable in Britain.

The exporter is well advised, before entering into a service agreement with an employee in an overseas country, to ascertain whether such legislation is in operation in that country. Thus, according to William Hedley,[93]

> in Switzerland, notice under these contracts (*contrats de travail*) is subject to specific statutory regulations: if the contract has not been in existence one year then either party can terminate it by giving at least one month's notice, though if the agreement has lasted more than 12 months the period of notice is to be at least two months.

Further, Hedley states that in Norway in agreements of this nature a period of notice of not less than three months is customary and in some instances, again depending on the facts, even up to six months.

Of particular importance in this connection are the various national provisions dealing with unfair dismissal.[94] The regulation of English law has already been indicated.[95] This branch of law is highly developed in the United States and is also known in France where the principle of *abus de droit* is applied, in Germany which knows protection against dismissal which is *sozial ungerechtfertigt*, and in Italy where dismissal without *giustificato motivo* has legal consequences.

The question whether the foreign legislation protecting security of employment can be contracted out by providing that the contract of employment shall be governed by English law is difficult to answer; it depends in every case on whether the foreign legislation in question is mandatory in character.[96]

---

[93] "Sales Representatives Abroad" [1958] J.B.L. 347, 350. See Swiss OR, ss. 336a and 336b.
[94] See G. de N. Clark, "Remedies for Unfair Dismissal: A European Comparison," (1971) 20 I.C.L.Q., 397.
[95] See p. 333, *ante*.
[96] On the discussion of this question in relation to the contract of agency, see p. 310, *ante*.

CHAPTER 18

JOINT VENTURES AND OTHER FORMS OF JOINT EXPORT ORGANISATION. THE EUROPEAN ECONOMIC INTEREST GROUPING.

MODERN cross-border business uses various forms of combined trading as an alternative to a full take-over or merger. The characteristics of combined trading are that a number of economically independent manufacturers or merchants set up a joint organisation for the purpose of co-ordinating specified parts or individual projects of their production and/or distribution but retain their liberty of action in other respects. The co-operation agreed upon between the members of a joint organisation may be close or relatively loose. In international trade, the three most important types of combined trading are the joint venture, the joint marketing organisation and the consortium. In the EC, a fourth form has been added, *viz.* the European Economic Interest Grouping (EEIG).

JOINT VENTURES

In the present climate of intensification of international trade noted earlier[1] the joint venture is the favoured form of cross-border co-operation.[2]

The joint venture is a common undertaking created by two or more participants for a specific purpose of commercial, financial or technical nature.[3] In international trade one or several participants are foreign, and others Tax indigenous enterprises. The common undertaking formed by

---

[1] See p. 317, *ante.*

[2] Clive M. Schmitthoff, "Joint Ventures in Europe" in *Commercial Operations in Europe* (ed. R. M. Goode and K. R. Simmonds), Sijthoff, 1978, p. 327; George A. Zaphiriou, "Methods of Co-operation between Independent Enterprises (Joint Ventures)" 26 Am.J.Comp.L. 245 (1978); Michael W. Gordon, "Joint Ventures in Eastern Europe," 9 Texas International L.J. 281 (1974); Aleksandar Goldštajn, "Yugoslav Foreign Trade Law: A General Survey" in 6 Rev.Soc.Law (1980) No. 3, 325, 337; Edgar Herzfeld, *Joint Ventures*, Bristol, 1983; Eric H. K. Lee, "The Chinese Joint Venture and its Taxation" in [1983] J.B.L. 521; UN Economic Commission for Europe, "*Guide on Drawing up International Contracts on Joint Ventures*, Preliminary Study," Note by the Secretariat, July 4, 1986 (Trade/GE.1/R.57).

[3] For a definition of the joint venture see Brodley, "Joint Ventures and Anti-Trust Policy" in (1982) 95 Harvard L.R. 1523; Claude Reymond "Le contrat de 'Joint Venture' " in *Innominatverträge. Festgabe zum 60. Geburtstag von Walter R. Schluerp*, Zürich 1988, 385.

the participants may, as we shall see, be carried on in various legal forms. Apart from the common project planned and executed as a joint venture, the participants remain separate and each pursues his own commercial objects. The joint venture may be intended to be of long or limited duration.

The joint venture is of particular importance in the trade with China,[4] in East–West Trade[5] and in the trade with developing countries. Most of these countries have adopted special legislation aimed at encouraging foreign investment and, at the same time, protecting their own essential interests.[6] This legislation sometimes grants the foreign investor tax privileges and safeguards his right to transfer the profits accrued to him from the joint venture and to repatriate his capital.

Legal aspects of joint ventures

It is essential to distinguish between the agreement whereby the parties agree to enter into a joint venture (co-operation agreement; *l'accord de base*), and the legal form which they intend to give to the joint venture.

The co-operation agreement

The co-operation agreement,[7] which has a certain similarity with the framework agreement in countertrade,[8] has to be drafted with great care. It should define the form which the joint venture is to take, the contributions of the parties, their participation in the profits and losses, the management structure of the joint venture, its termination and the disposal of its assets after dissolution. The disposal of assets may create particular difficulties if joint rights were vested in the joint venture company and on its dissolution have to be unscrambled. In one case[9] the joint rights were defined as meaning—

---

[4] In January to September 1988, 3100 joint ventures were approved by the authorities in China, see *Financial Times*, November 11, 1988.
[5] The USSR published on December 12, 1988 a decree on foreign trade and investment allowing joint ventures in which the foreign partner takes a majority interest. See also T. Várady, "On the Management Structure of Enterprises with Foreign Participation in Socialist Countries—with Special Reference to Yugoslavia" in *The Legal Structure of the Enterprise*, Budapest, 1985, (Vol. II), p. 473.
[6] See *ECE Guide*, preliminary study, quoted in n. 2.
[7] For a detailed treatment of the co-operation agreement see Edgar Herzfeld, "Co-operation Agreements in Corporate Joint Ventures," in [1983] J.B.L. 121.
[8] On framework agreements in countertrade see p. 163, *ante*. The similarity consists in the fact that both are *accords de base*. The co-operation agreement is sometimes referred to as the "joint operating agreement."
[9] *BICC Plc.* v. *Burndy Corporation* [1985] 2 W.L.R. 132, 136.

> all United Kingdom and overseas patents and registered designs and applications therefor, copyright in literary and artistic work and all other rights in inventions and discoveries, including information as to improvements, processes, formulae, trade secrets and other know-how relating thereto which were part of the assets of the [joint venture company] and used by it for the purposes of its business.

The co-operation agreement should also contain a choice of law clause and provide for arbitration if disputes arise between the parties. If in a joint venture the two co-operating parties hold equal portions of the venture's capital (50/50), a deadlock in the management may ensue if they disagree on management policy. The International Chamber of Commerce has devised the *ICC Rules for the Regulation of Contractual Relations* (1979) which provide for the prompt designation of a third party to resolve the deadlock and define the conditions under which he may perform his task.[10] If the co-operation agreement provides that one party shall make advance payments to finance the joint venture and the joint venture is never carried out, the payor can recover the advances from the payee on the ground of total failure of consideration.[11]

Forms of joint ventures

Two types of joint ventures are distinguished: equity ventures (also called corporate ventures) and contractual ventures.[12]

Equity ventures

The characteristic of this form of venture is that the common object is carried out in a corporate form. This form of the joint venture should be as flexible as possible.[13] Often the parties will choose the form of a private limited company and their interest in the joint venture will be determined

---

[10] ICC Brochure No. 326 (1979) on *Adaptation of Contracts*, see p. 750, *post*.

[11] *Films Rover International Ltd.* v. *Cannon Film Sales Ltd.*, *Financial Times*, June 10, 1988. (In this case the payor received some incidental benefit but not the benefit for which the joint venture was formed.)

[12] In the People's Republic of China, different laws apply to equity and contractual joint ventures. Equity joint ventures are governed by the Law on Joint Ventures of July 1, 1979, and contractual joint ventures by the Law of April 13, 1988. In addition, there exists a Law on wholly foreign owned subsidiaries of February 14, 1986.

[13] The form of the joint venture can be used not only in export and international construction transactions but also for other purposes. In *Multinational Gas and Petrochemical Co.* v. *Multinational Gas and Petrochemical Services Ltd.* [1983] Ch. 258 three oil companies, which were incorporated in the U.S.A., France and Japan respectively, formed a joint venture company for the purposes of trading in liquified gas: although at the beginning successful, in the end the venture was a failure. See also *Films Rover International Ltd.* v. *Cannon Film Sales Ltd.*, *Financial Times*, June 10, 1988.

by their equity shareholding. But other possibilities exist. Thus in France the *Groupement d'Intérêt Economique* (GIE) offers distinct advantages. This form was introduced into French law by ordinance of September 23, 1967. The GIE has a separate legal personality but no corporation tax is paid by it on its profits. It must have a name and is registered under it in the commercial register; it has to show the letters GIE on all documents addressed to third parties. It is represented by one or several directors (*administrateurs*). It need not have a capital and passes its profits on to its members who are liable for its obligations without limitation.

In Germany the form of GmbH & Co. or GmbH & Co. KG[14] is frequently used. These are partnerships consisting of several limited companies as partners. Such partnerships have no separate legal personality, unless they have to be classified as commercial partnerships[14a] and are not subject to corporation tax.

In the Eastern European orbit, equity joint ventures are admitted in Bulgaria, Czechoslovakia, Hungary, Poland, Romania[15] and Yugoslavia.[16]

Contractual ventures

In this type a corporate structure is not used as the vehicle for the joint enterprise and the parties rely only on their contractual arrangements. Two examples may be given.

(1) The cartellised industry in country A wishes to secure a steady supply of a particular mineral required for the production of its goods. The mineral is in plentiful supply in an undeveloped region of country B. The Government of B undertakes to finance mining operations of the mineral in the region in question in consideration of a long-term purchase contract of the mineral by the industry in B.[17]

(2) The country in which the joint venture is to be operative, does not admit a corporate structure comparable to a company limited by shares. This was the case in Yugoslavia.[18] before the new Foreign Investment Law came into operation on January 1989.[19] This law admits corporate as well as contractual joint ventures.

Joint ventures and competition law

The parties who wish to co-operate in a joint venture have to comply strictly with the relevant law relating to restrictive trade practices, and in

---

[14] KG stands for *Kommandit-Gesellschaft* which is a limited partnership.
[14a] *Offene Handelsgesellschaften,* see *Handelsgesetzbuch,* s.124.
[15] ECE Guide to Drawing up International Contracts of Joint Ventures, see n. 2, *ante.*
[16] See the Yugoslav Foreign Investment Law, which came into operation on January 8, 1989; in English in *Investing in Yugoslavia, Challenges and Opportunities,"* Jugoslavenski Pregled, 1989.
[17] Such a contract will contain elaborate price escalation clauses and a hardship clause, see p. 746 and 751, *post.*
[18] ECE Guide to Drawing up International Contracts of Joint Ventures, see n. 2, *ante.*
[19] See n. 16 above.

particular with the competition law of the EC[20] and American anti-trust law. The joint venture is no magic wand by which the dangers of contravention of the restrictive practices legislation can be dispelled. In the United States the Supreme Court held[21] that there was no "reason or authority for the proposition that agreements between legally separate persons and companies to suppress competition amongst themselves and others can be justified by labelling the project a joint ventue."[22]

Joint Marketing Organisations

Several United Kingdom companies may combine solely for the purpose of promoting their exports. They may either create a joint export organisation in this country or jointly use one of the marketing techniques discussed in the preceding chapters, viz. jointly appoint a sole distributor or self-employed agent, or form a company in the country to which the exports are targeted.

The choice of form for the joint marketing organisation depends on the nature and relationship of the member enterprises, the conditions of the overseas markets and, to no small extent, the personal susceptibilities of the manufacturers who agree to co-operate in the field of exports while remaining competitors in other respects. The form of the limited liability company provides the most adaptable instrument that the law can contribute when the co-ordination of conflicting economic interests is attempted.

United Kingdom enterprises which engage in any of these forms of joint exporting have to be very careful that their arrangements are compatible with, the competition law of the EC, which is very strict, and that of the United Kingdom which normally will not be difficult to comply with. These topics are treated in the next chapter.[23]

---

[20] See p. 346, *post*. The EC Commission intends to issue a Policy Notice indicating which joint venture arrangements are compatible with the EEC competition rules. The first draft of this Notice was published on December 23, 1985; the Guidelines were not available on August 1, 1987, see Bellamy and Child, *Common Market Law on Competition*, 3rd ed., 1987, para. 5–065, p. 224; see also p. 356, *post*.

In *General Electric Company plc and Siemens AG* v. *Plessey plc.*, *Financial Times*, December 21, 1988, Morritt J., when referring the case to the European Court of Justice, observed that the mere acquisition by one company of shares in another did not come within Article 85 but the potential effects of such an acquisition might do so.

See also the notices of the Commission in the three cases involving joint venture agreements between Air France and other air lines; these agreements concerned the sharing of air routes: [1989] 4 C.M.L.R. 974.

[21] In *Timken Roller Bearing Co.* v. *United States*, 341 U.S. 593, 598 (1951).

[22] In the U.S.A. the Webb-Pomerene Act of 1918 exempts from the prohibitions of the Sherman Act and of the Clayton Act, s.7, associations entered for the sole purpose of engaging in export trade and not affecting prices within the U.S.; see George A. Zaphiriou, *op. cit.* in n. 2, 257.

[23] See pp. 346 and 361 respectively.

Companies formed in the United Kingdom for the promotion of exports

Two useful forms of modern co-operative marketing abroad are the formation in the United Kingdom of—

(a) *A group sales company.* This company is incorporated as a company limited by shares by manufacturers whose products do not compete but which, when taken together, cover the whole range of products in a particular industry, *e.g.* machine tools: or

(b) *A wholly owned subsidiary export company.* This type of organisation is used by large manufacturing concerns consisting of interconnected companies under the same financial control. The export company is charged with the duty of handling all the exports of the group.

CONSORTIA

A consortium is "an organisation which is created when two or more companies co-operate so as to act as a single entity for a specific and limited purpose."[24] Consortia have been formed by British companies to build abroad nuclear power stations, steel works, tyre factories, blast furnaces and rolling mills, foundries, paper mills, oil refineries and general large-scale engineering projects. Similar organisations exist in France, Holland, Germany and Switzerland. Sometimes international consortia are formed by companies incorporated in different countries; they are particularly useful to carry out international development schemes sponsored by the International Bank for Reconstruction and Development, the European Development Fund of the EC or similar international bodies.

Most British consortia are formed as companies incorporated under the Companies Acts 1985, but sometimes a looser form of organisation bearing the characteristics of partnership is used. Particular attention has to be given to the financial structure, the profit distribution and the so-called superimposed obligation of the consortium.[25] The latter term denotes the responsibilities of the consortium as a whole to the overseas Government or other contracting party; here the question is how the liability amongst the members of the consortium shall be distributed if the common venture encounters difficulties due to the fault of one of the members; *e.g.* a complete electric power station has to be built but additional expense is incurred owing to the faulty design of machinery supplied by one of the members. The mutual rights and duties of the members have to be agreed beforehand and to be clearly defined in the

---

[24] A. H. Boulton, "Construction Consortia—Their Formation and Management" [1959] J.B.L. 234. See further A. H. Boulton, *Business Consortia* (Sweet & Maxwell, 1961).
[25] A. H. Boulton, "Finance in the 'Single Project' Consortium" [1961] J.B.L. 368.

documents constituting the consortium. The choice of an "independent chairman . . . of suitable stature and acceptability"[26] will greatly facilitate the settlement of internal differences in the consortium.

THE EUROPEAN ECONOMIC INTEREST GROUPING

The European Community permits the creation of a new legal form, the European Economic Interest Grouping (EEIG).[27] A Regulation admitting this measure was adopted by the Council of Ministers on July 25, 1985, The EEIG is a projection to the European level of the French *Groupement d'Intérêt Economique* which has met with a fair measure of success.[28] The EC regulation provides that an EEIG is formed by contract and has to be registered in the EC State in which it has its official address (Arts. 1 and 6).

In the United Kingdom, the application of the EC Regulation is carried out in accordance with the *European Economic Interest Grouping Regulations 1989* to which the EC Regulation is appended as a schedule and which came into operation[29] on July 1, 1989. The UK EEIG Regulations provide that an EEIG, according to the locality at which its official address will be situate, shall register with:

the Registrar of Companies for England and Wales (in Cardiff, branch office in London); or
the Registrar of Companies for Scotland (in Edinburgh); or
the Registrar of Companies for Northern Ireland (in Belfast).

An EEIG which has its official address outside Great Britain but establishes a place of business within this country has to register with the appropriate Registrar of Companies (Reg. 12).

The EEIG is a legal entity but it is not a company limited by shares. It can only be formed by companies, firms and individuals residing in different Member States of the Community. It has capacity to enter into contracts and to sue and be sued. The EC Regulation leaves it to every Member State to provide whether the status of legal personality shall be attached to EEIGs whose official address is in its territory. The UK EEIG Regulations provide that an EEGI whose official address is in Great Britain and which is duly registered shall be a body corporate, *i.e.* shall have legal personality (Reg. 3).

The EEIG need not have an initial capital, like a company, and shall not invite investment from the public. The contract by which the EEIG is

---

[26] A. H. Boulton [1959] J.B.L. 240.
[27] Council Regulation No. 213/85; O.J. 1985, L. 199, of July 31, 1985. The Regulation is founded on Art. 253 of the EEC Treaty.
[28] See p. 341, *ante*; and Burchard Bott and Wolfgang Rosener, "The Groupement d'Intérêt Economique" in [1970] J.B.L. 313.
[29] S.I. 1989 No. 638.

formed may, where appropriate, require the members to make contributions in cash or kind. The members of an EEIG are liable without limitation jointly and severally for the debts of the EEIG but the creditors of the Grouping shall not initiate proceedings against a member for repayment of an EEIG debt unless they have first given written notice to the Grouping and have not been paid.

The purpose of the Grouping is to facilitate or develop the businesses of the members and to improve or increase the results of those businesses. Its business must be related to those of the members, and be no more than ancillary to such businesses. The objects of the Grouping, within these requirements of the Regulation, shall be defined in the contract for the formation of the Grouping.

The form of the EEIG may, for instance, be used for the following activities:

Joint buying office. The EEIG would collect the various orders of its members for the same product or similar products and on the strength of the combined orders seek to secure a better price from the suppliers;

Joint sales office. Manufacturers of the same product or similar products would combine to study their market and, if necessary, adopt a joint trade mark which the ECG would undertake to market by means of an advertising campaign and by seeking buyers on behalf of the members. It would collect orders and allocate them among the members in accordance with arrangements laid down by themselves;

Administration of specialised services. Members wishing to make economies in certain operations essential to each of them would entrust the EEIG with administering these functions on their behalf. In this way the EEIG could take over the management of the pay section for the employees of its members or supervise the installation of a mechanised accounting system;

Representation of the members in individual transactions. Members interested in a contract whose scope exceeded the capacity of any of them to handle, would establish an EEIG to compete for the contract on their behalf and, if the contract has been awarded to them, allocate tasks and co-ordinate and supervise their execution.[30]

Co-ordination of certain technical activities of the members. The members would decide to entrust the EEIG with the co-ordination of their research activities relating to a new product, the prototype of a machine, etc.

---

[30] An EEIG formed for these purposes pursues aims similar to those of a consortium but the legal form is different, see p. 343, *ante*.

CHAPTER 19

THE COMPETITION LAW OF THE EUROPEAN COMMUNITY
AND OF THE UNITED KINGDOM

THE economy of the Member States of the European Community is founded on the tenets of the market philosophy. This economic system requires laws safeguarding legitimate competition and controlling restrictive trade practices and monopoly situations. Such legal regulation exists on two levels, that of the EC and that of the national law of the Member States. The former is of great practical importance to the exporter and this importance will be enhanced when the single market will be established in the Community on December 31, 1992. The latter, as far as the United Kingdom is concerned, is of minor significance to those engaged in international trade; the main aim of United Kingdom competition law is directed to the control of economic power concentrations, such as mergers and monopolies, in the domestic sphere.

In this chapter first the competition law of the EC and then that of the United Kingdom will be treated.

THE BASIC PROVISIONS OF EC COMPETITION LAW

The basic provisions on competition are contained in Articles 85 and 86 of the EC Treaty.[1] The former prohibits as incompatible with the common market certain restrictive trade practices which may affect trade between the Member States and have as their object or effect the prevention, restriction or distortion of competition in the common market. Agreements that fall within the prohibition and do not merit exemption are void (Art. 85(2)) and cannot be enforced in the courts of the Member States.[2] Article 86 contains a prohibition of the abuse of a

---

[1] The whole chapter of the EEC Treaty on the Rules on Competition comprises Articles 85 to 90. For further reading: Christopher Bellamy and Graham Child, *Common Market Law of Competition* (3rd ed., 1987); D. M. Raybould, *Comparative Law of Monopolies* (1988); von Kalinowski (Gen. Ed.), *Competition Law of the European Community*. See the excellent work by Lawrence Collins, *European Community Law in the United Kingdom* (3rd ed., 1984).

[2] See, *e.g. Brasserie de Haecht* v. *Wilkin (No. 2)* [1973] C.M.L.R. 287; *BRT* v. *SABAM* [1977] 2 C.M.L.R 238; *Lancôme-Cosparfrance* v. *Etos & Albert Heyn* [1981] 2 C.M.L.R. 164; *Pronuptia de Paris* v. *Schillgalis* [1986] 1 C.M.L.R. 414; *British-American Tobacco Co. Ltd.* v. *EC Commission* [1988] 4 C.M.L.R. 24; *Re Wood Pulp Cartel. A. Ahlström OY* [1988] 4 C.M.L.R. 901; *Bureau National Interprofessionnel du Cognac* v. *Yves Aubert* (Case 136/86).

dominant position within the common market, as far as it may affect trade between Member States. The following is the wording of these two articles:

Article 85

1. The following shall be prohibited as incompatible with the common market: all agreements between undertakings, decisions by associations of undertakings and concerted practices which may affect trade between Member States and which have as their object or effect the prevention, restriction or distortion of competition within the common market, and in particular those which:
   (a) directly or indirectly fix purchase or selling prices or any other trading conditions;
   (b) limit or control production, markets, technical development, or investment;
   (c) share markets or sources of supply;
   (d) apply dissimilar conditions to equivalent transactions with other trading parties, thereby placing them at a competitive disadvantage;
   (e) make the conclusion of contracts subject to acceptance by the other parties of supplementary obligations which, by their nature or according to commercial usage, have no connection with the subject of such contracts.
2. Any agreements or decisions prohibited pursuant to this Article shall be automatically void.
3. The provisions of paragraph 1 may, however, be declared inapplicable in the case of:
   — any agreement or category of agreements between undertakings;
   — any decision or category of decisions by associations of undertakings;
   — any concerted practice or category of concerted practices;
   which contributes to improving the production or distribution of goods or to promoting technical or economic progress, while allowing consumers a fair share of the resulting benefit, and which does not;
   (a) impose on the undertakings concerned restrictions which are not indispensable to the attainment of these objectives;
   (b) afford such undertakings the possibility of eliminating competition in respect of a substantial part of the products in question.

Article 86

Any abuse by one or more undertakings of a dominant position within the common market or in a substantial part of it shall be prohibited as incompatible with the common market in so far as it may affect trade between Member States. Such abuse may, in particular, consist in:
   (a) directly or indirectly imposing unfair purchase of selling prices or other unfair trading conditions;
   (b) limiting production, markets or technical development to the prejudice of consumers;
   (c) applying dissimilar conditions to equivalent transactions with other trading parties, thereby placing them at a competitive disadvantage;
   (d) making the conclusion of contracts subject to acceptance by the other parties of supplementary obligations which, by their nature or according to commercial usage, have no connection with the subject of such contracts.

These articles are amplified by secondary legislation[3] and other measures of the Community. They are interpreted by numerous decisions

---

[3] Mainly founded on Art. 87(1) of the EC Treaty.

of the Commission and the European Court of Justice. In the result a pattern of European competition law has emerged which, while admitting broad exceptions, is strict and effective and may expose an offender to heavy fines.[4]

The ambit of the Community regulation on competition is wide. It may affect horizontal as well as vertical arrangements,[5] concerted practices,[6] market-sharing agreements,[7] price-fixing agreements,[8] agreements with exclusive dealers,[9] forms of co-operation, joint ventures,[10] and patent,[11] trade mark,[12] franchising agreements,[13] copyright[14] or licensing agreements.[15] The Community regulation applies to the supply of services as well as goods.[16] Even inventors exploiting their inventions under a patent licence are "undertakings" within the competition rules.[17] Agreements with indirect effect on competition are also caught, such as agreements to exchange detailed information about prices, customers, turnover, capacity available, etc.[18] Even the acquisition of shares in order to influence the commercial conduct of a competitor may be within the prohibition of Article 85(1).[19]

---

[4] Arts. 15 and 16 of Reg. 17/62; see *I.C.I. and Others* v. *Commission* [1972] C.M.L.R. 557; *Commercial Solvents* v. *Commission* [1974] 1 C.M.L.R. 309; *Re Pioneer Hi-Fi* [1980] 1 C.M.L.R. 457 (the fine was reduced by the court); *Musique Diffusion Française* v. *EC Commission* [1983] 3 C.M.L.R. 221; *AEG* v. *EC Commission* [1983] E.C.R. 315; *Hasselblad (GB)* v. *EC Commission* [1984] 1 C.M.L.R. 559; *Re Polypropylene* O.J. 1986 L230/1.

[5] *De Geus* v. *Bosch* [1962] C.M.L.R. 1; *Consten and Grundig* v. *Commission* [1966] C.M.L.R. 418; *Italy* v. *Council and Commission* [1969] C.M.L.R. 39.

[6] *I.C.I. and Others* v. *EC Commission* [1972] C.M.L.R. 557; *Zuchner* v. *Bayerische Vereinsbank* [1982] 1 C.M.L.R. 313.

[7] *Re Polypropylene* O.J. 1988 L230/1.

[8] *Distillers Co.* v. *EC Commission* [1980] 3 C.M.L.R. 121. See also [1983] 3 C.M.L.R. 173; *Re Peroxygen Cartel, The Community* v. *Solvay et Cie and Others* [1985] 1 C.M.L.R. 481 (Commission decision).

[9] *Re Pioneer Hi-Fi (supra)*; *Hasselblad (GB)* v. *EC Commission (supra)*; *Ford Werke AG* v. *The Commission*, Cases 25 and 26/84, [1985] 3 C.M.L.R. 528.

[10] *Re Rockwell/Iveco* [1983] 3 C.M.L.R. 709.

[11] *Re Davidson Rubber Co.* [1972] C.M.L.R. D52. Patent licences may now benefit from the block exemption dealing with this subject and published in O.J. of August 16, 1984, L219/15; see n. 47, *post*.

[12] *Sirena S.R.L.* v. *Eda S.R.L.* [1971] C.M.L.R. 260; *Van Zuylen Frères* v. *Hag A.G.* [1974] 2 C.M.L.R. 127.

[13] *Pronuptia de Paris GmbH* v. *Schillgalis* (Case 161/84), [1986] 1 C.M.L.R. 414.

[14] See *Deutsche Grammophon GmbH* v. *Metro-SB-Grossmärkte GmbH & Co. K.G.* [1971] C.M.L.R. 631.

[15] Alan Dashwood, "Exclusive Licences in the Common Market" [1973] J.B.L. 205; Lewis, "Dealings with Patents and Know-How" [1979] E.I.P.R. 217; also Byrne [1980] E.I.P.R. 141.

[16] *Verband der Sachversicherer e.V.* v. *EC Commission* [1987] E.L.R. 265 on insurance.

[17] *A.O.I.P* v. *Beyrard* [1976] 1 C.M.L.R. D14.

[18] *Re Cobelyn* [1977] 2 C.M.L.R. D28; *Re Fatty Acids* O.J. 1987 L3117.

[19] *British-American Tobacco Co. Ltd.* v. *EC Commission* [1988] 4 C.M.L.R. 24.

Articles 85 and 86 have direct application in the national jurisdiction.[20] An agreement which is prohibited by Article 85(1) is void by virtue of Article 85(2) unless it has been duly notified and thus gained provisional validity until it is decided whether it is a prohibited agreement and, if so, whether it falls under an exemption within Article 85(3). A non-notifiable agreement is valid. If an agreement is void as being prohibited by Article 85(2), the question arises whether the offending clauses can be severed from the other clauses of the agreement. It is thought that this should be possible unless the severance would change the whole character of the agreement. An infringement of Article 85 or 86 may give rise in English law to an action for compensation by a person who suffered loss as the result of such infringement.[21]

In principle the prohibitions of Articles 85 and 86 apply only to arrangements which may affect trade between the Member States. This requirement appears to exclude from the application of Community law arrangements operative only outside the Community[22] or only inhibiting exports to countries outside the Community.[23] On the other hand, an arrangement restricted to one Member State might affect trade between Member States and be caught by Article 85(1) because it might hinder the economic penetration of the national market by competitors from other Member States.[24] Consequently, an arrangement operative only within one Member State is subject to Community law if it obstructs the importation of the goods in question into that country from the other Member States or otherwise affects imports and exports between the Member States. Further, as we shall see,[25] in certain circumstances the competition law of the Community claims to have extra-territorial effect.

Procedure

The procedure for the application of Articles 85 and 86 is set out in Council Regulation 17 of 1962, as amended.[26] In general, agreements, decisions and concerted practices of the kind described in Article 85(1)

---

[20] *BRT* v. *SABAM* [1974] 2 C.M.L.R. 238; *Garden Cottage* v. *Milk Marketing Board* [1984] A.C. 130 (H.L.), where an alleged breach of Art. 86 was held to be the alleged breach of a statutory duty in the United Kingdom; see Lawrence Collins, *op. cit.*, 77.
[21] *Garden Cottage Foods Ltd.* v. *Milk Marketing Board* [1984] A.C. 130 (H.L).
[22] *Rieckermann/AEG-Elotherm* [1968] C.M.L.R. D78.
[23] *Bulk Oil (Zug) AG* v. *Sun International (No. 2)* [1986] 2 C.M.L.R. 732.
[24] *Vereiniging van Cementhandelaren* v. *EC Commission* [1973] C.M.L.R. 7. See also *Vacuum Interrupters* [1977] 1 C.M.L.R. D67; *Salonia* v. *Poidmanis & Giglio* [1982] C.M.L.R. 1; *Re Deutsche Castrol Vertriebsgesellschaft* [1983] 3 C.M.L.R. 165; *Bureau National Interprofessionnel du Cognac* v. *Clair* (Case 123/83) [1985] 2 C.M.L.R. 430; *Remia* v. *EC Commission* [1987] 1 C.M.L.R. 1, 29.
[25] See p. 350, *post*.
[26] Reg. 17/62 was supplemented by Regs. 27/62, 99/63, 118/63, 1133/68, 2822/71, 1699/75.

must be *notified* to the Commission[27] and failure to notify intentionally or negligently may expose the offender to heavy fines.[28] There are exceptions from the duty to notify but in the excepted cases the arrangement may be notified in the discretion of the parties[29]: Each party to an arrangement described in Article 85(1) is entitled to notify the Commission.

For the purposes of Articles 85 and 86, an undertaking which is resident in a non-Member State but has in a Member State a subsidiary which must act according to its instructions, is regarded as being resident in the Common Market because it forms an economic unit with the subsidiary.[30] Conversely, a wholly-owned subsidiary which enjoys no real autonomy in the market is regarded as being part of the same economic unit as its parent company and agreements between those two companies do not fall within the ambit of Article 85(1).[31] If, however, the subsidiary is to some extent autonomous, it will be treated as a separate undertaking.[32] Furthermore, an undertaking established in a non-Member State which is a party to an agreement that may have *effect* in the Common Market is subject to the jurisdiction of the Community authorities.[33] In these respects the Community authorities claim extra-territorial jurisdiction.

THE CONTROL OF RESTRICTIVE ARRANGEMENTS IN EC COMPETITION LAW

The prohibitions of Article 85(1) are worded very widely. Their unmitigated application would lead to results which are unacceptable to the trade in the Community. For this reason Article 85(3) authorises the Commission to grant exemption from the prohibitions of Article 85(1), subject to certain conditions. These exemptions may be individual exemptions, which can be obtained by applying for a declaration of inapplicability of Article 85(1); or they may block exemptions, which apply to a whole class of commercial activities.

Negative clearance and declaration of inapplicability

If a party thinks that the arrangement to which he is a party is outside the prohibition of Article 85(1) and wishes to obtain official confirmation

---

[27] Reg. 17/62, Arts. 4 and 5.
[28] *Ibid.* Art. 15(2).
[29] *Ibid.* Art. 4(2). An agreement which could appreciably affect imports or exports cannot benefit from the exception: *IAZ International Belgium* v. *EC Commission* [1984] 3 C.M.L.R. 276.
[30] *I.C.I. and Others* v. *Commission* [1972] C.M.L.R. 557; *Commercial Solvents Corpn.* v. *Commission* [1974] 1 C.M.L.R. 309 (the *Zoja* case); *Liptons Cash Register & Business Equipment Ltd.* v. *Hugin Kassaregister AB* [1978] 1 C.M.L.R. D19, D33; *Hugin Kassaregister AB* v. *EC Commission* [1979] 3 C.M.L.R. 345.
[31] *Re Christiani and Nielsen* [1970] C.M.L.R. D19.
[32] *Eurim Pharm GmbH* v. *Johnson & Johnson* [1981] 2 C.M.L.R. 287.
[33] *Béguelin Import* v. *SAGL Import-Export S.A.* [1972] C.M.L.R. 81; *Re Pittsburgh Corning Europe-Formica-Belgium-Hertel* [1973] C.M.L.R. D2; *Re Wood Pulp Cartel. A. Ahlström OY* [1988] 4 C.M.L.R. 901.

of that view, he can apply to the Commission for *negative clearance* which, however, is only granted "on the basis of the facts in its possession."[34] If the agreement falls within Article 85(1) but the conditions of Article 85(3) are satisfied, the Commission, on the application of a party, can grant a *declaration of inapplicability* of Article 85(1).[35] This can only be done when the arrangement is duly notified.[36] Given the small numbers of formal decisions taken by the Commission, the more likely outcome, however, is a *comfort letter* from the Commission telling the parties either that, in its view the arrangement is not caught by Article 85(1) or that it is likely to satisfy the criteria for exemption under Article 85(3), and that it is closing its file; before doing this, it may ask the parties to abrogate certain anti-competitive provisions in their agreement. A case in which the Commission formally refused to grant a declaration of inapplicability of Article 85(1) concerned the British Net Book Agreement entered into by British publishers and aimed at collective retail price maintenance for books[37]; the decision of the Commission meant that the Net Book Agreement does not apply to the intra-Community book trade; the decision was remarkable because the Net Book Agreement was one of the few arrangements upheld by the United Kingdom Restrictive Practices Court.[37a]

The notification of an arrangement and applications for negative clearance or inapplicability of Article 85(1) are made on combined form A/B.[38]

Powers of Commission to obtain information and to conduct investigations

The Commission has wide powers to obtain information. It may request an undertaking to give it information necessary to the performance of its functions in enforcing the competition rules,[39] and may send an inspector to the premises of an undertaking for an "on the spot" investigation, such as to examine documents, ask oral questions, and so

---

[34] Reg. 17/62, Art. 2.

[35] It may, however, require the parties to modify their agreement. This can have unfortunate consequences when one of the parties is no longer able to negotiate with the other from a position of strength. This consideration, it is believed, has sometimes led parties to run the risk of a fine rather than notify. This is a dangerous course in view of the present level of fines.

[36] *Distillers Company* v. *EC Commission* [1980] 3 C.M.L.R. 121; *Zinc Cartel*, O.J. 1984, L220/17.

[37] Commission decision of December 13, 1988; see [1989] 4 C.M.L.R. 87.

[37a] See p. 367, *post*.

[38] The most recent version of the form is founded on Reg. 2526/85.

[39] Giving the Commission the wrong information is a ground for the maximum penalty being imposed under Reg. 17/62 Art. 15(1): *Community* v. *Comptoir Commercial D'Importation* [1982] 1 C.M.L.R. 440.

on.[40] In pursuing its investigation, the Commission must, however, have regard to the legitimate interests of undertakings that their business secrets should not be disclosed.[41]

Measures providing block exemption and notices

In order to eliminate obviously innocuous arrangements, the Community made use of its powers under Article 85(3) to declare inapplicable the prohibition of Article 85(1) to certain categories of arrangements, in brief, to grant them *block exemptions*. It also published *notices* specifying agreements which in its view did not fall within Article 85(1). The most important of these exemptions for our purposes relate to exclusive agency contracts, exclusive distribution agreements, exclusive purchasing agreements, patent licensing, specialisation agreements and research and development agreements. The Commission has also issued notices declaring its policy on co-operation agreements and agreements of minor importance. These measures require individual consideration.

Agreements of minor importance

The Commission stated as early as in 1964[42] that an agreement did not infringe the prohibition of Article 85 if it did not distort the Common Market to an "appreciable" extent. By subsequent notices,[43] the Commission has sought to attach a concrete meaning to the term "appreciable." In the latest, the Notice of September 3, 1986, *on Agreements of Minor Importance*,[44] it reasserts its desire "to facilitate co-operation between small and medium-sized enterprises."[45] The Notice then provides

---

[40] Reg. 17/62, Arts. 11 and 14.
[41] For the power to request information see Art. 11 of Regulation 17; for the power to conduct investigations see Art. 14. It was held by the European Court in *Hoechst AG* v. *Commission, The Times,* October 23, 1989 (Cases 46/87 and 227/88) that the Commission, when conducting an on spot investigation, does not require a search warrant even though such a warrant is prescribed for a national investigation under national competition law. On confidentiality see EC Treaty, Art. 214; Regulation 17 Art. 20; and *AKZO Chemie BV and AKZO Chemie UK Ltd.* v. *EC Commission* [1987] 1 C.M.L.R. 231; *BAT* v. *EC Commission* [1988] 4 C.M.L.R. 24, [1988] 4 C.M.L.R. 24.
[42] In *Grossfillex-Fillistorf* [1964] C.M.L.R. 237. In *Völk* v. *Etablissements Vervaecke S.P.R.L.* [1969] C.M.L.R. 273 the European Court held that an agreement may escape the prohibition of Article 85(1) if the position of the parties was too weak to influence trade between the Member States.
[43] A Notice of the Commission is a declaration of policy on the part of the Commission; it does not prevent the European Court from interpreting Article 85 differently.
[44] O.J. 1986 C.231/2.
[45] It had done so before in the notice of July 29, 1968, concerning co-operation agreements, J.O. C 75 of July 29, 1968.

that an agreement is not regarded as infringing Article 85(1) if it satisfies two cumulative tests, namely a market test and a turnover test. These tests are satisfied if—

> the goods or services which are the subject of the agreement (hereinafter referred to as "the contract products") together with the participation undertakings' other goods or services which are considered by users to be equivalent in view of their characteristics, price and intended use, do not represent more than five per cent. of the total market for such goods or services (hereinafter referred to as "products") in the area of the common market affected by the agreement and
> the aggregate annual turnover of the participating undertakings does not exceed 200 million ECU.

An excess by less than one tenth of each of these tests in the course of two consecutive years is admitted as being innocuous.

An agreement which satisfies these two tests need not be notified. A great number of agreements between small and medium-sized enterprises is thus in the view of the Commission, completely outside the operation of the competition law of the European Community.[45a]

Exclusive agency contracts

By an Announcement of December 24, 1962 on *Exclusive Agency Contracts made with Commercial Agents*[46] the Commission indicated that in certain circumstances restrictive provisions in agreements between principals and agents do not fall within Article 85. This applies only to dependent agents who accept no financial risk, do not act as independent dealers for other suppliers, and who are prepared to take detailed instructions from their principals.[47] Such an agent may be treated as an auxiliary organ, forming an integral part of the principal's business.[48] The definition of an agent by the Commission is closer to that used in the common law than to that in the European continental countries. The Commission understands by an agent a person who has acted on behalf of a principal, and regards it as irrelevant whether he has acted in the name of the principal or in his own name, provided that he does not accept the financial risk for the transaction.[49] The Announcement states:

> The Commission regards as the decisive criterion, which distinguishes the commercial agent from the independent trader, the agreement—express or implied—which deals

---

[45a] The Commission may, however, take into account not merely the market share at the time it is examining the agreement but also its likely development, *Service Master* [1989] 4 C.M.L.R. 581. The cautious approach now is to notify agreements which come within the notice in the hope of receiving a "comfort letter", see p. 351, *ante*.

[46] The Announcement is published in J.O. of December 24, 1962, 139/2921.

[47] *Pittsburgh Corning (Europe)* [1973] C.M.L.R. D2 and D7–8; *Suiker Unie* [1976] 1 C.M.L.R. 295.

[48] See Bellamy and Child, *Common Market Law of Competition* (3rd ed.), para. 6–004.

[49] The only financial risk which he may assume is the *del credere* risk; on *del credere* agents, see p. 294, *ante*.

with responsibility for the financial risks bound up with the sale or with the performance of the contract. Thus the Commission's assessment is not governed by the way the "representative" is described. Except for the usual *del credere* guarantee, a commercial agent must not, by the nature of his functions, assume any risk resulting from the transaction. If he does assume such risks his function becomes economically akin to that of an independent trader and he must therefore be treated as such for the purposes of the rules of competition.

An intermediary is regarded as an independent dealer, and not an agent within the meaning of the Announcement, if he—

—is required to keep or does in fact keep, as his own property, a considerable stock of the products covered by the contract, or

—is required to organise, maintain or ensure at his own expense a substantial service to customers free of charge, or does in fact organise, maintain or ensure such a service, or

—can determine or does in fact determine prices or terms of business.

Exclusive distribution agreements

A block exemption, Regulation 1983/83 of the Commission,[50] exempts certain *exclusive distribution agreements* from the prohibition of Article 85(1). This regulation is limited in time; the exemption is granted only until December 31, 1997.

The Regulation exempts the following agreements from the prohibition of Article 85(1)[51]: agreements to which only two undertakings are a party and whereby one party agrees with the other to supply certain goods for resale within the whole or a defined area of the Common Market[52] only to that other. Certain additional clauses may be included in the exempt agreement. The most important of them are as follows[53]:

(*a*) the obligation not to manufacture or distribute goods which compete with the contract goods;

(*b*) the obligation to obtain the contract goods for resale only from the other party;

(*c*) the obligation to refrain, outside the contract territory and in relation to the contract goods, from seeking customers, from establishing any branch and from maintaining any distribution depot.

The exemption is available notwithstanding that the exclusive distributor undertakes all or any of the following obligations:

(*a*) to purchase complete ranges of goods, or minimum quantities;

(*b*) to sell the contract goods under trade marks, or packed and presented as specified by the other party;

---

[50] O.J. of 22 June 1983, L. 173/1. See Korah "Exclusive Dealing Agreements in the EEC" E.L.C. (1984); also [1984] 21 C.M.L.R. 53; see also ICC *Guide To Drafting International Distributorship Agreements*, Chap. 17 (ICC Brochure No. 441, 1988).

[51] Art. 1.

[52] In *Compact/Hydrotherm's Agreement* [1981] 3 C.M.L.R. 670 the benefit of the equivalent exemption in Regulation 67/67, now replaced by Regulation 1983/83, was interpreted as extending to agreements which covered countries both inside and outside the EC. Nothing in the agreement hindered parallel imports.

[53] *Ibid*, Art. 2.

(c) to take measures for promotion of sales, in particular:
   — to advertise
   — to maintain a sales network or stock of goods
   — to provide customer and guarantee services
   — to employ staff having specialised or technical training.

On the other hand, an exclusive distribution agreement is not exempt in the following cases where[54]:

(a) manufacturers of identical goods or of goods which are considered by users as equivalent in view of their characteristics, price and intended use enter into reciprocal exclusive distribution agreements between themselves in respect of such goods;

(b) manufacturers of identical goods or of goods which are considered by users as equivalent in view of their characteristics, price and intended use enter into a non-reciprocal exclusive distribution agreement between themselves in respect of such goods unless at least one of them has a total annual turnover of no more than 100 million ECU;

(c) users can obtain the contract goods in the contract territory only from the exclusive distributor and have no alternative source of supply outside the contract territory;

(d) one or both of the parties makes it difficult for intermediaries or users to obtain the contract goods from other dealers inside the common market or, in so far as no alternative source of supply is available there, from outside the common market, in particular where one or both of them:

   1. exercises industrial property rights so as to prevent dealers or users from obtaining outside, or from selling in, the contract territory properly marked or otherwise properly marketed contract goods;

   2. exercises other rights or takes other measures so as to prevent dealers or users from obtaining outside, or from selling in, the contract territory contract goods.

Exclusive purchasing agreements

There is also a block exemption for certain kinds of *exclusive purchasing agreements*. This is under Regulation 1984/83. The Regulation has four Titles, the first is of general application and the next two are devoted respectively to beer and petrol products. The fourth Title contains miscellaneous provisions. The first Title sets out the general principles of exemption. The agreement must be one between two undertakings under which: ·

one party, the reseller, agrees with the other, the supplier, to purchase certain goods for sale only from the supplier or from a connected undertaking or from another undertaking the supplier has entrusted with the sale of his goods.

As in Regulation 1983/83, an agreement will not be exempt in certain cases where:

(a) manufacturers of identical goods or of goods which are considered by users as equivalent in view of their characteristics, price and intended use enter into reciprocal exclusive purchasing agreements between themselves in respect of such goods;

---

[54] *Ibid,* Art. 3.

    (*b*) manufacturers of identical goods or of goods which are considered by users as equivalent in view of their characteristics, price and intended use enter into a non-reciprocal exclusive purchasing agreement between themselves in respect of such goods, unless at least one of them has a total annual turnover of no more than 100 million ECU;

    (*c*) the exclusive purchasing obligation is agreed for more than one type of goods where these are neither by their nature nor according to commercial usage connected to each other;

    (*d*) the agreement is concluded for an indefinite duration or for a period of more than five years.

The scheme of Titles II and III is similar to Title I but there are some differences to take account of the peculiarities of the markets in question.[55]

Joint research and development, joint ventures and specialisation agreements

The Commission wishes to encourage enterprises, in particular of small and medium size, to co-operate with a view to enabling them to compete with stronger undertakings. In furtherance of this policy, which was mentioned earlier,[56] Regulations have been promulgated[57] granting block exemptions to research and development agreements[58] and specialisation agreements.[59] A notice or block exemption on joint ventures is also expected, it will indicate which joint ventures are compatible with Article 85(1) and which are not.

Exemptions have also been granted in individual cases.[60]

Patent and know-how licensing agreements

A Regulation of 1984 grants a block exemption to certain closely defined patent licensing agreements.[61] The Regulation contains a list of "white" clauses which fall under the exemption from the general prohibition of Article 85(1), and a list of "black" clauses which are not exempted and consequently are prohibited.

---

[55] Regulation 84/83 Recital 12. On the differences see Korah, *op. cit.*, Ch. 3.

[56] See p. 352, *ante*.

[57] For details of these Regulations see *Bellamy and Child*, (3rd ed.), Chap. 5.

[58] Regulation 418/85. This Regulation expires on December 31, 1997.

[59] Regulation 417/85. This Regulation expires on the same date as Regulation 418/85.

[60] Exemptions were granted in: *ACEC/Berliet* [1968] C.M.L.R. D35; *Henkel/Colgate* [1981] C.M.L.R. D31; *Re Davidson Rubber* [1972] C.M.L.R. D52; *Re European Music Satellite Venture* [1984] 3 C.M.L.R. 162; *Optical Fibres* O.J. 1986 L.236/30: *Mitchell Cotts Sofiltra* O.J. 1987 L.41/31; *Transocean Marine Paint Association* [1989] 4 C.M.L.R. 84.

[61] Reg. 2349/84.

The Regulation is too complex to be treated here. In drafting any licensing agreement, reference should be made to the text of the Regulation.

The text of a draft block exemption covering know-how licensing agreements has been published.[62]

Franchising agreements

On November 30, 1988 the Commission issued a block exemption concerning franchising agreements.[63] This exemption was considered in an earlier chapter.[63a]

Agreements relating to other intellectual property rights

Other block exemptions relating to intellectual property rights are in the course of preparation, in particular one covering trade mark licences.

Maritime transport and air transport

The application of Articles 85 and 86 to maritime transport is covered by a Regulation of 1986.[64] The Regulation sets out procedural rules governing investigations of the Commission into cases of suspected infringements and provides block exemption for agreements between members of liner conferences[65] complying with the provisions of the Regulation.

Regulations have also been promulgated on air transport.[66]

Agreements prohibiting parallel exports or imports

Prohibited by Article 85(1) is, in principle, a clause whereby a supplier imposes an obligation on an exclusive dealer not to sell the goods to which the agreement relates outside the assigned territory to another part of the common market or not to import into his territory the goods in question from another source in the common market. Thus, in *Consten*

---

[62] [1987] 3 C.M.L.R. 144.
[63] Regulation 4087/88; 1988 O.J. 1359/46.
[63a] See p. 274 *et seq.*, *ante*.
[64] Regulation 4056/86.
[65] See p. 549, *post*.
[66] Regulation 3975/87 and 3976/87.

and Grundig v. *Commission*[67] the German company Grundig appointed the French company Consten its sole dealer for France, the Saar and Corsica with respect to Grundig products. The agreement contained a clause according to which Consten undertook not to sell articles liable to compete with Grundig products and not to export the goods to which the contract related directly or indirectly to other countries. Grundig had imposed similar restrictions on the sole concessionaires in other countries, including Germany. Consten was permitted to register and use in France the trade mark GINT which was carried by all goods manufactured by Grundig. Another French company, UNEF, bought Grundig products from German dealers and sold them in France more cheaply than the goods marketed by Consten. Consten commenced proceedings against UNEF in the French courts and the matter was referred to the European Court. The European Court held that the restrictions on exports and imports imposed on Consten and the other sole concessionaires of Grundig infringed Article 85(1). The same decision was given with respect to the exercise and use of the trade mark GINT in France because that industrial property right was, in effect, used to create an artificial national division of the Common Market.

The Commission thus relies on the possibility of parallel imports to reduce national price differences. It hopes that where price differences are great it will pay someone to buy in the low priced market and sell in the higher. Restraints on exports or imports are so inimical to the Common Market that few have been exempted under Article 85(3). In *A. Bulloch & Co.* v. *The Distillers Co. Ltd.*[68] the Distillers' conditions of sale for United Kingdom trade customers prohibited these customers to sell outside the United Kingdom whisky and other liquor produced by the Distillers. The effect of this prohibition was that the Distillers could operate a double pricing policy, enabling them to charge less for the same brand of liquor in the United Kingdom than in the other EEC countries. The Commission held that the Distillers' conditions of sale for United Kingdom trade customers infringed article 85(1) and refused to declare

---

[67] [1966] C.M.L.R. 418. Further, *Technique Minière* v. *Maschinenbau Ulm GmbH* [1966] C.M.L.R. 357; *Béguelin Import Co.* v. *SAGL Import-Export S.A.* [1972] C.M.L.R. 81. *Procureur du Roi* v. *Dassonville* [1974] 2 C.M.L.R. 436 (*Scotch Whisky* case; British Customs Certificate of Origin as measure equivalent to a quantitative restriction within Art. 30 of the Treaty); *Centrafarm BV* v. *Sterling Drug Inc.* [1974] 2 C.M.L.R. 480; *Distillers Company* v. *EC Commission* [1980] 3 C.M.L.R. 121; *Eurim Pharm GmbH* v. *Johnson & Johnson* [1981] 2 C.M.L.R. 287; *Nungessor & Eisele* v. *EC Commission* [1983] 1 C.M.L.R. 278; *BAT Cigaretten-Fabriken GmbH* v. *The Commission*, (Case 35/83), [1985] 2 C.M.L.R. 470. *ETA Fabriques d'Ebauches* v. *DK Investment* (Case 31/85), Judgment of December 10, 1985; *The Times*, January 2, 1986; *R.* v. *Pharmaceutical Society of Great Britain* cases 266/87) [1989] 2 C.M.L.R. 751 ([UK legislation prohibiting pharmacists to supply equivalent imported medicines, if doctor prescribes a proprietary brand, valid).
[68] [1978] 1 C.M.L.R. 400 (the *Distillers' Case*).

the provision inapplicable under subsection (3) of that article.[69] It would appear, however, that in reaching their conclusion in this case, the Commission had failed to make a thorough appraisal of the facts, as the Court in *Grundig/Consten* had emphasised they should. The promotional needs in the several markets were very different.[70]

In the case of standard conditions agreed upon by a manufacturer with exclusive dealers who have special technical qualifications, the Commission may insist that clauses prohibiting the import and export to another Member State must be removed but will then approve the conditions.[71]

ABUSE OF DOMINANT POSITION IN EC COMPETITION LAW

The European Court has given Article 86 of the EC Treaty a wide interpretation. The "dominant position" referred to in that article relates to a position of economic strength which enables an enterprise to prevent effective competition being maintained in the relevant market by giving it the power to behave to an appreciable extent independently of its competitors, customers and ultimately the consumers.[72] An abuse of a dominant position may already exist where an undertaking of considerable strength in the market attempts further to increase its share in a particular market by taking over a rival enterprise.[73]

It is also an abuse of a dominant position if an undertaking which is in control of certain raw material cuts off the supply of that material to a customer who needs it for the production of goods which are in competition with goods produced by the enterprise that has a monopoly with respect to the raw material.[74] In this case a dominant position is abused although the measure objected to applies to different stages of the production.

In circumstances like these it is not easy to determine what is a *relevant market* in which an undertaking has a dominant position. The "relevant

---

[69] However, where a buyer dishonestly obtains goods from a manufacturer at the lower export price, intending to sell them in the home market at the higher price ruling there, a criminal offence has been committed although the double pricing policy of the manufacturer may contravene Article 85: *R.* v. *Dearlove. R.* v. *Druker, The Times*, January 28, 1988.

[70] *Distillers Company* v. *EC Commission* [1980] 3 C.M.L.R. 121.

[71] *Re Kodak* [1970] C.M.L.R. D19; *Re Omega* [1970] C.M.L.R. D49.

[72] *United Brands Co.* v. *Commission* [1978] 1 C.M.L.R. 429, 486–487; *Hoffman La Roche* v. *EC Commission* [1979] 3 C.M.L.R. 211; *Argyll Group plc.* v. *Distillers Co. plc.*, [1986] 1 C.M.L.R. 764 ("Abuse" must be an act having a significant and abnormal effect distorting the market).

[73] *Europemballage Corpn. and Continental Can Co. Inc.* v. *Commission* [1973] C.M.L.R. 199; *British-American Tobacco Co. Ltd.* v. *EC Commission* [1988] 4 C.M.L.R. 24.

[74] *Commercial Solvents Corpn.* v. *Commission* [1974] 1 C.M.L.R. 309 (the *Zoja* case). Abuse of a dominant position can occur on the demand, as well as the supply side: *Eurofima* [1973] C.M.L.R. 217. Predatory price undercutting by a large undertaking in order to keep a small competitor away from a particular market may be abuse of a dominant position: *ECS/AKZO* [1986] 3 C.M.L.R. 273.

market" is determined by two criteria: the particular features of the product in question and the geographical area in which it is marketed. The product market is determined by the application of a relatively narrow test. The court held in *United Brands Co.* v. *Commission*[75] that bananas constituted a market which was sufficiently distinct from that of other fresh fruit to form a separate relevant market for the purposes of Article 86. Even a relatively small company may enjoy a dominant position with respect to some of its products; thus, in one case[76] a Swedish enterprise supplied only 12 or 13 per cent. of cash registers in the common market countries and was found not to have a dominant position with respect to cash registers, but the parts of the cash registers marketed by that company were not interchangeable with those of other registers, so that the users of its cash registers were utterly dependent on the Swedish company with respect to the supply of spare parts; the Commission ruled that the Swedish company had a dominant position with respect to the spare parts of its cash registers, but the EC Court quashed this decision on the ground that trade between Member States was not affected.[77]

In another case[78] a UK car manufacturer, British Leyland, had to issue "certificates of conformity" required by Government regulations in order to enable dealers to sell the manufacturer's cars. It was alleged that, in order to prevent the reimportation of cars from another Member State (to which they were imported to save tax), the manufacturer refused certificates of conformity on reimported cars or charged excessive fees for the certificates. The European Court held that the manufacturer had an "administrative monopoly" and had abused its dominant position, contrary to Article 86.

Infringement of Article 86 of the EC Treaty can be a basis for the issue of an injunction or other relief in the national courts,[79] or a defence to an action for infringement.[80] Proceedings may however be suspended on a satisfactory undertaking being given.[81]

Speaking generally, the grant to its customers by a dominant enterprise of a quantity discount (which is linked solely to the volume of purchases) is not an abuse of its dominant position but a loyalty discount (which

---

[75] [1978] 1 C.M.L.R. 429, 483–484.

[76] *Liptons Cash Registers & Business Equipment Ltd.* v. *Hugin Kassaregister AB* [1978] 1 C.M.L.R. D19.

[77] *Hugin Kassaregister AB* v. *EC Commission* [1979] 3 C.M.L.R. 345.

[78] *British Leyland plc* v. *EC Commission* [1987] 1 C.M.L.R. 185.

[79] *Garden Cottage Foods Ltd.* v. *Milk Marketing Board* [1983] A.C. 130. See Friend and Shaw [1984] 100 L.Q.R. 188.

[80] *British Leyland Motor Corporation Ltd.* v. *TI Silencers* [1981] 2 C.M.L.R. 75; *I.C.I. Ltd.* v. *Berk Pharmaceuticals* [1981] 2 C.M.L.R. 91. But, if a Eurodefence is pleaded, a sufficient nexus between the alleged actions of the plaintiff and the alleged breaches of a dominant position must be particularised: *Ransburg-Gema AG* v. *Electrostatic Plant Systems, The Times,* February 22, 1989.

[81] *The Community* v. *I.B.M.* [1984] 3 C.M.L.R. 147.

tends to prevent the customers from obtaining their supplies from competing manufacturers) is an abuse under Article 86.[82]

THE COMPETITION LAW OF THE FREE TRADE AGREEMENTS

The EC has entered into bilateral Free Trade Agreements (FTAs)[83] with the member states of EFTA[84] which did not join the Community, namely with Austria,[85] Finland,[86] Iceland,[87] Norway,[88] Sweden,[89] and Switzerland.[90] All the FTAs contain provisions relating to competition. Typical is Article 23 of the FTA with Sweden:

> The following are incompatible with the proper functioning of the Agreement in so far as they may affect trade between the Community and Sweden:
>
> (i) all agreements between undertakings, decisions by associations of undertakings and concerted practices between undertakings which have as their object or effect the prevention, restriction or distortion of competition as regards the production of or trade in goods;
> (ii) abuse by one or more undertakings of a dominant position in the territories of the Contracting Parties as a whole or in a substantial part thereof;
> (iii) any public aid which distorts or threatens to distort competition by favouring certain undertakings or the production of certain goods.

If a practice is regarded to be incompatible with these provisions, a Contracting Party to the Agreement may complain to the Joint Committee constituted under the FTA and, if necessary, take unilateral measures designed to safeguard its position.[91]

The principles regulating competition in the European Community and the provisions of the block exemptions apply to the competition rules of the FTAs *mutatis mutandis*.

THE COMPETITION LAW OF THE UNITED KINGDOM

The competition law of the United Kingdom is at present[92] in a state of flux. The Government has published a White Paper entitled "Opening

---

[82] *Nederlandsche Banden-Industrie Michelin NV* v. *Commission* [1985] 1 C.M.L.R. 282.
[83] See pp. 370–371, *post.*
[84] European Free Trade Association.
[85] Austria: Cmnd. 5159 (January 1, 1973).
[86] Finland: O.J. 1973, L328/1 (October 5, 1973).
[87] Iceland: Cmnd. 5182 (April 1, 1973).
[88] Norway: O.J. 1973, L171/1 (May 14, 1973).
[89] Sweden: Cmnd. 5180 (January 1, 1973).
[90] Switzerland: Cmnd. 5181 (January 1, 1973).
[91] On the question of direct enforceability of Art. 23 see Neville March Hunnings, "Enforceability of the EEC–EFTA Free Trade Agreements" in (1977) 2 E.L.R. 163; M. Waelbroeck in (1978) 3 E.L.R. 27; and Neville March Hunnings in (1978) 3 E.L.R. 278; see also *Re Wood Pulp* [1985] 3 C.M.L.R. 474.
[92] October 1, 1989.

Markets: New Policy on Restrictive Trade Practices'"[93] in which it indicates the legislation that it intends to introduce. It is possible that a Bill relating to the proposed changes will be introduced into Parliament soon. The treatment of this subject is presented here under two headings, the present law and the intended reform.[94]

THE PRESENT COMPETITION LAW OF THE UNITED KINGDOM

The competition law of the United Kingdom is of two kinds: part of it designates certain *forms* of business practice thought to be anti-competitive, and another part focuses on the anti-competitive *effects* of business practices. The former are often referred to as *forms legislation* and the latter as *effects legislation*. The former legislation aims at the control of restrictive trade practices and the latter deals with mergers capable of creating a monopolies situation and other anti-competitive practices. The regulation provided by these two types of legislation is different. The forms legislation provides a judicial procedure before a special tribunal, the Restrictive Practices Court, and the effects legislation prescribes an administrative procedure which ultimately leaves the decision of intervention to the Secretary of State. It follows that the merger regulation has a stronger political element than the restrictive trade practices legislation.

The forms approach is adopted by the Restrictive Trade Practices Acts 1976 and 1977, and by the Resale Prices Act 1976. Proceedings under these enactments come before the Restrictive Practices Court.[95] The effects approach is adopted by the Fair Trading Act 1973 as amended,[95a] and the Competition Act 1980, both of which too are domestic measures. The common law doctrine of restraint of trade must not be forgotten either.[96]

As far as exports are concerned, four aspects of this legislation affect the exporter directly *viz.* the duty to notify restrictive trade agreements, monopoly situations in relation to exports, collective price maintenance agreements intended to operate abroad, and in proceedings before the Restrictive Practices Court the justification of a restrictive agreement intended to operate in the home market on the ground that its removal would cause a substantial reduction of exports.

Control of restrictive trade practices

Pre-notification of restrictive agreements

The Restrictive Trade Practices Act 1976, as amended, provides[97] that any agreement made between two or more persons carrying on business

---

[93] July 1989. Cm.727.
[94] See p. 372, *post.*
[95] Restrictive Practices Court Act 1976.
[95a] By the Companies Act 1989, ss. 146–153.
[96] See p. 371, *post, ante.*
[97] In s.6(1).

within the United Kingdom in the production or supply of goods or in the application to goods of any process of manufacture must be notified by any of them to the Director General of Fair Trading (DGFT) if restrictions are accepted by two or more parties[98] in respect of the following matters:

(*a*) the prices to be charged, quoted or paid for goods supplied, offered or acquired, or for the application of any process of manufacture to goods;

(*b*) the prices to be recommended or suggested as the prices to be charged or quoted in respect of the resale of goods supplied;

(*c*) the terms or conditions on or subject to which goods are to be supplied or acquired or any such process is to be applied to goods;

(*d*) the quantities or descriptions of goods to be produced, supplied or acquired;

(*e*) the processes of manufacture to be applied to any goods, or the quantities or descriptions of goods to which any such process is to be applied; or

(*f*) the persons or classes of persons to, for or from whom, or the areas or places in or from which, goods are to be supplied or acquired, or any such process applied.[99]

Under s.9(3), no account is to be taken of any term which relates exclusively to the goods supplied (or to which a process of manufacture is applied). In *Re Diazo Copying Materials*[1] it was held that a restriction on a party preventing it from making sales outside the United Kingdom related exclusively to the goods supplied and had therefore to be ignored.

The Act of 1976 extends to information agreements if they relate to the prices charged or quoted for selling or processing goods, or to the terms or conditions on which goods are supplied,[2] but agreements to inform each other or a third party only about the charges made for goods exported from the United Kingdom are exempted and need not be registered.[3] Further, the provisions of the 1976 Act have been extended to agreements relating to services,[4] and to information agreements relating to services.[5]

The Restrictive Practices Court, which was established by the Restrictive Trade Practices Act 1956 and now operates under the Restrictive Practices Court Act 1976, has jurisdiction to declare any registered agreement as contrary to the public interest, with the effect that the agreement is void (s.1(3) and s.2(1)).[6] In proceedings before the court it

---

[98] It was held in *Royal Institution of Chartered Surveyors* v. *Director-General of Fair Trading*, [1986] I.C.R. 550 (C.A.), that the Royal Charter and by-laws of the RICS constituted multilateral agreements between the members and that the 1976 Act could apply to it.

[99] It should be noted that the Act does not apply to restrictions relating to employees and the conditions of employment (s.9(6)); Restrictive Trade Practices (Information Agreements) Order 1969 (S.I. 1969/1842).

[1] [1984] I.C.R. 429.

[2] s.7.

[3] Restrictive Trade Practices Act 1976, Sched. 3, para. 6.

[4] s.11; see Restrictive Trade Practices (Services) Order 1976 (S.I. 1976 No. 98). See Restrictive Trade Practices Act 1977, s.1(3).

[5] *Ibid.* s.12.

[6] All further references are to the Restrictive Trade Practices Act 1976 unless stated otherwise.

is presumed that a registered agreement is contrary to the public interest but the presumption is rebutted if certain specified sets of circumstances, the so-called *gateways,* are present (ss.10(1), 19(1)).

As regards export agreements, three cases have to be distinguished: in some cases, agreements are not registrable at all and thus *completely excepted* from the operation of the Act; in other cases, where a restrictive agreement contains *exclusively restrictions applying to the export trade*, particulars of it have to be furnished to the Director General of Fair Trading but it does not have to be registered by him; and in a third category of cases in which the agreement contains *mixed restrictions, i.e.* restrictions applying to the home as well as to the export trade, it has to be registered by the Director.

Excepted agreements The most frequently met forms of export agreements, *viz.* exclusive selling or agency arrangements between United Kingdom manufacturers or merchants and their overseas representatives, are completely unaffected by, and outside, the United Kingdom restrictive trade practices legislation. This is because the Act applies only to agreements between two or more parties carrying on business within this country. Agreements providing only exclusive selling, distributing or agency rights, whether in the export or home market or both, are completely excepted from the operation of the Restrictive Trade Practices Acts, provided that no trade association[7] is a party to the agreement and the agreement is made by not more than *two* persons or companies, interconnected companies[8] being counted as one (Sched. 3, para. 2). This exception is not available if the restriction applies to topics other than the supply of goods of the *same* description; in that case the export agreement might fall into the category of exclusive or mixed export agreements which are treated later.

Furthermore, contracts relating only to the grant of licences of patents[9] or registered designs, the exchange of information on manufacturing processes ("know-how"), or the use of trade marks[10] are excepted from the operation of the Restrictive Trade Practices Acts (Sched. 3, paragraphs 3–5). It is to be noted that agreements can qualify for exemption only under *one* paragraph of Schedule 3; one cannot cumulate exemptions.

Exclusive export agreements. Agreements (other than excepted agreements) which would be registrable if relating to the home trade are exempt from registration by the DGFT if their restrictions relate *exclusively*—

   (*a*) to the supply of goods by export from the United Kingdom;

---

[7] As defined in s.43(1).
[8] Defined in Sched. 3, para. 6.
[9] Patent or design pooling agreements are, however, in principle, not excluded (Sched. 3, paras. 4, 5).
[10] Including certification trade marks, Sched. 3, para. 4.

(b) to the production of goods, or the application of any process of manufacture to goods, outside the United Kingdom;

(c) to the acquisition of goods to be delivered outside the United Kingdom and not imported into the United Kingdom for entry for home use; or

(d) to the supply of goods to be delivered outside the United Kingdom otherwise than by export from the United Kingdom.[11]

But particulars of agreements mentioned under (a) have to be furnished to the Director.[12]

Considerable advantages are derived from this concession. An agreement, particulars of which have merely to be filed with the Director, is not open to public inspection, but agreements which have formally to be notified and are registered by the DGFT can be freely inspected by members of the public, including competitors or representatives of overseas government departments. Further, an export agreement, particulars of which have merely to be furnished to the DGFT, cannot be challenged by him before the Restrictive Practices Court as being void on the ground that it is contrary to the public interest. On the other hand, the furnishing of particulars of an export agreement to the DGFT does not preclude a reference to the Monopolies and Mergers Commission, and the same is true of export agreements with respect to which no particulars have to be furnished.

It obviously is advantageous for manufacturers or distributors who wish to provide for restrictions applying to the supply of goods for the home and the export market to do so in two separate agreements, one applying to the home market and the other to the export market. The former might have to be registered, but the latter, would not be (though particulars of it would have to be furnished).

Mixed agreements. If an agreement containing restrictions which would make it registrable by virtue of section 6(1)[13] is intended to apply both to the home and the export market, it has to be notified to the DGFT; the mere furnishing of particulars would be insufficient. It is therefore suggested that separate agreements be drawn up.

Reduction of exports as defence in proceedings before the Restrictive Practices Court

It has already been observed that every registrable agreement is, in principle, capable of being challenged in the Restrictive Practices Court

---

[11] Sched. 3, para. 6.

[12] s.25. See also the Registration Trading Agreements (EEC Documents) Regulations 1973 (S.I. 1973 No. 950) which requires parties to inform the United Kingdom DGFT when notifying an agreement to the EC Commission, or when seeking negative clearance, or when proceedings are begun.

[13] See pp. 362–363, *ante.*

and that in proceedings before the court it is presumed that the agreement is contrary to the public interest, so that the burden of justifying it falls on the respondent, *i.e.* the party who wishes to uphold it.

A respondent who wishes to justify a restrictive agreement has to satisfy the court—

1. that one of the eight sets of circumstances listed in section 10(1) or 19(1) is present; and
2. that on balance the restriction is not unreasonable.[14]

One of the eight sets of circumstances listed in that provision is the likelihood that the removal of the restriction would cause a substantial reduction in the value or earnings of the export business. Section 10(1)(*f*) expresses this requirement as follows:

> that, having regard to the conditions actually obtaining or reasonably foreseen at the time of the application, the removal of the restriction or information provision would be likely to cause a reduction in the volume or earnings of the export business which is substantial either in relation to the whole export business of the United Kingdom or in relation to the whole business (including export business) of the said trade or industry.

The meaning of this complicated provision was considered by the Restrictive Practices Court in *Re Water-Tube Boilermakers' Agreement*.[15] The boilermakers who made or designed water boilers for use by power stations or factories had formed a trade association; their agreement provided that if a member received an inquiry a consultation had to be held between the members, the transaction would be allocated to one, or sometimes two, of them, and the price at which the order was to be carried out would be fixed. About 40 per cent. of the members' activities consisted of exports, and some members maintained offices and staffs abroad. The operations of the members had been highly successful in the past in securing orders against foreign competition. The association's attempt to justify its agreement under what is now section 10(1)(*f*) was successful. The court held that if the restriction on competition which the agreement imposed was removed a substantial reduction of export business of the trade was likely to result and that, on balance, the preservation of the capacity of this industry, engaged as it was in the manufacture of heavy capital goods, was in the national interest.

Further, section 10(1)(*f*) might protect an exporting association or a company which wishes to preserve for itself a share in the international market against stronger competitors, as, *e.g.* in the trade in tyres.[16]

Collective price maintenance agreements

Individual resale price maintenance is, in principle, unlawful in the United Kingdom. Any term or condition of a contract between a supplier

---

[14] s.10(1) refers to goods and s.19(1) to services; the two sections have a similar wording, *mutatis mutandis*.
[15] [1959] 1 W.L.R. 1118; L.R. 1 R.P. 285; [1959] J.B.L. 380.
[16] See *Pneumatic Tyres Report* (1955), p. 84, para. 1465.

and a dealer obliging the latter to charge minimum prices for the goods on resale in illegal and avoided by the Resale Prices Act 1976, s.9, unless the Restrictive Practices Court has ordered that the goods shall be exempt from this prohibition (s.14). Contravention of the provisions of the Act is not a criminal offence but a person affected by it can claim damages for breach of statutory duty (s.25). The Resale Prices Act 1976 applies, however, only to goods supplied for resale in the United Kingdom; it does not restrict the liberty of export suppliers to establish minimum prices for the resale of goods outside the United Kingdom.

The Resale Prices Act 1976 further makes, in principle, unlawful collective price maintenance agreements, including agreements whereby the enforcement of minimum prices is entrusted to a trade association (s.1). This general prohibition of collective price maintenance agreements does not apply to agreements which deal only with the supply of goods abroad, nor does it affect persons carrying on business abroad, but particulars of such agreements would have to be furnished to the DGFT as exclusive export agreements under sections 24 and 25.[17]

Overseas suppliers operating in the United Kingdom and, in particular, their resident sales representatives, have to comply with United Kingdom legislation; resale price maintenance conditions infringing the Resale Prices Act 1976 would be void.

Control of monopolies and other anti-competitive practices

Monopoly situations in relation to exports

The DGFT, as well as a minister may make a reference to the Monopolies and Mergers Commission where it appears to him that a *monopoly situation* exists or may exist.[18] The Fair Trading Act 1973 sets out several types of monopoly situations, and one of them relates to exports. It arises if one-quarter or more of goods of a particular description and destined for export are produced in the United Kingdom by the same producer or his group, or is subject to agreements distorting

---

[17] A curious position has arisen with respect to collective price maintenance of books. The UK Restrictive Trade Practices Court decided in 1962 in *The Net Book Agreement* that the agreement did not contravene public policy; the Court upheld the agreement [1962] L.R. 3 R.P. 246. But the EC Commission ruled in December 1988 that, as far as intra-Community trade was concerned, the agreement contravened Article 85(1) and that no exemption should be granted under Article 85(3) [1989] 4 C.M.L.R. 87. The present positon (unless changed) is that the Net Book Agreement is valid for the book trade within the UK but invalid outside the U.K. for the trade in British books between the EC countries, see [1989] J.B.L. 100.

[18] Fair Trading Act 1973, ss.50 and 51.

competition. This monopoly situation is set forth in section 8 of the 1973 Act which runs as follows:

(1) For the purposes of this Act a monopoly situation shall be taken to exist in relation to exports of goods of any description from the United Kingdom in the following cases, that is to say, if—

    (*a*) at least one-quarter of all the goods of that description which are produced in the United Kingdom are produced by one and the same person, or

    (*b*) at least one-quarter of all the goods of that description which are produced in the United Kingdom are produced by members of one and the same group of interconnected bodies corporate;

and in those cases a monopoly situation shall for the purposes of this Act be taken to exist both in relation to exports of goods of that description from the United Kingdom generally and in relation to exports of goods of that description from the United Kingdom to each market taken separately.

(2) In relation to exports of goods of any description from the United Kingdom generally, a monopoly situation shall for the purposes of this Act be taken to exist if—

    (*a*) one or more agreements are in operation which in any way prevent or restrict, or prevent, restrict or distort competition in relation to, the export of goods of that description from the United Kingdom, and

    (*b*) that agreement is or (as the case may be) those agreements collectively are operative with respect to at least one-quarter of all the goods of that description which are produced in the United Kingdom.

(3) In relation to exports of goods of any description from the United Kingdom to any particular market, a monopoly situation shall for the purposes of this Act be taken to exist if—

    (*a*) one or more agreements are in operation which in any way prevent or restrict, or prevent, restrict or distort competition in relation to, the supply of goods of that description (whether from the United Kingdom or not) to that market, and

    (*b*) that agreement is or (as the case may be) those agreements collectively are operative with respect to at least one-quarter of all the goods of that description which are produced in the United Kingdom.

Where the conditions of section 8(2) or (3) are satisfied, that is where two or more persons and their groups are involved, a *complex monopoly situation*[19] exists, which likewise may give rise to a reference to the Monopolies and Mergers Commission, "although as previously no account can be taken of a provision that renders an agreement registrable under the Restrictive Trade Practices Acts."[20] A reference may further be made where a monopoly situation is limited to a part of the United Kingdom.[21]

The reference results in a report of the Monopolies and Mergers Commission, which is made to the minister.[22] The minister may make such orders on the report as appear to be appropriate to him for the purpose of remedying or preventing the adverse effect of the monopoly.[23]

---

[19] *Ibid.* s.11.
[20] Valentine Korah, "The Fair Trading Act 1973 and the Functions of the Director General" in [1973] J.B.L. 305, 306.
[21] Fair Trading Act 1973, s.9.
[22] *Ibid.* s.54.
[23] *Ibid.* s.56.

Anti-competitive practices

A reference to the Monopolies and Mergers Commission can involve lengthy and expensive investigation. The need was therefore perceived for a more informal procedure. This was introduced by the Competition Act 1980. The "trigger" concept for the Act's application is an "anti-competitive practice." Under section 2(1):

> a person engages in an anti-competitive practice if, in the course of business, that person pursues a course of conduct which, of itself or when taken together with a course of conduct pursued by persons associated with him, has or is intended to have or is likely to have the effect of restricting, distorting or preventing competition in connection with the production, supply or acquisition of goods in the United Kingdom or any part of it. . . .

Under section 2(2) of the 1980 Act, agreements registrable under the Restrictive Trade Practices Act 1976 are excluded (because they are subject to the different machinery of that Act, as explained above). Moreover, under the Anti-Competitive Practices (Exclusions) Order 1980[24] practices carried out by firms with an annual turnover in the United Kingdom of less than £5 million and with less than a 25 per cent. share of the relevant market are excluded (provided the firms in question are not members of a group which exceeds those limits). The market share is numerically the same as that required for monopoly and merger references under the Fair Trading Act 1973, but that Act does not lay down a turnover figure. The method by which the annual turnover is calculated is set out in Schedule 2 to the Order. Article 1 and Schedule 1 of the Order exclude certain courses of conduct from constituting an anti-competitive practice. These include courses of conduct relating solely to the supply of goods outside the United Kingdom, including the refusal to supply goods outside the United Kingdom except on certain conditions.[25] They also include courses of conduct pursued by operators of international sea transport services in respect, inter alia, of goods, and pursued by any person solely in respect of securing international sea transport services. "Sea transport" includes mixed sea and land transport when forming part of the same service, and carriage by hovercraft. Courses of conduct pursued by international air transport undertakings in respect of carriage by air are also excluded. There is also an exemption for courses of conduct pursued by agricultural and forestry associations and fisheries associations falling within section 33 of the Restrictive Trade Practices Act 1976.

The Act introduces a two-tier system of investigation of suspected anti-competitive practices. The DGFT conducts a preliminary investigation,

---

[24] S.I. 1980 No. 979, made under the Competition Act 1980, s.2(2).
[25] If the country concerned is an EC Member this could, of course, infringe the Treaty of Rome see p. 346 *et seq., ante.*

and if at the end of it he concludes that a practice is anti-competitive, he can accept undertakings from the firm or firms in question. He may also make a "competition reference" to the Monopolies and Mergers Commission under s. 5 of the Competition Act 1980 where he has not accepted any undertaking, or where an undertaking appears to have been breached[26] and he has given notice to that effect as required. He can also require an undertaking to be varied, and if the variation is not forthcoming, make a reference to the Monopolies and Mergers Commission.

Relationship between United Kingdom regulation and the Competition Law of the European Community and the Free Trade Agreements

Relationship to EC law

Many agreements registrable by virtue of the Restrictive Trade Practices Acts 1976 and 1977 are unlikely to infringe the competition law of the European Community. In some circumstances, however, an agreement may be registrable under United Kingdom law and, at the same time, contravene the competition provisions of Community law. Here the *doctrine of the double barrier* applies.[27] According to that doctrine the agreement must satisfy both the requirements of Community and of national law. The European Court held in *Wilhelm* v. *Bundeskartellamt*[28] that the same agreement might be subject to two sets of proceedings, namely before the Community authorities under Article 85 of the EC Treaty and also before the national authorities in application of national law but if a conflict occurred between the two regulations, the Community regulation must take precedence. The Restrictive Trade Practices Act 1976, s.5(1), provides that it shall apply to an agreement notwithstanding that it is or may be void by reason of any directly applicable Community provision, or is expressly authorised by such a provision, but the Restrictive Practices Court may decline or postpone the exercise of its jurisdiction if it appears to the court right, having regard to a Community provision, and the DGFT may refrain from taking proceedings in court. This provision is designed to avoid a conflict between the United Kingdom and Community law. United Kingdom parties are required[29] to inform the DGFT when notifying an agreement to the Commission or seeking negative clearance for it and when proceedings are instituted and decisions given in respect of an agreement.

---

[26] s.4.
[27] Adrienne M. Page "The Double Barrier" [1973] J.B.L. 332.
[28] [1969] C.M.L.R. 100; *Boehringer Mannheim GmbH* v. *Commission* [1973] C.M.L.R. 864.
[29] By the Registration of Restrictive Trading Agreements (EEC Documents) Regulations 1973 (S.I. 1973 No. 950).

Relationship to FTAs

Before joining the European Community, the United Kingdom was a party to two free trade agreements, the EFTA Convention[30] and the Anglo-Irish Agreement.[31] Both agreements contained provisions relating to restrictive business practices. When the United Kingdom joined the European Community, the EFTA Convention ceased to have effect and, as regards the countries which, with the United Kingdom, joined the Community (Denmark and the Irish Republic), the Community regulation applies. As regards the countries which did not join the Community (Austria, Finland, Iceland, Norway, Portugal, Sweden and Switzerland), the enlarged European Community entered into free trade agreements (FTAs) with them which include virtually all the goods that were eligible for duty-free treatment under EFTA. The FTAs, which are bilateral agreements between the Community and the country in question, contain also provisions relating to restrictive trade practices.[32] Section 12(1) of the Restrictive Trade Practices Act 1968 has not been repealed[33] but has not been extended to the FTAs; it is thought that the section has spent its effect.

Restraint of Trade at Common Law

The doctrine of restraint of trade applies to agreements subject to English law. It is of considerable importance in domestic transactions.[34] Although the doctrine applies to restraints no matter whether they are intended to have worldwide or only domestic effect,[35] no cases have been reported in which it has been used to regulate transactions directly involved in the export trade, and it is unlikely that it would be necessary to invoke the doctrine in this context. Agreements relating to trade within the EC are subject to the provisions of the EC Treaty,[36] and agreements relating to trade elsewhere may also be subject to particular competition regulation.[37] Furthermore, such matters as the relative bargaining strength of the parties which are relevant considerations in the application of the

---

[30] Convention of 1959 establishing the European Free Trade Association.
[31] Agreement of 1965 between the Governments of the U.K. and the Republic of Ireland establishing a Free Trade Area between the two countries.
[32] See p. 360, *ante.*
[33] See Restrictive Trade Practices Act 1976, Sched. 6.
[34] Especially in the sole and exclusive distribution arrangements for petrol and fuel oil known as "solus" agreements. Restraints of trade are also frequently inserted in service contracts and agreements for the sale of gas.
[35] *Nordenfelt* v. *Maxim Nordenfelt Guns & Ammunition Co.* [1894] A.C. 835.
[36] See p. 346 *et seq. ante.*
[37] See p. 374, *post.*

doctrine,[38] will not usually give rise to problems in the context of the export trade which would cause the doctrine to be invoked. For these reasons, these problems are not dealt with here in detail.

THE REFORM OF COMPETITION LAW IN THE UNITED KINGDOM

In 1988 the Department of Trade and Industry published two consultative papers, one entitled "Review of Restrictive Practices Policy"[38a] and the other "Policy and Procedure of Merger Control."[39] This was followed in 1989 by a White Paper on "Opening Markets: New Policy on Restrictive Trade Practices."[40] This White Paper takes the reform indicated in the first of the consultative papers a stage nearer to implementation by legislation. The survey of the reform of United Kingdom restrictive practices law in the following section is founded on the White Paper but it should be borne in mind that the Bill which will be introduced into Parliament and the Act which will eventually emerge may contain different provisions. Most of the proposals discussed in the second consultative paper are embodied in the Companies Act 1989.[41]

The reform of restrictive practices law

The principal aim of this reform is to align the new law and procedure to those of Article 85 of the EEC Treaty. It is proposed that the pre-notification procedure[42] shall be abolished and that every agreement or arrangement falling within the prohibition of the intended legislation shall be void and unenforceable. The registration of agreements and the filing of export agreements are to be discontinued.

Like Article 85(1), the intended legislation will contain a general prohibition followed by a list of particular illustrations of prohibited arrangements. It is intended that block exemptions and individual exemptions may be granted, as is the case in EC competition law. The block exemptions are likely to be similar to those issued by the EC Commission. In addition, there will be an exception for *de minimis* agreements.

---

[38] See, *e.g. Esso Petroleum* v. *Harpers Garage* (*Stourport*) [1968] A.C. 269; *Texaco* v. *Mulberry Filling Station Ltd.* [1972] 1 W.L.R. 814; *Alec Lobb Garages Ltd.* v. *Total Oil Great Britain Ltd.* [1983] 1 W.L.R. 87. (These cases refer to so-called "solus" agreements between oil companies and petrol stations).
[38a] Cm. 331.
[39] No Cm. Number.
[40] Cm. 727.
[41] Companies Act 1989, ss. 146–153.
[42] See p. 362 *et seq., ante.*

They will generally be agreements made by parties to which have a combined UK turnover below £5 million. However, in a departure from this rule, the *de minimis* exceptions for vertical agreements (resale price maintenance excepted) will apply, provided no party to the agreement has a UK turnover in excess of £30 million.

The Restrictive Trade Practices Court will be abolished. Its place will be taken by a Restrictive Trade Practices Tribunal, which will be composed of members of the (enlarged) Mergers and Monopolies Commission: the Tribunal will sit in panels of three, and an appeal from its decisions to the High Court will be admitted. However, the actual administration of the new law will be in the hands of the DGFT, whose powers will be extended. He will be responsible for the investigation of anti-competitive agreements, for initial conclusions about whether an agreement infringes the prohibition and whether it qualifies for an exemption. He will also make recommendations to the Secretary of State for block exemptions. The new law will combine the legal treatment of restrictive trade practices and retail price maintenance there will be no difference between them in law.

A particular feature of the new law will be that it will admit a private action for damages against persons or enterprises operating a prohibited agreement. This action — a statutory remedy similar to an action in tort — may be commenced by anybody who has suffered loss as the result of operating a prohibited agreement. In addition, the law will provide penalties. The offender is thus exposed to two enforcement procedures, a civil and a penal remedy.

As the new legislation will be closely framed on the model of the EC law of competition, the decisions of the European Court of Justice may be relevant for those of the DGFT, the tribunal or the courts. The new legislation will therefore permit these national institutions to make use of those of the EC. The White Paper provides:[43]

> The legislation will share many (though not all) the objectives of Article 85 of the EEC Treaty and in many instances will be intended to achieve the same particular results. Much of the impact of Article 85 may be identified not directly from the Treaty or regulations made under it but through cases brought before the Court of Justice (ECJ). The Government believe that the decisions reached by the ECJ will be highly relevant to similar cases in this area in the UK competition legislation, despite the obvious difference that the EEC Treaty is additionally concerned with the creation of a common market. The new legislation will therefore permit EC jurisprudence to inform the decision-making of the DGFT, the tribunal and the courts, insofar as relevant. Decisions established in other countries may also provide useful insights into competition principles from time to time.

Although thus the proposed legislation does not abolish the rule of the double barrier,[43a] the practical situation will be greatly ameliorated by the alignment of UK competition law with that of the EC.

---

[43] White Paper, para. 2.31, on p. 12.
[43a] See p. 370, *ante*.

The reform of merger control

The changes discussed in the consultative paper published by the Department of Trade and Industry in 1988 and mentioned earlier have been largely implemented by the Companies Act 1989.[44] The main object of this legislation is to speed up and simplify the present procedure. It has introduced a voluntary scheme of pre-notification which in simple cases will lead to a speedy clearance of the intended merger without reference to the Monopolies and Mergers Commission but in complicated cases may take longer. It is further provided that legally binding undertakings of the companies concerned in the merger may be admitted, *e.g.* that the take-over bidder undertakes to divest himself of specified subsidiaries or other economic interests, and then the merger may be cleared without reference to the Monopolies and Merger Commission.

FOREIGN NATIONAL COMPETITION LEGISLATION

It would not be profitable here to review the foreign national legislation aiming at the protection of free and fair competition. Too many differences exist and no general pattern of legal rules emerges; moreover, in some countries the legislative effort is in marked contrast to economic experience and the prohibitions can easily—and lawfully—be avoided. The only practical conclusion which can safely be drawn is that an exporter who, on the broadest possible view, fears that the expansion of his exports might come into conflict with the restrictive practices legislation of a particular country should at once seek expert advice.

Of the countries of the EC, the most elaborate law relating to cartels and monopolies is that of West Germany.[45] Further, it should be noted that the anti-trust legislation of the United States assumes to have extraterritorial effect,[46] though in the United Kingdom this is limited by

---

[44] Companies Act 1989, ss. 146–153.

[45] On the competition law of the Member States of the European Community, see Lipstein, *The Law of the European Community*, 1974, 188 *et seq.* For the German cartel law, and described more shortly, that of the other Member States, see A. H. Bermann and Colin Jones, *Fair Trading in Europe* (1977). The OECD publish an accurate description of the way the Restrictive Practices laws of Member States operate, but it is usually very out of date. The UN Conference on Trade and Development produces a bulletin *Restrictive Business Practices Information*; it is published quarterly and lists recent developments abroad. See also D. M. Raybould, *Comparative Law of Monopolies* (loose leaf, 1988) which includes USA law, in addition to UK, German and other laws. The legislation of individual countries is kept up to date in *Competition Law in Western Europe and the USA* (eds. Gijlstra and Murphy), a loose-leaf book.

[46] *British Nylon Spinners Ltd.* v. *Imperial Chemical Industries Ltd.* [1953] Ch. 19; see further *U.S.* v. *Aluminium Co. of America*, 148 F. 2d 416 (1945); *U.S.* v. *Watchmakers of Switzerland Information Center*, 133 F.Supp. 40 (1955). The US Supreme Court decided in *Mitsubishi Motor Corpn.* v. *Soler Chrysler-Plymouth Inc.*, 473 U.S. 614, 105 S.Ct. Ed. 2d, 444 that in an international distribution agreement the parties may agree to submit a civil anti-trust claim to arbitration but that the arbitrators are expected to take cognisance of US anti-trust law.

the *Protection of Trading Interests Act* 1980.[47] The Act, which was considered earlier,[48] provides, *inter alia*, that a judgment of an overseas court for multiple damages—the U.S. courts have jurisdiction to award double, treble and other multiple damages in anti-trust proceedings—is not enforceable in the United Kingdom.[49] Moreover, a defendant who has paid such damages is entitled to recover in the United Kingdom courts[50] the excess over the part attributable to compensation.[51]

Consequently, a United Kingdom company which combines with an American corporation in a consortium or joint venture for the purpose of making or distributing goods in a third country, *e.g.* India, has to make certain that the agreement to which it is a party satisfies not only the laws of India and the United Kingdom but also does not infringe the anti-trust legislation of the United States.

---

[47] As amended, see p. 229, *ante*.

[48] See p. 229 *ante*.

[49] s.5.

[50] The defendant must be a citizen of the United Kingdom, a body corporate in the United Kingdom (or in an overseas territory for whose international relations the UK is responsible), or a person carrying on business in the United Kingdom (s.6(1)). But if the defendant was ordinarily resident in the overseas country in question or if he carried on business there and the foreign judgment exclusively concerned activities in that country, he is not entitled to recover excess damages (s.6(3) and (4)). The party who recovered the excess damages in the overseas jurisdiction may in the UK proceedings be outside the United Kingdom (s.6(5)).

[51] s.6. Overseas judgments directed to conteracting a judgment for multiple damages given in a third country may be made enforceable in the United Kingdom on a reciprocal basis: s.7, as amended by s.38 of the Civil Jurisdiction and Judgments Act 1982.

PART THREE

FINANCE OF EXPORTS

CHAPTER 20

BILLS OF EXCHANGE

In every contract for the sale of goods abroad, the clause dealing with the payment of the purchase price embodies four elements: time, mode, place and currency of payment. The various methods of paying for exports represent, in law, variations and permutations of these four elements.

The custom of the merchants has developed typical methods of payment whereby it is attempted to reconcile the conflicting economic interests involved in the export transaction. The interest of the exporter is to obtain the purchase price as soon as possible, but, if the transport documents are documents of title to the goods, not to part with the documents before having received payment or, at least, being certain that his draft has been accepted, while the buyer wishes to postpone payment of the price until the documents—and notably the bills of lading—are no longer in the disposition of the seller. To achieve a reconciliation of these conflicting interests, the interposition of a bank, or of banks, is necessary. The most frequent payment methods in which banks are involved are a *collection arrangement* or payment under a *letter of credit.* In a collection arrangement the bank receives its instructions from the seller; the exchange of the documents of title representing the goods and the payment of the price is normally effected at the place at which the buyer carries on business. In the case of a letter of credit, conversely, the instructions to the bank emanate usually from the buyer; the exchange of the documents and the price is normally effected at the seller's place. A considerable amount of business is transacted under letters of credit under which the banker, on the instructions of the buyer, promises to accept, honour or negotiate bills of exchange drawn by the seller. Both these methods, the collection arrangement and the letter of credit, enable the interposed bank or banks to use the documents of title as a collateral security.

Occasionally payment arrangements are made which do not require the interposition of banks. The buyer may transfer the price to the seller on open account or the seller may send the buyer a documentary bill of exchange, *i.e.* a bill of exchange to which the bill of lading is attached.[1]

In this chapter the methods of payment which do not necessarily involve the interposition of a bank will be considered. The chapter deals,

---

[1] See p. 389, *post.*

in particular, with bills of exchange. These instruments are, of course, not only used where the buyer makes direct payment to the seller but they are also used very frequently in collection and letter of credit arrangements.

In the following chapters will be considered collection arrangements,[2] letters of credit,[3] bank guarantees,[4] and factoring, forfaiting financial leasing and other forms of merchant finance for exports. [5]

PAYMENT ON OPEN ACCOUNT

In the simplest case, the parties agree on "cash with order" terms. An exporter, who is able to sell on these terms, reduces the financial risk of the export transaction to a minimum.

Sometimes the parties agree on "sight payment" either in sterling or in a foreign currency. Here the buyer has to remit the purchase price when presented with the documents of title to the goods sold.

Sight payment is arranged when the exporter is acquainted with the financial status of the buyer and entertains no doubt about his solvency. The exporter sends the documents to the buyer who remits the agreed price by telegraphic transfer (T/T) or mail (M/T). These remittances are usually carried out through the buyer's bank. Sight payment is further sometimes arranged when the exporter sells goods to his own overseas branch or subsidiary. Here "the seller ships to his branch and settlement is usually a matter of periodical remittance. There may even be a two-way trading, as where raw materials are drawn from the territory where the products are finally marketed, in which case settlement between parent and offspring is a matter of running accounts and periodical remittances of balances due."[6]

If the exporter is not acquainted with the financial status of the buyer or other circumstances demand it, he arranges that the purchase price shall be paid "cash against documents" or "cash on delivery." These clauses are particularly suitable when delivery of the goods sold is to take place ex works. "Cash on delivery" can also be arranged in transportation of goods by land under the CMR.[6a] In f.o.b. or c.i.f. contracts direct payment by the buyer is not the normal method of payment; usually payment is effected through a bank, either under a collection arrangement[7] or under a letter of credit.[8]

---

[2] See p. 395, *post.*
[3] See p. 400, *post.*
[4] See p. 446, *post.*
[5] See p. 453, *post.*
[6] W. W. Syrett, "Finance of Exports," in *Talks about Exports*, published by the Institute of Export, Pitman, p. 44; on countertrade see Chapter 10, on p. 154 *ante.*
[6a] See p. 641, *post.*
[7] See p. 395, *post.*
[8] See p. 400, *post.*

PAYMENT BY BILLS OF EXCHANGE

Normally the buyer does not remit the purchase price on open account, but allows the exporter to draw a bill of exchange[9] on him.[10] This arrangement offers obvious advantages to both parties; the exporter obtains a negotiable instrument which he can turn into cash by negotiation at once, and the buyer is allowed a definite time of credit for settlement unless the bill is payable at sight.[11] If the parties fail to make express arrangements, the custom prevailing in the particular trade determines whether the price is to be paid on open account or by bill, and on which terms the latter has to be drawn.

Nature of the bill of exchange

The law governing bills of exchange is codified in the Bills of Exchange Act 1882. This Act, which has been referred to by an eminent commercial judge[12] as "the best drafted Act of Parliament ever passed," should be carefully studied by everyone who has to deal with bills of exchange. The Act defines in section 3 a bill of exchange as

an unconditional order in writing, addressed by one person to another, signed by the person giving it, requiring the person to whom it is addressed to pay on demand or at a fixed or determinable future time a sum certain in money to or to the order of a specified person, or to bearer.

This definition can be expressed in graphic form as follows:

	London, January 10, 19....
£10,000	*On demand* pay Britannia Bank Limited or Order*** the sum of ten thousand pounds for value received.
	Exports Limited
To Imports Inc., Boston, U.S.A.	

*or—*On March* 10, 19....   **or—*Bearer*
or—*Ninety days after sight.*

---

[9] The expression "bill of exchange" and "draft" have the same meaning.
[10] For an example of such a transaction, see *Credito Italiano* v. *M. Birnhak & Sons Ltd.* [1967] 1 Lloyd's Rep. 314, 320. A similar arrangement was agreed upon by the parties to a c. and f. contract in *Leigh and Sillivan Ltd.* v. *Aliakmon Shipping Co. Ltd.* [1985] Q.B. 350 (C.A.), affd. [1986] A.C. 785 (H.L.), but in this case the bill of exchange was to be endorsed by the buyer's bank (in the events which happened the bank declined to back the bill).
[11] On sight bills and time bills see p. 384, *post.*
[12] MacKinnon L.J. in *Bank Polski* v. *K.J. Mulder & Co.* [1942] 1 K.B. 497, 500.

There are three original parties to a bill of exchange: the drawer, the drawee and the payee. They are, in the preceding example: Exports Ltd. (the drawer), Imports Inc. (the drawee), and Britannia Bank Ltd. (the payee). The drawer and the payee, or the drawee and the payee may be the same person, but where the drawer and the drawee are the same person the bill may be treated, at the option of the holder of the bill, as a promissory note or a bill of exchange (s.5).[13]

The characteristics of a bill of exchange are—

(1) Every obligation arising under the bill must be expressed in writing on the bill and signed by the party liable (s.23).

(2) The obligations stipulated in the bill can be transferred easily by "negotiation" of the bill, often in performance of the sale of the bill at a discount if the bill is a time bill *i.e.* contains a credit element. The negotiation is done, in case of a bill to bearer, by mere delivery of the bill, and, in case of a bill to order, both by delivery of the bill and indorsement (s.31).

(3) Performance of the obligations stipulated in the bill can only be claimed by a person holding the document. This person is called the holder of the bill and is defined, in section 2, as the payee or indorsee or bearer of the bill, who is in possession of the bill.

(4) The person to whom a bill is negotiated may acquire a better right under it than his predecessors possess. This is a remarkable exception to the common law principle that no transferee can acquire a better title than his transferor. The object of this rule is to facilitate the negotiation of bills.

Section 38(2) expresses the rule as follows:

> where he [*i.e.* the holder of a bill] is "holder in due course," he holds the bill free from any defect of title of prior parties, as well as from mere personal defences available to prior parties amongst themselves, and may enforce payment against all parties liable on the bill.

A *holder in due course* is a holder who took a bill, which is complete and regular on the face of it, in good faith and for value and without notice of any defect in the title of the person negotiating it to him, and before it was overdue and without notice that it was dishonoured (s.29(1)). A holder who derives his title through a holder in due course and who is not himself a party to any fraud or illegality affecting the bill, has all the rights of that holder in due course as regards the acceptor and all parties to the bill prior to that holder (s.29(3)). Consequently, where a bill is negotiated to a holder in due course but later on dishonour is returned into the possession of the drawer, the latter, by virtue of section 29(3), has all the rights of that holder in due course.[14] A holder of a bill is

---

[13] References here and on the following pages are to the Bills of Exchange Act 1882.

[14] *Jade International Steel Stahl und Eisen GmbH & Co. KG* v. *Robert Nicholas (Steels) Ltd.* [1978] Q.B. 917.

prima facie presumed to be a holder in due course, but if it is admitted or proved that the acceptance, issue or subsequent negotiation of the bill is affected by fraud,[15] duress or force and fear, or illegality, the burden of proof is shifted and the holder has to prove, first, that value was given at the relevant time and, secondly that he has acted in good faith (s.30(2)).[16]

It should be noted that a bill of exchange does not represent an individual obligation but it contains a number of obligations which, while being independent in many respects, are in others closely interconnected for the reason that they are embodied in the same document. All three original parties normally are liable to honour the bill; the drawer by drawing it (s.55); the drawee by writing his acceptance on, or usually across, the bill whereby he becomes the acceptor (s.17); and the payee by indorsing the bill when negotiating it whereby he becomes the indorser (s.52(2)(*a*)).

A bill is irregular on the face of it if, *e.g.* it bears an irregular indorsement. "When is an indorsement irregular? The answer is, I think, that it is irregular whenever it is such as to give rise to doubt whether it is the indorsement of the named payee. A bill of exchange is like currency. It should be above suspicion."[17]

On principle every person signing a bill of exchange, even the mere "backer" of the bill (s.56), incurs liability,[18] but the drawer or an indorser can negative his liability by adding the words "without recourse" (*sans recours*) to his signature.

Further, a person signing a bill as drawer, indorser or acceptor can negative his liability by adding words to his signature indicating that he signs for or on behalf of a principal or in a representative capacity[19]; but the addition of descriptive words, such as "commission agent" or "company director," may not be sufficient to exempt him from personal liability (s.26(1)).

The primary liability to pay the bill rests upon the drawee. The drawer and indorsers are only liable on recourse, *i.e.* if the drawee dishonours the bill and they have received notice of dishonour by the holder or a subsequent indorser. Return of the dishonoured bill is a sufficient notice of dishonour (s.49(6)).

A bill payable on demand (*sight bill*) is dishonoured if it is not paid on presentation. A *time bill* is dishonoured if it is not accepted by the drawee

---

[15] "Fraud" means here a common law fraud *i.e.* dishonesty: *Österreichische Länderbank* v. *S'Elite Ltd.* [1981] Q.B. 565.

[16] *Bank of Cyprus (London) Ltd.* v. *Jones* (1984) 134 N.L.J. 522.

[17] *Per* Denning L.J. in *Arab Bank Ltd.* v. *Ross* [1952] 2 Q.B. 216, 227.

[18] See p. 390, *post.*

[19] But where the bill was accepted by a company and later indorsed by a director "for and on behalf of the company" the director was held to be personally liable because the company was already liable on the acceptance and his intention must have been to bind himself (s.26(2)): *Rolfe Lubbell & Co.* v. *Keith and Greenwood* [1979] 2 Lloyd's Rep. 75; this decision rests on its facts and does not reveal a general principle.

when presented to him for acceptance (unless presentment is excused) or if not paid by him. Presentment for acceptance is required where the bill is payable a certain time after sight in order to fix the maturity of the bill (s.39(1)). There is, of course, no presentment for acceptance in the case of a sight bill. In the case of a time bill, United Kingdom law allows three days of grace unless the bill otherwise provides (s. 14), but the laws of most other countries have abolished the days of grace.

The drawer or any indorser may insert in the bill the name of a person to whom the holder may resort if the bill is dishonoured by non-acceptance or non-payment (s.15). Such person is called "the referee in case of need." The bill must be protested or noted[20] before it can be presented to the referee (s.67). In the United Kingdom presentment in case of need is optional, but in many overseas countries such presentment is obligatory.

The time of payment is normally inserted in the bill when it is drawn. The bill is either a sight bill or a time bill, in banking language also called a term bill or usance bill; the latter expression originally referred to a time bill drawn for a period customary in a particular trade. A sight bill is defined in section 10(1) of the Act, as a bill

> (a) *which is expressed to be payable on demand, or at sight, or on presentation, or*
> (b) *in which no time for payment is expressed.*

A time bill is payable at a fixed future time or a determinable future time (ss.10, 11). In the latter case it is usually payable a fixed period after date or sight, *e.g.* "ninety days after sight." A bill payable at an uncertain date or on a contingency is not a bill of exchange in the meaning of the law; consequently, a bill would be bad if payable "on or before" a certain date[21] "by" a certain date,[22] "after sight," or "on arrival of steamer . . . "[23]

The place of payment is specified in the bill by the drawer or, if the drawer fails to do so, by the acceptor when accepting the bill. Usually a bill is made payable at a banker's office, but this is not a requirement of the law. Where a particular place is specified as the place of payment, that place is not regarded as the exclusive place of payment (s.19(2)(c)), and the acceptor can be sued for payment at another place. But where it is expressly stated that the bill shall be paid at the particular place only and not elsewhere, the acceptor can only be sued at that place; where the acceptor adds an exclusive place of payment to his acceptance, the holder of the bill is entitled to treat the acceptance as qualified and the bill as dishonoured (s.44), but he cannot claim this right if the place of payment

---

[20] See pp. 385 and 398, *post.*
[21] *Williamson* v. *Rider* [1963] 1 Q.B. 89.
[22] *Claydon* v. *Bradley* [1987] 1 W.L.R. 521.
[23] It was held in *Korea Exchange Bank* v. *Debenhams (Central Buying) Ltd.* [1979] 1 Lloyd's Rep. 548, 551 (C.A.) that the words "At 90 days documents against acceptance . . . pay" were "gibberish" and the instrument was not payable at a fixed or determinable future time.

is not made exclusive. In one case[24] a Polish firm drew a bill on "X Y, Plantation House, Mincing Lane, London, payable in Amsterdam at the A B Bank"; the bill was drawn on May 1, 1939, and payable in Dutch florins on November 1, 1939. It was duly accepted by X Y, but could not be presented in Amsterdam owing to the outbreak of the Second World War. Although the place of payment was in Holland and the stipulated currency Dutch florins, the court held that the plaintiff was entitled to recovery from X Y in London because Amsterdam was not stipulated as the only place of payment.

Foreign bills

The Bills of Exchange Act 1882 contains important provisions dealing with foreign bills.[25] A foreign bill is a bill which:

(*a*) either is drawn by a person who is not resident in the British Islands,[26]

(*b*) or is drawn by a person resident in the British Islands on a person resident abroad *and* is payable abroad.

All other bills are inland bills (s.4). It should be noted that a bill is not necessarily a foreign bill if it is payable abroad or if the drawee resides abroad; only if these two elements are combined is the bill a foreign bill, while it is always a foreign bill if the drawer resides abroad. If it is uncertain whether a bill is an inland bill or a foreign bill, it is treated as an inland bill (s.4(2)). The main difference between inland bills and foreign bills is that the latter, as a rule, must be formally protested upon dishonour by non-acceptance or by non-payment (s.51), while no protest is required for inland bills. In this respect English law differs from many foreign laws which likewise prescribe a protest for inland bills. In view of these and other differences between English and foreign law, it is often important to know whether the obligation of a person who signed a bill is to be judged by English law or a particular system of foreign law. The Act contains, in section 72 detailed rules on the conflict of laws, so far as relating to bills of exchange.[27]

Where the bill is expressed in foreign currency, but is payable in England, judgment can be obtained in the English courts in foreign currency.[28]

---

[24] *Bank Polski* v. *K.J. Mulder & Co.* [1942] 1 K.B. 497.

[25] *Dicey and Morris on The Conflict of Laws* (11th ed., 1987) Vol. 2, pp. 1308 *et seq.*

[26] The term "British Islands" includes any part of the United Kingdom of Great Britain and Ireland, the Islands of Man, Guernsey, Jersey, Alderney and Sark, and the islands adjacent to any of them being part of the dominions of the Crown.

[27] This section is reproduced in Dicey and Morris, *op. cit.* in n. 23, as Rule 197, on pp. 1313 *et seq.* where it is commented upon.

[28] *Barclays Bank International Ltd.* v. *Levin Brothers (Bradford) Ltd.* [1977] Q.B. 270.

The UN Convention on International Bills of Exchange and International Promissory Notes (1988)

The law of bills of exchange in the world is divided into two legal families. The Geneva system, founded on the Geneva Conventions,[29] is accepted by 19 countries of the European Continent, including the USSR[30] and also by Brazil and Japan. The Anglo-American system applies in the United Kingdom, most countries of the Commonwealth, the United States and the other countries which found their law on the common law.

In order to reconcile these two systems, UNCITRAL prepared a Convention on International Bills of Exchange and Promissory Notes.[31] This Convention was approved by the General Assembly of the United Nations on December 9, 1988.

The aim of the Convention is to create special instruments which persons engaged in international trade might use in place of the existing instruments to make payment or to give credit. The Convention will apply only if the instrument in question is designated "International Bill of Exchange" or "International Promissory Note," both with the addition of a reference to the Convention; this designation must appear in the heading and the text of the instrument.

The Convention will come into operation twelve months after the date of deposit of the instrument of ratification or accession by ten States. As some time will elapse before this Convention will have practical effect, it is not treated here in detail.

The claused bill

The draft customary in the export trade is not normally in the simple form set out on p. 381, *ante*, but contains a number of additional clauses. The following is an example of a draft as used in export transactions:

---

[29] There are three Geneva Conventions on the Unification of the Law relating to Bills of Exchange of June 7, 1930, and three further Conventions signed at Geneva on the Unification of the Law relating to Cheques of March 19, 1931.
[30] The USSR has accepted the Geneva Conventions on Bills of Exchange, but not those on Cheques.
[31] See p. 65 *ante*.

No. 1285

Liverpool, February 15,
19....

Ninety days after sight of this our First of Exchange (Second and Third of the same date and tenor unpaid) pay Britannia Bank Limited or Order the sum of ten thousand Pounds Sterling, payable at the collecting Bank's selling rate for sight drafts on London, with interest at 12 per cent. per annum added thereto from date hereof to due date of payment, value received.

$10,000

Exports Limited.

To
Imports Inc.,
Boston,
U.S.A.

Particular regard should be had to the clauses providing for payment at a specific rate of exchange or adding, to the sum payable, interest or specified charges. Thus, payment is stipulated "at the collecting bank's selling rate for sight drafts on London" and it is provided that interest at twelve per cent. per annum . . . from date hereof to due date of payment" shall be added to the stipulated sum. Such clauses are very common, particularly when the bill is made payable in foreign currency because various rates of exchange normally exist for the currencies in force at the buyer's and seller's residence, and it is unavoidable, when the bill is negotiated, that incidental expenses, such as bankers' charges or foreign stamp duties, are incurred. Even where payment has to be made by sterling draft it is advisable to insert exchange and charges clauses in the bill in order to define with certainty the financial obligations of the parties in the case of any unforeseen fluctuations in the rate of exchange.

The following "floating" exchange clauses are found in drafts used in export transactions:

payable at the bank's drawing rate for demand drafts on London,
payable at collecting bank's selling rate for Telegraphic Transfer,
payable at collecting bank's selling rate for sight drafts on London,
payable at collecting bank's selling rate for ninety days after sight drafts on London,
payable by approved bank's draft on London, exchange per indorsement.

Some of these clauses are customary in the trade with particular overseas countries and others are used where the buyer intends to obtain finance in a particular manner; thus, "exchange as per indorsement" clauses are mainly used where the seller wishes to discount the bill to bank; the bank then includes its discount in the sum payable when converting the stipulated currency into the local currency of the drawee.[32]

As alternatives to the clause stated in the example, *supra,* the following clauses relating to charges and interest are found, sometimes combined with one another and added to an exchange clause:

---

[32] In view of the possibility of currency devaluations, it is advisable to specify the exchange calculation expressly in the indorsement and not to rely on the details on the front of the bill: *Tropic Plastic and Packaging Industry* v. *Standard Bank of South Africa Ltd.* 1969 (4) S.A. 108; see the note in [1970] J.B.L. 121–122.

payable with interest at . . . per cent. per annum from date hereof to due date of arrival of
remittance in London,
payable with exchange,
payable without loss in exchange,
payable with stamps,
payable with bankers' charges,
payable with collecting bank's charges,
payable with negotiating bank's charges.

If the bill does not provide for payment of interest from the date of the
bill, interest can only be demanded from the time of maturity of the bill
(s.57(1)(b)). If the bill does not provide that the incidental charges should
be borne by the drawee, they fall upon the drawer.

From the legal point of view, no objection exists to inserting in the bill
clauses regulating the rate of exchange or the payment of interest or
charges. The Bills of Exchange Act 1882 provides that the sum payable
by the bill has to be "a sum certain in money,"[33] but adds in section 9(1)
that—

the sum payable by a bill is a sum certain within the meaning of this Act, although it is
required to be paid—
 (a) with interest,
 (d) according to an indicated rate of exchange or according to a rate of exchange to
     be ascertained as directed by the bill.

The clause "payable with interest at . . . per cent. per annum from date
hereof to due date of arrival of remittance in London" is of doubtful legal
validity. It was held by the highest court in Australia[34] that the clause was
invalid on the ground of uncertainty, mainly because the terminal date of
interest could not be ascertained from anything appearing on the face of
the bill. It is submitted, with great respect, that this view is incorrect.
That the requirement of payment of interest does not invalidate the bill is
expressly provided by section 9(1)(a) of the Act of 1882. The payment of
interest is merely ancillary to the payment of the main sum, and it is
thought that the requirement of certainty does not extend to ancillary
sums, such as interest and exchange, with the same rigour as to the main
sum. But the rate of interest must be specified in the bill.[35] However,
banks in the City of London sometimes consider the clause under
examination as unacceptable on the ground of uncertainty, but the
English courts have not yet been called upon to give their ruling on the
clause.

The clause "payable without loss in exchange" is designed to protect
the drawer against loss caused by an adverse alteration of the rate of

---

[33] See p. 381, *ante*.
[34] *Commonwealth Bank of Australia* v. *Rosenhain & Co.* [1922] Vic.L.R. 155 (High Court of
Australia).
[35] The American Uniform Commercial Code, s.3–106(1)(b), even admits different specified
rates before and after default.

exchange, particularly during the time which might elapse between the deposit of the price by the buyer in local currency with his bank and the release of the currency of exchange by the latter—or the foreign central bank—to the seller after compliance with the foreign exchange control regulations.

A draft expressed in foreign currency need not contain an exchange clause, the provisions of section 9(1)(*d*) of the Act are purely permissive[36]; if no exchange clause is inserted and the rate of exchange cannot be ascertained by reference to the custom of the trade, it is calculated according to the rate of sight drafts at the place of payment on the day the bill is payable (s.72), but instead of claiming that rate of exchange, judgment may be obtained in the foreign currency in which the draft is expressed and the date of conversion into sterling is then the date on which enforcement of the judgment is sought, *i.e.* virtually the date of payment.[37]

The documentary bill

The seller often attaches to a bill of exchange which he has drawn on the buyer the bill of lading to the goods sold. Such a bill of exchange is known as a *documentary bill*. The purpose of issuing a documentary bill is mainly to ensure that the buyer shall not receive the bill of lading and, therewith the right of disposal of the goods, unless he has first accepted or paid the attached bill of exchange according to the arrangement between the parties. If the buyer fails to honour the bill of exchange, he has to return the bill of lading, and, if he wrongfully retains the latter, the law presumes that the property in the goods sold has not passed to him.[38]

Occasionally the tenor of the documentary bill contains a clear reference to the export transaction to which the bill relates. Such statements do not render the bill of exchange void though they are, of course, superfluous (s.3(4)(*b*)). The practice of inserting them is convenient, and facilitates the careful checking of bills and documents which is a paramount responsibility of those dealing with the financial aspects of the export trade.

Avalised bills

An aval is the signature on a bill of exchange by a person who wants to "back" it and to guarantee its payment to the holder in due course.[39] Lord

---

[36] *Cohn* v. *Boulken* (1920) 36 T.L.R. 767.
[37] *Barclays Bank International Ltd.* v. *Levin Brothers (Bradford) Ltd.* [1977] Q.B. 270; see p. 386, *ante.*
[38] Sale of Goods Act 1979, s.19(3); p. 120, *ante. Cf. Leigh and Sillivan Ltd.* v. *Aliakmon Shipping Co. Ltd.* [1985] Q.B. 350 (C.A.), affd. [1986] A.C. 785 (H.L.) (This case concerned, however, subs. (1), and not (3), of s.19.); on the *Aliakmon* case see p. 46, *ante.*
[39] See p. 383, *ante.*

Blackburn[40] described the term "aval" as an antiquated term signifying "underwriting." But, influenced by the continental practice, it has come again into use in the United Kingdom, particularly in connection with forfaiting.[41]

Section 56 provides:

> Where a person signs a bill otherwise than as drawer or acceptor, he thereby incurs the liabilities of an indorser to a holder in due course.

Although the avaliser incurs the liabilities of an indorser to a holder in due course, he is not in the position of an indorser.[42] He is, as observed, a guarantor of the liabilities of an immediate party to the bill. It depends on the wording of the aval on the instrument, whose liabilities the avaliser guarantees. He may guarantee payment by the acceptor, or by one of the indorsers, or payment by all immediate parties, the acceptor and those liable on recourse.

> In *G. & H. Montage GmbH* v. *Irvani*[43] the plaintiffs, a Germany company, sold in 1976 three cold stores to an Iranian company of which the defendant Irvani was chairman and managing director. The balance of the purchase price was payable in 30 semi-annual bills of exchange; these bills were in DM payable in London. It was further agreed that the defendant should guarantee the bills. The plaintiffs posted the 30 drafts to the Iranian buyers who duly accepted them and the defendant Irvani signed them on the back. When the plaintiffs sent the drafts to their bank in Germany—apparently for collection—the bank advised that the defendant should be asked to add the words "*bon pour aval pour les tirés*" (good as a guarantee for the drawees) above his signature. On the authority of the defendants, the plaintiffs added these words. After the Iranian revolution in February 1979 some of the outstanding bills were dishonoured No notice of dishonour was given with respect to these bills, and in the case of some of them the protest was not carried out in the time required by section 51 of the Bills of Exchange Act.
>
> The plaintiffs sued the defendant Irvani, who had fled from Iran, in the English courts on the aval. Saville J. and the Court of Appeal decided in favour of the plaintiffs, though on different grounds[44], but both courts agreed that section 56 did not apply. It is thought that in a case to which section 56 applies, notice of dishonour [44a] to the avaliser is required because this is a condition precedent of his liability.

Only a time bill, and not a sight bill, can be avalised. An original party to the bill of exchange, *e.g.* the drawer or the acceptor, cannot avalise a bill himself as he is liable on the bill in any event and the aval, by its nature, is the added liability of another person though he becomes "a

---

[40] In *Steele* v. *M'Kinlay* (1880) 5 App.Cas. 754, 772.

[41] See p. 453, *post*.

[42] He is sometimes described, not very happily, as a quasi-indorser.

[43] For the decision of Saville see [1988] 1 W.L.R. 1285; The case is reported in [1988] 1 Lloyd's Rep. 460 *sub nom. Grunzweig und Hartmann GmbH* v. *Irvani*; For the CA decision see *The Times,* August 11, 1989.

[44] Saville J. held that section 56 was not applicable because the plaintiffs were not holders in due course and the defendant was liable, by virtue of German law as a guarantor and not as an indorser; the Court of Appeal held that German law was the law governing the aval (although the bills were dishonoured in London) and under German law no notice of dishonour to the avaliser was required.

[44a] And compliance with other provisions of the Act for recourse to the indorser, such as timely protest.

party" to the bill.[45] But their own liability of an original party may be avalised by a third party.

As a rule a bill is avalised only after it has been accepted by the drawee. Usually bills are avalised by banks[46] but there is no rule of law to that effect and anybody, whose signature carries weight, may avalise a bill. Banks usually carry out the aval by stamping across the bill "per aval" or similar words; this notation must, of course, be signed by an authorised person.

Commercially the aval of a bank of good standing is of great value. As already observed, it is one of the forms of security which a finance house requires when providing non-recourse finance to an exporter by way of a forfaiting arrangement or a similar transaction.[47] The charges of the avaliser for adding his liability to the bill are likely to be high.

Avals can also be used in connection with the transport documents. Thus, if under a collection arrangement the documents are to be presented to the acceptor of the bill (who in the sales transaction will be the buyer) it may be a condition precedent of the release of the documents to him that he obtains a good aval. Or, conversely, the acceptor can make the procurement of the aval by him conditional on the documents being released to him first. This combination of the financial and the documentary aspects bears some similarity to a letter of credit transaction but it cannot replace the latter and does not give the export seller the same financial assurance as, *e.g.* an irrevocable and confirmed letter of credit.

Other legal systems emphasise the 'guarantee character' of the aval. The American equivalent to the aval is the notation "Payment guaranteed" on the bill of exchange.[48] In German law the avaliser is called *Wechselbürge*[49] and the French Commercial Code states[50] that the avaliser "guarantees" the payment of the bill.[51]

Bills drawn in a set

It has been seen earlier[52] that the seller usually presents the buyer with several sets of transport documents. In this case, the seller does not draw

---

[45] As the avaliser is a "party" to the bill, section 72 is applicable, Saville J. in *G. & H. Montage GmbH* v. *Irvani*, [1988] 1 E.L.R. 1285, 1295.
[46] The difference between a bank signing as avaliser and an acceptance credit by the bank is that in the former case the bank, as a stranger, adds its signature to that of the acceptor, but in the latter case the bill is drawn on the bank and the bank signs as one of the original parties to the bill.
[47] See p. 453, *post*.
[48] American Uniform Commercial Code, s. 3–416(1).
[49] German Bills of Exchange Act 1933, Art. 32.
[50] French Code de Commerce, Art. 130(1).
[51] The German and French enactments refer to the intention of the avaliser in so far as they provide that he is only liable for the obligations of the person for whom he has undertaken the aval.
[52] On p. 37, *ante*.

the bill of exchange as a "sola" but as "parts of a set" and attaches a part of the bill to every set of transport documents which he despatches. The tenor of every part indicates that the bill represents a part in a set, and states the number of parts existing in all. In the example on p. 387, *ante*, the words "First of Exchange (Second and Third of the same date and tenor unpaid)" indicate that the bill is drawn in triplicate. The Bills of Exchange Act 1882 regulates this practice by providing, in section 71(1), that

where a bill is drawn in a set, each part of the set being numbered, and containing a reference to the other parts, the whole of the parts constitute one bill.

The parts of the set may be indorsed to different persons, but only one part is accepted by the drawee. If he is so foolish as to write his acceptance on more than one part and the accepted parts reach different holders in due course, he is liable on each part as if it were a separate bill. In the normal case, payment of the accepted part discharges the whole bill and the acceptor is entitled to claim delivery of the accepted part.

Negotiation of bills by exporter

It is vital for the exporter as for every other businessman to turn over his capital as quickly as possible. The exporter therefore frequently asks his bank to make an advance on the security of a documentary bill handed to the bank for collection[53] or to discount or purchase bills which he is entitled to draw on the issuing or advising bank under an accepted letter of credit[54] opened by the buyer. A bill which bears a bank's acceptance is known in banking circles as a "fine trade bill."

In the case of advances, specific advances against individual bills are distinguished from general overdrafts allowed on security of a steady flow of bills for collection held by the bank. These advances are in law in the nature of bankers' loans to customers[55]; in case of the exporter's failure, the bank would be in the position of a secured creditor in respect of the documentary bills held by it and the proceeds thereof.

Where the buyer has agreed to pay the purchase price under a letter of credit, the exporter who wishes to obtain finance before delivery of the transport documents to the advising bank might negotiate the draft drawn on the buyer or the bank to another bank[56] for cash. Here bankers distinguish two transactions: bills are said to be discounted where the

---

[53] On collection arrangements, see p. 395, *post*.
[54] On letters of credit, see p. 400, *post*.
[55] *Plein & Co. Ltd.* v. *Inland Revenue Commissioners* (1946) 175 L.T.Rep. 453.
[56] On negotiation credits where the advising bank is authorised to negotiate the bill drawn by the seller, see p. 421 *post*.

exporter (drawer) pays the bank's interest; and they are said to be purchased where the drawee pays the bank's interest and the exporter receives the nominal value of the bill. Whether a bill is purchasable or discountable depends on the clauses in a bill.[57] The rates of discount are here of great practical importance. In law no difference is drawn between purchased and discounted bills. They are both negotiated to the bank by indorsement and delivery of the bill, and in both cases the bank which has become the indorsee is entitled to have recourse to the drawer. The UCP (1983 Revision)[58] recognise the single concept of negotiation, in harmony with the legal position.[59]

Different from the negotiation of a bill of exchange under a letter of credit is the discount of the letter of credit itself which may occur where the credit provides for deferred payment.[60] This subject is treated later on.[61]

Proceedings on bills of exchange

Where one of the parties to a bill of exchange defaults, *e.g.* the acceptor dishonours the bill by non-payment, a summary judgment may be obtained against him under the Rules of the Supreme Court 1965, Order 14.[62] This means that, if the plaintiff supports his application for judgment by an affidavit that the defendant has no defence to his claim, the court will give judgment against the defendant at once. In cases founded on bills of exchange the court will give the defendant leave to defend only in exceptional circumstances. It is stated in *The Supreme Court Practice* 1985[63]

> Bills of exchange are treated as cash and, unless there are exceptional circumstances, where there is an action between the immediate parties to a bill of exchange, judgment will not be held up by virtue of a counterclaim by the defendant and execution will not be stayed.

Lord Wilberforce referred in one case[64] to time bills, *i.e.* bills payable at future dates, as "deferred instalments in cash" and said that since a bill is

---

[57] See p. 387, *ante.*
[58] See p. 401, *post.*
[59] UCP 1974/1983 Revisions Compared and Explained, ICC Brochure No. 411, p. 23.
[60] See *European Asian Bank AG* v. *Punjab & Sind Bank (No. 2)* [1983] 1 W.L.R. 642.
[61] See p. 421, *post.*
[62] Most other countries provide also for summary proceedings in case of default under a bill of exchange.
[63] Note 14/3–4/17. The statement in the text is supported by reference to the following cases: *James Lamont & Co. Ltd.* v. *Hyland Ltd.* [1950] 1 K.B. 585; *Brown Shipley & Co. Ltd.* v. *Alicia Hosiery Ltd.* [1966] 1 Lloyd's Rep. 668 and *Nova (Jersey) Knit Ltd.* v. *Kammgarn Spinnerei GmbH* [1977] 1 W.L.R. 713 (H.L.). See also Lord Denning M.R. in *Power Curber International Ltd.* v. *National Bank of Kuwait S.A.K.* [1981] 2 Lloyd's Rep. 394, 398; *Continental Illinois National Bank & Trust Co. of Chicago* v. *John Paul Papanicolaou. The Fedora, Tatiana and Eretrea II.* [1986] 2 Lloyd's Rep. 441, 445.
[64] In *Nova (Jersey) Knit Ltd.* v. *Kammgarn Spinnerei GmbH* [1977] 1 W.L.R. 713, 721.

an "unconditional order in writing," as stated in section 3, "English law . . . does not allow cross-claims, or defences, except such limited defences as those based on fraud, invalidity or failure of consideration, to be made."

CHAPTER 21

COLLECTION ARRANGEMENTS

WHERE the parties have not arranged for payment of the purchase price to take place in the seller's country the following problem arises: who is to present the bill of exchange drawn by the seller on the buyer at his residence and, if it is a documentary bill,[1] to deliver the transport documents to him when he accepts or pays the draft? Normally, the exporter asks his bank to arrange for the collection of the price, *i.e.* the acceptance or payment of the bill, and the bank will carry out this task through its own branch office abroad or a correspondent bank in the buyer's country. Sometimes the seller entrusts these duties to his representative or subsidiary company, if he is represented at the buyer's place of business, or to his forwarders.

The documentary bill lodgment form

The seller's instructions to present for acceptance or for payment the bill drawn for the price pass through many hands and have to be carried out abroad. They have to be precise and complete and to deal with the various contingencies which may arise in the course of their execution. The banks ask their customers to issue instructions on a *documentary bill lodgment form* which is designed to obtain instructions for all eventualities. The form which should be obtained from the exporter's bank, is completed in duplicate. One copy is retained by the bank and the other is given to the customer. The details of the retained copy are at once fed into the bank's computer and for this purpose the form is suitably coded. The retained copy forms part of the bank's bill register.

In modern practice the documentary bill lodgment form is arranged in a tabular manner. The table contains all contingencies which occur in the ordinary course of business and the customer is requested to complete the form and to tick off the instructions which he wants to give the bank. This layout is followed by a space in which "Other instructions" may be given if desired.

In the form used by one of the clearing banks in London[2] are the "Conditions of Collection" printed on the reverse; they read:

---

[1] On documentary bills of exchange, see p. 389, *ante.*
[2] Midland Bank plc (August 8, 1989).

Conditions of Collection

1. The collection of bills payable outside the United Kingdom is undertaken only on the terms that the Bank is not liable for loss, damage, or delay, however caused, which is not directly due to the negligence or default of its own officials or servants.

2. Where, owing to exchange restrictions, prohibitions, or suspension of means to effect transmission, payment of a bill is effected in a currency other than that in which it is drawn, neither this Bank nor its agents can accept responsibility for any loss in exchange which may occur if and when subsequent conversion shall take place.
   Subject to the Uniform Rules for Collections, I.C.C. Brochure No. 322, January 1979, where they are applicable.

Uniform Rules for Collections

The banking practice relating to collection arrangements is standardised by the *Uniform Rules for Collections* (1978 Revision), sponsored by the International Chamber of Commerce.[3] The Uniform Rules apply only if embodied by the parties into their contract. This is widely done, particularly in the intercourse betweeen the remitting bank, instructed by the seller, and the collecting bank, which presents the bill to the buyer at his place on the instructions of the remitting bank. The following definitions of the Uniform Rules are of interest:

    (i) "Collection" means the handling by banks, on instructions received, of documents as defined in (ii) below, in order to—
        (*a*) obtain acceptance and/or, as the case may be, payment, or
        (*b*) deliver the commercial documents against acceptance and/or, as the case may be, against payment, or
        (*c*) deliver documents on other terms and conditions.
    (ii) "Documents" mean financial documents and/or commercial documents:
        (*a*) "financial documents" means bills of exchange, promissory notes, cheques, payment receipts or other similar instruments used for obtaining the payment of money;
        (*b*) "commercial documents" means invoices, shipping documents, documents of title or other similar documents, or any other documents whatsoever, not being financial documents.
    (iii) "Clean collection" means collection of financial documents not accompanied by commercial documents.
    (iv) "Documentary collection" means collection of—
        (*a*) financial documents accompanied by commercial documents;
    (*b*) commercial documents not accompanied by financial documents.

The Uniform Rules thus distinguish two types of collection arrangements, clean collections and documentary collections. In the latter type of arrangement the commercial documents are presented by the collecting bank to the buyer, together with the financial documents; it is this type of collection arrangement which is of interest to the exporter.

---

[3] ICC Brochure No. 322. The Uniform *Rules* for Collections should not be confused with the Uniform *Customs* and Practice for Documentary Credits; on the latter, see p. 401, *post*. The ICC has published a list of countries and territories in which banks have indicated on July 25, 1989 that they adhere to the Uniform Rules for Collection (ICC Doc.470/569).

The Uniform Rules provide that all remittances must be accompanied by a *collection order* to be sent by the remitting bank to the collecting bank. The collection order must give complete and precise instructions. The collecting bank is only permitted to act upon the instructions in the collection order; if it cannot do so, it must advise the remitting bank immediately. The collecting bank must advise the remitting bank of the fate of the collection immediately; the advice has to be sent by the quickest mail but in case of urgency may be sent by the collecting bank by a quicker method at the expense of the customer, *i.e*, the exporter.[4] Today advice by fax may be expected. Further, the Uniform Rules contain the following provision which, in its generality, is of doubtful validity in English law[5]:

> Banks concerned with a collection assume no liability or responsibility for the consequences arising out of delay and/or loss in transit of any messages, letters or documents, or for delay, mutilation or other errors in the transmission of cables, telegrams, telex, or communication by electronic systems, or for errors in translation or interpretation of technical terms.

In the case of a documentary collection, the exporter has to instruct the remitting bank on the lodgment form, and the latter the collecting bank in the collection order, whether the documents shall be delivered to the buyer on acceptance of the bill (D/A), on actual payment (D/P) or in accordance with special instructions (which have to be stated on the form); whether the documents shall be handed to a *representative in case of need*[6] and what the powers of the representative are; whether the buyer shall be allowed a rebate for payment before maturity; and, if the documents are not taken up, whether the goods are to be warehoused and what insurance is to be effected. Precise instructions must be given relating to the noting or protest by a notary public at the payee's residence if the bill of exchange is dishonoured by non-acceptance or non-payment. Noting means obtaining a minute on the bill by the notary public at the time of refusal of acceptance or payment; the minute which is dated and initialled by the notary is, in practice, a sufficient assurance for all parties concerned that the bill has been dishonoured, and only in particular cases, *e.g.* when the matter leads to litigation, is the notary public required to procure a formal protest. According to English law, which, of course, applies only if proceedings against the defaulting payee can be taken in England,[7] where a bill has been noted on the day of dishonour or the next succeeding business day, the protest may be drawn

---

[4] *Ibid.*, Art. 20(ii).

[5] *Ibid.* Art. 4. Different from this provision, British clearing banks, according to their "Terms on which collection is undertaken" (see p. 396, *ante*), accept liability in certain cases in which the loss, damage or delay is caused by the negligence of their own officers or servants.

[6] The Uniform Rules contain detailed provision on the representative in case of need and the protection of the goods (Arts. 18 and 19).

[7] See p. 384, *post*.

up subsequently and dated back to the date of noting (Bills of Exchange Act 1882, ss.51 and 93).

The instructions for collection may contain additional requests; the exporter may, *e.g.* require the collecting bank to "cable advice if not paid."

Delivery of documents contrary to instructions

If the collecting bank releases the documents to the buyer contrary to instructions, *e.g.* by not insisting on payment or the acceptance of a time bill, the bank is liable in damages to the seller for breach of contract[8] and for conversion of the documents.

Release under a trust receipt

Sometimes the collecting bank finds itself in a predicament. It realises that it takes a considerable risk if releasing the documents, and particularly the bill of lading, without insisting on the performance of the conditions set out in the collection order but, on the other hand, the buyer may be one of its customers. In these cases an indemnity by the buyer would not protect the bank if the buyer becomes insolvent. The bank may therefore be tempted to release the documents prematurely under a *trust receipt.* Under such a document a genuine trust is constituted, the buyer being the trustee, the bank the beneficiary, and the trust property being the bill of lading, the goods obtained by the buyer from the vessel and, if the buyer is authorised to sell them, the proceeds of sale.[9] Under this form of trust receipt the buyer undertakes to pay the bank—he may be able to do so out of the proceeds of sale of goods—and thus to discharge the condition imposed on the bank in the collection order. Under another form of trust receipt the buyer is not entitled to sell the goods obtained from the vessel but is obliged to warehouse them in the bank's name and to deliver the warehouse receipt to the bank. But, as observed, if the release under a trust receipt does not go according to plan, the collecting bank is liable to the seller unless it has first obtained his authority. Moreover, if a buyer who qualifies as a mercantile agent

---

[8] Privity of contract exists between the seller and the collecting bank because, when, in the collection order, the remitting bank passes on the seller's instructions, it acts as authorised agent of the seller, see *Calico Printers Association Ltd.* v. *Barclays Bank* (1930) 36 Com.Cas. 197 (C.A.).

[9] A trust receipt is not a bill of sale within the meaning of The Bills of Sale Act 1878 and consequently need not be registered as a charge under the Companies Act 1985, s.396(1)(c).

sells the bill of lading to a bona fide purchaser in breach of the trust constituted by the trust receipt, the title of the bona fide purchaser prevails over that of the bank.[10]

In *Midland Bank Ltd.* v. *Eastcheap Dried Fruit Co.*[11] the bank was instructed to release the documents, including the bill of lading, to the buyers against payment in cash.[12] The bank, which was in the position of the collecting bank, released the documents without insisting on cash payment, but did so under a "collection note," which stated that the documents were released only for inspection and were left with the buyers in trust and had to be returned to the bank if no immediate payment was made. The buyers sold the documents to a bona fide purchaser. The bank paid the seller and then sued the buyers. The Court of Appeal held that the buyers were liable to the bank for breach of contract and for conversion of the bill of lading.

---

[10] *Lloyd's Bank* v. *Bank of America National Trust and Savings Association* [1937] 2 K.B. 631; [1938] 2 K.B. 147; see p. 295, *ante*.
[11] [1962] 1 Lloyd's Rep. 359.
[12] This case did not involve a documentary bill of exchange but the collecting bank was instructed to deliver the documents against cash payment.

CHAPTER 22

LETTERS OF CREDIT

CHARACTERISTICS OF THE LETTER OF CREDIT

LETTERS of credit,[1] also called documentary credits, are the most frequent method of payment for goods in the export trade. They have been described by English judges as "the life blood of international commerce."[2] Donaldson L.J., with the concurrence of Ackner L.J., said[3]:

> Irrevocable letters of credit and bank guarantees given in circumstances such that they are equivalent to an irrevocable letter of credit have been said to be the life blood of commerce. Thrombosis will occur if, unless fraud is involved, the courts intervene and thereby disturb the mercantile practice of treating rights thereunder as being equivalent to cash in hand.

The feature common to all types of letters of credit is this: in accordance with the agreement between the seller and the buyer in the contract of sale ("the underlying contract"[4]), the buyer arranges that payment of the price is made by a bank, normally at the seller's place, on presentation of specified documents, which usually include the transport documents, and the performance of other conditions stated in the credit and advised by the bank to the seller. On presentation of the documents the bank pays the purchase price, according to the terms of the credit, by sight payment, deferred payment, or by acceptance or negotiation of a bill of exchange drawn by the seller.[5]

The essence of the letter of credit transaction is its documentary character, *i.e.*, where the goods are represented by a bill of lading, this

---

[1] For further reading: H. C. Gutteridge and Maurice Megrah, *The Law of Bankers' Commercial Credits* (6th ed., 1979); E. P. Ellinger, *Documentary Letters of Credit* (1970); F. M. Ventris, *Bankers' Documentary Credits*, (2nd ed., 1983); Michael Rowe, *Letters of Credit* (1985); William Hedley, *Bills of Exchange and Bankers' Documentary Credits* (1986); Lazar Sarna, *Letters of Credit. The Law and Current Practice* (2nd ed. 1986, Canada).
[2] Kerr L.J. in *R. D. Harbottle (Mercantile) Ltd.* v. *National Westminster Bank Ltd.* [1978] Q.B. 146, 155; Griffiths L.J. in *Power Curber International Ltd.* v. *National Bank of Kuwait S.A.K.* [1981] 2 Lloyd's Rep. 394, 400; Donaldson L.J. in *Intraco Ltd.* v. *Notis Shipping Corporation of Liberia. The Bhoja Trader* [1981] 2 Lloyd's Rep. 256, 257; Ackner L.J., *ibid.*; and Stephenson L.J. in *United City Merchants (Investments) Ltd.* v. *Royal Bank of Canada* [1982] Q.B. 208, 222; Hirst J. in *Hong Kong and Shanghai Banking Corporation* v. *Kloeckner & Co. AG*, [1989] 2 Lloyd's Rep. 323, 330.
[3] In *Intraco Ltd.* v. *Notis Shipping Corporation of Liberia. The Bhoja Trader, supra.*
[4] The underlying contract may be another type of contract, *e.g.* a construction contract or a contract for services.
[5] See p. 421, *post.*

document of title is used as a means of financing the transaction. Lord Wright[6] describes the function of the letter of credit as follows:

> The general course of international commerce involves the practice of raising money on the documents so as to bridge the period between the shipment and the time of obtaining payment against documents.

The documentary character of this type of bankers' credit, as used in international trade, cannot be over-emphasised: the paying bank is prepared to pay the exporter because it holds the documents as collateral security and, if necessary, can take recourse to the issuing bank which, in turn can take recourse to the buyer as instructing customer. Where the transport documents consist of bills of lading, the bank invariably asks for the delivery of a full set of original bills; otherwise a fraudulent shipper would be able to obtain payment under the letter of credit on one of them and advances from other bankers on the security of the other originals constituting the set.[7]

A comprehensive definition of the letter of credit is to be found in the *Uniform Customs and Practice for Documentary Credits (1983 Revision)*[8] where it is provided[9]:

For the purposes of these articles, the expressions "documentary credit(s)" and "standby letter(s) of credit"[10] used herein (hereinafter referred to as "credit(s)"), mean any arrangement, however named or described, whereby a bank (the issuing bank), acting at the request and on the instructions of a customer (the applicant for the credit),[11]

    (i) is to make a payment to or to the order of a third party (the beneficiary),[12] or is to pay or accept bills of exchange (drafts) drawn by the beneficiary, or

    (ii) authorises another bank[13] to effect such payment, or to pay, accept or negotiate such bills of exchange (drafts),

against stipulated documents, provided that the terms and conditions of the credit are complied with.

Uniform Customs and Practice for Documentary Credits

The banking practice relating to letters of credit is standardised by the *Uniform Customs and Practice for Documentary Credits (1983 Revision)*,

---

[6] In *T. D. Bailey, Son & Co.* v. *Ross T. Smyth & Co. Ltd.* (1940) 56 T.L.R. 825, 828.

[7] This passage was quoted with approval by Ackner L.J. in *United City Merchants (Investments) Ltd.* v. *Royal Bank of Canada* [1982] Q.B. 208, 247.

[8] ICC Brochure 400. The *Uniform Customs and Practice for Documentary Credits 1983* (Brochure 400) must not be confused with the *Uniform Rules for the Collection of Commercial Paper 1978* (Brochure 322), discussed on p. 396, *ante*. The ICC has published a list of countries and territories in which banks had notified their adherence to the UCP (1983) Revision by July 25, 1989 (ICC Doc. No. 470/568).

[9] In art. 2.

[10] On standby letters of credit, see p. 429 *post*.

[11] This is the buyer.

[12] This is the seller (exporter), but as the underlying contract may be another than a contract of sale, the neutral expression "beneficiary" is used.

[13] This is normally the advising bank at the seller's place.

which are sponsored by the International Chamber of Commerce.[14] They are commonly referred to as *UCP*. Letters of credit are the branch of law in which the attempts at unifying the law have been most successful. The UCP have practically universal effect. This success has been achieved after more than 50 years of effort.[15]

Application of the UCP

In principle, the UCP apply only if the parties have embodied them into their contract. Article 1 of the UCP makes this clear:

> These articles apply to all documentary credits, including, to the extent to which they may be applicable, standby letters of credit, and are binding on all parties thereto unless otherwise expressly agreed. They shall be incorporated into each documentary credit by wording in the credit indicating that such credit is issued subject to Uniform Customs and Practice for Documentary Credits, 1983 revision, ICC Publication No. 400.

In English law the UCP do not have the force of law or the status of a trade custom. In accordance with Article 1, they apply only if the parties have incorporated them into their contract. This is normally done by British banks, when contracting with a United Kingdom party, an overseas merchant or other banks. Consequently, the English courts are familiar with the provisions of the UCP and have frequently interpreted them.[16] Similar is the position in France.[17] In the State of New York the provisions of the Uniform Commercial Code on letters of credit[18] are replaced by the UCP where the parties have agreed to apply them or where they are customarily applicable. In countries, which have national banking associations, the general standard conditions[19] applied by the members of these associations often incorporate the UCP. If the automated international transfer system SWIFT[20] is used by banks in letter of credit transactions, the UCP apply to the contractual relations between the banks and between them and SWIFT.

---

[14] ICC Doc. 400. See also *Guide to Documentary Credit Operations*, ICC Publication No. 415 (1985).

[15] The first issue of the UCP was published in 1933, the second in 1951, the third in 1962, and the fourth in 1974. The present—fifth—Revision, *viz.* the 1983 Revision, came into operation on October 1, 1984.

[16] *e.g.* in *Banque de l'Indochine et de Suez SA* v. *J. H. Rayner (Mincing Lane) Ltd.* [1983] Q.B. 711; *European Asian Bank AG* v. *Punjab & Sind Bank (No. 2)* [1983] 1 W.L.R. 642; *Forestal Mimosa Ltd.* v. *Oriental Credit Ltd.*, [1986] 1 W.L.R. 631.

[17] *Cour de Cassation*, October 14, 1981, in *Receuil Sirey-Dalloz*, 1982, 301. In Belgium the *Tribunal de commerce de Bruxelles*, in a decision of November 16, 1978, *Revue de la Banque*, 1980, regarded the UCP as customary law but this decision is controversial.

[18] UCC, article 5.

[19] In the United Kingdom no general standard conditions for banks exist.

[20] For SWIFT see p. 78, *ante*. But SWIFT has not adopted the *ICC Uniform Rules for Collections*.

Even where the UCP are adopted specifically or generally, the parties are at liberty to contract out of some of them; this is clearly expressed in Article 1, quoted earlier.

The ICC has made an attempt to standardise the documentation relating to letters of credit; it has published the *Standard Documentary Credit Forms*,[21] which are based on the UN layout key proposed by the UN Economic Commission for Europe and this aligns with the other export documentation.[22] The ICC Banking Commission is sometimes asked to express its view on the interpretation and application of the UCP by the banks and the collection of its opinions[23] is valuable source material.

The stages of a letter of credit transaction

Where payment under a letter of credit is arranged, four stages can normally be distinguished—

(i) The exporter and the overseas buyer agree in the contract of sale that payment shall be made under a letter of credit.

(ii) The overseas buyer (acting as "applicant for the credit") instructs a bank at his place of business (known as the "issuing bank") to open a letter of credit for the United Kingdom exporter (known as "the beneficiary") on the terms specified by the buyer in his instructions to the issuing bank.

(iii) The issuing bank arranges with a bank at the locality of the exporter (known as the "'advising bank") to negotiate, accept or pay the exporter's draft upon delivery of the transport documents by the seller.

(iv) The advising bank informs the exporter that it will negotiate, accept or pay his draft upon delivery of the transport documents. The advising bank may do so either *without its own engagement* or it may *confirm* the credit opened by the issuing bank.[24]

---

[21] ICC Doc. No. 416. A shortened version containing only the Guidance Notes for Credit Applicants is No. 416A. Both documents were published in April 1986.

[22] See p. 77, *ante*.

[23] Decisions (1975–1979) of the ICC Banking Commission (ICC Doc. No. 371); Opinions (1980–1981) of the ICC Banking Commission (ICC Doc. No. 399), and Opinions of the ICC Banking Commission on Queries relating to Uniform Customs and Practice for Documentary Credits (1984–1986) (ICC Doc. No. 434). Opinions covering the period between 1981 and 1984 have not been published.

Another important ICC Document is "Case Studies on Documentary Credits. Problems, queries, answers," (ICC Doc. No. 459. 1989).

[24] Sometimes the situation is more complicated. The issuing bank may authorise another bank, (*e.g.* at a major trading centre in the seller's country) to confirm, and this bank may instruct a third bank, (*e.g.* in a small place at which the seller carries on business) to advise the irrevocable and confirmed credit. But no bank would confirm a credit if the issuing bank has not made it irrevocable; see UCP, art. 10(b). On confirmed and unconfirmed credits, see p. 423, *post*.

Sometimes, when the bank is represented at the overseas buyer's and the exporter's place, stages (iii) and (iv) are combined and the issuing bank advises the exporter of the credit opened in his favour, either directly or through a branch at the exporter's place.

Two points emerge from this analysis: first, stages (i) and (iv) are of singular importance to the exporter, *viz.* the arrangement, in his contract of sale with the overseas buyer, of the most appropriate type of credit; and the corresponding notification from the advising bank.

Secondly, provided the correct documents are tendered and this is done before the expiry of the credit, there is a binding undertaking of the issuing bank, if the credit is irrevocable, and also of the confirming bank, if it is confirmed, to the beneficiary to pay the purchase price. These undertakings are of contractual nature. A bank which has given such undertaking will refuse to accept instructions from the buyer not to pay a seller who has performed the conditions of the credit,[25] and will not accept a revocation of the credit.

The two fundamental principles

The law relating to letters of credit is founded on two principles:

  (i) The autonomy of the credit; and
  (ii) the doctrine of strict performance.

The autonomy of the letter of credit

According to this principle, the credit is separate from and independent of the underlying contract of sale or other transaction. A bank which operates a credit is only concerned with one problem: whether the documents tendered by the seller correspond to those specified in the instructions. The letter of credit transaction is thus a paper transaction. It is irrelevant to the bank whether the underlying contract concerns the purchase of timber, oil, machinery or whether it concerns another transaction. The only case in which—exceptionally—the bank should refuse to pay under the credit occurs if it is proved to its satisfaction that the documents, though apparently in order on their face, are fraudulent and the beneficiary (the seller) was involved in the fraud.[26] This case is sometimes referred to as the "fraud exception."

---

[25] *Hamzeh Malas & Sons* v. *British Imex Industries Ltd.* [1958] 2 Q.B. 127; see p. 426, *post.*
[26] *United City Merchants (Investments) Ltd.* v. *Royal Bank of Canada.* [1983] 1 A.C. 168; *Tukan Timber Ltd.* v. *Barclays Bank plc.* [1987] 1 Lloyd's Rep. 171, 174. On fraud affecting letters of credit, see p. 441, *post.*

The principle of autonomy of the credit is stated in Articles 3 and 4 of the UCP in these terms:

Article 3

Credits, by their nature, are separate transactions from the sales or other contract(s) on which they may be based and banks are in no way concerned with or bound by such contract(s), even if any reference whatsoever to such contract(s) is included in the credit.

Article 4

In credit operations all parties concerned deal in documents, and not in goods, services and/or other performances to which the documents may relate.

By virtue of its autonomous character, the letter of credit is approximated, to some extent, to the bill of exchange.[27] This development was noted by Lord Denning M.R. in *Power Curber International Ltd.* v. *National Bank of Kuwait*,[28] when he said[29]:

It is vital that every bank which issues a letter of credit should honour its obligations. The bank is in no way concerned with any dispute that the buyer may have with the seller. The buyer may say that the goods are not up to contract. Nevertheless the bank must honour its obligations. The buyer may say that he has a cross-claim in a large amount. Still the bank must honour its obligations. A letter of credit is like a bill of exchange given for the price of the goods. It ranks as cash and must be honoured. No set off or counterclaim is allowed to detract from it: see *Nova (Jersey) Knit Ltd.* v. *Kammgarn Spinnerei GmbH.*[30] All the more so with a letter of credit. Whereas a bill of exchange is given by buyer to seller, a letter of credit is given by a bank to the seller with the very intention of avoiding anything in the nature of a set off or counterclaim.

In this case distributors in Kuwait bought machinery from Power Curber, an American company carrying on business in North Carolina. The National Bank of Kuwait issued an irrevocable letter of credit, instructing the Bank of America in Miami to advise the credit to the sellers through a bank in Charlotte, North Carolina. The machinery was duly delivered but the Kuwaiti buyers raised a large counterclaim against the sellers in the courts of Kuwait and obtained from them a provisional attachment order which prevented the bank, which was willing to honour the irrevocable credit, from paying under it. The sellers sued the bank, which had a registered address in London, in the English courts and Parker J. gave

---

[27] This statement should not be misunderstood. The concept of a holder in due course (p. 382, *ante*) does not apply to letters of credit. Further, a letter of credit is not negotiable; if it is made transferable, it can be transferred only once (p. 435, *post*).

[28] [1981] 1 W.L.R. 1233. See also *Toprak Mahsulleri Ofisi* v. *Finagrain Compagnie Commerciale Agricole et Financière SA* [1979] 2 Lloyd's Rep. 98; *Intraco Ltd.* v. *Notis Shipping Corporation. The Bhoja Trader* [1981] 2 Lloyd's Rep. 256. It was held in *R.* v. *Benstead*, [1982] Crim.L.R. 456 (C.A.) that a letter of credit was a valuable security within the meaning of s.20 of the Theft Act 1968.

[29] [1981] 1 W.L.R., on p. 1241.

[30] [1977] 1 W.L.R. 713 (This case concerned bills of exchange, and not letters of credit).

summary judgment against the bank. The Court of Appeal upheld this decision. It held that the order of the court in Kuwait did not affect the obligation of the bank to honour the credit and, moreover, it could not have extraterritorial effect.

As can be seen from this case, a summary judgment[31] can in many instances be obtained against a bank which tries to negate its obligations under an irrevocable or irrevocable and confirmed credit. Moreover, the courts will normally refuse to issue a *Mareva* injunction, now authorised by the Supreme Court Act 1981, s.37(1) and (3),[32] against a bank preventing it from paying the credit.[33] But the courts are prepared in appropriate cases to issue such injunction against the beneficiary (the seller), attaching the proceeds which he has received from the bank under the credit. Lord Denning said in one case[34]:

> The injunction does not prevent payment under a letter of credit or under a bank guarantee, but it may apply to the proceeds as and when received by the defendant.
> On the other hand, it has been held[34a] that a bank may set off a claim for liquidated damages which has accrued to it, against its own letter of credit liability to the beneficiary in a case in which the claim for liquidated damages arose directly out of the same banking transaction to which the letter of credit related.

The doctrine of strict compliance

The legal principle that the bank is entitled to reject documents which do not strictly conform with the terms of the credit is conveniently referred to as the doctrine of strict compliance. The reason underlying this rule—which is not always appreciated by exporters—is that the advising bank is a special agent of the issuing bank and the latter is a special agent of the buyer; if such agent who has a limited authority acts outside his authority (in banking terminology: his mandate) the principal is entitled to disown the act of the agent, who cannot recover from him and has to bear the commercial risk of the transaction. In a falling market a buyer is easily tempted to reject documents which the bank accepted, on the ground that they do not strictly conform with the terms of the

---

[31] See p. 393, *ante*. See also *S.L. Sethia Liners Ltd.* v. *State Trading Corporation of India Ltd.* [1985] 1 W.L.R. 1398, 1401; *Forestal Mimosa Ltd.* v. *Oriental Credit Ltd.*, [1986] 1 W.L.R. 631; *Continental Illinois National Bank & Trust Company of Chicago* v. *John Paul Papanicolaou. The Fedora, Tatiana and Eritrea II* [1986] 2 Lloyd's Rep. 441 (C.A.) (This case concerned a guarantee).

[32] See pp. 701–702, *post*.

[33] *Intraco Ltd.* v. *Notis Shipping Corporation. The Bhoja Trader* [1981] 2 Lloyd's Rep. 256; *Bolivinter Oil SA* v. *Chase Manhattan Bank N.A.* [1984] 1 W.L.R. 392; [1984] 1 Lloyd's Rep. 251; see p. 442, *post*. If the fraud exception is established, the court may be persuaded to grant a *Mareva* injunction.

[34] *Z. Ltd.* v. *A-Z and AA-LL* [1982] Q.B. 558, 574.

[34a] *Hong Kong and Shanghai Banking Corporation* v. *Kloeckner & Co. AG,* [1989] 2 Lloyd's Rep. 323 (The decision is founded on exceptional facts).

credit. Moreover, the bank deals in finance, not in goods[35]; it has normally no expert knowledge of the usages and practices of a particular trade. If the documents tendered are not strictly in conformity with the terms of the credit and the bank refuses to accept them, the exporter should at once contact his overseas buyer and request him to instruct the bank to accept the documents as tendered; the refusal of the bank to depart even in a small and apparently insignificant matter not sanctioned by the instructions or the UCP, where applicable, from its instructions will, in the overwhelming majority of cases, be upheld by the courts if litigation ensues. Lord Sumner expressed the doctrine of strict compliance in the following classic passage: "There is no room for documents which are almost the same, or which will do just as well."[36]

The doctrine of strict compliance may be illustrated by the following examples.

In *Equitable Trust Company of New York* v. *Dawson Partners Ltd.*[37] the defendants bought vanilla beans from a seller in Batavia (now Jakarta). They instructed the plaintiff bank to open a confirmed letter of credit in favour of the seller and to make finance available thereunder on delivery of certain documents including a certificate of quality to be issued "*by experts.*" Owing to an ambiguity in the cabled codeword, the advising bank in Batavia informed the seller that the credit was available on the tender of a certificate "*by expert.*" The seller who was fraudulent shipped mainly rubbish and the expert failed to discover the fraud. The House of Lords held that the plaintiff bank was not entitled to be reimbursed by the buyers because, contrary to their instructions, it made available finance on the certificate of one expert only instead of at least two experts.

In *Soproma S.p.A.* v. *Marine & Animal By-Products Corporation*[38] the buyers, an Italian company, bought a quantity of Chilean fish full meal from a New York company. The contract, which was on a London Cattle Food Trade Association form, was c. and f. Savona and provided that the buyers should open a letter of credit with a New York bank. The documents to be presented by the sellers to that bank had to include bills of lading issued to order and marked "freight prepaid" and further an analysis certificate stating that the goods had a content of minimum 70 per cent. protein. The credit was subject to the UCP (1951 Revision). The sellers tendered to the advising bank in New York bills of lading

---

[35] See UCP, art. 4, quoted on p. 405, *ante.*
[36] In *Equitable Trust Co. of New York* v. *Dawson Partners Ltd.* (1927) 27 Ll.R. 49, 52; Devlin J. in *Midland Bank Ltd.* v. *Seymour* [1955] 2 Lloyd's Rep. 147. Parker J. in *Kydon Compania Naviera SA* v. *National Westminster Bank Ltd. The Lena.* [1981] 1 Lloyd's Rep. 68, 75.
[37] (1927) 27 Ll.L.R. 49. See also *Gian Singh & Co. Ltd.* v. *Banque de l'Indochine* [1974] 1 W.L.R. 1234.
[38] [1966] 1 Lloyd's Rep. 367.

which were not to order and consequently were not negotiable[39] and which did not bear the remark "freight prepaid" but, on the contrary, bore the remark "collect freight"; the analysis certificate showed only a protein content of 67 per cent. minimum; and the goods, although described in the invoice as "Fish Full Meal," were described in the bills of lading only as "Fishmeal." The buyers rejected the documents. Thereupon (the time of validity of the credit having expired) the sellers made a second tender of documents to the buyers directly,[40] adding a freight receipt showing that they had paid the freight and an analysis certificate of minimum 70 per cent. protein. The buyers likewise rejected the second tender and, after arbitration in London, the dispute came before the English court. McNair J. decided that the buyers had rightly rejected the documents, for the following reasons:

1. the second—direct—tender of documents was irrelevant[41] and had to be disregarded completely;
2. the first tender, *i.e.* the tender to the correspondent bank in New York, was defective because—
   (*a*) the bills of lading did not bear the remark "freight prepaid"[42] but were in fact marked "freight collect." Further, they were not negotiable as they were not to order and consequently were not proper bills which could be tendered under a c.i.f. or c. and f. contract;
   (*b*) the analysis certificate showed too low a minimum protein content;
   (*c*) but the description of the goods in the bill of lading in general terms (as "Fishmeal") was sufficient, since the goods were correctly described in the commercial invoice; the learned judge referred here to the UCP (1951 Revision), Art. 33,[43] where it is provided that a general description in the bills of lading is sufficient if the goods are correctly described in the commercial invoice.[44]

---

[39] See p. 571, *post*.
[40] Not to the advising bank in New York.
[41] For reasons discussed on p. 439, *post*.
[42] Nor was the freight deducted from the price or a freight receipt tendered with the bills.
[43] This provision of the 1951 edition is substantially the same as Art. 41(c) of the 1983 Revision.
[44] In cases to which the UCP apply, reliance can no longer be placed on *S.H. Rayner & Co. v. Hambros Bank Ltd.* [1943] 1 K.B. 37. In this case the correspondent bank advised the sellers that a letter of credit in their favour was available upon delivery of certain documents evidencing the shipment of "Coromandel groundnuts." The sellers tendered a bill of lading describing the goods as "machine shelled groundnut kernels" and having in its margin the letters "C.R.S." which were an abbreviation of "Coromandels," but in the invoice the goods were described correctly as "Coromandel groundnuts." The Court of Appeal held that the bank had rightly refused payment under the credit, in view of the doctrine of strict performance. McNair J. rightly distinguished the *Soproma* case from the *Rayner* case because the UCP applied to the former but not to the latter.

Where a bank pays under a confirmed letter of credit although the documents tendered are defective, the principal—the issuing bank or the buyer, as the case may be—forfeits his right to refuse reimbursement if he ratifies the unauthorised payment.[45] The intention to ratify may, in appropriate circumstances, even be inferred from prolonged inaction or silence.[46] In a c.i.f. contract the documents should be rejected by the principal on their face value; if, *e.g.* the buyer who is aware of their irregularity remains inactive and attempts to reject them after the arrival and inspection of the goods at the port of destination, he is likely to be deemed to have ratified the payment by the bank. In *Bank Melli Iran* v. *Barclays Bank D.C.O.*[47] an Iranian buyer purchased American trucks from English sellers. On the instructions of the buyer Bank Melli Iran opened a credit for the sellers, Barclays acting as the advising bank. The instructions of the issuing bank to the advising bank stated that the credit was for the price of "100 new Chevrolet trucks" and required the presentation of a certificate of the United States Government to that effect. The documents tendered to Barclays were ambiguous and contradictory. The invoice stated that the trucks were "in a new condition," the Government certificate referred to them as "new, good," and the delivery order described them as "new-good"(*sic!*). Barclays paid against these documents and passed them on to Bank Melli Iran. The latter informed Barclays that they considered the documents faulty but did not reject them. Indeed, later on they authorised Barclays to increase the credit and the buyer surveyed the first consignment of the goods on arrival in Iran. After approximately six weeks Bank Melli rejected the documents. McNair J. held (1) that the documents were faulty and should have been rejected by Barclays, (2) but in the circumstances Bank Melli had ratified the transaction and lost its right of rejection.

The documents tendered to the bank

According to the doctrine of strict compliance[48] the bank is within its rights when refusing documents tendered by the seller which do not

---

[45] *Bank Melli Iran* v. *Barclays Bank* (*Dominion, Colonial and Overseas*) [1951] 2 Lloyd's Rep. 367. *Cf.* also *Panchaud Frères S.A.* v. *Établissements General Grain Company* [1970] 1 Lloyd's Rep. 53, 57 (in this case payment was not to be made under a documentary credit).
[46] *Bank Melli Iran* v. *Barclays D.C.O.*, *ibid.* and the Canadian case *Michael Doyle & Associates Ltd.* v. *Bank of Montreal* [1982] 6 W.W.R.24 (bank unconditionally accepted draft drawn on it although the documents were defective; bank could not recover from beneficiary). See further Gerald T. McLaughlin, "Letters of Credit: Basic Principles and Current Controversies" in 17 *Australian Business Law Review* (1989) 302, 305.
[47] [1951] 2 Lloyd's Rep. 367.
[48] See p. 406, *ante.*

contain all the particulars specified in the credit.[49] But beyond this the bank is not obliged to go and should not go. In particular, it need not concern itself with the legal significance and value of the documents which it is instructed to demand. Even if their legal value appears to be questionable the documents in the required form may have some commercial value for the buyer and, as Devlin J. said,[50] "it is not for the bank to reason why." An illustration is the requirement of a credit that the bill of lading shall contain a specific description of the goods; the value of such description is nugatory in view of the—usual—clause in the bill that "weight, measure, marks, numbers, quality, contents and value if mentioned in the bill of lading are to be considered unknown"; nevertheless, the bank must insist that the bill contains the specified description but, unless instructed otherwise, need not reject such bill on the ground that the "weight, etc., unknown" clause is not deleted.[51] Speaking generally, in the absence of instructions to the contrary, banks are not under a duty to concern themselves with the clauses—the "small print"—on a bill of lading but all they have to do, in the words of Salmon J.,[52] is "to satisfy themselves that the correct documents are presented to them, and that the bills of lading bear no indorsement or clausing by the shipowners or shippers which could reasonably mean that there was, or might be, some defect in the goods or their packing."[53]

Discrepancy of the documents

The law on this subject is summed up by Sir John Donaldson M.R. in the following passage,[54] where he observed that the basis was:

---

[49] The bank is entitled to demand documentary evidence that the conditions in the instructions are complied with: *Floating Dock Ltd.* v. *Hongkong and Shanghai Banking Corporation* [1986] 1 Lloyd's Rep. 65, 80. See also *Banque de l'Indochine et de Suez SA* v. *J. H. Rayner (Mincing Lane) Ltd.* [1983] Q.B. 711 (C.A.); *Astro Exito Navegacion SA* v. *Chase Manhattan Bank NA The Messiniaki Tolmi* [1988] 2 Lloyd's Rep. 217 (C.A.) (Gas free certificate not endorsed by Taiwan authorities).
[50] In *Midland Bank Ltd.* v. *Seymour* [1955] 2 Lloyd's Rep. 147, 151. Also Donaldson J. in *Golodetz & Co. Inc.* v. *Czarnikow-Rionda Co. Inc. The Galatia.* [1979] 2 Lloyd's Rep. 450, 457; and Parker J. in *Kydon Compania Naviera SA* v. *National Westminster Bank Ltd. The Lena.* [1981] 1 Lloyd's Rep. 68, 75.
[51] See *ibid.*
[52] In *British Imex Industries Ltd.* v. *Midland Bank Ltd.* [1958] 1 Q.B. 542, 552.
[53] Sometimes the credit instructions incorporate unusual requirements. Thus, in *Astro Exito Navegacion SA.* v. *Southland Enterprise Co. Ltd.* (*No.* 2) [1982] 2 Q.B. 1248, which concerned the sale of a vessel intended to be broken up, the instructions required a certificate signed on behalf of the buyers that the vessel had arrived safely at its destination. Also *Gill & Guffus SA* v. *Berger & Co. Inc.* (*No.* 2) [1984] A.C. 382, where the shipping documents to be tendered under a c.i.f. contract were to include a certificate of quality of the goods on discharge; these instructions were obviously nonsense (see p. 40, *ante*). If the credit instructions prohibit transhipment and the UCP apply, art. 29 has to be considered; see pp. 48–49, *ante*.
[54] *Banque de l'Indochine et de Suez SA* v. *J. H. Rayner (Mincing Lane) Ltd.* [1983] Q.B. 711, 729–730. See also *Shamsher Jute Ltd.* v. *Sethia (London) Ltd.* [1987] 1 Lloyd's Rep. 388. Further, Clive M. Schmitthoff, "Discrepancy of Documents in Letter of Credit Transactions" [1987] J.B.L. 94, *Essays*, 431.

... that the banker is not concerned with why the buyer has called for particular documents,[55] that there is no room for documents which are almost the same, or which will do just as well, as those specified,[56] that whilst the bank is entitled to put a reasonable construction upon any ambiguity in its mandate, if the mandate is clear there must be strict compliance with that mandate,[57] that documents have to be taken up or rejected promptly and without opportunity for prolonged inquiry,[58] and that a tender of documents which properly read and understood calls for further inquiry or is such as to invite litigation is a bad tender.[59]

Two situations have thus to be distinguished: there may be an ambiguity in the credit instructions (mandate), or there may be an ambiguity with respect to the tendered documents.

If the credit instructions are ambiguous,[60] the best course for the bank is to ask for clarification but if this is not possible, the bank is protected if it has acted reasonably. Lord Diplock said[61]:

> ... where the banker's instructions from his customer are ambiguous or unclear he commits no breach of his contract with the buyer if he has construed them in a reasonable sense, even though upon the closer consideration which can be given to questions of construction in an action in a court of law, it is possible to say that some other meaning is to be preferred.

If the tendered documents are ambiguous, the tender is, in principle, a bad tender. But the bank, when examining the tendered documents, should not insist on the rigid and meticulous fulfilment of the precise wording in all cases. If, "properly read and understood," the words in the instructions and in the tendered documents have the same meaning, if they correspond though not being identical, the bank should not reject the documents. It was said in an Opinion of the Banking Commission of the ICC that "banks could not act like robots, but had to check each case individually and use their judgment".[62] But the margin allowed to the bank in interpreting the documents is very narrow and the bank will be at risk if it does not insist on strict compliance. In practice, the bank may in exceptional cases be prepared to accept an ambiguous document-at its risk-under reserve[63] or against indemnity.[64]

If the bank decides to reject the documents, it must specify the discrepancies in the notice of rejection. The reason for this rule is that the beneficiary shall have an opportunity of curing the defect if he can do so

---

[55] *Commercial Banking Co. of Sydney Ltd.* v. *Jalsard Pty. Ltd.* [1973] A.C. 279.
[56] *Equitable Trust of New York* v. *Dawson Partners Ltd.* (1926) 27 Ll.L. Rep. 49.
[57] *Jalsard's* case, *supra*.
[58] *Hansson* v. *Hamel and Horley Ltd.* [1922] 2 A.C. 36.
[59] *M. Golodetz & Co. Inc.* v. *Czarnikow-Rionda Co. Inc. The Galatia* [1980] 1 W.L.R. 495.
[60] Which would contravene art. 5 of the UCP. It is thought that any discrepancy between the underlying contract and the tendered documents should be disregarded by the banks because, in principle (and subject to the fraud exception) the banks are not concerned with the underlying contract; see *Siporex Trade SA* v. *Banque Indosuez* [1988] 2 Lloyd's Rep. 147, 161 (a performance bond case).
[61] In *Jalsard's* case, *supra*.
[62] Opinions (1980–1981) of the ICC Banking Commission (ICC Publications No. 399), 35.
[63] See p. 438, *post*.
[64] See p. 437, *post*.

before the expiry of the credit. If the documents are rejected by the issuing bank, it must notify the advising bank at once by telecommunication or, if this is not possible, by another expeditious means and the documents must be placed at its disposal.[65]

The issuing bank and, it is thought, also the advising or confirming bank, have a "reasonable time" to examine the documents for discrepancies.[66] The length of the reasonable time depends in each case on the circumstances, such as the complexity of the tendered documents, their language, the need for urgency in view of the early arrival of the vessel carrying the goods, and possible objections to payment by the buyer on the ground of a suspected or actual fraud by the seller. In United Kingdom banking practice five to six banking working days would be considered as reasonable and in exceptional cases eight banking days would satisfy this requirement. In normal cases United Kingdom banks keep well within these limits and usually aim at accepting or rejecting the documents within three days. In some countries, notably in the LDCs, banks require a longer time to examine the documents.[67]

Provisions relating to the documents in the UCP

When a question of sufficiency of documents under a letter of credit issued under the UCP arises and this question cannot be resolved by reference to the instructions to the bank, it is necessary to turn to the UCP which define in considerable detail the documents normally acceptable to the bank.

The UCP distinguish between two situations: if the credit instructions do not call for a marine bill of lading, the documents to be tendered are specified by Article 25; but if they call for a marine bill of lading, the required documents are specified by Article 26. The reasons for this distinction are the continuing revolution in transport technology, involving the geographical extension of containerisation and combined transport, and the communications revolution which aims at replacing paper as means of transmitting information data relating to a trading transaction by methods of automated or electronic data processing.[68]

---

[65] UCP, art. 16(d). The same duty falls on the issuing bank if the beneficiary has presented the documents directly to it. The issuing must then notify the beneficiary.

[66] The UCP, art. 16(c) stipulate the reasonable time requirement only for the issuing bank but, as observed in the text, it obviously likewise applies to the advising or confirming bank.

[67] On reasonable time for the examination of documents see E. P. Ellinger in [1985] J.B.L. 406. On the liability of the bank for delaying payment of the credit beyond a reasonable time without excuse, see p. 421, *post*.

[68] Unless otherwise stipulated in the credit, banks will accept as originals documents produced by a reprographic system, by an automated or computerised system, or carbon copies, if these documents are marked as originals and, if necessary, appear to have been authenticated (UCP, Art. 22(c)).

Consequently, in simple trading transactions, in which the buyer (consignee) intends to take delivery of the goods himself, less formal transport documents than quasi-negotiable bills of lading are sufficient. Examples of such documents of minor legal status are combined transport documents,[69] waybills or data freight receipts,[70] FIATA bills of lading,[71] or even post receipts. According to Article 25 the banks are authorised to accept such a transport document, if it satisfies the requirements of this article. But they must insist on a proper marine bill of lading if the instructions require so; this is provided in Article 26. The following is the wording of these two articles:

Article 25

Unless a credit calling for a transport document stipulates as such document a marine bill of lading (ocean bill of lading or a bill of lading covering carriage by sea), or a post receipt or certificate of posting:

(a) banks will, unless otherwise stipulated in the credit, accept a transport document which:
    (i) appears on its face to have been issued by a named carrier, or his agent, and
    (ii) indicates dispatch or taking in charge of the goods, or loading on board, as the case may be, and
    (iii) consists of the full set of originals issued to the consignor if issued in more than one original, and
    (iv) meets all other stipulations of the credit.

(b) Subject to the above, and unless otherwise stipulated in the credit, banks will not reject a transport document which:
    (i) bears a title such as "Combined transport bill of lading," "Combined transport document," "Combined transport bill of lading or port-to-port bill of lading," or a title or a combination of titles of similar intent and effect, and/or
    (ii) indicates some or all of the conditions of carriage by reference to a source or document other than the transport document itself (short form/blank back transport document), and/or
    (iii) indicates a place of taking in charge different from the port of loading and/or a place of final destination different from the port of discharge, and/or
    (iv) relates to cargoes such as those in containers or on pallets, and the like, and/or
    (v) contains the indication "intended," or similar qualification, in relation to the vessel or other means of transport, and/or the port of loading and/or the port of discharge.

(c) Unless otherwise stipulated in the credit in the case of carriage by sea or by more than one mode of transport but including carriage by sea, banks will reject a transport document which:
    (i) indicates that it is subject to a charterparty, and/or
    (ii) indicates that the carrying vessel is propelled by sail only.

(d) Unless otherwise stipulated in the credit, banks will reject a transport document issued by a freight forwarder unless it is the FIATA Combined Transport Bill of Lading approved by the International Chamber of Commerce or otherwise indicates that it is issued by a freight forwarder acting as a carrier or agent of a named carrier.

---

[69] See p. 615, *post.*
[70] See p. 578, *post.*
[71] See pp. 579–580, *post.*

Article 26

If a credit calling for a transport document stipulates as such document a marine bill of lading:

  (a) banks will, unless otherwise stipulated in the credit, accept a document which:
  (i) appears on its face to have been issued by a named carrier, or his agent, and
  (ii) indicates that the goods have been loaded on board or shipped on a named vessel, and
  (iii) consists of the full set of originals issued to the consignor if issued in more than one original, and
  (iv) meets all other stipulations of the credit.
  (b) Subject to the above, and unless otherwise stipulated in the credit, banks will not reject a document which:
  (i) bears a title such as "Combined transport bill of lading," "Combined transport document," "Combined transport bill of lading or port-to-port bill of lading," or a title or a combination of titles of similar intent and effect, and/or
  (ii) indicates some or all of the conditions of carriage by reference to a source or document other than the transport document itself (short form/blank back transport document), and/or
  (iii) indicates a place of taking in charge different from the port of loading, and/or a place of final destination different from the port of discharge, and/or
  (iv) relates to cargoes such as those in Containers or on pallets, and the like.
  (c) Unless otherwise stipulated in the credit, banks will reject a document which:
  (i) indicates that it is subject to a charterparty, and/or
  (ii) indicates that the carrying vessel is propelled by sail only, and/or
  (iii) contains the indication "intended," or similar qualification in relation to the vessel and/or the port of loading—unless such document bears an on board notation in accordance with Article 27(b) and also indicates the actual port of loading, and/or
  the port of discharge—unless the place of final destination indicated on the document is other than the port of discharge, and/or
  (iv) is issued by a freight forwarder, unless it indicates that it is issued by such freight forwarder acting as a carrier, or as the agent of a named carrier.

Articles 25 and 26 contain only the basic requirements of the documents to be tendered. For more specific details the other Articles of the UCP should be consulted.

Several documents to be read together

The bank is usually instructed to make finance available on tender of several documents in a set, normally the transport document, *e.g.* a bill of lading, the invoice and insurance policy or certificate. In that case, in the absence of instructions to the contrary, it is sufficient if all the documents in the set, taken together, contain the particulars required by the bank's mandate and it is not necessary that every document in the set should contain them. The goods must be fully described in the invoice, in accordance with the credit instructions, but in the other documents they may be described in general terms. This rule is now contained in Article 41(c) of the UCP[71a] which mitigates, to some extent, the effect of the doctrine of strict compliance.

[71a] This rule, in the version adopted by the 1951 edition, was applied in *Soproma S.p.A.* v. *Marine & Animal By-Products Corporation* [1966] 1 Lloyd's Rep. 367; see p. 407, *ante.*

The rule in Article 41(c) is founded on the English case of *Midland Bank Ltd.* v. *Seymour.*[72] In this case a merchant in England bought a quantity of ducks' feathers from sellers in Hong Kong c. and f. Hamburg; the instructions to the bank were that the documents had to evidence "shipment from Hong Kong to Hamburg of the undermentioned goods," and then, under "Description, Quantity and Price" it was stated "Hong Kong duck feathers—85 per cent. clean; 12 bales each weighing about 190 lb.; 5s. per lb." The bill of lading described the goods merely as "12 bales; Hong Kong duck feathers" but all the documents, namely the bills of lading, invoices, weight account and certificate of origin, when read together, contained a complete description of the goods. The seller shipped worthless goods and the buyer claimed that the bank was not entitled to debit him with the credit since the bill of lading did not contain a full description of the goods. Devlin J. rejected this contention and held that the bank had complied with its mandate.

Linkage of documents

While, as stated in the preceding section, some latitude is allowed in the description of the goods in the documents other than the invoice, all documents tendered to the bank must clearly and unequivocally relate to the same goods. This question of *identification* of the goods is different from that of their *description* in the documents. If the documents are not linked by an unambiguous reference to *the same goods*, the tender is bad. But it is not necessary that the *documents themselves* be linked by mutual references. In one case[73] concerning the sale of sugar the credit instructions required certificates of origin, EUR 1 certificates, and a full set of clean on board bills of lading evidencing shipment from an EC port to Djibouti in transit to Yemen. The bills of lading showed that shipment was made in the vessel *Markhor*. One of the certificates of origin referred to the goods as shipped in "m.v. *Markhor or* substitute" and the other to "*transport mixed à destination Djibouti Port in Transit Yemen.*" The Court of Appeal held that, although the requirements relating to description provided in what is now Article 41(c) of the 1983 UCP were satisfied, the linkage between the bills of lading and the certificate of origin was missing. "Clearly this [m.v. *Markhor* or substitute] *could* be a different vessel and accordingly refer to a different parcel of sugar."[74] Although the

---

[72] [1955] 2 Lloyd's Rep. 147; see also *Panchaud Frères S.A.* v. *Etablissements General Grain Co.* [1970] 1 Lloyd's Rep. 53 (C.A.), p. 41, *ante*.
[73] *Banque de l'Indochine et de Suez SA* v. *J. H. Rayner (Mincing Lane) Ltd.* [1983] Q.B. 711; another issue which arose in this case is treated on p. 438, *post*. The ruling of the court on the linkage of documents is in harmony with UCP, art. 23.
[74] *Per* Sir John Donaldson M.R., *ibid.* 732.

decision of the Court of Appeal was unanimous, it is respectfully thought that on this issue[75] the requirement of linkage was applied by the court too strictly.

Instructions communicated by teletransmission

The provisions of the UCP which deal with credit instructions communicated by teletransmission are contained in Article 12. The essence of these provisions is, as already observed,[76] that the telecommunication should clearly indicate whether it contains the operative instructions or whether the operative instructions will be contained in a subsequent confirming letter. This is of great importance if the two communications do not agree. Article 12 is worded as follows:

Article 12

(a) When an issuing bank instructs a bank (advising bank) by any teletransmission to advise a credit or an amendment to a credit, and intends the mail confirmation to be the operative credit instrument, or the operative amendment, the teletransmission must state "full details to follow" (or words of similar effect), or that the mail confirmation will be the operative credit instrument or the operative amendment. The issuing bank must forward the operative credit instrument or the operative amendment to such advising bank without delay.

(b) The teletransmission will be deemed to be the operative credit instrument or the operative amendment, and no mail confirmation should be sent, unless the teletransmission states "full details to follow" (or words of similar effect), or states that the mail confirmation is to be the operative credit instrument or the operative amendment.

(c) teletransmission intended by the issuing bank to be the operative credit instrument should clearly indicate that the credit is issued subject to Uniform Customs and Practice for Documentary Credits, 1983 revision, ICC Publication no. 400.

(d) If a bank uses the services of another bank or banks (the advising bank) to have the credit advised to the beneficiary, it must also use the services of the same bank(s) for advising any amendments.

(e) Banks shall be responsible for any consequences arising from their failure to follow the procedure set out in the preceding paragraphs.

Time of opening of credit

Often the contract of sale will make express provision as regards the date at which the credit has to be opened. Sometimes it is stated that the credit shall be opened by a certain date, sometimes it is provided that it

---

[75] There were other discrepancies on the documents and, having regard to them, the decision of the court was clearly correct.

[76] See pp. 93–94, *ante*.

shall be opened "immediately" which means that the credit has to be opened at once within such time as is required for a person of reasonable diligence to establish the credit,[77] or sometimes the opening of the credit is made dependent on an act by the seller relating to the delivery of the goods, *e.g.* the sending of a provisional invoice[78] or of an advice that the goods are, or will soon be, ready for shipment;[79] the opening of the credit may also be made dependent on the seller providing a performance guarantee.[79a] The credit is regarded as "opened" when the advice or the confirmation, as the case may be, is communicated to the beneficiary (the seller).[80]

Where the contract does not provide when the credit shall be opened, the parties are not normally entitled to assume that the existence of the contract of sale depends on the opening of the credit by the buyer. Although the parties are at liberty to agree that the contract shall be "subject to the opening of a credit" in which case the opening of the credit is a condition precedent to the *formation* of the contract and, in the words of Denning L.J., "if no credit is provided, there is no contract between the parties,"[81] such interpretation of the buyer's promise is only possible where the parties have expressly or impliedly agreed that this promise shall be subject to that condition. In the normal cases in which the contract is unqualified, the stipulation to open a letter of credit is only a condition precedent to the *performance* of the contract; it is the mechanism agreed upon for the payment of the price, the failure of the buyer to open the credit within the stipulated time may be treated by the seller as a breach of a condition of the contract and as repudiation of it.[82]

Where the contract of sale is unconditional but does not provide a date on which the credit shall be opened, the credit has to be opened within "a

---

[77] *Garcia* v. *Page & Co.* (1936) 55 Ll.L.R. 391. The seller may waive the rights arising from the delay in the opening of the credit expressly or impliedly: *Baltimex, etc.* v. *Metallo Chemical Refinery Co. Ltd.* [1956] 1 Lloyd's Rep. 450.

[78] *Knotz* v. *Fairclough, Dodd & Jones Ltd.* [1952] 1 Lloyd's Rep. 226.

[79] *Plasticmoda S.p.A.* v. *Davidsons (Manchester)* [1952] 1 Lloyd's Rep. 527. See also *Etablissements Chainbaux S.A.R.L.* v. *Harbormaster Ltd.* [1955] 1 Lloyd's Rep. 303.

[79a] *Cf. State Trading Corporation of India Ltd.* v. *M. Golodeetz Ltd. The Sara D* [1989] 2 Lloyd's Rep. 277: see p. 158, *ante*, and n. 80, *post*.

[80] *Bunge Corporation* v. *Vegetable Vitamin Foods (Pte) Ltd.* [1985] 1 Lloyd's Rep. 613, with reference to *Brinkibon Ltd.* v. *Stahag Stahl und Stahlwarenhandels GmbH* [1983] 2 A.C. 34, p. 23, *ante*. *State Trading Corporation of India* v. *M. Golodetz Ltd. The Sara D* [1988] 2 Lloyd's Rep. 182 (where Evans J. held that the "opening" of a bank guarantee required the person obliged to procure it to take "the appropriate steps" with the bank) rests on the facts of this case. Evans J. was overruled by the CA on other grounds [1989] 2 Lloyd's Rep. 277; see p. 158, *ante*. On the moment when an irrevocable or a confirmed credit becomes binding on the bank, see n. 423, *post*.

[81] *Trans Trust S.P.R.L.* v. *Danubian Trading Co. Ltd.* [1952] 2 Q.B. 297, 304; see also *United Dominions Trust (Commercial) Ltd.* v. *Eagle Aircraft Services Ltd.* [1968] 1 W.L.R. 74, 80, 82; *Gyllenhammar & Partners International Ltd.* v. *Sour Brodogradevna Industria,* [1989] 2 Lloyd's Rep. 403 ("subject to" obtaining a bank guarantee).

[82] *Nichimen Corporation* v. *Gatoil Overseas Inc.* [1987] 2 Lloyd's Rep. 46. (This repudiation, like every repudiation (see p. 264, *ante*), has, of course, to be accepted by the innocent party.

reasonable time."[83] This means a reasonable time calculated back from the first date of the shipment, not calculated forward from the date of the conclusion of the contract.[84] Taking the first date of shipment as the starting point, the buyer has, it is thought, to open the credit a sufficient time in advance of that event to enable the seller to know before he sends the goods to the docks that his payment will be secured by the credit for which it is stipulated. Where a certain period for shipment is stipulated in the contract, *e.g.* shipment in February, March or April, in the absence of a stipulation to the contrary, the buyer has to open the credit not when the seller is ready to ship but he has to give the seller the benefit of the whole shipment period; as Somervell L.J. observed in one case[85]:

> When a seller is given a right to ship over a period and there is machinery for payment, that machinery must be available over the whole of that period. If the buyer is anxious, as he might be if the period of shipment is a long one, not to have to put the credit machinery in motion until shortly before the seller is likely to want to ship, then he must insert some provision in the contract by which the credit shall be provided, *e.g.* fourteen days after a cable received from the seller.

These rules apply equally to c.i.f. contracts[86] and f.o.b. contracts in which the seller has to make arrangements for freight and marine insurance for the account of the buyer,[87] and there is at least a prima facie rule that they likewise apply to f.o.b. contracts of the strict type[88] although in that case the shipping period is arranged for the benefit of the buyer and not the seller, because only in that way, in the words of Diplock J.,[89] can one get "certainty into what is a very common commercial contract."

The expiry date of the credit

The letter of credit invariably stipulates a date when it will expire and after which the advising bank will refuse to accept the documents presented by the seller. Article 46(a) of the UCP provides:

---

[83] This is an implied term of the contract: *Diamond Cutting Works Federation* v. *Triefus & Co. Ltd.* [1956] 1 Lloyd's Rep. 216, 225.

[84] *Sinason-Teicher Inter-American Grain Corporation* v. *Oilcakes and Oilseeds Trading Co. Ltd.* [1954] 1 W.L.R. 935.

[85] *Pavia & Co. S.p.A.* v. *Thurmann-Nielsen* [1952] 2 Q.B. 84, 88; see also *Tsakiroglou & Co. Ltd.* v. *Transgrains S.A.* [1958] 1 Lloyd's Rep. 562 (shipping period and nomination of port of destination by buyers); *Margaronis Navigation Agency Ltd.* v. *H. W. Peabody & Co. of London Ltd.* [1964] 1 Lloyd's Rep. 173 (laydays under charterparty).

[86] *Pavia & Co. S.p.A.* v. *Thurmann-Nielsen* [1952] 2 Q.B. 84; *Sinason-Teicher Inter-American Grain Corporation* v. *Oilcakes and Oilseeds Trading Co. Ltd.* [1954] 1 W.L.R. 935.

[87] See p. 20, *ante; N.V. Handel My. J. Smits Import-Export* v. *English Exporters (London) Ltd.* [1957] 1 Lloyd's Rep. 517, 519.

[88] See p. 20, *ante.* Particularly when they are string contracts in which the credit of the ultimate buyer is of overriding character: *Ian Stach Ltd.* v. *Baker Bosley Ltd.* [1958] 2 Q.B. 130, 143.

[89] *Ibid.* at p. 144.

All credits must stipulate an expiry date for presentation of documents for payment, acceptance or negotiation.

The UCP further contains detailed provisions for the ascertainment of the expiry date and its extension in case of the expiry date falling on a day when the bank is closed[90] or in case of interruption of the bank's business owing to events beyond its control.[91]

The expiry date of the credit should not be confused with the shipment date. The shipment date is the—earlier—date shown in the bill of lading as the date when the goods were loaded. The credit sometimes stipulates, in addition to its expiry date, that the bills presented to the bank shall indicate a certain shipment date.[92] If the bills of lading presented by the seller to the bank show a later date or if the bills are stale,[93] the bank will refuse to accept the documents even if presented before the expiry date.

Exceptionally, in long-term transactions the credit may have to be kept open for a considerable time. Thus, in one case[94] the parties agreed that upon expiration of the period of three years the credit was considered automatically invalidated but in the event of the matter being submitted to arbitration it should be deemed automatically extended without amendment for one year from any expiry date. A letter of credit may also contain a provision under which it is automatically extended for another fixed period from the expiry date unless the bank notifies the beneficiary, *e.g.* 30 days prior to the expiry date by registered mail, that it has elected not to renew the credit. Such a provision is known as the *evergreen clause*. It has been developed by American Banks and there is no reason why it should not be used by banks in other countries in appropriate cases. The wording of the evergreen clause varies. An evergeen credit should not be confused with a revolving credit.[95]

The law applicable to the credit

It will rarely be necessary to ascertain the law governing a letter of credit because, as has been seen,[96] banks in most countries operate credits under the UCP and that uniformity excludes the possibility of a conflict of laws with respect to most legal problems.

However, if it is necessary to determine the law governing a letter of credit and the credit itself does not contain a choice of law clause, in

---

[90] UCP, art. 48(a).
[91] UCP, art. 19.
[92] The UCP contain detailed provisions on the ascertainment of the loading date in articles 47 to 50.
[93] See p. 582, *post.*
[94] *Offshore International S.A.* v. *Banco Central S.A.* [1976] 2 Lloyd's Rep. 402.
[95] See p. 430, *post.*
[96] See p. 402, *ante.*

accordance with general principle[97] it is incumbent on the lawyer to ascertain the system of law with which the credit has its closest and most real connection.[98] This question is, of course, entirely separate from the ascertainment of the law governing the relationship between the seller and the buyer, *i.e.* the underlying contract of sale. When attempting to ascertain the law governing the credit, it should be borne in mind that the credit involves several contractual relationships.

1. As between the buyer and the issuing bank, the law of the closest connection is likely to be that of the country in which the bank carries on business and has issued the credit. That relationship is founded on the customer-banker relationship and in such a contract there is always a—rebuttable—presumption in favour of the law of the bank.

2. Where the seller, *i.e.* the beneficiary under the credit, is involved, the law of the closest connection is likely to be that of the advising bank. That is true not only as between the seller and the advising bank but also as between him and the issuing bank. In one case[99] an irrevocable credit was opened by a Spanish bank in favour of an oil rig company incorporated in Panama but operating from Houston, Texas. The credit was advised by a New York bank but was not confirmed by it. The beneficiary sued the issuing bank in the English courts and the preliminary question arose whether the contract between the beneficiary and the issuing bank was governed by Spanish law (the law of the issuing bank) or by New York law (the law of the advising bank). Ackner J. decided in favour of New York law on the ground that this was the law with which the transaction had its closest and most real connection. The following observations of the learned judge are incontrovertible[1]:

The advising bank would have constantly to be seeking to apply a whole variety of foreign laws [if a different view were adopted].

3. The relationship between the issuing and advising bank causes the greatest difficulty. In these inter-bank transactions general conditions of business or a course of dealing may admit some conclusions as to the law of the closest connection. Where these indications are absent, it is thought, that the weight of facts will often point to the law of the advising bank because, as that law is likely to apply to the relationship with the seller-beneficiary, the application of different laws to two facets of the same commercial transaction would be undesirable.

---

[97] See p. 214, *ante.*
[98] *Offshore International S.A.* v. *Banco Central S.A.* [1976] 2 Lloyd's Rep. 402, 403.
[99] See n. 98.
[1] The observations of Ackner J. were approved by the Court of Appeal in *Power Curber International Ltd.* v. *National Bank of Kuwait SK* [1981] 2 Lloyd's Rep. 394, 399 and 400. See also *Toprak Mahsulleri Ofisi* v. *Finagrain Compagnie Commercial Agricole et Financière SA* [1979] 2 Lloyd's Rep. 98, 114; *Intraco Ltd.* v. *Notis Shipping Corporation. The Bhoja Trader* [1981] 2 Lloyd's Rep. 256, 258; *Attock Cement Company Ltd.* v. *Romanian Bank for Foreign Trade*, [1989] 1 Lloyd's Rep. 572.

Damages for failure to open or pay a credit

Where the buyer fails to open a credit as stipulated, the seller is entitled to claim damages for breach of that stipulation, which qualifies as a condition.[2] The amount of damages recoverable under this heading is sometimes higher than the amount which the seller can recover for breach of the buyer's obligation to accept delivery of the goods. In the latter case, if the goods have an available market, the presumption of section 50(3) of the Sale of Goods Act 1979 applies which provides that the measure of damages is prima facie the difference between the contract price and the market price at the date when the goods ought to have been accepted. In a rising market damages for non-acceptance of the goods are nominal but damages for failure to open a commercial credit are not subject to the restriction of section 50(3) and may, in appropriate cases, include the loss of profit which the seller would have made had the transaction been carried out.[3] Where the advising bank delays the payment of the credit without excuse beyond a reasonable time, although the documents were presented timely, it may be liable to the seller in damages.[4]

KINDS OF LETTERS OF CREDIT

Payment at sight, deferred payment, acceptance and negotiation credits

It is of importance to the seller to know in what manner he will obtain the moneys due to him under the credit. There exist four possibilities[5]: the credit may be available by sight payment, by deferred payment, by acceptance or by negotiation. The credit itself should state which of these four methods has been chosen by the parties and this point should be settled beforehand in the contract under which the credit is opened.

1. If the parties have arranged a *payment at sight credit*, the advising bank is instructed to pay, or arrange for payment, to the seller the moneys due on presentation of the documents. This is a case of payment against documents.

2. If the parties have arranged a *deferred payment credit*, the advising bank is authorised to pay, or make arrangements for payment, at some future date determinable in accordance with the terms of the credit.

---

[2] See p. 133, *ante.*

[3] *Trans Trust S.P.R.L.* v. *Danubian Trading Co. Ltd.* [1952] 2 Q.B. 297, 305.

[4] *Ozalid Group (Export) Ltd.* v. *African Continental Bank Ltd.* [1979] 2 Lloyd's Rep. 231. On the length of a "reasonable time" for the examination of the documents, see p. 412, *ante.*

[5] UCP, art. 10(a).

The deferred payment credit may, *e.g.* provide for payment 180 days from the date of the bill of lading. In this case an acceptance credit[6] providing for a time bill would be inappropriate because a bill of exchange cannot be made payable at a time which can only be determined by reference to the uncertain date of the issue of the bill of lading.[7]

If the seller requires cash before the deferred payment credit matures, he can only obtain it by negotiating the letter of credit.[8] The issuing bank sometimes provides in the credit that such negotiation shall be restricted to a specified bank, "perhaps because this [is] a bank with which [it has] a commercial relationship."[9] The negotiation of the deferred payment credit is normally done at a discount, which reduces the amount of the credit due to the seller.

3. If the credit is an *acceptance credit*, the seller draws the bill of exchange on the advising bank in the specified manner. The bill will normally be a time draft. By accepting the bill, the bank signifies its commitment to pay the face value on maturity to the party presenting it. The bill accepted by the advising bank provides the seller with a considerable degree of security. If he does not want to hold the bill until it matures, he may turn it into money by negotiating it, *e.g.* by discounting it or selling it to his own bank.[10] On negotiation he is unlikely to receive the full amount of money stated in the tenor of the bill because the negotiating bank will deduct a discount or interest and commission.

Another form of acceptance credit is a credit which, according to the arrangement of the parties to the contract of sale, shall be accepted by the issuing bank or by the buyer (the applicant for the credit). Where the issuing bank issues the credit as irrevocable, it holds itself under the UCP, Article 10 (a) (iii), responsible that the bill will be accepted and paid by the buyer. Where the advising bank confirms the credit, a similar obligation is placed on it by the UCP, Article 10 (b) (iii). It follows that, even if the arrangement of the parties is that only the buyer has to accept, if the credit is made irrevocable or irrevocable and confirmed and is made subject to the UCP, the seller has a considerable degree of security.[11]

There is no recourse by a bank which has accepted a bill, against the seller. If that bank dishonours the bill by non-payment, *e.g.* because it becomes insolvent, the seller has still his claim for the purchase price against the buyer because the acceptance credit is only a conditional performance of the buyer's obligation to pay.[12]

---

[6] For acceptance credit see next section in the text.
[7] See p. 384, *ante.*
[8] *European Asian Bank AG* v. *Punjab & Sind Bank (No. 2)* [1983] 1 W.L.R. 642. See E.P. Ellinger, "Discount of Letter of Credit," [1984] J.B.L. 379. The French term for deferred credit is *crédit documentaire à paiment différé*; see Michel Vasseur in *Recueil Dalloz Sirey*, 1987, 9e cashier-chronique.
[9] *Per* Robert Goff L.J. (handing down the judgment of the C.A.), in the *European Asian Bank AG* case, *supra*, n. 8, 655.
[10] See pp. 392–393, *ante.*
[11] See *Forestal Mimosa Ltd.* v. *Oriental Credit Bank Ltd.* [1986] 1 W.L.R. 631 (C.A.).
[12] See p. 439, *post.*

4. Under the *negotiation credit* the advising bank is only authorised to negotiate[13] a bill of exchange drawn by the seller on the buyer or the issuing bank. The advising bank will indorse the bill and negotiate it, subject to deduction of discount or interest and commission. The bill may be a sight draft or a time draft, according to the terms of the credit.

The negotiation credit is subject to recourse against the seller as drawer of the bill because the bank has become an indorser of the bill of exchange, but if the negotiating bank is the confirming bank (and the tender of the documents is in order), it cannot avail itself of this facility since it is liable to the seller on the confirmation.[14]

Sometimes the bank is only authorised to make an advance on the security of the documentary bill.[15]

Revocable and irrevocable credits; confirmed and unconfirmed credits

It is of great importance to distinguish between these types of credit. The quality of the credit as "revocable" and "irrevocable" refers to the obligation of the issuing bank to the beneficiary (the seller). The quality of the credit as "confirmed" or "unconfirmed"[16] refers to the obligation of the advising bank to the beneficiary. Of course, no advising or nominated bank would ever confirm a credit unless the issuing bank has made it irrevocable. The UCP contains detailed provisions entitling the advising bank, which has taken up the documents in accordance with the instructions, to reimbursement from the issuing bank[17]; these provisions apply to revocable as well as irrevocable credits.[18]

It is controversial at which moment the irrevocable credit becomes binding on the issuing bank and the confirmed credit on the advising bank.[19] It is thought that these obligations become binding on the banks

---

[13] See p. 392, *ante*.
[14] The treatment of a time draft as sight draft does not automatically operate as confirmation and does not prevent recourse: *Maran Road* v. *Austin Taylors Co. Ltd.* [1975] 1 Lloyd's Rep. 156, 161.
[15] *Plein & Co. Ltd.* v. *Inland Revenue Commissioners* (1946) 175 L.T. 453.
[16] The UCP use the term "without engagement" for "unconfirmed" credits: art. 8.
[17] Provided the documents have been taken up before the credit was revoked.
[18] UCP, arts. 9 and 10.
[19] The difficulty is due to the fact that the bank makes the beneficiary a unilateral offer of a contract and the question arises when this offer is accepted. Some authors, like Treitel, *The Law of Contract,* (7th ed., 1987) p. 117, think that the acceptance takes place when the beneficiary has "taken steps in the performance," *i.e.* the performance of the contract of sale. This view can refer to the statement of Rowlatt J. in *Urquhart Lindsay & Co. Ltd.* v. *Eastern Bank Ltd.* [1922] 1 K.B. 318, that the beneficiary must have "acted upon" the bank's undertaking. Other authors, like Gutteridge and Megrah, *The Law of Bankers' Commercial Credits* (1984) p. 34 take the view that the question is academic; they state that the bank becomes bound to the seller the moment the credit is communicated to him but its liability is unenforceable until the seller complies with the conditions of the credit. The controversy is treated admirably by P. N. Todd, "Sellers and Documentary Credits" in [1983] J.B.L. 468.

already before the tender of the documents, namely when the beneficiary receives the communication of the bank and accepts it.[20] The relationships between the banks which undertake these obligations and the beneficiary are, as already observed, contractual.

From the point of view of the exporter, a particularly important feature of the credit is whether it is irrevocable or irrevocable and confirmed. He has to arrange in the contract of sale (or other underlying contract) the most appropriate of these two types of credit and all the other details of it, including the mode of payment.[21] Later he has to check the notification sent to him by the bank; this notification should contain the terms of the credit, as arranged in the underlying contract.

Revocable and unconfirmed credits

A credit which does not state otherwise, is revocable (and, of course, unconfirmed). This legal principle is stated in the UCP, Article 7, as follows:

> (b) All credits . . . should clearly indicate whether they are revocable or irrevocable.
> (c) in the absence of such indication the credit shall be deemed to be revocable.

The UCP further provides in Article 9(a) that a revocable credit may be amended or cancelled by the issuing bank at any moment and without prior notice to the beneficiary; the Article further provides that the issuing bank has to reimburse another bank which has already paid the credit.

In practice, however, revocable credits are not widely used[22] but irrevocable credits, which may be confirmed or unconfirmed, which will be treated in the next sections,[23] are in frequent use.

If the credit is revocable its nature is reflected in the advice sent by the advising bank to the beneficiary (the seller) which also states expressly that the credit is not confirmed. The following clause in the advice note is typical:

> We have no authority from our clients to confirm this credit. The credit is therefore subject to cancellation or modification at any time without notice.

From the exporter's point of view, an unconfirmed credit is a very unsatisfactory method of finance, but unconfirmed credits are sometimes

---

[20] This is the view which the practice takes. It is in harmony with the UCC, s. 5–106. It is founded on the ruling that the credit is regarded as "opened" when the advice is communicated to the beneficiary; see p. 417, *ante*. See also Donaldson J. in *Elder Dempster Lines Ltd.* v. *Ionic Shipping Agency Inc.* [1968] 1 Lloyd's Rep. 529, 535.

[21] Whether by sight payment, deferred payment, acceptance or negotiation; see p. 421, *ante*.

[22] The Standard Documentary Credits Forms (ICC Docs. Nos. 416 and 416A (p. 403, *ante*), do not contain Forms for revocable credits but contain Forms for irrevocable credits which may be confirmed or unconfirmed.

[23] See p. 425, *post*.

preferred to confirmed credits because they are cheaper than the latter. The precarious nature of an unconfirmed credit is well illustrated by the facts in *Cape Asbestos Co.* v. *Lloyds Bank.*[24] Importers in Warsaw bought a consignment of asbestos sheets from the plaintiffs and opened an unconfirmed credit in favour of the latter with the defendants. The defendants duly advised the plaintiffs of the credit, adding the clause "this is merely an advice of opening of the above-mentioned credit and is not a confirmation of the same." The plaintiffs shipped part of the consignment and their draft on the bank was duly accepted. The plaintiffs then shipped the remainder, but, on presenting their draft to the bank, acceptance of the draft was refused. In the meantime the importers in Warsaw had cancelled the credit, but the defendant bank had failed to notify the plaintiffs of the cancellation. It was held that the bank was entitled to refuse the acceptance of the draft for the remainder and Bailhache J. said in the course of the judgment that "an unconfirmed credit is practically worthless."

This case was based on unusual facts because normally the bank will notify the creditor of the revocation of an unconfirmed credit. The exporter who sells under such a credit should at least ask the bank to insert a *notice clause* in the advice. Under this clause the bank is obliged to inform the exporter forthwith of the cancellation of the credit.

Irrevocable and unconfirmed credits

Where this type of credit[25] is used, the issuing bank cannot revoke its undertaking to the beneficiary, but the advising bank does not enter into its own obligation to make payment under the credit. The advice of an irrevocable and unconfirmed credit would state:

> This credit is irrevocable on the part of the above-mentioned issuing bank but we are not instructed to confirm it and therefore it does not involve any undertaking on our part.

These credits are sometimes issued by leading banks, particularly American and British banks, which consider a local confirmation as unnecessary.

While unconfirmed credits are somewhat cheaper than confirmed credits, they have the disadvantage that they do not localise the perfor-

---

[24] [1921] W.N. 274; see also Lord Denning M.R. in *W. J. Alan & Co. Ltd.* v. *El Nasr Export and Import Co.* [1972] 2 Q.B. 189, 207.
[25] For examples, see *Cie Continentale d'Importation* v. *Ispahani Ltd.* [1960] 1 Lloyd's Rep. 293, 301; *Maran Road* v. *Austin Taylor & Co. Ltd.* [1975] 1 Lloyd's Rep. 156; *Discount Records Ltd.* v. *Barclays Bank Ltd.* [1975] 1 W.L.R. 315; *Trendtex Trading Corporation* v. *Central Bank of Nigeria* [1977] 2 W.L.R. 356; *E. D. & F. Man Ltd.* v. *Nigerian Sweets & Confectionery Co. Ltd.* [1977] 1 Lloyd's Rep. 50.

mance of the contract of sale in the seller's country; if the advising bank refuses to pay on tender of the documents, the beneficiary might be compelled to institute proceedings overseas—a situation which largely defeats the main purpose of the commercial credit.[26]

Irrevocable and confirmed credits

This is the type of letter of credit most favourable to the exporter because the advising bank stipulates here in terms that it will honour the exporter's drafts provided they are drawn and presented in conformity with the terms of credit.

In the case of a confirmed credit, the engagement of the advising bank to the beneficiary is expressly stated in the letter of advice which that bank sends him. The following clause in the advice note is typical:

> We undertake to honour such drafts on presentation provided that they are drawn and presented in conformity with the terms of this credit.

The effect of a confirmed credit has been described by Diplock J.[27] as constituting "a direct undertaking by the banker that the seller, if he presents the documents as required in the required time, will receive payment." The bank cannot withdraw from its liability to the exporter even if instructed by the buyer to cancel the credit. This is illustrated by *Hamzeh Malas & Sons* v. *British Imex Industries Ltd.*[28] where the plaintiffs, a Jordanian firm, contracted to buy from the defendants, a British firm, a quantity of reinforced steel rods, to be delivered in two instalments. Payment was to be made under two confirmed credits, one for each instalment, to be opened with the Midland Bank, London. Both credits were duly opened and confirmed by the bank to the sellers and the first was realised on shipment of the first instalment but a dispute arose with respect to the second credit. The buyers complained that the first instalment was not of contract quality and applied to the court for an injunction restraining the sellers from drawing on the second credit or recovering any money under it. Donovan J. and the Court of Appeal refused to grant the injunction, on the grounds stated by Jenkins L.J. in a lucid judgment:

> It seems to be plain enough that the opening of a confirmed letter of credit constitutes a bargain between the banker and the vendor of the goods, which imposes upon the

---

[26] Clive M. Schmitthoff, "Confirmation in Export Transactions" in [1957] J.B.L. 17.
[27] In *Ian Stach Ltd.* v. *Baker Bosley Ltd.* [1958] 2 Q.B. 130.
[28] [1958] 2 Q.B. 127; a sequel of this litigation was the case of *British Imex Industries Ltd.* v. *Midland Bank Ltd.* [1958] 1 Q.B. 542, mentioned on p. 410, *ante*. See also *Urquhart Lindsay* v. *Eastern Bank* [1922] 1 K.B. 318; further, see *Stein* v. *Hambros Bank* (1921) 9 Ll.L.R. 507; *National Bank of South Africa* v. *Banca Italiana* (1922) 10 Ll.L.R. 531; *Discount Records Ltd.* v. *Barclays Bank Ltd.*, [1975] 1 W.L.R. 315.

banker an absolute obligation to pay, irrespective of any dispute there may be between the parties as to whether the goods are up to the contract or not. An elaborate commercial system has been built up on the footing that bankers' commercial credits are of that character, and, in my judgment, it would be wrong for this court in the present case to interfere with that established practice.

There is this to be remembered, too. A vendor of goods selling against a confirmed letter of credit is selling under the assurance that nothing will prevent him from receiving the price. That is no mean advantage when goods manufactured in one country are being sold in another.

Where the credit does not conform to the terms of the contract of sale, two courses are open to the seller. He may reject the non-conforming credit; thus, where under the terms of the contract of sale he is entitled to a confirmed credit but is only advised of the opening of an unconfirmed credit, he need not ship the goods.[29] Or he may accept the non-conforming credit, and if he does so without objection, he is treated as having waived irrevocably his right to a conforming credit.[30]

Recourse and reimbursement of confirming bank

Under a confirmed credit the paying bank does not have a right of recourse against the seller, even if the credit is only a negotiation credit,[31] except if the bank has paid "under reserve,"[32] or has obtained an indemnity from the seller,[33] or the seller has acted fraudulently.[34]

The confirming bank, which has paid the seller in accordance with the terms of the credit, is entitled to reimbursement from the issuing bank and/or the applicant for the credit (the buyer).[35]

Where the confirming bank pays the beneficiary under reserve but the issuing bank retains the documents beyond a reasonable time without electing whether to accept or reject them and in the end accepts them, the issuing bank is regarded to have waived the right to rely on

---

[29] *Panoutsos* v. *Raymond Hadley Corp.* [1917] 2 K.B. 473.

[30] *W. J. Alan & Co. Ltd.* v. *El Nasr Export and Import Co.* [1972] 2 Q.B. 189, 212 (*per* Lord Denning) (C.A.).

[31] See p. 423, *ante,* and *Maran Road* v. *Austin Taylor & Co.* [1975] 1 Lloyd's Rep. 156, 161. On the liability of the confirming bank under an acceptance credit, see *Forestal Mimosa Ltd.* v. *Oriental Credit Ltd., Financial Times,* February 19, 1986.

[32] See p. 438, *post.*

[33] p. 437, *post.*

[34] See p. 441, *post.* It is thought that, apart from the case of fraud or dishonesty on the part of the seller, a claim for restitution by the confirming bank against the seller is admissible if such claim is admitted under the general principles of the law; *e.g.* in the case of payment by the confirming bank under a common mistake; but this view is controversial, see Gutteridge-Megrah, 1984, pp. 86–87.

[35] See UCP, Art. 16(a).

discrepancies and has to reimburse the confirming bank for the financing charges (including interest) which arise from the late acceptance.[36]

The confirmation as localisation device

Confirmed credits are very popular in modern export trade because they act as a localisation device, localising the all-important payment incident of an export transaction in the seller's country. If he has obtained the confirmation of a bank of good standing in his own country, he can be sure of obtaining payment, acceptance of his draft or its negotiation, as arranged in the contract with his buyer, if he tenders the correct documents in good time. The export transaction is thus assimilated to a home transaction, as far as the payment incident is concerned, and the credit risk of the export transaction is practically eliminated. Confirmed letters of credit are in many trades the normal terms of settlement. The banks have made an invaluable contribution to the smooth discharge of export transactions by making available this type of commercial credit.[37]

Variants of confirmation

The practice has developed two variants of the advising bank's confirmation: the "seller's confirmation" and the "soft confirmation."

The *seller's confirmation* is an arrangement under which the bank charges for the confirmation have to be borne by the beneficiary (the seller), and not by the applicant for the credit (the buyer), as is normally the case.[38] This arrangement is made where the seller is anxious to minimise the risk of the sales transaction by obtaining an absolute undertaking of a respectable bank at his place of business, but the buyer is unwilling to bear the costs for providing the seller with this additional security.

---

[36] *Co-operative Centrale Raiffeisen-Boereleenbank BA (Rabobank Nederland)* v. *Sumitomo Bank Ltd. The Royan* [1987] 1 Lloyd's Rep. 345; see Art. 16 of the 1983 UCP. In the Canadian case of *Michael Doyle & Associates Ltd.* v. *Bank of Montreal* [1982] 6 W.W.R. 24, (which concerned an irrevocable but unconfirmed credit) the advising bank accepted a draft drawn on it by the sellers although the documents showed a discrepancy. The issuing bank rejected the documents. The Court of Appeal of British Columbia held that the advising bank could not take recourse on the sellers.

[37] Where the credit had to be confirmed by a first-class West European or U.S. bank, the fact that the opening of the credit was illegal under Turkish law (the law of the buyers) was immaterial because the sellers were not concerned with the machinery of providing the credit: *Toprak Mahsulleri Ofisi* v. *Finagrain Cie. Commerciale* [1979] 2 Lloyd's Rep. 98, 114.

[38] *British Imex Industries Ltd.* v. *Midland Bank Ltd.* [1958] 1 Q.B. 542, 544, concerned a seller's confirmation. In this case the seller agreed to pay the bank a confirming commission.

The *soft confirmation* is a conditional—and not a definite and absolute —undertaking of the advising bank. This practice has arisen where imports into a developing country are financed by loans granted by international institutions, such as the International Bank for Reconstruction and Development (the World Bank) or the International Development Association (IDA), or by a regional or national foreign aid institution. The advising bank in the exporter's country may find it difficult to obtain reimbursement from the issuing bank, if, *e.g.* the government of the importing country prohibits the reimbursement or exchange control regulations delay it. The advising bank, if apprehending that such a complication may arise, may make its confirmation conditional on being reimbursed by the financing institution. The advising bank would then qualify its confirmation *e.g.*, by stating:

> We clause our confirmation to the extent that we shall only be able to honour it after we have obtained reimbursement from. . . .

The ICC Banking Commission has ruled[39] that such qualified undertaking by the advising bank is admissible, providing that the conditions under which payment will be made are clearly indicated to the beneficiary. However, as far as the UCP are concerned, such credit does not rank as an "irrevocable credit" nor does the advising bank's undertaking constitute a "confirmation" within the meaning of the UCP.

Standby letters of credit

A standby letter of credit is an undertaking by a bank to make payment to a third party (the beneficiary) or to accept bills of exchange drawn by him, provided that he timely complies with the stipulations of the credit which, in international trade transactions, invariably include the tender of one or several documents. The bank may also be instructed to authorise another bank to pay, accept or negotiate bills of exchange against the stipulated documents. As observed earlier,[40] standby letters of credit are covered by the UCP, if the parties subject them to this regulation.

In international trade transactions the standby letter of credit, like the ordinary letter of credit, is activated by the tender of documents in accordance with the requirements of the credit. The difference between these two types of credit is this: the ordinary letter of credit is a payment instrument which normally[41] obliges the beneficiary to tender, together with other specified documents, the transport documents. The standby credit is intended to protect the beneficiary in case of default of the other

---

[39] Opinions (1980–1981) of the ICC Banking Commission, pp. 10–13 (Ref. 68).
[40] See p. 401, *ante*.
[41] But there may be other documents, see on packing credits, p. 431, *post*.

party to the (underlying) contract. Consequently in a standby credit the required documents need not include the transport documents but this type of credit may be activated by a document of any description, *e.g.* a demand by the beneficiary or a statement by him that the other party is in default. The standby letter of credit is thus often functionally similar in effect to a bank guarantee.[42]

The standby letter of credit originated in the United States. According to federal law and the laws of some States national banking associations are prohibited from issuing guarantees. These American banks have therefore extended the letter of credit concept to domestic banking but have varied it with respect to the documents to be tendered. In modern practice English banks have issued them not only for American beneficiaries but also in favour of enterprises in Australia, Libya, Portugal, Romania, Sweden and Switzerland.[43] But English banks, like those in other European countries,[44] prefer to issue demand guarantees[45] and ordinary letters of credit.

The principles relating to ordinary letters of credit likewise apply to standby credits, *mutatis mutandis*. In particular, the principles of the autonomy of the credit and the requirement of strict compliance also apply to this type of credit.

Revolving credits

Where the export sale is not an isolated transaction but the overseas buyer is a regular customer of the exporter, the buyer will arrange a revolving credit in favour of the latter. The buyer gives the bank standing instructions to arrange for a credit in favour of the exporter which at no time shall exceed a fixed maximum. The advantage of this arrangement is that no renewal is required and clerical labour is saved; a revolving credit is, *e.g.* a corollary to a sole distribution agreement.[46] The joint general manager of Lloyds Bank, when called in one case[47] as an expert witness to explain the meaning of this term, gave the following definition:

> A revolving credit is one for a certain sum which is automatically renewed by putting on at the bottom that which is taken off at the top. If you have a revolving credit for

---

[42] See p. 446, *post*.

[43] Rolf Eberth, "Der Standby Letter of Credit im Recht der Vereinigten Staaten von Amerika," in *Zeitschrift für Vergleichende Rechtswissenschaft,* 1980 (Vol. 80), 29, 35. A standby letter of credit was issued by a bank in *Hong Kong and Shanghai Banking Corporation* v. *Kloeckner & Co. AG,* [1989] 2 Lloyd's Rep. 323.

[44] European continental banks sometimes issue "documentary payment guarantees subject to the UCP (1983 Revision)." This practice is to be deprecated; these instruments should be entitled "standby letter of credit" instead of "guarantee" (see *Case Studies on Documentary Credits,* ICC Doc. 459, p. 16).

[45] See p. 451, *post*.

[46] See p. 259, *ante*.

[47] *Nordskog* v. *National Bank* (1922) 10 Ll.L.R. 652.

£50,000 open for three months to be operated on by drafts at 30 days' sight, as drafts are drawn they temporarily reduce the amount of the credit below the £50,000. As these drafts run off and are presented and paid they are added again to the top of the credit and restore it again to the £50,000. That is what is known technically as a revolving credit, and it is automatic in its operation and does not need renewal.

Several varieties of revolving credit are in use. The revolving credit should not be confused with the evergreen credit,[48] although both have in common that they are not limited to a single period of currency.

Packing credits; red clause credits

The packing credit, sometimes called anticipatory credit, is intended to assist the exporter in the production or procurement of the goods sold. The credit is here payable at a time prior to the shipment of the goods, and against a document other than a transport document. The bank is instructed to pay the purchase price, or part of it, on production of, *e.g.* a warehouse receipt (evidencing that the goods are in existence) or a forwarder's certificate of receipt (FCR)[49] (affirming that the goods have been received for shipment or have been shipped), or an air dispatch registered post receipt.[50]

The packing credit is a convenient method of finance for the small exporter who is not conversant with shipping practice; if he, *e.g.* sells cloth ex London store and arranges that the purchase price shall be paid under a letter of credit against delivery of a forwarder's receipt, he is not concerned with the actual shipping arrangements which will be made by the forwarder on instructions of the buyer. The buyer, on the other hand, is certain that the goods sold are no longer in the possession of the seller when receiving the purchase price. In more complicated transactions, which are nearer in nature to letters of credit proper, the bank when advising the exporter of the credit, inserts the so-called *red clause*[51] into the letter of advice and is prepared to honour the exporter's sight drafts to a certain amount against production of the stipulated documents, *e.g.* the warehouse receipts[52]; when the exporter ships the goods and delivers the transport documents to the bank, he presents a draft for the purchase price less the amount received by way of advance.

---

[48] See p. 419, *ante.*
[49] See pp. 578–579, *post.*
[50] *Diamond Cutting Works Federation* v. *Triefus & Co. Ltd.* [1956] 1 Lloyd's Rep. 216.
[51] Gutteridge and Megrah, *loc. cit.,* p. 12. This clause is called the red clause because it was originally written in red ink.
[52] In *Tukan Timber Ltd.* v. *Barclays Bank plc.* [1987] 1 Lloyd's Rep. 171 the red clause provided that no advance could be made on the credit without the countersignature of one of the directors of the buyers. In *Mitsui & Co. Ltd.* v. *Flota Mercante Granco lombiana SA* [1988] 1 W.L.R. 1145 the red clause provided that 80 per cent. of the price was payable "when the goods were available for consignment but before shipment."

In the case of a packing credit, the arrangement can be construed as an agreement that the buyer, through the bank, is to make an advance on the purchase price, the advance being payable on production of the stipulated documents, and the balance of the price being payable on delivery of the proper transport documents (and/or other specified documents).

Back-to-back and overriding credits

Back-to-back credits, also called countervailing credits, are mainly used in the *external trade* where a United Kingdom merchant buys goods in one overseas country and sells them in another, and in *string contracts*[53] where the same goods are sold or resold by several middlemen before being bought by the ultimate purchaser.

The characteristic feature of the back-to-back credit is that the confirmed credit opened by the ultimate purchaser in favour of his immediate seller is used by the latter as security for the credit which he has to open for his own supplier. If there are several middlemen, each will use the credit in his favour as security for the credit which he has to open for his predecessor in the chain of contracts until the first buyer in the chain opens a credit in favour of the original supplier. The terms of these credits are literally identical, except as far as relating to prices and invoices.

The easiest method of operating back-to-back credits is to have the various credits controlled by the same bank but they can also be operated when several banks are concerned. Back-to-back arrangements can also be operated by means of a transferable credit[54] or by combining a documentary credit with a collection arrangement.[55]

Of particular importance in these arrangements is the credit to be opened by the ultimate purchaser. That credit, known as the *overriding credit*, is, as the middlemen are usually aware, the foundation on which the whole financial structure of the arrangement rests. For this reason the courts pay special attention to the terms of that credit if issues involving the whole chain of contracts arise.[56]

---

[53] This type of trading is used particularly often in the commodity trade but is also found in other trades.
[54] See p. 433, *post*.
[55] See pp. 440–441, *post*.
[56] *Ian Stach Ltd.* v. *Baker Bosley Ltd.* [1958] 2 Q.B. 130, 138; *Baltimex etc.* v. *Metallo Chemical Refinery Co. Ltd.* [1956] 1 Lloyd's Rep. 450, 455.

Transferable credits

A more popular method of financing the supply transaction than the back-to-back credit is the practice of making a credit transferable.[57] The UCP provide in Article 54 that a transferable credit is automatically divisible, provided that partial shipments are not prohibited. To make a credit transferable, it is not necessary—though it would be desirable—for the parties to use the word "transferable" in it. They may use other phrases indicating their intention to make it transferable, *e.g.* by stating that it is "divisible" or that is is "unrestricted for negotiation.[58]

As has been observed earlier,[59] the letter of credit is not negotiable in the sense in which a bill of exchange or another negotiable instrument can be transferred to another person. The advising bank is not authorised, unless receiving instructions to the contrary, to pay the credit to *any* person satisfying the conditions of the credit; indeed, if it paid on tender of the stipulated documents by a person other than the named beneficiary (or his agent) it would contravene its mandate.

If it is intended to make the benefit of the credit available to a person other than the named beneficiary, two possibilities exist: the assignment of the benefit of the credit and the transfer of the credit as such with its attendant rights and duties but it should again be emphasised that the latter possibility only exists if the parties have made the credit transferable. These two possibilities require separate consideration.

The assignment of the benefits of the credit

A letter of credit is a thing in action.[60] Where it is an irrevocable credit or a confirmed credit, it is a conditional debt of the bank, which has undertaken an obligation to the seller, *i.e.* an obligation subject to the condition precedent that the seller tenders the stipulated documents

---

[57] See *e.g. Ian Stach Ltd.* v. *Baker Bosley Ltd.* [1958] 2 Q.B. 130; *W. J. Alan & Co. Ltd.* v. *El Nasr Export and Import Co.* [1972] 2 Q.B. 189; *Ets Soules & Cie* v. *International Trade Development Ltd.* [1979] 2 Lloyd's Rep. 122, 129; *European Asian Bank AG* v. *Punjab and Sind Bank (No. 2)* [1981] 2 Lloyd's Rep. 651, 129; [1983] 1 W.L.R. 642, 649 (C.A.); *Bank Negara Indonesia 1946* v. *Lariza (Singapore) Pte. Ltd.* [1988] A.C. 583. See also R. M. Goode, in [1981] J.B.L. 150; C. M. Schmitthoff, "The Transferable Credit" in [1988] J.B.L. 49.

[58] On the distinction between the negotiability of a transferable credit, *e.g.* to the supplier, and the negotiability of a deferred payment credit by the beneficiary (in order to obtain ready cash), see *European Asian Bank AG* v. *Punjab and Sind Bank (No. 2)* [1981] 1 W.L.R. 642, 654–655.

[59] See p. 405, *ante*.

[60] *Per* Denning L.J. in *Trans Trust S.P.R.L.* v. *Danubian Trading Co. Ltd.* [1952] 2 Q.B. 297, 305.

timely. The seller can assign this conditional debt, *viz.* the benefit accruing to him under the credit, without authority of the buyer or the paying bank, even though the credit is not advised to be transferable or assignable, provided that he complies with the requirements laid down for the assignment of things in action in section 136 of the Law of Property Act 1925, which are that the assignment has to be absolute and not in part, that it has to be in writing under the hand of the assignor, and that notice in writing of the assignment must be given to the debtor, *viz.* the bank. The assigned debt continues to be conditional and the condition can only be discharged by the seller (or his agent) but not by the assignee. This condition constitutes a *liability* which, according to general principles of law, cannot be assigned without consent of the other party, *viz.* the paying bank which, in that respect, has to act on the instructions of its principal, the issuing bank or the buyer. The UCP admit expressly the assignability of the benefit of a letter of credit even if the credit is not stated to be transferable,[61] but the assignability of such benefit may be excluded by a term to that effect in the credit. The usefulness of an assignment of the benefit of a credit is limited to the cases in which the seller himself intends to ship and to present the documents to the bank.

Other, less formal, methods of making the benefit of the credit available to the supplier are likewise in use. In *Trans Trust S.P.R.L.* v. *Danubian Trading Co. Ltd.*[62] the position was this: A gave B an option to buy; B sold to C; C sold to D. In the contract of sale between B and C, the latter undertook to procure a credit to be opened by D in favour of A, and B undertook to refund to C the difference between C's buying price and selling price which was thus disclosed to B. When D failed to open the credit, C was held to be liable to B for loss of profit.

A mere undertaking by the seller that he will pay the supplier out of the proceeds of the credit to be opened by the buyer affords little security to the supplier. This may operate as an equitable assignment but even if the seller notifies the bank of it, his interest in the credit may be defeated by a subsequent fraudulent transfer of the credit (if it is transferable) or a legal assignment of the benefit under it. Mere instructions by the seller to the bank to pay over the credit (or part of it) to the supplier on presentation of the proper documents by the seller likewise do not protect the supplier because they can be countermanded by the seller.

The transfer of the credit

The transfer of the credit as such is very different from the assignment of the benefit under it. It means that the seller transfers the rights and at

---

[61] UCP, art. 55.
[62] [1952] 2 Q.B. 297.

least certain of the duties arising under the credit to another person, usually his supplier, in such a manner that that person steps into the credit and in advance is assured payment out of funds made available by the ultimate buyer, provided that the conditions of the original credit are complied with. This is the type of arrangement which businessmen have in mind when they make a credit transferable. Such an arrangement requires the consent of the buyer (who is not obliged to provide a transferable credit unless he has agreed to do so) and of the issuing bank; the credit should be stated in terms to be transferable. Where a credit is made transferable, it can normally be transferred once only and, if it is issued under the UCP, to a person who resides in the same country as the original beneficiary or another country, unless the credit specifically states otherwise.

A transferable credit to which the UCP apply is, as already observed,[63] automatically divisible and can be transferred in fractions, provided that partial shipments are not excluded. A transferable credit governed by English law, which is not subject to this provision of the UCP, would not appear to be automatically divisible. If this effect is desired, the credit should, it is thought, expressly be subjected to the UCP and be made transferable.

The UCP provide in article 54:

(a) A transferable credit is a credit under which the beneficiary has the right to request the bank called upon to effect payment or acceptance or any bank entitled to effect negotiation to make the credit available in whole or in part to one or more other parties (second beneficiaries).

(b) A credit can be transferred only if it is expressly designated as "transferable" by the issuing bank. Terms such as "divisible," "fractionnable," "assignable," and "transmissible" add nothing to the meaning of the term "transferable" and shall not be used.

(c) The bank requested to effect the transfer (transferring bank), whether it has confirmed the credit or not, shall be under no obligation to effect such transfer except to the extent and in the manner expressly consented to by such bank.

(d) Bank charges in respect of transfers are payable by the first beneficiary unless otherwise specified. The transferring bank shall be under no obligation to effect the transfer until such charges are paid.

(e) A transferable credit can be transferred once only. Fractions of a transferable credit (not exceeding in the aggregate the amount of the credit) can be transferred separately, provided partial shipments are not prohibited, and the aggregate of such transfers will be considered as constituting only one transfer of the credit. The credit can be transferred only on the terms and conditions specified in the original credit, with the exception of the amount of the credit, of any unit prices stated therein, of the period of validity, of the last date for presentation of documents in accordance with article 47 and the period for shipment, any or all of which may be reduced or curtailed, or the percentage for which insurance cover must be effected, which may be increased in such a way as to provide the amount of cover stipulated in the original credit, or these articles. Additionally, the name of the first beneficiary can be substituted for that of the applicant for the credit, but if the name of the applicant for the credit is specifically required by the original credit to appear in any document other than the invoice, such requirement must be fulfilled.

---

[63] On p. 433, *ante*.

(f) The first beneficiary has the right to substitute his own invoices (and drafts if the credit stipulates that drafts are to be drawn on the applicant for the credit) in exchange for those of the second beneficiary, for amounts not in excess of the original amount stipulated in the credit and for the original unit prices if stipulated in the credit, and upon such substitution of invoices (and drafts) the first beneficiary can draw under the credit for the difference, if any, between his invoices and the second beneficiary's invoices. When a credit has been transferred and the first beneficiary is to supply his own invoices (and drafts) in exchange for the second beneficiary's invoices (and drafts) but fails to do so on first demand, the paying, accepting or negotiating bank has the right to deliver to the issuing bank the documents received under the credit, including the second beneficiary's invoices (and drafts) without further responsibility to the first beneficiary.

(g) Unless otherwise stipulated in the credit, the first beneficiary of a transferable credit may request that the credit be transferred to a second beneficiary in the same country, or in another country. Further, unless otherwise stipulated in the credit, the first beneficiary shall have the right to request that payment or negotiation be effected to the second beneficiary at the place to which the credit has been transferred, up to and including the expiry date of the original credit, and without prejudice to the first beneficiary's right subsequently to substitute his own invoices and drafts (if any) for those of the second beneficiary and to claim any difference due to him.

A transferable credit can be used in a back-to-back arrangement in the following manner. Company A in country (A) sells goods to company B in country (B) and B undertakes to pay by an irrevocable and confirmed credit. Company B then resells the goods to company C in country (C), and C undertakes to pay B by (another) irrevocable and confirmed credit, which is made transferable. B then transfers to A the part of the credit opened by C which corresponds to the purchase price due to A. In such a case it is of the utmost importance that the credit of C is expressed in the same currency as that opened by B because otherwise currency fluctuations may affect the arrangement. In one case[64] the credit opened by B was expressed in Kenyan shillings and that opened by C in United Kingdom shillings. At the time of the transfer the two currencies were equivalent and company A did not object when the credit in United Kingdom currency was transferred to it. Later the United Kingdom currency was devalued but the Kenyan currency remained at its original value. The Court of Appeal held that by accepting the credit in the United Kingdom currency, company A had lost its right to claim payment in the undevalued Kenyan currency although the latter was the currency of account of the transaction.

It would appear that a bank, which has issued or advised a transferable credit, may still refuse to effect the transfer although all the conditions of the credit are fulfilled. The UCP state in Art. 54 (a) that, if the credit is made transferable, "the beneficiary has the right *to request* the bank" to

---

[64] *W. J. Alan & Co. Ltd.* v. *El Nasr Export and Import Co.* [1972] 2 Q.B. 189. See also *Ets Soules et Cie.* v. *International Trade Development Co. Ltd.* [1979] 2 Lloyd's Rep. 122, 132 and *Ficom SA* v. *Socidad Cadex Limitada* [1980] 2 Lloyd's Rep. 118 (the terms of the contract of sale may be varied by the agreed terms of the letter of credit which is opened thereafter).

make it available to a second beneficiary (the transferee of the credit).[65] This, it is thought, means that the bank is *authorised* to accept the transfer of the credit, but it does not mean that it is *obliged* to do so. This interpretation is supported by para. (c) of Article 54, according to which the bank is "under no obligation" to effect the transfer "except where it has 'expressly consented' to it." It was held by the Privy Council in an appeal from Singapore[66] that the bank's consent "has to be an express consent made after the request [for transfer] and it has to cover both the extent and the manner of the transfer requested." This means that the designation of the credit as "transferable," when issued, is not a sufficient consent of the bank within Article 54(b) of the UCP (1983 Revision). This decision has been criticized as reducing the usefulness of the transferable credit for financing the supply transaction.[67] Fortunately major international banks do not in practice refuse to accept a request for transfer of a credit, which they have issued as "transferable," unless they think that there is good reason for doing so (but they are not bound in law to disclose this reason).

ANOMALOUS LETTER OF CREDIT SITUATIONS

Letters of credit and bank indemnities

Where the seller tenders non-conforming documents, as unfortunately sometimes happens, the advising bank, instead of refusing to accept them, as it is entitled to do, may ask the seller to supply an indemnity and, on the strength of such indemnity, may make the credit available. Sometimes, where the advising bank is not identical with the exporter's bank, it will ask for an indemnity by the exporter's bank. This procedure is adopted where there are discrepancies between the documents presented by the exporter and the instructions received by the advising bank, or when documents are presented after the expiry date of the credit and no arrangements have been made for its extension. An indemnity which the seller gives the advising bank cannot be transferred or extended by that bank to the issuing bank without the seller's consent.

The exporter, when giving an indemnity in order to avail himself of the credit, should be aware that the bank may have recourse against him and

---

[65] The corresponding Article 46 (a) of the 1974 Revision of the UPC stated that "the beneficiary has the right *to give instructions* to the bank" to effect the transfer. This formulation, was deliberately changed in the 1983 Revision.

[66] *Bank Negara Indonesia 1946* v. *Lariza (Singapore) Pte. Ltd.* [1988] A.C. 583 (This case arose under the 1974 Revision of the UCP).

[67] See C. M. Schmitthoff, in the article quoted on p. 433, *ante*, n. 57.

may hold him liable on the indemnity[68]; he should, therefore, endeavour to settle the point, which has given rise to the discrepancy, forthwith by agreement with the overseas buyer.

An alternative to giving the bank an indemnity is for the seller to ask the advising bank to forward the documents as *collection under protection of the credit*.[69] In this case the advising bank will pay the seller when the buyer has taken up the documents. This substitute arrangement, while avoiding the hazards of an indemnity by the seller, defeats the purpose of the letter of credit which the buyer was obliged to open by virtue of the underlying contract of sale.

If the buyer's refusal to amend the instructions to the bank is so serious as to amount to a repudiation of the buyer's undertaking to open the credit in accordance with the terms of the contract of sale, the seller has the further alternative of claiming damages from the buyer for breach of that contract.

Payment under reserve

Another possibility for a bank which has doubts whether the tendered documents conform to the instructions received by it but wishes to accommodate the beneficiary (the seller) is to make payment[70] "under reserve." The bank will do so when it considers the beneficiary to be of good standing and able to make repayment if a difficulty arises or when it thinks that the alleged discrepancy is unimportant and the issuing bank and the buyer are likely to take up the documents in spite of it. In particular, the bank will be prepared to make payment under reserve if the beneficiary is a valued customer and a genuine dispute has arisen with him whether the documents are in order.

The expression "payment under reserve" occurs in the UCP[71] but is not defined therein.[72] Its meaning was considered by the Court of Appeal in *Banque de l'Indochine et Suez SA* v. *J. H. Rayner (Mincing Lane) Ltd.*[73] In this case the bank advised the beneficiaries of an irrevocable credit opened by a bank in Djibouti and added its own confirmation. The bank considered the tendered documents to be defective on various specified grounds but, by arrangement with the beneficiaries, made payment under reserve. In the court proceedings the question arose whether the reserva-

---

[68] *Moralice (London) Ltd.* v. *E. D. & F. Man* [1954] 2 Lloyd's Rep. 526.

[69] On collection arrangements see p. 395, *ante*.

[70] Or to accept or negotiate.

[71] See UCP, art. 16(f).

[72] Sir John Donaldson M.R. in *Banque de l'Indochine et de Suez SA* v. *J. H. Rayner (Mincing Lane) Ltd.* [1983] Q.B. 711, 727 suggested that a future revision of the UCP should define this term.

[73] [1983] Q.B. 711.

tion entitled the bank to recover the money if the issuing bank refused to take up the documents or whether it could reclaim the money only if it was established that the tendered documents were genuinely defective. The court decided that, according to the intention of the parties, the expression "under reserve" had the former meaning. "What the parties meant," said Kerr L.J.[74] "was that payment was to be made under reserve in the sense that the beneficiary would be bound to repay the money on demand if the issuing bank should reject the documents, whether on its own initiative or on the buyer's instructions." The court did not have to decide[75] whether the advising bank could recover its money only if the issuing bank rejected the documents on the same grounds—or at least some of them—as those originally notified by the advising bank to the beneficiaries but it inclined to this view. It is thought that this is doubtful; the advising bank should be entitled to recover the money paid under reserve whenever the documents are rejected by the issuing bank or the buyer.

Short-circuiting of letter of credit

On principle, no short-circuiting

In principle, where the parties to the contract of international sale have arranged for the payment mechanism of a letter of credit, they must abide by their agreement and cannot short-circuit the credit by making direct claims connected with the payment of the price against each other. The letter of credit arrangement, said McNair J. in the *Soproma* case,[76]

> is of mutual advantage to both parties—of advantage to the seller in that by the terms of the contract he is given what has been called in the authorities a "reliable paymaster" generally in his own country whom he can sue, and of advantage to the buyer in that he can make arrangements with his bankers for the provision of the necessary funds. . . .

For this reason McNair J. in the *Soproma* case regarded the second-direct-tender of documents by the sellers to the buyers as ineffective.

The conditional character of the credit

Exceptionally, however, the short-circuiting of the letter of credit arrangement is admissible. In the ordinary way the credit operates as

---

[74] *Ibid.* 734.
[75] Because the documents were in fact defective; in particular there was no linkage between them; see p. 415, *ante.*
[76] *Soproma S.p.A.* v. *Marine & Animal By-Products Corporation* [1966] 1 Lloyd's Rep. 367, 385; see p. 407, *ante.*

conditional payment of the price; it does not operate as absolute payment.[77] If, *e.g.* the bank whom the parties have interposed as intermediary becomes insolvent, the seller normally can claim the price from the buyer directly, making a direct tender of documents to the latter.[78] The implied condition is discharged by the insolvency of the intermediary.

Thus, in one case[79] Nigerian buyers bought a quantity of sugar from London sugar merchants. Payment was to be made under an irrevocable letter of credit to be opened with Merchants' Swiss Ltd., a merchant bank most shares in which were owned by the Nigerian buyers. The credit was an acceptance credit providing for 90 days' drafts on the bank. The sugar was supplied and the buyers transferred the purchase price to Merchants' Swiss Ltd. Before the bank paid over the price to the London sellers, it went into a creditors' voluntary winding up. The sellers claimed the price from the buyers in arbitration in London which eventually resulted in court proceedings. Ackner J. held that the sellers could claim the price from the buyers although they had already transferred the money to the bank. Ackner J. said[80]:

> It follows from the finding that the letters of credits were given only as a conditional payment, that if they were not honoured the respondents' debt has not been discharged. This is because the buyers promised *to pay.* by letter of credit not to provide by a letter of credit the source of payment which did not pay . . . The respondents' liability to the sellers was a primary liability. This liability was suspended during the period available to the issuing bank to honour the drafts and was activated when the issuing bank failed.[81]

But if payment under the credit is not made because the seller is at fault, *e.g.* he tenders non-conforming documents, he cannot rely on the conditional character of the credit and the buyer is discharged.[82]

Other instances of short-circuiting

Similar considerations were applied in *Sale Continuation Ltd.* v. *Austin Taylor & Co. Ltd.*[83] In this case N, a timber exporter in Malaysia, used

---

[77] *W. J. Alan & Co. Ltd.* v. *El Nasr Export and Import Co.* [1972] 2 Q.B. 189 (C.A.). Also *Maran Road* v. *Austin Taylor & Co. Ltd.* [1975] 1 Lloyd's Rep. 156, 159; *E. D. & F. Man Ltd.* v. *Nigerian Sweets & Confectionery Co. Ltd.* [1977] 2 Lloyd's Rep. 50; *Shamsher Jute Mills Ltd.* v. *Sethia (London) Ltd.* [1987] 1 Lloyd's Rep. 388. The credit constitutes absolute payment only if the seller stipulates, expressly or impliedly, that it should be so.

[78] *Soproma S.p.A.* case [1966] 1 Lloyd's Rep. 367, 386.

[79] *E. D. & F. Man Ltd.* v. *Nigerian Sweets & Confectionery Co. Ltd.* [1977] 2 Lloyd's Rep. 50.

[80] *Ibid.* p. 56.

[81] The fact that the parties had agreed on a particular bank as issuing and correspondent bank, did not convert the conditional obligation into an absolute one.

[82] *Shamsher Jute Mills Ltd.* v. *Sethia (London) Ltd.* [1987] 1 Lloyd's Rep. 388.

[83] [1967] 2 Lloyd's Rep. 403.

the services of A, the defendant, as selling agent for the sale of timber. A sold N's timber to G, a Belgian timber importer. Payment was arranged by a back-to-back arrangement[84] which consisted of a combination of an irrevocable credit and a collection arrangement. A Belgian bank was instructed to collect the price from G against the documents, and A, through the plaintiffs, an English merchant bank which acted as issuing bank in this transaction, opened a credit in favour of N, the seller, who drew a bill of exchange on the plaintiffs; that bill was accepted by the latter. The plaintiffs then passed the documents to A under a trust receipt, and A handed them to G who paid the purchase price to A and received the timber. The plaintiffs then became insolvent and dishonoured the bill drawn by N on them. A thereupon transferred the purchase price received from G directly to N. The plaintiffs sued A, claiming that they were entitled to the price and that N had merely a claim in their insolvency. Paull J. rejected the plaintiffs' argument and held that the defendant A had rightly transferred the purchase price directly to N. Since the plaintiffs had evinced the intention not to honour the bill drawn by N on them, A was free from his obligation to put the plaintiffs in funds to enable them to meet N's bill. As to the effect of the trust receipt, N was entitled to cancel the contract of pledge of the documents with the plaintiffs when the latter intimated that they would not honour his bill. No doubt, this decision of Paull J. is clear common sense.

Fraud affecting letters of credits

It has been seen earlier[85] that one of the maxims on which the letter of credit system is founded is the autonomy of this institution. This means that the banks engaged in a letter of credit transaction are, in principle, not involved in a dispute arising between the parties to the underlying contract of sale or other contract. Only one exception is admitted to this rule: the fraud exception. This exception is available only in very limited circumstances. Where it can be pleaded successfully, the bank—the issuing bank under an irrevocable credit and the advising bank if it has added its confirmation—should refuse to honour the undertaking which it has given the beneficiary, *viz.* to pay, accept or negotiate according to the terms of the credit, if the correct documents are tendered before the expiry of the credit.

Unlike the case of discrepancy,[86] we are dealing here with a situation in which the documents appear to be in order on their face, but they or their

---

[84] See p. 432, *ante.*
[85] See p. 404, *ante.*
[86] See p. 410, *ante.*

tender are tainted by fraud. This fraud will usually relate to the documents themselves. They may be forged or untrue in relation to the goods to which they refer. But on their face they appear to be correct.

The allegation of fraud is normally raised by the buyer. He will attempt to prevent the bank from honouring the credit or the seller from drawing on it. The buyer may allege that the seller shipped rubbish instead of conforming goods or that he shipped no goods at all, or that the bills of lading were forged or fraudulently false,[87] in that they were antedated to show shipment within the stipulated shipping time whereas the goods were actually shipped out of time.

The bank is not obliged actively to ascertain whether the alleged fraud can be proved.[88] It may adopt a passive attitude and evaluate the evidence placed before it by the buyer. If court proceedings ensue, the issue whether a relevant fraud has occurred has to be decided according to the facts then known to the court and it is irrelevant that at an earlier stage the fraud was unknown to the bank.[89]

In ascertaining whether the fraud exception is admissible, three cases have to be distinguished.

First, there is only an allegation, communicated by the buyer to the bank, that fraud has occurred. This allegation may be founded on suspicion, even a grave one. Or the bank itself, without instigation by the buyer, may entertain such suspicion. If no more can be established, the bank should pay. Megarry J. said[90]: "I would be slow to interfere with bankers' irrevocable credits, and not least in the sphere of international banking, unless a sufficiently grave cause is shown," and the Court of Appeal stated in a case in which it refused an application for an injunction restraining the bank to pay[91]:

> The wholly exceptional case where an injunction may be granted is where it is proved that the bank knows that any demand for payment already made or which may

---

[87] The courts appear to draw no difference between forged and fraudulently false bills of lading in this respect but there may be a difference: in the case of the forged bill of lading it can be argued that it is a non-document but a false bill (even if fraudulent) is a genuine bill of lading having an untrue content; in the *United City Merchants* case (next page, text) the House of Lords dealt with a false bill of lading but did not deal with a forged bill.

[88] *Barclays Bank plc.* v. *Quincecare Ltd.*, *Financial Times*, March 1, 1989 (relating to the general duty of the bank to exercise care).

[89] *Bolivinter Oil SA* v. *Chase Manhattan Bank N.A.* [1984] 1 Lloyd's Rep. 251, 256.

[90] In *Discount Records Ltd.* v. *Barclays Bank Ltd.* [1975] 1 W.L.R. 315, 320. See also *Etablissement Esefka International Anstalt* v. *Central Bank of Nigeria* [1979] 1 Lloyd's Rep. 455 and *The American Accord* [1979] 1 Lloyd's Rep. 267; *Tukan Timber Ltd.* v. *Barclays Bank plc.* [1987] 1 Lloyd's Rep. 171 (the fact that two forgery attempts were made before did not support the assumption that on a future third occasion again forged documents would be tendered).

[91] *Bolivinter Oil SA* v. *Chase Manhattan Bank N.A.* [1984] 1 W.L.R. 392, 393. Also *Continental Illinois National Bank and Trust Company of Chicago* v. *John Paul Papanicolaou. The Fedora, Tatiana and Eretrea II.* [1986] 2 Lloyd's Rep. 441. The English courts have not adopted the practice of the American courts to grant temporary restraining orders on the basis of strong suspicion or fraud.

thereafter be made will be clearly fraudulent. But the evidence must be clear, both as to the fact of fraud and as to the bank's knowledge. It would certainly not normally be sufficient that this rests upon the uncorroborated statement of the customer, for irreparable damage can be done to a bank's credit in the relatively brief time which must elapse between the granting of such an injunction and an application by the bank to have it discharged.

Secondly, it is clearly established to the satisfaction of the bank that a fraud has occurred. There is unambiguous evidence before it, *e.g.* that the documents, or some of them, are fraudulent or forged. But there is no evidence before the bank which shows *that the beneficiary (the seller) knew of the fraud.* There is the possibility that the fraud was committed by a third party, *e.g.* a forwarder or loading broker, who intended to cover up the fact that the goods were shipped out of time, and that the beneficiary himself was unaware of this fraud. One should have thought that even in this case the rule applies that "fraud unravels all."[92] But not so. The House of Lords decided in *United City Merchants (Investments) Ltd.* v. *Royal Bank of Canada*[93] that in this case the bank must pay. The case concerned the purchase of a glass fibre manufacturing plant by Peruvian buyers from English sellers and at the request of the buyers the purchase price was doubled in the invoice in order to evade Peruvian exchange control regulations. The case raised two issues: the "Bretton Woods Agreement point," which was considered earlier,[94] and a letter of credit point. This point, which has to be examined here, arose in the following manner. The bills of lading were antedated. They showed as date of shipment December 15, 1976, which was the latest date of shipment required by the credit, but the goods were, in fact, loaded a day later, which was out of time. The bank (the Royal Bank of Canada), which had confirmed the credit, knew of this fraud because in the first tender of the bills of lading the date was blanked out and the date of December 15, 1976 was superimposed, but later, before the expiry of the credit, a second tender of unamended bills of lading was made which showed the date of December 15, 1976. The documents were thus correct on their face. The false date was inserted by an employee of the loading brokers and the sellers knew nothing about it. The House of Lords held, as observed, that the bank was obliged to pay, in spite of its knowledge of the fraud, because not only the bank and the buyers, but also the sellers, were deceived by the fraud of the third party. Lord Diplock observed[95]:

... what rational ground can there be for drawing any distinction between apparently conforming documents that, unknown to the seller, in fact contain a statement of fact that is inaccurate where the inaccuracy was due to inadvertence by the maker of the document,

---

[92] *Szteijn* v. *J. Henry Schroder Banking Corporation* (1941) 31 N.Y.S. 2d, 631, 634.
[93] [1983] 1 A.C. 168. Further, *Tukan Timber Ltd.* v. *Barclays Bank plc.* [1987] 1 Lloyd's Rep. 171. See also the important decision of the Supreme Court of Canada in *Bank of Nova Scotia* v. *Angelica-Whitewear Ltd.* (1987) 36 D.L.R. (4th) 161.
[94] See p. 112, *ante*.
[95] [1983] 1 A.C. 168, 187.

and the like document where the same inaccuracy had been inserted by the maker of the document with intent to deceive, among others, the seller/beneficiary himself?

The *United City Merchants* decision has caused unease in banking circles. It is contrary to the common sense of the ordinary banker to pay under a credit if he knows that the tendered documents,[96] though apparently correct on their face, are in fact fraudulent or forged. Moreover, he fears that, by doing so, he may incur legal liability. The beneficiary (seller) may raise a contractual claim on the ground that the bank has paid against a document which, as it knew, was a nullity, owing to its forgery or the fraud. It is thought that in some of these cases, if the credit is operated under the UCP, the bank is protected by Article 17, which provides:

> Banks assume no liability or responsibility for the form, sufficiency, accuracy, genuiness, falsification or legal effect of any documents. . . .

But these questions were not decided in *United City Merchants* and the legal position remains doubtful.[97]

Thirdly, the bank has positive proof that a fraud has been committed *and that the beneficiary knew of this fraud*. If both these facts are clearly established to the satisfaction of the bank, it must not honour its obligation under the credit. Such a case may arise, *e.g.* if the beneficiary (seller) himself tenders documents which, to his knowledge, are false or if somebody else does so with his knowledge or connivance. Another illustration would be if the seller tenders documents evidencing the transportation of the goods to the buyer, but the seller has recalled the goods from the person carrying out the transport and knows that the goods will not reach the buyer. The legal position is here clear from *United City Merchants* and other cases.[98]

Evidence of fraud

The courts require, in principle, that the facts, on which the fraud exception is pleaded, are established clearly and unambiguously. But, as

---

[96] On the possible differentiation in the treatment of forged and false bills of lading see p. 442 n. 87, *ante*.

[97] The Uniform Commercial Code, section 5–114(2)(b), gives the court of appropriate jurisdiction discretion to grant an injunction on "notification from the customer in case of fraud." The American courts do not require proof that the beneficiary was involved in the fraud. *United Bank* v. *Cambridge Sporting Goods Corpn.* (New York Court of Appeals, 41 N.Y. 2d 254, 360 N.E. 2d 943, 392 N.Y.S. 2d 265 (1976)); see Stephen J. Leacock in "Fraud in the International Transaction: Enjoining Payment of Letters of Credit in International Transactions" in *Vanderbilt Journal of Transnational Law*, Vol. 17 (1984), 885. But the American courts will grant an injunction only if its refusal would cause the plaintiff "irreparable injury," and if there is only a suspicion of fraud and fraud cannot be proved, this test is difficult to satisfy, see, *e.g. American Bell International Inc.* v. *Islamic Republic of Iran*, 474 F.Supp. 420 (S.D.N.Y. 1979).

[98] *Empresa Exportadora de Azucar* v. *Industria Azucarera Nacional SA (IANSA). The Playa Larga and the Marble Islands.* [1983] 2 Lloyd's Rep. 171. (This case did not involve the bank but arose between the buyer and the seller, but the facts are relevant to the discussion in the text); *Famouri* v. *Delacord Ltd. and Mayer*, 33 N.L.J. (1983), 153; *Tukan Timber Ltd.* v. *Barclays Bank plc.* [1987] 1 Lloyd's Rep. 171, 176.

Ackner L.J. pointed out in one case,[99] a requirement of excessive strictness with respect to the proof of fraud would make it impossible for the courts to apply this exception to the principle of autonomy of the credit at all. The learned judge gave the following guidance for the degree of proof required for establishing fraud[1]:

> We would expect the court to require strong corroborative evidence of the allegation, usually in the form of contemporary documents, particularly emanating from the buyer. . . . If the court considers that on the material before it the only realistic inference to draw is that of fraud, then the seller would have made out a sufficient case for fraud.

---

[99] *United Trading Corporation SA* v. *Allied Arab Bank Ltd.* (This case concerned a performance guarantee given by the seller, and not a letter of credit, but where fraud is alleged, the legal issues are the same.) [1985] 2 Lloyd's Rep. 554, 561, see E. P. Ellinger, [1985] J.B.L. 232; *Bolinvinter Oil SA* v. *Chase Manhattan Bank N.A.* [1984] 1 W.L.R. 392, 393; [1984] 1 Lloyd's Rep. 251, 255–257.

[1] *Ibid.*

CHAPTER 23

BANK GUARANTEES AND OTHER CONTRACT GUARANTEES

IN GENERAL

Guarantees in the common law and in international trade

In the common law the guarantee, or suretyship, is an arrangement involving three parties: the *creditor* who has a claim against the *principal debtor,* and a third party, the *guarantor* (the surety), who undertakes to be liable to the creditor if the principal debtor fails to discharge his obligation to him.[1] The arrangement between the creditor and the guarantor is the *contract of guarantee.* It is a secondary obligation, subsidiary to the contract between the creditor and the principal debtor.[2] If the principal contract is invalid, the guarantor is not liable to the creditor.[3] The same is true if the principal contract is varied without the guarantor's consent, *e.g.* if the creditor grants the principal debtor an extension of time or releases a co-surity.[4] The contract of guarantee has to be evidenced by a note or memorandum in writing signed by the guarantor or his agent, according to section 4 of the Statute of Frauds 1677.[5]

In international trade, a bank guarantee or another contract guarantee has often—though not always—a different meaning. It means a primary

---

[1] The creditor can claim against the guarantor if the principal debtor is in default. It is not necessary for the creditor first to make a claim against the principal debtor or first to sue him, but the parties may so provide in the contract of guarantee.

When the guarantor has paid the creditor, he has normally a claim for reimbursement against the principal debtor: *The Zuhal K and Selin* [1987] 1 Lloyd's Rep. 151. See also *Minories Finance Ltd.* v. *Daryanani, Financial Times,* April 26, 1989 (guarantee that the bank would be repaid in London in the same hard currency which it had advanced to the lender).

[2] On the other hand, the *contract of indemnity* is a two-parties arrangement. Under this contract the indemnor undertakes to hold somebody harmless if the latter suffers loss in his dealings with another. The contract of indemnity creates a *primary liability* for the indemnor and does not depend for its validity on the existence of a contract between the other parties. The contract of indemnity need not be evidenced by a writing under the Statute of Frauds 1677, s.4.

[3] *Associated Japanese Bank (International)* v. *Crédit du Nord* [1989] 1 W.L.R. 255.

[4] Unless the contract of guarantee provides that the creditor may allow the principal debtor such indulgence.

[5] But the consideration for the guarantor's undertaking need not be set out in the memorandum: Mercantile Law AmendmentAct 1856.

and independent undertaking by the guarantor to pay if the conditions of the guarantee are satisfied.[6] In the words of Somervell L.J.,[7] "the word 'guarantee' is often used in other than its legal sense." It simply means "undertaking."[8] This is the meaning attributed to the term "guarantee" in this chapter. And this is the meaning in which the term "guarantee" is used in the brochure *Uniform Rules for Contract Guarantees,* published by the ICC.[9] This brochure was published in 1978; a revision is at present[9a] in preparation and is likely to be published in 1990.

The Uniform Rules of the ICC deal only with guarantees, bonds, indemnities, sureties or similar undertakings ("guarantees") given on behalf of the seller or supplier but do not deal with those given on behalf of the buyer. They deal with three types of guarantees: the tender guarantee which in this work is treated later on in the chapter on the construction of works and installations abroad,[10] the performance guarantee and the repayment guarantee. The Uniform Rules are intended to regulate the case of guarantees given by banks, insurance companies or other third parties. The Uniform Rules apply only if the guarantee states that "it is subject to the Uniform Rules for Tender, Performance and Repayment Guarantees ('Contract Guarantees') of the International Chamber of Commerce (Publication No. 325)."[10a]

Kinds of guarantee

The main distinction is between demand and conditional guarantees. In the case of a *demand guarantee,* the guarantor must pay on first demand by the beneficiary. More will be said about this type of guarantee, which is frequently used in practice, later on.[11] In the case of a *conditional guarantee,* the obligation of the guarantor is normally activated by the

---

[6] In some civil law jurisdictions, this is called an "abstract guarantee."

[7] In *Heisler* v. *Anglo-Dal Ltd.* [1954] 1 W.L.R. 1273, 1276.

[8] In *Heisler* v. *Anglo-Dal Ltd.* [1954] 1 W.L.R. 1273 the seller gave the buyers a personal "guarantee" to pay them 10 per cent. of the value of the goods should he fail to deliver them. The buyers insisted on a bank or third-party guarantee. The Court of Appeal, affirming Devlin J., held that on the true construction of the contract the buyer was not entitled to a third-party guarantee and the seller's personal guarantee was sufficient. The Court of Appeal approved the statement of Devlin J. that, although to a lawyer a "guarantee" by a person to perform what he had undertaken was quite worthless, to a commercial man it had some value as underlining the promise which had been given. Moreover, it might be construed as a promise to pay the fixed amount by way of liquidated damages if the contract was not performed. See also *Newman Industries* v. *Indo-British Industries* [1957] 1 Lloyd's Rep. 211 and *Attock Cement Co. Ltd.* v. *Romanian Bank for Foreign Trade* [1989] 1 W.L.R. 1147 (autonomous character of performance bond).

[9] ICC Brochure No. 325 (1978).

[9a] September 1, 1989.

[10] See p. 742 *post.*

[10a] When the 1990 Uniform Rules will be operative this reference was to be suitably altered.

[11] See p. 451 *post.*

production of a document,[12] such as a judgment or award in favour of the beneficiary, the certificate of a neutral person that the money is due to be paid to the beneficiary, or even a mere statement of the beneficiary that the other party is in default.[13] Banks are sometimes disinclined to issue conditional guarantees because they do not want to be involved in disputes arising from the underlying contract. But other financial institutions, such as insurance or surety companies, are prepared to issue conditional guarantees.

Another classification is according to the purpose of the guarantee. In addition to the tender, performance and repayment guarantee,[14] defined in the ICC Uniform Rules for Contract Guarantees[15] and regulated by them, a great variety of guarantees are issued by banks, insurance companies and other third parties. Two of them may be mentioned here: the counterguarantee and the superguarantee. The *counterguarantee* arises in the following circumstances: the buyer (or employer in a construction contract) asks the seller (or contractor) to provide a performance guarantee. The seller obtains such a guarantee from a bank in his own country but the bank gives the guarantee to a local bank in the buyer's country, and not to the buyer directly. The local bank then gives the buyer a counterguarantee.[15a] It is of great importance that the terms of the counterguarantee are identical with those of the primary guarantee.[16] The position is similar to that in a back-to-back letter of credit.[17] A *superguarantee* is defined by Professor M. Hanžekovic[18] as follows:

> Superguarantee is a special kind of indirect guarantee and is in fact a guarantee's guarantee. A superguarantee is generally requested by the beneficiary who wants to

---

[12] In the case of a demand guarantee the demand must be made by a notice in a tangible form; ICC Uniform Rules state in art. 8(1) that the claim shall be made "in writing or by cable or telegram or telex"; fax counts as "writing."

[13] *State Trading Corporation of India* v. *E. D. & F. Man (Sugar)*, [1981] Com. L.R. 235; [1981] J.B.L. 383 (C.A.); *Esal (Commodities) Ltd.* v. *Oriental Credit Ltd.* [1985] 2 Lloyd's Rep. 546 (C.A.).

In *Chiswell Shipping Ltd.* v. *State Bank of India. The World Symphony* [1987] 1 Lloyd's Rep. 165 the bank guaranteed payment of the sums awarded in arbitration; the guarantee did not contain a provision for first demand by the beneficiary.

[14] A repayment guarantee for an advance payment made by the employer in a construction contract was in issue in *Muduroglu Ltd.* v. *T. C. Ziraat Bankasi* [1986] Q.B. 1225.

[15] In the ICC Uniform Rules, art. 2.

[15a] Sometimes the terminology is reversed and the gurantee given by the local bank is called "the guarantee" and that by the seller's bank the "counterguarantee", see *I.E. Contractors Ltd.* v. *Lloyd's Bank plc and Rafidain Bank* [1989] 2 Lloyd's Rep. 205. This is a purely terminological difference and does not affect the observations in the text.

[16] Counterguarantees were issued in *Edward Owen Engineering Ltd.* v. *Barclays Bank International Ltd.* [1978] Q.B. 159 and *United Trading Corporation S.A.* v. *Allied Arab Bank Ltd.*, [1985] 2 Lloyd's Rep. 554; *Muduroglu Ltd.* v. *T. C. Ziraat Bankasi* [1986] Q.B. 1225. Some overseas countries, particularly in the Middle East, *e.g.* Syria, Iraq and Egypt, require performance guarantees to be operated by way of counterguarantees.

[17] See p. 432, *ante*.

[18] M. Hanžekovic "Contracts involving (abstract) Bank Guarantees and Documentary Credit under Private International Law," in *International Contracts—Credit and Guarantee Financing*, "Hague-Zagreb Essays on the Law of International Trade," Vol. 6, ed. by C. C. A. Voskuil and J. A. Wade, 1986.

obtain besides the guarantee of the debtor bank—which itself might not be well known—also the guarantee of the better known bank. The request for a super-guarantee is submitted by the bank-guarantor which vouches that it will reimburse the superguarantor for sums he might be obliged to pay due to obligations arising from the superguarantee. The provisions of the superguarantee must in all details correspond to the obligations arising from the guarantee.

In major international contracts—"jumbo" contracts—tender, performance and other contract guarantees are of very large size. It then becomes sometimes necessary to resort to the syndication method in order to spread the risk of the guarantors and to issue these guarantees as *syndicated bond facilities.*[19]

Bank guarantees

Bank guarantees may be procured by the buyer or by the seller. If they are procured by the buyer, their aim is to secure the payment of the price to the seller by substituting a "reliable paymaster"[20] for the buyer. If they are procured by the seller, their purpose is to secure the buyer if he has a claim for damages against the seller for non-delivery of the goods, their defective delivery or other cases of non-performance; these guarantees are known as *performance guarantees.* But, as has been observed earlier, bank guarantees are also given to secure a great variety of other contingencies.

A bank guarantee is normally an absolute undertaking[21] by the bank to pay if the conditions for payment are satisfied. In this respect it is similar to a banker's confirmed letter of credit and many considerations applying to the latter likewise apply to the bank guarantee. In particular, the principles of the autonomy of the bank undertaking[22] and of strict compliance with the conditions stated in the bank's instructions (mandate)[23] apply, *mutatis mutandis,* to bank guarantees as well,[24] but the doctrine of strict compliance does not apply to the demand notice given by the beneficiary under an on demand performance guarantee. The obligation of the bank to honour its undertaking is subject to the fraud

---

[19] See Zouhair Kronfol, "The Syndication of Risk in Unconditional Bonds" in [1984] J.B.L. 13; also the same author, "Legal Theory and Practice of Guarantee Bonds in the Arabian Gulf" The IBK Papers No. 8, 1983, The Industrial Bank of Kuwait KSC.

[20] *Per* McNair J. in *Soprama, S.p.A.* v. *Marine & Animal By-Products Corporation* [1966] 1 Lloyd's Rep. 367, 385.

[21] A bank guarantee often contains a clause obliging the guarantor to pay "free of set-off or counterclaim" (see *The Fedora* [1986] 2 Lloyd's Rep. 441) sometimes this clause may be implied into a bank guarantee as a matter of construction, see the Singapore case *P. H. Grace Pte. Ltd.* v. *American Express International Banking Corp.* [1987] 1 M.L.J. 437.

[22] See p. 404, *ante.* See in particular *Siporex Trade S.A.* v. *Banque Indosuez* [1986] 2 Lloyd's Rep. 146.

[23] See p. 406, *ante.*

[24] Hirst J. in *Siporex,* see n. 22, *ante.* On this case see also p. 450, *post.*

exception in the same circumstances[25] as have been explained when letters of credit were treated[26]; indeed, some of those rules were developed in cases in which bank guarantees were involved.[27]

In international trade, in rare cases will the bank guarantee be a guarantee in the strict common law sense, *i.e.* an undertaking to pay only if the bank's customer is in default.

BANK GUARANTEES PROCURED BY THE BUYER

The Bank guarantee procured by the buyer for the benefit of the seller[28] may provide that the bank is liable to the seller for the guaranteed amount if no letter of credit is issued in his favour or no payment of the price is made in the manner and at the time stipulated in the underlying contract. In a case[29] in which the defendant bank provided a so-called performance guarantee obliging it to pay in the event that no letter of credit was issued in favour of the plaintiff sellers by a certain date, and no credit was, in fact, issued, Hirst J. held that the bank was liable on the guarantee because its obligation was an absolute undertaking; the learned judge said[30] in words reminiscent of the famours "life blood" passage relating to letters of credit[31]:

> The whole commercial purpose of a performance bond is to provide a security which is to be readily, promptly and assuredly available when the prescribed event occurs.

Devlin J. observed,[32] that "the bank guarantee is not a general performance guarantee but only a guarantee of a limited performance," *i.e.* of the payment of the price.

Where the buyer is obliged to obtain a confirmed letter of credit and the advising bank, instead of confirming the credit, absolutely guarantees payment of the price on the same conditions as were stipulated for the confirmed credit, it is thought that the bank guarantee is an adequate substitute for the confirmed credit. As far as the time for opening a bank guarantee by the buyer is concerned, the rules relating to letters of credits apply analogously.[32a]

---

[25] See p. 443, *ante.* But if the guarantee is a demand performance guarantee given by the seller, the question is whether the buyer (and not the seller, as under a letter of credit) has acted fraudulently, when making demand under the guarantee, see p. 451, *post.*

[26] See p. 441, *ante.*

[27] *United Trading Corporation S.A.* v. *Allied Arab Bank Ltd.* [1985] 2 Lloyd's Rep. 554; *Bolivinter Oil S.A.* v. *Chase Manhattan Bank N.A.* [1984] 1 W.L.R. 392; *Intraco Ltd.* v. *Notis Shipping Corporation. The Bhoja Trader.* [1981] 2 Lloyd's Rep. 256; *Potton Houses Ltd.* v. *Coleman Contractors (Overseas) Ltd., The Times,* February 28, 1984, [1984] B.L. 106.

[28] Or the beneficiary under another type of underlying contract.

[29] *Siporex Trade S.A.* v. *Banque Indosuez* [1986] 2 Lloyd's Rep. 146.

[30] *Ibid.*, 158.

[31] See p. 400, *ante.*

[32] In *Sinason-Teicher Inter-American Grain Corporation* v. *Oilcakes and Oilseeds Trading Co. Ltd.* [1954] 1 W.L.R. 935, 941; affirmed [1954] 1 W.L.R. 1394 (C.A.).

[32a] See Mark Lawson, "Performance Bonds—Irrevocable Obligations" in [1987] J.B.L. 259.

BANK GUARANTEES PROCURED BY THE SELLER

Demand performance guarantees

These guarantees,[33] sometimes also referred to as "on demand" bonds, are procured by the seller in order to protect the buyer against non-performance.[34] Similar in nature are repayment guarantees which have to be procured by the seller in order to secure a refund to the buyer in cases in which part or all of the purchase price has been paid in advance.[35]

The condition on which the bank is obliged to pay is usually a first demand[36] by the buyer. Here again, the bank enters into an absolute undertaking, similar to the confirmation of a letter of credit, and must meet its obligations even if the seller objects and there are circumstances strongly supporting his contention that the buyer's demand is unjustified. But if it is clearly established to the satisfaction of the bank that the demand is fraudulent and the buyer knew of the fraud,[37] the bank should not pay or at least it should interplead, *i.e.* apply to pay the money into court and leave it to the parties to litigate on who is entitled to it. Demand performance guarantees are often requested by Middle Eastern and African purchasers. In *Edward Owen Engineering Ltd.* v. *Barclays Bank International Ltd.*[38] the sellers in the United Kingdom agreed to supply greenhouses to a State enterprise in Libya. The buyers undertook to open an irrevocable confirmed credit in favour of the sellers through Barclays International. The sellers had to provide a demand performance guarantee of 10 per cent. of the purchase price. They instructed Barclays International to issue such guarantee to the Umma Bank in Libya which gave its own counterguarantee to the buyers. Barclays International's guarantee was payable "on demand without proof or conditions." The buyers failed to open a satisfactory credit, as stipulated in the contract,

---

[33] On the *Uniform Rules for Contract Guarantees* (1978) issued by the ICC, see p. 447, *ante*.
[34] *R. D. Harbottle (Mercantile) Ltd.* v. *National Westminster Bank Ltd.* [1978] Q.B. 146; *Edward Owen Engineering Ltd.* v. *Barclays Bank International Ltd.* [1978] Q.B. 159; *Potton Houses Ltd.* v. *Coleman Contractors (Overseas) Ltd., The Times,* February 28, 1984; *United Trading Corporation S.A.* v. *Allied Arab Bank Ltd.* [1985] 2 Lloyd's Rep. 554; *Siporex Trade S.A.* v. *Banque Indosuez* [1986] 2 Lloyd's Rep. 146; *Tukan Timber Ltd.* v. *Barclays Bank plc* [1987] 1 Lloyd's Rep. 171; *Gyllenhammar & Partners International Ltd.* v. *Sour Brodogradevna Industrija,* [1989] 2 Lloyd's Rep. 403 (where the builders of a ship agreed to obtain a bank guarantee in favour of the buyers of the ship but the bank never issued the guarantee).
[35] *Howe Richardson Scale Co. Ltd.* v. *Polimex Cekop and National Westminster Bank* [1978] 1 Lloyd's Rep. 161 C.C.A.
[36] The demand must be made strictly in the manner prescribed by the guarantee (or counterguarantee); otherwise it is invalid: *I.C. Contractors Ltd.* v. *Lloyd's Bank plc and Rafidain Bank* [1989] 2 Lloyd's Rep. 205. On the form of the demand, see p. 448, *ante,* n.12
[37] See pp. 443–444 *ante*.
[38] [1978] Q.B. 159.

and the sellers refused to supply the greenhouses. The buyers claimed under the demand guarantee from the Umma Bank and the latter claimed from Barclays International under their guarantee. The Court of Appeal refused an injunction by the sellers enjoining Barclays International to pay. The court treated payment under a demand guarantee as analogous to payment under a confirmed letter of credit. Lord Denning M.R. observed[39]:

> All this leads to the conclusion that the performance guarantee stands on a similar footing to a letter of credit. A bank which gives a performance guarantee must honour that guarantee according to its terms. It is not concerned in the least with the relations between the supplier and the customer: nor with the question whether the supplier has performed his contracted obligation or not; nor with the question whether the supplier is in default or not. The bank must pay according to its guarantee, on demand, if so stipulated, without proof or conditions. The only exception is when there is a clear fraud of which the bank has notice.

The bank will issue a demand performance guarantee normally only on the counter-indemnity of the seller. The guarantee will usually state the maximum liability of the bank and has an expiry date.

If the seller (or contractor under a construction contract) fails to perform the contract, the buyer (or employer) is entitled to recover full damages but, if he has called in the performance guarantee, he has to give credit for the amount of the guarantee in the computation of the damages.[40]

Unfair demand

The demand guarantee involves the exporter in a heavy risk. The beneficiary may make an unfair demand under the guarantee, *i.e.* a demand which is wholly unjustified in the circumstances, having regard to the mutual undertakings of the parties in the underlying contract. Kerr J. observed correctly[41] that "performance guarantees in such unqualified terms seem astonishing, but I am told that they are by no means unusual, particularly in transactions with customers in the Middle East." Competitive conditions of business make it necessary for the exporter to accept this risk. The Export Credit Guarantees Department is prepared, subject to certain conditions, to cover the risk of unfair demand.[42]

---

[39] *Ibid.* 171.
[40] *Baytur S.A.* v. *Moona Silk Mills* December 20, 1984 (Mustill J.), unreported, noted in [1985] J.B.L. 324. This case concerned the interpretation of a clause in GAFTA Form No. 62. The buyers claimed damages *in addition* to the performance guarantee but Mustill J. held, on the construction of the clause, that they had to give credit for the guarantee.
[41] In *R. D. Harbottle (Mercantile) Ltd.* v. *National Westminster Bank Ltd.* [1978] Q.B. 146, 150.
[42] See p. 484, *post.*

CHAPTER 24

FACTORING, FORFAITING, FINANCIAL LEASING AND OTHER FORMS OF MERCHANT FINANCE

IN addition to the financing methods described in the preceding chapters, a variety of other financing procedures are used in modern export trade. They have in common that finance is made available by banks or finance houses. Four of these additional financing methods call for treatment here, *viz.* factoring, forfaiting, financial licensing and non-recourse finance.

Two of these methods, international factoring and international financial leasing, form the subject matter of international Conventions, each dealing with the respective topic. The Conventions were prepared by Unidroit[1] and adopted by a Diplomatic Conference at Ottawa on May 28, 1988. The Conventions are not in force yet; they require ratification by at least three States.[2] They are examples of sound draftsmanship and, even before coming into operation, contribute to the understanding of the legal principles on which these financial transactions are founded. The main features of the Conventions will be reviewed later on.[3]

FACTORING

The essence of international factoring

The essence of export factoring[4] is that a finance house, called the factor, agrees to relieve the exporter of the financial burden of the export transaction, in particular the collection of the price due from overseas

---

[1] Unidroit is the short name of the International Institute for the Unification of Private Law in Rome.

[2] Leasing Convention, Art. 16(1); Factoring Convention, Art. 14(1).

[3] Factoring Convention, see p. 458, *post*; Leasing Convention, see p. 463, *post*. In January 1990 the Department of Trade and Industry published a Consultative Document on the Factoring Convention.

[4] See F. R. Salinger, *Factoring. A guide to factoring practice and law* (Tolley, 1984); Anthony N. Cox and John A. MacKenzie, *International Factoring* (Euromoney, 1986). R. M. Goode, "Some Aspects of Factoring Law" in [1982] J.B.L. 240, 338, 410, and 527; the same "Conclusion of the Leasing and Factoring Conventions" in [1988] J.B.L. 347, 510. The trading association of finance houses engaged in factoring is The Association of British Factors Ltd., Hind Court, 147 Fleet Street, London EC4A 2BU, Tel.: 071–353 1213.

buyers, so that the exporter can concentrate on his real business, the selling and marketing of his products. There is thus a division of work: the exportation, including the despatch of the goods, the documentation and the transfer of the transport documents, is done by the exporter (the seller), but the credit management, to the extent agreed upon, is the task of the factor. International factoring is of considerable importance in modern export trade. It helps to ease the cash flow of the exporter's business, an important consideration as most export transactions contain a credit element, and, if it is on a non-recourse basis,[5] it affords protection against bad debts.

When entering into a factoring agreement, two points, both of legal nature, are of particular importance to the exporter: what is the legal form of the factoring arrangement, is it disclosed or undisclosed; and does the factor have a claim of recourse against the exporter if the overseas buyer fails to pay or is the factoring arrangement on a non-recourse basis?

As regards the legal form, in *disclosed factoring* the overseas buyer is notified—or at least can be notified—of the financing arrangement, but the *undisclosed factoring* arrangement is confidential between the export seller and the finance house and no notification is given to the overseas buyer. In both cases the international factor is not a factor in the legal sense.[6]

Where the factoring agreement is on a non-recourse basis, the factor to whom the exporter's claim for the price is assigned, bears the credit risk and is not entitled to reimbursement, if the buyer defaults. But if the factoring agreement admits recourse, *e.g.* for unapproved receivables assigned to the factor,[7] the factor has a claim for indemnification.

Direct and indirect factoring

Factoring may be either direct or indirect.[7a] In direct factoring there is only one factor, the export factor in the exporter's (seller's) country, with whom the exporter has concluded the factoring agreement. In indirect factoring, there are two factors, the export factor and the import factor in the importer's (buyer's) country. Under a direct factoring arrangement, on assignment of the claim for the price, the export factor enters into

---

[5] See p. 455, *post.*
[6] On factors within the meaning of the Factors Act 1889 see p. 295, *ante.* Mocatta J. in *Hamilton Finance Co.* v. *Coverley Westray and Another* [1969] 1 Lloyd's Rep. 53, 58, described the expression "factoring" as somewhat confusing.
[7] See p. 456, *post.*
[7a] This distinction should not be confused with that between disclosed and undisclosed factoring.

direct contractual relations with the overseas buyer. In the case of indirect factoring, the overseas buyer, to whom this arrangement is disclosed, makes payment to an import factor in his country. The import factor will pay the export factor in the seller's country and the latter provides the arranged finance to the export seller. There is no contractual relationship between the exporter and the import factor. Indirect factoring has the advantage that each of the finance houses—the export factor and the import factor—deals with a local customer whose creditworthiness it can best appraise. The relationship between the export factor and import factor, who may be associated companies, is sometimes one of mutuality.

The factoring contract is, of course, separate from the export sales contract. The law governing the factoring contract is normally that of the place at which the factor carries on business.

As regards recourse, whether the factoring arrangement is with or without recourse to the export seller, is a matter of arrangement between the two parties to the agreement. If, to the knowledge of the seller, non-conforming goods are supplied or another condition of the sales contract is broken by the seller and the buyer rightly refuses to pay under the contract of export sale, the factor is normally entitled to recourse, even if the contract with him provides for non-recourse finance.

Legal forms of factoring

The legal structure of disclosed and undisclosed factoring is different. Disclosed factoring is, in essence, founded on a legal assignment of the exporter's claim for payment of the purchase price to the factor as assignee. The assignment has to comply with the requirements of section 136 of the Law of Property Act 1925 which regulates the assignment of debts. According to this provision the assignment must be in writing, signed by the assignee (the export seller), it must be absolute[8] and express notice in writing must be given to the debtor (the overseas buyer). In practice the notice is often given simply on the invoice.

The most common forms of undisclosed factoring constitute merely an equitable assignment of the seller's claim to the finance house. They do not satisfy the requirements of a legal assignment as no notice is given to the overseas buyer. Some foreign legal systems do not recognise an equitable assignment and for this reason finance houses are in some cases reluctant to agree to this form of factoring. Other forms of undisclosed factoring are likewise in use.[9]

---

[8] This means that the whole claim, and not only part of it, must be assigned, so that the debtor is not inconvenienced by having to deal with several creditors.
[9] See p. 458, *post*.

The overseas buyer (the debtor for the price) should be notified of the assignment to the factor as early as possible. Such notification may secure the factor priority over other secured creditors of the debtor. If several equitable interests compete, the order of notification to the debtor determines the priority.[10] In one case[11] a German wine producer sold a quantity of wine to an English wine merchant; the contract contained a reservation of title clause which was void against the creditors of the buyer because it was not registered as a charge under section 395 of the Companies Act 1985[12]; the unregistered charge was merely an equitable charge. Later the buyer resold the wine to a sub-purchaser and entered into a factoring agreement with the defendant factors,[13] to whom he assigned the claim for the sub-purchase price by way of a legal assignment. The sub-purchaser was notified of the assignment and made payments to the factors. When the original buyer ceased paying the German wine seller, the latter sued the factors for the moneys received from the sub-purchasers. Phillips J. felt compelled—rather surprisingly—to treat the legal assignment to the factors as an equitable assignment.[14] The learned judge held that the (later) equitable assignment to the factors took priority over the (earlier) equitable charge in favour of the German seller because *notification to the debtor* of the assignment to the factors was earlier in time.

Disclosed factoring

The *price collection service* in disclosed factoring transactions is carried out in this manner. The factor enters into the factoring contract with the exporter whereby he agrees to purchase from him certain specifically approved short-term debts ("approved receivables") owed by the overseas buyers. When the exporter sells goods abroad, the claim for the price is assigned to the factor and the overseas buyer is asked to pay to him. The buyer is thus notified of the fact that the price shall not be paid to the exporter. Assignments of approved receivables may—and often do—form the subject-matter of non-recourse finance. Receivables which are not approved by the factor ("unapproved receivables") are purchased by him on a recourse basis. Factoring arrangements are usually made on a

---

[10] Under the rule in *Dearle* v. *Hall* (1828) 3 Russ, 1.

[11] *E. Pfeiffer Weinkellerei-Weineinkauf GmbH* v. *Arbuthnot Factors Ltd.* [1988] 1 W.L.R. 150.

[12] On reservation of title clauses, see p. 121, *ante*.

[13] This was a home market factoring arrangement, and not an international factoring contract.

[14] If Phillips J. had treated the assignment as a legal assignment, he could have founded his decision in favour of the factors on this ground because a legal assignment takes normally priority over equitable interests.

"whole turnover" basis and the factor's commission is calculated accordingly. Under such an arrangement the export seller is obliged to offer all his receivables to the finance house for factoring.

In addition to the price collection service, the factor may carry out some functions of the exporter's *credit management.* What these functions are, is provided in the factoring agreement, and several possibilities exist here according to the arrangements of the parties. They may include the handling, by the factor, of the internal credit control and sales accounting ("*ledgering*") of the exporter. In these cases the exporter passes duplicate invoices to the factor to enable him to carry out these activities.

The factor may make payment to the exporter on a calculated average settlement date; this is called "*average maturity factoring.*" Under this arrangement the exporter receives an assured payment regularly on a specified date, instead of a number of small payments which fall due on the varying maturity dates of the purchase price from the overseas buyers. But if the exporter prefers, he may also arrange that the finance house pays him on those maturity dates; this is called "*pay as paid factoring.*"

If the exporter wants the factor to *finance* the transaction, in addition to providing price collection and/or credit management services, the factor will make an immediate payment to the exporter, usually up to 80 per cent. of the book value of approved invoices, while extending credit to the overseas buyer. Here again, the factor may assume the credit risk and make payment to the exporter for approved receivables on a non-recourse basis. Where an export factor finances the transaction, he will often use the services of an import factor in the overseas buyer's country; this enables the latter to pay the price in his own currency. If the factor provides immediate finance in addition to the debt collecting services, a charge will be made which varies with the money rates and is usually 3 to 4 per cent. per annum above the appropriate bank's base rate. The factor selects the exporters whom he accepts as clients with great care.

If the provision of finance by the factor is combined with the assignment of receivables under a price collection arrangement—a combination which is often met in practice—and the supplier is a company, the question arises whether the assignment of present and future receivables has to be registered as a book debt by virtue of section 396(1)(*e*) of the Companies Act 1985. It is thought that no registration under this section is required because the object of the assignment is debt collection and not the provision of security for a loan, and the assignment of the receivables is absolute, and not by way of a charge.[14a]

[14a] See *Lloyd's and Scottish Finance Ltd.* v. *Prentice* (1977) S.J. 147; see also *Lloyds and Scottish Finance Ltd.* v. *Cyril Lord Carpets Sales Ltd.* 130 N.L.J. 207 (H.L.).

In American law the combination described in the text may constitute a security interest.

Undisclosed factoring

The most common type of undisclosed factoring is known as *invoice discounting*. It is carried out in the form of an equitable assignment of the purchase price by the export seller to the factor. In this arrangement the factoring arrangement is not disclosed to the overseas buyer. He pays the purchase price to the export seller. The factoring contract will provide that the export seller receives the price as a trustee of the factor and has to place it into a separate account nominated by the latter. Where the contract so provides, the director of the exporting company would commit the tort of conversion and has to refund such payment to the factor if, on receipt of the payment, he puts it into the company's account.[15] Invoice discounting is usually on a recourse basis.

Some finance houses use other legal forms which do not involve the disclosure of the financing arrangement to the overseas buyer. They require the exporter to sell the goods to them outright for cash and then authorise the exporter to resell them to the overseas buyer as their undisclosed agent.[16] The resale to the overseas buyer is often on credit terms. In this arrangement the exporter receives the price from the overseas buyer as agent of the finance house and has to account for it to the latter. This arrangement is, *e.g.* used by EXFINCO.[17]

The Ottawa Convention on International Factoring

The Convention, when in force,[18] applies[19] whenever the receivables assigned pursuant to a factoring contract arise from a contract of sale of goods between a supplier (the seller) and a debtor (the buyer) whose places of business are in different States and:

   (a) these States and the State in which the factor has its place of business are Contracting States; or
   (b) both the contract of sale of goods and the factoring contract are governed by the law of a Contracting State.

The purpose of this provision is to align the International Factoring Convention with the Vienna Convention on Contracts for the International Sale of Goods.[20]

---

[15] *International Factors Ltd.* v. *Rodriguez* [1979] Q.B. 351.
[16] See p. 281, *ante.*
[17] See p. 487, *post.*
[18] See p. 453, *ante.*
[19] Art. 2(c).
[20] See p. 249, *ante.*

The Convention governs factoring contracts, and for its purposes a factoring contract must satisfy the following requirements[21]:

(a) the supplier may or will assign to the factor receivables arising from contracts of sale of goods made between the supplier and its customers (debtors) other than those for the sale of goods bought primarily for their personal, family or household use;

(b) the factor is to perform at least two of the following functions:
— finance for the supplier, including loans and advance payments;
— maintenance of accounts (ledgering) relating to the receivables;
— collection of receivables;
— protection against default in payment by debtors.

The Convention applies to undisclosed and disclosed factoring.

A difficult question is whether a prohibition of the assignment of the claim for the price in the supply contract prevents the supplier from assigning the claim to the factor. As already observed, the supply contract and the factoring contract are two different contractual relations. The solution which the Convention adopts is to provide[22] that the assignment of a receivable by the supplier to the factor shall be effective notwithstanding any agreement between the supplier and the debtor prohibiting such assignment. But a Contracting State may contract out of this provision by declaring that it shall not apply when, at the time of conclusion of the contract of sale of goods, the debtor has his place of business in the Contracting State[23] Further, the assignment to a factor in spite of a prohibition in the supply contract does not affect any obligation of good faith owed by the supplier to the debtor or any liability for breach of a term in the supply contract.[24]

As regards the notice of assignment, to the debtor, it is provided[25] that it shall be in writing and reasonably identify the factor to whom payment has to be made and the receivables to which the assignment relates. A notice relating to the assignment of receivables which form the subject-matter of a future supply contract is invalid,[26] and so is a general notice of assignment with respect to all future supply contracts.

Where the debtor has made payment to the factor and never receives the goods or receives non-conforming goods, he has, in principle, no right to recover payment from him but has only a claim against the supplier.[27] In two exceptional cases, however, the debtor may claim recovery against

---

[21] Art. 1(2).

[22] Art. 6(1).

[23] Arts. 6(2) and 18.

[24] Art. 6(3).

[25] Art. 8(1) (b) and (c).

[26] This statement applies only to the notice to be given to the debtor and to his position. The factoring contract (between the supplier and the factors) may provide for the supplier's obligation to assign future receivables (Art. 5(a)) and even for their assignment without a new act of transfer (Art. I).

[27] Art. 10(1).

the factor[28]: if the debtor has paid the factor but the factor has not paid the supplier in respect of the receivable in question, and if the factor paid the supplier with knowledge that the supplier had defaulted on his obligations to the debtor.

The Convention regulates also indirect factoring.[29] Where the supplier assigns to the export factor and the export factor makes a second assignment to the import factor, it happens often that the debtor is only notified of the second assignment, but not of the first one. The Convention provides[30] that notification of the second assignment shall also operate as notice of the first assignment. While in principle the Convention applies to subsequent assignments, this is not so if the (first) factoring agreement prohibits subsequent assignments.[31]

FORFAITING

Forfaiting,[32] or to use the French expression,[33] an *à forfait* transaction, is the purchase of a debt expressed in a negotiable instrument, such as a bill of exchange or a promissory note, from the creditor on a non-recourse basis, *i.e.* the purchaser, known as the forfaiter, undertakes to waive—to forfeit—his right of recourse against the creditor if he cannot obtain satisfaction from the debtor. But the forfaiter will purchase the negotiable instrument only if he is given security from a bank of good standing. This security is given either in the form of an aval on the negotiable instrument itself[34] or in the form of a separate bank guarantee[35] guaranteeing due and punctual observance of all obligations under the negotiable instrument. The purchase of the negotiable instrument by the forfaiter is, of course, at a discount. The forfaiter will be a bank, finance house or discount company.

---

[28] Art. 10(2).

[29] Art. 11.

[30] Art. 11(2).

[31] Art. 12.

[32] See M. C. Johns and J. M. Skelton, "Legal Considerations in a Forfait Market," A Presentation to the XI International Forfaiting Congress, September 28, 1984, published by Withers, 20 Essex Street, Strand, London WC2R 3AL (Tel.: 01–836 8400).

[33] Forfaiting has its origin on the European Continent and is said to have been first developed in Switzerland. Today London has become an important forfaiting market and forfaiting transactions are undertaken by most London banks engaged in international finance.

[34] See p. 389, *ante.*

[35] See p. 449, *ante.*, or a standby credit, on p. 429 *ante.*

The essence of forfaiting

The essence of the transaction is that the debtor's obligation, which matures at some future date, can be turned by the creditor at once into ready cash, by selling that obligation to the forfaiter who, however, agrees to the purchase of the obligation on a non-recourse basis only if it is secured by a third party. The forfaiting technique is used in two types of transactions: in a financial transaction, to make a long-term financial facility liquid; and in an export transaction, to help the cash flow of the exporter who has allowed the overseas buyer credit. We are here concerned only with the second type of forfaiting.

Avalised bills of exchange and bank guarantees as security for the forfaiter

In international trade, the export seller will obtain from the overseas buyer time bills of exchange or promissory notes maturing at specified future dates. These negotiable instruments will be avalised by a bank in the importer's country or that bank will guarantee their performance. The negotiable instruments, so secured, will then be negotiated by the export seller to his own bank, without recourse by that bank to him. The exporter's bank thus acts as the forfaiter. The forfaiting arrangement has to be agreed between the seller and the buyer in the contract of export sale and normally this is only done after first agreement is obtained with the banks, *i.e.* agreement between the seller and his bank that it will forfait the negotiable instruments, and agreement between the buyer and the bank in his country that it will avalise or guarantee them. Forfaiting is particularly appropriate to the export of capital goods where the contract of sale may provide for payment by instalments extending over two to five years. A typical transaction would be the sale of machinery to be paid by 10 promissory notes of the buyer maturing in six-monthly intervals over five years. Banks prefer promissory notes of the buyer but bills of exchange are also acceptable.

The forfaiter is naturally particularly interested in the effectiveness of the security supporting the negotiable instrument which he purchases. If it is an aval, it has already been observed[36] that such a commitment is valid in English law and the avaliser as a backer is under the same liability as an indorser of the document. If the security takes the form of a bank guarantee, it will state that it is a primary guarantee and the guarantor is in the position of a principal debtor, that it is irrevocable and unconditional, that it is divisible and assignable, and it will contain a statement such as:

---

[36] See p. 389, *ante*.

> Notice in writing of any default on the part of the said [acceptor/promissor] is to be given to us [the guaranteeing bank] and forthwith upon receipt of such notice payment shall be made by us of all sums then due from us under this guarantee.

The security for the negotiable instrument is abstract and does not depend on incidents concerning the underlying sale or other export transaction for which the overseas importer has given the negotiable instruments. In this respect the security is autonomous. The contract between the forfaiter and the export seller usually states so in express terms but nevertheless the forfaiter normally requests to be informed of the underlying transaction.

The contract between the export seller and the forfaiter usually contains a choice of law clause and a jurisdiction clause and, if the security is a guarantee, similar clauses are inserted into the guarantee which the bank in the importer's country gives the forfaiter. If the forfaiter is located in England and Wales, these contracts are normally governed by English law and there is a non-exclusive jurisdiction clause in favour of the English courts.

Primary and secondary forfaiting transactions

The forfaiter will often re-negotiate the negotiable instruments which he has purchased by way of a forfaiting transaction in order to put himself into funds or to spread the risk. Financial circles speak here of a primary and a secondary forfait market and refer to the original forfaiter as the introducing bank. Secondary market operations may raise complicated legal problems. Normally the exporter is not concerned with them but on occasion they may have repercussions concerning him. For this reason a leading bank having a forfaiting unit words the non-recourse clause in its forfait contract with the seller in these cautious terms:

> We confirm that we waive our right of recourse against you as drawer of these bills and will endeavour to obtain a similar undertaking from any subsequent purchaser from us.

Further, it has been argued that the non-recourse clause does not protect the seller if he fails to deliver the goods to the buyer without legal excuse. It is doubtful whether the courts will accept this argument in view of the autonomous character of the security (aval or bank guarantee), but it will certainly be successful if it can be proved that the seller was involved in a fraud.[37]

If the forfaiter is a bank operating export finance transactions, it will normally obtain the forfaitable paper through its documentary credit collection system.[38] Documents of title to the goods are transmitted to the

---

[37] On the principle accepted by the House of Lords in *United City Merchants (Investments) Ltd.* v. *Royal Bank of Canada* [1983] 1 A.C. 168; see p. 443, *ante*.
[38] See p. 395, *ante*.

importer's bank with instructions that they must only be released against acceptance of the bills of exchange or signature of the promissory notes plus the per aval indorsement or the issue of the letter of guarantee by the importer's bank, according to the previous arrangement with the forfaiter.

INTERNATIONAL FINANCIAL LEASING

The essence of the financial leasing transaction

Banks and finance houses are sometimes asked to provide financial assistance to international leasing transactions. These transactions concern normally capital goods, such as the leasing of ships or aircraft, containers, or heavy equipment for the exploration of oil or mineral resources. The lessee, who wants to use the equipment, pays the lessor a rental. As the period of the lease may be lengthy, the lessor incurs a considerable financial risk.

If the owner of the equipment is prepared to accept this risk, he will act as the lessor himself. The ordinary lease is thus a two-party agreement between the lessor and the lessee.[38a] If the owner does not want to accept the financial risk, a financial leasing transaction is entered into. Under such a transaction a bank or finance house is interposed between the owner and the user. The owner (known as the supplier) sells the goods outright to the finance house (known as the creditor), possibly on a cash basis, and the finance house acts as lessor *vis à vis* the user (the lessee, known as the debtor). This is a three-party transaction. It is an application, in the international sphere, of the principle on which, in the domestic sphere the concept of the hire-purchase contract and the debtor-creditor-supplier agreement under the Consumer Credit Act 1974[39] is founded.

Financial leasing agreements are of two types. In the pure leasing transaction, possession reverts to the lessor when the lease is terminated. Under other leasing agreements the lessee has the option of acquiring the property in the leased goods; in these cases a deferred price component is included in the rental. In both types of financial leasing agreements the rental payable by the lessee sometimes includes an amortisation element for the wear and tear of the equipment.

[38a] See p. 271, *ante*.
[39] Consumer Credit Act 1974, s.12.

The Ottawa Convention on International Financial Leasing

The Convention,[40] when in force, applies[41] if the lessor and the lessee have their places of business in different States and:

  *(a) these States and the State in which the supplier has its place of business are Contracting States; or
  (b) both the supply agreement and the leasing agreement are governed by the law of a Contracting State.

The Convention governs a transaction which includes the following characteristics[42]:

  (a) the lessee specifies the equipment and selects the supplier without relying primarily on the skill and judgment of the lessor;
  (b) the equipment is acquired by the lessor in connection with a leasing agreement which, to the knowledge of the supplier, either has been made or is to be made between the lessor and the lessee; and
  (c) the rentals payable under the leasing agreement are calculated so as to take into account in particular the amortisation of the whole or a substantial part of the cost of the equipment.

The Convention applies whether or not the lessee has the option to buy the equipment or to hold it on lease for a further period, and whether or not for a nominal price or rental.[43]

The Convention distinguishes between two agreements:

  (a) *the supply agreement* concluded between the lessor and the supplier, and
  (b) *the leasing agreement* between the lessor and the lessee.[44]

The main objective of the Convention is to remove, with respect to the equipment, liability from the lessor to the supplier, as the lessor has only a financial interest in the transaction.[45] Except as otherwise agreed, the lessor does not incur liability to the lessee in respect of the equipment, except if the loss is caused by the reliance of the lessee on the skill and judgment of the lessor or the lessor has intervened in the selection of the supplier or the equipment.[46] Further, the lessor, in his capacity as such, is not liable to third parties for death, personal injury or damage to property caused by the equipment,[47] though he may be liable in another capacity, *e.g.* as owner.[48]

Where the equipment is not delivered or is delivered late or does not conform to the terms of the supply contract, the rights of the parties to the leasing agreement are as follows:

---

[40] See p. 453, *ante.*
[41] Convention, Art. 3(1).
[42] Art. 1(2).
[43] Art. 1(3).
[44] Art. 1(1).
[45] R. M. Goode, "Conclusion of the Leasing and Factoring Conventions—I," [1988] J.B.L. 347.
[46] Art. 8(1)(a).
[47] Art. 8(1)(b).
[48] Art. 8(1)(c).

    (a) the lessee has the right as against the lessor to reject the equipment or to terminate the leasing agreement;[49] and

    (b) the lessor is entitled to remedy the failure by tendering equipment in conformity with the supply contract,[50]

    (c) the lessee may withhold payment of the rental until the lessor has made a remedial tender of the equipment.[51]

These rights are aligned with those of the seller and buyer under the Vienna Convention on Contracts for the International Sale of Goods.[52] The rights conferred on the lessor and lessee under the Convention are exercisable as if the lessee had agreed to buy the equipment from the lessor under the terms of the supply agreement.[53]

The Convention contains further safeguards for the protection of the lessor. It provides[54] that the lessor shall not be responsible for a default by virtue of non-delivery or misdelivery of the equipment to the lessee, except if it is due to an act or omission of the lessor,[55] and that the duties of the supplier under the supply contract shall also be owed to the lessee as if he were a party to the supply agreement.[56]

Only two of the other provisions of the Convention shall be mentioned here. First, in the case of default by the lessee the lessor may recover the accrued unpaid rentals, together with interest and damages[57]; where the default is substantial, the lessor may claim acceleration of future rentals or termination of the leasing agreement, and after termination he may recover possession of the equipment and damages[58]; but if he terminates the leasing agreement, he cannot claim accelerated rentals, though their value may be taken into account in computing the damages[59]; in any event, the damages which the lessor may claim are only compensatory; a contract clause providing for the payment of excessive liquidated damages is not enforceable against the lessee.[60]

Secondly, the lessor's real rights in the equipment are protected in the insolvency of the lessee; they are valid against the trustee in bankruptcy[61] and the creditors, including creditors who have obtained an attachment or execution.[62] Where a legal system recognises as valid in the lessee's insolvency real rights in the equipment only if a prescribed form of public

---

[49] Art. 12(1)(a).

[50] Art 12(1)(b)

[51] Art 12(3), or he—the lessee—has lost the right to reject the equipment.

[52] See p. 249, *ante*.

[53] Art. 12(2) and 12(1), end. This provision, and that of Art. 10, modifies, to some extent, the English doctrine of privity of contract.

[54] Art. 12(5).

[55] *Ibid.*.

[56] Art. 10. But the supplier is not liable to both the lessor and lessee for the same damage.

[57] Art. 13(1).

[58] Art. 13(2).

[59] Art. 13(2).

[60] Art. 13(2)(b) and (3)(b).

[61] Art. 7(1)(b) gives a wide definition of this term; it includes a liquidator and an administrator.

[62] Art. 7(1).

notice has been given, *e.g.* by registration of those rights, this requirement of the applicable law[63] has to be complied with.

OTHER FORMS OF MERCHANT FINANCE

Non-recourse finance

This type of finance occupies a half-way position between the facilities
offered by the confirming house[64] and by the confirming bank under a
letter of credit.[65] The typical transaction of this kind differs from the
activities of a confirming house in so far as the finance house does not
undertake to export the goods and does not concern itself with making
arrangements for transport, insurance or export documentation; and it
differs from the position of the confirming bank in so far as the exporter
is not required to undertake personal liability as the drawer of a bill of
exchange.[66] Consequently, in this type of transaction the finance house
accepts the financial risk of the transaction.

The terms on which finance houses make non-recourse finance available differ considerably and the rights and obligations of the exporter
depend largely on his arrangement with the finance house. In a typical
non-recourse transaction—always bearing in mind that other arrangements are possible—the finance house enters into two contracts, one with
the exporter and the other with the overseas buyer.

In the contract with the exporter the finance house undertakes to pay
him at once the purchase price in full, less a deposit paid by the overseas
buyer to the exporter,[67] such payment to be made on delivery of specified

---

[63] Art. 7(2). For the purposes of this provision, the applicable law is defined in Art. 7(3) as
the law of the State which, at the time when the lessor becomes entitled to invoke the rules
of Article 7 is:

   (a) in the case of a registered ship, the State in which it is registered in the name of the
        owner (for the purposes of this sub-paragraph a bare boat charterer is deemed not
        to be the owner);
   (b) in the case of an aircraft which is registered pursuant to the Convention on
        International Civil Aviation done at Chicago on December 7, 1944, the State in
        which it is so registered;
   (c) in the case of other equipment of a kind normally moved from one State to
        another, including an aircraft engine, the State in which the lessee has its principal
        place of business;
   (d) in the case of all other equipment, the State in which the equipment is situated.

[64] See p. 296, *ante*.
[65] See p. 426, *ante*.
[66] Under the terms of his contract with the finance house, the exporter will, however, be
liable to the finance house if the buyer refuses to pay for reasons for which the exporter is
responsible, *e.g.* if he has supplied goods not conforming to the contract.
[67] The payment of such a deposit is normal in this type of transaction.

transport documents to the finance house. Some finance houses, but not all, undertake this liability only after the name of the buyer is disclosed to them and they are satisfied as to his financial standing. Normally the finance house itself is covered by an ECGD policy[68] and further agrees in its contract with the exporter to relieve him of the credit and political risk attending the transaction, as far as it is itself covered by that policy.[69] The contract will then contain a clause making it clear that the finance house is not involved in the goods aspects of the transaction, *e.g.*:

> We shall not be responsible for any claim arising out of or in connection with your transactions with the buyer, on whatever legal ground such claim may be founded or whether it is for loss, damage or otherwise or made by you against the buyer or by the buyer against you.

The contract also provides for a particular and a general lien in favour of the finance house, for the application of English law and for London arbitration.

The second contract relating to the same transaction is concluded between the finance house and the overseas buyer. This contract provides an obligation on the part of the buyer to pay to the finance house the purchase price and the charges of the finance house, less the deposit paid directly to the exporter; usually the buyer, on presentation of the transport documents to him, has to accept drafts drawn on him by the finance house; this procedure enables the finance house to grant the buyer credit or to accept instalment payments from him. The contract does not, of course, refer to the ECGD policy of the finance house. Some finance houses request an indemnity from the buyer and ask for an affirmation that he has any necessary import licences and exchange control permissions for the transfer of funds to the finance house. In other respects the contract with the buyer contains similar clauses to those with the exporter.

---

[68] See p. 480, *post*.
[69] The policy must not be disclosed to the buyer.

PART FOUR

INSURANCE OF EXPORTS

Chapter 25

EXPORT CREDITS GUARANTEES

The Government provides insurance facilities covering risks which are peculiar to export transactions but are not normally covered by commercial insurance. The legislative basis for these so-called export credits guarantees[1] is the Export Guarantees and Overseas Investment Act 1978.

The Act authorises the Secretary of State, after consultation with the Advisory Council, to give *export guarantees* to an amount of 25,000 million pounds, and, in respect of foreign currency transactions, an amount of 10,000 million special drawing rights. Export guarantees are given for "the purpose of encouraging trade with other countries,"[2] and this definition includes any transaction involving a consideration in money or money's worth accruing from a person trading outside the United Kingdom, the Isle of Man and the Channel Isles to a person trading in the United Kingdom, the Isle of Man or the Channel Isles,[3] whether the transaction concerns "visible" or "invisible" exports or external trade. Guarantees are available to and for the benefit of persons carrying on business[4] in the United Kingdom "in connection with the export, manufacture, treatment or distribution of goods, the rendering of services or any other matter which appears to the Secretary of State conducive to the purpose of encouraging trade with other countries"[5] and to companies directly or indirectly controlled by any such person.[6]

The Secretary of State is further authorised by the same Act to give *guarantees in the national interest* for such purposes and "for the purpose of rendering economic assistance to countries outside the United Kingdom."[7] These guarantees are likewise available to, and for, persons carrying on business in the United Kingdom, the Isle of Man and the Channel Isles and their overseas and other subsidiaries.

The Secretary of State may also, with the consent of the Treasury, make arrangements for the purpose of insuring investment overseas against the risk of war, expropriation, restrictions on remittances and such other risks as appear to the Secretary of State not to be commercial risks.

---

[1] "Guarantee" includes any contract to indemnify, see s.15(1) of the Act of 1978.
[2] s.1(1).
[3] s.15(5).
[4] "Business" includes a profession: s.15(1).
[5] s.1(2).
[6] s.15(4).
[7] s.2.

The Export Credits Guarantee Department

The administration of the scheme of export credits guarantees is in the hands of the Exports Credits Guarantee Department (ECDG) which is in law a separate government department under the Secretary of State for Trade.[8] The insurance facilities offered by ECGD are extensive and enable the exporter to eliminate export risks which are not covered by the usual marine and war risks policies. The premium rates charged by ECGD vary according to the risks involved and to the countries to which the export is intended. As ECGD does not aim at making a commercial profit but merely at paying its way, actual premium rates are moderate. An exporter will find it easier to obtain advances from his bank for exports insured with ECGD than if the transactions are not so covered. Where ECGD issues one of its Bankers' Guarantees to a policy-holder's bank, the bank will provide finance at a lower interest rate than otherwise.

Exporters may approach ECGD either directly through one of its branch offices or through insurance brokers. By completing the appropriate proposal form, the exporter can obtain a quotation for the premium rates applicable to his class of business, free of charge and without an obligation to conclude an insurance. The headquarters of ECGD are at Crown Building, Cathays Park, Cardiff, CF1 2NH, and ECGD has regional offices in the main industrial centres.

Insurance Facilities offered by the Export Credits Guarantee Department

Most policies issued by ECGD provide that ECGD shall not be liable for loss in respect of any risk which was insured with any other government department or with commercial insurers at the date when the expected contract was made."

Insurance facilities offered by ECGD are available on a "declaration" basis where the overseas buyer is granted a short-term credit, normally not exceeding six months and this form of cover is extended by a supplemental guarantee for credit of up to 5 years, or in exceptional cases even longer, for engineering goods involving a recurring pattern of trade; for capital goods, constructional works or projects falling outside any regular pattern specific policies are available covering single contracts. In addition, other types of direct guarantees are available to banks providing finance for exports.

---

[8] s.12(1).

Short-term credits

These credits are normally covered by a standard policy, the *Comprehensive Short Term Guarantee*, generally known as the *CST Guarantee*.

The CST Guarantee is, in principle, on a "whole turnover" basis, *i.e.* it covers the whole overseas trade of the exporter for cash or on short-term credit, (*i.e.* up to 180 days credit), but it is a flexible insurance package which can be tailored to meet the customer's business needs. It is continuous, remaining in force until either ECGD or the exporter decides to terminate it, which either may do annually. The CST Guarantee protects the exporter from the time the goods are shipped to the time of receipt of payment, but can include the "pre-credit" risk as an optional extra. The basic policy is suitable for exporters who can readily dispose of the goods sold in the home, or other overseas markets in the event of the original overseas buyer becoming insolvent or the performance of the export contract being impossible.

A CST Guarantee is of importance to the United Kingdom exporter not only if he sells directly to an overseas buyer but also if he acts as sub-contractor to a foreign main contractor. In one case[9] German main contractors contracted with the Saudi Arabian Government to build two stadiums in Jeddah and Daman. The German main contractors then contracted with a United Kingdom company that the latter should supply certain metal work for the stadiums. The United Kingdom sub-contractors who wanted to cover the credit risk were advised by an officer of ECGD that, if the credit cover which the German main contractors obtained from Hermes Versicherung AG, the German counterpart to ECGD, included the United Kingdom sub-contractors, there was no need to take out additional cover with ECGD. The main contractors confirmed that their insurance included the sub-contractors but the Hermes cover did not extend to a claim by the sub-contractors against the main contractors, and the latter failed to pay the sub-contractors for the metal work supplied by him. The United Kingdom sub-contractors sued ECGD for negligent advice. Neill J. held that there were two risks involved, *viz.* the Saudi risk, which was covered by Hermes, and the German risk for which the sub-contractors were not covered and which should have been covered by appropriate ECGD Guarantee. The learned judge held that ECGD had failed in their duty of care on the basis of the principles laid down in *Hedley Byrne* v. *Heller and Partners*[10] and was therefore liable in negligence.

---

[9] *Culford Metal Industries Ltd.* v. *Export Credit Guarantee Department, The Times*, March 25, 1981.
[10] [1964] A.C. 465.

Extended terms

Over the years changes in credit terms have carried large categories of engineering goods outside the field of six months' credit normally covered by the CST Guarantee although the types of these goods and the size of the individual contracts would not make them eligible for individual "Specific Guarantees."[11] A CST Guarantee can be supplemented to cover this type of intermediate business transaction on terms of payment of up to five years' credit or sometimes longer, by a supplemental Extended Terms Guarantee.

The CST Guarantee

Under the basic guarantee the following risks, described in the guarantee as "causes of loss," are covered:

R.01 The insolvency of the buyer;

R.02 The failure of the buyer to pay to the insured within six months after the due date of payment the amount owing in connection with goods delivered to and accepted by the buyer;

R.03 The failure or refusal of the buyer to accept goods despatched, where such failure or refusal does not arise from any breach of contract on the part of the insured:

Provided that this cause of loss shall not apply unless the insurer has stated in writing that he is satisfied that no useful purpose would be served by the institution or continuation of legal proceedings against the buyer;

R.04 A general moratorium decreed by the government of the buyer's country or by that of a third country through which payment must be effected;

R.05 Any other measure or decision of the government of a foreign country which in whole or in part prevents performance of the contract;

R.06 Political events, or economic difficulties, arising outside the United Kingdom or legislative or administrative measures taken outside the United Kingdom, being events, difficulties or measures which prevent or delay the transfer of payments or deposits made in respect of the contract;

R.07 The operation of a law (including an order, decree or regulation having the force of law) in the buyer's country which has the effect of giving the buyer a valid discharge of the debt under the law (not being a valid discharge under the proper law of the contract) for payments made notwithstanding that, as a result of fluctuations in exchange rates, such payments when converted into the currency of the contract, are less than the amount of the debt at the date of transfer;

R.08 The occurrence outside the United Kingdom of war (including civil war, hostilities, rebellion and insurrection), revolution or riot, cyclone, flood, earthquake, volcanic eruption or tidal wave which in whole or in part prevents performance of the contract:

Provided that no liability shall arise under this cause of loss in respect of any risk which is normally insured with commercial insurers;

R.09

 (i) The cancellation or non-renewal of an export licence; or

 (ii) The operation, after the date of contract, of any law in the United Kingdom which prohibits or restricts the export of the goods to the buyer's country, other

---

[11] See p. 479 *post*.

than the refusal to grant an export licence in relation to goods which on the said date of contract were subject to licence; or

R.10 Where in respect of any contract the insurer has stated in writing that—

(i) the buyer under that contract is a public buyer, or
(ii) he is satisfied, in the case of a guarantee of payment and indemnity for breach of that contract, that the giver of the guarantee and indemnity is a national government authority,

and the insurer has confirmed that this cause shall apply (subject only to such conditions as the insurer may think fit), the failure or refusal on the part of the buyer to fulfil any of the terms of that contract.

If the buyer is an *associated or subsidiary company* of the seller (the insured), special conditions apply.[12] Associated or subsidiary companies are defined in the CST Guarantee; generally speaking, they are companies in whose profits the insured has an interest. Where the sale is to such a company, only causes of loss R.04 to R.08 apply; in short, ECGD is only liable in the cases of political risk specified in those paragraphs but it is not liable for risks connected with the buyer.

The normal percentages of the amount of any losses which are covered are:

90 per cent. in respect of causes of loss R.01, R.02 and R.03;
90 per cent. in respect of all other causes of loss where loss is ascertained under the pre-credit risk section;
95 per cent. in all other cases.

It should be noted that the guarantee does not give cover for loss sustained:

(*a*) by reason of any failure by the insured or by any person acting on his behalf to fulfil any of the terms and conditions of the contract or to comply with the provisions of any law (including any order, decree or regulation having the force of law) in so far as that law affects performance of the contract;
(*b*) by reason of the failure to obtain any import licence or any other authorisation necessary for the performance of the contract under any law (including any order, decree or regulation having the force of law) in force at the date on which the insurer's liability in respect of the contract commences under this guarantee;
(*c*) which provides that payment is to be made in a currency other than sterling if, on the date on which the insurer's liability in respect of that contract commences under this guarantee, the use of such currency for that payment would contravene any exchange control regulations in force at that date in the United Kingdom, the buyer's country, the country in whose currency payment is to be made, or any country through which under the terms of the contract payment is to be made;
(*d*) unless the insured gives to the insurer notice in writing of the insured's intention to make a claim in respect of the contract and states all available particulars of such claim within two years of the date of the occurrence of the cause of loss.

The insurer shall not, unless he otherwise agrees in writing (whether or not in a relevant section), be under any liability:

(*a*) in respect of any contract which does not specify—

---

[12] They are those in the Credit Risk Section D of the General Conditions of the CST Guarantee.

     (i) the nature and quantity of the goods sold or agreed to be sold, and
    (ii) the terms of payment, and
  (iii) the currency in which payment is to be made, being

        (a) sterling, or
        (b) any currency which, at the date on which the liability of the insurer in respect of that contract commences under this guarantee is specified in the Appendix of Overseas Currencies annexed to Schedule 2, or
        (c) such other currency as may be agreed in writing by the insurer; or

  (*b*) if the pre-credit risk section is applied to this guarantee, in respect of any contract in connection with which any goods have not been despatched within 12 months from date of contract; or

  (*c*) in respect of any contract if the insured consents to any extension of a due date of payment under that contract without the insurer's prior agreement in writing:
Provided that unless the insurer otherwise states in writing, the insured shall be entitled in the event of need arising at or shortly before the original due date of payment to extend that due date of payment for a period not exceeding 90 days, except—

     (i) in the case of a cash against documents, documentary sight draft or documents against payment transaction, or
    (ii) where the insured has either in the contract or otherwise agreed in advance to any such extension; or

  (*d*) in respect of any contract in connection with which goods are to be despatched to any person in any country other than the buyer's country:
Provided that this paragraph d shall not apply where—

     (i) under the terms of the contract, payment by the buyer is not dependent upon the goods being despatched to or imported into such other country and the cause of loss is specified in the relevant section and is either—
        (a) cause R.09; or
        (b) not such as prevent such despatch or importation; and
    (ii) on the date on which the insurer's liability in respect of such contract commences under this guarantee, this guarantee is not excluded by reason of any special condition contained in Schedule 2 from applying to all contracts made with buyers in such other country; or

  (*e*) in respect of any contract under which payment is to be made from a country other than the buyer's country; or

  (*f*) in respect of any contract in relation to which the relevant authorisation to import goods and to pay for them is made subject to conditions as to the export of other goods from any country or subject to conditions as to the payment of such other goods when so exported.

The policy contains detailed provisions regarding the ascertainment, payment and amount of loss, the payment of claims and the subrogation, after payment, of the guarantors to the rights of the exporter.[13]

The CST Guarantee contains a credit limit in respect of overseas buyers which shall determine the maximum amount as defined at any one time outstanding to which the guarantee shall apply in respect of goods sold or agreed to be sold on credit terms, after they have been delivered to and accepted by the buyer; and in respect of goods sold or agreed to be sold on payment terms of cash against documents, documentary sight draft, or documents against payment, after they have been placed at the buyer's disposal.

The amount of the *credit limit* for any particular buyer shall be:

---

[13] On the right of the Department to subrogation, see *Re Miller, Gibb & Co. Ltd.* [1957] 1 W.L.R. 703; on subrogation generally, see p. 531, *post.*

(*a*) where the insured has made a single contract of not more than £250 in value with a buyer with whom the insured has made no previous contract and at the date of contract the insured is not aware of any circumstances which would make it undesirable for him to enter into such a contract with that buyer, £250, or

(*b*) the amount on such terms and conditions, if any, which may be—

    (i) recommended in writing, not more than six months before the date of contract, or where the pre-credit risk section is not applied to this guarantee, the date of despatch of the goods, by a bank or credit information agency operating in the buyer's country or in the United Kingdom; or

    (ii) justified by information in writing about the buyer and his financial condition obtained from such a source not earlier than the said six months, subject in either case to a maximum of such amount as may be stated in Schedule 1 as the maximum discretionary limit, or, where no amount is so stated, £5,000; or

(*c*) the amount approved in writing by the insurer for the insured; or

(*d*) 25 per cent. more than the highest amount which has at any one time been owed by the buyer and has been paid to the insured during the two years preceding the date of contract or, where the pre-credit risk section is not applied to this guarantee, the date of despatch of the goods, no part of which was paid later than 60 days from the original due date of payment of that part, subject to a maximum of the greater of—

    (i) £20,000; and

    (ii) 25 per cent. more than the amount of the currently valid credit limit approved by the insurer;

Provided that if any amount so paid was secured by an irrevocable letter of credit, an independent guarantor or other surety, such amount may be used for the purpose of establishing a credit limit under this paragraph (*d*), but only if the credit limit is subject to the same terms of security.

It follows that the exporter may grant, under (*b*) above, a reasonable credit to the buyer up to a fixed maximum without further reference to the Department and under (*d*) above he may grant credit 25 per cent. over and above the highest amount he had had outstanding against the particular buyer previously, provided that such earlier debt has been paid satisfactorily.

Under the guarantee the exporter agrees to declare to the guarantors all contracts and exports made by him to which the provisions of the guarantee are, or may be, applicable including any insurance, freight and other charges paid by the exporter on the buyer's behalf; and all amounts which at the end of the previous month remained wholly or partly unpaid for more than three months from the original due date of payment in respect of exports previously declared.

The declarations are made on special forms which are simply constructed so that clerical labour is kept down to a minimum. An *Operational Guide*—form ECG 3001—is provided to each holder of an ECGD CST Guarantee.

The premium is payable on demand on each £100 of the face value of the contract or, as the case may be, on the gross invoice value of the exports to which the guarantee applies.

An invoice is sent to the exporter following each monthly declaration of contracts and exports.

The premium is payable in two parts. First, an annual amount, based on the export turnover, but not less than £150, is payable; this part of the premium is non-returnable. Secondly, a monthly amount based on a rate tailored to each customer's business is charged.

Before the ECGD issues a guarantee the exporter must complete a proposal form stating details of his export transactions, in particular the various countries where his exports are directed, the value of exports and bad debt experience. He must also give the approximate number of overseas accounts and the credit limits of such accounts. The proposal forms part of the guarantee.

Re-exports

Normally re-exports can be covered by indorsement under the CST Guarantee provided that the goods concerned do not compete with similar goods of United Kingdom origin.

Stocks held overseas

The CST Guarantee and the "pre-credit" variant may, by supplemental guarantee, also cover stocks of the exporter's goods held overseas by agents in readiness for quicker delivery to buyers. The cover provides against loss by confiscation of the goods held in stock, loss through civil disturbance or war or a ban on the re-export of the goods.

Constructional and engineering works and service policies

As well as providing insurance against certain risks incurred in the sale of goods (visible exports) to overseas buyers, ECGD offers cover against the non-payment of earnings from the rendering of services to overseas principals. The classes of "invisible" exports coming under this heading are varied but include, for instance, constructional work on the building of bridges, dams, airfields, etc.; services of engineering and other consultants, etc., refits, conversions, overhauls and repairs; processing; hiring; sale or lease of "know-how," etc.

The services policy like all specific guarantees, does not give cover for any loss due to the failure of the insured or the overseas principal to comply with any law of the United Kingdom or the principal's country relating to the performance of the service or making of payment in respect of it, and further does not give cover in cases where authorities have to be obtained and can be and are not obtained before the service is rendered, for the performance of the service and/or the making of payment in respect of it.

Services policies can be used to apply to individual transactions or a series of transactions under one or a number of contracts, depending upon the nature of the services involved.

The Constructional Works policies relate to contracts which provide for both the supply of goods and the performance of services. These policies have been drafted to provide for business done under the standard Conditions of Contract (International) recognised by the Export Group for the Constructional Industries, although they may be modified to apply to other contracts. Cover is given on a "Specific" basis.

Medium and long-term credits

To cover against loss in the "capital goods or services field" ECGD provides the *Specific Guarantee*: the terms of payment involved are unusually long. Terms of payment under the Specific Guarantee may extend to 10 years from completion or 15 years from date of contract, but five years from completion is more normal. The insurance can run from the date the export contract is completed until the date of final payment or alternatively (and at cheaper rates of premium) from the time the goods are shipped overseas until the time of receipt of final payment. Unlike the guarantees for short-term credit (where the exporter must insure the whole of his export trade or a good selection of it) the Specific Guarantee is given for an individual contract.

Where the buyer is an overseas government, the guarantee can be extended to cover the buyer's failure or refusal to fulfil the terms of the contract provided such action does not arise from any breach of contract on the part of the exporter.

Alternatively, long-term credit for capital goods or services may often be covered by a Buyer Credit Guarantee securing a loan direct to the buyer.[14]

ECGD and the provision of finance

The Department does not itself provide finance for exports, but it does assist customers to obtain the finance he requires in the following ways.

Hypothecation of insurance sum

By operating a simple form of hypothecation, rights to the proceeds of a valid claim can be transferred from the customer to the financing bank.

---

[14] See p. 481, *post.*

There are four ways in which this can be done: the first—by form ECG 3051—applies to individual transactions where the customer's authority is required for each transaction for which finance is provided; the second— by form ECG 3055—covers all transactions on one or more named markets; the third—by form ECG 3053—relates to all transactions covered under the customers policy; and the fourth—by form ECG 3057—relating to transactions with a specific buyer. The procedure is for the customer to complete and send to the financing bank the relevant "letter of authority" authorising ECGD to pay direct to the financing bank any moneys which may become due to him under his policy; the bank countersigns the form and forwards it to ECGD; the Department then returns the duplicate copy to the bank acknowledging the arrangement.

Direct guarantees to banks

The completeness of the protection afforded to the bank by assignment of a policy in this way is dependent on the extent to which the bank can rely on the customer to perform the contract and comply with the conditions of the policy.

Where the credit period is two years or more and particularly where the customer is seeking finance from a specialist bank, the bank is likely to look for the security afforded by an *ECGD Bank Guarantee*. Such a guarantee is an undertaking given direct by ECGD to the financing bank, promising to make good 100 per cent. of any payment under the contract in question which is more than six months overdue, irrespective of the cause of non-payment. Such Bank Guarantees usually become operative when the goods have been exported, the works completed or services satisfactorily performed. ECGD retains the right, wherever such a payment made against a Bank Guarantee would not have been made under its normal insurance cover, to take recourse against the customer for the recovery of such amount.[15]

The customer must provide the bank with specified documents proving shipment, and a warranty that the transaction is covered by valid ECGD insurance. Finance is available from approved banks in respect of ECGD insured business at favourable rates: a minimum of 9.85 per cent. for credit of two to five years; a minimum of 9.85 per cent. for credit over five years determined case by case, and governed by international

---

[15] The provision in the recourse agreement obliging the exporter to pay back to the Department the amounts which it has paid to the financing bank under the bank guarantee, is not in the nature of a penalty clause; consequently such provision is enforceable as against the exporter: *Export Credit Guarantees Department* v. *Universal Oil Products Co.*: [1983] 2 Lloyd's Rep. 152.

consensus guidelines on the category of the buyer's country as "relatively rich; intermediate; relatively poor."

Buyer credit guarantees

In many large contracts for which specific supplier credit insurance is available, an exporter may prefer to negotiate on cash terms and arrange a loan to the buyer on repayment terms equivalent to the credit he might expect from the supplier. ECGD *Buyer Credit Guarantees* are available to banks making such loans in respect of contracts of £1 million or more. They are expressed either in sterling or in foreign currency, usually in U.S. dollars.

Under a Buyer Credit Guarantee the overseas purchaser, out of his own resources, is normally required to pay direct to the supplier not less than 15 per cent. of the contract price, including an adequate down-payment on signature of the contract. The remainder is paid to the supplier direct from the loan made to the buyer or a bank in his country by a United Kingdom bank and guaranteed by ECGD, as to 100 per cent. of capital and interest, against non-payment for any reason. The contract may include some foreign goods and services, but the amount of the loan will normally be less than for British goods and services to be supplied.

The loan agreement covered by ECGD is separate from the contract of sale.

The contractual relationships involved are:

    (i) a supply contract between the British supplier and the overseas buyer;
   (ii) a loan agreement between a British lender and the overseas buyer or his bankers;
  (iii) Buyer Credit Guarantee given by ECGD to the British lender, in consideration of
  (iv) a premium agreement between the British supplier and ECGD.

The same favourable interest rates mentioned above apply to Buyer Credit Guarantees.

Foreign currency specific bank guarantee

This guarantee will enable export contracts concluded on a supplier credit basis—*i.e.* credit extended by the exporter to his overseas buyer—to be financed in foreign currency.

This guarantee is designed to help capital goods exporters who are recourse-worthy under supplier credit arrangements and who find supplier credit more appropriate to their business arrangements than buyer credit, or who are selling to those markets which prefer supplier credit. The guarantee is available for one-off United Kingdom export contracts with credit terms of two years or more normally in either US dollars or Deutsche Marks. Contracts will normally be expected to be worth at least £1m.

Under the terms of the foreign currency specific bank guarantee ECGD undertake to continue funding a loan should the lending bank be unable to raise sufficient funds on the Euromarket. This funding agreement is in line with that given under foreign currency buyer credits.

Cover for lines of credit

Many governments, or government agencies contemplating, for example, an electrification scheme, farm mechanisation, or development of one or more industries prefer to arrange the credit facilities without at the same time committing themselves to any one supplier. To meet this need, and to promote openings for British goods generally, ECGD will in many cases guarantee a *line of credit* offered by a British bank to the government or agency, and in some cases to private sector institutions.

How these are arranged varies from case to case, but, typically, ECGD will give a Buyer Credit Guarantee to one British bank which will have secured the backing of other banks and will undertake to provide credit up to a specified amount in respect of contracts for British goods or services falling within the terms of the credit agreement. A terminal date is specified by which contracts must be placed to qualify for the credit, and the decision as to what contracts should be made use of the credit usually lies with the foreign government or agency.

In order that such agreements should not lead to any lengthening of credit terms they are usually limited to purchases of a capital nature and the lengths of credit for individual contracts are usually related to specified minimum contract values, sometimes down to £20,000. The amount to be paid on or before shipment and the extent to which local costs in the buyer's country may be financed are also specified.

Finance contracts (overseas banks) and associated borrower endorsement

Alternative facilities to the lines of credit described above are available to United Kingdom export finance houses holding Comprehensive Extended Terms Guarantees.

The Finance Contracts (Overseas Banks) Endorsement to the basic guarantee (FINCOBE) provides 95 per cent. cover, regardless of performance under the supply contract, against the risk of non-repayment of a loan made to an overseas bank and tied to the purchase of United Kingdom capital goods. As with general purpose lines of credit, the exporter can receive up to 85 per cent. of the eligible value of his contract from the finance house.

Since this facility is being restricted to first class United Kingdom export finance houses and to first class overseas borrowers (usually banks), there is no longer the need, as there is under a line of credit, for ECGD to be involved in the negotiations of the loan agreement.

A parallel facility, the Associated Borrower Endorsement (ABE), is available where there is a connection between the United Kingdom finance house and the overseas borrower. The same terms and conditions apply but the borrower causes of loss, (*i.e.* insolvency and protracted default) are excluded.

A bank guarantee may be issued in parallel with these facilities on conditions similar to those applying to specific bank guarantees.

Premium for the FINCOBE facility is in line with that for specific business, assessed on the length of credit and the standing of the country of the borrower. A lower rate applies for ABE.

Insurance for overseas investments

All companies carrying on business in the United Kingdom and their overseas subsidiaries are in principle eligible for *cover for new investment overseas*, but UK-based subsidiaries or branches of foreign companies are excluded if they are merely acting as a conduit for an investment by their overseas parent. Investment is defined as a contribution of resources to an enterprise; this includes equity capital in the form of cash, plant or know-how, as well as loans to overseas enterprises; investments through debt/equity swaps can be considered. To qualify for cover, the investment must be new, *i.e.* investment which finances a new enterprise or is an injection of additional capital into an existing overseas enterprise; the investor must apply for cover before becoming irrevocably committed. Existing investment does not qualify.

The United Kingdom investor is offered insurance against losses arising from expropriation, nationalisation, confiscation (including discrimination against the investor or the overseas enterprise), inability to operate due to war, revolution or insurrection and damage to physical assets); and restrictions on remittances of capital, profits and interest. No insurance is given in respect of the commercial risk of the investment. The standard commitment of ECGD is normally for 15 years for 90 per cent. of any loss arising in respect of the three risks covered. An overall maximum insured amount will be determined at the outset, within which the investor proposes a current insured amount at the beginning of each 12 months of the contract of insurance. Cover is based on the initial investment earnings retained in the enterprise, and profits in the course of transfer to the UK. For loans cover is based on the total principal outstanding plus accrued interest.

Performance guarantees[16]

For contracts worth £250,000 or more on cash or near cash terms which are insured with ECGD against the normal credit risks, ECGD assists in suitable cases by providing support for the issue of performance guarantees, also called bonds. ECGD does not provide the bonds, but gives support by means of an indemnity to a bank or surety company which is willing to issue the bond. Under its indemnity, ECGD is unconditionally liable to reimburse the bond giver in full for the amount of bond call.

Any payment by ECGD to the bond holder becomes the subject of a claim by ECGD against the contractor under a related recourse agreement. ECGD will refund the contractor if it is established that he is not in default under the terms of the contract, or that his failure to comply is due to specified causes outside his control.

ECGD can also give similar support for tender, advance payment, and progress payment guarantees.

Cover against unfair calling of demand guarantees[17]

ECGD offers insurance to exporters against the unfair calling of demand bonds raised without ECGD support. This cover is available for any contract on cash or credit terms insured under a normal ECGD guarantee (except external trade and re-exports), provided the form of the bond is acceptable to ECGD and the buying country is considered suitable for this form of cover.

The insurance takes the form of an addendum to the basic guarantee. ECGD agrees to reimburse the exporter for 100 per cent. of any loss due to the calling of a bond if it is subsequently shown that the exporter was not in default in his performance of the contract, or if any failure on his part is due to specified events outside his control. However, tender bonds are insured within the framework of the Multiple Tender Bond Guarantee.

Projects insurance

Projects financing cover

ECGD provides a scheme in support of lenders prepared to finance large capital projects abroad. For the purposes of this scheme, "project

---

[16] See pp. 446, 451, *ante.*
[17] See pp. 451–452, *ante.*

financing" is defined as the lending in respect of a major capital project where security for repayment is restricted to charges on project assets and revenues with recourse to project owners or sponsors in limited or defined circumstances.

The scheme is available for capital projects with a minimum UK Export Credit Loan Value, (*i.e.* the principal amount covered by ECGD which will not exceed 85 per cent. of UK content and eligible foreign costs) of £20 million. When calculating the UK Export Credit Loan Value, any grant under ATP[18] will be deducted from the UK content and the ECGD cover will relate only to the balance.

The scheme is based on the Buyer Credit system[19] and offers lenders three options:

Option 1 covers the "standard" political risks;
Option 2 covers the "standard" political risks and provides cover against breach of specific government undertakings;
Option 3 covers political risks, under option 2, and commercial risks on a risk sharing basis.

Applicants for project financing cover will be required to bear the cost of any export/specialist advice and any external and overseas legal fees.

Project participants

British members of a consortium contracting overseas for a large project may be exposed to heavy losses which they are unable to bear arising from the insolvency of a member of a consortium.[20] ECGD can insure main contractors or consortium members participating in major export projects of £20 million or more for 90 per cent. of the loss arising from unavoidable costs, expenses or damages due to the insolvency of a sub-contractor or fellow consortium member. This facility is available to United Kingdom companies for joint venture or sub-contract relationships with either United Kingdom or non-United Kingdom companies in acceptable cases.

The main contractor or consortium member should nominate the amount and period for which cover is required. Since the liability of ECGD is related to the items for which the defaulting party is contractually liable, it is necessary for sub-contracts or joint venture agreements for which insurance is required to set out in detail all additional costs which would be faced by the contractor in completing an aborted contract.

Loss is ascertained on the basis of the expenditure incurred by the policyholder in continuing the sub-contract or work that would otherwise

---

[18] On ATP see p. 83, *ante*.
[19] On the Buyer Credit System see p. 481, *ante*.
[20] See p. 343, *ante*.

have been undertaken by the insolvent consortium member. Interim claims are accepted against an undertaking from the policyholder that amounts claimed are included in the ultimate claim lodged with the liquidator.

Joint and several cover

ECGD has also introduced a Joint and Several Facility, which is available selectively for such projects with a minimum contract value of £50 million, where they are judged to be of exceptional national interest. This will enable estimated sums in the tender price to cover such risks to be reduced to the level of the ECGD premiums, and thus make the bid more competitive.

The facility can be taken advantage of by main contractors in relation to United Kingdom sub-contracts amounting to 5 per cent. or more of the total project value, or it can be adapted to cover United Kingdom members of consortia or joint ventures. ECGD will indemnify the insured contractor against cost over-runs, which are judged by ECGD to be unavoidable and irrecoverable, incurred for reasons outside the insured's control in connection with sub-contracts. The causes of loss covered are:

> default by an insured sub-contractor which necessitates termination of his sub-contract and completion of his work by a replacement sub-contractor at a total cost exceeding the original sub-contract price provided for in the tender price;
>
> unavoidable additional cost incurred by the main contractor and attributable to an insured sub-contractor but not recoverable from him by reason of limitations imposed in his contract, other than that arising from an event occurring in the buyer's country.

The amount of ECGD's cover will be 80 per cent. of the admissible losses with a maximum liability of 20 per cent. of the total United Kingdom value of the project contract.

Unusually for ECGD, applications for this cover should be made to:

> Overseas Project Board,
> Department of Trade and Industry,
> 1 Victoria Street,
> London SW1H OET

on an application form obtainable from that address.

This board will select those projects suitable for this cover and pass them to ECGD for further consideration. A prerequisite of the issue of this facility is basic credit insurance cover with ECGD, which should be sought from ECGD in the normal way as early as possible in the negotiations.

PRIVATE CREDIT INSURANCE

Credit insurance is also offered to the exporter by private insurance and indemnity companies. They offer, in particular, cover of the commercial risk, including the insolvency of the overseas buyer, and some of them, *e.g.* Trade Indemnity plc, are also prepared to cover some cases of the political risk.[21]

Mention should be made in this connection of the facilities offered by the Export Finance Co. Ltd. (EXFINCO)[22] because they are linked with the CST Guarantee of ECGD. If an exporter holds such a guarantee with respect to the sale of specified goods to an overseas buyer, EXFINCO is prepared to pay him at the time of shipment 100 per cent. of the credit insured valued of the exported goods. In other words, the ECGD Guarantee is used as a security for the immediate payment to the exporter. The master agreement of EXFINCO provides that the exporter sells the goods, which he wishes to export, outright to EXFINCO and then resells them to the overseas buyer as an undisclosed agent of EXFINCO. The collection of the purchase price from the overseas buyer is the duty of the exporter who must not disclose his arrangement with EXFINCO to the buyer. The exporter has to arrange payment by the overseas buyer into a separate bank account opened by EXFINCO in his, the exporter's, name. He has further to arrange with ECGD that any monies payable by the Department under the Guarantee are paid directly to EXFINCO, and not to him. The legal structure of the contract between the exporter and EXFINCO has thus some features in common with undisclosed factoring[23] but there are important differences, the most important of them being the complete protection offered by EXFINCO against exchange risks from the time of the contract to that of payment by the buyer. EXFINCO also provides similar back-up services for the short term policy issued by Trade Indemnity plc.

---

[21] The address of Trade Indemnity plc is: 12–34 Great Eastern Street, London EC2A 3AX (Tel.: 01–739 4311); there are offices in other United Kingdom cities. The political risk cover is only available as an endorsement to the export credit whole turnover policy issued by the Company and cover can be obtained for non-payment arising from transfer delay, war, civil war, government action frustrating the contract or public buyer default. Cover can also be obtained against the failure or refusal of a buyer to take up goods despatched to him.

[22] Address: EXFINCO House, Sanford Street, Swindon, Wiltshire, SN1 1QQ (Tel.: (0793) 616333), London office: 5–8 Plantation House, Mincing Lane, EC3M 3DX.

[23] See p. 453 *et seq. ante.*

CHAPTER 26

MARINE AND AVIATION INSURANCE

IT is customary to insure goods sold for export against the perils of the journey. According to the method of transportation, a marine, aviation or overland insurance is effected.

The term "marine insurance" is somewhat misleading because the contract of marine insurance can, by agreement of the parties or custom of the trade, be extended so as to protect the assured against losses on inland waters or land which are incidental to the sea voyage.[1] In the export trade frequently—but not invariably—extended marine insurance arrangements are made in order to cover not only the sea voyage but also the transportation of goods from the warehouse of the seller to that of the overseas buyer.[2] Marine insurance is an institution of great antiquity; it was known in Lombardy in the fourteenth century, the first English statute dealing with it was passed in 1601, and Lloyd's Coffee House, the birthplace of Lloyd's of London, is first mentioned in the records in 1688. The law relating to marine insurance is codified in the Marine Insurance Act 1906.[3] The Schedule to this Act contains the standard form policy known as the *Lloyd's S.G. policy.* Since January 1, 1982 this has been replaced by the *Lloyd's Marine Policy,* and the Institute Cargo Clauses.[4] The three most important sets of clauses are known as Clauses A, B and C.

MARINE INSURANCE

Stipulations in the contract of sale

In an export transaction, the terms of the contract of sale provide normally whether the costs of marine insurance shall be borne by the

---

[1] Marine Insurance Act 1906, s.2(1).

[2] On the transit clause (incorporating the warehouse to warehouse clause) see p. 514. *post.*

[3] References to sections on the following pages relate to this Act. The regulation of insurance business in the United Kingdom is governed by the Insurance Act 1982, as amended by the Financial Services Act, 1986, and that of Lloyd's by Lloyd's Act 1982; both these enactments do not call for treatment in this work.

[4] See p. 512, *post.* The full text of the Institute Cargo Clauses is reproduced in the Reference Book of Marine Insurance Clauses, (56th ed., 1984, Witherby). A commentary on these, and the Lloyd's Marine Policy form by Dr. Samir Mankabady is contained in 13 Journ. Mar. L. & Com. 527 (1982) and in the article by Nicole Leloir, "The Lloyd's Marine Policy and the Institute Cargo Clauses" in [1985] J.B.L. 228 (Miss Leloir's article contains a useful comparative table).

seller or by the buyer. If the goods are sold on f.o.b. terms, these costs have to be paid by the buyer and that is even true if the f.o.b. seller, by request of the buyer, has taken out the policy.[5] If the goods are sold on c.i.f. terms, it is the duty of the seller to take out the policy and pay the costs of insurance.[6] In a c. and f. contract the seller need not insure, nor need the buyer (at whose risk the goods travel), but if the c. and f. contract contains a clause "insurance to be effected by the buyer," or a clause in similar terms, that will normally place the buyer under a contractual obligation to insure and has not merely declaratory effect; the obligation to insure is thereby "put into the reverse," and the buyer must take out the same policy which the seller would have been obliged to obtain if the contract had been a c.i.f. contract.[7]

The marine insurance policy or the marine insurance certificate[8] forms part of the shipping documents.[9] Where goods are sold c.i.f. the seller is obliged to take out a marine insurance policy or certificate which provides cover against the risks customarily covered in the particular trade in respect of the cargo and voyage in question, but he is not required to do more.[10] He need not take out an all risks[11] policy unless the parties have agreed thereon or it is demanded by the custom of the trade.

The assured, the insurer and the broker

The parties to a contract of marine insurance are known as the assured and the insurer. Insurers are either underwriting members of Lloyd's or marine insurance companies. The "Society of Lloyd's" has underwriting and non-underwriting members. The former, known as the "names," form groups called "syndicates," which conduct the actual underwriting through an underwriting agent; every member of a syndicate is liable for a proportionate fraction of the risk, and thus the aim of all insurance is achieved, namely to spread the risk to many persons while, at the same time, providing indemnity for one person, the assured, if a loss occurs. The underwriting agent is usually, but not necessarily, a member of the syndicate or syndicates for which he acts. The duty of an underwriting agent is to conduct the affairs of the syndicate in good faith and for the benefit of the syndicate as a whole.[12] Insurance at Lloyd's is effected in

---

[5] See p. 20, *ante*.
[6] See p. 35, *ante*.
[7] *Reinhart Co.* v. *Joshua Hoyle & Sons Ltd.* [1961] 1 Lloyd's Rep. 346; see p. 55, *ante*.
[8] See p. 501, *post*.
[9] See p. 37, *ante*.
[10] In the cotton trade the ordinary insurance policy to be taken out under a c.i.f. contract includes "country damage," *i.e.* pre-shipment damage to the goods: *Reinhart Co.* v. *Joshua Hoyle & Sons Ltd.* [1961] 1 Lloyd's Rep. 346, 353.
[11] On the meaning of "all risks" insurance, see p. 513, *post*.
[12] *Daly* v. *Lime Street Underwriting Agencies* [1987] 2 F.T.L.R. 277.

"The Room," which is situate in London, and underwriting members accept only risks offered through Lloyd's brokers (who have access to The Room). A person who wishes to effect an insurance at Lloyd's has thus to employ the services of such a broker. The marine insurance companies have been early competitors of Lloyd's in the field of marine insurance, and can be approached directly or through an agent of the company (sometimes called an "underwriting agent" though his functions are different from those of an underwriting agent at Lloyd's), or through an insurance broker.

In the normal course of business the exporter, who wishes to have his goods insured, does not approach the insurer directly but instructs an insurance broker to effect insurance on his behalf. Where the exporter is the regular client of an insurance broker, he forwards his instructions on a form supplied by the broker and gives the required particulars on that form. The broker, who is usually authorised to place the insurance within certain limits as to the rates of premium, writes the essentials of the proposed insurance in customary abbreviations on a document called "the slip"[13] which he takes to Lloyd's or a marine insurance company. An insurer, who is prepared to accept part of the risk, writes on the slip the amount for which he is willing to insure and adds his initials; this is known as "writing a line." The presentation of the slip by a broker to an underwriter constitutes an offer and "writing a line" constitutes an acceptance by the underwriter.[14] Hence each line written on a slip gives rise to an immediately binding contract between the underwriter and the assured or reinsured for whom the broker is acting when he presents the slip. The broker then takes the slip to other insurers who successively likewise write lines until the whole risk is covered.[15] More will have to be said about the legal character of the slip later on.

When the risk is covered, the broker sends the assured a memorandum of the insurance effected which is conveniently executed on a duplicate form of the instructions. According to the nature of insurance which the broker was instructed to obtain, the memorandum assumes the form of a closed or open cover note.[16] A closed cover note is sent if the assured, in his instructions, has given full particulars as to cargo and shipment and the insurance has, thus, been made definite. An open cover note is sent if the instructions of the assured are so general and indefinite that further instructions are required from him to define the cargo, voyage or interest shipped under the insurance; this happens where the assured requires an

---

[13] On the legal character of the slip, see p. 499 *et seq, post.*
[14] *General Re-insurance Corporation* v. *Forsakringsaktiebolaget Fennia Patria* [1983] Q.B. 856; on this case, see p. 500, *post.*
[15] *Ibid.*
[16] The open cover note should not be confused with the type of insurance known as the "open cover"; see p. 497, *post.*

"open cover"[17] or a "floating policy,"[18] or where he reserves the right to give "closing instructions."

The insurance broker should, as a matter of prudent business practice, notify the assured promptly of the terms of the insurance which he arranged for him and forward the cover note as soon as possible, but he is not under a legal duty to do so. In *United Mills Agencies Ltd.* v. *R. E. Harvey, Bray & Co.,*[19] the plaintiffs instructed the defendants, insurance brokers, to effect an open marine insurance on their goods, obtaining immediate cover. On April 2 the brokers reported that the cover was placed, and on April 4 they sent the assured the cover note which did not contain a clause covering the goods while at packers. In the night of April 4–5 goods of the value of £8,000 were destroyed by fire at a warehouse of packers. The action of the assured against the brokers for damages was dismissed. McNair J. held that the brokers had no knowledge that the goods in the hands of the packers were uninsured and that the brokers were not negligent by not insuring them in the hands of the packers or not informing the assured that they had not so insured them.[20] The learned judge likewise rejected the contention of the assured that the brokers were under a duty to notify the assured at once of the terms of the insurance:

> It was, no doubt, prudent to do so, both to allay the client's anxiety and possibly to enable the client to check the terms of insurance, but that was very different from saying it was part of the broker's duty.

The Standard Trading Conditions of the Institute of Freight Forwarders (1984 Edition) provide that forwarders, who in practice often act as packers or procure packing, are not obliged to arrange insurance unless expressly instructed by the customer and, when arranging insurance, act as agents of the customer; Article 21 of the Standard Trading Conditions states:

> (A) No insurance will be effected except upon express instructions given in writing by the Customer and all insurances effected by the Company are subject to the usual exceptions and conditions of the policies of the insurance company or underwriters taking the risk. Unless otherwise agreed in writing the Company shall not be under any obligation to effect a separate insurance on each consignment but may declare it on any open or general policy held by the Company.
> (B) Insofar as the Company agrees to arrange insurance, the Company acts solely as Agent for the Customer using its best endeavours to arrange such insurance and does so subject to the limits of liability contained in Clause 37 hereof.

---

[17] See p. 497, *post.*

[18] See p. 494, *post.*

[19] [1952] 1 T.L.R. 149.

[20] If they had acted negligently, the result would have been different; see *Osman* v. *J. Ralph Moss Ltd.* [1970] 1 Lloyd's Rep. 313 where, in the case of motor insurance, it was held that the brokers were under a duty to advise and protect their clients: similarly *McNealy* v. *Pennine Insurance Co. Ltd.* [1978] R.T.R. 285 (C.A.) (likewise a case of motor insurance).

The position of the insurance broker is anomalous in two respects: he is normally the agent of the assured but is paid by the insurer.[21] Even more remarkable is the fact that he is personally and solely responsible to the insurer for payment of the premium[22] while, as between insurer and assured, by a legal fiction the premium is regarded as paid. The historical origin of the rule is that underwriting members of Lloyd's refused, at an early date, to deal with assured persons directly, and accepted insurances only from brokers whom they knew personally as financially trustworthy.[23] Today, the rule is laid down, in respect of marine insurance effected at Lloyd's or elsewhere, in the Marine Insurance Act 1906, ss.53 and 54.

The anomalous position of the insurance broker, in the second respect mentioned above, has been repeatedly commented on by the Bench. Bayley J. said in an early case[24]:

> As between the assured and the underwriter the premiums are considered as paid. The underwriter, to whom, in most instances, the assured are unknown, looks to the broker for payment, and he to the assured. The latter pays the premium to the broker only, who is a middleman between the assured and the underwriter. But he is not merely an agent, he is a principal to receive the money from the assured, and to pay it to the underwriter.

The broker has a lien on the policy until the premium, commission and other charges due to him have been paid (s.53(2)).

Kinds of marine insurance

(i) *Valued and unvalued policies.*

The Marine Insurance Act 1906 distinguishes between valued and unvalued policies. A valued policy is a policy which specifies the agreed

---

[21] On his duties as agent, see *Anglo-African Merchants* v. *Bayley* [1970] 1 Q.B. 311; *North and South Trust Co.* v. *Berkeley* [1971] 1 W.L.R. 470, 480. Exceptionally, he may be the agent of the insurer; see *Stockton* v. *Mason*, [1978] 2 Lloyd's Rep. 430 (which concerned a provisional motor insurance cover granted by the broker orally over the telephone). See also *Amin Rasheed Corp.* v. *Kuwait Insurance* [1982] 1 W.L.R. 961, 967 where Bingham J., adopting *Anglo-African Merchants* v. *Bayley*, above, observed "There is most compelling authority for the proposition that in placing insurance the broker acts as agent of the assured and not of the underwriter." The broker is entitled to sue and to hold the proceeds as fiduciary for the assured, unless the agreement, construed as a whole, shows a contrary intention *Transcontinental Underwriting Agency* v. *Grand Union Insurance Co. Ltd.* [1987] 2 Lloyd's Rep. 409. See also *Daly* v. *Lime Street Underwriting Agencies* [1987] F.T.L.R. 277.
[22] In *Wilson* v. *Avec Audio-Visual Equipment Ltd.* [1974] 1 Lloyd's Rep. 81, the insurance broker who had effected burglary and transit insurances was held to have no authority to pay the premium, but the case rests on its own very special facts; the assured had expressly revoked the authority to pay the premium to the insurers after they had become insolvent.
[23] See p. 490, *ante.*
The unfortunate result of the antiquated position of the insurance broker is this: if the assured gives the broker full disclosure of all relevant facts but the broker, completing the proposal on behalf of the assured, omits some of them, the assured cannot recover from the insurer; in *Roberts* v. *Plaisted* [1989] 2 Lloyd's Rep. 341, 345 Purchas L.J. suggested that this anomaly might attract the attention of the Law Commission.
[24] *Power* v. *Butcher* (1829) 10 B. & Cr. 329, 340.

value of the subject-matter insured (s.27(2)); an unvalued policy[25] states merely the maximum limit of the sum insured and leaves the insurable value to be ascertained subsequently (s.28).

The main difference between these two types of policy is that in the case of a valued policy the value fixed by the policy is, in the absence of fraud, conclusive of the insurable value of the subject insured (s.27(3)), while in the case of an unvalued policy the value of the insured goods has to be proved by production of invoices, vouchers, estimates and other evidence. In the case of an unvalued policy, the insurable value of goods or merchandise is the prime cost of the goods, plus the expenses of and incidental to shipping and the charges of insurance upon the whole (s.16(3)).

The difference between valued and unvalued policies is of great practical importance. In a valued policy, the buyer's anticipated profits are normally included in the value declared by adding a percentage of, say, 10 or 15 per cent. to the invoice value and the incidental shipping and insurance charges of the goods. In an unvalued policy, the buyer's anticipated profits cannot be included in the insurable value.

In modern export practice, valued policies are the rule and unvalued policies are rarely used. This tendency goes so far that, in the case of floating policies and open covers where the assured cannot always declare the insurable value before arrival of the goods or notices of their loss, special provision is made for the valuation of such shipments.[26]

The "insured value" is the agreed value (if any) specified in the policy; the "shipping value" is defined in identical terms with the definition of insurable value for unvalued policies, as set out in section 16(3). If there is the possibility of rising market prices during the transit of the goods, the assured who has covered the goods under an ordinary policy can obtain a so-called *"increased value"* policy. In all three versions of the Institute Cargo Clauses A, B and C, clause 14 includes wording which takes this practice into account. Clause 14 is reproduced on p. 528, *post*.

(ii) *Voyage, time and mixed policies*

Another classification of policies is into voyage, time and mixed policies (s.25). Under a voyage policy the subject-matter is insured in transport from one point to another; under a time policy the subject-matter is insured for a fixed time. Under a mixed policy the subject-matter is insured both for a particular journey and a certain period of time.

---

[25] Unvalued policies are sometimes called open policies. This term should not be confused with the open cover; see p. 497, *post*.
[26] See p. 495, *post*.

In voyage policies, the duration of the insurance cover is governed by the transit clause in Institute Cargo Clauses A, B and C. Cover is provided from warehouse to warehouse and hence the transit clause extends the marine insurance to land risks incidental to the sea voyage. If the transit clause is deleted, the risk will commence and terminate at the sea ports. The transit clause is considered in more detail later in this chapter.[27]

Time policies[28] were rarely used in export transactions but are found more frequently in recent times. These policies may cover a period exceeding 12 months[29]; they often contain the "*continuation clause*" under which the parties agree that—

> should the vessel at the expiration of this policy be at sea, or in distress, or at a port of refuge or of call, she shall, provided previous notice be given to the underwriters, be held covered at a *pro rata* monthly premium to her port of destination.[30]

Mixed policies are issued in the frequent instances where goods are insured under a contract for both voyage and time. Here the insurer is only liable under the insurance when a loss occurs during the period of insurance and while the ship is on the specified voyage.

(iii) *Floating policies*

The floating policy lays down the general conditions of insurance, but not the particulars of the individual consignments intended to be covered. These particulars are usually unknown to the assured when effecting the insurance. Notwithstanding this element of uncertainty, the floating policy covers automatically all shipments made thereunder and the assured is obliged to "declare" the individual shipments to the insurer with due expedition. The floating policy might cover, say, shipments to stated destinations within 12 months to the aggregate amount of £50,000. When the assured ships and declares a shipment of £3,000, the available cover is reduced to £47,000, and when the policy is fully declared, it is written off.[31]

---

[27] See p. 514, *post*.

[28] For a discussion of the nature of a time policy, see *Compania Maritima San Basilio S.A. v. Oceanus Mutual Underwriting Association (Bermuda) Ltd*. [1977] Q.B. 49.

[29] s.25(2) of the Marine Insurance Act 1906, which, in principle, prohibited time policies exceeding 12 months, was repealed by the Finance Act 1959, s.30(5). S.23(2) to (5) of the Marine Insurance Act 1906 was likewise repealed by s.30(5) of the Finance Act 1959.

[30] Other forms of the continuation clause are in use; see Arnould. *The Law of Marine Insurance and Average* (British Shipping Laws), (16th ed., 1981), para. 514. The continuation clause in the Institute Time Clauses makes the prolongation of the risk dependent on notice being given to the insurer.

[31] Arnould, *op cit*, para. 165.

The use of the floating policy has diminished in recent years. Open covers have taken their place in many cases. Brokers have also effected time policies in their stead, and the informal "slip" policy has taken the place of the floating policy in Lloyd's market.[32] A consideration of the floating policy is, however, still required because that type of policy forms the model on which the frequently used informal open cover is framed.

Under the floating policy it is usual to supply the assured with a book of declaration forms or certificates of insurance on which he declares the shipments as they go forward.

The Marine Insurance Act 1906 contains, in section 29, the following provisions on floating policies:

(1) A floating policy is a policy which describes the insurance in general terms, and leaves the name of the ship or ships and other particulars to be defined by subsequent declaration.

(2) The subsequent declaration or declarations may be made by indorsement on the policy, or in other customary manner.

(3) Unless the policy otherwise provides, the declarations must be made in the order of dispatch or shipment. They must, in the case of goods, comprise all consignments within the terms of the policy, and the value of the goods or other property must be honestly stated, but an omission or erroneous declaration may be rectified even after loss or arrival, provided the omission or declaration was made in good faith.

(4) Unless the policy otherwise provides, where a declaration of value is not made until after notice of loss or arrival, the policy must be treated as an unvalued policy as regards the subject-matter of that declaration.

Section 29(4) discourages shippers from waiting until they have knowledge as to whether or not a particular shipment has arrived safely, before deciding whether or not to declare it. Were it not for this subsection, shippers could declare only losses. The effect of the subsection, however, is that such a practice would result in the subject-matter being treated as though the policy were an unvalued one. The value of the goods would accordingly be assessed by reference to the provisions of section 16(3).[33] However, the assured need not, and in fact sometimes cannot, declare the shipment before the ship sails. As seen above, section 29(3) of the Act provides that an omission or erroneous declaration may be rectified even after loss or arrival, provided the omission or declaration was made in good faith. Further, the insurer cannot refuse an individual risk which falls within the terms of the policy although he is entitled to refuse a risk which the policy was not intended to cover, or a declaration which is made dishonestly.

The floating policy often contains a clause obliging the assured to make declarations of shipment as early as possible. It has been held[34] that an

---

[32] V. Dover, *A Handbook of Marine Insurance* (8th ed.) London, H. F. and G. Witherby Ltd., 1975, p. 133.
[33] See p. 493, *ante*.
[34] In *Union Insurance Society of Canton Ltd.* v. *George Wills & Co.* [1916] 1 A.C. 281.

assured who, in breach of this undertaking, omitted to make a declaration at the earliest possible moment was not entitled to recover under the policy for loss suffered by him; the assured could not rely on section 29(3) because it was a case in which no declaration at all had been made within the express terms of the contract, and the insurer had, consequently, lost the opportunity of reinsuring the risk.

The floating policy is not a time policy but an aggregation of voyage policies. The assured, who desires to avoid leaving some of his shipments unprotected, has to take out a further floating policy before the expiration of the current policy. This is a disadvantage of the floating policy because, if an assured forgets to take out a new policy the goods may travel uninsured. This disadvantage is avoided if an *"always open"* open cover is taken out. In the case of a floating policy, the new policy which follows the old one, contains the clause—

to follow and succeed policy No. . . . dated . . .

The meaning of this clause is, in the words of Lord Blackburn,[35] "there being consecutive policies any loss declared is to be borne first by the earlier policies, and that it is not till after the earlier policy is exhausted, either by losses or declared adventures which have come in safe, that the underwriters on the policy which follows are to bear the loss, if any."

The floating policy often contains a clause limiting the risk per vessel, *e.g.* a policy granting cover for a total of £500,000 may provide—

limit per bottom, £50,000.

The assured who wishes to ship in excess of the limit per vessel, should make arrangements for a separate additional cover prior to shipment.

The per bottom clause is regularly supplemented by a location clause by which the insurer restricts to a fixed maximum sum his liability for accumulation of covered risks in one locality. The location clause is invariably inserted by underwriters where insuring land risks incidental to sea transit. The following is an example of the location clause:

> In the case of loss and/or damage before shipment to the insured interest in any one locality the underwriter, notwithstanding anything to the contrary contained in this contract, shall not be liable in respect of any one accident or series of accidents arising out of the same event for more than his proportion of an amount up to, but not exceeding, the sum of £ . . . . . . in all taken in conjunction with preceding and/or succeeding insurances. The conveyance of the insured interest upon interior waterways or by land transit shall not be deemed to be shipment within the meaning of this clause.

The individual location risk is often limited to the same amount as the per bottom risk. As a result of the location clause, if goods accumulated in

---

[35] In *Inglis* v. *Stock* (1885) 10 App.Cas. 263, 269.

one warehouse prior to shipment are destroyed by fire, the insurers are only liable to the sum stated in the location clause although the aggregate insurable value of the goods may far exceed that limit. Dover maintains[36] that the location clause limits only pre-shipment accumulations in one locality but not accumulations at the port of discharge or later; this view is supported by the present wording of the clause but the clause can, of course, be extended by agreement of the parties to limit the liability of the insurer for accumulations subsequent to the discharge from the overseas vessel.

The premium is often arranged at fixed rates for specified kinds of goods, *e.g.* textiles, hardware, motor-cars, etc. Sometimes a "held covered" clause[37] is added providing:

other interests held covered at rates to be arranged.

The effect of such a clause is to bring within the ambit of the insurance cover voyages or goods not specifically mentioned in the policy. The assured is bound to give notice to the underwriters immediately he becomes aware of facts which fall within the held covered clause, otherwise the voyage and goods will not be held covered.[38] An underwriter receiving notice is bound to give insurance cover at a reasonable premium, being the market rate for a particular risk. A floating policy describes the type of goods, gives the rates of premium, and the voyages to be undertaken, but it does not specify the names of the ships to be used. For his own protection, an insurer will insist that the vessels used be of a particular class in the shipping register. He will insist on the attachment of the Institute Maintenance of Class Clause, under which the assured warrants that all the ships used will be of the specified class. This clause is in the form of a warranty pursuant to section 33, and failure to comply with it discharges the underwriter as from the time of the breach.

(iv) *Open covers*

The open cover, combined with the issue of insurance certificates, has become the most common and most popular form of insurance used in the export trade. The open cover is another method of effecting a general insurance for recurring shipments, the details of which are unknown when the insurance is taken out. This method resembles, in many respects, the floating policy; in particular, the assured is likewise bound to declare all

---

[36] V. Dover, *loc. cit.*, p. 495, *ante.*

[37] The "held covered" clause is discussed on p. 505, *post.*

[38] *Thames and Mersey Insurance Co. Ltd.* v. *H. T. Van Laun & Co.* [1917] 2 K.B. 48 (note (1905)).

individual shipments effected thereunder unless the contract of insurance otherwise provides.

The open cover, like the slip,[39] is not an insurance policy but is a document by which the underwriter undertakes subsequently to issue duly executed floating or specific policies within the terms of the cover. Open covers sometimes embody the *Institute Standard Conditions for Open Covers*[40] which are similar in wording to the Institute Standard Conditions for Floating Policies, except that they use the words "open cover" instead of "floating policies."

The open cover may be limited in time or may be permanent while the floating policy is normally limited to twelve months. Where the open cover is perpetual in character ("always open"), a clause is inserted enabling both parties to give notice of cancellation of the cover within a stated time, *e.g.* thirty days or three months.

The open cover normally contains a maximum limit of the insurer's liability per bottom and a location clause like the floating policy.[41]

Frequently special conditions are laid down in the open cover for the determination of the insurable value. It is sometimes provided that, if the value of a consignment is declared before the loss occurs, the declaration of value shall be binding, but, where the loss occurs before the declaration, the basis of valuation shall be the prime cost of the goods plus expenses, freight, insurance and a fixed percentage of profit, usually 15 per cent.; and sometimes it is stated that this amount is to be increased by the value of any duty payable or paid on the goods.

From the practical point of view, the difference between the floating policy and the open cover may be stated as follows: in the case of a floating policy the assured receives a formal policy document. In case of an open cover no formal policy is issued and the arrangement is more informal, but the assured is entitled to demand a policy if he requires it, *e.g.* if litigation ensues. In both cases the cover is written off, as declarations are made.

A recital of the main terms of the open cover is normally found on certificates of insurance issued under the cover in respect of individual shipments declared thereunder.[42]

If the open cover contains unusual conditions which an assignee of a certificate of insurance issued under it might not expect to be included in the contract of insurance, they should be printed specifically on the certificate; a mere reference to the open cover does not embody them, particularly if other conditions contained in the open cover are reproduced in the certificate. Thus, in one case[43] an open cover issued by a

---

[39] See p. 499, *post.*
[40] On Institute Clauses, see p. 512, *post.*
[41] See p. 497, *ante.*
[42] See below in the text.
[43] *MacLeod Ross & Co. Ltd.* v. *Compagnie d'Assurances Générales L'Helvetia of St. Gall* [1952] W.N. 56.

Swiss insurance company to a French firm of forwarders contained a provision that the insurers could only be sued in the commercial tribunals of the place where the contract was entered into, *i.e.* in the Swiss courts. Customers of the French forwarders sold a quantity of canned ham to an English company, and asked the French forwarders to insure it. The forwarders sent declarations of the consignment to the insurers, who issued certificates of insurance which, though referring to the open cover and reprinting some of its terms, did not state, or refer to, the provision giving exclusive jurisdiction to the Swiss courts. The documents, including the insurance certificates, were accepted by the buyers who claimed under the insurance for damage which, as they alleged, was covered by the contract of insurance. In an action commenced by the buyers against the insurers in the English courts, the latter asked for a stay of proceedings on the ground that the Swiss courts had exclusive jurisdiction. The English Court of Appeal refused the stay because, on the construction of the documents, the open cover and the certificates were separate contracts and the buyers were not bound by the clause relating to the jurisdiction of the Swiss courts in the open cover. In support of this view the judges in the Court of Appeal referred to the rule in *Phoenix Insurance Co. of Hartford* v. *De Monchy*.[44]

(v) *Blanket policies*

In the case of floating policies and open covers the assured has normally to make declarations of the individual shipments falling under these insurances to the insurer. This is inconvenient to the exporter and requires a considerable amount of labour and costs where the various consignments are of small value or the voyage is of short duration. In these cases the assured will take out a "blanket policy" which usually provides that he need not advise the insurer of the individual shipments and that a lump sum premium—instead of a premium at several rates— shall cover all shipments.

The contract of insurance

We have now to consider the rights and duties of the parties to the contract of insurance.

The slip and the policy

The proposed assured and the broker decide on the particulars of the proposed cover. The broker then prepares a memorandum or slip. This

---

[44] (1929) 45 T.L.R. 543; see p. 501, *post*.

sets out details of the proposed insurable property, the voyage or period of time for which the insurance is to be provided, a valuation of the subject matter, an indication of which policy form (A, B, or C) is required, an indication of any standard clauses to be incorporated such as the Institute War Clauses, and any other special terms or warranties which are required. The broker presents this slip to underwriting syndicates, the first, known as "the leader," generally being a well established person of good reputation. The initialling of the slip by the underwriter amounts to an acceptance of risk by the underwriter and creates a binding contract between the parties in relation to the portion of the total risk accepted. In *General Reinsurance Corporation* v. *Forsakringsaktiebolaget Fennia Patria*,[45] a Finnish insurance company sought to amend its reinsurance of a particular risk at Lloyds, London. An amendment slip was accepted by General Reinsurance for part of the amount stated on it. Before the total amount was underwritten, a loss occurred. Fennia Patria wanted to cancel the amendment because in the circumstances the unamended cover was more favourable to it. It was held, however, that a valid contract had been concluded between Fennia Patria and General Reinsurance and hence Fennia Patria could not cancel the amendment on the ground that the insured risk on the amended slip was not completely covered.

Once the slip has been initialled fully, the total risk is covered. The broker takes the slip to the signing office at Lloyd's where it is signed, thereby executing the policy. A contract of marine insurance must be embodied in a policy before it is admissible in evidence.[46] If there is any discrepancy between the policy and the slip, reference may be made to the slip.[47] In such a case, it is the terms of the slip that prevail.[48] If insurers wish to make their obligations as expressed in the policy differ from the obligations undertaken in the slip, they must reserve the power to make such alteration in the slip.[49]

---

[45] [1983] Q.B. 856 (C.A.).

[46] Marine Insurance Act 1906, s.2.

[47] *Ibid.* s.89. Stamp Duty is no longer payable upon policies of marine insurance: Finance Act 1970, Sched. 7, para. 1(2)(*b*).

[48] *Symington & Co.* v. *Union Insurance Society of Canton Ltd.* (*No.* 2) (1928) 34 Com.Cas. 233, 235, *per* Scrutton L.J.

[49] In principle the contract of insurance is subject to identical terms for all underwriters who have signed the slip: *Jaglom* v. *Excess Insurance Co. Ltd.* [1972] 2 Q.B. 250, 257. The underwriters may also agree on "t.b.a. L/U" which means that they will be bound by "terms to be agreed with leading underwriters" without requiring further consultation: *Amercian Airlines Inc.* v. *Hope* [1973] 1 Lloyd's Rep. 233, 245.

On the liability of the broker to the underwriter if the broker indicates to reduce ("sign down") the underwriter's liability on the slip if the risk is oversubscribed, but the slip cannot be signed down, see *General Accident Fire and Life Assurance Co.* v. *Tanter, The Zephyr* [1985] 2 Lloyd's Rep. 529 (C.A.).

Certificates of insurance; *brokers' cover notes*; *letters of insurance*

In modern export practice, much use is made of documents which, though lacking the legal characteristics of an insurance policy and, therefore, being of a lower order than the latter, acknowledge that insurance cover has been obtained. The most important of these documents are certificates of insurance, but brokers' cover notes and letters of insurance issued by the seller of the insured goods are likewise occasionally used. The reasons for the popularity of these documents are explained by Bailhache J.[50] as follows:

> The preparation of a policy of insurance takes some little time, particularly if there are a number of underwriters or several insurance companies, and when documents require to be tendered with promptness on the arrival of a steamer in order that expense may not be incurred through delay in unloading, or through the buyer not being ready to take delivery, it is not always practicable to obtain actual policies of insurance. In order to facilitate business in circumstances such as these, buyers are accordingly in the habit of accepting brokers' cover notes and certificates of insurance instead of insisting on policies.

The certificate of insurance is particularly frequently used when an open cover has been obtained. It consists of two parts: the first part recites the main terms of the open cover under which the goods are insured[51]; the second part contains the declaration of the goods stating the value insured, the voyage and the marks, numbers and other particulars of the goods. The certificate is signed by the insurance broker who procured the open cover, or by the assured himself.

Certificates of insurance which are issued by an insurance broker or assured entitle the holder to demand the issue of a policy in the terms of the certificate and to claim for losses. According to older authorities[52] the buyer under a c.i.f. contract is not obliged, in English law, to accept a certificate of insurance in the place of an insurance policy unless he has agreed to do so or there is an established custom of the trade to that effect, but, as has been explained earlier,[53] the modern view is that an insurance certificate entitling the holder to demand the issue of a policy would be equivalent to the policy itself.

Brokers' cover notes are merely advice notes sent by brokers to their clients and informing them that insurance cover has been obtained.[54] Their practical value is smaller than that of certificates of insurance and, in the absence of stipulations to the contrary, the c.i.f. buyer need not accept a cover note in the place of a policy.

---

[50] In *Wilson, Holgate & Co.,* v. *Belgian Grain and Produce Co.* [1920] 2 K.B. 1, 8.
[51] See p. 498, *ante.*
[52] *Diamond Alkali Export Corporation* v. *Fl. Bourgeois* [1921] 3 K.B. 443; *Phoenix Insurance Co. of Hartford* v. *De Monchy* (1929) 45 T.L.R. 543.
[53] See pp. 39–40, *ante.*
[54] See p. 490, *ante.*

Letters of insurance, addressed by the seller (the assured) to the buyer, confirm that an insurance has been effected. Such an advice may or may not be correct; its value depends on the trust which the buyer reposes in the seller. Letters of insurance have no established status in law but are admissible in evidence against the seller (the assured) if litigation ensues between him and the buyer.

The duty to disclose

A contract of marine insurance, like every contract of insurance, is a contract based upon the utmost good faith (contract *uberrimae fidei*), and if the utmost good faith is not observed by either party[55] the contract may be avoided by the other party (s.17).[56] It follows from the confidential nature of the contract that the assured is bound to disclose to the insurer, before the contract is concluded, every material circumstance[57] which is, or in the ordinary course of business ought to be, known to him (s.18(1)). Every circumstance is regarded as material which would influence the judgment of a prudent insurer in fixing the premium or determining whether he will take the risk (s.18(2)).[58] Thus, in one case[59] the goods were leather jerkins ex government surplus and were manufactured at least 20 years earlier, but they were declared to the insurers simply as "new men's clothing in bales for export"; the court held that there was a failure to disclose material facts and the assured could not recover under the policy when the goods were stolen.

Section 20 deals with the effect of various representations. A material representation must be true, otherwise the insurer can avoid the contract.[60] A material representation is one which would influence the

---

[55] As to the insurer's duty see *Banque Keyser Ullman SA* v. *Skandia (U.K.) Insurance Ltd.* [1989] 3 W.L.R. 25 (C.A.). The duty to observe utmost good faith does not exist between the assignee of the benefit of the insurance and the insurer: *Bank of Nova Scotia* v. *Hellenic Mutual War Risks Association (Bermuda) Ltd. The Good Luck*, [1989] 2 Lloyd's Rep. 238 (C.A.).
[56] The duty of utmost good faith is a mutual duty, owed by the parties to each other.
[57] Circumstances are facts: they must be known, or should reasonably be known to the insured.
[58] See also *Container Transport International Inc.* v. *Oceanus Mutual Underwriting Association (Bermuda) Ltd.* [1984] 1 Lloyd's Rep. 476, 492 *per* Kerr L.J. In *Mayne Nickless Ltd.* v. *Pegler* [1974], 1 N.S.W.L.R. 228, 239, Samuels J. offered another test, namely that a fact is material if it would have *reasonably* affected the mind of a prudent insurer, and this formulation was approved by the P.C. in *Marlene Knitting Mills Pty. Ltd.* v. *Greater Pacific General Insurance Ltd.* [1976] 2 Lloyd's Rep. 631, 642; this is a preferable formulation.
[59] *Anglo-African Merchants* v. *Bayley* [1970] 1 Q.B. 311, 319–320. In *Woolcott* v. *Sun Alliance and London Insurance Ltd.* [1978] 1 W.L.R. 493 it was held that the insurance company could avoid a fire insurance policy on the ground of material non-disclosure because the assured had failed to disclose that he had been convicted of robbery. See also *Lambert* v. *Co-operative Insurance Society Ltd.* [1975] 2 Lloyd's Rep. 485.
[60] s.20(1).

judgment of a prudent insurer in fixing the premium or accepting the risk.[61] The section distinguishes between representations as to fact, and representations as to expectation or belief.[62] In the case of the former, the insurer cannot avoid the contract if the representation of fact is substantially correct.[63] In the case of the latter, the insurer cannot avoid the contract if the representation as to a matter of expectation or belief is made in good faith.[64]

Where the contract is concluded through an insurance broker or other agent, the agent must disclose to the insurer every material circumstance which is known to himself or has been communicated to him, or ought to be known by him, in addition to material circumstances that should be disclosed by the assured (s.19);[64a] but a policy effected by the agent in ignorance of a material fact known to the assured cannot be avoided if it has come too late to the knowledge of the assured to be communicated to the agent (s.19(*b*)). It therefore follows, that when sections 17 to 20 are read together, one way of formulating the test as to the duty of disclosure and fairness and accuracy of representation is to ask the following questions: "Having regard to all the circumstances known or deemed to be known to the assured and to his broker, and ignoring those which are expressly excepted from the duty of disclosure, was the presentation in summary form to the underwriter a fair and substantially accurate presentation of the risk proposed for insurance, so that a prudent insurer could form a proper judgment—either on the presentation alone or by asking questions if he was sufficiently put on inquiry and wanted further details whether or not to accept the proposal, and, if so, on what terms?"[65] In the absence of inquiry, the following circumstances need not be disclosed (s.18(3)):

(*a*) Any circumstance which diminishes the risk.
(*b*) Any circumstance which is known or presumed to be known to the insurer. The insurer is presumed to know matters of common notoriety or knowledge, and matters which an insurer in the ordinary course of his business, as such, ought to know.
(*c*) Any circumstance as to which information is waived by the insurer.
(*d*) Any circumstance which it is superfluous to disclose by reason of any express or implied warranty.

The exporter who wishes to insure goods sold for export will ask himself whether he has to give the insurer detailed information of the

---

[61] s.20(2).   [62] s.20(3).   [63] s.20(4).   [64] s.20(5).
[64a] If the assured gives the broker full disclosure but the latter fails to do so to the insurer, the contract is voidable but the insurer may have waived his right to have further disclosure: *Roberts* v. *Plaisted* [1989] 2 Lloyd's Rep. 341, see p. 492 *ante*. On the liability of the broker in such a case see, *Forsikringsaktieselskapei Vesta* v. *J.N.E. Butcher Bain Dawes Ltd.* [1989] 1 Lloyd's Rep. 331.
[65] *C.T.I. International Inc.* v. *Oceanus Mutual Underwriting Association (Bermuda) Ltd.* [1984] 1 Lloyd's Rep. 476, 496, *per* Kerr L.J.

nature of the cargo, and especially of an unusual and particularly dangerous propensity of the consignment. The following rules emerge from the decisions of the courts[66]:

(1) Where the goods are an ordinary species of lawful merchandise which may fairly be described as a parcel of ordinary cargo, the exporter need not, in strict law, disclose details of the insured risk to the insurer, but where there is the slightest doubt which a reasonable person can entertain, the exporter would be wise to disclose details.

(2) Where the goods are of an unusual and particularly dangerous kind, the duty of disclosure arises.[67]

(3) Where the cargo is tendered in such a manner—*e.g.* under a novel or unusual description—as to put an ordinary careful insurer on inquiry, and he fails to inquire, a waiver of information under section 18(3)(*c*) can be assumed.[68]

Once there is non-disclosure, be it fraudulent, negligent or innocent, the aggrieved party is entitled to elect whether he will avoid or affirm the contract.[68a] The right to avoid "exists from the time when the contract is made and continues until the underwriter, with full knowledge of the non-disclosure or misrepresentation, affirms or is deemed to have affirmed the contract . . . Full knowledge of the facts is essential before there can be any question of affirmation—being put on inquiry is insufficient . . . and even when the underwriter has full knowledge of the facts, he is entitled to a reasonable time in which to decide whether to affirm the contract. In a situation in which the underwriter has taken no action to affirm or repudiate the contract and a reasonable time for making up his mind has elapsed, he will be deemed to have affirmed the contract if either so much time has elapsed that the necessary inference is one of affirmation, or the assured has been prejudiced by the delay in making an election or the rights of third parties have intervened."[69] Avoiding the contract necessitates returning the premium unless there is fraud (s.84).

---

[66] *Greenhill* v. *Federal Insurance Co. Ltd.* [1927] 1 K.B. 65; see further *Mann, Macneal Boyd* v. *Dubois* (1811) 3 Camp. 133 and *Carter* v. *Boehm* (1766) 3 Burr. 1905, which have received a restricted interpretation in these modern cases.
[67] Arnould, *op. cit.*, para. 654.
[68] Sargant L.J. in *Greenhill* v. *Federal Insurance Co. Ltd.* [1927] 1 K.B. 65, 89.
[68a] Whether the aggrieved party is also entitled to claim damages is very doubtful. It was held in *Banque Keyser Ullman SA* v. *Skandia (U.K.) Insurance Ltd.* [1989] 3 W.L.R. 25 (C.A.) that such a claim could not be founded on contract or a statutory duty, but could only be brought in tort (the decision, although well reasoned, is not convincing). See also *Banque Financière de la Cité* v. *Westgate Insurance Co., Financial Times,* August 12, 1988. The claim cannot be founded on the Misrepresentation Act 1967, s.2, because the breach of duty consists merely of *silence* and not a positive act.
[69] *Liberian Insurance Agency* v. *Mosse* [1977] 2 Lloyd's Rep. 560, 565, *per* Donaldson J.

The Rules for Construction of Policy, which are appended to the Act, provide, that the term "goods" means goods in the nature of merchandise but, in the absence of any usage to the contrary, deck cargo and living animals must be insured specifically, and not under the general denomination of goods (r. 17). This definition still applies although the Lloyd's S. G. Policy appended to the Marine Insurance Act 1906 is no longer used.

The "held covered" clause

In practice goods are normally specified in detail, and the assured has to take great care to describe the goods correctly. A material misdescription of the goods in the policy enables the insurer to avoid the contract on the ground of misrepresentation. This is even true where the erroneous description was due to the fact that the assured failed to realise the materiality of the description, or where he acted under an innocent mistake or where the misdescription was due to an accident. In view of these serious consequences the parties sometimes insert a "held covered" clause into the contract which covers, at any rate, innocent misdescription of the goods but obliges the assured to pay an additional premium if necessary. The clause "held covered at premium to be arranged" places the insurer on risk.[70] The following illustration of such a clause is taken from the Institute Cargo Clauses A, B and C:[71]

> Where, after attachment of this insurance, the destination is changed by the Assured, *held covered at a premium and on conditions to be arranged subject to prompt notice being given to the Underwriters.*

Even without express provision, a "held covered" clause is always subject to an implied term that the assured will give prompt notice to the insurer of any event which affects the clause.[72]

In one case,[73] the assured described a case of second-hand machinery simply as machinery, innocently believing that that description was sufficient, and the insurance policy contained a "held covered" clause. The machinery suffered breakage during the voyage, and it was held that, while the description of the subject-matter was a material misrepresentation which normally would entitle the insurer to rescind the contract, this defect was cured by the "held covered" clause and the insurers had to pay

---

[70] *American Airlines Inc.* v. *Hope* [1973] 1 Lloyd's Rep. 233, 241.
[71] Clause 10 of Institute of Cargo Clauses A, B and C.
[72] *Thames and Mersey Marine Insurance Company Ltd.* v. *H. T. Van Laun & Co.* [1917] 2 K.B. 48 (note), (1905); *Greenock SS. Co.* v. *Maritime Insurance Co.* [1903] 1 K.B. 367.
[73] In *Hewitt Brothers* v. *Wilson* [1915] 2 K.B. 739. Further, *Kirby* v. *Consindit Società per Azioni* [1969] 1 Lloyd's Rep. 75.

for the loss suffered by the assured but were entitled to an additional premium.

The exporter can obtain the protection of the "held covered" clause only if he has acted with the utmost good faith towards the insurer, this being an obligation which rests on him throughout the currency of the policy. In one case[74] the assured imported canned pork butts from France to the United Kingdom and effected an "all risks" policy[75] covering inherent vice and hidden defects and the condemnation of the goods by the authorities; the policy provided that the assured warranted that all tins were marked by the manufacturers with an indication of the date of manufacture and it contained a "held covered" clause. Some of the tins were not properly marked, and when part of the consignment was rejected by the sub-purchasers of the assured, the assured claimed that, despite the inaccurate markings, they were protected by the "held covered" clause. McNair J. rejected the contention and decided in favour of the insurers on the ground that the assured had not been frank with their insurers and that the "held covered" clause could not have been invoked if, "at the time when the assured seeks to invoke the clause, they have been and are unable to correct the misdescription."[76]

In another instance, an assured failed to disclose that a cargo of enamelware he was exporting was an end of stock purchase bought at a very low price which had been touched up by overpainting. Further, it was not disclosed that the enamelware was packed in cartons, not wooden cases as stated. Here, the "held covered" clause contained in the policy was not applied in favour of the assured because the misdescription was of such a serious nature that no underwriter would have quoted a reasonable commercial rate for cover. The "held covered" clause was held to apply only where such a premium was applicable, but here, a very high extra premium would have been quoted.[77]

The insurable interest

It is a fundamental principle of insurance law[78] that the assured must have an insurable interest in the subject-matter insured at the time of the loss.[79] If he has such an interest, an assured can recover for an insured loss occurring during the period of insurance cover, notwithstanding that the loss occurred prior to the insurance contract being concluded, unless

---

[74] *Overseas Commodities Ltd.* v. *Style* [1958] 1 Lloyd's Rep. 553.
[75] The policy was actually an "all loss or damage" policy.
[76] *Overseas Commodities Ltd.* v. *Style* [1958] 1 Lloyd's Rep. 553, 559.
[77] *Liberian Insurance Agency Inc.* v. *Mosse* [1977] 2 Lloyd's Rep. 560.
[78] Marine Insurance Act 1906, s.6.
[79] The provisions of s.6 are reiterated by Clause 11.1 Institute Cargo Clauses A, B and C.

the assured was aware of the loss and the underwriters were not.[80] In *Lucena* v. *Craufurd*[81] Lawrence J. defined an insurable interest in the following terms: "To be interested in the preservation of a thing, is to be so circumstanced with respect to it as to have benefit from its existence, prejudice from its destruction. The property of a thing and the interest divisible from it may be very different: of the first the price is generally the measure, but by interest in a thing every benefit and advantage arising out of or depending on such thing, may be considered as being comprehended." Essentially, therefore, in order to have an insurable interest in property, a person must in some way suffer loss as a result of its damage, loss or destruction. The Marine Insurance Act 1906 states in section 5(1): "Subject to the provision of this Act, every person has an insurable interest who is interested in a marine adventure," and by section 5(2) it is provided that:

> In particular a person is interested in a marine adventure where he stands in any legal or equitable relation to the adventure or to any insurable property at risk therein, in consequence of which he may benefit by the safety or due arrival of insurable property or may be prejudiced by its loss or by damage thereto, or by detention thereof, or may incur liability in respect thereof.

If a person attempted to insure property in which he has no insurable interest, the contract is not one of insurance and is void. Such a contract is void both as being against public policy and also as being contrary to the statutory prohibition against contracts of marine insurance by way of gaming or wagering.[82] Such a contract is also void under the Gaming Act 1845, s.18. An underwriter may agree to insure goods without seeking proof that the proposer has an insurable interest in them and such a policy is known as a ppi (policy proof of interest) policy. Although a ppi policy carries no legal obligation under the Marine Insurance Act and other statutes, an underwriter will usually carry out his obligations in the usual way. Such a policy, being dependent on the underwriter's honour, is often referred to as an honour policy. Although it is unlikely that an underwriter would risk his reputation by refusing to pay out on such a policy, any action against a trustee in bankruptcy or receiver of such underwriter would fail.

If goods which are the subject matter of a contract of sale are insured, the question may arise whether the seller or the buyer has an insurable interest in them or whether both have such an interest. The answer

---

[80] Institute Cargo Clauses A, B and C, Clause 11.2.

[81] (1806) 2 Bos. & P. (N.S.) 269, 302.

[82] A policy effected "interest or no interest" or "without proof of interest other than the policy itself" or "without benefit of salvage to the insurer" or subject to any other like term, is deemed to be a gaming or wagering contract: Marine Insurance Act 1906, s.4(2). Provided there is no possibility of salvage, a policy may however be effected "without benefit of salvage," s.4(2).

depends on the terms of the contract of sale and the state of its performance. Clearly the party in whom the property in the goods is vested has an insurable interest. Possession of the goods, or the right to immediate possession, likewise constitutes an insurable interest.

In addition, it is thought that the party who bears the risk has likewise an insurable interest. The decision of the House of Lords in *Leigh and Sillivan Ltd.* v. *Aliakmon Shipping Co. Ltd.*[83] does not affect this position; the highest court decided in this case that a buyer on c.i.f. or c. and f. terms, to whom only the risk, but no proprietary or possessory interest had passed, could not bring an action in the tort of negligence against the carrier, but it did not deal with the question of the insurable interest (s.7(2)). The buyer has always an insurable interest in the profits which he would have made on resale if the goods had arrived safely.

The unpaid seller has a contingent interest in the goods because he may have to exercise his right of stoppage in transit. He has also a defeasible interest in them until the buyer is deemed to have accepted the goods and thus lost his right to reject them. Similarly an f.o.b. seller or a c. and f. seller, who has not received the price yet, has a contingent interest in the goods during transit. Contingent and defeasible interests constitute insurable interests within the law (s.7(1)). They can—and should—be covered by a *seller's contingency insurance;* it is obtainable from commercial insurance and is not covered by the E.C.G.D. guarantee.

Problems have arisen where unascertained goods are sold on f.o.b. terms and the buyer wishes to take out an insurance, *e.g.* when part of a bulk cargo is sold or unspecified goods of the same description are shipped to several unconnected buyers at the same place. Here the buyer does not acquire property in his portion of the goods before they are appropriated,[84] but normally the goods are carried at his risk and this has been held sufficient to given him an insurable interest.[85]

A carrier has an insurable interest in the goods entrusted to him since he is, in principle, liable to the cargo owner for loss of or damage to the goods; he may insure the owner's goods and sue on the policy as trustee of the owner.[86]

An agent who is instructed by an overseas principal to buy goods may order these goods in the home market in his own name. This procedure is sometimes adopted by confirming houses.[87] If in these cases the agent has

---

[83] [1986] A.C. 785. See p. 46, *ante.*

[84] Sale of Goods Act 1979, ss.16 and 18, r. 5(1).

[85] *Karlshamns Oljefabriker* v. *Eastport Navigation Co. The Elafi* [1981] 2 Lloyd's Rep. 679; *Leigh and Sillivan Ltd.* v. *Aliakmon Shipping Co. Ltd.* [1986] A.C. 785; also *Inglis* v. *Stock* (1855) App. Cas. 263. By s.8 of the Marine Insurance Act 1906 a partial interest of any nature is insurable.

[86] But if under the terms of the contract of carriage he has incurred no risk (which will be a rare case), he cannot recover under the policy because mere possession of another person's goods (without incurring liability for them) does not constitute an insurable interest: *Scott* v. *Globe Marine Insurance Co. Ltd.* (1896) 1 Com.Cas. 370.

[87] See p. 297 *ante.*

already shipped the goods and the insurance covering the transit risks has been arranged by the principal, the agent may find himself under a liability to the seller in the home market which would be onerous if the principal became insolvent. The agent would in this case have the right of stoppage in transit as if he were a seller,[88] but it is not always certain that the exercise of this right will lead to practical satisfaction. As a result of an agreement between the Institute of London Underwriters and the British Export Houses Association insurance cover is available to protect the agent against these eventualities. The facilities under this protection are only available on prior request to the underwriters concerned. The Export Credits Guarantee Department is likewise prepared to cover agents against these risks.[89]

Under section 26(2) of the Marine Insurance Act 1906, the nature and extent of the interest of the assured in the subject-matter insured need not be specified in the policy. The Act refers to a number of insurable interests. For example, the insurer under a contract of marine insurance who has an insurable interest, may reinsure in respect of it,[90] but the original assured has no rights or interest in respect of such reinsurance and so can only proceed against his original insurer.[91] Where advance freight is payable, the person advancing the freight has an insurable interest in so far as the freight is not repayable in case of loss.[92] An assured has an insurable interest in respect of his insurance costs.[93] The owner of insurable property has an insurable interest in respect of the full value of such property notwithstanding that some third party may have agreed, or be liable to indemnify him in the case of loss.[94]

The premium

The premium is payable to the insurer when he issues the policy unless another arrangement is agreed upon by the parties or required by trade custom (s.52). It has been explained earlier[95] that in normal cases the broker is responsible solely and directly to the insurer for payment of the premium.

A proportionate part of the premium can be reclaimed where the assured has over-insured under an unvalued policy (s.84(2)(e)), but not

---

[88] Sale of Goods Act 1979, s.38(2). See p. 298, *ante*.
[89] See p. 474 *ante*.
[90] Marine Insurance Act 1906, s.9(1).
[91] *Ibid*. s.9(2). On problems concerning the relationship between the insurer and reinsurer, see p. 500, *ante*.
[92] s.12; see p. 552, *post*.
[93] s.13.
[94] *Ibid*. s.14.
[95] See p. 492, *ante*.

where he has done so under a valued policy because here the agreed valuation is, as a rule, binding on both parties. Where an over-insurance has been effected by double insurance, the assured who is covered only to the value of the insured interest can reclaim a proportionate amount of the several premiums paid by him. In case of loss the assured can claim the whole payment due to him from any one of the several underwriters and leave it to them to adjust the loss amongst themselves rateably (s.32). In a few exceptional cases the assured is barred from recovering the overpaid portions of the premium—

1. If the double insurance was effected by the assured knowingly, or
2. If a claim has been paid for the full sum insured, or
3. If the policies were effected at different times and an earlier policy bore, at any time, the entire risk (s.84(3)(*f*), proviso).

Double insurance occurs only if the same insurable interest and the risk is insured twice or more frequently in excess of its value. It does not occur if two persons, *e.g.* the seller and the carrier, are interested in the same consignment and insure their (different) interests therein.[96]

The rates of premium require careful attention by the exporter who has to rely here on the expert advice of his broker. The rates quoted normally include the cover under the Institute Cargo Clauses.

Assignment

When insured goods are sold or transferred, the insurance effected in respect of them does not pass automatically to the buyer. The assured, when conveying the property in the insured goods to the buyer, does not automatically assign the "policy" (ss.15, 51). Insurance is not, as Arnould puts it, an "incident of the property insured."[97]

Normally, however, a contract to sell insured goods contains an express or implied condition that the seller shall assign the insurance to the buyer. In modern practice, the assignment is carried out by indorsing the policy in blank and delivering it to the buyer. This procedure is in accordance with the law (s.50(3)); the assignee of the policy is entitled to sue thereon in his own name (s.50(2)). The consent of the insurer is not necessary for an assignment. As already observed,[98] the relationship between the insurer and the assignee is not one of utmost good faith. The policy can be assigned after a loss. An insurance policy is not a negotiable instrument.

---

[96] See *A. Tomlinson (Hauliers) Ltd.* v. *Hepburn* [1966] A.C. 451.
[97] Arnould, *loc. cit.* para. 252.
[98] See p. 502, *ante.*

When insured goods are sold and the policy is assigned to the buyer, the buyer is entitled, in case of loss, to claim the full value of the insurance even if the cargo was sold at a price lower than the value insured; the seller cannot claim the difference between the insurance money and the purchase price.[99] The buyer, on the other hand, cannot claim the benefit of an insurance on "increased value" which the seller concludes as his own speculation and which he would not be bound to transfer to the buyer under the contract of sale.[1]

Risks covered and risks not covered ("exclusions")

The word "warranty" is used, in marine insurance, in a contradictory and confusing manner. "First, it is used to denote a condition to be fulfilled by the assured. Secondly, it is used to denote a mere limitation on, or exception from, the general words of the policy."[2]

The first type of warranty is known as *promissory warranty*. These warranties are promises by the assured that certain facts exist; they take the following form:

> warranted professionally packed,
> or
> warranted no iron ore.
> or
> that the adventure insured is a lawful one.[3]

They are, in general legal terminology, conditions[4] which, if not exactly complied with, whether material to the risk or not, entitle the insurer to disclaim liability from the date of their breach (s.33(3)).[5]

---

[99] *Ralli* v. *Universal Marine Insurance Co.* (1862) 31 L.J.Ch. 207; *Landauer* v. *Asser* [1905] 2 K.B. 184.

[1] *Strass* v. *Spiller and Bakers* (1911) 16 Com.Cas. 166. In this case the insurers had paid the insurance sum to the sellers and had not raised the question of an insurable interest remaining in the sellers after the sale; the buyers then claimed the insurance money from the sellers, but their claim was dismissed.

[2] Chalmers, *Marine Insurance*, 9th ed., 1983, p. 50.

[3] Marine Insurance Act 1906, s.41. However, a contract for the sale and return of diamonds in West Germany was not affected by a deliberate misstatement of the value of goods in an invoice in order to avoid the German equivalent to V.A.T.: *Euro-Diam* v. *Bathurst* [1987] 1 Lloyd's Rep. 178.

[4] Diplock J. in *Vaughan Motors & Sheldon Motor Services Ltd.* v. *Scottish General Insurance Co. Ltd.* [1960] 1 Lloyd's Rep. 479, 481. On conditions generally, see p. 133, *ante*. It should be noted that the term "warranty," as used in insurance law, has a different meaning from that term as used in the law of contract generally.

[5] Where a promissory warranty is broken, in English law the insurer may refuse to pay the insurance sum even if the breach of the condition is not causative for the loss suffered by the insurer; other legal systems adopt a more lenient attitude, as evinced by Norwegian law, see *Forsikringsaktieselskapet Vesta* v. *J. N. E. Butcher, Bain Dawes Ltd.* [1989] 1 Lloyd's Rep. 331; see p. 211, *ante*.

Breach of a promissory warranty entitles the insurer to treat the insurance contract as voidable but (in spite of the wording of s.33) does not render the contract void: *Bank of Nova Scotia* v. *Hellenic Mutual War Risks Association (Bermuda) Ltd. The Good Luck.* [1989] 2 Lloyd's Rep. 238 (C.A.).

Entirely different is the second type of warranty, known as an *exceptive warranty*, by which the insurer obtains exemption from liability in the indicated circumstances. These warranties are expressed by the words "warranted free . . . "; that means that the risk is not covered; *e.g.* the clause—

> warranted free of loss or damage caused by strikers, locked-out workmen or persons taking part in labour disturbances, riots or civil commotions

means that the insurer is not liable for any loss due to these causes.

The difference between "warranted" and "warranted free" is of fundamental importance for an exporter who wishes to obtain a clear idea of the protection which the policy provides for his shipments.

In modern practice this confusing antiquated terminology is usually avoided and it is stated that specified risks are covered and others are not covered. This terminology is used in the Institute Cargo Clauses A, B and C where the section dealing with the risks not covered is headed "Exclusions."

The Lloyd's Marine Policy and the Institute Cargo Clauses A, B and C

The form of policy is the *Lloyd's S.G. Policy*,[6] appended as a model form to the Marine Insurance Act 1906. This policy was adopted in 1779, and was a revision of earlier forms. It defied attempts to render it into a more modern and comprehensible form. The meaning of individual clauses had to be sought in numerous decisions of the courts over the two centuries during which it was in use. The existence of the guidelines to interpretation provided by these decisions was in itself a hindrance to redrafting the policy. Eventually change resulted from the strong criticism of the policy by the United Nations Commission on Trade and Development.[7] The Technical Clauses Committee of the Institute of London Underwriters succeeded in formulating a new policy, which was to replace the S.G. Policy, and five sets of clauses. The New Policy and Clauses were introduced on January 1, 1982 with a transitional period until March 31, 1983, the date set for the withdrawal of the old clauses. The new form is known as *Lloyd's Marine Policy* and the new cargo clauses are described as *Institute Cargo Clauses A, B and C* respectively. They are devised for use with the new policy form.

The Lloyd's Marine Policy form no longer contains the terms of insurance. It is simply a schedule into which the following information is

---

[6] "S.G." stands for ships and goods. There was formerly an S. Policy covering ships only and a G. Policy covering goods only, but they have fallen into disuse.
[7] UNCTAD Official Records TD/B/590.

to be inserted: the policy number; the names of the assured and the vessel; the voyage or period of insurance; the subject-matter insured and its agreed value (if any); the amount insured; the premium; clauses and endorsements to be attached; and a "catch-all" of special conditions and warranties.

The three new sets of cargo clauses reflect a decidedly new approach when compared to the old forms. In addition, there are various other new clauses such as the Institute War Clauses (Cargo) and the Institute Strikes Clauses (Cargo).

Institute Cargo Clauses A, B and C list the cover which they afford, together with losses which are excluded under the policy. Institute Cargo Clauses A are considered as replacing the "all risks" cover which was available under the old S.G. Policy. Institute Cargo Clauses B and C cover specific perils, with Clauses C being by far the narrowest, providing cover against major casualties only. All three clauses cover general average and salvage charges.

Institute Cargo Clauses A

Clause 1 of the Institute Cargo Clauses A defines the cover provided by this insurance. It states:

> This insurance covers all risks of loss of or damage to the subject-matter insured except as provided in Clauses 4, 5, 6 and 7 below.

The "all risks" cover provided by Institute Cargo Clauses A does not, however, cover loss or damage caused by an inherent defect of the goods or insufficient packing, or by delay.[7a]

Clauses 4, 5, 6 and 7 are exclusion clauses which will be considered later in detail.[8]

Institute Cargo Clauses B

The risks covered by this insurance are the following, except as provided in clauses 4, 5, 6 and 7:

1.1 loss of or damage to the subject-matter insured reasonably attributable to
1.1.1 fire or explosion,
1.1.2 vessel or craft being stranded ground sunk or capsized,
1.1.3 overturning or derailment of land conveyance,

[7a] See p. 517, *post.*
[8] See p. 516, *post.*

1.1.4 collision or contact of vessel craft or conveyance with any external object other than water,

1.1.5 discharge of cargo at a port of distress,

1.1.6 earthquake volcanic eruption or lightning,

1.2 loss of or damage to the subject-matter insured caused by

1.2.1 general average sacrifice,

1.2.2 jettison or washing overboard,

1.2.3 entry of sea lake or river water into vessel craft hold conveyance container liftvan or place of storage,

1.3 total loss of any package lost over board or dropped whilst loading on to, or unloading from, vessel or craft.

Exclusion Clauses 4, 5, 6 and 7 are the same as those in Cargo Clauses A but Clause 4.7 additionally excludes deliberate damage or destruction of the subject-matter insured.

Institute Cargo Clauses C

This insurance covers, except as provided by Clauses 4, 5, 6 and 7:

1.1 loss of or damage to the subject-matter insured reasonably attributable to

1.1.1 fire or explosion,

1.1.2 vessel or craft being stranded grounded sunk or capsized,

1.1.3 overturning or derailment of land conveyance,

1.1.4 collision or contact of vessel craft or conveyance with any external object other than water,

1.1.5 discharge of cargo at a port of distress,

1.2 loss of or damage to the subject-matter insured caused by

1.2.1 general average sacrifice,

1.2.2 jettison.

Exclusion Clauses 4, 5, 6 and 7 are again applicable and are identical to those in Institute Cargo Clauses B.

The Transit Clause

It is appropriate at this point to consider the Transit Clause which is present in Institute Cargo Clauses A, B and C, and is therefore applicable unless it is deleted. By this Clause, the liability of the insurer is extended to cover pre-shipment and post-shipment risks. The assured can, under this clause, for example, insure a consignment of goods from Birmingham to Paris, provided these places are named in the policy as the commencement and destination of the transit.[9] In Institute Cargo Clauses A, B and

---

[9] The clause does not cover damage to the goods before they reach the warehouse at the commencement of the transit: *Reinhart Co.* v. *Joshua Hoyle & Sons Ltd.* [1961] 1 Lloyd's Rep. 346, 354 and 358.

C the Transit Clause is supplemented by the Termination of Contract of Carriage Clause and these two Clauses are worded as follows:

8.1 This insurance attaches from the time the goods leave the warehouse or place of storage at the place named herein for the commencement of the transit, continues during the ordinary course of transit and terminates either

8.1.1 on delivery to the Consignees' or other final warehouse or place of storage at the destination named herein,

8.1.2 on delivery to any other warehouse or place of storage, whether prior to or at the destination named herein, which the Assured elect to use either

8.1.2.1 for storage other than in the ordinary course of transit or

8.1.2.2 for allocation or distribution,

or

8.1.3 on the expiry of 60 days after completion of discharge overside of the goods hereby insured from the oversea vessel at the final port of discharge, whichever shall first occur.

8.2 If, after discharge overside from the oversea vessel at the final port of discharge, but prior to termination of this insurance, the goods are to be forwarded to a destination other than that to which they are insured hereunder, this insurance, whilst remaining subject to termination as provided for above, shall not extend beyond the commencement of transit to such other destination.

8.3 This insurance shall remain in force (subject to termination as provided for above and to the provisions of Clause 9 below) during delay beyond the control of the Assured, any deviation, forced discharge, reshipment or transhipment and during any variation of the adventure arising from the exercise of a liberty granted to shipowners or charterers under the contract of affreightment.

If owing to circumstances beyond the control of the Assured either the contract of carriage is terminated at a port or place other than the destination named therein or the transit is otherwise terminated before delivery of the goods as provded for in Clause 8 above, then this insurance shall also terminate *unless prompt notice is given to the Underwriters and continuation of cover is requested when the insurance shall remain in force, subject to an additional premium if required by the Underwriters*, either

9.1 until the goods are sold and delivered at such port or place, or, unless otherwise specially agreed, until the expiry of 60 days after arrival of the goods hereby insured at such port or place, whichever shall first occur,

or

9.2 if the goods are forwarded within the said period of 60 days (or any agreed extension thereof) to the destination named herein or to any other destination, until terminated in accordance with the provisions of Clause 8 above.

Under the Transit Clause, with its additional Termination of Contract of Carriage Clause, the goods are covered from the time when they leave the warehouse at the place named in the policy for the commencement of the transit and continue to be covered until they are delivered to the final warehouse at the destination named in the policy or another warehouse, whether prior to or at the destination named in the policy, but the policy provides an overriding time limit of 60 days[10] after the completion of discharge overside the overseas vessel at the final port of discharge; on the expiration of that time limit cover ceases even though the goods may

---

[10] There exists also a so-called South American 60 day clause which appears to be similar to the Institute Clause except that it provides a 90 day extension for shipments via the Magdalena River.

not have reached a warehouse. If before the expiration of the 60 days but after discharge the goods are forwarded to a destination other than that named in the insurance, the cover terminates when the transit begins. The 60 days' cover is very valuable for the assured if, for some reason, the goods cannot proceed to the warehouse, for instance, if they are detained in the Customs shed because the buyer has not paid the import duties, and the assured cannot dispose of them quickly. The principle underlying these provisions is that the assured shall be covered until he or a buyer from him can reasonably be expected to have made further insurance arrangements for the goods. If under the contract of carriage the goods are unloaded at a place other than the contemplated place of destination, due to circumstances beyond the control of the assured, they continue to be insured[11] (subject to the overriding time limit of 60 days) until they are forwarded to the agreed or another destination and have arrived at the final warehouse, or until they are sold and delivered. The word "warehouse" has been given its ordinary and natural meaning.[12]

The risks covered

Except as excluded by Clauses 4, 5, 6 and 7, discussed below, Institute Cargo Clauses A cover all risks of loss or damage to the subject-matter insured, whereas Clauses B and C only cover risks which are specifically referred to. A detailed consideration of these specific risks would go beyond the ambit of this work.

The exporter who, in order to save on the premium, does not wish to insure under Clauses A but prefers to insure under Clauses B or C, should make sure that the specific risks to which his cargo may be exposed are expressly covered, and also are not excluded by the provisions of Clauses B and C.

Risks not covered (the Exclusion Clauses)

General Exclusion Clause. Clause 4 is the General Exclusion Clause and, except as regards one particular exclusion which will be considered later, it is present in Institute Cargo Clauses A, B and C.

Clause 4.1 excludes "loss damage or expense attributable to wilful misconduct of the Assured." This clause mirrors section 55(2)(*a*) which states:

> The insurer is not liable for any loss attributable to the wilful misconduct of the assured, but, unless the policy otherwise provides, he is liable for any loss prox-

---

[11] See *e.g. G. H. Renton & Co.* v. *Palmyra Trading Corporation of Panama* ("*The Caspiana*") [1957] A.C. 149.
[12] *Leo Rapp Ltd.* v. *McClure* [1955] 1 Lloyd's Rep. 292; *Reinhart Co.* v. *Joshua Hoyle & Sons Ltd.* [1961] 1 Lloyd's Rep. 346, 358.

imately[13] caused by a peril insured against, even though the loss would not have happened but for the misconduct or negligence of the master or crew.[14]

"Wilful misconduct" is essentially a question of fact, but drawing a proper inference from the facts involves a consideration of the law.[15]

Clause 4.2 excludes "ordinary leakage, ordinary loss in weight or volume, or ordinary wear and tear of the subject-matter insured." The word "ordinary" refers to the normal transit losses which may arise from various causes such as the nature of the goods or the loads exerted on them. When the ordinary leakage of one cargo damages a second cargo, the assured in respect of the second cargo can only recover if he is insured under Cargo Clauses A, but not if his insurance is based upon Clauses B or C only.

Clause 4.3 excludes "loss damage or expense caused by insufficiency or unsuitability of packing or preparation of the subject-matter insured (for the purpose of this Clause 4.3 'packing' shall be deemed to include stowage in a container or liftvan, but only when such stowage is carried out prior to attachment of this insurance or by the Assured or their servants)." The question of whether packing is suitable or sufficient is often determined according to what is customary in a particular trade. Where the packing is such that the cargo cannot withstand the usual conditions appertaining to a particular voyage, the assured cannot recover for any loss or damage caused or for any expenses incurred in replacing inadequate packing.[16] Loss of, or damage to, the contents of a container or liftvan will not be covered where such is loaded by the assured or his servants prior to or after the attachment of the insurance. This exclusion will not apply, however, when the stowing is done after the attachment of the insurance and without the assured or his servants being involved.

Clause 4.4 includes "loss damage or expense caused by inherent vice or nature of the subject-matter insured."[17] This exclusion clause covers situations where the goods insured are damaged or destroyed by an internal development. As an example, spontaneous combustion may occur within one cargo damaging a second cargo. The owner of the first cargo cannot recover where the spontaneous combustion is the result of inherent vice, such as may be the case in the cargo of grain, but the owner of the second cargo can recover for his own loss under Clauses A, B or C since the risk of loss or damage due to fire explosion is covered.

---

[13] On proximity, see p. 525, *post.*

[14] Including wilful misconduct, though an assured cannot take advantage of his own wrong see *Schiffshypotheken Bank zu Luebeck AG* v. *Compton The Alexion Hope* [1987] 1 Lloyd's Rep. 60.

[15] For the interpretation of "wilful misconduct" see *Horabin* v. *British Overseas Airways Corp.* [1952] 2 All E.R. 1016; *Coutlas* v. *K.L.M.* (S.D.N.Y. 1961) Transport Laws of the World iv/c/1 p. 303.

[16] *F. W. Berk* v. *Style* [1956] 1 Q.B. 180.

[17] *Soya GmbH Mainz Kommandit-Gesellschaft* v. *White* [1983] 1 Lloyd's Rep. 122.

A difficulty arises where the loss or damage is caused not by the goods themselves but by insufficient packing. Sellers J. held in *F. W. Berk & Co. Ltd.* v. *Style*[18] that insufficiency of packing was an inherent vice of the goods—kieselguhr packed in bags—themselves, but the learned judge had found as a fact that the goods in no circumstances would have withstood the necessary handling and transport, and for that reason refused the assured's claim for the costs of re-bagging. Where, on the other hand, the packing would have been sufficient to withstand ordinary handling and transit but failed to protect the goods as the result of an extraneous event, that event—and not the insufficiency of packing— would be the proximate cause of the damage or loss and the assured could, it is thought recover under the All Risks policy, now Clauses A.

Clause 4.5 excludes "loss damage or expense proximately caused by delay even though the delay be caused by a risk insured against (except expenses payable under [the general average] clause)." Therefore, although under the Transit Clause[19] the insurance will remain valid where a delay is beyond the control of the assured, the assured will not be protected in respect of any damage which is proximately caused by that delay. However, in the case of a general average act which causes a delay, the assured is entitled to recover his proportion of any expenses incurred during the period of the delay, such as, for example, his contribution to the wages of the crew.

Clause 4.6 excludes "loss damage or expense arising from insolvency or financial default of the owners managers charterers or operators of the vessel." If due to financial difficulties, the carrier has to stop short at a port, the insurer will not have to pay the forwarding expenses incurred by the assured. Further, these expenses cannot be recovered under Clause 12 which is applicable only to expenses incurred where a voyage is terminated as a result of the peril insured against.

Clause 4.7 in Clauses B and C excludes "deliberate damage to or deliberate destruction of the subject-matter insured or any part thereof by the wrongful act of any person or persons." This clause is not to be found in Institute Cargo Clauses A. Where this clause is present, the insurer will not be liable for loss or damage caused by arson, scuttling or any form of sabotage or any other malicious acts, by which the subject-matter insured is deliberately damaged or destroyed. Where an assured wishes to remove this exception, a Malicious Damage Clause should be added.

Clause 4.7 in Cargo Clauses A, which is identical to Clause 4.8 in Clauses B and C, excludes "loss damage or expense arising from the use of any weapon of war employing atomic or nuclear fission and/or fusion or other like reaction or radioactive force or matter."

---

[18] [1956] 1 Q.B. 180. See also *Gee & Garnham* v. *Whittall* [1955] 2 Lloyd's Rep. 562, where aluminium kettles insured under an "all risks" policy arrived damaged; Sellers J. dismissed the claim of the assured, treating again insufficient packing as inherent vice of the goods.
[19] See p. 514, *ante*.

By section 55(2)(c) of the Marine Insurance Act 1906 "unless the policy otherwise provides, the insurer is not liable for . . . any loss proximately caused by rats or vermin. Under Clauses A such loss is covered since it is not expressly excluded, but where Clauses B and C are used, such loss is not covered even though not specifically excluded under the general exclusions clause, since the risk is not expressly provided for in the risks clauses.

Unseaworthiness and Unfitness Exclusion Clause. When the insured cargo is shipped, the assured probably will have no control over the vessel used, but by virtue of section 39, the assured's cover may be invalid if the vessel is unseaworthy. By Clause 5.2 of the Cargo Clauses, however, the "Underwriters waive any breach of the implied warranties of seaworthiness of the ship and fitness of the ship to carry the subject-matter insured to destination, unless the Assured or their servants are privy to such unseaworthiness or unfitness."

Therefore, by Clause 5.2, the insurer is liable for any loss or damage which is insured against and which is not excluded where the assured or his servants have no knowledge of unseaworthiness or unfitness. Although not expressly stated, Clause 5.2 refers to the condition of the ship when it actually commences its voyage. This is made clear by the wording of Clause 5.1 which refers to the time of loading the cargo. It states:

> In no case shall this insurance cover loss damage or expense arising from unseaworthiness of vessel or craft, unfitness of vessel craft conveyance container or liftvan for the safe carriage of the subject-matter insured, where the Assured or their servants are privy to such unseaworthiness or unfitness, at the time the subject-matter insured is loaded therein.

Clause 5.1 is more comprehensive than Clause 5.2 in that it exempts the insurer as regards the unseaworthiness of a craft, for example a lighter, and also with respect to the unfitness of any conveyance or container used for carrying the goods, where the assured or his servants have knowledge of such unseaworthiness or unfitness. "Servants" in this context should not be confused with agents, and the knowledge of the assured's agents, such as stevedores, will not affect the insurer's liability.

War Exclusion Clause. Clause 6 is the War Exclusion Clause and is present in Cargo Clauses A, B and C. Deletion of Clause 6 will mean that war risks are covered in Clauses A, but not in Clauses B or C, since such perils are not present in the risks clause. Where an assured requires war risk cover, he should ask for the addition of the Institute War Clauses.

Strikes Exclusion Clause. This Clause 7 is present in all three Institute Cargo Clauses but its deletion would only enable an assured to recover for such risks where he is insured under Clauses A, since in Clauses B and C the peril is not within the specific risks covered.

Where an assured specifically wants cover for strikes and other labour disturbances, he should require the addition of the Institute Strikes Clauses.

Clause 7.3 excludes loss damage or expense "caused by any terrorist or any person acting from a political motive."

Minimising losses. The old S.G. Policy used to contain a "sue and labour" clause, which provided that it was lawful for an assured "to sue, labour and travel for, in and about the defence, safeguards, and recovery of the goods, ship, etc., without prejudice to this insurance." This clause has now been replaced by Clause 16 in Clauses A, B and C which states:

> It is the duty of the Assured and their servants and agents in respect of loss recoverable hereunder: to take such measures as may be reasonable for the purpose of averting or minimising such loss and to ensure that all rights against carriers, bailees or other third parties are properly preserved and exercised and the Underwriters will, in addition to any loss recoverable hereunder, reimburse the Assured for any charges properly and reasonably incurred in pursuance of these duties.

This clause is now called the Duty of Assured Clause. In conjunction with section 78 of the Act it enables an assured to recover from the insurer any expenses reasonably incurred pursuant to the clause, notwithstanding that the insurer has already paid for a total loss. Recovery depends upon the reasonableness of the assured's assessment of the situation and if he has in all the circumstances acted reasonably to avert a loss where there was a risk that the insurers might have to bear it, then the assured can recover.[20]

General average[21]

The law of general average pertains to general maritime law and affects two relationships in which the exporter stands, namely the contract of carriage by sea which he concludes with the carrier, and the contract of insurance which he concludes with the insurer.[22] The same general average act might affect both contracts, and the rights and duties of the exporter under the contract of carriage are different from those arising under the contract of insurance.

The general average act

A general average act occurs in the following circumstances. During the sea voyage, three interests are at risk: the ship, the cargo and the

---

[20] *Integrated Container Service Inc.* v. *British Traders Insurance Co.* [1984] 1 Lloyd's Rep. 154; *Netherlands Insurance Co. Est. 1845 Ltd.* v. *Karl Ljungberg & Co., AB* [1986] 2 Lloyd's Rep. 19 (P.C. on appeal from Singapore; reimbursement for litigation costs expended by assured to preserve time bar against carrier recoverable under "sue and labour" clause).

[21] See Lowndes and Rudolf's *Law of General Average* (British Shipping Laws, Vol. 7, 10th ed., 1975).

[22] The law of general average might even affect a third relationship, namely the right of a cargo owner to recover from another ship that negligently collided with the carrying ship, the general average contribution which the cargo owner paid to the carrying ship in consequence of the collision; *Morrison Steamship Co.* v. *Greystoke Castle* [1947] A.C. 265.

freight. They form a common adventure and they are exposed to the same risks. When these interests encounter a common peril, it may become necessary voluntarily to make an extraordinary sacrifice or to incur an extraordinary expenditure in order to preserve the property imperilled in the common adventure (s.66(2)). The ship may encounter heavy weather and it may be necessary to jettison part of the cargo or of the ship's equipment in order to lighten it; the sacrifice that is made here is made for the benefit of all concerned in the common adventure and it is only just and fair that the owners of all interests saved by a deliberate sacrifice of a co-adventurer's property should contribute proportionately to his loss. The situation which arises here is totally different from that arising, *e.g.* where the cargo deteriorates owing to sea water entering a container carried on a ship; this is a misfortune that befalls an individual interest and has to be borne by the owner of that interest alone, but he can cover this risk by taking out insurance under Institute Cargo Clauses A or B (though Cargo Clauses C would not cover him against this risk).

A general average act has thus to satisfy the following requirements (s.66(2)). It must be—

(1) an extraordinary sacrifice or expenditure,
(2) purposely resorted to,
(3) reasonably made or incurred,
(4) in time of peril,
(5) for the purpose of preserving the property imperilled in the common danger.

It must also appear

(6) that the sacrifice or the expenditure was judiciously incurred.
(7) that it is not included in those ordinary duties or expenses which are incidental to the navigation of the ship, and are paid out of the freight.
(8) that it was not due to any wrongful act, for which the claimant is responsible.

The general average loss

A general average loss is expenditure caused[23] or a sacrifice incurred as the result of a general average act (s.66(1)).

A general average loss may arise from a general average sacrifice, *e.g.* when cargo is jettisoned or, if the ship is in danger of foundering, where part of the cargo is loaded on boats and lost. Jettison of cargo does not constitute a general average act unless such cargo is carried in accordance with recognised customs of the trade.[24] A general average loss may also

---

[23] An indemnity paid to tugowners whose tugs were called in to tow a ship to safety is a "direct consequence" of a general average act and recoverable as general average expenditure; *Australian Coastal Shipping Commission* v. *Green* [1971] 1 Q.B. 456; see York-Antwerp Rules 1974, Rule VI.
[24] See York-Antwerp Rules 1974, Rule I.

arise from general average expenditure, *i.e.* extraordinary expenditure incurred for the common benefit to secure the physical safety of ship and cargo, *e.g.* the expense of making and entering a port of refuge.[25] Reasonable costs incurred at the port of refuge for repair of the ship, warehousing the cargo, etc., are likely to be regarded as general average expenditure; it is at least general English practice to allow costs of warehousing of the cargo at the port of refuge as general average expenditure, provided the ship put into the port of refuge in consequence of damage which was itself the subject of general average.[26]

The laws of maritime nations differ materially in their definition of general average. It has been said with justification that "no two of the leading maritime States of the world agree completely in their provisions regarding general average."[27] It is to the merit of the International Law Association to have secured some measure of uniformity in this confused situation. The Association drafted standard rules dealing with the adjustment of general average which in their present form are known as the York-Antwerp Rules 1974; they came into force on July 1, 1974.[28] These rules, though not having the force of law, are in practice frequently adopted by the parties. Sometimes the parties make other arrangements, *e.g.* they may provide that "average, if any, shall be adjusted according to the British Rule." Where the York-Antwerp Rules are not adopted and the parties have not made special arrangements, general average is adjusted in accordance with the law in force at the port of destination, and if the ship does not reach that port, at the port at which the journey is broken up.

General average and the contract of carriage by sea

It is now necessary to deal separately with the contracts of carriage by sea and insurance, so far as they are affected by the law of general average. In the law of maritime transport, where there is a general average loss, the party on whom it falls is entitled to a rateable[28a]

---

[25] Where a vessel suffering a breakdown in her diesel generator made a deviation to a port of refuge for repairs and the deviation was a reasonable deviation within the meaning of Art. IV r. 4 of the Hague Rules relating to Bills of Lading (see p. 600, *post*), the shipowners were entitled to claim general average from the cargo owners and their insurers; *Danae Shipping Corporation* v. *T.P.A.O. and Guven Turkish Insurance Co. Ltd. The Daffodil B* [1983] 1 Lloyd's Rep. 499.

[26] Rules of Practice of the Association of Average Adjusters, Rule 17.

[27] Lowndes and Rudolf, *op. cit.*, para. 277. There exists an International Convention on Salvage of 1989, reproduced in 20 *Journal of Maritime Law and Commerce* (1989), 589. This convention has nothing to do with general average loss or contribution but deals with the salvage award for the salvor; the Convention is not in force yet.

[28] The York-Antwerp Rules 1974 superseded the 1950 version, which in turn superseded the York-Antwerp Rules 1924.

[28a] The general average contributions of the shipowner and the cargo owner are calculated proportionally, according to the value of the interests involved: *The M Vatan, Financial Times*, January 17, 1990.

contribution from the other parties interested in the venture (s.66(3)). According to circumstances this contribution may be a right or a duty of the cargo owner. If he suffers a general average loss, he is entitled to claim contribution from the shipowner and the other cargo owners. If their interest is lost and his is saved by their sacrifice or expenditure, he is liable to make a contribution to them.[29] These rights and duties arise from the contract of carriage by sea. They have no immediate connection with insurance and exist whether the cargo owner is insured or not. The cargo owner is not liable to contribute to general average expenditure, if the York-Antwerp Rules were embodied in the bill of lading and ship and cargo were completely lost after the expenditure was incurred.[30] The shipowner has, at common law, a lien on the cargo for general average contributions as long as he continues to be in possession of the goods. He refuses sometimes to give up possession of the goods unless the persons entitled thereto have signed an *average bond,*[31] *i.e.* a formal undertaking that they will pay their respective general average contributions after they have been ascertained, and have paid a deposit into a bank in the joint names of trustees nominated by the shipowner and the cargo owners. The cargo owner who has paid the deposit receives a general average deposit receipt which states the name of the adjuster and which he has to produce when the refund found to be due to him is paid out. The average bond is normally concluded between the shipowner on the one hand and all cargo owners on the other hand. If, in an individual case, a cargo owner wishes to act on his own and to obtain possession of his cargo independently, he offers the shipowner an indemnity or guarantee issued by a bank. The adjustment of general average loss, *i.e.* the calculation of the individual contributions, is a complicated and often lengthy operation which is carried out by average adjusters.[32] The shipowner is entitled to appoint the average adjuster.

---

[29] Except where the claimant was at fault, *e.g.* the shipowner negligently failed to make the ship seaworthy; in that case the cargo owners do not lose their defences and counterclaims if they do not sue the shipowner within one year, as provided by the Hague Rules, Art. III, r. 6 (see p. 606, *post*): *Goulandris Brothers Ltd.* v. *B. Goldman & Sons Ltd.* [1958] 1 Q.B. 74 (interpreting the York-Antwerp Rules 1950, Rule D). Further, *The Aga* [1968] 1 Lloyd's Rep. 431.

[30] *Chellew* v. *Royal Commission on Sugar Supply* [1922] 1 K.B. 12.

[31] In principle the limitation period for a claim for general average contribution counts from the date of the sacrifice. But where the consignee of the cargo executes a Lloyd's standard form average bond in return for release of the cargo, he undertakes a new contractual obligation to contribute to general average and time begins to run from the date when the adjusters have completed their statement: *Castle Insurance Co. Ltd.* v. *Hong Kong Islands Shipping Co. Ltd. The Potoi Chau.* [1984] A.C. 226 (P.C. from Hong Kong.).

[32] For the Rules of Practice of the Association of Average Adjusters, see Lowndes and Rudolf, *The Law of General Average* (British Shipping Laws, Vol. 7, 10 ed., 1975), paras. 1041 *et seq.*

General average and the contract of insurance

The risks which may fall upon the cargo owner under the law of general average are normally fully covered by his marine insurance. They are twofold: either physical loss of, or damage to, his goods, or liability to pay a general average contribution. The Marine Insurance Act provides in section 66(4) and (5):

(4) Subject to any express provision in the policy, where the assured has incurred a general average expenditure, he may recover from the insurer in respect of the proportion of the loss which falls upon him; and in the case of a general average sacrifice, he may recover from the insurer in respect of the whole loss without having enforced his right of contribution from the other parties liable to contribute.

(5) Subject to any express provision in the policy, where the assured has paid, or is liable to pay, a general average contribution in respect of the subject insured, he may recover therefor from the insurer.

These provisions are implemented by the Institute Cargo Clauses. The General Average Clause in Cargo Clauses A, B and C is in identical terms.[33] It is worded as follows:

This insurance covers general average and salvage charges, adjusted or determined according to the contract of affreightment and/or the governing law and practice, incurred to avoid or in connection with the avoidance of loss from any cause except those excluded in Clauses 4, 5, 6 and 7 or elsewhere in this insurance.

It should be noted that a general average loss due to an event listed in one of the applicable Exclusion Clauses is not covered by this clause.[34]

By virtue of section 66(4) the cargo owner is enabled to claim, in respect of the loss suffered, payment of the insurance money from the insurer without becoming involved in the complications of the average adjustment. The underwriter, on payment of the insurance money, is subrogated to the rights of the assured under the contract of carriage by sea and is thus in a position to pursue the cargo owner's claim for contribution.[35] This is, of course, an eminently practical solution; provided that there was no underinsurance the exporter can recover his loss from the insurer forthwith and leave the technicalities of the general average adjustment to the latter. The exporter, when advised of such loss, should lose no time in notifying the insurer who is generally

---

[33] In Cargo Clauses A, general average sacrifice is covered by the all risks cover. In Cargo Clauses B and C this risk is covered by an express provision.

[34] Although claims for a general average contribution have their origin in the common law, if they relate to events during the operation of a charterparty, they are claims arising out of the charterparty and are subject to an arbitration clause in the charterparty: *Union of India* v. *E. B. Aaby's Rederi A/S* [1975] A.C. 797.

[35] See p. 531, *post*.

prepared to pay the deposit money and to sign the average bond or a similar undertaking. Where the exporter has already paid the deposit, the underwriter normally refunds it upon delivery of the general average deposit receipt, although in strict law he might not be bound to do so.[36]

Claims

Liability and causation

In order to recover for loss or damage under Institute Cargo Clauses A, B or C, it is not sufficient to show that the particular risk is covered by the Institute Cargo Clauses used. It must also be clear that liability has not been specifically excluded under Clauses 4, 5, 6 or 7.[37]

Initially, when it is intended to make a claim under the insurance, it must be considered whether the insurer is prima facie liable to reimburse the assured. It is stated in section 55(1) of the Marine Insurance Act 1906:

> Subject to the provisions of this Act and unless the policy otherwise provides, the insurer is liable for any loss proximately caused by a peril insured against, but, subject as aforesaid, he is not liable for any loss which is not proximately caused by a peril insured against.

With the use of Institute Cargo Clauses A, the proximate cause test is applied to all the risks. Where Clauses B or C are used, it is expressly stated that with regard to certain of the risks covered, it is only necessary to show that loss or damage is reasonably attributable to the risk insured against. These risks are set out in Clause 1.1 of the Institute Cargo Clauses B and C. Where a claim is made under Clause 1.2 of the Institute Cargo Clauses B and C, the "proximately caused by" test is still applicable.

The cause which is proximate is that which is proximate in terms of efficiency and is not necessarily the first in time.[38] The choice of which cause is proximate is made by applying commonsense standards. A good

---

[36] *Brandeis, Goldschmidt & Co.* v. *Economic Insurance Co. Ltd.* (1922) 38 T.L.R. 609.

[37] Normally the cargo owner is a party to the insurance contract (either an original party or a party by assignment) and raises his claim directly under that contract. In exceptional circumstances, however, he has to rely on the statutory transfer of the right against the insurer under the Third Parties (Rights against Insurers) Act 1930; thus, in *The Fanti. The Padre Island* (*No.* 2) [1989] 1 Lloyd's Rep. 239, a shipowning company was insured with a Protection and Indemnity (P. & I.) Club in respect of cargo damage; such damage occurred but the company was wound up; it was held that the cargo owners could recover from the P. & I. Club under the 1930 Act. (C.A.).

[38] *Leyland Shipping Company Limited* v. *Norwich Union Fire Insurance Society Limited* [1918] A.C. 350.

example is the case of *Reischer* v. *Borwick*.[39] Here a ship was insured against damage due to collision but not against perils of the sea. The ship ran against a snag[40] in a river and was holed. The leak was temporarily plugged and a tug was sent to tow the ship to the nearest dock for repairs. Unfortunately, whilst being towed, the motion of the ship through the water was such that the plug was dislodged and the ship began to sink. It was held that the proximate cause of the loss here was the collision with the snag and therefore the risk was covered by the insurance.

Where there are two dominant causes of damage, one covered by the Institute Cargo Clauses used and the other excluded under the clauses, the insurers can rely on the exclusion and hence avoid liability,[41] but if there is no exclusion, the insurers must indemnify the assured.[42]

Burden of proof

Where an assured wishes to recover under his insurance, the burden of proof is initially on him, to show that his loss or damage falls within a risk covered under the insurance, but if he relies, *e.g.* on "the perils of the sea," he must prove the cause of the loss or damage with some degree of particularity.[43] He must also prove that they were undamaged when the insurance began to cover them.[44] In one case[45] the assured, an English company, bought essential oils from an Indonesian firm in Jakarta. These oils were to be used in the manufacture of soap and perfumes. The goods were insured under an Institute of London Underwriters Companies Combined policy covering all risks and containing the usual warehouse to warehouse clause.[45] When the steel or iron drums containing the goods arrived they were found to contain water, with slight traces of essential oil. Mocatta J. dismissed the claim of the assured against the insurers. The learned judge held that the assured had not discharged the burden of proof upon them of establishing on the balance of probabilities that the oil in drums that they had agreed to buy ever started on the transit.

Once the assured has proved that the loss was due to an insured risk, the burden of proof shifts to the insurer and it is for him to show that the

---

[39] [1894] 2 Q.B. 548.
[40] This is a piece of timber embedded in a river or in the sea.
[41] *Wayne Tank and Pump Co. Ltd.* v. *Employers Liability Assurance Corporation Ltd.* [1974] Q.B. 57 *per* Lord Denning M.R. (67C), Cairns L.J. (69B) and Roskill L.J. (75D).
[42] *J. J. Lloyd Instruments Ltd.* v. *Northern Star Insurance Co. Ltd.* [1987] 1 Lloyd's Rep. 264.
[43] *Rhesa Shipping Co. S.A.* v. *Edmunds. The Popi M.* [1985] 1 W.L.R. 948 (H.L.).
[44] See p. 522, *ante*, where reference was made to *Reinhart Co.* v. *Joshua Hoyle & Sons* [1961] 1 Lloyd's Rep. 346, 354 and 358. Also *Fuerst Day Lawson Ltd.* v. *Orion Insurance Co. Ltd.* [1980] 1 Lloyd's Rep. 656, and *Electro Motion Ltd.* v. *Maritime Insurance Co. Ltd. and Bonner* [1956] 1 Lloyd's Rep. 420.
[45] *Fuerst Day Lawson Ltd.* v. *Orion Insurance Co. Ltd.*, *supra*; see also p. 128, n. 74.
[46] The case arose before Lloyd's Marine Policy and the Institute Cargo Clauses A, B and C came into use.

risk is not in fact covered or is actually excluded.[47] The insurer may be able to rely on an exclusion clause, even when there is prima facie liability under a risk covered clause.

Preparation of claims

If the assured learns, even unofficially, that the goods might possibly be lost or damaged in transit he should forthwith inform his insurance broker and act on his advice. It is customary to employ brokers not only for the conclusion of a contract of insurance but also for the settlement of claims. If the consignee is informed that the goods have arrived damaged, he should immediately notify Lloyd's local agent at the port of discharge who will survey the goods and issue a *survey report,* unless the claim is for less than £3; in this case no survey report is required. The assured should further try to ascertain whether the loss is due to particular average or general average. A particular average loss is a loss to be borne by the particular interest incurring it alone and if such a loss is recoverable under the policy, the assured requires the following documents to support his claim: the policy, invoice, bill of lading and survey report. Other documents have to be added if necessary in the circumstances, *e.g.* the weight notes on loading and discharge if the loss is due to short weight, an extract from the ship's log or the master's protest if the loss is due to the perils of the sea.[48] The *master's protest* is a formal statement made by the master, often supported by members of the crew, before a consul or notary public and explaining the cause of damage. In the case of general average loss, the procedure indicated earlier[49] should be followed. The broker acting for the assured should not be employed by the insurer for the purpose of obtaining the report of a claims assessor.[50]

Cargo policies payable abroad frequently embody a special red clause, known as the *"Important"* Clause (because it is headed by that word), specifying the requirements of the insurer as regards claims procedure. If the policy contains such a clause, the procedure set out therein must be followed punctiliously.

The Institute Cargo Clauses A, B and C all contain a set of clauses under the heading "Claims" and these are reproduced here:

11.1 In order to recover under this insurance the Assured must have an insurable interest in the subject-matter insured at the time of the loss.

11.2 Subject to 11.1 above, the Assured shall be entitled to recover for insured loss occurring during the period covered by this insurance, notwithstanding that the loss occurred before the contract of insurance was concluded, unless the Assured were aware of the loss and the Underwriters were not.

---

[47] *M. Golodetz and Co. Inc.* v. *Czarnikow-Rionda Co. Inc.* [1980] 1 W.L.R. 495 at 513.

[48] Dover, *A Handbook of Marine Insurance* (8th ed., 1975), p. 618.

[49] See p. 524, *ante.*

[50] *North and South Trust Co.* v. *Berkeley* [1971] 1 W.L.R. 471.

12. Where, as a result of the operation of a risk covered by this insurance, the insured transit is terminated at a port or place other than that to which the subject-matter is covered under this insurance, the Underwriters will reimburse the Assured for any extra charges properly and reasonably incurred in unloading storing and forwarding the subject-matter to the destination to which it is insured hereunder. This Clause 12, which does not apply to general average or salvage charges, shall be subject to the exclusions contained in Clauses 4, 5, 6 and 7 above, and shall not include charges arising from the fault negligence insolvency or financial default of the Assured or their servants.

13. No claim for Constructive Total Loss shall be recoverable hereunder unless the subject-matter insured is reasonably abandoned either on account of its actual total loss appearing to be unavoidable or because the cost of recovering, reconditioning and forwarding the subject-matter to the destination to which it is insured would exceed its value on arrival.

14.1 If any "Increased Value" insurance is effected by the Assured on the cargo insured herein the agreed value of the cargo shall be deemed to be increased to the total amount insured under this insurance and all Increased Value insurances covering the loss, and liability under this insurance shall be in such proportion as the sum insured herein bears to such total amount insured.

   In the event of claim the Assured shall provide the Underwriters with evidence of the amounts insured under all other insurances.

14.2 **Where this insurance is on Increased Value the following clause shall apply:** The agreed value of the cargo shall be deemed to be equal to the total amount insured under the primary insurance and all Increased Value insurances covering the loss and effected on the cargo by the Assured, and liability under this insurance shall be in such proportion as the sum insured herein bears to such total amount insured.

   In the event of claim the Assured shall provide the Underwriters with evidence of the amounts insured under all other insurances.

It can be seen that under Clause 12 the insurer undertakes to reimburse the assured for any charges, above the normal charges, which are properly and reasonably incurred in unloading, storing and forwarding the cargo to its destination and which result from the operation of a risk covered by the insurance.

The Corporation of Lloyd's has published *Lloyd's Survey Handbook* which, though primarily for the use of surveyors, contains valuable information for exporters and importers who wish to make a claim under cargo insurance policies.[51]

Total and partial loss

The law attaches a special technical meaning to the term "total loss," and treats every loss that is not total as partial loss. A partial loss occurs, for example, if 25 crated bicycles of a consignment of 100 are corroded by seawater, or if, owing to heating, a cargo of hay has to be sold at an intermediate port.

Total loss is either actual or constructive total loss. Actual total loss (sometimes called "absolute total loss") occurs:

---

[51] Compiled and edited by the Controller of Agencies, Lloyd's, obtainable from Lloyd's.

(1) where the subject-matter insured is destroyed, or
(2) where the assured has been irretrievably deprived thereof, or
(3) where the subject-matter has been so damaged that it has lost its commercial identity (s.57).

Constructive total loss, as far as goods are concerned, occurs:

where the costs of repairing the damage and forwarding the goods to their destination would exceed their value on arrival (s.60(2)(III)).

The difference between actual and constructive total loss is that, in the former case, the subject-matter is so completely and irretrievably lost that the only course open to the assured is to recover the loss from the insurer, whereas in the latter case, the damage is repairable, though at considerable cost, and the assured is put to his election either to treat the loss as partial loss or to abandon the subject-matter to the insurer and treat the loss as total loss (s.61). Consequently, where the total loss is actual, the assured need not give the insurer notice of abandonment as this would be an empty form; but, where total loss is constructive, the assured has to give notice of abandonment in order to indicate which course he elects to take, and, if he fails to give notice with reasonable diligence, the loss is treated as a partial loss only (s.62). If a constructive total loss of goods is followed by a justifiable sale by the master, this is treated as an actual total loss and no notice of abandonment is required because the goods are in this case irretrievably lost and no benefit would accrue to the insurer if notice were given to him (s.62(7)).[52]

It is not always easy to say whether a loss is an actual or constructive total loss. Numerous cases have been decided on this issue but have not yielded, so far, well-defined principles. The best illustration is provided by an old case[53] where a vessel on which dates had been shipped was sunk during the course of the voyage, and subsequently raised; on arrival at the port of discharge, the dates still retained the appearance of dates and were of value for distillation into spirits, but they were so impregnated with seawater and in such a condition of fermentation as to be no longer merchantable as dates. This was held to be an actual total loss of the dates.

Measure of indemnity

In case of a total loss, the assured is entitled, if the policy is a valued policy,[54] to recover the sum fixed in the policy, and, if the policy is an

---

[52] *Asfar & Co.* v. *Blundell* [1896] 1 Q.B. 123. See also *Terkol Rederierne* v. *Petroleo Brasileiro. The Badagry* [1985] 1 Lloyd's Rep. 395 (Effect of constructive total loss on substitution clause in charterparty).
[53] *Roux* v. *Salvador* [1836] 3 Bing, N.C. 266.
[54] See p. 493, *ante*.

unvalued policy, to recover the insurable value of the goods, subject to the limit of the sum insured (s.68). The assured who has insured the goods at their arrival value plus estimated sales profits of the buyer[55] receives in this case full indemnity.

In case of partial loss of the goods, the measure of damages is—

    (1) where part of the goods insured by a valued policy is lost, such proportion of the fixed value as the lost part bears to the whole insurable value of the insured goods;

    (2) where part of the goods insured by an unvalued policy is lost, the insurable value of the part lost;

    (3) where the whole or part of the goods insured arrives damaged, such proportion of the fixed value in case of a valued policy, or insurable value in the case of an unvalued policy, as the difference between the gross sound and damaged values at the place of arrival bears to the gross sound value (s.71).

In case of partial loss, where the goods are not lost but damaged, section 71 does not always give the assured full indemnity. As the percentage of the insurance sum which the insurer has to pay is calculated by comparison of the gross arrival value of the goods, if they had arrived sound, with the gross value of the damaged goods, the percentage remains constant and is independent of market fluctuations, while the result would be different if the calculation were based on net values, (*i.e.* values after deduction of freight charges).[56] The result of maintaining a constant measure of indemnity is that the assured in making a claim has a greater advantage in a falling market than in times of boom conditions. This effect of the calculation prescribed by section 71 will be seen from the following:

Illustration

Data
    (1) Goods insured by valued policy at £600
    (2) *Case I*: if arriving sound in gaining market, saleable at gross value of £800
    (3) *Case II*: if arriving in sound losing market, saleable at gross value of £400
    (4) In both cases, goods arrive damaged and are sold at gross price of 75 per cent. of their sound value

	Case I	Case II
(*a*) Sound gross value	£800	£400
(*b*) Damaged gross value	600	300
Difference	£200=	£100=
	25 per cent.	25 per cent.

In each case, the insurers have to pay 25 per cent. of £600=£150.

The measure of indemnity is not always ascertained so easily as in the preceding example. Where different species of property are insured under a single valuation and one species only is damaged, the value of the

_____

[55] See p. 493, *ante*.
[56] V. Dover, *loc. cit.*, p. 495.

damaged goods must first be apportioned in the proportion which the damaged item bears to the different species before the ordinary rules of calculation can be applied (s.72).

The insurer's right of subrogation[57]

On payment of the insurance money the insurer is entitled to be subrogated to all rights and remedies of the assured in respect of the interest insured in so far as he has indemnified the assured (s.79). The purpose of subrogation is to prevent the assured from recovering more than once for the same loss, *e.g.* where goods are lost owing to a collision, the assured cannot claim the insurance money from the insurer and then sue the owners of the ship that negligently caused the collision. Under the doctrine of subrogation the right to sue the owners of the negligent ship passes from the insured to the insurer on payment of the insurance money. The insurer is subrogated to all rights of the assured arising from tort or contract, *e.g.* the assured's rights against the carrier under the contract of carriage. If the assured has already recovered damages from the third party, the insurer can claim from the assured the moneys received.[58]

The right of subrogation is subject to two qualifications—

(1) the insurer can only claim to stand in the shoes of the assured, he cannot acquire a better right than the latter possessed,[59] and
(2) unless the parties have otherwise agreed by way of a contractual subrogation clause, the insurer can claim to be subrogated to the rights of the assured only in so far as he has indemnified him.

The insurer can claim to be subrogated to the rights and remedies of the assured in case both of total and partial loss, but in case of total loss he has an additional right, *viz.* he becomes the owner of whatever remains of the interest he paid for (even if the value of that interest on salvage is greater than the insurance money paid by him).[60] If the insurer

---

[57] See generally *Subrogation in Insurance Law* by S. R. Derham.
[58] See *Re R. Miller, Gibb & Co. Ltd.* [1957] 1 W.L.R. 703 (subrogation to ECGD of right to the price, after having paid the seller); *H. Cousins Ltd.* v. *D. & C. Carriers Ltd.* [1971] 2 Q.B. 230 (subrogation of interest after insurer had paid assured); *Pierce* v. *Bemis. The Lusitania* [1986] Q.B. 384 (insurers subrogated to hull and equipment of wrecked ship after having paid owners in respect of total loss). The insurer cannot, however, bring a second action in pursuance of a right of subrogation, where the insured has recovered in respect of the uninsured loss: *Hayler* v. *Chapman, The Times,* November 11, 1985.
[59] Consequently, if the assured no longer exists, the insurer cannot sue the third party directly: *M. H. Smith (Plant Hire)* v. *D. L. Mainwaring* [1986] 2 Lloyd's Rep. 244. It would seem, however, that a timely assignment by the insured would avoid this problem, see below.
[60] But if, owing to depreciation of currency, the assured recovers more from the person liable for the loss than the insurer paid, the assured is entitled to retain the excess:

pays for partial loss only, the title in the subject-matter insured remains vested in the assured and any benefits derived from salvage may be retained by him (s.79).

In practice, the insurer invariably asks the assured, on payment of the insurance money, to sign a letter of subrogation and retains the documents, including the bill of lading, in order to prosecute the rights subrogated to him.

The right of subrogation should not be confused with the right of the insurer, on abandonment, to take over the subject-matter insured (s.63). Abandonment has effect only where there is a constructive total loss,[61] whereas subrogation applies to all cases where loss is paid, whether the loss is total or partial. In case of abandonment, the property in the subject-matter passes but the claims for recovery of damages against third persons do not—as in the case of subrogation—pass. In case of subrogation, payment of the insurance money is a condition precedent to the passing of the assured's rights, but not so in the case of abandonment. This means in practice that, even in case of a constructive total loss, the insurer cannot pursue the assured's claims against third persons, *e.g.* negligent carriers, before he has paid the insurance money to the assured. But if the insurer has taken an assignment of the insured's rights, he can sue even before he has paid the insurance money.

AIR CARGO INSURANCE

There are two principal methods for the insurance of cargo sent by air:

(1) in the marine market via brokers, or
(2) mainly in the aviation market via the air waybill.

Of these two methods the first is the more usual because those who are in the air cargo business can arrange annual policies to suit their own specific requirements.

Marine Clauses

Air cargo insurance taken out in the marine market is obtained under special Institute Air Cargo Clauses. They are:

Institute Cargo Clauses (Air) (Cl. 259),
Institute War Clauses (Air Cargo) (Cl. 258), and
Institute Strikes Clauses (Air Cargo) (Cl. 260).

---

[61] See p. 529 *ante*.

The Institute Air Cargo Clauses are for use with Lloyd's Marine Policy form. They are modelled on the marine Institute Cargo Clauses, subject to suitable alterations. They came into effect likewise on January 1, 1982.

The Institute Cargo Clauses (Air) are the standard form. The risks covered by this form are:

> 1. This insurance covers all risks of loss of or damage to the subject-matter insured except as provided in Clauses 2, 3 and 4 below.

This standard policy is thus an all risks policy but Clauses 2, 3 and 4 contain 14 exceptions, including exceptions for war and strikes.

The Institute War Clauses (Air Cargo) cover the following risks, subject to nine exceptions stated in that clause:

> This insurance covers, except as provided in Clause 2 below, loss of or damage to the subject-matter insured caused by
> 1.1 war civil war revolution rebellion insurrection, or civil strife arising therefrom, or any hostile act by or against a belligerent power
> 1.2 capture seizure arrest restraint or detainment, arising from risks covered under 1.1 above, and the consequences thereof or any attempt thereat
> 1.3 derelict mines torpedoes bombs or other derelict weapons of war.

This policy thus covers the war risks excluded from the standard form. It neither includes nor excludes the risk of strikes or similar events. It is thought that these risks are not covered by this policy as they are not listed in the risks covered by this policy; Clause 2 contains the exceptions.

The Institute Strikes Clauses (Air Cargo) cover the following risks, subject to 11 exceptions stated in that clause:

> This insurance covers, except as provided in Clause 2 below, loss of or damage to the subject-matter insured caused by
> 1.1 strikers, locked-out workmen, or persons taking part in labour disturbances, riots or civil commotions
> 1.2 any terrorist or any person acting from a political motive.

These Clauses thus give also cover against terrorist or political attacks. Again the exceptions are contained in Clause 2.

A comprehensive cover is only provided by a combination of all three Air Cargo Clauses and this cover is rated accordingly. Professional cargo shippers will have annual policies on which individual and bulk shipments may be made on a basis of regular declarations.

The Cargo Clauses (Air) and the War Clauses (Air Cargo) exclude sendings by Post but the Institute Strikes Clauses (Air Cargo) are silent on this point. As these Clauses are normally used in combination with the standard form, the exclusion of postal sendings on this form would likewise make the Strikes Clauses inapplicable for postal sendings.

Air waybill cover

In practice there is no uniformity of cover offered via the air carrier's air waybill, indeed, not all airlines offer this. Those that do will include a rubric on the face of the air waybill whereby the shipper can choose to declare a value for the purpose of being insured via the air carrier's own policies which accept declarations from individual shippers. The terms of such policies are available on application to the carrier's principal offices and usually they will be based on the Institute Clauses noted above. Applying for insurance via the air waybill is obviously convenient for the non-professional or occasional shipper of cargo by air but it is seldom the choice of the professional cargo handler who will have his own annual policy in the marine market.

For this reason, insurance via the air waybill is not a large-volume business and does not seem to be a prominent part of air cargo marketing even though it has minor fringe benefits for the air carrier, such as generating a small commission and eliminating subrogation claims against the airline.

The air waybill in fact offers a cargo shipper three opportunities to declare a value:

(a) for carriage,
(b) for Customs,
(c) for insurance.

Declaring a value for carriage is unnecessary for cargo with a low value per kilogramme. If the value exceeds $20 kg or £13.80 kg then the shipment is eligible for a value declaration for which a supplementary charge will be made. However, in certain jurisdictions the value of the limitation will fluctuate according to the free market price of gold. Professional cargo shippers do not consider declarations of value as cost-effective because this is not a normal form of insurance. Declaring an excess value for carriage merely has the effect of raising the carrier's limit of liability to the declared value: it is still necessary to prove the amount of loss *and* that the airline is legally liable. Where no value is declared, it is common to leave the rubric for declaring the value blank or to insert "NVD" (no value declared). The best practice for occasional or professional cargo shippers is to rely on individual insurance arrangements, as outlined above.

PART FIVE

TRANSPORTATION OF EXPORTS

CHAPTER 27

CARRIAGE OF GOODS BY SEA

THE CARRIAGE OF GOODS IN EXPORT TRANSACTIONS

Unimodal and multimodal transport

GOODS which are the subject matter of an export transaction, whether a contract of sale or of construction, have to be moved from the place of dispatch to that of destination. This carriage has invariably an international character. It may be executed by sea, air or land or by a combination of these modes of transportation. If it is done by only one of them, the international transport is *unimodal* and if it is carried out by a combination of them, it is *multimodal* or combined transport. To give examples: a Swiss manufacturer sells watches to a store in London; the consignment is flown by air from Zurich to Heathrow; this would be a unimodal international transport. Further, a merchant in Bradford, England, sells knitwear to an importer in Canberra, Australia; the goods are loaded into a door-to-door container in Bradford, taken by lorry or trailer to Liverpool; there the container is loaded on a vessel which proceeds to Sydney where it is unloaded and taken by land to Canberra; here the international transport is multimodal as it consists of three stages, a land leg, a sea leg, and again a land leg.

Unimodal international transport is governed by international Conventions. They have been adopted by many countries and are of great practical effect. The most important of them are:

Sea transport: the Hague-Visby Rules relating to Bills of Lading.
Air transport: the Warsaw Convention; or the Warsaw Convention as amended.[1]
Land transport by road: the CMR.[2]

---

[1] In air transport, there exists, however, also non-Convention carriage, p. 631, *post.*
[2] The acronym CMR stands for *Convention relative au contrat de transport international des marchandises par route.* There exists also an international convention relating to transport of goods by rail; it is known as CIM, which stands for *Convention internationale concernant le transport des marchandises par chemin de fer.* The CIM is embodied in the Convention concerning International Carriage by Rail, known as COTIF, which stands for *Convention relative aux transports internationaux ferroviaires.* On international rail transport, see p. 634, *post.*

These Conventions will be considered later.[3]

There exists also an international Convention on multimodal transport. It is:

> The UN Convention on International Multimodal Transport of Goods, adopted at Geneva on May 24, 1980.

This Convention is not yet operative.

Traditional methods of transport and container transport

Traditionally the carriage of goods by sea is effected by two methods determined by the nature of the goods. If they are to be carried in bulk, *e.g.* grain, coal or oil, the shipper[4] may hire a whole vessel by means of a *charterparty.*[5] If individual packages of goods have to be carried, they are normally loaded in a ship's hold or on deck and are carried under *bills of lading.*[6] The traditional method of carriage of goods by air is done under *air consignment notes*[7] or *air waybills.*[8] In the international carriage by road *consignment notes*[9] are used.

In modern international transport goods other than bulk cargoes are often carried in containers.[10] Here the traditional transport documents may be used but more frequently other documents, which are variations of them, are used. The most important of them are *combined transport documents*[11] and *FIATA combined transport bills of lading.*[12] A high percentage of international cargoes is nowadays carried in containers under documents which are not traditional transport documents. For this reason the 1983 Revision of the UCP[13] provides that,

> Unless the credit stipulates otherwise, banks will not reject a transport document which bears a title such as "combined transport document" or is a FIATA combined transport bill of lading.[14]

---

[3] On the Hague-Visby Rules, see pp. 562–564, *post*; on the Warsaw Convention, see pp. 620, 625, *post*; on the CMR, see p. 635, *post*.

[4] This is the designation applied to the person who contracts with the carrier by sea. He will usually be the exporter, *i.e.* the seller, but he may also be the buyer or the buyer's agent.

[5] See p. 540, *post*. But bills of lading may be issued with respect to goods carried in chartered vessels: see p. 574, *post*.

[6] See p. 561, *post*.

[7] See p. 626, *post*.

[8] See p. 629, *post*.

[9] See p. 638, *post*.

[10] See p. 609, *post*.

[11] See p. 615, *post*.

[12] See p. 580, *post*.

[13] Art. 25 of the UCP (1983 Revision). See p. 413, *ante*.

[14] Suggestions for a *multimodal transport document* are made by the Geneva Convention on International Multimodal Transport of 1980; see Jan Ramberg in *International Carriage of Goods: Some Legal Problems and Possible Solutions*, ed. C. M. Schmitthoff and R. M. Goode, London, 1988.

Containerisation raises difficult legal problems, many of which are still unresolved by the courts.

It follows from the preceding observations that the international carriage of goods is, to a large extent, still conducted on the basis of paper work, *viz.* by using transport documents, as for the past 300 years, although, of course, the nature and form of these documents has changed greatly. One day the traditional written transport documentation will be superseded by the paperless electronic communication of trade data.[15] Although progress has been made in this direction,[16] the practical realisation of this aim lies still in the future.

The modern developments in transport technology can only be understood, when the exporter has a knowledge of the traditional methods of international transport. For this reason we shall consider in this chapter the law relating to the traditional carriage of goods by sea. This will be followed by a chapter dealing with the special legal aspects of container transport.[17] Then the law of carriage of goods by air[18] and by land[19] will be treated in separate chapters.

THE COURSE OF BUSINESS IN THE CARRIAGE OF GOODS BY SEA

The general course of business in traditional sea transport may be illustrated by the following example. Let us assume that a United Kingdom exporter is obliged, by his contract of sale with the overseas buyer, to arrange for the carriage of goods by sea to the place of destination and wishes to carry out this arrangement himself. Evidently he has to conclude a contract of carriage with a shipowner[20] whereby the latter undertakes to carry the goods in his ship from the United Kingdom port of dispatch to the overseas port of destination. This contract is known as the contract of carriage by sea[21]; the remuneration to be paid to

---

[15] See Alan Urbach, "The Electronic Presentation and Transfer of Shipping Documents" in *Electronic Banking* (ed. R. M. Goode), (1985). In June 1985 UNCITRAL adopted a recommendation to review the legal requirements for automatic data processing (adp) of international trade documents and is at present actively involved in the study of this project, see TDR (Transnational Data Report) (1985), Vol. 6, 306–308. Further, Kurt Grönfors, in *Internatonal Carriage of Goods: Some Legal Problems and Possible Solutions*, see preceding note n. 14; Ian Walden and Nigel Savage, "The Legal Problems of Paperless Transactions," in [1989] J.B.L. 102.

[16] On the electronic communication of export terms generally, see p. 78, *ante*.

[17] See p. 609, *post*.

[18] See p. 620, *post*.

[19] See p. 634, *post*.

[20] Or with a person who, for the time being, as against the shipowner has the right to enter into a contract of carriage of goods in his ship, *e.g.* a charterer. On the question whether the exporter as shipper contracts with the shipowner or charterer, if the ship is under charter, see pp. 560 and 574, *post*.

[21] Sometimes the old-fashioned expression "contract of affreightment" is still used.

the shipowner is the freight, the shipowner is the carrier, and the exporter, as a party to the contract of carriage by sea, is referred to as the shipper. The exporter has first to decide[22] whether the quantity of goods to be exported warrants the charter of a complete ship; in this case the terms of the contract of carriage are embodied in a document called the charterparty. In most cases, however, the goods form only part of the intended cargo of the ship; they are carried in the ship together with goods belonging to other shippers; here the terms of the contract of carriage are evidenced by a document called the bill of lading which, in effect, is a receipt by the shipowner acknowledging that goods have been delivered to him for the purpose of carriage[23] and reiterating the terms of the contact, but this document is issued generally only after the contract of carriage is well on its way to performance.[24]

Usually the shipper instructs a forwarder to procure freight space for the cargo. The shipowner, on the other hand, likewise employs an agent, the loading broker, to obtain cargoes for his ships. Devlin J. described the duties of these agents as follows[25]:

> The forwarding agent's normal duties are to ascertain the date and place of sailing, obtain a space allocation if that is required, and prepare the bill of lading. The different shipping lines have their own forms of bill of lading which can be obtained from stationers in the City, and it is the duty of the forwarding agent to put in the necessary particulars and to send the draft . . . to the loading broker. His duties include also arranging for the goods to be brought alongside, making the customs entry and paying any dues on the cargo. After shipment he collects the completed bill of lading and sends it to the shipper. All the regular shipping lines operating from the United Kingdom appear to entrust the business of arranging for cargo to a loading broker. He advertises the date of sailings in shipping papers or elsewhere, and generally prepares and circulates to his customers a sailing card. It is his business to supervise the arrangements for loading, though the actual stowage is decided on by the cargo superintendent who is in the direct service of the shipowner. It is the broker's business also to sign the bill of lading, and issue it to the shipper or his agent in exchange for the freight. His remuneration is by way of commission on freight[26] and that is doubtless an inducement to him to carry out his primary function, at any rate when shipping is plentiful, of securing enough cargo to fill the ship . . .
>
> The loading broker and the forwarding agent thus appear to discharge well-defined and separate functions, but in practice the same firm is often both the loading broker and the forwarding agent, though the two sets of dealings may be kept in two separate compartments of the business. The firm generally acts as loading broker only for one line and does all the line's business, so that it is free in respect of other business to act as it will.

The shipowner, through his loading broker, advises the shipper or his agent in due course of the name of the ship that is to carry the consignment, of the locality where the goods should be sent for loading

---

[22] The course of business in container transport is described on p. 609, *post*.

[23] Scrutton on *Charterparties and Bills of Lading* (19th ed., 1984), p. 2.

[24] See p. 542, *post*.

[25] In *Heskell* v. *Continental Express Ltd.* [1950] 1 All E.R. 1033, 1037.

[26] The commission of the loading broker is paid by the shipowner, while the commission of the forwarder is paid by the shipper.

and of the time when the ship is ready to receive the goods. This is often done by a printed notice, called the sailing card, which contains a reference to the closing date, *i.e.* the last date when goods are received by the ship for loading. The closing date is usually a few days in advance of the actual sailing date in order to give the ship an opportunity to get ready for the voyage. If the goods are not sent to the appointed locality in good time, *i.e.* if they arrive after closing date, the shipowner is entitled to shut them out even if the ship has not sailed.

When the goods are sent to the docks, the shipper sends to the shipowner shipping instructions which state briefly the particulars of the intended shipment, and a shipping note to the superintendent of the docks advising him of the arrival of the goods and stating their particulars and the name of the ship for which they are intended.

The place and mode of delivery of the goods to the shipowner are subject to agreement of the parties or fixed by the custom of the port. The law provides that, in the absence of special agreement or custom, the shipper has, at his own expense, to deliver the goods alongside the ship or within reach of her tackle. When the goods are delivered to the shipowner, the shipper receives a document known as the mate's receipt unless there are special customs of the port to the contrary. In the Port of London, for instance, the shipper receives a mate's receipt only if waterborne goods are delivered alongside the ship. Where goods are sent to the docks by land, they are stored in a shed of the Port of London Authority which issues a wharfinger's note or dock receipt and the mate's receipt is issued later when the goods are placed on board ship. In some foreign ports, mate's receipts are issued for all cargo whether received by water or land.

The *mate's receipt* is a document of some importance. When the goods are at the docks for loading on board ship, they are inspected by tally clerks who take down a "record or tally of their date of loading, identification marks, individual package, numbers, their weight and/or measurement, and any defect or comment about the condition in which the goods are received."[27] The tally clerks note, in particular, any damage to packages, lack of protection, old cases, ambiguous markings, etc. When the loading is completed, the ship's officer in charge of loading operations signs the mate's receipt which is based on the notes of the tally clerks and embodies any comments and qualifications in respect of the condition of the goods received. If the mate's receipt is qualified, it is said to be claused[28]; if it does not contain adverse observations, it is a clean receipt. The qualifications on the mate's receipt are later embodied in the

---

[27] *Harris & Son Ltd.* v. *China Mutual Steam Navigation Co. Ltd.* [1959] 2 Lloyd's Rep. 500, 501. See also *Naviera Mogor SA* v. *Société Metallurgique de Normandie. The Nogar Marin* [1988] 1 Lloyd's Rep. 412, 420 (C.A.).
[28] See *Cremer* v. *General Carriers S.A.* [1974] 1 W.L.R. 341. (In this case the qualifications on the mate's receipt were not transferred to the bill of lading which was issued clean.)

bill of lading and make that document a claused or clean bill respectively. In law, the issue of the mate's receipt has two consequences:

(1) The mate's receipt is an acknowledgement by the shipowner that he has received the goods in the condition stated therein, and that the goods are in his possession and at his risk. It sometimes contains a statement to the effect that

> these goods are received subject to the conditions contained in the bill of lading to be issued for the same,[29]

but it has been held[29a] that, even where no such clause is expressly inserted, the goods are held by the shipowner subject to the conditions and exemptions of his usual bill of lading.

(2) The mate's receipt is prima facie evidence of ownership of the goods. The shipowner may safely assume, unless he has knowledge to the contrary, that the holder of the receipt or the person named therein[30] is the owner of the goods and the person entitled to receive the bill of lading in exchange for the mate's receipt. But the mate's receipt is not a document of title; its transfer does not pass possession of the goods and it is, in so far, of a lower order than the bill of lading.[31] Consequently, the shipowner is within his rights if he issues a bill of lading without insisting on the return of the mate's receipt.[32]

The records of loading which the tally clerks take during the loading operation are handed to the shipowner's clerks who compare them with the draft bills of lading sent by the shipper to the shipowner's office. The shipping companies which run regular shipping services publish their printed forms of bills of lading which are revised from time to time and are obtainable from stationers. The shipper or his agent completes usually a set of two or three original bills of lading in respect of the consignment,[33] and when the particulars on the bills agree with the tally notes taken during the loading, the bills are signed by the loading broker or another agent on behalf of the shipowner and the completed and signed

---

[29] *De Clermont and Donner* v. *General Steam Navigation Co.* (1891) 7 T.L.R. 187.
[29a] *Ibid.*
[30] If a person is named; the majority of receipts do not name a person.
[31] Exceptionally, however, by local custom, the mate's receipt may be a document of title but the addition of the words "not negotiable" would destroy its character as a document of title: *Kum* v. *Wah Tat Bank Ltd.* [1971] 1 Lloyd's Rep. 439, 443 (such local custom was found to exist in the trade between Singapore and Sarawak).
[32] *Nippon Yusen Kaisha* v. *Ramjiban Serowgee* [1938] A.C. 420.
[33] In 1970 the OCL/ACL announced that they would no longer accept shipper-prepared container bills of lading but, for a small charge, would prepare the bills themselves; the reason given for this change was an endeavour to expedite the documentation.

bills are handed over to the shipper.[34] But a bill is not always clean; if it is disputed complications might arise because, where payment is arranged under a letter of credit, the advising bank is likely to refuse the shipper finance when he presents a claused, instead of a clean, bill of lading. These complications, and the proper and improper means of resolving them, will be considered later.[35]

The particulars of all bills of lading are entered on the *ship's manifest*. The manifest must contain full particulars of marks, numbers, quantity, contents, shipper, and consignee, with particulars required by the consular authorities of the country to which the goods are being forwarded. The ship's manifest is produced to naval, port, Customs or consular authorities; it contains details of the complete cargo of the ship.

Bills of lading are usually issued in a set of two or more original parts, all of the same tenor and date. If one of them is "accomplished," *i.e.* the goods are delivered against it, the others stand void. Unless payment is arranged under a letter of credit, the various parts of the set are forwarded to the consignee by subsequent air mails, preferably registered, to secure their speedy and safe arrival. It is of great importance that at least one part of the set should be in the consignee's hands before or at the time of the arrival of the goods because the shipowner is not bound to hand over the goods unless a bill of lading is delivered to him. Sometimes one part of the bill, together with the other papers forming the shipping documents,[36] is dispatched by letter in the ship's bag of the ship carrying the goods. Control of the contents of ship's bags is exercised in the United Kingdom by the Senior Naval Officer at the port of departure. The exporter sends the documents in the ship's bag in an unsealed envelope addressed to the overseas buyer or to his own representative or a referee in case of need.[37] Correspondence not relating to the cargo and remittances must not be included, and the dispatch is covered by a cover letter addressed to the master and asking him to deliver the dispatch to the addressee. On arrival, the master delivers the letter to the addressee who, if he has not received a part of the bill of lading before, delivers the bill of lading to the shipowner's representative or agent at the port of destination, known as the ship's agent.[38] The ship's

---

[34] In practice the bill of lading is sometimes handed over to the shipper only when the ship leaves port. Where the bill is issued under the Carriage of Goods by Sea Act 1971, as is mostly the case for consignments loaded in British ports (see p. 565, *post*), this practice is not in accordance with the law because the Hague-Visby Rules appended to the Act provide in Art. III(3) that the shipper can demand the issue of the bill after the carrier has received the goods into his charge. This means that the bill should be issued *immediately* after this event; see p. 570, *post* and Scrutton, *loc. cit.*, p. 54.

[35] See p. 594, *post*.

[36] See p. 37, *ante*.

[37] See p. 397, *ante*.

[38] The function of the ship's agent is described by Staughton J. in *A/S Hansen-Tangens Rederi III* v. *Total Transport Corporation. The Sagona.* [1984] 1 Lloyd's Rep. 194, 198–199. On arrival of the ship, he deals with the port, immigration and customs formalities and arranges its proper discharge. In law he is normally the agent of the shipowner but, if the ship is on a time charter, he is in general the agent of the charterer.

agent will then issue a *delivery order* which the holder presents to the ship's officer in charge of unloading.

If the exporter sells under a letter of credit, he normally hands all parts of the bill, together with the other required documents, to the advising or nominated bank, and that bank then forwards the documents by air mail to the issuing bank. Where various parts of a bill of lading are in the hands of different persons, the shipowner or the master (acting as the shipowner's agent) may hand over the cargo to the first person presenting a bill, "provided that he has no notice of any other claims to the goods, or knowledge of any other circumstances raising a reasonable suspicion that the claimant is not entitled to the goods. If he has any such notice or knowledge he must deliver at his peril to the rightful owner or must interplead. He is not entitled to deliver to the consignee named in the bill of lading without the production of the bill of lading, and does so at his risk if the consignee is not in fact entitled to the goods."[39]

On presentation of the delivery order, the goods are delivered from the ship to the person authorised by the order to take delivery. In the absence of agreement of the parties or a custom of the port of discharge to the contrary, the shipowner or master is not bound to notify the consignee of the arrival of the ship or his readiness to unload; it is the duty of the consignee to ascertain these facts. Where nothing else is arranged or customary, delivery has to take place over the ship's rail, and the consignee has to pay for lighters and stevedores to take delivery. The shipowner's responsibility for the goods does not cease when the ship arrives at the port of destination but only after he has duly delivered the goods to the consignee in accordance with the provisions of the contract of carriage, as evidenced by the bill of lading or as stipulated by law, but delivery does not necessarily mean transfer of the goods into the physical custody of the consignee; often delivery to a dock company or appropriate warehousing of the goods is sufficient. Normally the bill of lading contains detailed provisions about the methods of delivery and the cessation of the shipowner's liability. Where goods are imported from overseas into the United Kingdom, sections 492–501 of the Merchant Shipping Acts 1894 to 1988 apply. They contain detailed provisions for the delivery of the goods and the continuation of the shipowner's lien for freight after the landing of the goods.[40]

THE CONTRACT OF CARRIAGE BY SEA

Carriage covered by bill of lading or charterparty

The two types of contract of carriage by sea, *viz.* contracts evidenced by bills of lading and contracts contained in charterparties, have few points in common.

---

[39] Scrutton, *loc. cit.,* p. 296.
[40] See p. 556, *post.*

Charterparties are mainly governed by the rules of common law. The principle of liberty of contracting applies to them[41] and the shipowner may, by agreement with the charterer, modify his normal liability as a carrier without any limitations apart from those postulated by the general principles of common law. Contracts of carriage evidenced by bills of lading, on the other hand, are to a large measure regulated by statute law, in particular by the Carriage of Goods by Sea Act 1971[42] which qualifies the contractual liberty of the parties and especially restrains the shipowner from introducing exemptions from his liability beyond those admitted by the Rules relating to Bills of Lading—the Hague-Visby Rules—appended to the Act.

Charterparties are of little interest to the average exporter because only in exceptional cases is the quantity or bulk of his shipments such that the hire of a whole ship would be profitable for him; the exporter who has chartered a whole ship may issue bills of lading under the charterparty, but if payment is to be made under a banker's letter of credit, bills which contain a clause incorporating the terms of the charterparty will not be accepted by the bank unless it is authorised to accept charterparty bills of lading.[43]

The following observations deal only with contracts of carriage covered by bills of lading.

Conclusion of the contract of carriage by sea

It has been seen earlier that the contract of carriage by sea is concluded prior to the issue of the bill of lading, and that the latter merely evidences the terms of a contract which has already been partly performed.[44] Consequently a special term of the contract of carriage, even if agreed upon only orally, may override the general clauses printed in the bill of lading. This proposition can hardly be illustrated better than by reference to *The Ardennes*.[45] In this case a shipper of mandarins in Spain orally

---

[41] By virtue of their liberty of contracting, the parties to a charterparty often adopt a standard form, such as the Gencon Charter, the Baltmore 1939 Charter or the New York Product Exchange form, but sometimes they vary the clauses in the standard form to suit their own requirements, see *Compagnie Tunisienne de Navigation S.A.* v. *Compagnie d'Armement Maritime S.A.* [1971] A.C. 572; see p. 217, *ante*.

[42] See p. 564, *post*.

[43] UCP (1983 Revision), Art. 26(c)(i). On the incorporation of charterparty clauses into bill of lading, see p. 574, *post*.

[44] See p. 541, *ante*. A *draft* bill of lading sent by the shipper to the carrier is often an offer but the contract of carriage is only concluded when the carrier accepts this offer by receiving the shipper's goods for carriage: *Burke Motors Ltd.* v. *Mersey Docks and Harbour Co.* [1986] 1 Lloyd's Rep. 155.

[45] [1951] 1 K.B. 55; also Hobhouse J. in *Bergerco U.S.A.* v. *Vegoil Ltd.* [1984] 1 Lloyd's Rep. 440, 443. But bill of lading clauses which have not been varied by an overriding special agreement remain effective: *The Arawa* [1980] 2 Lloyd's Rep. 135, 138.

agreed with a carrier that the goods should be shipped directly to England so that they would reach this country before December 1, 1947, when the import duty on these goods was to be raised. The bill of lading covering the consignment contained the usual clause providing that the carrier was at liberty to proceed by any route and to carry the goods directly or indirectly to the port of destination. The ship proceeded first to Antwerp and then to London which it did not reach until December 4. Lord Goddard C.J. held that the contract of carriage was concluded before the issue of the bill of lading, that it was an express warranty in the contract of carriage that the carrier would not rely on a liberty which otherwise would have been open to him, and that that oral warranty overrode the terms set out in the bill of lading, and accordingly he awarded the consignor damages.

If the vessel carrying the goods is let by the owner to a charterer who makes it available as a general ship, the question arises whether the party with whom the shipper enters into the contract of carriage is the shipowner or the charterer. This question is considered later.[46]

Shutting out goods

When the goods of a shipper are shut out by the shipowner for want of room, though the goods were sent to the appointed place of loading before the closing date, two cases have to be distinguished: if, in reliance on the statement in the sailing card, the shipper sends the goods to the docks without previous agreement with the shipowner, he cannot claim damages because no contract has been concluded. The notification on the sailing card is in the nature of an invitation to make an offer, the dispatch of the goods to the docks is the offer, and the shipowner is free to accept or refuse this offer. But the position is different if, as is the modern practice, the shipper has booked freight space in advance; here "the contract of affreightment is prima facie broken and an action will lie against the shipowner."[47] Even in this case, actions are rarely brought for damage caused by "shutting out." There are several reasons for this. First, shipowners' notifications of closing dates usually contain the reservation that—

last day for goods is . . . unless the ship is previously full.

Secondly, in such a case the shipowner normally refunds without dispute freight if already paid, and loss of profits on goods shut out cannot usually be recovered.[48]

---

[46] See p. 560, *post.*
[47] Scrutton, *loc. cit.*, p. 121.
[48] Bigham J. in the unreported case of *Hecker* v. *Cunard S.S.*, July 1898 (referred to by Scrutton, *loc. cit.*, p. 121 n. (2)).

Freight

"Freight is the reward payable to the carrier for the safe carriage and delivery of the goods; it is payable only on the safe carriage and delivery; if the goods are lost on the voyage, nothing is payable."[49] This definition clearly indicates that, in law, the shipowner is not entitled to claim freight unless he is ready to deliver the cargo to the consignee at the port of destination, except if he is prevented by the cargo owner from so doing. Two rules are based on this proposition: first, the shipowner cannot claim freight if the cargo is lost. "If the goods are lost on the way, *no matter how*, no freight is earned. The excepted perils afford the shipowner a good excuse for non-delivery of the goods, but he cannot earn freight by virtue of one of them."[50] If the cargo arrives, though damaged, the shipowner is entitled to freight unless the damage is so serious that the goods have completely lost their merchantable character.[51] Secondly, freight is not payable before the goods have arrived at the port of destination and the shipowner is ready to deliver them. In practice, both rules are invariably abrogated by the terms of the contract of carriage as evidenced in the bill of lading.

Calculation of freight

Freight payable under bills of lading is calculated by weight, measurement or on an *ad valorem* basis. The shipowner is entitled to elect the mode of calculation most favourable to him. However, the customary bases of freight calculation are at present in a state of transition, in view of the increased use of combined transport and containerisation.

Bills of lading sometimes provide that if the shipper fails to make a correct or sufficient declaration of the cargo the shipowner shall be entitled to charge double freight calculated according to the true contents, value or nature of the goods, such double freight being liquidated damages and not a penalty.[52]

Freight rates fixed by shipping conferences

The standard freight rates for shipments in liner vessels are often fixed by so-called *shipping conferences*. These are combinations or pools of

---

[49] *Kirchner* v. *Venus* (1859) 12 Moore P.C. 361, 390; *Compania Naviera General S.A.* v. *Kerametal Ltd. The Lorna I* [1983] 1 Lloyd's Rep. 373, 374. On prepaid freight and "freight collect" see p. 553.
[50] Payne and Ivamy, *Carriage of Goods by Sea* (13th ed., 1989) p. 260.
[51] On the meaning of "merchantable character" in this connection, see Donaldson J. in *Montedison SpA* v. *Icroma SpA* [1980] 1 W.L.R. 48, 53. It follows from the statement in the text that, where it is alleged that the goods are damaged in transit, no deduction from the freight is admissible; see p. 558, *post.*
[52] On the measurement of goods for freight, see *Carver's Carriage by Sea* (13th ed., 1982) Vol. 2, para. 1705, p. 1195.

shipowners maintaining regular liner services to particular parts of the world, *e.g.* ports of the River Plate, South Africa, or Australia. The rates which they offer are frequently lower than those which non-conference shipowners are able to quote, but regular services can only be profitably maintained if supported by regular freight bookings. The members of the conference have, therefore, to guard against the defection of their regular clients who may transfer their custom occasionally to tramp steamers or other outsiders if offered freight space at cheaper rates than the conference rates.

In modern practice shipping conferences have evolved two systems of granting their regular clients preferential rates: they may use the system of deferred rebates of varying amounts up to 10 per cent. on the total freight; these rebates are retained by the shipping company for three or six months when they are payable, provided that during that period the shipper has not sent goods to the area in question in non-conference ships; if he has used the services of a non-conference shipowner, the percentage, which is sometimes inaccurately described as primage,[53] is forfeited.

The other method which they may use is the so-called contract system under which a shipper signs a contract whereby he undertakes to ship only by conference lines; he is then entitled to receive an immediate—not a deferred—rebate on the freight or—what amounts to the same—to ship at lower tariff rates; the immediate rebate is usually lower than the deferred rebate, *e.g.* $9\frac{1}{2}$ per cent. instead of 10 per cent. The contract normally provides that a shipper who breaks his undertaking has to pay an amount equivalent to the immediate rebate by way of liquidated damages. Sometimes a shipping conference offers shippers both systems of rebates according to their choice.

The rebate will be paid only to the shipper named in the bill of lading. This is a point to which attention should be paid in the relationship between the exporter and his forwarding agent. If the intention is that the rebate shall be passed on to the exporter it is advisable that the bills of lading are taken out in his name, and not in that of the forwarding agent.

The validity, in common law, of a conference arrangement was upheld in the famous *Mogul* case,[54] where a non-conference shipowner sued members of the conference formed for the shipment of tea from China to Europe; it was held that the conference arrangement was not illegal as being a conspiracy because its members pursued the lawful object of protecting and extending their own trade and had not employed unlawful means to achieve this object.

The arrangements which the owners combined in a shipping conference make between themselves and with their customers have undoubtedly a

---

[53] See pp. 555–556, *post.*
[54] *Mogul Steamship Co.* v. *McGregor, Gow & Co.* [1892] A.C. 25.

restrictive element which, however, can be justified in view of the benefit which the international trading community derives from the maintenance of scheduled liner services to distant places. This restrictive element came under review in the EC and in the U.S.A. In the EC a Regulation of the Council of Ministers of 1986[55] exempts, subject to certain conditions, shipping conference arrangements from the prohibitions of Articles 85 and 86 of the EC Treaty. In the U.S.A. the Bonner Act of 1961 imposes stringent conditions on the admission of the conference system[56]; the Federal Maritime Commission sought to probe in the United Kingdom into some of the conference arrangements; this was regarded as an attempt to infringe the territorial sovereignty of the United Kingdom and led to the enactment of preventive legislation[57] which today is contained, in a much wider ambit, in the Protection of Trading Interests Act 1980[58]; the dispute about shipping conference contracts between the Federal Maritime Commission and the United Kingdom and other maritime nations was later amicably settled.[59]

The liner conference system was also criticised by some of the less developed countries which claimed that in some instances it operated in a discriminatory fashion against their shipowners, shippers and foreign trade. On the suggestion of UNCTAD a *Convention on a Code of Conduct for Liner Conferences* was signed at Geneva on April 6, 1974 and became effective on October 6, 1983,[60] the aims of the Convention have been described thus[61]:

> The Code . . . aims at striking a just and fair balance between many interests. Discrimination between the members of a liner conference and non-members which are recognised national shipping lines shall be avoided; this provision,[62] it is thought, modifies the ruling of the House of Lords in the *Mogul* case.[63] The relations between the members of a liner conference, who often have disputes among themselves, are regulated. Transactions between conference members and shippers, including the grant of loyalty rebates, are covered. Important rules for freight determination, including promotional freight rates for non-traditional exports, are laid down. Altogether, this is a very comprehensive code.

The Code also provides a mandatory conciliation procedure for certain specified disputes. Already before the Convntion came into effect, the

---

[55] Council Regulation 4056/86 (EEC) of December 22, 1986, known as the Maritime Transport (Antitrust) Regulation 1986, see [1986] O.J. L 378/4 (December 31, 1986); [1989] 4 C.M.L.R. 451.

[56] John P. Gorman, "Shipping Conferences and the Bonner Act 1961" in [1962] J.B.L. 24.

[57] The Shipping Contracts and Commercial Documents Act 1964; see on this Act David A. Godwin Sarre in [1964] J.B.L. 293. The 1964 Act was repealed and superseded by the 1980 Act mentioned in the text.

[58] See p. 229, *ante.*

[59] David A. Godwin Sarre, "Shipping Conferences and the Federal Maritime Commission" in [1965] J.B.L. 93.

[60] See Lawrence Juda, "The UNCTAD Liner Code: A Preliminary Examination of the Implications of the Code of Conduct for Liner Conferences," in 16 *Journ. of Maritime Law and Commerce*, 1985, 181.

[61] In an Editorial in [1982] J.B.L. 441.

[62] Art. 1 of the Code.

[63] *Mogul Steamship Co.* v. *McGregor, Gow & Co.* [1892] A.C. 25; see p. 548, *ante.*

United Kingdom had passed enabling legislation, *viz.* the *Merchant Shipping (Liner Conferences) Act* 1982, to which the Code was appended in the Schedule. The Act came into force on March 14, 1985.[64]

By whom freight is payable

From the point of view of the exporter, the question to whom freight is payable normally causes little difficulty, except if the vessel is under charter and the question arises whether the shipper is in contract with the shipowner or the charterer.[65] On the other hand, the question from whom the shipowner may demand payment of the freight is of great practical significance. This question cannot be answered by reference to the contract of sale under which the exporter sold and shipped the goods. That contract regulates the ultimate responsibility for freight between the two parties to the sale but is irrelevant as far as the liability for freight to the shipowner is concerned.

The liability for freight is often expressly regulated by the bill of lading. The following clause, which provides for prepayment of the freight,[66] is typical:

> Freight for the said goods with primage, if any, shall be due and payable by the shipper on shipment at port of loading in cash, without deduction, and shall not be repayable, vessel or goods lost or not lost.

Where the bill of lading does not contain express provisions, the following rules apply:

(1) The shipper is primarily liable for payment of the freight because he is the person with whom the shipowner concludes the contract of carriage. This liability is purely contractual; it is irrelevant, in this respect, whether the shipper was at the time of the shipment the owner of the goods or not, or whether under the bill of lading the goods were made deliverable to the shipper or his order, or to a third person.

(2) The consignee is an entirely different position. He is not liable for freight under the contract of carriage because he is not a party thereto unless, of course, he is himself the shipper[67] or the shipper

---

[64] Merchant Shipping (Liner Conferences) Act 1982 (Commencement) Order 1985 (S.I. 1985 No. 182). The following S.I.s have also been issued: Merchant Shipping (Liner Conferences) (Conditions for Recognitions) Regulations (S.I. 1985 No. 405); and Merchant Shipping (Liner Conferences) Regulations 1985 (S.I. 1985 No. 406).

[65] See p. 560, *post.*

[66] See p. 552, *post.*

[67] It should be recalled that under an f.o.b. (buyer contracting with carrier) contract the consignee (the buyer) is the contracting party to the contract of carriage; see pp. 20–21, *ante.*

concluded the contract as his agent. Notwithstanding this fact, the shipowner may demand freight from him in either of the following cases:

(a) where he is named in the bill of lading as consignee or where the bill of lading is indorsed to him, *and* he has acquired the property in the goods by reason of such consignment or indorsement.[68] The liability which attaches only if these two conditions concur is of statutory character, being laid down by the *Bills of Lading Act 1855,* s.1.[69] The consignee is not liable if he does not acquire the property in the goods in this manner.[70] For this reason, a banker who accepts the bill of lading as security for an advance, or an agent who accepts delivery of the goods for their owner, is normally not liable for freight; or

(b) where he undertakes, even by implication, to pay the freight. Such undertaking is readily inferred from his course of dealing with the shipowner. If the agent of the owner of the goods persuades the master to deliver the goods to him and thereby to give up the shipowner's lien on the goods, the courts, applying the rule in *Brandt* v. *Liverpool, Brazil and River Plate Steam Navigation Co.*[71] are likely to hold that he (being the consignee) concluded a new contract with the shipowner whereby he promised payment of the freight in consideration of delivery of the goods to him.

(3) An indorsee who is liable for freight by virtue of the Bills of Lading Act 1855, s.1 (above No. (2)(a)), ceases to be liable when reindorsing the bill *and* transferring the property in the goods to the person to whom he reindorses the bill, provided that the bill is reindorsed while the goods are in transit and before they are delivered. Here again, both conditions of reindorsement and transfer of property under a contract in pursuance of which the bill of lading is reindorsed have to be satisfied; the indorsee, who became liable for freight by virtue of the Act, remains liable if he merely resells the goods but retains the bill of lading, or indorses the bill, *e.g.* as a security, but retains the goods. Where both aforesaid conditions are satisfied and the transferor of the bill of lading ceases to be liable for the freight, the transferee becomes liable for it by virtue of section 1 of the 1855 Act.

---

[68] *K/S A/S Seateam & Co.* v. *Iraq National Oil Co. The Sevonia Team* [1983] 2 Lloyd's Rep. 640, 643.

[69] On the transfer of the right to sue under the Bills of Lading Act 1855, see p. 558, *post.*

[70] *Gardano and Ciampieri* v. *Greek Petroleum George Mamidakis & Co.* [1962] 1 W.L.R. 40. The consignee will normally acquire property (and thus the right to sue) by indorsement and delivery of the bill of lading to him or his agent: *The San Nicholas* [1976] 1 Lloyd's Rep. 8, 11.

[71] [1924] 1 K.B. 575, as interpreted in *The Aramis* [1989] 1 Lloyd's Rep. 213; see pp. 44–45, *ante.*

(4) The seller, who exercises his right of stoppage in transit,[72] is liable to pay the freight to the shipowner, even if not liable under Rule 1.

Prepaid freight

It has been seen[73] that, in law, the shipowner is not entitled to claim freight before the cargo has arrived and he is ready to deliver it. The parties are at liberty to modify these rules by agreement, and their discretion is not qualified by the Carriage of Goods by Sea Act 1971.

In respect of freight payable under a bill of lading, the rules of law are, in practice, invariably abrogated by express agreement of the parties. Clauses in bills of lading stipulating prepayment of freight vary considerably; the clause referred to on p. 550, *ante,* is fairly typical.

Most freight clauses in bills of lading contain the words "ship lost or not lost," often supplemented by the words "freight deemed to have been earned on shipment." Where words to this effect are inserted in the bill of lading, the nature of prepaid freight is beyond dispute: it is, in legal terminology, *advance freight*. Such freight is due and earned when the stipulated event happens, *e.g.* on the signing of the bill of lading.[74] Apart from exceptional cases, the right of the shipowner to claim freight is not affected by the subsequent loss of the goods, and the shipowner is not only entitled to retain the full amount of prepaid freight but may even sue the shipper for it, if, for one reason or another, due prepaid freight has not been paid.[75] These rules are subject to three exceptions: the shipowner has to return advance freight:

(1) if "the ship never earned freight and never began to earn freight,"[76] *e.g.* because she did not sail, or
(2) if the goods are lost before advance freight becomes due,[77] or
(3) if the goods are lost by an event other than an excepted peril.[78]

If the bill of lading omits to state when advance freight shall become payable, it appears to be payable on the final sailing of the ship. As the

---

[72] See p. 150, *ante.*
[73] See p. 547, *ante.*
[74] It is due if, under the terms of the contract (in this case the charterparty) it is payable at a later date and even if before it is payable, the contract is terminated by acceptance of a repudiatory breach; the claim for advance freight, when it has become due, survives such termination: *Bank of Boston Connecticut* v. *European Grain and Shipping Ltd. The Dominique* [1989] 2 W.L.R. 442 (H.L.).
[75] *Oriental Steamship Co. Ltd.* v. *Tylor* [1893] 2 Q.B. 518.
[76] *Per* James L.J. in *Ex p. Nyholm, re Child* (1873) 43 L.J.Bk. 21, 24.
[77] If, *e.g.*, the advance freight is payable, say, five days after the master signed the bill, and the cargo is lost by a frustrating event within the five days and the bill does not contain an "earned upon shipment" or similar clause, the carrier cannot demand payment of the (unpaid) advance freight: *Compania Naviera General SA* v. *Kerametal Ltd. The Lorna I.* [1983] 1 Lloyd's Rep. 373. But see *The Dominique,* noted in n. 74, *ante.*
[78] *Dufourcet* v. *Bishop* (1886) 18 Q.B.D. 373; *Rodocanachi* v. *Milburn* (1886) 18 Q.B.D. 67.

shipper bears the risk in respect of prepaid freight, he has an insurable interest therein which he may cover by marine insurance.[79]

In modern practice the wording of freight clauses in the bill of lading or charterparty puts it normally beyond doubt that prepaid freight is intended by the parties to be advance freight. In older days it was sometimes doubtful whether prepaid freight was in the nature of advance freight or merely a loan by the shipper on account of freight payable in accordance with the general rules of the common law, namely, on safe arrival of the cargo. The difference in the interpretation of the prepayment clause is considerable when the goods are lost in transit. The prepaid sum, if advance freight, cannot normally be recovered, but if paid as a loan can be recovered by the shipper. The interpretation of the clause depends entirely on the intention of the parties which it is not always easy to ascertain; the courts have evolved the rule that, when freight has to be insured by the shipowner, the prepayment is likely to be a loan, but if it has to be insured by the shipper it is likely to be advance freight.

Freight prepaid and freight collect bills of lading

We have so far considered the obligations arising from the contract of carriage by sea, as far as they concern the questions who has to pay the freight and when freight is payable. Another problem arises between the seller and the buyer under a c.i.f. contract. It is obvious that the c.i.f. price includes a freight element but the question is whether that freight element has to be paid by the seller by way of prepaid freight or by the buyer on arrival of the goods, in which case the seller has to give the buyer credit for the freight, by deducting the freight element from the invoice price. Whether the one or the other method is used, depends on the agreement of the parties. "When the first method is used the seller provides *freight prepaid bills of lading*. When the second method is used he provides what have been conveniently called *freight collect bills of lading,* that is to say, bills of lading under which freight is payable by the receiver (who may be the buyer himself or a sub-buyer from the buyer) to the ship at the port of discharge."[80]

The distinction is of considerable commercial importance. If freight collect bills are used, the buyer's obligation to pay freight to the shipowner is conditional on the arrival of the goods, but notwithstanding this condition, the contract is a true c.i.f. contract.[81]

---

[79] See p. 506, *ante.*
[80] Brandon J. in *The Pantanassa* [1970] 1 Lloyd's Rep. 153, 163. See also *Federal Commerce and Navigation Ltd.* v. *Molena Alpha Inc., The Nanfri* [1979] A.C. 757 (H.L.).
[81] *Ibid.*

Dead freight

Where the shipper fails to load the cargo or the full cargo after arranging with the shipowner for its carriage, he has broken the contract of carriage and is liable to pay the agreed freight as damages (dead freight). But the shipowner who uses the freight space which would have been taken up by the goods of the defaulting shipper and carries therein goods of other shippers has to deduct the earned freight when claiming damages. He may claim from the defaulting shipper the difference between the agreed and actually earned freight, *e.g.* if he had to accept cargo which earned a lower rate of freight.[82]

Lump sum freight

While freight is normally arranged according to weight, measurement or value,[83] the shipper may agree to pay a lump sum as freight for the use of the entire ship or a portion thereof.[84] In this case, the amount of freight payable by the shipper is fixed and invariable and, if the shipowner is ready to perform his contract, is payable whether the shipper uses the hired space to full capacity, or loads below capacity or does not load at all. Moreover, in the absence of agreement to the contrary, the whole lump sum freight is payable if only part of the loaded cargo is delivered by the shipowner at the port of destination and the remainder is lost,[85] but the shipowner cannot claim lump sum freight if he is unable to deliver at least part of the cargo.

Lump sum freight is not customary in a contract of carriage evidenced by bills of lading, but is sometimes arranged under charterparties when the shipper is uncertain of the quantity or species of the goods which he has to ship.

Back freight

The shipper is liable to pay back freight where the goods shipped are carried, on his instructions or in his interest, to a place other than the port of destination. Where the shipper, in his capacity of unpaid seller,

---

[82] *Cf. Total Transport Corporation of Panama* v. *Amoco Transport Co. The Altus* [1985] 1 Lloyd's Rep. 423, 436.
[83] See p. 547, *ante.*
[84] Scrutton, *loc. cit.*, p. 339.
[85] *William Thomas & Sons* v. *Harrowing Steamship Co.* [1915] A.C. 58.

exercises his right of stoppage in transit[86] and instructs the shipowner to deliver the goods at a port other than the port of destination named in the bill of lading, the shipper is liable for any additional freight and, if he instructs the shipowner to deliver the goods short of the original port of destination, he has to pay the total original freight as damages because, by giving notice of stoppage, he broke the contract of carriage concluded with the shipowner and prevented the latter from earning the freight.[87] Where the master, in the interest of the shipper, considers it advisable to carry the goods to another place than the bill of lading destination, *e.g.* because that port is strikebound,[88] the shipper is liable to pay the additional freight as "back freight."

Pro rata freight

Pro rata freight is payable in exceptional circumstances only, namely, where the parties to the contract of carriage conclude a new contract[89] to the effect that the goods shall be delivered at an intermediate port, and not the port of destination named in the bill of lading. Such agreement, unless concluded expressly, is only inferred from the circumstances where the shipper has a genuine choice of having his goods carried to the destination originally agreed upon. The shipper is, therefore, not obliged to pay *pro rata* freight where the shipowner leaves the goods at an intermediate port and is unable or unwilling to carry them to the port of destination. The shipowner is likewise entitled to *pro rata* freight where he loads only part of the agreed cargo or delivers only part of the total loaded cargo, the delivery of the remainder having become impossible through excepted perils.[90]

Primage

Some bills of lading refer to the remuneration payable to the shipowner as

freight and primage (if any).

Primage was originally a small payment made by the shipper to the master in consideration of the care and attention which he was to give

---

[86] See p. 150, *ante.*
[87] *Booth Steamship Co. Ltd.* v. *Cargo Fleet Iron Co. Ltd.* [1916] 2 K.B. 570.
[88] *G. H. Renton & Co. Ltd.* v. *Palmyra Trading Corporation of Panama; The Caspiana* [1957] A.C. 149.
[89] *St. Enoch Shipping Co. Ltd.* v. *Phosphate Mining Co.* [1916] 2 K.B. 624, 627.
[90] Scrutton, *loc. cit.*, p. 343; on excepted perils, see p. 600, *post.*

during the voyage to the shipper's cargo, but such payment is no longer customary.

In modern practice, primage is not normally charged. Where it is claimed, it means hardly more than a percentage added to the freight and is payable to the shipowner. Where primage is charged, it is normally 10 per cent. of the net freight.

Sometimes the deferred rebate payable to the shipper under conference arrangements[91] is referred to as primage.

Shipowner's lien

The shipowner has a lien on the goods of the shipper which are in his possession. The shipowner's lien is derived from common law or based on express agreement.

At common law the shipowner has a lien:

(1) for freight which is payable on delivery of the goods, but not for advance freight,[92] dead freight,[93] or freight payable after delivery of the goods;

(2) for general average contributions. This lien has been considered earlier[94];

(3) for "expenses incurred by the shipowner or master in protecting and preserving the goods."[95]

The common law lien of the shipowner is a possessory lien; it can be exercised only as long as the goods are in the shipowner's possession on board ship or, subject to the notice of lien discussed below, in a warehouse ashore. This shipowner's lien is lost when the goods are duly delivered or the shipowner agrees to accept freight subsequent to delivery. Where goods are imported into the United Kingdom from overseas, the shipowner's lien for freight and other charges is subject to the provisions of the Merchant Shipping Acts 1894 to 1988, Pt. VII, ss.492 to 501. The Acts provide that the lien is maintained when the shipowner, on landing the goods and placing them into the custody of a warehouseman, gives the warehouseman notice in writing that the goods are to remain subject to the lien to an amount stated in the notice, but the owner of the goods is entitled to deposit with the warehouseman the claimed sum and thereupon to receive possession of the goods. The deposit takes the place of the goods and, if there is a dispute about the freight between the parties to the contract of carriage, the right to the deposit is ascertained by arbitration[96] or litigation.

---

[91] See p. 548, *ante.*
[92] See p. 552, *ante.*
[93] See p. 554, *ante.*
[94] See p. 523, *ante.*
[95] Scrutton, *loc. cit.,* p. 386.
[96] See Arbitration Act 1950, s.29.

Where the shipowner's lien is not discharged and no deposit is made, and the shipowner instructs the warehouseman to sell the goods by public auction, such auction may not take place until 90 days after the goods were placed in the warehouseman's custody: only if they are perishable may they be auctioned before that period. The provisions of the Merchant Shipping Acts 1894 to 1988 do not apply to the lien of the shipowner for outward voyages. At common law the shipowner's lien attaches to all goods carried to the same consignee on the same voyage under the same contract; and it is immaterial that several bills of lading have been issued in respect of them. If part of the goods is delivered without payment of freight the shipowner may still claim his lien on the remainder of the goods for the whole freight due to him. But the position is different where goods are shipped under different contracts of carriage. Where *e.g.* the shipowner carries goods under one contract of carriage and delivers them without insisting on payment of freight, and later ships goods of the same shipper to the same consignee under another contract of carriage, he cannot in common law claim a lien on these goods for the unpaid freight due under the previous contract.

The lien of the shipowner is usually extended beyond the limits of the common law lien by agreement of the parties. Bills of lading normally contain special clauses dealing with the shipowner's lien. The following clause is typical:

> The carrier, his servants or agents shall have a lien on the goods and a right to sell the goods whether privately or by public auction for all freight (including additional freight payable as above stipulated), primage, dead freight, demurrage, detention charges, salvage, average of any kind whatsoever, and for all other charges and expenses whatsoever, which are for account of the goods or of the shipper, consignee or owner of the goods under this bill of lading, and for the costs and expenses of exercising such lien and of such sale and also for all previously unsatisfied debts whatsoever due to him by the shipper, consignee or owner of the goods. Nothing in this clause shall prevent the carrier from recovering from the shipper, consignee or owner of the goods the difference between the amount due from them or any of them to him and the amount realised by the exercise of the rights given to the carrier under this clause.

The shipowner's lien is often extended by these special clauses to cover dead freight,[97] advance freight,[98] freight payable after delivery of the goods, unsatisfied previous freight, inland or forwarding charges, porterage, fines, costs and other charges or amounts due from the shippers or consignees, to the shipowners or their agents.[99] The clauses dealing with the shipowner's lien usually authorise the shipowner to realise the lien by sale of the goods by public auction or otherwise.

---

[97] See p. 554, *ante.*
[98] See p. 552, *ante.*
[99] *Whinney* v. *Moss Steamship Co. Ltd.* (1910) 15 Com.Cas. 114. It was held by Nourse J. in *In Re Welsh Irish Ferries Ltd.* [1985] 3 W.L.R. 610, that a shipowner's lien on sub-freight constituted a charge registrable under what is now s.396 of the Companies Act 1985, but it is doubtful whether this decision is correct.

No deduction from freight in respect of cargo claim

It has been seen[1] that the carrier is entitled to the full freight if he delivers the goods at their destination, even though they are damaged.[2] It follows that the cargo owner is not entitled to make a deduction from the freight for the damage to the goods or delay in the delivery or to set off his claim for damages against the carrier's claim for freight.[3] But the cargo owner is entitled to pursue such a claim for damages by way of action or counterclaim.[4]

Proceedings by cargo owner

The right to sue

The contract of carriage by sea is often concluded by the consignor, particularly where he has sold the goods on delivery terms such as strict f.o.b., f.o.b. with additional services, or c.i.f. terms. If it is necessary to bring an action against the carrier, the question arises who is entitled to sue, the consignor or the consignee.

If the bill of lading has been transferred to the consignee or indorsee of the bill and the property has passed by reason of such consignment or indorsement, by virtue of section 1 of the Bills of Lading Act 1855[5] such consignee or indorsee:

> shall have transferred to and vested in him all rights of suit, and be subject to the same liabilities in respect of such goods as if the contract contained in the bill of lading had been made with himself.

In other words, this provision operates as a statutory transfer of the right to sue and the consignee or indorsee is clearly entitled to bring an action against the carrier for damages for any loss of or damage to the cargo, as he has suffered these damages himself as the owner of the goods.[6]

---

[1] See p. 547, *ante.*
[2] Provided that they have not lost their merchantable character.
[3] *Aries Tanker Corporation* v. *Total Transport Ltd.* [1977] 1 W.L.R. 185, 189 (H.L.); *Bank of Boston Connecticut* v. *European Grain and Shipping Ltd., The Dominique*, [1989] 2 W.L.R. 440 (H.L.). Also *R. H. & D. International Ltd.* v. *I. A. S. Animal Air Services Ltd.* [1984] 1 W.L.R. 573 (application to CMR freight).
[4] Scrutton, *loc. cit.*, p. 341.
[5] See Andrew P. Bell, "The Bills of Lading Act 1855 Today" in [1985] J.B.L. 124.
[6] See *The San Nicholas* [1976] 1 Lloyd's Rep. 8. But the right of suit does not pass to the consignee under the Bills of Lading Act 1855 if the property in the goods has passed to him otherwise than on consignment or endorsement of the bill of lading, *e.g.* if it has passed to him before shipment; *Hispanica de Petroleos SA (Hispanoil)* v. *Vencedora Oceanica Navegacion SA. The Kapetan Markos* [1986] 1 Lloyd's Rep. 211, 213 and *The Kapetan Markos (No. 2)* [1987] 2 Lloyd's Rep. 321, 329.

Where quantified parcels of a bulk cargo are sold under separate bills of lading, the consignee of such a bill cannot sue the shipowner by virtue of the 1855 Act because the goods being unascertained goods, no property can pass in them[7].

The consignor cannot normally sue the carrier for substantial damages suffered by the consignee or indorsee of the bill of lading because he has not suffered these damages himself and under section 1 of the 1855 Act, in the words of Lord Diplock[8]:

> the right of suit against the shipowner in respect of obligations arising under the contract of carriage passes to [the consignee or indorsee] from the consignor. Furthermore, a holder of a bill for valuable consideration in exercising his own right of suit has the benefit of an estoppel not available to the consignor that the bill of lading is conclusive evidence against the shipowner of the goods described in it.

Occasionally, however, in cases to which the Bills of Lading Act 1855 does not apply, the consignor may recover from the carrier substantial damages suffered by the consignee or indorsee to whom the property in the goods has passed, on the ground that privity of contract exists between him and the carrier.[9] He has, of course, to hand over the damages recovered to the person who suffered them (or his insurer). It may be added that a bailee of goods, such as a carrier or warehouseman, can recover substantial damages suffered by his bailor in respect of the goods of the latter, if the loss or damage was caused by negligence or another tort was committed by a third party;[10] provided that the bailor's proprietary interest in the goods was insured by the bailee, the latter can recover the insurance money for the benefit of the bailor.[11]

So far the right of suit under the *contract of carriage* has been examined. An entirely different question is whether the consignee to whom the bill of lading has not been transferred and who therefore cannot avail himself of the benefit of the Bills of Lading Act 1855 is entitled to bring an action in *tort* against the carrier if the goods are lost or damaged as the result of the carrier's negligence. This question has been considered earlier.[12]

---

[7] *The Aramis* [1989] 1 Lloyd's Rep. 213, 218 (C.A.); *Enichem Anic SpA* v. *Ampelos Shipping Co. Ltd. The Delfini. The Times*, August 11, 1989; on the passing of property, see p. 116, *ante*. The requirement of the transfer of property by s.1 of the Bills of Lading Act 1855 is discussed with a view to possible reform, in working paper No. 112 of the (English) Law Commission and discussion paper No. 83 of the Scottish Law Commission on Rights to Goods in Bulk, both published in 1989.

[8] *Albacruz (Cargo Owners)* v. *Albazero (Owners)* [1977] A.C. 774, 847. But the Bills of Lading Act 1855 does not transfer the benefit or burden of an estoppel operative for or against the consignor to the consignee: *Government of Swaziland Central Transport Administration* v. *Leila Maritime Co. Ltd. The Leila* [1985] 2 Lloyd's Rep. 172, 177.

[9] *Dunlop* v. *Lambert* (1837) 6 Bl. & F. 600, as interpreted in *The Albazero*; *Pan Atlantic Insurance Co. Ltd.* v. *Pine Top Insurance Co. Ltd.* [1988] 2 Lloyd's Rep. 505, 511.

[10] *The Winkfield* [1902] P. 42.

[11] *A. Tomlinson (Hauliers) Ltd.* v. *Hepburn* [1966] A.C. 451; *Petrofina (U.K.) Ltd.* v. *Magnaload Ltd.* [1983] 2 Lloyd's Rep. 91, 95.

[12] See p. 45, *ante*.

If the carrier wrongly delivers the goods to a person not entitled thereto, the cargo owner can sue the carrier in *tort* for conversion.[13] This situation arises, in particular, if the consignee has resold the goods to a further purchaser and has transferred the bill of lading to the latter but prevails on the carrier to deliver the goods to him—the consignee—on arrival without return of the bill of lading.[14]

Whom to sue, the shipowner or the charterer

Where the shipowner has let the ship to a charterer and the latter employs it as a general ship, it is sometimes difficult to determine whether the contract of carriage is made with the shipowner or the charterer, in short, who the carrier is.[15]

If the charter is a bareboat charter,[16] under which the charterer employs his own master and crew, it is probable that the master has signed the bills of lading as agent of the charterer and the latter would be the carrier.

But if the charter is not a bareboat charter—and this is the normal case—the master and crew are the employees of the shipowner and the contract of carriage is usually made with the shipowner. This will even be the case if the charter provides that the master shall sign the bills of lading as agent of the charterer and the shipper does not know that the charterparty contains such a clause.[17] Sometimes the bill of lading contains a clause stating expressly that the party contracting with the shipper shall be the shipowner (or demise charterer), and not the (ordinary) charterer.[18] But the circumstances vary and each case has to be judged on its own facts.

If the shipper erroneously makes a claim for loss of or damage to the cargo against the charterer, thinking that he is the shipowner, the charterer cannot be regarded as agent of the owner, except if he has authority from the latter,[19] and a later claim against the owner would fail if the action against him is brought outside the time limit of the Hague-Visby Rules.[20]

---

[13] See *Chabbra Corporation Pte. Ltd.* v. *Jag Shakti (Owners). The Jag Shakti* [1986] 2 W.L.R. 87 (P.C.) (the issue concerned the measure of damages for conversion).

[14] *Ibid.*

[15] See Scrutton, *loc. cit.*, p. 68.

[16] Also called a charterparty by demise.

[17] *Manchester Trust* v. *Furness, Withy & Co.* [1895] 2 Q.B. 539.

[18] This clause is usually referred to as the "demise clause," *Kenya Railways* v. *Antares Co. Pte. Ltd. The Antares (No. 2)* [1986] 2 Lloyd's Rep. 633; *Ngo Chew Hong Edible Oil Pte. Ltd.* v. *Scindia Steam Navigation Co. Ltd. The Jalamohan* [1988] 1 Lloyd's Rep. 443.

[19] In *The Antares (No. 2)* he had no authority but in *The Jalamohan* he had such authority.

[20] *The Antares (Nos 1 and 2)* [1987] 1 Lloyd's Rep. 424 (C.A.); on the time limits under the Hague-Visby Rules, see p. 606, *post.*

The charterparty usually provides that the charterer shall indemnify the shipowner against all liabilities that may arise from the signing of the bills of lading in accordance with the directions of the charterer; consequently, even if the shipowner is liable to the holder of the bill of lading, he can pass on this liability under the indemnity clause in the charterparty to the charterer.[21]

CARRIAGE COVERED BY BILLS OF LADING

Nature of the bill of lading

The principal purpose of the bill of lading is to enable the owner of the goods, to which it relates, to dispose of them rapidly although the goods are not in his hands but are in the custody of a carrier. When goods are on the high seas in transit from London to Singapore and the bill of lading has been airmailed to the buyer in Singapore and the buyer thus has become the owner of the goods, the bill of lading representing the goods enables the buyer to pledge the goods with his bank in Singapore or to resell them to a repurchaser in New York. The bill of lading is a creation of mercantile custom, a typical institution of international trade. It came into use in the sixteenth century. A book on mercantile law, published in 1686, stated that "bills of lading are commonly to be had in print in all places and several languages."[22] The character of the bill of lading as a document of title was first recognised by the courts in 1794 in *Lickbarrow* v. *Mason*.[23]

From the legal point of view, a bill of lading[24] is—

(1) a formal receipt by the shipowner acknowledging that goods alleged to be of the stated species, quantity and condition are shipped to a stated destination in a certain ship, or at least are received in the custody of the shipowner for the purpose of shipment;

---

[21] The claim for indemnification of the shipowner against the charterer frequently gives rise to disputes; a consideration of these cases is outside the ambit of this work.

[22] Malynes, *Lex Mercatoria* (3rd ed., 1686), p. 97.

[23] (1794) 5 T.R. 683.

[24] The most frequently used format of the bill of lading today is that known as the "Model B" bill of lading. This format was first developed as the result of international co-operation under the auspices of the UN Economic Commission for Europe (ECE), which devised the so-called ECE layout key. In this work the ECE was greatly assisted by the International Chamber of Shipping which acted in consultation with the International Chamber of Commerce. This form of bill of lading is used as a model in the SITPRO aligned series, *System Export Documentation* (see p. 77, *ante*).

(2) a memorandum of the contract of carriage, repeating in detail the terms of the contract which was in fact concluded prior to the signing of the bill; and

(3) a document of title to the goods enabling the consignee to dispose of the goods by indorsement and delivery of the bill of lading.

The international Rules relating to bills of lading

Although the clauses contained in a duly tendered and signed bill of lading represent, in law, the terms of agreement between the shipper and the carrier, the shipper has little discretion in the negotiation of these terms. The terms of the contract which he concludes,[25] are fixed in advance, and his position is not unlike that of a railway passenger who, when buying a ticket, concludes an elaborate standard contract with the railway authority for the carriage of his person from one locality to another. The shipper, like the railway passenger, is protected by Act of Parliament against abuse of the greater bargaining power of the other party. As far as the shipper is concerned, this protection is contained in the *Carriage of Goods by Sea Act 1971*. The legislative intention is, in the words of Lord Sumner,[26] to "replace a conventional contract, in which it was constantly attempted, often with much success, to relieve the carrier from every kind of liability, by a legislative bargain, under which . . . his position was to be one of restricted exemption."

The Act of 1971 was preceded by the *Carriage of Goods by Sea Act 1924* which has an interesting history.[27] The clauses in bills of lading exempting the carrier from liability had become so complex and diffuse that the usefulness of bills of lading as "currency of trade"[28] was seriously threatened. This was particularly unsatisfactory to holders of bills of lading who were not the original parties to the contract of carriage and consequently had no influence on its formation, such as further purchasers of goods, bankers who accepted the bills as security for advances, or insurers who were subrogated to the rights of the shipper. On the initiative of the International Law Association the *Hague Rules 1921 relating to Bills of Lading* were formulated and diplomatic conferences held in Brussels in 1922, 1923 and 1924[29] recommended their international

---

[25] See p. 545, *ante.*

[26] In *Gosse Millard Ltd.* v. *Canadian Government Merchant Marine* [1929] A.C. 223, 236 (in respect of the Carriage of Goods by Sea Act 1924, which preceded the 1971 Act).

[27] See the excellent account in Chap. 1, "Historical Antecedents," of Raoul P. Colinvaux, *The Carriage of Goods by Sea Act 1924* (Stevens, 1954).

[28] Scrutton, *loc. cit.,* p. 409.

[29] The final conference was in 1924, after the United Kingdom Act, which was based on an earlier draft, had been adopted.

adoption. In the United Kingdom, effect was given to the Hague Rules by the Carriage of Goods by Sea Act 1924. The Hague Rules imposed on the carrier certain minimum responsibilities which he could not reduce, *e.g.* to exercise due diligence to provide a seaworthy ship, to load, handle, stow, carry, keep, care for and discharge the goods and to issue a bill of lading in a particular form, and put upon him the liability for the proper and careful conduct of these operations while giving him certain maximum exemptions which he could not increase.

The Hague Rules were revised by the Brussels Protocol of 1968.[30] The revised Rules, known as the *Hague-Visby Rules,* are appended to the Carriage of Goods Act 1971 and form part of it. That Act came into operation on June 23, 1977.[31] It has repealed the Carriage of Goods by Sea Act 1924 and is the enactment in force at present. The Hague-Visby Rules have been accepted by the following States which are "Contracting States" within section 2(1)(*a*) of the Act[32]:

> United Kingdom (which extended the application of the Hague-Visby Rules to The Isle of Man, Bermuda, British Antarctic Territory, British Virgin Islands, Cayman Islands, Falkland Islands, Falkland Islands Dependencies, Gibraltar, Hong Kong, Montserrat, and Turks and Caicos Islands), Belgium, Denmark, Ecuador, Egypt, Finland, France, German Democratic Republic, Lebanon, The Netherlands (in Europe), Norway, Poland, Singapore, Spain, Sri Lanka, Sweden, Switzerland, Syria and Tonga.

The Hague-Visby Rules were fundamentally revised by the United Nations Convention on the Carriage of Goods by Sea 1978, which accepted the so-called *Hamburg Rules.* They were prepared by UNCITRAL and adopted by a United Nations conference at Hamburg on March 30, 1978. They have been ratified or acceded to by sixteen States.[33] The major alterations proposed by the Hamburg Rules are: they shall apply to all contracts for the carriage of goods by sea between two different States, except charterparties, even if the carriage is not carried out under a bill of lading; the period of responsibility of the carrier is extended so as to cover the whole period during which the goods are in his charge; the exclusion of the carrier's liability in case of error in

---

[30] Another international measure was the Protocol of December 21, 1979, which provided that the various limitation amounts expressed in gold francs in the Hague-Visby Rules should be replaced by equivalent amounts expressed in special drawing rights (SDRs) as defined by the International Monetary Fund. The United Kingdom gave effect to this Protocol by the Merchant Shipping Act 1981 and this regulation came into operation on November 29, 1984 (The Merchant Shipping Act 1981 (Commencement No. 3) Order 1984 (S.I. 1984 No. 1695 (C.39)). For the ascertainment of the sterling equivalents of the SDRs, see p. 602, *post.*

[31] The Carriage of Goods by Sea Act 1971 (Commencement) Order 1977 (S.I. 1977 No. 98 (c. 35)).

[32] The Carriage of Goods by Sea (Parties to Convention) Order 1985 (S.I. 1985 No. 443). Position: April 1, 1989. More States may be added by Statutory Instrument.

[33] Position: October 9, 1989. The Convention will come into force if 20 States have ratified it or acceded to it.

navigation is abolished; a distinction is drawn between the contractual carrier and actual carrier, the contractual carrier being liable for the actual carrier and, in principle, both being liable to the shipper jointly and severally; the maximum limits of the carrier's liability are greatly increased and fixed by reference to the Special Drawing Rights of the International Monetary Fund (SDRs); and the Rules may apply to transport documents other than bills of lading.[34]

The present position is this: the Hamburg Rules are not in force yet and may, therefore, be disregarded for the purposes of this treatise. The Hague-Visby Rules are law in the United Kingdom and the other Contracting States referred to earlier. A number of States have not adopted the Hague-Visby Rules yet but still adhere to the original Hague Rules, amongst them, in particular, the United States of America.[35] The original unity of international regulation in the law relating to bills of lading is thus lost, at least temporarily, until all sea-going States will have adopted again uniform Rules.[36] The following treatment is founded on the United Kingdom Carriage of Goods by Sea Act 1971 and the Hague-Visby Rules contained in the Schedule to that Act.

But it should be noted that the original Hague Rules may still be relevant in proceedings before arbitrators or in the courts in the United Kingdom, *e.g.* if a dispute concerns a bill of lading relating to a shipment from a State which is not a Contracting State under the Hague-Visby Rules but still adheres to the original Hague Rules; such a bill would not be governed by the 1971 Act.

Application of the Carriage of Goods by Sea Act 1971

Documentary application

The Act, including the Hague-Visby Rules, applies to all shipments where "the contract expressly or by implication provides for the issue of a bill of lading or any similar document of title."[37]

The carrier can thus escape from the application of the Act and the Rules if his contract with the shipper does not provide for the issue of a bill of lading and shipment is carried out under a non-negotiable liner waybill, data freight receipt or a similar transport document acknowledg-

---

[34] There exists also a United Nations Convention on International Multimodal Transport. It was sponsored by UNCTAD and adopted by a United Nations Conference at Geneva on May 24, 1980. The Convention is not in operation yet. See further p. 613, *post.*
[35] See U.S. Carriage of Goods by Sea Act 1936.
[36] It may take some time before this happens.
[37] s.1(4).

ing only the receipt of the goods[38]; such non-negotiable receipts are invariably issued instead of bills of lading by English cross-channel operators.[39] These non-negotiable receipts can, however, be subjected to the application of the Act and the Rules by marking the receipt that the Rules shall apply "as if the receipt were a bill of lading."[40]

The Rules do not normally apply to deck cargo or live animals,[41] but if the bill of lading or other receipt refers to such cargo, it may state expressly that the Rules shall apply.[42]

Territorial application

Article X of the Rules provides:

> The provisions of these Rules shall apply to every bill of lading relating to the carriage of goods between ports in two different States if:
> - (a) the bill of lading is issued in a Contracting State; or
> - (b) the carriage is from a port in a Contracting State; or
> - (c) the contract contained in or evidenced by the bill of lading provides that these Rules or legislation of any State giving effect to them are to govern the contract.
>
> whatever may be the nationality of the ship, the carrier, the shipper, the consignee, or any other interested person.

The Rules thus apply by force of law to outward bills of lading relating to all goods exported from ports in Great Britain and Northern Ireland and any other Contracting State and also to bills issued in these countries, but they do not normally apply to the transportation of live animals,[43] and deck cargo which is carried on deck in pursuance of the contract of carriage.[44] But where cargo is carried on deck without specific agreement between the parties as to the carriage on deck, and no statement appears on the face of the bill of lading that goods carried on deck are in fact so carried, the carriage is subject to the Rules. Where the bill of lading contains the usual clause that the shipowner shall be at liberty to carry on deck, he is free to do so but is not relieved, by that clause, of his obligations under Article III, r. 2, *e.g.* to stow diligently.[45] The Hague-

---

[38] See p. 578, *post.*

[39] *Browner International Transport Ltd.* v. *Monarch S.S. Company Ltd.,* [1989] 2 Lloyd's Rep. 185.

[40] Carriage of Goods by Sea Act 1971, s.1(6)(*b*).

[41] See the definition of "goods" in Art. 1(*c*). In this footnote and the following footnotes the references to Articles are to the Hague-Visby Rules contained in the Schedule to the Carriage of Goods by Sea Act 1971. The references to sections are to the 1971 Act itself.

[42] s.1(7).

[43] As the carriage of live animals is not subject to the Act, shipowners are entitled to insert the "mortality" clause in the bill of lading.

[44] Art. 1(*c*).

[45] *Svenska Traktor Akt.* v. *Maritime Agencies (Southampton) Ltd.* [1953] 2 Q.B. 295.

Visby Rules apply to bills of lading relating to coastal as well as to international voyages.[46] They apply by force of law only "in relation to and in connection with the carriage of goods by sea"[47]; they do not apply to the preceding and subsequent land transport. Thus, in one case[48] the carrier contracted to take frozen chicken in a refrigerated container from Uckfield in Sussex to Jeddah in Saudi Arabia. A bill of lading evidencing shipment from an English port to Jeddah was issued. But, without the knowledge of the shipper, the carrier, after having taken the container by land from Uckfield to Shoreham, shipped it from there to Le Havre, stored it for five or six days, and then shipped it from Le Havre in another vessel to Jeddah. When the goods arrived, they were found to be contaminated, owing to heating in the container. It was clear that they could not have thawed on the short land journey from Uckfield to Shoreham but they could have deteriorated on the voyage from there to Le Havre. Bingham J. held (1) that the Hague-Visby Rules did not apply to the land journey from Uckfield to Shoreham, (2) but that the sea voyage, according to the contract of carriage, began in Shoreham, and not in Le Havre, and (3) that the short storage on land in Le Havre was "in connection with" the sea voyage. The learned judge held that the Rules applied when the goods were loaded in Shoreham and that the shipper could recover damages under the Rules.

Carriers cannot contract out of their liability for loss of or damage to, or in connection with, goods arising from their negligence, fault or failure in their duties imposed by the Rules; a clause in the contract of carriage purporting to relieve them of these obligations would be null and void and without effect.[49] In *The Hollandia*, also known as *The Morviken*,[50] the House of Lords had to consider the ambit of this provision in the following circumstances. A road-finishing machine was shipped from the Scottish port of Leith on board a Dutch vessel, *The Haico Holwerda*, to Bonaire, in the Dutch West Indies. The bill of lading contained a clause providing that the contract of carriage by sea should be governed by the law of the Netherlands and that all actions should be brought in the court of Amsterdam. The machine was transshipped in Amsterdam into a Norwegian vessel, *The Morviken*. When the machine was unloaded in Bonaire, it was damaged, as the owners alleged, by the negligence of the carrier's employees. In the United Kingdom under the Hague-Visby Rules the cargo owners could recover about £11,000, if they could prove

---

[46] The original Hague Rules did not apply to coastal transport (Carriage of Goods by Sea Act 1924, s.4; see 1971 Act, s.1(3)).

[47] s.1(3).

[48] *Mayhew Foods Ltd.* v. *Overseas Containers Ltd.* [1984] 1 Lloyd's Rep. 317.

[49] Art. III(8).

[50] [1983] A.C. 565. See also *The Saudi Prince (No. 2)* [1988] 1 Lloyd's Rep. 1 (Art. III, r. 8 applied under Italian Law); *The Amazona. The Yayamaria*, [1989] 2 Lloyd's Rep. 130. (Construction of Art. III s.8 in the light of *The Hollandia*.)

their case, but in the Netherlands, where at that time[51] the unamended Hague Rules applied, the maximum liability of the carrier was limited to about £250. In proceedings in the English courts on the preliminary point whether they had jurisdiction[52] the House of Lords held that the choice of law in favour of Netherlands law was ineffective, under Article III, r. 8, as far as it would lead to the lessening of the carrier's liability under the Hague-Visby Rules because otherwise a carrier could avoid this liability by the simple device of opting in the bill of lading for a law which did not apply these Rules.[53] The court also held that the choice of jurisdiction clause in favour of the court of Amsterdam was likewise ineffective, but only in so far as it would lead to the reduction of the carrier's liability; it would remain valid if the dispute did not concern his liability, *e.g.* if it concerned a claim for unpaid freight.[54] It should be noted that the decision in *The Hollandia* concerned a situation in which a clause in the bill of lading adopted a legal system which had not given effect to the enlarged liability of the carrier under the Hague-Visby Rules. It is thought that, where the reference in the bill of lading is to a foreign law which has adopted these Rules but the cargo owner would receive less by way of damages because the foreign currency in which the damages are awarded is worth less than the pound sterling, the choice of law clause in the bill of lading is fully effective.

The clause paramount

The Carriage of Goods by Sea Act 1924 provided[55] that every bill of lading to which it applied must contain an express statement that it was to have effect subject to the provisions of the original Hague Rules. Such a statement was frequently referred to in bills of lading as the *clause paramount*. The 1971 Act has discontinued this requirement and consequently there is no longer a legal obligation to insert a clause paramount into the bill.

Nevertheless, in practice in many instances a clause paramount is inserted into the bill of lading. The following is an example of the clause:

---

[51] The Netherlands have now adopted the Hague-Visby Rules, see p. 563, *ante.*
[52] The case arose in the English jurisdiction because a sister ship of *The Haico Holwerda, The Hollandia,* was arrested in the English jurisdiction.
[53] But it was held in *The Benarty* [1985] Q.B. 325 that a foreign jurisdiction clause in favour of the court of Jarkarta was valid although that court would apply the Indonesian Commercial Code which provided for a *tonnage* liability of the charterer that was lower than the *package* liability of the Hague-Visby Rules. The United Kingdom provision on tonnage liability is s.503 of the Merchant Shipping Act 1894, as amended by the Merchant Shipping Acts 1981, s.1, 1984, s.12.
[54] It was further decided in The *Hollandia* that the time at which to ascertain whether a choice of jurisdiction clause had the effect of reducing the liability of the carrier, contrary to the Hague-Visby Rules, was the time when the carrier sought to rely on the relieving clause.
[55] In s.3.

All the terms, provisions and conditions of the Carriage of Goods by Sea Act 1971 and the Schedule thereto are to apply to the contract contained in this bill of lading, and the company are to be entitled to the benefit of all privileges, rights and immunities contained in such Act, and the Schedule thereto as if the same were herein specifically set out. If anything herein contained be inconsistent with the said provisions it shall, to the extent of such inconsistency and no further, be null and void.

Lord Denning M.R. described the effect of the clause paramount as follows[56]:

When a paramount clause is incorporated into a contract, the purpose is to give the Hague Rules contractual force; so that, although the bill of lading may contain very wide exceptions, the Rules are paramount and make the shipowners liable for want of due diligence to make the ship seaworthy and so forth.

Sometimes bills of lading embodying the clause paramount are used for homeward shipping from States other than Contracting States and the question arises whether the Act applies in that case to such a bill. The answer depends on the wording of the clause; the Act applies if the clause is intended to subject such bills to the Act,[57] and it does not apply if the clause is only intended to restate the position as existing under the Act.[58] Generally speaking, the Hague Rules have shown a remarkably expansive character and are often adopted by contract, *i.e.* by insertion of a clause paramount, to shipping to which they do not apply by statute.[59] The Rules are even adopted, as far as applicable, by charterparties[60] and, as has already been observed,[61] by non-negotiable transport documents.[62]

Where a dispute arises whether English or foreign law governs the contract of carriage, the law referred to in the clause paramount is normally regarded to be the proper law of the contract, subject, of course, to Article III(8) of the Hague-Visby Rules which prohibits contract clauses reducing or eliminating the carrier's liability imposed by the Rules.[63]

In modern law, very little weight is attributed to the presumption that the contract of carriage by sea is governed by the law of the flag of nationality which the ship carries because, as Willmer J. said in *The*

---

[56] *Adamastos Shipping Co. Ltd.* v. *Anglo-Saxon Petroleum Co. Ltd.* [1957] 2 Q.B. 233, 266; *Nea Agrex S.A.* v. *Baltic Shipping Co. Ltd.* [1976] Q.B. 933.

[57] *Golodetz* v. *Kersten, Hunik & Co.* (1926) 24 Ll.L.R. 374; *Silver* v. *Ocean Steamship Co.* [1930] 1 K.B. 416, 424.

[58] *Tudor Accumulator Co. Ltd.* v. *Ocean Steam Navigation Co. Ltd.* (1924) 41 T.L.R. 81.

[59] K. Grönfors, "The Mandatory and Contractual Regulation of Sea Transport" [1961] J.B.L. 46.

[60] *Adamastos Shipping Co. Ltd.* v. *Anglo-Saxon Petroleum Co. Ltd.* [1959] A.C. 133; *The Merak* [1964] 2 Lloyd's Rep. 527, 536; *Seven Seas Transportation Ltd.* v. *Pacifico Union Marina Corporation*; *The Satya Kailash and Oceanic Amity* [1984] 1 Lloyd's Rep. 588.

[61] See p. 565, *ante.*

[62] Such as, *e.g.* a commercial vehicle movement order, see *McCarren* v. *Humber International Transport Ltd. The Vechscroon* [1982] 1 Lloyd's Rep. 301.

[63] See pp. 566–567, *ante.*

Assunzione,[64] "in modern times there are a number of ships sailing the seas wearing the flags of countries with which their owners have no association at all." That presumption is, as Hodson L.J. observed in the Court of Appeal, in the same case,[65] available "only as a last resort, when the evidence is so evenly balanced that the court cannot otherwise reach a fair and just conclusion." Sometimes a charterparty bill of lading[66] incorporates a choice of law clause; in that case that clause applies in principle to the bill of lading issued under the charterparty and the contract represented by the bill.[67]

Kinds of bills of lading

"Shipped" and "received" bills

Unless the goods are shipped in containers, bills of lading are usually "shipped" bills but sometimes "received for shipment" bills (also called "alongside" bills) are used.

The difference between these types of bills may be seen from the following examples:

Shipped in apparent good order and condition by . . . on board the steam or motor vessel . . .

and

Received in apparent good order and condition from . . . for shipment on board the ship . . .

A "shipped" bill is also called an "on board" bill, particularly in the United States. United Kingdom businessmen buying in the United States of America usually call for an "on board ocean" bill of lading if they wish to get a "shipped bill of lading," as understood in this country. The practical difference between the shipped and received form is considerable.

Where the shipowner issues a "shipped" bill, he acknowledges that the goods are loaded on board ship. Where he issues a "received for shipment" bill, he confirms only that the goods are delivered into his custody; in this case the goods might be stored in a ship or warehouse

---

[64] [1953] 1 W.L.R. 929, 938.
[65] [1954] p. 150, 194.
[66] See p. 574, *post.*
[67] *The San Nicholas* [1976] Lloyd's Rep. 8, 12.

under his control. The "received" bill is, thus, less valuable than the "shipped" bill because it does not confirm that the shipment has already begun. The buyer under a c.i.f. contract need not accept a "received for shipment" bill as part of the shipping documents but may insist on a "shipped" bill, unless the contrary is expressly agreed upon by the parties to the contract of sale or is customary in a particular trade.[68] In *Yelo* v. *S. M. Machado & Co. Ltd.*,[69] the terms of the credit provided for "shipped" bills; Sellers J. held that the tender of "received" bills (which were not indorsed with the date of shipment) was insufficient.

The shipper is entitled, in all cases to which the Carriage of Goods by Sea Act 1971 applies,[70] to demand from the shipowner—

(1) The issue of a bill of lading after the goods have been received into the charge of the shipowner (Art. III, Rule 3). At this stage the shipowner is only obliged to issue a "received" bill, but if the goods are actually loaded he will, of course, issue a "shipped" bill.

(2) The issue of a "shipped" bill, after the goods are loaded (Art. III, Rule 7). The Rules provide that where formerly another document of title, *e.g.* a "received" bill, was issued relating to the same goods, the shipowner may notate the document at the port of shipment with the name of the ship upon which the goods are shipped and the dates of shipment, stating that the goods are now on board, and when so notated, the document shall have the same functions as a "shipped" bill. The notation of "received" bills is not a customary practice in the United Kingdom, but it is used in the United States.

A container bill of lading issued at an inland loading depot of the container shipping line is invariably a "received" bill of lading.[71]

Where payment is arranged under a letter of credit, the terms of the credit may provide that the bills of lading to be tendered have to be

clean, on board, to order and blank indorsed.

A "received" bill does not satisfy these terms because it is not an "on board" bill, but the UCP, like the Hague-Visby Rules, equate a "received" bill which has been duly notated to a "shipped" bill. The UCP (1983 Revision) provide in article 27(b)[72]:

---

[68] See pp. 37–38, *ante,* and *Diamond Alkali Export Corporation* v. *Fl. Bourgeois* [1921] 3 K.B. 443. On the wording of a "received for shipment" bill of lading see Lloyd J. in *Ishag* v. *Allied Bank International, Fuhs and Kotalimbora* [1981] 1 Lloyd's Rep. 92, 97.

[69] [1952] 1 Lloyd's Rep. 183.

[70] See p. 564, *ante.*

[71] See p. 616, *ante.*

[72] In *Westpac Banking Corporation* v. *South Carolina National Bank* [1986] 1 Lloyd's Rep. 311 a bill of lading was issued in the "received for shipment" form but was notated "Shipped on Board," "Freight pre-paid," and the intended vessel was stated to be *The Columbus America.* The advising bank accepted the bill as a properly notated bill but the issuing bank rejected it. The Privy Council, on appeal from New South Wales, held that the bill was a properly notated bill and that there was no inconsistency between the statements on the bill.

Loading on board or shipment on a vessel may be evidenced either by a transport document bearing wording indicating loading on board a named vessel or shipment on a named vessel, or, in the case of a transport document stating "received for shipment," by means of a notation of loading on board on the transport document signed or initialled and dated by the carrier or his agent, and the date of the notation shall be regarded as the date of loading on board the named vessel or shipment on the named vessel.

Freight prepaid and freight collect bills of lading

These two types of bills of lading have already been considered.[73]

Clean and "claused" bills

The difference between these types of bills and the consequences attending the issue of a qualified or "claused" bill of lading are dealt with elsewhere.[74]

It may be added that a clause which does not refer to *the state of the goods when loaded* but refers to the subsequent fate of the goods and their state when discharged does not make a bill a claused bill. It was held in one case[75] that the clause on the bill "Cargo covered by this bill of lading has been discharged . . . damaged by fire and/or water used to extinguish fire for which general average declared" did not deprive the bill of its character of a clean bill.[76]

Negotiable and non-negotiable bills

Bills of lading can perform their principal function of enabling a person to dispose of goods which are no longer in his possession only if they are, at least to some extent, negotiable. But mercantile custom has mobilised cargoes to a smaller, extent than credit, and consequently the negotiability of bills of lading is less developed in law than that of bills of exchange.

---

[73] See p. 553, *ante*.
[74] See pp. 542–543, *ante*, and p. 585, *post*.
[75] *Golodetz & Co. Inc.* v. *Czarnikow-Rionda Co. Inc. The Galatia* [1980] 1 W.L.R. 495 (C.A.).
[76] Sometimes a charterparty bill of lading (which refers to the terms of the charterparty) is described as a "claused" bill, but this terminology is confusing and should be avoided, see *Federal Commerce and Navigation Ltd.* v. *Molena Alpha Inc., The Nanfri, The Benfri, The Lorfri* [1979] A.C. 757.

Bills of lading, like bills of exchange, may be made out to bearer, or to a particular person or his order. If made out to bearer, they are transferred by delivery while, if made out to order, they are transferred by indorsement and delivery of the bill. In practice, bills of lading made out to bearer are rarely used, as the bill of lading is a document of title which is a symbol of the goods represented by the bill[77]; a transfer of the bill of lading passes such rights in the goods as the parties wish to pass, *e.g.* the property if the goods are sold and the parties intend to pass the property on delivery of the bill, or a charge if the goods are pledged. It is the quality of the bill of lading as a document of title which, though logically distinct from its mode of transfer,[78] confers great practical significance on the latter: by making the bill of lading "negotiable" the cargo is, in fact, made negotiable. It follows that a buyer who in the contract of sale has stipulated for "negotiable" bills of lading is entitled to reject non-negotiable bills.[79]

In two aspects, the negotiability of bills of lading is less developed than that of bills of exchange. First, while a bill of exchange is negotiable *unless* its negotiability is expressly *excluded*, a bill of lading is only negotiable if *made* negotiable. The shipper, when making out the draft bill, has the choice of creating a transport document that can generally be used by the consignee as a medium of transfer of the goods represented by the bill, or of merely obtaining from the shipowner a formal receipt stipulating delivery to a named person.

In the modern bill of lading a box on the left-hand corner of the bill usually provides:

Consignee (if "Order" state Notify Party).

If the shipper intends to obtain a negotiable bill he completes this box by inserting "order" and adding as "notify party" the name of the consignee.[80]

A shipper who wishes to obtain a bill of lading which is not negotiable does not insert the word "order" in the appropriate box of the bill but inserts the name of the consignee in the following box.[81] The effect of this procedure is that, although the shipper can transfer title in the goods to

---

[77] See p. 590, *post.*
[78] *Cf. Wah Tat Bank Ltd.* v. *Kum* [1967] 2 Lloyd's Rep. 437; *sub. nom. Kum* v. *Wah Tat Bank Ltd.* [1971] 1 Lloyd's Rep. 439 (P.C.). See p. 593, *post.*
[79] *Soproma SpA* v. *Marine & Animal By-Products Corporation* [1966] 1 Lloyd's Rep. 367, see p. 408, *ante.*
[80] The shipper may name himself as consignee.
[81] These bills are referred to in the American practice as *straight bills of lading*. The U.S. Bills of Lading Pomerene Act 1916 (which, unlike the U.S. Carriage of Goods by Sea Act 1936, applies only to outward bills of lading) appears in Art. 9 to authorise a carrier to deliver the cargo to a consignee named in a straight bill of lading, without requiring the return of a bill.

the consignee by delivering the bill of lading to him, the consignee cannot further pass on title in them to a third party by transfer of the bill of lading.

The second aspect in which the negotiability of bills of lading varies from that of bills of exchange is that a holder of a bill of lading, unlike the holder in due course of a bill of exchange, cannot acquire a better title than his predecessor possessed.[82] He does not take "free of equities." This is a significant difference; it means that, where a negotiable bill of lading is obtained by fraud and indorsed to a bona fide indorsee for value, the latter does not acquire a title to the goods represented by the bill, while, if the same happens in case of a bill of exchange which is regular on its face, and not overdue or dishonoured, the indorsee is entitled to all rights arising under the bill of exchange. In view of this difference, some authorities deny the bill of lading the character of a negotiable instrument and classify it as "quasi-negotiable."

In two exceptional cases, however, statutory provisions enable the bona fide indorsee of a bill of lading to acquire, upon certain carefully defined conditions, a better title than his predecessor possessed: The Factors Act 1889, s.2(1), protects an indorsee who takes a bill from a factor acting in excess of his authority[83]; and the Sale of Goods Act 1979, s.47(2), provides that the unpaid seller's rights of lien and of stoppage in transit are defeated by a previous transfer of a bill from the buyer to an indorsee who takes the bill in good faith and for valuable consideration.[84]

The traditional form of negotiable bills of lading is preferred in some kinds of international business but in others the non-negotiable form is favoured. Negotiable bills are normally used in the commodity trade, such as trade in grain or oil, where bills of lading relating to goods in transit are purchased and sold in string contracts[85] under which the intermediaries do not intend to take delivery and only the last purchaser in the string will take physical delivery of the goods from the ship on its arrival. Negotiable bills of lading are also used if the buyer intends, or at least contemplates, to pledge the bills as a collateral security to a bank before the goods arrive, and there are other cases in which a negotiable bill of lading is stipulated in the contract between the exporter and the overseas importer. On the other hand, where it is anticipated that the consignee himself will take delivery of the goods on arrival of the ship and will not deal in the bills of lading, a non-negotiable bill is perfectly sufficient. Non-negotiable transport documents will be considered later.[86]

---

[82] See p. 382, *ante.*
[83] See pp. 295–296, *ante.*
[84] See p. 153, *ante.*
[85] A string contract is a series of contracts of sale under which the same goods or bills of lading relating to them are sold by A to B, by B to C, and so forth, possibly through the whole alphabet.
[86] See p. 578, *post.*

Steamship and charterparty bills of lading

It is, as has been explained in the preceding section, an important feature of the bill of lading that it is quasi-negotiable. This implies that the bill itself shall contain all essential terms of the contract of carriage and a third party, such as an indorsee or other holder of the bill shall be able to gather them from the document itself. A steamship bill of lading, sometimes abbreviated as S.S. Co.'s bill of lading, satisfies that requirement but a charterparty bill, as we shall see, does not do so.[87]

A charterparty bill of lading is a bill which incorporates, by reference, some of the terms of the charterparty, so that they might have effect against the consignee or the indorsee of the bill. But a bill, though issued under a charterparty, which does not incorporate the terms of the charterparty into the contract with the consignee or indorsee, is not a charterparty bill of lading in the technical sense. In *Enrico Furst & Co.* v. *W. E. Fischer Ltd.*[88] the buyers bought a quantity of cast iron piping f.o.b. London; they chartered a tramp ship which proceeded to London and issued bills in the form authorised by the London Short Sea Traders' Association; these bills did not contain any reference to the terms of the charterparty; Diplock J. held that they fulfilled the requirements of a letter of credit stipulating for the tender of either "bills of lading" or "S.S. Co.'s bills of lading."

Sometimes the charterparty provides that bills of lading issued under it shall be charterparty bills, incorporating all or any of the clauses of the charterparty. Such a provision is inserted in the interest of the shipowner who wants to preserve the protection of the charterparty against the shipper (cargo owner).[89] A charterparty bill of lading may be issued in the negotiable or non-negotiable form.

The importance of the distinction between steamship and charterparty bills is that, according to universal banking practice, a bank, unless instructed to the contrary, will refuse to accept a charterparty bill of lading as good tender under a letter of credit. The UCP (1983 Revision) state in articles 25(c)(i) and 26(c)(i) that, unless otherwise stipulated in the credit, banks will reject a document which "indicates that it is subject to a charterparty."

---

[87] On charterparty bills of lading, see Scrutton, *op. cit.,* Art. 34 *et seq.*; and Carver's *Carriage by Sea,* 13th ed., 1982, Vol. I, paras. 699 *et seq.* The American law on incorporation of charterparty arbitration clauses in bills of lading appears to be less exacting than English law, see John P. McMahon, "The Hague Rules and Incorporation of Charterparty Arbitration Clauses into Bills of Lading" in 2 *Journ. Maritime Law and Commerce* (1970), 1.

[88] *Enrico Furst & Co.* v. *W. E. Fischer Ltd.* [1960] 2 Lloyd's Rep. 340.

[89] *Federal Commerce and Navigation Ltd.* v. *Molena Alpha Inc. The Nanfri, The Benfri, The Lorfri* [1979] A.C. 757; *Paros Shipping Corporation* v. *Nafta (G.B.) Ltd. The Paros* [1987] 2 Lloyd's Rep. 269 (in this case the bills of lading, in breach of the charterparty, were not issued as charterparty bills).

Where the bill is a charterparty bill of lading in the technical sense, the question arises which terms of the charterparty are incorporated into the bill by reference. Here the observations of Sir John Donaldson M.R.[90] should be borne in mind that "the starting point . . . must be the contract contained in or evidenced by the bill of lading, for this is the only contract to which the shipowners and consignees are both parties. What the shipowners agreed with the charterers, whether in the charterparty or otherwise, is wholly irrelevant, save in so far as the whole or part of any such agreement has become part of the bill of lading contract." Two possibilities exist: the incorporation clause may expressly refer to one or several specific terms in the charterparty, or the reference may be in a general manner, *e.g.* by stating that "all the terms, provisions and exceptions of the aforesaid charterparty are deemed to be incorporated into this bill of lading."[91] In the former case a problem can hardly arise; the specific charterparty clause has been brought to the notice of the consignee or indorsee and has to be regarded as duly incorporated in the bill of lading. It was held in one case,[92] in which the incorporation clause contained a specific reference to the arbitration clause in the charterparty, that a dispute arising under the bill of lading contract had to be resolved by arbitration. The second case, in which the incorporation clause in the bill of lading is couched in general terms, is more frequent in practice. Here it is often difficult to determine which charterparty clauses are incorporated in the contract contained in or evidenced by the bill of lading. The House of Lords[93] categorically rejected the view formerly widely held that clauses in the charterparty which were directly germane to the shipment, carriage or delivery of goods were presumed to be incorporated in the bill of lading. It is thought that the problem is one of interpretation of the incorporation clause and, as such, makes it necessary to ascertain the intention of the parties, including a consignee or indorsee of the bill of lading. For the purposes of interpretation it has to be assumed that the consignee or indorsee is acting in a diligent and reasonable manner and is unaware of the terms of the charterparty. What charterparty clauses would such a person expect to find in the bill of lading in consequence of the incorporation clause? Some points have emerged from the decided cases. A clause in the charterparty providing for personal liability of the charterer for demurrage is not incorporated in the bill of lading and consequently the consignee or indorsee is not

---

[90] *Skips A/S Nordheim* v. *Syrian Petroleum Co. Ltd. The Varenna* [1984] Q.B. 599, 615.

[91] There exists a great variety in the wording of incorporation clauses and their width varies accordingly; see Scrutton, *op. cit.,* art. 36.

[92] Branson J. in *The Rena K* [1978] 1 Lloyd's Rep. 545, 551. See also *Oriental Maritime (Pte) Ltd.* v. *Ministry of Food of Bangladesh,* [1989] 2 Lloyd's Rep. 371 (cargo owner as indorsee of bill of lading in contract with head owner of vessel, and not with subcharterer).

[93] In *Miramar Maritime Corp.* v. *Holborn Oil Trading Ltd. The Miramar* [1984] A.C. 676.

personally liable for demurrage[94] because, as Lord Diplock observed,[95] "no businessman who has not taken leave of his senses would intentionally enter into a contract which exposed him to potential liability of this kind." Further, an arbitration clause in the charterparty is not normally incorporated in the bill of lading by a general incorporation clause.[96]

In any event, when the question of incorporation of charterparty terms into the bill of lading arises, terms which "one might describe as 'surplus,' 'insensible' 'inconsistent' provisions fall to be disincorporated."[97]

Through bills of lading

Where the ocean shipment forms only part of the complete journey and, subsequent[98] thereto, the goods have to be carried by other land or sea carriers, it is more convenient for the shipper to take out a through bill of lading than to contract with the various carriers who have to carry the goods at the consecutive stages of the journey. The necessity for a through bill arises, *e.g.* where goods have to be carried from the United Kingdom to such places as Baghdad. Through bills of lading are also used where "the sea transit itself [is] divided into separate stages to be performed by different shipowners by a process of transhipment;"[99] but whether the contract of carriage, as evidenced by the bill of lading, allows transshipment is a different question which has been considered earlier.[1] Through bills of lading are increasingly used in modern transport.

---

[94] *Miramar Maritime Corp.* v. *Holborn Oil Trading Ltd. The Miramar* [1984] A.C. 676.

[95] *Ibid.*, on p. 685. The House of Lords left it open in the *Miramar* case whether the lien clause in the charterparty was incorporated in the bill of lading by a general incorporation clause. Mustill J. had answered this question in the affirmative, when deciding the case in the Commercial Court but the matter is not free from doubt.

[96] *Skips A/S Nordheim* v. *Syrian Petroleum Co. Ltd. The Varenna* [1984] Q.B. 599; also *The Annefield* [1971] P. 168; *Astro Valiente Compania Naviera S.A.* v. *Government of Pakistan Ministry of Food and Agriculture (No. 2). The Emmanuel Colocotronis* [1982] 1 W.L.R. 1096; see also *The Merak* [1965] P. 223; *Navigazione Alta Italia SpA* v. *Svenska Petroleum AB. The Nai Matteini* [1988] 1 Lloyd's Rep. 452; *Federal Bulk Carriers Inc.* v. *C. Itoh & Co. Ltd. The Federal Bulker* [1989] 1 Lloyd's Rep. 103. It was held by the Court of Appeal in *The San Nicholas* [1976] 1 Lloyd's Rep. 8 that a choice of law clause (in favour of English law) in the charterparty was incorporated in the bill of lading by a general incorporation clause but this decision is not easily reconcilable with the House of Lords decision in *The Miramar*.

[97] Sir John Donaldson M.R. in *Skips A/S Nordheim* v. *Syrian Petroleum Co. Ltd. The Varenna, supra,* n. 96.

[98] Through bills are also used where the on-carriage occurs prior to shipment, *e.g.* if goods are shipped from Chicago to the U.K. The observations in the text apply to such bills *mutatis mutandis*.

[99] Scrutton, *op. cit.*, art. 179, p. 377.

[1] See pp. 48–49, *ante*, where the rules of the UCP relating to the acceptability by banks of bills of lading prohibiting transshipment (Art. 29 of the UCP) are likewise discussed.

The following clauses are usually found in through bills; they illustrate clearly the points arising here:

> The freight received is inclusive of the cost of forwarding to . . . which will be arranged through the present carrier acting as agent for the shipper and/or consignees of the goods without any liability whatsoever, the conditions of such forwarding to be covered by the current lawful forms of contract.
>
> To avoid the tendering of separate documents at each stage of the journey delivery at destination will be given only on due presentation of one of these sets of bills of lading unto . . . or to his or their assigns and notice to this effect shall be included in the on-carrier's bill of lading or other freight contracts.

The shipper, who takes out a through bill, has only to deal with the carrier who signs the through bill. This carrier undertakes to arrange the transshipment with the on-carriers. The carrier charges an inclusive freight,[2] which, if prepayable, is due on the stipulated event[3] and governed by the rules explained earlier in respect of prepaid freight.[4] The goods are only delivered by the last on-carrier upon delivery of one original part of the through bill which has to be dispatched to the consignee.

The principal contract of sea carriage is superimposed upon the contracts with the on-carriers, and this fact is sometimes expressed by a clause in the through bill adopting:

> all conditions expressed in the regular forms of bills of lading in use by the steamship company performing the ocean carriage.

Through bills frequently contain a clause exempting the carrier arranging on-carriage from all liability or stating that transhipment is at owner's risk, or that the responsibility of the shipowner shall cease on delivery of the goods to the on-carrier.

Where legal difficulties arise between the shipper and an on-carrier, it may become relevant to ascertain, whether the on-carrier is a party to a contract with the shipper or not. The answer depends, in the first instance, on the construction of the terms of the through bill. If the shipper contracted exclusively with the carrier, and the on-carrier is merely the carrier's servant, the carrier alone can claim against the on-carrier in contract, he alone is responsible to the shipper and the direction of the on-carriage rests solely with him. If, on the other hand, the carrier, when contracting with the shipper, acts as agent of the on-carrier, a direct contract of carriage has come into existence between the shipper and the on-carrier. Both alternatives are used in practice.

The Carriage of Goods by Sea Act 1971 and the Rules adopted by the Act apply to through bills issued in respect of goods dispatched from a port in the United Kingdom and Northern Ireland, or of any other

---

[2] As freight is charged at a higher rate than in normal cases, through bills are sometimes printed in red.

[3] See p. 552, *ante.*

[4] *Ibid.*

Contracting State or issued in those countries, even after the goods have been transshipped at a foreign port. If and when the Hamburg Rules become law, the relationship between the shipper and the contractual and actual carrier will be fundamentally altered.[5]

Through bills of lading covering on-carriage by air

This type of through bill is used where the goods, after having been unloaded at the port of discharge, are carried to their ultimate inland destination by air; this method is used, *e.g.* in East and Central Africa where inordinate delay would occur if inland transport were used for the on-carriage.

There is no reason why a through bill should not cover on-carriage by air. The legal difficulty is that the bill of lading is a document of title[6] but the air consignment note is not.[7] It is thought that a combination of these two documents does not give the combined through bill the character of a document of title. While in practice the goods might sometimes not be delivered to the consignee at the final place of destination without surrender of the through bill of lading by him, no commercial custom exists to that effect; the exporter cannot rely on this practice and has no legal remedy if it is not observed.

Container bills of lading

These bills are issued by container shipping lines to cover the multimodal transport of goods in a container from an inland place of dispatch to the final place of arrival. Container bills have features not present in other bills; they are considered later in this work.[8]

Non-negotiable liner waybills; data freight receipts, shipping certificates

In modern times the use of non-negotiable transport documents issued by the carrier has greatly increased, especially as the result of the growth of ocean container transport. It has already been observed[9] that a non-

---

[5] See pp. 563–564, *ante.*
[6] See p. 590, *post.*
[7] See pp. 626–627, *post.*
[8] See p. 615, *post.*
[9] See pp. 571–572, *ante.*

negotiable document is sufficient where the intention is that the consignee shall take delivery of the goods on arrival of the ship but that in some kinds of business, in which bills of lading are traded, or certain financial arrangements are contemplated, a negotiable bill of lading is required.

A non-negotiable transport document may be a non-negotiable bill of lading or it may simply be a receipt by the carrier, acknowledging that he has received the goods in his charge or that he has shipped them.[10] If the document is a non-negotiable bill of lading, the Hague-Visby Rules apply to the contract of carriage, provided that the conditions for the application of the Carriage of Goods by Sea Act 1971 are satisfied.[11] If the transport document is merely a receipt, the Rules do not apply except if the document expressly states that they shall apply.[12]

The non-negotiable receipt is called a *liner waybill*[13] or a *data freight receipt*[14] but other designations are also used. Non-negotiable documents of this character are used in ordinary as well as in container transport and are usually issued in the "received for shipment" form. They have this in common that they embody the terms of the contract of carriage by sea only by reference to the bills of lading issued by the carriers in question, but do not state these terms in detail on the reverse, as is customary in the case of ordinary bills of lading; for this reason these documents are sometimes colloquially referred to as "blank back bills of lading."

Shipping certificates are of two kinds. They are issued either by a carrier, especially on short sea routes, or by a forwarder (who is not the carrier). In both cases they are merely receipts confirming that the person who has issued them has taken the goods in his charge.

House bills of lading; groupage bills of lading; delivery orders

House bills of lading[15] are issued by freight forwarders who consolidate several cargoes belonging to different owners or forming the subject-matter of different export transactions in one consignment shipped under a groupage bill of lading issued by the carrier to the forwarder. Such a

---

[10] To give examples: in an f.o.b. (buyer contracting with carrier) contract (see p. 20, *ante*) the non-negotiable document, even if described as a bill of lading, is merely a receipt of the carrier, but in a strict f.o.b. contract, an f.o.b. contract with additional services, or a c.i.f. contract the non-negotiable bill of lading may well be a true bill of lading.

[11] See p. 564, *ante*.

[12] See 1971 Act, s.1(6)(*b*) and p. 565, *ante*.

[13] *e.g.* the standard non-negotiable liner waybill, sponsored by SITPRO, with the support of General Council of British Shipping. This form of liner waybill has a further advantage in that it can be used for all shipping lines supporting this scheme.

[14] *e.g.* the instrument issued by ACL or Intercargo.

[15] Sometimes called shipping certificates.

consolidation of cargoes is particularly frequent in the case of groupage containers.[16] An example of such a document is the *FIATA Combined Transport Bill of Lading (FBL)*[93]; this document states in its title that it is "negotiable" and, in its amended version of 1987 (8.87), is approximated in form and layout to a real bill of lading[18]; it satisfies the requirements of an ICC Combined Transport Document[19] and is recognised as a "transport document" for the purpoes of article 25 of the UCP, but not as a "marine bill of lading" within article 26 of the UCP.[20]

A house bill of lading is a misnomer because such a document is not a bill of lading in the technical legal sense.[21] It is not a document of title giving the consignee or assignee a right to claim the goods from the carrier. The provisions of the Bills of Lading Act 1855[22] which make bills of lading quasi-negotiable do not apply to it. It follows that a house bill of lading cannot be tendered under a c.i.f. contract as a proper bill of lading and, if the contract allows such a tender, the contract cannot be regarded as a proper c.i.f. contract.[23]

The FIATA Combined Transport Bill of Lading is recognised by the ICC and, according to the UCP (1983 Revision), Art. 25(d),[24] may be accepted by banks in letter of credit transactions, unless the credit stipulates that the beneficiary must tender a marine bill of lading. A transport document (other than a FIATA bill) issued by a freight forwarder, *e.g.* a house bill of lading, will be rejected by banks unless the document indicates that the forwarder is acting as a carrier or as an agent of a carrier, or, of course, the credit instructions otherwise provide.

---

[16] See p. 610, *post.*

[17] FIATA stands for *Fédération Internationale des Associations de Transitaires et Assimilés*; its headquarters are at 24, Baumackerstrasse, P.O. Box 8493, Zurich, Switzerland, CH–8050. Three FIATA documents are in use: the FIATA FCR (Forwarder's Certificate of Receipt), the FIATA FCT (Forwarder's Certificate of Transport) and the FBL (Negotiable FIATA Combined Transport Bill of Lading). The former two documents have on the reverse the Standard Trading Conditions of the Institute of Freight Forwarders, but the third document has special conditions attached to it, with a liability in excess of the Institute Standard Trading Conditions.

[18] It is not "negotiable" in the same manner as a bill of lading; the bill of lading derives its negotiable character from the Bills of Lading Act 1855 which does not apply to FIATA Combined Transport Documents; the "negotiability" of the FIATA documents means merely assignability of the rights under the contract of carriage but not transfer of obligations. The FIATA Combined Transport Bill of Lading is further not a document of title, but contractually the surrender of the duly endorsed document is a condition precedent for the delivery of the goods; for the difference between a combined transport document and a genuine bill of lading see C. M. Schmitthoff, "The Development of the Combined Transport Document," *Essays,* 369.

[19] See p. 615, *post.*

[20] See pp. 413–414, *ante.*

[21] The definition of "bill of lading" in the UCC, 1–102(6), is wider than the English definition; the definition of the UCC includes receipts of good for shipment issued by persons engaged in the business of transporting and forwarding goods, including airbills.

[22] See pp. 551, 558–559, *ante.*

[23] *Comptoir d'Achat* v. *Luis de Ridder* [1949] A.C. 293.

[24] For the wording of Art. 25(d), see p. 413, *ante.*

The splitting up of a consignment shipped under one bill of lading into smaller parcels sold to different buyers can be achieved by the use of delivery orders relating to specified portions of the whole consignment. Such delivery orders may be of two kinds,[25] and from the legal point of view this distinction is important: they may either be directed to an agent of the seller or they may be directed to the carrier; the latter type are called *ship's delivery orders*. "[Ship's delivery orders] must . . . be documents issued by or on behalf of shipowners while the goods are in their possession or at least under their control and containing some form of undertaking that they will be delivered to the buyers (or perhaps to the bearer) on presentation of the documents."[26] The issue of delivery orders directed to an agent of the seller is similar to the issue of house bills of lading. In this case the whole consignment is consigned to a freight forwarder or to another person acting as agent of the seller at the port of destination, and the order directs the agent to deliver the portion or quantity of the goods stated in it to the holder of the order.

An order such as the one issued in *Comptoir d'Achat* v. *Luis de Ridder*,[27] does not give the buyer a direct right against the carrier.[28] Where it is provided in a contract described by the parties as being on c.i.f. terms that the seller may tender such a delivery order instead of a bill of lading the contract is not a true c.i.f. contract but is an "ex ship" or "arrival" contract.[29]

Ship's delivery orders are addressed to the carrier and instruct him to deliver the goods specified in them to the holder. They are of a higher legal quality than delivery orders addressed to an agent of the seller in so far as they give the holder in certain circumstances a direct right of action against the carrier, and, where it is stipulated in a c.i.f. contract of sale that the seller may tender them in the place of bills of lading, the contract is regarded in law as creating the typical effect attributed to a c.i.f. contract, *viz.* that in certain respects the tender of the shipping documents constitutes the performance of the contract.

But even a delivery order to the ship is not of the same order and quality as a bill of lading, as was pointed out by Denning L.J. in one case[30] in the following passage:

---

[25] An excellent explanation of the various types of delivery orders is contained in the judgment of Kerr J. in *Cremer* v. *General Carriers S.A.* [1974] 1 W.L.R. 341, 349.

[26] Kerr J. in *Waren Import Gesellschaft Krohn & Co.* v. *Internationale Graanhandel Thegra N.V.* [1975] 1 Lloyd's Rep. 146, 155.

[27] [1949] A.C. 293; see p. 52, *ante.* Further, *Margarine Union GmbH* v. *Cambay Prince Steamship Co. Ltd. The Wear Breeze* [1969] 1 Q.B. 219.

[28] Nor does it render the buyer liable to the shipowner for discharging port demurrage: *Tradax Internacional S.A.* v. *R. Pagnan & Fratelli* [1968] 1 Lloyd's Rep. 244 (in this case, on the terms of the contract of sale, the buyers likewise were not liable to the sellers for the demurrage which the latter as charterers had to pay to the shipowners).

[29] See pp. 51, 56, *ante.*

[30] *Colin & Shields* v. *Weddel & Co. Ltd.* [1952] 2 All E.R. 337, 343.

A seller often only has one bill of lading for the whole consignment, and he cannot deliver that one bill of lading to each of the buyers because it contains more goods than the particular contract of sale, so in each of his contracts of sale the seller stipulates the right to give a ship's delivery order . . . The ship's delivery order is not as good a protection for the buyer as a separate bill of lading would be, because it gives no cause of action against the ship unless the master attorns to the buyer and then it gives a different cause of action which may not be as favourable as a bill of lading. To overcome these drawbacks so far as possible, the contract provides for the ship's delivery order "to be countersigned by a banker, shipbroker, captain, or mate, if so required."

"Stale" bills of lading

The expression "stale bill of lading" is used in banking practice. A bank which is instructed by, or on behalf of, a buyer to make finance available under a letter of credit upon presentation, by the seller, of a bill of lading (and of other documents) might feel obliged, in order to safeguard the interest of its principal, to reject the bill as being "stale." By that is meant that the bill, though conforming in all respects with the requirements of the credit, is presented so late that, as the result of the delay in its presentation, the consignee might become involved in legal or practical complications or might have to pay additional costs, *e.g.* for the warehousing of goods.

The UCP (1983 Revision) provide in article 47(a) that transport documents must be presented within a specified time after issuance and that, if no time is specified, banks may refuse documents if presented to them later than 21 days after issuance of the bill of lading or other transport document. In many instances the introduction of a definite time limit has reduced the uncertainty inherent in the concept of the stale bill.

Often the bank will accept a bill of lading or other transport document which it might regard as stale on an indemnity given by the seller.

The date of the bill of lading

The correct dating of the bill of lading is a matter of great importance. The correct date of a "shipped" bill is the date when the goods are taken on board[31] and that of a "received for shipment" bill is the date when they are taken into the charge of the carrier.[32] If a "received for shipment" bill

---

[31] In the case of a "shipped" bill it is not the earlier date when the goods are placed into a "full load" container at an inland container collection depot: Mocatta J. in *United City Merchants (Investments) Ltd.* v. *Royal Bank of Canada* [1979] 1 Lloyd's Rep. 267, 271–273.
[32] By virtue of the Hague-Visby Rules, Art. III(3), the shipper is entitled to demand a bill of lading after the carrier has received the goods into his care; see p. 570, *ante.* If the bill is issued by the carrier only when the ship leaves port, it should show the correct date of the bill, as stated in the text above.

is notated "shipped," the date of shipment of the goods is that of the notation,[33] and not that of the receipt of the goods by the carrier. Where the loading extends over several days, the bill should be dated when the loading is completed[34] but there may be a trade custom admitting the insertion of the date when the loading commences.

The date of the bill of lading is material in three legal relationships: in the contract of carriage, in the contract of sale, and in relation to the banks if payment is arranged under a letter of credit.

As to the contract of carriage, it has already been observed that the shipper is entitled to demand that the bill of lading should be dated correctly. If the master (or another agent of the carrier) negligently misdates the bill, the carrier as principal is liable in damages, provided that the shipper can prove that he has suffered a loss as the result of the misdating, because there is an implied obligation that due care should be exercised in the dating of the bill,[35] but the position may be different if the misdating is due to want of care on the part of the shipper.[36]

The date of the bill of lading may also be relevant in the contract of sale. The tender of a wrongly dated bill of lading qualifies, at least in a c.i.f. contract, as breach of a condition and entitles the buyer to reject the bill and to treat the contract as repudiated,[37] even if the goods are in fact shipped in contract time.[38] In *The Almak*[39] it was agreed that the purchase price of the goods—gas oil—should be the price ruling at the date of the bill of lading. The goods were loaded on June 27 but the bill bore the date of June 22, and the master signed it without noticing that it was incorrectly dated. The price was calculated by reference to June 22, instead of June 27. The market fell by £7 between these two dates, with the result that the buyer paid the seller more than he would have done if the bill had been correctly dated. The action of the buyer (who had chartered the ship to carry the goods which he had purchased) against the disponent owner of the ship failed because the inclusion of the wrong date in the bill of lading was due to want of care on his part as he—the buyer—had tendered the (inadvertently) incorrectly dated bill to the master for signature.

---

[33] On notating, see p. 510, *ante.*

[34] *Rudolf A. Oetker* v. *IFA International Frachtagentur AG. The Almak* [1985] 1 Lloyd's Rep. 557, 558.

[35] *Stumore Weston & Co.* v. *Michael Breen* (1886) 12 A.C. 698 (and the carrier may have a claim against the master to be indemnified). Also *The Saudi Crown* [1986] 1 Lloyd's Rep. 261.

[36] *The Almak,* quoted in n. 34, *ante,* 560.

[37] Unless the breach can be regarded as a breach of an innominate term; see p. 135, *ante.*

[38] *Re an Arbitration between the General Trading Co. (Ltd.)* v. *van Stolk's Commissiehandel* (1911) 16 Com.Cas. 95; *Procter & Gamble Philippine Manufacturing Corporation* v. *Kurt A. Becher GmbH & Co. KG* [1988] 2 Lloyd's Rep. 21 (C.A.).

[39] See n. 34, *ante.*

Where payment is arranged under a letter of credit, the credit often states a date for shipment of the goods, in addition to the expiry date which every credit contains.[40] Here the date of the bill of lading is likewise relevant. An issuer of a bill of lading, who deliberately backdates it in order to bring it within the shipment time in the credit, acts fraudulently, and, as far as the *issue* of the bill is concerned, there is no difference between the case where he has forged the bill and where he has deliberately backdated it. But, in the hands of an innocent person, the fraudulently backdated bill is far from being a nullity; in fact, it is perfectly valid. In *United City Merchants (Investments) Ltd.* v. *Royal Bank of Canada*[41] the bill was backdated by an employee of the forwarder but the shipper had no knowledge of the fraud and it was held that the bank, which had confirmed the credit, was bound to pay on tender of the backdated bill.

Description of the goods in the bill of lading

The bill of lading, being a receipt of the shipowner for the goods, contains in its free space, known as the margin, a description of the goods. This description is perhaps the most vital part of the whole bill because the consignee or indorsee of the bill, who wishes to buy the goods by having the bill indorsed to him, normally has no opportunity of verifying the representations of the buyer as to their quantity and quality by examining them, and parts with the purchase price in reliance upon the shipowner's description of the goods in the bill of lading. In numerous cases disappointed buyers have tried, often successfully, to hold the shipowner responsible for an inaccurate description of the goods in the bill and ingenious clauses have been devised by shipowners to restrict that liability.

By the provisions of the Rules,[42] the shipper is entitled to demand that the bill of lading which the owner is obliged to issue to him should contain the following leading marks and other particulars:

(a) The leading marks necessary for identification of the goods as the same are furnished in writing by the shipper before the loading of such goods starts, provided such marks are stamped or otherwise shown clearly upon the goods if uncovered, or on the cases or coverings in which such goods are contained, in such a manner as should ordinarily remain legible until the end of the voyage;

(b) Either the number of packages or pieces, or the quantity, or weight, as the case may be, as furnished in writing by the shipper;

(c) The apparent order and condition of the goods:

---

[40] See p. 418, *ante*.
[41] [1983] A.C. 168; see p. 443, *ante*.
[42] Hague-Visby Rules, Art. III, r. 3.

Provided that no carrier, master or agent of the carrier, shall be bound to state or show in the bill of lading any marks, number, quantity, or weight which he has reasonable ground for suspecting not accurately to represent the goods actually received, or which he has had no reasonable means of checking.

When the shipowner affirms that the goods received are in "apparent good order and condition," he issues a "clean" bill; when this statement is qualified the bill is "claused."[43] The following definition of a clean transport document of lading is provided by the UCP (1983 Revision), Art. 34(a)[44]:

A clean transport document is one which bears no superimposed clause or notation which expressly declares a defective condition of the goods and/or the packaging.

The words "in apparent good order and condition" denote that "apparently, and so far as met the eye, and externally [the goods] were placed in good order on board this ship,"[45] but the statement does not extend to qualities of the goods "which were not apparent to reasonable inspection having regard to the circumstances of loading."[46] The statement does not constitute a promise or undertaking by the shipowner, but is merely a statement of fact, an affirmation that certain facts are correct.[47] The shipowner who gives a clean bill does not promise to deliver goods "in apparent good order and condition" to the consignee, and may prove that the goods were damaged subsequent to the issue of the bill by an excepted peril, but he is prevented ("estopped") from denying that he received the goods in apparent good order and condition and cannot escape liability by alleging that an excepted peril existed prior to the issue of the clean bill, *e.g.* insufficient packing.[48] This estoppel operates only in favour of a consignee who *relies* on the statement in the bill that goods were in apparent good order and condition, but, as was said by Scrutton L.J.,[49]

the mercantile importance of clean bills is so obvious and important that I think the fact that he (*i.e.* the consignee) took the bill of lading which in fact is clean, without objection, is quite sufficient evidence that he relied on it.

---

[43] See pp. 542–543, 571, *ante,* and Salmon J. in *British Imex Industries Ltd.* v. *Midland Bank Ltd.* [1958] 2 Q.B. 542, 551.

[44] See also "The Problem of Clean Bills of Lading" ICC Brochure 223 (1963). This brochure gives a list of superimposed clauses in current use for reference and optional use.

[45] *Per* Sir R. Phillimore in *The Peter der Grosse* (1875) 1 P.D. 414, 420.

[46] *Per* Branson J. in *Re National Petroleum Co., The Athelviscount* (1934) 39 Com.Cas. 227, 236; *Harris & Son Ltd.* v. *China Mutual Steam Navigation Co. Ltd.* [1959] 2 Lloyd's Rep. 500, 501 (inherent defect); see also Art. IV, r. 2, of the Rules.

[47] Channel J. in *Compañia Naviera Vascongada* v. *Churchill & Sim* [1906] 1 K.B. 237, 247.

[48] *Silver* v. *Ocean Steamship Co.* [1930] 1 K.B. 416; *Cremer* v. *General Carriers S.A.* [1974] 1 W.L.R. 341, 500; *Naviera Mogor SA* v. *Société Métallurgique de Normandie, The Nogar Marin* [1988] 1 Lloyd's Rep. 412 (clean bill issued although wire coils, which were to be shipped, were obviously rusty; shipowner held to be liable).

[49] In *Silver* v. *Ocean Steamship Co.* [1930] 1 K.B. 416.

In one case[50] the master, who was instructed to sign bills of lading "as presented," refused to sign a bill which showed a larger quantity of goods—fuel oil shipped in Saudi Arabia—than actually loaded.[51] This necessitated a further survey[52] and caused delay in the departure of the vessel. Evans J. held that the "as presented" clause did not mean that the master was obliged to sign irregular bills. "There is a basic and implied requirement that the bills as presented should relate to goods actually shipped, and that they should not contain a misdescription of the goods which was known to be incorrect.[53]

The carrier, when asked to issue a clean bill contrary to the facts, is in an evident predicament. If he obliges, he may be liable to the consignee; if he refuses, he inconveniences his client, the shipper, who might have difficulties in negotiating the bill. This explains why sometimes a—dangerous—attempt is made to induce the carrier upon receipt of an indemnity from the shipper or his bank to issue a clean bill contrary to facts.[54] It further explains the tendency of clausing the bill in an apparently innocent form which, while protecting the carrier, does not frighten off the unwary consignee. This accounts for vague qualifying remarks such as "weight unknown," "quality unknown," or "condition unknown" which are occasionally found in the margin of the bill. Some forms of bills of lading have the following or similar words imprinted in their context:

> Measurement, weight, quantity, brand, contents, condition, quality and value as declared by shipper but unknown to the carrier.

The protective value, from the point of view of the carrier, of qualifying clauses is greatly diminished in the cases to which the Carriage of Goods by Sea Act 1971 applies because under this Act the shipper is entitled to demand a clear statement in the bill of lading as to some of the particulars in question.[55] Where the required particulars are stated they cannot be negatived or contradicted by a clause that they are "unknown" to the shipowner; such a qualifying clause is ineffective in law.

It should, however, be noted that the carrier is only obliged, by Art. III(3)(*b*) of the Rules, to state in the bill *either* the number of packages or pieces, *or* the quantity *or* the weight, but not *all* these particulars.[56]

---

[50] *Boukadoura Maritime Corporation* v. *SA Marocaine de' Industrie rt du Raffinage Boukadoura* [1989] 1 Lloyd's Rep. 393.

[51] The reason may have been that the shore measurements differed from the loading measurements.

[52] The measurements of the master proved to be approximately correct.

[53] *Per* Evans J., in *The Boukadoura, supra*, 399.

[54] See pp. 594–595, *post.*

[55] See p. 584, *ante.*

[56] As regards air transport under the Warsaw Convention 1929, compare *Corocraft Ltd. and Vendome Jewels Ltd.* v. *Pan American Airways Inc.* [1969] 1 Q.B. 616 (C.A.); see p. 627, n. 21.

Where he states the number of packages, and adds a qualifying clause in respect of other particulars, *e.g.* "weight and quality unknown," the qualifying clause affords him protection in respect of the latter particulars.[57] But the "unknown" clause does not provide absolute protection; a shipowner who acknowledges having received the goods in apparent good order and condition cannot nullify this admission by adding "condition unknown," as was held in one case[58] where the cargo consisted of timber which was loaded in a deteriorated condition; the master recorded in his log that the timber was "very black, wet and partly musty" but issued a clean bill qualified only by the words "condition unknown." Langton J. held that the clause was insufficient to convey to the consignee that the timber was damaged. The learned judge said[59]:

> The straightforward thing to do was surely to put upon the bill of lading, in the ample margin which is apparently provided for that purpose, a clause which would clearly advertise to any buyer of a particular bill of lading that the goods he was going to receive were not in good order and condition. It would not have been beyond the master's power to take the entry from his own log and to put upon the bill of lading "very black, wet and partly musty." If he could see it for the purposes of his log, he could with the same eyes have seen it for the purposes of the bill of lading.

Another question is whether the shipowner can escape from the effect of the estoppel created by a clean bill of lading by pleading that under the terms of the contract of sale the consignee was bound to accept the defective goods in any event.[60] Kerr J.[61] rejected this contention because the consequences of the issue of a clean bill of lading arise from the contract of carriage, and a party thereto cannot avail himself of a defence which originates in quite a different contract, namely the contract of sale.[62]

The shipper is deemed to have guaranteed to the carrier the accuracy of the marks, number, quantity and weight as furnished by him, and the shipper has to indemnify the carrier against loss or damage arising from inaccuracies in such particulars; the right of the carrier to be indemnified by the shipper in these circumstances cannot be pleaded by the carrier in

---

[57] *New Chinese Antimony Co.* v. *Ocean Steam Ship Co.* [1917] 2 K.B. 664; *Pendle & Rivet* v. *Ellerman Lines* (1927) 33 Com.Cas. 70, 77; *Re National Petroleum Co., The Athelviscount* (1934) 39 Com.Cas. 227; *Rederiaktiebolaget Gustav W. Erikson* v. *Dr. Fawzi Ahmed Abou Ismail. The Herroe and The Askoe* [1986] 2 Lloyd's Rep. 281, 283; *The Boukadoura* [1989] 1 Lloyd's Rep. 393, 399.

[58] *The Skarp* [1935] P. 134; in *The Herroe and The Askoe, supra,* the effect of the "unknown" clause was superseded by the master expressly attaching his signature and stamp against the number of potato bags stated to be loaded in the bill of lading.

[59] *The Skarp, supra,* at p. 142.

[60] Essentially this is a question of reliance on the estoppel. In *The Skarp* [1935] P. 134 Langton J. held, on the facts of the case before him, that the consignee would have accepted the goods even in their defective condition.

[61] In *Cremer* v. *General Carriers S.A.* [1974] 1 W.L.R. 341, 353.

[62] This would be *res inter alios acta* (a transaction between other parties).

defence against a consignee who tries to hold him responsible.[63] Where the shipowner is hesitant to issue a clean bill, the shipper sometimes gives him an express indemnity in order to induce him to issue a clean bill, but such indemnity might be illegal and in that case does not protect the carrier.[64] Bills of lading sometimes contain clauses providing that in case of incorrect or insufficient declaration of the cargo the shipper shall be obliged to pay double freight by way of liquidated damages.[65]

A bill of lading issued under the Carriage of Goods by Sea Act 1971 is *prima facie evidence* of the receipt of the goods by the carrier as described in accordance with Article III(3)(*a*)–(*c*); this provision[66] applies to "shipped" and "received" bills alike. The Hague-Visby Rules—different from the original Hague Rules—further provide[67] that the bill shall be *conclusive evidence* regarding those particulars in the hands of a third party acting in good faith; such a third party, it is thought, would be the consignee, to whom the bill is transferred, and an indorsee. As far as these persons are concerned, the Rule goes further than the Bills of Lading Act 1855, s.3, which provides that a "shipped" bill of lading in the hands of a consignee or indorsee for valuable consideration is conclusive evidence of such shipment—*but not of the leading marks and other particulars of the goods as stated in the bill*—as against the master or other person signing the bill, even if the goods or part of them have not been shipped; but the person signing the bill is exonerated by showing that the consignee had actual notice of the true position, or that the misrepresentation was due to a fraud of the shipper, the consignee or a person under whom the consignee claims. It is obvious that the bill is conclusive evidence of shipment against the person who actually signed it, *e.g.* the master of the ship, but the question is whether the carrier as principal is also liable if the master (or another agent) signs an inaccurate bill and its holder suffers a loss in consequence of the misrepresentation in the bill. The master has actual authority to sign correct bills, but as regards incorrect bills, the question is whether he has acted within his *ostensible authority*; if so, the carrier is liable for misstatements in the bill according to general principles of agency law,[68] unless, of course, the shipper was aware of the lack of the master's authority. In one case,[69] where plywood was shipped from Port Kelang in Malaysia to Newport in United Kingdom, the bill of lading stated that the goods were shipped below deck whereas they were actually shipped on deck. The plywood was

---

[63] Hague-Visby Rules, Art. III(5).

[64] See p. 594, *post.*

[65] See p. 129, *ante.*

[66] Rules, Art. III(4); *Att.-Gen. of Ceylon* v. *Scindia Steam Navigation Co. India.* [1962] A.C. 60 (but the bill is not even prima facie evidence as to the weight or contents of the packages; see p. 586, *ante*); see also *The Frank Pais* [1986] 1 Lloyd's Rep. 529, 533.

[67] Rules, Art. III(4), second sentence.

[68] See p. 282, *ante.*

[69] *The Nea Tyhi* [1982] 1 Lloyd's Rep. 606.

damaged by rain water. The buyers contended that they would never have accepted bills claused "shipped on deck" because it was essential that the goods should be kept dry during the voyage. The buyers' claim for damages against the carrier was successful. Sheen J. said[70]:

> ... the charterers' agents had ostensible authority to sign bills of lading on behalf of the master. Accordingly that signature binds the shipowners as principals to the contract contained in or evidenced by the bills of lading.

But if it is clear that the master (or other agent) has acted outside his ostensible authority, the carrier is not liable; thus, if, *e.g.* the master issues a bill which states that goods have been shipped whereas they were never loaded, the carrier is not liable on the master's (or other agent's) signature.[71] The—unauthorised—agent himself may be liable for breach of an implied warranty of authority.[72]

Bills of lading sometimes contain a clause cautioning shippers against shipping dangerous or damaging goods[73]; *e.g.*:

> Shippers are cautioned against shipping goods of a dangerous or damaging nature as by so doing they may become responsible for all consequential damage and also render themselves liable to penalties imposed by statute.

The liability of the shipper for damage done by his goods to the ship or other cargoes arises from an implied warranty on his part that the goods are fit for carriage in the ordinary way.[74] The shipper warrants not only that the goods will not cause physical injury or damage but also that the goods can be discharged without delay due to import restrictions or prohibitions.[75] The shipper is not liable under the warranty if he duly informs the shipowner of the nature of the goods or if the shipowner knows, or ought to know, that they are dangerous or that delay in the discharge may be encountered. Under the Merchant Shipping Acts 1894 to 1988[76] a shipper is liable to fines for shipping in any vessel, British or foreign, explosives, petrol or other goods scheduled as "dangerous" without giving the shipowner due notice in writing and distinctly marking the nature of the goods on the outside of the packages, or for knowingly sending dangerous goods under false description of the goods or the sender. In addition, shippers are required to furnish, prior to shipment, a statement in writing of the identity of the goods and nature of the danger

---

[70] *Ibid.*, 611. Also *The Saudi Crown* [1986] 1 Lloyd's Rep. 261.
[71] *Grant* v. *Norway* (1851) 10 C.B. 665; *Heskell* v. *Continental Express* [1950] W.N. 210; *V/O Rasnoimport* v. *Guthrie & Co. Ltd.* [1966] 1 Lloyd's Rep. 1, 8.
[72] *V/O Rasnoimport* v. *Guthrie & Co. Ltd.* [1966] 1 Lloyd's Rep. 1, 8.
[73] The clauses are also found in charterparties: *Micada Confedria S.A.* v. *Texim* [1968] 2 Lloyd's Rep. 57.
[74] Art. IV, r. 6.
[75] *Mitchell, Cotts & Co.* v. *Steel Brothers & Co. Ltd.* [1916] 2 K.B. 610.
[76] ss.446–450.

to which the goods give rise and of other particulars.[77] Further, the nature of the danger and the identity of the goods has to be marked clearly with specified distinctive labels or stencils on the outside of each package of dangerous cargo. Failure to comply with these regulations will result in the cargo being refused for shipment and renders the sender liable to heavy penalties. Goods of inflammable, explosive or dangerous nature may be rendered innocuous by the carrier or his agent without liability on his part; if they are carried without the carrier's consent, this right can be exercised at any time; if they are carried with his consent, this right can only be exercised if the goods endanger the ship or cargo and subject to liability for general average, if any.[78]

The bill of lading as a document of title

It has been seen[79] that the principal purpose of the bill of lading is to enable the person entitled to the goods represented by the bill to dispose of the goods while they are in transit. By mercantile custom, possession of the bill is in many respects equivalent to possession of the goods[80] and the transfer[81] of the bill of lading has normally the same effect as the delivery of the goods themselves. The bill of lading is, in so far, a symbol of, or a key to, the goods themselves. We have this function of the bill of lading in mind when referring to it as a document of title.

Two points should be noted in this connection: first, the transfer of the bill of lading is merely deemed to operate as a symbolic transfer of possession of the goods, but not necessarily as a transfer of the property in them. The transfer of the bill passes such rights in the goods as the parties intend to pass. Where the consignee or indorsee of the bill is the

---

[77] Merchant Shipping (Dangerous Goods) Rules 1981 (S.I. 1981 No. 1747 amended by S.I.s 1982 No. 715 and 1986 No. 1069). These Rules were made under the Merchant Shipping (Safety Convention) Act 1949, s.23 and the Merchant Shipping Act 1979, s.47(1).

The carriage of dangerous or hazardous goods also forms the subject matter of the IMDG (International Maritime Dangerous Goods) Code, published by the International Maritime Organisation in 1990, and the so-called Blue Book, which is the 1978 Report of the Department of Trade's Standing Committee on the Carriage of Dangerous Goods in Ships. Special precautions have to be taken when such goods are packed in groupage containers with other goods; here the "segregation rules" apply; see *Understanding the Freight Business* (3rd ed., 1984), published by Thomas Meadows & Co. Ltd., Chapter 6 on Hazardous Goods by Sea. By virtue of the Dangerous Vessels Act 1985 a harbour master may prohibit the entry of a vessel into an area where she may present a grave risk to the safety of persons or property or obstruct navigation.

[78] Art. IV, r. 6.

[79] See p. 561, *ante.*

[80] The holder of the bill of lading has constructive possession of the goods; the actual possession is with the carrier as long as the goods are in his charge.

[81] On the transfer of the bill of lading, see p. 572, *ante.*

agent of the shipper at the port of destination, it is evident that the parties, by transferring the bill of lading, intend only to pass the right to claim delivery of the goods from the carrier upon arrival of the goods, but not the property in them. Where the consignee or indorsee is a banker who advances money on the security of the goods represented by the bill, the parties are likely to intend, by the transfer of the bill, the creation of a charge or pledge on the goods in favour of the banker, but not the transfer of the property in them to him. In the seller and buyer relationship, the rules relating to the passing of property, which have been reviewed earlier,[82] apply. Where the goods are unascertained, *e.g.* where they are part of a bulk cargo, property cannot normally pass on transfer of the bill of lading. Where the goods are ascertained, it depends on the intention of the parties whether the property in the goods shall pass on the transfer of the bill of lading; often this will be the case as the seller in a c.i.f. contract—and often also in other types of international sales—will have this intention but it may be recalled that taking out a bill of lading in the name of the buyer does not necessarily reveal the seller's intention of passing the property to him.[83]

Secondly, only a person holding a bill of lading is entitled to claim delivery of the goods from the carrier. The carrier is protected if he delivers the goods to the holder of the first original bill presented to him—though it is only one in a set[84]—and need not inquire into the title of the holder of the bill or the whereabouts of the other parts of the bill. The bill of lading retains its character of document of title until the contract of carriage by sea is discharged by delivery of the goods against the bill,[85] and the carrier is not responsible for wrongful delivery of the goods against the bill unless he knows of the defect in the title of the holder. If the carrier (or his agent) delivers the goods to a person who is not the holder of the bill of lading, he does so at his peril. If that person is not the true owner, the carrier is liable to the latter for conversion of the goods. In practice, carriers normally rigorously insist on the production of a bill of lading, but, where the bill is produced and the identity of the consignee is in doubt or in other exceptional cases,[86] they sometimes deliver the goods against letters of indemnity which, in some instances, have to be provided by a bank.

---

[82] See p. 116, *ante.*

[83] *The Kronprinsessan Margareta* [1921] 1 A.C. 486, 517. For the right of the consignor to sue when the bill of lading has been transferred to the consignee or an indorsee, see p. 558, *ante.*

[84] See p. 543, *ante.*

[85] *Barclays Bank Ltd.* v. *Commissioners of Customs and Excise* [1963] 1 Lloyd's Rep. 81 (the bill does not lose its character of document of title by "exhaustion," *i.e.* by non-presentation immediately on arrival of the ship).

[86] In the oil trade the goods sometimes arrive before the bills of lading are in the hands of the last indorsee. The reason is that the bills are traded in string contracts. In these cases the carrier may release the goods against a bank indemnity but he does so at his risk.

The difficulties which might arise when the carrier releases the goods without insisting on the production of the bill of lading are demonstrated by *Sze Hai Tong Bank* v. *Rambler Cycle Co. Ltd.*[87] In that case an English company had sold bicycle parts to importers in Singapore; the goods were shipped in the *SS. Glengarry* which belonged to the Glen Line Ltd. The sellers instructed the Bank of China to collect the proceeds and release the bills of lading to the buyers on payment. The buyers, however, induced the carriers to deliver the goods to them without bills of lading, on an indemnity given by the buyers and their bank, the Sze Hai Tong Bank. When the sellers discovered what had happened they brought proceedings in the courts of Singapore against the carriers for damages for breach of contract and conversion, and the carriers brought in as third parties the Sze Hai Tong Bank against which the carriers claimed a declaration of indemnity. The High Court of Singapore held the carriers to be liable and held further that the bank was obliged to indemnify them. The bank appealed without success to the Court of Appeal in Singapore and eventually to the Judicial Committee of the Privy Council. Lord Denning who gave the judgment of the court said[88]:

> It is perfectly clear that a shipowner who delivers without production of the bill of lading does so at his peril. The contract is to deliver, on production of the bill of lading, to the person entitled under the bill of lading. . . . The shipping company did not deliver the goods to any such person. They are therefore liable for breach of contract unless there is some term in the bill of lading protecting them. And they delivered the goods, without production of the bill of lading, to a person who was not entitled to receive them. They are, therefore, liable in conversion unless likewise protected.

The Judicial Committee rejected the argument that the carriers—and consequently the bank—were relieved from liability by a clause in the bill of lading that the responsibility of the carriers should cease absolutely after the goods were discharged from the ship, because that exemption clause was not intended to protect a carrier who deliberately disregarded his obligation and committed a fundamental breach of contract by releasing the goods without production of a bill of lading.

On the other hand, even the true owner of the goods cannot claim the goods if unable to produce a bill of lading. In one case[89] a Canadian company bought six trucks and certain spare parts from a seller in England. The seller shipped the goods from Southampton to Montreal and paid the freight but the carriers refused to deliver the bills of lading

---

[87] [1959] A.C. 576. See also *Chabbra Corporation Pte. Ltd.* v. *Jag Shakti (Owners). The Jag Shakti* [1986] A.C. 337; see p. 560, *ante*.

[88] [1959] A.C. 576, on p. 586.

[89] *Trucks & Spares Ltd.* v. *Maritime Agencies (Southampton) Ltd.* [1951] 2 All E.R. 982.

(which were duly drawn up and signed) to the seller until he paid them certain shipping charges incurred in respect of previous shipments. The carriers who alleged to have a general lien on the bills of lading forwarded them to their agents at Montreal with instructions to hold them until they sanctioned their release. The Canadian company claimed to be the owners of the goods and applied to the English court for an interim injunction ordering the carriers to deliver the goods to them without production of a bill of lading. The Court of Appeal refused to make such an order. Denning L.J. said[90]: "Whether the property has passed or not, in my opinion, they [the buyers] ought to produce the bills of lading duly endorsed in order to make a good title at this stage," and Lloyd-Jacob J. observed[91]: "A decision affirming title at this stage may create grave injustice to some person or persons acquiring a title through the bills of lading in ignorance of the circumstances with which this action is concerned."

In the oil cargo trade the strict requirement that an original bill of lading must be produced on arrival of the goods appears sometimes to be treated with laxity. If in this case the tanker is on a time charter and the charterer instructs the master to deliver the cargo to a party who cannot produce a bill of lading, the master is entitled to refuse compliance with the instructions but if, without reason for suspecting that anything is wrong, he complies with them and the owner of the cargo suffers a loss, the shipowner, who normally would have to bear responsibility as principal of the master, can claim indemnity from the charterer who has given the unlawful order.[92]

In some foreign countries, notably Venezuela and other South American countries, a consignee may obtain delivery of the cargo without actual tender of the bill of lading.

Logically the function of the bill of lading as a document of title is distinct from its quality as a negotiable instrument.[93] Even a bill of lading which is not made negotiable, operates as a document of title because the consignee named therein can only claim delivery of the goods from the shipowner if able to produce the bill of lading. But the great practical value of the bill of lading as a means of making goods in transit rapidly transferable is due to the customary combination of the two features of the bill, *viz.* its quasi-negotiability and its function as a document of title.

---

[90] *Ibid.*, on p. 983.
[91] *Ibid.*, on p. 984.
[92] *A/S Hansen-Tangens Rederi III* v. *Total Transport Corporation. The Sagona* [1984] 1 Lloyd's Rep. 194.
[93] See p. 572, *ante.* The quality of the bill of lading as a document of title originates in the custom of the merchants and was first recognised by the courts in *Lickbarrow* v. *Mason* (1794) 5 T.R. 683; the character of the bill of lading as a quasi-negotiable instrument is derived from the Bills of Lading Act 1855.

Indemnities and bills of lading

It has already been observed[94] that a difficult situation develops if the carrier feels compelled to refuse the issue of a clean bill of lading. Where payment is arranged under a letter of credit, the exporter will be unable to obtain finance from the bank if he presents a claused, instead of a clean, bill, and, on the other hand, the carrier who issues a clean bill although he knows that the goods are not in apparent good order and condition, when shipped or received for shipment, is estopped from denying as against the bona fide consignee or assignee that he received the goods in such condition and might be liable to him.[95]

The obvious way out of this difficulty is for the exporter to offer the carrier an indemnity under which the exporter will recompense him for any loss sustained as the result of the issue of a clean bill of lading. Such indemnity, however, does not provide a solution in all circumstances. If both parties, the exporter and the carrier, know that the clean bill for which the indemnity is given, should never have been issued, in view of the condition of the cargo, they have conspired to defraud the bona fide consignee or indorsee who will take up the bill and part with his money, thinking that the goods did not show any defect when shipped or received for shipment. Such fraud vitiates the indemnity and renders it illegal; the carrier cannot claim under it against the exporter and, from the carrier's point of view, such indemnity is completely worthless.

Not all indemnities given for clean bills of lading are illegal. Two cases have to be distinguished: the clausing of the bill may concern a technicality which, as the exporter well knows, does not entitle the buyer to reject the goods; in this case the tender of an indemnity is legitimate and convenient. Only if the clausing of the bill concerns a serious matter which would entitle the buyer to reject the goods, is the indemnity tainted by fraud[96] and invalid; the proper course for the exporter is here to inform the buyer at once of the true facts and to ask him to amend the credit and to authorise the bank to pay against the bills of lading as issued. These principles were stated in *Brown, Jenkinson & Co. Ltd.* v. *Percy Dalton (London) Ltd.*[97] where the majority of the Court of Appeal held that an indemnity was invalid which was given by the exporters (the defendants) to the plaintiffs who were loading brokers for the shipowners; the cargo

---

[94] On p. 586, *ante*.

[95] See pp. 586–587, *ante*.

[96] A consignee or indorsee of a fraudulently issued clean bill of lading can sue for fraudulent misrepresentation: *Cordova Land Co. Ltd.* v. *Victor Brothers Inc.* [1966] 1 W.L.R. 793, 800.

[97] [1957] 2 Q.B. 621. Referred to with approval in the Indian case of *Ellerman & Bucknall Steamship Co.* v. *Sha Misrimal* [1966] All India Rep. 1892.

consisted of 100 barrels of orange juice and the tally clerk had described the casks on his tally card as "old and frail" and recorded some leaking, but the plaintiffs, on the request of the defendants, had issued clean bills of lading against the defendant's indemnity. Pearce L.J. said[98]:

> Trust is the foundation of trade; and bills of lading are important documents . . . In trivial matters and in cases of bona fide dispute where the difficulty of ascertaining the correct state of affairs is out of proportion to its importance, no doubt the practice [of accepting indemnities] is useful. But here the plaintiffs went outside those reasonable limits . . . Recklessness is sufficient to make a man liable in damages for fraud. Here the plaintiffs intended their misrepresentation to deceive, although they did not intend that the party deceived should ultimately go without just compensation.

London banks have for some time past by mutual consent refused to issue and countersign indemnities required to obtain clean bills of lading.[99]

An indemnity given to the carrier in order to induce him to deliver the goods to the consignee without production of the bill of lading, although in some instances equally reprehensible, is valid and enforceable by the carrier, as has been seen from the discussion of *Sze Hai Tong Bank* v. *Rambler Cycle Co. Ltd.*[1]

The limitation period for an action for an indemnity is not one year from the date of the delivery of the goods but such action can be brought within the time allowed by the law of the court seized of the case.[2] In English law the limitation period for a claim founded on a simple contract is six years after the cause of action accrued.[3]

LIABILITY OF SHIPOWNER FOR LOSS OF OR DAMAGE TO THE GOODS

General rules of liability

The liability of the carrier for goods exported from the United Kingdom is governed by the Carriage of Goods by Sea Act 1971 which, it

---

[98] [1957] 2 Q.B. 621, 639.
[99] [1957] J.B.L. 173.
[1] [1959] A.C. 576; see p. 592, *ante*.
[2] Art. III, r. 6 (bis), p. 607, *post*; but the time must not be less than three months. As far as the limitation period is concerned, Art. III, r.6(bis) is independent of r. 6; r.6(bis) applies if shipowner A, being under actual or potential liability to cargo-owner B, claims an indemnity by way of damages against ship or shipowner C: *China Ocean Shipping Co.* (*owners of Xingcheng*) v. *Andros* (*Owners of The Andros*) [1987] 1 W.L.R. 1213.
[3] Limitation Act 1980, s.5. If the indemnity is given by deed, it would be 12 years (Limitation Act 1980, s.8).

will be remembered,[4] applies to all outward shipments under bills of lading, from any port of the United Kingdom or a Contracting State, except in a few relatively unimportant cases, and of which the parties cannot contract out.[5] The Rules relating to Bills of Lading, as appended to the Act, are further often adopted by the clause paramount[6] for journeys not covered by the Act. Where the Rules do not apply by force of law[7] or voluntary agreement, the liability of the carrier is determined by the contract of the parties as evidenced in the bill of lading which, as a rule, will contain stipulations exempting the carrier from liability in case of loss of or damage to the goods entrusted to his care. In the absence of contractual stipulations the rules of common law apply to contracts of carriage by sea not governed by the statutory Rules; according to common law, the carrier impliedly undertakes the same liability as a common carrier, namely to carry the goods at his own absolute risk, except if the goods are lost or damaged by act of God, the Queen's enemies, inherent defect of the goods themselves or the shipper's default.[8] For practical purposes, it is sufficient to consider in the following paragraphs the carrier's liability under the Carriage of Goods by Sea Act 1971.

The responsibilities of the carrier in respect of the safety of the goods entrusted to his care are described in detail in the Rules,[9] Article III:

1. The carrier shall be bound, before and at the beginning of the voyage, to exercise due diligence to—
   (*a*) Make the ship seaworthy.
   (*b*) Properly man, equip and supply the ship.
   (*c*) Make the holds, refrigerating and cool chambers, and all other parts of the ship in which goods are carried, fit and safe for their reception, carriage and preservation.
2. Subject to the provisions of Article IV, the carrier shall properly and carefully load, handle, stow, carry, keep, care for and discharge the goods carried.

The principle underlying these provisions is that the shipowner is only liable if acting negligently. This is clearly expressed by the words, in paragraph 1, enjoining the shipowner "to exercise due diligence," and, in paragraph 2, postulating that he should act "properly and carefully." The responsibilities of the shipowner under the Act are thus lighter than they

---

[4] See p. 565, *ante.*
[5] Rules, Art. III(8).
[6] The Rules, including the time limit of Article III, r. 6, do not apply to actions against the shipowner founded on the tort of conversion of goods by misdelivery: *The Captain Gregos,* [1989] 2 Lloyd's Rep. 63.
[7] See p. 566, *ante.*
[8] Halsbury's *Laws of England* (4th ed.), Vol. 43, "Shipping and Navigation," para. 447.
[9] The Rules are commented upon in detail in Scrutton, *op. cit.*, chapter XX.

are at common law though this is compensated for by the provision that he cannot contract out of the Act. In particular, at common law the shipowner is under an absolute obligation to provide a seaworthy ship, *i.e.* a ship that in all respects is fit to load, carry and discharge the cargo safely, having regard to the ordinary perils encountered on the voyage. Under the Act, he is only responsible if he fails, upon reasonable inspection, to discover the lack of seaworthiness of his ship.[10] "Under the old rule, the only relevant question was whether the ship was seaworthy or unseaworthy. That rule was no doubt well adapted to more simple days when ships were not very complicated wooden structures . . . but in modern times, when ships are complicated steel structures full of complex machinery, the old unqualified rule imposed too serious an obligation on carriers by sea . . . he is to be liable for all such duties as appertain to a prudent and careful carrier acting as such by the servants and agents in his employment."[11] Seaworthiness, within the meaning of Article III, Rule 1(a) (and in common law) includes cargoworthiness; consequently the vessel is unseaworthy if its condition before loading the cargo constitutes a major and permanent obstacle to the completion of the contract voyage. A vessel is unseaworthy if before loading it is infested with insects and for this reason the discharge of the cargo is prohibited by the authorities at the port of destination.[12] The vessel is likewise unseaworthy if it is provided with navigational charts which are out of date.[13]

The obligation of the carrier to use due diligence in the cases stated in Article III(1) and (2) is not limited to his personal diligence; he is liable if servants and agents[14] in his employment fail to act with due diligence[15] and he was even held to be liable for a reputable independent contractor whom he instructed to repair his ship and whose workman acted

---

[10] Carriage of Goods by Sea Act 1971, s.3. On the duty of the carrier to use due diligence to make the ship seaworthy see Sheen J. in *The Tilia Gorthon* [1985] 1 Lloyd's Rep. 552.

[11] *Per* Wright J. in *W. Angliss & Co. (Australia) Proprietary* v. *Peninsular and Oriental Steam Navigation Co.* [1927] 2 K.B. 456, 461; *Ministry of Food* v. *Lamport and Holt Line Ltd.* [1952] 2 Lloyd's Rep. 371; *International Packers London Ltd.* v. *Ocean S.S. Co. Ltd.* [1955] 2 Lloyd's Rep. 218, 236; *Riverstone Meat Co. Pty. Ltd.* v. *Lancashire Shipping Co. Ltd. The Muncaster Castle* [1961] A.C. 807; *Union of India* v. *N.V. Reederij Amsterdam, The Amstelslot* [1963] 2 Lloyd's Rep. 223; *Albacora S.R.L.* v. *Westcott & Laurance Line Ltd. The Maltasian* [1966] 2 Lloyd's Rep. 53; *The Flowergate* [1967] 1 Lloyd's Rep. 1, 7; *The Torenia* [1983] 2 Lloyd's Rep. 210.

[12] *Empresa Cubana Importadora de Alimentos "Alimport"* v. *Iasmos Shipping Co. S.A. The Good Friend* [1984] 2 Lloyd's Rep. 586. But there is no unseaworthiness within the Rules where the vessel, as such, is seaworthy and had only to be lightened to get through the Panama Canal: *Actis Co. Ltd.* v. *The Sanko Steamship Co. Ltd. The Aquacharm* [1982] 1 Lloyd's Rep. 7.

[13] *Cf. Grand Champion Tankers Ltd.* v. *Norpipe A/S. The Marion* [1984] A.C. 563. (This case did not concern the question of unseaworthiness under the Rules.)

[14] On the protection of servants and agents by the Rules, see p. 604, *post.*

[15] See the cases referred to in n. 11, above.

negligently although the shipowner himself, or his servants and agents, were not guilty of any negligence.[16] That under Article III(1) and (2) the carrier is liable for the negligence of his servants and agents is an important extension of his liability and should be contrasted with Article IV(2)(*a*) which provides that the carrier is not liable for the neglect or the fault of his servants or agents in the navigation or management of the ship. On the other hand, a servant or agent of the carrier—but not an independent contractor[17]—if sued, is entitled to the same defences and limits of liability which the carrier may invoke under the Rules.[18]

The liability of the carrier for the negligent acts or omissions of his servants exists not only in the cases listed in Article III(1) but also in those mentioned in Article III(2). Thus, carriers were held liable to owners of a cargo of maize for damage caused by bad stowage. Above the maize, which was carried mostly in bulk in a lower hold, a cargo of tallow in casks was carried. During the voyage some of the casks were broken and the tallow which became heated began to leak and penetrate to the hold in which the maize was stowed, causing it damage.[19] Carriers were likewise held liable for damage caused during the loading operation by the negligence of their servants,[20] for the destruction, by negligently caused fire of the goods after they were loaded but before the ship sailed,[21] and for the loss of a tractor carried on deck without specific agreement with the shipper that it should be deck cargo, and washed overboard because it was not properly secured.[22] On the other hand, carriers did not act negligently and were not held to be responsible when in an intermediate port, in spite of a careful watch, the cover plate of a storm valve in a hold was stolen by stevedores during unloading and loading and sea water damaged the cargo in the hold on the continued voyage.[23] But if the master, when stowing the goods, follows strictly the instructions of the shipper's agent (who acts within his authority), the shipper may be estopped by conduct from asserting that the stowage was defective.[24]

The carrier is practically bound to play some part in the loading operation but the scope and area of the part which he has to play is determined by the contract of the parties, and may further depend upon

---

[16] *Riverstone Meat Co. Pty. Ltd.* v. *Lancashire Shipping Co. Ltd. The Muncaster Castle* [1961] A.C. 807; *Empresa Cubana Importadora de Alimentos "Alimport"* v. *Iasmos Shipping Co. S.A. The Good Friend.* [1984] 2 Lloyd's Rep. 586.

[17] See p. 604, *post.*

[18] Art. IVbis.

[19] *Ministry of Food* v. *Lamport and Holt Line Ltd.* [1952] 2 Lloyd's Rep. 371.

[20] *Pyrene Co. Ltd.* v. *Scindia Navigation Co. Ltd.* [1954] 2 Q.B. 402; see p. 21, *ante.*

[21] *Maxine Footwear Co. Ltd.* v. *Canadian Government Merchant Marine Ltd.* [1959] A.C. 589.

[22] *Svenska Traktor Akt.* v. *Maritime Agencies (Southampton) Ltd.* [1953] 2 Q.B. 295.

[23] *Leesh River Tea Co. Ltd.* v. *British India Steam Navigation Co. Ltd. The Chyebassa* [1966] 1 Lloyd's Rep. 450.

[24] *Ismael* v. *Polish Ocean Lines* [1976] Q.B. 893.

the custom and practice of the port and the nature of the cargo. The phrase "shall properly and carefully load" in Article III(2) is not designed to define the scope and area of the carrier's part in the loading operation but defines the terms on which that service is to be performed.[25] Thus, where goods sold under an f.o.b. contract and loaded from the quay in the ship's tackle onto the ship were damaged by the negligence of the carrier's servants before they crossed the ship's rail, *viz.* they were dropped on the quay, the carriers were liable because *under the contract of carriage* in question they were responsible for the *whole* of the loading, and not only for the part following the crossing of the rail.[26]

The duty of the carrier properly and carefully to discharge the goods carried, which is stipulated in Article III(2), is normally ended when the goods are delivered from the ship to a person entitled to receive them[27] in the same apparent order and condition as on shipment,[28] but where they are discharged into a lighter, the shipowner continues to be liable if the goods loaded into the lighter are damaged by other cargoes stowed negligently on top of them.[29] Since these words of Article III(2) likewise define the terms on which the contract of carriage is to be performed and have no geographical connotation, they do not invalidate a clause according to which the carrier is entitled, if the port of discharge is strikebound, to discharge the goods at any other safe and convenient port[30]; the costs of on-carriage to the agreed port of discharge have to be borne by the shipper.

An attempt of the carrier in a case to which the Hague-Visby Rules apply[31] to contract out of his responsibilities under Article III, rules 1 and 2, is void by virtue of rule 8 of this Article.[32]

---

[25] *G. H. Renton & Co. Ltd.* v. *Palmyra Trading Corporation of Panama, The Caspiana* [1957] A.C. 149.
[26] *Pyrene Co. Ltd.* v. *Scindia Navigation Co. Ltd.* [1954] 2 Q.B. 402; see p. 21, *ante.*
[27] *Sze Hai Tong Bank Ltd.* v. *Rambler Cycle Co. Ltd.* [1959] 2 Lloyd's Rep. 114, 120.
[28] Wright J. in *Gosse Millard* v. *Canadian Government Merchant Marine; American Can Co.* v. *Same* [1927] 2 K.B. 432, 434.
[29] Roche J. in *Goodwin, Ferreira & Co. Ltd.* v. *Lamport and Holt Ltd.* (1920) 34 Ll.L.R. 192, 194; see also *East & West Steamship Co.* v. *Hossain Brothers* [1968] 2 Lloyd's Rep. 145, 149 (Pakistan Sup.Ct.).
[30] *G. H. Renton & Co. Ltd.* v. *Palmyra Trading Corporation of Panama. The Caspiana* [1957] A.C. 149.
[31] Or the unamended Hague Rules.
[32] *The Saudi Prince (No.* 2) [1988] 1 Lloyd's Rep. 1. But in the case of a freight receipt, which is not governed by the Hague-Visby Rules, such exclusion might be possible if the general law so allows; see *Browner International Transport Ltd.* v. *Monarch SS Company Ltd. The European Enterprise* [1989] 2 Lloyd's Rep. 185.

Excepted perils

The Rules contain, in Article IV,[33] a "long list of matters in respect of loss or damage arising or resulting from which the carrier is not liable."[34] This Article provides in Rules 1 and 2:

> 1. Neither the carrier nor the ship shall be liable for loss or damage arising or resulting from unseaworthiness unless caused by want of due diligence on the part of the carrier to make the ship seaworthy, and to secure that the ship is properly manned, equipped and supplied, and to make the holds, refrigerating and cool chambers and all other parts of the ship in which goods are carried fit and safe for their reception, carriage and preservation in accordance with the provisions of paragraph 1 of Article III. Whenever loss or damage has resulted from unseaworthiness the burden of proving the exercise of due diligence shall be on the carrier or other person claiming exemption under this article.
>
> 2. Neither the carrier nor the ship shall be responsible for loss or damage arising or resulting from—
>
> (a) Act, neglect, or default of the master, mariner, pilot, or the servants of the carrier in the nevigation or in the management of the ship.
>
> (b) Fire, unless caused by the actual fault or privity of the carrier.
>
> (c) Perils, dangers and accidents of the sea or other navigable waters.
>
> (d) Act of God.
>
> (e) Act of war.
>
> (f) Act of public enemies.
>
> (g) Arrest or restraint of princes, rulers or people, or seizure under legal process.
>
> (h) Quarantine restrictions.
>
> (i) Act or omission of the shipper or owner of the goods, his agent or representative.
>
> (j(Strikes or lockouts or stoppage or restraint of labour from whatever cause, whether partial or general.
>
> (k) Riots and civil commotions.
>
> (l) Saving or attempting to save life or property at sea.
>
> (m) Wastage in bulk or weight or any other loss or damage arising from inherent defect, quality or vice of the goods.
>
> (n) Insufficiency of packing.
>
> (o) Insufficiency or inadequacy of marks.
>
> (p) Latent defects not discoverable by due diligence.
>
> (q) Any other cause arising without the actual fault or privity of the carrier, or without the fault or neglect of the agents or servants of the carrier, but the burden of proof shall be on the person claiming the benefit of this exception to show that neither the actual fault or privity of the carrier nor the fault or neglect of the agents or servants of the carrier contributed to the loss or damage.

The burden of proof

The burden of proof rests upon the shipowner who wants to rely on one of the excepted perils.[35] He has to prove that the goods were lost

---

[33] Article IV (which comprises six Rules and is followed by Article IVbis) is too long to be produced here in full; the solution of a practical problem requies the examination of the whole Article.

[34] Wright J. in *Gosse Millard* v. *Canadian Government Merchant Marine* [1927] 2 K.B. 432, 434.

[35] Scrutton, *op. cit.*, 220. Also *Phillips Petroleum Co.* v. *Cabaneli Naviera SA The Theodegmon, The Times,* June 15, 1989.

without his fault[36] and, if he wishes to claim exemption from his liability on the ground that the damage or loss of the cargo is due to one of the excepted perils he has to establish this fact also.[37] Among the grounds on which the shipowner will frequently try to rely, is inherent defect of the cargo (Art. IV(2)(*m*)).[38]

The burden of proof causes problems in cases of short delivery, *i.e.* if a smaller quantity of a cargo is unloaded than was loaded according to a (clean) bill of lading. This is an event not uncommon in the transportation of oil in bulk.[39] In such a case the onus of proving the shortage falls on the cargo owner who will normally be the plaintiff,[40] but he need not prove the cause of the shortage, which, in any event, may be speculative.[41]

Excepted perils and insurance

From the point of view of the shipper, the catalogue of exceptions is not so disconcerting as it would appear at the first glance. A comparison of the catalogue with Lloyd's Marine Policy and the Institute Cargo Clauses A, B and C supplementing it[42] shows that some exceptions, which are not based on the carrier's neglect (such as fire damage to the cargo aboard), are covered by these standard clauses. If they are not covered by them, additional insurance, at the cost of a further premium, can always be obtained. It is of great practical importance for the shipper to make certain that the clauses of his contract of carriage and contract of marine insurance are duly co-ordinated. Risks which the shipper has to bear under the contract of carriage should be covered by his marine insurance policy.

Sometimes bills of lading contain a clause drawing the attention of the shipper to the necessity of obtaining adequate insurance cover. The following is an example of such a clause:

> Shippers are requested to note particularly the terms and conditions of this bill of lading with reference to the validity of their insurance upon their goods.

---

[36] *The Torenia* [1983] 2 Lloyd's Rep. 210.
[37] *Per* Wright J. in *Gosse Millard* v. *Canadian Government Merchant Marine; American Can Co.* v. *Same* [1927] 2 K.B. 432, 435; *Svenska Traktor Akt.* v. *Maritime Agencies (Southampton) Ltd.* [1953] 2 Q.B. 295.
[38] *Albacora S.R.L.* v. *Westcott & Laurance Line Ltd. The Maltasian* [1966] 2 Lloyd's Rep. 53; *The Flowergate* [1967] 1 Lloyd's Rep. 1, 7; *Chris Foodstuffs (1963) Ltd.* v. *Nigerian National Shipping Line. The Amadu Bello* [1967] 1 Lloyd's Rep. 293 (concealed pre-shipment damage).
[39] See *The Herroe and The Askoe,* [1986] 2 Lloyd's Rep. 281, see p. 587, n. 57, *ante.*
[40] *Amoco Oil Co.* v. *Parpada Shipping Co. Ltd. The George S.* [1987] 2 Lloyd's Rep. 69.
[41] *BP International Ltd.* v. *Surena Delmar Navegacion SA, The Irini M* [1988] 1 Lloyd's Rep. 253.
[42] See p. 512, *ante.*

Maximum limits of shipowner's liabilities

The Hague-Visby Rules provide in Article IV(5) the following maximum limits for the carrier's liability for damage to or loss of the goods shipped:

(a) Unless the nature and value of such goods have been declared by the shipper before shipment and inserted in the bill of lading, neither the carrier nor the ship shall in any event be or become liable for any loss or damage to or in connection with the goods in an amount exceeding 666.67 units of account[43] per package or unit or 2 units of account[43] per kilogramme of gross weight of the goods lost or damaged, whichever is the higher.

(b) The total amount recoverable shall be calculated by reference to the value of such goods at the place and time at which the goods are discharged from the ship in accordance with the contract or should have been so discharged.

The value of the goods shall be fixed according to the commodity exchange price, or, if there be no such price, according to the current market price, or, if there be no commodity exchange price or current market price, by reference to the normal value of goods of the same kind and quality.

(c) Where a container, pallet or similar article of transport is used to consolidate goods, the number of packages or units enumerated in the bill of lading as packed in such article of transport shall be deemed the number of packages or units for the purpose of this paragraph as far as these packages or units are concerned. Except as aforesaid such article of transport shall be considered the package or unit.

(d) The unit of account mentioned in this Article is the special drawing right as defined by the International Monetary Fund. The amounts mentioned in sub-paragraph (a) of this paragraph shall be converted into the national currency on the basis of the value of that currency on a date to be determined by the law of the court seized of the case.[44]

(e) Neither the carrier nor the ship shall be entitled to the benefit of the limitation of liability provided for in this paragraph if it is proved that the damage resulted from an act or omission of the carrier done with intent to cause damage, or recklessly and with knowledge that damage would probably result.

(f) The declaration mentioned in sub-paragraph (a) of this paragraph, if embodied in the bill of lading, shall be prima facie evidence, but shall not be binding or conclusive on the carrier.

In the United Kingdom the value of the SDRs mentioned in sub-paragraph (a) of Article IV Rule 5 is ascertained by conversion into pounds sterling on a daily basis.[45]

---

[43] The units of account are the SDRs of the International Monetary Fund, as is stated in Art. IV(5)(d), see below in the text.

[44] These references to units of account were substituted for provisions relating to the "Poincaré gold franc" by section 2 of the Merchant Shipping Act 1981, which gave effect to the 1979 Protocol; referred to on p. 563, n. 30, *ante*.

It was held in *The Rosa S* [1989] 2 W.L.R. 162, that the original reference to gold franc in the Rules was to the gold value converted into sterling.

[45] Merchant Shipping Act 1981, s.2, brought into force on November 29, 1984 (Merchant Shipping Act 1981 (Commencement No. 3) Order 1984; S.I. 1984 No. 1695 (.39)).

The conversion value of an SDR on a particular day can be ascertained from a bank or by reference to the financial press. If necessary, a certificate by or on behalf of the Treasury can be obtained which shall be conclusive evidence of the equivalent sterling value on a particular day (Merchant Shipping Act 1981, s.3).

The maximum limits provided by the Rules for the carrier's liability are not of an absolute character. They may be increased by agreement of the parties or by adoption of the following procedures.[46]

(1) A declaration of the nature and value of the shipped goods by the shipper before shipment, *and*

(2) insertion of the declaration in the bill of lading.

The maximum limits for the liability of the carrier cannot, by agreement, be reduced below the limits provided in rule 5(*a*) of Article IV.[47]

Where the declared value of the goods is embodied in the bill, the shipper may, in case of damage or loss due to other than excepted perils, claim damages in excess of the maximum limits. The measure of damages is the loss actually suffered by the shipper, and it is open to the carrier to prove that that loss is smaller than the value of the goods stated in the bill.

The shipper, who wishes to hold the carrier liable in excess of the statutory maximum limit, should note that two conditions have to be satisfied, *viz.* the declaration of the nature and value of the goods, and the insertion of these particulars in the bill. In one case,[48] the shipper had satisfied the first condition, but the value of the goods was not embodied in the bill. MacKinnon J. said: "Though the plaintiffs did declare the value of the goods before shipment, that was not inserted in the bill of lading; and in those circumstances only one of the conditions on which the defendants could be liable for more than £100 was fulfilled," and ruled that the maximum limits applied.[49] Where the parties arrange for the carrier's liability in excess of the maximum limits, the freight rate is higher than in the case where the limits apply.

The carrier can plead the maximum limits of liability not only against the party to the contract of carriage by sea and his assignee but, in the case of an f.o.b. (buyer contracting with carrier) contract,[50] also against the seller who loads the goods on board a ship contracted for and nominated by the buyer, if the goods are damaged by the negligence of the shipowner's servants before they cross the ship's rail.[51]

The package limitation of Article IV r. 5(a) cannot be relied upon by the shipowner if, without agreement of the cargo owner, he carries delicate equipment of the latter on deck (and not below it) and as the result of this breach of his obligations the cargo is damaged.[52]

---

[46] Art. IV(5)(*a*) and (*f*).

[47] Art. IV(5)(*g*). See also Art. III(8) and *The Hollandia (also called The Morviken)* [1983] A.C. 565; see p. 566, *ante*.

[48] *Pendle & Rivet Ltd.* v. *Ellerman Lines Ltd.* (1927) 33 Com.Cas. 70, 78.

[49] On the date when this case was decided £100 was the maximum limit of the carrier's liability under the Hague Rules.

[50] See p. 22, *ante*.

[51] *Pyrene Co. Ltd.* v. *Scindia Navigation Co. Ltd.* [1954] 2 Q.B. 402; see p. 22, *ante*.

[52] *The Chanda*, [1989] 2 Lloyd's Rep. 494 the learned judge—Hirst J.—distinguished this case from *The Antares* (*Nos. 1 and 2*), see p. 607, n. 71, *post*.

Where the maximum limits apply, the liability of the carrier may be calculated per package or unit or per gross weight, whichever is higher. " 'Package'," in the words of a former Lord Chief Justice,[53] "must indicate something packed"; therefore, a car put on a ship without a box, crate or any form of covering is not a package.[54] The reference to "unit" is to freight units in use in various trades, *e.g.* in case of bulk shipment of grain. If the measure of damages is calculated on the number of packages or units, their weight is irrelevant.

In two cases the protective provisions of the Rules do not operate: *as against the carrier,* he (and the ship) cannot rely on the maximum limits of liability if it is proved that the damage resulted from an act or omission of the carrier done with intent to cause damage, or recklessly and with knowledge that damage would probably result[55] or, at least, might result; *e.g.* if on arrival he hands over the cargo to somebody who cannot produce an original bill of lading; in fact "misdelivery whether dishonest, honestly intentional or merely mistaken is entirely outside the scope of the rule."[55a]. And as *against the shipper* who has knowingly misstated in the bill of lading the nature or value of the goods; in this case the shipper cannot hold the carrier or the ship responsible for loss or damages to these goods.[56] unless the master, on inspection, could have noticed the misstatement and failed to clause the bill of lading.[57]

Protection of servants and agents, but not independent contractors

The question arises whether persons whom the carrier employs in the performance of his duties can, when sued by the cargo owner (*e.g.* for negligent damage to the cargo), plead the protection of the maximum limits of liability and other defences which the carrier could have pleaded under the Rules if he had been sued. The Hague-Visby Rules admit the extension of these protective provisions to servants and agents of the carrier but do not admit their extension to independent contractors.[58] The Rules provide in Article IVbis (2) to (4):

---

[53] Goddard J. (as he was then) in *Studebaker Distributors Ltd.* v. *Charlton Steam Shipping Co. Ltd.* [1938] 1 K.B. 459, 467.
[54] *Ibid.*
[55] Art. IV(5)(*e*); see *The Chanda*, p. 603, n. 52, *ante.*
[55a] *Per* Hirst J. in *Compania Portorafti Commerciale SA* v. *Ultramar Panama Inc., The Captain Gregos.* [1989] 2 Lloyd's Rep. 63, 69.
[56] Art. IV(5)(*h*).
[57] See *Naviera Mogor SA* v. *Société Métallurgique de Normandie. The Nogar Marin* [1988] 1 Lloyd's Rep. 412; in this case the negligence of the master (who was the servant of the shipowner) broke the chain of causation and the shipowner was estopped from raising this defence.
[58] The original Hague Rules did not even admit the extension to servants and agents and the only way to protect these auxiliary persons was to insert into the bill of lading the *Himalaya* clause described *infra* in the text.

2. If such an action is brought against a servant or agent of the carrier (such servant or agent not being an independent contractor), such servant or agent shall be entitled to avail himself of the defences and limits of liability which the carrier is entitled to invoke under these Rules.

3. The aggregate of the amounts recoverable from the carrier, and such servants and agents, shall in no case exceed the limit provided for in these Rules.

4. Nevertheless, a servant or agent of the carrier shall not be entitled to avail himself of the provisions of this article, if it is proved that the damage resulted from an act or omission of the servant or agent done with intent to cause damage or recklessly and with knowledge that damage would probably result.

That independent contractors employed by the carrier are not protected by the Rules was decided in *Midland Silicones Ltd.* v. *Scruttons Ltd.*[59] In that case the House of Lords held that stevedores (employed by the carrier) who negligently damaged cargo when unloading it, in an action for negligence brought against them by the cargo owners, could not claim the maximum limitation of liability under the contract of carriage which embodied the Hague Rules[60] because there was no privity of contract between the stevedores and the cargo owners.

If it is intended, in addition to the carrier's servants and agents, to protect independent contractors employed by the carrier or, in the case of a bill of lading governed by the original Hague Rules, to provide protection to all three categories of auxiliary persons, it is necessary to insert into the bill of lading the so-called *Himalaya* clause[61] which provides that the *carrier*, as agent of his own servants and agents (including independent contractors from time to time employed by the carrier), contracts with the cargo owner that these servants, agents and independent contractors shall be protected by the limits of liability and other defences arising from the contract of carriage. A majority of the Privy Council in *New Zealand Shipping Co. Ltd.* v. *A. M. Satterthwaite & Co. Ltd., The Eurymedon*[62] held that such a clause achieved the desired

---

[59] *Scruttons Ltd.* v. *Midland Silicones Ltd.* sub nom. *Scruttons* v. *Midland Silicones Ltd.* [1962] A.C. 446. Stevedores and ship's agents may be liable to the owner for loss of goods on mere acceptance of the goods for bailment; no contract or attornment is necessary: *Gilchrist Watt and Sanderson Pty. Ltd.* v. *York Products Pty. Ltd.* [1970] 1 W.L.R. 1262.
[60] By virtue of the U.S. Carriage of Goods by Sea Act 1936.
[61] *Adler* v. *Dickson. The Himalaya* [1955] 1 Q.B. 158 where in a case concerning personal injury to a passenger (she travelled in *The Himalaya*) it was held that an exclusion clause in favour of the carrier did not bar an action in negligence against the master of the ship. According to Pearce L.J. in the *Midland Silicones* case [1961] 1 Q.B. 106, 128 the principles governing the liability of carriers under contracts of passage and of carriage of goods by sea are, in that respect, the same. The object of the *Himalaya* clause is to remedy the difficulties resulting from *Adler* v. *Dickson* for the carrier's servants, agents and independent contractors.
[62] [1975] A.C. 154; N. E. Palmer, "The Stevedore's Dilemma: Exemption Clauses and Third Parties" [1974] J.B.L. 101.

effect. The decision has been criticised,[63] but has been confirmed by high authority[64] and is undoubtedly in harmony with commercial thinking.[65]

Notice of claim and time limit for claims for loss of or damage to the goods

The Rules provide in Article III(6) and (6*bis*) strict requirements for a claim against the carrier for loss of or damage to the goods. They require notice in writing of such loss or damage to be given to the carrier or his agent at once, and for suit founded on such a claim to be brought within a year of the delivery or intended delivery of the goods. The following are the provisions of rules 6 and 6*bis*:

> 6. Unless notice of loss or damage and the general nature of such loss or damage be given in writing to the carrier or his agent at the port of discharge before or at the time of removal of the goods into the custody of the person entitled to delivery thereof under the contract of carriage, or, if the loss or damage be not apparent, within three days, such removal shall be prima facie evidence of the delivery by the carrier of the goods as described in the bill of lading.
>
> The notice in writing need not be given if the state of the goods has at the time of their receipt been the subject of joint survey or inspection.
>
> Subject to paragraph 6*bis* the carrier and the ship shall in any event be discharged from all liability whatsoever in respect of the goods, unless suit[66] is brought within one year of their delivery or of the date when they should have been delivered.[67] This period may, however, be extended if the parties so agree after the cause of action has arisen.

---

[63] See *Salmond and Spraggen (Australia) Pty. Ltd.* v. *Port Jackson Stevedoring Pty. Ltd. The New York Star* [1979] 1 Lloyd's Rep. 298 (High Ct. of Australia).

[64] *Ibid., nom. rev.* [1981] 1 W.L.R. 138, 143 (P.C.); *Godina* v. *Patrick Operations Pty. Ltd.* [1984] 1 Lloyd's Rep. 333 (Austr. case; CA of NSW). See also *Burke Motors Ltd.* v. *Mersey Docks & Harbour Co.* [1986] 1 Lloyd's Rep. 155 (The *Himalaya* clause can only protect after the contract of carriage has been concluded); see also *The Kapetan Markos* [1986] 1 Lloyd's Rep. 211.

[65] See P. J. Davies and N. E. Palmer, "The Eurymedon Five Years On" in [1979] J.B.L. 337; Philip H. Clarke, "The Reception of the Eurymedon Decision in Australia, Canada and New Zealand," in 29 I.C.L.Q. (1980) 132.

[66] The limitation period of one year is only interrupted if "suit" is brought by a competent plaintiff (*i.e.* a plaintiff who has title to the goods) in a competent court (which, however, may be a foreign court): *The Nordglimt* [1988] Q.B. 183. "Suit" includes arbitration proceedings, *The Merak* [1965] P. 223; *Ch. E. Rolimpex Ltd.* v. *Aura Shipping Co. Ltd. The Angeliki* [1973] 2 Lloyd's Rep. 226, 229; *Nea Agrex S.A.* v. *Baltic Shipping Co. Ltd.* [1976] Q.B. 933. In court proceedings, where suit is brought within one year but the statement of claim is amended after the year, according to general principles of the English law of procedure the amendment relates back and is treated as taking effect at the date of the writ: *Empresa Cubana Importadora de Alimentos* v. *Octavia Shipping Co. S.A. The Kefalonia Wind* [1986] 1 Lloyd's Rep. 273.

[67] For cases in which the period of limitation does not operate against the cargo owners, see *Goulandris Brothers* v. *B. Goldman & Sons Ltd.* [1958] 1 Q.B. 74; noted on p. 523, n. 29, *ante*, and *Rambler Cycle Co.* v. *P. & O. Steam Navigation Co.* [1968] 1 Lloyd's Rep. 42 (Malaysia Fed.C. (Appellate)). "Delivery" within Art. III(6) occurs when the goods are landed on the quay or at least placed at the consignee's disposal: *The Beltana* [1967] 1 Lloyd's Rep. 531 (Aust.).

> In the case of any actual or apprehended loss or damage the carrier and receiver shall give all reasonable facilities to each other for inspecting and tallying the goods.
>
> 6bis. An action for indemnity against a third person may be brought even after the expiration of the year provided for in the preceding paragraph if brought within the time allowed by the law of the court seized of the case. However, the time allowed shall be not less than three months, commencing from the day when the person bringing such action for indemnity has settled the claim or has been served with process in the action against himself.

These provisions are sometimes modified in slight but significant detail by clauses in the bill of lading. Thus, the bill of lading might provide:

> The ship's protest[68] relating to facts and circumstances exempting carriers from liability duly sworn by the captain and/or one or more members of the crew will be deemed sufficient proof by parties to this bill of lading of such facts and circumstances.

The time limit of Article III(6) applies only to claims for loss of or damage to the goods;[68a] it does not apply to other claims against the carrier, such as a claim founded on delay in the delivery.[69]

If it is intended to extend the limitation period provided in the Rules or in the bill of lading by agreement, great care has to be taken to establish that a clear agreement on the extension has been reached. Mere inactivity or silence by one of two parties may lead to an ambiguous situation and may raise difficult questions of estoppel.[70]

If a bill of lading issued under the Rules contains an arbitration clause, an apparent conflict occurs between the Rules and arbitration law. The Rules provide the one year time limit but the Arbitration Act 1950 provides in section 27 that the High Court shall have power to extend a time limit agreed upon in the arbitration agreement "if it is of opinion that . . . undue hardship would otherwise be caused." The conflict is apparent because the power of the court to extend the time limit applies only to *contractual* time limits but the time limit in Article III, r. 6 is a *statutory* time limit which is imposed by force of law; consequently the discretionary power under section 27 of the Arbitration Act 1950 does not enable the court to extend the one-year time limit of Article III(6).[71]

---

[68] Also called the master's protest, see p. 527, *ante.*

[68a] Article III (6) also bars actions founded on the tort of conversion alleged to have been committed on delivery: *The Captain Gregos, Financial Times,* December 22, 1989.

[69] *Interbulk Ltd.* v. *Ponte dei Sospiri Shipping Co. The Standard Ardour* [1988] 2 Lloyd's Rep. 159 (This case arose under section 3(6) of the U.S. Carriage of Goods by Sea Act 1936.)

[70] *K. Lokumal & Sons (London) Ltd.* v. *Lotte Shipping Co. Pte. Ltd. The August Leonhardt* [1985] 2 Lloyd's Rep. 28 (C.A.).

[71] *Kenya Railways* v. *Antares Co. Pte. Ltd., The Antares (Nos. 1 and 2)* [1987] 1 Lloyd's Rep. 424 (C.A.). It was also held in this case that the carrier was not deprived of his right to rely on the time limit by his unauthorised act of stowing the goods on deck; but see *The Chanda,* on p. 603, n. 52, *ante.* See also *Government of Sierra Leone* v. *Marmaro Shipping Co. Ltd., The Times,* March 24, 1988.

GENERAL AVERAGE CLAIMS AND CONTRIBUTIONS

The law of general average, so far as it affects the rights and duties of the shipper under the contract of carriage by sea, has been discussed in the chapter on insurance,[72] as a necessary preliminary to an explanation of the rules of insurance law protecting the shipper in case of general average loss or expenditure.

Bills of lading regularly contain a clause providing that general average shall be adjusted in acccordance with the York-Antwerp Rules 1974. Sometimes it is added that the practice of English Average Adjusters shall apply to all points on which the Rules do not contain provisions.

---

[72] See p. 522, *ante*. If the limitation period is agreed to be extended but the last day of the extension is a Sunday, the writ is timely served on the next Monday; if the last day is another *dies non juridicus*, the time limit is further extended to the next available day: *The Clifford Maersk* [1982] 1 W.L.R. 1292.

CHAPTER 28

CONTAINER TRANSPORT

THE transportation of export goods is nowadays frequently carried out in containers. "Scheduled ocean container operations now provide the key liner cargo services between the main markets of the industrialised world. . . . Roll-on/roll-off operations are also flourishing on long-haul routes due to their 'flexibility,' while this same factor is similarly contributing to the important growth of unitised services to developing areas of the world."[1] Other forms of unitised services, such as pallets and LASH barges,[2] are also used.

Containers are particularly suitable for multimodal transport.[3] If, as in the example given earlier,[3] the goods have to pass through three stages of transportation, *viz.* they are first carried by land, then by sea, and finally again by land, they will travel in the same container from the place of loading to that of discharge and the physical labour as well as the cost of conveying them from one vehicle of transportation to the next is saved. In addition, the danger of theft and pilferage is reduced.[4]

Container transport raises, as will be seen, difficult and largely unsolved legal problems. The failure to achieve so far a widely accepted international regulation[5] on multimodal transport does not make the task of finding solutions more easy.

THE COURSE OF BUSINESS IN CONTAINER TRANSPORT

The course of business in container transport is that the exporter, having made arrangements with a forwarder or directly with the office of a

---

[1] *Understanding the Freight Business*, (3rd ed., 1984), published by Thomas Meadows & Co. Ltd., p. 33. On containers generally, see Mark D. Booker, *Containers*, Conditions, Law and Practice of Carriage and Use, Twickenham, England, 1987. See also Malcolm Clarke, "Containers: Proof that Damage occurred during Carriage," in *International Carriage of Goods: Some Legal Problems and Possible Solutions* (ed. C. M. Schmitthoff and R. M. Goode), 1988, 64.

In the United States a proliferation of multimodal services, under such names as landbridge, minibridge and microbridge, has been developed, see Le T. Thuong and Frederick M. Collison, "In Search of a Coherent Policy on Intermodal Transportation" in (1985) 16 Journ. Mar. Law and Com. 397.

[2] LASH stands for "Lighter-aboard-ship".

[3] See p. 537, *ante*.

[4] But not entirely avoided as the whole container may be stolen.

[5] See p. 613, *post*.

container shipping line, sends his goods to the nearest container loading depot of the forwarder or shipping line. These depots, called *container freight stations* (CFSs), are situate in all major industrial centres inland or at the ports.[6]

If the exporter intends to fill a full container load (FCL), the forwarder or shipping line will be prepared to send an empty container to the exporter for loading. If the exporter has arranged for the delivery of the goods to the overseas buyer's place of business, the container would be a *door-to-door container*. It is important that the door-to-door container is properly sealed with the carrier's seal, this is sometimes done by the shipper, and in other cases by the driver of the collecting vehicle. The exporter should make sure of this because, if there is a claim for shortage of or damage to the cargo carried in the container, the state of the carrier's seal may allow an inference of what has happened. If it is broken, it would indicate that the cargo has been tampered with during the transport.

If the cargo is less than a full container load (LCL), the exporter sends it to the container freight station, where it will be consolidated with the goods of other exporters in a *groupage container*. On arrival at the place of destination it will be taken to a container freight station, where it will be "degrouped," *i.e.* the parcels contained therein will be separated and delivered to the various consignees. In *The Emeralda I*,[7] decided by the Supreme Court of New South Wales, the plaintiff, an importer in Australia, bought a quantity of cutlery from a manufacturer in Brazil. The goods were to be carried in an FCL container on *The Emeralda I*, a vessel chartered to the defendant carrier and loading in Rio Grande. The container was taken to the seller's premises and, after the goods were placed into it, the carrier's seal was affixed and the container was secured by a padlock. When the container arrived in Sydney, it was taken to the buyer's premises. There the seal, which was intact, was removed and the padlock forced. Of the 437 cardboard boxes of cutlery, allegedly loaded in the container, 118 cartons were missing. The plaintiff (the consignee) sued the defendant (the carrier) for damages. The bill of lading, which was a clean "shipped on board" bill, contained on its face the letters "FCL/FCL" and the following statement:

> quantity . . . contents . . . if mentioned in the bill of lading were furnished by the shippers and were not and could not be ascertained or checked by the Master unless the contrary has been expressly acknowledged and agreed to.

There were further similar notices on the bill. The bill described the goods as "one 20ft. container said to contain 437 cardboard boxes." The

---

[6] Leggatt J. held in *Burke Motors Ltd.* v. *Mersey Docks & Harbour Co.* [1986] 1 Lloyd's Rep. 155 that a shipping line instructed to carry goods from England to Canada, which had stored them in a CFS prior to the arrival of the vessel, had acted as forwarder, and not yet as carrier; it is respectfully doubted that this decision is correct.

[7] *Ace Imports Pty. Ltd.* v. *Companhia de Navegacão Lloyd Brasileiro. The Emeralda I* [1988] 1 Lloyd's Rep. 206.

action was dismissed. The clauses on the face of the bill of lading defeated the consignee's argument that the carrier was estopped from denying that he had received 437 cardboard boxes for shipment. The court accepted expert evidence that in the letters FCL/FCL the first reference to FCL meant that the shipper wanted to ship whatever could go into a full container, and the second reference to this acronym meant that it was the importer who would unpack the whole container. The court also held that "the goods" referred to in the bill of lading within the meaning of the Hague Rules Article III r. 4 were the container, and not the cardboard boxes carried therein.[8]

Container leasing agreements

The containers are not necessarily owned by the carrier. There exist container companies which own containers and let them to carriers[9]; in fact, container letting is a business of considerable size.

The container leasing contract usually provides that, if the lessee retains the container beyond the stipulated time, he has to pay "demurrage," *i.e.* liquidated damages.[10]

When the forwarder or shipping line has taken charge of the goods loaded in a full container or sent for groupage in a groupage container,[11] a receipt is issued. If the recipient is a shipping line, it may issue a container bill of lading.[12] If he is a forwarder, he may issue a FIATA combined transport bill of lading,[13] or a combined transport document,[14] or a house bill of lading,[15] or any other form of receipt. No uniform practice exists in this respect.

---

[8] The court found as a fact that the pilfering took place in Brazil before the FCL container was sealed and locked.

[9] In *The River Rima* [1988] 2 Lloyd's Rep. 193 the House of Lords held that containers supplied to a vessel were not "goods or materials supplied to a ship for her operation or maintenance" within the meaning of section 20(m) of the Supreme Court Act 1981 and that consequently the court could not exercise Admiralty jurisdiction *in rem* (arrest of the ship) in a claim arising from a leasing agreement between a container leasing company and a vessel.

[10] There exists a trade usage in England according to which a Customs clearance agent appointed by an importer is responsible to the forwarder for demurrage for retention of the forwarder's container if the return of the container is unreasonably delayed through the fault of the clearance agent: *Kuehne and Nagel Ltd.* v. *W. B. Woolley (Scotland) Ltd.* (unreported, Westminster County Court, August 15, 1973, Plaint. No. 73 50487).

[11] See p. 610, *ante.*

[12] See p. 615, *post.*

[13] See p. 580, *ante.*

[14] See p. 615, *post.*

[15] See p. 579, *ante.*

LEGAL PROBLEMS OF CONTAINER TRANSPORT

The contract of export sale and container transport

If the parties to a contract of international sale agree on container transport, the "critical point" for the delivery of the goods and the passing of the risk is different from that under a ontract in which the traditional method of sea transport is envisaged. In the traditional forms of export contract, such as f.a.s., f.o.b., c.i.f. or c. and f., the critical point is in the port of shipment, and in an arrival contract it is in the port of destination.[16] But if container transport is contemplated, the critical point is the place at which the carrier (or his agent) takes charge of the goods this place may well be a container freight station inland.[17]

Incoterms take account of this situation. They suggest that if the parties to the contract of sale contemplate shipment in a container, they should adopt the appropriate container trade term, and not one of the traditional trade terms.[17a] The container trade terms which Incoterms define are "free carrier," "freight/carriage and insurance paid to," and "freight/carriage paid to." They were considered earlier.[18]

The liability of the container operator

Containers, as we have seen, are largely used in multimodal transport. If the goods conveyed in the container are lost or damaged in transport or delay occurs and it is sought to hold the container operator liable, a difficulty arises. The international Conventions applying to the various modes of international transport[19] differ considerably with respect to the conditions of liability of the carrier and the maximum limits of his liability. This difficulty is particularly marked in the European trade. Here the liability for loss in sea transport is usually governed by the Hague-Visby Rules, for air transport by the Warsaw Convention, and for land transport by the CMR or CIM. The Hague-Visby Rules hold the carrier only liable if he has acted negligently. On the other hand, the

---

[16] See Chapter 2, p. 9, *ante*. The position is different if the contract is on terms ex works, delivered carrier, delivered at frontier, or delivered free.

[17] If the parties to the contract of sale, though agreeing on container transport, have provided for delivery at the buyer's place (door-to-door container), the position would be different.

[17a] This reference is to Incoterms 1980 (see p. 10, *ante*). Incoterms 1990 no longer draw a distinction between traditional and container terms but retain the terms themselves.

[18] See p. 59, *ante*.

[19] See p. 537, *ante*.

Warsaw Convention, and CMR as well as CIM provide, in principle, strict liability but differ on the defences which the carrier may plead; in the case of air carriage he is not liable if he proves that he has taken all "necessary" measures to avoid the damage, and under CMR and CIM a few specified defences, including inherent vice or force majeure, are admitted. This difficulty is increased if it is impossible to ascertain during which phase of the multimodal transport the loss or damage occurred; at present an international regulation which provides a solution of this problem is not yet generally accepted.

The continuance of this legal tower of Babel is indefensible in modern circumstances, in which the multimodal transport plays an almost dominating role in the international transport of goods, and, in the eyes of the exporter, a multimodal transport operation constitutes one business transaction, irrespective of the various stages of the carriage of goods. The obvious solution is that a *uniform system of liability* should be adopted for the multimodal transport operator.[20] Such an arrangement would make it unnecessary to inquire at which stage the loss of or damage to the goods occurred.[21] This system of liability is, in fact, accepted by the *UN Convention on International Multimodal Transport of Goods*, adopted at Geneva on May 24, 1980.[22] At the date of writing,[23] the Convention is not in force yet and does not form United Kingdom law. The principle of uniform liability is expressed in Article 16 of the Convention as follows:

Basis of liability

1. the multimodal transport operator shall be liable for loss resulting from loss of or damage to the goods, as well as from delay in delivery, if the occurrence which caused the loss, damage or delay in delivery took place while the goods were in his charge as defined in Article 14, unless the multimodal transport operator proves that he, his servants or agents or any other person referred to in Article 15 took all measures that could reasonably be required to avoid the occurrence and its consequences.

---

[20] The problems which arise in this connection are discussed by Anthony Diamond in "Liability of the Carrier in Multimodal Transport," published in *International Carriage of Goods* (ed. C. M. Schmitthoff and R. M. Goode), 1988, p. 35.

[21] This solution was already advocated in May 1972 by an international seminar on intermodal transport held in Genoa; see Lord Diplock, "A Combined Transport Document" in [1972] J.B.L. 269.

[22] UN Doc. TD/MT/Conf/16.

[23] Position: October 1, 1989. The Convention will come into force one year after 30 countries have ratified it or have acceded to it—necessarily a slow process.

UNCITRAL is at present working on a Draft Convention on the Liability of Operators of Transport Terminals; this work is still in a preparatory stage.

There exist, however, some technical Conventions relating to containers which are already in operation, notably the International Convention on Safe Containers (CSC); this Convention, UK Statutory Instruments relating to safety standards, and other material are produced in Mark D. Booker, *Containers*, Conditions, Law and Practice of Carriage and Use, Twickenham, England, 1987.

2. Delay in delivery occurs when the goods have not been delivered within the time expressly agreed upon or, in the absence of such agreement, within the time which it would be reasonable to require of a diligent multimodal transport operator, having regard to the circumstances of the case.
3. If the goods have not been delivered within 90 consecutive days following the date of delivery determined according to paragraph 2 of this Article, the claimant may treat the goods as lost.

As regards the maximum liability of the multimodal transport operator, the Convention provides in Article 19(1) that his liability is limited to 920 units of account (SDRs) per package or other shipping unit or 2.75 units of account per kilogramme of gross weight of the goods lost or damaged, whichever is the higher, but it adds in Article 19(3) that, notwithstanding this provision, if the international multimodal transport does not, according to the contract, include carriage by sea or inland waterways, his liability is limited to 8.33 units of account per kilogramme of gross weight of the goods lost or damaged. This latter limitation is similar to the— rather low—limitation provided by the CMR.

Until the Convention comes into operation and is given effect in the various national jurisdictions—and it may be some time before this is achieved—a regulation of the liability of the multimodal transport operator has to be provided on a contractual basis. As most international Conventions regulating the various modes of transportation are of mandatory character,[24] the contractual regulation has to proceed in two stages. It has to provide, first, that if it is known at which stage of the multimodal transport the loss occurred, the international Convention governing that mode of transport shall apply; and, secondly, if this cannot be ascertained, another regime specified in the contract shall apply, *e.g.* the regulation of the Hague-Visby Rules or of the CMR.[25] This arrangement of the liability of the multimodal transport operator is known as the *network liability system.*

The documents used in container transport

It has already been observed[26] that documents which differ in character and effect are used by multimodal transport operators and that no uniform practice has emerged yet.

---

[24] The Warsaw Convention, *e.g.*, contains in Article 31 an express provision dealing with combined carriage, which includes an air leg. It states that in the case of combined carriage the parties may insert in the document of air carriage conditions relating to other modes of transport, provided that the provisions of the Convention are observed as regards the air carriage.

[25] The CMR so provide in Art. 2(1); see p. 636, *post.*

[26] See p. 611, *ante.*

The combined transport document

The ICC has sponsored *Uniform Rules for a Combined Transport Document*[27] which can be embodied into the contract of combined transport by agreement of the parties. The combined transport document, known as the CT document, is intended to be a "start-to-finish" document and to make it unnecessary to issue separate documents for every stage of the multimodal transport. The CT document may be issued in a negotiable or non-negotiable form, as the parties desire. By issuing a CT document, the combined transport operator accepts full responsibility for the performance of the combined transport, as well as liability, on the terms stated in the Uniform Rules, for loss or damage, and delay, throughout the entire combined transport.

The Uniform Rules do not apply automatically. They have to be embodied into the contract between the exporter and the combined transport operator and the CT document shall state that it is issued "subject to Uniform Rules for a Combined Transport Document (ICC Brochure No. 298)." The Negotiable FIATA Combined Transport Bill of Lading FBL, in its amended version (8.87),[28] satisfies these requirements.

As the Uniform Rules are applied by contract, they cannot avoid adopting the system of network liability, but they provide their own maximum limits of compensation when the stage of transport where the loss or damage occurred is not known and consequently none of the international Conventions can be resorted to.

The importance of the Uniform Rules for a Combined Transport Document is enhanced by the fact that according to the UCP (1983 Revision) such a document may be accepted by banks under a letter of credit unless the instructions state that a marine bill of lading shall be tendered.[29]

Container bills of lading

If a shipping line engages in combined transport, it may issue container bills of lading. Such documents are genuine bills of lading. They are subject to the Hague-Visby Rules by force of law, as far as the carriage by sea is concerned[30]; indeed, these Rules contain express provisions

---

[27] ICC Brochure 298, 1975 (Reprinted March 1985); see F. J. J. Cadwallader, "Uniform Rules for Combined Transport" in [1974] J.B.L. 193. On the multipurpose transport document (mpt), see p. 538, *ante*.

[28] See p. 580, *ante*.

[29] Art. 25(b)(i); see p. 413, *ante*.

[30] But by contract they are normally extended to situations in which it cannot be ascertained at which stage of the transport the loss or damage occurred; see text.

applying to the carriage of goods in a container, pallet or similar article of transport.[31]

All container bills of lading are normally "received for shipment" bills and not "shipped on board" bills; it could not be different where the goods are received at a container freight station inland.

All container bills of lading adopt the network liability system. They usually provide that, when the stage where the loss of or damage to the goods cannot be ascertained, the liability of the carrier shall be determined by the Hague-Visby Rules. The most elaborate of these clauses is found in the bill used by the Atlantic Container Line (ACL).[32] This clause has also taken account of American law; its relevant part runs as follows:

3. Responsibility

I . . . .
II. When either the place of receipt or place of delivery set forth herein is an inland point in the USA or Europe, the responsibility of ACL with respect to the transportation to and from the sea terminal ports will be as follows:

    a) Within countries in Europe, to transport the goods in accordance with any mandatory national law or in the absence thereof, subject to the inland carrier's own contracts and tariffs.
    b) Between countries in Europe, to transport the goods
        (1) if by road, in accordance with the Convention on the Contract for the International Carriage of Goods by Road, dated 19th May 1956 (CMR)
        (2) if by rail, in accordance with the International Agreement on Railway Transports, dated 25th February 1961 (CIM)
        (3) if by air, in accordance with the Convention for the Unification of Certain Rules relating to International Carriage by Air, signed Warsaw 12th October, 1929, as amended by the Hague Protocol, dated 28th September 1955.
    c) Between points in the USA or Canada, to procure transportation by carriers (one or more) authorized by competent authority to engage in transportation between such points, and such transportation shall be subject to the inland carrier's contracts of carriage and tariffs. ACL guarantees the fulfilment of such inland carriers' obligations under their contracts and tariffs.

III. As to services incident to through transportation, ACL undertakes to procure such services as necessary. All such services will be subject to the usual contracts of persons providing the services. ACL guarantees the fulfilment of the obligations of such persons under the pertinent contracts.
IV. When the goods have been damaged or lost during through transportation and it cannot be established in whose custody the goods were when the damage or loss occurred, the damage or loss shall be deemed to have occurred during the carriage by water and the Hague Rules as defined above shall apply.[33]

---

[31] Hague-Visby Rules, Art. IV Rule 5(c); see p. 602, *ante*.
[32] The ACL Bill of Lading is issued by Atlantic Container Line BV, Rotterdam. But the bill provides (in cl. 17) that disputes shall be determined, at the option of the "merchant" (defined as including the shipper, consignee, holder of the bill of lading and the owner of the goods), by the Commerical Court in London according to English law or by the U.S. District Court for the Southern District of New York according to the law of the United States but for the traffic to or from Canada jurisdiction is only in the Commercial Court in London.
[33] The definition of "the Hague Rules" is contained in paragraph I of this clause. The definition is very complicated because, as far as the U.K. and other countries which have given effect to the amended Rules are concerned it refers to the Hague-Visby Rules, but as far as the U.S.A. is concerned, it refers to the (unamended) original Hague Rules because the U.S.A. have not given effect to the amended Rules.

A container bill states, usually in the Terms and Conditions printed on the reverse, that the shipowner shall be entitled to carry the goods on deck in containers. This, however, is only a liberty, it is not a statement that the shipowner has made use of it and that the goods are, in fact, carried on deck. If this is the case, the bill has to be marked accordingly on its face, so that a purchaser of the bill is aware that the goods are deck cargo. In an American case[34] which concerned the shipment of books frrom New York to Yokohama the container in which the books were carried was stowed on deck but the bill of lading did not contain an indication on its face to that effect; the ship encountered heavy weather when crossing the Pacific and the books were damaged by sea water; the court held that the shipowner had forfeited the defence of pleading the limitation of liability under the Hague Rules by stowing the cargo on deck; one of the reasons which the court gave was that "no consignee or assignee could tell from the bill whether it was below deck or on deck cargo."[35] In an English case[36] a forwarder promised an importer orally to ship a container containing his goods below deck. Contrary to his promise he shipped them on deck and when the ship met a slight swell the container fell of and went to the bottom of the sea. The Court of Appeal held the forwarder liable for the loss.

The UCP (1983 Revision) provide that a combined transport bill of lading or a document of similar intent and effect is acceptable to banks in a letter of credit transaction unless the bank is instructed only to accept a shipped marine bill of lading; this applies even if the bill is in blank back form.[37]

FIATA combined transport bills of lading and house bills of lading

These documents are likewise used as container transport documents. They have been considered earlier.[38]

Definition of "package or unit" in container transport

The container itself, as distinguished from the individual cargoes contained therein, is normally shipped under an ordinary "shipped" bill

---

[34] *Encyclopaedia Britannica Inc.* v. *The Hong Kong Producer and Universal Marine Corpn.* [1969] 2 Lloyd's Rep. 536, 542.

[35] *Ibid.* p. 542.

[36] *J. Evans & Sons (Portsmouth) Ltd.* v. *Andrea Merzario Ltd.* [1976] 1 W.L.R. 1078; see p. 98, *ante*, where the case is treated fully.

[37] UCP (1983 Revision), Art. 25(b)(i) and (ii); see p. 413, *ante*.

[38] See p. 580, *ante*.

of lading. As far as the transport by sea is concerned, it is important to ascertain whether the whole container or each of the individual cargoes contained therein constitutes a "package or unit" within the meaning of the Hague-Visby Rules, Art. IV, r. 5, which provides a maximum limit of liability in favour of the carrier in case of loss or damage to such a package or unit.[39] The Rules attempt to solve this problem by providing in Article IV(5)(c) a container clause which was already cited earlier.[40]

In other words, according to the Hague-Visby Rules, the wording of the bill of lading issued by the carrier by sea is prima facie decisive. If the bill only refers to "one container said to contain (specified merchandise)," then the container itself shall be considered as the package or unit, but if it enumerates the cargoes included in the container separately, each of those cargoes shall constitute a separate package or unit. If the bill mentions specifically one or two cargoes but not the other contents of the container, the separately mentioned items are regarded as separate packages for the purposes of maximum limitation of liability, and the rest of the container falls under the general limitation. The English courts have not considered the interpretation of that clause yet.

The American courts held in *The Mormaclynx*[41] that bales of leather packed in a container were separate packages; the bill of lading referred to "1 container s.t.c. 99 bales of leather."[42] In *The Kulmerland*,[43] on the other hand, the American courts treated the container as the package or unit; in that case the bill of lading stated "1 container said to contain machinery," without "indication to the carrier of the number of cartons or the intention of the shipper to contract on that basis."[44]

It is thought that the English courts, if this question has to be decided by them, would be likely to consider the description of the goods in the bill of lading as the decisive element. This would be in accordance with the Hague-Visby Rules, Article IV, r. 5(c); it is the test applied by the

---

[39] See p. 602, *ante*.

[40] See p. 616, *ante*.

[41] *Leather's Best Inc.* v. *The Mormaclynx* [1970] 1 Lloyd's Rep. 527. This decision was followed in the Canadian case *The Tindefjell* [1973] 2 Lloyd's Rep. 253.

[42] The abbreviation "s.t.c." signifies "said to contain."

[43] *Royal Typewriter Co., Division Litton Business Systems Inc.* v. *M.V. Kulmerland and Hamburg-Amerika Linie* [1973] 2 Lloyd's Rep. 428. In *The Kulmerland* the American court did not consider the declaration of the goods in the bill of lading as the decisive criterion but attributed weight to the fact that the goods in the container were not packed for export ("the functional test") but Collier J. in *The Tindefjell* rightly referred to the vague declaration of the cargo in the bill issued in *The Kulmerland*. In another American case, *Insurance Company of North America* v. *S/S Brooklyn Maru, Japan Line Ltd.*; *The Brooklyn Maru* [1975] 2 Lloyd's Rep. 512, the court likewise applied the "functional economics" (*sic!*) test, but in later decisions, *e.g.* *Mitsui & Co. Ltd.* v. *American Lines* 1981 A.M.C. 331, 2nd Circuit (1981) the American courts abandoned the functional test because it penalised shippers who took advantage of the container by using lighter packaging for the goods carried therein; see Timothy J. Armstrong, "Packaging Trends and Implications in the Container Revolution" in 1981 *Journ. of Maritime Law and Commerce*, Vol. 12, p. 427.

[44] *Per* Collier J. in *The Tindefjell, supra*, p. 259.

Supreme Court of New South Wales in *The Esmeralda I*, and it probably reflects the intention of the parties. In other words, if the bill describes the goods as "a container s.t.c. (specified merchandise)," the container is the package, but if it refers to the goods, adding that they are packed in a container, "the goods" are the individual packages for the purposes of the Hague-Visby Rules.

An empty container was held to be a "consignment of goods" within the Conditions of Carriage of the Road Haulage Association (RHA).[45]

A roll-on/roll-off lorry or trailer or a LASH barge is not likely to be considered a "package" within Article IV r. (5)(c).[46]

---

[45] *Acme Transport Ltd.* v. *Betts* [1981] 1 Lloyd's Rep. 131.
[46] Scrutton, *op. cit.*, p. 455, n. 33.

Chapter 29

CARRIAGE OF GOODS BY AIR

THE air law relating to the carriage of goods has reached a considerable measure of international uniformity.

History of the Carriage by Air Acts 1932, 1961 and 1962

These three enactments, like the Carriage of Goods by Sea Acts 1924 and 1971, are the outcome of international negotiations. The Act of 1932 gave statutory effect, in the United Kingdom, to a Convention for the unification of certain rules relating to international air carriage which was signed in Warsaw in 1929.

Over the years it became evident that the Warsaw Convention required amendment. In particular, the limitation of liability in the event of death or injury of a passenger was found to be too low.[1] For that reason an amendment was agreed at The Hague, on September 28, 1955; the amendment is known as the Hague Protocol. The "Warsaw Convention, as amended at the Hague 1955" is scheduled to the Carriage by Air Act 1961 and came into force on June 1, 1967, in the United Kingdom, the Channel Isles, the Isle of Man and twenty British territories overseas.

The 1961 Act repeals the Carriage by Air Act 1932, but by means of an ingenious use of section 10 of the 1961 Act, provision is made to give effect to the unamended Convention in applicable cases.

The basic Convention regulates the legal liabilities and relationships between carriers by air on the one hand, and passengers as well as cargo consignors and consignees on the other. But neither the original nor the amended Warsaw Convention makes it clear whether the "carrier" referred to therein is the carrier in contractual relationship with the passenger or consignor, or whether it is the carrier who actually performs the carriage. It was therefore necessary to supplement the Warsaw Convention by a further Convention which was signed in 1961 at Guadalajara in Mexico. This supplementary Convention aims at the unification of certain rules relating to international carriage performed by a person other than the contracting carrier. The Guadalajara Convention

---

[1] See Harold Caplan, "Ratification of Hague Protocol by United Kingdom" in [1961] J.B.L. 170.

is embodied in the Carriage by Air (Supplementary Provisions) Act 1962 which applies to carriage governed by the original and the amended Warsaw Convention.[2]

The Carriage by Air and Road Act 1979 substitutes the Special Drawing Rights (SDRs) of the International Monetary Fund for the gold francs used in the Convention as determining the maximum limits of the air carrier's liability. This Act contains in Schedule 1 the text of the Warsaw Convention, as amended by the Hague Protocol of 1955 and Protocols Nos. 3 and 4 signed at Montreal in 1975, and in Schedule 2 the consequential amendments of the Acts of 1961 and 1962 but, at the date of writing[3] neither the 1979 Act, as far as air carriage is concerned, nor the two Schedules are in force yet; as far as non-Convention carriage is concerned, SDRs were substituted for gold francs with effect from October 4, 1985, but by virtue of the Carriage by Air Act 1961, and not by virtue of the 1979 Act.

Based on these international agreements, English statute law now provides a comprehensive but complex code of reasonable uniformity for the carriage of goods by air, so far as actions in the English courts are concerned, not only for so-called international carriage, which is the subject of the Conventions, but also for what will be referred to below as non-Convention carriage,[4] which includes carriage which in the ordinary sense of words is international but is not governed by the Conventions.

General introduction

The basic scheme of carrier's liability is uniform in all the three regimes recognised by English law which apply equally well to carriage for reward as to gratuitous carriage by an air transport undertaking. It is therefore convenient first to describe the basic system of liability and then to note the differences which exist in each of the three regimes, *viz.*—

1. carriage governed by the original Warsaw Convention;
2. carriage governed by the amended Convention;
3. non-Convention carriage.

Basic system of liability

The carrier of goods by air is automatically liable for destruction or loss of, or damage to or delay of cargo if it occurs during the carriage by air.

---

[2] The text of the unamended Warsaw Convention is contained in Sched. 2. to the Carriage by Air Acts (Application of Provisions) Order 1967 (S.I. 1967 No. 480) the Amended Convention, (*i.e.* the Warsaw Convention as amended by the Hague Protocol) and the Guadalajara Convention, with the exceptions, adaptations and modifications made in this Order are set out in Sched. 1 to the Order.

[3] Position: October 1, 1989.

[4] Often called "non-international carriage" because it is not "international" as defined in the Convention, see pp. 625 *post.*

The Convention, to which effect is given in the UK by the Carriage by Air Acts, creates a statutory right of action.[5] The carrier has the right to use specified defences if he can, but he cannot contract out of liability or for a lower limit of liability. In return for this liability the carrier can rely on the benefit of maximum limits for his liability, and even that liability arises only if the claimant can prove damage to that extent. The maximum limits of the air carrier's liability are—

250 gold francs per kilogramme; or

the value declared by the shipper for which any supplementary charge has been paid.

The franc, also known as the Poincaré gold franc, consists of $65\frac{1}{2}$ milligrammes of "gold of millesimal fineness nine hundred" and the current value of 250 francs is declared to be £13.63.[6]

When the relevant provisions of the Carriage by Air and Rail Act 1979 will have become operative, the maximum liability of the carrier will be limited to 17 Special Drawing Rights (SDRs) of the International Monetary Fund per kilogramme.[6a]

The carrier loses the benefit of the limits in the event of certain kinds of misconduct.

The persons who have rights of action are the consignor and the consignee, but the owner of the damaged or lost goods is likewise entitled to sue the carrier as his right of action is not expressly excluded by the Warsaw Convention.[7] It is thought, however, that the Convention provisions limiting the rights of the consignor and consignee to sue likewise apply to the right of action of the owner. In the absence of fraud by the carrier, these rights of action are only exercisable provided that written complaints are made to the carrier within specified time limits in cases of damage or delay. The right to damages is extinguished if an action is not brought within two years reckoned from the date of actual or expected arrival at destination, or the date on which carriage stopped. Receipt of cargo by the person entitled to delivery without complaint is prima facie evidence of delivery in good condition.

Damage during "carriage by air"

So far as the destruction, loss of or damage to cargo is concerned, "carriage by air" comprises the whole period during which the cargo is in

---

[5] Lloyd J. in *American Express Co* v. *British Airways Board* [1983] 1 W.L.R. 701, 707–708.
[6] The Carriage by Air (Sterling Equivalents) Order 1986 (S.I. 1986 No. 1778); it will be necessary to watch for further Sterling Equivalent Orders. Near note *4a*.
[6a] Carriage by Air and Road Act 1979, Schedule 1. This Schedule contains the Warsaw Convention as amended by the Hague Protocol of 1955 and by Protocols No. 3 and No. 4 signed at Montreal in 1975; Article 22A of the Convention deals with the maximum liability of the carrier, as expressed in SDRs. When the provisions of the Act have been put into operation with respect to carriage by air (see p. 621 *ante*), the conversion of SDRs into sterling on a particular day is done by obtaining a certificate relating to the converted sterling value from the Treasury (1979 Act, s.5).
[7] *Gatewhite Ltd.* v. *Iberia Lineas Aereas de Espana Sociedad* [1989] 1 Lloyd's Rep. 160.

the charge of the carrier, whether in an aerodrome or on board an aircraft, or in the case of landing outside an aerodrome in any place whatsoever. If surface carriage takes place outside an aerodrome for the purpose of loading, delivery or transhipment of air cargo, any damage is presumed to have taken place during the carriage by air, subject to contrary proof.

Carrier's defences

The carrier is not liable if he proves that he and his servants or agents[8] have taken all necessary[9] measures to avoid the damage or that it was impossible for him or them to take such measures.

If the carrier proves that the damage was caused or contributed to by the negligence of the injured person the court may exonerate the carrier wholly or partly.

There is nothing to prevent a carrier from refusing to enter into a contract of carriage or from making rules which do not conflict with the applicable law.

Carriers who may be sued

(a) *a successive carrier.* He is deemed to be a party to the original contract of carriage so far as is relevant to the carriage performed under his supervision.

(b) *the contracting carrier.* He, as a principal, makes an agreement for carriage with the consignor or the consignor's agent. In many cases the contracting carrier will be the first or sometimes the only carrier by air, but the contracting carrier may also be one who merely issues a waybill, or an aircraft charterer, or a cargo consolidator or forwarder.

(c) *the actual carrier.* By virtue of authority from the contracting carrier, he performs the whole or part of the carriage and is neither a successive carrier nor a contracting carrier.[10]

---

[8] s.29 of the Air Navigation Act 1936 substituted "servants and agents" for "agents" in the English text of the Warsaw Convention scheduled to the Carriage by Air Act 1932, thereby correcting an error in the translation of *préposés* which appeared in the authentic French text of the Convention. The correction has been continued in force by the Carriage by Air Act 1961 and Orders made thereunder.

[9] Interpreted as reasonably necessary by Greer L.J. in *Grein* v. *Imperial Airways Ltd.* [1937] 1 K.B. 50, 69–71.

[10] See p. 620, *ante.*

Who may sue

(a) The consignor has a right of action against the first carrier and the carrier who performed the carriage during which destruction, loss, damage or delay took place (the performing carrier) unless the first carrier has expressly assumed liability for the whole carriage.

(b) The consignee has a right of action against the last carrier and the performing carrier.

(c) The owner of the damaged, or lost goods has a right of action against the performing carrier.

(d) The first carrier, the performing carrier and the last carrier are jointly and severally liable respectively to the consignor and the consignee.

(e) The contracting carrier is liable for the whole of the carriage.

(f) The actual carrier is only liable for the part performed by him.

(g) At the plaintiff's option, written complaints may be made and actions may be brought against either the actual carrier or the contracting carrier or against both together or separately.

Servants and agents of the carrier acting within the scope of their employment can claim the benefit of the limits of liability applicable to the carrier.[11] Acts and omissions of the actual carrier, including his servants and agents, are deemed to be those of the contracting carrier and vice versa, but the actual carrier's liability cannot exceed 250 gold francs per kilogramme or, when the 1979 Act will be operative, 17 SDRs per kilogramme by reason of—

(i) any act or omission of the contracting carrier;
(ii) any special agreement entered into by the contracting carrier; or
(iii) special declarations of value made to the contracting carrier,

unless in cases (ii) and (iii) the actual carrier has agreed to be bound.

When do the various regimes apply?

It is no longer a straightforward matter to determine when the various regimes apply, but the following may assist. Carriage of cargo for reward by aircraft or gratuitous air carriage by an air transport undertaking is governed by:

---

[11] Internationally this is a feature of the amended Convention, but it was applied to actions arising in the English courts by s.4 of the Carriage by Air (Supplementary Provisions) Act 1962, now continued for this purpose in Art. 25A of Part B of Sched. 2 to the Carriage of Air Acts (Application of Provisions) Order 1967 (S.I. 1967 No. 480).

1. *The original Warsaw Convention*[12]

When, according to the contract between the parties, the places of departure and destination (regardless of breaks, miscarriage,[13] transshipment or numbers of consecutive contracts or successive carriers) are located—

> either in the territories of two State parties to the original Convention; or
> in the territory of a single such State with an agreed stopping place anywhere outside that State.

However, the original Convention does not apply to carriage "with a view to the establishment of a regular line of air navigation" or carriage "in extraordinary circumstances outside the normal scope of an air carrier's business."[14]

2. *The amended Convention*[15]

When, according to the agreement between the parties, the places of departure and destination (regardless of breaks, transshipment or numbers of consecutive contracts or successive carriers) are located—

> either in the territories of two States both of which are parties to the amended Convention;
> or in the territory of a single State party to the amended Convention with an agreed stopping place anywhere outside that State.

Difficulties can arise when, *e.g.* the place of departure is in the territory of a State party to the original Convention, (*e.g.* USA) whilst the place of destination is in the territory of a State which is not only a party to the original Convention but has also become a party to the amended Convention (*e.g.* the UK). In such circumstances, the only obligations which bind both of the States concerned are those contained in the original Convention.

For the purposes of actions in the English courts, the Carriage by Air (Parties to Conventions) Orders[16] certify those States and their associated

---

[12] Sched. 2 to the Carriage by Air Acts (Application of Provisions) Order 1967.
[13] See *Rotterdamsche Bank N.V.* v. *B.O.A.C.* [1953] 1 W.L.R. 493.
[14] There is no similar reservation of such a wide scope in the amended Convention.
[15] s.1 and 1st Sched. to the Carriage by Air Act 1961.
[16] The Carriage by Air (Parties to Convention) Order 1977 (S.I. 1977, No. 240); the Carriage by Air (Parties to Convention) (Supplementary) Order 1977 (S.I. 1977 No. 1631); and the Carriage by Air (Parties to Convention) (Supplementary) Order 1978 (S.I. 1978 No. 1058). These Orders are too lengthy to be reproduced here.

territories which are parties to either or both the original and the amended Conventions.[17]

3. *The non-Convention rules*

When the carriage of cargo is governed neither by the original nor by the amended Convention, *e.g.* if the place of destination is in Peru (party to neither Convention) and there is no agreed stopping place in another State then, whatever the place of departure, no part of the carriage would, as a matter of law, be governed by either of the two Conventions, and in an action before the English courts the carriage would be governed by the non-Convention rules, even though the carriage is international in the ordinary meaning of that word but not within the technical meaning which governs the applicability of the two Conventions. But the non-Convention rules do not apply to purely internal flights, *i.e.* flights where the contract of carriage is made and to be performed wholly within the territory of one State.[18] In these cases the law of the country in question applies or, where that law allows, the law chosen by the parties as the proper law of the contract.

The non-Convention rules also govern[19] carriage of mail or postal packages[20] presumably of both a domestic and an international character.

Each regime contains variations on the basic system of liability as follows:

Carriage governed by the original Warsaw Convention

Document of carriage

The document of carriage is called the *air consignment note* (ACN). The carrier has the right to require the consignor to make out an air consignment note and to require a separate one for each package, and the carrier is required to accept it. Nevertheless, the absence, irregularity or loss of the document does not affect the validity of the contract or the operation of the Convention rules. The ACN is not a document of title.

---

[17] *Phillipson* v. *Imperial Airways Ltd.* [1939] A.C. 332 has very little practical application today.
[18] *Holmes* v. *Bangladesh Biman Corporation* [1989] 2 W.L.R. 481 (passenger killed in air crash on purely internal Bangladesh flight; the House of Lords held that the contract of carriage was govered by Bangladesh law and that the Order of 1967 did not apply).
[19] Sched. 1 to the Carriage by Air Acts (Application of Provisions) Order 1967.
[20] Art. 4 of the Carriage by Air Acts (Application of Provisions) Order 1967.

Each air consignment note must be in three original parts and handed over with the goods. The First Part is marked "for the carrier" and signed by the consignor; the Second Part, marked "for the consignee," is signed by the consignor and accompanies the goods; the Third Part is signed by the carrier and handed to the consignor after the goods have been accepted for carriage. The consignor must furnish the additional information and documents necessary for Customs and police purposes before the goods can be delivered to the consignee and the consignor is liable to the carrier for any damage arising out of the absence or irregularity of such information or documents. This obligation of the consignor extends also to particulars and statements inserted by him in the air consignment note, and if the carrier makes out the air consignment note at the request of the consignor, he is deemed to have done so as the consignor's agent.

But if the carrier accepts goods without an air consignment note or if the air consignment note does not contain any of the following particulars, then he cannot take advantage of the provisions of the Convention which would otherwise exclude or limit the carrier's liability:

(*a*) place and date of execution of the air consignment note;
(*b*) places of departure and destination;
(*c*) agreed stopping places (which the carrier may alter in case of necessity);
(*d*) name and address of consignor;
(*e*) name and address of first carrier;
(*f*) name and address of consignee "if the case so requires" [*sic*];
(*g*) nature of the goods;
(*h*) number of packages, method of packing and the particular marks or numbers on them;
(*i*) either the weight, quantity, volume or dimensions of the goods,[21]
(*j*) a statement that the carriage is subject to the rules relating to liability established by the Convention.[22]

The air consignment note and the statements therein are prima facie evidence of the conclusion of the contract, receipt of the goods, the conditions of carriage, the weight, dimensions, packing and number of goods. Statements relating to quantity, volume or condition are not evidence against the carrier unless expressly stated on the air consignment note to have been either checked in the presence of the consignor or they relate to apparent condition.

Basic liability

In addition to the two basic defences, the carrier is not liable if he can prove that "the damage was occasioned by negligent pilotage or negli-

---

[21] The Court of Appeal decided to follow the original French text and the American translation and concluded that only *one* of these particulars need be given: *Corocraft Ltd.* v. *Pan American World Airways Inc.* [1969] 1 Q.B. 616.

[22] The formula used in IATA tickets and waybills is "Carriage hereunder is subject to the rules relating to liability established by the Warsaw Convention unless such carriage is not 'international carriage' as defined by the Convention." This formula has been approved in an American case, *Seth* v. *B.O.A.C.* [1964] 1 Lloyd's Rep. 268, and an English case, *Samuel Montagu & Co. Ltd.* v. *Swissair* [1965] 2 Lloyd's Rep. 363.

gence in the handling of the aircraft or in navigation and that in all other respects he and his agents have taken all necessary measures to avoid the damage." This defence is never used because it is not available in case of injury or death of passengers, and to raise this defence for cargo might give rise to unlimited liability for passengers under Article 25. This Article, as worded in the unamended Warsaw Convention, denies the carrier reliance on the maximum limits of liability if he or his servants or agents were guilty of "wilful misconduct."[23] The exception of Article 25 is also important for the air carriage of goods. In one case[24] two boxes of platinum were sent by air from South Africa to Philadelphia. The contract of air carriage was governed by the unamended Warsaw Convention. The platinum was transferred at Heathrow, London, from a South African plane to a plane bound for the USA. On this occasion, as the trial judge found, one of the boxes of platinum was stolen by one or several of the loaders. The Court of Appeal held that the plaintiffs, who were the owners, consignors and consignees, were entitled by way of damages to the full value of the platinum and that the carriers could not rely on the maximum limits of the Convention because the theft of the platinum by the loaders was "wilful misconduct" on the part of the loaders for which the carriers were liable.

When calculating the carrier's limits of liability (250 gold francs [or, when the 1979 Act will be operative, 17 SDRs] per kilogramme) under the unamended Warsaw Convention, the weight of the damaged package ("Package weight") alone is decisive, whereas under the amended Convention[25] the weight of other parts of the cargo covered by the same air waybill and affected by the value of the damaged package ("affected weight") may also be taken into account.[26]

Special rights of consignor and consignee

Unless varied by express provision in the air consignment note, the consignor and the consignee have the following rights:

The consignor—

(a) has the right of disposal prior to delivery to the consignee, subject to the production of the consignor's copy of the air consignment note to the carrier and payment of all expenses involved; and

---

[23] The wording of Article 25 in the amended Warsaw Convention is different and the term "wilful misconduct" in not used therein.
[24] *Rustenburg Platinum Mines Ltd. etc.* v. *South African Airways, etc.* [1979] 1 Lloyd's Rep. 19. For the definition of "recklessness" (which term is used in Art. 25 of the amended Convention but which does not appear in the unamended Convention) see *Goldman* v. *Thai Airways International Ltd.* [1983] 1 W.L.R. 1186 (C.A.).
[25] By virtue of Art. 22(2) of the amended Convention.
[26] *Datacard Corpn.* v. *Air Express International Corpn.* [1984] 1 W.L.R. 198.

(*b*) may enforce rights in his own name even if acting in the interests of another, subject to the fulfilment of all obligations of the consignor under the contract of carriage.

The consignee—

(*a*) has the right to require the carrier to hand over goods and the air consignment note on arrival at the destination on payment of proper charges and compliance with any other conditions set out in the air consignment note; and
(*b*) may enforce rights in his own name even if acting in the interests of another, subject to the fulfilment of all obligations of the consignor under the contract of carriage.

Complaints and actions

(*a*) Unless otherwise stated in the air consignment note the consignee can exercise his rights if the carrier admits loss of the goods or if they have not arrived seven days after they should have arrived.
(*b*) Complaints by the person entitled to delivery must be made in writing either upon the air consignment note or separately:

in cases of damage: forthwith after discovery, or at the latest within seven days of receipt,[27]
in cases of delay: within 14 days from the date on which the goods were placed at his disposal.[28]

Carriage governed by the amended Warsaw Convention

Document of carriage

The document of carriage is called an *air waybill* (AWB). All the provisions of the original Convention relating to the air consignment note apply to the air waybill under the amended Convention with the most important exception of the particulars to appear therein and the penalties for omission.

If, *with the consent of the carrier,* cargo is loaded on board[29] without an air waybill or if the air waybill does not contain a notice to the consignor

---

[27] "damage" includes partial loss: *Fothergill* v. *Monarch Airlines Ltd.* [1981] A.C. 251. *Cf.* also *Rothmans of Pall Mall (Overseas) Ltd.* v. *Saudi Arabian Airlines Corpn.* [1981] Q.B. 368.
[28] On the calculation of damages for delay see *Panalpina International Transport Ltd.* v. *Densil Underwear Ltd.* [1981] 2 Lloyd's Rep. 187.
[29] The unamended Convention, as scheduled to the Carriage by Air Act 1932, says "accepted."

"to the effect that, if the carriage involves an ultimate destination or stop in a country other than the country of departure, the Warsaw Convention may be applicable and that the Convention governs and in most cases limits the liability of carriers in respect of loss of or damage to cargo,"[30] then, in either of these circumstances, the carrier cannot take advantage of the limits of liability. The carrier will not suffer these consequences if the carriage is "performed in extraordinary circumstances outside the normal scope of an air carrier's business."

It is stated expressly in the amended Convention that nothing therein "prevents the issue of a negotiable air waybill," but equally well there was nothing in the original Convention to prevent the issue of a negotiable air consignment note. The fact is that the speed of air transport has largely eliminated the need for a negotiable document of carriage, and waybills in practice are printed "not negotiable."

Basic liability

There are no defences in addition to the basic two: the defence of negligent pilotage has been dropped.

Servants and agents of the carrier enjoy the benefit of the same limits of liability as the carrier if they have acted in the course of their employment. The aggregate liability of a carrier, his servants and agents cannot exceed the limit (if a limit applies).

When calculating the limits of liability, the weight to be used is the weight of the package or packages concerned, and not necessarily the weight of all packages recorded on the same air waybill, unless the loss, damage or delay of one package affects the value of others on the same air waybill.[31]

The carrier may insert contractual provisions relieving him of liability or fixing a lower limit in respect of inherent defect, quality or vice of the cargo carried. Arbitration clauses are allowed if arbitration is to take place within one of the jurisdictions allowed by the Convention.

The nature of the misconduct which will disentitle the carrier from relying on the limits of liability has been re-defined.[32]

Special rights of consignor and consignee

These have not been varied in the amended Convention.

---

[30] Amended Convention, Arts. 8(c) and 9. The notice quoted in the text appears on the reverse side of the latest IATA air waybill, on the face of it is stated in large letters: "Subject to the conditions of contract on the reverse hereof. The shipper's attention is drawn to the notice concerning the carrier's limitation of liability."

[31] See pp. 628 *ante*. On the calculation of weight when part of a passenger's baggage is lost and the weight of the lost part is unknown, see *Bland* v. *British Airways* [1981] 1 Lloyd's Rep. 289.

[32] See p. 628 *ante*.

Complaints and actions

The time limits for written complaints by the person entitled to delivery have been varied as follows:

in cases of damage: the maximum is increased from 7 to 14 days,[33]
in cases of delay: the maximum is increases from 14 to 21 days.

Non-Convention carriage

The basic system of liability including limits and times within which written complaint must be made for non-Convention carriage[34] is exactly the same as those in the amended Convention, but there are no provisions whatsoever relating to documents of carriage or what has been described above as Special Rights of Consignor and Consignee.

The non-Convention rules were also applied to the *carriage of mail or postal packages* because it became clear that at common law the sender of an airmail package had a right of direct action without any limitation of liability against the air carrier[35]; the particular case involved carriage between London and Kuwait which would not have been governed by the original Warsaw Convention even if the package had been ordinary cargo instead of airmail because Kuwait was not then a party to the Convention. In any event, the unamended Convention "does not apply to carriage performed under the terms of any international postal Convention" and the amended Convention "shall not apply to carriage of mail and postal packages." The point has now been dealt with by section 29(3) of the Post Office Act 1969 which protects the Post Office, its officers and persons "engaged in or about the carriage of mail" from civil liability for loss of or damage to a postal packet.[36] It has been held that an airline, which carried mail, could claim the protection of this section; in this case[37] American Express sent a postal packet containing travellers' cheques from Brighton, England, to a bank in Swaziland. The Post Office sent a sealed mailbag containing this consignment to British Airways at Heathrow airport in London for carriage to Johannesburg and on carriage to

---

[33] On partial loss, see *Fothergill* v. *Monarch Airlines Ltd.* [1981] A.C. 25 and p. 629 *ante*.
[34] The rules applicable here are contained in Sched. 1 to the Carriage by Air Acts (Application of Provisions) Order 1967.
[35] *Moukataff* v. *B.O.A.C.* [1967] 1 Lloyd's Rep. 396, in which the senders of £20,000 in bank notes to Kuwait recovered the missing balance of over £17,000 from B.O.A.C. by reason of the theft of the money from a sealed mailbag by a B.O.A.C. employee who was convicted of the offence.
[36] Section 33 of the Post Office Act 1969 imposes a limited liability in respect of registered inland packets.
[37] *American Express Co.* v. *British Airways Board* [1983] 1 W.L.R. 701.

Swaziland. The packet containing the traveller's cheques was stolen at the airport by a loader who was later convicted of theft. In proceedings by the American Express the defendant airline pleaded successfully the protection of section 29(3). As the immunity from suit provided by this section is total, it cannot be said that this regulation is satisfactory but it should not be overlooked that it is laid down in an Act of Parliament.

For non-convention carriage, Special Drawing Rights (SDRs) are already substituted for gold francs.[38]

IATA carriage

A further measure of uniformity in the rules relating to cargo is introduced by the practices of members of the International Air Transport Association (IATA) who have for over 40 years been using a common form of air waybill and associated conditions of contract which appear on the reverse of the three Original copies, all of which have been revised from time to time. The IATA style of waybill and conditions of contract are used by IATA members for interline and online carriage, and also by non-members who either participate in interline carriage involving IATA members or merely wish to adopt the international standards set by IATA members. The format of the IATA air waybill is designed, amongst other things, to facilitate production of a copy air waybill which can easily be transmitted by electronic means but is not a document of significance for legal purposes.

IATA conditions of contract cannot in any way derogate from the provisions of either the original or the amended Convention. Sample copies of the latest forms are freely made available to exporters on application to the leading IATA airlines.

Condition No. 4 of the IATA Conditions provides that in non-Convention situations, except as otherwise provided in the carrier's tariffs or the conditions of carriage, the carrier's liability shall not exceed US $20.00 or the equivalent per kilogramme of goods lost, damaged or delayed, in the absence of any declared value. The maximum limit of US $20.00 is intended to be an approximation to the Convention limit of 250 gold francs per kilogramme. Thus, for all practical purposes, the Convention limits prevail in all but the most rare of situations internationally and are applied by law and by contract to all actions in the English courts, except if the flight is a purely internal flight[39] Thus, a contract for the carriage of passengers or cargo from London to Manchester would be

---

[38] The Carriage by Air Acts (Application of Provisions) (Second Amendment) Order 1979 (S.I. 1979 No. 931).
[39] See p. 626, *ante*.

governed neither by the Convention (in its amended or unamended form), nor by the non-Convention Rules, but it would be governed by its contractual terms which would be subject to the provisions of the Unfair Contract Terms Act 1977.

Extension to territories overseas

By means of a series of Orders in Council, the system of law for carriage by air described above for the United Kingdom has been extended to[40]—

the Channel Isles, the Isle of Man, Bermuda, British Antarctic Territory, Belize (British Honduras), British Indian Ocean Territory, British Virgin Islands, Cayman Islands, Central and Southern Line Islands, Cyprus (only in the sovereign base areas of Akrotiri and Dhekelia), Falkland Islands and Dependencies, Gilbert and Ellice Islands Colony, Hong Kong, Montserrat, St. Helena and Ascension, Turks and Caicos Islands (now Kiribati).

---

[40] Position: October 1, 1989. The substitution of SDRs for gold francs in non-international carriage was done by the Carriage by Air (Sterling Equivalents) (No. 2) Order 1985 (S.I. 1985/1428), which was made under s.10 of the 1961 Act and came into operation on October 4, 1985. For overseas territories SDRs were likewise substituted; see Carriage by Air Acts (Application of Provisions) (Overseas Territories) (Amendment) Order 1984 (S.I. 1984 No. 701).

CHAPTER 30

CARRIAGE OF GOODS BY LAND

CARRIAGE BY RAIL AND ROAD

THE international transport of goods overland is carried out by rail or road. Both modes of transport are regulated by international Conventions.

International transport of goods by rail is governed by the International Convention concerning the Carriage of Goods by Rail (CIM)[1] of February 25, 1961. This Convention was given statutory force in the United Kingdom by the Carriage by Railway Act 1972 but this Act was repealed by the *International Transport Conventions Act 1983* which continued to give effect to the CIM as part of the Convention Concerning International Carriage by Rail (COTIF) signed at Berne on May 9, 1980; CIM is appended to this Convention as *Uniform Rules concerning the Contract for International Carriage of Goods by Rail (CIM).*[2] The 1983 Act and, as far as the United Kingdom is concerned, COTIF, came into operation on May 1, 1985.[3]

International transport of goods by road is governed by the *Convention on the Contract for the International Carriage of Goods by Road (CMR),*[4] signed at Geneva on May 19, 1956. Effect was given to it in the United Kingdom by the *Carriage of Goods by Road Act 1965* which embodies the CMR in its Schedule.[5] The 1965 Act came into operation on June 5, 1967.[6]

The Parties to COTIF include practically all European countries, with the notable exception of the Soviet Union, and also some Asian and African countries.[7]

---

[1] For the meaning of this acronym, which is derived from the French title of the Convention, see p. 537, *ante.*
[2] The 1983 Act incorporates Cmnd. 8535 (1982), which contains COTIF; CIM is Appendix B of the COTIF, reproduced in Cmnd. 8535 on pp. 107 *et. seq.*
[3] The International Transport Conventions Act 1983 (Certification of Commencement of Convention) Order 1985 (S.I. 1985 No. 612).
[4] See *supra,* n.1.
[5] The 1965 Act is amended by the Carriage by Air and Road Act 1979 which replaces the references to gold francs in the CMR by references to SDRs.
[6] Carriage of Goods by Road Act 1965 (Commencement) Order 1967 (S.I. 1967 No. 819). The application of the 1965 Act has been extended by virtue of section 9 of the Act to Gibraltar, the Isle of Man and Guernsey.
[7] Position: October 1, 1989.

It is not intended in this work to discuss the CIM. It is, however, necessary to give an account of the main provisions of the CMR, and this for two reasons. First, the carriage of export goods overland in lorries or trailers[8] is of frequent occurrence. Secondly, the CMR has often given rise to legal disputes, and cases concerning the interpretation of its provisions or its application have often been considered by the courts.

THE CMR

Scope of application

The CMR[9] applies to every contract for the carriage of goods by road in vehicles[10] for reward, when the place of taking over the goods and the place designed for delivery, as specified in the contract, are situated in two different countries[11] of which at least one is a Contracting Party,[12] *i.e.* a State which has accepted the Convention. All the Contracting Parties are Euopean States. The are[13]:

> Austria, Belgium, Bulgaria, Czechoslovakia, Denmark, Finland, France, Federal Republic of Germany, German Democratic Republic, Greece, Hungary, Italy, Luxembourg, The Netherlands, Norway, Poland, Portugal, Romania, Spain, Sweden, Switzerland, United Kingdom of Great Britain and Northern Ireland and Yugoslavia.

It should be noted that the Convention does not require that both the countries of despatch and of destination should be Contracting Parties. A contract for the consignment by road of goods from the United Kingdom (a Contracting Party) to Saudi Arabia (not a Contracting Party) is governed by the CMR.

The Convention also applies where the carriage is carried out by States or by governmental institutions or organisations.[14] For the purposes of

---

[8] The various types of trailers, semi-trailers, super trailers and road trains are described in *Understanding the Freight Business,* (3rd ed., 1984), pp. 43 *et seq.,* published by Thomas Meadows & Co. Ltd.

[9] For further reading: D. J. Hill and A. D. Messent, *CMR: Contracts for the International Carriage of Goods by Road* (1984); Malcolm A. Clarke, *International Carriage of Goods by Road: CMR* (1982); Malcolm A. Clarke, "Containers; Proof that Damage occurred during Carriage," in *International Carriage of Goods: Some Legal Problems and Possible Solutions* (ed. C. M. Schmitthoff and R. M. Goode), 1988, 64; David A. Glass and Chris Cashmore, *Introduction to the Carriage of Goods,* 1989, ch. 3.

[10] "Vehicles" includes articulated vehicles, trailers and semi-trailers; Art. 1(2).

[11] For the purposes of the Convention, Jersey is not a "different country" from the United Kingdom: *Chloride Industrial Batteries Ltd.* v. *F. & W. Freight Ltd.* [1989] 1 W.L.R. 45.

[12] Art. 1(1).

[13] s.2 of the Act and Carriage of Goods by Road (Parties to the Convention) (Amendment) Order 1980 (S.I. 1980 No. 697). The Soviet Union became a Contracting Party of the CMR on September 2, 1983 but no S.I. has been made in the UK amending in this respect, the S.I. of 1980. (But the Soviet Union is not a member of COTIF).

[14] Art. 1(3) and s.6 of the Act.

any proceedings brought in a court in the United Kingdom under the Convention, a party to a contract of carriage to which the CMR applies is deemed to have submitted to the jurisdiction of the court,[15] and the same applies as regards submission to arbitration.[16] The Crown is bound by the Act.[17] The CMR does not apply to traffic between the United Kingdom and the Irish Republic.[17] Further, the CMR does not apply[18]:

   (*a*) to carriage performed under an international postal Convention;
   (*b*) to funeral consignments; or
   (*c*) to furniture removal.

The CMR further provides that, where the vehicle containing the goods is carried over part of the journey by sea, rail, inland waterways or air and, except in cases of emergency, the goods are not unloaded from the vehicle, the CMR shall apply to the whole of the carriage. The CMR thus applies in the frequent cases in which a container, particularly a groupage container, is taken by road on a trailer or similar vehicle from the territory of a Contracting Party to another country. But if the loss, damage or delay has occurred during the carriage by the other means of transport and was not caused by an act or omission of the carrier by road, the liability of the carrier by road is determined not by the CMR but by the applicable international Convention[19]; if there is no such Convention, the CMR applies. These provisions were applied in *Thermo Engineers Ltd.* v. *Ferrymasters Ltd.*,[20] a case which was discussed earlier.[21]

Successive carriers

The CMR provides in Article 34 that, if the carriage by road is governed by a single contract but performed by successive road carriers, each shall be responsible for the performance of the whole operation, the second and each successive carrier becoming a party to the contract of

---

[15] s.7 and Art. 33.
[16] s.13.
[17] Protocol of Signature, attached to the Act.
[18] Art. 1(4).
[19] Art. 2(1).
[20] [1981] 1 Lloyd's Rep. 200.
[21] See p. 22, *ante*.

carriage, under the terms of the consignment note,[22] but, except in the case of a counterclaim or set-off, legal proceedings in respect of liability for loss, damage or delay may only be brought against the first carrier, the last carrier or the carrier who was in control of the goods when the event which caused the loss, damage or delay occurred, but several carriers may be sued at the same time.[23] In the case of successive carriers the one responsible for the loss or damage is, as between the carriers, solely liable for compensation but if it cannot be ascertained to which carrier liability is attributable, the compensation has to be borne by them proportionally.[24] If one of the carriers is insolvent, the share of compensation due from him has to be paid by the other carriers in proportion to the share of the payment for the carriage due to them.[25]

It is not always easy to decide whether the person with whom the owner of the goods contracts undertakes only to *procure* carriage, *i.e.* to act as a forwarder, or whether he contracts to *carry*, *i.e.* to act as carrier, even if he sub-contracts the actual carriage to somebody else.[26] In the former case the CMR does not apply to him but in the latter case it does. If a person has contracted to carry the goods to their destination by a single contract but does not take the goods into charge himself and arranges for them to be delivered directly to the actual carrier to whom he has sub-contracted the job, he is nevertheless the first carrier and the actual carrier is the successive carrier within article 34 of the CMR. Apart from the contract of carriage with the first carrier, in the words of Megaw L.J.,[27] "the CMR Convention then sets out to create an artifical statutory

---

[22] Art. 34. A "single contract performed by successive carriers" within Art. 34 is a contract under which a *single* consignment note is issued. If a consignment is split into several parcels and separate consignment notes are issued, one for each parcel, the carriers carrying these separate parcels are not "successive carriers" within Art. 34: *Arctic Electronics Co. (UK) Ltd.* v. *McGregor Sea & Air Services Ltd.* [1985] 2 Lloyd's Rep. 510. This issue is of particular importance if the question of jurisdiction of the English courts under Art. 39(2) arises; see later in the text.

"Where there are successive CMR carriers, a CMR carrier successfully sued by the sender or consignee can recover against a CMR carrier responsible for the loss or damage, but that carrier cannot escape liability by showing that he has delegated or sub-contracted performance to a non-CMR carrier who was actually responsible": Bingham L.J. in *ITT Schaub-Lorenz Vertriebsgesellschaft mbH* v. *Birkart Johann Internationale Spedition GmbH & Co. KG.* [1988] 1 Lloyd's Rep. 487, 493.

[23] Art. 36. Despite of the wording of Art. 36, the general rule, known as the rule in *Aries Tanker Corporation* v. *Total Transport Ltd.* [1977] 1 W.L.R. 185 (see p. 558, *ante*), that a claim in respect of loss of or damage to the cargo cannot be asserted by way of deduction from freight, likewise applies to freight due under a contract of carriage to which the CMR applies: *R. H. & D. International Ltd.* v. *I.A.S. Animal Air Services Ltd.* [1984] 1 W.L.R. 573.

[24] Art. 37.

[25] Art. 38. Art. 39(2) deals with the forum in which the carrier who has paid the goods owner can bring proceedings for recovery against the carriers concerned, who were responsible for the loss, damage or delay, see *Cummins Engine Co. Ltd.* v. *Davis Freight Forwarding (Hull) Ltd.* [1981] 1 W.L.R. 1363, (C.A.).

[26] For a discussion of this question and the relevant decisions of the courts see "The forwarder acting as principal or as agent," on p. 302, *ante*.

[27] In *Ulster Swift Ltd.* v. *Taunton Meat Haulage Ltd.* [1977] 1 Lloyd's Rep. 346, 360–361.

contract between the actual carrier and the owner of the goods." The learned judge continued:

> Looking at article 1(1), I think that the CMR Convention must have contemplated that for this purpose the company, or individual, with whom the owner of the goods contracts is the first carrier, whether or not he himself takes possession of the goods, and that all subsequent carriers are the successive carriers within the meaning of these provisions.

On the other hand, if the owner of the goods himself contracts with several contractors, each for a part of the journey, there is no single contract of carriage with the first contractor and the rules of the CMR on successive contractors do not apply, although the Convention may apply to the individual carriers.

The consignment note

The CMR provides that the contract of carriage by road shall be confirmed by a consignment note but that the absence of, or any irregularity in, the note shall not affect the validity of the contract which will remain subject to the Convention.[28] The consignment note has to be made out in three original copies signed by the sender and the carrier. The first copy is handed to the sender, the second accompanies the goods, and the third is retained by the carrier. When goods are carried in different vehicles or are of a different kind or are divided into different lots the seller or the carrier is entitled to require a separate consignment note for each vehicle or each kind or lot of goods.[29] The consignment note is not a negotiable instrument, nor a document of title.

The consignment note is prima facie evidence of the making of the contract of carriage, the conditions of the contract and the receipt of the goods by the carrier.[30] If the consignment note does not contain a clausing relating to the condition of the goods, when received by the carrier, it is presumed—though not irrebuttably—that the goods and their packaging appeared to be in good order and condition and that, when the carrier took them over, their marks and numbers corresponded with the statements in the consignment note.[31]

For the purposes of the Customs or other formalities which have to be completed before delivery of the goods, the sender shall attach the necessary documents to the consignment note or place them at the

---

[28] Art. 4. The consignment note is sometimes described by the parties inaccurately as "shipping certificate" or even as "bill of lading."
[29] Art. 5.
[30] Art. 9(1).
[31] Art. 9(2).

disposal of the carrier and shall furnish him with all the information which he requires.[32]

The sender is entitled to dispose of the goods, in particular by asking the carrier to stop the goods in transit, to change the place at which delivery is to take place, or to deliver the goods to a person other than the consignee designated in the consignment note,[33] but that right ceases when the second copy of the consignment note has been handed over to the designated consignee or that consignee has required the carrier, against his receipt, to deliver up to him the second copy of the consignment note and the goods.[34] Furthermore, the consignee is entitled to dispose of the goods already from the time when the consignment note is drawn up, if the sender has made an entry to that effect on the consignment note.[35] If the sender, in exercising his right of disposal, has ordered the delivery of the goods to another person, that person is not entitled to name another consignee.[36] The sender who wishes to exercise the right of disposal, has to produce the first copy of the consignment note to the carrier and the new instructions must be entered thereon; he must further give the carrier an indemnity and a division of the cargo on such a diversion is not permissible.[37] The right of the sender to stop the goods in transit given by these provisions should not be confused with the right of stoppage in transit of the seller under the contract of sale.[38] The right under the CMR exists against the carrier and is not dependent on the insolvency of the buyer but the right under the Sale of Goods Act 1979 exists against the buyer and can be exercised only if the buyer has become insolvent.

When circumstances prevent delivery of the goods after their arrival at the place of destination, the carrier shall ask the sender for his instructions. If the consignee refuses to accept the goods, the sender is entitled to dispose of them without being obliged to produce the first copy of the consignment note, but in spite of his refusal the consignee may still require delivery as long as the carrier has not received instructions to the contrary from the seller.[39]

Liability of the carrier

The carrier is liable for the total or partial loss[40] of the goods and for damage thereto occurring between the time when he takes over the goods

---

[32] Art. 11.
[33] Art. 12(1).
[34] Art. 12(2) and Art. 13.
[35] Art. 12(3).
[36] Art. 12(4).
[37] Art. 12(5).
[38] See p. 150, *ante.*
[39] Art. 15.
[40] On the meaning of "total loss" in the CMR see p. 642, *post.*

and the time of delivery, as well as for delay in the delivery.[41] But the carrier is relieved of liability if the loss, damage or delay was caused:

1. by the wrongful act or neglect of the claimant; or
2. by the instructions of the claimant given otherwise than as the result of a wrongful act or neglect on the part of the carrier; or
3. by inherent vice of the goods; or
4. through circumstances which the carrier could not avoid and the consequences of which he was unable to prevent.[42]

If the carrier wishes to rely on the fourth of these relieving grounds, it is not sufficient for him to show that he did not act negligently; he has to show that the loss *could not be avoided*.[43] In one case[44] the carrier, who was driving a consignment of shoes from Milan to England, parked the lorry in an unguarded lorry park in Milan in order for him and his assistant to have a meal. The only guarded lorry park was two hours away and to drive there would have involved breaking the driving period regulations. The alarm on the lorry was left on but thieves managed to by-pass it and to steal the lorry and its load. The carrier was held to be liable to the owner of the shoes because the loss was avoidable; he and his assistant could have taken turns to guard the lorry.

The carrier cannot rely on any of the relieving events if the loss, damage or delay is caused by the defective condition of the vehicle,[45] *e.g.* if the tilt cover of the vehicle is porous and, as a result of it, the load is damaged by rain.[46] Further, the carrier is not relieved of liability by reason of the wrongful act or neglect of the person from whom he may have hired the vehicle or of the agents or servants of the latter.[47]

In addition, the CMR contains a catalogue of special risks which relieve the carrier from liability; among them are the use of open unsheeted vehicles when their use has been expressly agreed and specified in the consignment note.[48] The burden of proving that loss, damage or delay was due to one of the exempting causes specified in article 17(2) rests on the carrier.[49] If the carriage is performed in vehicles specially equipped to protect the goods from the effects of heat, cold, variation in temperature or the humidity of the air, the carrier cannot claim the benefit of the special risks exemptions otherwise applicable unless he proves that all steps incumbent on him in the circumstances with respect to the choice,

---

[41] Art. 17(1).
[42] Art. 17(2).
[43] The burden of proving that the loss could not be avoided rests on the carrier: Art. 18(1).
[44] *Michael Galley Footwear Ltd. (in liq.)* v. *Laboni* [1982] 2 All E.R. 200. Also *J. J. Silber Ltd.* v. *Islander Trucking Ltd.* [1985] 2 Lloyd's Rep. 243 (armed robbery in Italy; carriers liable because they failed to discharge burden of proof imposed by Art. 18).
[45] Art. 17(3).
[46] *Walek & Co.* v. *Chapman and Ball (International) Ltd.* [1980] 2 Lloyd's Rep. 279.
[47] See n.44, *supra*.
[48] Art. 17(4).
[49] Art. 18(1).

maintenance and use of such equipment were taken and he complied with any special instructions issued to him.[50]

The fact that the goods have not been delivered within 30 days following the expiry of the agreed time limit or, if no time limit has been agreed, within 60 days from the time when the carrier took over the goods, shall be conclusive evidence of the loss of the goods, and the person entitled to make a claim may thereupon treat them as lost.[51]

If the goods are sent on a "cash on delivery" (c.o.d.) term and the carrier hands them over without insisting on payment in cash, he is liable for compensation not exceeding the amount of the charge defined in the term without prejudice to his right of action against the consignee.[52]

The compensation which the carrier is liable to pay in respect of total or partial loss of the goods is subject to a maximum limitation of liability. It is 8.33 SDRs per kilogramme of gross weight short[53]; in addition, the carrier has to refund in full the carriage charges incurred, Customs duties and other charges incurred in respect of the carriage of the goods.[54] In *James Buchanan & Co. Ltd.* v. *Babco Forwarding and Shipping (U.K.) Ltd.*[55] a consignment of whisky for export from Glasgow to Iran was stolen from a lorry park in Woolwich. The export value of the whisky was some £7,000 but the Customs authorities demanded from Buchanan, the owners and consignors, excise duty of about £30,000. According to Customs law Buchanan had to pay that duty. Buchanan then tried to recover that amount from the carriers. The House of Lords considered that claim as justified. The court decided that the excise duty constituted "other charges incurred in respect of the carriage of goods" within Article

---

[50] Art. 18(4) and *Ulster Swift Ltd.* v. *Taunton Meat Haulage Ltd.* [1977] 1 Lloyd's Rep. 346.

[51] Art. 20.

[52] Art. 21. The carrier is, in principle, not authorised to accept a cheque instead of cash but, it is thought, he has implied authority to release the goods to the consignee if he has an unqualified binding undertaking of the consignee's bank that the cheque will be honoured. Sometimes the carrier is instructed to release the goods *contre attestation de blocage des fonds* (CABF arrangement); such a certificate would have to be given by the consignee's bank.

If the carrier fails to comply with the c.o.d. instructions, the goods owner is entitled to recover damages from him, and these damages may exceed the maximum limits of Article 23(3).

[53] Art. 23(3). The SDRs were introduced as "units of account" by the Carriage by Air and Road Act 1979, s.4(2), with effect from December 28, 1980 (Carriage by Air and Road Act 1979 (Commencement No. 1) Order 1980 (S.I. 1980 No. 1966 C.84)). The conversion of the SDRs into sterling for a particular day is ascertained from the Treasury and a certificate on the conversion value given by or on behalf of the Treasury is conclusive evidence of this value (1979 Act, s.5).

Before the introduction of the SDRs the maximum limitation of liability was expressed as 25 gold francs; the reference to the gold franc was here to the Latin Union gold franc; the ascertainment of the value of this gold franc was uncertain. See L. Bristow, "Gold franc—Replacement of unit of account" in [1978] 1 MCLQ 31.

[54] Art. 23(4). The fee for the survey of the damaged goods is recoverable as "other charges": *I.C.I. plc.* v. *MAT Transport Ltd.* [1987] 1 Lloyd's Rep. 354, 362.

[55] [1978] A.C. 141.

23(4) and held that the carriers were liable for the full £37,000 because there was no limit placed on the items mentioned in paragraph 4 but, on the contrary, it was provided that the carrier had to pay them "in full."

In the case of delay, the measure of damages is limited to the carriage charges if the claimant can prove that he has suffered damage to that amount.[56]

The defences which exclude or limit the liability of the carrier are also available if the action is founded on tort and not on contract.[57] The agents and servants and any other persons of whose services the carrier makes use for the performance of the carriage may avail themselves of the same defences, if they have acted within the scope of their employment.[58]

Time limits

If the consignee takes delivery of the goods and does not in the case of apparent loss or damage, at the time of delivery, or in the case of loss or damage which is not apparent, within seven days of delivery, send the carrier a *notice of reservations*, giving a general indication of the loss or damage, the fact of taking delivery is prima facie evidence that he received the goods in the condition described in the consignment note.[59] No compensation is payable for delay in delivery unless a notice of reservations has been sent in writing to the carrier within 21 days from the time that the goods were placed at the disposal of the consignee.[60]

The period of limitation for bringing an action arising out of the contract of carriage under the CMR is one year. Nevertheless, in the case of wilful misconduct or such default as in accordance with the law of the court or tribunal dealing with the case is considered equivalent to wilful misconduct, the period of limitation is three years.[61] According to Article 32(1), time begins to run:

(*a*) in the case of partial loss, damage or delay in delivery from the date of delivery;
(*b*) in the case of total loss,[62] from the 30th day after the expiry of the agreed time limit or, where no time limit is agreed, from the 60th day from the date when the goods were taken over by the carrier; or
(*c*) in all other cases on the expiry of three months after the making of the contract.

---

[56] Art. 23(5).
[57] Art. 28.
[58] Art. 28(2).
[59] Art. 30(1).
[60] Art. 30(3).
[61] Art. 32(1). On "wilful misconduct" see *Sidney G. Jones Ltd.* v. *Martin Bencher Ltd.* [1986] 1 Lloyd's Rep. 54. (Driver falling asleep on wheel).
[62] "Total loss" in Article 32(1) of the CMR means in the terminology of the Marine Insurance Act 1906, "actual total loss"; it does not include "constructive total loss": *I.C.I. plc.* v. *MAT Transport Ltd.* [1987] 1 Lloyd's Rep. 354.

Paragraph (a) of this provision applies only if two conditions are satisfied: there must be a partial loss, damage or delay, and the goods must have been delivered. Where the goods are not delivered within the time limits stated in Article 20(1),[63] they are conclusively presumed to be lost and consequently the starting point for the one year limitation period is determined by paragraph (b). If the case cannot be brought under either paragraph (a) or (b) of Article 32(1), the starting point for the one year period of limitation is determined by paragraph (c).[64]

The CMR allows the normal limitation period of one year, which is rather short, to be suspended if a written claim is made by the goods owner or somebody on his behalf against the carrier. But this suspension operates only until the date on which the carrier rejects the claim by notification in writing.[65] The object of this suspension is to enable the carrier to decide whether the claim is justified. Where there are successive carriers, the claimant must notify the carrier against whom he wants to make the claim; it is not sufficient for the claimant only to notify the first carrier and to leave it to him to notify the successive carriers because each of the carriers concerned must know that a claim is intended against him and be given the opportunity of stopping the suspension of the limitation period by rejecting the claim.[66]

Nullity of stipulations contrary to the Convention

Apart from the internal arrangements between successive carriers,[67] any stipulation which would directly or indirectly derogate from the provisions of the CMR is null and void.[68] In particular, a benefit of insurance in favour of the carrier or any other similar clause or any clause shifting the burden of proof is null and void.[69]

---

[63] These times limits are 30 days following the expiry of the agreed time limit or, if there is no agreed time limit, 60 days from the time the carrier took over the goods.
[64] *Worldwide Carriers Ltd.* v. *Ardtran International Ltd.* [1983] 1 Lloyd's Rep. 61, 65. *Cf. William Tatton & Co. Ltd.* v. *Ferrymaster Ltd.* [1974] 1 Lloyd's Rep. 203.
[65] Art. 32(2).
[66] *Worldwide Carriers Ltd.* v. *Ardtran International Ltd., supra.,* 66; *Sidney G. Jones Ltd.* v. *Martin Bencher Ltd.* [1986] 1 Lloyd's Rep. 54; *Poclain SA* v. *S.C.A.C. SA* [1986] 1 Lloyd's Rep. 404 (authority of liability insurer of carrier to receive written claim); *I.C.I. plc.* v. *MAT Transport Ltd.* [1987] 1 Lloyd's Rep. 354.
[67] But in their internal arrangements carriers cannot abrogate Articles 37 and 38.
[68] Art. 41(1).
[69] Art. 41(2).

PART SIX

INTERNATIONAL COMMERCIAL DISPUTE SETTLEMENTS

CHAPTER 31

INTERNATIONAL COMMERCIAL ARBITRATION

EXTRAJUDICIAL DISPUTE SETTLEMENT AND COURT PROCEEDINGS

THE contingency of legal disputes is never absent in international trade transactions. The reasonable exporter who, in spite of the care which he has taken in the preparation of the contract of sale, has to contemplate resort to the law against the buyer who has broken the contract, might, in appropriate circumstances, prefer to cut his losses rather than to engage in costly and protracted proceedings. There are, however, circumstances where this solution is out of the question. The subject-matter in issue might be too valuable to accept the loss, interests of third parties might be involved, the breach might appear too flagrant to allow it to pass unchallenged. Here the question is what is the most convenient, speediest and cheapest machinery to settle the dispute.

The exporter should consider this question *before* entering into the contract of export sale. When he has made his choice from the available procedures, he should insist that a term giving full expression to the chosen procedure is inserted into the contract. Experience has shown that it is easier to obtain agreement on this point when the contract is negotiated than when a dispute has arisen; in the latter case the aggrieved party has no means of compelling the other party to agree to an extrajudicial procedure of dispute settlement and resort to the court is the only way open to him.

If the exporter decides in favour of extrajudicial dispute settlement, he may insert into the contract a *conciliation* clause or an *arbitration* clause. The difference between conciliation, also called mediation, and arbitration lies in the different aims of these procedures. It has been stated[1]:

> If the parties agree on conciliation, they want an amicable settlement of their dispute with the active assistance of a third person, the conciliator, or they hope at least that an amicable settlement can be achieved. But if they agree on arbitration, they intend to adopt an adversary stance and will demand the resolution of their dispute by a decision, though a decision of private judges of their choice and not judges appointed by the State. Arbitration is thus closer to court proceedings than conciliation.

It is obvious that conciliation is preferable to arbitration. But conciliation can only succeed if the climate is right for it. Normally the parties

---

[1] Clive M. Schmitthoff, "Extrajudicial Dispute Settlement," *Forum internationale*, No. 6, May 1985, 10–11, also in the *Essays*, 1988, pp. 637, 647.

will insert a conciliation clause into their contract only if their relationship is sufficiently friendly to hold out the prospect of an amicable settlement. The usual choice of parties who desire an extrajudicial method of dispute settlement is to agree on arbitration.

GENERAL ASPECTS OF ARBITRATION

Comparison of arbitration and litigation

In the view of international businessmen, arbitration offers distinct advantages. First, the parties to an international contract can entrust the resolution of their dispute to judges of their own choice; as the parties live in different countries, which sometimes found their laws on legal concepts having a different traditional and cultural background, they may be disinclined to go to the national courts although in most countries the commercial courts function well and administer justice efficiently. Secondly, businessmen prefer finality to meticulous legal accuracy. The arbitration award is, at least in principle, final but a court case may go to appeal and to further appeal to the highest court and a long time may pass before the final word is spoken. Thirdly, arbitration is in private and does not take place in open court, and in sensitive matters this is a distinct advantage. Lastly, international Conventions, which will be considered later,[2] facilitate the recognition and enforcement of foreign arbitral awards and thus render their international execution relatively easy.

It is sometimes claimed that arbitration is more speedy and cheaper than court proceedings. This may be true in many cases but in others experienced businessmen and lawyers will treat these claims with a degree of scepticism.

Questions of fact and questions of law

In principle questions of fact are decided by the arbitrator; he also decides, of course, questions of law arising in the course of the arbitration. But in the limited cases in which a judicial review is admitted in English law by virtue of the Arbitration Act 1979,[3] the court will accept the facts, as found by the arbitrator, and restrict its review to questions of law.

---

[2] See p. 687, *post.*
[3] See p. 666, *post.*

Where the dispute concerns only facts, *e.g.* whether the goods are of the stipulated quality or description, or are in accordance with sample, arbitration offers overwhelming advantages over litigation. Most of these so-called *quality arbitrations*, particularly those arranged under the rules of the great trade associations,[4] are expeditiously and cheaply disposed of and it happens rarely that a dispute arising from them is later taken to court.

On the other hand, where the facts of the matter are not in dispute, *viz.* where the dispute concerns the construction of a document or another purely legal question, it is often cheaper and more expeditous[5] for the parties to submit their dispute to the court. In these so-called *technical arbitrations* it is often to the advantage of the parties to waive arbitration by mutual agreement and to go straightaway to the Commercial Court. In one case[6] Singleton L.J. observed in respect of a contract embodying the arbitration clause of the London Jute Association:

> This dispute was referred to arbitration, and subsequently there was an appeal to the committee. Thereafter a special case was stated by the committee and came before Lord Goddard C.J. Most respectfully, I would point out that this procedure adds greatly to the cost and trouble which the parties have to encounter in a case of this kind. It would, I think, be better that a dispute such as this should go direct to the Commercial Court, and there be dealt with, as it would be a saving of costs for the parties. If the issue concerns a point of general importance in a particular trade and it is desired to obtain an authoritative ruling on it, it is generally better to waive the arbitration agreement and to take the case to the Commercial Court.[7]

Frequently the dispute concerns both questions of fact and of law. In these *mixed arbitrations* the arbitrator's decision on legal questions is subject to judicial review[8] but his decision on the facts is not unless it is obviously absurd. A typical example of a problem in which both questions of fact and law are involved is that of frustration. The circumstances alleged to have led to frustration raise questions of fact but the issue whether these facts are sufficient to satisfy the legal test of frustration and thus to lead to the termination of the contract is purely a question of law. Lord Diplock observed[9]:

> . . . the question of frustration . . . is never a pure question of fact but does in the ultimate analysis involve a conclusion of law as to whether the frustrating event or

---

[4] See p. 73, *ante.*

[5] In *British Imex Industries Ltd.* v. *Midland Bank Ltd.* [1958] 1 Q.B. 542 (see p. 426, *ante*) the Commercial Court gave judgment eleven days after the issue of the writ.

[6] *K. C. Sethia (1944) Ltd.* v. *Partabmull Rameshwar* [1950] 1 All E.R. 51, 58; affd. [1951] 2 All E.R. 352. Also *Macpherson Train & Co. Ltd.* v. *J. Milhem & Sons* [1955] 2 Lloyd's Rep. 59, 64 (Singleton L.J.); *J. H. Vantol Ltd.* v. *Fairclough Dodd & Jones Ltd.* [1955] 1 W.L.R. 642, 648 (McNair J.), 1302 (C.A.); *Compagnie Tunisienne de Navigation S.A.* v. *Compagnie d'Armement Maritime S.A.* [1971] A.C. 572, 600 (Lord Wilberforce).

[7] See also Lord Donaldson in *Seaworld Ocean Line Co. SA* v. *Catseye Maritime Co. Ltd. The Kelaniya* [1989] 1 Lloyd's Rep. 30, 32.

[8] See p. 666, *post.*

[9] *Pioneer Shipping Ltd.* v. *B.T.P. Tioxide Ltd. The Nema* [1982] A.C. 724, 738.

series of events has made performance of the contract a thing radically different from
that which was undertaken by the contract.

Since the division of functions between the arbitrator and the court can
lead to delay and additional costs, the parties may, if they so desire,
appoint a judge of the Commercial Court as sole arbitrator or as umpire[10];
the appointment of a *judge-arbitrator* avoids the procedure by judicial
review and the splitting up of questions of fact and of law. An appeal
from the judge-arbitrator lies to the Court of Appeal.[11]

The characteristics of arbitration

Arbitration has a contractual and a judicial element.

The contractual element of arbitration

There can never be arbitration without an agreement of the parties to
submit to this method of dispute settlement.[12] This is a very fundamental
proposition. The agreement of the parties may take the form of an
arbitration clause in the original contract, *e.g.* in the contract of export
sale, in which case it refers to future disputes, or there may be a separate
arbitration agreement subsequent to the conclusion of the original contract, particularly after the dispute has arisen. The agreement of the
parties determines the *jurisdiction* of the arbitrator. He must not go
beyond the powers which the parties have conferred upon him.[13]

The contractual nature of arbitration determines two questions which
are not free from controversy. The first is whether the arbitrator himself
can decide conclusively whether he has jurisdiction over a particular issue
if the parties are in disagreement whether he has such jurisdiction.[14] It is

---

[10] Administration of Justice Act 1970, s.4. The award of a judge-arbitrator does not carry
the same weight as the decision of a judge given in court: *The Kelaniya, supra* n. 7, on p. 32
of the law report.

[11] *Ibid.* s.4(5).

[12] *Compagnie Européenne de Ceréals SA* v. *Tradax Export SA* [1986] 2 Lloyd's Rep. 301,
306: *Kenya Railways* v. *Antares Pte Ltd. The Antares (Nos. 1 and 2)* [1987] 1 Lloyd's Rep.
424, 432.

[13] *Phoenician Express SARL* v. *Garware Shipping Corporation, The Times,* November 23,
1983 (finding of arbitrator that respondent company had changed its name and reference to
a company trading under the new name may be excess of jurisdiction and was deleted from
the award).

[14] See Clive M. Schmitthoff, "The Jurisdiction of the Arbitrator" in *The Art of Arbitration*,
(1982) pp. 285 *et seq,* also in the *Essays,* 1988, pp. 628 *et seq.* In continental jurisprudence
the question whether the arbitrator may determine his own jurisdiction is described as the
question of *compétence compétence*.

thought that this question has to be answered in the negative. He may express a view on this point[15] but, even if the parties leave it to him to decide the limits of his jurisdiction, ultimately, *i.e.* when the enforcement of the award is sought, a court will have to decide whether he has exceeded the powers which the parties conferred on him by their agreement.[16]

The second question—which is different from the first one—is whether, if the arbitration clause is contained in the original contract, the arbitrator may decide whether the original contract is void *ad initio*, *e.g.* on the ground of misrepresentation or relevant mistake.[17] The question is here whether the arbitration clause constitutes a severable contract which is not affected by the challenge to the main contract, in which case the arbitrator would have jurisdiction to decide this issue, or whether it forms an inseparable part of it, in which case, if the challenge is justified, the arbitration clause would fall to the ground with the main contract and the arbitrator would have no jurisdiction to deal with this issue. The answer to the question is essentially a matter of construction of the parties' intention, which has to be gathered from the wording of the arbitration clause or has to be inferred by necessary implication.[18] An older English decision[19] favoured the latter view but in a later decision[20] Lord Scarman expressed himself in favour of the former view when he observed.[21]

> Such a contract is often to be found as an arbitration clause in a commercial, industrial or other type of contract. Where so found, it is, in strict analysis, a separate contract, ancillary to the main contract.

According to modern English cases,[22] Lord Scarman's analysis normally accords with the intention of the parties. In one case[23] where the arbitration clause gave the arbitrator jurisdiction to decide issues "arising [under the contract]" or "in connection therewith," the court held that allegations of mistake and misrepresentation were within the scope of the arbitration clause.

---

[15] Devlin J. in *Christopher Brown Ltd.* v. *Genossenschaft Oesterreichischer Waldbesitzer Holzwirtschaftsbetriebe* [1954] 1 Q.B. 8, 12.
[16] *Dalmia Dairy Industries* v. *National Bank of Pakistan* [1978] 2 Lloyd's Rep. 223 (The decision dealt with Indian law but it was held that on this issue Indian law was the same as English law): see pp. 677–678, *post*; *Ashville Investments Ltd.* v. *Elmer Contractors Ltd.* [1988] 3 W.L.R. 867, 873.
[17] In an English arbitration, if it is alleged that a party is guilty of fraud, the court has power to order that this issue is determined by the court and that the arbitration agreement shall cease to have effect in so far (Arbitration Act 1950, s.24(2) and (3); see p. 665, *post*.
[18] *Ashville Investments Ltd.* v. *Elmer Contractors Ltd.* [1988] 3 W.L.R. 867.
[19] *Heyman* v. *Darwins Ltd.* [1942] A.C. 356, 371.
[20] *Bremer Vulkan Schiffbau und Maschinenfabrik* v. *South India Shipping Corporation Ltd.* [1981] A.C. 909.
[21] *Ibid.* p. 998.
[22] *Ashville Investments Ltd.* v. *Elmer Contractors Ltd.* [1988] 3 W.L.R. 867; *Overseas Union Insurance Ltd.* v. *AA Mutual International Insurance Co. Ltd.* [1988] 2 Lloyd's Rep. 63.
[23] The *Ashville Investments* case, see *supra*.

It has always been non-contenious that, if it is alleged that the contract has come to an end in consequence of an event *subsequent to its valid conclusion*, the arbitration clause remains alive and the arbitrator has jurisdiction; such issues are, *e.g.* whether the contract has been frustrated, or repudiated or duly terminated in accordance with its terms.[24]

A different question arises where it is alleged that the arbitration clause itself was obtained by fraud, misrepresentation or relevant mistake or where it is contended that the parties were never in agreement on the insertion of the arbitration clause into the main contract. Here the objection is directed to the arbitration agreement and not to the main contract. To leave this decision to the arbitrator means that he would have power to decide on his own jurisdiction. An attack on the validity of the arbitration clause itself, from which the arbitrator derives his jurisdiction, can only be settled conclusively by the court.

The contractual nature of arbitration has also to be borne in mind when it is contended that the prolonged inactivity of the parties in the prosecution of the arbitration resulted in "frustration" of the arbitration by delay on the ground that owing to lapse of time a fair trial is no longer possible.[25] It has already been observed[26] that this is not a case of "frustration" in the legal sense. Prolonged inactivity by both parties may prompt the conclusion that the parties have agreed to abandon the arbitration or that one of them has repudiated the arbitration agreement and the other has accepted the repudiation.[27] Both these conclusions are within the contractual ambit of the arbitration agreement. In both cases the obligation to submit to arbitration has come to an end. The judge, unlike his position in court proceedings, has in arbitrations at present no jurisdiction to dismiss a claim for want of prosecution.[28] The arbitrator may apply to the court under section 5(1) of the Arbitration Act 1979 to

---

[24] See the cases referred to in note 22, *ante*.

[25] In *Bremer Vulkan Schiffbau und Maschinenfabrik* v. *South India Shipping Corporation* [1981] A.C. 909, 938, Lord Diplock held that in an arbitration both parties were under a mutual obligation to keep the arbitration moving but this view was criticised by Lord Goff in *Food Corporation of India* v. *Antclizo Shipping Corporation* [1988] 1 W.L.R. 603, 607. It was suggested in this case by the House of Lords that in arbitrations which have gone to sleep for many years, the court should be empowered by legislation to dismiss the arbitration for want of prosecution.

[26] See pp. 183, *ante*.

[27] *Bremer Vulkan Schiffbau und Maschinenfabrik* v. *South India Shipping Corporation* [1981] A.C. 909; *Paal Wilson & Co. A/S* v. *Partenreederei Hannah Blumenthal. The Hannah Blumenthal* [1983] 1 A.C. 854; *Allied Marine Transport Ltd.* v. *Vale do Rio Doce Navegačao S.A., The Leonidas D* [1985] 1 W.L.R. 925, 936 (C.A.); *Tracomin S.A.* v. *Anton C. Nielson A/S* [1984] 2 Lloyd's Rep. 195; *K. Lokumal & Sons (London) Ltd.* v. *Lotte Shipping Co. Pte. Ltd.. The August Leonhardt* [1985] 2 Lloyd's Rep. 28, 35; *Cie Française d'Importation et de Distribution SA.* v. *Deutsche Continental Handelsgesellschaft* [1985] 2 Lloyd's Rep. 592; *Excomm Ltd.* v. *Guan Guan Shipping (Pte) Ltd. The Golden Bear* [1977] 1 Lloyd's Rep. 330; *Gebr. van Weelde Scheepvaartkantor BV* v. *Compania Naviera Sea Orient SA. The Agrabele* [1987] 2 Lloyd's Rep. 223.

[28] See the suggestions of the House of Lords in the *Antclizo* case, n. 25, above.

obtain an order compelling a party to comply with his directions[29] but it is unlikely that the court will make an order compelling a party to proceed with the arbitration.

The judicial element of arbitration

The arbitrator, as a private judge chosen by the parties or appointed in accordance with the arbitration agreement, must approach the issues before him in the same spirit as a judge appointed by the State. He must be absolutely impartial. He must not show bias in favour of one of the parties, nor must he conduct himself in a manner which would lead a reasonable man to conclude that he is biased.[30]

The arbitrator must conduct the arbitration not only in accordance with the procedural rules applicable to it but he must strictly observe the requirements of natural justice.[31] He must give the parties a fair hearing. If he receives from one party a communication which has not been sent to the other party, he must inform the latter and will normally send him a copy of the communication. The arbitrator, like the judge, has power to order the inspection of the object in dispute, *e.g.* a cargo or a vessel,[32] but he should give the parties an opportunity of being present at the inspection. The arbitrator may make his award in a foreign currency in appropriate circumstances.[33] He may order that the sum awarded should bear interest up to the date of the award and he has a discretion to fix the rate of such interest, but he has no power to order the payment of interest after the date of the award at a rate other than that applicable to a judgment debt.[34] Unlike a judge, the arbitrator has no power to order

---

[29] Arbitration Act 1979, s.5.

[30] The appearance of bias, as contrasted with actual bias, is called imputed bias. The test of imputed bias is an objective one, *i.e.* the inference which a reasonable man would draw from the conduct of the arbitrator: *Tracomin S.A.* v. *Gibbs Nathaniel (Canada) Ltd.* [1985] 1 Lloyd's Rep 586; *cf. Bremer Handelsgesellschaft mbH* v. *Ets Soules et Cie.* [1985] 2 Lloyd's Rep. 199 (C.A.); *Cook International Inc.* v. *B.V. Handelsmaatschappij Jean Delvaux* [1985] 2 Lloyd's Rep. 225.

[31] For a discussion of the requirements of natural justice, though not in connection with arbitration, see *Mahon* v. *Air New Zealand Line* [1984] A.C. 808, 820–821; *Reg.* v. *Monopolies and Mergers Commission, ex parte Matthew Brown plc.* [1987] 1 W.L.R. 1235, 1239. The court may remit the case to the arbitrator if, owing to a "procedural mishap", he has failed to hear argument on the costs: *Harrison* v. *Thompson* [1989] 1 W.L.R. 1325.

[32] Lloyd J. in *The Vasso* [1983] 1 W.L.R. 838.

[33] See p. 225, *ante*.

[34] This follows from section 20 of the Arbitration Act 1950; see *Timber Shipping Co. S.A.* v. *London & Overseas Freighters Ltd.* [1972] A.C. 1 (But the arbitrator may refuse any interest after the award); see also *Rocco Giuseppe & Figli* v. *Tradax Export S.A.* [1984] 1 W.L.R. 742. The arbitrator has power to award interest on a sum paid with delay but before the award (1950 Act, s.19A, added by the Administration of Justice Act 1982, sched. 1, Part IV). On the award of interest see further Lord Brandon of Oakbrook in *President of India* v. *La Pintada Compania Navigacion* [1985] A.C. 104, 113–131, and *Edmunds* v. *Lloyds Italico etc.* [1986] 1 W.L.R. 492.

security for costs but in arbitration proceedings an application for security may be made to the court.[35]

If an irregularity (other than one of trifling character or a clerical error) occurs in the conduct of the arbitration or in the award, the proceedings are a nullity and the court will set them aside. The irregularity may be due to misconduct[36] of the arbitrator or it may be a purely technical error, *e.g.* if he receives inadmissible evidence which goes to the root of the case or makes an award on a point which was not before him.[37]

Ad hoc and institutional arbitration

In their arbitration agreement the parties may opt for ad hoc arbitration or for institutional arbitration. If they decide in favour of the former, they may agree on the person of the arbitrator or leave his appointment to a third person, *e.g.* the president of the Law Society in London.[38] In major contracts the arbitration clause will sometimes provide for a three-person arbitration tribunal, each party appointing his arbitrator and the two arbitrators electing the chairman. In ad hoc arbitrations it is advisable to provide for the application of the UNCITRAL Arbitration Rules[39] in order to minimise procedural disputes and to enable a deadlock to be broken if the respondent fails to appoint his arbitrator or the two arbitrators cannot agree on the chairman.[39]

Often the parties will agree on arbitration under the rules of one of the institutions which provide facilities for the arbitral settlement of disputes

---

[35] By virtue of the Arbitration Act 1950, s.12(6)(*a*); see Supreme Court Practice 1985 para. 23/1–3/20. In ICC arbitrations (p. 676, *post*) the courts, in the exercise of their discretion, will normally be disinclined to make an order for security for costs: *Bank Mellat* v. *Helleniki Techniki S.A.* [1984] Q.B. 291. But in arbitrations, which are regularly held in London, such as maritime and commodity arbitrations, it is generally appropriate to make an order for security for costs; in the case before the court two shipbuilding contracts were in issue; both parties were non-resident in the United Kingdom but the contracts provided that English law should apply: *K/S A/S Bani and K/S A/S Havbulk I* v. *Korea Shipbuilding and Engineering Corporation*: [1987] 2 Lloyd's Rep. 445.

[36] In the older decisions the term "misconduct" was used to cover not only deliberate or careless breach of duty but also a purely technical error.

[37] *Société Franco-Tunisienne d'Armement-Tunis* v. *Government of Ceylon* [1959] 1 W.L.R. 787; *E. Rotheray & Sons Ltd.* v. *Carlo Bedarida & Co.* [1961] 1 Lloyd's Rep. 220 (material documents in a foreign language placed before arbitrator who decides without knowing the foreign language and without proper translations); *Giacomo Costa Fu Andrea* v. *British Italian Trading Co. Ltd.* [1963] 1 Q.B. 201 (only misconduct of arbitration appeal board, but not of arbitrator of first instance, is relevant); *European Grain and Shipping Ltd.* v. *Johnston* [1983] Q.B. 520 (arbitrator signs the award form in blank without taking part in the decision process); *K/S A/S Bill Biakh and K/S A/S Bill Biali* v. *Hyundai Corporation* [1988] 1 Lloyd's Rep. 187 (a mere error in relation to the admissibility of evidence in an arbitrator's ruling does not amount to misconduct).

[38] If the third person fails to make the appointment, the court may make it: Arbitration Act 1950, s.10(2), added by the Arbitration Act 1979, s.6(4).

[39] See p. 673, *post*.

arising in international trade transactions. The major international arbitration institutions are considered later.[40] Institutional arbitration offers some advantages over ad hoc arbitration. The institution usually offers administrative assistance with respect to the conduct of the arbitration and its rules contain a code of procedure for the conduct of the arbitration.

Whether the arbitration agreement provides for ad hoc or institutional arbitration, it should always specify the venue and the language of the arbitration.

The law governing the arbitration procedure

The adoption of an English arbitration clause often supports the assumption that the parties intend to submit their contract to the rules of English law,[41] but the law applicable to the arbitration procedure, sometimes referred to as the curial law, may be different from the law governing the contract; thus, in a case[42] in which the law governing the contract was English law, the parties held their arbitration in Scotland in accordance with the Scots law applicable to arbitration; the House of Lords decided that Scots law regulated the arbitration procedure whilst the arbitrator had to apply English law as the law governing the contract.

If the parties have adopted an international code of arbitration procedure, such as the UNCITRAL Arbitration Rules or the Rules for the ICC Court of Arbitration, there will often be no need to go beyond it and to resort to a national law in order to ascertain the rules of arbitration procedure. In this — restricted — sense one can talk of arbitration which is "transnational," or "anational," or "floating." But if the international regulation contains *a gap*, reference will have to be made to the national legal system applicable to the arbitration procedure. This will normally be the law of the place where the arbitration is held but exceptionally another legal system may apply or may at least govern certain aspects of the curial law. Thus, in one case[43] (which was not concerned with the filling of gaps in the agreed arbitration rules) an English court had to decide whether an award made by the Iran–United

---

[40] See pp. 672 *et seq., post.*
[41] See p. 218, *ante.*
[42] *Whitworth Street Estates (Manchester) Ltd.* v. *James Miller & Partners Ltd.* [1970] A.C. 583. Also *International Tank and Pipe S.A.K.* v. *Kuwait Aviation Fuelling Co. K.S.C.* [1975] Q.B. 224. See also *Dalmia Dairy Industries Ltd.* v. *National Bank of Pakistan* [1978] 2 Lloyd's Rep. 223, 228.
[43] *Dallal* v. *Bank Mellat* [1986] Q.B. 441. On transnational arbitration see Sir Michael John Mustill, "Transnational Arbitration in English Law," in *Current Legal Problems*, (1984), p. 133. See also Jan Paulsson, "Arbitration unbound: Award detached from the law of its country of origin" in 30 I.C.L.Q. (1981) 358 and the references on p. 655, n. 45, *post.*

States International Arbitration Tribunal at The Hague was valid and should be recognised in the United Kingdom. The Tribunal derived its authority from the Iran–United States Declaration of Algiers of January 19, 1981 which ended the dispute between the United States and Iran following the deposition of the Shah. The Dutch Government had consented to the constitution of the Tribunal in the Netherlands but if Dutch law was the curial law the arbitration agreement was invalid as not conforming with the provisions of Dutch law. Hobhouse J. held that the Tribunal derived its jurisdiction and authority from the Algiers Declaration, which was an international treaty between two sovereign States and that that jurisdiction was recognised by their municipal laws. They constituted the curial law for the purposes of giving jurisdiction to the Tribunal and its award had to be recognised in England.

The Foreign Limitation Periods Act 1984, under which a foreign limitation period is treated as pertaining to substantive law, applies to arbitration proceedings.[44]

Application of the lex mercatoria *in arbitration proceeding*

The "transnational" or "anational" character of the legal regulation may extend to the substantive law of the contract, as applied by the arbitrator. The parties may authorise him to decide the substantive issues before him according to the "internationally accepted principles of law governing contractual relations," which briefly are referred to as the *lex mercatoria* (the law merchant)[45] or, if they leave the choice of the proper law to him, he may opt for the *lex mercatoria*. In one case,[46] which arose from an oil exploration agreement between an enterprise in a Middle Eastern State (the enterprise was Rakoil and the State was R'As el-Khaimah) and a German company (D.S.T.), the arbitration clause provided for ICC arbitration to be held in Geneva; the ICC Rules of Arbitration authorised the arbitrators, in the absence of any indication as to the proper law, to apply the law which they deemed to be appropriate; the arbitration tribunal held that it would be inappropriate in the case

---

[44] See p. 221, *ante*.
[45] The Rt. Hon. Lord Justice Mustill, "The new Lex Mercatoria: The First Twenty-Five Years," in *Liber Amicorum for Lord Wilberforce* (ed. Bos and Brownlie), 1987, 149; Ole Lando, "The Lex Mercatoria in International Commercial Arbitration," 34 I.C.L.Q. (1985), 747; Clive M. Schmitthoff, "International Trade Usages," Inst. Internl. Bus. Law and Practice, 1987, ICC Publication No. 440/4. See also Felix Dasser, *Internationale Schiedsgerichte und lex mercatoria*, Zürich, 1989. The practice of international commercial arbitrators, if so authorised, to resort to the *lex mercatoria* as an anational system of law, is growing.
[46] *Deutsche Schachtbau-und Tiefbohrgesellschaft mbH.* v. *R'As al-Khaima National Oil Co.* [1987] 3 W.L.R. 1023.

before it to apply a national system of law but that the substantive law governing the obligations of the parties was the "internationally accepted principles of law governing contractual relations." In English proceedings for the enforcement of the award the Court of Appeal rejected the argument that the choice of an anational system of law contravened public policy; Sir John Donaldson M.R. said[47]:

> I can see no basis for concluding that the arbitrators' choice of proper law—a common denominator of principles underlying the laws of various nations governing contractual relations—is outwith the scope of the choice which the parties left to the arbitrators.

Arbitration ex aequo et bono.

The parties sometimes authorise the arbitrator to decide *ex aequo et bono*. Such "equity" clauses are worded differently; sometimes they provide that the arbitrator shall apply equitable considerations and in other cases they state that the agreement shall be interpreted "as an honourable engagement."[48]

An equity clause does not mean that the arbitrator may disregard the law; a clause purporting to give him this power would be void. It means that, in interpreting the law and the contract between the parties, the arbitrator should take a common sense view and should not be bound by legal technicalities. In one case[49] in which the Court of Appeal interpreted an equity clause as authorising the arbitrator to take "the lenient view"[50] Lord Denning M.R. said of such a clause[51]:

> It only ousts technicalities and strict constructions. That is what equity did in the old days. And it is what arbitrators may properly do today under such a clause as this.

Where the arbitration agreement contains an equity clause, the arbitrator's liberty to interpret legal rules more leniently extends to the substantive law as well as to arbitration procedure. Thus, under such a clause the arbitrator in an English arbitration is not bound to apply the strict English rules on the examination of witnesses.

ENGLISH ARBITRATION

The statutory framework

The statutory law relating to arbitration is contained in three enactments, the Arbitration Acts 1950, 1975 and 1979. The 1950 Act is the

---

[47] *Ibid.* 1035.

[48] "Honourable engagement" provisions are often found in arbitration clauses of reinsurance agreements.

[49] *Eagle Star Insurance Co. Ltd.* v. *Yuval Insurance Co. Ltd.* [1978] 1 Lloyd's Rep. 357. See also *Overseas Union Insurance Ltd.* v. *AA Mutual International Insurance Co. Ltd.* [1988] 2 Lloyd's Rep. 63; *Home and Overseas Insurance Co. Ltd.* v. *Mentor Insurance Co. (UK) Ltd.,* [1989] 1 Lloyd's Rep. 473.

[50] Goff J. in the *Eagle Star* case, *supra.*

[51] *Eagle Star,* 362.

principal Act; it applies to England and Wales and, with slight modifications, to Scotland and Northern Ireland. The 1975 Act gives effect, in the United Kingdom, to the New York Convention on the Recognition and Enforcement of Foreign Arbitral Awards of June 10, 1958.[52] The 1979 Act has introduced a far-reaching reform of the law of arbitration; it extends the principle of finality of the award by admitting the exclusion of judicial review.[53] The 1979 Act forms part of the law of England and Wales but does not apply in Scotland.

The statutory regulation of arbitration law is at present under review and there may be a single enactment in the near future.[54]

The arbitration agreement and the arbitrators

The form of the arbitration agreement

The Arbitration Acts 1950 to 1979[55] define an arbitration agreement as a "written agreement to submit present or future differences to arbitration whether an arbitrator is named therein or not" (s.32); written agreements within the meaning of the Acts need not be signed by the parties; it is sufficient that the clause is expressed in writing and the contract wherein the clause appears has been accepted or acted upon by the parties, nor need the agreement be contained in one and the same document. Lloyd L.J. said in one case concerning a GAFTA arbitration[56]:

> For an agreement to be a written agreement to arbitrate it is unnecessary for the whole of the contract, including the arbitration agreement to be contained in the same document. It is sufficient that the arbitration agreement is itself in writing; indeed it is sufficient if there is a document which recognises the existence of an arbitration agreement between the parties . . . I would hold that an arbitration agreement need not be signed and that the definition of s.32 of the Act is satisfied provided there is a document or documents in writing . . .

An exchange by telex communications satisfies this test and constitutes an arbitration agreement in writing.[57]

Oral arbitration agreements, which are rare in practice, are valid at common law, but not governed by the Arbitration Acts 1950 to 1979 and

---

[52] See p. 689, *post.*
[53] See p. 666, *post.*
[54] Position: October 1, 1989.
[55] All references are to the 1950 Act unless stated otherwise.
[56] *Excomm Ltd.* v. *Ahmed Abdul-Qawi Bamaodah. The St. Raphael.* [1985] 1 Lloyd's Rep. 403, 408 and 409. See also *Zambia Steel & Building Supplies Ltd.* v. *James Clark & Eaton Ltd.* [1986] 2 Lloyd's Rep. 225.
[57] *Arab African Energy Corp. Ltd.* v. *Olieprodukten Nederland BV* [1983] 2 Lloyd's Rep. 419.

import, consequently, an element of uncertainty with respect to the implications and enforcement of the arbitration agreement. It is, therefore, desirable that the arbitration clause should always be in the written form. If there is an arbitration clause in a contract of sale or of partnership, it does not extend to the submission of claims under bills of exchange given by merchants in performance of those contracts unless there is a clear intention of both parties to that effect.[58]

Examples of arbitration clauses

The following are examples of arbitration clauses[59]:

EXAMPLE 1

If any dispute, difference or question shall at any time hereafter arise between the parties in respect of or in connection with the present contract,[60] the same shall be referred to the arbitration of a person to be agreed upon by the parties, or, failing agreement, to be nominated by . . . (*e.g.* the London Court of International Arbitration) . . . in accordance with and subject to the provisions of the Arbitration Acts 1950 to 1979 or any statutory modification thereof for the time being in force.

EXAMPLE 2

If any dispute, difference or question shall at any time hereafter arise between the parties in respect of or in connection with the present contract, the same shall be referred to the arbitration of two arbitrators, one to be appointed by each party. This arbitration agreement shall be deemed to be a submission to arbitration within the meaning of the Arbitration Acts 1950 to 1979 or any statutory modification thereof for the time being in force.

On comparing these two examples, it will be observed that in the first case the arbitration is to be held by a single arbitrator, while in the

---

[58] *Nova (Jersey) Knit.* v. *Kammgarn Spinnerei GmbH* [1977] 1 Lloyd's Rep. 463, 467 (H.L.).
[59] A clause worded "suitable arbitration clause" in an English contract is not void on the ground of uncertainty because, if the parties fail to agree, the court will appoint an arbitrator under s.6 of the Arbitration Act 1950: *Hobbs Padgett & Co. (Reinsurance) Ltd.* v. *J. C. Kirkland Ltd.* [1969] 2 Lloyd's Rep. 547. A clause providing for arbitration to be settled "in the customary manner" in a charterparty was not invalid but meant that, as was usual in maritime disputes, two arbitrators should be appointed, one by each party: *Laertis Shipping Corporation* v. *Exportadora Española de Cementos Portland S.A.* [1982] 1 Lloyd's Rep. 613.
[60] On the meaning of "arising out of contract" and "under the contract" see pp. 661–662, *post.*

second case it is to be held by two arbitrators.[61] In the former case the arbitrator may be appointed by concurrence of the parties or by a third person. If a third person has to make the appointment and refuses or fails to do so within the specified time or a reasonable time, any party to the arbitration agreement may give him notice to make the appointment and, if he fails to do so within seven days, the court will make the appointment in his place (s.10(2)).[62] When the parties have to concur in the appointment of the arbitrator and fail to reach agreement, the court has power to appoint the arbitrator (s.10(1)(*a*)). In the case illustrated by example 2, the usual arrangement is that each party is entitled to appoint one arbitrator; the two arbitrators may then appoint an umpire forthwith who has to decide alone when the arbitrators fail to agree (s.8), but the two arbitrators are also entitled to appoint the umpire after they have conferred and disagreed.[63] If the arbitrators cannot agree on the person of the umpire, the court will appoint him (s.10(1)(*c*)). It may happen that one party desires to go to arbitration and appoints his arbitrator while the other party is unwilling to do so. Here the former party may serve the defaulting party with notice to appoint the arbitrator, and, if the defaulting party has not done so within seven clear days after the notice was served, the party who appointed the arbitrator may direct him to act as sole arbitrator and his award is binding on the parties (s.7(*b*)).[64] The arbitrator must consent to act in this capacity before the appointment is effective.[65]

It is more convenient to arrange for arbitration by two arbitrators than by one arbitrator because if one party desires to proceed to arbitration and the other fails to co-operate, in the event of two arbitrators the arbitrator appointed by the willing party may be directed by that party to act as sole arbitrator while, when arbitration by one arbitrator is

---

[61] On the appointment of a judge of the Commercial Court as arbitrator, see p. 649, *ante*.

[62] Added by the Arbitration Act 1979, s.6(4).

[63] Arbitration Act 1950, s.8, as amended by the 1979 Act, s.6(1)(a).

[64] Many arbitration clauses contain a time limit for the appointment of arbitrators by the parties; in the event of non-compliance with such a time limit the court has a discretion to give relief if otherwise "undue hardship" is caused (s.27); *Liberian Shipping Corporation* v. *A. King & Gough Ltd.* [1967] 1 Lloyd's Rep. 302. The court has power to extend the time limit even if the arbitrators are given discretion to extend the time, as, *e.g.* the arbitration clause in GAFTA standard contract forms does: *European Grain and Shipping Ltd.* v. *Dansk Landbrugs Grovvareselskab* [1986] 1 Lloyd's Rep. 163; *Irish Agricultural Wholesale Society Ltd.* v. *Partenreederei M.S. Eurotrader. The Eurotrader.* [1987] 1 Lloyd's Rep. 418; *Comdel Commodities Ltd.* v. *Siporex Trade SA*, (No. 2) [1989] 2 Lloyd's Rep. 13. It was held in *Kenya Railways* v. *Antares Co. Pte Ltd. The Antares (Nos. 1 and 2)* [1987] 1 Lloyd's Rep. 424 that the court's power under section 27 to extend the contractual time limit in arbitrations did not entitle it to extend a statutory time limit, such as provided by the Hague-Visby Rules under the Carriage of Goods by Sea Act 1971. The discretion exists if the substantive law of the arbitration clause is English law: *International Tank and Pipe* v. *Kuwait Aviation Fuelling Co.* [1975] Q.B. 224; *Sioux Inc.* v. *China Salvage Co., Kwangchow Branch* [1980] 1 W.L.R. 996.

[65] *Tradax Export S.A.* v. *Volkswagenwerk A.G.* [1970] 1 Q.B. 537.

arranged, the willing party would have to apply to the court for the appointment of the arbitrator (s.10(1)(*a*)). The two arbitrators in a commercial arbitration have often an unusual dual role in so far as they are judges and advocates in the same person as may be seen from the following observations of Diplock J.[66]:

> once the arbitrators have disagreed and appointed an umpire they are *functus officio* as arbitrators. If they attend, as they do, the hearing before the umpire, it is as advocates for the parties who appointed them, for unless they attend in that capacity as representatives of the parties, they have no right to discuss the matter with the umpire at all.

In their capacity as advocates the arbitrators are authorised to waive minor irregularities of procedure in the hearing before the umpire.[67] It is, however, also possible to appoint the third arbitrator as *chairman*, and not as *umpire*; in this case the majority of arbitrators decide.

The arbitration tribunal

In major international contracts it is usual for the arbitration clause to provide for the constitution of an *arbitration tribunal* consisting of three arbitrators. Each party appoints one and the two arbitrators then choose the third arbitrator, who normally acts as the chairman. The mode of constituting the arbitration tribunal should be stated in the arbitration clause with particularity.

The Arbitration Acts contain provisions for the constitution and procedure of an arbitration tribunal. The 1950 Act, as amended, provides[68] that, if the reference is to three arbitrators, the chairman procedure (and not the umpire procedure) is presumed to apply unless a contrary intention is expressed. If one party appoints his arbitrator but the other fails to do so within the time specified in the agreement or within a reasonable time, the party who has initiated the arbitration may notify the party in default to make his appointment within seven days and if that party fails to do so, the initiating party may apply to the court for the appointment of the arbitrator on behalf of the party in default; the arbitrator appointed by the court is empowered to co-operate with the arbitrator appointed by the initiating party in appointing the third

---

[66] *Wessanen's Koninklijke Fabrikien* v. *Isaac Modiano & Sons Ltd.* [1960] 1 W.L.R. 1243.

[67] *Wessanen's* case, *ibid.* Where the arbitration clause provides that the arbitrators and the umpire shall be "commercial men," a practising member of the Bar cannot be appointed umpire by the arbitrators who have no authority to waive these provisions of the arbitration clause: *Rahcassi Shipping Co. S.A.* v. *Blue Star Line Ltd.* [1969] 1 Q.B. 173. A professional maritime arbitrator is a "commercial man": *Pando Compania Naviera S.A.* v. *Filmo S.A.S.*, *The Times*, February 12, 1975.

[68] Arbitration Act 1950, s.9, as substituted by the 1979 Act, s.6(2).

arbitrator who will normally act as chairman (s.10(3)).[69] If the two arbitrators cannot agree on the person of the third arbitrator, the court will appoint him (s.10(1)(c)).

Implied provisions

The following provisions are implied by the law in every written arbitration agreement unless a contrary intention is expressed therein:

(1) If no other mode of reference is provided, the reference shall be to a single arbitrator (s.6).

(2) If the reference is to two arbitrators, the two arbitrators may appoint an umpire at any time after they are themselves appointed and shall do so forthwith if they cannot agree (s.8(1)).

(3) If the arbitrators have delivered to any party to the submission or the umpire a notice in writing, stating that they cannot agree, the umpire may forthwith enter on the reference in lieu of the arbitrators (s.8(2)).

(4) The parties to the reference, and all persons claiming through them respectively, shall, subject to any legal objection, submit to be examined by the arbitrators or umpire, on oath or affirmation, in relation to the matters in dispute and shall, subject as aforesaid, produce before the arbitrators or umpire all books, deeds, papers, accounts, writings and documents within their possession or power respectively which may be required or called for, and do all other things which during the proceedings on the reference the arbitrators or umpire may require (s.12(1)).

(5) The witnesses on the reference shall, at the discretion of the arbitrators or umpire, be examined on oath or affirmation (s.12(2)).

(6) The award to be made by the arbitrators or umpire shall be final and binding on the parties and the persons claiming under them respectively (s.16).

(7) The costs of the reference and award shall be in the discretion of the arbitrators or umpire who may direct to and by whom and in what manner those costs or any part thereof shall be paid, and may tax or settle the amount of costs to be paid or any part thereof, and may award costs to be paid as between solicitor and client (s.18).

(8) The arbitrators or umpire shall have the same power as the court to order specific performance of any contract other than a contract relating to land or any interest in land (s.15).

(9) The arbitrators or umpire may, if they think fit, make an interim award (s.14).

Disputes covered by the arbitration agreement

The arbitration agreement determines which disputes are submitted to the jurisdiction of the arbitrator. The ambit of arbitration clauses varies and much depends on the wording of the clause which should not be defective.[70] A formulation which is frequently adopted is that "all disputes

---

[69] Added by the Administration of Justice Act 1985, s.58.
[70] Clive M. Schmitthoff, "Defective Arbitration Clauses," in [1975] J.B.L. 9; also in *Essays*, p. 608.

arising out of the contract or in connection with it" shall be submitted to arbitration. The intention of the parties, when agreeing on such a wording, is that claims concerning an alleged relevant mistake or misrepresentation as well as extracontractual claims, such as for a *quantum meruit* or unjust enrichment,[71] or even in tort, if these claims are connected with the contract, are subject to the jurisdiction of the arbitrator. Asquith L.J. said in a case where the claim was founded on tort[72]:

> We are of opinion that, even if the claim in negligence is not a claim arising "under the contract," yet there is a sufficiently close connection between that claim and the transaction to bring the claim within the arbitration clause even though technically framed in tort

A counterclaim is admissible in arbitration if it is within the ambit of the arbitration clause.[73]

In the case of frustration the arbitrator may make an adjustment under the Law Reform (Frustrated Contracts) Act 1943.[74] An arbitrator has discretion under the Misrepresentation Act 1967, s.3, as amended by the Unfair Contract Terms Act 1977, s.8, to admit an exemption clause excluding liability for misrepresentation only if it satisfies the reasonableness test, as stated in the Unfair Contract Terms Act, and the onus of showing that it does is on the party claiming the exemption.

Domestic and non-domestic arbitrations

The Arbitration Acts draw a distinction between domestic and non-domestic arbitrations.

---

[71] *Ashville Investments Ltd.* v. *Elmer Contractors Ltd.* [1988] 2 Lloyd's Rep. 73 (arbitration in a building contract; claim for rectification of contract arbitrable under "in connection" clause).
[72] In *Woolf* v. *Collis Removal Service* [1947] 2 All E.R. 260, 263; see also Sellers J. in *Government of Gibraltar* v. *Kenney* [1956] 2 Q.B. 410, 422–423. The older view, expressed by Lord Porter in *Heyman* v. *Darwins Ltd.* [1942] A.C. 356, 399, that "arising out of the contract" had a wider meaning than "arising under contract" has now been rightly abandoned, at least as far as commercial arbitration clauses are concerned, see Lord Salmon in *Union of India* v. *E. B. Aaby's A/S* [1974] 3 W.L.R. 269, 282. These phrases were also considered, in another connection, in *The Antonis P. Lemos* [1985] A.C. 771 (interpretation of Admiralty jurisdiction under the Supreme Court Act 1981, s.20(2)(*h*)); *Overseas Union Insurance Ltd.* v. *AA Mutual International Insurance Co. Ltd.* [1988] 2 Lloyd's Rep. 63; *Ashville Investments Ltd.* v. *Elmer Contractors Ltd.* [1988] 2 Lloyd's Rep. 73 (see preceding note); *Fillite (Runcorn) Ltd.* v. *Aqualift, The Times,* February 28, 1989 ("arising under" could not be read as including "and in connection with the contract"); *Ethiopian Oilseeds and Pulses Export Corporation* v. *Rio del Mar Foods Inc., Financial Times,* August 9, 1989, *The Times,* August 11, 1989 ("arising out of" to be interpreted widely, it gives the arbitrator jurisdiction to decide on rectification of contract).
[73] Alan Redfern and Martin Hunter, *Law and Practice of International Commercial Arbitration,* 1986, 242.
[74] *Government of Gibraltar* v. *Kenney* [1956] 2 Q.B. 410.

A domestic arbitration agreement is defined in the Arbitration Act 1979[75] as an arbitration agreement:

> which does not provide, expressly or by implication, for arbitration in a State other than the United Kingdom and to which neither—
>
> (*a*) an individual who is a national of, or habitually resident in, any State other than the United Kingdom; nor
>
> (*b*) a body corporate which is incorporated in, or whose central management and control is exercised in, any State other than the United Kingdom;
>
> is a party at the time the arbitration agreement is entered into.

The definition of a domestic arbitration in the Arbitration Act 1975 is in identical terms, except that the relevant time is the time the proceedings are commenced.[76]

All other arbitrations are non-domestic, *i.e.* international. The distinction is important in two respects, as we shall see later, *viz.* with respect to the power of the court to break an arbitration clause[77] and as regards the right of the parties to exclude the judicial review of the arbitration award.[78]

The reasoned award

The Arbitration Acts do not require the arbitrator to state reasons for his award. But the Arbitration Act 1979 provides that the arbitrator or umpire shall state reasons if one of the parties notifies him that they are required.[79] If he fails to do so or if the reasons given are not set out in sufficient detail to enable the court to consider a question of law arising out of the award, the judge may remit the case to the arbitrator or umpire and order him to supply sufficient reasons,[80] but this jurisdiction should be exercised sparingly and remission should be refused if the award is inherently consistent and on the assumption that later an application was made for its judicial review it is likely that such review would be refused on the principles of *The Nema* and *The Antaios*.[81] Even if a party has not asked the arbitrator to state the reasons for his award, he may do so on

---

[75] Arbitration Act 1979, s.3(7).

[76] Arbitration Act 1975, s.1(4).

[77] See p. 665, *post*.

[78] See p. 669, *post*.

[79] Arbitration Act 1979, s.1(6)(*a*). The practice for obtaining a reasoned award is explained by Staughton J. in *Michael L. Warde* v. *Feedex International Inc.* [1984] 1 Lloyd's Rep. 310, 315. See also *Trave Schiffahrtsgesellschaft mbH & Co. KG* v. *Ninemia Maritime Corporation* [1986] Q.B. 802.

[80] Arbitration Act 1979, s.1(5).

[81] *Universal Petroleum Co. Ltd.* v. *Handels und Transport GmbH* [1987] 1 W.L.R. 1178. On *The Nema* and *The Antaios* see p. 667, *post*. See also *Hansa General Insurance Co. Ltd.* v. *Bishopsgate Insurance plc.* [1988] 1 Lloyd's Rep. 503.

his own accord. The reasons should not be unduly long and need not set out the law exhaustively. Donaldson L.J. said[82]:

> All that is necessary under the Act of 1979 is that the arbitrators should give a "reasoned award," *i.e.* the arbitrators should set out what, in their view of the evidence, did or did not happen, and should explain succinctly why in the light of what happened they had reached their decision and what that decision was. They are not expected to analyse the law and the authorities.

As already observed, the award may be expressed in a foreign currency.[83] It carries the same interest as a judgment unless the arbitrator orders that it should not carry interest.[84]

On principle the arbitrator should award the costs of arbitration to the successful party. If he wishes to depart from this rule, he should set out the reasons which caused him to depart from the usual order.[85]

The important question of the enforcement of an award will be considered later.[86]

The function of the courts in arbitrations

Although the courts, as a matter of principle, refrain from interfering with the arbitral process and leave it to the arbitrator to conduct the proceedings, to hear the evidence and to arrive at his decision, they have an important role to play in arbitrations. They have to ensure that the arbitration is conducted properly and the intention of the parties is carried out. The functions of the courts in arbitrations can be summed up as follows:

1. The courts assist in the constitution of the arbitral tribunal and make available to it the judicial measures which are not at the disposal of the arbitrator.[87]
2. They intervene if the arbitrator commits an irregularity or misconducts himself.[88]
3. They allow access to the courts if it is appropriate to stay the arbitration proceedings.

---

[82] In *Westzucker GmbH* v. *Bunge GmbH* [1981] Com. L.R. 179 (the wording in [1981] 2 Lloyd's Rep. 132–133 differs in inessential details); Lord Diplock in *Antaios Compania Naviera S.A.* v. *Salen Rederierna AB* [1984] 3 W.L.R. 592, 597.
[83] See p. 225, *ante.*
[84] See p. 652, *ante.*
[85] *Smeaton Hanscomb & Co. Ltd.* v. *Sassoon I. Setty, Son & Co.* (*No.* 2) [1953] 1 W.L.R. 1481; *Lewis* v. *Haverfordwest Rural District Council* [1953] 1 W.L.R. 1486; *Centrala Morska* v. *Cie. Nacional de Navegaĉao* [1975] 2 Lloyd's Rep. 69, 71–72.
[86] See p. 687, *post.*
[87] See pp. 659–660, *ante.* The court may, *e.g.* order security for costs in arbitation proceedings, an order which the arbitrator cannot make; see p. 653, n. 35, *ante.*
[88] See p. 652, *ante.*

4. Subject to certain—strict—conditions, they admit a judicial review on issues of law.
5. They control the enforcement of domestic and foreign awards.

The functions of the courts listed under the first two headings have already been reviewed. Those under the third and fourth heading will be examined in the following sections. The control over the enforcement of awards will be considered later.[89]

Stays in arbitration proceedings

If the parties agree to abandon the arbitration and to take the dispute to the court, no problem arises.[90] The original arbitration agreement is abrogated by a further agreement of the parties and the court will hear the case if it has jurisdiction.

Usually, however, the position is different. One of the parties may commence proceedings in court, contrary to the arbitration agreement, and the other, who wishes to abide by the agreement, applies to the court for a stay of court proceedings, so that the arbitration may take its course. The question is here whether the court has jurisdiction to allow the court proceedings to continue, thus breaking the arbitration agreement, and, if it has jurisdiction, in which circumstances it will exercise it.[91]

Here the distinction between domestic and non-domestic arbitrations drawn by the Arbitration Act 1975[92] is relevant. In domestic arbitrations the court has discretion to order a stay of court proceedings, thus allowing the arbitration to proceed, or to refuse a stay, thus allowing the court proceedings to continue (s.4(1)). Normally the English courts will exercise their discretion in favour of arbitration, thus holding the parties to their agreement.[93] Only in exceptional cases will they allow the court

---

[89] See p. 687, *post.*
[90] On the question whether inactivity of the parties amounts to abandonment, see p. 183, *ante.*
[91] If there is an allegation of fraud, the court has power, by virtue of section 24(2) and (3) of the 1950 Act, to order that this issue be tried by the court and the arbitration agreement shall cease to have effect in so far. The court may be willing to exercise this power (and to refuse a stay of court proceedings) on the application of the party charged with the fraud but it will be reluctant to use this power if the true motive of the person charging the fraud is to discontinue the arbitration: *Cunningham-Reid* v. *Buchanan-Jardine* [1988] 1 W.L.R. 678.
[92] See p. 662, *ante.*
[93] *Unterweser Reederei GmbH* v. *Zapata Off-Shore Co.* [1968] 2 Lloyd's Rep. 158; *The Eleftheria* [1969] 1 Lloyd's Rep. 237, 242; *The Makefjell* [1976] 2 Lloyd's Rep. 29; *The Adolf Warski* [1976] 2 Lloyd's Rep. 241; *The Kislovodsk* [1980] 1 Lloyd's Rep. 183; *The El Amria* [1980] 1 Lloyd's Rep. 190; *The Star of Luxor* [1981] 1 Lloyd's Rep. 139; *The Blue Wave* [1982] 1 Lloyd's Rep. 151; *The Benarty* [1995] Q.B. 325; *Cunningham-Reid* v. *Buchanan-Jardine* [1988] 1 W.L.R. 678. It should be noted that many of these cases do not deal with the stay of an arbitration clause but deal with the stay of a foreign jurisdiction clause but the legal considerations are the same, except that the provisions of the Arbitration Act 1975 do not, of course, apply to foreign jurisdiction clauses.

proceedings to continue by refusing a stay of the court proceedings.[94] It is not easy to persuade the court that the agreed method of dispute settlement, *i.e.* arbitration, should not be applied. Sheen J. said in one case[95] that "the plaintiffs must show strong reasons why the court should not give effect to the agreement." The burden of proving these strong reasons is on the party who has commenced the court proceedings.[96] Matters which the court will take into consideration are the situation of the evidence and the convenience of and cost to the parties.

In non-domestic arbitrations the position is different. Here the discretion of the courts is severely curtailed.[97] In these arbitrations the court is *bound* to stay the court proceedings unless satisfied that the arbitration agreement is null and void, inoperative or incapable of being performed, or that there is not in fact any dispute between the parties with regard to the matter referred to arbitration (Arbitration Act 1975, s.1(1)).[98]

The application to stay court proceedings must be made timely. This means that the party who wishes to apply for a stay, must do so "at any time after appearance, and before delivering any pleadings or taking any steps in the proceedings."[99]

Judicial review

The Arbitration Act 1979 admits the judicial review of arbitration awards on questions of law, but this review is severely restricted and admitted only subject to stringent conditions. If they are not satisfied the court has no power to review the award on its merits.[1] In certain well-

---

[94] *The Fehmarn* [1958] 1 W.L.R. 159; *Carvalho* v. *Hull, Blyth (Angola) Ltd.* [1979] 1 W.L.R. 1228.

[95] *The El Amria* [1980] 1 Lloyd's Rep. 390, 391; [1981] 2 Lloyd's Rep. 619 (C.A.); *The Frank Pais* [1986] 1 Lloyd's Rep. 529 (jurisdication clause, stay refused); *The Sidi Bishr* [1987] 1 Lloyd's Rep. 42 jurisdiction clause, stay refused).

[96] Brandon J. in *The Eleftheria* [1969] 1 Lloyd's Rep. 237, 242.

[97] In consequence of the New York Convention on the Recognition and Enforcement of Foreign Arbitral Awards of 1958, to which effect was given in the United Kingdom by the Arbitration Act 1975.

[98] That the provisions of s.1(1) of the Arbitration Act 1975 are mandatory was decided in *Roussel-Uclaf* v. *G. D. Searle & Co. Ltd.* [1978] 1 Lloyd's Rep. 225. On the enforcement of a Convention Award within the meaning of the 1975 Act see 687 *post.* There is no "dispute" within section 1 of the 1975 Act if the plaintiff is plainly right in law and the court is not prevented by that section from at once giving judgment in his favour; but if the defendant has a strongly arguable case, there is a "dispute" and the court is bound to send the matter to arbitration: *S.L. Sethia Liners Ltd.* v. *State Trading Corporation of India Ltd.* [1985] 1 W.L.R. 1398; *Comdel Commodities Ltd.* v. *Siporex Trade SA* [1987] 1 Lloyd's Rep. 325, 329, [1989] 2 Lloyd's Rep. 13 (C.A.).

[99] 1950 Act, s.4(1) and 1975 Act s.1(1). It is controversial what "any other step" in the court proceedings means. It is unnecessary to refer to the many cases dealing with this question.

[1] This system is described as "a system of filtered appeals" by Kerr L.J. in *Universal Petroleum Co. Ltd.* v. *Handels und Transport GmbH* [1987] 1 W.L.R. 1178, 1189.

defined cases the parties may even exclude the judicial review completely. The 1979 Act, in common with the general international trend, thus leans heavily in favour of the finality of the arbitral award, as indicated by Lord Diplock[2]:

> . . . in weighing the rival merits of finality and meticulous legal accuracy there are, in my view, several indications in the Act itself of a parliamentary intention to give effect to the turn of the tide in favour of finality in arbitral awards (particularly in non-domestic arbitrations . . .), at any rate where this does not involve exposing arbitrators to a temptation to depart from "settled principles of law."

Judicial review procedure

The procedure for a review of the award by the court is as follows. An appeal may be brought to the High Court on any question of law arising out of the award by any party to the arbitration—

(a) with the consent of all other parties; or
(b) by leave of the court, but the court shall not grant leave unless it considers that "the determination of the question of law concerned could substantially affect the rights of one or more of the parties to the arbitration agreement."[3]

The judicial review procedure can, of course, be applied only if the award states reasons in sufficient detail. Otherwise the judge would be unable to form an opinion on the question of law which is the subject-matter of the appeal.[4]

The Nema guidelines

It happens rarely that all the parties will ask for judicial review. Normally only one party, the loser in the arbitration, will take the award to court and ask that the award be reviewed. The applicant cannot claim judicial review as of right[5]; it is in the court's discretion whether it will be admitted.

The House of Lords has indicated in the so-called *Nema* guidelines[6] that the court's discretion in allowing judicial review should be exercised

---

[2] In *Pioneer Shipping Ltd.* v. *B.T.P. Tioxide Ltd. The Nema* [1982] A.C. 724, 739–740.
[3] Arbitration Act 1979, s.1(3) and (4).
[4] On reasoned awards see p. 663, *ante.*
[5] The Arbitration Act 1979, s.1(1) abolished the "special case" procedure under the Arbitration Act 1950, s.21. The 1979 Act also abolished the common law principle that the court had jurisdiction to set aside an award on the ground that it showed an error of fact or law on its face.
[6] *Pioneer Shipping Ltd.* v. *B.T.P. Tioxide Ltd. The Nema* [1982] A.C. 724. The *Nema* guidelines were explained in *Antaios Companie Naviera S.A.* v. *Salen Rederierna B.A.* [1985] A.C. 191. In *Petraco (Bermuda) Ltd.* v. *Petromed International SA* [1988] 1 W.L.R. 896 the Court of Appeal laid down some additional guidelines for cases in which the judge was asked to allow judicial review on a point of law not argued before the arbitrator.

sparingly and, as far as possible, the parliamentary intention in favour of finality of the arbitral award should be given effect. However, these guidelines "are not intended to be all-embracing or immutable, but subject to adaptation to match changes in practices . . .".[7]

In the *Nema* guidelines the House of Lords distinguishes between *one-off contracts, i.e.* contracts of singular occurrence, and *contracts involving a question of general importance.* A stricter test has to be applied to the former than to the latter. In the former class of cases the judge should allow judicial review only if, on a perusal of the reasoned award or after brief argument by counsel, he comes to the conclusion that the decision of the arbitrator on the point of law is "obviously wrong."[8] The latter class of case includes the interpretation of clauses in standard contract forms and events of general character that affect similar transactions between many other persons engaged in the same commercial activity; Lord Diplock gave as examples "the closing of the Suez Canal, the United States soya bean embargo, the war between Iraq and Iran."[9] Here judicial review should be admitted if "a strong prima facie case has been made out that the arbitrator was wrong in his construction."[10]

Preliminary points of law

An application may be made to the High Court to determine a question of law arising in the course of the arbitration. The High Court shall not entertain the application unless—

> (*a*) the determination might produce substantial savings in costs; and
> (*b*) the conditions on which the court may give leave to appeal from an arbitration award on a point of law are satisfied.[11]

The application for the determination of a preliminary point of law by the court is made by a party either with the consent of the arbitrator or with the consent of the other parties.[12]

Appeals from the decision of the High Court

These appeals are also severely restricted. There is no appeal from the decision of the High Court to allow or to refuse judicial review or the

---

[7] *Antaios, per* Lord Diplock, 200.

[8] *Nema,* p. 742. In *The Kerman* [1982] 1 Lloyd's Rep. 62, 65. Parker J. formulated this test as follows: " . . . in a one-off case, in the absence of special circumstances, leave should not be given unless on the conclusion of argument on the application for leave the court has formed the provisional view that the arbitrator was wrong and considers that it would need a great deal of convincing that he was right."

[9] *Nema,* p. 744.

[10] *Antaios, per* Lord Diplock, 203; see also *Ipswich Borough Council* v. *Fisons plc.* [1990] 2 W.L.R. 108 (A.C.).

[11] 1979 Act, s.2(2). For these conditions see pp. 667, *ante.*

[12] 1979 Act, s.2(1).

determination of a preliminary point of law unless the High Court gives leave.[13]

If the High Court has given its decision in a judicial review case or a case involving a preliminary point of law, no appeal is admitted to the Court of Appeal unless—

(a) the High Court or the Court of Appeal gives leave; and
(b) it is certified by the High Court that the question of law to which the decision relates either is one of general public importance or is one which for some other special reason should be considered by the Court of Appeal.[14]

Exclusion agreements

As already observed, in certain circumstances the parties may exclude judicial review completely. Where they have entered into a valid *exclusion agreement,* no appeal on a point of law is admitted to the court nor has the court power to determine a preliminary point of law.

For the admissibility of exclusion agreements, arbitrations can be arranged into:

domestic arbitrations;
non-domestic arbitrations; and
special category arbitrations.

The distinction between domestic and non-domestic arbitrations has been considered earlier.[15] It has been seen that the definitions of these two terms are identical in the Arbitration Acts of 1975 and 1979, with the exception that under the 1979 Act the relevant requirements must be satisfied at the time when the arbitration agreement is entered into[16] but under the 1975 Act they must be satisfied when the arbitration proceedings are commenced.[17]

Special category arbitrations concern:

(a) a question or claim falling within the Admiralty jurisdiction of the High Court; or
(b) a dispute arising out of a contract of insurance; or
(c) a dispute arising out of a commodity contract.[18]

A "commodity contract" is defined as a contract—

(a) for the sale of goods regularly dealt with on a commodity market or exchange in England or Wales which is specified for the purposes of this section by an order made by the Secretary of State; and
(b) of a description so specified.[19]

---

[13] 1979 Act, ss.1(6A) and 2(2A), added by the Supreme Court Act 1981, s.148. See *Aden Refinery Co. Ltd.* v. *Ugland Management Co. Ltd.* [1987] Q.B. 650.
[14] 1979 Act, ss.1(7) and 2(3).
[15] See p. 662, *ante.*
[16] 1979 Act, s.3(7).
[17] 1975 Act, s.1(4).
[18] 1979 Act, s.4(1).
[19] 1979 Act, s.4(2).

By a statutory instrument[20] the leading commodity markets and exchanges in England and Wales are specified as falling under this provision. They include, *e.g.* GAFTA, FOSFA and the London Metal Exchange. Every contract concluded on these markets and, as specified in the statutory instrument, governed by the arbitration rules of the listed trade associations is a "commodity contract" within the meaning of the 1979 Act.

Exclusion agreements are admitted on the following conditions:

Domestic arbitrations

The parties may exclude the judicial review by an exclusion agreement entered into only *after* the commencement of the arbitration.[21]

Non-domestic arbitrations

The parties may make an exclusion agreement validly *before* or *after* the commencement of the arbitration.[22]

Special category arbitrations

An exclusion agreement is admitted only:

(a) *after* the commencement of the arbitration; or
(b) if the contract is governed by a law other than that of England and Wales.[23]

International arbitrations fall into the categories of non-domestic and special arbitrations. The regulation of non-domestic arbitrations makes it possible for the parties to include an advance exclusion agreement already into the arbitration clause in their main contract.

If was held in *Marine Contractors Inc.* v. *Shell Petroleum Development Co. of Nigeria Ltd.*[24] that the adoption of an ICC arbitration clause in the main contract operated as an advance exclusion agreement; Ackner L.J. said[25]:

> . . . when parties agree to arbitration by the ICC they deliberately accept an alternative tribunal to the courts because the ICC rules prohibit resort to municipal courts, so far as such prohibition may be lawful.

The main reason on which the Court of Appeal founded its decision was Article 24 of the Rules for the ICC Court of Arbitration (1988 edition) which provides:

---

[20] The Arbitration Act 1979 (Commencement) Order 1979 (S.I. 1979 No. 750 (C.16)).
[21] 1979 Act, s.3(6).
[22] *Ibid.*
[23] Arbitration Act 1979, s.4(1)(i) and (ii).
[24] [1984] 2 Lloyd's Rep. 77; *Arab African Energy Corporation Ltd.* v. *Olieprodukten Nederland B.V.* [1983] 2 Lloyd's Rep. 419. In ICC arbitrations the English courts will not normally order security for costs: *Bank Mellat* v. *Helliniki Techniki S.A.* [1984] Q.B. 281, see p. 678, *post.*
[25] [1984] 2 Lloyd's Rep. 77, at 82.

Finality and enforceabiliy of award

(1) The arbitral award shall be final.
(2) By submitting the dispute to arbitration by the International Chamber of Commerce, the parties shall be deemed to have undertaken to carry out the resulting award without delay and to have waived their right to any form of appeal insofar as such waiver can validly be made.

As the same or similar provisions are found in the rules of most arbitral institutions and also in the UNCITRAL Arbitration Rules,[26] the English courts will recognise the finality of arbitration awards in all "one-off" contracts, in which the arbitration clause in the main contract contains such a provision. Thus, in a wide area of international commercial arbitration even the "filtered" system of judicial review admitted by the 1979 Act can be excluded, if the parties so desire, and the award can be made final.

As far as international contracts falling into the special category are concerned, the reason for the denial of advance exclusion clauses, at least for the time being,[27] is that in this type of contract the decision of the courts may affect not only the parties but also traders in a similar position, and that the certainty of commercial law is promoted if the court retains a limited degree of control.[28]

EC law and arbitration

In arbitration proceedings Community law, where relevant, has to be taken into account. If it becomes necessary to make a reference to the European Court of Justice in Luxembourg under article 177 of the EC Treaty, *e.g.* in order to obtain a ruling on the interpretation of the Treaty, the arbitrator cannot do so because he is not a national "court or tribunal" deriving its authority from a Member State.[29]

Where such a reference becomes necessary, an application for judicial review has to be made under the Arbitration Act 1979 from the award to

---

[26] UNCITRAL Arbitration Rules (1977), Art. 32(2).
[27] The 1979 Act provides in s.4(3) that the exception to the non-domestic regulation in the case of special category arbitrations may be discontinued if an order is made to that effect by the Secretary of State (s.4(3)).
[28] Even before the 1979 Act adopted the principle of finality of the arbitral award (subject to exceptions), the courts admitted an agreement by the parties that no action should be brought in court until an award was made. Such a clause, known as the *Scott* v. *Avery* clause, after an early case of this name ((1856) 25 L.J. Ex. 308), was commonly stipulated in submissions to commercial arbitration in England and Wales and is still widely used; see *Tracomin S.A.* v. *Sudan Oil Seeds Co. Ltd.* [1983] 1 W.L.R. 1026, 1033.
[29] See *Bulk Oil (Zug) Ltd.* v. *Sun International Ltd.* [1984] 1 W.L.R. 147, 151; [1986] 2 C.M.L.R. 732 (European Court). This follows from the decision of the European Court in *Widow Vaassen Göbbels* v. *Beambtenfonds* (Case 61/65) [1966] E.C.R. 261, [1966] C.M.L.R. 508. See further Clive M. Schmitthoff, "Arbitration and EEC Law" in 24 C.M.L.R. (1987), p. 1, and also in the *Essays*, p. 663.

the High Court and the judge may then make the reference.[30] The judge may likewise make a reference to the European Court if asked to determine a preliminary point of law. The European Court stated[31]:

> Community law must be observed in its entirety throughout the territory of all the Member States; parties to a contract are not, therefore, free to create exceptions to it. In that context attention must be drawn to the fact that if questions of Community law are raised in an arbitration resorted to by agreement the ordinary courts may be called upon to examine them either in the context of their collaboration with arbitration tribunals, in particular in order to assist them in certain procedural matters or to interpret the law applicable, or in the course of a review of an arbitration award . . . which they may be required to effect in case of an appeal or objection, in proceedings for leave to issue execution or by any other method of recourse available under the relevant national legislation.

INTERNATIONAL ARBITRATION

The various national laws on arbitration[32] differ in material aspects. Many countries adopt a liberal attitude to international commercial arbitration. Thus, the Supreme Court of the United States rejected already in 1974 the "parochial" approach to the interpretation of an arbitration clause in an international agreement[33] and in 1985 held in the *Mitsubishi* case[34] that even an issue of United States antitrust law could be validly submitted to arbitration. French law, as amended in 1981,[35] provides[36] that arbitral awards shall be recognised in France if their existence is proven by the party relying thereon and if such recognition is not manifestly contrary to international public policy (*ordre public international*). In Belgium, according to a law of March 27, 1985 which came into operation on May 13, 1985, the courts have no jurisdiction to annul an arbitral award unless one of the parties is an individual who has Belgian nationality or is

---

[30] *Ibid.* 154 (*per* Ackner L.J.).

[31] *Nordsee Deutsche Hochseefischerei GmbH* v. *Reederei Mond Hochseefischerei Nordstern AG & Co. KG* (Case 102/81) [1982] E.C.R. 1095, 1111.

[32] *International Commercial Arbitration* (Clive M. Schmitthoff, ed.) (3rd ed., 1985), Oceana; *International Handbook on Commercial Arbitration* (Pieter Sanders, ed.), also in *Essays*, on p. 637. Kluwer; *Commercial Arbitration Yearbook* (since 1976); see also Clive M. Schmitthoff, "Extrajudicial Dispute Settlement," *Forum Internationale*, No. 6, 1985.

[33] In *Scherk* v. *Alberto-Cuver Co.* 417 U.S. 506, rehearing denied 419 U.S. 885 (1974).

[34] *Mitsubishi Motors Corporation* v. *Soler Chrysler-Plymouth Inc.* 473 U.S. 614 (decided on July 2, 1985). Also *Shearson/American Express* v. *Eugene McMahon* 107 S.Ct. 2332 (1987) claims founded on allegations of securities fraud and infringement of the Racketeer Influenced and Corrupt Organisations Act (RICO) are arbitrable); *Rodriguez de Ouijas* v. *Shearson/American Express Inc.* 49 CCH S Ct,Bull. p. B2432 (allegation of infringement of the Securities Act arbitrable).

[35] By the Decree of May 12, 1981, published in the *Journal Officiel* of May 12, 1981. The provisions introduced by this Decree are incorporated into the French Code of Civil Procedure as articles 1492–1507.

[36] French Code of Civil Procedure, Art. 1498.

resident in Belgium, or a company which is constituted under Belgian law or has its seat or a branch in Belgium.[37] In Switzerland, the Private International Law Statute adopted by Parliament on December 18, 1987, which came into operation on January 1, 1989, contains a federal regulation of international arbitration which is very liberal;[38] it applies to all arbitrations if the seat of the arbitration tribunal is situated in Switzerland and if, at the time when the arbitration agreement was concluded, at least one of the parties had neither its domicile nor its habitual residence in Switzerland.[39]

Various attempts have been made to devise an international procedure of commercial arbitration which commends wide acceptance. The most important of them will be considered here under the following headings[40]:

UNCITRAL;
The ICC Court of Arbitration;
The London Court of International Arbitration;
American arbitration;
The International Centre for Settlement of Investment Disputes;
Arbitration in the socialist countries.

UNCITRAL

UNCITRAL itself does not provide arbitration facilities but has sponsored several measures which have made a notable contribution to the unification of the law of international arbitration.

The UNCITRAL Arbitration Rules

These Rules were adopted by UNCITRAL in 1976 and their use was recommended by the General Assembly of the United Nations on

---

[37] Amending the Belgian *code judiciaire*, Art. 1717, see M. Storme and B. Demeulenaere, *International Commercial Arbitration in Belgium, 1989*.

[38] In Chapter 12; see Pierre A. Karrer, "Switzerland's New Law of International Arbitration" in [1989] J.B.L. 169. Mark Blessing, "The New International Arbitration Law in Switzerland. A Significant Step Towards Liberalism" in 5 J.I.A. (1988), on p. 9. For a detailed commentary on the new Swiss international arbitration law and the Swiss Concordat on Arbitration see P. Lalive, J.-F. Poudret and C. Reymond, *Le Droit de L'Arbitrage Interne et International de Suisse*, 1989.

[39] Article 176 of the Swiss PIL Statute. Apart from the cases stated in Art. 176, the parties may, of course, prorogate Swiss arbitration law as the law governing the arbitration procedure.

[40] Another attempt which is not treated here is the European Convention providing a Uniform Law on Arbitration, sponsored by the Council of Europe; European Treaty Series No. 56, opened for signature on January 20, 1966.

December 15, 1976. They have become very popular. They are almost indispensible in ad hoc arbitrations and many arbitral institutions, which have adopted their own rules, allow the parties to use the UNCITRAL Rules in preference or refer to them in order to fill any gaps in their own rules.

The UNCITRAL Arbitration Rules do not have the force of law in any country. They may be adopted by the contracting parties. The following model clause is recommended for their adoption:

> Any dispute, controversy or claim arising out of or relating to this contract, or the breach, termination or invalidity thereof, shall be settled by arbitration in accordance with the UNCITRAL Arbitration Rules as at present in force.
> *Note—Parties may wish to consider adding*:
>   (a) The appointing authority shall be . . . (name of institution or person);
>   (b) The number of arbitrators shall be . . . (one or three);
>   (c) The place of arbitration shall be . . . (town or country);
>   (d) The language(s) to be used in the arbitral proceedings shall be. . . .

The main characteristic of the UNCITRAL Arbitration Rules is that no arbitration shall fail on the ground that the parties cannot agree on an arbitrator or for any other reason no arbitrator can act. If no appointing authority has been agreed by the parties or if the appointing authority refuses to act or fails to appoint an arbitrator within 60 days of the receipt of a party's request, either party may request the Secretary-General of the Permanent Court of Arbitration at the Hague to designate an appointing authority.[41] Unless the parties have agreed upon the place where the arbitration is to be held, such place is determined by the arbitration tribunal.[42] It is further provided by Article 21(1) and (2) that the arbitration tribunal shall have the power to rule on objections that it has no jurisdiction and to determine the existence or the validity of a contract of which the arbitration clause forms part; for the purposes of this provision the arbitration clause is treated as independent of the other terms of the contract and a decision that the contract is null and void shall not entail *ipso facto* the invalidity of the arbitration clause. The attitude of English law to these problems has been discussed earlier.[43]

Many national chambers of commerce and arbitration institutions have agreed to act as "appointing authority" under the UNCITRAL Arbitration Rules.

The UNCITRAL Conciliation Rules

In view of the practical difference between conciliation and arbitration[44] UNCITRAL has prepared and in 1980 adopted the UNCITRAL Concil-

---

[41] UNCITRAL Arbitration Rules, Art. 6(2).
[42] *Ibid.* Art. 16(1).
[43] See p. 649, *ante*.
[44] See p. 646, *ante*.

iation Rules which were recommended by the United Nations General Assembly on December 4, 1980.

The UNCITRAL Conciliation Rules, like the Arbitration Rules, apply only if the parties have adopted them.

The Rules suggest the following Model Conciliation Clause:

> Where in the event of a dispute arising out of or relating to this contract, the parties wish to seek an amicable settlement of that dispute by conciliation, the conciliation shall take place in accordance with the UNCITRAL Conciliation Rules as at present in force.
> (The parties may agree on other conciliation clauses).

The conciliation commences when the invitation to conciliate under the Rules is accepted by the other party.[45] There may be one conciliator, or two or three.[46] If the parties do not agree on the person or persons of the conciliator they may enlist the assistance of an appropriate institution[47] but, unlike the UNCITRAL Arbitration procedure, there is no compulsory procedure for the appointment of a conciliator. The conciliator may make a proposal for a settlement agreement which the parties may either accept or reject.[48]

The parties undertake not to initiate, during the conciliation proceedings, any arbitral or judicial proceedings in respect of a dispute that is the subject of the conciliation proceedings, except in so far as is necessary to preserve the rights of a party.[49] The Rules do not provide what should happen if the conciliation attempt fails. The parties may have provided in their contract that in this case the dispute should go to arbitration; otherwise an aggrieved party is at liberty to take the matter to the court.

A person who has acted as conciliator shall not act as arbitrator if after the failure of the conciliation attempt the matter goes to arbitration,[50] but it is thought that this rule can be dispensed with if all parties agree.

The UNCITRAL Model Law on International Commercial Arbitration

In view of the great divergency of national arbitration laws, which has already been alluded to,[51] UNCITRAL has prepared and adopted in 1985 this Model Law. The General Assembly of the United Nations recommended on December 11, 1985 that all States should give consideration to

---

[45] UNCITRAL Conciliation Rules, Art. 2.
[46] *Ibid.* Art. 3.
[47] *Ibid.* Art. 4(2).
[48] *Ibid.* Arts. 7(4) and 13.
[49] *Ibid.* Art. 16.
[50] *Ibid.* Art. 19.
[51] See pp. 672–673, *ante.*

the Model Law, in view of the needs of international commerce. It is to be hoped that the countries of the world will frame their national laws on this model and that thus uniformity of national legislations relating to arbitral procedure will be achieved.[52] Even if followed by a country as a pattern for its own legislation, the Model Law as such does not have direct legal effect in a national jurisdiction. It has been stated[53]:

> The idea is that the countries of the world should frame their own national arbitration laws on the UNCITRAL model, that they should know from it what the consensus of international lawyers is on controversial questions which arise when they draft or reform their own arbitration laws and that thus a degree of uniformity of the various arbitration regulations used in the world will be established.

The ICC Court of Arbitration

The ICC Court of Arbitration is the most important institution for the arbitral settlement of international trade disputes.[54] It is widely used and enjoys the confidence and respect of businessmen all over the world and is also frequently resorted to in East-West trade.

The ICC Court of Arbitration is not a governmental institution but is created by the International Chamber of Commerce. It has its seat at the headquarters of the ICC in Paris.[55] The present Rules of the ICC Court of Arbitration have been in force since June 1, 1975, they were amended with effect from January 1, 1988.[56]

The following arbitration clause is recommended by the ICC when it is intended to submit differences to arbitration by its Court of Arbitration:

> All disputes arising in connection with the present contract shall be finally settled under the Rules of Conciliation and Arbitration of the International Chamber of Commerce by one or more arbitrators appointed in accordance with the said Rules.

> *Note*:

> Parties are reminded that it may be desirable for them to stipulate in the arbitration clause itself the law governing the contract, the number of arbitrators and the place

---

[52] *Ibid.*

[53] Clive M. Schmitthoff, "Extrajudicial Dispute Settlement," *Forum Internationale*, No. 6, 1985, 15, also in *Essays*, 1988, on p. 637. Legislation based on the Model Law has been enacted in Australia, Canada (by the Federal Parliament and by the legislatures of all Provinces and Territories), Cyprus, Nigeria and the State of California (U.S.A.). (Position: May 17, 1989). Further, the Scottish Advisory Committee on Arbitration Law has recommended the adoption of the Model Law for Scotland, subject to certain modifications, and the Lord Advocate has accepted this recommendation *(Scottish Law Gazette, Vol. 57 No. 4, 100, Dec. 1989).*

[54] In *Bank Mellat* v. *GAA Development and Construction Co.* [1988] 2 Lloyd's Rep. 44, 48 Steyn J. referred to ICC arbitration as "the most truly international of all arbitral systems."

[55] Address: 38 Cours Albert 1ᵉ, 75008 Paris, France. (Tel.: 562.34.56).

[56] The 1975 Rules were contained in ICC Brochure No. 291 which was superseded by Brochure 447. This Brochure contains the Rules in force as from January 1, 1989.

and language of the arbitration. The parties' free choice of the law governing the contract and the place and language of the arbitration is not limited by the ICC Rules of Arbitration.

Attention is called to the fact that the laws of certain countries require that parties to contracts expressly accept arbitration clauses, sometimes in a precise and particular manner.

Arbitration under the Rules of the ICC is open to members and non-members. A procedure for optional conciliation may be adopted. An Administrative Commission for Conciliation is constituted at the ICC and for each dispute a Conciliation Committee of three members is set up by the President of the ICC. The party requesting conciliation may apply either through his National Committee or to the international headquarters of the ICC directly.

If no request for conciliation is made or the conciliation has failed, the dispute proceeds to arbitration. No person having sat on the Conciliation Committee for the settlement of the dispute in question may be appointed as arbitrator. The Court of Arbitration does not itself settle disputes but if the parties have not agreed on the arbitrator(s), the Court chooses a National Committee of the ICC and requests it to propose the arbitrator(s); usually the National Committees have lists of competent and suitable persons to serve in that capacity. The sole arbitrator or the chairman of an arbitration tribunal shall be chosen from a country other than those of which the parties to the dispute are nationals. The arbitration is initiated by a request for arbitration to the Secretariat of the ICC Court of Arbitration, either through the National Committee of the applicant or to Headquarters directly, and the date when the request is received by the Secretariat is deemed to be the date of the commencement of the arbitral proceedings.[57] Article 8(3) and (4) of the ICC Court of Arbitration Rules provide:

(3) Should one of the parties raise one or more pleas concerning the existence or validity of the agreement to arbitrate, and should the Court be satisfied of the prima facie existence of such an agreement, the Court may, without prejudice to the admissibility or merits of the plea or pleas, decide that the arbitration shall proceed. In such a case any decision as to the arbitrator's jurisdiction shall be taken by the arbitrator himself.

(4) Unless otherwise provided, the arbitrator shall not cease to have jurisdiction by reason of any claim that the contract is null and void or allegation that it is inexistent provided that he upholds the validity of the agreement to arbitrate. He shall continue to have jurisdiction, even though the contract itself may be inexistent or null and void, to determine the respective rights of the parties and to adjudicate upon their claims and pleas.

These provisions constitute an agreement of the parties to empower the arbitrator to decide on his own jurisdiction and to have jurisdiction even

---

[57] ICC Court of Arbitration Rules (1975), Art. 3(1). A—prior—nomination of the arbitrator does not "commence" the arbitration: *Offshore International S.A.* v. *Banco Central S.A.* [1976] 2 Lloyd's Rep. 402, 407.

if the contract containing the arbitration clause is "inexistent," *i.e* void *ab initio* or invalid or illegal when he gives his award. The first of these provisions was considered in *Dalmia Dairy Industries Ltd.* v. *National Bank of Pakistan*,[58] a case concerning Indian law which on the relevant issues was held by the Court of Appeal to be the same as English law.[59] The court held unanimously that in Indian and English law the arbitrator could not be allowed finally to determine his own jurisdiction.[60]

The ICC Rules of Arbitration "provide a code that is intended to be self-sufficient in the sense that it is capable of covering all aspects of arbitrations conducted under the rules, without the need for any recourse to any municipal system of law or any application to the courts of the forum."[61] The three main characteristics of ICC arbitration are:

1. Before proceeding with the arbitration, the arbitrator shall draw up the *terms of reference* and, if possible, obtain the signature of the parties thereto.[62]
2. Before the arbitrator signs the award, he shall submit it in draft form to the ICC Court of Arbitration in Paris for *scrutiny*[63]; and
3. The costs of arbitration shall be covered by a *deposit* which the parties normally have to pay to the Court in advance in equal parts.[64]

The object of the statement of the terms of reference is to determine with certainty the issues which are in dispute before the arbitrator. The scrutiny of the draft award by the ICC Court of Arbitration is intended to ensure that the award is enforceable in the country in which enforcement is sought. The Court may suggest modifications as to the form, without affecting the arbitrator's liberty of decision, and also draw his attention to points of substance.[65] The requirement of a deposit will normally make it unnecessary for a national court to order in ICC arbitrations that a foreign claimant should provide security for costs.[66]

---

[58] [1978] 2 Lloyd's Rep. 223. In that case the provisions of Article 13(3) and (4) of the 1955 Rules were considered by the court; they were substantially the same as those of Article 8(3) and (4) of the 1975 Rules.
[59] In the *Dalmia* case the question was whether certain guarantees which the Bank of Pakistan had given to Dalmia in 1962 and 1964 were enforceable although allegedly a state of war existed between India and Pakistan in 1965 and 1971. The guarantees provided for ICC arbitration. The Swiss arbitrator made two awards in favour of the plaintiffs Dalmia who brought an action in the English Courts for the enforcement of these awards. Kerr J. and the Court of Appeal decided in favour of the plaintiffs. The Court of Appeal ruled that in English law an arbitration clause between "enemies" was not abrogated on the outbreak of war, if the main contract in which it was contained was not abrogated and if no dispute requiring arbitration had then arisen.
[60] For a discussion of the general aspects of the problems raised by this decision, see p. 649, *ante*.
[61] Per Kerr L.J. in *Bank Mellat* v. *Helliniki Techniki S.A.* [1984] Q.B. 291, 304.
[62] Rules for the ICC Court of Arbitration, Art. 13.
[63] *Ibid*. Art. 21.
[64] *Ibid*. Art. 9.
[65] The scrutiny procedure is not an appeal or review procedure; the scrutiny procedure under the ICC Rules of Arbitration is explained by Steyn J. in *Bank Mellat* v. *GAA Development and Construction Co.* [1988] 2 Lloyd's Rep. 44, 48.
[66] *Bank Mellat* v. *Helliniki Techniki S.A.* [1984] Q.B. 291; see p. 670, *ante*.

The award is deemed to be made at the place of the arbitration proceedings.[67] The Rules provide[68] that "the arbitral award shall be final" and in view of this provision the English courts have held[69] that the adoption of the ICC Rules of Arbitration may be treated as an advance exclusion agreement within the Arbitration Act 1979, excluding the judicial review on points of law. In normal circumstances the finality of the ICC arbitration award is thus accepted by the English courts.

As a new source of the *lex mercatoria*,[70] the ICC intends to publish extracts from past awards given in arbitration proceedings held under the Rules of the ICC Court of Arbitration. The published extracts will be carefully edited to ensure the anonymity of the parties.

Other ICC dispute settlement measures

The ICC and the *Comité Maritime International* (CMI) have jointly established an *International Maritime Arbitration Committee* with its seat at the headquarters of the ICC in Paris. This Committee applies the *ICC-CMI Rules of Arbitration*, first issued in March 1979.[71]

Under its rules for *Adaptation of Contracts*, issued in 1978, the ICC has constituted a *Standing Committee for the Regulation of Contractual Relations*. Its activities are considered later in the chapter dealing with the Construction of Works and Installations Abroad.[72]

In December 1976 the ICC constituted an *International Centre for Technical Expertise*.[73] The need for this Centre arises primarily in cases where a technical dispute has become unavoidable during the performance of an international contract, such as a long term contract for the construction of works and installations. A neutral expert can be appointed by the Centre and may assist in the solution of the problems which have arisen. Such assistance is not in the nature of an arbitration.

The ICC has also prepared *Rules for Arbitral Referee Procedure*.[74] The function of the arbitral referee is to give a rapid decision in cases of urgency, without prejudice to the final settlement of the dispute by arbitration or litigation. This procedure is particularly useful in long-term transactions or construction projects, where a decision on the site is

---

[67] Rules for the ICC Court of Arbitration, Art. 22.
[68] *Ibid.* art. 24(1). The full text of this article is reproduced on p. 671, *ante.*
[69] *Marine Contractors Inc.* v. *Shell Petroleum Development Co. of Nigeria Ltd.* [1984] 2 Lloyd's Rep. 77; *Arab African Energy Corporation Ltd.* v. *Olieprokukten Nederland B.V.* [1983] 2 Lloyd's Rep. 419; see p. 670, *ante.*
[70] See p. 655, *ante.*
[71] ICC Brochure No. 324 (1979).
[72] ICC Brochure No. 326 (1978).
[73] See pp. 750, *et seq. post.*
[74] Provisional version, 1989.

required. The position of the arbitral referee is similar to that of the engineer appointed under the FIDIC contract,[75] but the arbitral referee is appointed by agreement of the parties or, failing such agreement, by the chairman of the ICC Court of Arbitration, whereas the engineer is appointed by the employer.[76] The arbitral referee shall act in subsequent arbitration proceedings as an arbitrator only with the written agreement of the parties.

The ICC has established an *ICC Liaison Committee with Chambers of Commerce in Socialist Countries*. The Liaison Committee is under the joint chairmanship of an Eastern and Western representative. Terms of reference of the Liaison Committee were published in April 1975.[77] The Committee is known as the East/West Committee.

The London Court of International Arbitration

The London Court of International Arbitration is a tripartite organisation, sponsored by the London Chamber of Commerce, the City of London Corporation, and the Chartered Institute of Arbitrators, and is administered by the latter. Its seat is at the International Arbitration Centre in London.[76] The Rules of the London Court of International Arbitration are known as the LCIA Rules.[79]

The Court recommends the adoption of the following arbitration clause:

> Any dispute arising out of or in connection with this contract, including any question regarding its existence, validity or termination, shall be referred to and finally resolved by arbitration under the Rules of the London Court of International Arbitration, which Rules are deemed to be incorporated by reference into this clause.

The following provisions may be suitable:

> The governing law of this contract shall be the substantive law of . . .
> The tribunal shall consist of . . . (a sole or three) arbitrators). (In the case of a three member tribunal, the following words may be added . . . two of them shall be nominated by the respective parties).
> The place of the arbitration shall be . . . (city).
> The language of arbitration shall be . . .

The Court has prepared several panels of arbitrators which contain the names of many prominent international personalities. A scale of arbitration fees is provided which are within moderate limits.

---

[75] See p. 745, *post.*
[76] See p. 745, *post.*
[77] ICC Brochure No. 307 (1977).
[78] Address: 75 Cannon Street, London EC4N 5BH. There exists also The London International Arbitration Trust Ltd. which aims at promoting arbitration in London. It has published a pamphlet entitled "Arbitration in London" (1983) which contains a collection of arbitration clauses.
[79] 1985 edition.

A number of trade associations provide their own machinery for international commercial arbitration. The most important are those listed earlier[80] when the standard contract forms issued by trade associations were discussed; these standard contracts normally embody an arbitration clause providing for arbitration under the rules of the association in question.

American arbitration

In the United States, "most commercial arbitrations are governed by the United States Arbitration Act, which applies to all transactions in interstate or foreign commerce or Admiralty and which preempts local laws on the subject."[81] The Act referred to is the United States Arbitration Act 1925, as amended.[82] In addition there exists the Uniform Arbitration Act[83] which, sometimes with variations, on May 1, 1984 was adopted by 46 American jurisdictions.

The major United States arbitration institution is the American Arbitration Association (AAA) which has its seat in New York.[84] It has published various sets of arbitration rules. In international trade transactions the *Commercial Arbitration Rules*,[85] supplemented by the *Supplementary Procedures for International Commercial Arbitration*, are relevant. The AAA recommends the inclusion of the following arbitration clause into the parties' agreement:

> Any controversy or claim arising out of or relating to this contract, or the breach thereof, shall be settled by arbitration in accordance with the Commercial Arbitration Rules of the American Arbitration Association, and judgment upon the award rendered by the Arbitrator(s) may be entered in any court having jurisdiction thereof.

The Commercial Arbitration Rules provide that the AAA shall establish a national panel of arbitrators.[86] The Rules further adopt the so-called list procedure if the parties have not appointed an arbitrator and have not agreed on another method of appointment; under this procedure the AAA submits simultaneously to each party an identical list of persons

---

[80] See p. 73, *ante*.

[81] J. Gillis Wetter, *The International Arbitral Process: Public and Private*, Vol. II 1979, 6. On the liberal attitude of the Supreme Court to arbitration, see p. 672, *ante*.

[82] Title 9. US Code paras. 1–14, enacted February 12, 1925 (43 Stat. 883), codified July 30, 1947 (61 Stat. 669), and amended September 3, 1954 (68 Stat. 1233), Chapter 2 added July 31, 1970 (84 Stat. 692).

[83] Adopted by the National Conference of the Commissioners on Uniform State Laws in 1955 and amended in 1956.

[84] Address: 140 West 51st Street, New York, N.Y. 100120.

[85] As amended and in effect from April 1, 1985.

[86] AAA Commercial Arbitration Rules, Art. 5.

chosen from the panel and the parties may cross off names to which they object or indicate the order of preference; the AAA then invites the person approved on both lists according to the order of preference to act as arbitrator.[87] Each arbitrator is required before the first hearing to take an oath of office.[88]

The AAA has also published separate rules on *Procedure for Cases under the UNCITRAL Arbitration Rules*, if the parties prefer arbitration under these Rules.

The International Centre for Settlement of Investment Disputes

An attempt has been made to approach the protection of foreign investors from the procedural angle by providing machinery for the settlement of international investment disputes. This approach has been successful. In 1965 a *Convention on the Settlement of Investment Disputes between States and Nationals of Other States* was concluded in Washington.[89] This Convention has become effective. On June 30, 1988, it had been ratified by 89 countries, among them the United States, the United Kingdom, France and West Germany. The United Kingdom gave effect to it by the *Arbitration (International Investment Disputes) Act 1966*,[90] as amended.[91]

The Convention, which was sponsored by the International Bank for Reconstruction and Development, provides for the formation of an *International Centre for Settlement of Investment Disputes (ICSID)* at the principal office of the Bank in Washington.[92] The ICSID makes available facilities to which contracting States and foreign investors who are nationals of other contracting States have access on a voluntary basis for the settlement of investment disputes between them in accordance with rules laid down in the Convention. The method of settlement might be conciliation or arbitration, or conciliation followed by arbitration in case

---

[87] *Ibid.* Art. 13.

[88] *Ibid.* Art. 27.

[89] The Convention entered into force on October 14, 1966. David M. Sassoon, "Convention on the Settlement of Investment Disputes" in [1965] J.B.L. 334; Joy Cherian, *Investment Contracts and Arbitration, The World Bank Convention on the Settlement of Investment Disputes,* Sijthoff, 1975.

On the *Multilateral Investment Guaranty Agency (MIGA)* see next page text. The MIGA Convention was approved by the Board of Governors of the World Bank in Seoul on October 10, 1985.

[90] The Convention entered into force for the U.K. on January 18, 1967 (Treaty Series No. 25/1967); Cmnd 3255. The Convention has been extended to various colonies and other territories; see S.I.s 1967 Nos. 159, 249, 585 in particular.

[91] By the Evidence (Proceedings in Other Jurisdictions) Act 1975, s.8(2) and Sched. 2 and the Supreme Court Act 1981, Sched. 5.

[92] The address of the ICSID is: 1818 H Street, N.W. Washington, D.C., 20433, U.S.A.

the conciliation effort fails. The initiative for such proceedings might come from a State as well as from an investor. The ICSID itself does not act as conciliator or arbitrator but maintains panels of specially qualified persons from which conciliators or arbitrators can be selected by the parties, and provides the necessary facilities for the conduct of the proceedings. Once a State and a foreign investor have agreed to use the facilities of the ICSID, they are required to carry out their agreement, to give due consideration to the recommendations of a conciliator and to comply with an arbitral award. In addition, all contracting States, whether parties to the dispute or not, are required to recognise arbitral awards rendered in accordance with the Convention as binding and to enforce the pecuniary obligations imposed thereby.

The United Kingdom Arbitration (International Investment Disputes) Act 1966, as amended, sets out the Convention in a schedule.[93] The Act itself provides that a person seeking recognition or enforcement of an award made under the Convention is entitled to have it registered in the High Court. The Act came into force on January 18, 1967.[94]

The *Convention establishing the Multilateral Investment Guarantee Agency* (MIGA) to which the United Kingdom has given effect by the Multilateral Investment Guarantee Agency Act 1988, provides an arbitration procedure for certain disputes; it further provides that, if the arbitration tribunal is not constituted within 60 days. the arbitrator or the president of the arbitration tribunal shall be appointed, at the joint request of the parties, by the Secretary General of ICSID.[94a]

The ICSID has published four sets of Rules, *viz.* the Administrative and Financial Regulations, the Institution Rules, the Arbitration Rules and the Conciliation Rules. They, together with the Convention, are published in a document entitled "ICSID Basic Documents."[95]

European arbitration

A *European Convention on International Commercial Arbitration* was signed on April 21, 1961, in Geneva and came into force on January 7, 1964.[96] The Convention was sponsored by the UN Economic Commission for Europe. The Convention has been ratified or adhered to by:

---

[93] Act of 1966, s.1(2).
[94] *Ibid.* s.9(2); see n. 90, *ante.*
[94a] Convention, Annex II, Art. 4(b). The Convention is reproduced as schedule to the Multilateral Investment Guarantee Agency Act 1988.
[95] Published in January 1985 (the pamphlet contains the documents as revised on September 26, 1984). The pamphlet also contains a flyleaf setting out the Schedule of Costs, as in January 1985.
[96] The Convention was complemented by the *Agreement relating to the Application of the European Convention on International Commercial Arbitration* signed in Paris on December 17, 1962. There exist also *Arbitration Rules for Certain Categories of Perishable Agricultural Products* of July 1979, sponsored by the UN Economic Commission for Europe (ECE/AGRI/43).

Austria, Bulgaria, Byelorussian S.S.R., Czechoslovakia, Cuba, France, Germany (Federal), Hungary, Italy, Poland, Romania, Ukrainian S.S.R., Upper Volta, U.S.S.R. and Yugoslavia.

In addition the following States have signed the Convention:

Belgium, Denmark, Finland, Spain, Turkey.

The United Kingdom has neither signed nor ratified the Convention. The Convention attempts to overcome difficulties in the constitution of arbitral tribunals and in arbitration procedure, particularly in trading relations between countries of different economic order. The Convention provides that the parties to an arbitration agreement shall be free to submit their dispute to a permanent arbitral institution or to an ad hoc constituted tribunal. It further contains rules for the arrangement of arbitration if the parties cannot agree on the composition or venue of the arbitral tribunal or one party fails to co-operate with another in making the necessary arrangements for the arbitration. In particular, a *Special Committee* is constituted which consists of three members, one designated by the International Chamber of Commerce, the other by the countries in which no national committees of the ICC exist, *i.e.* mainly the socialist countries, and the chairman being a member of one of these two groups in rotation; the chairmanship changes every two years. The function of the Special Committee is to appoint the arbitrator or umpire and to settle procedural details of the arbitration if the contract is silent or the parties cannot agree. The Special Committee constitutes a bridge between Eastern and Western arbitration.

Other provisions of the Convention which should be mentioned are that foreign nationals may be designated as arbitrators, that the arbitrators shall act as *amiable compositeurs* if the parties so decide and if they may do so under the law applicable to the arbitration, and that "legal persons of public law," such as foreign trade corporations of the countries of state-planned economy, have the right to conclude valid arbitration agreements.

The UN European Commission for Europe has also sponsored the *Economic Commission for Europe's Arbitration Rules* of January 20, 1966. These Rules may be adopted by the parties to a contract. The Rules,[97] like the Convention of 1961, aim at assisting the parties to constitute an arbitration tribunal if there exists uncertainty or the defendant fails to co-operate. They designate certain "appointing authorities" which in principle are national chambers of commerce. They provide that if within a specified period the arbitration tribunal is not constituted, the claimant may apply to the competent appointing authority for the appointment of the arbitrator or umpire. The competent

---

[97] United Nations reference: Ref. E/ECE/625/Rev. 1 (1970).

appointing authority is that designated in the contract, failing such designation the one operating at the place of arbitration defined in the contract, and if the contract neither designates an appointing authority nor defines the venue of arbitration, the claimant may apply to the Special Committee constituted under the Convention of 1961 for the appointment of the arbitrator or umpire. In the United Kingdom the Association of British Chambers of Commerce has been designated as appointing authority.

Arbitration in the socialist countries

In the socialist countries arbitration tribunals are constituted for dealing with commercial disputes between the indigenous foreign trade organisations and business enterprises of other countries, with which they enter into export and import transactions.[98] In the Soviet Union two international arbitration tribunals exist, both constituted at the USSR Chamber of Commerce and Industry in Moscow, *viz.* the Arbitration Court and the Maritime Arbitration Court which has jurisdiction over claims arising from contracts of carriage of goods by sea, bills of lading, charterparties, marine insurance policies and further, speaking generally, over claims which in England would fall within the province of Admiralty jurisdiction.[99] Similar arbitration tribunals exist in Poland, Czechoslovakia, East Germany, Romania, Hungary, Yugoslavia and China.[1] In their negotiations with business enterprises of the Western countries, the foreign trade organisations of the socialist countries will attempt to obtain agreement to clauses submitting disputes to the arbitration tribunals of their own country. Since these tribunals have a reputation for fair and impartial dealings in purely commercial matters, some exporters in the Western countries do not object; others who object will normally find that the foreign trade organisation with which they negotiate is willing to agree to arbitration under the rules of the ICC Court of Arbitration, or to "neutral" arbitration, *e.g.* in Sweden or Switzerland. In Yugoslavia there is no difficulty in obtaining the consent of the indigenous trade corpora-

---

[98] See *International Commercial Arbitration*, 3rd ed. (1985), Vol. I, Pt. III; also D. F. Ramzaitsev and Denis Tallon on "The Law applied by Arbitration Tribunals" in *The Sources of the Law of International Trade*, (Schmitthoff, ed.) (London, 1964), pp. 138 *et seq*. See further Pavel Kalinsky, "Le droit international privé comparé des états socialistes dans leur coopération économique," *Academy of International Law, Recueil des cours*, Vol. 208 (1988–I), 173.

[99] There exists a maritime arbitration tribunal for Poland, East Germany and Czechoslovakia; its seat is in Gdynia (Poland) and its jurisdiction is similar to that of the USSR Maritime Arbitration Court.

[1] Thomas W. Hoya, *East-West Trade. Comecon Law. American-Soviet Trade* (1984) pp. 324–325 (with much further material on pp. 329 *et seq*).

tions, which enjoy considerable independence from the State, to arbitration outside the country.

Arbitration in the socialist countries differs in some respects from that in the countries of free economy, but following the liberalisation policy of many Eastern countries, these differences are diminishing and likely to disappear completely in course of time. The rules governing the constitution of and procedure in the arbitration courts in the Eastern countries are published and most of them are available in English.

The countries of the Council of Mutual Economic Assistance (CMEA) adopted on May 26, 1972 a revised *Convention on the Settlement by Arbitration of Civil Law Disputes resulting from Economic, Scientific and Technical Co-operation*. Further, in 1975 the Executive Committee of CMEA approved revised *Uniform Rules for Arbitration Tribunals* of the CMEA countries, these Uniform Rules were amended from time to time.

The particular character of foreign trade arbitration in the socialist countries has raised difficult problems in the courts of the Western countries. In the Swiss courts the question arose[2] whether awards of the Arbitration Court of the Czechoslovak Chamber of Commerce in Prague were enforceable in Switzerland under the Geneva Convention of 1927[3] to which both Czechoslovakia and Switzerland were parties; the Federal Supreme Court of Switzerland held that the fact that the members of the arbitration court were nominated by the President of the Czechoslovak Chamber of Commerce was not against Swiss public policy and that the enforcement of the Czech award could not be refused on that ground. In the English and American courts proceedings have been stayed so that arbitration in Moscow could proceed.[4] The Soviet Foreign Trade Commission—the predecessor of the Moscow Arbitration Court—itself had to consider the plea that the Soviet tribunal and the Soviet party were, in fact, one and the same person and rejected it.[5] In all these cases the courts attached decisive importance to the fact that the defendant, when accepting the arbitration clause, had voluntarily submitted to the jurisdiction of a tribunal in a socialist country; to relieve him of that obligation on the ground that the tribunal was composed in a particular manner, would be contrary to the principle that contracts have to be performed

---

[2] *Ligna Aussenhandelsunternehmen* v. *Baumgartner & Co. A.G.*, BGE 1958 (84), I, 39; *Compagnie Continentale d'Importation* v. *Eberle*, BGE 1958 (84), I, 56; see H.-P. Friedrich in [1960] J.B.L. 468.

[3] See p. 688, *post.*

[4] In England: *May & Hassell Ltd.* v. *Exportles* (1940) 66 Ll.L.R. 103; *The Kislovodsk* [1980] 1 Lloyd's Rep. 183. In U.S.A.: *Amtorg Trading Corpn.* v. *Camden Fibre Mills Inc.* (1952) 304 N.Y. 519.

[5] *Exportles* v. *Compagnie Commerciale de Bois à Papier*, quoted by Pisar in "Treatment of Communist Foreign Trade Arbitration in Western Courts," *International Trade Arbitration* (Domke, ed.), 1958, 101, 104. That the Polish State and a Polish foreign trade corporation were different persons was decided in *C. Czanikow Ltd* v. *Rolimpex* [1979] A.C. 351; see p. 188, *ante.*

(*pacta sunt servanda*). Differences in legal concepts between countries of a different economic order have been considered by the English courts in another connection[6] and have been held not to infringe English public policy.

ENFORCEMENT OF AWARDS

The decision of the arbitrator or umpire is called the award.[7] In many cases the award is carried out faithfully by the parties, but sometimes it is necessary to ascertain the means by which the award can be enforced in law.

In England an English award is normally enforced in the same manner as a judgment; the only difference is that leave of the court must first be obtained for the execution of an award. Leave is granted by a master of the court in a simple and inexpensive procedure which is commenced by originating summons. In exceptional cases, *e.g.* when the submission was oral, an action for the enforcement of the award has to be brought which is heard by the judge.[8]

More important in international trade relations is the question whether an English award can be enforced in a foreign country where property of the debtor is situate, or, *vice versa,* whether a foreign award can be enforced in the English jurisdiction. As matters stand at present, it can be stated that in many cases the enforcement of a foreign award is possible, but the legal method of enforcement varies. As far as the enforcement of a foreign award in England is concerned—and the same applies to the enforcement of an English award in the respective foreign countries—one distinguishes between the enforcement under the Geneva Protocol and Convention and that under the New York Convention. Both aim at making the enforcement of a foreign award as simple as that of an award made within the jurisdiction and to admit it to execution under the same conditions. Enforcement under the Geneva Protocol and Convention is regulated by the Arbitration Act 1950 and these awards are known as *foreign awards*. Enforcement under the New York Convention of 1958 is possible under the Arbitration Act 1975 and these awards are referred to as *Convention awards*. The New York Convention is designed to supersede the Geneva Protocol and Convention by one instrument and, at the same time, to make more effective the international recognition of arbitration agreements and foreign arbitral awards and the enforcement of the latter. At present these two methods of enforcement overlap with respect to some countries. Where that is the case, the enforcement as

---

[6] *Luther* v. *Sagor* [1921] 3 K.B. 532, 539; *Re Trepca Mines Ltd.* [1960] 1 W.L.R. 1273, 1278.
[7] In French it is called *la sentence*, the same word as is used for a court decision.
[8] Arbitration Act 1950, s.26.

Convention award is preferable because it is the easier method of enforcement. Both methods will be considered below. In addition to these two methods, a foreign arbitral award made in a country to which the Foreign Judgments (Reciprocal Enforcement) Act 1933 is made applicable, can be enforced in England and Wales upon registration, provided that it is enforceable in the country in which it was made, in the same manner as a judgment.[9] Speaking generally, it is more easy to enforce a foreign arbitral award than it is to enforce a foreign judgment, particularly if the recognition and enforcement is governed by the New York Convention.

An arbitration award can be enforced against foreign State property for the time being in use or intended for use for commercial purposes.[10]

The Geneva Protocol and Convention

Two international agreements have been concluded in Geneva, the Protocol on Arbitration Clauses of 1923, and the Convention on the Execution of Foreign Arbitral Awards of 1927.[11] Both agreements have been ratified by a number of countries, amongst them the United Kingdom. By the Arbitration Act 1950 statutory effect is given in the United Kingdom to the Protocol on Arbitration Clauses of 1923 by sections 4(2) and 35, and to the Convention of the Execution of Foreign Arbitral Awards of 1927 by section 35. The Protocol is contained in the First Schedule and the Convention in the Second Schedule to the Act of 1950.

Under the Convention a foreign award can be enforced in the English jurisdiction in the same manner as an English award, provided the arbitration agreement is valid under its proper law and certain other requirements have been satisfied, but the enforcement will be refused if the award is contrary to English public policy. The application of these provisions depends on reciprocity being granted by the country where the award is made. Awards are mutually enforceable under the Convention in the following countries[12]:

> Antigua and Barbuda, Austria, Bahamas, Bangladesh, Belguim, Belize, Czechoslovakia, Denmark, Dominica, Finland, France, Federal Republic of Germany, German Democratic Republic, Greece, Grenada, Guyana, India, Republic of Ireland, Israel, Italy, Japan, Kenya, Luxembourg, Malta, Mauritius, Netherlands, New Zealand, Pakistan, Portugal, Romania, Saint Christopher and Nevis, St. Lucia, Spain, Sweden,

---

[9] Foreign Judgments (Reciprocal Enforcement) Act 1933, s.10A, added by the Civil Jurisdiction and Judgments Act 1982, Sched. 10, para. 4; see 709, *post*.
[10] State Immunity Act 1978, s.13; see p. 228, *ante*.
[11] They were sponsored by the League of Nations.
[12] Arbitration (Foreign Awards) Order 1984 (S.I. 1984 No. 1168).

Switzerland, Tanzania, Thailand, United Kingdom of Great Britain and Northern Ireland, Western Samoa, Yugoslavia, Zambia.

The Geneva Protocol applies to the following countries[12]:

Anguilla, British Virgin Islands, Cayman Islands, Falkland Islands, Falkland Islands Dependencies, Gibraltar, Hong Kong, Montserrat, Turks and Caicos Islands, Antigua and Barbuda, Austria, Bahamas, Bangladesh, Belgium, Belize, Czechoslovakia, Denmark, Dominica, Finland, France, Federal Republic of Germany, German Democratic Republic, Greece, Grenada, Guyana, India, Republic of Ireland, Israel, Italy, Japan, Kenya, Luxembourg, Malta, Mauritius, Netherlands (including Curacao), New Zealand, Pakistan, Portugal, Romania, Saint Christopher and Nevis, St. Lucia, Spain, Sweden, Switzerland, Tanzania, Thailand, United Kingdom of Great Britain and Northern Ireland, West Samoa, Yugoslavia, Zambia.

The New York Convention

On June 10, 1958, a *Convention on the Recognition and Enforcement of Foreign Arbitral Awards* was approved by a United Nations Conference at New York.[13] New York Convention has been given effect in the United Kingdom by the Arbitration Act 1975. The following 70 States have agreed to be bound by the Convention[14] but some States have ratified or acceded subject to reservations, notably specifying that the Convention's application is subject to reciprocity (the reciprocity reservation) or that it is limited to business and commercial transactions (the commercial reservation)[15]:

Australia (including all the external territories for the international relations of which Australia is responsible), Austria, Belgium, Belize, Benin, Botswana, Bulgaria, Byelorussian Soviet Socialist Republic, Cambodia, Central African Republic, Chile, China, People's Republic, Colombia, Cuba, Cyprus, Czechoslovakia, Denmark (including Greenland and the Faroe Islands), Djibouti, Ecuador, Egypt, Finland, France (including all the territories of the French Republic), Federal Republic of Germany, German Democratic Republic, Ghana, Greece, Guatemala, Haiti, Holy See, Hungary, India, Indonesia, Republic of Ireland, Israel, Italy, Japan, Jordan, Korea, Kuwait, Luxembourg, Madagascar, Mexico, Monaco, Morocco, Netherlands (including the Netherlands Antilles), New Zealand, Niger, Nigeria, Norway, Philippines, Poland, Romania, San Marino, Singapore, South Africa, Spain, Sri Lanka, Sweden, Switzerland, Syria, Tanzania, Thailand, Trinidad and Tobago, Tunisia, Ukrainian Soviet Socialist Republic, Union of Soviet Socialist Republics, United Kingdom of Great Britain and Northerm Ireland, United States of America (including

---

[13] The text of the Convention is reproduced in [1958] J.B.L. 396, and its provisions are explained by Samuel Pisar, "The United Nations Convention on Foreign Arbitral Awards," in [1959] J.B.L. 219. For an excellent treatment of the New York Convention see Albert Jan van den Berg, *The New York Arbitration Convention of 1958*. T. M. C. Asser Institute, The Hague, 1981.

[14] Arbitration (Foreign Awards) Order 1984 (S.I. 1984 No 1168) and Arbitration (Foreign Awards) Order 1987 (S.I. 1987 No. 1029). According to the UNCITRAL Publication on *Status of Conventions* (October 9, 1989), 83 States have ratified the Convention or acceded to it.

[15] These reservations are made by virtue of Art. I(3) of the New York Convention.

all the territories for the international relations of which the United States of America is responsible), Uruguay, Yugoslavia.

The New York Convention represents great progress in the field of international arbitration, when compared with the Geneva provisions. They were founded on the requirement of reciprocity which made it necessary to conclude bilateral agreements between States before the Geneva provisions could become operative in their jurisdictions. The requirement of reciprocity guaranteed by bilateral treaties is abandoned by the New York Convention which applies, in principle, to every foreign award, *i.e.* an award made in the territory of any State other than that in which its recognition and enforcement is sought, but, as already observed, when ratifying the Convention or acceding to it some States have limited the application of the Convention to awards made in the territory of other Member States (Art. I).[16] It has rightly been said[17] that that reservation is self-liquidating since its effect will abate as more and more States ratify the Convention.

Further, whilst the application of the Geneva Protocol of 1923 depended on the parties to the agreement being subject to the jurisdiction of different States which were members of the Protocol, the New York Convention no longer stipulates that requirement and applies to all agreements in writing under which the parties undertake to submit to arbitration (Art. II).

The Arbitration Act 1975 provides[18] that in principle, enforcement of a Convention award shall not be refused.[19] Exceptionally the enforcement may be refused if the person against whom it is invoked proves[20]:

(a) that a party to the arbitration agreement was (under the law applicable to him) under some incapacity; or

(b) that the arbitration agreement was not valid under the law to which the parties subjected it or, failing any indication thereon, under the law of the country where the award was made; or

(c) that he was not given proper notice of the appointment of the arbitrator or of the arbitration proceedings or was otherwise unable to present his case; or

(d) . . . that the award deals with a difference not contemplated by or not falling within the terms of the submission to arbitration or contains decisions on matters beyond the scope of the submission to arbitration; or

(e) that the composition of the arbitral authority or the arbitral procedure was not in accordance with the agreement of the parties or, failing such agreement, with the law of the country where the arbitration took place; or

---

[16] References are to the New York Convention.

[17] By Samuel Pisar, *loc. cit.*, p. 225.

[18] Arbitration Act 1975, s.5(1).

[19] The 1975 Act is applicable if the foreign country where the award was made was a party to the Convention at the time when the enforcement proceedings were commenced in England even though it was not a party to the Convention when the award was made: *Government of the State of Kuwait* v. *Sir Frederick Snow and Partners* [1984] A.C. 426 (H.L.).

[20] *Ibid.* s.5(2). These provisions of the 1975 Act aim at giving effect, in the United Kingdom, to article V of the 1958 Convention, although there are considerable differences in the wording of the Act and the Convention.

(f) that the award has not yet become binding on the parties, or has been set aside or suspended by a competent authority of the country in which, or under the law of which, it was made.

Enforcement of a Convention award may also be refused if the award is in respect of a matter which is not capable of settlement by arbitration, or if it would be contrary to public policy to enforce the award.[21] A Convention award which contains decisions on matters not submitted to arbitration may be enforced to the extent that it contains decisions on matters submitted to arbitration and separable from the matters not so submitted.[22] A Convention award is enforceable in the manner provided for by section 26 of the Arbitration Act 1950, *i.e.* normally by leave of the master or the judge, in the same manner as an English judgment.[23]

Enforcement of awards in the absence of international regulation

In countries which do not adhere to the international regulation, the position is the following: An arrangement for the reciprocal enforcement of money judgments has been made with some Commonwealth countries under the Administration of Justice Act 1920[24] and this arrangement is extended to arbitral awards which, under the law in force where they are made, are enforceable in the same manner as judgments.[25] A similar provision is contained in the Foreign Judgments (Reciprocal Enforcement) Act 1933.[26] In these cases the enforcement of the award is by simple registration in the country in which enforcement is sought. This method is satisfactory because it is inexpensive and requires the observation of few formalities. The method of registration is available in Australia, New Zealand, the Canadian Provinces of Newfoundland and Saskatchewan and Gibraltar, and many other parts of the Commonwealth.[27] In those parts which do not admit the system of registration, *e.g.* Canada (with the exception of Newfoundland and Saskatchewan), and in the foreign countries outside the Commonwealth which have not ratified the Geneva or New York Conventions with effect to the United Kingdom, the enforcement of English awards depends entirely on private international law and might meet with considerable difficulties.[28]

---

[21] *Ibid.* s.5(3).

[22] *Ibid.* s.5(4).

[23] *Ibid.* s.3(1)(a) see p. 687, *ante.*

[24] See p. 706 *post.*

[25] 1920 Act, s.12(1).

[26] 1933 Act, s.10A, added by the Civil Jurisdiction and Judgments Act 1982, Sched. 10, para. 4; see p. 709, *post.*

[27] This method is alternative to those admitted by the Geneva Convention of 1927 or the New York Convention of 1958.

[28] A foreign award which, for one reason or another, cannot be enforced in the United Kingdom by registration may be enforced by action (which may be *in personam* or *in rem*) but the cause of the action is the agreement of the parties to submit to arbitration and not the award itself: *The Saint Anna* [1983] 1 W.L.R. 895.

CHAPTER 32

INTERNATIONAL COMMERCIAL LITIGATION

If the exporter feels compelled to take court proceedings against a customer abroad, he is faced with a difficult choice. His first inclination will be to commence proceedings in the debtor's country and to obtain a judgment which he can execute into the debtor's assets situate there.[1] He has, however, an alternative course. If certain conditions are satisfied the English courts are prepared to assume jurisdiction over persons and companies not resident in England and Wales even if those parties are unwilling to submit to the English jurisdiction; if these conditions are satisfied, the exporter may consider obtaining a judgment in the English courts and trying to enforce it against the debtor's assets in the United Kingdom or abroad.

In the following, first the ordinary jurisdiction of the English courts over foreign litigants will be considered, then a general survey of the law relating to the reciprocal enforcement of foreign judgments—English judgments abroad and foreign judgments in the English jurisdiction—will be given, and eventually the special position under the *Brussels Convention on Jurisdiction and Enforcement of Judgments in Civil and Commercial Matters* of September 27, 1968 (in this chapter referred to as "the *Convention*"), to which effect is given in the United Kingdom by the Civil Jurisdiction and Judgments Act 1982, will be considered.

THE JURISDICTION OF THE ENGLISH COURTS OVER FOREIGN LITIGANTS

Jurisdiction of the English courts

The English courts have jurisdiction over claims arising from contractual relations if—

1. the defendant is in England and Wales and is served with a writ there;
2. if, though he is not in England or Wales,
   (a) he has submitted to the jurisdiction of the English courts; or
   (b) the courts assume jurisdiction over him in accordance with the Rules of the Supreme Court, Order 11[2]; these Rules are made by the judges under statutory authority.

---

[1] If the debtor has assets in a third country, the exporter may consider commencing proceedings there, provided that the rules of procedure of that country so allow.
[2] And Order 75 which deals with Admiralty proceedings.

The jurisdiction of the English courts under No. 1 above does not require further consideration in this work, but the situations under No. 2 call for further explanation.

Submission to the English jurisdiction

Where a foreign defendant in an action for breach of contract voluntarily submits to the jurisdiction of a local court, the court is normally prepared to exercise jurisdiction over him.[3] It is not regarded as a voluntary submission if the defendant appears before the court solely to contest its jurisdiction. In proceedings in the English courts the defendant may dispute the jurisdiction of the court by virtue of R.S.C., Ord. 12, r. 8(1). Rule 8(6) of this Order states expressly[4]:

> A defendant who makes an application under paragraph (1) shall not be treated as having submitted to the jurisdiction of the court by reason of his having given notice to defend [in order to dispute the jurisdiction].

Conversely, it is provided in section 33(1) of the Civil Jurisdiction and Judgments Act 1982 that the English courts shall not treat an appearance in a foreign court as voluntary submission to its jurisdiction if the defendant appeared only—

(a) to contest the jurisdiction of the court;
(b) to ask the court to dismiss or stay the proceedings on the ground that the dispute in question should be submitted to arbitration or to the determination of the courts of another country; or
(c) to protect, or obtain the release of, property seized or threatened with seizure in the proceedings.

But if the defendant does more than merely contest the jurisdiction, *e.g.* if he takes any steps to defend on the merits, he is treated as having submitted to the jurisdiction of the court. An application to the English court for a stay of proceedings pending the outcome of proceedings in a foreign court does not amount to submission to the English jurisdiction,[5] nor does an application to discharge a *Mareva* injunction issued against

---

[3] Except in so far as by virtue of the Convention the court of another Contracting State has exclusive jurisdiction, see p. 714, *post*.
[4] *Cf. Carmel Exporters (Sales) Ltd.* v. *Sea-Land Services Inc.* [1981] 1 W.L.R. 1068; *Amanuel* v. *Alexandros Shipping Co.* [1986] Q.B. 464 (submission can be made before proceedings commence).
[5] *Williams & Glyn's Bank plc* v. *Astro Dinamico Compania Naviera S.A.* [1984] 1 W.L.R. 438.

the defendant constitute a submission to the jurisdiction over the main action.[6]

Service out of the jurisdiction

There exist two regimes for the exercise of the assumed jurisdiction by the English courts over persons not present in England and Wales and not having submitted to the English jurisdiction. If the defendant is domiciled[7] in a Convention State and the requirements of the Convention are satisfied,[8] service out of the jurisdiction may be carried out *without leave* of the court, but if these conditions are not fulfilled and the defendant is domiciled in a non-Convention country, service out of the jurisdiction requires *the leave* of the court.

Both regimes are regulated by the Rules of the Supreme Court, Order 11. Paragraph (1) of this Order deals with service on a person in a non-Convention country, and paragraph (2) with service on a person in a Convention country. Order 11 is of such importance that it is set out here in full, as far as relevant.

The two regimes of Order II compared

There exist remarkable differences between the two regimes. In particular, if service in a non-Convention country is contemplated, leave of the court can be obtained not only if the contract is to be performed in the English jurisdiction but also if it is made in England and Wales or is governed by English law. But if service has to be carried out in a Convention country, only the place of performance is relevant and it is irrelevant where the contract was concluded and which law applies to it. The admission of service out of the jurisdiction in Convention cases is

---

[6] *Obikoya* v. *Silvernorth Ltd.*, *The Times*, July 6, 1983. The adoption of English law as the proper law of the contract does not necessarily mean submission to the jurisdiction of the courts of this country: *Dundee Ltd.* v. *Gilman & Co. (Australia) Pty. Ltd.* [1968] 2 Lloyd's Rep. 394 (Sup. Ct. of N.S.W.). Where a foreign plaintiff has commenced proceedings in the English courts, he is regarded as having submitted to a counterclaim by the defendant: *Derby & Co. Ltd.* v. *Larsson* [1976] 1 W.L.R. 202. See also *The Kapitan Markos* [1986] 1 Lloyd's Rep. 211, 229. A foreign defendant who applies to the court for an order that the plaintiff should provide security for costs solely for the dispute on the preliminary issue of the court's jurisdiction does not thereby submit to the jurisdiction, but if he applies for security for the whole proceedings that may well be interpreted as a submission to the jurisdiction of the court; see Dicey and Morris on *The Conflict of Laws*, 11th ed., 1987, comment to Rule 26, on p. 301, n. 19.
[7] On the "domicile" for the purposes of the Convention, see p. 710, *post*.
[8] On these requirements, see p. 710, *post*.

thus more limited than that in non-Convention cases; in the former category, "exorbitant" jurisdiction situations are not admitted.

The list in Order 11(1) should be compared with the Convention jurisdiction listed on pp. 712–714, *post*.

Order 11

1.—(1) Provided that the writ does not contain any claim mentioned in Order 75, r. 2(1) and is not a writ to which paragraph (2) of this rule applies, service of a writ out of the jurisdiction is permissible with the leave of the Court if in the action begun by the writ—

    (*a*) relief is sought against a person domiciled[9] within the jurisdiction;

    (*b*) an injunction is sought ordering the defendant to do or refrain from doing anything within the jurisdiction (whether or not damages are also claimed in respect of a failure to do or the doing of that thing);

    (*c*) the claim is brought against a person duly served within or out of the jurisdiction and a person out of the jurisdiction is a necessary or proper party thereto;

    (*d*) the claim is brought to enforce, rescind, dissolve, annul or otherwise affect a contract, or to recover damages or obtain other relief in respect of the breach of a contract, being (in either case) a contract which—

        (i) was made within the jurisdiction, or

        (ii) was made by or through an agent trading or residing within the jurisdiction on behalf of a principal trading or residing out of the jurisdiction,[10] or

        (iii) is by its terms, or by implication, governed by English law,[11] or

        (iv) contains a term to the effect that the High Court shall have jurisdiction to hear and determine any action in respect of the contract;

    (*e*) the claim is brought in respect of a breach committed within the jurisdiction of a contract made within or out of the jurisdiction, and irrespective of the fact, if such be the case, that the breach was preceded or accompanied by a breach committed out of the jurisdiction that rendered impossible the performance of so much of the contract as ought to have been performed within the jurisdiction;

    (*f*) the claim is founded on a tort and the damage was sustained, or resulted from an act committed, within the jurisdiction[12];

---

[9] For the definition of "domicile" see para. 4 of Order 11 (on p. 697, *post*) and p. 710, *post*.

[10] If the representative is doing his own business in the jurisdiction, and not the principal's, he is not an agent within the meaning of this provision: *Vogel* v. *R. and A. Kohnstamm Ltd.* [1973] Q.B. 133.

[11] Where the contract is governed by English law, service out of the jurisdiction may be granted for a claim for relief under the Law Reform (Frustrated Contracts) Act 1943: *B.P. Exploration Co. (Libya) Ltd.* v. *Hunt* [1976] 1 W.L.R. 788.

[12] When deciding where a tort was committed, the courts apply the so-called substantive test, *i.e.* they ask where in substance did the cause of action arise? If they conclude that substantially the tort was committed within the jurisdiction, the conflict of law rules developed in *Boys* v. *Chaplin* [1971] A.C. 356 or any defences arising under foreign law are irrelevant: *Metall und Rohstoff AG* v. *Donaldson Lufkin & Jenrette Inc.*, [1989] 3 W.L.R. 563. Leave may be given if either the act causing damage was done within the jurisdiction or damage was caused here, wherever the damage-causing act was committed. Negligent misrepresentation is committed where the representation is received and acted upon: *Diamond* v. *Bank of London and Montreal Ltd.* [1979] Q.B. 333. In *Cordoba Shipping Co. Ltd.* v. *National State Bank, Elizabeth, New Jersey. The Albaforth* [1984] 2 Lloyd's Rep. 91 the alleged negligent misrepresentation was contained in a telex received in London and the court held that there was a good arguable case in the English courts.

(*g*) . . . [13]

(*h*) the claim is brought to construe, rectify, set aside or enforce an act, deed, will, contract, obligation or liability affecting land situate within the jurisdiction;

(*i*) the claim is made for a debt secured on immovable property or is made to assert, declare or determine proprietary or possessory rights, or rights of security, in or over movable property, or to obtain authority to dispose of movable property, situate within the jurisdiction;

(*j*) the claim is brought to execute the trusts of a written instrument being trusts that ought to be executed according to English law and of which the person to be served with the writ is a trustee, or for any relief or remedy which might be obtained in any such action;

(*k*) . . . [14]

(*l*) . . . [14]

(*m*) the claim is brought to enforce any judgment or arbitral award;

(*n*) the claim is brought against a defendant not domiciled in Scotland or Northern Ireland in respect of a claim by the Commissioners of Inland Revenue for or in relation to any of the duties or taxes which have been, or are for the time being, placed under their care and management;

(*o*) the claim is brought under the Nuclear Installations Act 1965 or in respect of contributions under the Social Security Act 1975;

(*p*) the claim is made for a sum to which the Directive of the Council of the European Communities dated 15th March 1976 No. 76/308/EEC applies, and service is to be effected in a country which is a Member State of the European Economic Community[15];

(*q*) the claim is made under the Drug Trafficking Offences Act 1986.

(2) Service of a writ out of the jurisdiction is permissible without the leave of the Court provided that each claim made by the writ is either:—

    (*a*) a claim which by virtue of the Civil Jurisdiction and Judgments Act 1982 the Court has power to hear and determine,[16] made in proceedings to which the following conditions apply—

        (i) no proceedings between the parties concerning the same cause of action are pending in the courts of any other part of the United Kingdom or of any other Convention territory, and

        (ii) either—

the defendant is domiciled in any part of the United Kingdom or in any other Convention territory, or

the proceedings begun by the writ are proceedings to which Article 16 of Schedule 1 or of Schedule 4 refers, or the defendant is a party to an agreement conferring jurisdiction to which Article 17 of Schedule 1 or of Schedule 4 to that Act applies,

    or

    (*b*) a claim which by virtue of any other enactment the High Court has power to hear and determine notwithstanding that the person against whom the claim is made is not within the jurisdiction of the Court or that the wrongful act, neglect or default giving rise to the claim did not take place within its jurisdiction.

(3) Where a writ is to be served out of the jurisdiction under paragraph (2), the time to be inserted in the writ within which the defendant served therewith must acknowledge service shall be—

    (*a*) 21 days where the writ is to be served out of the jurisdiction under paragraph (2)(*a*) in Scotland, Northern Ireland or in the European territory of another Contracting State, or

---

[13] Relates to land only.

[14] Relates to administration and probate of estates of deceased persons only.

[15] This Directive relates to the recovery of sums due under the European Agricultural Guidelines and Guarantee Fund and for agricultural levies and Customs duties.

[16] See p. 709, *post*.

> (b) 31 days where the writ is to be served under paragraph (2)(a) in any other territory of a Contracting State, or
>
> (c) limited in accordance with the practice adopted under r. 4(4) where the writ is to be served under paragraph (2)(a) in a country not referred to in sub-paragraphs (a) or (b) or under paragraph (2)(b).
>
> (4) For the purposes of this rule, and of r. 9 of this Order, domicile is to be determined in accordance with the provisions of sections 41 to 46 of the Civil Jurisdictions and Judgments Act 1982 and "Convention territory" means the territory or territories of any Contracting State, as defined by s.1(3) of that Act, to which the Conventions as defined in s.1(1) of that Act apply.

Non-Convention service out of the jurisdiction

The assumed jurisdiction of the court over persons who are not domiciled in a Contracting State of the Convention will be exercised only if two conditions are satisfied: the plaintiff who makes the application must have a good arguable case, and the court, in the exercise of its discretion, is satisfied that it is appropriate that leave to serve abroad should be granted.[17]

When exercising its discretion, the court is "exceedingly careful before it allows a writ to be served out of the jurisdiction."[18] Even where the application is clearly within the terms of the assumed jurisdiction of the court, the court will refuse the application when, in the circumstances of the case, it thinks that it is not proper that a foreigner should be put to the inconvenience of contesting his rights in this, instead of his own, country.[19] In particular, if the only ground on which the assumed jurisdiction of the English courts is claimed to be founded is that English law is the law governing the contract, "the exorbitance of the jurisdiction sought to be invoked . . . is an important factor to be placed in the balance against granting leave."[20]

In every case, a full and fair disclosure of all surrounding circumstances is demanded by the court, and the order for service out of the jurisdiction will be set aside when afterwards material facts transpire which were not disclosed in the application for the order.[21]

---

[17] *Islamic Arab Insurance Co.* v. *Saudi Egyptian American Reinsurance Co.* [1987] 1 Lloyd's Rep. 315. *E. F. Hutton & Co. (London) Ltd.* v. *Mofarru* [1989] 1 W.L.R. 488; *Attock Cement Company Ltd.* v. *Romanian Bank for Foreign Trade,* [1989] 1 Lloyd's Rep. 572. *Unilever plc* v. *Gillette UK Ltd., Financial Times,* June 28, 1989.

[18] *Per* Pearson J. in *Société Générale de Paris* v. *Dreyfus Bros.* (1885) 29 Ch.D. 239, 243, and du Parcq L.J. in *George Monro Ltd.* v. *American Cyanamid & Chemical Corporation* (1944) 60 T.L.R. 265; also *Aaronson Bros. Ltd.* v. *Maderera del Tropico S.A.* [1967] 2 Lloyd's Rep. 159, 162.

[19] See *The Atlantic Star* [1974] A.C. 436 (H.L.).

[20] *Per* Lord Diplock in *Amin Rasheed Shipping Corporation* v. *Kuwait Insurance Co.* [1984] A.C. 50, 68; also *Spiliada Maritime Corporation* v. *Cansulex Ltd. The Spiliada* [1985] 2 Lloyd's Rep. 116.

[21] What constitutes full and fair disclosure is discussed in numerous cases, *e.g. Bloomfield* v. *Serenyi* [1945] 2 All E.R. 646; *The Andria now renamed Vasso* [1984] Q.B. 477; *Lloyds Bowmaker Ltd.* v. *Britannia Arrow Buildings plc* [1988] 3 W.L.R. 1337; *Dormeuil Frères S.A.* v. *Nicolian International (Textiles) Ltd.* [1988] 1 W.L.R. 1362; *Brink's-Mat Ltd.* v. *Elcombe* [1988] 3 W.L.R. 1350.

Where the English courts assume jurisdiction over persons or companies abroad and the service is duly effected, the defendant is in the same position as a defendant within the jurisdiction; he may appear before the court by counsel or in person and defend the case, or he may not appear, in which case the plaintiff will sign judgment by default against him, if able to establish his case.

How service abroad is effected

Service abroad is effected in accordance with R.S.C., Ord. 11, r. 5 and r. 6, usually by a British consular authority in the country in which the defendant resides, or by the procedure provided by the Hague Convention on the Service Abroad of Judicial and Extra-judicial Documents in Civil and Commercial Matters of November 15, 1965, (known as the Service Convention),which came into effect on February 10, 1969 and of which the United Kingdom is a Contracting State; under this Convention each Contracting State has appointed a central authority[21a] designated to receive requests for service coming from other Contracting States and to execute them.[21b]

In addition to the multilateral Hague Convention, the United Kingdom has concluded a number of bilateral conventions on the facilitation of service of court documents abroad with some overseas countries and these conventions are still in force. The USA is neither a party to the Hague Convention nor to a bilateral convention with the United Kingdom on this subject; legal proceedings in the English courts have to be served in the United States by the British consular authorities, by private agents or under an order of a district court.

Concurrent proceedings

Situations may arise in which several national courts, according to their rules of procedure, have jurisdiction to try the same case. Here the plaintiff may engage in *forum shopping, i.e.* he may select the forum which offers him the greatest advantages. Modern law disapproves of

---

[21a] In England and Wales the central authority is the High Court of Justice in London; in Scotland it is the Crown Agents in Edinburgh.
[21b] Service without leave out of the jurisdiction under R.S.C. 0.11 r. 1(2) is regulated by a Practice Note issued in November 1989; see 139, N.L.J. 1989, p. 1527.

forum shopping[22] but the English courts are well aware that the problem exists and accept the realities of the situation.[23]

Where a plaintiff legitimately[24] commences litigation in the English and a foreign court, the defendant, faced with this multiplicity of proceedings, may ask the English court for two kinds of relief; either for an injunction that the English proceedings be stayed or for an injunction that the plaintiff be restrained from proceeding in the foreign court.[25] The rules of English procedure applying to these two forms of injunction are not the same, but in both cases an issue can only arise if the English court is satisfied that some other forum having competent jurisdiction is clearly available. In the former case the English court will order a stay of its own proceedings and refuse to exercise its—undoubted—jurisdiction if, in its judgment, the foreign court is the "natural and appropriate forum" to deal with the dispute. In this case the English court would consider itself as *forum non conveniens*.[26] In principle the English courts reject as improper a comparison of the justice which they administer with that obtainable in the courts of other countries.[27] Lord Diplock said[28]:

> The essential change in the attitude of the English courts to pending or prospective litigation in foreign jurisdictions that has been achieved step-by-step during the past ten years . . . is that judicial chauvinism has been replaced by judicial comity . . .

If the defendant applies for an injunction to restrain the plaintiff from proceeding in the foreign jurisdiction, the English courts apply a much stricter test. In principle they refuse to arrogate the foreign court's jurisdiction to decide whether it will entertain the plaintiff's claim, but exceptionally, if justice so demands, they will make a restraint order, *e.g.* if it would be vexatious or oppressive on the defendant to allow the foreign proceedings to continue.

---

[22] See Lord Reid in *The Atlantic Star* [1974] A.C. 436, 454, *Saipem SpA* v. *Dredging VO2 BV. The Volvox Hollandia* [1988] 2 Lloyd's Rep. 363, 364 (Kerr L.J.). The Convention, to which effect is given in the United Kingdom by the Civil Jurisdiction and Judgments Act 1982, tries to reduce the possibility of forum shopping in the EC but is not wholly successful; see p. 710, *post.*

[23] See *Castanho* v. *Brown & Root (U.K.) Ltd.* [1981] A.C. 557; *Smith Kline & French Laboratories Ltd.* v. *Bloch* [1983] 1 W.L.R. 730; *British Airways Board* v. *Laker Airways Ltd.* [1985] A.C. 58; *Société Nationale Industrielle Aérospatiale* v. *Lee Kui Jak* [1987] A.C. 871. In *South Carolina Insurance Co.* v. *Assurantie Maatschappij "De Zeven Provincien" NV* [1987] A.C. 24 the H.L. allowed a party in English proceedings to obtain pre-trial discovery of documents by order of a U.S. court from a party resident in the USA, the documents to be used in the English proceedings.

[24] In accordance with the rules of procedure of the English and the foreign court.

[25] The defendant may, of course, also apply to the foreign court to stay its own proceedings; this application is governed by the rules of procedure of the foreign court.

[26] *The Abidin Daver* [1984] A.C. 398, 411. *Cordoba Shipping Co. Ltd.* v. *National State Bank, Elizabeth, New Jersey, The Albaforth* [1984] 2 Lloyd's Rep. 91.

[27] *Aratra Potato Co. Ltd.* v. *Egyptian Navigation Co. The El Amria* [1981] 2 Lloyd's Rep. 119; *Amin Rasheed Shipping Corporation* v. *Kuwait Insurance Co.* [1984] A.C. 50; *The Abidin Daver, supra.*

[28] In *The Abidin Daver, supra,* 411.

The first of these rules—*forum non conveniens*—was established in *The Abidin Daver*,[29] the second was first indicated in *Spiliada*[30] and was fully developed in the *Aerospatiale* case.[31]

In *The Abidin Daver*, a vessel owned by a Turkish State corporation, collided in the Bosphorous with a Cuban vessel piloted by a Turkish pilot. Each ship blamed the other for the collision. The owners of the Turkish vessel commenced proceedings in the competent Turkish Admiralty court where the owners of the Cuban vessel could have lodged a cross-claim if they had wished to do so. A few months later the Cuban owners started proceedings in the Admiralty Court of England and arrested a sister ship of *The Abidin Daver*. The Turkish owners applied to the English court for a stay of proceedings on the ground that their claim and any cross-claim by the Cubans should be adjudicated by the Turkish court. The House of Lords held that the Turkish Admiralty Court was the natural and appropriate forum for the litigation and that the English proceedings should be stayed.

Aerospatiale[32] was concerned with the consequences of a helicopter crash in Brunei, the law of which was in all material respects the same as English law. The helicopter was built by *Société Nationale Industrielle Aérospatiale* (SNIAS), a French company; it was owned by a UK company and operated and serviced by Bristow Helicopters Malaysia Sdn Bhd, an associated company of another UK company, Bristow Helicopters Ltd.; the helicopter was under contract to Sarawak Shell Bhd.

All passengers on board the helicopter were killed, amongst them Mr. Yong Joon San, a wealthy businessman. His personal representatives initiated proceedings in Brunei, France and Texas, the latter being founded on the Texas Wrongful Death Statute, which was asserted to give the Texas courts jurisdiction on the ground that SNIAS were doing business in Texas. The proceedings in France were discontinued and the claims against all defendants, except SNIAS, were settled. The only

---

[29] *The Abidin Daver* [1984] A.C. 398 (H.L.); *Muduroglu Ltd.* v. *T. C. Ziraat Bankasi* [1986] 3 W.L.R. 606; *The Sidi Bishr* [1987] 1 Lloyd's Rep. 42; *The Adhiguna Mercanti* (C.A. of Hong Kong) [1988] 1 Lloyd's Rep. 384; *Cleveland Museum of Art* v. *Capricorn International SA, Financial Times,* October 17, 1989. See also the cases referred to in the next note.
[30] *Spiliada Maritime Corporation* v. *Cansulex Ltd.* [1987] A.C. 460 (H.L.); *Charm Maritime Inc.* v. *Minos Xenophon Kyriakou* [1987] 1 Lloyd's Rep. 433; *The Falstra* [1988] 1 Lloyd's Rep. 495, 499; *Bibby Bulk Carriers Ltd.* v. *Cansulex Ltd.* [1989] 2 W.L.R. 182 (a sequel to *Spiliada*); *Roneleigh Ltd.* v. *MII Exports Inc., The Times,* February 23, 1989 (cost advantage may be taken into account); *Irish Shipping Ltd.* v. *Commerical Union Assurance Co. plc. The Irish Rowan,* [1989] 2 Lloyd's Rep. 144. See also the Australian case *Oceanic Sun Line Special Shipping Co. Inc.* v. *Fay* 79 ALR 9 (HC of A, 1988).
[31] *Société Nationale Industrielle Aérospatiale* v. *Lee Kui Jak* [1987] A.C. 871 (P.C.); *Saipem SpA* v. *Dredging VO2 BV, The Volvox Hollandia* [1988] 2 Lloyd's Rep. 361, 374; *E. I. Du Pont de Nemours & Co. Ltd.* v. *I.C. Agnew (No. 2)* [1988] 2 Lloyd's Rep. 240.
[32] See the preceding note.

outstanding claim, that against SNIAS, was pending in two jurisdictions, that of Brunei and that of Texas. SNIAS first tried to obtain an order from the Texas courts stopping proceedings before them but was unsuccessful. It then applied to the Brunei court for an injunction restraining the plaintiffs from pursuing their claim in the Texas courts. The Court of Appeal of Brunei refused the injunction.

SNIAS appealed to the Privy Council. This court reversed the Brunei Court of Appeal and granted the injunction. The judgment of the court was delivered by Lord Goff who had also given the leading judgment in *Spiliada*.[30] The Privy Council held that Brunei was the natural forum for this litigation and that SNIAS would suffer oppression if it were sued in Texas because it would then lose the opportunity of claiming over in the same proceedings against Bristow Helicopters Malaysia for indemnity and compensation.

Foreign limitation periods

It has been observed earlier[32a] that in English private international law, by virtue of the Foreign Limitation Periods Act 1984, the rules relating to limitation periods are regarded as pertaining to the substantive law of the contract, and not to the law of procedure.

The Mareva injunction[33]

Its nature

If the English courts have jurisdiction over a dispute, whether proceedings in the English courts are pending or contemplated,[34] it is possible to obtain an interlocutory injunction against the defendant freezing his assets and ordering him not to dispose of or remove them. This type of injunction is known as the *Mareva* injunction.[35] It is now granted by virtue

---

[32a] See p. 221, *ante*.
[33] For further reading: Steven Gee and Geraldine Andrews, *Mareva Injunctions*, 1986; Mark Hoyle, *The Mareva Injunction and related Orders*, 2nd ed., 1989.
[34] If proceedings are contemplated but not commenced within a reasonable time, the *Mareva* injunction will be discharged: *Siporex Trade S.A.* v. *Comdel Commodities Ltd.* [1986] 2 Lloyd's Rep. 428, 436. A post-judgment *Mareva* injunction freezing the assets of the defendant may be obtained: *Babanaft International Co. S.A.* v. *Bassatne* [1989] 2 W.L.R. 232. A *Mareva* injunction can be obtained in the English courts freezing the assets of the defendant in the English jurisdiction (or even worldwide), if proceedings are pending or contemplated in the courts of another EC Member State (and not in the English courts), see pp. 703–704, *post*.
[35] Named after *Mareva Compania Naviera S.A.* v. *International Bulkcarriers S.A.*; *The Mareva* [1975] 2 Lloyd's Rep. 509 (C.A.); see David G. Powles, "The Mareva Injunction" [1978] J.B.L. 11. See also *Third Chandris Shipping Corp.* v. *Unimarine S.A.* [1979] 2 All E.R. 972.

of section 37(3) of the Supreme Court Act 1981. Like the grant of all injunctions, it is discretionary and is granted on the balance of convenience. The purpose of the *Mareva* injunction is "simply to prevent the injustice of a defendant removing or dissipating his assets so as to cheat the plaintiff of the fruits of his claim"[36]; it is not to improve the position of the plaintiff as against the other creditors.[36a] The plaintiff has to satisfy the court on two points, *viz.* that he has a good arguable case against the defendant, and that there is danger of removal or dissipation of the defendant's assets.[37]

The *Mareva* injunction is thus essentially an interim conservation order. This is a developing jurisdiction.[38] The *Mareva* injunction is granted invariably against an undertaking by the applicant to indemnify the other party if he—the applicant—loses the action and, in the retrospective, the injunction was unjustified.[39]

The plaintiff will normally apply for a *Mareva* injunction *ex parte*, but if, in support of his application, he fails to give full and fair disclosure of all relevant facts, the injunction will be discharged or, if limited in time, will not be continued.[40]

The *Mareva* injunction cannot be used to found the jurisdiction of the English court in cases in which it does not have jurisdiction according to its rules of procedure and in so far as it is an ancillary remedy.[41] But a *Mareva* injunction may also be granted by the English courts in support of proceedings pending, contemplated or concluded in the court of another Member State of the EC; this follows from article 24 of the Convention and section 25 of the Civil Jurisdiction and Judgments Act 1982.[42]

The *Mareva* injunction is particularly useful against a defendant residing abroad against whom the English courts, in the exercise of their

---

[36] *Per* Lloyd J. in *P.C.W. (Underwriting Agencies) Ltd.* v. *P. S. Dixon* [1983] 2 Lloyd's Rep. 197, 202.

[36a] *Town and Country Building Society* v. *Daisystar Ltd. The Times,* October 16, 1989 (abuse of *Mareva* procedure not to prosecute action but to use the injunction for the purpose of improving one's position against the other creditors).

[37] Guidelines for the grant of a Mareva injunction are contained in *Z Ltd.* v. *A-Z and AA -LL* [1982] Q.B. 558. The earlier history and gradual extension of the Mareva injunction is discussed by Lloyd J. in *The Niedersachsen* [1983] 2 Lloyd's Rep. 600, 602. See also *Avant Petroleum Inc.* v. *Gatoil Overseas Inc.* [1986] 2 Lloyd's Rep. 236.

[38] The court decisions on the various aspects of the *Mareva* injunction are very numerous; it is not intended to deal with all of them.

[39] On undertakings see *In re D.P.R. Futures Ltd.* [1989] W.L.R. 778.

[40] On disclosure see *Ali and Fahd Shobokshi Group Ltd.* v. *Moneim* [1989] 1 W.L.R. 710; *Behbehani* v. *Salem* [1989] 1 W.L.R. 723; *O'Regan* v. *Iambic Productions Ltd.*, 130 N.L.7 (1989) 1378.

[41] *The Siskina* [1979] A.C. 210. But the defendant need not be foreign-based and, if the conditions on which a Mareva injunction is granted are present, it may be granted against a person based in England and Wales: *Barclay-Johnson* v. *Yuill* [1980] 1 W.L.R. 1259, 1264–1265.

[42] *Republic of Haiti* v. *Duvalier* [1989] 2 W.L.R. 261; *X* v. *Y* [1989] 3 W.L.R. 910. (In these two cases the English courts granted worldwide *Mareva* injunctions in support of French proceedings.) The *Siskina* rule does not apply in these cases.

assumed jurisdiction, have granted leave of service out of the jurisdiction. It prevents such a defendant from removing assets out of the jurisdiction and thus rendering an English judgment against him difficult to enforce.

Orders supporting the Mareva injuncton

In order to make the *Mareva* injunction as effective as possible, the courts are prepared to grant ancillary orders supporting the *Mareva* injunction. Two of these ancillary orders may be mentioned.

First, the court may order that the defendant or other persons, who have knowledge of the whereabouts of the defendant's assets, shall give information about the nature, location and value of the assets of the defendant.[43] Such a disclosure order is of particular importance in worldwide *Mareva* injunctions. Where the *Mareva* injunction is obtained *ex parte*, as is usual, and the disclosure order is directed to parties other than the defendant himself, the judge may even order that the fact that such an order is made shall not be communicated to the defendant until the order is complied with.[44] But these orders, like the *Mareva* injunction itself, should contain a proviso that the rights of persons other than the defendant shall not be affected by the order; this proviso is known as the *Babanaft* proviso.[45]

Secondly, the court may order that the defendant shall surrender his passport and shall not leave the jurisdiction until the case is decided.[46]

Assets which can be frozen by a Mareva injunction

In principle only assets within the jurisdiction are frozen but the courts can issue a *Mareva* injunction freezing assets situate, or suspected to be situate, abroad.[47] Although the courts assert that they exercise jurisdiction to freeze foreign assets only rarely, they have in fact made worldwide *Mareva* injunctions in several cases.[48] This is a natural reaction to the

---

[43] *A. J. Bekhor & Co. Ltd.* v. *Bilton* [1981] Q.B. 923, 940; *Allied Arab Bank Ltd. Hajjar* [1988] Q.B. 746, 787; *Maclaine Watson & Co. Ltd.* v. *International Tin Council (No. 2)* [1988] 3 All E.R. 257, 381; *O'Regan* v. *Iambic Productions Ltd.*, *Financial Times*, August 2, 1989 (this case concerned an *Anton Piller* injunction).

[44] *Republic of Haiti* v. *Duvalier* [1989] 2 W.L.R. 261, 265.

[45] See p. 704, *post*.

[46] *Bayer AG* v. *Winter* [1986] 1 W.L.R. 497.

[47] See Peter Kaye, "Powers of Disclosure of Foreign Assets in the English Courts" in (1989) 139 N.L.J. 875.

[48] *Babanaft International Co. Ltd.* v. *Bassatne* [1989] 2 W.L.R. 232; *Republic of Haiti* v. *Duvalier* [1989] 2 W.L.R. 261; *Derby & Co. Ltd.* v. *Weldon* [1989] 2 W.L.R. 276; *Derby & Co. Ltd.* v. *Weldon (Nos. 3 and 4)* [1989] 2 W.L.R. 412.

international financial situation which enables parties to transfer money and other assets from one country to another rapidly and sometimes anonymously. A worldwide *Mareva* injunction was *e.g.* granted in *Republic of Haiti* v. *Duvalier*[49]; in this case the Republic of Haiti alleged—the court did not have to consider whether the allegations were true—that the defendant Jean-Claude Duvalier, who was president of the Republic for some years, and members of his family had embezzled US $120 million from the Republic; the Republic started proceedings against some members of the Duvalier family in France, where they were resident; the Republic then applied to the English court for a worldwide *Mareva* injunction and a disclosure order; the Court of Appeal granted these orders; the judgment of that court was delivered by Staughton L.J.; it contains, *inter alia*, interesting observations on the application of Article 24 of the Convention and the *Babanaft* proviso.

There appears, however, to exist a difference between pre-judgment *Marevas* and post-judgment *Marevas*. In the former case the courts appear to be more inclined to exercise their jurisdiction of granting worldwide *Marevas*, but in the latter case they are more reluctant to do so. This distinction finds its explanation in the fact that pre-judgment *Marevas* are clearly of protective character whereas post-judgment *Marevas* serve attachment purposes in relation to judgments already given.[50] In any event, a post-judgment *Mareva* injunction over foreign assets has to be qualified by an appropriate *Babanaft* proviso.

The Babanaft proviso

It has already been stated that a *Mareva* injunction or a supporting order for disclosure of the whereabouts of the defendant's assets should invariably contain a clause safeguarding, in general terms, the rights of third parties (to whom the order is directed). Such a clause, known as the *Babanaft* proviso,[51] would, *e.g.* protect a bank which wishes to claim a set-off against the frozen assets, or a solicitor who wishes to exercise his lien on documents which he has to surrender in compliance with the order.

The *Babanaft* proviso is usually a lengthy clause. In the *Duvalier* case[52] it began as follows:

> Provided always that no person other than the defendants themselves shall in any wise be affected by the terms of this order . . .

---

[49] [1989] 2 W.L.R. 261.
[50] *Derby & Co. Ltd.* v. *Weldon* [1989] 2 W.L.R. 276.
[51] Named after *Babanaft International Co. Ltd.* v. *Bassatne* [1989] 2 W.L.R. 232.
[52] [1989] 2 W.L.R. 261, 274. Another illustration is provided in *Derby & Co. Ltd.* v. *Weldon (Nos. 3 and 4)* [1989] 2 W.L.R. 412, 426.

The Anton Piller injunction

This is an injunction which authorises the applicant to enter the premises of the respondent and to inspect and take away specified documents or other specified property. The injunction is often granted to the applicant *ex parte*. It takes its name from a case decided in 1975[53] and is now granted by virtue of the Supreme Court Act 1981, s.33. The *Anton Piller* injunction has been discussed earlier.[54]

ENFORCEMENT OF JUDGMENTS ABROAD

There are two methods of enforcing a judgment outside the jurisdiction of the court which pronounced it: a new action, founded on the judgment, has to be commenced in the foreign country in which it is sought to enforce the judgment; or it may be possible to register the judgment in the foreign country and then to enforce it directly in the same manner as a judgment given in the courts of that country.

Action founded on the foreign judgment

This method is dilatory and cumbersome because the plaintiff is compelled to conduct two lawsuits in order to obtain satisfaction. But if an action is brought in an English court on a judgment given by a foreign court, the English judge will not normally reopen the case and hear the case anew on its merits; he will apply the doctrine of *issue estoppel*.[55] The conditions on which this doctrine can be applied are[56]: the earlier judgment must have been given by a foreign court which, according to the principles of private international law,[57] had jurisdiction to pronounce

---

[53] *Anton Piller K.G.* v. *Manufacturing Processes Ltd.* [1976] Ch. 55.

[54] See p. 286, *ante*.

[55] Issue estoppel should be distinguished from action estoppel. The latter occurs if a party brings an action on a particular cause and judgment is given, and he later brings an action founded on the same cause; he is then normally estopped from doing so. Issue estoppel occurs if in a case before the court an issue is raised which in previous proceedings before a competent court, including a foreign court, the same issue has been finally decided; if the conditions explained in the text for issue estoppel are satisfied, the issue cannot be litigated again in the subsequent proceedings: *Charm Maritime Inc.* v. *Minas Xenophon Kyriakou* [1987] 1 Lloyd's Rep. 433, 440–441.

[56] *Carl Zeiss Stiftung* v. *Rayner & Keeler Ltd.* (*No. 2*) [1967] 1 A.C. 853, 909; *The Sennar* (*No. 2*) [1985] 1 W.L.R. 490; *The Speedlink Vanguard* v. *European Gateway* [1986] 2 Lloyd's Rep. 265, 269; *S.C.F. Finance Co. Ltd.* v. *Masri* (*No. 3*) [1987] 2 W.L.R. 81, 96.

[57] According to English law, a court has international jurisdiction if, at the commencement of the suit, the defendant is resident in its jurisdiction or has submitted to it. If the jurisdiction of the foreign court is solely founded on the situation of assets or the residence of a subsidiary in the jurisdiction, the foreign judgment is not enforceable in the English jurisdiction: *Adams* v. *Cape Industries plc*, *The Times*, August 5, 1989.

it; it must have been final; there must have been identity of the parties; and the subject matter must have been the same in the earlier and later litigation. Issue estoppel operates regardless of whether an English court would consider the reasoning of the foreign judgment as open to criticism.[58]

A foreign judgment obtained by fraud against the foreign court is not enforceable in the English jurisdiction.[59]

Registration of foreign judgments

This method is more satisfactory than that of bringing an action on the foreign judgment. It is much favoured in modern law. The direct enforcement of judgments by registration is not regulated by general international agreements like the conventions on the execution of foreign arbitral awards,[60] but on the regional level some degree of uniformity exists. In the United States, according to the "full faith and credit" clause of the Constitution,[61] each State shall recognise the judgments of the other States of the Federation. In the EC, the *Brussels Convention on Jurisdiction and the Enforcement of Judgments in Civil and Commercial Matters* of 1968, known as the "Judgments Convention," contains similar principles; more will be said about this Convention later on.[62]

The direct enforcement of foreign judgments by registration is admitted in the United Kingdom only under statutory powers. The enactments which admit this procedure are[63]:

> The Administration of Justice Act 1920, Part II;
> The Foreign Judgments (Reciprocal Enforcement) Act 1933; and
> The Civil Jurisdiction and Judgments Act 1982 (which gives effect to the Brussels Convention of 1968 in the United Kingdom and will be considered later).[64]

The Administration of Justice Act 1920, Part II.

Under the provisions of this enactment money judgments given in a part of the Commonwealth outside the United Kingdom can be enforced in

---

[58] *Per* Lord Diplock in *The Sennar (No. 2), supra,* 493.
[59] *Jet Holdings Inc.* v. *Patel* [1988] 3 W.L.R. 295. But if the fraud is not directed against the foreign court, *e.g.* by presenting to it perjured witnesses or forged documents, and is only pleaded in the foreign proceedings on the subject matter but rejected by the foreign court, the judgment of the foreign court would normally be capable of enforcement in the English jurisdiction, even if the English court considers that the decision of the foreign court on this point was wrong.
[60] See p. 687, *ante.*
[61] Article IV, section 1.
[62] See p. 709, *post.*
[63] There exists also the Judgments Extension Act 1868 which deals with the enforcement of Scottish and Northern Irish judgments in England and Wales.
[64] See p. 709, *post.*

the United Kingdom upon registration, provided the territory in question has extended reciprocity to England and Wales. Under this arrangement, English judgments are enforceable, *inter alia,* in all States of Australia, New Zealand, the Canadian Provinces of Newfoundland and Saskatchewan, Ghana, Malawi, Nigeria, Singapore, Zambia and Zimbabwe, the West Indies, Gibraltar, Hong Kong and other parts of the Commonwealth. Notable exceptions are the other Provinces of Canada.

The 1920 Act is being faded out. The Foreign Judgments (Reciprocal Enforcement) Act 1933 provides[65] that the 1933 Act may be applied by Order in Council to a Commonwealth country and, if this is done, Part II of the 1920 Act shall cease with respect to that country. Such Orders in Council have, in fact, been made for some Commonwealth countries. But where no Orders under the 1933 Act have been made, the Orders made under the 1920 Act are still operative; indeed, these Orders were consolidated in 1984[66] and according to the consolidation Order Part II of the 1920 Act still applies to 56 territories.

The Foreign Judgments (Reciprocal Enforcement) Act 1933.[67]

Broadly speaking, this Act applies to money judgments, *i.e.* judgments under which is payable a sum of money (not being in respect of taxes or other charges of a like nature or in respect of a fine or other penalty), provided that the judgment has become final and conclusive between the parties.[68]

Under the 1933 Act the direct enforcement of such foreign judgments is admitted in the United Kingdom by a number of bilateral treaties which are based on the principle of reciprocal treatment. When a foreign country grants substantial reciprocity in the United Kingdom, the benefits of the 1933 Act are extended to it by Order in Council. Under this Act foreign judgments are admitted to direct enforcement in England upon registration in the English courts on compliance with certain conditions. In fact, enforcement upon registration is in these cases the only way in which the foreign judgment can be executed in England and Wales (s.6).[69] The Act has so far been applied to:

---

[65] In section 7(2).

[66] By the Reciprocal Enforcement of Judgments (Administration of Justice Act 1920, Part II) (Consolidation) Order 1984 (S.I. 1984 No. 129); this Order was made by virtue of the Civil Jurisdiction and Judgments Act 1982, s.35(3).

[67] As amended by the Civil Jurisdiction and Judgments Act 1982, s.35(1) and Sched. 10.

[68] 1933 Act, s.1, as amended.

[69] Bankruptcy proceedings may be instituted on the basis of a registered judgment: *Re a Judgment Debtor* (No. 2176 of 1938) (1939) 160 L.T. 92. A French judgment awarding damages as *résistance abusive* is registrable under the Foreign Judgments (Reciprocal Enforcement) Act 1933 because the award is for compensatory damages and not for a penalty and its enforcement is not against English public policy: *S.A. Consortium General Textiles* v. *Sun & Sand Agencies Ltd.* [1978] Q.B. 279.

the Australian Capital Territory, Austria, *Belgium*, Canada (the following provinces and territories: Federal Court of Canada, British Colombia, Manitoba, New Brunswick, Nova Scotia, Ontario, Yukon Territory, Prince Edward Island, Saskatchewan, the Northwest Territories),[70] *France, Germany (West) and Berlin (West)*, Guernsey, Jersey, India, Israel, *Italy*, Man (Isle of), *Netherlands* and Netherlands Antilles, Norway, Pakistan, Surinam, Tonga,

[the bilateral treaties with the countries printed in *italics* were superseded, subject to a qualification stated on p. 710, *post*, by the Brussels Convention to which effect was given by the Civil Jurisdiction and Judgments Act 1982

Judgments given by the recognised courts of those countries are admitted to direct enforcement in England and, *vice versa*, judgments of the High Court in England, the Court of Session in Scotland and the High Court in Northern Ireland can be enforced upon registration in those countries. A Draft Convention for the Reciprocal Recognition and the Enforcement of Judgments in Civil Matters between the United Kingdom and the United States was published in 1977 but has not been signed or ratified yet,[71] as regards the United States it is still necessary to bring an action upon the judgment.

A foreign judgment duly registered in an English court under the 1933 Act is enforced in the English jurisdiction in the same manner as an English judgment. In particular, the judgment debtor, on an examination under R.S.C., Order 48, has to answer questions relating to his assets outside as well as within the jurisdiction.[72] A foreign judgment which is registrable under the 1933 Act is treated by the English courts as conclusive in circumstances similar to those explained when the question of issue estoppel was discussed.[73] Section 8(1) of the 1933 Act provides:

> Subject to the provisions of this section, a judgment to which Part I of this Act applies or would be applied if a sum of money had been payable thereunder, whether it can be registered or not, and, whether, if it can be registered, it is registered or not, shall be recognised in any court of the United Kingdom as conclusive between the parties thereto in all proceedings founded on the same cause of action and may be relied on by way of defence or counterclaim in any such proceedings.

But this provision should not be misunderstood. The foreign judgment is made by the Act only conclusive in the English jurisdiction for the purposes of its *enforceability*, but not for other purposes, such as a defence by a defendant. Lord Reid said[74]:

---

[70] The Reciprocal Enforcement of Foreign Judgments (Canada) Order 1987 (S.I. 1987 No. 468, as amended by S.Is. 1987 No. 2211, 1988 Nos. 1304 and 1853 and 1989 No. 987.
[71] Cmnd. 6771 (1977).
[72] *Interpool Ltd.* v. *Galani* [1988] Q.B. 738.
[73] See pp. 705, *ante*.
[74]; In *Black-Clawson Internation Ltd.* v. *Papierwerke Waldhof-Aschaffenburg AG* [1975] A.C. 591, 616; it was held in this case that a German judgment dismissing a claim by an English company against a German defendant on the preliminary ground that it was barred by limitation of time (which in Germany was shorter than in England) was not conclusive under s.8(1). Today the matter would be affected by the Foreign Limitation Periods Act 1984; see p. 221, *ante*.

I now turn to the Act. Clearly its principal purpose—dealt with in Part I—was to facilitate the enforcement here of rights given by foreign judgments to recover sums of money . . . But Part I has no application to defendants' judgments which entitle them to nothing but merely protect them against claims made against them. It would be a misuse of language to say that such a judgment can be enforced. It can only be used as a shield or defence.

The provisions of the 1933 Act apply, with a few exceptions, to an arbitral award made in a country to which the Act had been made applicable if the award has become enforceable in that country in the same manner as a judgment.[75]

The Civil Jurisdiction and Judgments Act 1982[76]

The main object of this Act[76] is to give effect in the United Kingdom to the *Brussels Convention on Jurisdiction and Enforcement of Judgments in Civil and Commercial Matters* of September 27, 1968, to which Denmark, Ireland and the United Kingdom acceded on October 9, 1978.[77] This Convention was promoted by the EC in accordance with Article 220 of the EC Treaty. The adoption of the Brussels Convention in the United Kingdom raised two problems which the 1982 Act has tried to resolve. First, in the United Kingdom three jurisdictions exist, one in England and Wales, another in Scotland, and another in Northern Ireland, and the Convention had to be adapted to each of them. Secondly, the Convention uses in part civil law[78] concepts which had to be assimilated to the concepts with which common law jurists are familiar.

---

[75] 1933 Act, s.10A, added by the Civil Jurisdiction and Judgments Act 1982, Sched. 10, para. 4.

[76] For further reading: Peter Kaye, *Civil Jurisdiction and Enforcement of Foreign Judgments*, 1987; *Private International Litigation* (ed. Sir Jack I. H. Jacob), 1988.

[77] In addition to the Brussels Convention and the Accession Convention, there exists the so-called 1971 Protocol, signed at Luxembourg on June 3, 1971. This Protocol gives the EC Court of Justice jurisdiction to interpret the Brussels Convention. This jurisdiction extends likewise to the Accession Convention. When Greece became a member of the EC, it acceded to the Brussels Convention and the Luxembourg Protocol by the Accession Convention of 1982. The 1982 Convention necessitated amendments of the first-mentioned two documents and also of the UK Civil Jurisdiction and Judgments Act 1982; the latter were carried out by the *Civil Jurisdiction and Judgments Act (Amendment) Order 1989* (S.I. 1989 No. 1346), which came into operation on October 1, 1989. The amended Brussels Convention and the amended Luxembourg Protocol, as well as an extract of the 1982 Accession Convention, are attached as schedules to the 1989 amending S.I. An accession Convention for the remaining two States, Spain and Portugal, was signed on May 26, 1989; this will require further amendments of the 1982 Act.

The 1982 Act relates originally only to Belgium, Germany (Federal Republic), France, Italy, Luxembourg, the Netherlands, and to Denmark, Ireland and the United Kingdom, but, as explained in the first paragraph, has been extended to Greece and is likely to be further extended to Spain and Portugal.

In the Republic of Ireland the Brussels Convention came into operation on June 1, 1988.

[78] On the distinction between the civil law and common law systems, see p. 293, *ante*.

Area of application of the Convention

The EC Judgments Convention intends to provide what has been described—loosely and not very happily—as "the free movement of judgments" between the Contracting States. It pursues two aims: to reduce the possibility of forum shopping, *i.e.* the multiplicity of jurisdictions in which a plaintiff, according to his choice, may commence proceedings; and to make the judgments to which it applies enforceable in all Member States of the EC.[78a]

The Convention applies to civil and commercial matters,[79] whatever the nature of the court or tribunal, but it does not extend to revenue, Customs or administrative measures.[80] It also does not apply to[80]:

1. the status or legal capacity of natural persons, rights in property arising out of matrimonial relationship, wills and succession;
2. bankruptcy, proceedings relating to the winding up of insolvent companies or other legal persons, judicial arrangements, compositions and analogous proceedings;
3. social security:
4. arbitration.[81]

On the coming into operation of the 1982 Act and consequently of the Convention,[82] the bilateral treaties concluded by the United Kingdom with the other Member States of the EC under the Foreign Judgments (Reciprocal Enforcement) Act 1933[83] were superseded[84] The countries in question are:

Belgium, France, Germany (West) and Berlin (West), Italy and the Netherlands.

But the bilateral treaties became ineffective only with respect to matters to which the Brussels Convention applies; in other respects they remain valid.[85]

[78a] It is doubtful whether security for costs can be ordered under R.S.C. 023 r.1 against a plaintiff resident in another Member State of the EC.; see *Berkeley Administration Inc.* v. *Arden C. McClelland, Financial Times,* January 23, 1990; in most cases English judges will refuse to do so in the exercise of their discretion.

[79] For a definition of the term "civil or (*sic!*) commercial matters" in another connection see Lord Goff in *In Re State of Norway's Application* (*Nos. 1 and 2*) [1989] 2 W.L.R. 458, 462.

[80] Brussels Convention Art. 1.

[81] This provision which excludes the application of the Convention, applies to all aspects of arbitration. Consequently, the Convention does not deprive an English court of its jurisdiction to appoint an arbitrator under section 10(3) of the Arbitration Act 1950 although the case is already pending in the court of another Contracting State: *Marc Rich & Co. AG* v. *Societa Italiana Impiantio PA. The Atlantic Emperor,* [1989] 1 Lloyd's Rep. 548

[82] On January 1, 1987.

[83] See p. 708, *ante*.

[84] Brussels Convention, Art. 55. Art. 60 defines the territories of the Member States to which the Convention shall, or shall not, apply.

[85] *Ibid.* Art. 56, first para.

Domicile for the purposes of the Convention

The Convention uses, as we shall see, the "domicile" of a person as the connecting factor with a locality. But the term "domicile" has a different meaning in the Convention from that ascribed to it in the common law.[86] For this reason the 1982 Act goes to considerable length to define the meaning of "domicile" for the purposes of the Convention.

An individual is domiciled in the United Kingdom if:

(a) he is resident in the United Kingdom; and
(b) the nature and circumstances of his residence indicate that he has a substantial connection with the United Kingdom.[87]

This definition excludes a residence which is only fleeting, *e.g.* on occasion of a brief visit, but is less stringent than the requirement of habitual residence; a "substantial" connection is sufficient.

As regards a company or another corporation or association, the Act provides[88] that its "seat" shall be treated as its domicile, and it then goes on to define the "seat" of the corporation thus[89]:

A corporation or association has its seat in the United Kingdom if and only if—

(a) it was incorporated or formed under the law of a part of the United Kingdom and has its registered office or some other official address in the United Kingdom; or
(b) its central management and control is exercised in the United Kingdom.

There are corresponding provisions for corporations which have their "seat" in another Contracting State.[90]

Jurisdiction clauses

The Convention admits in Article 17 a contract clause conferring exclusive jurisdiction on a particular court of a Contracting State but requires that:

such an agreement conferring jurisdiction shall be either in writing or evidenced in writing or, in international trade or commerce, in a form which accords with practices in that trade or commerce of which the parties are or ought to have been aware.

---

[86] The reason for this conceptual discrepancy is that the Convention was originally drafted by the original Member States which were all civil law countries.
[87] 1982 Act, s.41(2).
[88] *Ibid.* s.42(1).
[89] *Ibid.* s.42(3). A company may satisfy the test for the location of its seat, within the meaning of the Act, in relation to more than one State: *The Deichland* [1989] 3 W.L.R. 478, 488.
[90] *Ibid.* s.42(6).

Such *express prorogation clauses* are, as has been seen,[91] frequently inserted into international trade contracts if the parties prefer to go to the court rather than to arbitration, should a dispute develop.[92]

The Convention also admits in Article 18 an *implied prorogation* by appearing before a court of a Contracting State which would not normally have jurisdiction but this Article provides expressly that an appearance solely to contest the jurisdiction shall not be regarded as conferring jurisdiction on that court. In English law[93] the principle of Article 18 is spelt out in precise terms by section 33(1) of the 1982 Act which has already been considered.[94]

If the exclusive jurisdiction clause was inserted for the benefit of only one of the parties, he may waive that benefit and bring proceedings in any other court which has jurisdiction by virtue of the Convention (Art. 17, last para.).[95]

Jurisdiction where there is no jurisdiction clause

The Convention regulates the jurisdiction of the courts, if there is no express or implied prorogation, in the following manner.[96] The courts may exercise—

    (a) general jurisdiction;
    (b) special jurisdiction;
    (c) additional jurisdiction; or
    (d) exclusive jurisdiction.

General jurisdiction. The fundamental principle which the Convention has adopted is that, as far as individuals or corporations domiciled in the EC are concerned, there shall be only *one* court competent to entertain claims in civil and commercial matters. This is the court of domicile of the defendant. This principle is expressed in Article 2 as follows:

---

[91] See p. 76, *ante*.

[92] In *Iveco Fiat SpA* v. *Van Hool SA* (Case 313/85) [1988] 1 C.M.L.R. 57 a written agreement between an Italian and a Dutch company provided for exclusive jurisdiction of the District Court of Turin. The agreement further provided that it could be renewed only in writing but that, after expiry, it should be the legal basis for the relations of the parties, notwithstanding that it was not in writing. The EC Court of Justice held that the formal requirements of Art. 17 were satisfied for a dispute which arose after expiry of the original agreement (which was not renewed in writing) and that the Turin Court had exclusive jurisdiction.

[93] For an interpretation of Art. 18 by the EC Court of Justice see *Spitzley* v. *Sommer Exploitation S.A.* (Case 48/84) [1985] E.C.R. 787.

[94] See p. 693, *ante*.

[95] The fact alone that the prorogated forum is that of one of the parties to the contract does not support the conclusion that the jurisdiction clause was inserted for the benefit of that party only: *Rudolf Anterist* v. *Crédit Lyonnais* (No. 22/85) [1987] 1 C.M.L.R. 333.

[96] This arrangement in the text follows that adopted by the Convention.

> Subject to the provisions of this Convention, persons domiciled in a Contracting State shall, whatever their nationality, be sued in the courts of that State.

It should be noted that the nationality of the parties is irrelevant. Moreover, if proceedings involving the same cause of action between the same parties are pending in the courts of one Contracting State (*lis pendens*), any court in another Contracting State shall decline jurisdiction over that case *on its own motion*.[97] If "related actions" are brought in the courts of different Member States, the second court has a discretion to order a stay. Actions are "related" if there is a risk of irreconcilable judgments of the two courts concerned with the matter (Art. 22).[97a]

Special jurisdiction. The Convention has not been able to avoid forum shopping completely. It has to admit in some instances fora alternative to the forum of the defendant. These alternative fora are listed in Article 5. Those relevant in the context of international trade are:

1. In matters relating to a contract, the courts for the place of performance of the obligation in question[98];

---

[97] Art. 21 applies equally to defendants who are domiciled in Contracting States and to those who are not: *Overseas Union Insurance Ltd.* v. *New Hampshire Insurance Ltd.*, *The Times*, September 27, 1988.

The question which of several competing national courts was first seized with the case, depends on when the case became pending in the courts according to the rules of their procedure: *Kloeckner & Co. AG* v. *Gatoil Overseas Inc.*, *The Times*, August 23, 1989.

Where the (German) seller sued the (Italian) buyer in a competent German court for payment of the price and later the buyer commenced proceedings in the Italian court for annulment of the contract, the EC Court of Justice held that the definition of *lis pendens* in Art. 21 covered the situation and the dispute involved the same subject-matter, as in both proceedings the enforceability of the contract was the central issue. Consequently, the German court was competent to try the case: EC Court of Justice in *Gubisch Maschinenfabrik KG* v. *Giulio Palumbo* (Case 144/86), *The Times*, January 12, 1988.

[97a] *Virgin Aviation* v. *CAD Aviation*, *The Times*, February 2, 1990 (In the exercise of judicial discretion, a juridical advantage, such as the opportunity of obtaining summary judgment under R.S.C., 0.14, is only of subordinate importance).

[98] The place of performance has to be determined according to the rules of private international law of the national court seized with the matter: *Industrie Tessili Italiana Como* v. *Dunlop A.G.* [1977] 1 C.M.L.R. 26, 52.

The place of performance, for the purposes of Art. 5(1), is the place at which the contractual obligation on which the action is founded has to be performed; *Shenavai* v. *Kreischer* (Case 255/85) [1987] 3 C.M.L.R. 782; *Medway Packaging Ltd.* v. *Meurer Maschinen GmbH, Financial Times,* October 20, 1989. See also *Jesam Distribution Ltd.* v. *Schuk Mode Team GmbH, The Times,* October 24, 1989 (court has jurisdiction under Art. 5(1) if the existence of the contract which was not performed is in dispute).

The phrase "matters relating to a contract" in Art. 5(1) has to be interpreted by reference to the objectives of the Convention; thus, the claims of an independent agent for commission and compensation in case of wrongful repudiation of the agency agreement fall under this concept; *Arcado Sprl* v. *Haviland SA* (Case 9/87).

2. . . .
3. In matters relating to tort, delict or quasi-delict, the courts for the place where the harmful event occurred[99];
4. . . .
5. as regards a dispute arising out of the operation of a branch, agency or other establishment, the courts for the place in which the branch, agency or other establishment is situated[1];
6. . . .
7. as regards a dispute concerning the payment of remuneration claimed in respect of the salvage of a cargo or freight the court under the authority of which the cargo or freight in question:
    (a) has been arrested to secure such payment, or
    (b) could have been so arrested, but bail or other security has been given;
    provided that this provision shall apply only if it is claimed that the defendant has an interest in the cargo or freight or had such an interest at the time of the salvage.

It is of particular importance that the courts of the place of performance of a contractual obligation are alternative fora to the forum at which the defendant is domiciled.

Additional jurisdiction. Additional fora are also provided in matters relating to insurance and to consumer transactions involving the grant of credit to the consumer.

In a claim arising from, or in connection with, an insurance contract, proceedings may be taken in the courts of the State in which the insurer is domiciled or in those of another Contracting State where the policyholder is domiciled.[2] As far as consumer transactions involving a credit element are concerned, the Convention provides that in instalment sales (or loans) the seller (or lender) can, in principle, be sued in the seller's (or lender's) or the buyer's (or borrower's) courts.[3]

Exclusive jurisdiction. The cases in which the national courts of the Contracting States have exclusive jurisdiction, regardless of domicile, are listed in Article 16 of the Convention.

---

[99] Cf. *Bier* v. *Mines de Potasse D'Alsace* (case 21/76) [1976] E.C.R. 1735. See also *Minster Investments Ltd.* v. *Hyundai Precision and Industry Co. Ltd.*, *The Times*, June 26, 1987 (allegedly negligent issue of inspection certificate by defendant being domiciled abroad but certificate relied upon by plaintiff in England; the "harmful event" occurred in England). The phrase "tort, delict or quasi-delict' in Art. 5(3); (like the phrase "matters relating to contract" in Art 5(1); see n. 96), has to be interpreted with reference to the system and objectives of the Convention, and not with reference to national law; that term includes any action in which a claim for civil liability of the defendant is pursued and which does not fall under Art. 5(1): EC Court of Justice in *Kalfelis* v. *Schröder, Münchmeyer, Hengst and Others* (Case 189/87), *The Times*, October 5, 1988.
[1] An agent who has merely to solicit orders is not a "branch agency or establishment" within this provision: *Blanckaert & Willems PVBA* v. *Trost* (Case 139/80) [1982] 2 C.M.L.R. 1.
  Art. 5(5) applies where a company, without being a "branch, agency or other establishment," behaves as if it were such an undertaking; the principle of apparent authority is applied here: EC Court of Justice in *Schotte GmbH* v. *Parfums Rothschild Sarl, Paris* (Case 218/86).
[2] Convention, Art. 8.
[3] *Ibid.* Arts. 13–15.

They include, in particular, proceedings concerning immovable property situate in the Contracting State of the court in question[4]; the constitution, nullity or dissolution of companies or other legal persons or associations; the registration of patents, trade marks, designs or similar rights of intellectual property; and proceedings concerning the enforcement of foreign judgments.

Recognition

A judgment given in a Contracting State shall be recognised in the other Contracting States without any special procedure being required.[5]
However, a judgment shall not be recognised[6]:

1. if such recognition is contrary to public policy in the State in which recognition is sought;
2. where it was given in default of appearance, if the defendant was not duly served with the document which instituted the proceedings or with an equivalent document in sufficient time to enable him to arrange for his defence;
3. if the judgment is irreconcilable with a judgment given in a dispute between the same parties in the State in which recognition is sought;
4. if the court of the State in which the judgment was given, in order to arrive at its judgment, had decided a preliminary question concerning the status or legal capacity of natural persons, rights in property arising out of a matrimonial relationship, wills or succession in a way that conflicts with a rule of the private international law of the State in which the recognition is sought, unless the same result would have been reached by the application of the rules of private international law of that State;
5. if the judgment is irreconcilable with an earlier judgment given in a non-Contracting State involving the same cause of action and between the same parties, provided that this latter judgment fulfils the conditions necessary for its recognition in the State addressed.

Under no circumstances may a foreign judgment be reviewed as to its substance.[7]

Enforcement

A judgment given in one Contracting State shall be enforced in another Contracting State by order for enforcement made in the latter; in the United Kingdom the proper procedure — is — to have the foreign

---

[4] This exclusive jurisdiction extends to all lettings of immovable property, even for a short term, such as the use for a holiday home only: *Rösler* v. *Rottwinkel* (Case 241/83) [1985] 3 W.L.R. 898.
[5] *Ibid.* Art. 26.
[6] *Ibid.* Art. 27.
[7] *Ibid.* Art. 29.

judgment registered for enforcement in the relevant part of the United Kingdom.[8] In brief, the enforcement procedure of the judgment of another court in the EC is similar to the well-established registration procedure under the Foreign Judgments (Reciprocal Enforcement) Act 1933.

The Parallel Convention[9]

On September 16, 1988, at a diplomatic conference held in Lugano, the EFTA countries (Austria, Finland, Iceland, Norway, Sweden and Switzerland) entered into a Convention on Jurisdiction and the Enforcement of Judgments in Civil and Commercial Matters with the Member States of the EC.[10] The aim of the Lugano Convention, known as the *Parallel Convention,* is to make the advantages of mutual recognition and enforcement of judgments in civil and commercial matters, which the Contracting States of the Brussels Convention enjoy, available to the EFTA countries. This could not be done by the EFTA countries simply becoming 'Contracting States' of the Brussels Convention because the EFTA countries were unwilling to accept the role of the EC Court of Justice in interpreting the Brussels Convention. It therefore became necessary to devise a further Convention which runs parallel to the Brussels Convention but omits this feature and contains also a few other amendments.

Many provisions of the Lugano Convention are the same as those of the Brussels Convention but there exist important differences.[11] Two features of the Lugano regulation may be mentioned.

First, the Lugano Convention provides[12] that it shall not prejudice the operation of the Brussels Convention. Consequently, if the dispute concerns persons in two Contracting States of the Brussels Convention, this Convention applies and if it involves persons in two EFTA countries the Lugano Convention is applicable. Where one of the parties is domiciled in a Brussels Convention State and the other in a Lugano Convention country, no difficulty should arise as the rules of application are the same in both Conventions. If, *e.g.* an English exporter sells goods to an importer in Sweden, and the seller wants to commence proceedings

---

[8] *Ibid.* Art. 31. A provisional or protective measure authorised in the absence of the other party (attachment of assets, *saisie conservatoire*, *ex parte* Mareva injunction) does not come within the system of recognition and enforcement provided by Title III of the Convention: *Denilauler* v. *SNC Couchet Frères* (Case 125/79) [1981] 1 C.M.L.R. 62.

[9] See James Fawcett, "The Lugano Convention" in 14 *European Law Review* (1989), 105.

[10] The Lugano Convention is published in 1988 O.J. L319/9 of November 25, 1988.

[11] These differences are well explained by Professor Fawcett in the article referred to on p. 715, *supra.*

[12] In Art. 54B.

in the buyer's domicile, the Swedish court has jurisdiction by virtue of the Lugano Convention.

Secondly, in spite of the absence of a *forum commune*, similar as the European Court of Justice for the interpretation of the Brussels Convention, the Lugano Convention attempts to safeguard a uniform interpretation of the two Conventions. The provisions dealing with this subject are contained in a protocol and some declarations to the Lugano Convention. They provide that there shall be an exchange of information concerning relevant judgments; such an exchange of information has to take place between the EC Court of Justice and the designated courts in the EFTA countries, as well as between the EFTA courts themselves. It is further provided that the EFTA courts shall pay due regard to the principles laid down in the courts of the other Contracting States and that the EC Court of Justice, when interpreting the Brussels Convention, shall pay due regard to the decisions of the EFTA courts. By this mechanism it is hoped to establish uniformity of interpretation of the Brussels and Lugano Conventions.

At the date of writing,[13] the United Kingdom has not given effect to the Parallel Convention.

Judgments of the Court of the European Communities

The judgments and orders of the Court of Justice of the EC and other "Community judgments"[14] and orders of the Community institutions are directly enforceable in the United Kingdom, subject to certain conditions.[15] Such enforcement is done by registration in the High Court but it is necessary that first the Secretary of State appends an order of enforcement. These European measures are then enforceable in the United Kingdom, subject to the Treaties, as if they were judgments or orders of the court in which they are registered.

---

[13] October 1, 1989.
[14] This strange expression includes the decision of certain other organs of the EC.
[15] European Communities (Enforcement of the Community Judgments) Order 1972 (S.I. 1972 No. 1590), made under the European Communities Act 1972.

CHAPTER 33

THE DISPUTE SETTLEMENT PROCEDURE OF GATT

THE general nature of the General Agreement on Tariffs and Trade (GATT) is succinctly indicated by the present Director-General of this organisation, Mr. Arthur Dunkel.[1]

> The General Agreement on Tariffs and Trade is a multilateral treaty that lays down general rules, accepted by over 120 States,[2] for the conduct of international trade relations. Since 1948,[3] GATT has been the main forum for the liberalisation of trade barriers and for the settlement of international trade disputes.[4]

Although the provisions of GATT are detailed and complex, three fundamental principles by which it seeks to achieve its aim of global trade liberalisation can be discerned:

> 1. The principle of non-discrimination expressed in the so-called general Most Favoured Nations (MFN) clause of Article I of GATT. The significance of this provision is that if a Contracting Party in bi-lateral negotiations grants another Party a tariff concession, such concession can in principle be claimed by all other contracting parties.

---

[1] In his Foreword to Edmond McGovern, *International Trade Regulation—GATT, The United States and the European Community*, Exeter, 1986.

[2] At present, 97 Contracting Parties, one further country has acceded provisionally and 28 countries apply GATT Rules on a *de facto* basis (September 1, 1989).

[3] GATT was established on October 30, 1947, to become effective on January 1, 1948. It was intended to be a temporary measure. Its institutional functions were to be exercised on a permanent basis by the proposed International Trade Organisation (ITO) which was to be created by the so-called Havana Charter. When the ITO failed to materialise, the institutional element of GATT was developed. Today GATT, although essentially a multilateral international treaty, is backed by a full institutional organisation. Its highest body is called the Contracting Parties, it has a Council of Representatives, several Standing Committees, a Director-General and Secretariat, the address of which is at the Centre William Rappard, 154 rue de Lausanne, 1211 Geneva 21, Switzerland.

[4] The original GATT of 1948 has been much amended by a series of multilateral trade negotiations which have become known as "Rounds". They are:

> 1947 Geneva
> 1949 Annecy
> 1950–51 Torquay
> 1955–56 Geneva
> 1961–62 Geneva (The Dillon Round)
> 1963–67 Geneva (The Kennedy Round)
> 1973–79 Geneva (The Tokyo Round)
> 1986– Punta del Este (The Uruguay Round; this Round is still in progress; (October 1, 1989)).

(ICC Brochure *International Trade Negotiations ICC Business Guide to the new GATT Round*, ICC Brochure 446, 1987).

2. A Contracting Party shall rely only on import tariffs where the protection of its domestic industry is necessary. Non-tariff measures, such as quantitative restrictions (quotas) or standards requirements discriminating against imports, are in principle prohibited. The prohibition of quotas is often bypassed by voluntary restraint agreements (VRAs).

3. An elaborate system for the resolution of trade disputes is provided.

These GATT principles, in their application, are subject to many exceptions, particularly in favour of Customs unions and free trade areas,[5] in emergency situations.[6] and in the interest of the developing countries.[7] GATT also contains special provisions on anti-dumping and countervailing duties.[8]

GATT, as a treaty concerning international trade concluded by States, forms part of *international economic law*, which is a branch of public international law. Strictly speaking, a discussion of GATT is outside the ambit of this work which deals with *international trade law*, a topic of private law.[9] But these academic distinctions must give way to practical considerations.[10] It happens from time to time—more often today than before—that the exporter feels that he is discriminated against by legislative regulation or administration practice in the country to which his exports are directed. In such a situation, his legal adviser has to consider whether the dispute settlement procedure of GATT offers redress. These considerations make it necessary to include a brief account of this subject in the present work.

The trade policy of States with respect to imports varies. It moves between the two opposite tendencies of free trade and protectionism. Most national economies adopt an amalgam of these tendencies but, despite their global interdependence, there exists no agreement on how these two tendencies should be reconciled. Some are, with respect to imports, more liberal and others more protectionist. The trading policies of States thus lead frequently to conflict situations. GATT, which attempts to maintain the ideal of world trade liberalisation in the face of a rising tide of national protectionism,[11] provides rules for the resolution of these conflicts. From rudimentary beginnings in 1948, these rules have been refined from time to time and have been further improved by a resolution of the Uruguay Round in 1989, reference to which will be made in the following.

---

[5] GATT, Art. XXIV.

[6] *Ibid.*, Art. XIX.

[7] *Ibid.*, Art. XVIII.

[8] *Ibid.*, Art. VI.

[9] On the distinction between international economic law and international trade law, see Clive M. Schmitthoff, "The Concept of Economic Law in England" [1966] J.B.L. 309; *Essays*, 38.

[10] Moreover, as Lord Goff pointed out in the *State of Norway's Application* cases [1989] 2 W.L.R. 458, 471, the distinction in the civil law between public and private law is by no means clear cut; the same considerations apply, *mutatis mutandis*, to the distinction between public and private international law.

[11] See the ICC Brochure 446, referred to in n. 4, *ante*.

The exporter's standing in GATT disputes

The first hurdle, which the exporter desirous of making use of the GATT dispute procedure encounters, is this. GATT, as has been seen, is an international treaty pertaining to public international law. It is normal in this branch of law—although there are exceptions[12]—that only States which have acceded to the treaty may raise complaints about its breach but that such complaints cannot be lodged by private persons—individuals or companies resident in one of the contracting States—although they may be affected by a breach of the international treaty. In principle only States are "Contracting Parties" of GATT.

It follows that the ordinary exporter has no standing (*locus standi*) under GATT and cannot set into motion its dispute settlement machinery but he may approach the competent Ministry of his country—in the UK the Department of Trade and Industry—with the request to take up his case and to raise a complaint in accordance with the rules of GATT. Whether the Minister will accede to this request is a matter of his discretion. This is a policy decision. As such, it is normally not subject to review by the courts.

The EC has *locus standi* under GATT although it is not a "State." The Community has been accepted as a signatory to the protocols incorporating the results of the Kennedy and Tokyo Rounds and other GATT agreements.[13] It has been involved as a party in various trade disputes.[14] This is of importance to the exporter. If a discriminatory measure of a contracting State affects traders in several EC Member States, *e.g.* unfair pre-shipment certificate requirements are postulated by a particular State,[15] the EC Commission may be inclined to lodge a complaint under GATT.

The complaint procedure of GATT is adversarial; the complaint must be raised by a Contracting Party. The procedure is not inquisitorial, the GATT organisation does not act on its own initiative, even if its attention is drawn by a person who has no *locus standi* to an obvious breach of GATT obligations by a Contracting Party.[16]

---

[12] A notable exception is the European Convention of Human Rights which gives individuals direct access to the Commission.

[13] McGovern, *op.cit.* in n. 1, para 2.34, p. 100.

[14] *e.g.* EC refunds on exports of sugar—Complaint by Brazil (1981); EC tariff treatment on imports of citrus (1985).

[15] See p. 128, *ante*.

[16] Jeffrey M. Waincymer "Revitalising GATT, Article XXIII—Issues in the Context of the Uruguay Round" in 17 *Australian Business Law Review* (1989) 3, 12.

The law relating to GATT disputes

The procedure for the settlement of GATT disputes is now fairly precise. McGovern (whose book was published in 1986) refers to the legal sources under three headings.[17]

> 1. Articles XXII and XXIII of GATT;
> 2. the provisions in GATT dealing with specific subject areas, such as Article XIX;
> 3. resolutions of the Tokyo Round, in particular the decision on an Understanding regarding Notification, Consultation, Dispute Settlement and Surveillance (the 1979 Understanding), with an annex, an agreed description of the customary practice of GATT in the field of dispute settlement.[18]

A fourth heading should be added in consequence of the resolutions of the Uruguay Round. On April 12, 1989, the GATT Council adopted a further measure, *viz*:

> 4. Improvements to the GATT Dispute Settlement Rules and Procedures (1989) adopted by the Uruguay Round.[19] The purpose of this measure is to streamline[20] the settlement procedure.[20A] But the 1989 measure is, at least for the time being, only temporary; it is to be applied from May 1, 1989 to the end of the Uruguay Round.

The coordination of these texts is unusual. Articles XXII and XXIII of the original GATT have not been amended; they are still in operation as the fundamental text. But they are of little practical assistance as they are expressed in general terms. The other texts are precise and, *inter alia*, contain time limits for the various procedural steps. These other texts should be read together with the venerable text of 1948. The whole regulation provides a workable code of procedure for the settlement of disputes under GATT.

The stages of the GATT settlement procedure

It is now intended to consider the various stages of the GATT disputes procedure. This will be done under the following headings:

---

[17] McGovern, *op.cit.* in n. 1, para. 1–16, pp. 32–33. Also Kenneth R. Simmonds and Brian H.W. Hill, *Law and Practice under the GATT and other Trading Arrangements*, Dobbs Ferry, NY, 1987.

[18] Doc. BISD 26S/210 (1980).

[19] *Focus*, No. 61 (May 1989) p. 9, and No. 62 (June 1989), pp 1 and 4. (*Focus* is the monthly Newsletter of GATT).

[20] See Jeffrey M. Waincymer, *op.cit.* in n. 16, *ante*.

[20a] The Uruguay Round of negotiations is considered a single undertaking and all agreements of the various negotiating groups are provisional until they will be approved as part of the final package at the end of the Round. The deliberations of the negotiating group on dispute settlement are continuing. It is therefore possible that the final version of the streamlined dispute settlement procedure which will be adopted by the Uruguay Round will be different from that provisionally approved and treated in the text.

Notification
Consultation.
Arbitration.
Panels and working parties.
The report.
Implementation of recommendations and rulings.

The GATT procedure is widely used. In 1988 the number of panels examining complaints has doubled, as compared with the number for 1987.[21]

Notification

If a Contracting Party, on its own initiative or as the result of representation by an enterprise in its territory, concludes that another Contracting Party has committed a breach of its obligations under GATT, it may approach the other Party informally or though diplomatic channels and may attempt in negotiations to obtain redress, *e.g.* by a tariff concession of the other Party.

If these negotiations are successful, the result shall be notified to GATT. The resolution accepted by the Uruguay Round states so expressly. The main purpose of notification is to inform the other Contracting Parties who are not involved in the dispute and to make them aware that a problem has arisen (and has been settled).

Consultation

The consultative process is more formal than informal negotiations.[22] Consultation is already recommended as a means of dispute settlement by Article XXII of the original GATT. The implementing procedure adopted by the Uruguay Round introduces into the rules on consultation the time limits which are characteristic for modern GATT procedures; they are aimed at expediting the settlement process.

The GATT complaint procedure normally commences with the request of the complaining Party for conciliation. The aim of the GATT procedure is thus to achieve an amicable compromise between the parties in dispute. Only if it is not possible to achieve a settlement by conciliation, more formal measures, such as arbitration or the constitution of a panel, are admitted.

---

[21] Ambassador Alan Oxley (Australia) at the session of the GATT Contracting Parties at Montreal on November 7 and 8, 1988.
(*Focus*, No. 58, December 1988, p. 1).
[22] On the consultation process in general, see Clive M. Schmitthoff, "Extrajudicial Dispute Settlement," in *Forum Internationale* (No. 6), The Netherlands, 1985, *Essays*, 637).

The resolution adopted by the Uruguay Round provides that, if a request is made under Article XXII.I or XXIII.I for conciliation, the respondent party shall, unless otherwise agreed, reply to the request within ten days after the receipt and shall enter into consultation with the complaining party in good faith within 30 days from the day of the request. If the respondent party fails to comply with these obligations, the complaining party may proceed directly to request the establishment of a panel or a working party.

If the consultations fail to achieve a settlement of the dispute within 60 days after the request, the complaining party may request the establishment of a panel or a working party.[23]

In cases of urgency, including perishable goods en route, these time limits are reduced.

It is also provided[24] that the parties may agree that a third party should assist them by providing his *good offices, conciliation or mediation*. The Director-General of GATT, acting *ex-officio* may also offer this assistance. If this procedure is adopted, the complaining party is bound to allow 60 days from the date of the request for consultations before asking for a panel or a working party.

Arbitration

Arbitration is not the normal means of GATT dispute settlement if conciliation fails (or is not attempted). The normal method in this contingency is the establishment of a panel or a working party. In practice, GATT arbitrations are rare,[25] for reasons explained under the next heading.

But if the parties so agree, they may have arbitration. The GATT code does not provide for the application of rules of procedure for arbitration, such as the UNCITRAL Arbitration Rules.

Moreover, arbitration under GATT is very different from normal commercial arbitration. In GATT arbitration, the judicial element[26] is largely absent and the aim is prevalent to achieve a just and fair compromise (rather than to decide the issue according to the law).

---

[23] The complaining party may request a panel or working party at once if before the expiration of 60 days the parties jointly consider that the consultation has failed.

[24] In the Uruguay Round resolution, under D.

[25] In February 1989 the EC requested arbitration in a dispute with the USA and nominated the Director-General of GATT as sole arbitrator. The dispute concerned the US transposition of its tariff schedule to the Harmonised System (HS). The USA objected to arbitration as a measure of dispute settlement and the EC stated that it would look at alternative options, *Focus*, No. 62, (June 1989), p. 4.

[26] See p. 652 *ante*. Apart from the requirements of natural justice which, it is thought, likewise apply to GATT arbitrations.

The parties are required to agree beforehand that they will abide by the arbitration award. Third Contracting Parties may become parties to the arbitration if the complaining and respondent parties agree.

Panels and working parties

The disputes which arise under GATT concern mainly economic questions or technical problems pertaining to Customs law. The ordinary means for the resolution of legal disputes, *viz.* arbitration and litigation, are not suitable for the settlement of these disputes. For this reason, GATT has developed it own method of settlement procedure, *viz.* the panel and working party procedure. But this procedure tends to have some legalistic aspects. McGovern observes[27]:

> Although GATT participants are notoriously wary of appearing legalistic, many aspects of panel behaviour suggest that its character is essentially judicial.

In support of this view, McGovern refers, *inter alia*, to the common practice of citing previous panel rulings as precedents and to the occasional reference to principles of general international law regarding the interpretation of treaties.

Panels and working parties are appointed by the Council on behalf of the Contracting Parties. Where a party raises a complaint, claiming that the benefits of the Agreement are nullified or impaired by the behaviour of another party (Article XXIII), the establishment of a panel is the normal course. A working party is constituted where the subject-matter is of more general and usually less contentious character, such as requests for accession to GATT, verification that agreements concluded by member countries are in conformity with GATT, or studies of issues on which member countries will later wish to take a common stand. The object of both bodies, working parties as well as panels, is to produce a report for the consideration of the Contracting Parties.

The request for a panel or a working party has to be made in writing. It shall indicate whether consultations were held and shall provide a brief summary of the factual and legal issues. The Council has to decide on the request at its next meeting, if the complaining party so wishes.

The panel consists of three members unless the parties to the dispute agree, within ten days from the establishment of the panel, that a panel should be composed of five members.[28] The members of the panel are

---

[27] McGovern, *op.cit.* in no. 1, p. 36.
[28] Uruguay Round Document F(c), 4.
(It should be borne in mind that the 1989 resolution on improvement of the settlement procedure is, for the time being, only temporary; see text, p. 721, *ante.*)

well qualified governmental and/or non-governmental individuals[29] and the Contracting Parties shall permit their representatives to serve as panel members.[29] The Secretariat keeps a roster of non-governmental panelists for the choice of the disputing parties. If there is no agreement on the members of the panel within 20 days from the establishment of the panel, the Director-General of GATT, in consultation with the Chairman of the Council, appoints the panel.[30]

The standard terms of reference of a panel are the following but the parties to the dispute may agree on other terms within 20 days from the establishment of the panel.[31]

> To examine, in the light of the relevant GATT provisions, the matter referred to Contracting Parties . . . and to make such findings as will assist the Contracting Parties in making the recommendations or in giving the rulings provided for in Article XXIII.2.

All Contracting Parties have to be informed about the constitution of a panel and the progress of its proceedings. Any third Contracting Party having a substantial interest in the matter before the panel shall have an opportunity of being heard by the panel and of making written submissions to it.[32]

The Report

The deliberations of the panel or the working party result, as already observed, in a report to the Contracting Parties. As a general rule, the final report shall be submitted to the parties in dispute not later than six months, in cases of urgency (including complaints relating to perishable goods) this time is reduced to three months. If the panel considers that it cannot submit its report within these time limits, it shall inform the Council in writing of the reasons for the delay but in no circumstances shall the final report be submitted later than nine months.[33]

In order to give the members of the Council sufficient time to examine panel reports, they shall not be considered for adoption by the Council until 30 days after they have been issued to the Contracting Parties.[34] A Contracting Party which has an objection to the panel report shall give written reasons for these objections for circulation at least ten days prior to the Council meeting at which the panel report will be considered.[35] The

---

[29] *Ibid.*, F(c), 1 and 2.
[30] *Ibid.*, F(c), 5.
[31] *Ibid.*, F(b), 1.
[32] *Ibid.*, F(e).
[33] *Ibid.*, F(f), 5.
[34] *Ibid.*, G.1.
[35] *Ibid.*, G.2.

parties in dispute are entitled fully to participate in the deliberations of the report by the Council and their views shall be fully regarded.[36] The decision of the Council on the adoption of the panel report shall not be given later than 15 months after the request for conciliation by the complaining party, unless the parties otherwise agree.[37]

The decision of the Council on the adoption of a panel report shall be taken "by consensus".[38] Consent is the normal procedure in the GATT organisation.

Implementation of recommendations and rulings

GATT has devised a mechanism of surveillance in order to make certain that the recommendations and rulings of the panels are carried out. If it is impracticable to carry them out immediately, the affected party is granted a reasonable time to do so. Normally this should not be longer than six months. Thereafter, the issue of implementation remains on the agenda of the Council meetings until it is resolved.[39]

If a party fails to carry out the recommendations or rulings adopted by the Contracting Parties, the ultimate remedy provided in Article XXIII.2 is for the Contracting Parties to authorise the aggrieved party (or other Contracting Parties) to suspend, as far as the offending party is concerned, the application of such concessions or other obligations under GATT as seem to be appropriate. This remedy is applied in very rare circumstances. The only reported case in which this retaliatory measure was sanctioned was the complaint of the Netherlands against the USA in 1952.[40]

A party against whom suspensory action is taken, may withdraw from GATT. This is done by written notice to the executory secretary. The notice can only be given within 60 days after the suspension. The notice becomes effective 60 days following the day on which the executory secretary received notice of withdrawal.[41]

AMERICAN TRADE LEGISLATION

A short note on the US trade legislation has to be added because the US *Omnibus Trade and Competitiveness Act of 1988*[42] has raised a contro-

---

[36] *Ibid.*, G.3.
[37] *Ibid.*, G.4.
[38] *Ibid.*, G.4 but the rather mysterious proviso is added: "without prejudice to the GATT provisions on decision-making."
[39] *Ibid.*, I.2 and 3.
[40] BISD IS/32 (1953) Report of Working Party on Netherlands action under Article XXIII.2 to suspend obligations to the US.BISD IS/62 (1953).
[41] Article XXIII.2.
[42] Pub. No. 100–418.

versy. Some authors consider this enactment as an indication that the USA intends to pursue a unilateral policy of protectionism.[43] Others take the view that the enactment is wholly reconcilable with the multilateral philosophy of GATT. The latter is the official view in the United States. In fact, even after the passing of the 1988 Act the US has continued to take an active part in the deliberations and activities of GATT.

The pre-1988 position

The 1988 Act has, *inter alia*, greatly extended the field of application of section 301 of the Trade Act 1974.[44]

Section 301 actions, also known as retaliatory or unfair trade actions, enable an interested person, such as an exporter, domestic manufacturer or investor, to bring administrative proceedings in the USA contesting the legality or reasonableness of foreign trade practices which allegedly restrict US exports, investment or business abroad. The United States Trade Representative (USTR) may also initiate these proceedings.

If the action is successful, the USA can take certain retaliatory action, including restricting imports from the offending country into the USA or, more frequently, imposing a surcharge on its imports.

The purpose of section 301 actions is thus to force open foreign markets for US exports. The 301 action is intended to assist the US exporter in expanding his business abroad. Its purpose is not to protect domestic production.

Before the coming into operation of the 1988 Act, relatively little use was made of the section 301 action.

The 1988 Act

The 1988 Act provides a great strengthening of the section 301 action. The new section 301 transfers the power to determine whether the foreign action is in violation of section 301 from the President to the USTR. In many cases, action by the USTR is now mandatory. Some of the definitions are extended; thus, an "unjustifiable" foreign country act now includes an act in violation of or inconsistent with the international legal rights of the USA.

---

[43] See the observations of the Director-General in *GATT Activities 1988*, obtainable from the GATT Secretariat in Geneva (The Director-General does not refer to the USA expressly but states his view in general terms).
[44] As amended. Section 301 (unamended by the 1988 Act) is reproduced in Folsom, Gordon and Spanogle, Jr., *International Business Transactions*, St. Paul (USA), p. 1011.

The 1988 Act contains a link with the GATT disputes procedure. It provides that there is no violation of the mandatory provisions of the Act when GATT determines that the foreign practice does not violate a trade agreement.

The extension of the section 301 action by the 1988 Act should be seen as an addition to the armoury of the USA if that country unfortunately gets involved in a trade war. It is intended to act more as a threat of the possibility of retaliatory action than as an aggressive measure. A distinguished American scholar, Professor Stuart S. Malawer, comments on the 1988 Act thus[45]:

> The intent behind the legislation to open foreign markets by imposing import restrictions in the United States, seems paradoxical. The preferred way is the multilateral route through the expansion of GATT and not unilateral trade restrictions or bilateral management of trade investment flows. This will only work against the United States in the long run.

Professor Malawer considers trade litigation like that provided by section 301 as essentially unnecessary. He continues:

> Revamping the dispute-resolution mechanism of the GATT and expanding its substantive coverage (to include investment and services) are more attractive alternatives.

---

[45] Stuart S. Malawer "The 1988 Trade Act: Expanding Retaliatory Actions," in *Virginia Bar Association Journal,* Winter 1989, p.4.

PART SEVEN

CONSTRUCTION AND LONG TERM CONTRACTS

CHAPTER 34

THE CONSTRUCTION OF WORKS AND INSTALLATIONS
ABROAD

THE contract for the construction of works and installations abroad has
certain typical characteristics. The parties to this international contract
are often a foreign government department or government corporation as
employer and a company—or several companies jointly—incorporated in
another country as *contractor*. Often, but not necessarily, the employer is
an organisation in a country in the course of development and the
contractor is incorporated in an industrialised country. Legally, this type
of international contract is a contract for work, the supply of goods, for
services or a combination of these forms of contract; economically, it is a
contract for the transfer of technology from one country to another.
Illustrations of this type of contract are the undertaking of a contractor to
build and equip in the country of the employer a hospital, a factory, an
airport or a pipeline but in some cases contractors are known to have
undertaken to build whole ports or cities for the employer. The contract
may be a turn-key contract under which the contractor undertakes to
hand over the installation ready for use, or it may proceed by stages when
each stage has to be tested and accepted by the employer.

Another feature of an international procurement contract is that it
involves usually considerable amounts of money.[1] Often the employer,
particularly if he is an organisation in a developing country, cannot or will
not finance the undertaking out of his own resources and it has to be
financed by public international bodies, such as the International Bank
for Reconstruction and Development (IBRD, the World Bank), the
International Development Association (IDA), both in Washington,
D.C., or the European Investment Bank (EIB) or the European
Development Fund (EDF), both of the European Community. While
these financial institutions are loath to decree the terms on which their
borrower, the employer, has to contract, some of them have established
guidelines which they expect the parties to the international procurement

---

[1] In the Department of Trade and Industry an *Overseas Projects Board* (see p. 83, *ante*)
provides an identifiable central point to which industrialists, bankers and consultants can
look for co-ordination on government and official support for capital projects overseas. The
Board administers the Aid and Trade Provisions Fund from which contributions may in
certain circumstances be made towards the cost of a wide range of activities preceding the
main contract, but such contributions are repayable in the event of the contract being
secured.

contract to respect. Another aspect of the financial magnitude of these transactions is that they have given rise to various kinds of contract guarantees, such as, *e.g.* tender guarantees, performance guarantees and repayment guarantees,[2] some of which are dealt with in the ICC brochure on *Uniform Rules for Contract Guarantees.*[3]

A third feature of international procurement contracts is that their performance often extends over a considerable period of time. During that time the economic situation may change. For this reason it is usual to insert into this type of contract, in addition to the ordinary currency and *force majeure* clauses, special clauses, aimed at reducing the economic risk inherent in long term contracts, such as price adjustment and hardship clauses.

The UNCITRAL Legal Guide

The *UNCITRAL Legal Guide on Drawing Up International Contracts for the Construction of Industrial Works* was adopted by that organisation in August 1987. It was published by the United Nations in 1988.[4]

The UNCITRAL Legal Guide is a comprehensive and detailed manual[5] intended to be of benefit to those charged with the task of drawing up international construction contracts. Its observations and the suggestions made in it aim at striking a just and fair balance between the interests of the employer and the contractor. The UNCITRAL Legal Guide deals with construction contracts on a global and not a regional level.

TYPES OF PROCUREMENT

Procurement by inviting tenders and by negotiation

From the legal point of view, there exist two methods of international procurement, *viz.* by inviting tenders from companies prepared to

---

[2] See p. 446, *ante.*
[3] ICC Brochure No. 325 (August 1978).
[4] The UNCITRAL Legal Guide may be obtained through mail order, quoting sales number E.87.V.10, document A/CN.9/SER.B/2, by readers in Europe, Africa and northern Asia from United Nations Publications, Palais des Nations, CH–1211 Geneva 10, Switzerland, and by readers in North, Central and South America, southern Asia and the Pacific from United Nations Publications, Room DC2–0853, United Nations Headquarters, New York, New York 10017, U.S.A. The UNCITRAL Legal Guide may also be purchased from bookshops and distributors throughout the world that stock United Nations publications. UNCITRAL is also working on a *Model Law on Procurement.*
[5] The preparation of the UNCITRAL Legal Guide took approximately seven years. The chairman of the Working Group was Mr. Leif Sevon of Finland.

contract with the employer (*appels d'offres*) or by negotiating the contract of work or supply with the contractor directly or through agents, without previously requiring competitive bids from intending contractors (*marchés de gré à gré*). Of these two methods, procurement by tender, *i.e.* by competitive bid, is the preferred method. It has been said[6]:

> Competitive tender has certain obvious advantages over other methods of contractor selection . . . Not only is it an effective means of getting the needed goods or service at lowest cost, but the resulting fixed price contract, under which increased cost must normally be absorbed by the contractor, is easy to administer. Competitive tender also diminishes the risk of bias or favouritism in contract awards and tendering firms will feel that they have an equal chance of getting the contract.

It is therefore understandable that the World Bank requires this method as the normal method of procurement; it is stated in the Bank's *Guidelines*[7]:

> The Bank has found that, in most cases,[8] these needs and interests can best be realized through international competitive bidding, properly administered, and with suitable allowance for preferences for local or regional manufacturers and, where appropriate, for local contractors under prescribed conditions. In such cases, therefore, the Bank requires its borrowers to obtain goods and works through international competitive bidding open to eligible suppliers and contractors.

Open and selective tenders

There are two types of tender: the open and the selective. Under the open (or public) procedure "tenders are invited through advertisements or other forms of public notice from any eligible party. In the case of selective tenders a limited number of firms are invited by the [employer's] contracting agency to submit offers. The agency can select the tenderers either through its previous knowledge of the market or after a pre-qualification procedure, in which elegible firms are invited to provide evidence of their ability to perform the services or produce the goods desired by the agency."[9] The prevalent method is selective competitive bidding preceded by a prequalification procedure.

If the procurement is done without competitive bidding, the observations discussed in the previous chapters apply to the contract between the employer and the contractor, but sometimes some of the special clauses noted in this chapter, *e.g.* the hardship clause, are added.

---

[6] Colin Turpin, *Government Contracts* (London, Penguin, 1972), 135.
[7] *Guidelines for Procurement under IBRD Loans and IDA Credits* (3rd ed., May 1985), art. 1.3.
[8] The Bank admits in appropriate cases other methods of procurement, see *ibid*, pp. 28–32.
[9] Gösta Westring, *International Procurement*, (2nd revised ed., International Trade Centre UNCTAD/GATT, 1985). See also the *GATT Agreement on Government Procurement*, Geneva, 1979.

The following observations deal only with the procurement by competitive tender.

The EC Directives on public procurement

The EC has issued several Directives dealing with the procurement procedures of government departments and government agencies of the Member States.[10] The most important of these Directives are:

> the 1971 Directive on public works and construction contracts[11];
> the 1977 Directive on government procurement of supplies of goods and equipment[12];
> the 1988 Directive clarifying the EC rules on public procurement of supplies and equipment.[13]
> A similar clarifying draft on public works and construction contracts has been before the Council of Ministers since 1986.[14]

The main purpose of these EC measures is to provide equal opportunities in bidding for public sector contracts for suppliers and contractors from all EC countries and so to discourage discrimination against non-indigenous firms; further, tendering and award procedures should be open and above board. Excluded from the application of the EC Directives are public water and energy utilities and public transport and telecommunications services (telecommunications only from the procurement rules for supplies and equipment, but not from the public works provisions).

The 1988 amending Directive deals mainly with the problem of transparency; in particular, it obliges the authority which wishes to commission construction work or to invite tenders for supply to publish advance information about its procurement programme for the following year.

The EC had to align its public procurement measures with the GATT Agreement on Government Procurement,[15] known as the GATT Code,[16]

---

[10] Procurement procedures, such as invitations of tenders for construction work or the supply of goods, occur, of course, also in the private sector of business but the EC has not extended its regulation to that sphere.

[11] Directive 71/305/EEC; O.J. 1971 L 185, p. 5.

[12] Directive 77/62/EEC; O.J. 1977 113, p. 1.

[13] Directive 88/295/EEC; O.J. 1988 L 127, p. 1.

[14] *Public Procurement and Construction—Towards an Integrated Market*, 2nd ed., 1988 (obtainable from the Luxembourg Office for Official Publications of the European Communities, 1989; catalogue No. CB–PP–88–002–EN–C). See also DTI, *Pyblic Purchasing*, 1989; Friedl Weiss, "Public Procurement in the EEC—Public Supply Contracts" in 13 *European Law Review* (1988), 318.

[15] For the GATT Code see p. 733, n. 9, *ante*.

[16] The list of authorities falling under the GATT Code is contained as Appendix II in the publication referred to in n. 14.

because the EC has accepted the Code. The GATT Agreement contains a lengthy list of public authorities to which it applies; the list includes, as far as the United Kingdom is concerned, apart from the obvious ministries and government agencies, inter alia, the British Museum, the Supreme Court, and the Royal Botanic Gardens at Kew.

Only contracts exceeding a certain threshold value fall under these regulations. The threshold value for the GATT Code procurement contracts is lower than the general threshold under the EC regulation. The general threshold is ECU 200,000 (in 1988 £142,938), and the GATT Code threshold is ECU 130,000 (in 1988 £92,325); both amounts are exclusive of VAT.

PROCUREMENT BY TENDER

The course of dealing

Where a foreign government department or corporation intends to invite tenders, the normal course of business is as follows. The employer, *i.e.* the foreign government organisation, publishes *an announcement of preliminary selection* in leading newspapers of the world. This advertisement states, apart from the nature of the work, the name and address of the employer and the time limit for the applications, the conditions of the *prequalification procedure, i.e.* the conditions of technical and financial capability which applicants have to satisfy in order to be allowed to tender; normally the applicants are required to pay a small fee for the tender documents. Interested firms from various parts of the world, which think that they satisfy the prequalification conditions, will then apply to the employer for the *tender documents*. The employer will send the documents to those applicants who is his opinion satisfy the prequalification conditions. The tender documents are usually voluminous, setting out the technical specifications, the contract terms, the amount of the tender guarantee and the instructions on how and when to submit the tender. The employer will also appoint a *consulting engineer*,[17] if he has not done so before; his function is to advise him impartially on the suitability of the tenderers; he is not one of the competing bidders. The firms which have received the tender documents will consider them and, if they are interested, submit a formal *tender*. Sometimes formalities are prescribed for such a submission, *e.g.* it has to be submitted in a sealed

---

[17] See *Guidelines for the Use of Consultants by World Bank Borrowers and by the World Bank as Executing Agency*, (August 1981; reprinting 1988). *ECE Guide for Drawing up International Contracts on Consulting Engineering, including some related aspects of Technical Assistance*, (UN, New York, 1983).

envelope in order to safeguard the confidentiality of the tender. At the same time each tenderer will provide a *tender guarantee* (*tender bond*) in the prescribed amount. The tender guarantee is usually provided by means of a bank guarantee. It indicates to the employer that the tenderer is seriously interested in the proposition and that his submission is not frivolous.

The next step is the *opening of the tenders by the employer*. In some cases this is done in a ceremonious manner: all tenders, which are contained in sealed envelopes, are opened on the same day and publicly read out. In other cases a less formal procedure is followed and the tenders are opened and read as they are received. The employer then proceeds to the *evaluation of the tenders*, on the advice of his consulting engineer. At this stage, under the terms of the tender documents, he may negotiate with one or the other of the tenderers, but that should be done only to clarify points in their tenders; it would be unfair if the terms of the other tenders were disclosed at this stage. The employer will then decide to accept the most advantageous tender, which need not be the lowest, and will send a *letter of acceptance* to the contractor whom he has selected. Eventually the formal *contract* is signed by both parties. It is normally a short document, referring to, and embodying, the tender, the drawings, the conditions of contract, the specifications, the bills of quantities, the letter of acceptance, etc. Often the tender guarantees of the unsuccessful bidders are released only after the signature of the formal contract, because before that event there is no certainty that a binding contract has been concluded.

The parties will then proceed to the *performance of the contract*. The contractor will usually give the employer a *performance guarantee* from a bank and in some cases the employer will give the contractor a *payment guarantee* of a bank. Sometimes the tender guarantee of the successful bidder is converted to form part of the performance guarantee which he has to provide. Under some contracts the employer will appoint the so-called *engineer*,[18] he is a technical expert whose duty it is to resolve any differences which may arise in the course of performance; he is not an arbitrator and he may be a person other than the consulting engineer who advised in the evaluation of the tenders. The contract usually provides for the rough work to be done by local labour and for the technical work to be executed by the contractor's staff, but it is important that a representative of the contractor be present at the site from the beginning to supervise the co-ordination of the foundations and the installation of the machinery. The contract also sometimes provides for the training of the employer's personnel in the country of the contractor and for the adequate housing of the contractor's personnel employed on the site in the country of the employer.

---

[18] On the legal position of the engineer see p. 745 *post*.

The terms of payment vary according to the nature of the work to be done or the goods to be supplied. Sometimes, when goods have to be supplied, they are the terms usual in c.i.f. or other contracts concluded on the familiar trade terms,[19] in other cases they depend on the progress of the work and payment is made in stages on the certificate of the engineer. Here complicated procedures are sometimes arranged for the *acceptance of the work* and it is not unusual to distinguish between provisional and final acceptance. The contract may also provide for the payment of liquidated damages in cases of delayed performance and bonus payments in case of performance in advance of the stipulated time.

When the work or installation is completed, it is unusual for the employer to release the final balance of the price at once. Normally he is entitled to *retention money, i.e.* he may retain the balance for a specified time, sometimes as long as a year, in order to be assured that the installation operates satisfactorily.

The standard contract forms

Contracts for the construction of works and installations abroad are usually concluded in the form of standard forms which are adapted to the requirements of the transaction in question. The most important of these standard contract forms were listed earlier[20] but reference may be made again to those whose terms will be considered here from time to time. They are:

1. *Conditions of Contract (International) for Works of Civil Engineering Construction,* (4th ed., 1987). This standard form is sponsored by FIDIC, the *Fédération Internationale des Ingénieurs-Conseils.* This form is known as the *FIDIC Contract.*[21]
2. *The Guidelines for Procurement under IBRD Loans and IDA Credits* (3rd ed., May 1985), known as the *World Bank Guidelines.*[22]
3. *General Conditions for Public Works and Supply Contracts* financed by the European Development Fund of the EEC (Brussels, February 14, 1972). These Conditions are known as the *EDF Conditions.*[23]

The FIDIC Contract

Of particular interest is the FIDIC Contract because this standard contract form is of global importance.

---

[19] See p. 9, *ante.*

[20] See p. 74, *ante*; other standard contract forms are set out in Gösta Westring, *op. cit.*

[21] The FIDIC contract can be obtained from the Association of Consulting Engineers, Alliance House, 12 Caxton Street, London, SW1H 0QL or from the headquarters of FIDIC, P.O. Box 86, CH–1000 Lausanne, 12–Chailley, Switzerland.

[22] Obtainable from the Headquarters of the World Bank, 1818 H Street, N.W., Washington D.C. 20433, USA.

[23] Obtainable from the Commission of the European Communities Directorate-General for Development, Direction Finance, rue de la Loi 200, Brussels, Belgium. These conditions are at present subject to negotiations between the Community and the ACP States. Three sets of General Conditions are being prepared: for works, services and supplies. In addition, Rules of Arbitration for EDF-financed contracts have been prepared.

The FIDIC Contract is arranged in two parts:–

Part I: General Conditions with Forms of Tender and Agreement.
Part II: Conditions of Particular Application with Guidelines for Preparation of Particular Clauses.[24]

Parts I and II are published in separate volumes. The General Conditions of Part I include 72 clauses which are divided into sub-clauses. They are intended to be of universal application and do not contain any reference to the names of the parties of the particular work in hand. The Conditions of Particular Application in Part II contain the terms which apply to the particular transaction in question. They are variable and are intended as as *aide-memoire* for the adaption of Part I to the particular contract. The clauses of Part II are linked to those of Part I by the same numbers. They contain, *inter alia*, the names of the employer and contractor, as well as that of the engineer, the language(s) of the contract and the ruling language, and the law to which the contract shall be subject. The clauses in Part II are usually followed by an explanation and in many instances by examples. This kind of presentation enhances the practical usefulness of the standard form for the draftsman who has to adapt it to the agreement in hand.

The form of the tender suggested by the FIDIC contract is contained in Part I. Appended to it are the financial details, such as the amounts of the performance guarantee, in the FIDIC contract called "the performance security," of liquidated damages, of the retention money, and the time limits, *e.g.* the period for the commencement of the work, of completion, of maintenance, and the time within which payment is to be made after the issue of the certificate by the engineer. These financial (and other) details have to be signed or initialled by or on behalf of the contractor. The FIDIC contract does not provide a standard form for the letter of acceptance by the employer.

The form of agreement set out in the FIDIC contract is likewise contained in Part I. It is extremely short. It contains only four clauses but it incorporates by reference:

(a) the letter of acceptance;
(b) the tender;
(c) the Conditions of Contract (Parts I and II);
(d) the specification;
(e) the drawings; and
(f) the bill of quantities.

The FIDIC Contract suggests that the agreement is executed in the form of a deed, duly signed, sealed and delivered by both parties in the presence of witnesses.

---

[24] Part II contains in its Introduction observations drawing attention to clauses of particular importance for dredging and reclamation work.

A typical feature of the FIDIC Contract is that it requires the employer to appoint *an engineer* whose name is inserted into Part II of the Conditions of Contract.[25] He is a technical expert whose function includes the decision of disputes which may arise in the execution of the work, the issue of certificates of satisfactory completion of certain stages or of the whole work, and the giving of orders, particularly with respect to alterations, additions and omissions of the agreed work.

Parts I and II of the FIDIC Contract contain full indices.

The pre-contractual stage

The prequalification procedure

There exists no standard procedure for prequalification requirements. Sometimes the requirements are kept in general terms, *e.g.*:

> In order to obtain the necessary application form, interested companies which can prove their fitness, technical and financial capacity, experience and tradition in such field of the . . . industry, are requested to contact . . .

Sometimes the employer, if so requested, sends applicants a prequalification questionnaire. Where tenders are invited for work already begun, it is usual to exempt applicants who have already prequalified for previous stages from further prequalification.

Transactions financed by World Bank loans or IDA credits will normally require a prequalification procedure for bidders. The World Bank Guidelines provide[26]:

> Prequalification is advisable for large or complex works and, exceptionally, for custom designed equipment and specialized services to ensure, in advance of bidding, that invitations to bid are extended only to those who are capable. The Loan Agreement with the Bank will specify if prequalification is required for particular contracts. Prequalification may also be useful to determine a contractor's eligibility for domestic preference where this is allowed. Prequalification should be based entirely upon the capability of prospective bidders to perform the particular contract satisfactorily, taking into account, *inter alia*, their (i) experience and past performance on similar contracts, (ii) capabilities with respect to personnel, equipment, and plant and (iii) financial position. The invitation to prequalify for bidding on specific contracts should be advertised and notified. . . . The scope of the contract and a clear statement of the requirements for qualification should be sent to all those that wish to be considered for prequalification. As soon as prequalification is completed, the bidding documents should be issued to the qualified bidders. All such bidders that meet the specified criteria should be allowed to bid.

The World Bank and IDA will normally wish to review prequalification procedures and to be notified of the list of prequalified firms and any

---

[25] On the legal status of the engineer see p. 745, *post*.
[26] World Bank Guidelines, Art 2.10.

reasons for exclusion of any applicant for prequalification. This has to be done before applicants are invited.[27] These international financial institutions thus wish to safeguard industry against arbitrary exclusion from prequalification and to ensure that fair play is observed.

The invitation to tender

The contracting agency of the employer will send those applicants who have qualified the tender documents. From the legal point of view they constitute an invitation to bid, *i.e.* to make an offer. Although in the legal context this is still a preliminary step, the tender documents are of the utmost importance because they constitute the basis of any contract which may result. They are usually incorporated into the tender and again into the contract, when it is made, by reference.

The tender documents are usually divided into three parts, one which contains the conditions of contract, another which contains the technical details, such as the drawings, specifications and bill of quantities, and a third one which contains detailed instructions to the intending bidder on how to submit his tender.

Four clauses which are often found in invitations to bid may be mentioned here.

First, the invitation will state that the employer is not bound to accept the lowest bid or any bid at all. Even without the addition of this clause the employer would not be bound to do so. Secondly, the employer may reserve the right to seek clarification of the bid from a bidder. The principle which applies here is defined in the World Bank Guidelines thus[28]:

> The [employer] should ask any bidder for clarification needed to evaluate his bid but should not ask or permit any bidder to change the substance or price of his bid after the bid opening.

Thirdly, if it is intended to give certain bids preference for non-commercial reasons, *e.g.* where domestic, political or regional preference is intended to be given, that should be stated clearly in the invitation to tender.[29] Fourthly, the invitation should state that the employer shall be entitled to avoid the contract if it is proved that the contractor or any of his employees were engaged or involved in any form of bribery or corruption in connection with the contract.[30]

---

[27] *Ibid.* Appendix 1.
[28] *Ibid.* 2.46.
[29] *Ibid.* Appendix 2.
[30] ICC Brochure No. 315 (1977) on *Extortion and Bribery in Business Transactions*, para. 3, pp. 10–11.

Furthermore, since bids are usually invited from tenderers in different countries, the tender documents should clearly state the currency or currencies in which bid prices may be expressed and the contract price will be paid.[31]

The tender

This is the offer made by the contractor to enter into a binding contract with the employer on the terms of the tender documents. In English law and the laws of many other countries the tender can be withdrawn by the contractor before it is accepted but normally the right of withdrawal is restricted. The EDF Conditions restrict it to the end of the tendering time[32]:

> Any tender may be withdrawn, supplemented or amended prior to the date fixed for the receipt of tenders.

The FIDIC Contract goes further than that and its form of tender excludes the right of withdrawal for a specified time after the expiration of the tendering time[33]:

> We agree to abide by this tender for the period of . . . days from the date fixed for receiving the same and it shall remain binding upon us and may be accepted at any time before the expiration of that period.

In English law these restrictions of the right of withdrawal do not prevent the tenderer from withdrawing the tender after the expiration of the specified period (and also before its expiration[34]), provided that the withdrawal communication reaches the employer's contracting agency before acceptance. Here, however, the mechanism of the tender guarantee operates: if the tenderer withdraws the tender contrary to his undertaking to be bound by it, it is thought that the bond is forfeit.

The tender incorporates the tender documents by reference and consequently both the conditions of contract and the technical details become part of the tender. The form of tender suggested by the FIDIC Contract also contains the following significant provision which excludes the "subject to (formal) contract" interpretation:[35]

> Unless and until a formal agreement is prepared and executed this tender, together with your written acceptance thereof, shall constitute a binding contract between us.

---

[31] World Bank Guidelines, Art. 2.21–2.26.
[32] EDF Conditions, Art. 40(1).
[33] FIDIC Contract, Part I. Tender form, cl. 4..
[34] On firm offers, see p. 90, *ante*.
[35] FIDIC contract, Part I, Tender form, cl. 5.

The tender guarantee

It is customary to ask the tenderer to support his tender by a tender guarantee (tender bond) given by a bank, insurance company or other third party. The object of the tender guarantee is twofold: to indicate to the employer that the tenderer is in earnest and to protect the employer against the breach of any obligations which the tenderer undertakes by submitting his tender. As far as the banks, insurance companies and other third parties are concerned, the *Uniform Rules for Contract Guarantees,* published by the ICC,[36] provide a useful regulation which applies, however, only if adopted by the parties. The Uniform Rules define a tender guarantee thus[37]:

> "tender guarantee" means an undertaking given by a bank, insurance company or other party ("the guarantor") at the request of a tenderer ("the principal") or given on the instructions of a bank, insurance company, or other party so requested by the principal ("the instructing party") to a party inviting tenders ("the beneficiary") whereby the guarantor undertakes—in the event of default by the principal in the obligations resulting from the submission of the tender—to make payment to the beneficiary within the limits of a stated sum of money.

Under the Uniform Rules the tender guarantee expires:

(*a*) six months from the date of the guarantee[38]

(*b*) on acceptance of the tender by the employer by the award of a contract to the tenderer[39];

(*c*) by the award of the contract to another tenderer[40]; or

(*d*) if the employer expressly declares that he does not intend to place a contract.[41]

According to the Uniform Rules, a tender guarantee is valid only in respect of the original tender and does not cover any amendments not approved by the guarantor.[42] The Rules further provide that the employer who wishes to make a claim under the tender guarantee has to submit documentation supporting his claim within a specified time.[43] If the guarantee does not specify the documentation, a declaration from the employer is required that the contractor's tender has been accepted but he has failed either to sign the contract or to submit a performance guarantee. In addition, a declaration is required, addressed to the contractor, to have any dispute settled by arbitration, if not otherwise specified, in accordance with the Rules of the ICC Court of Arbitration

---

[36] ICC Brochure No. 325 (1978) see p. 447, *ante.*

[37] *Ibid.* Art. 2(*a*).

[38] *Ibid.* Art. 4(*a*).

[39] *Ibid.* Art. 5(2)(*a*).

[40] *Ibid.* Art. 5(2)(*b*).

[41] *Ibid.* Art. 5(2)(*c*).

[42] *Ibid.* Art. 7(1).

[43] *Ibid.* Arts. 8 and 9.

or the UNCITRAL Arbitration Rules, at the option of the contractor. The Uniform Rules for Contract Guarantees fail to deal with a claim under the guarantee by the employer if the contractor withdraws the tender contrary to his undertaking to be bound by it. The Uniform Rules provide[44] that, if a guarantee does not indicate the law applicable, it shall be governed by the law of the guarantor's place of business, and if he has several places of business by the law of the place of the branch which issued the guarantee.

The World Bank Guidelines provide[45] that bid bonds or guarantees shall be released to unsuccessful bidders as soon as possible after it is determined that they will not be awarded the contract.

Opening of tenders

Both the World Bank Guidelines[46] and the EDF Conditions[47] require the bids which are formally in order to be opened in public session, but the EDF Conditions do so only with respect to contracts for the supply of goods and not with respect to contracts for work. The World Bank Guidelines state:

> Bids should be opened in public; *i.e.* bidders or their representatives should be allowed to be present. The name of the bidder and the total amount of each bid, and of any alternative bids, if they have been requested or permitted, should be read aloud and recorded, when opened . . .

Acceptance of tender

It has already been observed that the employer normally reserves in the tender documents the right not to accept the lowest or any bid and to negotiate with tenderers about the clarification of their bids or even to invite alternative bids. This is necessary in order to have a basis for comparison. The FIDIC Contract form of tender provides expressly:

> We understand that you are not bound to accept the lowest or any tender you may receive.

The World Bank Guidelines provide similarly[48]:

> The bid with the lowest evaluated cost, but not necessarily the lowest submitted price, should be selected for the award [of the contract].[49]

---

[44] *Ibid.* Art. 10.
[45] World Bank Guidelines, Art. 2.14.
[46] World Bank Guidelines, Art 2.45.
[47] EDF Conditions, Art. 4.2.
[48] World Bank Guidelines, Art. 2.49.
[49] On the proceedings of an unsuccessful bidder in the EC Court of Justice concerning the Amarti River project, to be be financed by the EDF, see *CMC Cooperativa Muratori e Cementisti* v. *Commission* (Case 118/83). [1985] E.C.R. 2325.

The contract

The international contract for the construction of works and installations abroad contains many of the terms which have been discussed in the previous chapters, particularly as far as the supply of machinery and equipment for the installations to be built is concerned. However, some terms peculiar to construction contracts require attention.

Inspection and acceptance

The acceptance of the progressive stages of the work or the completed work is an important incident in the performance of the contract because often payment, or part payment, is made dependent on it. This topic is usually regulated in the contract with some particularity. Sometimes the contract provides for provisional acceptance and final acceptance. According to the arrangement of the parties, the engineer will issue his certificate on provisional or final acceptance of part of the works, and on such certificate a further instalment of the price will become payable.

Great difficulty arises in practice with respect to alterations, additions and omissions because it is rarely possible to execute a major building operation strictly according to the original drawings. Here the FIDIC Contract provides[50]:

> [Varied work[51]] shall be valued at the rates and prices set out in the contract if, in the opinion of the engineer, the same shall be applicable. If the contract does not contain any rates or prices applicable to the varied work, rates and prices in the contract shall be used as the basis for valuation so far as may be reasonable, failing which, after due consultation by the Engineer with the Employer and Contractor, suitable rates or prices shall be agreed upon between the Engineer and the Contractor. In the event of disagreement the Engineer shall fix such rates or prices as are, in his opinion, appropriate and shall notify the Contractor accordingly, with a copy to the Employer. Until such time as rates or prices are agreed or fixed, the Engineer shall determine provisional rates or prices to enable on-account payments to be included in certificates issued in accordance with clause 60.

Sub-contracting

While the contractor is prohibited from assigning the contract or any part of it without the prior consent of the employer,[52] it is not unusual to

---

[50] FIDIC Contract, cl. 52.1. This contract form contains further more detailed rules on the fixing of rates and prices.
[51] A definition of "varied work" is provided in cl. 52.2.
[52] *Ibid.* cl. 3.1.

allow him to sub-contract certain parts of the contract. Where, *e.g.,* a hospital has to be built by a construction firm, it is probable that they will sub-contract x-ray and other clinical equipment to specialists. The FIDIC Contract refers to sub-contractors, who are approved by the employer or the engineer as "nominated sub-contractors,"[53] and provides that, before the engineer issues his certificate of completion of work or a stage thereof, he may ask the contractor to furnish proof that the sub-contractors in question have been paid and, failing such proof, the employer may pay the sub-contractors directly.[54] The parties may, of course, agree that the employer shall pay the sub-contractors directly in any event, *e.g.* on the certificate of the engineer or the main contractor.

The FIDIC Contract further provides[55] that the main contractor shall be responsible for the acts, defaults or neglects of any sub-contractor, his agents, servants or workmen.

The employer may entrust the work not to a single contractor, who then sub-contracts, but may contract directly with several contractors, each being responsible for a specific part of the whole work. It is also possible for the employer to contract separately for consecutive phases of the work; this is called "fast track" contracting; in such a case several contracts, each for the completion of an individual phase, are concluded by him; this method may reduce the total period of time needed for the completion of the whole work but it requires careful planning and may lead to technical difficulties in the co-ordination of the various phases of the work.

The legal status of the engineer

The functions which the engineer has to perform in a construction contract have already been described.[56]

The engineer is appointed by the employer, unless the contract between the latter and the contractor otherwise provides. He is thus in a contractual relationship with the employer only, and not with the contractor. But he is not the employer's representative[57] in the sense that he has to take into account only the employer's interests. His contract obliges him to act as an impartial mediator between the employer and the contractor: the FIDIC contract states[58] that "he shall exercise [his]

---

[53] *Ibid.* cl. 59.1. See Edgar Herzfeld, "Sub-Contracts in Long-term Construction Contracts" in [1984] J.B.L. 226; the same "Nominated Sub-contractors" in [1985] J.B.L. 386.
[54] *Ibid.* cl. 59(5).
[55] *Ibid.* cl. 4.2.
[56] See p. 739, *ante.*
[57] He may be the employer's agent, in the strictly legal sense.
[58] In cl. 2.6.

discretion impartially within the terms of the contract [between employer and contractor] and having regard to all the circumstances."

If the contractor is aggrieved by the decision of the engineer and the latter was appointed under a FIDIC contract, the proper course is for the contractor to go to arbitration under article 67 of the FIDIC contract. An action for negligence—even if negligence can be proved—is unlikely to succeed because, if the claim is for the recovery of economic loss, the "proximity test," in the restrictive sense in which it is applied today,[59] is unlikely to be satisfied.[60]

Adjustment of price

In a construction or long term contract various methods of pricing are used. Three may be mentioned; the lump sum method, the cost reimbursable method, and the unit price method.[61]

The lump sum method is widely favoured because it introduces an element of certainty into the price mechanism, but, particularly in long term contracts, it can create great distortion unless sophisticated price adjustment and revision mechanisms are built into the contract.

The cost reimbursable method, also known as the "cost *cum*" (profits) method, requires the contractor to present to the employer vouchers of the production costs, to which is added an agreed fee which constitutes the profit of the contractor. This method lacks the element of certainty. It means that the employer (as purchaser) bears the whole risk of increase in the costs of the construction. Financial institutions do not favour this pricing method.

"Under the unit price method, the parties agree on a rate for a construction unit, and the total price to be paid is dependent upon the number of construction units used for the construction. The rate fixed for a construction unit should include an increment representing the contractor's profit."[62] The construction unit may be calculated on a materials basis, *e.g.* the quantity of cement for concrete or a labour basis *e.g.* the time of labour for a specified work. Obviously this pricing method is not suitable for all types of construction or long term contracts.

It is of great importance in the type of contract discussed here to provide a detailed mechanism for price adjustment. Here two problems arise. Some variations in prices are foreseeable, and others are beyond the normal course of events that might be expected.

As regards the former, the usual procedure is to provide an index-based price adjustment mechanism. In some long term contracts a basket

---

[59] See p. 174, *ante*.
[60] *Pacific Associates Inc.* v. *Baxter*, [1989] 3 W.L.R. 1150 (C.A.).
[61] See *UNCITRAL Legal Code* (*ante*, p. 732), pp. 78 *et seq*.
[62] *Ibid* p. 82.

of indices is used. In one case, which has come to the author's knowledge,[63] a combination of indices representing the Diesel Fuel component, the labour component and the materials and supplies component was used; this was combined in a mathematical formula which indicated whether an addition to the base price was necessary. Such a revision procedure has to be carried out at regular intervals.

As regards unforeseeable events influencing the price, it is necessary to include in the contract a hardship clause which can be invoked if a party can justifiably claim that the contractual arrangement, if not amended, would cause substantial hardship. The hardship clause constitutes, in the words of Donaldson L.J.[64] "the ultimate safety net." The hardship clause will be considered later.[65]

Performance and repayment guarantees

It is usual for the contractor to provide a *performance guarantee* which is issued by a bank, insurance company or other third party. The guarantee is intended to safeguard the employer against the failure of the contractor to perform his obligations under the contract. This type of guarantee is sometimes combined with a *repayment guarantee*, which is intended to protect the employer if he has paid advances on the contract price and fears that the contractor may not fulfil the terms of the contract. Sometimes the employer will be asked to provide a payment guarantee, *e.g.* by a bank in a neutral country such as Switzerland, in order to safeguard any claims by the contractor against the employer, but where the employer is a public authority and in the last resort the credit of a foreign State is involved, payment guarantees are rarely demanded. These types of contract guarantees have been considered earlier.[66]

Retention Money

It is usual in international construction contracts to provide for *retention money*. The employer is entitled, under the terms of such a contract, to retain, *e.g.* 5 to 10 per cent. of the total price for a specified length of time, *e.g.* six or 12 months, in order to be satisfied that the installation operates as promised. The World Bank Guidelines provide[67]:

---

[63] In connection with an arbitration.
[64] In *Superior Overseas Development Corporation and Phillips Petroleum (U.K.) Co. Ltd.* v. *British Gas Corporation* [1982] 1 Lloyd's Rep. 262, 269.
[65] See p. 751, *post.*
[66] See pp. 446 *et seq., ante.*
[67] World Bank Guidelines, Art 2.34.

Contracts may provide for a percentage of the total payment to be held as retention money to secure full compliance by the contractor. Security should extend sufficiently beyond the estimated date for completion of the works to cover the warranty or maintenance period specified in the contract. Alternatively, a separate security may be obtained for that period.

In the FIDIC Contract, the percentage of the retention money and its limit are stated in the appendix to the form of tender.

Currency clauses

Particular attention has to be paid to the *currency clauses*,[68] especially if the employer has to make payment to joint contractors in different countries or to sub-contractors carrying on business in countries other than that of the main contractor. Both the World Bank Guidelines[69] and the FIDIC Contract[70] contain elaborate provisions relating to payment in foreign currency. In appropriate cases the separation of the money of account and the money of payment, which was discussed earlier,[71] may provide a solution. The contract price would be expressed in the employer's currency which is the money of account, and payment is made in the various currencies of the joint contractors or the main contractor and the sub-contractors, and these are the currencies of payment. Where this device is used, it has to be stated at which rate the exchange shall be carried out, *e.g.* the rate governing the exchange shall be that ruling at the date of payment.

Insurance and indemnity clauses

The contract will also have to make provision for insurance and indemnity. The World Bank Guidelines require the types and terms of insurance already to be specified in the bidding documents.[72] According to the FIDIC Contract, the contractor has to take out insurance of workmen and for third party risks,[73] but if he fails to do so the employer may insure himself for the account of the contractor.[74]

The FIDIC Contract also provides for indemnities to be given by the contractor as well as by the employer.[75]

---

[68] See *Exchange Rate Risks in International Contracts* (ed. Bruno Oppetit), ICC Publications 440/3, 1987.
[69] World Bank Guidelines, Arts. 2.21–2.26.
[70] FIDIC Contract, cls. 71 and 72.
[71] See p. 224, *ante*.
[72] World Bank Guidelines, Art. 2.36.
[73] FIDIC Contract, cls. 23 to 25.
[74] *Ibid.* cl. 25.3.
[75] *Ibid.* cls. 22, 24(1).

Post-contractual problems

An international construction contract normally incorporates many of the clauses discussed earlier[76] in this work, in particular:

the force majeure clause,[77]
the choice of law clause,[78]
the arbitration clause,
the waiver of immunity clause.[79]

Some of these clauses, such as the arbitration clause, have to be adapted to the special requirements of a long-term construction contract.

The arbitration clause

The position with respect to arbitration is complicated by the fact that many of these contracts, particularly those concluded in the FIDIC Contract form, provide for the office of an engineer, an official mediator or intervener who is not an arbitrator but whose functions include the duty of resolving difficulties of technical and similar nature which may arise almost daily. The FIDIC Contract, in its clause on the settlement of disputes,[80] adopts a detailed procedure which can be summarised as follows. Any dispute or difference between the employer and the contractor or the engineer and the contractor shall be settled by the engineer within 84 days after being requested by either party to do so. If the engineer fails to give written notice of his decision in writing within those 84 days to the employer and the contractor, or if either party is dissatisfied with his decision, the matter may be referred to arbitration, but the reference must be made within 70 days from the expiration of the period of 84 days, or from the date after receiving the engineer's decision, as the case may be. Where notice of intention to commence arbitration is given, arbitration shall not be commenced unless an attempt has first been made by the parties to settle the dispute amicably, but, unless the parties otherwise agree, arbitration may be commenced on or after the 56th day after the day on which notice to commence arbitration was given, whether an attempt at an amicable settlement has been made or not. The arbitration shall be held under the Rules of Conciliation and

---

[76] See pp. 75–76, *ante*.
[77] See p. 199, *ante*.
[78] See p. 711, *ante*.
[79] State Immunity Act 1978, ss 2(2) and 9; see pp. 226–229, *ante*.
[80] FIDIC Contract, cl. 67.

Arbitration of the ICC Court of Arbitration.[80a] If, after the engineer has given his decision, no application is made for arbitration, the engineer's decision becomes final. As far as possible, work on the installations shall continue, despite the arbitration.

The European Development Fund (EDF) has drafted a detailed *Regulation on the Arbitration of Public Contracts financed by the EDF,*[81] which, however, has not been adopted by the EC yet. This Draft Regulation does not adopt ICC arbitration but proposes the setting up of an arbitration board, the President of which shall be the President of the Court of Justice of the European Communities at Luxembourg, and the secretary of which shall be an official of that Court. It is proposed that there shall be a panel of arbitrators from which the arbitrator(s) in a particular dispute shall be elected. A sole or a third arbitrator shall not be of the same nationality as the parties to the proceedings. An application maay be made in certain circumstances to have the award set aside; such application is made to an arbitration court consisting of three members chosen from the panel of arbitrators and appointed by the President of the arbitration board.

Third person intervention. The arbitral referee

Experience has shown that in long term contracts the intervention of a third person mediator, such as the engineer appointed under a FIDIC Contract, can be helpful. A contract may, in the light of circumstances appearing after it has been signed, show defects. There may be lack of precision, the existence of gaps, the possibility of different interpretations, and similar deficiencies. The ICC has set up procedure enabling the parties to a contract to call upon a third person to facilitate the implementation of their contract. These proposals are contained in an ICC Brochure entitled *Adaptation of Contracts.*[82] A Standing Committee for the Regulation of Contractual Relations is constituted at the ICC. At any time during their contractual relations, the parties may ask the Standing Committee for the appointment of a third person or a board of three, to fulfil the task which has been contractually assigned to them. These third person interveners do not act as arbitrators. The third person or board must formulate a recommendation or take a decision within 90 days after the file is delivered to them.

In order to make this facility available, the parties have to insert into their contract an appropriate clause. Before so doing, they have to

---

[80a] See p. 676, *ante.*
[81] EEC Doc. VIII/119/77–E.
[82] ICC Brochure No. 326 (1979).

ascertain the legality and effectiveness of third person intervention under the law which is applicable. They have also to agree on whether they wish the third party to make only a recommendation or to give a binding decision. The following are the two model standard clauses suggested by the ICC:

> In the event that the parties are unable to agree to apply all or any of the provisions of article . . . of this contract (or any other appropriate wording chosen by the parties in the particular circumstances of the contract) . . . , they shall apply to the Standing Committee for the Regulation of Contractual Relations of the International Chamber of Commerce (ICC) in order that a third person* who shall be appointed in accordance with the Rules on the Regulation of Contractual Relations of the ICC, and who shall carry out his mission in accordance with the said Rules—
> *may issue a recommendation***or
> *may on their behalf make a final decision which shall be binding on the parties and shall be deemed to be incorporated in the contract.***
> *Should the parties wish to have the decision or recommendation made by a board of three persons instead of by one person, they should make this clear in the clause.
> **Only one of these alternatives can be adopted.

The ICC provides also another procedure by which a third person, known as the *arbitral referee*.[83] assists the parties in the performance of their contractual duties. The arbitral referee is appointed by the parties. The purpose of such an appointment is to empower a neutral person to make temporary—interlocutory—orders for the conservation of property, the preservation and recording of evidence, and other measures. The functions of the arbitral referee are, in some respects, similar to those of the engineer under the FIDIC contract; he should act rapidly in situations of urgency. The arbitral referee may expect his rulings to be generally accepted by the parties, as he is appointed by their mutual consent, and not by one party (the employer) only, as is the engineer under the FIDIC contract.

The use of the arbitral referee procedure does not preclude resort to arbitration or to the courts but the arbitral referee shall not act later as an arbitrator.

Hardship clauses

A problem which is typical for international long term contracts is this: After the conclusion of the contract, there may have been a fundamental change in the economic or political circumstances, which occurred beyond the control of the parties, and yet the parties are anxious to continue their contractual relations. This fundamental change in the situation is similar to that which gives rise to frustration[84] or the application of a *force*

---

[83] ICC Brochure No. 480 (1990).
[84] See p. 181, *ante*.

majeure clause,[85] but the intention of the parties is different: they do not wish to dissolve the contract but, on the contrary, wish to continue it. Sometimes the parties are compelled by economic circumstances to consider the continuation rather than the dissolution of their contract, in spite of the changed circumstances. The construction of the factory has to be completed, or the supply of crude oil or natural gas has to be continued, in spite of those changes.

To meet this situation, the parties sometimes insert into their contract a so-called *hardship clause*,[86] sometimes called the "iniquity clause." Under this clause the parties are obliged, if such change in circumstances occurs, to enter into negotiations and to seek an amicable adaptation of their contract, such as an adjustment of the price, an extension of time for the completion of the work, or other changes in the contract terms as originally arranged. Legally the hardship clause is merely an agreement to agree and, as such, without legal effect, except that it obliges the parties to negotiate. It has therefore to be complemented by a further clause which provides for the contingency of the parties not reaching agreement within a specified time. The complementary clause usually provides for arbitration but it would also be possible to provide that in this contingency either party shall be entitled to give notice of termination of the contract or for another resolution of the deadlock.

The following is an illustration of a hardship clause which is contained in a contract for the supply of natural gas[87]:

> Substantial hardship shall mean if at any time or from time to time during the term of this agreement, without default of the party concerned, there is the occurrence of an intervening event or change of circumstances beyond the said party's control, when acting as a reasonable and prudent operator, such that the consequences and effects of which are fundamentally different from what was contemplated by the parties at the time of entering into this agreement . . . the party claiming that it is placed in such a position as aforesaid may by notice request the other for a meeting to determine if said occurrence has happened and, if so, agree upon what, if any, adjustment in the price then in force under this agreement and/or other terms and conditions thereof is justified in the circumstances, in fairness to the parties to alleviate said consequences and effects of said occurrence . . .
>
> If the seller(s) and the buyer(s) have not agreed a mutually acceptable solution within 60 days after the notice requesting a meeting . . . either party may request the matter to be submitted to arbitration. . . . The arbitrators shall determine whether the aforesaid occurrence has happened, and if so what adjustments, if any, in the said price or in the other terms and conditions should be made . . . having due regard to the interest of the other party, and any revised prices or other conditions so

---

[85] See p. 199, *ante*.

[86] B. Oppetit, *L'adaptation des contrats internationaux aux changements de circonstances: la clause "hardship,"* in *Journal du droit international* (1974), pp. 794 *et seq.*; M. J. Bonell, *Arbitration as a means for the Revision of Contracts*, in Italian National Reports to the Xth International Congress of Comparative Law, Budapast 1978, Milan, Giuffré, 1978, 221; M. Fontaine, "Hardship Clauses" in (1976) 2 P.D.C.I. 51; Clive M. Schmitthoff, "Hardship and Intervener Clauses" in [1980] J.B.L. 82, *Essays*, p. 465.

[87] Oppetit, *loc. cit.*, 812. Bonell, *loc. cit.*, 226. The clause is not phrased particularly elegantly.

determined by said arbitrators shall take effect on the date when notice of arbitration was first given. . . .

The English Court of Appeal had to consider the concept of substantial hardship in connection with a hardship clause inserted into a contract between suppliers of North Sea natural gas and the British Gas Corporation; the contract had a duration of 25 years.[88] The court rejected a mathematical approach to this concept and preferred a common sense approach. Donaldson L.J. said[89]:

> What is meant by "substantial" on this view of the parties' intentions? It is a simple English word. The parties could, if they had wished, have produced a [mathematical] formula to define it . . . but they have not done so. In my view it was not for the experts to do so. Their task was akin to that of Lord Mansfield's jury of merchants—in this case a "special jury of experts." They had to find the economic facts, both as to the causative change or changes in economic circumstances and the effects of that change or changes on the economic fortunes of the parties. Having found the facts, they had to ask themselves two jury questions: "Has there been any substantial change in the economic circumstances relating to this agreement?" and "Has that change or changes caused either and which party to suffer substantial economic hardship?" They should not have concerned themselves with insubstantial change or insubstantial hardship.

The ICC treats hardship clauses in its brochure *Force Majeure and Hardship*.[90] It wisely refrains from suggesting a standard hardship clause but makes a number of drafting suggestions. For the case of the parties failing to settle the controversy by mutual consultation within 90 days of the request for revision, several alternatives are suggested.

Liquidated damage and bonus clauses

International construction contracts often contain clauses providing for the payment of liquidated damages by the contractor if the work is not carried out within the stipulated times. The amount of the liquidated damages should be a reasonable estimate of the loss likely to be suffered; it should not be of punitive character because in this case it would be a penalty and may be set aside as such. Further, the clause should provide that no liquidated damages are payable if the contractor is prevented by an event beyond his control from completing the work. The FIDIC Contract also states[91] that if, before the completion of the whole of the works, any part or section of the works has been certified by the engineer

---

[88] *Superior Overseas Development Corporation* v. *British Gas Corporation* [1982] 1 Lloyd's Rep. 262. On "undue Hardship (in another connection) see *Jones* v. *Trollope Colls Cementation Overseas Ltd., The Times,* January 26, 1990 see p. 222, *ante.*
[89] *Ibid.* 269.
[90] ICC Brochure No. 421 (March 1985).
[91] FIDIC Contract, cl. 47.2.

as completed and occupied or used by the employer, the liquidated damages for delay shall be reduced in the proportion which the value of the part or section so certified bears to the value of the whole of the works.

That a clause stipulating liquidated damages is appropriate in this type of contract, is indicated in the World Bank Guidelines[92]:

> Provisions for liquidated damage or similar clauses in an appropriate amount should be included in bidding documents when delays in completion of works or delivery of goods, or failure of the works or goods, to meet performance requirements would result in extra cost, loss of revenue or loss of other benefits to the borrower. Provision may also be made for a bonus to be paid to contractors or suppliers for completion of works or delivery of goods ahead of the times specified in the contract when such earlier completion or delivery would be of benefit to the borrower.

Clauses providing for bonus payments to the contractor, if he completes the work before the time agreed, are less frequently found than clauses stipulating liquidated damages; they are not provided for in the General Conditions (Pt. I) of the FIDIC Contract but may, of course, be specified in the Conditions of Particular Application (Pt. II) and in the Appendix to the Tender.

---

[92] World Bank Guidelines, Art. 2.40.

PART EIGHT

CUSTOMS LAW

CHAPTER 35

GOVERNMENT REGULATION OF EXPORTS

THE United Kingdom regulation of exports extends to three topics:

    (1) the requirement of export licences for the exportation of certain goods;
    (2) Customs formalities to be complied with on the exportation of goods; and
    (3) EC regulation of free movement of goods.

In addition, the exporter has to bear in mind the provisions applying to value added tax (VAT) which are likewise administered by Customs and Excise.[1] These provisions are explained in certain Customs Notices.[2] Goods exported direct by a taxable person to a customer overseas are relieved from VAT by zero-rating. Further, retail export schemes, notably the Personal Export Scheme and the Over-the-Counter Scheme, are free from VAT, subject to certain conditions.

EXPORT LICENSING

The legislation relating to export licensing deals with "goods" only. This term does not include banknotes, treasury bills, bills of exchange, promissory notes, shares, stock, debentures and similar things in action, and gold bullion; These were exclusively governed by exchange control regulations before these regulations were abolished in the United Kingdom.[3]

The present system of export licensing controls the exportation, from the United Kingdom, of specified goods which cannot be exported without the provision of an export licence by the Department of Trade and Industry (DTI). As regards strategic goods, the DTI was formerly empowered to exercise extraterritorial control but these powers appear to have lapsed.[4] The Nato States carry out a supernational vetting procedure

---

[1] The law relating to VAT is not treated in this work.
[2] The most important of them are Customs Notices No. 703 on Value Added Tax—Exports (revised March 1987); No. 704—Retail Export Schemes (revised March 1985); No. 704/1—VAT Refunds for Visitors to the UK (revised March 1985); No. 704/2—Refunds for UK Residents Going Abroad (revised January 1987). Should the EC Commission's proposals for the harmonization of indirect taxation in relation to the Single European Market be adopted after 1992 the system of VAT collection for exports is likely to change substantially.
[3] Exchange Control Act 1947, s.22. See p. 110 *ante.*
[4] See p. 762, *post.*

for strategic goods through CoCom but the suggestions of this body, although published in the United Kingdom, are effective in this country only if embodied into United Kingdom law.[5]

The general control of exports

The general powers of the DTI to regulate the exportations of goods are based on the Import, Export and Customs Powers (Defence) Act 1939, which authorises the Department to make "such provisions as the Department think expedient" for the regulation of the importation into, or exportation from, the United Kingdom of all goods of a specified description. In exercise of these powers, the Secretary of State has issued the Export of Goods (Control) Order 1987.[6]

The provisions of the Export of Goods (Control) Order apply to goods intended to be exported from the United Kingdom but have no extraterritorial effect on goods situate outside the UK.

The exporter who wishes to ascertain whether an export licence is required in respect of the particular goods which he intends to export, should obtain a copy of the Order and all amendments to date, or inquire of the Export Licensing Branch of the DTI[7] or his trade association.

The regulation provided by the Order may be summed up as follows:

Goods—this expression includes used and unused goods unless otherwise specified (Art. 1(2))—are divided by the Order into two categories:

1. Goods which do not require an export licence. Hereunder fall most types of consumer goods of ordinary character.
2. Goods, the exportation of which is prohibited or restricted and which require an export licence if their export is intended. Here it is provided (Art. 2):—
   (i) scheduled goods[8] indicated by the letter "A" are prohibited to be exported to any destination;
   (ii) scheduled goods indicated by the letter "T " are prohibited to be exported to any destination except that when in relation to such goods the provisions of Regulation (EC) 1062/87,[9] as amended by Regulation (EC) 2823/87,[10] relating to the use of Community transit documents requiring anything to be done at or before the time of exportation have been complied with, the goods may be exported to a destination in another Member State:

---

[5] *Ibid.*
[6] S.I. 1987 No. 2070. This Order revokes and replaces the Export of Goods (Control) Order 1985 and the subsequent amendments thereto. It came into force on January 1, 1988. It has been amended by S.I. 1988 No. 1487, S.I. 1989 Nos. 246, No. 354, 1270 and 1914. After going to press the Export of Goods (Control) Order 1989 (S.I. 1989 No. 2376) was issued; this Order is not noted in the text.
[7] Address: Kingsgate House 66–74 Victoria Street, London SW1E 6SW. (Enquiries: 01–215 7877.)
[8] "Scheduled goods" are described in Sched. 1 to the Export of Goods (Control) Order 1987.
[9] O.J. No. L107, 22.4.87 p. 1.
[10] O.J. No. L270, 23.9.87 p. 1.

(iii) scheduled goods indicated by the letter "E" are prohibited to be exported to any destination except a destination in another Member State;

(iv) scheduled goods consisting of classes of ships indicated by the letter "S" are prohibited to be exported to any destination after delivery or for the purpose of delivery, directly or indirectly, to a person in Afghanistan, Albania, Bulgaria, China, Czechoslovakia, the German Democratic Republic, Hungary, Mongolia, North Korea, Poland, Romania, the Union of Soviet Socialist Republics or the Socialist Republic of Vietnam;

(v) scheduled goods indicated by the letter "I" are prohibited to be exported to any destination in Iran or Iraq;

(vi) scheduled goods indicated by the letters "E (S)" are prohibited to be exported to any destination except that when in relation to such goods the provisions of Regulation (EC) 1062/87, as amended, relating to the use of Community transit documents requiring anything to be done at or before the time of exportation have been complied with, the goods may be exported to a destination in another Member State, other than Spain;

(vii) scheduled goods indicated by the letters "E(PS)" are prohibited to be exported to any destination except that when in relation to such goods the provisions of Regulation (EC) 1062/87, as amended, relating to the use of Community transit documents requiring anything to be done at or before the time of exportation have been complied with, the goods may be exported to a destination in another Member State, other than Portugal or Spain;

(viii) scheduled goods indicated by the letter "L" are prohibited to be exported to any destination in Libya;

(ix) scheduled goods indicated by the letter "Z" are prohibited to be exported to any destination in South Africa or Namibia;

(x) all goods in relation to the export of which from any country an international import certificate has been issued and which have been imported into the United Kingdom are prohibited to be exported to any destination;

(xi) specialised components of any of the apparatus, appliances or equipment falling within a description in Group 1 of Part II of Schedule 1 hereto, whether or not such components are specified in the description, are prohibited to be exported to any destination in South Africa or Namibia;

(xii) goods of a description specified in Group C of Part I of Schedule 1 hereto are prohibited to be exported to any destination in the United States of America or the Commonwealth of Puerto Rico;

(xiii) technological documents, other than documents generally available to the public, and other than applications for the grant of patents (or any other forms of protection for inventions) or for the registration of designs, in either case under the law of the United Kingdom or of any other country or under any treaty or international convention, and documents necessary to enable such applications to be filed, or made and pursued, the information contained in which relates to any goods specified in Groups 1 to 3 of Part II of Schedule 1 hereto or to any goods, technologies or processes specified in Group 4 of Part II of Schedule 1 hereto are prohibited to be exported to any destination in any country specified in paragraph (iv) above;

Schedule 1, also known as the *Prohibition List*, is too lengthy and technical to be produced here and, besides, is subject to frequent amendments; it is arranged as follows:

Part I   Group A   Goods specified by reference to headings and subheadings of the Combined nomenclature[11]

         Group B   Photographic Material, Antiques, Collectors' Items etc.

---

[11] See Council Regulation (EEC) No. 2658/87 O.J. No. L256, 7.9.87, p. 1.

	Group C	Steel products prohibited to be exported to the United States of America or the Commonwealth of Puerto Rico
Part II	Group 1	Military aircraft, Arms and related material, Ammunition, Military Stores and Appliances, and Security and Para-military Police Equipment
	Group 2A	Atomic Energy Minerals and Materials
	Group 2B	Nuclear Facilities, Equipment and Appliances
	Group 3A	Metal Working Machinery and Associated Equipment
	Group 3B	Chemical and Petrolium Equipment
	Group 3C	Electrical and Power-Generating Equipment
	Group 3D	General Industrial Equipment
	Group 3E	Aircraft, Spacecraft, Compasses, Gyroscopic Apparatus, Marine Equipment and Ships (other than Warships and Naval Equipment)
	Group 3F	Electronic Equipment including Communications and Radar
	Group 3G	Scientific Instruments and Apparatus, Servo-Mechanisms and Photographic Equipment
	Group 3H	Metals, Minerals and their Manufactures
	Group 3I	Chemicals, Metalloids and Petroleum Products
	Group 4	Goods, Technologies and Processes in respect of which the export of technological documents, other than documents generally available to the public, is prohibited to any destination in any country specified in Article 2(iv)

The Export Control Organisation of the DTI will advise whether an export licence is required and provide the appropriate application form. There are two principal forms of licence. The usual type is an Individual Licence applied for by a particular exporter and relating to particular goods. The second type is the newly introduced Open General Export Licence which came into force on April 28, 1989 (OGEL). The OGEL removes the need to apply for individual licences for exports to scheduled destinations in Western Europe, North America, Japan and Australia, over a wide range of industrial equipment and technology which is subject to control under the Export of Goods (Control) Order. The products eligible for export under the OGEL are any goods which fall within Group 3 of Part II of Schedule 1 to the Order, except for goods referred to in Schedule 2 of the OGEL. Such excepted goods remain subject to the requirement of an individual export licence.

Even in the case of goods which, as a rule, require an export licence, exceptions are admitted. They are stated in article 4 of the Export of Goods (Control) Order 1987.

Any licence or other permission for the exportation of goods may be modified or revoked at any time by the Secretary of State (Art. 9(1)).

Goods are exported within the Order although, when they are taken out of the country, it is intended to bring them back later. Thus, a traveller in possession of jewellery which she intends to wear abroad, "exports" them and has to declare them on leaving the country, in compliance with what is now article 7(1), although she intends to bring them back and has insured them for the return journey.[12]

---

[12] *R.* v. *Berner* (1953) 37 Cr.App.R. 113.

The exporter is not entitled to assign the authority to export goods which he is granted by licence, unless he is expressly authorised by the licence to do so. Normally the licence is not transferable, but in case of bulk shipments or similar exceptional cases the licence may be granted to "X Y or any person or firm authorised in writing by them."

Antiques are works of art manufactured or produced more than 50 years before the date of exportation; they are subject to the requirement of export licensing. The provisions relating to photographic positives or negatives and other items are obscure. They are worded thus[13]:

> Any photographic positive or negative produced more than 60 years before the date of exportation or any album or other assemblage containing such photographs, the value of which, as required by the Commissioners to be declared, is £400 or more, except any photographic positive or negative or album exported by, and being the personal property of, the manufacturer or producer thereof, or the spouse, widow or widower of that person.
>
> Any goods manufactured or produced more than 50 years before the date of exportation except
>
> (1) photographic positives and negatives, and albums or assemblages thereof;
> (2) postage stamps and other articles of philatelic interest;
> (3) birth, marriage or death certificates or other documents relating to the personal affairs of the exporter or the spouse of the exporter;
> (4) letters or other writings written by or to the exporter or the spouse of the exporter; and
> (5) any goods exported by, and being the personal property of the manufacturer or producer thereof, or the spouse, widow or widower of that person.

The items under (1) to (5) do not appear to require a licence but the items under (5) include only the general household goods of exporter.

The export licence does not authorise the exporter to do an act prohibited by other enactments or regulations, such as regulations relating to Customs or postal matters. The grant of the export licence in the United Kingdom does not relieve the exporter from his duty to obtain an import licence in the country of importation if such licence is required there and he has undertaken, by the contract of sale, to procure the import licence.

Control of strategic goods

Until recently there existed a separate system of controls over disposals of strategic goods situated outside the United Kingdom. These were contained in the Strategic Goods (Control) Order 1967.[14] The Order provided

---

[13] Group B of Sched. 1 to the Export of Goods (Control) Order 1987.
[14] S.I. 1967 No. 983.

that no person in the United Kingdom, or ordinarily residing therein, could dispose of goods specified as strategic goods in the Order, to any government, government agency or other authority or person, where the goods were situate outside the United Kingdom. This provision introduced an element of extraterritoriality to British export controls.

The 1967 Order was made in pursuance of the powers conferred upon the predecessor to the DTI, the Board of Trade, under ss.3(1) and 22(3) of the Emergency Laws (Re-enactments and Repeals) Act 1964. That statute expired at the end of 1974 and was later repealed. It appears that, as a result, the 1967 Order is "spent."[15] The Order has not been replaced. Therefore it seems that control of strategic goods has now been assimilated into the system of export controls described above. The most important consequence of this is that British export controls no longer have any extraterritorial effect over goods situate outside the United Kingdom and are restricted to exports of goods from the United Kingdom.

CoCom

Controls over international trade in strategic goods exist on the supranational level. The Member States of NATO less Iceland plus Japan participate in the *Co-ordinating Committee on Multilateral Export Controls (CoCom)*.[16] This body vets the transfer of sensitive Western technology to the Eastern bloc. It produces lists of goods and technologies which should be controlled for strategic reasons. These lists have no direct force in English law. Their contents will, however, appear in the lists of controlled goods and technologies drawn up under the Export of Goods (Control) Order. China has, since 1985, been treated more favourably by CoCom than other Eastern bloc States. However, CoCom operates on the basis of a regular review of all controlled items every four years. It thus retains a discretion over its policy.

Powers of inquiry and search; penalties

The Customs authorities which are charged with the execution of the export licensing regulations exercise wide powers of inquiry and search.[17]

---

[15] See Halsbury's Statutory Instruments (4th Ed.) (Vol. 23) War & Emergency Part I "Note" at p. 11.
[16] On CoCom controls see *British Business* Supplement 3 March 1989 "Security Export Control". Updated information on such controls appears from time to time in *British Business*. For further information contact the CoCom Licensing Unit Room 640, at the address given in note 21 below.
[17] Export of Goods (Control) Order 1987 Arts. 5 and 7.

Contraventions of the licensing control may constitute criminal offences.[18]

Transhipment licences

Where goods are brought from overseas to the United Kingdom for transhipment or transit to another overseas country, the regulations in force for transhipment licences have to be complied with.

The current version of these regulations can be found in the Open General Transhipment Licence dated March 19, 1979.[19] Subject to certain formalities, the following goods may be imported for transhipment and subsequently exported:

(a) goods which are not subject to export control;
(b) aircraft, arms and other military goods to any destination named in the Schedule to the Licence other than South Africa or Namibia;
(c) atomic energy minerals, materials and appliances to any destination named in Part I of the Schedule to the Licence;
(d) any industrial goods of strategic significance named in Part II of Schedule 1 to the Export of Goods (Control) Order to any destination named in the Schedule to the Licence.

One of the formalities which the Open Licence requires is that the goods are, at the time of their importation, entered with the Commissioners of Customs and Excise for transit or transhipment and exportation; a transhipment bond note and a transhipment SAD[20] must be completed and produced to the Customs authorities at the place of importation.

Where a licence is required, application should be made to the Import Licensing Branch[21] of the DTI, from which application forms for transhipment licences can be obtained. Application should be made before shipment and must be made by a firm or individual responsible in the United Kingdom.

CUSTOMS REGULATIONS

The principal purpose of Customs legislation is to secure the payment of Customs duties in the interest of the revenue. This explains why the Customs formalities, which have to be observed on the exportation of

---

[18] *Ibid.* Art. 5.
[19] Obtainable from HMSO. A revised version is expected soon.
[20] Single Administrative Document. See pp. 764 and 774, *post.*
[21] Address: Dean Bradley House 52 Horseferry Road, London SW1P 2AG. Telephone: 01 –276 2580/2581.

goods from the United Kingdom, depend to some degree on the dutiable character of the goods intended to be exported. Where the exportation does not involve the payment or refund of Customs duties, these formalities are relatively simple, but, where the payment or refund of Customs duties is involved, as in the case of bonded and drawback goods, the procedure is more complicated.

Since January 1, 1988 a simplified Customs documentation procedure has been introduced whereby the different Customs declarations for import, export and transit have been replaced by the Single Administrative Document (SAD).[22] Furthermore, a new computerised processing facility for Customs Handling of Import and Export Freight ("CHIEF") is being phased in to extend existing computerised facilities for the handling of Customs documentation.[23]

In addition to the task of collecting and safeguarding Customs duties, the Customs authorities are charged with administering the executive side of the export licensing system described earlier.[23a] The Customs requirements have normally to be complied with strictly.

The Customs requirements to be complied with on exportation of goods from the United Kingdom are laid down in the Customs and Excise Act 1979[24] and in the statutory instruments having effect thereunder. The Customs authorities have published a number of important *Customs Notices* which give detailed information on special subjects and can be obtained from the Secretary, Customs and Excise,[25] and any officer of Customs and Excise.

An "exporter," according to the Customs and Excise Management Act 1979, s.1(1), includes "the shipper of . . . goods and any person performing in relation to an aircraft functions corresponding with those of a shipper."

Entry and pre-entry of goods

The exporter is required, on exportation of goods which are not Community transit goods,[26] to deliver to the proper Customs officer a

---

[22] On the SAD see Customs Notice 484 (July) 1987. For guidance on how to use the SAD see Tony Symes *How to Complete Your SAD—Happily* (Exportlink 1987).

[23] The CHIEF system will become available from May 28, 1990 and will become mandatory on October 31, 1991.

[23a] See p. 757, *ante*.

[24] The "Customs and Excise Act 1979" is defined in section 1(1) of the Customs and Excise Management Act 1979 as meaning that Act, the Customs and Excise (General Reliefs) Act 1979, the Alcoholic Liquor Duties Act 1979, the Hydrocarbon Oil Duties Act 1979, the Matches and Mechanical Lighters Duties Act 1979, and the Tobacco Products Duty Act 1979.

[25] Address: HM Customs and Excise, New Kings Beam House, 22 Upper Ground, London SE1 9PJ.

[26] For the definition of "Community transit goods" see p. 667 *post*.

document giving particulars of the goods exported.[27] Where nothing else is required than the delivery of such document on or after the exportation of the goods, the procedure is called "the entry" of goods, but it would be more correct to call it "post-entry" as it need only be completed after exportation of the goods. Where the document has to be delivered before the exportation of the goods and the goods must not be exported until the Customs authorities have approved of it, the procedure is called "the pre-entry" of goods. The clearance for entry is effected by the signature of the proper Customs Officer on the document in question.

The documents required under the standard "pre-entry" procedure are an export SAD completed accurately by exporters or their agents and a load-list, to be completed by loaders, describing the name of the ship or flight number as the case may be, the expected date of departure, the destination of the goods, the number of packages and their distinguishing marks and numbers.

Pre-entry

The Customs and Excise Management Act 1979, s.53, requires "dutiable and restricted goods" to be pre-entered. Section 52 of the Act defines these goods as follows;

    (a) goods from warehouse, other than goods which have been kept, without being warehoused, in a warehouse by virtue of section 92(4) below;
    (b) transit goods;
    (c) any other goods chargeable with any duty which has not been paid;
    (d) drawback goods;
    (e) goods with respect to the exportation of which any restriction is for the time being in force under or by virtue of any enactment;
    (f) any goods required by or under any provision of this Act other than a provision of this Part of by or under a provision of any other Act to be entered before exportation or before shipment for exportation or as stores.

"Other" provisions of the Act of 1979 which require the pre-entry of goods are sections 75 and 76. The goods referred to therein are explosives within the meaning of the Explosives Act 1875.

Entry

In all cases in which a pre-entry is not required, a post-entry after exportation of the goods is sufficient. The Customs and Excise Manage-

---

[27] For an explanation of the main Customs procedures for exports and the documents required see Customs Notice 275 (Current ed: January 1988).

ment Act 1979 provides in section 54(2) that "the form of entries . . . , the particulars to be contained therein and the manner of their delivery shall be such as the Commissioners may from time to time direct."

Goods exported by post need not be entered or pre-entered by means of SAD but are subject to special rules,[28] unless a drawback is claimed in respect of them.[29]

The entry and pre-entry of goods should not be confused with the entry outwards of the ship. This is a declaration which the master of the ship has to make to the Customs authority on a prescribed form before commencing to load an export cargo. The purpose of the entry outwards of the ship is to warn the Customs authorities of the intended departure of the ship. The exporter has nothing to do with the completion of that form.

Tariff requirements for exports

The exporter is required to enter or pre-enter exported goods on the SAD in accordance with the description of the goods in the Integrated Tariff of the United Kingdom briefly known as the *Tariff*.[30]

The current version of the *Tariff* was implemented on January 1, 1988. It incorporates both the European Community's Common Customs Tariff and statistical nomenclature system, and the Harmonised Commodity Description and Coding System developed under the auspices of the Customs Co-operation Council.[31] The combined effect is to expand the United Kingdom's Tariff Trade Code numbers to nine, the first eight of which represent the combined nomenclature of the European Communities. The first six digits refer to the Harmonised Commodity Description Code (to which the EC itself adheres). The seventh and eighth digits refer to the specialised EC classifications. The ninth digit is for use in national breakdowns for trade and statistical purposes. In this way the *Tariff* conforms to the internationally agreed classification of all the goods of international commerce and ensures that each article is classified in one place and one place only within its scheme.

In the introductory part of the *Tariff* the general requirements of Customs export documentation are explained. Reference is made to the Customs Registered Number (CRN) which the exporter can obtain and the use of which greatly simplifies the Customs procedure.[32] That part of

---

[28] See p. 770, *post.*
[29] See p. 768, *post.*
[30] HMSO (loose leaf, with frequent Supplements).
[31] The new harmonised system was adopted by Convention on June 14, 1983. The EC and all the Member States have ratified this Convention.
[32] Customs and Excise Management Act 1979, s.55. Customs Notice No. 275 explains how a CRN number can be obtained and used. (para. 11).

the *Tariff* gives detailed information on trade statistics, the forms to be used and the significance of CRN mixed goods, the particulars to be given on the forms, where to lodge export documents, Common Agricultural Policy (CAP) licences, and CAP export refunds and export levies.

Under particulars to be given on the Customs forms the following items are explained: CRN Tariff heading number, EC trade, ship/flight etc., country of destination, final destination, description of goods, port/airport of export, inland clearance depot (ICD), goods in containers, roll on/roll off road traffic (known as ro/ro), packages, marks and numbers etc., Tariff/Trade Code number, quantities, value, licence particulars.

The value to be declared on export documents is the f.o.b. value of the goods although it is no longer described as such.[33] The description which the *Tariff* gives is this:

> The value to be declared on Customs documents is the cost, to the nearest pound sterling, of the goods to the purchaser abroad (or if there is no sale, the price which the goods would fetch if sold to a purchaser abroad), including packing, inland and coastal transport in the United Kingdom, dock dues, loading charges and all other costs, profits, charges and expenses (*e.g.* insurance and commission) accruing up to the point where the goods are deposited on board the exporting vessel or aircraft or at the land boundary of Northern Ireland. For goods re-exported after process in the United Kingdom the value to be declared must include the charge for the process and the value of the goods when imported.
>
> In all cases, outwards sea or air freight and marine or air insurance should be excluded, and cash and trade discounts to the purchaser abroad deducted.

Goods other than bonded or drawback goods[34]

It has been seen that these goods were, and in some instances still are, privileged in comparison with bonded or drawback goods in so far as they require merely an entry and not a pre-entry.

The procedure applicable to such goods has been recently reformed. The first change has been to introduce the Simplified Clearance Procedure (SCP). This allows approved exporters or their agents to clear goods for export with simplified export documentation consisting of either a standard commercial document approved for this purpose by Customs,[35] or of a partially completed SAD. The exporter wishing to use SCP must be issued with a CRN. He can obtain this by submitting a standard

---

[33] The import value of goods traded in the United Kingdom under a trade name includes the "uplift": *Rolex Watch Co. Ltd.* v. *Commissioners of Customs and Excise* [1956] 1 W.L.R. 612.

[34] Export goods other than bonded or drawback goods are sometimes referred to as "free goods," but this term is avoided here because, in present-day circumstances, it is liable to be misunderstood.

[35] Among the standard commercial documents approved are the national standard shipping note, the air waybill and the CMR note. See further Customs Notice 275 para. 11.

application form, C274 (SCP) to his local Customs and Excise officer. The main benefit of this system is that the exporter of non-dutiable and unrestricted goods can export such goods with a minimum of information. However, the exporter must provide full information within 14 days of shipment either by completing Copies 2 and 3 of the SAD, or by completing a schedule on Form C&E 1187, and sending the document to the Controller of the Customs and Excise Statistical Office.[36]

The second major change permits the exporter of single consignments of goods that are not dutiable or restricted, and whose value is less than £475 and whose weight is 1000 kg or less, to export using the same simplified documentation as under the SCP. The document must be clearly marked with a reference to this second new procedure and to the value of the goods. No post-shipment declaration is required under this system. If the goods require an export licence then the standard pre-entry procedure, briefly mentioned above, applies. In this case the exporter must present the licence along with the pre-shipment SAD.

Thirdly, certain procedures designed to assist the large-scale exporter should be mentioned. The first is Local Export Control. Here the exporter with regular unit loads can have his goods cleared at his premises by local Customs officers. This is done by periodic review of exporter's records and occasional visits during packing for export.[37] Finally, should the goods that are being exported have been temporarily imported, either for use or for processing, the exporter may be entitled to relief from Customs duty and/or VAT if he was also the importer.[38] In such a case the standard pre-entry procedure applies and he must fill in his SAD accordingly.[39]

Bonded and drawback goods

Bonded goods are goods liable to import duties which are imported without payment of duties and kept in an approved warehouse until payment of the duties; the keeper of the warehouse gives a bond to the Customs authorities as a security for his obligations. Many dutiable commodities are stored in such bonded warehouses where they can be inspected by customers of the importer; when the goods are sold for home consumption, duties are paid and they are released from bond; when they are unsaleable in this country, the importer tries to export them to another country. No manufacturing process is allowed on the goods while lying in a bonded warehouse.[40]

---

[36] Address: The Controller, Statistical Office (Unit 23) HM Customs and Excise, Portcullis House, 27 Victoria Avenue, Southend on Sea, Essex SS2 6AL.
[37] See Customs Notice 482.
[38] See Customs Notice 278.
[39] See Customs Notices 200, 201, 221, 235, 266 and 702.
[40] See Customs Notice 232.

Drawback goods are goods on which import duties or excise duties have been paid but which are entitled to a refund of the whole or part of the duties when the goods are exported in accordance with certain conditions. In some cases drawback is granted where the goods are exported in the same state as imported or have undergone a process which has not changed their form or character. In other cases, drawback is granted when the goods have been used for a specified purpose of manufacture, *e.g.* leather has been used for the manufacture of shoes for export, or sugar for beer brewed for export. The law relating to drawback is contained in the Import Duties Act 1958,[41] s.9 and Sched. 5, and general provisions relating to drawbacks are contained in the Customs and Excise Management Act 1979, ss.119 *et seq.* The rates of drawback for the various species of goods are stated in the *Tariff.* General information as to the procedure to be followed by exporters claiming drawback for exported goods is published in various Customs Notices obtainable from any collector of Customs and Excise.

The Customs requirements for the exportation of goods ex bonded warehouse or subject to drawback claims have been affected by the introduction of the SAD. Removals from a bonded warehouse for export must be declared on a SAD under the standard pre-entry procedure. The same applies to goods for which excise drawback or repayment of duty is claimed. The exporter may be required to present additional information on the SAD in accordance with the applicable Customs requirements.

In relation to shipments from a bonded warehouse the exporter must enter on his SAD the name of the warehouse. He must also enter any other details, statements or authorisation and/or document numbers required under this procedure. This would include a declaration by the exporter of the goods to be moved. The duly completed SAD is then presented to the warehouse keeper, who must note the removal on his stock records. An officially stamped copy of the SAD is then sent to the warehouse keeper as evidence that the goods have been exported. If the warehouse keeper does not receive this document within two months of removal he must inform his Customs officer.

In the case of drawback goods the exporter must enter on his SAD any required "notice to pack". This is a notice to the Customs officer informing him at least twenty-four hours before packing is to commence of the impending export transaction, so that he may examine the goods before they are packed. This notice must be in writing. The SAD must also be accompanied by a separate claim form. This must be presented along with the SAD at the place of export clearance, usually the port of shipment. The Customs official in attendance at the port must provide an official certificate of shipment on Copy 1 of the SAD for each consignment exported. This is a condition precedent to the drawback claim.

---

[41] The Import Duties Act 1958 is, in part, repealed by the Customs and Excise (General Reliefs) Act 1979 but the provisions referred to in the text are not repealed.

Goods exported by parcel post

Goods other than drawback goods may be exported by parcel post without being pre-entered or post-entered for Customs. A Customs declaration has to be completed which can be obtained from a post office. The form, together with the postal dispatch note, has to be handed to the post office when the goods are posted. The exporter has to state, on the Customs declaration, whether the goods are exported under an export licence (in which case the licence has to be attached), whether the goods are exported under a general licence (number and date of which has to be given), or whether they are not prohibited to be exported.

Two kinds of Customs declarations are in use, namely,

(*a*) an adhesive form which is affixed to the parcel; an alternative tie-on version of the adhesive form may be used in appropriate cases. This form is mainly used for parcels to destinations in the EC, the Irish Republic and some other designated countries, including those in the Commonwealth[42];

(*b*) a non-adhesive form. This form is prescribed for other foreign countries. It requires more details of the consignment than the adhesive form; thus, the description of outer packing and of any special marks and the country of production or manufacture have to be stated on the non-adhesive form, and a postal despatch note has to be sent with it.

The adhesive form thus simplifies the Customs requirements and where it is possible to use it the exporter has to complete one form only instead of two. For letters and small parcels the green label statement of contents is sufficient.

Where goods on which drawback is claimed are sent by parcel post, full export documents must be filled out. When goods are subject to special controls a certificate of posting is required on Form C&E 132.

Return of unused imports

An importer is entitled[43] to claim from the Commissioners repayment of any import duty, subject to such conditions as the Commissioners may impose, where it is shown—

(a) that goods were imported in pursuance of a contract of sale and that the description, quality, state or condition of the goods was not in accordance with the contract or that the goods were damaged in transit; and

---

[42] The countries for which the adhesive form may be used are listed in the current *Post Office Guide*.

[43] By virtue of the Customs and Excise Management Act 1979, s.123.

(b) that the importer with the consent of the seller either—

   (i) returned the goods unused to the seller and for that purpose complied with the provisions of section 53 of this Act as to [pre-entry] in like manner as if they had been dutiable or restricted goods for the purposes of Part V of this Act;[44] or

   (ii) destroyed the goods unused.

No repayment of import duties can be claimed for goods imported on approval, or on sale or return, or on similar terms.[45]

Goods in transit

Special provisions exist for goods consigned from an overseas destination to another place overseas and being in transit in the United Kingdom. If the goods are Community transit goods,[46] the observations made later[47] apply. But goods in transit may also be goods which have not been imported from another Community country or are not destined for such a country. Often these goods are shipped on a through bill of lading; sometimes they are exported in the same vessel that imported them, but sometimes they are transhipped in the same port or another port. These provisions likewise apply where goods in transit pass through an approved airport or over the land frontier of Northern Ireland. Goods imported for transit or transhipment are not liable to import duty.

Strict Customs formalities are provided to ensure that the same goods that were imported are, in fact, exported. Lighters and vehicles which are licensed to carry transhipment goods are secured by Crown locks and accompanied by Customs officials, and transit goods removed from one port to another have to be conveyed in bonded railway trucks or lorries. Goods must be removed from the place of importation to that of exportation with all reasonable dispatch, and a time limit may be set for this. As a general rule, transit and transhipment operations should be completed within one month of the importation of the goods, but an extension may be granted if sufficient cause is shown.

In some instances, an export licence is required for transhipment goods.[48] The licence has to be produced together with the SAD. The licence number must be entered in Box 44 of the SAD.

FREE MOVEMENT OF COMMUNITY GOODS

The EC Treaty provides for the free movement of goods in the Community territory.[49] This aim entails the operation of a Customs union.

---

[44] *i.e.* by filling in the SAD giving full details of the goods to be returned.

[45] In the case of a non-trader, the value of goods for import duties is the price paid abroad by a non-trader for such goods, plus freight and expenses, see *Salomon* v. *Customs and Excise Commissioners* [1967] 2 Q.B. 116.

[46] For a definition of Community transit goods see p. 773 *post.*

[47] See p. 774, *post.*

[48] See p. 763, *ante.*

[49] EEC Treaty, Arts. 9–37.

Within the territory of that Customs union there shall be a free circulation (*libre pratique*) of Community goods from one Member Country to another which shall not be impeded by internal tariffs or other obstacles and the whole territory of the union is protected against imports from other countries by a common external tariff (CET), usually referred to as the *Common Customs Tariff* (CCT).

The main measures concerning Community transit of goods are:

Council Regulation of December 13, 1976 on Community Transit (222/77)[50];

Council Regulation of December 22, 1976 on provisions for the implementation of the Community transit procedure and for simplifications of that procedure (223/77)[51]

Council Regulation of February 18, 1985 on simplifying Formalities in Trade in Goods within the Community, which introduces the SAD for inter-Community trade, (678/85)[52] and

Commission Regulation of March 27, 1987 on provisions for the implementation of the Community transit procedure and for certain simplifications of that procedure. (1062/87)[53]

The Customs and Excise Duties (General Reliefs) Act 1979, s.1(2), provides that goods may be relieved from Customs duty in the United Kingdom if that is necessary or expedient with a view to:

(*a*) conforming with any Community obligations; or

(*b*) otherwise affording relief provided for, by or under the Community Treaties or any decisions of the representatives of the governments of the Member States of the Coal and Steel Community meeting in Council.

Customs and Excise have published a series of informative Customs Notices on Community transit.[54]

Central concepts

The free movement of goods in the EC is founded on three central concepts which require further consideration, *viz.* those of Community goods, the free circulation of goods, and the Common Customs Tariff.

---

[50] O.J. 1977/L 38/1.
[51] O.J. 1977/L 38/20.
[52] O.J. 1985/L 79/1.
[53] O.J. 1987/L 107/1.
[54] The most important of these Customs Notices are: Nos. 750 and 750B (Community Transit), No. 750A (List of Community Transit Offices), No. 751(1) Completion of Community Transit forms, (2) Use of loading lists as parts of Community Transit documents, No. 755 (Special Control Procedures), No. 827 (EC Exports Preference Procedures), No. 828 (EC Preferences; Rules of Origin).

Community goods

They are defined[55] as:

(a) goods which wholly originate in the Community, and

(b) goods satisfying the conditions of Articles 9 and 10 of the EC Treaty, being goods coming from a non-Community country which have been put into free circulation in the Community.

Community goods are entitled to Community treatment in any Member State of the EC.

There exists a definition of *Community transit goods*.[56] The term means:

(a) in relation to imported goods,
   (i) goods which have been imported under the internal or external Community transit procedure for transit through the United Kingdom with a view to exportation where the importation was and the transit and exportation are to be part of one Community operation; or
   (ii) goods which have, at the port or airport at which they were imported, been placed under the internal or external Community transit procedure for transit through the United Kingdom with a view to exportation where the transit and exportation are to be part of one Community transit operation;

(b) in relation to goods for exportation,
   (i) goods which have been imported as mentioned in paragraph (a)(i) of this definition and are to be exported as part of the Community transit operation in the course of which they were imported; or
   (ii) goods which have, under the internal or external Community transit procedure, transited the United Kingdom from the port or airport at which they were imported and are to be exported as part of the Community transit operation which commenced at that port or airport.

Free circulation

This means:

the ability of goods to move within the EC without liability to Customs import charges. Goods imported into the Community are in free circulation if all the import formalities in the Member State where they are imported are completed and all the Customs import charges due are paid and not repaid in whole or part.[57]

By applying the concept of free circulation status the Community avoids, in the great majority of cases, the need for certificates of origin for Community goods—a considerable simplification of export documentation.[58]

---

[55] In Customs Notice No. 750, Appendix D and para. 10(b).

[56] Customs and Excise Management Act 1979, s.1(1). Community transit goods do not require a Customs pre-entry or entry; see p. 764, *ante*.

[57] Customs Notice No. 750, Appendix A.

[58] There exists Council Regulation 802/68 of June 27, 1968 on the Common Definition of the Concept of the Origin of Goods (J.O. 1968 L 148/1; O.J. 1968, 165).

The Common Customs Tariff

The CCT is founded on the Harmonised System of goods nomenclature which has been considered earlier.[59] This has been accepted by all the Member States and by the Community itself.

Community transit procedure

The movement of goods in the Community across frontiers of the Member States is carried out on the basis of Community Transit (CT) documents.[60] The purpose of these documents is to prove to the Customs authorities of the importing country that the goods are entitled to free circulation status. These documents must, therefore, be certified by the Customs of the exporting Member State. The basis for this documentation is the SAD, known outside the United Kingdom as the "Single document" or the "COM document". It replaces the so-called T Forms except the control copy T5 (C1125) which deals with goods subject to a Community special control on use, destination or exportation,[61] and Form T2M (C1135) which concerns the Community status of fish landed in one Member State by a vessel registered in another Member State.[62]

Single administrative document

The SAD is an eight part document but only copies 1, 3, 4, 5 and 7 are used to form a CT document. The SAD acts not only as a dispatch and transit document, it also acts as a declaration of the status of the goods. The SAD is used as follows for CT purposes:

---

[59] See p. 766, *ante*.
[60] The law regulating the movement of goods in the EC is contained in Regulations and decisions of the Community authorities. The most important of them are Regulations 222/77, 223/77, and amending Regulations. The movement procedure is explained in the Customs Notices referred to in n. 54 *ante*. The Community transit system was extended from March 1, 1986 to include movements of goods between Spain and Portugal and the other Member States. The Transit Advance Note (TAN) is abolished as from July 1, 1990, except where goods leave the Community in the course of a Community transit operation, *viz* when they cross Switzerland or Austria.

The European Court considered problems relating to the free movement of goods in *Commission* v. *Council* (Case 218/82) [1983] E.C.R. 4063; *Commission* v. *Ireland* (Case 288/83) [1985] 3 C.M.L.R. 152; *Procuratore della Republica* v. *Migliorini* (Case 199/84) [1987] 2 C.M.L.R. 841.
[61] See Notice 755.
[62] See Notice 754.

Copy 1—is retained by the office of departure;

Copy 3—is kept by the exporter;

Copy 4—accompanies the goods to their destination and is for the use of the office of destination; it also acts as the Community status declaration (T2L)[63];

Copy 5— is the return copy, and

Copy 7—is provided for import statistical purposes.

The remaining copies are used as follows:

Copy 2—the export statistical copy;

Copy 6—the import entry;

Copy 8—the consignee's copy.

Copies of the SAD can be obtained from Customs either as full sets of eight or as sets of the copies needed for CT purposes. Copies 1 and 4 can be obtained separately where only a declaration of status is required.

Declaration of status on the SAD

The CT document must note the status of the goods either as "T1," "T2," "T2ES," or "T2PT." The completed document is then referred to as a "T1 declaration" or "T2 declaration" etc.

The "T1" declaration must be given for goods which are, or which include, goods originating in a non-Community country, and which:

(i) on importation into the UK or another member state were not subject to full import formalities; *i.e.* payment of customs duty, CAP and equivalent charges; or

(ii) on importation into the UK or another member state were subject to full import formalities including payment of customs duty, CAP and equivalent charges but that such duty and/or charges has been or is to be repaid in whole or in part; or

(iii) although otherwise entitled to be treated as Community goods, are, or will be, subject to customs export formalities for the grant of CAP export refunds on export from the Community; or

(iv) come under the Treaty establishing the European Coal and Steel Community (ECSC) and thereby are not in free circulation in the Community.[64]

The "T2ES" declaration must be given when the goods have been in free circulation in Spain and the "T2PT" when the goods have been in free circulation in Portugal. These declarations will continue during the transitional period to the full obligations of membership of the Community on the part of Spain and Portugal.[65]

The "T2" declaration may be given for Community goods. It must not be used where T1, T2ES or T2PT status is appropriate.

Goods covered by Community status documents

In addition there exist Community status documents. Their only function is to provide evidence of Community status. They have no effect

---

[63] See below in text.

[64] Notice 750 (February 1989) para. 30.

[65] See further Notice 750B.

on normal Customs requirements for the movement of goods and need not accompany goods during their movement. However, it may be convenient to send them with the goods.

The Community status document consists of Copies 1 and 4 of the SAD upon which the "T2L" declaration is placed and which is authenticated at the office of departure together with the required export documentation.

The "T2L" declaration may be used only for movements of Community goods directly transported, *i.e.* if they do not pass through the territory of a non-Community country, except Austria and Switzerland, or if they pass through the territory of a non-Community country under cover of a single transport document made out in a Member State; further, the "T2L" declaration can only be used if the use of the full CT procedure is not obligatory.[66]

The "T2L" declaration is also used for Community goods (with certain exceptions) consigned to a non-Community country, other than Austria or Switzerland, and expected to be reconsigned to a Member State. No process may be carried out on the goods and they must be re-imported into the Community in exactly the same state in which they were exported. This declaration may be issued for this purpose if the goods are to travel under the full CT procedure to the point at which they leave Community territory.

TIR and ATA carnets

The full CT procedure need not be used for goods travelling under ATA carnet.[67] It must not be used for goods covered by TIR carnet.[68]

The TIR procedure must not be used for movements wholly within the Community territory. It may be used for movements involving Member States if:

  (i)   the movement begins or ends outside the Community, Austria or Switzerland; or
  (ii) the goods leave and re-enter the Community in the course of the movement; or
  (iii) the consignment is for split delivery to destinations in the Community and in Austria or Switzerland; or
  (iv) the consignment is for split delivery to destinations both in the Community, Austria or Switzerland and in another non-Community country.

A TIR movement must be covered by a T2L declaration if delivery of the goods is intended in a Community country, Austria or Switzerland, but such a declaration is not to be used for goods intended for export outside the Community and covered by the TIR procedure.

---

[66] See Notice 750 *op. cit.* paras 20–22.
[67] On ATA carnets see p. 314 *ante*. See too Customs Notice 104.
[68] See Customs Notice 464.

The full CT procedure

The full CT procedure is an intra-Community transit procedure to facilitate the movement of goods between Member States by reducing border formalities and avoiding the use of different national transit procedures. The SAD, which is used here, acts both as a transit document and as evidence as to whether or not the goods are entitled to intra-Community rates of import charge. If it is used for goods which are not entitled to intra-Community rates but are entitled to some other preferential rate, (*e.g.* under a Free Trade Agreement with a non-Community country) the appropriate evidence of entitlement, such as a certificate of origin, must be produced with the SAD when Customs entry is made for the goods in the Member State of destination. The use of the full CT procedure as a transit system is in principle obligatory, but in some circumstances, which are explained in Customs Notice No. 750, its use is optional.[69]

In the full CT procedure the various copies of the SAD are used in the manner described above.

The CT movement commences when the CT documents have been presented and authenticated and the goods have been cleared at the office of departure. The goods are then under CT Customs control until they are properly presented at the CT office of destination. During transit appropriate advice notes must be lodged with the relevant office of transit. If some unforeseen incident befalls the goods in transit, such as the breakage of seals, theft or accidental destruction, the nearest Customs authority must be informed. The CT transit terminates upon the goods and the CT documents being presented at the office of destination within the time limit laid down for the completion of the CT movement.

There also exists the article 41 procedure.[70] It is available when export entry is made before exportation at the point of exit from the United Kingdom and the goods are to be entered through Customs at the point of importation into the next Member State. This procedure is appropriate for goods crossing the Irish land boundary or goods crossing a sea that forms an internal frontier between the UK and the Member State in which the goods are entered to Customs. The exporter need only use Copies 1 and 4 of the SAD. Copy 4 is returned to the exporter, duly authenticated, by the office of departure. It is then presented to Customs immediately on entering the next Member State.

---

[69] Customs Notice No. 750, para. 22.
[70] *Ibid.*, para. 48.

Full CT procedure guarantees

Exporters starting an operation under the full CT procedure must, except in the cases listed in Customs Notice No. 750,[71] have guarantee cover in respect of the duty and similar charges which may become payable on the goods in the course of the transit operation as the result of any irregularity. This is required whether or not the goods are in free circulation. The guarantee will normally take the form of a written contract of guarantee given by a person or organisation other than the exporter. Where a CT guarantee covers the movement of the goods in the United Kingdom, any security which might normally be required for that movement under a United Kingdom national procedure need not be provided.

Various types of guarantees are in use, such as individual guarantees, comprehensive guarantees, and flat-rate guarantees.[72]

Transit through Austria and Switzerland

The Community Transit (CT) system and its various subsidiary and simplified procedures are available for movements of goods which;

    (*a*) cross Austria or Switzerland during a movement between two points in the Community; or

    (*b*) are reconsigned from Austria or Switzerland after deposit, up to a limited period, in a bonded warehouse; or

    (*c*) move to Austria or Switzerland from a point in the Community, or vice versa.

These arrangements are intended to facilitate the passage of goods which cross Austria or Switzerland en route from one point in the Community to another or which cross part of the Community to or from Austria or Switzerland. Austria and Switzerland are not members of the European Community and the use of Community transit documentation for trade through or with these two countries does not confer any entitlement to preferential duty rates upon Community goods entering Austria or Switzerland or on Austrian or Swiss goods entering the Community.[73]

EC preference arrangements

Some countries which are not members of the EC grant imports from an EC country preferential tariff treatment. These countries are:

---

[71] Customs Notice No. 750, para. 35. These exceptions include passage by sea and passage by air by an approved airline (most airlines operating frequent flights between the UK and other Member States are approved for this purpose; if in doubt, the Customs office should be consulted). Part of the EC Commission's 1992 proposals involves the eventual abolition of the CT guarantee procedure.

[72] The UK flat-rate guarantors are listed in Appendix H of Customs Notice No. 750.

[73] See Customs Notice No. 750.

(a) the EFTA countries which have not joined the EC, *viz.* Austria, Finland, Iceland, Norway, Sweden and Switzerland (including Liechtenstein);
(b) Cyprus;
(c) Israel;
(d) Malta;
(e) Ceuta, Melilla and the Canary Islands;
(f) some of the African, Caribbean and Pacific States (ACP countries), and Overseas Countries and Territories (OCT countries), which receive preferences from the EC and which, though not required to do so, give a preference to EC originating goods.

The exporter in the EC country has to comply with certain requirements to enable his customer in the preference-giving non-EC country to claim preferential treatment.[74] The basic condition is that the exported goods must comply with the origin rules governing the particular preference. Those origin rules vary in the preference-giving countries and the exporter must satisfy himself that the goods he is exporting comply with the rules for the particular country of destination. The rules of origin are set out in Customs Notice No. 828. The exporter has to supply his customer with a prescribed certificate of origin which will normally be movement certificate EUR1 (C1299); that form is endorsed by the Customs authority of the exporting country. A different form can be used for certain low-value or postal exportations; in those cases Form EUR2 (C1297), which does not require endorsement by the Customs authority, is sufficient. In the case of private exportations of small value no form is required at all. It should, however, be emphasised that the use of forms is not obligatory. Their use is necessary only if the exported goods qualify as originating and preferential admission into the importing country is to be claimed. Often the certificate of origin can be certified by the local chamber of commerce. A movement certificate must normally be produced for the Customs authorities of the importing country within a specified period after endorsement in the exporting country. For the EFTA countries certificates are valid for four months, and for Cyprus, Israel and Malta five months.[75]

The exporter may be called upon to give supporting evidence showing that the particulars of the certificate of origin are correct. Untrue information given to Customs and Excise may in certain circumstances be a Customs offence. If no verifying evidence is forthcoming, when required, the Customs authorities of the importing country will normally require the importer to pay the full non-preferential duties and may also impose a penalty.

The range of goods admissible for preference in the preference-giving countries, the preferential rates of duty, the application of quota requirements and the consignment rules vary considerably in the preference-giving countries. Information about the availability of a preference and

---

[74] These requirements are stated in Customs Notice No. 827.
[75] *Ibid.*, para. 20.

the preferential rate should, if required by the exporter, be sought from the customer in the country concerned or from the DTI, Overseas Trade Division.[76]

As a general rule there can be no entitlement to both export relief in the EC and preferential tariff treatment, at least not in an EFTA country. Such export relief is sometimes available in the EC; it means the suspension or reimbursement of import duties on goods which are exported in the form of compensating products from an inward processing relief arrangement but it does not include relief from CAP levies and variable charges, payment of export refunds, or relief from, or repayment of, excise duties.[77] As an exception to the general rule, export relief can be claimed as follows:

(a) *Exports to EFTA countries*. When the relief claim is restricted to;
  (i) materials originating in the EC or the EFTA countries and imported from those countries;
  (ii) materials imported from other countries of a kind which are not covered by the EC–EFTA Agreements; and
  (iii) packing regarded as forming a whole with the goods it contains, except packing in which goods are put up for retail sale.
(b) *Exports to other countries*. A declaration that goods are originating can be made even if export relief is being claimed.

CUSTOMS OFFENCES

The concept of Customs offences

The Commissioners of Customs and Excise administer, in addition to the regulation of the Customs, the executive provisions of the law relating to export and import licensing, the EC regulation of the free movement of goods, and VAT taxation. The measures dealing with these topics contain in many instances criminal provisions requiring that offences against them should have consequences similar to Customs offences. The concept of the Customs offence is thus much wider than merely constituting an infringement of the Customs and Excise Acts and the regulations made thereunder.[78]

Fines and forfeiture of goods

The Customs Acts provide heavy fines and terms of imprisonment for persons contravening the Customs regulations.[79] The goods in respect of

---

[76] Address: 1 Victoria Street, London SW1H OET. Tel: 01–215 7877.
[77] Customs Notice No. 827, para. 10.
[78] Thus the theft of export quotas may amount to a Customs offence: *Attorney-General of Hong Kong* v. *Daniel Chan Nai-Keung* [1987] 1 W.L.R. 1339 (PC).
[79] On the burden of proof in Customs prosecutions, see p. 783, *post*.

which the offence is committed may be treated as "prohibited goods" and declared as forfeited.[80] In particular, section 68 of the Customs and Excise Management Act 1979 provides that a person who exports, or brings to any place in the United Kingdom for the purpose of export, goods, the exportation of which is prohibited or restricted, shall be liable to a penalty of three times the value of the goods[81] or £400, whichever is the greater, and the goods shall be liable to forfeiture. If the offence is committed knowingly, the penalty may be imprisonment.[82] The Customs authorities may also seize and subject to forfeiture any ship, aircraft or vessel that has been used to carry goods liable to forfeiture, provided that the owner is aware of the carriage of the prohibited goods or that he could have discovered the goods had he used due diligence.[83] As regards forfeiture a number of points should be noted.

First, the Court of Appeal held[84] that Krugerrand coins were "goods" within the Customs legislation. Persons who smuggled them into the country could be convicted for having committed a Customs offence and the coins were liable to forfeiture. Krugerrands are gold coins minted in South Africa. They can be used as a means of payment in South Africa but their use in the international field is that they are bought and kept as an investment in view of their intrinsic gold value. The decision of the Court of Appeal is in contrast with that of the Court of the European Communities which had held[85] that Krugerrand coins were not "goods" but "capital." It is thought that, at least for the purposes of Customs law, the decision of the Court of Appeal is correct.

Secondly, the forfeiture of smuggled goods is only possible if the Customs authorities have lawfully seized them. This was decided in *Attorney-General of New Zealand* v. *Ortiz.*[86] In this case a New Zealand enactment was in issue but the ruling of the House of Lords applies with equal force to United Kingdom Customs law. In the *Ortiz* case a valuable Maori carving consisting of five wooden panels was exported from New Zealand without permission of the New Zealand Government and

---

[80] On service abroad in condemnation proceedings under what is now Sched. 3 to the Customs and Excise Management Act 1979, see *Commissioners of Customs and Excise* v. *I.F.S. Irish Fully Fashioned Stockings Ltd.* [1957] 1 W.L.R. 397. Forfeiture proceedings are procedures *in rem*; this means that the only question is whether the goods are liable to forfeiture; it is irrelevant who has imported them or whether they were unsolicited goods; *Denton* v. *Jones* [1971] 1 W.L.R. 1426 (Rhodesian stamps).

[81] On the calculation of the value of the goods, see *Byrne* v. *Low* [1972] 1 W.L.R. 1282.

[82] What is now s.68 (then s.56 of the Customs and Excise Act 1952) was applied to an illicit export to Rhodesia, when exportation to that country was prohibited, but in the case before the court the offence was not committed knowingly: *Superheater Co. Ltd.* v. *Commissioners of Customs and Excise* [1969] 1 W.L.R. 858.

[83] S.141(1)(*a*) of the Customs and Excise Management Act 1979 as interpreted in *Customs and Excise Commissioners* v. *Air Canada* [1989] 2 W.L.R. 589.

[84] *Allgemeine Gold und Silberscheideanstalt* v. *Customs and Excise Commissioners* [1980] Q.B. 390.

[85] *Reg.* v. *Ernest Thompson* (Case 7/78) [1980] Q.B. 229.

[86] *Attorney-General of New Zealand* v. *Ortiz* [1984] A.C. 1.

eventually purchased by Mr. Ortiz who acquired it in good faith. The exportation contravened the New Zealand Historic Articles Act 1962 which declared that articles exported without permission "shall be forfeited" to the Crown. The Attorney-General of New Zealand claimed in the English courts that the carving was forfeited automatically to the Crown and had become Crown property. The House of Lords dismissed the claim. Lord Brightman said[87] that "there being no seizure in the instant case, the conclusion is inescapable that the ownership of the carving and the right of possession have not become vested in the Crown." In United Kingdom Customs law this is even clearer because the Customs Act uses the expression "shall be liable to forfeiture," and not, as the New Zealand Act, "shall be forfeited."

Thirdly, the powers of the Customs authorities in relation to the forfeiture of goods are capable of review under the provisions relating to the free movement of goods under the EC Treaty[88] and under Art. 1 of the First Protocol to the European Convention of Human Rights, which protects the peaceful enjoyment of one's possessions. However, in each case the State authorities are permitted to control the free circulation of goods and, if necessary, to forfeit those goods where this can be justified on the ground of public interest which is specifically mentioned in the relevant provisions of the EC Treaty and the European Convention.[89]

Other aspects

Section 68(2) extends criminal liability to any person knowingly "concerned in the exportation" of goods which require an export licence. Activities which amount to being "concerned with exportation" are not limited to those of actually taking the goods out of the country, but a person can be "concerned in the exportation" by doing things in advance of the time when the ship or aircraft leaves, *e.g.* by handing over the goods to the buyer's agent the night before the ship or aircraft leaves,

---

[87] *Ibid.* 817.
[88] Arts. 30, 36.
[89] See *R.* v. *Bow Street Metropolitan Stipendiary Magistrate Ex Parte. Noncyp Ltd.* [1988] 3 W.L.R. 827 (DC) and *R.* v. *Henn* (Case 34/79) [1981] A.C. 850 on the application of the EC Treaty to seizures by Customs of books alleged to contravene the Obscene Publications Act 1959 but in free circulation in other Member States; and on Art. 1 Protocol 1 ECHR see *Allgemeine Gold und Silberscheideanstalt AG* v. *United Kingdom* (Case No. 14/1984/86/133) Judgment European Court of Human Rights October 24, 1986. (1987) 9 EHRR 1

The Court held that the forfeiture of the Krugerrands smuggled into the UK by the applicants did not violate Art 1 Protocol 1 as the means used were lawful and proportionate to the public interest sought to be protected.

knowing that the agent will take the goods out of the country without licence.[90] However, the Privy Council has held in an appeal from Hong Kong that the offence of "causing" goods to be taken outside Hong Kong in violation of local Customs requirements could not be committed by a person who handed over the goods inside Hong Kong territory to another who would take the goods outside the territory even if the former knew that the goods would be smuggled out.[91]

Where patented goods, without being licensed by the owner of the patent, are imported into the United Kingdom, the Customs authorities must disclose the names of the importers to the owner of the patent because the illicit importation constitutes a tort against the owner of the patent and every person who, though innocently, becomes involved in tortious acts of others, comes under a duty to assist the injured person by giving him full information by way of discovery, although he personally may not be liable in damages to the third person.[92] Where whisky worth £7,000 (not including excise duty) in transit to a destination abroad was stolen from the transporting vehicle in the United Kingdom, the owner had to pay the (unpaid) excise duty of some £30,000.[93]

The burden of proof that the goods have been lawfully imported and Customs duties have been paid on them, rests on the importer[94]; he has to establish his innocence in all cases where he is prosecuted, and not merely in those cases where the goods have been seized by the Customs authorities.[95] The offence of dealing with uncustomed goods with intent to defraud the revenue of import duties or purchase tax can be committed anywhere in the realm and not merely at the port of entry.[96] But if on importation of goods a Customs officer mistakenly undervalues the goods, without having been misled by an untrue statement of the

---

[90] *Garrett* v. *Arthur Churchill (Glass) Ltd.* [1970] 1 Q.B. 92.

[91] *Attorney-General of Hong Kong* v. *Tse Hung-lit and another* [1986] 3 W.L.R. 320 (P.C.).

[92] *Norwich Pharmacal Co.* v. *Customs and Excise Commissioners* [1974] A.C. 133. Where a party has obtained an Anton Piller injunction (see p. 286, *ante*) and his solicitors have retained documents, which they have taken away, in safe custody, they must refuse the Customs and Excise Commissioners inspection of the documents, if the Commissioners investigate an alleged non-payment of VAT, until the court grants the Commissioners leave to inspect the documents: *Customs and Excise Commissioners* v. *A.E. Hamlin & Co.* [1984] 1 W.L.R. 509.

[93] *James Buchanan & Co. Ltd.* v. *Babco Forwarding and Shipping (U.K.) Ltd.* [1978] A.C. 141. See also the decision of the Court of the European Communities in *Ministero delle Finanze* v. *Esercizio Maggazzini Generali SpA* (Cases 186 and 187/82). [1984] 3 C.M.L.R. 217.

[94] Customs and Excise Management Act 1979, s.154(2).

[95] *R.* v. *Fitzpatrick* [1948] 1 All E.R. 769. Where goods are seized there is no overriding duty on the Customs to preserve the goods. Customs could rely on secondary evidence relating to the goods where this was available and could put it before a jury: *R.* v. *Uxbridge Justices Ex Parte Sofaer and another,* [1987] 85 Cr.App.R. 367.

[96] *Beck* v. *Binks* [1949] 1 K.B. 250.

importer (who realises that the officer made a mistake), no Customs offence is committed.[97]

Finally, Customs offences may arise as a result of the operation of international agencies and Conventions. Thus, under the EC Common Agricultural Policy, where an agricultural product has not entered the importing State for home use, but for the purposes of illegal "carousel trading" by the purchaser, the exporter may be refused any compensation payment due to him even if he has acted in good faith.[98] In other cases an international Convention may create a Customs offence. For example, there exists a Convention on the means of prohibiting and preventing the illicit Import, Export and Transfer of Ownership of Cultural Property adopted on November 14, 1970; this Convention requires international co-operation in the control of such trade and obliges States party to the Convention to prohibit the import of cultural property stolen from a museum or a church or similar secular public monument or institution.[99] Further, the Single Convention on Narcotic Drugs, signed at New York on March 30, 1961, obliges the United Kingdom to co-operate with the other Convention countries in the fight against the abuse of dangerous drugs; to perform these obligations, a Customs officer may produce to the authorities of another Convention country copies—but not the originals— of documents seized by him by virtue of the relevant dangerous drugs legislation.[1]

---

[97] *Customs and Excise Commissioners* v. *Tan* [1977] A.C. 650 (Customs officer asked importer at airport what two jade pendants which she had bought in China for £8,300 were worth and she replied that she did not know. The officer valued them £50 and charged the duty at £12.50. She sold one pendant for £8,400. No Customs offence was committed). See also *R.* v. *Commissioners of Customs and Excise; ex p. Tsahl, The Times*, December 12, 1989 (When restoring seized goods, Customs may take into account drop in value of the goods).

[98] See *Irish Grain Board (Trading) Ltd.* v. *Minister for Agriculture* (Case 254/85) [1987] 1 C.M.L.R. 727 (E.C.)

[99] See the description of this Convention (to which the United Kingdom has not acceded) in *Kingdom of Spain* v. *Christie Manson and Woods Ltd* [1986] 1 W.L.R. 1120 (Ch.D.).

[1] *R.* v. *Southwark Crown Court.; ex Parte Customs and Excise, Financial Times*, June 7, 1989. The relevant UK legislation was the Drug Trafficking Offences Act 1986 and the Misuse of Drugs Act 1971 (the case concerned the disclosure of documents seized at a bank in London to the USA authorities; the documents were alleged to relate to transactions by General Noriega, then ruler of Panama).

INDEX

*(References in **bold** type indicate the page where the subject is treated fully)*